AN INTRODUCTORY
ANTHOLOGY OF WORLD DRAMA

Edited with
historical introductions
by
NORMAN A. BERT

MERIWETHER PUBLISHING LTD.
Colorado Springs, Colorado

Meriwether Publishing Ltd., Publisher
PO Box 7710
Colorado Springs, CO 80933-7710

Editor: Arthur L. Zapel, Rhonda Wray
Cover design: Tom Myers

© Copyright MCMXCV Meriwether Publishing Ltd.
Printed in the United States of America
First Edition

Library of Congress Cataloging-in-Publication Data

Theatre alive! : an introductory anthology of world drama / edited with
  historical introductions by Norman A. Bert.
     p.   cm.
  ISBN 10: 1-56608-008-8
  ISBN 13: 978-1-56608-008-8
    1. Drama --Collections.   I. Bert, Norman A.
  PN6112.T437   1994
  808.82--dc20   94-41533
                                          CIP

5   6   7   06 07 08

PERMISSIONS ACKNOWLEDGEMENTS

PERMISSIONS ACKNOWLEDGMENTS (cont'd)

For my parents
Eldon and Harriet Bert

CONTENTS

Asian Theatre

Early Twentieth-Century Theatre

Political Drama

Mid-Twentieth Century American Drama

Absurdist Drama

African-American Drama

The Sixties and After

ACKNOWLEDGMENTS

Many thanks to Eastern Montana College for providing time for this project through a sabbatical leave and reassigned time and to the Communication Arts Department for providing clerical support. I also want to thank Mindy Askelson, Tabitha Bert, and Teresa Hedegaard for bibliographical and research assistance and Debra Bonogofsky and Julie Guardipee for clerical help. My special thanks to Rhonda Wray, editorial assistant at Meriwether, for her liaison work with publishers. And my continuing gratitude and appreciation to my wife Deb for her direct assistance on the anthology as well as for helping to keep my life both interesting and serene. Finally, I want to thank my parents, Eldon and Harriet Bert, for their nurture and financial assistance during my preparatory years and their continued interest and moral support. May they live long and well.

Norman A. Bert
Eastern Montana College
Billings, Montana

Introduction

THEATRE:
The Now-Art
with a Past

Theatre does its work by bringing a live audience in contact with a living work of art. In this work of art, the play, theatre artists create a new world which is usually similar in at least some respects to the everyday world outside the theatre. By watching what happens in this created world, the audience gains new perspectives on the real world. At its best, this shared experience of a created world excites, enlivens, and gives pleasure to the artists and the audience alike. At its best, this new perspective, gained in the theatre, gives one's life fullness, enjoyment, and direction.

Theatre focuses on the importance of the moment. No matter how many times they have repeated a play, in each performance, the players strive to create the illusion of freshness, to play their roles in such a way that their characters appear to be encountering these situations, doing these actions, and saying these words for the first time. Furthermore, since the composition of the audience (one-half of the performer-spectator relationship) changes from night to night, each performance differs subtly from every other performance; when you watch a play, you participate in a one-of-a-kind, unrepeatable art work.

While readers perceive novels as having happened in the past, audience members perceive plays as happening in the present — even if the events are set in the remote past such as prehistoric Greece. And finally, a live theatre performance always occurs between artists and audience members who are sharing an identical moment in history; theatre differs in this respect from the visual arts such as painting and sculpture in which a late-twentieth-century American may view a portrait by an artist who painted primarily to please the tastes of a sixteenth-century Italian aristocrat. Even if a theatre group today decides to stage a sixteenth-century Italian play such as Machiavelli's *Mandragola*, they are still modern artists performing for their contemporaries; they and their audience members will focus on aspects of the play which they find meaningful today, regardless of the interests of the original playwright and audience. In theatre, the moment — the *present* moment — is all-important. Theatre is the now-art.

Why then — if the present moment is so important — study the

1

theatre of the past? Because the theatre of the past is one of the elements which determine which choices today's theatre artists will make. A performed play is the result of thousands of choices, large and small. For instance, in producing Shakespeare's play *Julius Caesar*, the director and designers will need to decide whether to costume the characters in Roman clothing of the first century BC when the play's action occurs, or in English Renaissance costumes (which is probably the way the actors dressed in the first production of the play), or in twentieth-century American clothing, or in the costumes of some other time or place. This major decision will have an immense effect on the play's production. Of the many factors which affect such decisions, an important one is the director's and designers' knowledge and understanding of the theatre of the past.

Furthermore, the more audience members know about the theatre of the past, the better they are prepared to enjoy the plays they watch. This is true not only in the case of plays from the past, such as *Julius Caesar,* but also in the case of new plays by current writers, plays which form the latest moment in the on-going history of theatre.

To create theatre, and to fully appreciate theatre, we need to be familiar with theatre's past.

Theatre: A Developing Art Form

We often speak of theatre as an art which has *developed* into its present form. We notice, for instance, vast differences between *Oedipus the King* and *Othello,* and also vast differences between *Othello* and *Children of a Lesser God.* It doesn't surprise us that theatre has changed over the past twenty-five hundred years, that plays from such different times and places would be different. In other ways, however — and perhaps more surprisingly — these three plays have remarkable similarities. Over time, theatre has not only changed but it has also remained the same; the plays of most eras have drawn some elements from plays of the past, have rejected other elements of former drama, and have invented some new elements of their own. The plays in this anthology trace the development of Western theatre from its origin in ancient Athens to its current stage in late-twentieth-century America.

The idea of "development," however, has some traps that can trick us into misunderstanding history, the plays of the past, and the manner in which theatre artists work. In the first place, for instance, focusing on the development of theatre may cause us to ignore the intrinsic value of each play or each theatrical period in and of itself. Our interest in tracing out the developing strands of theatre may lead us to value individual plays only for how they relate to our theatre or, at least, some later theatre. For a long time, for instance, scholars studied medieval theatre only as a prelude to Shakespeare. Because their real interest lay in Shakespeare rather than the medieval plays they studied, they tended to ignore or denigrate aspects of those plays which did not develop into Shakespeare's plays. As a result, these scholars closed their eyes to the power and genius of the medieval plays and tended to see them as inartistic, primitive, unsophisticated, and simplistic — in other words, as bad art.

Furthermore, seeing theatre as development wrongly suggests the existence of an independent "spirit of the theatre" that determines theatre's development regardless of the theatre artists; instead of theatre artists being the shapers of theatre, they tend to be seen as puppets in the process. In reality, however, the work of theatre artists determines how the tradition will develop.

Finally, seeing theatre as development can lead us to misunderstand the idea of "influence." Influence is a way of understanding the relationship between earlier and later art works which have similarities to each other. For instance, when students notice that the plays of both Seneca (a first-century Roman playwright) and Shakespeare use epigrammatic sentences called "sententia," they commonly say that Shakespeare's plays were influenced by Seneca. The problem comes when we speak of an earlier play "exerting an influence" on later playwrights, as if the early work was so powerful that the later artists, almost in spite of themselves, *had* to write plays in the same way. In fact, in cases of "influence," the similarities are almost *always* a matter of the later artist *choosing* to use elements of the earlier drama; "influence" depends on the choices of the later artist, not the power of the earlier art work.

Even with these dangers, the concept of theatre history as developmental is valid and useful because it helps us understand the similarities and differences between plays of different periods of history. The idea of theatre history as development is basic to this collection of plays. To avoid the pitfalls of this concept, however, we should keep in mind that (1) each play is valuable in and of itself, (2) the work of theatre artists shapes the development of theatre, not vise versa, and (3) "influence" is a matter of later artists *choosing* to use aspects of earlier works, not earlier works "exerting an influence" on later artists.

Theatre: The Responsive Art

Besides the plays of the past, dramatists of all ages have been alert to a wide variety of practices and ideas both within theatre and in the world at large. Their responses to these artistic, philosophical, and political realities and concepts helped determine the shape of their plays. The shaping elements they responded to include each era's performance conventions, stagecraft, theatre architecture, thea-

3

trical organization, theory of drama, and political/social/philosophical viewpoints. Since these elements are essential to a clear understanding of drama and since the introductions to the individual plays discuss them, it is worthwhile to introduce each of them here.

The *performance conventions* — the manner in which actors play their roles — help determine how the playwrights construct their plots. In a Japanese Noh play, for instance, the actors speak and move in a very slow, extremely stylized manner. Because of this performance approach, Zeami naturally kept his scripts relatively short in terms of the number of words. Even though the play *Izutsu* occupies relatively few pages of script, in performance it would last well over an hour. Furthermore, Zeami wrote nonrealistic, stylized dialog to match the style of the acting.

Stagecraft

Current approaches to stagecraft also help shape the plays of each era. In medieval theatre, for instance, the setting usually consisted of an open space surrounded by a number of "mansions," or set pieces, each of which represented a different place. All of the mansions were in plain view of the audience throughout the play. The writer of *Everyman*, therefore, could easily move the action from heaven to Everyman's counting house to the church to Everyman's grave without ever needing to insert a "scene break." In contrast with this, the late-nineteenth-century design practice of representing only a single place on stage at one time and doing so with a lot of complicated, realistic scenery led the playwrights of Ibsen's day to confine the action of their plays to a limited number of places — or even a single room, such as Nora and Helmer's living room in *A Doll's House.*

Architecture

Various kinds of theatre architecture also have an effect on the writing of plays. The theatre building of Shakespeare's day, for instance, provided a large stage with a permanent background which included several doors and acting areas. This kind of theatre building made it natural for Shakespeare to construct his plays in numerous short scenes in which all the characters in one scene vacated the stage as the characters of the next scene entered; this kind of plot construction would be less suitable in a theatre like Molière's which provided a single, small playing area and very few places for the actors to enter or exit.

Theatrical Companies

The organization of theatrical companies also conditions playwriting. For example, since Athenian theatre practices limited the number of speaking actors to three, the list of characters for a play by Sophocles is relatively short. In contrast, the Elizabethan acting

4

company consisted of 10 to 15 major actors, all of whom expected to have a role in almost every play; as a result, the cast lists of Shakespeare's plays tend to be long. Interestingly, today the expense of hiring actors at union wages has led many late-twentieth-century playwrights to return to the ancient Greek practice of writing small-cast plays.

Dramatic Theory

Current dramatic theory also helps shape the plays of each period. The rules of French neoclassicism, for instance, required "legitimate" plays to have five acts, to limit their action to a single location and a single day's events, and to provide for "poetic justice," with good characters being rewarded and evil characters being punished. Neoclassicism also dictated that comedy should be kept strictly separate from tragedy. Comedies had to focus on middle-class life, while tragedies focused on royalty and the nobility. Comedies were to avoid serious subject matter and scenes, while tragedies were to avoid comic scenes. In keeping with these expectations, Molière's *Hypochondriac (The Imaginary Invalid)* focuses on the foolish behavior of a middle-class man, limits the action to Argon's room, and observes unity of time. The play concludes with a farcical ritual in which Argon receives the ridicule his foolishness has earned him.

Finally, the shape of a play is affected by the *political, social, and philosophical viewpoints* of its author and its period. Peter Weiss, for instance, was deeply committed to the Marxist concept of revolution. The main Marxist countries of his day, however — the USSR and East Germany — committed their energies to repressing the revolutionary impulse for freedom among their people. Moved by the contrast between his political ideals and the political realities of his time, Weiss wrote his chaotic play *Marat/Sade,* which calls for revolution while equating the Communist regimes of his day with the politically and economically conservative French Empire of the early nineteenth century. Another sample of the effect of political and social viewpoints on drama is provided by the contrasting treatments of racial conflict in the plays *Uncle Tom's Cabin,* written prior to the Civil War, and *Dutchman,* written in the 1960s.

Theatre Scripts: Blueprints for Art Works

Strictly speaking, the word "play" denotes not a written document, but rather a performed theatre piece. Only in performance before a live audience does a piece of dramatic art reach completion. A written text, made up of the words to be spoken by the characters and stage directions describing the characters and their actions, is properly called a script. Scripts — including the 15 samples in this anthology — provide blueprints for acted plays, and unless viewed in production on stage, they remain incomplete. The peculiar nature of

5

play scripts demands a reading approach different from that used in reading poems, essays, and fiction. The key principle of script-reading is that readers should do everything they can to visualize the produced play in action. Here are some suggestions:

First, read the script straight through in one sitting. Novelists expect that readers will spend an hour or so with their book and then put it down for several hours or a day and then come back to it. But playwrights expect that audiences will view their play in one concentrated, continuous experience. You, the script reader, should approximate this kind of contact with the play as nearly as possible. Read at a steady pace without turning back to re-read portions. Since playwrights know that theatre audiences can't "turn back the page," they are careful to point up items which are crucial to the play's meaning. Give yourself a brief "intermission" between acts, then return to the play. The total reading time for a play — even a Shakespearian play — should not exceed three hours; ideally, it should take the same time, or slightly less time, to read a play than it would to watch it in a theatre.

Second, imagine the play's events happening on a stage, not in real life. Theatre tends to heighten and intensify life rather than imitate it with photographic realism. If you visualize the play as happening in real life, you are likely to miss some of the play's values and, at the same time, add things to your perception of the play that don't really come from it. In order to visualize the play, pay attention to any details the script may contain about the arrangement of the set, and see if you can picture this environment in your mind's eye. Also, notice staging details in the play's introduction and keep them in mind as you read the play. For instance, picturing the central characters in *Oedipus the King* as masked actors or Desdemona in *Othello* as being played by an adolescent boy will help you grasp an image of the effect these plays must have had on their first audiences. Most of us have seen a huge number of television dramas and movies by the time we start reading plays. Since most movies and television shows do attempt a photographic imitation of reality, this background can make it difficult for readers to picture a script coming to life on a stage. Correct this problem by taking every opportunity to attend live stage plays.

Third, as you read, focus on the *action* of the play. The action is the social, psychological event that gives the play its essential unity. Find the action by asking yourself, "What is *happening* in this play?" Keeping your answer to this question short — one simple sentence — will help you cut through peripheral *activities* and penetrate to the central *action*. The action of a play is the main change in the human situations portrayed. Because of this, you will most easily discover the play's action by focusing on character identities and relationships, changes in characters and relationships, and the play's sequence of situation-event-situation.

Other less important aspects of a play include such things as word-play, symbolism, and philosophical ideas. These elements are usually not important in themselves, but instead serve to unify the play and give power to its action. The play does not exist for these elements; rather they exist for the sake of the play.

Fourth, if you are going to take notes on the play, do so after completing the reading. Don't interrupt the play by underlining or taking notes during the initial reading of the script. And keep your notes brief; one or two pages should be ample. Brevity will help you focus on what is important, while a long, detailed narrative may cause you to obscure the thread of the play's action with a lot of unimportant details.

And finally, before you even begin to read a script, decide that you will accept the play on its own terms. In the history of world drama, millions of plays have been written. The 15 scripts in this book have been selected from this huge body of material as being the best, the most characteristic, or the most important plays ever written. They have been read, studied, and produced repeatedly from the time they were written down to the present day. Your job as a student, therefore, is not to decide whether or not you like the play you are reading, but rather to discover why it excited its original audience and held the stage ever since. Frequently teachers and students criticize plays before they understand them. They suggest that if the playwrights had just been a little more intelligent or artistic or cultured or skilled, the plays could have been a lot better. They fail to realize that, long after their criticisms — and they themselves — have disappeared from memory, these plays will still live on to thrill their audiences. Wise script readers, therefore, have a different approach. They begin by assuming that the playwrights knew what they were doing and were in control of their materials and their art. They go on to understand the plays and, in the process, they gain a new perspective on what it means to be human. And that, after all, is what theatre is all about.

7

THE CLASSICAL PERIOD: The Theatre of Ancient Greece and Rome

European theatre began in Athens in the sixth century BC, spread throughout the classical world, and developed in an unbroken tradition until the sixth century AD when Germanic invasions put an end to both the Roman Empire and public theatre. During this period of almost twelve hundred years, theatre evolved from a celebration of religious and cultural values into a debased, escapist form of entertainment. Production-wise, classical theatre began as a relatively simple event performed in an open area; by its conclusion, it had developed into a spectacle staged in monumental theatres. In the beginning, plays were staged infrequently and were written and performed by amateurs — true expressions of community theatre in which the plays were done by, for, and about the total population. By the end of the classical period, plays were staged frequently and were done by professionals for a shrinking, jaded audience. When theatre began again, many years after the last play was performed in Rome, people looked back to the classical period to learn about drama; as a result, the theatre of ancient Greece and Rome provided the basis for everything that has happened since in theatre and drama in Europe and the New World.

Political/Social/Philosophical Backgrounds

When it began in the sixth century BC, theatre played an important role in Athens' religious and political life. All free-born citizens participated in governing the "polis," or city of Athens. The Athenians, therefore, recognized the necessity of educating the populace so that they could carry out their civic responsibilities. Traditionally, the duty of education belonged to the poets; Athenians learned about their history and their values by reading the poetry of Homer and others. At religious festivals, which typically focused on a particular god, the recitation of poems played an important part.

Dithyrambs

The festivals of the god Dionysus, for instance, included the competitive performance of poems called *dithyrambs*. Dionysus was a fertility god whose cult had come into Athens from Asia Minor. The myth of Dionysus said that he was the son of the chief god Zeus and the woman Semele, and that Dionysus was murdered, dismembered, and then came back to life again. Dithyrambs, narrative poems in Dionysus' honor, were recited by choruses of 50 men or boys. As the choruses sang the stories of the gods, they moved in rank formation. The effect must have been similar to Handel's *Messiah* being sung by a chorus who would, while singing, perform a routine like a marching band at half-time in a football game.

Legend has it that a dithyrambic chorus leader named Thespis (6th century BC) originated the idea of using make-up or masks to disguise himself as various characters in the story. When a performer impersonated a character instead of telling about the character, a new poetic form — drama — came into existence. Of course, it was not uncommon for priests and worshipers in ancient religions to impersonate gods during the act of worship because they believed that they were thereby unified with the deities. The difference between religious ritual and dramatic performance seems to be that, while worshipers imitate the gods in order to become one with them, actors imitate the gods (or other characters) on behalf of an audience who wants to see how the characters might behave. Although we cannot know how clearly Thespis himself recognized this difference at first, we do know that in 534 BC he won the first competition for tragic drama. Theatre had been born.

Warfare in Athens

The fifth century in Athens, during which Greek drama came to maturity, was one of the high points of Western civilization. It was also a time of great turmoil. Throughout the century, in their attempt to establish an empire, the Athenians engaged in almost continuous warfare. Politicians wrangled for control and even assassinated one another. Devotees of the newly invented process of philosophy struggled to wrest from the poets the right to educate Athens' youths. All the while, theatre continued to play an important role. Through their tragedies, the Athenians relived the myths which told them who they were, where they had come from, and what was expected of them. Through their comedies, they ridiculed their own shortcomings and lambasted the controversial policies of their leaders.

In the fourth century BC, however, this all changed. The long Peloponnesian War between Athens and Sparta weakened both sides before it ended with the defeat of Athens in 404 BC. The Macedonians soon came south to fill the power vacuum left there. Although Philip of Macedon and his son Alexander the Great (356-323 BC) admired Athenian culture, as conquering tyrants they would not tolerate the kind of freedom of thought and speech which had nurtured Greek drama. As a result, theatre as a celebration of community came to an end. Few tragedies of note were written after the death of Euripides in 406 BC, the tragic competitions came to focus on acting performances rather than new plays, and comedy centered on romantic escapades rather than social criticism.

Roman Theatre

As the Hellenistic Empire, which Alexander had founded, fell apart, Rome came to dominate the Mediterranean world. Similar to the manner in which the Macedonians had admired Athenian culture, many Romans admired and imitated parts of Hellenistic culture, including theatre. Like the festivals of Dionysus in old Athens, the Roman festivals or *ludi* which included theatrical performances were civic events. As time passed, however, the celebration of Roman ideals at these dramatic festivals gave way to the desire of the rulers to entertain their subjects so they would forget their economic woes and their lack of political power. By the Augustan Period, the golden age of Roman art and literature (27 BC to AD 14), cultured Romans considered theatre to be fit only for rabble.

Furthermore, as Christianity grew, Roman theatre — especially mime — ridiculed the beliefs and practices of the new religion. The church responded by castigating the theatre, which in turn responded by becoming more aggressively anti-Christian. Meanwhile, theatre, in its attempt to compete with such entertainments as circuses and gladiatorial combats, became more and more sensationalistic. There are even stories of actual crucifixions taking place as part of dramatic performances. As a result, when newly Christianized Germanic tribes, who had little interest in classical culture, invaded from the north and took over Rome, theatre came to an end.

Dramatic Literature

Today, from the whole eleven-century period of classical theatre, only seventy scripts survive.[1] While it is typical to speak of "classical drama" as if all plays of the period were alike, they actually demonstrate considerable variety.

Tragedy

The dramatic form which developed out of dithyramb was tragedy. The Greek word *tragoidia,* from which our word "tragedy" comes, means "goat song." Scholars speculate that this kind of play carried this name because the prize won by the best set of tragedies at the Festival of Dionysus may have been a goat. Although the Greek tragedies displayed considerable variety, most were serious plays based on myths and most of them focused on the darker emotions such as pride, anger, fear, and shame. Greek tragedies usually started with a prologue in which the characters clarified the situation. During the next portion of the tragedy, the *parados,* the chorus entered, dancing and singing. The main body of the play consisted of episodes

[1]Seven tragedies by Aeschylus, seven tragedies and substantial fragments of a satyr play by Sophocles, sixteen tragedies and a satyr play by Euripides, eleven Greek Old Comedies by Aristophanes, one Greek New Comedy by Menander, twenty Roman comedies by Plautus, and six Roman comedies by Terence.

which alternated with choric segments called *stasimons*. The tragedy concluded with a scene called the *exodus* during which the characters and chorus made their exits.

Since tragedy developed out of the dithyramb, the earliest tragedies naturally focused primarily on the chorus. These plays, in fact, probably only had one actor in addition to the chorus. While the actor could represent different characters by changing masks, only one of these characters could be on stage at a given time. These early tragedies held the audience's interest, therefore, not by conflict between characters but rather by the force of poetry and the situation of a hero facing his destiny.

Aeschylus

The Suppliants by Aeschylus (525/4-456 BC) provides a sample of this kind of tragedy; although *The Suppliants* uses two actors, the scenes with dialogue between individual characters are few and the chorus itself emerges as the most important character.

Tradition says that Aeschylus introduced the use of a second speaking actor. The addition of a second actor made it easier to develop a story line in which a series of events take place. These tragedies also focused more attention on the actors and conflict between them and began to diminish the role of the chorus. Aeschylus' play *Prometheus Bound* is the best sample we have of this kind of tragedy.

Sophocles

Sophocles (496-406 BC) took the next step in tragedy's development by adding a third speaking actor. With this innovation, playwrights could present full, action-oriented stories; and again, this expansion of the importance of the speaking characters diminished the focus on the chorus. All seven of Sophocles' extant plays provide samples of this kind of tragedy.

Euripides

The third great Athenian tragedian, Euripides (484-406 BC), further decreased the importance of the tragic chorus. In his plays, the chorus frequently has very little part in the action of the play, and the choric songs often have so slight a connection with the events in the play that the chorus is almost superfluous. Furthermore, while some of Euripides' plays like *The Trojan Women* (415 BC) and *The Bacchae* are heart-wrenching in their pathos, others like *Helen* (412 BC) and *Alcestis* (438 BC) are almost like romantic comedies.

Seneca

Although the Romans also wrote tragedies, the only samples we have — those written by Lucius Annaeus Seneca (c. 4 BC-AD 65) — were intended for reading, not for staging. Seneca's tragedies, many of which he adapted from Euripides' plays, focus on sensational violence, bitter emotion, and flamboyant speeches. Although Seneca's plays were not theatre pieces, they became important to the stage when Renaissance writers, who greatly admired Roman literature, used Senecan techniques in their own plays.

Comedy

Comedy developed later than tragedy. Our word "comedy" comes from the Greek *komoidia,* which meant "revel song." The earliest form of Greek comedy we know of, represented by the plays of Aristophanes (c. 448-c. 380 BC), is known as "old comedy." Old comedy differed greatly from the tragedies of its day and also from our present-day comedies. Rather than using existing episodes from myth or history like the tragic poets, Aristophanes created his own stories. And rather than focusing on timeless human problems like the struggle against fate or the problems caused by ignorance, Aristophanes' plays dealt with topical issues from the political and social life of his day.

The didactic plot construction of old comedy provided an ideal vehicle for commenting on current events. The play usually started with a *prologue,* where the comic hero proposed a wildly improbable solution to a current problem. After the *parados,* (the entrance of the chorus) came the *agon* or "argument"; during this part of the play, antagonists attacked the idea of the protagonist who always managed to win the debate. After the agon, the chorus would lay aside their costumes and their dramatic identities and, using the playwright's words, would address the audience directly in their own persons; during this part of the comedy, called the *parabasis,* the chorus and their leader applied the theme of the play to present-day life. The parabasis used ridicule, satire, and invective to roast current politicians and heap scorn on Aristophanes' competitors. After the parabasis, the actors would perform a series of loosely related episodes in which they put into practice the wild "happy idea" of the protagonist. The comedy concluded with *komos* and *gamos,* a bawdy dance in which the characters and chorus exited, supposedly to indulge in drinking and debauchery.

Greek New Comedy

When Macedonian tyranny replaced the spirit of toleration which permitted this kind of play, old comedy came to an end. Greek new comedy, which replaced it, carried over from Aristophanes' theatre the tendency to invent story lines. In its approach to plot structure, however, it adopted the form of Euripides' romantic dramas. This combination resulted in comedies which focused on the humorous predicaments of young lovers, foolish old men, cowardly soldiers, and crafty slaves. The plots of these plays followed a chronological, cause-and-effect order, and the chorus contributed little more than entertaining scene breaks. *The Grouch* by Menander (c. 342-293 BC) is the only complete existing sample of Greek new comedy.

The Roman playwrights Titus Maccus Plautus (c. 254-184 BC) and Terence (c. 190-159 BC) adapted Greek New Comedies into Roman comedies. The plays of the two writers differ slightly; Plautus's plays are simple in plot, bawdy, and more varied in their poetic meter while Terence's are more refined and eloquent and tend to have somewhat more complicated plots. The plays of both, however, present stereotypical characters in stereotypical plots doing stereotypical comic bits. Entertainment for the masses, Roman comedies have much in common with television sitcoms.

Satyr Plays and Mime

In addition to tragedy and comedy, classical theatre also produced a variety of lesser forms. Greek tragic poets, for instance, wrote a satyr play to accompany each of their trilogies. These plays took their name from their choruses, who were costumed to represent the half-man, half-goat creatures called satyrs. They presented parodies of stories from mythology. Extant samples of satyr plays include Euripides' *Cyclops* and the fragmentary *Trackers* of Sophocles. Another theatrical form, common to both Greece and Rome, was mime. While the Romans began to put mimes into written form in the first century BC, the form was primarily an improvisational farce based on everyday life. It focused on adultery and other socially objectionable practices and used obscene language and stage business. No written samples of mime survive, but some scholars believe that mime, performed by itinerant troupes, lived on through the Dark Ages and helped spark the rebirth of theatre in the late Middle Ages and Renaissance.

Theatrical Organization

Compared with today, when most Americans watch numerous dramatic presentations every week on television and in movie theatres, the ancient Greeks had relatively few opportunities to see plays.

The City Dionysia Festival

The worship of Dionysus centered on four annual festivals. Three of these occasionally included theatrical events, and the fourth, the great City Dionysia, always featured dramatic competitions as the central element of the celebration. Poets competed for the opportunity to stage their plays. The three successful competitors were each assigned three actors and a *choregos,* a wealthy citizen who financed the production and recruited and rehearsed the chorus. Since the choice of the *choregoi* for the next festival took place just a month after the previous one, the rehearsal time for the productions lasted nearly a year. None of the people involved in the productions — playwrights, choregoi, chorus members, or actors — received enough money for their work to depend on theatre for their living. They were, therefore, amateurs who practiced their art for reasons other than monetary remuneration.

At the City Dionysia, one day was given to comedy, when five comic playwrights presented their plays. The following three days focused on tragedy; on each of these days, one of the tragic poets presented a trilogy of tragedies plus a satyr play. After the performance days, prizes were awarded and the community evaluated the conduct of the festival. The Athenians considered these events so important that they ceased all legal proceedings during the festival and even set prisoners free so they could participate. Men and women of all racial groups and social classes attended the theatre where they were given seating in accordance with their tribe, sex, and social status.

Acting as a Profession

When Alexander the Great spread Greek culture throughout the known world, many cities constructed theatres. The plays performed in these theatres had little relation to religion and were presented more often than in fifth-century Athens. Frequent productions created a demand for a regular supply of actors and led to the development of acting as a profession. Actors during this period earned their living by practicing their art. They belonged to touring theatre companies and formed guilds which regulated their behavior and terms of performance. As "servants of Dionysus," they were exempt from military duty. While some held respected places in society, actors as a group were considered disreputable characters.

Roman Theatre

As the Romans came to dominate the Mediterranean, they too began to stage plays. In Rome, as in ancient Athens, drama was at first limited to certain civic and religious festivals. As time went on, however, theatrical presentations increased in number until Romans could attend plays many days of the year. Wealthy citizens often underwrote the production expenses as an act of civic duty, personal pride, or to win popularity. Rather than overseeing the productions themselves, however, they hired professional managers. Playwrights sold the theatre managers scripts which then became the managers' property. The managers supervised companies of actors (frequently slaves), who staged the plays. Theatre in Rome had become a completely commercialized system.

Performance Conventions

In fifth-century Greece, four types of performers appeared in a dramatic production: Chorus members, speaking actors, non-speaking actors or "supernumeraries," and musicians.

The Chorus

In the beginning, the tragic chorus may have consisted of 50 men, but by Euripides' day it had diminished in number to 12 or 15. In old comedy, the chorus numbered 24. The chorus sang the portions of the script assigned to it while dancing in a rectangular formation. Sometimes the chorus would sing as a total group, while other times they divided into two semi-choruses who answered each other antiphonally. In some performances the chorus leader, functioning almost like a speaking actor, would sing or speak by himself. After the fifth century, the chorus rapidly became less important to the drama. By the time of Roman theatre, comedies frequently had no chorus at all, and the shrunken tragic choruses did little more than provide entr´act entertainment.

Speaking Actors

The speaking actors, limited in number to three men, each played several roles; they indicated changes in character by wearing different masks. The first actor, or "protagonist," focused primarily on playing the role of the play's central character. The second actor, the "antagonist," played major secondary characters, and the third actor played other speaking roles. Comedy may not have adhered quite as rigidly to the three-actor limit or may have permitted the supernumeraries more lines. With masks hiding their faces, and with large audiences seated a considerable distance away, the actors necessarily relied primarily on their voices and large, stylized gestures for characterization. Tragic actors probably used fewer and more graceful gestures, while the livelier movements of comedians included slapstick bits. Some records suggest that, as interest shifted to virtuoso acting, actors may have entertained their audiences with radically stylized vocal patterns and even orally-produced sound effects in imitation of machinery and animals.

Supernumeraries

Supernumeraries played nonspeaking roles such as the servant of Teiresias and Oedipus' children in *Oedipus the King*. Occasionally, these actors also played the roles of otherwise silent characters who had short speeches.

Musicians

Solo flute players provided music for both tragedy and comedy. These musicians stood near the chorus and played while the chorus sang and danced.

Costumes

The chorus members did not wear masks, but did wear costumes which indicated their dramatic identity. In comedy, therefore, they were costumed as animals, and in the satyr plays, as satyrs. Tragic actors wore long, close-fitting robes and a high-topped boot called a *kothurnos;* their masks indicated their characters and were not, at this point, horrible and exaggerated. The comic actors wore tights and short tunics, grotesque masks, and the phallus, an exaggerated, stylized imitation of male genitals.

During the Hellentistic Period, the actors became more demonstrative in their characterization; furthermore, their costume became more and more exaggerated. In tragedy, for instance, they wore elevated *kothurnoi,* heavy padded robes, and large masks with exaggerated features. Tradition has it that this costume so encumbered them that, if they fell down, they might have difficulty standing up again without assistance.

Roman comedy placed fewer restrictions on the number of actors. In these plays, the actors wore full head masks and costumes stereotyped to match the type of character represented — young lover, old man, courtesan, and so on. On their feet, they wore a slipper called a *soccus.* Since the plays call for a great deal of action such as running, hiding, pounding on doors, and beating other characters, these actors necessarily performed their roles with much more physical movement than their earlier Greek counterparts. Roman comedy also included flute music and songs sung by the actors.

Theatre Architecture

Temporary Theatres

In the beginning, the Athenians staged their tragedies on an open area near the temple of Dionysus. This area, called the *orchestra,* meaning "dancing place," had an altar in the center, and for the festival, the people erected a temporary tent or booth nearby in which the actors changed their costumes and masks. Audience members sat on the ground on the hillside surrounding the orchestra.

Semipermanent Theatres

In the fifth century, the Athenians constructed wooden seats for the audience; these benches, which encircled most of the orchestra, were called the *theatron,* meaning the "seeing place." On the segment of the orchestra not enclosed by audience seating, they erected a semipermanent wooden structure called the *skene.* The *skene* proper was a building which formed a backing for the actors. This structure had one or more doors which the actors used for entrances and exits. In front of the skene, raised perhaps one meter above the ground, was a flat acting area termed the *logion,* or "speaking place," which functioned as a stage for the actors. The logion had an altar, which was probably used for sacrifices which were part of the plays action, and several broad stairs, which made it easy for actors to descend to the orchestra or for the chorus to come up to the logion. Aeschylus,

17

Sophocles, and Euripides staged their plays in this simple performance area.

Permanent Theatres

In the fourth century, stone benches replaced the wooden seating of the *theatron*; this permanent theatre could seat about 14,000 spectators. The orchestra which the theatron surrounded measured about 65 feet in diameter. Next, a stone structure replaced the wooden *skene*. The roof of this stone skene was used as an acting area for the portrayal of gods. The height of the main stage area was probably about the same as in the old wooden building. The skene building still was not united with the theatron; the open areas at each end of the skene, separating it from the theatron, were called the *paradoi,* and were used for the entrance and exit of the chorus.

Theatres built during the Hellenistic period had a *logion* which was elevated about ten feet above the orchestra and was supported by a pillared structure called the *proskenion* because it was in front of the skene. High upon this elevated stage, their statures augmented with stilted kothurnoi, their bodies enlarged with padded costumes, and their trained voices issuing from behind grotesque masks, the Hellenistic actors must have been spectacular indeed.

Roman Theatres

Due in large part to conservative elements in the Roman Republic who mistrusted and resisted all things Greek, including theatre, Rome did not build its first permanent theatre until 55 BC. Prior to this time, during the lives of Plautus and Terence, the Romans constructed temporary structures for their dramatic productions. The permanent Roman theatres differed considerably from their Greek predecessors. Unlike the Greeks who used hillsides to elevate their audiences, the Romans built their theatres on flat ground and constructed steeply raked stadium seating. Since the importance of the chorus had greatly diminished, the Romans shrunk the diameter of the orchestra area and moved the stage area toward the audience so that the orchestra was now semicircular. As the orchestra diminished, the stage grew; in the Roman theatre, the stage, or *proscaenium,* elevated about five feet above the orchestra, measured 100 to 300 feet in length and 20 to 40 feet in depth. The Romans attached the *scaenae* building to the auditorium so that, unlike its Greek predecessors, these theatres were unified buildings. The Romans also fitted their theatres with awnings to protect actors, audience, and scenery from the sun and rain.

In the late Roman Empire period, theatres were sometimes designed as multipurpose amphitheatres. In these buildings, high walls enclosed the orchestra so that it could be used as an arena for gladiatorial combat, and sometimes the orchestra was even sealed so that it could be flooded and used for water ballet or imitation sea battles using small ships.

Stagecraft

Scenery

As far as we know, the Greeks and Romans used very little scenery in staging their plays. In almost every case, the action of these plays occurs out of doors in front of a single palace or row of houses. The permanent architectural facade of the Greek skene or the Roman *scaenae frons,* each with its sets of doors, provided adequate backing for these plays, and lines in the plays themselves identified the action's location.

Devices

During the fifth century, the Greeks used two technical devices. The *ekkyklema* was a platform with wheels that could be pushed out through the large central doors in the skene. The ekkyklema was used to bring on stage the bodies of characters who had been killed off-stage. The *mechane,* or "machine," was a crane-like device mounted on the skene and used to lower divine characters onto the stage. The Latin term for this effect, *deus ex machina,* meaning "the god from the machine," has come to indicate any plot device which unexpectedly rescues a hero from an otherwise impossible situation.

During the Hellenistic period, tradition says that the Greeks also used *periaktoi,* scenic devices consisting of three panels joined at the edges and mounted on a turntable. Viewed from above, the periaktoi would have looked like triangles. Artists would paint different scenes on each side of the periaktoi, and by rotating them to present a different scene to the audience, theatre technicians could suggest a different setting.

Theory of Drama

Three classical theorists made a particular impact on Western drama throughout its history: Plato (c. 427-347 BC), Aristotle (384-322 BC), and Horace (65-8 BC).

Plato

The Greek philosopher Plato argued that theatre should not be permitted in an ideal society for two reasons — it is false and it has no principles for evaluation. In the first place, Plato believed that true reality resided in ideas or ideals and that what *appears* to us to be real — animals, vegetation, manufactured goods, and even human beings — really only *imitates* the ideal animal, tree, chair, and so on. Plays, which imitate human life, are even further removed from the Truth and are therefore likely to confuse the people who watch them. In fact, Plato said, poetry — including theatre — tells lies about the gods. He insisted, for instance, that God is unchanging and not moved by anything like desire, and he therefore found it objectionable that poetry represented Zeus and the other gods as being moved by lust and changing themselves into human or other forms in order to appear to men and women.

In the second place, Plato argued that poets and actors produce their art not by logical, understandable techniques but rather by inspiration from the muses; since, he said, we cannot know whether these inspiring divinities are good or bad, and since the products — the plays and poems — move us strongly, to watch a play is to make ourselves vulnerable to potentially destructive forces.

Plato focused primarily on the relationship between theatre and society and between theatre and reality. In other words, he had an external perspective on theatre. Throughout history, many theoreticians have adopted his external viewpoint; theatre's opponents have repeated his objections to the art, and theatre's supporters have worked to refute them.

Aristotle

Plato's student, Aristotle, in his treatise on tragedy titled *The Poetics,* approached theatre from an *internal* perspective and set forth principles by which theatre could be judged. Like Plato, Aristotle considered theatre to be an imitation of human action, but unlike Plato, Aristotle defended imitation as good because the mimetic impulse is part of human nature and because people learn by imitating. In *The Poetics,* he went on to explain how plots are constructed, what kind of characters are most suitable to tragedy, and how tragedies can be evaluated. The main evaluative principle he set forth was that a play must make sense within itself. He said, for instance, that representing events on stage which are impossible in real life is not a fault as long as the playwright presents them in a way that makes them probable. Aristotle seems to have based his ideas about theatre on a careful study of existing tragedies — especially those by Sophocles. His *Poetics* established a vocabulary for discussing drama, and theorists ever since have tried to apply his ideas to the plays of their own ages. Renaissance theorists, for instance, redefined his concepts of the unities of time and action and made them fundamental principles of neoclassicism, and many twentieth-century teachers consider his concept of the "tragic flaw" basic to an understanding of tragic character.

Horace

Horace, the Roman poet and satirist, wrote a work on playwriting called *On the Poetic Art.* Whereas Aristotle primarily *explained* the workings of a play, Horace instead *prescribed* how a playwright should go about constructing a successful drama. Furthermore, rather than basing his work on a study of existing plays, Horace simply reformulated many traditional ideas about drama. As a result, while urbane and witty, *The Poetic Art* lacks the insightful authenticity of Aristotle's work. However, because most Europeans felt a greater affinity for Rome than for Greece, they gave Horace's ideas precedence over Aristotle's. Renaissance theoreticians, for instance, based most of the neoclassical approach to drama on Horace, and even today some of his concepts, such as the idea that the purpose of theatre is "to teach and to entertain," are basic to the popular understanding of drama.

Sophocles

Sophocles was born to a wealthy Athenian in Colonus, a suburb of Athens, where a local cult honored Oedipus who was believed to be buried there. Sophocles was a youth when the Greeks defeated the Persians at Marathon, and he led a chorus of boys celebrating the Greek victory over the Persians at Salamis in 480 BC.

When he entered his first tragic competition in 468 BC, he defeated Aeschylus to win first prize. Throughout his life he wrote over 120 plays. He won first place 24 times and never finished lower than second place. Of all his plays, only seven remain: *Ajax*, probably written in the early 440s BC, *Antigone*, written around 442 BC, *The Women of Trachis*, written in the 430s BC, *Oedipus the King* (for which he had to settle for second prize), first produced in 427 BC, *Electra*, written some time after 420 BC, *Philoctetes*, in 409 BC, and *Oedpius at Colonus*, produced in 401 BC after Sophocles' death.

In addition to practicing his dramatic art, Sophocles participated fully in civic affairs. He held office as imperial treasurer from 443 BC to 442 BC, and in 441 BC he became one of Athens' 10 generals, the highest elective office in the polis. He also was a priest in the cult of at least one of Athens' gods, and, when in his 80s, he served as special state commissioner. He earned himself a reputation for being successful, sociable, witty, charming, and good-tempered.

Besides popularizing a kind of tragedy which focused on the depiction of realistic characters, Sophocles is also credited with introducing painted scenery and increasing the number of principal actors in tragedy from two to three. After his death in 406 BC, the comic writer Phrynichus paid him this tribute: "Blessed is Sophocles, a happy and fortunate man who died after a long life; author of many beautiful tragedies, he came to a beautiful end and lived to see no evil day."

Oedipus the King

The Story

Sophocles' audience already knew the story of Oedipus because it had been told in two of their now-lost epics, called the *Oedipodeia* and the *Thebaid,* and had also been alluded to in the *Iliad* and the *Odyssey.* Although some details vary from version to version, the Oedipus legend goes as follows: Oedipus' ancestor, Cadmus, founded the city of Thebes. Located in central Greece, Thebes became the capital of Boeotia, which had Mount Parnassus on its northern border and Mount Cithaeron on its southern border. In the process of founding Thebes, Cadmus offended Ares, the god of war, by killing a dragon sacred to him. Ares later punished Cadmus, but the goddesses Athena and Artemis befriended him and became patrons of Thebes.

Like each of his forefathers, Laius, the great-grandson of Cadmus, became king of Thebes. An oracle warned Laius not to have any children because, if he did so, his child would murder him. Laius disregarded the warning and had a son by his wife, Jocasta. He became frightened, however, and decided to destroy the baby to avoid his prophesied fate. He pierced the infant's ankles with a spike, tied his feet together, and had Jocasta give him to a shepherd with orders to expose the child in the wilds of Mount Cithaeron. The shepherd, however, took pity on the baby and gave it to one of his friends, a shepherd of King Polybus of Corinth. The Corinthian shepherd gave the baby to the king and his wife Merope because they had no children of their own. Polybus and Merope named the baby Oedipus — "swollen foot" — because of his wounds, and raised him as their own son.

When Oedipus was a young man, someone told him he wasn't really Polybus' son. Disturbed by this accusation, Oedipus went to Apollo's shrine at Delphi on the north slopes of Mount Parnassus to inquire about his identity. The Greeks worshiped Apollo as god of music, poetry, and healing, as the Punisher of offenders, and as the Revealer of the future. Famed for his youthfulness and beauty, this mighty god was associated with the rays of the sun. The oracle ignored Oedipus' question about his parentage, but instead warned him that he would murder his father and marry his mother. Horrified, Oedipus decided never to return to Corinth, the home of his supposed parents. After leaving Delphi, Oedipus approached a crossroads at the same time as an old man who was riding in a chariot. The old man arrogantly ordered Oedipus to give way and, when the young man refused, commanded one of his servants to strike him. Enraged, Oedipus killed the old man and all of his servants except for one who escaped; the arrogant stranger was Laius, King of Thebes, and Oedipus' own father.

Oedipus traveled on to Thebes and there encountered the Sphinx — a winged monster with a woman's head and a lion's body. The Sphinx preyed on the citizens by posing a riddle, which no one could answer, and eating them when they couldn't solve it. One version of the story says that the Thebans would gather every day to try to answer the riddle, and every day they failed, and had to feed one of their number to the Sphinx. The riddle was, "What walks on four feet in the morning, two feet at noon, and three feet in the evening?" The Sphinx met her match in Oedipus, who answered that man crawls on all fours as an infant, walks on two legs as an adult, and hobbles on two legs and a cane in old age; vanquished, the Sphinx fell off a cliff and died. Jubilant at their deliverance and having recently lost their king, the Thebans rewarded Oedipus by making him king and giving him Queen Jocasta in marriage. Jocasta's brother, Creon, who had been ruling Thebes since Laius' death, graciously gave way to the newcomer. Oedipus and Jocasta had two daughters, Antigone and Ismene, and two sons, Polynices and Eteocles. Unbeknownst to Oedipus, the oracle's prophecy had come true.

Eventually, a terrible plague fell on Thebes and Oedipus sent Creon to Delphi to seek a remedy from Apollo. The oracle sent back the answer: "Find and punish the murderer of Laius." Having already delivered Thebes from the Sphinx, Oedipus eagerly took on this new challenge. In the process, however, he discovered not only the identity of the old man he killed at the crossroads, but also that he was the son of the man he had murdered and Jocasta, who had borne his children. When she learned the truth, Jocasta hanged herself, and Oedipus, having committed the two most heinous sins of patricide and incest, gouged out his eyes and, guided by his daughter Antigone, went voluntarily into exile.

Eventually, the gods decreed that they would protect the land where Oedipus was buried. Angry at Creon and his own sons who had spurned him, Oedipus refused to return to Thebes and eventually died in Colonus, where he was buried in a grove sacred to the Fates (avenging spirits and protectoresses of Athens).

Back in Thebes, it was decided that Polynices and Eteocles would rule the city in alternate years, but after the first year Eteocles refused to give way to his brother. Polynices brought an army against Thebes and the two brothers killed each other in combat. When Antigone disobeyed Creon's orders that Polynices' body be left unburied, Creon sentenced her to death. Oedipus' remaining daughter, Ismene, disappeared from legend, and the line of Cadmus came to an end.

The Plot:

In presenting the story of Oedipus, Sophocles used a late point-of-attack, a compressed time frame, a cause-and-effect relationship between scenes, and tight unity. Sophocles begins his play after many of the events of the total story have already occurred; this late point of attack means that he must fill in many background details through exposition, but it also makes the play more compact, more climactic, and therefore more exciting. To further increase the play's focus, he confines the play's action to one day in Oedipus' life, the day on which he learns his true identity. Each scene in the play occurs as a causal result of the previous scenes, and each in turn causes the next scene to occur. And all the events, characters, ideas, dialog, and spectacle in the play unify tightly around the play's one, central action: The identification and punishment of Laius' murderer. Judging from the many favorable references to *Oedipus the King* in Aristotle's *Poetics*, its strict dramatic economy made this play Aristotle's favorite tragedy.

Oedipus the King also demonstrates the typical arrangement of Greek tragedy. It begins with a prologue in which Oedipus, in conversation with two other characters, discovers what he must do to deliver Thebes from the plague. Next comes the parodos or entrance of the chorus who invoke the gods and pray for the end of the plague. Then comes the first episode during which Oedipus interviews the blind prophet Tiresias. After a choral ode (the first stasimon) follows the second episode in which Oedipus accuses Creon of conspiring against him with Tiresias and then begins to suspect that he himself may have murdered Laius. There follows the second choral stasimon and then the third episode in which Jocasta and Oedipus learn Oedipus' true identity and the enormity of their situation. After the third stasimon, in the fourth episode, the blind Oedipus carries out his promised sentence against Laius' murderer by voluntarily going into exile. The play concludes with the exodos during which all actors and the chorus exit.

Sophocles' use of the chorus in *Oedipus the King* provides a good example of a middle point in the development of classical tragedy. Unlike earlier Greek plays, such as Aeschylus' *Suppliants,* the chorus in *Oedipus* is not the central focus of the play, but unlike the later plays of Euripides, the chorus is still integral to the play's action. It functions as a character in the drama, helps intensify the mood of pathos, and — through its comments on the action — guides the audience in thinking about the events portrayed; with its dance movements and its singing it also added spectacle and beauty to the experience of its audience.

The Ideas:

Although the story of Oedipus may raise questions about fate and the relationship between human beings and the gods, and although the severity of Oedipus' punishment for committing crimes that he not only was ignorant of but even tried his best to avoid may offend our modern sense of justice, none of these ideas are central to *Oedipus the King.*

Instead, Sophocles handles the story so that it focuses on questions about knowledge and ignorance and their effect on human life. In the first place, everyone in the play is either trying to learn the truth or, in the case of Jocasta and Tiresias, to cover up the truth; and once the facts are known, Sophocles devotes the last episode to showing how knowledge affects Oedipus and the others. Furthermore, although the play mentions Athena, Artemis, Ares, and Dionysus, still Apollo, god of prophesy, dominates the play. Sophocles also uses motifs having to do with knowledge and ignorance. In the beginning, for instance, blind Tiresias knows the truth while sighted Oedipus is ignorant. In the end, however, Oedipus has become like the prophet both in his knowledge and his blindness. Furthermore, Sophocles laces the play with continual references to light and darkness, metaphors for knowledge and ignorance, and frequently alludes to sunbeams — symbols of all-knowing Apollo.

Finally, the play makes particularly effective use of "dramatic irony," the effect that occurs when an audience knows more about the characters than the characters themselves know. Since Sophocles' audience already knew the Oedpius story, they had an Apollo-like relationship to the events in the play. When we watch a mystery drama, we usually know as little as the hero and we enjoy the exercise of trying to figure out what is happening and how the story will end. In contrast, the first audience of this play had full knowledge of Oedipus' dire situation and the play's probable outcome. This knowledge permitted them to focus all their attention on the characters' behavior as conditioned by knowledge or ignorance.

During the classical period, dramatists displayed little interest in specific, idiosyncratic details about individuals; Sophocles, for instance, gives no physical description of his characters and doesn't even mention the obvious difference in age between Oedipus and his mother/wife. These dramatists focused instead on universals — those things which are true of all people in all places in all times. Oedipus, as portrayed in Sophocles' play, stands as a representative of humankind — doing our best in spite of our limited knowledge of our identities and destinies. Because of Sophocles' masterful presentation of this story, *Oedipus the King,* written two and a half millennia ago, still has power to move us.

For **Classical Theatre Timeline** see page 71 at the end of this chapter.

OEDIPUS THE KING

CHARACTERS

OEDIPUS
king of Thebes

A PRIEST
of Zeus

CREON
brother of Jocasta

A CHORUS
of Theban citizens and their LEADER

TIRESIAS
a blind prophet

JOCASTA
the queen, wife of Oedipus

A MESSENGER
from Corinth

A SHEPHERD

A MESSENGER
from inside the palace

ANTIGONE, ISMENE
daughters of Oedipus and Jocasta

Guards and attendants

Priests of Thebes

TIME AND SCENE: *The royal house of Thebes. Double doors dominate the*
facade; a stone altar stands at the center of the stage.
Many years have passed since OEDIPUS solved the riddle of the Sphinx
and ascended the throne of Thebes, and now a plague has struck the city. A
procession of priests enters; suppliants, broken and despondent, they carry
branches wound in wool and lay them on the altar.
The doors open. Guards assemble. OEDIPUS comes forward, majestic
but for a telltale limp, and slowly views the condition of his people.[1]
OEDIPUS: Oh my children, the new blood of ancient Thebes,
    why are you here? Huddling at my altar,
    praying before me, your branches wound in wool.
    Our city reeks with the smoke of burning incense,
    rings with cries for the Healer and wailing for the dead.[2]
    I thought it wrong, my children, to hear the truth
    from others, messengers. Here I am myself —
    you all know me, the world knows my fame:
    I am Oedipus.

Helping a Priest to his feet.

    Speak up, old man. Your years,
    your dignity — you should speak for the others.
    Why here and kneeling, what preys upon you so?
    Some sudden fear? some strong desire?
    You can trust me. I am ready to help,
    I'll do anything. I would be blind to misery
    not to pity my people kneeling at my feet.
PRIEST: Oh Oedipus, king of the land, our greatest power!
    You see us before you now, men of all ages
    clinging to your altars. Here are boys,
    still too weak to fly from the nest,
    and here the old, bowed down with the years,
    the holy ones — a priest of Zeus myself — and here[3]
    the picked, unmarried men, the young hope of Thebes.
    And all the rest, your great family gathers now,
    branches wreathed, massing in the squares,
    kneeling before the two temples of queen Athena[4]
    or the river-shrine where the embers glow and die
    and Apollo sees the future in the ashes.[5]
    Our city —
    look around you, see with your own eyes —
    our ship pitches wildly, cannot lift her head
    from the depths, the red waves of death . . .
    Thebes is dying. A blight on the fresh crops

[1]The stage directions have been added by the translator. The original play had very
few stage directions; they usually indicated no more than the entrance or exit of characters. The footnotes have been added by the editor.
[2]Healer: Apollo, god of healing.
[3]Zeus: King of the gods.
[4]Athena: Goddess of wisdom, daughter of Zeus, and patroness of both Athens and Thebes.
[5]Apollo: This high god was also worshipped as foreteller of the future; analyzing ashes
was a fortune-telling technique similar to reading tea leaves.

and the rich pastures, cattle sicken and die,
and the women die in labor, children stillborn,
and the plague, the fiery god of fever hurls down
on the city, his lightning slashing through us —
raging plague in all its vengeance, devastating
the house of Cadmus! And black Death luxuriates[6]
in the raw, wailing miseries of Thebes.
Now we pray to you. You cannot equal the gods,
your children know that, bending at your altar.
But we do rate you first of men,
both in the common crises of our lives
and face-to-face encounters with the gods.
You freed us from the Sphinx, you came to Thebes
and cut us loose from the bloody tribute we had paid
that harsh, brutal singer. We taught you nothing,
no skill, no extra knowledge, still you triumphed.
A god was with you, so they say, and we believe it —
you lifted up our lives.
So now again,
Oedipus, king, we bend to you, your power —
we implore you, all of us on our knees:
find us strength, rescue! Perhaps you've heard
the voice of a god or something from other men,
Oedipus . . . what do you know?
The man of experience — you see it every day —
his plans will work in a crisis, his first of all.

Act now — we beg you, best of men, raise up our city!
Act, defend yourself, your former glory!
Your country calls you savior now
for your zeal, your action years ago.
Never let us remember of your reign:
you helped us stand, only to fall once more.
Oh raise up our city, set us on our feet.
The omens were good that day you brought us joy —
be the same man today!
Rule our land, you know you have the power,
but rule a land of the living, not a wasteland.
Ship and towered city are nothing, stripped of men
alive within it, living all as one.
OEDIPUS: My children
I pity you. I see — how could I fail to see
what longings bring you here? Well I know
you are sick to death, all of you,
but sick as you are, not one is sick as I.
Your pain strikes each of you alone, each
in the confines of himself, no other. But my spirit

[6]Cadmus: Founder of Thebes; all the subsequent kings of Thebes, down to the time of
this story, were his descendants.

29

grieves for the city, for myself and all of you.
I wasn't asleep, dreaming. You haven't wakened me —
I have wept through the nights, you must know that,
groping, laboring over many paths of thought.
After a painful search I found one cure:
I acted at once. I sent Creon,
my wife's own brother, to Delphi —[7]
Apollo the Prophet's oracle — to learn
what I might do or say to save our city.

Today's the day. When I count the days gone by
it torments me . . . what is he doing?
Strange, he's late, he's gone too long.
But once he returns, then, then I'll be a traitor
if I do not do all the god makes clear.
PRIEST: Timely words. The men over there
are signaling — Creon's just arriving.
OEDIPUS:

Sighting CREON, then turning to the altar.

Lord Apollo,
let him come with a lucky word of rescue,
shining like his eyes!
PRIEST: Welcome news, I think — he's crowned, look,
and the laurel wreath is bright with berries.
OEDIPUS: We'll soon see. He's close enough to hear —

Enter CREON from the side; his face is shaded with a wreath.

Creon, prince, my kinsman, what do you bring us?
What message from the god?
CREON: Good news.
I tell you even the hardest things to bear,
if they should turn out well, all would be well.
OEDIPUS: Of course, but what were the god's *words*? There's no hope
and nothing to fear in what you've said so far.
CREON: If you want my report in the presence of these people . . .

Pointing to the priests while drawing OEDIPUS toward the palace

I'm ready now, or we might go inside.
OEDIPUS: Speak out,
speak to us all. I grieve for these, my people,
far more than I fear for my own life.
CREON: Very well,
I will tell you what I heard from the god.
Apollo commands us — he was quite clear —
"Drive the corruption from the land,
don't harbor it any longer, past all cure,

---

[7]Delphi: Located near Mount Parnassus in Phocis, an area northwest of Thebes, this was the location of a major shrine of Apollo. Apollo was believed to speak through the Delphian priests, his oracles.

don't nurse it in your soil — root it out!"
OEDIPUS: How can we cleanse ourselves — what rites?
What's the source of the trouble?
CREON: Banish the man, or pay back blood with blood.
Murder sets the plague-storm on the city.
OEDIPUS: Whose murder?
Whose fate does Apollo bring to light?
CREON: Our leader,
my lord, was once a man named Laius
before you came and put us straight on course.
OEDIPUS: I know —
or so I've heard. I never saw the man myself.
CREON: Well, he was killed, and Apollo commands us now —
he could not be more clear,
"Pay the killers back — whoever is responsible."
OEDIPUS: Where on earth are they? Where to find it now,
the trail of the ancient guilt so hard to trace?
CREON: "Here in Thebes," he said.
Whatever is sought for can be caught, you know,
whatever is neglected slips away.
OEDIPUS: But where,
in the palace, the fields or foreign soil,
where did Laius meet his bloody death?
CREON: He went to consult an oracle, Apollo said,
and he set out and never came home again.
OEDIPUS: No messenger, no fellow-traveler saw what happened?
Someone to cross-examine?
CREON: No,
they were all killed but one. He escaped,
terrified, he could tell us nothing clearly,
nothing of what he saw — just one thing.
OEDIPUS: What's that?
One thing could hold the key to it all,
a small beginning give us grounds for hope.
CREON: He said thieves attacked them — a whole band,
not single-handed, cut King Laius down.
OEDIPUS: A thief,
so daring, so wild, he'd kill a king? Impossible,
unless conspirators paid him off in Thebes.
CREON: We suspected as much. But with Laius dead
no leader appeared to help us in our troubles.
OEDIPUS: Trouble? Your *king* was murdered — royal blood!
What stopped you from tracking down the killer
then and there?
CREON: The singing, riddling Sphinx.
She . . . persuaded us to let the mystery go
and concentrate on what lay at our feet.
OEDIPUS: No,
I'll start again — I'll bring it all to light myself!

Apollo is right, and so are you, Creon,
to turn our attention back to the murdered man.
Now you have *me* to fight for you, you'll see:
I am the land's avenger by all rights,
and Apollo's champion too.
But not to assist some distant kinsman, no,
for my own sake I'll rid us of this corruption.
Whoever killed the king may decide to kill me too,
with the same violent hand — by avenging Laius
I defend myself.

To the priests.

Quickly, my children.
Up from the steps, take up your branches now.

To the guards.

One of you summon the city here before us.
tell them I'll do everything. God help us,
we will see our triumph — or our fall.

OEDIPUS and CREON enter the palace, followed by the guards.

PRIEST: Rise, my sons. The kindness we came for
Oedipus volunteers himself.
Apollo has sent his word, his oracle —
Come down, Apollo, save us, stop the plague.

The priests rise, remove their branches and exit to the side.
Enter a CHORUS, the citizens of Thebes, who have not heard the news that
CREON brings. They march around the altar, chanting.

CHORUS: Zeus!
Great welcome voice of Zeus, what do you bring?
What word from the gold vaults of Delphi
comes to brilliant Thebes? Racked with terror —
terror shakes my heart
and I cry your wild cries, Apollo, Healer of Delos
I worship you in dread ... what now, what is your price?
some new sacrifice? some ancient rite from the past
come round again each spring? —
what will you bring to birth?
Tell me, child of golden Hope
warm voice that never dies!

You are the first I call, daughter of Zeus
deathless Athena — I call your sister Artemis,[8]
heart of the market place enthroned in glory,
guardian of our earth —
I call Apollo, Archer astride the thunderheads of heaven —

[8]Artemis: Twin sister of Apollo, in whom were duplicated the feminine aspects
of his power; Artemis was goddess of deadly diseases and healing. She was also
goddess of hunting.

O triple shield against death, shine before me now!
If ever, once in the past, you stopped some ruin
launched against our walls
you hurled the flame of pain
far, far from Thebes — you gods
come now, come down once more!
No, no
the miseries numberless, grief on grief, no end —
too much to bear, we are all dying
O my people . . .
Thebes like a great army dying
and there is no sword of thought to save us, no
and the fruits of our famous earth, they will not ripen
no and the women cannot scream their pangs to birth —
screams for the Healer, children dead in the womb
and life on life goes down
you can watch them go
like seabirds winging west, outracing the day's fire
down the horizon, irresistibly
streaking on to the shores of Evening
Death
so many deaths, numberless deaths on deaths, no end —
Thebes is dying, look, her children
stripped of pity . . .
generations strewn on the ground
unburied, unwept, the dead spreading death
and the young wives and gray-haired mothers with them
cling to the altars, trailing in from all over the city —
Thebes, city of death, one long cortege
and the suffering rises
wails for mercy rise
and the wild hymn for the Healer blazes out
clashing with our sobs our cries of mourning —
O golden daughter of god, send rescue
radiant as the kindness in your eyes!
Drive him back! — the fever, the god of death
that raging god of war[9]
not armored in bronze, not shielded now, he burns me,
battle cries in the onslaught burning on —
O rout him from our borders!
Sail him, blast him out to the Sea-queen's chamber
the black Atlantic gulfs
or the northern harbor, death to all
where the Thracian surf comes crashing.
Now what the night spares he comes by day and kills —
the god of death.

O lord of the stormcloud,

---

[9]god of war: This seems to be a reference to Ares, god of war, whom Cadmus offended
during the founding of Thebes.

you who twirl the lightning, Zeus, Father,
thunder Death to nothing!

Apollo, lord of the light, I beg you —
whip your longbow's golden cord
showering arrows on our enemies — shafts of power
champions strong before us rushing on!

Artemis, Huntress,
torches flaring over the eastern ridges —
ride Death down in pain!

God of the headdress gleaming gold, I cry to you —[10]
your name and ours are one, Dionysus —
come with your face aflame with wine
your raving women's cries
your army on the march! Come with the lightning
come with torches blazing, eyes ablaze with glory!
Burn that god of death that all gods hate!

OEDIPUS enters from the palace to address the CHORUS, as if addressing the entire city of Thebes.

OEDIPUS: You pray to the gods? Let me grant your prayers.
Come, listen to me — do what the plague demands:
you'll find relief and lift your head from the depths.

I will speak out now as a stranger to the story,
a stranger to the crime. If I'd been present then,
there would have been no mystery, no long hunt
without a clue in hand. So now, counted
a native Theban years after the murder,
to all of Thebes I make this proclamation:
if any one of you knows who murdered Laius,
the son of Labdacus, I order him to reveal
the whole truth to me. Nothing to fear,
even if he must denounce himself,
let him speak up
and so escape the brunt of the charge —
he will suffer no unbearable punishment,
nothing worse than exile, totally unharmed.

OEDIPUS pauses, waiting for a reply.

Next,
if anyone knows the murderer is a stranger,
a man from alien soil, come, speak up.
I will give him a handsome reward, and lay up
gratitude in my heart for him besides.

Silence again, no reply.

[10]God . . . Dionysus: Dionysus, god of wine, fertility, and ecstasy, was also patron god of theatre.
OEDIPUS THE KING was first performed in Dionysus' temple precincts during a major festival
of this god.

But if you keep silent, if anyone panicking,
trying to shield himself or friend or kin,
rejects my offer, then hear what I will do.
I order you, every citizen of the state
where I hold throne and power: banish this man —
whoever he may be — never shelter him, never
speak a word to him, never make him partner
to your prayers, your victims burned to the gods.
Never let the holy water touch his hands.
Drive him out, each of you, from every home.
He is the plague, the heart of our corruption,
as Apollo's oracle has just revealed to me.
So I honor my obligations:
I fight for the god and for the murdered man.

Now my curse on the murderer. Whoever he is,
a lone man unknown in his crime
or one among many, let that man drag out
his life in agony, step by painful step —
I curse myself as well . . . if by any chance
he proves to be an intimate of our house,
here at my hearth, with my full knowledge,
may the curse I just called down on him strike me!
These are your orders: perform them to the last.
I command you, for my sake, for Apollo's, for this country
blasted root and branch by the angry heavens.
Even if god had never urged you on to act,
how could you leave the crime uncleansed so long?
A man so noble — your king, brought down in blood —
you should have searched. But I am the king now,
I hold the throne that he held then, possess his bed
and a wife who shares our seed . . . why, our seed
might be the same, children born of the same mother
might have created blood-bonds between us
if his hope of offspring had not met disaster —
but fate swooped at his head and cut him short.
So I will fight for him as if he were my father,[11]
stop at nothing, search the world.
to lay my hands on the man who shed his blood,
the son of Labdacus descended of Polydorus,[12]
Cadmus of old and Agenor, founder of the line:
their power and mine are one.
Oh dear gods,

[11]"So I will . . . father": The audience knows that Laius was indeed Oedipus'
father, but Oedipus does not know it. The resulting dramatic irony adds interest
to the play.
[12]Labdacus . . . Agenor: Laius was the son of Labdacus who was the son of
Polydorus who was the son of Cadmus, founder of Thebes, who was the son of
Agenor. Agenor's parents were Libya and Poseidon, god of the sea; Libya was
the daughter of the woman Io and the god Zeus.

my curse on those who disobey these orders!
Let no crops grow out of the earth for them —
shrivel their women, kill their sons,
burn them to nothing in this plague
that hits us now, or something even worse.
But you, loyal men of Thebes who approve my actions,
may our champion, Justice, may all the gods
be with us, fight beside us to the end!
LEADER: In the grip of your curse, my king, I swear
I'm not the murderer, I cannot point him out.
As for the search, Apollo pressed it on us —
he should name the killer.
OEDIPUS: Quite right,
but to force the gods to act against their will —
no man has the power.
LEADER: Then if I might mention
the next best thing . . .
OEDIPUS: The third best too —
don't hold back, say it.
LEADER: I still believe . . .
Lord Tiresias sees with the eyes of Lord Apollo.
Anyone searching for the truth, my king,
might learn it from the prophet, clear as day.
OEDIPUS: I've not been slow with that. On Creon's cue
I sent the escorts, twice, within the hour.
I'm surprised he isn't here.
LEADER: We need him —
without him we have nothing but old, useless rumors.
OEDIPUS: Which rumors? I'll search out every word.
LEADER: Laius was killed, they say, by certain travelers.
OEDIPUS: I know — but not one can find the murderer.
LEADER: If the man has a trace of fear in him
he won't stay silent long,
not with your curses ringing in his ears.
OEDIPUS: He didn't flinch at murder,
he'll never flinch at words.

Enter TIRESIAS, the blind prophet, led by a boy with escorts in attendance.
He remains at a distance.

LEADER: Here is the one who will convict him, look,
they bring him on at last, the seer, the man of god.
the truth lives inside him, him alone.
OEDIPUS: O Tiresias,
master of all the mysteries of our life,
all you teach and all you dare not tell,
signs in the heavens, signs that walk the earth!
Blind as you are, you can feel all the more
what sickness haunts our city. You, my lord,
are the one shield, the one savior we can find.

We asked Apollo — perhaps the messengers
haven't told you — he sent his answer back:
"Relief from the plague can only come one way.
Uncover the murderers of Laius,
put them to death or drive them into exile."
So I get you, grudge us nothing now, no voice,
no message plucked from the birds, the embers[13]
or the other mantic ways within your grasp.
Rescue yourself, your city, rescue me —
rescue everything infected by the dead.
We are in your hands. For a man to help others
with all his gifts and native strength:
that is the noblest work.
TIRESIAS: How terrible — to see the truth
when the truth is only pain to him who sees![14]
I knew it well, but I put it from my mind,
else I never would have come.
OEDIPUS: What's this? Why so grim, so dire?
TIRESIAS: Just send me home. You bear your burdens,
I'll bear mine. It's better that way,
please believe me.
OEDIPUS: Strange response . . . unlawful,
unfriendly too to the state that bred and reared you —
you withhold the word of god.
TIRESIAS: I fail to see
that your own words are so well-timed.
I'd rather not have the same thing said of me . . .
OEDIPUS: For the love of god, don't turn away,
not if you know something. We beg you,
all of us on our knees.
TIRESIAS: None of you knows —
and I will never reveal my dreadful secrets,
not to say your own.
OEDIPUS: What? You know and you won't tell?
You're bent on betraying us, destroying Thebes?
TIRESIAS: I'd rather not cause pain for you or me.
So why this . . . useless interrogation?
You'll get nothing from me.
OEDIPUS: Nothing! You,
you scum of the earth, you'd enrage a heart of stone!
You won't talk? Nothing moves you?
Out with it, once and for all!
TIRESIAS: You criticize my temper . . . unaware
of the one *you* live with, you revile me.

---

[13]birds: Analyzing the flight patterns of birds was another way of foretelling the future.
Because of this relationship between birds and discovering truth, Sophocles uses birds
and flight as another unifying motif. Even the Sphinx was, in part, a monstrous bird.
[14]"How terrible . . . who sees": This speech of the blind prophet combines some of the
central ideas and motifs of the play: sight contrasted with blindness, knowledge contrasted with ignorance, and pain contrasted with comfort.

OEDIPUS: Who could restrain his anger hearing you?
    What outrage — you spurn the city!
TIRESIAS: What will come will come.
    Even if I shroud it all in silence.
OEDIPUS: What will come? You're bound to *tell* me that.
TIRESIAS: I will say no more. Do as you like, build your anger
    to whatever pitch you please, rage your worst —
OEDIPUS: Oh I'll let loose, I have such fury in me —
    now I see it all. You helped hatch the plot,
    you did the work, yes, short of killing him
    with your own hands — and given eyes I'd say
    you did the killing single-handed!
TIRESIAS: Is that so!
    I charge you, then, submit to that decree
    you just laid down: from this day onward
    speak to no one, not these citizens, not myself.
    You are the curse, the corruption of the land!
OEDIPUS: You, shameless —
    aren't you appalled to start up such a story?
    You think you can get away with this?
TIRESIAS: I have already.
    The truth with all its power lives inside me.
OEDIPUS: Who primed you for this? Not your prophet's trade.
TIRESIAS: You did, you forced me, twisted it out of me.
OEDIPUS: What? Say it again — I'll understand it better.
TIRESIAS: Didn't you understand, just now?
    Or are you tempting me to talk?
OEDIPUS: No, I can't say I grasped your meaning.
    Out with it, again!
TIRESIAS: I say you are the murderer you hunt.
OEDIPUS: That obscenity, twice — by god, you'll pay.
TIRESIAS: Shall I say more, so you can really rage?
OEDIPUS: Much as you want. Your words are nothing —
    futile.
TIRESIAS: You cannot imagine . . . I tell you,
    you and your loved ones live together in infamy,
    you cannot see how far you've gone in guilt.
OEDIPUS: You think you can keep this up and never suffer?
TIRESIAS: Indeed, if the truth has any power.
OEDIPUS: It does
    but not for you, old man. You've lost your power,
    stone-blind, stone-deaf — senses, eyes blind as stone!
TIRESIAS: I pity you, flinging at me the very insults
    each man here will fling at you so soon.
OEDIPUS: Blind,
    lost in the night, endless night that nursed you!
    You can't hurt me or anyone else who sees the light —
    you can never touch me.
TIRESIAS: True, it is not your fate
    to fall at my hands. Apollo is quite enough,

and he will take some pains to work this out.
OEDIPUS: Creon! Is this conspiracy his or yours?
TIRESIAS: Creon is not your downfall, no, you are your own.
OEDIPUS: O power —
    wealth and empire, skill outstripping skill
    in the heady rivalries of life,
    what envy lurks inside you! Just for this,
    the crown the city gave me — I never sought it,
    they laid it in my hands — for this alone, Creon,
    the soul of trust, my loyal friend from the start
    steals against me . . . so hungry to overthrow me
    he sets this wizard on me, this scheming quack,
    this fortune-teller peddling lies, eyes peeled
    for his own profit — seer blind in his craft!

    Come here, you pious fraud. Tell me,
    when did you ever prove yourself a prophet?
    When the Sphinx, that chanting Fury kept her deathwatch here,[15]
    why silent then, not a word to set our people free?
    There was a riddle, not for some passer-by to solve —
    it cried out for a prophet. Where were you?
    Did you rise to the crisis? Not a word,
    you and your birds, your gods — nothing.
    No, but I came by, Oedipus the ignorant,
    I stopped the Sphinx! With no help from the birds,
    the flight of my own intelligence hit the mark.

    And this is the man you'd try to overthrow?
    You think you'll stand by Creon when he's king?
    You and the great mastermind —
    you'll pay in tears, I promise you, for this,
    this witch-hunt. If you didn't look so senile
    the lash would teach you what your scheming means!
LEADER: I would suggest his words were spoken in anger,
    Oedipus . . . yours too, and it isn't what we need.
    The best solution to the oracle, the riddle
    posed by god — we should look for that.
TIRESIAS: You are the king no doubt, but in one respect,
    at least, I am your equal: the right to reply.
    I claim that privilege too.
    I am not your slave. I serve Apollo.
    I don't need Creon to speak for me in public.
    So,
    you mock my blindness? Let me tell you this.
    You with your precious eyes,
    you're blind to the corruption of your life,
    to the house you live in, those you live with —
    who *are* your parents? Do you know? All unknowing
    you are the scourge of your own flesh and blood,

---

[15]Fury: Oedipus likens the Sphinx to the Furies, avenging spirits.

the dead below the earth and the living here above,[16]
and the double lash of your mother and your father's curse
will whip you from this land one day, their footfall
treading you down in terror, darkness shrouding
your eyes that now can see the light!
Soon, soon
you'll scream aloud — what haven won't reverberate?
What rock of Cithaeron won't scream back in echo?[17]
That day you learn the truth about your marriage,
the wedding-march that sang you into your halls,
the lusty voyage home to the fatal harbor!
And a crowd of other horrors you'd never dream
will level you with yourself and all your children.

There. Now smear us with insults — Creon, myself
and every word I've said. No man will ever
be rooted from the earth as brutally as you.
OEDIPUS: Enough! Such filth from him? Insufferable —
what, still alive? Get out —
faster, back where you came from — vanish!
TIRESIAS: I would never have come if you hadn't called me here.
OEDIPUS: If I thought you would blurt out such absurdities,
you'd have died waiting before I'd had you summoned.
TIRESIAS: Absurd, am I! To you, not to your parents:
the ones who bore you found me sane enough.
OEDIPUS: Parents — who? Wait . . . who is my father?
TIRESIAS: This day will bring your birth and your destruction.
OEDIPUS: Riddles — all you can say are riddles, murk and darkness.
TIRESIAS: Ah, but aren't you the best man alive at solving riddles?
OEDIPUS: Mock me for that, go on, and you'll reveal my greatness.
TIRESIAS: Your great good fortune, true, it was your ruin.
OEDIPUS: Not if I saved the city — what do I care?
TIRESIAS: Well then, I'll be going.

To his attendant.

Take me home, boy.
OEDIPUS: Yes, take him away. You're a nuisance here.
Out of the way, the irritation's gone.

Turning his back on TIRESIAS, moving toward the palace.

TIRESIAS: I will go,
once I have said what I came here to say.
I will never shrink from the anger in your eyes —
you can't destroy me. Listen to me closely:
the man you've sought so long, proclaiming,
cursing up and down, the murderer of Laius —
he is here. A stranger,

---

[16]"dead below the earth": Hades, the abode of the dead, was believed to be underground.
[17]Cithaeron: A mountain south of Thebes, between Thebes and Corinth.

40

you may think, who lives among you,
he soon will be revealed a native Theban
but he will take no joy in the revelation.
Blind who now has eyes, beggar who now is rich,
he will grope his way toward a foreign soil,
a stick tapping before him step by step.

OEDIPUS enters the palace.

Revealed at last, brother and father both
to the children he embraces, to his mother
son and husband both — he sowed the loins
his father sowed, he spilled his father's blood!

Go in and reflect on that, solve that.
And if you find I've lied
from this day onward call the prophet blind.

TIRESIAS and the boy exit to the side.

CHORUS: Who —
who is the man the voice of god denounces
resounding out of the rocky gorge of Delphi?
The horror too dark to tell,
whose ruthless bloody hands have done the work?
His time has come to fly
to outrace the stallions of the storm
his feet a streak of speed —
Cased in armor, Apollo son of the Father[18]
lunges on him, lightning-bolts afire!
And the grim unerring Furies[19]
closing for the kill.
Look,
the word of god has just come blazing
flashing off Parnassus' snowy heights![20]
that man who left no trace —
after him, hunt him down with all our strength!
Now under bristling timber
up through rocks and caves he stalks
like the wild mountain bull —
cut off from men, each step an agony, frenzied, racing blind
but he cannot outrace the dread voices of Delphi
ringing out of the heart of Earth,
the dark wings beating around him shrieking doom
the doom that never dies, the terror —
The skilled prophet scans the birds and shatters me with terror!
I can't accept him, can't deny him, don't know what to say,
I'm lost, and the wings of dark foreboding beating —

[18]Apollo: Son of Father Zeus, this god also over-saw the punishment of offenders.
[19]Furies: Winged, female avenging spirits who punished murderers.
[20]Parnassus: This mountain, located next to Delphi, was sacred to the Muses (goddesses of the arts), Apollo, and Dionysus.

I cannot see what's come, what's still to come . . .
and what could breed a blood feud between
Laius' house and the son of Polybus?[21]
I know of nothing, not in the past and not now,
no charge to bring against our king, no cause
to attack his fame that rings throughout Thebes —
not without proof — not for the ghost of Laius,
not to avenge a murder gone without a trace.

Zeus and Apollo know, they know, the great masters
of all the dark and depth of human life.
But whether a mere man can know the truth,
whether a seer can fathom more than I —
there is no test, no certain proof
though matching skill for skill
a man can outstrip a rival. No, not till I see
these charges proved will I side with his accusers.[22]
We saw him then, when the she-hawk swept against him,[23]
saw with our own eyes his skill, his brilliant triumph —
there was the test — he was the joy of Thebes!
Never will I convict my king, never in my heart.

Enter CREON from the side.

CREON: My fellow-citizens, I hear King Oedipus
    levels terrible charges at me. I had to come.
    I resent it deeply. If, in the present crisis,
    he thinks he suffers any abuse from me,
    anything I've done or said that offers him
    the slightest injury, why, I've no desire
    to linger out this life, my reputation in ruins.
    The damage I'd face from such an accusation
    is nothing simple. No, there's nothing worse:
    branded a traitor in the city, a traitor
    to all of you and my good friends.
LEADER: True,
    but a slur might have been forced out of him,
    by anger perhaps, not any firm conviction.
CREON: The charge was made in public, wasn't it?
    I put the prophet up to spreading lies?
LEADER: Such things were said . . .
    I don't know with what intent, if any.
CREON: Was his glance steady, his mind right
    when the charge was brought against me?
LEADER: I really couldn't say. I never look
    to judge the ones in power.

The doors open. OEDIPUS enters.

[21]Polybus: King of Corinth, Oedipus' supposed father.
[22]his: Oedipus'.
[23]she-hawk: The Sphinx.

Wait,
here's Oedipus now.
OEDIPUS: You — here? You have the gall
to show your face before the palace gates?
You, plotting to kill me, kill the king —
I see it all, the marauding thief himself
scheming to steal my crown and power!
Tell me,
in god's name, what did you take me for,
coward or fool, when you spun out your plot?
Your treachery — you think I'd never detect it
creeping against me in the dark? Or sensing it,
not defend myself? Aren't you the fool,
you and your high adventure. Lacking numbers,
powerful friends, out for the big game of empire —
you need riches, armies to bring that quarry down!
CREON: Are you quite finished? It's your turn to listen
for just as long as you've . . . instructed me.
Hear me out, then judge me on the facts.
OEDIPUS: You've a wicked way with words, Creon,
but I'll be slow to learn — from you.
I find you a menace, a great burden to me.
CREON: Just one thing, hear me out in this.
OEDIPUS: Just one thing,
don't tell *me* you're not the enemy, the traitor.
CREON: Look, if you think crude, mindless stubborness
such a gift, you've lost your sense of balance.
OEDIPUS: If you think you can abuse a kinsman,
then escape the penalty, you're insane.
CREON: Fair enough, I grant you. But this injury
you say I've done you, what is it?
OEDIPUS: Did you induce me, yes or no,
to send for that sanctimonious prophet?
CREON: I did. And I'd do the same again.
OEDIPUS: All right then, tell me, how long is it now
since Laius . . .
CREON: Laius — what did *he* do?
OEDIPUS: Vanished,
swept from sight, murdered in his tracks.
CREON: The count of the years would run you far back . . .
OEDIPUS: And that far back, was the prophet at his trade?
CREON: Skilled as he is today, and just as honored.
OEDIPUS: Did he ever refer to me then, at that time?
CREON: No,
never, at least, when I was in his presence.
OEDIPUS: But you did investigate the murder, didn't you?
CREON: We did our best, of course, discovered nothing.
OEDIPUS: But the great seer never accused me then — why not?
CREON: I don't know. And when I don't, *I* keep quiet.
OEDIPUS: You do know this, you'd tell it too —

if you had a shred of decency.
CREON: What?
If I know, I won't hold back.
OEDIPUS: Simply this:
if the two of you had never put heads together,
we would never have heard about *my* killing Laius.
CREON: If that's what he says . . . well, you know best.
But now I have a right to learn from you
as you just learned from me.
OEDIPUS: Learn your fill,
you never will convict me of the murder.
CREON: Tell me, you're married to my sister, aren't you?
OEDIPUS: A genuine discovery — there's no denying that.
CREON: And you rule the land with her, with equal power?
OEDIPUS: She receives from me whatever she desires.
CREON: And I am the third, all of us are equals?
OEDIPUS: Yes, and it's there you show your stripes —
you betray a kinsman.
CREON: Not at all.
Not if you see things calmly, rationally,
as I do. Look at it this way first:
who in his right mind would rather rule
and live in anxiety than sleep in peace?
Particularly if he enjoys the same authority.
Not I, I'm not the man to yearn for kingship,
not with a king's power in my hands. Who would?
No one with any sense of self-control,
not a fear in the world. But if I wore the crown . . .
there'd be many painful duties to perform,
hardly to my taste.
How could kingship
please me more than influence, power
without a qualm? I'm not that deluded yet,
to reach for anything but privilege outright,
profit free and clear.
Now all men sing my praises, all salute me,
now all who request your favors curry mine.
I am their best hope: success rests in me.
Why give up that, I ask you, and borrow trouble?
A man of sense, someone who sees things clearly
would never resort to treason.
No, I have no lust for conspiracy in me,
nor could I ever suffer one who does.

Do you want proof? Go to Delphi yourself,
examine the oracle and see if I've reported
the message word-for-word. This too:
if you detect that I and the clairvoyant[24]

[24]clairvoyant: One who sees what most people can't; in this case, Tiresias.

have plotted anything in common, arrest me,
execute me. Not on the strength of one vote,
two in this case, mine was well as yours.
But don't convict me on sheer unverified surmise.
How wrong it is to take the good for bad,
purely at random, or take the bad for good.
But reject a friend, a kinsman? I would as soon
tear out the life within us, priceless life itself.
You'll learn this well, without fail, in time.
Time alone can bring the just man to light —
the criminal you can spot in one short day.
LEADER: Good advice,
my lord, for anyone who wants to avoid disaster.
Those who jump to conclusions may go wrong.
OEDIPUS: When my enemy moves against me quickly,
plots in secret, I move quickly too, I must,
I plot and pay him back. Relax my guard a moment,
waiting his next move — he wins his objective,
I lose mine.
CREON: What do you want?
You want me banished?
OEDIPUS: No, I want you dead.
CREON: Just to show how ugly a grudge can . . .
OEDIPUS: So,
still stubborn? You don't think I'm serious?
CREON: I think you're insane.
OEDIPUS: Quite sane — in my behalf.
CREON: Not just as much in mine?
OEDIPUS: You — my mortal enemy?
CREON: What if you're wholly wrong?
OEDIPUS: No matter — I must rule.
CREON: Not if you rule unjustly.
OEDIPUS: Hear him, Thebes, my city!
CREON: My city too, not yours alone!
LEADER: Please, my lords.

Enter JOCASTA from the palace

Look, Jocasta's coming,
and just in time too. With her help
you must put this fighting of yours to rest.
JOCASTA: Have you no sense? Poor misguided men,
such shouting — why this public outburst?
Aren't you ashamed, with the land so sick,
to stir up private quarrels?

To OEDIPUS.

Into the palace now. And Creon, you go home.
Why make such a furor over nothing?
CREON: My sister, it's dreadful. Oedipus, your husband,
he's bent on a choice of punishments for me,

45

banishment from the fatherland or death.
OEDIPUS: Precisely. I caught him in the act, Jocasta,
plotting, about to stab me in the back.
CREON: Never — curse me, let me die and be damned
if I've done you any wrong you charge me with.
JOCASTA: Oh god, believe it, Oedipus,
honor the solemn oath he swears to heaven.
Do it for me, for the sake of all your people.

The CHORUS begins to chant.

CHORUS: Believe it, be sensible
give way, my king, I beg you!
OEDIPUS: What do you want from me, concessions?
CHORUS: Respect him — he's been no fool in the past
and now he's strong with the oath he swears to god.
OEDIPUS: You know what you're asking?
CHORUS: I do.
OEDIPUS: Then out with it!
CHORUS: The man's your friend, your kin, he's under oath —
don't cast him out, disgraced
branded with guilt on the strength of hearsay only.
OEDIPUS: Know full well, if that is what you want
you want me dead or banished from the land.
CHORUS: Never —
no, by the blazing Sun, first god of the heavens![25]
Stripped of the gods, stripped of loved ones,
let me die by inches if that ever crossed my mind.
But the heart inside me sickens, dies as the land dies
and now on top of the old griefs you pile this,
your fury — both of you!
OEDIPUS: Then let him go,
even if it does lead to my ruin, my death
or my disgrace, driven from Thebes for life.
It's you, not him I pity — your words move me.
He, wherever he goes, my hate goes with him.
CREON: Look at you, sullen in yielding, brutal in your rage —
you will go too far. It's perfect justice:
natures like yours are hardest on themselves.
OEDIPUS: Then leave me alone — get out!
CREON: I'm going.
You're wrong, so wrong. These men know I'm right.

Exit to the side. The CHORUS turns to JOCASTA.

CHORUS: Why do you hesitate, my lady
why not help him in?
JOCASTA: Tell me what's happened first.
CHORUS: Loose, ignorant talk started dark suspicions
and a sense of injustice cut deeply too.

[25]Sun: The sun god was Helius, but Apollo was associated with the sun's rays.

JOCASTA: On both sides?
CHORUS: Oh yes.
JOCASTA: What did they say?
CHORUS: Enough, please, enough! The land's so racked already
    or so it seems to me . . .
    End the trouble here, just where they left it.
OEDIPUS: You see what comes of your good intentions now?
    And all because you tried to blunt my anger.
CHORUS: My king,
    I've said it once, I'll say it time and again —
    I'd be insane, you know it,
    senseless, ever to turn my back on you.
    You who set our beloved land — storm-tossed, shattered —
    straight on course. Now again, good helmsman,
    steer us through the storm!

The CHORUS draws away, leaving OEDIPUS and JOCASTA side by side.

JOCASTA: For the love of god,
    Oedipus, tell me too, what is it?
    Why this rage? You're so unbending.
OEDIPUS: I will tell you, I respect you, Jocasta,
    much more than these men here . . .

Glancing at the CHORUS.

    Creon's to blame, Creon schemes against me.
JOCASTA: Tell me clearly, how did the quarrel start?
OEDIPUS: He says *I* murdered Laius — I am guilty.
JOCASTA: How does he know? Some secret knowledge
    or simply hearsay?
OEDIPUS: Oh, he sent his prophet in
    to do his dirty work. You know Creon,
    Creon keeps his own lips clean.
JOCASTA: A prophet?
    Well then, free yourself of every charge!
    Listen to me and learn some peace of mind:
    no skill in the world,
    nothing human can penetrate the future.
    Here is proof, quick and to the point.

    An oracle came to Laius one fine day
    (I won't say from Apollo himself
    but his underlings, his priests) and it declared
    that doom would strike him down at the hands of a son,
    our son, to be born of our own flesh and blood. But Laius,
    so the report goes at least, was killed by strangers,
    thieves, at a place where three roads meet . . . my son —
    he wasn't three days old and the boy's father
    fastened his ankles, had a henchman fling him away
    on a barren, trackless mountain.
    There, you see?
    Apollo brought neither things to pass. My baby

no more murdered his father than Laius suffered —
his wildest fear — death at his own son's hands.
That's how the seers and all their revelations
mapped out the future. Brush them from your mind.
Whatever the god needs and seeks
he'll bring to light himself, with ease.

OEDIPUS: Strange,
hearing you just now . . . my mind wandered,
my thoughts racing back and forth.

JOCASTA: What do you mean? Why so anxious, startled?

OEDIPUS: I thought I heard you say that Laius
was cut down at a place where three roads meet.

JOCASTA: That was the story. It hasn't died out yet.

OEDIPUS: Where did this thing happen? Be precise.

JOCASTA: A place called Phocis, where two branching roads,[26]
one from Daulia, one from Delphi,
come together — a crossroads.

OEDIPUS: When? How long ago?

JOCASTA: The heralds no sooner reported Laius dead
than you appeared and they hailed you king of Thebes.

OEDIPUS: My god, my god — what have you planned to do to me?

JOCASTA: What, Oedipus? What haunts you so?

OEDIPUS: Not yet.
Laius — how did he look? Describe him.
Had he reached his prime?

JOCASTA: He was swarthy,
and the gray had just begun to streak his temples,
and his build . . . wasn't far from yours.

OEDIPUS: Oh no, no,
I think I've just called down a dreadful curse
upon myself — I simply didn't know!

JOCASTA:What are you saying? I shudder to look at you.

OEDIPUS: I have a terrible fear the blind seer can see.
I'll know in a moment. One thing more —

JOCASTA: Anything,
afraid as I am — ask, I'll answer, all I can.

OEDIPUS: Did he go with a light or heavy escort,
several men-at-arms, like a lord, a king?

JOCASTA: There were five in the party, a herald among them,
and a single wagon carrying Laius.

OEDIPUS: Ai —
now I can see it all, clear as day.
Who told you all this at the time, Jocasta?

JOCASTA: A servant who reached home, the lone survivor.

OEDIPUS: So, could he still be in the palace — even now?

JOCASTA: No indeed. Soon as he returned from the scene
and saw you on the throne with Laius dead and gone,

[26]"A place . . . a crossroads": At this spot in the central Greek province of Phocis, roads met which led to Delphi, to Daulis located northeast of Delphi, and to Thebes located to the southeast.

he knelt and clutched my hand, pleading with me
to send him into the hinterlands, to pasture,
far as possible, out of sight of Thebes.
I sent him away. Slave though he was,
he earned that favor — and much more.
OEDIPUS: Can we bring him back, quickly?
JOCASTA: Easily. Why do you want him so?
OEDIPUS: I am afriad,
Jocasta, I have said too much already.
that man — I've got to see him.
JOCASTA: Then he'll come.
But even I have a right, I'd like to think,
to know what's torturing you, my lord.
OEDIPUS: And so you shall — I can hold nothing back from you,
now I've reached this pitch of dark foreboding.
Who means more to me than you? Tell me,
whom would I turn toward but you
As I go through all this?

My father was Polybus, king of Corinth.
My mother, a Dorian, Merope. And I was held[27]
the prince of the realm among the people there,
till something struck me out of nowhere,
something strange . . . worth remarking perhaps,
hardly worth the anxiety I gave it.
Some man at a banquet who had drunk too much
shouted out — he was far gone, mind you —
that I am not my father's son. Fighting words!
I barely restrained myself that day
but early the next I went to mother and father,
questioned them closely, and they were enraged
at the accusation and the fool who let it fly.
So as for my parents I was satisfied,
but still this thing kept gnawing at me,
the slander spread — I had to make my move.
And so,
unknown to mother and father I set out for Delphi,
and the god Apollo spurned me, sent me away
denied the facts I came for,
but first he flashed before my eyes a future
great with pain, terror, disaster — I can hear him cry,
"You are fated to couple with your mother, you will bring
a breed of children into the light no man can bear to see —
you will kill your father, the one who gave you life!"
I heard all that and ran. I abandoned Corinth,
from that day on I gauged its landfall only
by the stars, running, always running

[27]a Dorian: Doris was an area in central Greece between Mt. Parnassus on the south
and Mt. Oeta on the north.

toward some place where I would never see
the shame of all those oracles come true.
And as I fled I reached that very spot
where the great king, you say, met his death.
Now, Jocasta, I will tell you all.
Making my way toward this triple crossroad
I began to see a herald, then a brace of colts
drawing a wagon, and mounted on the bench . . . a man,
just as you've described him, coming face-to-face,
and the one in the lead and the old man himself
were about to thrust me off the road — brute force —
and the one shouldering me aside, the driver,
I strike him in anger! — and the old man, watching me
coming up along his wheels — he brings down
his prod, two prongs straight at my head!
I paid him back with interest!
Short work, by god — with one blow of the staff
in this right hand I knock him out of his high seat,
roll him out of the wagon, sprawling headlong —
I killed them all — every mother's son!

Oh, but if there is any blood-tie
between Laius and this stranger . . .
what man alive more miserable than I?
More hated by the gods? *I* am the man
no alien, no citizen welcomes to his house,
law forbids it — not a word to me in public,
driven out of every hearth and home.
And all these curses I — no one but I
brought down these piling curses on myself!
And you, his wife, I've touched your body with these,
the hands that killed your husband cover you with blood.

Wasn't I born for torment? Look me in the eyes!
I am abomination — heart and soul!
I must be exiled, and even in exile
never see my parents, never set foot
on native ground again. Else I am doomed
to couple with my mother and cut my father down . . .
Polybus who reared me, gave me life.
But why, why?
Wouldn't a man of judgment say — and wouldn't he be right —
some savage power has brought this down upon my head?

Oh no, not that, you pure and awesome gods,
never let me see that day! Let me slip
from the world of men, vanish without a trace
before I see myself stained with such corruption,
stained to the heart.
LEADER: My lord, you fill our hearts with fear.
But at least until you question the witness,

do take hope.
OEDIPUS: Exactly. He is my last hope —
　I am waiting for the shepherd. He is crucial.
JOCASTA: And once he appears, what then? Why so urgent?
OEDIPUS: I will tell you. If it turns out that his story
　matches yours, I've escaped the worst.
JOCASTA: What did I say? What struck you so?
OEDIPUS: You said *thieves* —
　he told you a whole band of them murdered Laius.
　So, if he still holds to the same number,
　I cannot be the killer. One can't equal many.
　But if he refers to one man, one alone,
　clearly the scales come down on me:
　I am guilty.
JOCASTA: Impossible. Trust me,
　I told you precisely what he said,
　and he can't retract it now;
　the whole city heard it, not just I.
　And even if he should vary his first report
　by one man more or less, still, my lord,
　he could never make the murder of Laius
　truly fit the prophecy. Apollo was explicit:
　my son was doomed to kill my husband . . . my son,
　poor defenseless thing, he never had a chance
　to kill his father. They destroyed him first.

　So much for prophecy. It's neither here nor there.
　From this day on, I wouldn't look right or left.
OEDIPUS: True, true. Still, that shepherd,
　someone fetch him — now!
JOCASTA: I'll send at once. But do let's go inside.
　I'd never displease you, least of all in this.

OEDIPUS and JOCASTA enter the palace.

CHORUS: Destiny guide me always
　Destiny find me filled with reverence
　pure in word and deed.
　Great laws tower above us, reared on high
　born for the brilliant vault of heaven —
　Olympian Sky their only father, [28]
　nothing mortal, no man gave them birth,
　their memory deathless, never lost in sleep:
　within them lives a mighty god, the god does not
　grow old.

　Pride breeds the tyrant
　violent pride, gorging, crammed to bursting

[28]Olympian Sky: Mount Olympus, in northeastern Greece, was the home of the gods.
The Chorus says that the laws of justice, order, and destiny come from an impersonal
source that is even above the gods themselves.

with all that is overripe and rich with ruin —
clawing up to the heights, headlong pride
crashes down the abyss — sheer doom!
No footing helps, all foothold lost and gone.
But the healthy strife that makes the city strong —
I pray that god will never end that wrestling:
god, my champion, I will never let you go.
But if any man comes striding, high and mighty
in all he says and does,
no fear of justice, no reverence
for the temples of the gods —
let a rough doom tear him down,
repay his pride, breakneck, ruinous pride!
If he cannot reap his profits fairly
cannot restrain himself from outrage —
mad, laying hands on the holy things untouchable!

Can such a man, so desperate, still boast
he can save his life from the flashing bolts of god?
If all such violence goes with honor now
why join the sacred dance?

Never again will I go reverent to Delphi,
the inviolate heart of Earth
or Apollo's ancient oracle at Abae[29]
or Olympia of the fires —
unless these prophecies all come true
for all mankind to point toward in wonder.
King of kings, if you deserve your titles
Zeus, remember, never forget!
You and your deathless, everlasting reign.

They are dying, the old oracles sent to Laius,
now our masters strike them off the rolls.
Nowhere Apollo's golden glory now —
the gods, the gods go down.

Enter JOCASTA from the palace, carrying a suppliant's branch wound in wool.

JOCASTA: Lords of the realm, it occurred to me,
just now, to visit the temples of the gods,
so I have my branch in hand and incense too.

Oedipus is beside himself. Racked with anguish,
no longer a man of sense, he won't admit
the latest prophecies are hollow as the old —
he's at the mercy of every passing voice
if the voice tells of terror.
I urge him gently, nothing seems to help,
so I turn to you, Apollo, you are nearest.

[29]Abae: One of Apollo's many minor shrines.

Placing her branch on the altar, while an old herdsman enters from the side, not the one just summoned by the King but an unexpected MESSENGER from Corinth.

> I come with prayers and offerings . . . I beg you,
> cleanse us, set us free of defilement!
> Look at us, passengers in the grip of fear,
> watching the pilot of the vessel go to pieces.

MESSENGER:

Approaching JOCASTA and the CHORUS.

> Strangers, please, I wonder if you could lead us
> to the palace of the king . . . I think it's Oedipus.
> Better, the man himself — you know where he is?

LEADER: This is his palace, stranger. He's inside.
> But here is his queen, his wife and mother
> of his children.

MESSENGER: Blessings on you, noble queen,
> queen of Oedipus crowned with all your family —
> blessings on you always!

JOCASTA: And the same to you, stranger, you deserve it
> such a greeting. But what have you come for?
> Have you brought us news?

MESSENGER: Wonderful news —
> for the house, my lady, for your husband too.

JOCASTA: Really, what? Who sent you?

MESSENGER: Corinth.
> I'll give you the message in a moment.
> You'll be glad of it — how could you help it? —
> though it costs a little sorrow in the bargain.

JOCASTA: What can it be, with such a double edge?

MESSENGER: The people there, they want to make your Oedipus
> king of Corinth, so they're saying now.

JOCASTA: Why? Isn't old Polybus still in power?

MESSENGER: No more. Death has got him in the tomb.

JOCASTA: What are you saying? Polybus, dead? — dead?

MESSENGER: If not,
> if I'm not telling the truth, strike me dead too.

JOCASTA:

To a servant.

> Quickly, go to your master, tell him this!

> You prophecies of the gods, where are you now?
> This is the man that Oedipus feared for years,
> he fled him, not to kill him — and now he's dead,
> quite by chance, a normal, natural death,
> not murdered by his son.

OEDIPUS:

Emerging from the palace.

Dearest,
what now? Why call me from the palace?
JOCASTA:

Bringing the MESSENGER closer.

Listen to *him,* see for yourself what all
those awful prophecies of god have come to.
OEDIPUS: And who is he? What can he have for me?
JOCASTA: He's from Corinth, he's come to tell you
your father is no more — Polybus — he's dead!
OEDIPUS:

Wheeling on the MESSENGER.

What? Let me have it from your lips.
MESSENGER: Well,
if that's what you want first, then here it is:
make no mistake, Polybus is dead and gone.
OEDIPUS: How — murder? sickness? — what? what killed him?
MESSENGER: A light tip of the scales can put old bones to rest.
OEDIPUS: Sickness then — poor man, it wore him down.
MESSENGER: That,
and the long count of years he'd measured out.
OEDIPUS: So!
Jocasta, why, why look to the Prophet's hearth,
the fires of the future? Why scan the birds
that scream above our heads? They winged me on
to the murder of my father, did they? That was my doom?
Well look, he's dead and buried, hidden under the earth,
and here I am in Thebes, I never put hand to sword —
unless some longing for me wasted him away,
then in a sense you'd say I caused his death.
But now, all those prophecies I feared — Polybus
packs them off to sleep with him in hell![30]
They're nothing, worthless.
JOCASTA: There.
Didn't I tell you from the start?
OEDIPUS: So you did. I was lost in fear.
JOCASTA: No more, sweep it from your mind forever.
OEDIPUS: But my mother's bed, surely I must fear —
JOCASTA: Fear?
What should a man fear? It's all chance,
chance rules our lives. Not a man on earth
can see a day ahead, groping through the dark.
Better to live at random, best we can.
And as for this marriage with your mother —
have no fear. Many a man before you,
in his dreams, has shared his mother's bed.

---

[30]hell: In Greek myth, the land of the dead, though not a pleasant place, was not the place of agonizing torment described in Christian teachings.

Take such things for shadows, nothing at all —
Live, Oedipus,
as if there's no tomorrow!
OEDIPUS: Brave words,
and you'd persuade me if mother weren't alive.
But mother lives, so for all your reassurances
I live in fear, I must.
JOCASTA: But your father's death,
that, at least, is a great blessing, joy to the eyes!
OEDIPUS: Great, I know . . . but I fear *her* — she's still alive.
MESSENGER: Wait, who is this woman, makes you so afraid?
OEDIPUS: Merope, old man. The wife of Polybus.
MESSENGER: The queen? What's there to fear in her?
OEDIPUS: A deadful prophecy, stranger, sent by the gods.
MESSENGER: Tell me, could you? Unless it's forbidden
other ears to hear.
OEDIPUS: Not at all.
Apollo told me once — it is my fate —
I must make love with my own mother,
shed my father's blood with my own hands.
So for years I've given Corinth a wide berth,
and it's been my good fortune too. But still,
to see one's parents and look into their eyes
is the greatest joy I know.
MESSENGER: You're afraid of that?
That kept you out of Corinth?
OEDIPUS: My *father,* old man —
so I wouldn't kill my father.
MESSENGER: So that's it.
Well then, seeing I came with such good will, my king,
why don't I rid you of that old worry now?
OEDIPUS: What a rich reward you'd have for that!
MESSENGER: What do you think I came for, majesty?
So you'd come home and I'd be better off.
OEDIPUS: Never, I will never go near my parents.
MESSENGER: My boy, it's clear, you don't know what you're doing.
OEDIPUS: What do you mean, old man? For god's sake, explain.
MESSENGER: If you ran from *them,* always dodging home . . .
OEDIPUS: Always, terrified Apollo's oracle might come true —
MESSENGER: And you'd be covered with guilt, from both your parents.
OEDIPUS: That's right, old man, that fear is always with me.
MESSENGER: Don't you know? You've really nothing to fear.
OEDIPUS: But why? If I'm their son — Merope, Polybus?
MESSENGER: Polybus was nothing to you, that's why, not in blood.
OEDIPUS: What are you saying — Polybus was not my father?
MESSENGER: No more than I am. He and I are equals.
OEDIPUS: My father —
how can my father equal nothing? You're nothing to me!
MESSENGER: Neither was he, no more your father than I am.

OEDIPUS: Then why did he call me his son?
MESSENGER: You were a gift,
    years ago — know for a fact he took you
    from my hands.
OEDIPUS: No, from another's hands?
    Then how could he love me so? He loved me, deeply . . .
MESSENGER: True, and his early years without a child
    made him love you all the more.
OEDIPUS: And you, did you . . .
    buy me? find me by accident?
MESSENGER: I stumbled on you,
    down the woody flanks of Mount Cithaeron.
OEDIPUS: So close,
    what were you doing here, just passing through?
MESSENGER: Watching over my flocks, grazing them on the slopes.
OEDIPUS: A herdsman, were you? A vagabond, scraping for wages?
MESSENGER: Your savior too, my son, in your worst hour.
OEDIPUS: Oh —
    when you picked me up, was I in pain? What exactly?
MESSENGER: Your ankles . . . they tell the story. Look at them.
OEDIPUS: Why remind me of that, that old affliction?
MESSENGER: Your ankles were pinned together. I set you free.
OEDIPUS: That dreadful mark — I've had it from the cradle.
MESSENGER: And you got your name from that misfortune too,
    the name's still with you.[31]
OEDIPUS: Dear god, who did it? —
    mother? father? Tell me.
MESSENGER: I don't know.
    The one who gave you to me, he'd know more.
OEDIPUS: What? You took me from someone else?
    You didn't find me yourself?
MESSENGER: No sir,
    another shepherd passed you on to me.
OEDIPUS: Who? Do you know? Describe him.
MESSENGER: He called himself a servant of . . .
    if I remember rightly — Laius.

JOCASTA turns sharply.

OEDIPUS: The king of the land who ruled here long ago?
MESSENGER: That's the one. That herdsman was *his* man.
OEDIPUS: Is he still alive? Can I see him?
MESSENGER: They'd know best, the people of these parts.

OEDIPUS and the MESSENGER turn to the CHORUS.

OEDIPUS: Does anyone know that herdsman,
    the one he mentioned? Anyone seen him
    in the fields, here in the city? Out with it!
    The time has come to reveal this once for all.

[31]name: "Oedipus" means swollen foot.

56

LEADER: I think he's the very shepherd you wanted to see,
    a moment ago. But the queen, Jocasta,
    she's the one to say.
OEDIPUS: Jocasta,
    you remember the man we just sent for?
    Is *that* the one he means?
JOCASTA: That man,
    why ask? Old shepherd, talk, empty nonsense,
    don't give it another thought, don't even think —
OEDIPUS: What — give up now, with a clue like this?
    Fail to solve the mystery of my birth?
    Not for all the world!
JOCASTA: Stop — in the name of god,
    if you love your own life, call off this search!
    My suffering is enough.
OEDIPUS: Courage!
    Even if my mother turns out to be a slave,
    and I a slave, three generations back,
    you would not seem common.
JOCASTA: Oh no,
    listen to me, I beg you, don't do this.
OEDIPUS: Listen to you? No more. I must know it all,
    must see the truth at last.
JOCASTA: No, please —
    for your sake — I want the best for you!
OEDIPUS: Your best is more than I can bear.
JOCASTA: You're doomed —
    may you never fathom who you are!
OEDIPUS:

To a servant.

Hurry, fetch me the herdsman, now!
    Leave her to glory in her royal birth.
JOCASTA: Aieeeeee —
    man of agony —
    that is the only name I have for you,
    that, no other — ever, ever, ever!

Flinging through the palace doors. A long, tense silence follows.

LEADER: Where's she gone, Oedipus?
    Rushing off, such wild grief . . .
    I'm afraid that from this silence
    something monstrous may come bursting forth.
OEDIPUS: Let it burst! Whatever will, whatever must!
    I must know my birth, no matter how common
    it may be — I must see my origins face-to-face.
    She perhaps, she with her woman's pride
    may well be mortified by my birth,
    but I, I count myself the son of Chance,[32]

[32]Chance: Perhaps Tyche, goddess of good luck, a daughter of Zeus.

the great goddess, giver of all good things —
I'll never see myself disgraced. She is my mother!
And the moons have marked me out, my blood-brothers,
one moon on the wane, the next moon great with power.
That is my blood, my nature — I will never betray it,
never fail to search and learn my birth!
CHORUS: Yes — if I am a true prophet
if I can grasp the truth,
by the boundless skies of Olympus,
at the full moon of tomorrow, Mount Cithaeron
you will know how Oedipus glories in you —
you, his birthplace, nurse, his mountain-mother!
And we will sing you, dancing out your praise —
you lift our monarch's heart!
Apollo, Apollo, god of the wild cry
may our dancing please you!
Oedipus —
son, dear child, who bore you?
Who of the nymphs who seem to live forever[33]
mated with Pan, the mountain-striding Father?[34]
Who was your mother? who, some bride of Apollo
the god who loves the pastures spreading toward the sun?
Or was it Hermes, king of the lightning ridges?[35]
Or Dionysus, lord of frenzy, lord of the barren peaks —
did he seize you in his hands, dearest of all his lucky finds? —
found by the nymphs, their warm eyes dancing, gift
to the lord who loves them dancing out his joy!

OEDIPUS strains to see a figure coming from the distance. Attended by palace guards, an old SHEPHERD enters slowly, reluctant to approach the king.

OEDIPUS: I never met the man, my friends . . . still,
if I had to guess, I'd say that's the shepherd,
the very one we've looked for all along.
Brothers in old age, two of a kind,
he and our guest here. At any rate
the ones who bring him in are my own men,
I recognize them.

Turning to the LEADER.

But you know more than I,
you should, you've seen the man before.
LEADER: I know him, definitely. One of Laius' men,
a trusty shepherd, if there ever was one.
OEDIPUS: You, I ask you first, stranger,
you from Corinth — is this the one you mean?

[33]nymphs: Minor nature deities, beautiful maidens who lived in the mountains and waters.
[34]Pan: Nature god of woodlands and pastures; Pan is portrayed in art as half-man, half-goat.
[35]Hermes: Herald and messenger of the gods.

MESSENGER: You're looking at him. He's your man.
OEDIPUS:

To the SHEPHERD.

> You, old man, come over here —
> look at me. Answer all my questions.
> Did you ever serve King Laius?

SHEPHERD: So I did . . .
> a slave, not bought on the block though,
> born and reared in the palace.

OEDIPUS: Your duties, your kind of work?

SHEPHERD: Herding the flocks, the better part of my life.

OEDIPUS: Where, mostly? Where did you do your grazing?

SHEPHERD: Cithaeron sometimes, or the foothills round about.

OEDIPUS: This man — you know him? ever see him there?

SHEPHERD:

Confused, glancing from the MESSENGER to the King.

> Doing what? — what man do you mean?

OEDIPUS:

Pointing to the MESSENGER

> This one here — ever have dealings with him?

SHEPHERD: Not so I could say, but give me a chance,
> my memory's bad . . .

MESSENGER: No wonder he doesn't know me, master.
> But let me refresh his memory for him.
> I'm sure he recalls old times we had
> on the slopes of Mount Cithaeron;
> he and I, grazing our flocks, he with two
> and I with one — we both struck up together,
> three whole seasons, six months at a stretch
> from spring to the rising of Arcturus in the fall,[36]
> then with winter coming on I'd drive my herds
> to my own pens, and back he'd go with his
> to Laius' folds.

To the SHEPHERD.

> Now that's how it was,
> wasn't it — yes or no?

SHEPHERD: Yes, I suppose . . .
> it's all so long ago.

MESSENGER: Come, tell me,
> you gave me a child back then, a boy, remember?
> A little fellow to rear, my very own.

SHEPHERD: What? Why rake up that again?

MESSENGER: Look, here he is, my fine old friend —
> The same man who was just a baby then.

[36]Arcturus: A bright star located in the Herdsman, a northern constellation.

SHEPHERD: Damn you, shut your mouth — quiet!
OEDIPUS: Don't lash out at him, old man —
    you need lashing more than he does.
SHEPHERD: Why,
    master, majesty — what have I done wrong?
OEDIPUS: You won't answer his question about the boy.
SHEPHERD: He's talking nonsense, wasting his breath.
OEDIPUS: So, you won't talk willingly —
    then you'll talk with pain.

The guards seize the SHEPHERD.

SHEPHERD: No dear god, don't torture an old man!
OEDIPUS: Twist his arms back, quickly!
SHEPHERD: God help us, why? —
    what more do you need to know?
OEDIPUS: Did you give him that child? He's asking.
SHEPHERD: I did . . . I wish to god I'd died that day.
OEDIPUS: You've got your wish if you don't tell the truth.
SHEPHERD: The more I tell, the worse the death I'll die.
OEDIPUS: Our friend here wants to stretch things out, does he?

Motioning to his men for torture.

SHEPHERD: No, no, I gave it to him — I just said so.
OEDIPUS: Where did you get it? Your house? Someone else's?
SHEPHERD: It wasn't mine, no, I got it from . . . someone.
OEDIPUS: Which one of them?

Looking at the citizens.

    Whose house?
SHEPHERD: No —
    god's sake, master, no more questions!
OEDIPUS: You're a dead man if I have to ask again.
SHEPHERD: Then — the child came from the house . . .
    of Laius.
OEDIPUS: A slave? or born of his own blood?
SHEPHERD: Oh no,
    I'm right at the edge, the horrible truth — I've got to say it!
OEDIPUS: And I'm at the edge of hearing horrors, yes, but I must hear!
SHEPHERD: All right! His son, they said it was — his son!
    But the one inside, your wife,
    she'd tell it best.
OEDIPUS: My wife —
    she gave it to you?
SHEPHERD: Yes, yes, my king.
OEDIPUS: Why, what for?
SHEPHERD: To kill it.
OEDIPUS: Her own child,
    how could she?
SHEPHERD: She was afraid —
    frightening prophecies.

OEDIPUS: What?
SHEPHERD: they said —
　he'd kill his parents.
OEDIPUS: But you gave him to this old man — why?
SHEPHERD: I pitied the little baby, master,
　hoped he'd take him off to his own country,
　far away, but he saved him for this, this fate.
　If you are the man he says you are, believe me,
　you were born for pain.
OEDIPUS: O god —
　all come true, all burst to light!
　O light — now let me look my last on you!
　I stand revealed at last —
　cursed in my birth, cursed in marriage,
　cursed in the lives I cut down with these hands!

*Rushing through the doors with a great cry. The Corinthian MESSENGER,
the SHEPHERD and attendants exit slowly to the side.*

CHORUS: O the generations of men
　the dying generations — adding the total
　of all your lives I find they come to nothing . . .
　does there exist, is there a man on earth
　who seizes more joy than just a dream, a vision?
　And the vision no sooner dawns than dies
　blazing into oblivion.

　You are my great example, you, your life
　your destiny, Oedipus, man of misery —
　I count no man blest.

　You outranged all men!
　Bending your bow to the breaking-point
　you captured priceless glory, O dear god,
　and the Sphinx came crashing down,
　the virgin, claws hooked
　like a bird of omen singing, shrieking death —
　like a fortress reared in the face of death
　you rose and saved our land.

　From that day on we called you king
　we crowned you with honors, Oedipus, towering over all —
　mighty king of the seven gates of Thebes.
　But now to hear your story — is there a man more agonized?
　More wed to pain and frenzy? Not a man on earth,
　the joy of your life ground down to nothing
　O Oedipus, name for the ages —
　one and the same wide harbor served you
　son and father both
　son and father came to rest in the same bridal chamber.
　How, how could the furrows your father plowed
　bear you, your agony, harrowing on

in silence O so long?

But now for all your power
Time, all-seeing Time has dragged you to the light,
judged your marriage monstrous from the start —
the son and the father tangling, both one —
O child of Laius, would to god
I'd never seen you, never never!
Now I weep like a man who wails the dead
and the dirge comes pouring forth with all my heart!
I tell you the truth, you gave me life
my breath leaps up in you
and now you bring down night upon my eyes.

Enter a MESSENGER from the palace.

MESSENGER: Men of Thebes, always first in honor,
what horrors you will hear, what you will see,
what a heavy weight of sorrow you will shoulder . . .
if you are true to your birth, if you still have
some feeling for the royal house of Thebes.
I tell you neither the waters from the Danube
nor the Nile can wash this palace clean.
Such things it hides, it soon will bring to light —
terrible things, and none done blindly now,
all done with a will. The pains
we inflict upon ourselves hurt most of all.

LEADER: God knows we have pains enough already.
What can you add to them?

MESSENGER: The queen is dead.

LEADER: Poor lady — how?

MESSENGER: By her own hand. But you are spared the worst,
you never had to watch . . . I saw it all,
and with all the memory that's in me
you will learn what that poor woman suffered.

Once she'd broken in through the gates,
dashing past us, frantic, whipped to fury,
ripping her hair out with both hands —
straight to her rooms she rushed, flinging herself
across the bridal-bed, doors slamming behind her —
once inside, she wailed for Laius, dead so long,
remembering how she bore his child long ago,
the life that rose up to destroy him, leaving
its mother to mother living creatures
with the very son she'd borne.
Oh how she wept, mourning the marriage-bed
where she let loose that double brood — monsters —
husband by her husband, children by her child.
And then —
but how she died is more than I can say. Suddenly
Oedipus burst in, screaming, he stunned us so

we couldn't watch her agony to the end,
our eyes were fixed on him. Circling
like a maddened beast, stalking, here, there,
crying out to us —
Give him a sword! His wife,
no wife, his mother, where can he find the mother earth
that cropped two crops at once, himself and all his children?
He was raging — one of the dark powers pointing the way,
none of us mortals crowding around him, no,
with a great shattering cry — someone, something leading him on —
he hurled at the twin doors and bending the bolts back
out of their sockets, crashed through the chamber.
And there we saw the woman hanging by the neck,
cradled high in a woven noose, spinning,
swinging back and forth. And when he saw her,
giving a low, wrenching sob that broke our hearts,
slipping the halter from her throat, he eased her down,
in a slow embrace he laid her down, poor thing . . .
then, what came next, what horror we beheld!

He rips off her brooches, the long gold pins
holding her robes — and lifting them high,
looking straight up into the points,
he digs them down the sockets of his eyes, crying, "You,
you'll see no more the pain I suffered, all the pain I caused!
Too long you looked on the ones you never should have seen,
blind to the ones you longed to see, to know! Blind
from this hour on! Blind in the darkness — blind!"
His voice like a dirge, rising, over and over
raising the pins, raking them down his eyes.
And at each stroke blood spurts from the roots,
splashing his beard, a swirl of it, nerves and clots —
black hail of blood pulsing, gushing down.

These are the griefs that burst upon them both,
coupling man and woman. The joy they had so lately,
the fortune of their old ancestral house
was deep joy indeed. Now, in this one day,
wailing, madness and doom, death, disgrace,
all the griefs in the world that you can name,
all are theirs forever.

LEADER: Oh poor man, the misery —
has he any rest from pain now?

A voice within, in torment.

MESSENGER: He's shouting,
"Loose the bolts, someone, show me to all of Thebes!
My father's murderer, my mother's —"
No, I can't repeat it, it's unholy.
Now he'll tear himself from his native earth,
not linger, curse the house with his own curse.

But he needs strength, and a guide to lead him on.
This is sickness more than he can bear.

The palace doors open.

Look
He'll show you himself. The great doors are opening —
you are about to see a sight, a horror
even his mortal enemy would pity.

Enter OEDIPUS, blinded, led by a boy. He stands at the palace steps, as if surveying his people once again.

CHORUS:
O the terror —
the suffering, for all the world to see,
the worst terror that ever met my eyes.
What madness swept over you? What god,
what dark power leapt beyond all bounds,
beyond belief, to crush your wretched life? —
godforsaken, cursed by the gods!
I pity you but I can't bear to look.
I've much to ask, so much to learn,
so much fascinates my eyes,
but you . . . I shudder at the sight.

OEDIPUS: Oh, Ohh —
the agony! I am agony —
where am I going? where on earth?
where does all this agony hurl me?
where's my voice —
winging, swept away on a dark tide —
My destiny, my dark power, what a leap you made!

CHORUS: To the depths of terror, too dark to hear, to see.

OEDIPUS: Dark, horror of darkness
my darkness, drowning, swirling around me
crashing wave on wave — unspeakable, irresistible
headwind, fatal harbor! Oh again,
the misery, all at once, over and over
the stabbing daggers, stab of memory
raking me insane.

CHORUS: No wonder you suffer
twice over, the pain of your wounds,
the lasting grief of pain.

OEDIPUS: Dear friend, still here?
Standing by me, still with a care for me,
the blind man? Such compassion,
loyal to the last. Oh it's you,
I know you're here, dark as it is
I'd know you anywhere, your voice —
it's yours, clearly yours.

CHORUS: Dreadful, what you've done . . .
how could you bear it, gouging out your eyes?

What superhuman power drove you on?
OEDIPUS: Apollo, friends, Apollo —
he ordained my agonies — these, my pains on pains!
But the hand that struck my eyes was mine,
mine alone — no one else —
I did it all myself!
What good were eyes to me?
Nothing I could see could bring me joy.
CHORUS: No, no, exactly as you say.
OEDIPUS: What can I ever see?
What love, what call of the heart
can touch my ears with joy! Nothing, friends.
Take me away, far, far from Thebes,
quickly, cast me away, my friends —
this great murderous ruin, this man cursed to heaven,
the man the deathless gods hate most of all!
CHORUS: Pitiful, you suffer so, you understand so much . . .
I wish you had never known.
OEDIPUS: Die, die —
whoever he was that day in the wilds
who cut my ankles free of the ruthless pins,
he pulled me clear of death, he saved my life
for this, this kindness —
Curse him, kill him!
If I'd died then, I'd never have dragged myself,
my loved ones through such hell.
CHORUS: Oh if only . . . would to god.
OEDIPUS: I'd never have come to this,
my father's murderer — never been branded
mother's husband, all men see me now! Now,
loathed by the gods, son of the mother I defiled
coupling in my father's bed, spawning lives in the loins
that spawned my wretched life. What grief can crown this grief?
It's mine alone, my destiny — I am Oedipus!
CHORUS: How can I say you've chosen for the best?
Better to die than be alive and blind.
OEDIPUS: What I did was best — don't lecture me,
no more advice. I, with *my* eyes,
how could I look my father in the eyes
when I go down to death? Or mother, so abused . . .
I have done such things to the two of them,
crimes too huge for hanging.
Worse yet,
the sight of my children, born as they were born,
how could I long to look into their eyes?
No, not with these eyes of mine, never.
Not this city either, her high towers,
the sacred glittering images of her gods —
I am misery! I, her best son, reared
as no other son of Thebes was ever reared,

65

I've stripped myself, I gave the command myself
All men must cast away the great blasphemer,
the curse now brought to light by the gods,
the son of Laius — I, my father's son!

Now I've exposed my guilt, horrendous guilt,
could I train a level glance on you, my countrymen?
Impossible! No, if I could just block off my ears,
the springs of hearing, I would stop at nothing —
I'd wall up my loathsome body like a prison,
blind to the sound of life, not just the sight.
Oblivion, what a blessing . . .
for the mind to dwell a world away from pain.

O Cithaeron, why did you give me shelter?
Why didn't you take me, crush my life out on the spot?
I'd never have revealed my birth to all mankind.

O Polybus, Corinth, the old house of my fathers,
so I believed — what a handsome prince you raised —
under the skin, what sickness to the core.
Look at me! Born of outrage, outrage to the core.
O triple roads — it all comes back, the secret,
dark ravine, and the oaks closing in
where the three roads join . . .
You drank my father's blood, my own blood
spilled by my own hands — you still remember me?
What things you saw me do? Then I came here
and did them all once more!
Marriages! O marriage,
you gave me birth, and once you brought me into the world
you brought my sperm rising back, springing to light
fathers, brothers, sons — one murderous breed —
brides, wives, mothers. The blackest things
a man can do, I have done them all!
No more —
it's wrong to name what's wrong to do. Quickly,
for the love of god, hide me somewhere,
kill me, hurl me into the sea
where you can never look on me again.

Beckoning to the CHORUS as they shrink away.

Closer,
it's all right. Touch the man of grief.
Do. Don't be afraid. My troubles are mine
and I am the only man alive who can sustain them.

Enter CREON from the palace, attended by palace guards.

LEADER: Put your requests to Creon. Here he is,
just when we need him. He'll have a plan, he'll act.
Now that he's the sole defense of the country

in your place.
OEDIPUS: Oh no, what can I say to him?
How can I ever hope to win his trust?
I wronged him so, just now, in every way.
You must see that — I was so wrong, so wrong.
CREON: I haven't come to mock you, Oedipus,
or to criticize your former failings.

Turning to the guards.

You there,
have you lost all respect for human feelings?
At least revere the Sun, the holy fire
that keeps us all alive. Never expose a thing
of guilt and holy dread so great it appalls
the earth, the rain from heaven, the light of day!
Get him into the halls — quickly as you can.
Piety demands no less. Kindred alone
should see a kinsman's shame. This is obscene.
OEDIPUS: Please, in god's name . . . you wipe my fears away,
coming so generously to me, the worst of men.
Do one thing more, for your sake, not mine.
CREON: What do you want? Why so insistent?
OEDIPUS: Drive me out of the land at once, far from sight,
where I can never hear a human voice.
CREON: I'd have done that already, I promise you.
First I wanted the god to clarify my duties.
OEDIPUS: The god? His command was clear, every word:
death for the father-killer, the curse —
he said destroy me!
CREON: So he did. Still, in such a crisis
it's better to ask precisely what to do.
OEDIPUS: So miserable —
you would consult the god about a man like me?
CREON: By all means. And this time, I assume,
even you will obey the god's decrees.
OEDIPUS: I will,
I will. And you, I command you — I beg you . . .
the woman inside, bury her as you see fit.
It's the only decent thing,
to give your own the last rites. As for me,
never condemn the city of my fathers
to house my body, not while I'm alive, no,
let me live on the mountains, on Cithaeron,
my favorite haunt, I have made it famous.
Mother and father marked out that rock
to be my everlasting tomb — buried alive.
Let me die there, where they tried to kill me.

Oh but this I know: no sickness can destroy me,
nothing can. I would never have been saved

from death — I have been saved
for something great and terrible, something strange.
Well let my destiny come and take me on its way!
About my children, Creon, the boys at least,
don't burden yourself. They're men,
wherever they go, they'll find the means to live.
But my two daughters, my poor helpless girls,
clustering at our table, never without me
hovering near them . . . whatever I touched,
they always had their share. Take care of them,
I beg you. Wait, better — permit me, would you?
Just to touch them with my hands and take
our fill of tears. Please . . . my king.
Grant it, with all your noble heart.
If I could hold them, just once, I'd think
I had them with me, like the early days
when I could see their eyes.

ANTIGONE and ISMENE, two small children, are led in from the palace by a nurse.

What's that?
A god! Do I really hear you sobbing? —
my two children. Creon, you've pitied me?
Sent me my darling girls, my own flesh and blood!
Am I right?
CREON: Yes, it's my doing.
I know the joy they gave you all these years,
the joy you must feel now.
OEDIPUS: Bless you, Creon!
May god watch over you for this kindness,
better than he ever guarded me.
Children, where are you?
Here, come quickly —

Groping for ANTIGONE and ISMENE, who approach their father cautiously, then embrace him.

Come to these hands of mine,
your brother's hands, your own father's hands
that served his once bright eyes so well —
that made them blind. Seeing nothing, children,
knowing nothing, I became your father,
I fathered you in the soil that gave me life.

How I weep for you — I cannot see you now . . .
just thinking of all your days to come, the bitterness,
the life that rough mankind will thrust upon you.
Where are the public gatherings you can join,
the banquets of the clans? Home you'll come,
in tears, cut off from the sight of it all,
the brilliant rites unfinished.

68

And when you reach perfection, ripe for marriage,
who will he be, my dear ones? Risking all
to shoulder the curse that weighs down my parents,
yes and you too — that wounds us all together.
What more misery could you want?
Your father killed his father, sowed his mother,
one, one and the selfsame womb sprang you —
he cropped the very roots of his existence.

Such disgrace, and you must bear it all!
Who will marry you then? Not a man on earth.
Your doom is clear: you'll wither away to nothing,
single, without a child.

Turning to CREON.

Oh Creon,
you are the only father thay have now . . .
we who brought them into the world
are gone, both gone at a stroke —
Don't let them go begging, abandoned,
women without men. Your own flesh and blood!
Never bring them down to the level of my pains.
Pity them. Look at them, so young, so vulnerable,
shorn of everything — you're their only hope.
Promise me, noble Creon, touch my hand!

Reaching toward CREON, who draws back.

You, little ones, if you were old enough
to understand, there is much I'd tell you.
Now, as it is, I'd have you say a prayer.
Pray for life, my children,
live where you are free to grow and season.
Pray god you find a better life than mine,
the father who begot you.
CREON: Enough.
You've wept enough. Into the palace now.
OEDIPUS: I must, but I find it very hard.
CREON: Time is the great healer, you will see.
OEDIPUS: I am going — you know on what condition?
CREON: Tell me. I'm listening.
OEDIPUS: Drive me out of Thebes, in exile.
CREON: Not I. Only the gods can give you that.
OEDIPUS: Surely the gods hate me so much —
CREON: You'll get your wish at once.
OEDIPUS: You consent?
CREON: I try to say what I mean; it's my habit.
OEDIPUS: Then take me away. It's time.
CREON: Come along, let go of the children.
OEDIPUS: No —
don't take them away from me, not now! No no no!

Clutching his daughters as the guards wrench them loose and take them through the palace doors.

CREON: Still the king, the master of all things?
No more: here your power ends.
None of your power follows you through life.

Exit OEDIPUS and CREON to the palace. The CHORUS comes forward to address the audience directly.

CHORUS: People of Thebes, my countrymen, look on Oedipus.
He solved the famous riddle with his brilliance,
he rose to power, a man beyond all power.
Who could behold his greatness without envy?
Now what a black sea of terror has overwhelmed him.
Now as we keep our watch and wait the final day,
count no man happy till he dies, free of pain at last.

Exit in procession.

Classical Theatre Timeline

- 1st TRAGIC COMPETITION (534 B.C.)
- AESCHYLUS (525-456 B.C.)
- SOPHOCLES (497-406 B.C.)
- EURIPIDES (484-406 B.C.)
- SOCRATES (c. 469-399 B.C.)
- ARISTOPHANES (c. 448-c. 380 B.C.)
- PELOPONNESIAN WAR (c. 431-404 B.C.)
- PLATO (c. 427-347 B.C.)
- ARISTOTLE (384-322 B.C.)
- ALEXANDER THE GREAT (356-323 B.C.)
- MENANDER (c. 342-293 B.C.)
- HELLENISTIC PERIOD (336 B.C. INTO 1st CENTURY)
- PLAUTUS (c. 254-184 B.C.)
- TERENCE (c. 190-159 B.C.)
- HORACE (65-8 B.C.)
- 1st PERMANENT THEATRE IN ROME (55 B.C.)
- AUGUSTAN AGE (27 B.C.-A.D. 14)
- ROMAN EMPIRE (27 B.C.-A.D. 476)
- SENECA (c. 4 B.C.-A.D. 65)
- LAST RECORDED THEATRE PERFORMANCE IN ROME (A.D. 533)

500 B.C. 400 B.C. 300 B.C. 200 B.C. 100 B.C. 0 A.D. 100 A.D. 200 A.D. 300 A.D. 400 A.D. 500

THE MEDIEVAL PERIOD: The Rebirth of Theatre in the Middle Ages

The Middle Ages cover the period from the end of the Roman Empire until the fifteenth- and sixteenth-century explosion of cultural and technological advances which we call the Renaissance. The Middle Ages in general, and medieval theatre in particular, have long suffered from bad press. This antimedieval attitude began during the Renaissance. The people of this period, in a kind of adolescent spirit of rebellion, tended to denigrate their "parent age" as old-fashioned, primitive, and embarrassing. They wanted to reject everything medieval and reach back instead to the Classical Age for their inspiration.

Cultural Darwinism

During the past hundred years, this attitude was reinforced by "Cultural Darwinism." Cultural Darwinism is the attempt to apply to cultural and social developments the principles of Charles Darwin's theory of biological evolution. It holds, for instance, that early forms are necessarily simpler, smaller, and more primitive than later forms, and it uses those terms — "simple," "small," "primitive" — disparagingly, in contrast with praise-terms such as "complex," "sophisticated," and "advanced." Although Cultural Darwinism has gone out of style, it remains difficult to lay it aside when looking at medieval drama. And finally, the theatre of the Middle Ages has suffered from being compared to Shakespeare. Many scholars and theatre people have developed such an overpowering admiration for Shakespeare that all other drama — and especially that which immediately preceded him — seems weak by comparison. However, those who succeed in laying aside these antimedieval prejudices and who succeed in understanding the impulses and techniques which underlie medieval drama will find that the theatre of this period is wonderfully diverse and peculiarly sophisticated.

Political/Social/Philosophical Backgrounds

The thousand years between the end of the Roman Empire and the Renaissance saw fantastic changes take place in Europe. During this period, the Germanic peoples who invaded Western Europe finished displacing the older Celtic culture, stopped their migrations, and settled down. They, along with the rest of the Europeans, laid aside many of their folkways and most aspects of their old religions and took on a veneer of Roman culture and Christian religion. The Christian church, centered in Rome, played a powerful role in this transformation. In many ways, the church's domination of Europe paralleled the earlier colonization of the Mediterranean world by the Roman Empire. Often whole tribes became Christian at once with the leaders, not the group as a whole, making the decision to convert, and frequently the new Christians had little or no grasp of the principles of their new faith. The absence of a strong, systematic government created feudalism with its two classes of peasant and gentry and its hierarchy of allegiances based on force. In the later Middle Ages, this system in turn produced a middle class of merchants and tradesmen.

Christianity's Influence

The thought patterns of the Middle Ages grew out of an uneasy marriage between biblical, Christian beliefs and Platonic, classical philosophy. The world view of Christianity as expressed in the New Testament — like that of Judaism in the Old Testament — was God-centered, unified, and relational. God was the supreme being, the creator, sustainer, and controller of *everything*. The sun rose and set because God made it do so, and if God decided it should stand still — or even go backwards — it would. Since God was supreme, the world was essentially unified. Even the forces of evil, sometimes personified as Satan and his emissaries, were ultimately under God's control. And, since God was a personal being rather than an impersonal force, human beings could relate to him like they related to each other. Having a strong relationship with God was the supreme good — ideally the all-consuming goal of every person.

Classicism's Influence

Classical thought, dominated by Plato's philosophy, was, in contrast, human-centered, dualistic, and logical. The universe was governed not by God but by the principle of *diké*, or "justice." The real duty and business of human beings was to know themselves, come to understand the laws of the universe (justice), and wisely manage their behavior in the light of this knowledge. Plato's contrast between that which is ideal and that which we experience came to be understood as separation between the spiritual and the physical. In this duality, the spirit was good while the body was bad, and the two were locked in endless warfare. And since a principle, not a personal being, ruled the universe, the best way to be fully human was to think and behave in logical patterns. Relational thinking, like Hebrew-Christian thought, accepts paradox — the simultaneous existence of mutually contradictory truths, but logical thought cannot tolerate paradox.

Christianity and Classicism Combined

Medieval scholars blended their commitment to Christian beliefs with their admiration for classical thought. According to the resulting world view, people lived in an open universe; at any time, God or his messengers or lucky coincidence might break in and change the course of events. Humankind's whole purpose for living was to achieve a right relationship with God, a goal which the forces of evil constantly threatened. These demons used a powerful tool to ensnare their victims — the temptations of fleshy indulgence — and all God's forces appealed to people to turn their backs on physical needs and desires and instead seek spiritual rewards. The stakes were high in this war of spirit against flesh: Those who failed were doomed to spend eternity in hell where Satan and his demons would subject them to endless torments, and those who succeeded won a place in heaven where they lived in eternal bliss with God, the angels, and the saints.

The cosmos, therefore, was pictured in three layers — heaven above, earth beneath, and hell under the earth. Furthermore, medieval people understood time as a pool rather than a stream; instead of seeing themselves separated from the biblical stories by a chronology of events, they felt that they shared the same moment with the biblical characters. And, to a far greater extent than we are capable of, medieval folk accepted paradox. They could believe without question, for instance, that at the high moment of the Catholic Mass, the bread of communion really became two things at once — wholly bread and wholly the body of Christ who, in his turn, had simultaneously been wholly God and wholly man. Twentieth-century rationalists may sneer at the medieval mind as naive and superstitious but, in the process, they are apt to lose sight of the layered sophistication and the sense of wonder with which medieval people viewed their world.

Because of the dominant influence of the church during this period, most medieval drama is religious. With the advent of the Renaissance, however, various forces combined to eliminate religious drama from most areas in Europe. The Renaissance interest in science, technology, exploration, and humanistic studies led people to view the subject matter of these plays as old-fashioned. In England, Italy, and France, a new secular drama grew in popularity. Furthermore, since during the Reformation Protestants and Catholics used morality plays against each other as propaganda tools, rulers like Elizabeth I of England, in an effort to unify their countries and stamp out religious wars, outlawed all religious drama. Medieval drama gave way to the theatres of Shakespeare, Moliére, and Racine.

Dramatic Literature

In the tenth century, after a gap of about 400 years, formal theatre began again in Europe, almost as if for the first time. It began because the people had a motive for doing plays, they had material to base the plays on, and they had models for dramatic form. The church's need to teach Christian doctrines to the illiterate masses and the people's desire to celebrate the Christian festivals of Easter, Christmas, and Corpus Christi motivated them to use drama. The Bible, legends about the saints, and doctrinal writings furnished the material for these plays. Popular folk rituals which reached back to pagan times, tournaments, mimes, and the plays of Terence and Plautus provided them with ideas of how to construct and stage plays.

Although the plays of the Middle Ages demonstrate considerable variety, they all shared two characteristics: First, they tended to be episodic. That is, they tended to be presented in segments which were complete within themselves and were not related by cause and effect. In this respect, they resembled succeeding episodes in a TV sitcom. Even sections within single episodes or plays didn't always have a strong causal relationship. Furthermore, they tended to blend popular tastes, such as the love for comedy and spectacle, with classical form and Christian subject matter. To later people, therefore, medieval plays seem to be poorly unified.

The Middle Ages had a variety of semidramatic events including mime, folk rituals, tournaments, and royal processions. The major dramatic forms, however, were Latin imitations of classical plays, Latin liturgical drama, and four varieties of vernacular dramas: Mystery plays, miracle plays, morality plays, and secular interludes and farces.

The best samples we have of Latin classical imitations are the works of the Canoness Hrotsvitha who lived in tenth-century Gandersheim in German Saxony. Because she apparently modeled her six prose plays on those of Terence, she is sometimes referred to as the Christian Terence. The short plays use simple plot structure, humor, and emotion to tell the stories of Christian saints. Probably intended for a reading audience rather than for staging, Hrotsvitha's plays demonstrate the medieval impulse to imitate and Christianize classical drama.

Tropes

Also in the tenth century, dramatic elements in the church's liturgy developed into plays. Liturgical drama grew out of *tropes,* words sung antiphonally by choirs to embellish portions of the Mass. The first trope (c. AD 92), called "Quem Quaeritis" after the first two Latin words of the text, portrays the conversation between the angels and the women who came to Jesus' empty tomb on the first Easter morning:

QUESTION (by ANGELS): Whom do you seek in the sepulcher, O followers of Christ?

ANSWER (by the MARYS): Jesus of Nazareth who was crucified, O heavenly ones.

ANGELS: He is not here; he is risen, just as he foretold. Go, announce that he is risen from the sepulcher.

The clergy eventually realized the dramatic potential of tropes. They removed some of them from the Mass and put them in the service of morning prayers where they were free to grow into fully-staged plays complete with simple scenery, stylized costumes, and individualized characters played by clergymen. The texts of these Latin liturgical plays focused on the Easter and Christmas stories, and the church's sanctuary provided the location. The earliest of these plays which still exists comes from the *Regularis Concordis* (965-975) compiled by Bishop Ethelwold of Winchester, England.

The Mystery Play

A much fuller kind of drama, called "mystery plays" and performed in the vernacular languages of the people, grew up around the festival called Corpus Christi. This feast, instituted in 1311 to celebrate the mystery of the Catholic Eucharist in which the bread was turned into the body of Christ (Corpus Christi), took place in May or June. From early on, people celebrated Corpus Christi by outdoor dramas which told the entire narrative of biblical history. Corpus Christi plays took different forms in different countries. In England, each episode was written by a clergyman and then assigned for staging to a particular trade or craft guild which were sometimes called mysteries because of their trade secrets. The guildsmen constructed stages for their plays on wagons called pageants. During the festival, they moved the pageants, one after another, to specified locations in the town, and there performed their plays. Each play in the cycle presented a single episode in religious history, starting with the creation of the world, portraying the fall of mankind, detailing Jesus' birth, life, death, and resurrection, and concluding with the last judgment day. The plays combined the biblical stories with popular humor, spectacle, and social criticism. The best known of these playlets is a Christmas play from the Wakefield Cycle. The second version of a script belonging to the Shepherds' Guild, it is therefore called *The Second Shepherds' Play.*

Miracle plays[1], another form of vernacular drama, focused on the lives and miracles of various saints. The lengthy *Mary Magdalene* is one of the few surviving English samples of this kind of play.

The Morality Play

The most important dramatic form of the Middle Ages, at least from the perspective of its contributions to the development of later drama, was the vernacular morality play. The morality plays dramatized materials from Christian doctrinal writings and teachings. Unlike previously discussed medieval plays which took their stories from the Bible or Christian history, morality plays used invented story lines. Their plots tended to follow a limited number of patterns. These included the debate of soul and body, the parliament in heaven, and the summons of death. *Everyman,* printed in this anthology, is the best sample of the last-named type. In the Middle Ages, however, by far the most common form of morality was the *psychomachia* play. This form, named after a fourth-century allegory, featured a conflict between evil and good over the soul of the central character. Psychomachia moralities personified the forces of evil as the Vice and the forces of good as Virtues and Graces. The Vice, whose antics the audiences loved, became the forerunner of evil characters like Shakespeare's Shylock and Iago and of the villains of nineteenth-century melodrama. Samples of psychomachia moralities include *Mankind* and *The Castle of Perseverance.*

Interludes and Farces

On the eve of the Renaissance, writers combined aspects of the morality play, elements of classical drama, and other comic devices to create secular forms called interludes and farces. Although people of the time tended to use these terms interchangeably, interludes were more didactic and took their name from the practice of performing them between courses of a banquet. Farces, with less educational intent, ridiculed typical human follies such as greed and dishonesty. Samples of interludes include *The Play of the Weather* and *The Four PP,* by John Heywood. The anonymous French *Pierre Patelin* is a good sample of medieval farce.

---

[1]In medieval times, the English used the term "miracle plays" for Corpus Christi dramas and called the type of play discussed in this paragraph "saint plays."

Theatrical Organization

With the exception of the mimes, itinerant performers who eked out a living performing their improvised entertainments in towns and manor houses, all the people involved in medieval theatre were amateurs. Monks and other clergy wrote most of the scripts, and the performers were either clergymen or trade guild members. While moralities, farces, and interludes might be performed at any time, the other plays were all attached to particular church festivals. Since the festivals and the accompanying plays drew large crowds to town, with obvious benefits to local merchants, the town councils often took an active hand in planning the productions and sometimes produced detailed production manuals. Like Greek theatre fifteen centuries earlier, medieval theatre was true community theatre.

Play Production

Found Spaces

Medieval actors performed their plays in churches, in the remains of Roman theatres, in the banquet halls of manor houses, in the courtyards of inns, and in town squares. In other words, they produced their plays in "found spaces," or areas which already existed and weren't built specifically for the purpose of staging their plays. Regardless of the space used, two principles characterized the staging of medieval plays: The use of simultaneous sets and an intimate relationship between the performers and the audience.

Simultaneous Staging

In "simultaneous staging," all the locations for the play's action are in continual view of the audience. Medieval stage sets usually consisted of a number of set pieces arranged around an open playing area. The set pieces, called *mansions,* each represented a particular place. Places called for in *Everyman,* each of which would be represented by a mansion, include heaven, Everyman's house, the house of Penitence, and Everyman's tomb. The open space between the mansions, called the *platea,* represented the area surrounding the mansion currently in use; so when the focal mansion was Everyman's house, the platea represented his house and courtyard, and when the focal mansion was his grave, the platea represented the graveyard.

Intimate Theatre

"Intimate Theatre" implies a close spatial relationship between the performers and the audience. Since medieval audiences typically stood to watch their plays, and since no clear distinction existed between the audience area and the stage, the audience was free to approach the playing area as closely as the actors would permit and also to surround the players on all sides.

Medieval scripts call for a great deal of realistic, physical movement on the part of the actors. Some typical characters in particular, such as the Vice in moralities and King Herod in the mysteries, became legendary for the furious ranting and raving with which they were played. Since the players were all amateurs and since players and audiences alike believed plays should indeed be *play,* it is probably accurate to assume that the acting was exuberant and made up in passion what it might have lacked in refinement.

Medieval Costumes

The plays also called for specific costuming, based on the normal clothing practices of the day. Characters such as demons probably wore costumes designed to accent their horrific and comic nature. The medieval love of spectacle led the performers to devise special effects for their plays. The machinery for these secrets, as they were called, was sometimes quite complicated and the effects could be truly impressive. Spectacular costuming and stage effects probably reached their peak in semidramatic events such as tournaments and royal processions. In the latter events, the royal personages would progress along the route of their procession and stop at monuments erected in their honor. The monuments, usually depicting some mythological scene, featured amazing special effects and people costumed as mythical beings.

Everyman

The Didactic Element

Like all medieval morality plays, *Everyman* is a didactic or rhetorical play, a play which endeavors to teach its audience and move them to a particular course of action. All plays contain ideas, insights, and questions about life. But while most plays subordinate the idea content to the action, didactic plays focus on ideas to the extent that they become the most important element in the drama. *Everyman,* for example, concentrates completely on Christian teachings about the alienation between God and humankind, the causes for the problem, and the means for reconciling God and man. The action is shaped to communicate these ideas and to encourage the audience to apply the remedies to their own lives. Like many didactic plays, *Everyman* uses various rhetorical devices — methods usually reserved for speeches and essays. For instance, the writer organizes the play like a speech which might be outlined as follows:

Introduction (the Messenger's speech)

I. The problem (Death's scenes with God and Everyman)

II. Bad solutions to the problem (Everyman's scenes with Fellowship, Cousin and Kindred, and Goods)

III. Good solutions to the problem (the rest of the play, except for the last speech)

Conclusion (the Doctor's speech)

Other rhetorical devices in *Everyman* include direct audience address (the introduction and conclusion) and summary speeches, such as Everyman's soliloquy just before he turns for help to Good Deeds.

The Ideas

Like most didactic plays, *Everyman* presents not just a single thesis, but a complex of related ideas. For instance, it presents a list of the Seven

Deadly Sins, explains the dangers of bad companions and of relying on family or wealth for security, shows step-by-step the church's process for attaining salvation, and clarifies the proper valuation of human faculties such as strength and intelligence. It ties these ideas together with a motif drawn from the growing commercial life of Europe: The play repeatedly represents Everyman's life as an account book which is out-of-balance and which must be corrected before he faces God, the Great Auditor.

Production History

Everyman was an English translation of a Dutch play dating from about 1495 titled *Elckerlyc*. The fact that *Everyman* was reprinted at least four times before 1540 gives some indication of the play's popularity in its own time. In 1903, William Poel, an English director whose Elizabethan Stage Society sparked an interest in historically accurate performances of Shakespeare's plays, presented a successful production of *Everyman*. And in 1920, Max Reinhardt presented a German version of the play by Hugo von Hofmannsthal, titled *Jedermann*, at the first Salzburg festival in Austria. It is likely that these productions helped stimulate such diverse twentieth-century approaches to theatre as Expressionism, the British verse drama movement, and Bertolt Brecht's Epic Theater. Whether because of *Everyman's* playing upon the universal fear of death, its comic portrayal of the Vices, its genuine portrayal of Everyman's emotions, or the way it succeeds in making the central character's death a joyful event, the play has appealed to widely different audiences and retains a great deal of its original power today.

A Note on the Editing

The editor based the following version of *Everyman* on transcriptions of four copies of the play dating from between 1508 and 1537. W. W. Greg published the transcriptions in the early 1900s[2]. To produce the present version, the editor first compared the four copies and chose the variant readings which would be meaningful to a late-twentieth century audience[3]. He then modernized spelling and punctuation, inserted a few explanatory notes, and added minimal stage directions. For those who would like to sample *Everyman* without this editorial work, the first ten lines of the Britwell Court edition of Skot read as follows:

[2]*Everyman, Reprinted by W. W. Greg from the edition by John Skot. Preserved at Britwell Court*. Vol. 4 of "Materialien zur Kunde des Älteren Englischen Dramas." Louvain: Uystpruyst, 1904. And *Everyman, Reprinted by W. W. Greg from the fragments of two editions by Pynson. Preserved in the Bodleian Library and the British Museum, together Critical Apparatus*. Vol. 28 of the same series, 1910. The critical apparatus in this latter book includes a table of textual variants which also covers the "Huth" copy of a Skot edition; Greg published the full text of the Huth copy in the 24th volume of "Materialien," 1909.

[3]One of the principles for establishing the most *authoritative* text is that the rougher, more difficult reading is to be chosen over the smoother, easier one. This principle assumes that scribes and printers tend to amend texts to make them more understandable, so a scholar who wants to establish the earliest reading will choose the least understandable one. With the aim of introducing modern students to *Everyman*, however, the editor took the position that the understandable reading is preferable to the obscure one, regardless of authenticity.

I Pray you all gyue your audyence   Messenger[4]
And here this mater with reuerence
By fygure a morall playe
The somonynge of every man called it is
That of our lyues and endynge shewes
How transytory we be all daye
This mater is wonders precyous
But the entent of it is more gracyous
And swete to here awaye
The story sayth man in the begynnynge . . .

---

[4]In Greg's edition, this is spelled Messeger with ∼ over the second e, and "man" in line 4 is spelled ma with ∼ over the a.

Medieval Theatre Timeline

◆ QUEM QUAERITIS TROPE (92)

● LAST RECORDED ROMAN PLAY PERFORMANCE (533)

CHARLEMAGNE (742-814)

HROTSUITHA (c. 935-1001)

COMPILATION OF ETHELWOOD'S *REGULARIS CONCORDIS* (965-975)

● NORMAN CONQUEST OF ENGLAND (1066)

THE GREAT CRUSADES (11th-13th CENTURIES)

FOUNDING OF FEAST OF CORPUS CHRISTI (1311) ●

JOAN OF ARC (c. 1412-31)

"THE CASTLE OF PERSEVERANCE" (c. 1425) ●

"MANKIND" (c. 1475) ●

"PIERRE PATELIN" FIRST PRINTED (1490) ●

"EVERYMAN" (c. 1500) ●

JOHN HEYWOOD (c. 1497-1580)

WILLIAM SHAKESPEARE (1564-1616)

| 500 | 600 | 700 | 800 | 900 | 1000 | 1100 | 1200 | 1300 | 1400 | 1500 | 1600 |

THE SUMMONING OF EVERYMAN

Playwright Unknown
Edited by Norman A. Bert

CAST OF CHARACTERS

MESSENGER/DOCTOR	GOOD DEEDS
GOD	KNOWLEDGE
DEATH	CONFESSION
EVERYMAN	DISCRETION
FELLOWSHIP	STRENGTH
KINDRED	FIVE WITS
COUSIN	BEAUTY
GOODS	AN ANGEL

TIME AND SCENE: *The play's action takes place in heaven and in a medieval European town.*

SETTING: *The play, which demands almost nothing by way of scenery or furniture, could be staged in any open area. Heaven might be represented by a raised area containing God's throne. There could also be two "mansions" — one representing a confessional booth and one representing a church — and a grave for the play's concluding scene. At the opening of the play, two forms lie on the stage, covered with cloths.*

> Here beginneth a treatise how the high
> Father of heaven sendeth death to sum-
> mon every creature to come and
> give account of their lives
> in this world, and is in manner
> of a moral play.[1]

MESSENGER: *(He enters wearing the robes of a scholar.)*[2] I pray you
all give your audience
And hear this matter with reverence,
By figure a moral play.
The Summoning of Everyman called it is,
That of our lives and ending shows   5
How transitory we be all day.
This matter is wondrous precious,
But the intent of it is more gracious
And sweet to hear always.
This story saith, "Man, in the beginning   10
Look well and take good heed to the ending,
Be you never so gay.
Ye think sin in the beginning full sweet,
Which in the end causeth thy soul to weep
When the body lieth in clay."   15
Here shall you see how fellowship and jollity,
Both strength, pleasure, and beauty,
Will fade from thee as flower in May;
For ye shall hear how our heaven King
Calleth everyman to a general reckoning.   20

(He indicates GOD on a throne in an elevated place.)

Give audience and hear what he doth say:

(The MESSENGER exits.)

GOD: I perceive here in my majesty
How that all creatures be to me unkind,
Living without dread in worldly prosperity.
Of ghostly sight the people be so blind;   25

---

[1]This paragraph, along with a woodcut showing Everyman and Death, forms the title page of the original copy.
[2]All stage directions in this version have been added by the editor. The original script has only four stage directions: Prior to line 22: "God speaketh." Prior to line 64: "Death." Prior to line 87: "Everyman." Prior to line 206: "Fellowship speaketh."

Drowned in sin, they know me not for their God.
In worldly riches is all their mind.
They fear not my righteousness, that sharp rod.
My law that I showed when I for them died
They forget clean, and shedding of my blood so red.   30
I hanged between two thieves, it cannot be denied;
To get them life, I suffered to be dead.
I healed their feet; with thorns hurt was my head.[3]
I could do no more than I did truly.
And now I see the people do clean forsake me;   35
They use the seven deadly sins damnable,
As pride, covetousness, wrath, and lechery[4]
Now in the world be made commendable.
And thus they leave of angels the heavenly company.
Everyman liveth so after his own pleasure,   40
And yet of their life they be not sure.
I see the more that I them forbear,
The worse they are from year to year.
All that liveth appeareth fast;
Therefore I will in all the haste   45
Have a reckoning of everyman's person.
For and I leave the people thus alone
In their life and wicked tempests,
Verily they will become much worse than beasts.
For now one would by envy another up eat;   50
Charity they all do clean forget.
I hoped well that everyman
In my glory should make his mansion,
And thereto I had them all elect;
But now I see, like traitors deject,   55
They thank me not for the pleasure that I to them meant
Nor yet for their being that I them have lent.
I proffered the people great multitude of mercy,
And few there be that asketh it heartily.
They be so cumbered with wordly riches,   60
That needs on them I must do justice —
On everyman living without fear.
Where art thou, Death, thou mighty messenger?
DEATH: *(Costumed like a skeleton draped with a cloth, he enters.)*
Almighty God, I am here at your will
Your commandment to fulfill.   65
GOD: Go thou to Everyman,
And show him in my name

---

[3]In good medieval fashion, this line combines several references in a single strong image. The allusions include the following: God's words to the serpent after the fall of Adam and Eve: "I will put enmity between thee and the woman, and between thy seed and her seed; it shall bruise thy head, and thou shalt bruise his heel" (Genesis 3.15); a line from the Messianic poem in Isaiah 53. 5: ". . . and with his stripes we are healed"; and, of course, the reference to the crown of thorns Jesus wore when he was crucified.
[4]The three deadly sins not mentioned in this list are gluttony, envy, and sloth.

A pilgrimage he must on him take
Which he in no wise may escape,
And that he bring with him a sure reckoning[5]   70
Without delay or any tarrying.
DEATH: Lord, I will in the world go run over all
And truly out-search both great and small.

(He leaves GOD's throne and descends to the stage.)

Everyman I will beset that liveth beastly
Out of God's laws and dreadeth not folly.   75
He that loveth riches I will strike with my dart,
His sight to blind and from heaven to depart —
Except that alms be his good friend —
In hell for to dwell, world without end.

(EVERYMAN, dressed as a prosperous merchant, strolls on stage.)

Lo! Yonder I see Everyman walking.   80
Full little he thinketh on my coming;
His mind is on fleshly lusts and his treasure,
And great pain it shall cause him to endure
Before the Lord, heaven King.
Everyman! Stand still! Whither art thou going   85
Thus gaily? Hast thou thy maker forgotten?
EVERYMAN: Why askest thou?
Wouldst thou wit?[6]
DEATH: Yea, sir I will show you:
In great haste I am sent to thee   90
From God out of his majesty.
EVERYMAN: What? Sent to me?
DEATH: Yes, certainly.
Though thou have forgotten him here,
He thinketh on thee in the heavenly sphere,   95
As ere we depart thou shalt know.
EVERYMAN: What desireth God of me?
DEATH: That shall I show thee:
A reckoning he will needs have
Without longer respite.   100
EVERYMAN: To give a reckoning, longer leisure I crave.
This blind matter troubleth my wit.
DEATH: On thee thou must take a long journey;
Therefore thy book of count with thee thou bring,
For turn again thou cannot by no way.   105
And look thou be sure of thy reckoning,

---

[5]A reckoning is a balance sheet. Note that this image, taken from the world of business as opposed to agricultural, technical, religious, military, or political life, dominates the play.
[6]In the original "wete" = know. Note that the final word in line 86 of the original was "forgete" which created a rhyme with "wete." Such rhymes are lost in this modernized edition.

For before God thou shalt answer and show
Thy many bad deeds and good but a few,
How thou hast spent thy life and in what wise,
Before the chief Lord of paradise.   110
Have ado that we were in that way,
For wit thou well: Thou shalt make none attorney.
EVERYMAN: Full unready I am such reckoning to give.
I know thee not. What messenger art thou?
DEATH: I am Death that no man dreadeth,[7]
For everyman I rest[8] and no man spareth,
For it is God's commandment
That all to me should be obedient.
EVERYMAN: O Death, thou comest when I had thee least in mind.
In thy power it lieth me to save;   120
Yet of my good[9] will I give thee if thou will be kind.
Yea, a thousand pound shalt thou have,
And defer this matter till another day.
DEATH: Everyman, it may not be by no way.
I set not by gold, silver, nor riches,   125
Nor by pope, emperor, king, duke nor princes.
For and I would receive gifts great,
All the world I might get,
But my custom is clean contrary.
I give thee no respite. Come hence, and not tarry.   130
EVERYMAN: Alas, shall I have no longer respite?
I may say, Death giveth no warning.
To think on thee it maketh my heart sick,
For all unready is my book of reckoning.
But twelve year and I might have abiding,[10]   135
My counting book I would make so clear
That my reckoning I should not need to fear.
Wherefore, Death, I pray thee, for God's mercy,
Spare me till I be provided of remedy.
DEATH: Thee availeth not to cry, weep, and pray.   140
But haste thee lightly that thou were gone that journey,
And prove thy friends, if thou can,
For wit you well: The tide abideth no man,
And in the world each living creature
For Adam's sin must die of nature.   145
EVERYMAN: Death, if I should this pilgrimage take
And my reckoning surely make,
Show me, for Saint Charity,
Should I not come again shortly?
DEATH: No, Everyman, and thou be once there,   150
Thou mayst nevermore come here.

[7]That is, ". . . Death, who dreads no one."
[8]arrest
[9]Everyman attempts to bribe Death: ". . . [some] of my good[s] I'll give you . . ."
[10]But, if I might have a stay of twelve years, . . .

Trust me verily.
EVERYMAN: O gracious God, in high seat celestial,
    Have mercy on me in this most need!
    Shall I have no company from this vale terrestrial   155
    Of mine acquaintance, that way me to lead?
DEATH: Yea, if any be so hardy
    That would go with thee and bear thee company.
    Hie thee, that thou were gone to God's magnificence,
    Thy reckoning to give before his presence.   160
    What? Weenest[11] thou thy life is given thee,
    And thy worldly goods also?
EVERYMAN: I had weened so, verily.
DEATH: Nay! Nay, it was but lent thee;
    For as soon as thou art gone,   165
    Another awhile shall have it and then go there from,
    Even as thou hast done.
    Everyman, thou art mad: Thou hast thy wits five,
    And here on earth will not amend thy life?
    For suddenly I do come   170
EVERYMAN: O wretched caitiff! Whither shall I flee
    That I might escape this endless sorrow?
    Now, gentle Death, spare me till tomorrow
    That I may amend me
    With good advisement.   175
DEATH: Nay, thereto I will not consent,
    Nor no man will I respite,
    But to the heart suddenly I shall smite
    Without any advisement.
    And now out of thy sight I will me hie.   180
    See thou make thee ready shortly,
    For thou mayst say, this is the day
    That no man living may escape away.

(DEATH exits.)

EVERYMAN: Alas! I may well weep with sighs deep!
    Now have I no manner of company   185
    To help me in my journey and me to keep.
    And also my writing is full unready.
    How shall I do now for to excuse me?
    I would to God I had never begot:[12]
    To my soul a great profit it had been,   190
    For now I fear pains huge and great.
    The time passeth! Lord, help, that all wrought!
    For though I mourn, it availeth nought.
    The day passeth and is almost ago!
    I wot not well what to do.   195

[11]imagine
[12]been begotten. In the original, this word, "begete," rhymes with the final word in line 191: "grete."

To whom were I best my complaint to make?
What and[13] I to Fellowship thereof spake
And showed him of this sudden chance?
For in him is all mine affiance.
We have in the world, so many a day,   200
Been good friends in sport and play.

(FELLOWSHIP, decked out in lively costuming, saunters on stage.)

I see him yonder certainly.
I trust that he will bear me company;
Therefore to him will I speak to ease my sorrow.
Well met, good Fellowship, and good morrow!   205
FELLOWSHIP: Everyman! Good morrow by this day!
Sir, why lookest thou so piteously?
If anything be amiss, I pray thee me say,
That I may help to remedy.
EVERYMAN: Yea, good Fellowship, yea.   210
I am in great jeopardy.
FELLOWSHIP: My true friend, show to me your mind.
I will not forsake thee to my life's end,
In the way of good company.
EVERYMAN: That is well spoken and lovingly.   215
FELLOWSHIP: Sir, I must needs know your heaviness.
I have pity to see you in any distress.
If any have you wronged, ye shall revenged be
Though I on the ground be slain for thee,
Though that I know before that I should die.   220
EVERYMAN: Verily, Fellowship, gramercy.
FELLOWSHIP: Tush! By thy thanks I set not a straw.
Show me your grief and say no more.
EVERYMAN: If I my heart should to you break,
And then you to turn your mind from me   225
And would not me comfort when you hear me speak,
Then should I ten times sorrier be.
FELLOWSHIP: Sir, I say as I will do in deed.
EVERYMAN: Then be you a good friend at need;
I have found you true here before.   230
FELLOWSHIP: And so ye shall evermore,
For in faith, and thou go to hell
I will not forsake thee by the way.
EVERYMAN: Ye speak like a good friend, I believe you well.
I shall deserve it and I may.[14]
FELLOWSHIP: I speak of no deserving by this day,
For he that will say and nothing do
Is not worthy with good company to go;
Therefore show me the grief of your mind,
As to your friend most loving and kind.   240

---

[13]Here and at many other places in the play, "and" = "if."
[14]In modern idiom, the line means, "I owe you one."

EVERYMAN: I shall show you how it is:
Commanded I am to go a journey —
A long way, hard and dangerous —
And give a straight count without delay
Before the high judge Adonai.   245
Wherefore I pray you bear me company,
As ye have promised, in this journey.
FELLOWSHIP: That is matter indeed! Promise is duty,
But and I should take such a voyage on me,
I know it well, it should be to my pain.   250
Also it makes me afraid, certain.
But let us take counsel here, as well as we can,
For your words would fear[15]a strong man.
EVERYMAN: Why, ye said if I had need,
Ye would me never forsake, quick nor dead,   255
Though it were to hell truly.
FELLOWSHIP: So I said certainly,
But such pleasures be set aside, the sooth to say.
And also — if we took such a journey,
When should we come again?   260
EVERYMAN: Nay never again till the day of doom.
FELLOWSHIP: In faith? Then will not I come there!
Who hath you these tidings brought?
EVERYMAN: Indeed, Death was with me here.
FELLOWSHIP: Now by God that all hath bought,   265
If Death were the messenger,
For no man that is living today
I will not go that loathsome journey —
Not for the father that begot me!
EVERYMAN: Ye promised me otherwise, pardie![16]
FELLOWSHIP: I wot well, I said so truly.
And yet if thou wilt eat and drink and make good cheer,
Or haunt to women, that lusty company,
I would not forsake you while the day is clear.
Trust me, verily.   275
EVERYMAN: Yea, thereto ye would be ready —
To go to mirth, solace, and play.
Your mind to folly will sooner apply.
Than to bear me company in my long journey.
FELLOWSHIP: Nay, in good faith, I will not that way.   280
But and thou will murder or any man kill,
In that I will help thee with a good will.
EVERYMAN: Oh, that is a simple advise, indeed.
Gentle Fellow, help me in my necessity;
We have loved long, and now I need,   285
And now, gentle Fellowship, remember me.
FELLOWSHIP: Whether ye have loved me or no,

[15]frighten
[16]From Old French "par Dé" = by God.

90

By Saint John, I will not with thee go.
EVERYMAN: Yet I pray thee, take the labor and do so much for me:
  To bring me forward, for Saint Charity,   290
  And comfort me till I come without the town.
FELLOWSHIP: Nay, and thou would give me a new gown
  I will not one foot with thee go.
  But and thou had tarried, I would not have left thee so.
  And as now, God speed thee in thy journey,   295
  For from thee I will depart as fast as I may.

(He starts to leave.)

EVERYMAN: Whither away? Fellowship, will thou forsake me?
FELLOWSHIP: Yea, by my faith. To God I betake thee.
EVERYMAN: Farewell, good Fellowship. For thee my heart is sore.
  Adieu, for I shall never see thee no more.   300
FELLOWSHIP: In faith, Everyman, farewell now at the end.
  For you I will remember that parting is mourning.

(He exits.)

EVERYMAN: Alack! Shall we thus depart indeed?
  O Lady, help! Without any more comfort,
  Lo, Fellowship forsaketh me in my most need.   305
  For help in this world, whither shall I resort?
  Fellowship here-before with me would merry make,
  And now little sorrow for me doth he take.
  It is said: In prosperity, men friends may find
  Which in adversity be full unkind!   310
  Now whither for succor shall I flee,
  Since that Fellowship hath forsaken me?
  To my kinsmen I will, truly,
  Praying them to help me in my necessity.
  I believe that they will do so,   315
  For kind will creep where it may not go.
  I will go say, for yonder I see them go.
  Where be you now, my friends and kinsmen?

(KINDRED a man, and COUSIN, a young woman, enter.)

KINDRED: Here we be now at your commandment.
  Cousin, I pray you show us your intent   320
  In any wise, and do not spare.
COUSIN: Yea, Everyman, and to us declare
  If ye be disposed to go anywhere;
  For wit you well, we will live and die together.
KINDRED: In wealthy and woe, we will with you hold,   325
  For over his kin, a man may be bold.
EVERYMAN: Gramercy,[17] my friends and kinsmen kind!
  Now shall I show you the grief of my mind:
  I was commanded by a messenger,

[17]From Middle French "grand merci" = great thanks.

That is a high king's officer. 330
He bade me go on pilgrimage to my pain,
And I know well I shall never come again.
Also I must give a reckoning straight,
For I have a great enemy that hath me in wait,
Which intendeth me for to hinder. 335
KINDRED: What account is that which ye must render?
That would I know.
EVERYMAN: Of all my works, I must show
How I have lived and my days spent.
Also of ill deeds that I have used 340
In my time since life was me lent,
And of all virtues that I have refused.
Therefore, I pray you, go thither with me
To help to make mine account, for Saint Charity.
COUSIN: What? To go thither? Is that the matter? 345
Nay, Everyman, I had liefer fast bread and water
All this five year and more!
EVERYMAN: Alas that ever I was born!
For now shall I never be merry,
If that you forsake me. 350
KINDRED: Ah, sir! What? Ye be a merry man.
Take good heart to you, and make no moan.
But one thing I warn you, by Saint Anne:
As for me, ye shall go alone!
EVERYMAN: My cousin, will you not with me go?
COUSIN: No, by our Lady! I have the cramp in my toe.
Trust not to me, for — so God me speed —
I will deceive you in your most need.

KINDRED: It availeth you not us to tice[18]
Ye shall have my maid, with all my heart. 360
She loveth to go to feasts, there to be nice,
And to dance, and abroad to start.
I will give her leave to help you in that journey,
If that you and she may agree.
EVERYMAN: Now show me the very effect of your mind: 365
Will you go with me, or abide behind?
KINDRED: Abide behind! Yea, that will I, and I may.
Therefore farewell till another day.

(He exits hurriedly.)

EVERYMAN: How should I be merry or glad?
For fair promises men to me make 370
But when I have most need, they me forsake.
I am deceived! That maketh me sad.
COUSIN: Cousin Everyman, farewell now,
For verily, I will not go with you.

---

[18]entice

Also of my own an unready reckoning   375
I have to account; therefore I make tarrying.
Now God keep thee, for now I go.

(And she is gone.)

EVERYMAN: Ah Jesus! Is all come here-to?
Lo, fair words make fools fain.
They promise much, and nothing will do, certain.   380
My kinsmen promised me faithfully
For to abide with me steadfastly,
And now fast away do they fly.
Even so Fellowship promised me.
What friend were best me of to provide?   385
I lose my time here, longer to abide.
Yet in my mind a thing there is:
All my life I have loved riches.
If that my good[19] now help me might,
He would make my heart full light.   390
I will speak to him in this distress.
Where art thou, my goods and riches?

*(EVERYMAN uncovers a pile lying to one side of the stage. The pile
turns out to be GOODS, an obese person loaded down with treasure
chests and money bags. GOODS awakens from a sound sleep.)*

GOODS: Who calleth me? Everyman? What? Hast thou haste?
I lie here in corners trussed and piled so high,
And in chests I am locked so fast —   395
Also sacked in bags, thou mayst see with thine eye.
I cannot stir — in packs low I lie.
What would ye have? Lightly me say.
EVERYMAN: Come hither Good in all the haste thou may,
For of counsel I must desire thee.   400
GOODS: Sir, and ye in the world have trouble or adversity,
That can I help you to remedy shortly.
EVERYMAN: It is another disease that grieveth me.
In this world it is not — I tell thee so.
I am sent for another way to go   405
To give a straight account general
Before the highest Jupiter of all.
And all my life I have had joy and pleasure in thee.
Therefore, I pray thee, go with me.
For peradventure thou mayst before God almighty   410
My reckoning help to clean and purify;
For it is said ever among,
That money maketh all right that is wrong.
GOODS: Nay, nay! Everyman, I sing another song.
I follow no man in such voyages,   415
For and I went with thee,

[19]goods

93

Thou shouldst fare much the worse for me.
For because on me thou did set thy mind,
Thy reckoning I have made blotted and blind
That thine account thou cannot make truly —   420
And that hast thou for the love of me.
EVERYMAN: That would grieve me full sore,
When I should come to that fearful answer.
Up! Let us go thither together.
GOODS: Nay, not so! I am too brittle — I may not endure.   425
I will follow no man one foot, be ye sure.
EVERYMAN: Alas I have thee loved, and had great pleasure
All my life days on my good and treasure.
GOODS: That is to thy damnation without leasing,
For my love is contrary to the love everlasting.   430
But if thou had me loved moderately during,
As to the poor to give part of me,
Then shouldst thou not in this dolor be,
Nor in this great sorrow and care.
EVERYMAN: Lo now! I was deceived or I was ware,   435
And all I may wite[20] my spending of time.
GOODS: What? Weenest thou that I am thine?
EVERYMAN: I had weened so.
GOODS: Nay, Everyman, I say no.
As for a while I was lent thee —   440
A season thou hast had me in prosperity.
My condition is man's soul to kill:
If I save one, a thousand I do spill.
Weenest thou that I will follow thee
From this world? Nay, verily!   445
EVERYMAN: I had weened otherwise.
GOODS: Therefore, to thy soul, Good is a thief,
For then thou art dead, this is my guise:
Another to deceive in this same wise
As I have done thee, and all to his soul's reproof.   450
EVERYMAN: O false Good! Cursed thou be!
Thou traitor to God! Thou hast deceived me
And caught me in thy snare.
GOODS: Mary, thou brought thyself in care,
Whereof I am glad —   455
I must needs laugh! I cannot be sad.
EVERYMAN: Ah, Good, thou hast had my hearty love —
I gave thee that which should be the Lord's above.
But wilt thou not go with me indeed?
I pray thee truth to say.   460
GOODS: No! So God me speed,
Therefore farewell, and have good day.

(And GOODS pulls the covers back up and goes back to sleep.)

---

[20]blame

EVERYMAN: Oh, to whom shall I make my moan,
    For to go with me in that heavy journey?
    First Fellowship said he would with me go —   465
    His words were very pleasant and gay —
    But afterward he left me alone.
    Then spake I to my kinsmen, all in despair,
    And also they gave me words fair;
    They lacked no fair speaking,   470
    But all forsook me in the ending.
    Then went I to my Goods that I love best,
    In hope to have found comfort, but there had I least,
    For my Goods sharply did me tell
    That he bringeth many into hell!   475
    Then of myself I was ashamed,
    And so I am worthy to be blamed.
    Thus may I well myself hate —
    Of whom shall I now counsel take?
    I think that I shall never speed   480
    Till that I go to my Good Deed.
    But else, she is so weak
    That she can neither go nor speak.
    Yet will I venture on her now —
    My Good Deeds where be you?   485

(EVERYMAN uncovers GOOD DEEDS, lying to one side of the stage. She is emaciated and bound hand and foot.)

GOOD DEEDS: Here I lie, cold on the ground.
    Thy sins have me so sore bound
    That I cannot stir.
EVERYMAN: O Good Deeds, I stand in fear!
    I must you pray of counsel,   490
    For help now should come right well.
GOOD DEEDS: Everyman, I have understanding
    That thou art summoned account to make
    Before Messias of Jerusalem king.
    And you do by me, that journey with you will I take.   495
EVERYMAN: Therefore I come, to you my moan to make.
    I pray thee to go with me.
GOOD DEEDS: I would full fain, but I cannot stand, verily.
EVERYMAN: Why? Is there anything on you fall?
GOOD DEEDS: Yea, sir! I may thank you of all!   500
    If ye had perfectly cheered me,
    Your book of account now full ready had been.
    Look: The books of your works and deeds, eke —
    Behold how they lie here under feet,
    To your soul's heaviness.   505

(EVERYMAN picks up the book which she indicates and opens it.)

EVERYMAN: Our Lord Jesus help me,
    For one letter here I cannot see.
GOOD DEEDS: Here is a blind[21]reckoning in time of distress.
EVERYMAN: Good Deeds, I pray you help me in this need,
    Or else I am forever damned indeed   510
    Therefore help me to make my reckoning
    Before the Redeemer of all thing,
    That king is and was and ever shall.
GOOD DEEDS: Everyman, I am sorry of your fall
    And fain would I help you, and I were able.
EVERYMAN: Good Deeds, your counsel, I pray you, give me.
GOOD DEEDS: That shall I do verily,
    Though that on my feet I may not go.
    I have a sister that shall with you also,
    Called Knowledge, which shall with you abide   520
    To help you to make that dreadful reckoning.
KNOWLEDGE: *(She enters from the wings)* Everyman, I will go with thee
    and be thy guide,
    In thy most need to go by thy side.
EVERYMAN: In good condition I am now in everything,
    And am wholly content with this good thing.   525
    Thanked be God, my creator!
GOOD DEEDS: And when he hath brought you there,
    Where thou shalt heal thee of thy smart,
    Then go you with your reckoning and your Good Deeds together
    For to make you joyful at heart   530
    Before the blessed trinity.
EVERYMAN: My Good Deeds, I thank thee heartfully!
    I am well content, certainly,
    With your words sweet.
KNOWLEDGE: Now go we together lovingly   535
    To Confession, that cleansing river.
EVERYMAN: For joy I weep! I would we were there!
    But I pray you give me cognition:
    Where dwelleth that holy virtue, Confession?
KNOWLEDGE: In the house of salvation.   540

(As she speaks, they cross to a small booth.)

    We shall find him in that place,
    That shall us comfort, by God's grace.

(She opens the door, revealing CONFESSION, dressed in the robes of a priest.)

    Lo, this is Confession. Kneel down and ask mercy,
    For he is in good conceit with God almighty.
EVERYMAN: *(Kneeling)* A glorious Fountain that all uncleanness
    doth clarify,   545
    Wash from me the spots of unclean vices
    That on me no sin may be seen.

---

[21]Blind can mean both sightless and defective.

I come with Knowledge for my redemption,
Repent with hearty and full contrition.
For I am commanded a pilgrimage to take   550
And great accounts before God to make.
Now I pray you, Shrift, mother of salvation,
Help my Good Deeds, for my piteous exclamation.
CONFESSION: I know your sorrow well, Everyman.
Because with Knowledge ye come to me,   555
I will you comfort as well as I can,
And a precious jewel I will give thee
Called penance, voider of adversity.
Therewith shall your body chastised be,
With abstinence and perseverance in God's service.   560
Here shall you receive that scourge of me,
Which is penance strong that ye must endure.
Remember, thy Savior was scourged for thee
With sharp scourges and suffered it patiently.
So must thou ere thou escape that painful pilgrimage.   565

(CONFESSION hands EVERYMAN the scourge of penance.)

Knowledge, keep him in this voyage,
And by that time Good Deeds will be with thee.
But in any wise, be sure of mercy,
For your time draweth fast and ye will saved be.
Ask God mercy, and he will grant it thee: 570
When with the scourge of penance man doth him bind,
The oil of forgiveness then shall he find.
EVERYMAN: *(Standing and examining the whip.)* Thanked be God for his
gracious work,
For now I will my penance begin.
This hath rejoiced and lighted my heart,   575
Though the knots be painful and hard within.
KNOWLEDGE: Everyman, look your penance that ye fulfill,
What pain that ever it to you be,
And I shall give you counsel at will
How your account ye shall make clearly.   580
EVERYMAN: *(He gives the scourge to KNOWLEDGE and kneels again.)*
O eternal God! O heavenly Figure!
O Way of righteousness! O goodly Vision,
Which descended down in a virgin pure,
Because he would Everyman redeem
Which Adam forfeited by his disobedience —   585
O blessed Godhead elect and high divine,
Forgive my grievous offense.
Here I cry thee mercy in this presence,
O ghostly Treasure. O merciful Redeemer,
Of all the world hope and conductor,   590
Mirror of joy, Foundation of mercy,
Which illumineth heaven and earth thereby:

Hear my clamorous complaint, though it late be.
Receive my prayers unworthy in this heavy life.
Though I be a sinner most abominable,   595
Yet let my name be written in Moses' table.
O Mary, pray to the Maker of all things
Me for to help at my ending,
And save me from the power of my enemy,[22]
For Death assaileth me strongly.   600
And Lady, that I may, by means of thy prayer,
Of your son's glory to be partaker,
By the means of his passion I it crave.
I beseech you, help my soul to save.

(He turns to KNOWLEDGE.)

Knowledge, give me the scourge of penance;   605
My flesh therewith shall have acquaintance.
I will now begin, if God give me grace.
KNOWLEDGE: *(She hands him the scourge.)* Everyman, God give
    you time and space.
Thus I bequeath you in the hands of our Savior.
Now may you make your reckoning sure!   610
EVERYMAN: In the name of the holy Trinity,
My body punished sore shall be.
Take this body, for the sin of the flesh!

(He strikes his back with the whip.)

Also thou delightest to go gay and fresh,
And in the way of damnation thou did me bring;   615
Therefore, suffer now strokes of punishing.

(He strikes himself again.)

Now of penance I will wade the water clear
To save me from hell and from the fire.

(He strikes again.)

GOOD DEEDS: *(She throws off her fetters and stands up.)* I thank God, now
    I can walk and go.
I am delivered of my sickness and woe.   620
Therefore, with Everyman I will go and not spare;
His good works I will help him to declare.
KNOWLEDGE: Now, Everyman, be merry and glad!
Your Good Deeds cometh; now ye may not be sad.
Now is your Good Deeds whole and sound,   625
Going upright on the ground.
EVERYMAN: My heart is light and shall be evermore.
Now will I smite faster than I did before.

(He gives himself three more strokes.)

---

[22]Everyman refers here to Satan; as God's messenger, Death is not likely to be considered
Everyman's enemy.

GOOD DEEDS: Everyman, pilgrim, my special friend,
    Blessed be thou without end!   630
    For thee is prepared the eternal glory.
    Ye have me made whole and sound;
    Therefore, I will abide with thee in every stound.[23]
EVERYMAN: Welcome, my Good Deeds! Now I hear thy voice,
    I weep for very sweetness of love.   635
KNOWLEDGE: *(She takes the whip from him and hands him a purple
    robe.)* Be no more sad but ever more rejoice;
    God seeth thy living in his throne above.
    Put on this garment to thy behalf,
    Which is wet with your tears,
    Or else before God you may it miss   640
    When you to your journey's end come shall.
EVERYMAN: *(Taking the robe.)* Gentle Knowledge, what do you it
    call?
KNOWLEDGE: It is the garment of sorrow;
    From pain it will you borrow.
    Contrition, it is,   645
    That getteth forgiveness.
    It pleaseth God passing well.
GOOD DEEDS: Everyman, will you wear it for your healing?
EVERYMAN: *(Putting on the robe.)* Now blessed be Jesu, Mary's son,
    For now have I on true contrition.   650
    And let us go now without tarrying.
    Good Deeds, have we clear our reckoning?
GOOD DEEDS: *(Showing him the book.)* Yea, indeed. I have it.
EVERYMAN: Then I trust we need not fear,
    Now friends, let us not part in twain.   655
KNOWLEDGE[24]: Nay, Everyman, that will we not certain.
GOOD DEEDS: Yet must thou lead with thee
    Three persons of great might.
EVERYMAN: Who should they be?
GOOD DEEDS: Discretion and Strength they hight,   660
    And thy Beauty may not abide behind.
KNOWLEDGE: Also ye must call to mind
    Your Five Wits as for your counselors.
GOOD DEEDS: You must have them ready at all hours.
EVERYMAN: How shall I get them hither?   665
KNOWLEDGE: You must call them all together,
    And they will hear you incontinent.
EVERYMAN: My friends, come hither and be present,
    Discretion, Strength, my Five Wits, and Beauty.

(The four named virtues, all female, enter.)

BEAUTY: Here at your will we be all ready.   670

[23]time
[24]In the original, this speech and the one in lines 666-667 were assigned to KINDRED;
assuming these designations were printer's errors, I have assigned the speeches to
KNOWLEDGE.

What will ye that we should do?
GOOD DEEDS: That ye would with Everyman go
And help him in his pilgrimage.
Advise you: Will ye with him go, or not, in this voyage?
STRENGTH: We will bring him all thither   675
To help and comfort him. Ye may believe me.
DISCRETION: So will we go with him all together.
EVERYMAN: Almighty God, loved may thou be!
I give thee laud that I have hither brought
Strength, Discretion, Beauty, and Five Wits. Lack I nought.   680
And my Good Deeds with Knowledge clear
All be in my company at my will here,
I desire no more to my business.
STRENGTH: And I, Strength, will stand by you in distress,
Though thou would in battle fight on the ground²⁵   685
FIVE WITS: And though it were through the world round,
We will not depart for sweet nor for sour.
BEAUTY: No more will I unto death's hour,
Whatsoever thereof befall.
DISCRETION: Everyman, advise you first of all.   690
Go with a good advisement and deliberation.
We all give you virtuous monition
That all shall be well.
EVERYMAN: My friends, hearken what I will tell:
I pray God reward you in his heavenly sphere.   695
Now hearken all that be here,
For I will make my testament.
Here, before you all present,
In alms, half my good I give with my hands twain
In the way of charity with good intent,   700
And the other half still shall remain.
I it bequeath to be returned where it ought to be.
This I do in despite of the Fiend of hell
To go quite out of his peril,
Ever after this day.   705
KNOWLEDGE: Everyman, hearken what I say:
Go to Priesthood, I you advise,
And receive of him in any wise
The holy sacrament and ointment together,
Then shortly see ye turn again hither.   710
We will all abide you here.
FIVE WITS: Yea, Everyman, hie you that ye ready were.
There is no Emperor, King, Duke, nor Baron
That of God hath commission
As hath the least priest in the world being.   715
For of the blessed sacraments, pure and benign,
He beareth the keys and thereof hath the cure
For man's redemption — it is ever sure —

---

²⁵To do battle on the ground instead of on horseback was to be at a definite disadvantage.

Which God for our souls' medicine
Gave us out of his heart with great pain. 720
Here, in this transitory life, for thee and me
The blessed sacraments seven there be:
Baptism, confirmation, with priesthood good,
And the sacrament of God's precious flesh and blood,
Marriage, the holy extreme unction, and penance; 725
These seven be good to have in remembrance —
Gracious sacraments of high divinity.
EVERYMAN: Fain would I receive that holy body,
And meekly to my ghostly[26] father I will go.
FIVE WITS: Everyman, that is the best that ye can do 730
God will you to salvation bring,
For Priesthood exceedeth all other thing.
To us holy scripture they do teach,
And converteth man from sin, heaven to reach.
God hath to them more power given 735
Than to any angel that is in heaven.
With five words he may consecrate
God's body in flesh and blood to make
And handleth his Maker between his hands.
The priest bindeth and unbindeth all bands, 740
Both in earth and in heaven.
Thou ministers all the sacraments seven.
Though we kiss thy feet, thou were worthy.
Thou art the surgeon that cureth sin deadly.
No remedy we find under God 745
But all only Priesthood.
Everyman, God gave priests that dignity
And setteth them in his stead among us to be,
Thus be they above angels in degree.

(As KNOWLEDGE and FIVE WITS continue their discussion of priesthood, EVERYMAN enters a mansion which represents a church.)

KNOWLEDGE: If priests be good, it is so surely. 750
But when Jesu hanged on the cross with great smart,
There he *gave* us out of his blessed heart
The same sacrament in great torment;
He sold them not to us, that Lord omnipotent.
Therefore, Saint Peter the apostle doth say 755
That Jesus' curse have all they
Which God their savior do buy or sell,
Or they for any money do take or tell.[27]
Sinful priests giveth the sinners example bad.
Their children sitteth by other men's fires, I have heard, 760

[26]spiritual
[27]A reference to Peter's rebuke of Simon the sorcerer who offered to pay for the power to bestow the Holy Spirit. Acts 8:9-24.

101

And some haunteth women's company
With unclean life, as lusts of lechery.
These be with sin made blind.
FIVE WITS: I trust to God, no such may we find.
    Therefore, let us Priesthood honor   765
    And follow their doctrine for our souls' succor.
    We be their sheep, and they shepherds be,
    By whom we all be kept in surety.

(EVERYMAN emerges from the church.)

    Peace, for yonder I see Everyman come,
    Which hath made true satisfaction.   770
GOOD DEEDS: Methink it is he, indeed.
EVERYMAN: Now Jesu be our elder speed!
    I have received the sacrament for my redemption
    And mine extreme unction.
    Blessed be all they that counseled me to take it!   775
    And now, friends, let us go without longer respite.
    I thank God that ye have tarried so long.
    Now set each of you on this rod your hand,
    And shortly follow me.

(He extends to them his pilgrim's staff which they all grasp.)

    I go before there I would be. God, be our guide.   780
STRENGTH: Everyman, we will not from you go
    Till ye have gone this voyage long.
DISCRETION: I, Discretion, will bide by you also.
KNOWLEDGE: And, though this pilgrimage be never so strong,
    I will never part you from.   785
STRENGTH: Everyman, I will be as sure by thee
    As ever I was by Judas Macabee.
EVERYMAN: *(He takes only a few steps which bring him near his grave.)*
    Alas, I am so faint I may not stand.
    My limbs under me do fold.
    Friends, let us not turn again to this land,   790
    Not for all the world's gold,
    For into this cave must I creep
    And turn to the earth and there to sleep.
BEAUTY: What? Into this grave? Alas!
EVERYMAN: Yea, there shall we consume, more and less.   795
BEAUTY: And what? Should I smother here?
EVERYMAN: Yea, by my faith, and never more appear.
    In this world live no more we shall,
    But in heaven before the highest Lord of all.
BEAUTY: I cross out all this! Adieu, by Saint John!   800
    I take my cap in my lap and am gone.

(She starts off.)

EVERYMAN: What? Beauty, whither will ye?
BEAUTY: Peace! I am deaf! I look not behind me,

Not and thou would give me all the gold in thy chest.

(She's gone.)

EVERYMAN: Alas! Whereto may I trust? 805
Beauty goeth fast away from me.
She promises with me to live and die.
STRENGTH: Everyman, I will thee also forsake and deny.
Thy game liketh me not at all.
EVERYMAN: Why, then ye will forsake me all? 810
Sweet Strength, tarry a little space.
STRENGTH: Nay, sir, by the rod of grace![28]
I will hie me from thee fast,
Though thou weep till thy heart burst.
EVERYMAN: Ye would ever bide by me, ye said. 815
STRENGTH: Yea, I have you far enough conveyed.
Ye be old enough, I understand,
Your pilgrimage to take on hand.
I repent me that I hither came.
EVERYMAN: Strength, you to displease I am to blame. 820
Will you break promise that is debt?
STRENGTH: In faith, I care not.
Thou art but a fool to complain.
You spend your speech and waste your brain.
Go thrust thee into the ground! 825

(And she exits without looking back.)

EVERYMAN: I had weened surer I should you have found.
He that trusteth in his Strength,
She him deceiveth at the length.
Both Strength and Beauty forsaketh me,
Yet they promised me steadfast to be. 830
DISCRETION: Everyman, I will after Strength be gone;
As for me, I will leave you alone.
EVERYMAN: Why Discretion! Will ye forsake me?
DISCRETION: Yea, in faith, I will go from thee,
For when Strength is gone before, 835
I follow after evermore.
EVERYMAN: Yet I pray thee, for love of the Trinity,
Look in my grave once piteously.
DISCRETION: Nay! So nigh I will not come!
Now farewell, fellows, everyone. 840

(She exits.)

EVERYMAN: Oh! All thing faileth save God alone —
Beauty, Strength, and Discretion —
For when Death bloweth his blast,
They all run away from me fast.
FIVE WITS: Everyman, my leave now of thee I take. 845

[28]the cross

I will follow the other, for here I thee foresake.
EVERYMAN: Alas! Then may I wail and weep,
    For I took you for my best friend.
FIVE WITS: I will no longer thee keep.
    Now farewell, and there an end.   850

(She exits.)

EVERYMAN: O Jesu, help! All hath forsaken me.
GOOD DEEDS: Nay, Everyman, I will abide with thee.
    I will not forsake thee, indeed;
    Thou shalt find me a good friend at need.
EVERYMAN: Gramercy, Good Deeds. Now may I true friends see.   855
    They have forsaken me everyone.
    I loved them better than my Good Deeds alone.
    Knowledge, will ye forsake me also?
KNOWLEDGE: Yea, Everyman, when you to Death shall go,
    But not yet, for no manner of danger.   860
EVERYMAN: Gramercy, Knowledge, with all my heart!
KNOWLEDGE: Nay, yet I will not from hence depart,
    Till I see where ye shall be come.
EVERYMAN: Methink, alas, that I must be gone
    To make my reckoning and my debts pay.   865
    For I see my time is nigh spent away.
    Take example, all ye that this do hear or see,
    How they that I love best now forsake me,
    Except my Good Deeds — that bideth truly.
GOOD DEEDS: All earthly things is but vanity.   870
    Beauty, Strength, and Discretion do man forsake,
    Foolish Friends and Kinsmen that fair spake.
    All fleeth save Good Deeds, and that am I.
EVERYMAN: Have mercy on me, God most mighty,
    And stand by me, thou mother and maid Mary.   875
GOOD DEEDS: Fear not. I will speak for thee.
EVERYMAN: Here I cry God mercy.
GOOD DEEDS: Short our end and minish our pain;[29]
    Let us go and never come again.
EVERYMAN: *(As he speaks, he climbs into his grave.)* Into thy hands,
    Lord, my soul I commend.   880
    Receive it, Lord, that it be not lost.
    As thou me boughtest so me defend,
    And save me from the Fiend's boast,
    That I may appear with that blessed host
    That shall be saved at the day of doom.   885
    In manus tuas of mights most,
    Forever *commendo spiritum meum.*[30]

(He lies back and disappears in the grave.)

[29]Shorten our end and diminish our pain.
[30]In manus tuas commendo spiritum meum = Latin for "Into your hands I commend my spirit." Everyman quotes Jesus' last words. See Luke 23:46.

KNOWLEDGE: Now hath he suffered that we all shall endure.
Thy Good Deeds shall make all sure.
Now hath he made ending. 890
Methinketh that I hear angels sing
And make great joy and melody
Where Everyman's soul received shall be.
ANGEL: *(The ANGEL enters from heaven. As he speaks, he takes EVERY-*
MAN by the hand, helps him from the grave, and leads him to the
throne where God welcomes him.) Come, excellent elect spouse to
Jesu.
Here above thou shalt go 895
Because of thy singular virtue.
Now thy soul is taken thy body from;
Thy reckoning is crystal clear.
Now shalt thou into the heavenly sphere,
Unto the which all ye shall come 900
That liveth well before the day of doom.
DOCTOR: *(He enters and addresses the audience.)* This moral men may have
in mind:
Ye hearers, take it of worth, old and young,
And forsake pride, for he deceives you in the end.
And remember, beauty, five wits, strength, and discretion — 905
They all at last do everyman forsake,
Save his good deeds there doth he take.
But beware: And they be small,
Before God he hath no help at all.
None excuse may be there for everyman. 910
Alas, how shall he do then?
For after death, amends may no man make,
For then mercy and pity doth him forsake.
If his reckoning be not clear when he doth come,
God will say, *"Ite, maledicti, in ignem eternum."*[31] 915
And he that hath his account whole and sound,
High in heaven he shall be crowned,
Unto which place God bring us all thither,
That we may live body and soul together.
Thereto help the Trinity. 920
Amen, say ye, for Saint Charity.

---

[31]Latin for "Go, you cursed, into eternal fire." The Doctor quotes from Jesus' teaching
about the day of judgment. See Matthew 25:41.

THE RENAISSANCE
PERIOD: The Re-Creation
of Classical Theatre

During the fifteenth, sixteenth, and seventeenth centuries, most of western Europe experienced an ideological upheaval that so transformed life that people ever since have referred to it as the Renaissance — "the rebirth." The effects of this change touched all aspects of life — religion, politics, science, and philosophy. Such a powerful movement could not help but change the now-art, theatre.

The people of the Renaissance thought they had rediscovered — and were re-establishing — the classical world of ancient Greece and Rome. In reality, they recaptured part of the classical ideal, combined it with certain aspects of the medieval tradition, and created a new world which was different from any period before and which, more significantly than either the classical or medieval worlds, laid the foundations for the present age.

While the Renaissance began in Italy and reached its purest expression in Italy and France, this introduction focuses primarily on the English Elizabethan[1] theatre of the late sixteenth and early seventeenth centuries, the theatre that produced the most important English language playwright of all times, William Shakespeare.

Political/Social/Philosophical Backgrounds

For a century or more, internal pressures, new developments, and Muslim expansion from the east and south had threatened to destroy the community of thought and practices which characterized medieval Europe.

The Renaissance Begins

Two events in the middle of the fifteenth century finally touched off the explosion of the Renaissance: First, in 1453, Constantinople fell to the Muslims, with the result that many Greek scholars fled to Italy, bringing with them the writings of ancient Greek writers. This event triggered intense interest in pre-Christian Greek and Roman traditions. And in 1465, the movable-type printing press, invented by Johannes Gutenberg (1390-1468), was imported to Italy. This invention made possible the quick, wide-spread publication of the classics and the ideas they triggered.

While Renaissance people knew about the Greek writers, they considered Rome to be the pinnacle of classical ideals. As a result, the plays of Plautus and Terence and the dramatic theories of Horace held

---

[1]This period of time in England is often called the Elizabethan age because it was dominated by the policies of Queen Elizabeth I who ruled England from 1558 until her death in 1603.

more importance for them than the Greek playwrights and Aristotle.
Today we usually oversimplify the changes which occurred during the
Renaissance by saying that the Middle Ages were religious, while the new
era was secular. Indeed, Renaissance folk did focus on current human en-
deavor as important in itself instead of as a preparation for the hereafter.
But Europeans continued a deep interest in religion as evidenced by the
Protestant Reformation, the Catholic Counter-Reformation, and the religi-
ous wars which grew out of this conflict.

Renaissance Changes

Furthermore, the new perspectives developed by the Renaissance had
considerable variety. In politics, for instance, nationalism replaced
feudalism. In religion and politics, pluralism began to replace community
of thought and belief, and classical samples took precedence over tradition
as the supreme authority. The discovery of the New World by Columbus in
1492 provided a new source of wealth and a vastly expanded world view.
And the discovery of Galileo Galilei (1564-1642) that the sun, planets, and
rest of the universe did not revolve around the earth expanded people's
concept of the world even further. These changes were reflected in the theatrical practices and the drama of the Renaissance.

The Puritans

Political and social revolution spread across England through the first
half of the seventeenth century as the Puritans championed the rights of
the common man against the aristocracy. While the Puritans succeeded in
instituting many democratic reforms, they also opposed theatre, and when
Parliament finally had the power in 1642, they closed down the theatres.
London would not see regular theatre performances again until after the
Restoration of the monarchy in 1660, and by then it was a new world all
over again.

Theatrical Organization

In contrast with medieval practice, Renaissance theatre was primarily
professional theatre — theatre in which the performers earned their living
by doing their art. Exceptions included the English inns of court where law
students staged plays as an exercise in learning public speaking, the Italian
academies (club-like groups organized for the purpose of studying various
topics such as classical theatre), and the child acting companies of England
in which choirmasters exploited the talents of the boys in their care by
having them perform plays. Important professional theatre groups of the
Renaissance included the Italian commedia dell'arte troupes, which toured
all over Europe doing popular improvisational theatre, and the English
acting companies.

English Acting Companies

The typical English acting company was licensed by a royal "patent,"
and functioned under the patronage of a royal person or aristocrat whose name
they bore; Shakespeare's company, for instance, was the Chamberlain's Men
and later became the King's Men. An acting company included three kinds

of participants: Patent-holding members, hired men, and apprentices.

Patent Members

The "patent members," who usually numbered about twelve, were the primary stockholders in the company. Their main task, along with making operational decisions, was performing the major roles in plays. Some of the patent members were also "householders," who owned a share in the theatre building itself. After paying expenses, the patent members divided between them whatever profits remained.

Hired Men

The company employed "hired men" to play music, assist backstage, act walk-on roles, clean the theatre, collect fees, and so on. Hired men earned wages similar to those of unskilled laborers.

Apprentices

Some patent members accepted apprentices, boys whose fathers paid to have them live with the master artist and learn his craft. Apprentices played the roles of children and women. These companies experienced very little turnover in personnel, and when a patent member died, his apprentice frequently inherited his place in the company (and also, often, his house and wife). Shakespeare came to London as an adult, joined the Chamberlain's Men, and became a patent member by 1595; he was also a householder who owned a share in the Globe Theatre.

Scripts

Acting companies usually bought scripts outright from playwrights, after which the scripts were the sole property of the company. Because there were no copyright laws, companies jealously guarded their scripts; it would be an unwise business practice to make their plays easily available to the competition by publishing them.

Theatre Architecture

The large Elizabethan public theatres were located on the south bank of the Thames River, just outside London's city limits and the jurisdiction of London's conservative city council. Although some variety existed among these theatres and a great deal of controversy surrounds their specific features, they seem to have shared certain basic characteristics. They were open-air structures with several stories of galleries surrounding a roofless courtyard. A large platform stage, attached to one side of the building, thrust out into the courtyard and provided the primary acting space. The facade which backed the stage probably had a small inner stage area, which could be curtained off from view, and one or more levels of balconies, which could be used as elevated acting areas or places for musicians. This part of the building, called the "tiring house," was used for off-stage actors, costume changes, and storage. The stage probably had a canopy roof called the "heavens" which covered most of it, and which may have contained machinery for flying in actors and prop items. The stage probably had one or more traps giving access to a low-ceilinged, cellar-like space called the "hell."

109

This relatively simple stage area provided an excellent performance space. It easily accommodated the large casts of Elizabethan plays, provided several levels for performers, and facilitated the unbroken flow of multi-scened plays.

Diverse Audiences

Audience members surrounded the stage on three sides and arranged themselves according to social status and finances. The least well-to-do audience members, such as servants and laborers, stood around the stage in the courtyard and were, therefore, known as "groundlings." More wealthy folk paid extra to sit in the covered galleries which surrounded the courtyard. And young men-about-town, who were at least as interested in being seen as they were in seeing the play, managed to buy themselves spaces right on the stage. During the performances, which always occurred in the afternoon, people visited, orange-girls hawked their wares, and prostitutes plied their trade.

This informal, cosmopolitan audience presented a real challenge to Elizabethan playwrights and actors. The plays needed to have enough simple action and bawdy humor to hold the interest of the "groundlings," while still providing intellectual stimulation for the more refined audience members. Judging from the enthusiasm of the audiences, who numbered 1,600 to 2,000 on a good day, the performers and plays met the challenge.

Theatres

During the winter, acting companies performed in "private" indoor theatres. The private theatres, which were usually existing halls remodeled as performance spaces, provided stages roughly similar to the public theatres, but because admission prices were higher, they catered to a smaller, more upper-class audience. And occasionally the actors gave a command performance for the king or queen in a hall in the palace.

While the Dutch and Spanish staged plays in buildings similar to the English public theatres, the other Europeans used different kinds of performance spaces. The Italians, for instance, developed the proscenium arch stage which could accommodate perspective scenery and satisfy the growing demand for spectacular sets. In France, the typical sixteenth-century theatre was a remodeled tennis court with a stage constructed at one end.

During the civil war between the Puritans and the crown in 1642, Parliament closed down the public theatres. Subsequently the buildings burned, gave way to other construction, or were converted into warehouses which, in turn, burned. By the end of the seventeenth century, none remained.

Stagecraft

Scenery

Backed by the unchanging facade of the tiring house, Elizabethan actors performed their plays using little or no scenery. They did this partly because the plays consisted of many scenes, set in different places, which followed each other in rapid succession. Encumbering this kind of plot construction with multiple scenery shifts would have badly slowed down the action. Furthermore, although many of the plays were set in remote periods of history or distant places, Elizabethans were not nearly as interested in historical details of time and place as they were in the behavior of people — actions and words were important; scenery was not.

Lighting

And since plays were staged outside in the afternoon on fair days only, they used no artificial stage lighting. When the actors performed in private theatres or at court, the entire room — stage and audience areas alike — were illuminated with candles and lamps.

Costume

The lack of interest in historical and cultural differences which made specific scenery unnecessary also carried over into costuming with a similar effect. Most costumes were owned and provided by the actors themselves. Since they often purchased second-hand garments of courtiers to use on stage, the costumes, while fancy, were all contemporary; actors might wrap a length of white cloth around their shoulders to indicate a Roman setting for plays about classical times, but they made no attempt to realistically imitate clothing styles different from their own.

The Court Masque

The simple scenic and costuming practices used in Elizabethan plays, however, were abandoned for another kind of drama — the court masque. Masques were dramatic extravaganzas staged by the royalty for themselves and guests of state. The texts for masques consisted of elaborate poetic treatments of mythical subjects. The courtiers and royalty themselves played the roles in masques, and fantastic scenery and costumes were designed for them by people like the famous London architect, Inigo Jones.

Meanwhile, in France, plays utilized simultaneous staging similar to the "mansion-and-platea" settings of the Middle Ages, and in Italy, painted perspective scenery was being developed for plays and opera alike.

Performance Conventions

Elizabethan Theatre

"Speak the speech . . . trippingly on the tongue. But if you mouth it, as many of our players do, I had as lief the town crier spoke my lines. Nor do not saw the air too much with your hand, thus, but use all gently, for in the very torrent, tempest, and . . . whirlwind of your passion, you must acquire and beget a temperance that may give it smoothness . . . . Be not too tame neither . . . . Suit the action to the word, the word to the action, with this special observance: That you o'erstep not the modesty of nature. For anything so o'erdone is [far] from the purpose of playing, whose end, both at the first and now, was and is, to hold as 'twere, the mirror up to nature . . . ."

These lines of *Hamlet* (Act III, Scene ii) demonstrate the dual goals

111

of the Elizabethan actor: Nature and artifice. On the one hand, audiences praised actors for their ability to imitate actual human behavior, or "nature." On the other hand, various conventions of Elizabethan theatre encouraged an artistic modification of reality. First, the practice of assigning female roles (such as Juliet, Ophelia, and Desdemona) to adolescent boy apprentices militated against realism. Also, actors apparently studied the rather stilted gestures and speech modes of contemporary rhetoricians, a practice which certainly facilitated their ability to deal with blank verse and long speeches, but which lent a kind of artificiality to their acting. Furthermore, each actor had a particular "line of business" or type of character he played, such as the heroic lead, the heavy lead or villain, the young lover, and in the case of Shakespeare himself, the noble elder such as the Duke in *Othello* and the Ghost in *Hamlet*. These lines of business "belonged" to the particular actors and they would play them until retirement; this practice would occasionally present an older actor in a youthful role, such as Romeo.

This combination — aspiring to imitate nature while using artificial techniques — gave Elizabethan acting a kind of heightened realism which the audiences loved.

Theory of Drama

Renaissance theorists and dramatists believed that theatre was an imitative art. They believed it should imitate nature and also the works of great masters of the past. However, rather than just duplicate reality and other works, they believed their drama should improve on the models. Plays should not just show the world as it was but rather as it should be, and they should not just translate source materials (such as classical drama, history, and romances) into plays, but should both clarify them and also make them more interesting.

Dramatists had to deal with the problem, however, of whether to adapt their imitations to scholarly ideals or to popular tastes. Theorists drew their scholarly principles primarily from Horace's *On the Poetic Art,* and they considered Horace's opinions to be the laws or rules of drama. These laws can be summarized under five headings:

1. *Form* — A play was to be either a pure tragedy or a pure comedy with no comic elements in the tragedies and no serious elements in the comedies.

2. *Unity* — The action of a play was to occupy only one day (unity of time), to be set in only one locale (unity of place), and to focus on a single story line (unity of action).

3. *Presentation* — A play was to have five acts.

4. *Decorum* — Characters were to adhere to the manner of speaking and behaving considered appropriate to their sex and social status.

5. *Purpose* — A play was supposed to teach good morals.

Legitimate and Illegitimate Drama

Popular tastes inherited from the enjoyment of medieval plays, however, demanded the mingling of comic and tragic elements, sprawling plots with the intermingling of multiple story lines, characters who behaved contrary to expectations, and plays which entertained, regardless of obvious moral value.

Renaissance people arrived at two solutions for this problem of contradictory standards. First, they developed two categories of plays: "Legitimate" or "regular" drama, which obeyed the rules, and "illegitimate" or "irregular" drama, which did not. While scholars considered plays in this latter category, which included such forms as opera, tragicomedy, and the commedia dell'arte, beneath the consideration of cultured folk, the theatre-going public loved them. The second solution was to bend the rules as far as possible in legitimate plays and, if necessary, construct elaborate arguments to demonstrate that, contrary to appearance, the plays really did fit the laws after all.

Dramatic Literature

In addition to Shakespeare, many other playwrights were writing during the Elizabethan period. The most important of these included Christopher Marlowe, Ben Jonson, Francis Beaumont, and John Fletcher.

Christopher Marlowe

Marlowe (1564-93) wrote history plays such as *Dr. Faustus* and *Edward II* which focused on the rise and fall of a strong central character. He perfected blank verse (unrhymed iambic pentameter) as a poetic form suitable for drama.

Ben Jonson

Jonson (1572-1637) aimed to recapture the spirit of the Greek comic dramatist Aristophanes; his satirical comedies such as *Volpone, or The Fox* and *The Alchemist* bitterly criticized human follies such as greed and lechery. Jonson also wrote a number of scripts for court masques.

Beaumont and Fletcher

The romantic comedies and tragedies of the team of Beaumont (1584-1616) and Fletcher (1579-1625), plays such as *Philaster, or Love Lies Bleeding,* had a popularity in the seventeenth century rivaling that of Shakespeare.

Lifestyle of the Playwrights

These playwrights tended to be very busy men. Shakespeare, for instance, who wrote at least thirty-six plays in about twenty years, also participated in the business of theatre as a householder and a patent member of a theatre company, acted regularly, and still found time to write sonnets and long narrative poems. Nor did they live tranquil lives; Jonson was in and out of jail on suspicion of holding treasonous opinions and Marlowe died before the age of thirty in a barroom brawl, perhaps assassinated because of his secret service activities.

Living these kinds of lives, they wrote their plays fast. They took all their story lines from romances or histories, and they let their sources determine how they would develop their plots. They frequently collaborated with other playwrights. And both they and their audiences loved complicated stories embellished with rich language and convoluted ideas. As a result, their plays tend to be sprawling, loosely structured compositions.

They unified their plays by focusing on a strong central character, by taking care to entangle and then unravel their story lines, and by lacing the scenes together with repetitive elements such as themes and motifs.

Although the convoluted plots, the large casts, and the unfamiliarity of the language make these plays challenging reading today, those who rise to the challenge find the plays fresh and rewarding, and those who are fortunate enough to see well-produced Elizabethan plays find them vastly exciting and entertaining.

Shakespeare

Although William Shakespeare was the most important English-language writer of all time, and although he was highly appreciated during his own lifetime, the documented facts about his life are extremely few. He was born in Stratford in 1564 to John Shakespeare and his wife Mary Arden. A glover by trade, John became an alderman the year after William's birth and by 1568 was bailiff, or mayor, of Stratford. At the age of 18, William married Anne Hathaway who, half a year later, bore their daughter, Susanna. Two years later the couple became the parents of twins, Hamnet and Judith.

In 1592, Shakespeare was in London, already busily engaged in his career as actor and playwright. By 1597 he had amassed enough wealth to buy a large house, New Place, in Stratford, but he continued to live and work in London. Although he apparently took up full-time residence at New Place in 1610, he continued to pursue business interests in London almost up to his death on his fifty-second birthday in 1616.

The natural desire to know more lively details about Shakespeare's life has led to the accumulation of a sizable body of legends, traditions, conjectures, and rumors. He may, for instance, have taught school at Stratford and been forced to leave town due to a deer-stealing incident. The warm terms with which he dedicated his poems *Venus and Adonis* and *The Rape of Lucrece* to the Earl of Southampton has led people to believe he at least enjoyed the nobleman's patronage and that they may have been lovers. And tradition says his death resulted from the strain of an evening of drinking with Ben Jonson and the poet Michael Drayton.

Although Shakespeare's plays mingle the serious with the comic and fiction with fact, scholars and editors have traditionally categorized them as histories, comedies, and tragedies. Among his best known history plays are the study of the rise and fall of the fiendish *Richard III* and *Parts I and II* of *Henry IV,* which feature the debauched comic knight Falstaff. His comic masterpieces include *The Taming of the Shrew, A Midsummer Night's Dream, Much Ado About Nothing, As You Like It,* and *Twelfth Night.* And his best-known tragedies are *Romeo and Juliet, Julius Caesar, Hamlet, Macbeth, King Lear,* and of course, *Othello.*

The large amount of space and time given to Shakespeare and his works in libraries, literary encyclopedias, and college curricula gives rise to the question: What is it about this writer that makes him so great? Part of the answer lies in the size and variety of the body of his works. While most writers specialize in one form, Shakespeare seemed equally adept at comedy and tragedy, and while some writers have been more prolific (such as Shakespeare's Spanish contemporary Lope de Vega [1562-1635] who claimed to have written 1,500 plays), Shakespeare's output of nearly 40 long theatre pieces is still monumental.

Furthermore, Shakespeare's plays contain philosophical observations and questions of considerable depth and variety combined with entertainment values of horror, comedy low and high, and human tragedy. They also combine high literary quality with great theatricality that makes them play well on stage. And finally, his historical moment makes Shakespeare important. He was able to intertwine the legacy of medieval drama with the new insights of the Renaissance. Many theatre artists and critics have loved and admired Shakespeare. Some have hated and despised him; few have been able to ignore him.

Othello

The Source

As usual, Shakespeare took the story of this tragedy from an existing romance and adapted it for his own purposes. Giovanni Battista Giraldi, known as "Il Cinthio" (1504-73) wrote the novelle from which *Othello* comes, "The Unfaithfulness of Husbands and Wives," and included it in his *Hecatommithi* (1565) from which Shakespeare also took the story for his *Measure for Measure*. Among other modifications in Cinthio's tale, Shakespeare changed the name of the heroine from Disdemona to the similar Desdemona, and her means of death from being bludgeoned to death with a stocking full of sand to being smothered in bed.

The Plot

Like his contemporary English Renaissance dramatists, Shakespeare constructed the plot of *Othello* with apparent disregard for the principles of classical theory. Unlike the climactic structure of *Oedipus the King,* Shakespeare's play starts with an early point of attack near the beginning of Othello and Desdemona's life together. As a result, the play does not observe unity of time or place but instead spreads the action out over weeks or months of time and across the Mediterranean world. Compared with many of Shakespeare's other plays, however, *Othello* does have relatively strong unity of action. It focuses on the corrupting and destruction of Othello and closely relates the secondary stories, those of Roderigo and Cassio, to this central action.

Shakespeare lends unity to his plot by focusing on themes of love and hate, trust and jealousy, and honesty and deception, and by repeating motifs such as racism, warfare, and hunting. He also unifies the play by designing his secondary characters to mirror and simultaneously contrast with the hero and heroine; the folly and weaknesses of Roderigo and Cassio throw light upon Othello's character, and Emilia and Bianca are both, in their own ways, innocent and suspect like Desdemona and, like her, they are mistreated by their men.

Although legitimate plays were to have five acts — unbroken sequences separated from each other by intermissions — Shakespeare constructed his play in a series of relatively short scenes with no breaks in the flow of the performance. Early editors divided the play into five acts, as in the present version, in order to bring Shakespeare's work into line with classical expectations.

Unlike classical tragedy, in which the fall of kings and queens causes the destruction of political order, *Othello* is a domestic tragedy, in which middle-class folk focus on normally private problems where their personal fates do not bring about tragedies of state.

Othello demonstrates clearly the transformation of the medieval religious psychomachia morality play into Renaissance secular tragedy. Like the central Mankind character of psychomachia plays, Othello starts out as a naive, innocent figure who is led toward damnation. The cunning Iago, whose evil intent has only the flimsiest motivation, differs from the psychomachia Vice primarily by being human rather than personifying some wicked quality, such as Mischief, Folly, or Love-Lust. And Desdemona, pure and good, stands in the place of the Graces who finally rescue the hero in morality plays. In *Othello,* however, human Desdemona does not have the divine powers of her psychomachia counterparts and so cannot save either Othello or herself. Later in dramatic history, nineteenth-century writers had only to add a happy ending to this kind of plot in order to turn it into melodrama.

Production History of Othello

The first recorded performance of *Othello* occurred at the King's court in 1604. Judging from the number of subsequent performances recorded, *Othello* was one of Shakespeare's most popular plays prior to the closing of the theatres in 1642. When theatre returned to London after the Restoration in 1660 and producers imported the French custom of casting actresses instead of boys in female roles, tradition says that *Othello* was the first play to employ actresses. In the eighteenth century, producers radically modified many of Shakespeare's scripts to bring them in line with the tastes of the day. In *The Merchant of Venice,* for instance, Shylock was played as a clownish fool, the witch sequences in *Macbeth* were turned into song and dance routines, and *Romeo and Juliet* was given a happy ending. Probably due to its simple, straightforward plot development, *Othello* was spared this kind of mutilation. The greatest actors throughout theatrical history counted Othello and Iago among their best roles, and the play continues to excite and move audiences today.

Renaissance Theatre Timeline

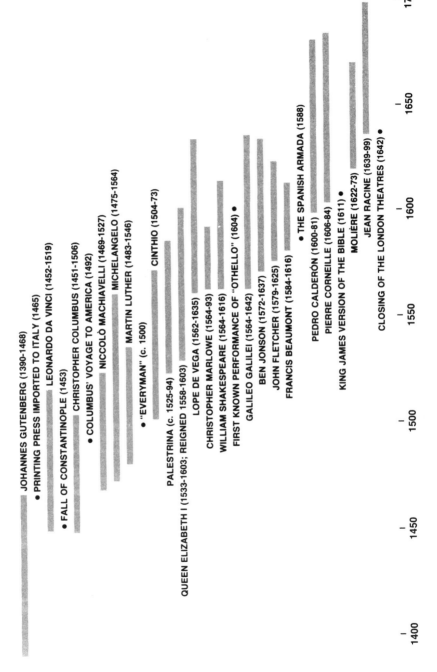

JOHANNES GUTENBERG (1390-1468)
• PRINTING PRESS IMPORTED TO ITALY (1465)
LEONARDO DA VINCI (1452-1519)
• FALL OF CONSTANTINOPLE (1453)
CHRISTOPHER COLUMBUS (1451-1506)
• COLUMBUS' VOYAGE TO AMERICA (1492)
NICCOLÒ MACHIAVELLI (1469-1527)
MICHELANGELO (1475-1564)
MARTIN LUTHER (1483-1546)
• "EVERYMAN" (c. 1500)
CINTHIO (1504-73)
PALESTRINA (c. 1525-94)
QUEEN ELIZABETH I (1533-1603; REIGNED 1558-1603)
LOPE DE VEGA (1562-1635)
CHRISTOPHER MARLOWE (1564-93)
WILLIAM SHAKESPEARE (1564-1616)
FIRST KNOWN PERFORMANCE OF "OTHELLO" (1604) •
GALILEO GALILEI (1564-1642)
BEN JONSON (1572-1637)
JOHN FLETCHER (1579-1625)
FRANCIS BEAUMONT (1584-1616)
• THE SPANISH ARMADA (1588)
PEDRO CALDERÓN (1600-81)
PIERRE CORNEILLE (1606-84)
KING JAMES VERSION OF THE BIBLE (1611) •
MOLIÈRE (1622-73)
JEAN RACINE (1639-99)
CLOSING OF THE LONDON THEATRES (1642) •

1400   1450   1500   1550   1600   1650   1700

THE TRAGEDY OF OTHELLO, THE MOOR OF VENICE

by William Shakespeare

The action of the first act takes place in Venice;
the rest of the play is set in a seaport in Cyprus.

CAST OF CHARACTERS[1]

Duke of Venice

BRABANTIO, a Senator

Two other Senators

GRATIANO, Brother of Brabantio

LODOVICO, Kinsman to Brabantio

OTHELLO, the Moor

CASSIO, Othello's Lieutenant

IAGO, Othello's Ancient[2]

RODERIGO, a Venetian Gentleman

MONTANO, Othello's Predecessor in the
Government of Cypress

Clown, Servant to Othello

Herald

DESDEMONA, Daughter to Brabantio,
and Wife to Othello

EMILIA, Wife to Iago

BIANCA, a Courtesan, Mistress to Cassio

Officers, Gentlemen, Messengers, Musicians,
Sailors, Attendants, etc.

---

[1]In keeping with tradition, this cast list presents the characters in descending hierarchical order; the main characters are listed from the highest noble (in this case, the Duke) down to the lowest woman (the prostitute Bianca), followed by a listing of the extras.
[2]ancient: ensign or standard-bearer — a lower rank.

ACT I

Scene i

At night on a street in Venice.

(RODERIGO and IAGO enter.[3])

RODERIGO: Tush, never tell me: I take it much unkindly,
That thou, Iago, — who hast had my purse,
As if the strings were thine, — shouldst know of this.
IAGO: 'Sblood,[4] but you will not hear me. —
If ever I did dream of such a matter,
Abhor me.
RODERIGO: Thou told'st me, thou didst hold him in thy hate.
IAGO: Despise me, if I do not. Three great ones of the city,
In personal suit to make me his lieutenant,
Off-capped[5] to him, — and, by the faith of man,
I know my price, I am worth no worse a place;
But he, as loving his own pride and purposes
Evades them, with a bombast circumstance,
Horribly stuffed with epithets of war;[6]
And in conclusion, nonsuits
My mediators; for, "Certes," says he,
"I have already chose my officer."
And what was he?
Forsooth, a great arithmetician,[7]
One Michael Cassio, a Florentine,
A fellow almost damned in a fair wife;[8]
That never set a squadron in the field,
Nor the division of a battle knows
More than a spinster; unless the bookish theoric,

[3]The Globe Theatre did not have a curtain to open and did not have the capability of dimming out lights to darken the theatre and catch the attention of the audience. Furthermore, large numbers of the audience members had no seats but stood to watch the play and so were free to mill around in "the yard" surrounding the stage. As a result, it likely took several speeches before the players could catch the attention of all the audience members; many spectators probably did not hear the first lines of the play. As Iago and Roderigo enter, they are already in the middle of a conversation. The situation seems to be that Iago has learned that Desdemona, whom Roderigo has courted without success, has eloped with Othello, a Moorish General in the Venetian army. Roderigo is embarrassed that his trusted confidant, Iago, learned this before he did. They are discussing this situation and Iago's hatred of Othello as they hurry along the street toward the house of Desdemona's father, Brabantio.
[4]'Sblood: An oath, an abbreviation of "God's blood," referring to the blood of Jesus Christ. Note that the first word spoken by Iago is a curse.
[5]Off-capped: Took off their hats in order to respectfully recommend to Othello that he make Iago his lieutenant.
[6]bombast . . . war: Iago pictures Othello as responding to the Venetian elders with rough, puffed-up speech.
[7]In this and the following lines, Iago claims that while he, Iago, has proved his worth in actual battle, Cassio is nothing but a military theoretician with no actual fighting experience.
[8]damned . . . wife: The meaning of this line is obscure; some have suggested that "wife" was originally "life," in which case Iago is making a comment on Cassio's character.

Wherein the togèd consuls[9] can propose
As masterly as he. Mere prattle, without practice,
Is all his soldiership. But he, sir, had the election.
And I — of whom his[10] eyes had seen the proof
At Rhodes, at Cyprus, and on other grounds,
Christian and heathen — must be be-lee'd and calmed[11]
By debitor-and-creditor, this counter-caster;[12]
He, in good time, must his lieutenant be,
And I (God bless the mark!) his Moorship's ancient.
RODERIGO: By Heaven, I rather would have been his hangman.
IAGO: But there's no remedy; 'tis the curse of service:
Preferment goes by letter, and affection,
Not by the old gradation, where each second
Stood heir to the first.[13] Now, sir, be judge yourself,
Whether I in any just term am affined
To love the Moor.
RODERIGO: I would not follow him, then.
IAGO: O sir, content you;
I follow him to serve my turn upon him.
We cannot all be masters, nor all masters
Cannot be truly followed. You shall mark
Many a duteous and knee-crooking knave,
That, doting on his own obsequious bondage,
Wears out his time, much like his master's ass,
For nought but provender; and, when he's old, cashiered;
Whip me such honest knaves.[14] Others there are,
Who, trimmed in forms and visages of duty,
Keep yet their hearts attending on themselves;
And, throwing but shows of service on their lords,
Do well-thrive by them, and, when they have lined their coats,
Do themselves homage: these fellows have some soul;[15]
And such a one do I profess myself.
For, sir,
It is as sure as you are Roderigo,
Were I the Moor, I would not be Iago.[16]
In following him, I follow but myself;

[9]togèd consuls: Civilian leaders wearing togas.
[10]his: Othello's
[11]be-leed and calmed: In a race, when a sailing ship comes between the wind and its competitor, the competitor is said to be in the other ship's lee; since it loses its wind, it is becalmed and loses headway.
[12]debitor-and-creditor: a term for bookkeeping; counter-caster: an accountant. Iago again demeans Cassio's theoretical, book knowledge of warfare.
[13]Preferment . . . the first: Iago complains that, in the army, advancement has more to do with the whims of the generals than with the more natural and traditional method of advancement by seniority.
[14]Many a duteous . . . honest knaves: Iago despises followers who serve their leaders loyally and expect to get nothing out of their service but a living and retirement.
[15]Others there are . . . some soul: He admires followers who, while pretending to be loyal to their leaders are really interested only in serving their own purposes.
[16]Were I . . . Iago: If Iago were Othello, he wouldn't want a follower like Iago.

Heaven is my judge, not I for love and duty,
But seeming so, for my peculiar end:
For when my outward action doth demonstrate
The native act and figure of my heart
In compliment extern, 'tis not long after
But I will wear my heart upon my sleeve
For daws[17] to peck at. I am not what I am.
RODERIGO: What a full fortune does the thick-lips owe,[18]
    If he can carry't thus![19]
IAGO: Call up her father,
    Rouse him, make after him, poison his delight,
    Proclaim him in the streets; incense her kinsmen,
    And, though he in a fertile climate dwell,
    Plague him with flies: though that his joy be joy,
    Yet throw such changes of vexation on't,
    As it may lose some color.
RODERIGO: Here is her father's house; I'll call aloud.
IAGO: Do; with like timorous accent, and dire yell,
    As when, by night and negligence, the fire
    Is spied in populous cities.
RODERIGO: What, ho! Brabantio! Signior Brabantio! Ho!
IAGO: Awake! What, ho! Brabantio! Thieves! Thieves! Thieves!
    Look to your house, your daughter, and your bags![20]
    Thieves! Thieves!

(BRABANTIO appears above[21] at a window.)

BRABANTIO: What is the reason of this terrible summons?
    What is the matter there?
RODERIGO: Seignior, is all your family within?
IAGO: Are your doors locked?
BRABANTIO: Why, wherefore ask you this?
IAGO: 'Zounds,[22] sir, you are robbed; for shame, put on your gown;
    Your heart is burst, you have lost half your soul;
    Even now, now, very now, an old black ram
    Is tupping your white ewe. Arise, arise;
    Awake the snorting citizens with the bell,
    Or else the devil will make a grandsire of you.

---

[17]daws: jackdaws; crow-like birds. Iago says he believes that honestly revealing his real intent by his deeds would be as foolish as exposing his heart to the destructive beaks of scavenger birds.
[18]owe: own.
[19]Roderigo returns to his obsession with Desdemona eloping with Othello. This prompts Iago, in the next speech, to goad him on to arousing Brabantio.
[20]bags: money bags. Note that Iago, throughout the play, uses monetary images; Shakespeare thus uses the New Testament teaching that "the love of money is the root of all evil" to help characterize Iago.
[21]above: the English Renaissance theatre had an acting area above the main level of the stage; some reconstructions portray this upper area as similar to the upstairs window of a Tudor house.
[22]'Zounds: an abbreviated form of "His wounds," an oath referring to the wounds of Jesus Christ.

Arise, I say.[23]
BRABANTIO: What, have you lost your wits?
ROGERIGO: Most reverend seignior, do you know my voice?
BRABANTIO: Not I; what are you?
RODERIGO: My name is — Roderigo.
BRABANTIO: The worse welcome;
    I have charged thee not to haunt about my doors.
    In honest plainness thou hast heard me say,
    My daughter is not for thee; and now, in madness,
    Being full of supper, and distempering draughts,
    Upon malicious bravery, dost thou come
    To start[24] my quiet.
RODERIGO: Sir, sir, sir, sir, —
BRABANTIO: But thou must needs be sure,
    My spirit, and my place, have in them power
    To make this bitter to thee.[25]
RODERIGO: Patience, good sir.
BRABANTIO: What tell'st thou me of robbing? This is Venice:
    My house is not a grange.[26]
RODERIGO: Most grave Brabantio,
    In simple and pure soul I come to you.
IAGO: 'Zounds, sir, you are one of those that will not serve God if the
    devil bid you. Because we come to do you service, you think
    we are ruffians. You'll have your daughter covered with a
    Barbary horse; you'll have your nephews neigh to you; you'll
    have coursers for cousins, and genets for germans.[27]
BRABANTIO: What profane wretch art thou?
IAGO: I am one, sir, that comes to tell you your daughter and the Moor
    are now making the beast with two backs.
BRABANTIO: Thou art a villain.[28]
IAGO: You are — a senator.[29]
BRABANTIO: This thou shalt answer. I know thee, Roderigo.[30]
RODERIGO: Sir, I will answer any thing.[31] But I beseech you,

[23]In this and his next speech, Iago makes racial and sexual slurs against Othello, comparing him to a rutting black ram, the devil, and an Arabian horse.
[24]start: startle.
[25]My spirit . . . to thee: Brabantio says that he has both the will and the power, as a senator, to punish Roderigo for continuing to frequent his premises.
[26]grange: an isolated farmhouse.
[27]courser: a spirited horse; genets: Spanish or Arabian horses; german: another word for relative.
[28]villain: here, the word denotes a low, uncultured, worthless person, not necessarily a scoundrel.
[29]You are a senator: Iago returns insult for insult. The line might be spoken with pause where the dash is so that Iago seems to say, "No, *you* are (a villain)," but then concludes his taunt with a factual statement for which he can't really be faulted: "a Senator." Or, it might be spoken without the pause in which case it means that a Senator is no better than a villain.
[30]This . . . Roderigo: Brabantio says Iago will be made to answer for his insolence; since he doesn't know Iago's identity and can't see him in the dark, he warns the pair that, since he does know Roderigo, he will find Iago through him or make Roderigo pay for Iago's taunts.
[31]I will answer any thing: Roderigo accepts responsibility for Iago's insults.

If't be your pleasure, and most wise consent,
(As partly, I find, it is,) that your fair daughter
At this odd-even and dull watch o' the night,
Transported — with no worse nor better guard,[32]
But with a knave of common hire, gondolier —
To the gross clasps of a lascivious Moor, —
If this be known to you and your allowance,
We then have done you bold and saucy wrongs;
But if you know not this, my manners tell me,
We have your wrong rebuke.[33] Do not believe,
That, from the sense of all civility,
I thus would play and trifle with your reverence.
Your daughter, — if you have not given her leave, —
I say again, hath made a gross revolt;
Tying her duty, beauty, wit, and fortunes,
In an extravagant and wheeling stranger,
Of here and every where.[34] Straight satisfy yourself;
If she be in her chamber, or your house,
Let loose on me the justice of the state
For thus deluding you.
BRABANTIO: Strike on the tinder, ho!
Give me a taper; — call up all my people. —
This accident is not unlike my dream;
Belief of it oppresses me already. —[35]
Light, I say! Light!

(He exits from above.)

IAGO: Farewell; for I must leave you.
It seems not meet, nor wholesome to my place,
To be produced (as, if I stay, I shall)
Against the Moor. For, I do know, the state —
However this may gall him with some check —[36]
Cannot with safety cast him![37] For he's embarked
With such loud reason to the Cyprus wars,
(Which even now stand in act), that, for their souls,
Another of his fathom they have not,[38]
To lead their business; in which regard,

[32]As partly . . . worse nor better: Roderigo seems to be padding out his sentence with redundant language in order to increase Brabantio's suspense.
[33]my manners . . . rebuke: my understanding of good manners tells me that you have wrongly rebuked us.
[34]extravagant . . . every where: Both "extravagant" and "wheeling" mean "wandering"; Roderigo suggests that, since Othello is not a Venetian citizen but instead a mercenary soldier of fortune, he cannot be depended upon to stay in Venice.
[35]This accident . . . already: Brabantio seems to have already had suspicions about his daughter and Othello.
[36]this: the business with Brabantio. check: rebuke or restraint.
[37]It seems not meet . . . cast him: Iago means that he can't yet afford to reveal himself as Othello's enemy; he knows Venice needs Othello's services badly enough that the state will not release and banish him for his affair with Desdemona.
[38]fathom: capacity or ability.

Though I do hate him as I do hell-pains,
Yet, for necessity of present life,
I must show out a flag and sign of love,
Which is, indeed, but sign. That you shall surely find him,
Lead to the Sagittary the raised search;[39]
And there will I be with him. So farewell.

(He exits. BRABANTIO and his servants enter below[40] with torches.[41])

BRABANTIO: It is too true an evil; gone she is;
And what's to come of my despised time,[42]
Is nought but bitterness. — Now, Roderigo,
Where didst thou see her? — O, unhappy girl! —
With the Moor, say'st thou? — Who would be a father? —[43]
How didst thou know 'twas she? O, thou deceiv'st me[44]
Past thought! — What said she to you? — Get more tapers;
Raise all my kindred. — Are they married, think you?
RODERIGO: Truly, I think they are.
BRABANTIO: O Heaven! — How got she out? — O treason of the
blood! —
Fathers, from hence trust not your daughters' minds
By what you see them act. — Are there not charms,
By which the property of youth and maidhood
May be abused? Have you not read, Roderigo,
Of some such thing?[45]
RODERIGO: Yes, sir; I have indeed
BRABANTIO: Call up my brother. — O that you had had her! —[46]
Some one way, some another. — Do you know[47]
Where we may apprehend her and the Moor?
RODERIGO: I think I can discover him; if you please
To get good guard, and go along with me.
BRABANTIO: 'Pray you, lead on. At every house I'll call;

[39]Sagittary: Archer, probably the name of an inn.
[40]below: on the main level of the stage which, in this scene, represents the street.
[41]torches: props used to indicate a night scene; since the Globe Theatre was an open air theatre, and since plays were performed there only during the day and only during fair weather, Shakespeare's company had no way to create actual darkness for nighttime scenes as is the usual practice today.
[42]my despised time: my old age; Brabantio fears entering old age without his daughter to care for him.
[43]Who . . . father?: Who would ever want to be a father? Note how Brabantio's agitation over Desdemona causes him to jump back and forth between ideas, sometimes without even finishing his thoughts, and to address now Roderigo, now his servants, now himself, and now even the absent Desdemona — all in a jumble.
[44]thou . . . thou: by the first "thou," Brabantio means Roderigo; by the second, he means Desdemona.
[45]charms . . . thing: Brabantio suspects Othello used magic to steal Desdemona's affections.
[46]O . . . her: Brabantio has completely changed his attitude toward Roderigo; moments earlier, he was threatening him with legal action for being outside his house; now he is asking his advice and saying he wishes Roderigo had married Desdemona.
[47]some one way, some another: Brabantio tells his servants to spread out in their search.

I may command at most.[48] —Get weapons, ho!
And raise some special officers of night. —[49]
On, good Roderigo, — I'll deserve your pains.[50]

(They exit.)[51]

[48]I may command at most: Most householders will be willing to help me.
[49]Get weapons . . . night: Brabantio directs these two commands to his servants.
[50]I'll deserve your pains: I'll reward you for your efforts.
[51]exit: note that, since the Globe Theatre had no curtain or stage lighting to dim, there was no way to indicate a scene break like this on stage; instead, as Brabantio and his group exited in one direction, Othello and his companions entered from the other side of the stage; the action would continue without a pause, and the audience would simply realize that the stage now represented a different place and a later time; the effect was much the same as quick dissolve from one scene to the next in a present-day motion picture.

ACT I

Scene ii

Later the same night on another street in Venice.

(OTHELLO, IAGO, and attendants enter.)

IAGO: Though in the trade of war I have slain men,
    Yet do I hold it very stuff o' the conscience,
    To do no contrived murder;[1] I lack iniquity
    Sometimes, to do me service.[2] Nine or ten times
    I had thought to have yerked[3] him here under the ribs.
OTHELLO: 'Tis better as it is.
IAGO: Nay, but he prated,
    And spoke such scurvy and provoking terms
    Against your honor,
    That, with the little godliness I have,
    I did full hard forbear him.[4] But, I pray, sir,
    Are you fast married?[5] For, be assured of this, —
    That the magnifico is much beloved;
    And hath, in his effect, a voice potential
    As double as the duke's.[6] He will divorce you;
    Or put upon you what restraint and grievance
    The law (with all his might to enforce it on)
    Will give him cable.[7]
OTHELLO: Let him do his spite;
    My services, which I have done the signory,[8]
    Shall out-tongue his complaints. 'Tis yet to know
    — Which, when I know that boasting is an honor,
    I shall promulgate — I fetch my life and being
    From men of royal siege[9]; and my demerits[10]
    May speak, unbonneted,[11] to as proud a fortune
    As this that I have reached. For know, Iago,
    But that I love the gentle Desdemona,
    I would not my unhoused, free condition
    Put into circumscription and confine
    For the sea's worth.[12] But, look! What lights come yonder?

[1]contrived: planned.
[2]I lacked . . . service: If I weren't such a principled person, I could be more effective. Notice how Iago parades his phony virtues before Othello.
[3]yerked: attacked.
[4]I did . . . him: I could just hardly put up with him.
[5]fast: securely.
[6]hath . . . the duke's: the effect of his word is as powerful as that of the duke's, whose power is double that of the individual senators.
[7]Or put . . . cable: will punish you to the full extent of the law.
[8]signory: the senate of the city-state of Venice.
[9]siege: throne or rank.
[10]demerits: merits; in Elizabethan usage, "demerit" could mean either positive or negative deserts.
[11]unbonneted: humbly, without insisting.
[12]But that . . . sea's worth: If I didn't love Desdemona I'd never give up my freedom as a bachelor.

(CASSIO enters with officers carrying torches.)

IAGO: These are the raised father, and his friends.
　　You were best go in.
OTHELLO: Not I; I must be found;
　　My parts,[13] my title, and my perfect soul,
　　Shall manifest me rightly. Is it they?
IAGO: By Janus, I think no.[14]
OTHELLO: The servants of the duke, and my lieutenant.
　　The goodness of the night upon you, friends!
　　What is the news?
CASSIO: The duke does greet you, general,
　　And he requires your haste-post-haste appearance,
　　Even on the instant.[15]
OTHELLO: What is the matter, think you?
CASSIO: Something from Cyprus, as I may divine;
　　It is a business of some heat. The galleys
　　Have sent a dozen sequent messengers
　　This very night at one another's heels;
　　And many of the consuls, raised, and met,
　　Are at the duke's already. You have been hotly called for;
　　When, being not at your lodging to be found,
　　The senate hath sent about three several quests,[16]
　　To search you out.
OTHELLO: 'Tis well I am found by you.[17]
　　I will but spend a word here in the house,
　　And go with you.

(He exits into the house.)

CASSIO: Ancient, what makes he here?
IAGO: 'Faith, he tonight hath boarded a land carrack;[18]
　　If it prove lawful prize, he's made forever.[19]
CASSIO: I do not understand.
IAGO: He's married.
CASSIO: To who?

(OTHELLO re-enters.)

IAGO: Marry, to — come, captain, will you go?

[13]parts: merits or natural gifts.
[14]Janus: This Roman god of doors and beginnings was portrayed as having two faces, one on each side of his head; he is therefore associated with duplicity and is therefore an appropriate deity to associate with Iago.
[15]haste-post-haste: In Shakespeare's time, these words were written on the outside of letters sent by express mail.
[16]three several quests: three different search parties.
[17]The emphasis is on the final word of the sentence; Othello is happy to have Cassio's be the search party that found him.
[18]carrack: a broad sailing ship used for hauling cargo; Iago's imagery equates Othello's lovemaking with Desdemona with the seizing of a ship at sea.
[19]Cassio's "What makes he here?" meant "What's he doing here?" Iago echoes Cassio's choice of words; "He's made" is equivalent to our "He's got it made."

OTHELLO: Have with you.
CASSIO: Here comes another troop to seek for you.

(BRABANTIO, RODERIGO, and officers of night enter with torches and weapons.)

IAGO: It is Brabantio. — General, be advised;
    He comes to bad intent.
OTHELLO: Hola! Stand there!
RODERIGO: Seignior, it is the Moor.
BRABANTIO: Down with him, thief!

(Both sides draw their weapons.)

IAGO: You, Roderigo! Come, sir, I am for you.
OTHELLO: Keep up your bright swords, for the dew will rust them. —[20]
    Good seignior, you shall more command with years,
    Than with your weapons.
BRABANTIO: O thou foul thief, where hast thou stowed my daughter?
    Damned as thou art, thou hast enchanted her;
    For I'll refer me to all things of sense,
    If she in chains of magic were not bound,
    Whether a maid — so tender, fair, and happy;
    So opposite to marriage, that she shunned
    The wealthy, curled darlings of our nation —
    Would ever have, to incur a general mock,
    Run from her guardage to the sooty bosom
    Of such a thing as thou, to fear, not to delight.
    Judge me the world, if 'tis not gross in sense,
    That thou hast practised on her with foul charms;
    Abused her delicate youth with drugs, or minerals,
    That weaken motion. — I'll have it disputed on,[21]
    'Tis probable, and palpable to thinking.
    I therefore apprehend and do attach thee,
    For an abuser of the world, a practiser
    Of arts inhibited and out of warrant. —[22]
    Lay hold upon him; if he do resist,
    Subdue him at his peril.
OTHELLO: Hold your hands,
    Both you of my inclining, and the rest.
    Were it my cue to fight, I should have known it
    Without a prompter. — Where will you that I go,
    To answer this your charge?
BRABANTIO: To prison; till fit time
    Of law, and course of direct session,
    Call thee to answer.
OTHELLO: What if I do obey?
    How may the duke be therewith satisfied,

[20]Keep up: put away.
[21]motion: emotion.
[22]inhibited: prohibited.

Whose messengers are here about my side,
Upon some present business of the state,
To bring me to him?
OFFICER: 'Tis true, most worthy seignior,
The duke's in council; and your noble self,
I am sure, is sent for.
BRABANTIO: How! The duke in council!
In this time of the night? — Bring him away.
Mine's not an idle cause; the duke himself,
Or any of my brothers of the state,
Cannot but feel this wrong, as 'twere their own.
For if such actions may have passage free,
Bond-slaves, and pagans, shall our statesmen be.

(They all exit.)

ACT I

Scene iii

Later the same night in Venice's council chamber.

(The DUKE and SENATORS are sitting at a table with OFFICERS in attendance on them.)

DUKE: There is no composition in these news,
That gives them credit.[1]
FIRST SENATOR: Indeed, they are disproportioned;
My letters say a hundred and seven galleys.
DUKE: And mine, a hundred and forty.
SECOND SENATOR: And mine, two hundred.
But though they jump not on a just account[2]
— As in these cases where the aim reports,[3]
'Tis oft with difference — yet do they all confirm
A Turkish fleet, and bearing up to Cyprus.
DUKE: Nay, it is possible enough to judgement;
I do not so secure me in the error[4]
But the main article I do approve
In fearful sense.
SAILOR: *(Off-stage)* What, ho! What, ho! What, ho!
OFFICER: *(Entering with the SAILOR)* A messenger from the galleys.
DUKE: Now; the business!
SAILOR: The Turkish preparation makes for Rhodes;[5]
So I was bid to report here to the state,
By Seignior Angelo.
DUKE: *(To the SENATORS.)* How say you by this change?
FIRST SENATOR: This cannot be,
By no assay of reason; 'tis a pageant,[6]
To keep us in false gaze. When we consider
The importancy of Cyprus to the Turk;[7]
And let ourselves again but understand,
That, as it more concerns the Turk than Rhodes,
So may he with more facile question bear it,
For that it stands not in such warlike brace,
But altogether lacks the abilities
That Rhodes is dressed in;[8] — if we make thought of this,
We must not think the Turk is so unskillful,

[1]composition: agreement.
[2]just: equal.
[3]aim: guess or estimate.
[4]so secure me: take comfort.
[5]Rhodes: A small island off the southern coast of Turkey.
[6]pageant: pretense.
[7]the Turk: probably Suleiman the Magnificent, sultan of the Turkish/Ottoman Empire from 1520 to 1566.
[8]as it more concern . . . is dressed in: not only is Cyprus of more strategic importance to the Turk than is Rhodes, but it is also less prepared for war and so would be easier to conquer than heavily fortified Rhodes.

To leave that latest which concerns him first;[9]
Neglecting an attempt of ease and gain,
To wake, and wage a danger profitless.[10]
DUKE: Nay, in all confidence, he's not for Rhodes.
OFFICER: Here is more news.
MESSENGER: *(Enters)* the Ottomites, reverend and gracious,
    Steering with due course to the isle of Rhodes,
    Have there injointed them with an after-fleet.[11]
FIRST SENATOR: Ay, so I thought. — How many, as you guess?
MESSENGER: Of thirty sail; and now do they restem[12]
    Their backward course, bearing with frank appearance
    Their purposes toward Cyprus. — Seignior Montano,
    Your trusty and most valiant servitor,[13]
    With his free duty recommends you thus,
    And prays you to believe him.
DUKE: 'Tis certain then for Cyprus. —
    Marcus Lucchesé, is he not in town?
FIRST SENATOR: He's now in Florence.
DUKE: Write from us; wish him post-post-haste. Dispatch!
FIRST SENATOR: Here comes Brabantio, and the valiant Moor.

*(BRABANTIO, OTHELLO, IAGO, RODERIGO, and OFFICERS
enter.)*

DUKE: Valiant Othello, we must straight employ you
    Against the general enemy Ottoman.

(Noticing BRABANTIO.)

    I did not see you; welcome, gentle seignior;
    We lacked your counsel and your help tonight.
BRABANTIO: So did I yours. Good your grace, pardon me;
    Neither my place, nor ought I heard of business,
    Hath raised me from my bed; nor doth the general care[14]
    Take hold on me; for my particular grief
    If of so floodgate and o'erbearing nature,
    That it engluts and swallows other sorrows,
    And it is still itself.[15]
DUKE: Why, what's the matter?
BRABANTIO: My daughter! O my daughter!
A SENATOR: Dead?
BRABANTIO: Aye, to me;
    She is abused, stolen from me, and corrupted

[9]latest: to the last.
[10]To wake . . . profitless: To awaken and take on a risk with little promise of reward.
[11]after-fleet: reinforcement fleet.
[12]restem: retrace.
[13]servitor: servant.
[14]the general care: the matters concerning the state at large.
[15] These lines perhaps allude to Pharaoh's dream in the Bible (Genesis 41.14-31) in which seven starved cattle symbolizing famine consumed seven fat cattle representing prosperity and were still as thin as before.

By spells and medicines bought of mountebanks.[16]
For nature so preposterously to err,
Being not deficient, blind, or lame of sense,
Sans witchcraft could not . . .[17]
DUKE: Whoe'er he be, that, in this foul proceeding,
Hath thus beguiled your daughter of herself,
And you of her, the bloody book of law
You shall yourself read in the bitter letter,
After your own sense;[18] yea, though our proper son[19]
Stood in your action.
BRABANTIO: Humbly I thank your grace.
Here is the man, this Moor; whom now, it seems,
Your special mandate, for the state affairs,
Hath hither brought.
DUKE and SENATORS: We are sorry for it.[20]
DUKE: *(To OTHELLO)* What, in your own part, can you say to this?
BRABANTIO: Nothing, but this is so.
OTHELLO: Most potent, grave, and reverend seigniors,
My very noble and approved good masters:
That I have ta'en away this old man's daughter,
It is most true; true, I have married her;
The very head and front of my offending
Hath this extent, no more. Rude am I in my speech,
And little blessed with the set phrase of peace;
For since these arms of mine had seven years' pith,
Till now some nine moons wasted, they have used[21]
Their dearest action in the tented field;
And little of this great world can I speak,
More than pertains to feats of broil and battle;
And therefore little shall I grace my cause,
In speaking for myself. Yet, by your gracious patience,
I will a round, unvarnished tale deliver
Of my whole course of love; what drugs, what charms,
What conjuration, and what mighty magic,
— For such proceeding I am charged withal —
I won his daughter with.
BRABANTIO: A maiden never bold —
Of spirit so still and quiet, that her motion
Blushed at herself; and she — in spite of nature,
Of years, of country, credit, everything —[22]

[16]mountebanks: sellers of quack medicines.
[17]sans: French for "without."
[18]The Duke says he will permit Brabantio to punish the offender to the full extent of the law, as interpreted by Brabantio himself.
[19]proper: own, or very.
[20]They are sorry to hear the accused is Othello.
[21]For since . . . nine moons wasted: for since I was seven years old until just nine months ago, during which time I've been idle . . .
[22]in spite of . . . everything: Brabantio says that, for Desdemona to fall in love with Othello, she would have to overcome natural inclinations, the difference in years between her youth and his mature age, their different ethnic origins, their difference in social standing — everything.

To fall in love with what she feared to look on!
It is a judgement maimed, and most imperfect,
That will confess perfection so could err
Against all rules of nature; and must be driven
To find out practices of cunning hell,
Why this should be. I therefore vouch again
That with some mixtures powerful o'er the blood,
Or with some dram conjured to this effect,[23]
He wrought upon her.
DUKE: To vouch this, is no proof,
Without more certain and more overt test,
Than these thin habits, and poor likelihoods
Of modern seeming, do prefer against him.[24]
FIRST SENATOR: But, Othello, speak.
Did you by indirect and forced courses
Subdue and poison this young maid's affections?
Or came it by request, and such fair question
As soul to soul affordeth?
OTHELLO: I do beseech you,
Send for the lady to the Sagittary,
And let her speak of me before her father.
If you do find me foul in her report,
The trust, the office, I do hold of you,
Not only take away, but let your sentence
Even fall upon my life.
DUKE: *(To attending officers.)* Fetch Desdemona hither.
OTHELLO: Ancient, conduct them, you best know the place.

(IAGO exits with attendants.)

And till she come, as truly as to heaven
I do confess the vices of my blood,
So justify to your grave ears I'll present
How I did thrive in this fair lady's love,
And she in mine.
DUKE: Say it, Othello.
OTHELLO: Her father loved me, oft invited me,
Still questioned me the story of my life,
From year to year, the battles, sieges, fortunes,
That I have passed.
I ran it through, even from my boyish days,
To the very moment that he bade me tell it.
Wherein I spoke of most disastrous chances,
Of moving accidents, by flood and field;[25]
Of hair-breadth 'scapes i' the imminent deadly breach;
Of being taken by the insolent foe,
And sold to slavery; of my redemption thence,

[23]dram: a small portion of something to drink.
[24]thin habits . . . modern seeming: typical expectations and current prejudices. Motivated by his need for Othello's services, the Duke seems exceptionally broad-minded for his time.
[25]Of moving . . . field: Of exciting mishaps on sea and battlefield.

And portance in my travel's history;[26]
Wherein of antars vast, and deserts wild,[27]
Rough quarries, rocks, and hills whose heads touch heaven,
It was my hint to speak — such was the process;
And of the cannibals that each other eat,
The Anthropophagi,[28] and men whose heads
Do grow beneath their shoulders.[29] These things to hear,
Would Desdemona seriously incline;
But still the house affairs would draw her thence;
Which ever as she could with haste dispatch,
She'd come again, and with a greedy ear,
Devour up my discourse; which I, observing,
Took once a pliant hour,[30] and found good means
To draw from her a prayer of earnest heart,
That I would all my pilgrimage dilate,
Whereof by parcels she had something heard,
But not intentively. I did consent;
And often did beguile her of her tears,
When I did speak of some distressful stroke,
That my youth suffered. My story being done,
She gave me for my pains a world of sighs;
She swore in faith, 'twas strange, 'twas passing strange;
'Twas pitiful, 'twas wondrous pitiful;
She wished she had not heard it; yet she wished
That heaven had made her such a man; she thanked me,
And bade me, if I had a friend that loved her,
I should but teach him how to tell my story,
And that would woo her. Upon this hint I spake:
She loved me for the dangers I had passed;
And I loved her that she did pity them.
This only is the witchcraft I have used.
Here comes the lady; let her witness it.

(DESDEMONA, IAGO, and their attendants enter.)

DUKE: I think this tale would win my daughter too.
Good Brabantio,
Take up this mangled matter at the best.
Men do their broken weapons rather use,
Than their bare hands.[31]
BRABANTIO: I pray you, hear her speak;
If she confess that she was half the wooer,
Destruction on my head, if my bad blame

[26]portance: behavior.
[27]antars: caves, or adventures.
[28]Anthropophagi: Man-eaters.
[29]Various travelers in this age of discovery, including Sir Walter Raleigh, reported stories of people who had no heads but instead had eyes in their shoulders and their mouths in the middle of their chests.
[30]pliant: easily influenced.
[31]Men do . . . bare hands: A "sententia" or proverb meaning "make the best of a bad situation."

Lights on the man! *(To DESDEMONA.)* Come hither, gentle mistress.
Do you perceive in all this noble company,
Where most you owe obedience?
DESDEMONA: My noble father,
I do perceive here a divided duty.
To you I am bound for life and education;[32]
My life and education both do learn me
How to respect you: You are the lord of duty;
I am hitherto your daughter. But here's my husband,
And so much duty as my mother showed
To you, preferring you before her father,
So much I challenge that I may profess
Due to the Moor, my lord.
BRABANTIO: *(To DESDEMONA.)* God be with you! *(To OTHELLO.)* I have
done.
(To the DUKE.) Please it your grace, on to the state affairs;
I had rather to adopt a child, than get it.[33]
(Turning again to OTHELLO.) Come hither, Moor.
I here do give thee that with all my heart,
Which, but thou hast already, with all my heart
I would keep from thee. *(To DESDEMONA.)* For your sake, jewel,
I am glad at soul I have no other child;
For thy escape would teach me tyranny
To hang clogs on them.[34] *(Turning again to the DUKE.)* I have done,
my lord.
DUKE: Let me speak like yourself; and lay a sentence,
Which as a grise, or step, may help these lovers
Into your favor.[35]
When remedies are past, the griefs are ended,
By seeing the worst, which late on hopes depended.[36]
To mourn a mischief that is past and gone,
Is the next way to draw new mischief on.
What cannot be preserved when Fortune takes,
Patience, her injury a mockery makes.
The robbed, that smiles, steals something from the thief;
He robs himself, that spends a bootless grief.[37]
BRABANTIO: So let the Turk of Cyprus us beguile;
We lose it not, so long as we can smile.[38]
He bears the sentence well, that nothing bears
But the free comfort which from thence he hears;[39]

[32]for life and education: because you gave me life and educated me.
[33]get: beget.
[34]clogs: weights attached to animals to hinder their movements.
[35]Notice that with the next line, the Duke launches into a series of four sententiae which he frames in rhymed couplets; when Brabantio replies, he echoes the Duke's speech mode, and then with his final line in the speech be breaks out of the rhymed couplet mode and they get on with the business of the war.
[36]late: lately.
[37]spends a bootless grief: gives himself over to useless grieving.
[38]Note the irony with which Brabantio gives the Duke a dose of his own medicine.
[39]comfort: advice.

But he bears both the sentence and the sorrow,
That, to pay grief, must of poor Patience borrow.
These sentences, to sugar, or to gall,
Being strong on both sides, are equivocal;
But words are words; I never yet did hear
That the bruised heart was pierced through the ear.[40]
I humbly beseech you, proceed to the affairs of state.

DUKE: The Turk with a most mighty preparation makes for Cyprus. —
Othello, the fortitude[41] of the place is best know to you; and though
we have there a substitute[42] of most allowed sufficiency yet opinion,
a sovereign mistress of effects, throws a more safer voice on you; you
must therefore be content to slubber[43] the gloss of your new fortunes
with this more stubborn and boisterous expedition.

OTHELLO: The tyrant Custom, most grave senators,[44]
Hath made the flinty and steel couch of war
My thrice-driven bed of down. I do agnize[45]
A natural and prompt alacrity[46]
I find in hardness, and do undertake
These present wars against the Ottomites.
Most humbly therefore bending to your state,
I crave fit disposition for my wife:
Due reverence of place, and exhibition,[47]
With such accommodation, and besort,[48]
As levels with her breeding.

DUKE: If you please,
Be't at her father's.

BRABANTIO: I'll not have it so.

OTHELLO: Nor I.

DESDEMONA: Nor I; I would not there reside,
To put my father in impatient thoughts,
By being in his eye. Most gracious duke,
To my unfolding lend a gracious ear;
And let me find a charter in your voice,[49]
To assist my simpleness.

DUKE: What would you, Desdemona?

DESDEMONA: That I did love the Moor to live with him,
My downright violence and storm of fortunes[50]
May trumpet to the world; my heart's subdued
Even to the very quality of my lord.[51]

---

[40]pierced: taken by most commentators to mean "healed."
[41]fortitude: fortifications.
[42]substitute: deputy — the governor.
[43]slubber: stain.
[44]Custom: Habit.
[45]agnize: acknowledge.
[46]alacrity: cheerful response.
[47]exhibition: (monetary) allowance
[48]besort: proper retinue.
[49]charter: pledge or guarantee
[50]violence . . . fortunes: unacceptable behavior and acceptance of the consequences.
[51]very quality: characteristic nature.

I saw Othello's visage in his mind;[52]
And to his honors, and his valiant parts,
Did I my soul and fortunes consecrate.
So that, dear lords, if I be left behind
A moth of peace, and he go to the war,
The rights, for which I love him, are bereft me,
and I a heavy interim shall support
By his dear absence. Let me go with him.[53]

OTHELLO: Your voices, lords; — 'beseech you, let her will
Have a free way.
Vouch with me, heaven: I therefore beg it not
To please the palate of my appetite,
Nor to comply with heat the young affects,
In me defunct, and proper satisfaction;[54]
But to be free and bounteous to her mind.[55]
And heaven defend your good souls, that you think[56]
I will your serious and great business scant,
For she is with me.[57] No! When light-winged toys[58]
Of feathered Cupid seel with wanton dullness[59]
My speculative and active instruments,
That my disports corrupt and taint my business,[60]
Let housewives make a skillet of my helm,[61]
And all indign and base adversities[62]
Make head against my estimation![63]

DUKE: Be it as you shall privately determine,
Either for her stay, or going; the affair cries haste,
And speed must answer it; you must hence tonight.

DESDEMONA: Tonight, my lord?

DUKE: This night.

OTHELLO: With all my heart.

DUKE: *(To the SENATORS.)* At nine i' the morning here we'll meet again.
Othello, leave some officer behind,
And he shall our commission bring to you,
With such things else of quality and respect,
As doth import you.

OTHELLO: Please your grace, my ancient.[64]
A man he is of honesty and trust.[65]

---

[52]visage: face. She means that his mind was more important to her than the color of his face.
[53]dear: costly.
[54]heat . . . defunct: urgent sexual drives which affect the young, by me brought under control.
[55]I therefore beg . . . her mind: He says he requests them to grant her request, not because of his own desires, but rather to give her what she desires.
[56]that: if.
[57]For: If.
[58]light-winged toys: arrows.
[59]seel: blind. wanton: lustful.
[60]disports: pleasures.
[61]helm: helmet.
[62]indign: unworthy.
[63]estimation: reputation.
[64]Please . . . ancient: If it pleases your grace, let the man be my ensign (Iago).
[65]Note Othello's ironically inaccurate evaluation of Iago.

To his conveyance I assign my wife,
With what else needful your good grace shall think
To be sent after me.
DUKE: Let it be so.
Goodnight to everyone. *(He turns to BRABANTIO.)* And noble seignior,
If virtue no delighted beauty lack,
Your son-in-law is far more fair than black.
FIRST SENATOR: Adieu, brave Moor! Use Desdemona well.
BRABANTIO: Look to her, Moor; have a quick eye to see:[66]
She has deceived her father, and may thee.

(He leaves, along with the DUKE, SENATORS, and OFFICERS.)

OTHELLO: *(To BRABANTIO.)* My life upon her faith. Honest Iago,
My Desdemona must I leave to thee.
I pr'ythee, let thy wife attend on her;
And bring them after in the best advantage.
Come, Desdemona. I have but an hour
Of love, of worldly matters and direction,
To spend with thee; we must obey the time.

(He leaves with DESDEMONA.)

RODERIGO: Iago . . .
IAGO: What say'st thou, noble heart?
RODERIGO: What will I do, thinkest thou?
IAGO: Why, go to bed, and sleep.
RODERIGO: I will incontinently drown myself.[67]
IAGO: Well, if thou dost, I shall never love thee after it.
    Why, thou silly gentleman!
RODERIGO: It is silliness to live, when to live is a torment; and then have
    we a prescription to die, when death is our physician.
IAGO: O, villainous! I have looked upon the world for four times seven
    years, and since I could distinguish between a benefit and an injury,
    I never found a man that knew how to love himself. Ere I would say
    I would drown myself for the love of a Guinea-hen,[68] I would change
    my humanity with a baboon.
RODERIGO: What should I do? I confess it is my shame to be so fond;[69] but
    it is not in virtue to amend it.[70]
IAGO: Virtue? A fig! 'Tis in ourselves that we are thus or thus. Our bodies
    are our gardens, to the which our wills are gardeners; so that if we
    will plant nettles or sow lettuce, set hyssop and weed up thyme,[71]
    supply it with one gender of herbs, or distract it with many, either to
    have it sterile with idleness, or manured with industry — why, the
    power and corrigible authority of this lies in our wills. If the balance
    of our lives had not one scale of reason to poise another of sensuality,[72] the

[66]Look to her: Keep an eye on her.
[67]incontinently: without delay.
[68]Guinea-hen: whore.
[69]fond: foolish.
[70]virtue: my power.
[71]hyssop: a bitter herb; thyme: a favorite English herb.
[72]reason . . . sensuality: Iago says that rational thinking should balance and control emotions.

blood and baseness of our natures would conduct us to most preposterous conclusions. But we have reason to cool our raging motions, our carnal stings, our unbitted lusts,[73] whereof I take this, that you call "love," to be a sect, or scion.[74]

RODERIGO: It cannot be.

IAGO: It is merely a lust of the blood, and a permission of the will. Come, be a man. Drown thyself! Drown cats, and blind puppies! I have professed me thy friend, and I confess me knit to thy deserving with cables of perdurable toughness;[75] I could never better stead thee than now. Put money in thy purse; follow these wars; defeat thy favor with an usurped beard;[76] I say, put money in thy purse.[77] It cannot be, that Desdemona should long continue her love to the Moor — put money in thy purse — nor he his to her. It was a violent commencement, and thou shalt see an answerable sequestration — put but money in thy purse.[78] These Moors are changeable in their wills — fill thy purse with money. The food that to him now is as luscious as locusts, shall be to him shortly as bitter as coloquintida.[79] She must change for youth;[80] when she is sated with his body, she will find the error of her choice.[81] She must have change, she must; therefore, put money in thy purse. If thou wilt needs damn thyself, do it in a more delicate way than drowning. Make all the money thou canst. If sanctimony and a frail vow, betwixt an erring barbarian and a supersubtle Venetian, be not too hard for my wits and all the tribe of hell, thou shalt enjoy her; therefore, make money. A pox of drowning thyself! It is clean out of the way; seek thou rather to be hanged in compassing thy joy, than to be drowned and go without her.

RODERIGO: Wilt thou be fast to my hopes, if I depend on the issue?[82]

IAGO: Thou art sure of me. Go make money. I have told thee often, and I retell thee again and again, I hate the Moor. My cause is hearted; thine hath no less reason. Let us be conjunctive in our revenge against him; if thou canst cuckold him, thou dost thyself a pleasure, and me a sport. There are many events in the womb of time, which will be delivered. Traverse; go; provide thy money. We will have more of this tomorrow. Adieu.

RODERIGO: Where shall we meet i' the morning?

IAGO: At my lodging.

RODERIGO: I'll be with thee betimes.

IAGO: Go to; farewell. Do you hear, Roderigo?

[73]unbitted: unbridled.

[74]scion: off-shoot. Iago says that what Roderigo calls love is really just a kind of lust.

[75]perdurable: very durable.

[76]defeat . . . beard: disguise your face with a false beard.

[77]Put money in thy purse: Iago's constant repetition of this refrain throughout the rest of the scene demonstrates his complete confidence in his ability to manipulate Roderigo; Roderigo's decision at the end of the scene to turn his estate into cash demonstrates both his foolishness and the accuracy of Iago's self-perception.

[78]sequestration: sequel.

[79]locusts/coloquintida: two medicines — the first sweet, the other bitter.

[80]for youth: because of her immaturity.

[81]sated: satisfied.

[82]fast/depend on the issue: true/have confidence in the outcome.

RODERIGO: What say you?
IAGO: No more of drowning; do you hear?
RODERIGO: I am changed. I'll sell all my land.
IAGO: Go to; farewell; put money enough in your purse.

(RODERIGO exits.)

Thus do I ever make my fool my purse;
For I mine own gained knowledge should profane,
If I would time expend with such a snipe,[83]
But for my sport and profit. I hate the Moor;
And it is thought abroad, that 'twixt my sheets
He has done my office.[84] I know not if't be true;
But I, for mere suspicion in that kind,
Will do, as if for surety. He holds me well;
The better shall my purpose work on him.
Cassio's a proper man.[85] Let me see now;
To get his place, and to plume up my will;[86]
A double knavery. How? How? Let me see.
After some time, to abuse Othello's ear.
That he is too familiar with his wife.[87]
He hath a person; and a smooth dispose[88]
To be suspected; framed to make women false.
The Moor is of a free and open nature,
That thinks men honest that but seem to be so,
And will as tenderly be led by the nose,
As asses are.
I have't; it is engendered. Hell and night
Must bring this monstrous birth to the world's light.

(He exits.)

---

[83]snipe: contemptible person.
[84]'twixt . . . office: he has taken my place in bed with my wife.
[85]proper: handsome and dignified.
[86]to plume up: to put a feather in the cap of.
[87]he/his: Cassio/Othello's.
[88]person/dispose: personality/disposition.

ACT II

Scene i

Days later in a seaport on Cyprus.

MONTANO: *(Entering with two GENTLEMEN.)* What from the cape can
    you discern at sea?
FIRST GENTLEMAN: Nothing at all. It is a high-wrought flood;
    I cannot, 'twixt the heaven and the main,[1]
    Descry a sail.
MONTANO: Methinks the wind hath spoke aloud at land;
    A fuller blast ne'er shook our battlements.
    If it hath ruffianed so upon the sea,
    What ribs of oak, when mountains melt on them,
    Can hold the mortise? What shall we hear of this?
SECOND GENTLEMAN: A segregation of the Turkish fleet.
    For do but stand upon the foaming shore,
    The chiding billow seems to pelt the clouds;
    The wind-shaked surge, with high and monstrous mane,
    Seems to cast water on the burning bear,
    And quench the guards of the ever-fixèd pole.[2]
    I never did like molestation view
    On the enchafèd flood.
MONTANO: If that the Turkish fleet
    Be not ensheltered and embayed, they are drowned;
    It is impossible they bear it out.

(Enter a third GENTLEMAN.)

THIRD GENTLEMAN: News, lords! our wars are done;
    The desperate tempest hath so banged the Turks,
    That their designment halts. A noble ship of Venice
    Hath seen a grievous wreck and sufferance
    On most part of their fleet.
MONTANO: How! is this true?
THIRD GENTLEMAN: The ship is here put in,
    A Veronesé; Michael Cassio,
    Lieutenant to the warlike Moor, Othello,
    Is come on shore. The Moor himself's at sea,
    And is in full commission here for Cyprus.
MONTANO: I am glad on't; 'tis a worthy governor.
THIRD GENTLEMAN: But this same Cassio, though he speak of comfort,
    Touching the Turkish loss, yet he looks sadly,
    And prays the Moor be safe; for they were parted
    With foul and violent tempest.
MONTANO: 'Pray Heaven, he be,
    For I have served him, and the man commands
    Like a full soldier. Let's to the seaside, ho,

---

[1]main: sea.
[2]burning bear/guards: Big Dipper/the two stars in the Big Dipper that point to the pole or North
Star.

As well to see the vessel that's come in,
As to throw out our eyes for brave Othello,
Even till we make the main, and the aerial blue,
An indistinct regard.[3]
THIRD GENTLEMAN: Come, let's do so;
    For every minute is expectancy
    Of more arrivance.

(CASSIO enters in time to overhear the last few lines.)

CASSIO: Thanks to the valiant of the warlike isle,
    That so approve the Moor. O, let the heavens
    Give him defense against the elements,
    For I have lost him on a dangerous sea!
MONTANO: Is he well shipped?
CASSIO: His bark is stoutly timbered, and his pilot
    Of very expert and approved allowance;
    Therefore my hopes, not surfeited to death,[4]
    Stand in bold cure.
VOICE: *(Off-stage)* A sail, a sail, a sail!

(Enter another GENTLEMAN.)

CASSIO: What noise?
FOURTH GENTLEMAN: The town is empty; on the brow o' the sea
    Stand ranks of people, and they cry, "A sail!"
CASSIO: My hopes do shape him for the governor.

(Guns are heard off-stage.)

SECOND GENTLEMAN: They do discharge their shot of courtesy;
    Our friends, at least.
CASSIO: I pray you, sir, go forth,
    And give us truth who 'tis that is arrived.
SECOND GENTLEMAN: I shall. *(He exits.)*
MONTANO: But, good lieutenant, is your general wived?
CASSIO: Most fortunately. He hath achieved a maid
    That paragons description and wild fame,
    One that excels the quirks of blazoning pens,
    And in the essential vesture of creation
    Does bear all excellently.

(Re-enter SECOND GENTLEMAN.)

    How now? who has put in?
SECOND GENTLEMAN: 'Tis one Iago, ancient to the general.
CASSIO: He has had most favorable and happy speed.
    Tempests themselves, high seas, and howling winds,
    The guttered rocks, and congregated sands,
    Traitors ensteeped to clog the guiltless keel,[5]

---

[3]till . . . regard: until we've waited until nightfall when the horizon line between sky and sea
disappears.
[4]surfeited: over-fed.
[5]ensteeped: hidden under water.

As having sense of beauty, do omit
Their mortal natures, letting go safely by
The divine Desdemona.
MONTANO: What is she?
CASSIO: She that I spake of, our great captain's captain,
Left in the conduct of the bold Iago,
Whose footing here anticipates our thoughts
A se'en-night's speed.[6] Great Jove, Othello guard,
And swell his sail with thine own powerful breath,
That he may bless this bay with his tall ship,
Make love's quick pants in Desdemona's arms,
Give renewed fire to our extincted spirits,
And bring all Cyprus comfort! Oh, behold!

(Enter DESDEMONA, EMILIA, IAGO, RODERIGO, and attendants.)

The riches of the ship is come on shore!
Ye men of Cyprus, let her have your knees.
Hail to thee, lady! And the grace of heaven,
Before, behind thee, and on every hand,
Enwheel thee round!
DESDEMONA: I thank you, valiant Cassio.
What tidings can you tell me of my lord?
CASSIO: He is not yet arrived; nor know I aught
But that he's well, and will be shortly here.
DESDEMONA: O, but I fear! How lost you company?
CASSIO: The great contention of the sea and skies
Parted our fellowship.

(An off-stage voice cries, "A sail, a sail!" Then guns are heard.)

But, hark! a sail.
SECOND GENTLEMAN: They give their greeting to the citadel;
This likewise is a friend.
CASSIO: See for the news.

(Exit GENTLEMAN. CASSIO speaks to IAGO.)

Good ancient, you are welcome. *(To EMILIA.)* Welcome, mistress.

(He kisses her.)

Let it not gall your patience, good Iago.
That I extend my manners; 'tis my breeding
That gives me this bold show of courtesy.
IAGO: Sir, would she give you so much of her lips
As of her tongue she oft bestows on me,
You'd have enough.
DESDEMONA: Alas, she has no speech.
IAGO: In faith, too much;
I find it still, when I have lust to sleep.
Marry, before your ladyship, I grant,

[6]whose footing . . . speed: who has landed here a week sooner than we expected.

143

She puts her tongue a little in her heart,
And chides with thinking.
EMILIA: You have little cause to say so.
IAGO: Come on, come on! You are pictures out of doors,[7]
Bells in your parlors, wild-cats in your kitchens,
Saints in your injuries,[8] devils being offended,
Players in your housewifery, and housewives in your beds.[9]
DESDEMONA: O, fie upon thee, slanderer!
IAGO: Nay, it is true, or else I am a Turk;
You rise to play, and go to bed to work.
EMILIA: You shall not write my praise.
IAGO: No, let me not.
DESDEMONA: What wouldst thou write of me, if thou shouldst praise me?
IAGO: O gentle lady, do not put me to't;
For I am nothing, if not critical.
DESDEMONA: Come on, assay.[10] There's one gone to the harbor?
IAGO: Aye, madam.
DESDEMONA: I am not merry; but I do beguile[11]
The thing I am, by seeming otherwise.
Come, how wouldst thou praise me?
IAGO: I am about it; but, indeed, my invention
Comes from my pate, as birdlime does from frieze,[12]
It plucks it out brains and all. But my Muse labors,
And thus she is delivered:[13]
If she be fair and wise, fairness and wit;
The one's for use, the other useth it.[14]
DESDEMONA: Well praised! How if she be black and witty?[15]
IAGO: If she be black, and thereto have a wit,
She'll find a white that shall her blackness fit.[16]
DESDEMONA: Worse and worse.
EMILIA: How, if fair and foolish?
IAGO: She never yet was foolish that was fair,
For even her folly helped her to an heir.[17]

[7]You are pictures out of doors: Iago quickly broadens his remarks about Emilia to cover all women. The idea of this first accusation is that they paint their faces, thereby becoming as inappropriate as a painting put on display out in the weather.
[8]saints in your injuries: pretending to be saintly when actually giving insults.
[9]Players . . . beds: You don't take your housekeeping seriously, and you're hussies in bed. (Hussy, meaning sluttish comes from the contraction of "housewife" spelled "huswif" and pronounced "husif.")
[10]assay: try.
[11]beguile: cheat.
[12]birdlime: a sticky substance which is smeared on branches to catch birds; frieze: a coarse cloth with a rough surface.
[13]is delivered: gives birth.
[14]This and the following sententia of Iago on the subject of women display his cynical attitude toward women and the relationships between the sexes. The present couplet means that a woman's beauty is only to be used and that wits — either hers or those of a man — will know how best to make use of her beauty.
[15]black: brunette, in contrast with fair, meaning blond.
[16]white: white person.
[17]This couplet refers to the contemporary legal principle that one's ability to marry and parent a child proved that one was not an idiot. Iago's proverb says that since a fair woman will likely be able to attract a husband and have a child, she can never be counted foolish.

DESDEMONA: These are old, fond paradoxes,[18] to make fools laugh I'the alehouse. What miserable praise has thou for her that's foul and foolish?

IAGO: There's none so foul, and foolish thereunto,
But does foul pranks which fair and wise ones do.

DESDEMONA: O heavy ignorance! Thou praisest the worst best. But what praise couldst thou bestow on a deserving woman indeed! One, that in the authority of her merit, did justly put on the vouch of very malice itself?[19]

IAGO: She that was ever fair, and never proud;
Had tongue at will, and yet was never loud;[20]
Never lacked gold, and yet went never gay;
Fled from her wish, and yet said, "Now I may";[21]
She that, being angered, her revenge being nigh,
Bade her wrong stay, and her displeasure fly;
She, that in wisdom never was so frail,
To change the cod's head for a salmon's tail;[22]
She that could think, and ne'er disclose her mind,
See suitors following, and not look behind;
She was a wight, if ever such wight were —[23]

DESDEMONA: To do what?

IAGO: — To suckle fools, and chronicle small beer.[24]

DESDEMONA: O, most lame and impotent conclusion! Do not learn of him, Emilia, though he be thy husband. How say you, Cassio? is he not a most profane and liberal counselor?[25]

CASSIO: *(As he speaks to her, he takes her hand.)* He speaks home, madam;[26] you may relish him more in the soldier, than in the scholar.[27]

IAGO: *(Aside)* He takes her by the palm. Aye, well said, whisper. With as little a web as this, will I ensnare as great a fly as Cassio. *(Watching CASSIO with DESDEMONA.)* Aye, smile upon her, do; I will gyve thee in thine own courtship.[28] You say true; 'tis so, indeed. If such tricks as these strip you out of your lieutenantry, it had been better you had not kissed your three fingers so oft, which now again you are most apt to play the sir in.[29] Very good! Well kissed! An excellent courtesy![30] 'Tis so, indeed. Yet again your fingers to your lips? 'Would

---

[18]fond: foolish.
[19]did justly . . . itself: could without fear accept even malicious testimony to her virtue.
[20]Had tongue at will: was capable of ready, intelligent conversation.
[21]Fled from . . . "I may": Did not act on mere whims, and yet could take wise, self-directing action when she wanted to.
[22]To change . . . tail: to give up a good thing for something worse.
[23]wight: person.
[24]to suckle . . . beer: to nurse babies and keep track of household expenses; in other words, to be a housewife.
[25]profane and liberal: obscene and licentious.
[26]home: directly to the point.
[27]relish him more in the: prefer him in the role of a soldier rather than in that of a scholar.
[28]gyve: fetter or shackle; courtship: courtesy. As Iago watches them, Cassio and Desdemona carry on a conversation. Cassio's actions, described by Iago, are courteous gestures; the two are not flirting, but Iago sees that the actions could be misconstrued.
[29]the sir: the gentleman.
[30]courtesy: curtsy.

they were clyster-pipes for your sake![31] *(Off-stage, a trumpet sounds.*
IAGO speaks out loud.) The Moor! I know his trumpet.
CASSIO: 'Tis truly so.
DESDEMONA: Let's meet him, and receive him.
CASSIO: Lo, where he comes! *(Enter OTHELLO and attendants.)*
OTHELLO: O my fair warrior!
DESDEMONA: My dear Othello!
OTHELLO: It gives me wonder, great as my content,
   To see you here before me.
   O my soul's joy!
   If after every tempest come such calms,
   May the winds blow till they have wakened death!
   And let the laboring bark climb hills of seas,[32]
   Olympus-high; and duck again as low
   As hell's from heaven! If it were now to die,
   'Twere now to be most happy; for, I fear,
   My soul hath her content so absolute,
   That not another comfort like to this
   Succeeds in unknown fate.[33]
DESDEMONA: The Heavens forbid
   But that our loves and comforts should increase,
   Even as our days do grow!
OTHELLO: Amen to that, sweet powers!
   I cannot speak enough of this content;
   It stops me here; it is too much of joy.
   And this — *(He kisses her.)* — and this — *(He kisses her again.)* — the
      greatest discords be,
   That e'er our hearts shall make!
IAGO: *(Aside)* O' you are well tuned now!
   But I'll set down the pegs that make this music,[34]
   As honest as I am.[35]
OTHELLO: *(To DESDEMONA.)* Come, let's to the castle.

(To the group.)

   News, friends: Our wars are done; the Turks are drowned.
   How does my old acquaintance of this isle?[36]
   Honey, you shall be well desired in Cyprus;[37]
   I have found great love amongst them. O my sweet,
   I prattle out of fashion, and I dote
   In mine own comforts. I pr'ythee, good Iago,
   Go to the bay, and disembark my coffers.[38]

[31]clyster-pipes: enema tubes.
[32]bark: boat.
[33]Succeeds . . . fate: Will come in the unknown future.
[34]set down: lower the pitch (as of a violin).
[35]As honest as I am: If I can be trusted.
[36]acquaintance: Montano.
[37]well desired: welcome.
[38]coffers: trunks.

Bring thou the master to the citadel;[39]
He is a good one, and his worthiness
Does challenge much respect. Come, Desdemona;
Once more, well met at Cyprus.

(OTHELLO, DESDEMONA and their attendants exit.)

IAGO: *(To RODERIGO.)* Do thou meet me presently at the harbor. Come hither. *(He speaks confidentially.)* If thou be'st valiant, as they say base men, being in love, have then a nobility in their natures more than is native to them, list me.[40] The lieutenant tonight watches on the court of guard. First, I must tell thee this: Desdemona is directly in love with him.

RODERIGO: With him! Why, 'tis not possible.

IAGO: Lay thy finger thus *(He puts his finger to his lips.)* and let thy soul be instructed. Mark me with what violence she first loved the Moor, but for bragging, and telling her fantastical lies;[41] and will she love him still for prating?[42] Let not thy discreet heart think it. Her eye must be fed; and what delight shall she have to look on the devil? When the blood is made dull with the act of sport, there should be — again to inflame it, and to give satiety a fresh appetite — loveliness in favor, sympathy in years, manners, and beauties — all which the Moor is defective in. Now, for want of these required conveniences, her delicate tenderness will find itself abused, begin to heave the gorge, disrelish and abhor the Moor;[43] very nature will instruct her in it, and compel her to some second choice. Now, sir, this granted, as it is a most pregnant and unforced position, who stands so eminently in the degree of this fortune, as Cassio does? A knave, very voluble;[44] no further conscionable, than in putting on the mere form of civil and humane seeming, for the better compassing of his salt and most hidden loose affection?[45] Why, none; why, none. A slippery and subtle knave, a finder-out of occasions, that has an eye can stamp and counterfeit advantages, though true advantage never present itself: A devilish knave! Besides, the knave is handsome, young; and hath all those requisites in him that folly and green minds look after: A pestilent, complete knave.[46] And the woman hath found him already.

RODERIGO: I cannot believe that in her; she is full of most blessed condition.

IAGO: Blessed fig's end! The wine she drinks is made of grapes; if she had been blessed, she would never have loved the Moor. Blessed pudding! Didst thou not see her paddle with the palm of his hand? Didst not mark that?

RODERIGO: Yes, that I did; but that was but courtesy.

IAGO: Lechery, by this hand; an index, and obscure prologue to the history

[39]master: ship's captain.
[40]list: listen to.
[41]mark me: notice; but for . . . lies: because he bragged and told her lies.
[42]prating: chattering meaninglessly.
[43]heave the gorge: retch.
[44]knave: deceitful person; voluble: fickle.
[45]salt: lustful.
[46]green: immature.

of lust and foul thoughts.[47] They met so near with their lips, that their breaths embraced together. Villainous thoughts, Roderigo! When these mutualities so marshal the way, hard at hand comes the master and main exercise, the incorporate conclusion. Pish! But, sir be you ruled by me. I have brought you from Venice. Watch you tonight; for the command, I'll lay't upon you.[48] Cassio knows you not; I'll not be far from you. Do you find some occasion to anger Cassio, either by speaking too loud, or tainting his discipline; or from what other course you please, which the time shall more favorably minister.

RODERIGO: Well.

IAGO: Sir, he is rash, and very sudden in choler; and haply, with his truncheon may strike at you.[49] Provoke him that he may; for even out of that will I cause these of Cyprus to mutiny, whose qualification shall come into no true taste again, but by the displanting of Cassio.[50] So shall you have a shorter journey to your desires, by the means I shall then have to prefer them, and the impediment most profitably removed, without the which there were no expectation of our propserity.

RODERIGO: I will do this, if you can bring it to any opportunity.

IAGO: I warrant thee. Meet me by and by at the citadel; I must fetch his necessaries ashore. Farewell.

RODERIGO: Adieu. *(He exits.)*

IAGO: That Cassio loves her, I do well believe it;
That she loves him, 'tis apt, and of great credit.[51]
The Moor, howbeit that I endure him not,
Is of a constant, loving, noble nature,
And, I dare think, he'll prove to Desdemona
A most dear husband. Now I do love her too —
Not out of absolute lust, though, peradventure,
I stand accountant for as great a sin —
But partly led to diet my revenge,[52]
For that I do suspect the lusty Moor
Hath leaped into my seat; the thought whereof
Doth, like a poisonous mineral, gnaw my inwards;
And nothing can or shall content my soul,
Till I am even with him, wife for wife,
Or, failing so, yet that I put the Moor
At least into a jealousy so strong
That judgement cannot cure. Which thing to do —
If this poor trash of Venice, whom I trace[53]
For his quick hunting, stand the putting on —[54]

---

[47]Indexes used to be placed at the beginnings of books.
[48]for the command . . . you: I'll let you take the lead.
[49]haply: with luck.
[50]whose qualification . . . Cassio: who will not be appeased again until Cassio is replaced (with Iago).
[51]apt: suited to the purpose; great credit: easily believable.
[52]diet: feed.
[53]trash: a poor hunting dog.
[54]whom I trace . . . hunting: whose footsteps I follow to make him hunt better.

I'll have our Michael Cassio on the hip;[55]
Abuse him to the Moor in the right garb —[56]
For I fear Cassio with my night-cape too —
Make the Moor thank me, love me, and reward me,
For making him egregiously an ass[57]
And practicing upon his peace and quiet,
Even to madness. 'Tis here, but yet confused;
Knavery's plain face is never seen, till used.

(He exits.)

[55]have . . . on the hip: either to throw him down (as in wrestling) or to have him all but dead — an image taken from hunting in which the dogs frequently attacked a deer's hip.
[56]in the right garb: in whatever manner turns out to be appropriate.
[57]egregiously: flagrantly.

ACT II

Scene ii

Later that afternoon, on a street in Cyprus.

HERALD: *(He enters carrying a proclamation. A crowd follows him.)* It is Othello's pleasure, our noble and valiant general, that, upon certain tidings now arrived, importing the mere perdition of the Turkish fleet,[1] every man put himself into triumph; some to dance, some to make bonfires, each man to what sport and revels his addition leads him;[2] for, besides these beneficial news, it is the celebration of his nuptials. So much was his pleasure should be proclaimed. All offices are open;[3] and there is full liberty of feasting, from this present hour of five, till the bell hath told eleven. Heaven bless the isle of Cyprus, and our noble general, Othello!

(He exits.)

---

[1]mere: complete.
[2]addition: disposition. This strange word choice, combined with the peculiar phrase "put himself into triumph" suggests that the herald is a pompous character who loves the sound of his own voice and his way with words.
[3]offices: rooms appointed for the use of upper servants of great households.

ACT II

Scene iii

That evening, in a hall in the castle

(OTHELLO enters with DESDEMONA, CASSIO, and attendants.)

OTHELLO: Good Michael, look you to the guard tonight.
Let's teach ourselves that honorable stop,
Not to out-sport discretion.

CASSIO: Iago hath direction what to do;
But, notwithstanding, with my personal eye
Will I look to't.

OTHELLO: Iago is most honest.
Michael, good night; tomorrow, with your earliest,
Let me have speech with you. *(To DESDEMONA.)* Come, my dear love,
The purchase made, the fruits are to ensue;
That profit's yet to come 'twixt me and you.

(To CASSIO.)

Good night.

(OTHELLO, DESDEMONA, and their attendants exit. IAGO enters.)

CASSIO: Welcome, Iago; we must to the watch.

IAGO: Not this hour, lieutenant; 'tis not yet ten o'clock. Our general cast us thus early,[1] for the love of his Desdemona, whom let us not therefore blame; he hath not yet made wanton the night with her; and she is sport for Jove.[2]

CASSIO: She's a most exquisite lady.

IAGO: And, I'll warrant her, full of game.

CASSIO: Indeed, she is a most fresh and delicate creature.

IAGO: What an eye she has! Methinks it sounds a parley of provocation.

CASSIO: An inviting eye; and yet, methinks, right modest.

IAGO: And when she speaks, is it not an alarum to love?

CASSIO: She is, indeed, perfection.

IAGO: Well, happiness to their sheets! Come, lieutenant, I have a stoup of wine; and here without are a brace of Cyprus gallants, that would fain have a measure to the health of black Othello.[3]

CASSIO: Not tonight, good Iago; I have very poor and unhappy brains for drinking. I could well wish courtesy would invent some other custom of entertainment.

IAGO: Oh, they are our friends. But one cup; I'll drink for you.

CASSIO: I have drunk but one cup tonight; and that was craftily qualified too, and, behold, what innovation it makes here.[4] I am unfortunate in

---

[1]cast: dismissed.
[2]sport: a plaything. Note that in the sequence beginning here, Iago speaks of Desdemona in suggestive, lustful terms while Cassio almost worships her with his respect and admiration.
[3]measure: portion of wine.
[4]craftily qualified: secretly watered down (apparently by Cassio himself) to keep from getting drunk. With the word "here" Cassio might indicate his flushed face.

the infirmity, and dare not task my weakness with any more.
IAGO: What, man? 'Tis a night of revels! The gallants desire it.
CASSIO: Where are they?
IAGO: Here at the door; I pray you, call them in.
CASSIO: I'll do it, but it dislikes me. *(He exits.)*
IAGO: If I can fasten but one cup upon him,
    With that which he hath drunk tonight already,
    He'll be as full of quarrel and offense
    As my young mistress' dog. Now my sick fool, Roderigo,
    Whom love has turned almost the wrong side outward,
    To Desdemona hath tonight caroused
    Potations pottle-deep;[5] and he's to watch.
    Three lads of Cyprus, noble swelling spirits
    That hold their honors in a wary distance —[6]
    The very elements of this warlike isle —
    Have I tonight flustered with flowing cups,
    And they watch too. Now, 'mongst this flock of drunkards,
    Am I to put our Cassio in some action
    That may offend the isle. But here they come.
    If consequence do but approve my dream,
    My boat sails freely, both with wind and stream.[7]

(CASSIO returns with MONTANO and gentlemen. CASSIO carries a wine cup.)

CASSIO: 'Fore heaven, they have given me a rouse already.
MONTANO: Good faith, a little one; not past a pint, as I am a soldier.
IAGO: *(He calls for the servants.)* Some wine, ho!

(He sings.)

    And let me the canakin clink, clink;
    And let me the canakin clink;
    A soldier's a man,
    A life's but a span;
    Why, then, let a soldier drink.

(He calls.)

    Some wine, boys!

(Servants bring in wine. As the scene continues, CASSIO and the Cypriots share cup after cup of wine.)

CASSIO: 'Fore heaven, an excellent song.
IAGO: I learned it in England, where, indeed, they are most potent in potting.[8] Your Dane, your German, and your swag-bellied Hollander — *(He shouts for more wine.)* Drink, ho! — are nothing to your English.

[5]To Desdemona . . . pottle-deep: has drunk huge amounts of wine toasting Desdemona tonight. A pottle is a measure of two quarts.
[6]hold . . . distance: are quick to take offense at a supposed insult.
[7]both with wind and stream: pushed along by a tail-wind and the current as well.
[8]potting: drinking.

CASSIO: Is your Englishman so expert in his drinking?

IAGO: Why, he drinks you, with facility, your Dane dead drunk; he sweats not to overthrow your Almain;[9] he gives your Hollander a vomit, ere, the next pottle can be filled.

CASSIO: To the health of our general.

MONTANO: I am for it, lieutenant; and I'll do you justice.

IAGO: O, sweet England!

(He sings.)

> King Stephen was and-a worthy peer,
> His breeches cost him but a crown;
> He held them sixpence all too dear,
> With that he called the tailor, lown.[10]

> He was a wight of high renown,[11]
> And thou art but of low degree;
> 'Tis pride that pulls the country down;
> Then take thine auld cloak about thee.

(He calls.)

> Some wine, ho!

CASSIO: Why, this is a more exquisite song than the other.

IAGO: Will you hear it again?

CASSIO: No, for I hold him to be unworthy of his place, that does those things. Well, Heaven's above all, and there be souls that must be saved, and there be souls must not be saved.

IAGO: It's true, good lieutenant.

CASSIO: For mine own part, no offense to the general or any man of quality, I hope to be saved.

IAGO: And so do I too, lieutenant.

CASSIO: Aye, but, by your leave, not before me; the lieutenant is to be saved before the ancient. Let's have no more of this; let's to our affairs. Forgive us our sins! Gentlemen, let's look to our business. Do not think, gentlemen, I am drunk; this is my ancient; this is my right hand, and this is my left hand.[12] I am not drunk now; I can stand well enough, and speak well enough.

ALL: Excellent well.

CASSIO: Why, very well, then; you must not think then, that I am drunk.

(He staggers out.)

MONTANO: To the platform, masters; come, let's set the watch.

IAGO: You see this fellow, that is gone before?

> He is a soldier fit to stand by Caesar
> And give direction. And do but see his vice:
> 'Tis to his virtue a just equinox,[13]

[9]Almain: German.
[10]lown: lout.
[11]wight: person.
[12]. . . right hand . . . left: An English soldier was considered sober as long as he could go through his facings (right-face, left-face, etc.)
[13]just equinox: equal counterpart.

The one as long as the other; 'tis pity of him.
I fear the trust Othello puts in him,
On some odd time of his infirmity
Will shake this island.
MONTANO: But is he often thus?
IAGO: 'Tis evermore the prologue to his sleep.
He'll watch the horologe a double set[14]
If drink rock not his cradle.
MONTANO: It were well
The general were put in mind of it.
Perhaps he sees it not, or his good nature
Prizes the virtue that appears in Cassio,
And looks not on his evils. Is not this true?

(RODERIGO enters.)

IAGO: How now, Roderigo? *(He speaks quietly to him:)*
I pray you: After the lieutenant! Go!

(RODERIGO exits.)

MONTANO: And 'tis great pity, that the noble Moor
Should hazard such a place, as his own second,
With one of an ingraft infirmity.
It were an honest action to say
So to the Moor.
IAGO: Not I, for this fair island.
I do love Cassio well, and would do much
To cure him of this evil.

(From off-stage comes a cry: "Help! Help!")

But hark! What noise?

(RODERIGO comes running in with CASSIO chasing him.)

CASSIO: You rogue! You rascal!
MONTANO: What's the matter, lieutenant?
CASSIO: A knave! Teach me my duty!
I'll beat the knave into a twiggen bottle.[15]
RODERIGO: Beat me?
CASSIO: Dost thou prate, rogue?

(He begins to beat RODERIGO. MONTANO steps in and tries to stop him.)

MONTANO: Nay, good lieutenant!
I pray you, sir, hold your hand.
CASSIO: Let me go, sir,
Or I'll knock you o'er the mazard.[16]
MONTANO: Come, come! You're drunk.

[14]horologe: clock. Since some clocks of the time were marked for 12 hours and some for 24, it is unclear whether Iago's "double set" means 24 hours or 48.
[15]twiggen-bottle: straw-wrapped bottle, like a Chianti bottle; Cassio threatens to slash Roderigo until his skin resembles the woven straw on a wine bottle.
[16]mazard: head.

CASSIO: Drunk!

(CASSIO draws his sword and attacks MONTANO who is therefore forced to draw and defend himself. As they fight, IAGO speaks quietly to RODERIGO:)

IAGO: Away, I say! Go out, and cry, "A mutiny!"

(RODERIGO runs out. IAGO turns his attention to the brawling pair.)

> Nay, good lieutenant! Alas, gentlemen!
> Help, ho! Lieutenant! Sir Montano!
> Help, masters! Here's a goodly watch, indeed!

(A bell starts to ring.)

> Who's that that rings the bell? Diablo, ho![17]
> The town will rise! God's will, lieutenant! Hold!
> You will be shamed forever!

(OTHELLO enters with attendants just as CASSIO runs his sword through MONTANO, the island's previous governor.)

OTHELLO: What is the matter here?
MONTANO: I bleed still! I am hurt to the death! He dies!

(He renews his attack on CASSIO.)

OTHELLO: Hold, for your lives!
IAGO: Hold! Hold, lieutenant! Sir Montano! Gentlemen!
> Have you forgot all sense of place and duty?
> Hold! Hold! The general speaks to you! Hold, for shame!
OTHELLO: Why, how now! Ho! From whence ariseth this?
> Are we turned Turks, and to ourselves do that
> Which heaven hath forbid the Ottomites?
> For Christian shame put by this barbarous brawl.
> He that stirs next to carve for his own rage,
> Holds his soul light; he dies upon his motion.

(To attendants.)

> Silence that dreadful bell; it frights the isle
> From her propriety. (He turns his attention back to the brawl.)
> What is the matter, masters?
> Honest Iago, that look'st dead with grieving,
> Speak! Who began this? On thy love, I charge thee.
IAGO: I do not know; friends all but now, even now,
> In quarter,[18] and in terms like bride and groom
> Divesting them for bed; and then, but now,
> As if some planet had unwitted men,
> Swords out, and tilting one at other's breast,
> In opposition bloody. I cannot speak
> Any beginning to this peevish odds;

[17]Diablo: the Devil.
[18]in quarter: at peace; or perhaps on duty (as in "at their quarters").

And 'would in action glorious I had lost
These legs, that brought me to a part of it!
OTHELLO: How comes it, Michael, you are thus forgot?
CASSIO: I pray you, pardon me. I cannot speak.
OTHELLO: Worthy Montano, you were wont to be civil;
The gravity and stillness of your youth
The world hath noted, and your name is great
In mouths of wisest censure.[19] What's the matter,
That you unlace your reputation thus,[20]
And spend your rich opinion, for the name
Of a night brawler? Give me answer to it.
MONTANO: Worthy Othello, I am hurt to danger.
Your officer, Iago, can inform you —
While I spare speech, which something now offends me —[21]
Of all that I do know. Nor know I aught
By me that's said or done amiss this night —
Unless self-charity be sometime a vice,
And to defend ourselves it be sin,
When violence assails us.
OTHELLO: Now by Heaven,
My blood begins my safer guides to rule,[22]
And passion, having my best judgement collied,[23]
Assays to lead the way. If I once stir,
Or do but lift this arm, the best of you
Shall sink in my rebuke. Give me to know
How this foul rout began, who set it on;
And he that is approved in this offense,[24]
Though he had twinned with me, both at a birth,
Shall lose me. What! in a town of war
Yet wild, the people's hearts brimful of fear,
To manage private and domestic quarrel,
In night, and on the court of guard and safety!
'Tis monstrous. Iago, who began it?
MONTANO: If partially affined, or leagued in office,[25]
Thou dost deliver more or less than truth,
Thou art no soldier.
IAGO: Touch me not so near.
I had rather have this tongue cut from my mouth,
Than it should do offense to Michael Cassio;
Yet, I persuade myself, to speak the truth
Shall nothing wrong him. Thus it is, general:

[19]censure: judgement.
[20]unlace: loosen.
[21]something: somewhat. He wishes he had the ability to speak, but his wound prevents him.
[22]My blood . . . to rule: The blood was sometimes considered the seat of the emotions. Othello recognizes here that reason is the "safer guide," but says he feels his emotions, especially frustration and anger, taking over.
[23]collied: darkened.
[24]approved: convicted by proof.
[25]partially affined: bound by partiality.

Montano and myself being in speech,
There comes a fellow, crying out for help;
And Cassio following with determined sword,
To execute upon him. Sir, this gentleman *(Meaning MONTANO.)*
Steps in to Cassio, and entreats his pause;
Myself the crying fellow did pursue,
Lest, by his clamor, as it so fell out,
The town might fall in fright. He, swift of foot,
Outran my purpose, and I returned the rather
For that I heard the clink and fall of swords,
And Cassio high in oath, which till tonight,
I ne'er might say before. When I came back,
For this was brief, I found them close together,
At blow and thrust, even as again they were
When you yourself did part them.
More of this matter can I not report,
But men are men; the best sometimes forget.
Though Cassio did some little wrong to him,
As men in rage strike those that wish them best,
Yet, surely, Cassio, I believe, received
From him that fled, some strange indignity,
Which patience could not pass.
OTHELLO: I know, Iago,
Thy honesty and love doth mince this matter,[26]
Making it light to Cassio.[27] Cassio, I love thee,
But never more be officer of mine . . .

(DESDEMONA enters with attendants.)

Look, if my gentle love be not raised up!

(Turning back to CASSIO.)

I'll make thee an example.
DESDEMONA: What's the matter, dear?
OTHELLO: All's well now, sweeting; come away to bed.

(Turning to MONTANO.)

Sir, for your hurts,
Myself will be your surgeon. *(To attendants.)* Lead him off.
Iago, look with care about the town,
And silence those whom this vile brawl distracted.
Come, Desdemona; 'tis the soldiers' life,
To have their balmy slumbers waked with strife.

(All but IAGO and CASSIO exit.)

IAGO: What, are you hurt, lieutenant?
CASSIO: Ay, past all surgery.

[26]mince: minimize.
[27]light to: easy on.

157

IAGO: Marry, heaven forbid![28]

CASSIO: Reputation, reputation, reputation! Oh, I have lost my reputation! I have lost the immortal part, sir, of myself, and what remains is bestial. My reputation, Iago, my reputation.

IAGO: As I am an honest man, I thought you had received some bodily wound; there is more offense in that, than in reputation. Reputation is an idle and most false imposition, oft got without merit, and lost without deserving.[29] You have lost no reputation at all, unless you repute yourself such a loser. What, man! There are ways to recover the general again. You are but now cast in his mood, a punishment more in policy than in malice;[30] even so as one would beat his offenseless dog, to affright an imperious lion. Sue to him again, and he's yours.

CASSIO: I will rather sue to be despised, than to deceive so good a commander with so slight, so drunken, and so indiscreet an officer.[31] Drunk? And speak parrot?[32] And squabble? Swagger? Swear? And discourse fustian with one's own shadow?[33] O thou invisible spirit of wine, if thou hast no name to be known by, let us call thee — devil!

IAGO: What was he that you followed with your sword? What had he done to you?

CASSIO: I know not.

IAGO: Is it possible?

CASSIO: I remember a mass of things, but nothing distinctly — a quarrel, but nothing wherefore.[34] Oh that men should put an enemy in their mouths, to seal away their brains! That we should, with joy, revel, pleasure, and applause, transform ourselves into beasts!

IAGO: Why, but you are now well enough. How came you thus recovered?

CASSIO: It hath pleased the devil, drunkenness, to give place to the devil, wrath; one unperfectness shows me another, to make me frankly despise myself.

IAGO: Come, you are too severe a moraler. As the time, the place, and the condition of this country stands, I could heartily wish this had not befallen; but, since it is as it is, mend it for your own good.

CASSIO: I will ask him for my place again; he shall tell me I am a drunkard! Had I as many mouths as Hydra, such an answer would stop them all.[35] To be now a sensible man, by and by a fool, and presently a beast! Oh, strange! Every inordinate cup is unblessed, and the ingredient is a devil.[36]

---

[28]Marry. Iago uses this light oath, referring to the Virgin Mary, as an emphasizer.

[29]imposition: deception.

[30]cast in his mood: ejected in his anger. More in policy than in malice: Iago goes on to suggest that Othello punished Cassio, not because he dislikes him but in order to restore peace to the nervous town.

[31]deceive: disgrace; slight: small.

[32]speak parrot: babble without meaning.

[33]discourse fustian: hold a pretentious conversation.

[34]wherefore: why.

[35]Hydra was a many-headed serpent in Greek mythology which Hercules killed. As each of its heads was cut off, two more immediately grew in its place.

[36]Every inordinate . . . a devil: While inordinate may merely mean excessive, it might also mean unordained in which case Cassio, apparently a very pious man, may be making a contrast between wine used as a beverage and the wine of holy communion which, far from containing a devil, embodies the blood of Christ.

IAGO: Come, come, good wine is a familiar good creature, if it be well used; exclaim no more against it.[37] And, good lieutenant, I think you think I love you.

CASSIO: I have well approved it, sir. I drunk!

IAGO: You, or any man living, may be drunk at some time, man. I'll tell you what you shall do. Our general's wife is now the general. I may say so in this respect, for that he hath devoted and given up himself to the contemplation, mark, and denotement of her parts and graces. Confess yourself freely to her; importune her; she'll help to put you in your place again. She is of so free, so kind, so apt, so blessed a disposition, that she holds it a vice in her goodness not to do more than she is requested. This broken joint between you and her husband, entreat her to splinter;[38] and, my fortunes against any lay worth naming, this crack of your love shall grow stronger than it was before.[39]

CASSIO: You advise me well.

IAGO: I protest, in the sincerity of love and honest kindness.[40]

CASSIO: I think it freely; and betimes in the morning, I will beseech the virtuous Desdemona to undertake for me.[41] I am desperate of my fortunes, if they check me here.[42]

IAGO: You are in the right. Good night, lieutenant; I must to the watch.

CASSIO: Good night, Honest Iago. *(CASSIO exits.)*

IAGO: And what's he, then, that says I play the villain?
     When this advice is free I give, and honest,
     Probal to thinking, and indeed the course
     To win the Moor again?[43] For 'tis most easy
     The inclining Desdemona to subdue
     In any honest suit; she's framed as fruitful
     As the free elements. And then for her
     To win the Moor — were't to renounce his baptism,
     All seals and symbols of redeemed sin,
     His soul is so enfettered to her love,
     That she may make, unmake, do what she list,
     Even as her appetite shall play the god
     With his weak function. How am I then a villain
     To counsel Cassio to this parallel course,
     Directly to his good? Divinity of hell!
     When devils will their blackest sins put on,
     They do suggest at first with heavenly shows,
     As I do now; for while this honest fool
     Plies Desdemona, to repair his fortunes,
     And she for him pleads strongly to the Moor,
     I'll pour this pestilence into his ear:

---

[37]creature: creation.
[38]splinter: put a splint on.
[39]lay: wager.
[40]"I protest" is equivalent here to "you're welcome."
[41]betimes: early.
[42]I am desperate . . . here. I despair of my future if it stops me here.
[43]probal: sensible.

159

That she repeals him for her body's lust.[44]
And, by how much she strives to do him good,
She shall undo her credit with the Moor.
So will I turn her virtue into pitch;
And out of her own goodness make the net
That shall enmesh them all. *(RODERIGO enters.)* How now, Roderigo?
RODERIGO: I do follow here in the chase, not like a hound that hunts, but
one that fills up the cry. My money is almost spent; I have been tonight
exceedingly well cudgelled; and, I think, the issue will be: I shall have
so much experience for my pains, and so, with no money at all, and
a little more wit, return to Venice.
IAGO: How poor are they that have not patience!
What wound did ever heal but by degrees?
Thou know'st we work by wit, and not by witchcraft;
And wit depends on dilatory time.
Does't not go well? Cassio hath beaten thee,
And thou, by that small hurt, hath cashiered Cassio.
Though other things grow fair against the sun,
Yet fruits that blossom first, will first be ripe.
Content thyself awhile. By the mass 'tis morning!
Pleasure, and action, make the hours seem short.
Retire thee; go where thou art billeted.
Away, I say; thou shalt know more hereafter.
Nay, get thee gone. *(RODERIGO exits.)* Two things are to be done:
My wife must move for Cassio to her mistress;
I'll set her on.
Myself, the while, to draw the Moor apart,
And bring him jump when he may Cassio find
Soliciting his wife. Ay, that's the way;
Dull not device by coldness and delay.[45] *(He exits.)*

---

[44]repeals him: calls Cassio back to his office.
[45]device: the plot.

ACT III

Scene i

The next morning, in front of the castle.

(CASSIO enters with some musicians.)

CASSIO: Master, play here — I will content your pains —
Something that's brief; and bid, good morrow, general.[1]

(The musicians play. While they play, a CLOWN enters.)[2]

CLOWN: Why, masters, have your instruments been at Naples, that they
speak i' the nose thus?[3]
LEAD MUSICIAN: How, sir, how!
CLOWN: Are these, I pray you, called wind instruments?
LEAD MUSICIAN: Ay, marry, are they, sir.
CLOWN: Oh, thereby hangs a tail.[4]
LEAD MUSICIAN: Whereby hangs a tale, sir?
CLOWN: Marry, sir, by many a wind instrument that I know. But masters,
here's money for you; *(He gives them money.)* and the general so likes
your music, that he desires you of all loves, to make no more noise
with it.
LEAD MUSICIAN: Well, sir, we will not.
CLOWN: If you have any music that may not be heard, to't again; but, as
they say, to hear music, the general does not greatly care.[5]
LEAD MUSICIAN: We have none such, sir.
CLOWN: Then put up your pipes in your bag, for I'll away.
Go; vanish into air; away. *(He chases the musicians off.)*
CASSIO: Dost thou hear, my honest friend?
CLOWN: No, I hear not your honest friend; I hear you.
CASSIO: Pr'ythee, keep up thy quillets.[6] There's a poor piece of gold for
thee; *(He gives the CLOWN a coin.)* if the gentlewoman that attends
the general be stirring, tell her, there's one Cassio entreats her a little
favor of speech. Wilt thou do this?
CLOWN: She is stirring, sir; if she will stir hither, I shall seem to notify
unto her.

(The CLOWN exits, and IAGO enters.)

CASSIO: In happy time, Iago.
IAGO: You have not been a-bed, then?
CASSIO: Why, no; the day had broke before we parted.

[1] I will content your pains: I'll pay you for your work. It was a custom for friends to provide
music for a couple to awaken to after their marriage night.
[2] CLOWN: court jester, a type of servant who was a traditional part of noble households.
[3] Naples: Either a joke about the nasal accent of Neapolitans or else a reference to syphilis which
supposedly plagued Naples and which destroyed the nose.
[4] "Thereby hangs a tale" means, "There's a story connected to that." The clown, however, is
making a pun which draws a parallel between the musicians' wind instruments and the anus,
located next to the tail, which produces its own kind of windy sound.
[5] "To't may be a pun (toot). "General" may also be a pun referring simultaneously to General
Othello and also to the general public who have little interest in music.
[6] quillets: puns or fine distinctions.

I have made bold, Iago, to send in to your wife.
My suit to her is that she will to virtuous Desdemona
Procure me some access.
IAGO: I'll send her to you presently.
And I'll devise a mean to draw the Moor
Out of the way, that your converse and business
May be more free. *(IAGO exits.)*
CASSIO: I humbly thank you for't. *(To himself)* I never knew
A Florentine more kind and honest.

(EMILIA enters.)

EMILIA: Good morrow, good lieutenant; I am sorry
For your displeasure; but all will soon be well.
The general and his wife are talking of it,
And she speaks for you stoutly. The Moor replies
That he you hurt, is of great fame in Cyprus,
And great affinity,[7] and that, in wholesome wisdom,
He might not but refuse you. But, he protests, he loves you,
And needs no other suitor but his likings
To bring you in again.
CASSIO: Yet I beseech you,
If you think fit, or that it may be done,
Give me advantage of some brief discourse
With Desdemona alone.
EMILIA: Pray you come in.
I will bestow you where you shall have time
To speak your bosom freely.
CASSIO: I am much bound to you. *(They exit.)*

[7]great affinity: a leading family.

ACT III

Scene ii

Later that morning, in a room in the castle.

(OTHELLO enters together with IAGO and some gentlemen.)

OTHELLO: These letters give, Iago, to the pilot,[1]
  And, by him, do my duties to the state.
  That done — I will be walking on the works —[2]
  Repair there to me.[3]
IAGO: Well, my good lord, I'll do't.
OTHELLO: This fortification, gentlemen, shall we see't?
A GENTLEMAN: We'll wait upon your lordship. *(They all exit.)*

[1]pilot: captain (of a ship bound back to Venice).
[2]works: breastworks or fortifications.
[3]repair: return, go.

ACT III

Scene iii

Later the same day, in front of the castle.

(DESDEMONA enters with CASSIO and EMILIA.)

DESDEMONA: Be thou assured, good Cassio, I will do
    All my abilities in thy behalf.
EMILIA: Good madam, do; I know it grieves my husband,
    As if the case were his.
DESDEMONA: Oh, that's an honest fellow. Do not doubt, Cassio,
    But I will have my lord and you again
    As friendly as you were.
CASSIO: Bounteous madam,
    Whatever shall become of Michael Cassio,
    He's never anything but your true servant.
DESDEMONA: O sir, I thank you. You do love my lord;
    You have known him long; and be you well assured
    He shall in strangeness stand no further off
    Than in a politic distance.[1]
CASSIO: Aye, but, lady,
    That policy may either last so long,
    Or feed upon such nice and waterish diet,
    Or breed itself so out of circumstance,
    That, I being absent, and my place supplied,
    My general will forget my love and service.
DESDEMONA: Do not doubt that;[2] before Emilia here,
    I give thee warrant of thy place. Assure thee,[3]
    If I do vow a friendship, I'll perform it
    To the last article. My lord shall never rest;
    I'll watch him tame, and talk him out of patience;[4]
    His bed shall seem a school, his board a shrift;[5]
    I'll intermingle everything he does
    With Cassio's suit. Therefore be merry, Cassio;
    For thy solicitor shall rather die,
    Than give thy cause away.

(OTHELLO and IAGO enter on the other side of the stage.)

EMILIA: Madam, here comes my lord.
CASSIO: Madam, I'll take my leave.
DESDEMONA: Why, stay, and hear me speak.
CASSIO: Madam, not now; I am very ill at ease;
    Unfit for mine own purposes.
DESDEMONA: Well, do your discretion. *(CASSIO exits.)*

[1]politic distance: distance dictated by political necessity.
[2]doubt: fear.
[3]assure thee: Be assured.
[4]I'll watch him tame: I'll keep him awake until he's tame. Keeping a wild animal or hawk awake until it was exhausted was considered a good way to tame it.
[5]his board a shrift: his table (shall seem to be) a confessional booth.

IAGO: Ha! I like not that.
OTHELLO: What dost thou say?
IAGO: Nothing, my lord, or if — I know not what.
OTHELLO: Was not that Cassio, parted from my wife?
IAGO: Cassio, my lord? No, sure, I cannot think it,
 That he would steal away so guilty-like,
 Seeing you coming.
OTHELLO: I do believe 'twas he.
DESDEMONA: How now, my lord?
 I have been talking with a suitor here,
 A man that languishes in your displeasure.
OTHELLO: Who is't you mean?
DESDEMONA: Why, your lieutenant, Cassio. Good my lord,
 If I have any grace or power to move you,
 His present reconciliation take;
 For, if he be not one that truly loves you,
 That errs in ignorance, and not in cunning,
 I have no judgement in an honest face.
 I pr'ythee call him back.
OTHELLO: Went he hence now?
DESDEMONA: Aye, sooth, so humbled[6]
 That he hath left part of his grief with me;
 I suffer with him. Good love, call him back.
OTHELLO: Not now, sweet Desdemona; some other time.
DESDEMONA: But shall't be shortly?
OTHELLO: The sooner, sweet, for you.
DESDEMONA: Shall't be tonight at supper?
OTHELLO: No, not tonight.
DESDEMONA: Tomorrow dinner, then?
OTHELLO: I shall not dine at home;
 I meet the captains at the citadel.
DESDEMONA: Why then, tomorrow night, or Tuesday morn,
 Or Tuesday noon, or night, or Wednesday morn —
 I pray thee, name the time, but let it not
 Exceed three days. In faith, he's penitent.
 And yet his trespass, in our common reason —
 Save that, they say, the wars must make examples
 Out of the best — is not almost a fault
 To incur a private check.[7] When shall he come?
 Tell me, Othello. I wonder in my soul,
 What you could ask me, that I should deny,
 Or stand so mammering on.[8] What? Michael Cassio,
 That came a-wooing with you, and so many a time,
 When I have spoke of you dispraisingly,

---

[6]sooth: in truth.
[7]not almost: scarcely. Desdemona says that, according to normal opinion, Cassio's offense of getting drunk and brawling would hardly even require a private rebuke, much less public censure and loss of rank.
[8]mammering: hesitating.

165

Hath ta'en your part — to have so much to do
To bring him in! Trust me, I could do much . . .
OTHELLO: 'Pr'ythee, no more. Let him come when he will;
    I will deny thee nothing.
DESDEMONA: Why, this is not a boon.[9]
    'Tis as I should entreat you wear your gloves,
    Or feed on nourishing dishes, or keep you warm,
    Or sue to you to do peculiar profit
    To your own person. Nay, when I have a suit,
    Wherein I mean to touch your love indeed,
    It shall be full of poize and difficulty,[10]
    And fearful to be granted.
OTHELLO: I will deny thee nothing;
    Whereon, I do beseech thee, grant me this:
    To leave me but a little to myself.
DESDEMONA: Shall I deny you? No. Farewell, my lord.
OTHELLO: Farewell, my Desdemona. I'll come to thee straight.
DESDEMONA: Emilia, come. *(Speaking again to OTHELLO.)* Be as your
        fancies teach you;
    Whate'er you be, I am obedient.

(She exits with EMILIA.)

OTHELLO: Excellent wretch![11] Perdition catch my soul,
    But I do love thee! And when I love thee not,
    Chaos is come again.
IAGO: My noble lord.
OTHELLO: What dost thou say, Iago?
IAGO: Did Michael Cassio, when you wooed my lady,
    Know of your love?
OTHELLO: He did, from first to last. Why dost thou ask?
IAGO: But for a satisfaction in my thought;
    No further harm.
OTHELLO: Why of thy thought, Iago?
IAGO: I did not think he had been acquainted with her.
OTHELLO: Oh yes, and went between us very oft.
IAGO: Indeed?
OTHELLO: Indeed? Aye, indeed. Discern'st thou aught in that?
    Is he not honest?
IAGO: Honest, my lord?
OTHELLO: "Honest?" Aye, honest.
IAGO: My lord, for aught I know.
OTHELLO: What dost thou think?
IAGO: Think, my lord?
OTHELLO: "Think, my lord?"
    By heaven, thou echoest me,
    As if there were some monster in thy thought

[9]boon: favor.
[10]poize: balance, or weight.
[11]"Wretch" may be either a term of endearment here or else an early misprint intended as "wench."

Too hideous to be shown. Thou dost mean something.
I heard thee say even now thou likest not that,
When Cassio left my wife. What didst not like?
And, when I told thee, he was of my counsel
In my whole course of wooing, thou criedst, "Indeed?"
And didst contract and purse thy brow together
As if thou then hadst shut up in thy brain
Some horrible conceit.[12] If thou dost love me,
Show me thy thought.
IAGO: My lord, you know I love you.
OTHELLO: I think thou dost;
And — for I know thou art full of love and honesty,
And weight'st thy words before thou giv'st them breath —
Therefore these stops of thine fright me the more;
For such things, in a false, disloyal knave,
Are tricks of custom, but in a man that's just,
They are close denotements, working from the heart,
That passion cannot rule.
IAGO: For Michael Cassio:
I dare be sworn, I think that he is honest.
OTHELLO: I think so too.
IAGO: Men should be what they seem,
Or, those that be not, 'would they might seem none!
OTHELLO: Certain, men should be what they seem.
IAGO: Why then, I think Cassio's an honest man.
OTHELLO: Nay, yet there's more in this.
I pray thee, speak to me as to thy thinkings,
As thou dost ruminate; and give thy worst of thoughts
The worst of words.
IAGO: Good my lord, pardon me;
Though I am bound to every act of duty,
I am not bound to that all slaves are free to.[13]
Utter my thoughts? Why, say they are vile and false —
As where's that palace, whereinto foul things
Sometimes intrude not? Who has a breast so pure,
But some uncleanly apprehensions
Keep leets and law-days and in session sit[14]
With meditations lawful?
OTHELLO: Thou dost conspire against thy friend, Iago,
If thou but think'st him wronged, and mak'st his ear
A stranger to thy thoughts.
IAGO: I do beseech you:
Though I, perchance, am vicious in my guess —
As, I confess, it is my nature's plague
To spy into abuses, and oft, my jealousy

[12]conceit: thought
[13]Iago says that even slaves are free to keep their thoughts to themselves and, even though he's under orders, he should at least have a slave's freedom.
[14]"Leets" is synonymous for "law-days," appointed times when the law courts hold session.

shapes faults that are not — I entreat you, then,
from one that so imperfectly conjects,[15]
You'd take no notice, nor build yourself a trouble
Out of his scattering and unsure observance.
It were not for your quiet, nor your good,
Nor for my manhood, honesty, or wisdom,
To let you know my thoughts.
OTHELLO: What dost thou mean?
IAGO: Good name, in man and woman, dear my lord,
Is the immediate jewel of their souls.
Who steals my purse, steals trash; 'tis something — nothing.
'Twas mine, 'tis his, and has been slave to thousands.
But he that filches from me my good name
Robs me of that which not enriches him,
And makes me poor indeed.
OTHELLO: By Heaven, I'll know thy thought!
IAGO: You cannot, if my heart were in your hand;
Nor shall not, whilst 'tis in my custody;
OTHELLO: Ha?
IAGO: Oh, beware, my lord, of jealousy.
It is the green-eyed monster, which doth make
The meat it feeds on. That cuckold lives in bliss,
Who, certain of his fate, loves not his wronger;[16]
But, oh, what damned minutes tells he o'er,
Who dotes, yet doubts — suspects, yet fondly loves!
OTHELLO: Oh misery!
IAGO: Poor and content is rich, and rich enough;
But riches, fineless, is as poor as winter[17]
To him that ever fears he shall be poor.[18]
Good heaven, the souls of all my tribe defend
From jealousy!
OTHELLO: Why! Why is this?
Think'st thou, I'd make a life of jealousy,
To follow still the changes of the moon
With fresh suspicions?[19] No. To be once in doubt
Is once to be resolved.[20] Exchange me for a goat,[21]
When I shall turn the business of my soul
To such exsufflicate and blown surmises,[22]
Matching thy inference. 'Tis not to make me jealous

[15]conjects: conjectures, or forms assumptions.
[16]cuckold: man whose wife is unfaithful. Iago says that a man who knows for a fact that his wife is unfaithful but who dislikes her is far better off than a man who loves his wife and only suspects that she's unfaithful.
[17]fineless: infinite.
[18]ever: always.
[19]Because of its obvious changes, the moon is a symbol of emotional moodiness.
[20]To be ... resolved: If I ever have reason to doubt, I'll take measures to solve the matter once for all.
[21]The goat is a symbol for sexual obsession. Othello says he has more important things to worry about.
[22]exsufflicate: bubble-like.

To say my wife is fair, feeds well, loves company,
Is free of speech, sings, plays, and dances well;
Where virtue is, these are more virtuous.
Nor from mine own weak merits will I draw
The smallest fear or doubt of her revolt;
For she had eyes, and chose me. No, Iago.
I'll see, before I doubt; when I doubt, prove;
And, on the proof, there is no more but this:
Away at once with love, or jealousy.

IAGO: I am glad of this, for now I shall have reason
To show the love and duty that I bear you
With franker spirit; therefore, as I am bound,
Receive it from me. I speak not yet of proof.
Look to your wife; observe her well with Cassio.
Wear your eye thus: Not jealous, nor secure.
I would not have your free and noble nature,
Out of self-bounty, be abused. Look to't.
I know our country disposition well:
In Venice they do let heaven see the pranks
They dare not show their husbands; their best conscience
Is not to leave undone, but keep unknown.

OTHELLO: Dost thou say so?

IAGO: She did deceive her father, marrying you.
And, when she seemed to shake, and fear your looks,[23]
She loved them most.

OTHELLO: And so she did.

IAGO: Why, go to, then;
She that, so young, could give out such a seeming,[24]
To seel her father's eyes up, close as oak;[25]
He thought 'twas witchcraft — But I am much to blame;
I humbly do beseech you of your pardon,
For too much loving you.

OTHELLO: I am bound to thee forever.

IAGO: I see this hath a little dashed your spirits.

OTHELLO: Not a jot, not a jot.

IAGO: Trust me, I fear it has.
I hope you will consider, what is spoke
Comes from my love — But I do see you are moved.
I am to pray you not to strain my speech
To grosser issues, nor to larger reach,
Than to suspicion.

OTHELLO: I will not.

IAGO: Should you do so, my lord,
My speech should fall into such vile success[26]

[23]seemed to: gave the appearance of.
[24]a seeming: an external appearance which hides one's true character.
[25]Seeling is a method used in training a hawk to hunt whereby the hunter ties the bird's eyelids shut in order to accustom it to wearing a hood.
[26]success: consequence.

As my thoughts aim not at. Cassio's my worthy friend —
My lord, I see you are moved.
OTHELLO: No, not much moved.
    I do not think but Desdemona's honest.
IAGO: Long live she so! And long live you to think so!
OTHELLO: And yet, how nature, erring from itself . . .
IAGO: Ay, there's the point. As, to be bold with you:
    Not to affect many proposed matches,
    Of her own clime, complexion, and degree,[27]
    Whereto, we see, in all things nature tends:
    Foh! One may smell, in such, a will most rank,[28]
    Foul disproportion, thoughts unnatural.
    But pardon me. I do not, in position,
    Distinctly speak of her; though I may fear[29]
    Her will, recoiling to her better judgement,
    May fail to match you with her country forms,
    And, happily, repent.[30]
OTHELLO: Farewell, farewell.
    If more thou dost perceive, let me know more.
    Set on thy wife to observe. Leave me, Iago.
IAGO: My lord, I take my leave. *(He starts to leave.)*
OTHELLO: *(To himself.)* Why did I marry? This honest creature, doubtless,
    Sees, and knows more, much more, than he unfolds.
IAGO: *(Returning)* My lord, I would I might entreat your honor
    To scan this thing no further. Leave it to time.
    And though it be fit that Cassio have his place,
    For, sure, he fills it up with great ability,
    Yet, if you please to hold him off a while,
    You shall by that perceive him and his means.
    Note if your lady strain his entertainment[31]
    With any strong or vehement importunity;[32]
    Much will be seen in that. In the mean time,
    Let me be thought too busy in my fears —
    As worthy cause I have to fear I am —
    And hold her free. I do beseech your honor.
OTHELLO: Fear not my government.
IAGO: I once more take my leave. *(He exits.)*
OTHELLO: This fellow's of exceeding honesty,
    And knows all qualities with a learned spirit
    Of human dealings. If I do prove her haggard,
    Though that her jesses were my dear heart-strings,
    I'd whistle her off, and let her down the wind,

---

[27]not to affect . . . degree: not to be attracted to suitors of her own country, race, and social class.
[28]rank: overgrown or foul.
[29]distinctly: specifically. Iago says he's speaking of generalities, not Desdemona in particular.
[30]happily: perhaps. Iago says he worries that this willful woman may do the more natural thing and, seeing that her marriage to Othello doesn't match up with her country's expectations. change her mind and leave him.
[31]"Entertainment" was the term for admission of soldiers to service or rank.
[32]importunity: excessive persistence.

To prey at fortune.[33] Haply, for I am black
And have not those soft parts of conversation
That chamberers have — or, for I am declined
Into the vale of years, yet that's not much —
She's gone.[34] I am abused, and my relief
Must be to loathe her. Oh, curse of marriage,
That we can call these delicate creatures ours,
And not their appetites! I had rather be a toad,
And live upon the vapor of a dungeon,
Than keep a corner in the thing I love,
For others' use. Yet 'tis the plague of great ones;
Prerogatived are they less than the base.[35]
'Tis destiny unshunnable like death.
Even then this forkèd plague is fated to us,[36]
When we do quicken.[37] Desdemona comes.

(DESDEMONA and EMILIA enter.)

If she be false, oh then heaven mocks itself!
I'll not believe it.
DESDEMONA: How now, my dear Othello?
Your dinner and the generous islanders
By you invited do attend your presence.
OTHELLO: I am to blame.
DESDEMONA: Why is your speech so faint? Are you not well?
OTHELLO: I have a pain upon my forehead here.[38]
DESDEMONA: 'Faith, that's with watching; 'twill away again.[39]
Let me but bind it hard, within this hour
It well be well. *(She starts to tie her handkerchief around his head.)*
OTHELLO: Your napkin is too little.

(He pushes the handkerchief away, and it drops.)

Let it alone. Come, I'll go in with you.
DESDEMONA: I am very sorry that you are not well.

(OTHELLO and DESDEMONA exit.)

EMILIA: *(Picking up the handkerchief.)* I am glad I have found this napkin.

[33]If I do prove . . . prey at fortune: Othello uses several terms here taken from the sport of falconry: A "haggard" hawk is a wild, untamed bird. A "jess" is a short strap, fastened to a hawk's leg, with a ring for attaching a leash. Falconers would send their birds to hunt against the wind, because if the hawk flew with the wind, it seldom returned; therefore, if a hunter wanted to be rid of a bird, he'd send it downwind and it would then have to depend on its own luck for a living, or "prey at fortune." Shakespeare's frequent use of terms taken from this sport gives the play the atmosphere of a hunt.
[34]Haply, for I am black . . . she's gone: What if she leaves me, perhaps, because I'm black and, as a soldier, don't have smooth speech like courtiers, or because I'm getting a little old?
[35]Yet 'tis the plague . . . the base: Having unfaithful wives is the curse of nobility; nobles, in this respect, have fewer rights than common folk.
[36]"Forked" refers to the horns which were supposed to decorate the cuckold's forehead.
[37]do quicken: are born.
[38]Another reference to the cuckold's horns.
[39]with watching: from lack of sleep.

This was her first remembrance from the Moor.
My wayward husband hath a hundred times
Wooed me to steal it, but she so loves the token —
For he conjured her she would ever keep it —[40]
That she reserves it evermore about her
To kiss and talk to. I'll have the work ta'en out,[41]
And give't Iago.
What he'll do with it heaven knows, not I;
I nothing but to please his fantasy.[42]

(Enter IAGO.)

IAGO: *(He enters.)* How now! What do you here alone?
EMILIA: Do not you chide. I have a thing for you.
IAGO: A thing for me? It is a common thing . . .
EMILIA: Ha![43]
IAGO: . . . to have a foolish wife.
EMILIA: Oh, is that all? What will you give me now
    For that same handkerchief?
IAGO: What handkerchief?
EMILIA: What handkerchief?
    Why, that the Moor first gave to Desdemona —
    That which so often you did bid me steal.
IAGO: Hast stolen it from her?
EMILIA: No, faith, she let it drop by negligence,
    And to advantage I, being here, took't up.
    Look, here it is.
IAGO: A good wench; give it to me.

(He grabs for it, but she quickly pulls it out of his reach.)

EMILIA: What will you do with it that you have been so earnest
    To have me filch it?
IAGO: Why, what's that to you?

(He snatches it away from her.)

EMILIA: If it be not for some purpose of import,
    Give it me again. Poor lady! She'll run mad
    When she shall lack it.
IAGO: Be not acknowen on't. I have use for it.[44]
    Go! Leave me! *(EMILIA exits.)*
    I will in Cassio's lodging lose this napkin,
    And let him find it. Trifles light as air,
    Are, to the jealous, confirmations strong
    As proofs of holy writ. This may do something.
    The Moor already changes with my poison.

[40]he conjured her: Othello made her swear.
[41]the work: the identifying embroidery.
[42]I nothing . . . fantasy: I know nothing but to please his whims.
[43]Emilia takes Iago's comment to mean — as he no doubt intended it — that her sexual organ is an object enjoyed in common by many.
[44]Be not acknowen on't: Don't acknowledge you know about it.

Dangerous conceits are in their nature's poisons,[45]
Which, at the first, are scarce found to distaste.
But, with a little act upon the blood,
Burn like the mines of sulphur. I did say so . . .[46]

(He sees OTHELLO coming.)

Look, where he comes! Not poppy or mandragora[47]
Nor all the drowsy syrups of the world
Shall ever medicine thee to that sweet sleep
Which thou ow'dst yesterday.[48]

OTHELLO: Ha! ha! False to me?
To me?

IAGO: Why, how now, general? No more of that.

OTHELLO: Avaunt! Be gone! Thou hast set me on the rack.[49]
I swear 'tis better to be much abused,
Than but to know't a little.

IAGO: How now, my lord?

OTHELLO: What sense had I of her stolen hours of lust?
I saw it not, thought it not. It harmed not me.
I slept the next night well, as free and merry.
I found not Cassio's kisses on her lips.
He that is robbed, not wanting what is stolen,[50]
Let him not know it, and he's not robbed at all.

IAGO: I am sorry to hear this.

OTHELLO: I had been happy if the general camp,
Pioneers and all, had tasted her sweet body,[51]
So I had nothing known. Oh now forever,
Farewell the tranquil mind! Farewell content!
Farewell the plumèd troop, and the big wars,
That make ambition virtue! Oh farewell!
Farewell the neighing steed, and the shrill trump,
The spirit-stirring drum, the ear-piercing fife,
The royal banner, and all quality,
Pride, pomp, and circumstance of glorious war!
And, O you mortal engines, whose rude throats
The immortal Jove's dread clamors counterfeit,[52]
Farewell! Othello's occupation's gone!

IAGO: Is it possible! My lord . . .

OTHELLO: Villain, be sure thou prove my love a whore!
Be sure of it. Give the ocular proof,[53]

(He takes IAGO by the throat.)

[45]conceits: opinions.
[46]mines: fireworks.
[47]poppy: opium; mandragora is another herb which induces sleep.
[48]ow'dst: owned.
[49]A rack is an instrument of torture.
[50]wanting: missing.
[51]pioneers: low ranking soldiers who did construction work.
[52]immortal Jove's dread clamors: thunders.
[53]ocular: eyewitness.

Or by the worth of mine eternal soul,
Thou hadst been better have been born a dog,
Than answer my waked wrath.
IAGO: Is it come to this?
OTHELLO: Make me see it, or at the least, so prove it
That the probation hear no hinge nor loop[54]
To hang a doubt on, or woe upon thy life!
IAGO: My noble lord . . .
OTHELLO: If thou dost slander her and torture me,
Never pray more. Abandon all remorse,
On horror's head horrors accumulate,
Do deeds to make heaven weep, all earth amazed.
For nothing canst thou to damnation add
Greater than that.
IAGO: O grace, O heaven, defend me!
Are you a man? Have you a soul or sense?
God be wi' you. Take mine office. O wretched fool,[55]
That liv'st to make thine honesty a vice!
O monstrous world! Take note, take note, O world,
To be direct and honest is not safe.
I thank you for this profit, and from hence
I'll love no friend, since love breeds such offense.
OTHELLO: Nay, stay! Thou shouldst be honest.
IAGO: I should be wise, for honesty's a fool,
And loses that it works for.
OTHELLO: By the world,
I think my wife be honest and think she is not.
I think that thou art just and think thou art not.
I'll have some proof! My name, that was as fresh
As Dian's visage, is now begrim'd and black[56]
As mine own face. If there be cords or knives,
Poison or fire or suffocating streams —[57]
I'll not endure it! Would I were satisfied!
IAGO: I see, sir, you are eaten up with passion.
I do repent me that I put it to you.
You would be satisfied?
OTHELLO: Would? Nay, I will!
IAGO: And may. But how? How satisfied, my lord?
Would you be supervisor? Grossly gape on?
Behold her topped?
OTHELLO: Death and damnation! Oh!
IAGO: It were a tedious difficulty, I think,
To bring them to that prospect. Damn them then,
If ever mortal eyes do see them bolster,[58]

---

[54]probation: examination.
[55]Iago addresses "O wretched fool . . ." to himself, not Othello.
[56]Dian's: Diana's (virgin goddess of the moon).
[57]Cords, knives, poison, fire, and drowning were all "ordeals" which suspected felons were subjected to; surviving an ordeal was taken as proof of the suspect's innocence.
[58]bolster: bed down.

More than their own! What then? How then?
What shall I say? Where's satisfaction?
It is impossible you should see this,
Were they as prime as goats, as hot as monkeys,
As salt as wolves in pride, and fools as gross
As ignorance made drunk. But yet, I say,
If imputation and strong circumstances —
Which lead directly to the door of truth —
Will give you satisfaction, you may have it.
OTHELLO: Give me a living reason she's disloyal.
IAGO: I do not like the office.
But sith I am entered in this cause so far,[59]
Pricked to it by foolish honesty and love,
I will go on. I lay with Cassio lately,[60]
And being troubled with a raging tooth,
I could not sleep.
There are a kind of men so loose of soul,
That in their sleeps will mutter their affairs;
One of this kind is Cassio.
In sleep I heard him say, "Sweet Desdemona,
Let us be wary, let us hide our loves!"
And then, sir, would he gripe and wring my hand,[61]
Cry, "O sweet creature!" and then kiss me hard,
As if he plucked up kisses by the roots
That grew upon my lips, then laid his leg
Over my thigh, and sighed, and kissed, and then
Cried, "Cursed fate, that gave thee to the Moor!"
OTHELLO: Oh monstrous! Monstrous!
IAGO: Nay, this was but his dream.
OTHELLO: But this denoted a foregone conclusion,
    'Tis a shrewd doubt, though it be but a dream.
IAGO: And this may help to thicken other proofs,
    That do demonstrate thinly.
OTHELLO: I'll tear her all to pieces.
IAGO: Nay, but be wise. Yet we see nothing done.
She may be honest yet. Tell me but this:
Have you not sometimes seen a handkerchief
Spotted with strawberries in your wife's hand?
OTHELLO: I gave her such a one. 'Twas my first gift.
IAGO: I know not that, but such a handkerchief —
    I am sure it was your wife's — did I today
    See Cassio wipe his beard with.
OTHELLO: If it be that . . .
IAGO: If it be that or any that was hers,
    It speaks against her with the other proofs.

[59]sith: since.
[60]lay: bunked.
[61]gripe: grab.

OTHELLO: Oh that the slave had forty thousand lives!
    One is too poor, too weak for my revenge!
    Now do I see 'tis true. Look here, Iago:
    All my fond love thus do I blow to heaven.
    'Tis gone.
    Arise, black vengeance, from thy hollow cell!
    Yield up, O love, thy crown and hearted throne,
    To tyrannous hate! Swell, bosom, with thy fraught;[62]
    For 'tis of aspics' tongues![63]
IAGO: Pray, be content.
OTHELLO: Oh blood, Iago, blood!
IAGO: Patience, I say. Your mind, perhaps, may change.
OTHELLO: Never, Iago. Like to the Pontic sea,[64]
    Whose icy current and compulsive course
    Ne'er feels retiring ebb, but keeps due on
    To the Propontic and the Hellespont;[65]
    Even so my bloody thoughts, with violent pace,
    Shall ne'er look back, ne'er ebb to humble love,
    Till that a capable and wide revenge
    Swallow them up. *(Othello kneels.)* Now, by yond' marble heaven,
    In the due reverence of a sacred vow
    I here engage my words.
IAGO: Do not rise yet. *(He kneels with OTHELLO.)*
    Witness, you ever-burning lights above!
    You elements that clip us round about!
    Witness, that here Iago doth give up
    The execution of his wit, hands, heart,
    To wronged Othello's service! Let him command
    And to obey shall be in me remorse,[66]
    What bloody work soever.
OTHELLO: I greet thy love,
    Not with vain thanks, but with acceptance bounteous,
    And will upon the instant put thee to't:
    Within these three days let me hear thee say
    That Cassio's not alive.
IAGO: My friend is dead; 'tis done, at your request.
    But let her live.
OTHELLO: Damn her, lewd minx; O, damn her![67]
    Come, go with me apart; I will withdraw
    To furnish me with some swift means of death

[62]fraught: load, or freight.
[63]aspics: asps.
[64]Pontic sea: Black Sea.
[65]Propontic and the Hellespont: The Propontic Sea, now known as the Sea of Marmara, is the relatively small body of water separated from the Black Sea by the Bosporos and from the Agean and Mediterranean Seas by the Dardanelles; this latter straight was formerly known as the Hellespont.
[66]remorse: pity, compassion.
[67]minx: lustful woman.

For the fair devil. Now art thou my lieutenant.[68]

IAGO: I am your own forever.

(They exit.)

---

[68]my lieutenant: A lieutenant is a person empowered to act on behalf of another. With this line, Othello seems not only to bestow on Iago the military rank Iago wanted, but also to make him his representative in his personal affairs.

ACT III

Scene iv

Later the same day, again in front of the castle.

(DESDEMONA enters with EMILIA and the CLOWN.)

DESDEMONA: Do you know, sirrah, where lieutenant Cassio lies?

CLOWN: I dare not say he lies anywhere.

DESDEMONA: Why, man?

CLOWN: He is a soldier, and for me to say a soldier lies is stabbing.

DESDEMONA: Go to! Where lodges he?

CLOWN: To tell where he lodges is to tell you where I lie.

DESDEMONA: Can anything be made of this?

CLOWN: I know not where he lodges. And for me to devise a lodging, and say, "He lies here," or "He lies there," were to lie in my own throat.

DESDEMONA: Can you inquire him out, and be edified by report?[1]

CLOWN: I will catechize the world for him; that is, make questions, and by them answer.

DESDEMONA: Seek him, bid him come hither. Tell him I have moved my lord in his behalf, and hope all will be well.

CLOWN: To do this is within the compass of man's wit, and therefore I will attempt the doing it. *(The CLOWN exits.)*

DESDEMONA: Where should I lose that handkerchief, Emilia?

EMILIA: I know not, madam.

DESDEMONA: Believe me, I had rather have lost my purse
Full of cruzadoes.[2] And, but my noble Moor[3]
Is true of mind and made of no such baseness
As jealous creatures are, it were enough
To put him to ill thinking.

EMILIA: Is he not jealous?

DESDEMONA: Who, he? I think the sun, where he was born,
Drew all such humors from him.[4]

EMILIA: *(Pointing out OTHELLO's arrival.)* Look where he comes.

DESDEMONA: I will not leave him now till Cassio
Be called to him. *(As OTHELLO enters, she addressed him.)* How is't with you, my lord?

OTHELLO: Well, my good lady. *(Then speaking to himself.)* Oh, hardness to dissemble!
(Addressing DESDEMONA.) How do you, Desdemona?

DESDEMONA: Well, my good lord.

OTHELLO: Give me your hand. *(She does so.)* This hand is moist, my lady

DESDEMONA: It yet has felt no age, nor known no sorrow.

OTHELLO: This argues fruitfulness, and liberal heart..
Hot, hot and moist. This hand of yours requires
A sequester from liberty, fasting, and prayer,[5]

---

[1]edified: enlightened. The word usually has a religious or moral connotation.
[2]A cruzado was a Portuguese coin with a cross stamped on it.
[3]but: if it were not that
[4]In medieval physiology, body fluids called humors were believed to determine a person's disposition.
[5]sequester: separation.

Much castigation, exercise devout;
For here's a young and sweating devil here,
That commonly rebels. 'Tis a good hand —
A frank one.
DESDEMONA: You may indeed say so,
For 'twas that hand that gave away my heart.
OTHELLO: A liberal hand. The hearts of old, gave hands;
But our new heraldry is: "Hands, not hearts."[6]
DESDEMONA: I cannot speak of this. Come, now: Your promise.
OTHELLO: What promise, chuck?[7]
DESDEMONA: I have sent to bid Cassio come speak with you.
OTHELLO: I have a salt and sullen rheum offends me;[8]
Lend me thy handkerchief.
DESDEMONA: *(She offers him a handkerchief.)* Here, my lord.
OTHELLO: That which I gave you.
DESDEMONA: I have it not about me.
OTHELLO: Not?
DESDEMONA: No, indeed, my lord.
OTHELLO: That is a fault.
That handkerchief
Did an Egyptian to my mother give.
She was a charmer, and could almost read
The thoughts of people. She told her while she kept it
'Twould make her amiable and subdue my father
Entirely to her love, but if she lost it
Or made a gift of it, my father's eye
Should hold her loathly, and his spirits should hunt
After new fancies. She, dying, gave it me,
And bid me, when my fate would have me wived,
To give it her. I did so, and take heed of't.
Make it a darling, like your precious eye;
To lose or giv't away, were such perdition,
As nothing else could match.
DESDEMONA: Is it possible?
OTHELLO: 'Tis true; there's magic in the web of it.
A sibyl, that had numbered in the world[9]
The sun to make two hundred compasses,
In her prophetic fury sewed the work.
The worms were hallowed that did breed the silk,
And it was dyed in mummy, which the skillful[10]
Conserved of maidens' hearts.
DESDEMONA: Indeed! Is't true?

[6]In this speech, Othello suggests that modern women make an outward show of affection (hands) without inner commitment (hearts). The reference to heraldry may allude to the joining of the coats of arms of noble husbands and wives; "Hands, not hearts" is similar to the cryptic mottoes attached to coats of arms.
[7]Chuck was a term of affection.
[8]rheum: watering of the eyes.
[9]sibyl: female prophet.
[10]mummy: magic potion made from dead bodies.

OTHELLO: Most veritable; therefore look to't well.
DESDEMONA: Then would to heaven that I had never seen it.
OTHELLO: Ha! Wherefore?[11]
DESDEMONA: Why do you speak so startingly and rash?
OTHELLO: Is't lost? Is't gone? Speak, is it out of the way?
DESDEMONA: Heaven bless us!
OTHELLO: Say you?
DESDEMONA: It is not lost, but what an if it were?
OTHELLO: Ha!
DESDEMONA: I say it is not lost.
OTHELLO: Fetch't! Let me see it.
DESDEMONA: Why, so I can, sir, but I will not now.
    This is a trick to put me from my suit.
    I pray, let Cassio be received again.
OTHELLO: Fetch me that handkerchief. My mind misgives.
DESDEMONA: Come, come;
    You'll never meet a more sufficient man.
OTHELLO: The handkerchief.
DESDEMONA: I pray, talk me of Cassio.
OTHELLO: The handkerchief!
DESDEMONA: A man that all his time
    Hath founded his good fortune on your love,
    Shared dangers with you . . .
OTHELLO: The handkerchief!
DESDEMONA: In sooth, you are to blame . . .
OTHELLO: Away! *(OTHELLO exits in a rage.)*
EMILIA: Is not this man jealous?
DESDEMONA: I ne'er saw this before.
    Sure, there's some wonder in this handkerchief.
    I am most unhappy in the loss of it.
EMILIA: 'Tis not a year or two shows us a man.
    They are all but stomachs, and we all but food.
    They eat us hungrily, and when they are full
    They belch us. Look you! Cassio, and my husband.

(CASSIO enters with IAGO urging him on.)

IAGO: There is no other way. 'Tis she must do't,
    And, lo, the happiness! Go, and importune her.[12]
DESDEMONA: How now, good Cassio? What's the news with you?
CASSIO: Madam, my former suit. I do beseech you.
    That, by your virtuous means, I may again[13]
    Exist, and be a member of his love,
    Whom I, with all the duty of my heart,
    Entirely honor. I would not be delayed.
    If my offense be of such mortal kind,

[11]Here, as in Juliet's balcony speech (Romeo, Romeo! Wherefore art thou Romeo), wherefore means why, not where.
[12]importune: beg.
[13]virtuous: powerful.

That neither service past, nor present sorrows,
Nor purposed merit in futurity,
Can ransom me into his love again,
But to know so must be my benefit.
So shall I clothe me in a forced content,
And shut myself up in some other course
To fortune's alms.
DESDEMONA: Alas! Thrice gentle Cassio,
My advocation is not now in tune.
My lord is not my lord; nor should I know him,
Were he in favor, as in humor, altered.[14]
So help me every spirit sanctified
As I have spoken for you all my best,
And stood within the blank of his displeasure[15]
For my free speech! You must awhile be patient.
What I can do I will, and more I will
Than for myself I dare. Let that suffice you.
IAGO: Is my lord angry?
EMILIA: He went hence but now,
And, certainly, in strange unquietness.
IAGO: Can he be angry? I have seen the cannon,
When it hath blown his ranks into the air
And, like the devil, from his very arm
Puffed his own brother. And can he be angry?
Something of moment, then.[16] I will go meet him.
There is matter in't indeed if he be angry.
DESDEMONA: I pr'ythee, do so. *(IAGO exits.)* Something, sure, of state —
Either from Venice, or some unhatched practice[17]
Made demonstrable here in Cyprus to him —
Hath puddled his clear spirit. And, in such cases,
Men's natures wrangle with inferior things,
Though great ones are their object. 'Tis even so,
For let our finger ache, and it endues
Our other healthful members even to that sense
Of pain. Nay, we must think men are not gods;
Nor of them look for such observances
As fit the bridal . . . Beshrew me much, Emilia,
I was, unhandsome warrior as I am,
Arraigning his unkindness with my soul.
But now I find I had suborned the witness,[18]
And he's indicted falsely.
EMILIA: Pray Heaven it be state matters, as you think,
And no conception nor no jealous toy[19]

---

[14]nor . . . altered: and if his appearance were as altered as his mood, I wouldn't recognize him.
[15]blank: bull's eye. The blank is the white spot at the center of a target.
[16]moment: importance (as in "momentous").
[17]unhatched practice: treasonous plot which has not yet been acted upon.
[18]suborned: pried false testimony from.
[19]toy: pastime.

Concerning you.
DESDEMONA: Alas the day! I never gave him cause.
EMILIA: But jealous souls will not be answered so.
They are not ever jealous for the cause,
But jealous for they are jealous. 'Tis a monster
Begot upon itself, born on itself.
DESDEMONA: Heaven keep that monster from Othello's mind!
EMILIA: Lady, amen.
DESDEMONA: I will go seek him. Cassio, walk here about;
If I do find him fit, I'll move your suit
And seek to effect it to my uttermost.
CASSIO: I humbly thank your ladyship.

(DESDEMONA exits with EMILIA as BIANCA, CASSIO's mistress enters.)

BIANCA: Save you, friend Cassio!
CASSIO: What make you from home?
How is it with you, my most fair Bianca?
I'faith, sweet love, I was coming to your house.
BIANCA: And I was going to your lodging, Cassio.
What! Keep a week away? Seven days and nights?
Eightscore hours? And lovers' absent hours,
More tedious than the dial eightscore times?[20]
Oh weary reckoning!
CASSIO: Pardon me, Bianca.
I have this while with leaden thoughts been pressed.
But I shall, in a more continuate time,[21]
Strike off this score of absence. Sweet Bianca,

(Giving her DESDEMONA's handkerchief.)

Take me this work out.[22]
BIANCA: O Cassio, whence came this?
This is some token from a newer friend.
To the felt absence now I feel a cause.
Is it come to this? Well, well.
CASSIO: Go to! Woman,
Throw your vile guesses in the devil's teeth
From whence you have them. You are jealous, now,
That this is from some mistress — some remembrance.
No, in good troth, Bianca.
BIANCA: Why, whose is it?
CASSIO: I know not, sweet. I found it in my chamber.
I like the work well. Ere it be demanded,
As like enough it will, I'd have it copied.
Take it and do't, and leave me for this time.
BIANCA: Leave you! Wherefore?

[20]More tedious than the dial: Slower than the clock.
[21]continuate: uninterrupted.
[22]As soon becomes clear, Cassio is not asking Bianca to remove the identifying monogram but rather to copy the handkerchief's embroidery.

CASSIO: I do attend here on the general;
    And think it no addition, nor my wish,[23]
    To have him see me woman'd.
BIANCA: Why, I pray you?
CASSIO: Not that I love you not.
BIANCA: But that you do not love me.
    I pray you, bring me on the way a little,
    And say if I shall see you soon at night.
CASSIO: 'Tis but a little way that I can bring you,
    For I attend here, but I'll see you soon.[24]
BIANCA: 'Tis very good. I must be circumstanced.[25]

(They exit.)

---

[23]addition: credit.
[24]attend: wait.
[25]I must be circumstanced.: I must give way to circumstances.

ACT IV

Scene i

Later, in front of the castle.

(OTHELLO and IAGO enter in conversation.)

IAGO: Will you think so?

OTHELLO: Think so, Iago?

IAGO: What?

To kiss in private?

OTHELLO: An unauthorized kiss.

IAGO: Or to be naked with her friend abed,

An hour or more, not meaning any harm?

OTHELLO: Naked abed, Iago, and not mean harm?

It is hypocrisy against the devil.

They that mean virtuously and yet do so,

The devil their virtue tempts, and they tempt Heaven.

IAGO: If they do nothing, 'tis a venial slip;[1]

But if I give my wife a handkerchief . . .

OTHELLO: What then?

IAGO: Why then, 'tis hers, my lord, and being hers,

She may, I think, bestow't on any man.

OTHELLO: She is protectress of her honor too.

May she give that?

IAGO: Her honor is an essence that's not seen.

They have it very oft, that have it not.

But, for the handkerchief . . .

OTHELLO: By Heaven, I would most gladly have forgot it.

Thou saidst — Oh, it comes o'er my memory

As doth the raven o'er the infected house

Boding to all — he had my handkerchief.

IAGO: Aye, what of that?

OTHELLO: That's not so good, now.

IAGO: What if I had said I had seen him do you wrong?

Or heard him say — as knaves be such abroad,

Who having, by their own importunate suit,

Or voluntary dotage of some mistress,

Convinced or supplied them, cannot choose

But they must blab . . .

OTHELLO: Hath he said anything?

IAGO: He hath, my lord, but be you well assured,

No more than he'll unswear.

OTHELLO: What hath he said?

IAGO: 'Faith, that he did — I know not what he did.

OTHELLO: What? What?

IAGO: Lie . . .

OTHELLO: With her?

IAGO: With, on her — what you will.

[1]venial: forgivable.

OTHELLO: Lie with her! Lie on her! We say lie on her, when they belie her. Lie with her! That's fulsome.[2] Handkerchief . . . Confessions . . . Handkerchief . . . to confess, and be hanged for his labor. First to be hanged, and then to confess. I tremble at it. Nature would not invest herself in such shadowing passion, without some instruction. It is not words that shake me thus.[3] Pish! Noses, ears, and lips.[4] Is it possible? Confess? Handkerchief? O devil! *(Overcome with emotion, OTHELLO falls in a trance.)*

IAGO: Work on,
My medicine, work! Thus credulous fools are caught,
And many worthy and chaste dames, even thus,
All guiltless meet reproach.

(He hears someone approaching and pretends to try to awaken OTHELLO.)

What, ho! my lord!

(CASSIO enters.)

My lord, I say! Othello! *(Pretending to notice CASSIO for the first time.)*
How now, Cassio?

CASSIO: What is the matter?

IAGO: My lord is fallen into an epilepsy.
This is his second fit; he had one yesterday.

CASSIO: Rub him about the temples.

IAGO: No, forbear.
The lethargy must have his quiet course.
If not, he foams at mouth, and by and by
Breaks out to savage madness. Look, he stirs.
Do you withdraw yourself a little while.
He will recover straight. When he is gone,
I would on great occasion speak with you.

(CASSIO exits and OTHELLO revives.)

How is it, general? Have you not hurt your head?

OTHELLO: Dost thou mock me?[5]

IAGO: I mock you? No, by Heaven.
'Would you would bear your fortunes like a man.

OTHELLO: A horned man's a monster, and a beast.

IAGO: There's many a beast, then, in a populous city,
And many a civil monster.

OTHELLO: Did he confess it?

IAGO: Good sir, be a man.
Think every bearded fellow that's but yoked
May draw with you.[6] There's millions now alive,

---

[2]fulsome: disgusting.
[3]I tremble . . . me thus: In the midst of his ranting, Othello seems to feel himself fainting, and he tells himself there must be more to the affair than just words for him to be so affected.
[4]Noses . . . lips: Othello may be visualizing Cassio and Desdemona making love, or he may be thinking of punishing them by mutilation.
[5]Dost thou mock me?: In Iago's previous line, Othello thinks he hears a reference to the horns which were imagined to sprout from the foreheads of cuckolds (husbands of adulterous women).
[6]yoked . . . with you: Iago mixes two metaphors here; "yoked" means married but also pictures Othello yoked together with all his fellow cuckolds, drawing carts like a bunch of horned oxen.

That nightly lie in those unproper beds,
Which they dare swear peculiar.[7] Your case is better.
Oh 'tis the spite of hell, the fiend's arch-mock,
To lip a wanton in a secure couch,
And to suppose her chaste![8] No, let me know,
And knowing what I am, I know what she shall be.
OTHELLO: Oh thou art wise. 'Tis certain.
IAGO: Stand you awhile apart.
Confine yourself but in a patient list.[9]
Whilst you were here, o'rewhelmed with your grief,
(A passion most unsuiting such a man)
Cassio came hither. I shifted him away,
And laid good 'scuse upon your ecstasy,
Bade him anon return and here speak with me,
The which he promised. Do but encave yourself,
And mark the fleers, the gibes, and notable scorns[10]
That dwell in every region of his face.
For I will make him tell the tale anew:
Where, how, how oft, how long ago, and when
He hath, and is again to cope your wife.[11]
I say, but mark his gesture. Marry, patience![12]
Or I shall say you are all in all in spleen,[13]
And nothing of a man.
OTHELLO: Dost thou hear, Iago?
I will be found most cunning in my patience,
But — dost thou hear? — most bloody.
IAGO: That's not amiss.
But yet keep time in all.[14] Will you withdraw?

(OTHELLO withdraws to a place on stage where he can watch without CASSIO seeing him.)

Now will I question Cassio of Bianca,
A housewife that, by selling her desires,[15]
Buys herself bread and clothes. It is a creature
That dotes on Cassio, as 'tis the strumpet's plague
To beguile many and be beguiled by one.
He, when he hears of her, cannot refrain

[7]unproper/peculiar: That which is "proper" is one's own; that which is "unproper" is shared with others. "Peculiar" means unique, belonging to one alone.
[8]to lip . . . chaste: to be deluded into thinking a loose woman is faithful just because one has kissed her in a marriage bed.
[9]list: limit.
[10]fleers: derisive looks. gibes: taunts.
[11]cope: cover (as with a priest's vestment — a cope).
[12]Marry, referring to the Virgin Mary, is an interjection used for emphasis.
[13]in spleen: in the grip of your passions. In the classical perception of character, men — particularly heroic men — were expected to stay always in control of their emotions, never to be controlled by them.
[14]keep time in all: each thing in its own time.
[15]"Housewife," in the original, is spelled "huswife." Pronounced "husif," it carries the meaning "hussy."

From the excess of laughter! *(Seeing CASSIO returning.)* Here he comes.
As he shall smile, Othello shall go mad,
And his unbookish jealousy must construe[16]
Poor Cassio's smiles, gestures, and light behavior
Quite in the wrong. *(CASSIO returns.)* How do you now, lieutenant?
CASSIO: The worser, that you give me the addition,[17]
Whose want even kills me.
IAGO: Ply Desdemona well, and you are sure of't.
Now, if this suit lay in Bianca's power,
How quickly should you speed?[18]
CASSIO: Alas, poor caitiff![19]
OTHELLO: *(In his hiding place, speaking to himself.)*
Look, how he laughs already!
IAGO: I never knew a woman love man so.
CASSIO: Alas, poor rogue! I think, i'faith, she loves me.
OTHELLO: Now he denies it faintly and laughs it out.
IAGO: Do you hear, Cassio?
OTHELLO: Now he importunes him
To tell it o'er. Go to! Well said, well said!
IAGO: She gives it out that you shall marry her.
Do you intend it?
CASSIO: Ha, ha, ha!
OTHELLO: Do you triumph, Roman? Do you triumph?
CASSIO: I marry her! What? A customer? I pr'ythee, bear
Some charity to my wit. Do not think it so unwholesome.
Ha, ha, ha!
OTHELLO: So, so, so, so. They laugh that win.
IAGO: 'Faith, the cry goes that you shall marry her.
CASSIO: Pr'ythee, say true.
IAGO: I am a very villain else.
OTHELLO: Have you scored me? Well.[20]
CASSIO: This is the monkey's own giving out. She is persauded I will marry
her out of her own love and flattery, not out of my promise.

(Without letting CASSIO see it, IAGO gestures to OTHELLO to pay close attention.)

OTHELLO: Iago beckons me; now he begins the story.
CASSIO: She was here even now. She haunts me in every place. I was, the
other day, talking on the sea-bank with certain Venetians, and thither
comes this bauble, and falls me thus about my neck . . .

(As he speaks, CASSIO imitates BIANCA, hugging and pulling at IAGO.)

OTHELLO: Crying, "O dear Cassio!" as it were: his gesture imports it.

[16]unbookish: ignorant or uncultured.
[17]addition: rank.
[18]The actor of Iago needs to speak Desdemona's name loudly so that Othello thinks they are talking about her, and then keep the rest of his words private between himself, Cassio, and (of course) the audience.
[19]caitiff: despicable one.
[20]scored: branded.

CASSIO: So hangs, and lolls, and weeps upon me, so hales, and pulls me. Ha, ha, ha! —

OTHELLO: Now he tells how she plucked him to my chamber. Oh I see that nose of yours, but not that dog I shall throw it to.

CASSIO: Well, I must leave her company.

IAGO: Before me! Look where she comes.

(BIANCA enters.)

CASSIO: 'Tis such another fitchew! Marry, a perfumed one.[21]
(Speaking to BIANCA.) What do you mean by this haunting of me?

BIANCA: Let the devil and his dam haunt you![22] What did you mean by that same handkerchief you gave me even now? I was a fine fool to take it. I must take out the whole work? A likely piece of work that you should find it in your chamber and not know who left it there! This is some minx's token, and I must take out the work![23] There! *(She throws it in his face.)* Give it to your hobby-horse. Wheresoever you had it, I'll take out no more work on't.

CASSIO: How now, my sweet Bianca? How now? How now?

OTHELLO: By Heaven, that should be my handkerchief.

BIANCA: If you'll come to supper tonight, you may;
If you will not, come when you are next prepared for.

(She exits in a huff.)

IAGO: After her, after her.

CASSIO: 'Faith, I must. She'll rail in the street else.[24]

IAGO: Will you sup there?

CASSIO: 'Faith, I intend so.

IAGO: Well, I may chance to see you; for I would very fain speak with you.

CASSIO: *(Trying to get IAGO to accompany him.)* Pr'ythee, come. Will you?

IAGO: Go to; say no more. *(CASSIO exits, and OTHELLO comes from his hiding place.)*

OTHELLO: How shall I murder him, Iago?

IAGO: Did you perceive how he laughed at his vice?

OTHELLO: Oh, Iago!

IAGO: And did you see the handkerchief?

OTHELLO: Was that mine?

IAGO: Yours, by this hand. And to see how he prizes the foolish woman, your wife! She gave it him, and he hath given it his whore.

OTHELLO: I would have him nine years akilling. A fine woman! A fair woman! A sweet woman!

IAGO: Nay, you must forget that.

OTHELLO: Aye, let her rot, and perish, and be damned tonight, for she shall not live. No, my heart is turned to stone. I strike it, and it hurts my hand. Oh the world hath not a sweeter creature! She might lie by an emperor's side, and command him tasks.

[21]fitchew: polecat (a metaphor for a loose woman).
[22]dam: wife.
[23]minx: loose woman.
[24]rail: rant and rave.

188

IAGO: Nay, that's not your way.[25]

OTHELLO: Hang her! I do but say what she is. So delicate with her needle! An admirable musician! Oh she will sing the savageness out of a bear! Of so high and plenteous wit and invention!

IAGO: She is the worse for all this.

OTHELLO: Oh a thousand, a thousand times. And then, of so gentle a condition!

IAGO: Aye, too gentle.

OTHELLO: Nay, that's certain. But yet the pity of it, Iago! O Iago, the pity of it, Iago!

IAGO: If you are so fond over her iniquity, give her patent to offend; for if it touch not you, it comes near nobody.[26]

OTHELLO: I will chop her into messes! Cuckold me!

IAGO: Oh 'tis foul in her.

OTHELLO: With mine officer!

IAGO: That's fouler.

OTHELLO: Get me some poison, Iago, this night. I'll not expostulate with her, lest her body and beauty unprovide my mind again. This night, Iago.

IAGO: Do it not with poison. Strangle her in her bed, even the bed she hath contaminated.

OTHELLO: Good, good! The justice of it pleases. Very good.

IAGO: And for Cassio, let me be his undertaker. You shall hear more by midnight. *(Off-stage, a trumpet sounds.)*

OTHELLO: Excellent good. What trumpet is that same?

IAGO: Something from Venice, sure. 'Tis Lodovico,
Come from the duke, and, see: Your wife is with him.

(LODOVICO enters with DESDEMONA and attendants.)

LODOVICO: 'Save you, worthy general!

OTHELLO: With all my heart, sir.

LODOVICO: The duke and senators of Venice greet you.

(He gives him a packet.)

OTHELLO: I kiss the instrument of their pleasure.

(He kisses the packet then opens it and reads.)

DESDEMONA: And what's the news, good cousin Lodovico?

IAGO: I am very glad to see you, seignior.
Welcome to Cyprus.

LODOVICO: I thank you. How does lieutenant Cassio?

IAGO: Lives, sir . . .

DESDEMONA: Cousin, there's fallen between him and my lord
An unkind breach; but you shall make all well.

OTHELLO: Are you sure of that?

DESDEMONA: My lord?

OTHELLO: *(Reading the papers.)* This fail you not to do, as you will . . .

---

[25]Iago warns Othello that if he dwells on Desdemona's good points, he'll lose his nerve.
[26]fond: foolish.

LODOVICO: He did not call. He's busy in the paper.
　　Is there division 'twixt thy lord and Cassio?
DESDEMONA: A most unhappy one. I would do much
　　T'atone them for the love I bear to Cassio.
OTHELLO: Fire and brimstone!
DESDEMONA: My lord?
OTHELLO: Are you wise?
DESDEMONA: What, is he angry?
LODOVICO: Maybe the letter moved him,
　　For, as I think, they do command him home.
　　Deputing Cassio in his government.[27]
DESDEMONA: By my troth, I am glad on't.
OTHELLO: Indeed!
DESDEMONA: My lord?
OTHELLO: I am glad to see you mad.
DESDEMONA: How, sweet Othello?
OTHELLO: Devil! *(He strikes her.)*
DESDEMONA: I have not deserved this.
LODOVICO: My lord, this would not be believed in Venice,
　　Though I should swear I saw it. 'Tis very much . . .
　　Make her amends, she weeps.
OTHELLO: O devil, devil!
　　If that the earth could teem with woman's tears,[28]
　　Each drop she falls would prove a crocodile.
　　Out of my sight!
DESDEMONA: I will not stay to offend you. *(She begins to exit.)*
LODOVICO: Truly, an obedient lady.
　　I do beseech your lordship, call her back.
OTHELLO: Mistress.
DESDEMONA: My lord?
OTHELLO: What would you with her sir?
LODOVICO: Who, I, my lord?
OTHELLO: Aye. You did wish that I would make her turn.
　　Sir, she can turn, and turn, and yet go on,
　　And turn again. And she can weep, sir, weep.
　　And she's obedient, as you say, obedient,
　　Very obedient. *(To DESDEMONA.)* Proceed you in your tears.

(To LODOVICO, referring the letter.)

　　Concerning this, sir . . . *(Back to DESDEMONA.)* O well-painted passion!
　　(Back to LODOVICO.) . . . I am commanded home. *(To DESDEMONA.)*
　　Get you away.
　　I'll send for you anon. *(To LODOVICO.)* Sir, I obey the mandate,
　　And will return to Venice. *(To DESDEMONA.)* Hence, avaunt!

(DESDEMONA exits.)

　　Cassio shall have my place. And, sir, tonight

---

[27]deputing . . . government: appointing Cassio to govern Cyprus in his place.
[28]the earth . . . woman's tears: woman's tears could impregnate the earth.

I do entreat that we may sup together.
You are welcome, sir, to Cyprus. Goats and monkeys!

(He exits.)

LODOVICO: Is this the noble Moor whom our full senate
Call "all in all sufficient?" This the noble nature
Whom passion could not shake? Whose solid virtue
The shot of accident, nor dart of chance,
Could neither graze, nor pierce?
IAGO: He is much changed.
LODOVICO: Are his wits safe? Is he not light of brain?
IAGO: He is that he is. I may not breathe my censure.
What he might be, if what he might, he is not,
I would to Heaven he were.
LODOVICO: What, strike his wife!
IAGO: 'Faith, that was not so well. Yet 'would I knew
That stroke would prove the worst.
LODOVICO: Is it his use?[29]
Or did the letter work upon his blood,
And new-create this fault?
IAGO: Alas, alas!
It is not honesty in me to speak
What I have seen and known. You shall observe him,
And his own courses will denote him so
That I may save my speech. Do but go after,
And mark how he continues.
LODOVICO: I am sorry that I am deceived in him.

(They all exit.)

---

[29]use: usual behavior.

ACT IV

Scene ii

A room in the castle.

(OTHELLO enters with EMILIA.)

OTHELLO: You have seen nothing, then?
EMILIA: Nor ever heard nor ever did suspect.
OTHELLO: Yes, you have seen Cassio and she together.
EMILIA: But then I saw no harm, and then I heard
    Each syllable that breath made up between them.
OTHELLO: What, did they never whisper?
EMILIA: Never, my lord.
OTHELLO: Nor send you out o' the way?
EMILIA: Never.
OTHELLO: To fetch her fan, her gloves, her mask, nor nothing?
EMILIA: Never my lord.
OTHELLO: That's strange.
EMILIA: I durst, my lord, to wager she is honest —
    Lay down my soul at stake. If you think other,
    Remove your thought; it doth abuse your bosom.
    If any wretch hath put this in your head,
    Let heaven requite it with the serpent's curse!
    For if she be not honest, chaste, and true,
    There's no man happy; the purest of their wives is foul as slander.
OTHELLO: Bid her come hither. Go!

(EMILIA exits.)

    She says enough. Yet she's a simple bawd
    That cannot say as much.[1] This is a subtle whore.
    A closet-lock-and-key of villainous secrets,
    And yet she'll kneel, and pray — I have seen her do't.

(EMILIA returns with DESDEMONA.)

DESDEMONA: My lord, what is your will?
OTHELLO: 'Pray, chuck, come hither.
DESDEMONA: What is your pleasure?
OTHELLO: Let me see your eyes; look in my face.
DESDEMONA: What horrible fancy's this?
OTHELLO: *(Speaking to EMILIA.)* Some of your function, mistress.[2]
    Leave procreants alone, and shut the door.[3]
    Cough, or cry, "Hem!" if anybody come.
    Your mystery, your mystery! — nay, despatch![4]

(EMILIA exits.)

[1]Yet she's . . . as much: Yet it would be a very stupid madam of prostitutes who could not think as quickly as this.
[2]Some of your function: Do your normal duty.
[3]procreants: those engaged in sex.
[4]mystery: special skill.

192

DESDEMONA: Upon my knees, what doth thy speech import?
    I understand a fury in your words,
    But not the words.
OTHELLO: Why, what art thou?
DESDEMONA: Your wife, my lord; your true
    And loyal wife.
OTHELLO: Come, swear it! Damn thyself,
    Lest, being like one of heaven, the devils themselves
    Should fear to seize thee. Therefore be double-damned:
    Swear thou art honest.
DESDEMONA: Heaven doth truly know it.
OTHELLO: Heaven truly knows that thou art false as hell.
DESDEMONA: To whom, my lord? With whom? How am I false?
OTHELLO: O Desdemona! Away! Away! Away!
DESDEMONA: Alas, the heavy day! Why do you weep!
    Am I the occasion of these tears, my lord?
    If, haply, you my father do suspect
    An instrument of this your calling back,
    Lay not your blame on me. If you have lost him,
    Why, I have lost him too.
OTHELLO: Had it pleased heaven
    To try me with affliction, had they rained
    All kinds of sores and shames on my bare head,
    Steeped me in poverty to the very lips,
    Given to captivity me and my utmost hopes —
    I should have found in some part of my soul
    A drop of patience. But, alas, to make me
    A fixed figure, for the time of scorn
    To point his slow, unmoving finger at!
    Yet could I bear that too, well, very well.
    But there, where I have garnered up my heart,
    Where either I must live or bear no life,
    The fountain from the which my current runs
    Or else dries up — to be discarded thence,
    Or keep it as a cistern for foul toads
    To knot and gender in! Turn thy complexion there,
    Patience, thou young and rose-lipped cherubim!
    Aye, there, look grim as hell![5]
DESDEMONA: I hope my noble lord esteems me honest.
OTHELLO: Oh, aye, as summer flies are in the shambles,[6]
    That quicken even with blowing.[7] O thou weed,
    Who art so lovely fair and smell'st so sweet,
    That the sense aches at thee!
    'Would thou hadst ne'er been born!
DESDEMONA: Alas, what ignorant sin have I committed?[8]

[5]Turn thy . . . as hell: It's enough to make Patience herself turn pale.
[6]shambles: meat markets.
[7]That quicken even with the blowing: that spring to life as the meat bloats with rot.
[8]what ignorant sin have I committed: what sin have I committed without knowing it.

OTHELLO: Was this fair paper, this most goodly book,
    Made to write "whore" upon? "What committed?"
    Committed! O thou public commoner!
    I should make very forges of my cheeks
    That would to cinders burn up modesty,
    Did I but speak thy deeds. "What committed!"
    Heaven stops the nose at it, and the moon winks.
    The bawdy wind that kisses all it meets
    Is hushed within the hollow mine of earth
    And will not hear it. "What committed!"
    Impudent strumpet!
DESDEMONA: By Heaven, you do me wrong.
OTHELLO: Are you not a strumpet?
DESDEMONA: No, as I am a Christian.
    If to preserve this vessel for my lord,
    From any other foul, unlawful touch
    Be not to be a strumpet, I am none.
OTHELLO: What, not a whore?
DESDEMONA: No, as I shall be saved.
OTHELLO: Is it possible?
DESDEMONA: O Heaven, forgive us!
OTHELLO: I cry you mercy, then.
    I took you for that cunning whore of Venice,
    That married with Othello.
    (EMILIA returns, and OTHELLO speaks to her.) You mistress,
    That have the office opposite to Saint Peter,
    And keep the gate of hell — You! You! Aye, you!
    We have done our course. There's money for your pains.

(He tosses her a coin.)

    I pray you, turn the key, and keep our counsel. *(He exits.)*
EMILIA: Alas, what does this gentleman conceive?
    How do you, madam? How do you, my good lady?
DESDEMONA: 'Faith, half asleep.
EMILIA: Good madam, what's the matter with my lord?
DESDEMONA: With who?
EMILIA: Why, with my lord, madam.
DESDEMONA: Who is thy lord?
EMILIA: He that is yours, sweet lady.
DESDEMONA: I have none. Do not talk to me, Emilia.
    I cannot weep, nor answer I have none,
    But what should go by water.⁹ 'Pr'ythee, tonight
    Lay on my bed my wedding-sheets. Remember.
    And call thy husband hither.
EMILIA: Here is a change indeed! *(She exits.)*
DESDEMONA: 'Tis meet I should be used so, very meet.
    How have I been behaved, that he might stick
    The smallest opinion on my least misuse?

⁹water: tears.

(EMILIA returns with IAGO.)

IAGO: What is your pleasure, madam? How is it with you?
DESDEMONA: I cannot tell. Those that do teach young babes
  Do it with gentle means and easy tasks.
  He might have chide me so; for, in good faith,
  I am a child to chiding.
IAGO: What's the matter, lady?
EMILIA: Alas, Iago, my lord hath so bewhored her,
  Thrown such despite and heavy terms upon her,
  As true hearts cannot bear.
DESDEMONA: Am I that name, Iago?
IAGO: What name, fair lady?
DESDEMONA: Such as she says my lord did say I was.
EMILIA: He called her whore. A beggar in his drink
  Could not have laid such terms upon his callet.[10]
IAGO: Why did he so?
DESDEMONA: I do not know. I am sure I am none such.
IAGO: Do not weep, do not weep. Alas, the day!
EMILIA: Has she forsook so many noble matches,
  Her father and her country and her friends,
  To be called whore? Would it not make one weep?
DESDEMONA: It is my wretched fortune.
IAGO: Beshrew him for it!
  How comes this trick upon him?
DESDEMONA: Nay, heaven doth know.
EMILIA: I will be hanged if some eternal villain —
  Some busy and insinuating rogue,
  Some cogging, cozening slave — to get some office,[11]
  Have not devised this slander. I'll be hanged else.
IAGO: Fie, there is no such man. It is impossible.
DESDEMONA: If any such there be, heaven pardon him!
EMILIA: A halter pardon him! And hell gnaw his bones![12]
  Why should he call her whore? Who keeps her company?
  What place? What time? What form? What likelihood?
  The Moor's abused by some most villainous knave,
  Some base, notorious knave, some scurvy fellow.
  O Heaven, that such companions thou'dst unfold,[13]
  And put in every honest hand a whip,
  To lash the rascal naked through the world,
  Even from the east to the west!
IAGO: Speak within door.
EMILIA: Oh fie upon him! Some such squire he was,
  That turned your wit the seamy side without,[14]
  And made you to suspect me with the Moor.

[10]callet: prostitute.
[11]"Cogging" and "cozening" are both synonyms for "cheating" or "deceiving."
[12]halter: hangman's noose.
[13]unfold: reveal.
[14]the seamy side without: inside out.

IAGO: You are a fool. Go to.
DESDEMONA: O good Iago,
What shall I do to win my lord again?
Good friend, go to him; for by this light of heaven,
I know not how I lost him. Here I kneel. *(She kneels.)*
If e'er my will did trespass 'gainst his love,
Either in discourse of thought, or actual deed,
Or that mine eyes, mine ears, or any sense
Delighted them in any other form,
Or that I do not yet, and ever did,
And ever will — though he do shake me off
To beggarly divorcement — love him dearly,
Comfort forswear me![15] Unkindness may do much.
And his unkindness may defeat my life,
But never taint my love. I cannot say "whore."
It does abhor me, now I speak the word.
To do the act that might the addition earn,[16]
Not the world's mass of vanity could make me.
IAGO: I pray you, be content.
(He helps her to her feet.) 'Tis but his humor.[17]
The business of the state does him offense,
And he does chide with you.
DESDEMONA: If 'twere no other . . .
IAGO: It is but so, I warrant you. *(Trumpets sound off-stage.)*
Hark, how these instruments summon to supper!
And the great messengers of Venice stay.
Go in, and weep not; all things shall be well.

(DESDEMONA and EMILIA exit, and RODERIGO enters.)

How now Roderigo?
RODERIGO: I do not find that thou deal'st justly with me.
IAGO: What in the contrary?
RODERIGO: Every day thou doff't me with some device, Iago,[18] and rather, as it seem to me now, keep'st from me all conveniency, than suppliest me with the least advantage of hope. I will, indeed, no longer endure it, nor am I yet persuaded to put up in peace what already I have foolishly suffered.
IAGO: Will you hear me Roderigo?
RODERIGO: 'Faith, I have heard too much, for your words and performances are no kin together.
IAGO: You charge me most unjustly.
RODERIGO: With naught but truth. I have wasted myself out of my means. The jewels you have had from me to deliver to Desdemona would half have corrupted a votarist.[19] You have told me she has received them and returned me expectations and comforts of sudden respect and acquittance, but I find none.

[15]forswear: renounce.
[16]addition: title.
[17]humor: mood.
[18]doff: put off.
[19]votarist: devout worshiper.

196

IAGO: Well, go to. Very well.

RODERIGO: Very well? Go to? I cannot go to, man, nor 'tis not "very well." By this hand, I say, it is very scurvy, and begin to find myself fobbed in it.[20]

IAGO: Very well.

RODERIGO: I tell you 'tis not very well. I will make myself known to Desdemona. If she will return me my jewels, I will give over my suit and repent my unlawful solicitation. If not, assure yourself I will seek satisfaction of you.

IAGO: You have said now.

RODERIGO: Aye, and I have said nothing but what I protest intendment of doing.

IAGO: Why, now I see there's mettle in thee and even from this instant do build on thee a better opinion than ever before. Give me thy hand, Roderigo. Thou hast taken against me a most just exception, but yet I protest I have dealt most directly in thy affair.

RODERIGO: It hath not appeared.

IAGO: I grant, indeed it hath not appeared, and your suspicion is not without wit and judgement. But, Roderigo, if thou hast that within thee, indeed, which I have greater reason to believe now than ever — I mean purpose, courage, and valor — this night show it. If thou the next night following enjoyest not Desdemona, take me from this world with treachery, and devise engines for my life.[21]

RODERIGO: Well, what is it? Is it within reason and compass?[22]

IAGO: Sir, there is especial commission come from Venice to depute Cassio in Othello's place.

RODERIGO: Is that true? Why, then Othello and Desdemona return again to Venice.

IAGO: Oh no. He goes into Mauritania[23] and takes away with him the fair Desdemona — unless his abode be lingered here by some accident, wherein none can be so determinate, as the removing of Cassio.

ROGERIGO: How do you mean "removing of him?"

IAGO: Why, by making him uncapable of Othello's place. Knocking out his brains.

RODERIGO: And that you would have me do?

IAGO: Aye, if you dare do yourself a profit and a right. He sups tonight with a harlot, and thither will I go to him. He knows not yet of his honorable fortune. If you will watch his going thence, which I will fashion to fall out between twelve and one, you may take him at your pleasure. I will be near to second your attempt, and he shall fall between us. Come, stand not amazed at it, but go along with me. I will show you such a necessity in his death that you shall think yourself bound to put it on him. It is now high supper-time, and the night grows to waste. About it!

[20]fobbed: cheated.
[21]engines for my life: cunning devices to destroy my life.
[22]compass: practicability.
[23]Mauritania is a country on the Atlantic coast of north-west Africa.

RODERIGO: I will hear further reason for this.[24]
IAGO: And you shall be satisfied.

(They exit.)

---

[24]will: want to.

ACT IV

Scene iii

(OTHELLO enters with LODOVICO, DESDEMONA, EMILIA, and attendants.)

LODOVICO: I do beseech you, sir, trouble yourself no further.
OTHELLO: Oh pardon me. 'Twill do me good to walk.
LODOVICO: Madam, good night. I humbly thank your ladyship.
DESDEMONA: Your honor is most welcome.
OTHELLO: Will you walk, sir?
    Oh, Desdemona?
DESDEMONA: My lord?
OTHELLO: Get you to bed on the instant. I will be returned forthwith.
    Dismiss your attendant there. Look it be done.
DESDEMONA: I will, my lord.

(OTHELLO, LODOVICO, and their attendants exit.)

EMILIA: How goes it now? He looks gentler than he did.
DESDEMONA: He says he will return incontinent.[1]
    He hath commanded me to go to bed
    And bade me to dismiss you.
EMILIA: Dismiss me!
DESDEMONA: It was his bidding; therefore, good Emilia,
    Give me my nightly wearing, and adieu.[2]
    We must not now displease him.
EMILIA: I would you had never seen him!
DESDEMONA: So would not I. My love doth so approve him,
    That even his stubborness, his checks, and frowns —
    Pr'ythee, unpin me — have grace and favor in them.
EMILIA: I have laid those sheets you bade me on the bed.
DESDEMONA: All's one. Good father! How foolish are our minds!
    If I do die before thee, 'pr'ythee, shroud me
    In one of those same sheets.
EMILIA: Come, come! You talk . . .
DESDEMONA: My mother had a maid called Barbara.
    She was in love, and he she loved proved mad
    And did forsake her. She had a song of "Willow."
    An old thing 'twas but it expressed her fortune,
    And she died singing it. That song, tonight,
    Will not go from my mind I have much to do
    But to go hang my head all at one side[3]
    And sing it like poor Barbara. 'Pr'ythee, dispatch.
EMILIA: Shall I go fetch your nightgown?
DESDEMONA: No. Unpin me here.
    This Lodovico is a proper man.
EMILIA: A very handsome man.

[1]incontinent(ly): immediately.
[2]nightly wearing: night clothes.
[3]I have much to do but to go hang: I can hardly keep from hanging.

DESDEMONA: And he speaks well.
EMILIA: I know a lady in Venice, who would have walked barefoot to
Palestine for a touch of his nether lip.
DESDEMONA: *(Singing)* The poor soul sat sighing by a sycamore tree.
Sing all a green willow.
Her hand on her bosom, her head on her knee.
Sing willow, willow, willow.
The fresh streams ran by her and murmured her moans.
Sing willow, willow, willow.
Her salt tears fell from her, and softened the stones . . .
Lay by these. *(Speaking this line, she gives EMILIA some of her things
to put away for the night, then she continues her song:)*
Sing willow, willow, willow . . .
(Speaking) Pr'ythee, hie thee; he'll come anon.[4]
(Singing) Sing all a green willow must be my garland.
Let nobody blame him, his scorn I approve . . .
(Speaking) Nay, that's not next — Hark! Who is it that knocks?
EMILIA: It is the wind.
DESDEMONA: *(Singing)* I called my love false love but what said he then?
Sing willow, willow, willow.
If I court mo women, you'll couch with mo men . . .
(Speaking to EMILIA.) So get thee gone. Good night. Mine eyes do itch.
Doth that bode weeping?
EMILIA: 'Tis neither here nor there.
DESDEMONA: I have heard it said so. Oh these men, these men!
Dost thou in conscience think — tell me, Emilia —
That there be women do abuse their husbands
In such gross kind?
EMILIA: There be some such, no question.
DESDEMONA: Wouldst thou do such a deed for all the world?
EMILIA: Why, would not you?
DESDEMONA: No, by this heavenly light!
EMILIA: Nor I neither by this heavenly light.
I might do't as well i' the dark.
DESDEMONA: Wouldst thou do such a deed for all the world?
EMILIA: The world is a huge thing. 'Tis a great price
For a small vice.
DESDEMONA: Good troth, I think thou wouldst not.
EMILIA: By my troth, I think I should, and undo't when I had done. Marry,
I would not do such a thing for a joint-ring,[5] nor for measures of lawn,[6]
nor for gowns, petticoats, nor caps, nor any petty exhibition.[7] But for
the whole world? Who would not make her husband a cuckold to make
him a monarch? I should venture purgatory for't.
DESDEMONA: Beshrew me, if I would do such a wrong for the whole world.
EMILIA: Why, the wrong is but a wrong i' the world, and having the world

[4]hie: hurry. anon: soon.
[5]A joint-ring is a ring that divides into two parts so that lovers can each wear half of it.
[6]lawn: fine, sheer fabric.
[7]exhibition: pension.

for your labor, 'tis a wrong in your own world, and you might quickly
make it right.
DESDEMONA: I do not think there is any such woman.
EMILIA: Yes, a dozen; and as many,
To the vantage, as would store the world they played for.[8]
But I do think it is their husbands' faults
If wives do fall. Say that they slack their duties
And pour our treasures into foreign laps,
Or else break out in peevish jealousies,
Throwing restraint upon us; or, say, they strike us,
Or scant our former having in despite.[9]
Why, we have galls, and though we have some grace,
Yet we have some revenge. Let husbands know
Their wives have sense like them: They see, and smell,
And have their palates both for sweet and sour,
As husbands have. What is it that they do,
When they change us for others? Is it sport?
I think it is. And doth affection breed it?[10]
I think it doth. Is't frailty, that thus errs?
It is so too. And have not we affections,
Desires for sport, and frailty as men have?
Then let them use us well, else let them know:
The ills we do, their ills instruct us to.
DESDEMONA: Good night, good night! Heaven me such uses send,[11]
Not to pick bad from bad, but by bad, mend!

(They both exit.)

[8]to the vantage as would store: in addition that would fill.
[9]scant our former having in despite: cut back the support we've become accustomed to in order
to spite us.
[10]affection: lust.
[11]uses: characteristic practices.

ACT V

Scene i

Later that night, on a street in town.

(IAGO enters with RODERIGO.)

IAGO: Here, stand behind this bulk.[1] Straight will he come.
Wear thy good rapier bare, and put it home.
Quick, quick! Fear nothing. I'll be at thy elbow.
It makes us, or it mars us. Think on that,
And fix most firm thy resolution.
RODERIGO: Be near at hand. I may miscarry in't.
IAGO: Here, at thy hand. Be bold, and take thy sword.

(IAGO retires a small distance from RODERIGO.)

RODERIGO: I have no great devotion to the deed,
And yet he has given me satisfying reasons.
'Tis but a man gone. *(He draws his sword.)* Forth, my sword. He dies!

(He hides as IAGO instructed him.)

IAGO: I have rubbed this young quat almost to the sense,[2]
And he grows angry. Now, whether he kill Cassio,
Or Cassio him, or each do kill the other,
Every way makes my gain. Live Roderigo,
He calls me to a restitution large
Of gold and jewels that I bobbed from him[3]
As gifts to Desdemona.
It must not be! If Cassio do remain,
He hath a daily beauty in his life,
That makes me ugly. And besides, the Moor
May unfold me to him. There stand I in much peril.
No, he must die. But so: I hear him coming.

(CASSIO enters.)

RODERIGO: *(To himself)* I know his gait. 'Tis he.
(To CASSIO.) Villain, thou diest!

(He rushes from hiding, and makes a pass at CASSIO with his sword.)

CASSIO: That thrust had been mine enemy indeed,
But that my coat is better than thou think'st.
I will make proof of thine.

(He draws and wounds RODERIGO.)

RODERIGO: Oh I am slain!

(IAGO rushes from hiding and cuts CASSIO behind in the leg then exits.)

CASSIO: I am maimed forever. Help, ho! Murder! Murder!

[1]bulk: pillar of a house.
[2]quat: pimple; to the sense: until it hurts.
[3]bobbed: took by trickery.

202

(He falls. OTHELLO enters at a distance.)

OTHELLO: The voice of Cassio. Iago keeps his word.
RODERIGO: Oh villain that I am!
OTHELLO: Hark! 'Tis even so.
CASSIO: Oh help! Ho! Light! A surgeon!
OTHELLO: 'Tis he! O brave Iago, honest and just,
That hast such noble sense of thy friend's wrong!
Thou teachest me. Minion, your dear lies dead,[4]
And your fate hies apace.[5] Strumpet, I come.
Forth of my heart those charms, thine eyes, are blotted.
Thy bed, lust-stained, shall with lust's blood be spotted.

(OTHELLO exits. On the other side of the stage, at a distance, LODOVICO and GRATIANO enter.)

CASSIO: What, ho! No watch? No passage?[6] Murder! Murder!
GRATIANO: 'Tis some mischance! The cry is very direful.
CASSIO: Oh help!
LODOVICO: Hark!
RODERIGO: Oh wretched villain!
LODOVICO: Two or three groans. It is a heavy night.[7]
These may be counterfeits. Let's think't unsafe
To come into the cry without more help.
RODERIGO: Nobody come? Then I shall bleed to death.

(IAGO enters with a light.)

LODOVICO: Hark!
GRATIANO: Here's one comes in his shirt, with light and weapons.
IAGO: Who's there? Whose noise is this, that cries on murder?
LODOVICO: We do not know.
IAGO: Did you not hear a cry?
CASSIO: Here, here! For Heaven's sake, help me.
IAGO: What's the matter?
GRATIANO: This is Othello's ancient, as I take it.
LODOVICO: The same, indeed. A very valiant fellow.
IAGO: What are you here that cry so grievously?
CASSIO: Iago! Oh I am spoiled, undone by villains!
Give me some help.
IAGO: Oh me, lieutenant! What villains have done this?
CASSIO: I think that one of them is hereabout,
And cannot make away.
IAGO: O treacherous villains!

(Calling to LODOVICO and GRATIANO.)

What are you there? Come in, and give some help.
RODERIGO: O, help me here!

---

[4]minion: servile dependent; Othello addresses Desdemona in her absence.
[5]hies apace: rushes on quickly.
[6]passage: one passing by.
[7]heavy: cloudy or dark.

CASSIO: That's one of them.
IAGO: O murderous slave! O villain!

(IAGO stabs RODERIGO.)

RODERIGO: O damned Iago! O inhuman dog!
    Oh! Oh! Oh!
IAGO: Kill men i' the dark! Where be these bloody thieves?
    How silent is this town! How! Murder! Murder!
    What may you be? Are you of good, or evil?
LODOVICO: As you shall prove us, praise us.
IAGO: Seignior Lodovico!
LODOVICO: He, sir.
IAGO: I cry you mercy. Here's Cassio hurt
    By villains.
GRATIANO: Cassio?
IAGO: How is it, brother?
CASSIO: My leg is cut in two.
IAGO: Marry, heaven forbid!
    Light, gentlemen! I'll bind it with my shirt.

(BIANCA enters.)

BIANCA: What is the matter, ho? Who is't that cried?
IAGO: Who is't that cried?
BIANCA: O my dear Cassio! My sweet Cassio!
    O Cassio! Cassio! Cassio!
IAGO: O notable strumpet! Cassio, may you suspect
    Who they should be, that have thus mangled you?
CASSIO: No.
GRATIANO: I am sorry to find you thus. I have been to seek you.
IAGO: Lend me a garter. *(He binds up CASSIO's leg.)* So, for a chair,
    To bear him easily hence!
BIANCA: Alas, he faints! O Cassio! Cassio! Cassio!
IAGO: Gentlemen all, I do suspect this trash
    To be a party of this injury.
    Patience awhile, good Cassio. Come, come!
    Lend me a light. *(Peering at RODERIGO.)* Know we this face, or no?
    Alas! My friend and my dear countryman,
    Roderigo? No! Yes, sure. O heaven! Roderigo.
GRATIANO: What, of Venice?
IAGO: Even he, sir. Did you know him?
GRATIANO: Know him? Aye.
IAGO: Seignior Gratiano? I cry you gentle pardon.
    These bloody accidents must excuse my manners
    That so neglected you.
GRATIANO: I am so glad to see you.
IAGO: How do you, Cassio? Oh a chair, a chair!
GRATIANO: Roderigo!
IAGO: He, he, 'tis he. Oh that's well said. The chair.

(People bring in a chair.)

Some good man bear him carefully from hence.
I'll fetch the general's surgeon. *(Speaking to BIANCA.)* For you, mistress,
Save you your labor. He that lies slain here, Cassio,
Was my dear friend. What malice was between you?
CASSIO: None in the world; nor do I know the man.
IAGO: *(To BIANCA.)* What, look you pale? Oh bear him out o' the air.

(CASSIO and RODERIGO are borne off.)

Stay you, good gentlemen. Look you pale, mistress?
Do you perceive the gastness of her eye?[8]
Nay, if you stare, we shall hear more anon.
Behold her well. I pray you, look upon her.
Do you see, gentlemen? Nay, guiltiness will speak,
Though tongues were out of use.

(EMILIA enters.)

EMILIA: 'Las, what's the matter? What's the matter, husband?
IAGO: Cassio hath here been set on in the dark,
By Roderigo and fellows that are 'scaped.
He's almost slain, and Roderigo dead.
EMILIA: Alas, good gentleman! Alas, good Cassio!
IAGO: This is the fruit of whoring. 'Pr'ythee, Emilia,
Go know of Cassio where he supped tonight.
(To BIANCA.) What, do you shake at that?
BIANCA: He supped at my house, but I therefore shake not.
IAGO: Oh did he so? I charge you, go with me.
EMILIA: Fie, fie upon thee, strumpet!
BIANCA: I am no strumpet, but of life as honest
As you that thus abuse me.
EMILIA: As I? Foh! Fie upon thee!
IAGO: Kind gentlemen, let's go see poor Cassio dressed.
Come, mistress, you must tell us another tale.
Emilia, run to the citadel,
And tell my lord and lady what has happened.
Will you go on, I pray? *(To himself.)* This is the night,
That either makes me, or foredoes me quite.

(All exit.)

---

[8]gastness: terror.

ACT V

Scene ii

Later that night in a bedchamber in the castle.

(DESDEMONA is in bed asleep. A light is burning. OTHELLO enters.[1])

OTHELLO: It is the cause, it is the cause, my soul.[2]
Let me not name it to you, you chaste stars!
It is the cause. Yet I'll not shed her blood,
Nor scar that whiter skin of hers than snow,
And smooth as monumental alabaster.

(He takes off his sword and lays it to one side.)

Yet she must die, else she'll betray more men.
Put out the light, and then — put out the light.
(Speaking to the lamp.) If I quench thee, thou flaming minister,
I can again thy former light restore,
Should I repent me — *(Turning to DESDEMONA.)* But once put out thine,
Thou cunning'st pattern of excelling nature,
I know not where is that Promethean heat[3]
That can thy light relume.[4] When I have plucked thy rose,
I cannot give it vital growth again.
It needs must wither. I'll smell it on the tree. *(He kisses her.)*
O balmy breath that dost almost persuade
Justice to break her sword! One more, one more. *(He kisses her again.)*
Be thus when thou are dead, and I will kill thee,
And love thee after. One more, and this the last. *(He kisses her again.)*
So sweet was ne'er so fatal. I must weep,
But they are cruel tears.[5] This sorrow's heavenly:
It strikes where it doth love.[6] She wakes!
DESDEMONA: Who's there? Othello?
OTHELLO: Aye, Desdemona.
DESDEMONA: Will you come to bed, my lord?
OTHELLO: Have you prayed tonight, Desdemona?
DESDEMONA: Aye, my lord.
OTHELLO: If you bethink yourself of any crime,

[1]Note that this is the first scene in the play that has begun with an actor already on stage. Many scholars believe that Shakespeare's stage had a recessed area in the tiring-house wall which backed the stage platform; this area could be curtained off from the audience's view. Desdemona's bed was probably located in this alcove and the curtain drawn aside to begin the scene.
[2]Scholars and producers have debated the meaning of these lines without arriving at a common solution. "It" might refer to Desdemona's supposed infidelity: "Her unfaithfulness is the reason why I'm doing this." Or "cause" might be the service of justice: "It is in the cause of justice that I must do this." One production had Othello looking in a mirror before the lines which give them the sense, "My race is the reason for her infidelity."
[3]In Greek mythology, Prometheus was a titan who befriended humankind and stole the fire of the gods to give to human beings.
[4]relume: re-light.
[5]His tears are cruel because he will not permit them to sway his purpose.
[6]This sorrow's . . . doth love: My passion is holy because I am striking not out of anger but out of love.

Unreconciled as yet to heaven and grace,
Solicit for it straight.
DESDEMONA: Alas, my lord, what may you mean by that?
OTHELLO: Well, do it, and be brief. I will walk by.
I would not kill thy unprepared spirit.
No, heaven forfend![7] I would not kill thy soul.
DESDEMONA: Talk you of killing?
OTHELLO: Aye, I do.
DESDEMONA: Then, heaven
Have mercy on me!
OTHELLO: Amen, with all my heart!
DESDEMONA: If you say so, I hope you will not kill me.
OTHELLO: Humph!
DESDEMONA: And yet I fear you, for you are fatal then
When your eyes roll so. Why I should fear, I know not,
Since guiltiness I know not. But yet I feel I fear.
OTHELLO: Think on thy sins.
DESDEMONA: They are loves I bear to you.
OTHELLO: Aye, and for that thou diest.
DESDEMONA: That death's unnatural, that kills for loving.
Alas, why gnaw you so your nether lip?[8]
Some bloody passion shakes your very frame.
These are portents. But yet I hope, I hope,[9]
They do not point on me.
OTHELLO: Peace, and be still!
DESDEMONA: I will so. What's the matter?
OTHELLO: That handkerchief which I so loved and gave thee,
Thou gav'st to Cassio.
DESDEMONA: No, by my life and soul.
Send for the man, and ask him.
OTHELLO: Sweet soul, take heed,
Take heed of perjury. Thou'rt on thy deathbed.
DESDEMONA: Aye, but not yet to die.
OTHELLO: Yes, presently.
Therefore confess thee freely of thy sin,
For to deny each article with oath,
Cannot remove nor choke the strong conception
That I do groan withal.[10] Thou art to die.
DESDEMONA: Then Lord have mercy on me!
OTHELLO: I say, amen.
DESDEMONA: And have you mercy too! I never did
Offend you in my life — never loved Cassio,
But with such general warranty of heaven[11]
As I might love. I never gave him token.

[7]forfend: forbid.
[8]nether: lower.
[9]portents: omens.
[10]the strong conception that I do groan withal: Using childbirth as a metaphor, Othello says that he is groaning with the labor pains of bringing to birth Desdemona's execution.
[11]warranty: authorization.

OTHELLO: By Heaven, I saw my handkerchief in his hand.
   O perjured woman! Thou dost stone my heart,[12]
   And mak'st me call what I intend to do
   A murder, which I thought a sacrifice.
   I saw the handkerchief.
DESDEMONA: He found it, then.
   I never gave it him. Send for him hither,
   And let him confess a truth.
OTHELLO: He hath confessed.
DESDEMONA: What, my lord?
OTHELLO: That he hath — used thee.
DESDEMONA: How? Unlawfully?
OTHELLO: Aye.
DESDEMONA: He'll not say so.
OTHELLO: No, his mouth is stopped.
   Honest Iago hath ta'en order for't.
DESDEMONA: My fear interprets. What, is he dead?
OTHELLO: Had all his hairs been lives, my great revenge
   Had stomach for them all.
DESDEMONA: Alas! He is betrayed, and I undone.
OTHELLO: Out, strumpet! Weep't thou for him to my face?
DESDEMONA: Oh banish me, my lord, but kill me not.
OTHELLO: Down, strumpet! *(OTHELLO attacks her, and she resists.)*
DESDEMONA: Kill me tomorrow. Let me live tonight.
OTHELLO: Nay, if you strive . . .
DESDEMONA: But half an hour.
OTHELLO: Being done,
   There is no pause.
DESDEMONA: But while I say one prayer.
OTHELLO: It is too late. *(He smothers her.)*
EMILIA: *(Off-stage)* My lord, my lord! What, ho! My lord! My lord!
OTHELLO: What noise is this?
   (DESDEMONA moves.) Not dead? Not quite dead?
   I that am cruel am yet merciful.
   I would not have thee linger in thy pain.
   So, so.[13]
EMILIA: *(Off-stage)* What, ho! My lord, my lord!
OTHELLO: Who's there?
EMILIA: *(Off-stage)* O good my lord, I would speak a word with you.
OTHELLO: *(Calling)* Yes. *(To himself.)* 'Tis Emilia. *(Calling)* By and by.
   (To himself.) She's dead.
   'Tis like she comes to speak of Cassio's death.
   The noise was high. Ha! No more moving?

---

[12]stone my heart: turn my heart to stone.
[13]Scholars, actors, and even physicians have argued long over what Othello does during the words "So, so." Some solutions: He stabs her, which would easily explain her paleness about which he later comments. Or, he removes the pillow he had tried to use before and presses her larynx with his hands, breaking it; she subsequently dies from the damage to her larynx. Or, he presses on the pillow again and assumes, erroneously, that she is dead; after she speaks, she dies of heart failure.

208

Still as the grave. Shall she come in? Were't good?
I think she stirs again. No. What's the best?
If she come in, she'll sure speak to my wife.
My wife! My wife! What wife? I have no wife.
Oh insupportable! Oh heavy hour!
Methinks it should be now a huge eclipse
Of sun and moon, and that the affrighted globe
Should yawn at alteration.[14]
EMILIA: *(Off-stage)* I do beseech you I may speak with you.
 O good my lord!
OTHELLO: I had forgot thee. Oh come in, Emilia.
 Soft! By and by. Let me the curtain draw.
 Where art thou? *(He unlocks the door, and EMILIA enters.)*
 What's the matter with thee now?
EMILIA: O good my lord, yonder's foul murder done.
OTHELLO: What? Now?
EMILIA: But now, my lord!
OTHELLO: It is the very error of the moon.
 She comes more near the earth than she was wont,
 And makes men mad.
EMILIA: Cassio, my lord, has killed a young Venetian
 Called Roderigo.
OTHELLO: Roderigo killed!
 And Cassio killed?
EMILIA: No, Cassio is not killed.
OTHELLO: Not Cassio killed? Then murder's out of tune,
 And sweet revenge grows harsh.
DESDEMONA: Oh falsely, falsely murdered!
EMILIA: Alas! What cry is that?
OTHELLO: That! What?
EMILIA: Out and alas! That was my lady's voice.

(She pulls the curtain open.)

 Help! Help! Ho! Help! O sweet mistress, speak!
DESDEMONA: A guiltless death I die.
EMILIA: Oh who hath done
 This deed?
DESDEMONA: Nobody — I myself. Farewell.
 Commend me to my kind lord. Oh farewell. *(She dies.)*
OTHELLO: Why, how should she be murdered?
EMILIA: Alas, who knows?
OTHELLO: You heard her say herself, it was not I.
EMILIA: She said so. I must needs report the truth.
OTHELLO: She's like a liar gone to burning hell.
 'Twas I that killed her.

---

[14]These lines ("it should now be a huge eclipse . . . at alteration") may be an allusion to the biblical description of the crucifixion of Jesus Christ: "Now from the sixth hour there was darkness over all the land until the ninth hour . . . and the earth shook, and the rocks were split." (Matthew 27.45 & 51).

EMILIA: Oh the more angel she,
  And you the blacker devil!
OTHELLO: She turned to folly, and she was a whore.
EMILIA: Thou dost belie her, and thou art a devil.
OTHELLO: She was false as water.
EMILIA: Thou art rash as fire to say
  That she was false. Oh she was heavenly true!
OTHELLO: Cassio did tup her. Ask thy husband else.
  Oh I were damned beneath all depth in hell,
  But that I did proceed upon just grounds
  To this extremity. Thy husband knew it all.
EMILIA: My husband?
OTHELLO: Thy husband.
EMILIA: That she was false to wedlock?
OTHELLO: Aye, with Cassio.
  Nay, had she been true,
  If heaven would make me such another world
  Of one entire and perfect chrysolite,[15]
  I'd not have sold her for it.
EMILIA: My husband?
OTHELLO: Aye, 'twas he that told me first.
  An honest man he is, and hates the slime
  That sticks on filthy deeds.
EMILIA: My husband?
OTHELLO: What needs this iterance, woman?[16] I say, thy husband . . .
EMILIA: O mistress, villainy hath made mocks with love!
  My husband say that she was false?
OTHELLO: He, woman.
  I say, thy husband. Dost understand the word?
  My friend, thy husband, honest, honest Iago.
EMILIA: If he say so, may his pernicious soul
  Rot half a grain a day! He lies to the heart.
  She was too fond of her most filthy bargain.
OTHELLO: Ha!
EMILIA: Do thy worst.
  This deed of thine is no more worthy heaven,
  Than thou wast worthy her.
OTHELLO: Peace, you were best.[17]
EMILIA: Thou hast not half the power to do me harm,
  As I have to be hurt. O gull! O dolt!
  As ignorant as dirt! Thou hast done a deed —
  I care not for thy sword.[18] I'll make thee known
  Though I lost twenty lives. Help! Help, ho! Help!
  The Moor has killed my mistress. Murder! Murder!

(MONTANO, GRATIANO, and IAGO enter.)

[15]Chrysolite is a greenish stone which was once thought to be very valuable.
[16]iterance: repetition.
[17]Peace, you were best: You had better shut up.
[18]Apparently Othello is threatening her with his sword.

MONTANO: What is the matter? How now, general?
EMILIA: Oh, are you come, Iago? You have done well,
    That men must lay their murders on your neck.
GRATIANO: What is the matter?
EMILIA: Disprove this, villain, if thou beest a man.
    He says thou told'st him that his wife was false.
    I know thou didst not. Thou'rt not such a villain.
    Speak, for my heart is full.
IAGO: I told him what I thought, and told no more
    Than what he found himself was apt and true.
EMILIA: But did you ever tell him she was false?
IAGO: I did.
EMILIA: You told a lie, an odious, damned lie.
    Upon my soul, a lie, a wicked lie —
    She false with Cassio! Did you say with Cassio?
IAGO: With Cassio, mistress. Go to, charm your tongue.[19]
EMILIA: I will not charm my tongue; I am bound to speak.
    My mistress here lies murdered in her bed.
ALL: O heavens forfend!
EMILIA: And your reports have set the murder on.
OTHELLO: Nay, stare not, masters. It is true, indeed.
GRATIANO: 'Tis a strange truth.
MONTANO: Oh monstrous act!
EMILIA: Villainy, villainy, villainy!
    I think upon't — I think — I smell't — Oh villainy!
    I thought so then. I'll kill myself for grief.
    Oh villainy, villainy!
IAGO: What, are you mad? I charge you, get you home.
EMILIA: Good gentlemen, let me have leave to speak.
    'Tis proper to obey him, but not now.
    Perchance, Iago, I will ne'er go home.
OTHELLO: *(Hanging over his wife.)* Oh! Oh! Oh!
EMILIA: Nay, lay thee down and roar,
    For thou hast killed the sweetest innocent
    That e'er did lift up eye.
OTHELLO: Oh she was foul!
    (Addressing GRATIANO.) I scarce did know you, uncle. There lies
        your niece
    Whose breath, indeed, these hands have newly stopped.
    I know this act shows horrible and grim.
GRATIANO: Poor Desdemona! I am glad thy father's dead.
    Thy match was mortal to him, and pure grief
    Shore his old thread in twain. Did he live now,
    This sight would make him do a desperate turn —
    Yea, curse his better angel from his side,
    And fall to reprobation.
OTHELLO: 'Tis pitiful. But yet Iago knows
    That she with Cassio hath the act of shame

---

[19]charm: control (by enchantment).

A thousand times committed. Cassio confessed it.
And she did gratify his amorous works
With that recognizance and pledge of love
Which I first gave her. I saw it in his hand.
It was a handkerchief, an antique token
My father gave my mother.
EMILIA: O heaven! O heavenly powers!
IAGO: Come, hold your peace.
EMILIA: 'Twill out, 'twill out. I hold my peace, sir? No!
No, I will speak as liberal as the air.[20]
Let heaven, and men, and devils, let them all,
All, all, cry shame against me, yet I'll speak.
IAGO: Be wise and get you home.
EMILIA: I will not.

(IAGO attempts to stab his wife.)

GRATIANO: *(Stopping him.)* Fie!
Your sword upon a woman?
EMILIA: O thou dull Moor! That handkerchief thou speak'st of,
I found by fortune, and did give my husband,
For often, with a solemn earnestness —
More than, indeed, belong to such a trifle —
He begged of me to steal it.
IAGO: Villainous whore!
EMILIA: She give it to Cassio? No, alas. I found it,
And I did give't my husband.
IAGO: Filth, thou liest.
EMILIA: By heaven, I do not. I do not, gentlemen.
O murderous coxcomb![21] What should such a fool
Do with so good a wife!

(IAGO stabs EMILIA, then runs out.)

OTHELLO: Are there no stones in heaven,
But what serve for the thunder?[22] Precious villain![23]
GRATIANO: The woman falls. Sure he has killed his wife.
EMILIA: Aye, aye. Oh lay me by my mistress' side!
GRATIANO: He's gone, but his wife's killed.
MONTANO: 'Tis a notorious villain.

(With a quick movement, he takes OTHELLO's sword.)

Take you this weapon,
Which I have here recovered from the Moor.
Come, guard the door without. Let him not pass,
But kill him rather. I'll after that same villain,
For 'tis a damned slave.

[20]liberal: freely.
[21]coxcomb: fool. The coxcomb was the headdress worn by a court jester.
[22]Are there no stones . . . thunder: Although the specific reasons for these word choices are obscure, Othello is calling upon heaven to punish Iago.
[23]precious: great.

(MONTANO and GRATIANO exit.)

OTHELLO: I am not valiant neither,
    But every puny whipster gets my sword.
    But why should honor outlive honesty?
    Let it go all.
EMILIA: What did thy song bode, lady?
    Hark, canst thou hear me? I will play the swan,
    And die in music. *(She sings.)* Willow, willow, willow —
    (Speaking) Moor, she was chaste. She loved thee, cruel Moor,
    So come my soul to bliss, as I speak true![24]
    So speaking as I think, I die — I die. *(She dies.)*
OTHELLO: I have another weapon in this chamber.
    It is a sword of Spain, the ice-brook's temper.
    Oh, here it is. *(Calling to GRATIANO.)* Uncle, I must come forth.
GRATIANO: *(Off-stage)* If thou attempt it, it will cost thee dear.
    Thou hast no weapon and perforce must suffer.
OTHELLO: Look in upon me, then, and speak with me,
    Or naked as I am, I will assault thee.[25]

(GRATIANO re-enters.)

GRATIANO: What is the matter?
OTHELLO: Behold! I have a weapon!
    A better never did itself sustain
    Upon a soldier's thigh. I have seen the day
    That, with this little arm and this good sword,
    I have made my way through more impediments
    Than twenty times your stop. But oh, vain boast!
    Who can control his fate? 'Tis not so now.
    Be not afraid, though you do see me weaponed.
    Here is my journey's end, here is my butt,[26]
    And very seamark of my utmost sail.[27]
    Do you go back dismayed? 'Tis a lost fear.
    Man but a rush against Othello's breast,
    And he retires. Where should Othello go?

(He looks at DESDEMONA.)

Now, how dost thou look now? O ill-starred wench!
Pale as thy smock! When we shall meet at compt,[28]
This look of thine shall hurl my soul from heaven,
And fiends will snatch at it. *(He touches her.)* Cold, cold, my girl?
Even like thy chastity.
O, cursed, cursed slave! Whip me, ye devils,
From the possession of this heavenly sight!
Blow me about in winds! Roast me in sulphur!

[24]bliss: heaven.
[25]naked: unarmed.
[26]butt: goal (taken from the meaning of "butt" as a earthen mound against which a target is set).
[27]A seamark is a mark on the beach made by the farthest reach of waves at high tide.
[28]compt: judgement.

Wash me in steep-down gulfs of liquid fire!
O Desdemona! Desdemona! Dead?
Dead? Oh! Oh! Oh!

(LODOVICO and MONTANO enter together with CASSIO being carried on a chair and Officers who have IAGO prisoner.)

LODOVICO: Where is this rash and most unfortunate man?
OTHELLO: That's he that was Othello. Here I am.
LODOVICO: Where is that viper? Bring the villain forth.
OTHELLO: *(Looking at IAGO.)* I look down towards his feet — but that's a
    fable.
    If that thou be'st a devil, I cannot kill thee.

(OTHELLO wounds IAGO with his sword.)

LODOVICO: Wrench his sword from him.

(The Officers take away OTHELLO's sword.)

IAGO: I bleed, sir, but not killed.
OTHELLO: I am not sorry, neither. I'd have thee live,
    For in my sense, 'tis happiness to die.
LODOVICO: O thou Othello, that was one so good,
    Fallen in the practice of a cursed slave,
    What shall be said to thee?
OTHELLO: Why, anything —
    An honorable murderer, if you will,
    For nought I did in hate, but all in honor.
LODOVICO: This wretch hath part confessed his villainy.
    Did you and he consent in Cassio's death?
OTHELLO: Aye.
CASSIO: Dear general, I never gave you cause.
OTHELLO: I do believe it, and I ask your pardon.
    Will you, I pray you, demand that demi-devil,[29]
    Why he hath thus ensnared my soul and body.
IAGO: Demand me nothing. What you know, you know.
    From this time forth I never will speak word.
LODOVICO: What? Not to pray?
GRATIANO: Torments will ope your lips.[30]
OTHELLO: *(To IAGO)* Well, thou dost best.
LODOVICO: Sir, you shall understand what hath befallen,
    Which, as I think, you know not. Here is a letter,
    Found in the pocket of the slain Roderigo,
    And here another. The one of them imports
    The death of Cassio to be undertook
    By Roderigo.
OTHELLO: O villain!
CASSIO: Most heathenish and most gross!
LODOVICO: Now, here's another discontented paper,

[29]demi-: half-.
[30]torments: torture.

Found in his pocket too, and this, it seems,
Roderigo meant to have sent this damned villain,[31]
But that belike, Iago, in the interim,[32]
Came in and satisfied him.[33]
OTHELLO: Oh the pernicious caitiff!
How came you, Cassio, by that handkerchief
That was my wife's?
CASSIO: I found it in my chamber,
And he himself confessed, but even now,
That there he dropped it for a special purpose
Which wrought to his desire.
OTHELLO: *(Addressing himself.)* O fool! Fool! Fool!
CASSIO: There is, besides, in Roderigo's letter
How he upbraids Iago that he made him
Brave me upon the watch, whereon it came
That I was cast.[34] And even but now he spake,
After long seeming dead — Iago hurt him —
Iago set him on.
LODOVICO: You must forsake this room, and go with us.
Your power and your command is taken off,
And Cassio rules in Cyprus. For this slave,[35]
If there be any cunning cruelty
That can torment him much and hold him long,[36]
It shall be his. You shall close prisoner rest,[37]
'Till that the nature of your fault be known
To the Venetian state. *(To the Officers.)* Come, bring him away.
OTHELLO: Soft you! A word or two, before you go.[38]
I have done the state some service, and they know it.
No more of that. I pray you, in your letters,
When you shall these unlucky deeds relate,
Speak of me as I am — nothing extenuate,
Nor set down aught in malice. Then must you speak
Of one that loved not wisely but too well,
Of one not easily jealous but, being wrought,
Perplexed in the extreme, of one whose hand
Like the base Judean threw a pearl away
Richer than all his tribe, of one whose subdued eyes,
Albeit unused to the melting mood,
Drop tears as fast as the Arabian trees
Their medicinal gum. Set you down this,
And say besides that in Aleppo once,[39]

[31]this damned villain: Othello.
[32]but that belike: except that probably.
[33]satisfied him: finished him off.
[34]cast: demoted.
[35]this slave: Iago.
[36]torment him much and hold him long: torture him for a long time without killing him quickly.
[37]rest: stay.
[38]soft you: not so quickly.
[39]Aleppo was a city in the Near East where, according to legend, any Christian who struck a Muslim was to suffer immediate death.

Where a malignant and a turbaned Turk
Beat a Venetian and traduced the state,[40]
I took by the throat the circumcised dog,
And smote him — *(Drawing a hidden dagger.)* — thus! *(He stabs himself.)*
LODOVICO: O bloody period![41]
GRATIANO: All that's spoke is marred.
OTHELLO: I kissed thee ere I killed thee. No way but this —

(He falls upon DESDEMONA.)

Killing myself, to die upon a kiss. *(He dies.)*
CASSIO: This did I fear, but thought he had no weapon,
For he was great of heart.
LODOVICO: *(Speaking to IAGO.)* O Spartan dog,[42]
More fell than anguish, hunger, or the sea![43]
Look on the tragic loading of this bed!
This is thy work. The object poisons sight.[44]
Let it be hid.

(Officers cover the bodies of DESDEMONA, EMILIA, and OTHELLO.)

Gratiano, keep the house,[45]
And seize upon the fortunes of the Moor,
For they succeed to you. *(To CASSIO.)* To you, lord governor,
Remains the censure of this hellish villain —
The time, the place, the torture. Oh enforce it!
Myself will straight aboard and to the state
This heavy act with heavy heart relate.

(All exit.)

---

[40]traduced: poured lying shame upon.
[41]A period is not only the punctuation at the end of a sentence but also a sentence structured as the last speech of Othello in which the speaker makes the hearers wait until the last word to understand the complete meaning of the line.
[42]Spartan dogs were reputed to be exceptionally savage; also, Spartans were famed for remaining silent under suffering.
[43]fell: deadly.
[44]the object: the picture.
[45]keep: guard.

NEOCLASSICAL DRAMA: The Theatre of Rationalism

$\mathbf{T}$oward the end of the sixteenth century, the creative exuberance of the Renaissance gave way to a period of consolidation and regularization. This era was known as the baroque period in music, art, and architecture, and as the age of rationalism in philosophy and religion. In theatre, this period (which lasted into the eighteenth century) is known as the neoclassical era. During this period, theatre architects created the type of building which would dominate theatre until the end of the twentieth century, theoreticians turned theatre criticism into a science of its own, and playwrights produced some of the great masterpieces of European drama.

Philosophical and Political Backgrounds

During the three centuries between 1500 and 1800, Europeans shifted their understanding of authority. In the Middle Ages, people believed that final authority was in the hands of the Church, with its on-going traditions and hierarchy. During the early part of the Renaissance, people rejected medieval churchly authority and reached back past the Middle Ages to the Greek philosophers and the biblical writers. For these people, truth rested with ancient authorities. As the Renaissance continued, however, people began to think for themselves. Rather than simply trust the teachings of ancient philosophers and prophets, they believed that they could best find truth by using reason and logic. They believed that rationalism, carefully followed, would show them what was true for all people in all places at all times. Toward the end of the eighteenth century, people began to lose confidence in the appeal to logic. They realized that rationalism, carried to extremes, became silly, that concentrating on the brain blinded them to the importance of the heart, and that differences among human beings were at least as important as their similarities. No longer willing to accept the rationalist laws of neoclassicism as trustworthy definitions of beauty, these people considered cultural standards to be a matter of good taste. In the early part of the 1800s, philosophers and artists would turn their backs on the entire classical world view and create a new cultural mode: Romanticism.

During the seventeenth and eighteenth centuries, three great political revolutions changed the governing systems of European peoples. Prior to this time, most people believed that monarchs reigned by divine right, that they represented the supreme human authority, and that they owed responsibility only to God. After this time, people believed that the ultimate political authority rested in the common folk themselves.

English Civil Wars

The first of the revolutions which brought about this change culminated in the English Civil Wars of the 1640s. In these wars, the Parliamentary

217

forces under Oliver Cromwell defeated the Royalist forces and, in 1649, executed Charles I. The English aristocrats who did not swear allegiance to Parliament went into exile in the court of France. Since Puritan England, under Cromwell's Commonwealth, considered theatre part of the trappings of the old order, public theatre ceased to exist in the 1640s, and most actors who wished to practice their craft went into exile with the court or toured Europe in itinerant troupes. Touring English actors helped spark the birth of German theatre, and Englishmen in Paris came to admire French neoclassicism. When England restored the monarchy in 1660, King Charles II had to acknowledge the supremacy of Parliament. During the period which followed, called the Restoration, English theatre artists attempted to adapt their native vision to the neoclassical modes they had learned on the Continent.

The American Revolution (1775-83) and the French Revolution (1789-99) clarified and extended the democratic principles established in the English Civil Wars.

France: Europe's Cultural Center

During the middle of the seventeenth century, France became the cultural center of Europe. Far from being an accident, France's cultural dominance resulted largely from the efforts of Cardinal Richelieu (1585-1642). As chief minister of Louis XIII, Richelieu strengthened the French monarchy by defeating numerous conspiracies of the nobles and eliminating divisive threats from the French Protestants or Huguenots. Not satisfied with a politically unified and powerful France, Richelieu also aimed to make it culturally strong. Accepting the Italian Renaissance as a standard, he sought to replace vestiges of medieval culture with neoclassicism. He invited Italian artists, actors, and scene designers to France, established a permanent, professional theatre company in Paris, constructed the first French proscenium arch theatre, the Palais-Royal, in his own palace, pressured the major Parisian theatres to eliminate the old mansion-and-platea staging, and helped establish the French Academy, which regulated matters of French literature and language.

Dramatic Theory

The principles of drama developed by the Renaissance theorists hardened into "rules" in the neoclasiscal period. These principles included:

The acceptability of only two fixed forms (tragedy and comedy);
Adherence to the unities of time, place, and action;
The five-act rule;
The insistence on decorum of character and language;
The expectation that theatre would teach good morals by demonstrating poetic justice.

The French classical dramatists, especially Racine and Molière, seemed to write naturally within these strictures, and the "rules" produced in their plays a classical focus of great power and beauty.

In England, however, the neoclassical system resulted in controversy. While in exile on the continent, the English intelligentsia learned to admire French classicism, and when they returned to England, they brought neoclassical concepts with them. Shakespeare and his contemporaries, however, had previously established an English mode of drama which continued to have great popular support and which was decidedly contrary to the neoclassical rules. This situation put the playwrights at odds with the critics and critics at odds with each other.

Drama theorists, during the seventeenth and eighteenth centuries, argued over the following topics: Are modern plays or ancient ones better? Are restoration plays or Shakespearean plays better? Are French plays or English plays better? Is reason or taste the better critical guide? Should drama appeal more to the head or to the heart? Do the neoclassical rules, supposedly based on logic, really make sense?

Among the great literary figures of the period who struggled with these questions were the Englishmen John Dryden (1631-1700), Alexander Pope (1688-1744), and Samuel Johnson (1709-84), the Frenchmen Boileau-Despréaux (1636-1711), Voltaire (1694-1778), and Denis Diderot (1713-84), and the German Gotthold Ephraim Lessing (1729-81). These theoreticians demonstrated the philosophical value of the study of dramatic principles and established the foundations of a modern critical tradition.

Dramatic Literature

The major playwrights of French neoclassicism were Pierre Corneille (1606-84), Molière (1622-73), and Jean Racine (1639-99). Molière's life and works are described later in this introduction, but the work of the two great French tragedians will be discussed here.

Pierre Corneille

Corneille began to write at about the same time that the neoclassical rules were gaining favor in France. His earliest plays, mostly comedies, gained him enough attention that Richelieu chose him as one of five playwrights who were to draft plays for him. Unwilling to subordinate his vision to Richelieu's demands, however, Corneille soon offended the cardinal and went his own way. *The Cid* (1637), his drama about a Spanish hero, triggered a noisy debate and marked the beginning of the crowning era of French classical drama. The controversy focused on the relationship between *The Cid* and the rules. The play violated the pure-form principle by concluding a serious action with a happy ending and compromised the principle of decorum because the heroine decides to marry her father's killer. It did obey the unities of time and place, but crowded so many incidents into a single day that it strained believability. And, unfortunately for the critics who favored the new rules, it was wildly popular. The furor of the debate served to draw attention to the neoclassical laws, and in subsequent plays, even Corneille managed to bring his sprawling imagination under their control. Besides *The Cid,* Corneille's best-known plays — all tragedies on Greek and Roman subjects — were *Horace* (1640), *Cinna* (1641), and *Polyeucte* (1642). After Torelli came to Paris in 1645, Corneille also wrote some "machine plays" to show off the Italian scene designer's technical devices. He was elected to the French Academy in 1647. During the last decades of his life, he collaborated in productions with Molière and developed an acrimonious competition with Racine.

Jean Racine

Jean Racine, a playwright who combined great poetry with complete mastery of the neoclassical principles, epitomizes French classical drama. Soon after coming to Paris from the religious community of Port-Royal, he made the acquaintance of Molière who, in 1664, staged his first play, *The Thébaïde*. After Molière produced Racine's second play, however, scandals, intrigue, and competition came between the two, and Racine went his own way. His plays *Andromaque* (1667) and *Iphigénie* (1674) were both successes, but his acknowledged masterpiece was his tragedy of guilty love, *Phèdre* (1677), a play which is to the French what *Hamlet* is to the English-speaking world. As fate would have it, however, Racine's many enemies arranged to have a second-rate playwright produce a play on the same subject at the same time and further contrived its greater success. Disgust over this affair, plus a court appointment as royal historiographer, led Racine to retire from theatre. He married, had seven children, and wrote only two plays after this, both biblical dramas written for private productions.

Racine's genius for depicting powerful, psychologically believable characters in the moment of their greatest inner conflict fit perfectly with the strictures of neoclassical drama. He was especially adept at creating great female characters who provided roles for many great French actresses including Mlle. Clairon (1723-1803), Rachel (1820-58), and Sarah Bernhardt (1844-1923).

Subsequent to the careers of Corneille, Molière, and Racine, French drama seemed to lose its creative edge. Trapped by the demands of neoclassicism and haunted by the giants of the mid-seventeenth century, French theatre would not exert world leadership again until the nineteenth century.

Restoration Comedy

But with the Restoration of the monarchy in London, English drama gained new life. English dramatists combined their native love for intricate plots with French cynicism and elements of neoclassicism. The re-established English upper-class provided them with both scandalous subject matter and an audience. Out of this mix came Restoration comedy. Restoration comedy, with its apparent aim of correcting social absurdities through the use of ridicule, was a kind of comedy of manners. It used witty, artificial language and plots with several intertwined story lines to depict the pretensions, follies, and immorality of well-to-do Londoners. The supporters of Restoration comedy argued that these plays punished immorality by ridiculing it and that they thus fulfilled the classical expectations of comedy. The Puritan critics of the genre were probably correct, however, in countering that the sexual intrigues portrayed in the plays titillated the audiences more than they corrected their morals. Three important playwrights of Restoration comedy were Sir George Etherege (1634-91) who wrote *The Man of Mode* (1676), William Wycherley (1640-1715) who wrote *The Country Wife* (1675), and William Congreve (1670-1729) who wrote *The Way of the World* (1700).

Incensed by the sexual hanky-panky in Restoration comedy, the Puritan elements in English society maintained a steady outcry against the form. Jeremy Collier finally brought Restoration comedy to an end with his pamphlet, "A Short View of the Immorality and Profaneness of the English Stage" (1698). Collier used the method of stating the neoclassical principles — especially those which required drama to contribute to moral improvement — and then showing that, although the restoration comedians claimed to support those principles, they violated them in their plays. His attack succeeded, in part, because of a shift in fashion away from cynicism toward what came to be known as "sensibility."

Sentimental Comedy and Domestic Tragedy

Restoration comedy gave way to sentimental comedy and domestic tragedy. Sentimental comedy, which dominated English playwriting throughout the eighteenth century and which had its French counterpart in *comédie larmoyante,* dealt with honorable, middle-class lovers who suffered through stressful situations and eventually found happiness. Comic only in the sense that they ended happily, sentimental comedies aimed to stir the higher passions and move their audiences to tears. Perhaps the best sample of sentimental comedy is *The Conscious Lovers* (1772) by Sir Richard Steele (1672-1729) in which a highly principled young man avoids a duel and eventually marries his beloved, a decent but poor woman, who turns out to be the long-lost daughter of a wealthy man. Domestic tragedy turned away from the traditional tragic focus on royalty to deal instead with the temptations and disasters of middle-class folk. For instance, *The London Merchant, or The History of George Barnwell* (1731) by George Lillo (1693-1739) tells the story of a young apprentice who is seduced and corrupted by a high-class prostitute. These eighteenth-century forms blurred the distinctions between comedy and tragedy and led directly into the development, in the next century, of melodrama.

Stagecraft and Theatre Architecture

Perspective Scenery

Italian Renaissance artists rediscovered and developed the principles of perspective painting. The technique of painting a scene on a two-dimensional surface so that it appeared to have actual depth became wildly popular and was soon applied to stage settings. Perspective scenery differed completely from the medieval mansion-and-platea scenery and also the architectural-facade staging of Elizabethan plays. Unlike these older approaches, which it eventually replaced, perspective scenery gave the illusion of a real-life location and also represented a single place instead of simultaneously depicting a variety of locations.

Giacomo Torelli

The specialized construction and painting skills demanded by perspective scenery provided work for a new theatre specialist, the scene designer. The most influential of the classical scene designers, Giacomo Torelli (1608-78) began work in Italy where his invention of scenic effects earned him the title, "The Great Magician." Cardinal Mazarin, Richelieu's successor, invited him to Paris in 1645. There he worked at Molière's theatre, the

Petite-Bourbon, and designed stage machinery which became standard scenic equipment.

Perspective scenery called for a specialized stage. In order to create the effect of ground rising to meet a horizon line in the distance, theatre architects raked the stage floor upward towards the rear. At the side of the stage, designers painted scenic elements on a series of wing flats which stood parallel with the front of the stage. Each succeeding pair of wings was shorter than the set in front of it, and scenery was painted on it in a smaller scale. Overhead scenic elements such as ceilings or clouds were painted on borders which corresponded to the pairs of wings. A drop or pair of shutter flats completed the scene at the rear of the stage. Since an actor standing beside an upstage flat would ruin the illusion by dwarfing the small-scale scenery, acting was confined to a level apron area downstage of the set. In order to hide the off-stage areas and the stage machinery from the audience, theatre architects separated the auditorium from the stage with a proscenium wall.

Torelli devised an ingenious system for changing perspective scenery. Originally, wings rested in grooves, and technicians changed settings by sliding the flats off stage to reveal the next set of wings with the next scene painted on them. These shifts occurred without closing the curtain, and the change from scene to scene provided part of the enjoyment of watching a play. A smooth scene shift, however, required many stage hands and a good deal of coordination. To solve this problem, Torelli designed machinery called the "chariot-and-pole" system. He attached the flats to poles which extended beneath the stage through slots and rested on wheeled components called chariots. The chariots rode on tracks and were connected to a winch with an intricate mechanism of pulleys and gears; by turning the winch, a few stagehands could shift an entire set with perfect synchronization.

New and Improved Theatres

New theatres were built to accommodate perspective staging. These proscenium arch theatres not only provided the necessary stage environment and equipment, but also reorganized the audience. The new auditorium was a compromise between the demands of perspective staging and the social expectations of audiences. Perspective scenery created its illusion most effectively for viewers located along the center line as it extended into the audience. Auditoriums, therefore, became deeper and narrower so that a greater portion of the audience could sit near this axis. At the same time, many people attended the theatre to be seen and to see each other. To accommodate this desire, theatre architects arranged the audience in three sections: a more-or-less flat area directly in front of the stage, surrounded on three sides by tiers of private boxes, above which was located an open gallery. These areas, called the "pit," the "boxes," and the "gallery," were occupied respectively by the middle classes, the upper classes, and the servants. The proscenium arch theatre became standard in Europe and America, and although theatre buildings changed size, audience arrangement, and stage detail, they remained essentially the same throughout the next four centuries.

Performance Conventions

Commedia Dell'arte

During the Renaissance, Italians created a dramatic form called the *commedia dell'arte*. The distinction "dell'arte," meaning "professional," differentiated this kind of theatre from the "commedia erudita" produced by intellectual amateurs. Commedia dell'arte was an improvisational form. Rather than performing a memorized script, the actors worked from sketchy "scenarios" which were posted backstage.

A commedia troupe consisted of about a dozen actors and actresses. Each performer specialized in playing a single character, complete with costume, make-up, personality, and behavior patterns; and each scenario, regardless of subject matter, setting, or situation, was designed for the same group of stock characters. Commedia characters included young, romantic lovers, saucy servant girls like "Columbine," old men like "Pantalone" and the lawyer "Dottore," and masked male servants or "zanni" like "Arlecchino," "Pedrolino," and "Pulcinella." With the exception of the young lovers, most of the characters wore masks. The characters of the zanni are more familiar to English speakers as Harlequin, Pierrot, and Punch.

Commedia dell'arte became extremely popular, and the troupes toured all over Europe. Some of the most famous of the companies during the sixteenth century were the Gelosi, the Confidenti, and the Uniti. The influence of commedia is evident in other theatres of the period. Shakespeare's *Comedy of Errors,* for instance, uses *lazzi* ("routines") from Italian comedy, and Molière, who shared the Petite-Bourbon Theatre with an Italian troupe, uses commedia-like characters in his plays.

The actresses of commedia dell'arte were likely the first female theatre professionals in Europe. Perhaps as a result of the Italian example, professional French troupes included actresses from the beginning, and when the English stage was re-established during the Restoration, it imported the practice of assigning female roles to women.

Theatrical Organization

Realizing that theatre had great potential for forming public opinion, both the French and the English governments attempted to control dramatic art. They did this in part by licensing only a limited number of theatres. In Paris, during Molière's time, there were four theatres: the Hôtel de Bourgogne, the Marais, the Petite-Bourbon, and the Palais-Royal. By 1680, under the influence of Louis XIV, these had been reduced to one theatre, the Comédie-Francaise. In England, the patent theatres were Drury Lane and Covent Garden. The governments also practiced censorship. In England, the Licensing Act of 1737 required that all plays given in public had to be licensed by the Lord Chamberlain's office. To receive a license, a play had to meet a variety of standards regarding language and subject matter. The Licensing Act was finally rescinded in 1968 under pressure from changing social mores and concepts of artistic freedom.

Influential English Actors

In England, the eighteenth century was the age of the great classic actors. Typically during this period, a theatre would be the home of a single acting company who would present plays in revolving repertory. Since relatively few new scripts were produced, audiences knew most of the plays and went to see how their favorite actors would perform familiar roles. James Quin (1693-1766) set the pace for the earlier part of the century with a powerful, declamatory style. As was typical of the period, he made no attempt at historical accuracy in costume or make-up, but instead played all his characters, regardless of era or nationality, in current English dress. David Garrick (1717-79), the greatest of English actors, introduced a much more natural style than Quin's. Through his astute management of Drury Lane and a two-year tour of the Continent, he did much to elevate the reputation of English theatre. John Philip Kemble (1757-1823) managed both Drury Lane and Covent Garden and earned respect for his controlled acting style. He also began to introduce historical accuracy in costume and setting, a trend which continued throughout the next two centuries.

Molière

A popular actor, capable theatre manager, and prolific playwright, Molière dominated French theatre in the middle of the seventeenth century and wrote some of the best comedies in the history of world drama. Jean-Baptiste Poquelin, born in 1622, studied law and was expected to succeed his father who had a position in the king's court. In 1643, however, he turned his back on the life of a courtier, took the stage name Molière, and joined with a group of actors to found a new theatre. This venture soon failed, and when Molière was released from debtor's prison, he joined some of his former colleagues and toured the provinces for thirteen years, writing and acting comedies and learning his craft. In 1658, he returned to Paris where his company performed Corneille's tragedy *Nicomède* for the king. The performance disappointed the court, but at its conclusion, Molière requested permission to present one of the comedies his troupe had been touring. The ensuing performance of his farce *Le Docteur amoureux* so pleased the king that Molière's company was allowed to share the Petite-Bourbon with the resident Italian troupe there.

By 1661, Molière had become the acknowledged master comedian of Paris and his company moved into the Palais-Royal. He won the continuing patronage of Louis XIV who stood as godfather to his child and protected him in the succession of conflicts that plagued his private life and career. This patronage carried a price, however, for Molière had to write and produce many court entertainments in which the king and courtiers joined Molière and his company as performers. By 1673, overwork, intrigue, and an unhappy marriage had exhausted Molière. He collapsed on stage while playing the title role in *The Hypochondriac,* and died soon thereafter. Because of the Church's rules against acting, Molière was refused Christian burial.

Molière wrote over thirty scripts which still exist, plus other plays, written during his touring years, which are lost. Among the best of his works are the short farces *The Affected Young Ladies* (1658) and *Sganarelle,* or *The Imaginary Cuckold* (1660) and the full-length comedies *The Misanthrope* (1666) and *The Miser* (1668). He wrote *Tartuffe,* a biting satire about a puritanical fanatic, in 1664, but the religious community put up such an outcry that it could not be presented publicly until 1667. Subsequently it became one of his most loved plays.

Molière made comedy the equal of tragedy in neoclassical France, and in later centuries his plays were produced more frequently than those of his tragic contemporaries. He raised comedy above the level of farce and made it a vehicle for social criticism. Entertaining, beautifully constructed, and insightful about human nature, Molière's comedies demonstrate the potential of the neoclassical mode.

The Hypochondriac (The Imaginary Invalid)

Dramaturgy

This play gives an example of the major features of comedy, a form that remained essentially the same from Menander in fourth-century-BC Greece to Neil Simon in twentieth-century America.

Comedy has a rising action. That is, comedies typically begin with the central characters stuck in a ridiculous situation, then trace the development of a series of foolish schemes, and conclude by resolving everything happily, often with a marriage. Unlike tragedians, comic writers usually invent their story lines rather than taking them from history or legend and almost always focus on middle-class life rather than royalty. Comedy usually uses a common style in contrast with the elevated style traditional in tragedy. Finally, comedy focuses on the ridiculous and the grotesque partly for the purpose of entertaining the audience and partly for the purpose of criticizing and correcting social aberrations and human folly. Comedy celebrates human resilience and our ability to weasel out of the predicaments we repeatedly get ourselves into.

Molière's play starts out with Argan's household in the throes of a mess of Argan's own making, traces the hare-brained plans of Argan, his daughter's lover, his maid, and his brother, and results in his happiness and the union of the young lovers. The characters, who all come from the middle or lower classes, include many of the types common in Molière's other plays and in many comedies throughout dramatic history — the foolish older man, the saucy servant, the romantic lovers, the wise brother, the shrewish wife, and the greedy, incompetent professional. The dialog is written in everyday prose and spiced up with occasional songs.

In the midst of the entertainment, Molière takes care to do his duty as a serious comedian: He ridicules the foolish human tendencies to be overly concerned with one's health and to use one's children for selfish purposes, he lambastes ineptitude and greed in the medical profession, and he debates current theoretical topics like the ancients-versus-the-moderns debate and the relative values of tradition and authority. He even has his characters discuss the proper purposes of comedy and comment on his own writing.

Molière also follows most of the neoclassical rules in *The Hypochondriac.* For instance, he confines the play's action to a single room and to a single day, and he also concentrates on a single story-line, the betrothal of Argan's daughter. The result is a strongly unified play that makes its impact with more focus than, for instance, a comedy by Shakespeare.

Molière increased the entertainment values of *The Hypochondriac* by adding song and dance routines to the play. In its original, it began with a short spoken prologue and a semidramatic song and dance sequence featuring shepherds, shepherdesses, and mythic characters common in pastoral entertainments. Between Acts 1 and 2, there was a musical interlude featuring Toinet's suitor, Polichinello, who comes to serenade his mistress and is beaten for his efforts. And between Acts 2 and 3, singers and dancers in Moorish costume entertain the audience. These three interludes, having little connection with the comedy's story, are typically omitted from printed texts of the play, but some versions, such as the one printed here, include the final interlude after Act 3, Argan's farcical initiation into the medical profession.

In typical French fashion, the script makes a numbered scene break every time a character exits or enters. Because of this practice, a segment of a play delineated by the entrance or exit of a character is called a French scene. Dividing a play this way differs from the practice in Shakespearean theatre where a scene break indicates a change in time and/or place.

Production History

Le Malade Imaginaire was first performed at the Palais-Royal on the tenth of February in 1673 with Molière in the role of Argan. During the fourth performance, Molière took ill, and he died later the same evening. The company continued to present the play for a while and then again revived it the next year when they presented it fifty-eight times with great success. The first authoritative edition of the play was published in 1682. This edition titled the play a "comedy combined with music and dances." The present version of the play was part of the first complete English translation of Molière's works. Done in 1739 by English playwrights H. Baker and J. Miller, the translation is a good sample of neoclassical theatre. The play has frequently been translated into English under titles such as *The Hypochondriac* and *The Imaginary Invalid*.

As long as people use their illnesses to wring pity from others, as long as laymen stand in awe of professionals, as long as parents manipulate their children to their own ends, as long as human greed and foolishness exist, Molière's *Hypochondriac* will have a place in the theatre.

Neoclassical Theatre Timeline

WILLIAM SHAKESPEARE (1564-1616)
LOUIS XIII (1601-43; KING 1610-43)
CARDINAL RICHELIEU (1585-1642)
RENÉ DESCARTES (1596-1650)
PIERRE CORNEILLE (1606-84)
GIACOMO TORELLI (1608-78)
MOLIÈRE (1622-73)
"THE HYPOCHONDRIAC" (1673)
JOHN DRYDEN (1631-1700)
GEORGE ETHEREGE (c. 1634-91)
● FRENCH ACADEMY ORGANIZED (1636)
BOILEAU-DESPRÉAUX (1636-1711)
WILLIAM WYCHERLEY (1640-1715)
LOUIS XIV (1638-1715; KING 1643-1715)
JEAN RACINE (1639-99)
● PALAIS-ROYAL THEATRE CONSTRUCTED (1641)
ENGLISH COMMONWEALTH (1649-60)
WILLIAM CONGREVE (1670-1729)
RICHARD STEELE (1672-1729)
JOHANN S. BACH (1685-1750)
ALEXANDER POPE (1688-1744)
GEORGE LILLO (1693-1739)
JAMES QUIN (1693-1766)
VOLTAIRE (1694-1778)
COLLIER'S "SHORT VIEW OF THE IMMORALITY..." (1698) ●
SAMUEL JOHNSON (1709-84)
DENIS DIDEROT (1713-84)
DAVID GARRICK (1717-79)
GOTTHOLD EPHRAIM LESSING (1729-81)
LICENSING ACT, ENGLAND (1737) ●
WOLFGANG AMADEUS MOZART (1756-91)
JOHN PHILIP KEMBLE (1757-1823)
AMERICAN REVOLUTION (1775-83)
FRENCH REVOLUTION (1789-99)
NAPOLEON BONAPARTE (1769-1821)

- 1830
- 1820
- 1810
- 1800
- 1790
- 1780
- 1770
- 1760
- 1750
- 1740
- 1730
- 1720
- 1710
- 1700
- 1690
- 1680
- 1670
- 1660
- 1650
- 1640
- 1630
- 1620
- 1610
- 1600
- 1590
- 1580
- 1570
- 1560

THE HYPOCHONDRIAC
(Le Malade Imaginaire)

by Molière
translated by H. Baker and J. Miller

The action of the play takes place in Paris in the sickroom of a citizen named Argan.

CAST OF CHARACTERS[1]

ARGAN
the hypochondriac

BELINA
Argan's second wife

ANGELICA
Argan's daughter, in love with Cleanthes

LOUISON
Argan's young daughter, Angelica's sister

BERALDO
Argan's brother

CLEANTHES
in love with Angelica

MR. DIAFOIRUS
a physician

THOMAS DIAFOIRUS
Mr. Diafoirus' son, Angelica's suitor

MR. PURGON
a physician

MR. FLEURANT
an apothecary

MR. BONNEFOY
a notary

TOINET
Argan's servant

[1]The cast is presented in a compromise between social order and dramatic importance. Argan, as the central character in the play, is presented before the physicians, and his family follows in hierarchial social order from oldest to youngest. Toinet, who is extremely important to the play, comes last because she is a servant. Several of the character names have symbolic meaning: "Diafoirus" is a play on the word for feces, "Purgon" refers to laxatives, "Fleurant" alludes to the typical practice of pharmacists in Molière's time who adjusted their prescriptions by *sniffing* the urine and feces of their clients, and "Bonnefoy" means good-faith.

ACT I

Scene I

Scene: Argan's Chamber

ARGAN: *(Sitting with a table before him, casting up his apothecary's bills with counters.)* Three and two make five, and five makes ten, and ten makes twenty. Three and two make five. Item, the twenty-fourth, a little insinuative, preparative and emollient clyster[1] to mollify, moisten, and refresh his worship's bowels. What pleases me in Mr. Fleurant, my apothecary, is that his bills are always extremely civil. His worship's bowels, thirty sous. Ay, but Mr. Fleurant, being civil isn't all, you ought to be reasonable too, and not fleece your patients. Thirty sous for a clyster! Your servant, I have told you of this already. You have charged me in your other bills but twenty sous, and twenty sous in the language of an apothecary is as much as to say ten sous; there they are, ten sous.[2] Item, the said day, a good detersive clyster composed of double cathlolicum, rhubarb, *mel rosatum*, etc., according to prescription, to scour, wash and cleanse his honour's abdomen, thirty sous; with your leave ten sous. Item, the said day at night, an hepatic, soporific, and somniferous julep, composed to make his honour sleep, thirty-five sous; I don't complain of that, for it made me sleep well. Ten, fifteen, sixteen, seventeen sous, six deniers. Item, the twenty-fifth, a good purgative[3] and corroborative medicine composed of *cassia recens* with *senna levantina*, etc., according to the prescription of Mr. Purgon to expel and evacuate his honour's choler, four livres. How! Mr. Fleurant, you jest sure, you should treat your patients with some humanity. Mr. Purgon did not prescribe you to set down four livres; put down, put down three livres if you please — fifty sous. — Item, the said day, an anodyne and astringent potion to make his honour sleep, thirty sous. Good — fifteen sous. Item, the twenty-sixth, a carminative clyster to expel his honour's wind, thirty sous. Ten sous, Mr. Fleurant. Item, his honour's clyster repeated at night as before, thirty sous. Ten sous, Mr. Fleurant. Item, the twenty-seventh, a good medicine composed to dissipate and drive out his honour's ill humours, three livres. Good, fifty sous; I'm glad you are reasonable. Item, the twenty-eighth, a dose of clarified, dulcified milk, to sweeten, lenify, temper and refresh his honour's blood, twenty sous. Good, ten sous. Item, a cordial preservative potion, composed of twelve grains of bezoar, syrup of lemons, pomegranates, etc., according to prescription, five livres. Oh! Mr. Fleurant, softly, if you please, if you use people in this manner, one would be sick no longer, content yourself with four livres; sixty sous. Three and two make five, and five makes ten, and ten makes twenty. Sixty-three livres, four sous and six deniers. So then in this month I have taken one, two, three, four, five, six, seven, eight purges; and one, two, three, four, five, six, seven, eight, nine, ten, eleven, twelve

---

[1]clyster: enema.
[2]there they are, ten sous: As Argan adds up what he owes the pharmacist, he also decides to pay less than the pharmacist is charging.
[3]purgative: laxative.

229

clysters; and the last month there were twelve purges, and twenty clysters. I don't wonder if I am not so well this month as the last. I shall tell Mr. Purgon of it, that he may set this matter to rights. Here, take me away all these things. There's nobody there, 'tis in vain to speak, I'm always left alone; there's no way to keep 'em here. *(He rings a bell.)* They don't hear; my bell's not loud enough. *(Rings.)* No. *(Rings again.)* They are deaf. Toinet! *(Making as much noise with his bell as possible.)* Just as if I did not ring at all. Jade! Slut! *(Finding he still rings in vain.)* I'm mad. Drelin, drelin, drelin,[4] the deuce take the carrion. Is it possible they should leave a poor sick creature in this manner! Drelin, drelin, drelin, oh! lamentable! Drelin, drelin, drelin. Oh! Heavens, they'll let me die here. Drelin, drelin, drelin.

Scene II

Toinet, Argan.[5]

TOINET: *(Entering.)* Here I am.

ARGAN: Oh, ye jade! O carrion!

TOINET: *(Pretending to have hurt her head.)* The deuce take your impatience, you hurry one so much that I've knocked my head against the window-shutter.

ARGAN: *(Angrily.)* Ah! baggage —

TOINET: *(Interrupting him.)* Oh!

ARGAN: 'Tis a

TOINET: Oh!

ARGAN: 'Tis an hour —

TOINET: Oh!

ARGAN: Thou hast left me —

TOINET: Oh!

ARGAN: Hold your tongue, you slut, that I may scold thee.

TOINET: Very well, i'faith, I like that, after what I've done to myself.

ARGAN: Thou hast made me bawl my throat sore, gipsy.

TOINET: And you have made me break my head, one's as good as t'other; so we are quit, with your leave.

ARGAN: How, hussy —

TOINET: If you scold, I'll cry.

ARGAN: To leave me, you jade —

TOINET: *(Still interrupting him.)* Oh!

ARGAN: Impudence! thou wouldst —

TOINET: Oh!

ARGAN: What! must not I have the pleasure of scolding her neither?

TOINET: Have your pennyworth of scolding with all my heart.

ARGAN: You hinder me from it, hussy, by interrupting me at every turn.

TOINET: If you have the pleasure of scolding, I must on my part, have the pleasure of crying: everyone to his fancy is but reasonable. Oh!

ARGAN: Come, I must pass over this. Take me away this thing, minx, take

[4]Drelin, drelin, drelin: Argan imitates the sound of his bell, "Tinkle, tinkle, tinkle."
[5]In typical French style, this script does not indicate the entrance or exit of a character by means of stage directions; instead a scene break indicates a change in the number of characters on stage, and the names immediately after the scene number tell which characters are present.

me away this thing. *(Rising out of his chair.)* Has my clyster worked well today?

TOINET: Your clyster!

ARGAN: Yes, have I voided much bilious matter?

TOINET: I'faith, I don't trouble myself about those matters. 'Tis for Mr. Fleurant to have his nose in 'em, since he has the profit of 'em.

ARGAN: Take care to get me some broth ready, for the other I'm to take by and by.

TOINET: This Mr. Fleurant and Mr. Purgon divert themselves finely with your carcass; they have a rare milch-cow of you. I would fain ask 'em what distemper you have, that you must take so much physic.

ARGAN: Hold your tongue, ignorance, 'tisn't for you to control the decrees of the faculty. Bring my daughter Angelica to me, I have something to say to her.

TOINET: Here she comes of herself; she has guessed your intention.

Scene III

Angelica, Toinet, Argan.

ARGAN: Come hither, Angelica, you come opportunely, I want to speak with you.

ANGELICA: I am ready to hear you, sir.

ARGAN: Stay. *(To TOINET.)* Give me my cane, I'll come again presently.[6]

TOINET: Go quick, sir, go. Mr. Fleurant finds us in business.

Scene IV

Angelica, Toinet.

ANGELICA: Toinet.

TOINET: Well.

ANGELICA: Look upon me a little.

TOINET: Well, I do look upon you.

ANGELICA: Toinet.

TOINET: Well, what would you have with Toinet?

ANGELICA: Don't you guess who I would speak of?

TOINET: I much suspect of our young lover; for 'tis on him that our conversation has entirely turned for these six days past, and you're not well unless you are talking of him every moment.

ANGELICA: Since you know that, why are not you the first then to talk of him to me, and spare me the pains of forcing you on this discourse?

TOINET: You don't give me time to do it; you have such a care about that matter, that 'tis difficult to be beforehand with you.

ANGELICA: I own to thee that I am never weary of talking of him to thee, and that my heart eagerly takes advantage of every moment to disclose itself to thee. But tell me, dost thou condemn, Toinet, the sentiments I have for him?

TOINET: Far from it.

ANGELICA: Am I in the wrong to abandon myself to these soft impressions?

TOINET: I don't say that.

[6]Argan exits quickly to respond to his pharmacist's effective laxative.

ANGELICA: And wouldst thou have me insensible to the tender protesta-
tions of that ardent passion he expresses for me?

TOINET: Heaven forbid!

ANGELICA: Tell me a little, dost not thou perceive as well as I something
of Providence, some act of destiny in the unexpected adventure of our
acquaintance?

TOINET: Yes.

ANGELICA: Dost not thou think that action of engaging in my defence,
without knowing me, was perfectly gallant?

TOINET: Ay.

ANGELICA: That 'twas impossible to make a more generous use of it?

TOINET: Agreed.

ANGELICA: And that he did all this with the best grace in the world?

TOINET: Oh, yes.

ANGELICA: Dost not thou think, Toinet, that he's well made in his person?

TOINET: Certainly.

ANGELICA: That he has the best air in the world?

TOINET: Undoubtedly.

ANGELICA: That his discourse, as well as actions, has something noble in it?

TOINET: That's sure.

ANGELICA: That never anything was heard more affectionate than all that
he says to me?

TOINET: 'Tis true.

ANGELICA: And that there's nothing more vexatious than the restraint
I'm kept under, which hinders all communication of the soft transports
of that mutual ardour which Heaven inspires us with?

TOINET: You're in the right.

ANGELICA: But, dear Toinet, dost thou think he loves me so much as he
tells me?

TOINET: Um — Those kind o' things are sometimes not absolutely to be
trusted to. The show of love is very much like the reality; and I have
seen notable actors of that part.

ANGELICA: Ah! Toinet, what sayest thou? Alas! in the manner he speaks,
is it really possible that he should not tell me the truth?

TOINET: Be it as it will, you'll shortly be made clear in that point; and the
resolution which he wrote you yesterday he had taken to ask you in
marriage, is a ready way to discover to you if he spoke truth or not.
That will be a thorough proof of it.

ANGELICA: Ah! Toinet, if this man deceives me, I'll never believe a man
as long as I live.

TOINET: Here's your father come back.

Scene V

Argan, Angelica, Toinet.

ARGAN: *(Sitting down.)* So, daughter, I'm going to tell you a piece of news,
which you little expect perhaps. You are asked of me in marriage.
How's this? You laugh. That's pleasant enough, ah! that word marriage. There's nothing so merry to young girls. Ah, nature! nature!
for what I can see then, child, I have no occasion to ask you if you are

willing to be married.

ANGELICA: 'Tis my duty, sir, to do whatever you shall please to enjoin me.

ARGAN: I'm glad to have such a dutiful daughter; the thing is fixed then, and I have promised you.

ANGELICA: 'Tis for me, sir, blindly to follow all your resolutions.

ARGAN: My wife, your stepmother, had a desire I should make a nun of you, and your little sister Louison likewise; and has always persisted in it.

TOINET: *(Aside.)* The sly beast had her reasons for it.

ARGAN: She would not consent to this match, but I have carried it, and my word is given.

ANGELICA: Ah! sir, how much am I obliged to you for all your goodness!

TOINET: Troth, I take this well of you now, this is the wisest action you ever did in your life.

ARGAN: I have not yet seen the person, but they tell me I shall be satisfied with him, and thou too.

ANGELICA. Most certainly, sir.

ARGAN: How! hast thou seen him?

ANGELICA: Since your consent authorises me to open my heart to you, I'll not conceal from you, that chance brought us acquainted about six days since, and that the request which has been made to you, is the effect of an inclination which we conceived for one another at first sight.

ARGAN: I was not told of that, but I'm very glad of it, and 'tis so much the better that things go in that manner. They say that he's a jolly, well-made young fellow.

ANGELICA: True, sir.

ARGAN: Well shaped.

ANGELICA: Without doubt.

ARGAN: Agreeable in his person.

ANGELICA: Most certainly.

ARGAN: Of a good countenance.

ANGELICA: Extremely good.

ARGAN: Discreet, and well born.

ANGELICA: Perfectly.

ARGAN: Very genteel.

ANGELICA: The most genteel in the world.

ARGAN: Speaks Latin and Greek well.

ANGELICA: I don't know that.

ARGAN: And will be admitted doctor in three days' time.

ANGELICA: He, sir!

ARGAN: Yes. Has not he told thee so?

ANGELICA: No indeed. Who told you so?

ARGAN: Mr. Purgon.

ANGELICA: Does Mr. Purgon know him?

ARGAN: A fine question! He must needs know him since he's his nephew.

ANGELICA: Cleanthes, Mr. Purgon's nephew!

ARGAN: What Cleanthes? We are speaking of the person you are asked for in marriage.

ANGELICA: Well, ay.

ARGAN: Very well, and that's the nephew of Mr. Purgon, who is the son of his brother-in-law, the physician Mr. Diafoirus; and this son's name is Thomas Diafoirus, not Cleanthes; and Mr. Purgon, Mr. Fleurant, and I, concluded the match this morning, and tomorrow this intended son-in-law is to be brought to me by his father. What's the matter? you look quite astonished.

ANGELICA: 'Tis because I find, sir, that you have been speaking of one person, and I understood another.

TOINET: What, sir, would you entertain so burlesque a design? And with so much wealth as you have, would you marry your daughter to a physician?

ARGAN: Yes. What business have you, hussy, to concern yourself, impudence as thou art?

TOINET: Good now, softly, sir, you fly immediately to invectives. Can't we reason together without falling into a passion? Come, let's talk in cool blood. What is your reason, pray, for such a marriage?

ARGAN: My reason is, that seeing myself infirm, and sick as I am, I would procure me a son-in-law, and relations physicians, in order to depend on good assistance against my distemper, and to have in my family sources of remedies which are necessary for me, and to be myself at consultations and prescriptions.

TOINET: Very well, that's giving a reason, and there's a pleasure in answering one another calmly. But, sir, lay your hand on your heart. Are you really sick?

ARGAN: How, jade, am I sick? am I sick, impudence?

TOINET: Well, yes, sir, you are sick, let us have no quarrel about that. Yes, you are very sick, I agree to't, and more sick than you think; that's over. But your daughter is to marry a husband for herself, and not being sick, it isn't necessary to give her a physician.

ARGAN: 'Tis for my sake that I give her this physician, and a girl of good-nature should be overjoyed to marry for the benefit of her father's health.

TOINET: Lookee, sir, will you let me as a friend give you a piece of advice?

ARGAN: What's that advice?

TOINET: Not to think of this match.

ARGAN: And the reason, pray?

TOINET: The reason's this, that your daughter won't consent to it.

ARGAN: She won't consent to it?

TOINET: No.

ARGAN: My daughter?

TOINET: Your daughter. She'll tell you that she has nothing to do with Mr. Diafoirus, nor with his son, Thomas Diafoirus, nor all the Diafoirus's in the world.

ARGAN: But I have something to do with 'em. Besides, the match is more advantageous than you think for. Mr. Diafoirus has only this son to inherit all he has, and moreover, Mr. Purgon, who has neither wife nor children, gives him all his estate in favour of this marriage, and Mr. Purgon is a man that hath a good eight thousand livres a year.

TOINET: He must have killed a world of people to become so rich.

ARGAN: Eight thousand livres a year is something, without reckoning the father's estate.

TOINET: All this, sir, is fair and fine. But I still return to the same story. I advise you between ourselves to choose another husband for her, for she's not made to be Madame Diafoirus.

ARGAN: But I'll have it be so.

TOINET: Oh! fie, don't say that.

ARGAN: How! not say that?

TOINET: No.

ARGAN: And why shall I not say it?

TOINET: They'll say you don't know what you talk of.

ARGAN: They may say what they please; but I tell you, I'll have her make good the promise I have given.

TOINET: No, I am sure that she'll not do it.

ARGAN: I'll force her to it then.

TOINET: She'll not do it, I tell ye.

ARGAN: She shall do it, or I'll put her into a convent.

TOINET: You?

ARGAN: I.

TOINET: Good!

ARGAN: How, good?

TOINET: You shall not put her into a convent.

ARGAN: I shall not put her into a convent?

TOINET: No.

ARGAN: No!

TOINET: No.

ARGAN: Hey-day, this is pleasant enough; I shall not put my daughter into a convent, if I please?

TOINET: No, I tell you.

ARGAN: Who shall hinder me from it?

TOINET: Yourself.

ARGAN: Myself?

TOINET: Yes, you would not have the heart.

ARGAN: I shall.

TOINET: You jest.

ARGAN: I don't jest.

TOINET: Fatherly tenderness will hinder you.

ARGAN: It won't hinder me.

TOINET: A little tear or two, her arms thrown about your neck, a dear papa pronounced tenderly, will be enough to move you.

ARGAN: All that will do nothing.

TOINET: Yes, yes.

ARGAN: I tell ye that I won't 'bate an inch on't.

TOINET: You trifle.

ARGAN: You shall not say that I trifle.

TOINET: Lack-a-day, I know you, you are good-natured.

ARGAN: *(Angrily.)* I am not good-natured, I'm ill-natured when I please.

TOINET: Softly, sir, you don't remember that you are sick.

ARGAN: I command her absolutely to prepare to take the husband I speak of.

TOINET: And I absolutely forbid her to do it.

ARGAN: Whereabouts are we then? and what boldness is this for a slut of a servant to talk at this rate before her master?

TOINET: When a master does not consider what he does, a sensible servant is in the right to inform him better.

ARGAN: *(Running after TOINET.)* Ah! insolence, I'll knock thee down.

TOINET: *(Running from him and putting the chair between her and him.)* 'Tis my duty to oppose anything that would disgrace you.

ARGAN: *(Running after her in a passion round the chair with his cane in his hand.)* Come here, come here, that I may teach thee how to speak.

TOINET: *(Saving herself on the opposite side of the chair to where Argan is.)* I interest myself as I ought, to hinder you from doing such a foolish thing.

ARGAN: Jade!

TOINET: No, I'll never consent to this match.

ARGAN: Baggage!

TOINET: I'll not have her marry your Thomas Diafoirus.

ARGAN: Carrion!

TOINET: And she'll obey me sooner than you.

ARGAN: Angelica, won't you lay hold of that slut for me?

ANGELICA: Alas, sir, don't make yourself sick.

ARGAN: If thou dost not lay hold of her for me, I'll refuse thee my blessing.

TOINET: And I'll disinherit her, if she does obey you.

ARGAN: *(Throwing himself in his chair.)* Oh! oh! I can bear it no longer. This is enough to kill me.

Scene VI

Belina, Argan.

ARGAN: Ah! wife, come hither.

BELINA: What's the matter, my poor spouse?

ARGAN: Come hither to my assistance.

BELINA: What is it then that's the matter, my dear child?

ARGAN: My love.

BELINA: My soul.

ARGAN: They have been putting me in a passion.

BELINA: Alas! my poor little love! and how then, my soul?

ARGAN: Your slut Toinet is grown more insolent than ever.

BELINA: Don't put yourself in a passion then.

ARGAN: She has made me mad, my life.

BELINA: Softly, my child.

ARGAN: She has been thwarting me this hour about things that I'm resolved to do.

BELINA: There, there, softly.

ARGAN: And has had the impudence to tell me that I'm not sick.

BELINA: She's an impertinent gipsy.

ARGAN: You know, my heart, how the matter is.

BELINA: Yes, my heart, she's in the wrong.

ARGAN: My love, that slut will kill me.

BELINA: Oh so, oh so!

ARGAN: She's the cause of all the choler I breed.

BELINA: Don't fret yourself so much.

ARGAN: And I have bid you, I know not how many times, turn her away from me.

BELINA: Alas, child, there are no servants, men or women, who have not their faults. We are sometimes forced to bear with their bad qualities for the sake of their good ones. This wench is dexterous, careful, diligent, and above all honest; and you know that at present there's need of great precaution with regard to those we take. Harkee, Toinet.

Scene VII

Argan, Belina, Toinet.

TOINET: Madam.

BELINA: What's the reason that you put my dear in this passion?

TOINET: *(In a soft tone.)* I, madam? Alas! I don't know what you mean, I think of nothing but to please my master in everything.

ARGAN: Ah! Traitress!

TOINET: He told us that he intended to give his daughter in marriage to the son of Mr. Diafoirus; I answered him that I thought the match was very advantageous for her; but believed he would do better to put her into a convent.

BELINA: There's no great harm in that, and I think she's in the right.

ARGAN: Ah! my love, dost thou believe her? she's a wicked jade. She said a hundred insolent things to me.

BELINA: Very well, I believe you, my soul. Come, recover yourself. Harkee, Toinet, if you vex my jewel ever again, I'll turn you out of doors. So, give me his fur cloak, and the pillows that I may set him easy in his chair. You are I don't know how. Pull your nightcap well over your ears; there's nothing gives people so much cold, as letting the air in at their ears.

ARGAN: Ah! my life, I'm vastly obliged to you for all the care you take of me.

BELINA: *(Adjusting the pillows which she puts round him.)* Raise yourself up that I may put this under you. Let us put this to keep you up, and this on the other side. Let's place this behind your back, and this other to support your head.

TOINET: *(Clapping a pillow hard on his head.)* And this to keep you from the damp.

ARGAN: *(Rising up in a passion, and throwing all the pillows after TOINET as she runs away.)* Ah! jade, thou wouldst stifle me.

Scene VIII

Argan, Belina.

BELINA: Oh so, oh so! What's the the the matter then?

ARGAN: *(Throwing himself into his chair.)* Oh! oh! oh! I can hold it no longer.

BELINA: Why do you fly into such passions? she meant to do well.

ARGAN: You don't know, my love, the malice of that baggage. Oh! she has put me beside myself; and there'll be need of more than eight doses of physic, and twelve clysters to set all this to rights again.

BELINA: So, so, my little dearie, pacify yourself a little.

ARGAN: My life, you are all my comfort.

BELINA: Poor little child.

ARGAN: That I may endeavour to requite the love you have for me, as I told you, my heart, I'll make my will.

BELINA: Ah! my soul, don't talk of that, pray now, I can't bear the thought of it; the very word of will makes me leap for grief.

ARGAN: I desired you to speak of it to your notary.

BELINA: He's within there, I brought him with me.[7]

ARGAN: Let him come here then, my love.

BELINA: Alas! my soul, when one loves a husband well, one's scarce in a condition to think of these things.

Scene IX

Mr. Bonnefoy, Belina, Argan.

ARGAN: Come hither, Mr. Bonnefoy, come hither. Take a chair pray. My wife has told me, sir, that you are a very honest man, and altogether one of her friends; and I have ordered her to speak to you about a will.

BELINA: Alas! I'm not capable of speaking about those things.

MR. BONNEFOY: She has unfolded your intentions to me, sir, and what you design for her; and I have to tell you upon that subject, that you cannot give your wife anything by will.

ARGAN: But why so?

MR. BONNEFOY: Custom is against it. If you were in a country of statute-law, it might be done; but at Paris, and in countries for the most part governed by custom, 'tis what can't be; and the disposition would be null. All the advantage that a man and woman joined by wedlock can give each to the other is by mutual gift during life; moreover there must be no children, either of the two conjuncts, or of one of them, at the decease of the first that dies.

ARGAN: Then 'tis a very impertinent custom that a husband can't leave anything to a wife, by whom he's tenderly beloved, and who takes so much care of him. I should desire to consult my counsellor to see what I could do.

MR. BONNEFOY: 'Tis not to counsel that you must apply, for they are commonly severe in these points, and imagine it a great crime to dispose of anything contrary to law. They are difficult people, and are ignorant of the by-ways of conscience. There are other persons to consult who are much fitter to accommodate you; who have expedients of passing gently over the law, and of making that just which is not allowed; who know how to smooth the difficulties of an affair, and to find means of eluding custom by some indirect advantage. Without that where should we always be? There must be a facility in things, otherwise we should do nothing, and I would not give a sou for our business.

ARGAN: My wife indeed told me, sir, that you were a very skilful and a very honest man. How then can I do, pray, to give her my estate, and to deprive my children of it?

MR. BONNEFOY: How can you do? You must secretly choose an intimate friend of you wife's, to whom you may bequeath in due form by your

---

[7]Note how well prepared Belina is to record Argan's will which, she hopes, will be in her favor.

will, all that you can, and this friend shall afterwards give up all to her. You may further sign a great many bonds, without suspicion, payable to several creditors, who shall lend their names to your wife, and shall put into her hands a declaration, that what they had done in it was only to serve her. You may likewise in your lifetime put into her hands ready money, or bills which you may have payable to the bearer.

BELINA: Alas! you must not torment yourself with all these things. If I should lose you, child, I'll stay no longer in the world.

ARGAN: My soul!

BELINA: Yes, my dear, if I'm unfortunate enough to lose you —

ARGAN: My dear wife!

BELINA: Life will be no longer anything to me.

ARGAN: My love!

BELINA: And I'll follow you, to let you see the tenderness I have for you.

ARGAN: My life, you break my heart; be comforted, I beg of thee.

MR. BONNEFOY: These tears are unseasonable, and things are not yet come to that.

BELINA: Ah! sir, you don't know what 'tis to have a husband that one tenderly loves.

ARGAN: All the concern I shall have, if I die, my soul, is that I never had a child by thee. Mr. Purgon told me that he'd make me able to get one.

MR. BONNEFOY: That may come still.

ARGAN: I must make my will then, my love, after the manner the gentleman says; but by way of precaution I'll put into your hands twenty thousand livres in gold, which I have in the ceiling of my alcove, and two notes payable to the bearer, which are due to me, one from Mr. Damon, and the other from Gérante.

BELINA: No, no, I'll have none of it. Ah! — how much do you say that there is in your alcove?

ARGAN: Twenty thousand livres, my love.

BELINA: Don't speak to me of riches, I beseech ye. Ah! — how much are the two notes for?

ARGAN: They are my life, one for four thousand livres, and the other for six.

BELINA: All the wealth in the world, my soul, is nothing to me in comparison of thee.

MR. BONNEFOY: *(To ARGAN.)* Would you have us proceed to make the will?

ARGAN: Yes, sir, but we shall be better in my little closet. My love, lead me pray.

BELINA: Come, my poor dear child.

Scene X

Angelica, Toinet.

TOINET: They are got with a scrivener there, and I heard 'em talk of a will. Your stepmother does not sleep, and 'tis certainly some contrivance against your interest that she's pushing your father upon.

ANGELICA: Let him dispose of his estate as he pleases, provided he does not dispose of my heart. Thou seest, Toinet, the violent designs they have against it. Don't abandon me, I beseech thee, in the extremity I'm in.

TOINET: I abandon you! I'll die sooner. Your stepmother in vain makes me her confidante, and strives to bring me into her interest; I never had any inclination for her, and have been always of your side. Let me alone, I'll make use of everything to serve you; but to serve you more effectually I'll change my battery, conceal the zeal I have for you, and pretend to enter into the sentiments of your father and stepmother.

ANGELICA: Endeavour, I conjure thee, to give Cleanthes notice of the marriage they have concluded on.

TOINET: I have nobody to employ in that office but the old usurer Polichinello, my lover, and 'twill cost me some kind words to have him do't, which I'll willingly disburse for you. Today 'tis too late, but very early tomorrow I'll send to seek for him, and he'll be overjoyed to —

BELINA: *(In the house.)* Toinet.

TOINET: *(To ANGELICA.)* I'm called. Good night. Rely upon me.[8]

ACT II

Scene I

Toinet, Cleanthes.

TOINET: *(Not knowing CLEANTHES.)* What do you want, sir?

CLEANTHES: What do I want?

TOINET: Ah, hah! is it you? surprising! what come you to do here?

CLEANTHES: To know my destiny; to speak to the amiable Angelica, consult the sentiments of her heart; and demand of her, what her resolutions are in respect to the fatal marriage they have given me intelligence of.

TOINET: Yes, but Angelica is not to be spoken with thus point blank; there must be intrigue to manage that point, and you have been told under how strict a guard she is kept. That they allow her not to stir abroad, or speak to anybody, and that 'twas the curiosity of an old aunt only, which favoured us with the liberty of going to that play, which gave birth to your passion; and we are very much upon our guard lest we speak of that adventure.

CLEANTHES: Accordingly I come not here as Cleanthes, and under the appearance of her lover, but as a friend of her music-master, who has given me leave to say that he sent me in his room.

TOINET: Here's her father. Retire a little, and let me tell him you are there.

Scene II

Argan, Toinet.

ARGAN: *(Thinking himself alone, and not seeing TOINET.)* Mr. Purgon told me I should walk in my chamber twelve times to and again in a morning; but I forgot to ask him, whether it should be longways or broadways.

TOINET: Sir, there is one —

ARGAN: Speak low, hussy, thou hast just split my brains, and thou never

---

"An act break indicates that all characters leave the stage; at this point, the scenery changes and performers present an interlude featuring Polichinello, introduced in Toinet's next to the last speech. After the interlude, the scenery changes back to Argan's bedroom.

considerest that sick folks should not be spoken so loud to.
TOINET: I would tell you, sir —
ARGAN: Speak low, I say.
TOINET: Sir — *(She makes as if she spoke.)*
ARGAN: Hey?
TOINET: I tell you that — *(She still makes as if she spoke again.)*
ARGAN: What is it you tell me?
TOINET: *(Aloud)* I tell you here is a man wants to speak with you.
ARGAN: Let him come. *(TOINET beckons to CLEANTHES to come near.)*

Scene III

Argan, Cleanthes, Toinet.

CLEANTHES: Sir —
TOINET: *(To CLEANTHES.)* Don't speak so loud, for fear of splitting my master's brains.
CLEANTHES: Sir, I am exceedingly glad to find you up, and to see that you are better.
TOINET: *(Pretending to be in a passion.)* How better? 'tis false, my master is always ill.
CLEANTHES: I had heard the gentleman was better, and I perceive he looks well.
TOINET: What d'ye mean with your looks well? He looks very ill, and they are impertinent people who told you he was better. He never was so ill in his life.
ARGAN: She's in the right on't.
TOINET: He walks, sleeps, eats, and drinks like other folks; but that does not hinder him from being sick.
ARGAN: That's true.
CLEANTHES: Sir, I am heartily sorry for it. I come from the young lady your daughter's music-master. He was obliged to go into the country for a few days; and, as I am one of his intimate friends, he sent me in his place, to go on with her lessons, for fear, that if they were discontinued, she might forget what she has already learnt.
ARGAN: Very well. *(To TOINET.)* Call Angelica.
TOINET: I fancy, sir, it would be better to show the gentleman to her chamber.
ARGAN: No. Bid her come hither.
TOINET: He can't teach her her lesson as he should do, if they are not by themselves.
ARGAN: Yes, yes.
TOINET: Sir, 'twill only stun you, and you had need to have nothing to disturb you, or split your brains, in the condition you are.
ARGAN: No, no, I love music, and I shall be glad to — hoh! here she comes. *(To TOINET.)* Do you go see if my wife be dressed.

Scene IV

Argan, Angelica, Cleanthes.

ARGAN: Come, daughter; your music-master is gone into the country, and here's a person he has sent to teach you in his place.

ANGELICA: *(Knowing CLEANTHES.)* Oh, Heavens!
ARGAN: What's the matter? Whence this surprise?
ANGELICA: 'Tis —
ARGAN: What? Who disturbs you in this manner?
ANGELICA: 'Tis a surprising accident, sir, that I meet with here.
ARGAN: How?
ANGELICA: I dreamt last night that I was in the greatest distress in the world, and that a person exactly like this gentleman, offered himself to me, of whom I demanded succour, and he presently freed me from the trouble I was in; and my surprise was very great to see unexpectedly, upon my coming in here, what I had in idea all night.
CLEANTHES: 'Tis no small happiness to have a place in your thoughts, whether sleeping or waking; and my good fortune would be undoubtedly very great, were you in any trouble from which you should judge me worthy to deliver you; and there is nothing I would not do to —

Scene V

Argan, Angelica, Cleanthes, Toinet.

TOINET: *(To ARGAN.)* Troth, sir, I'm o' your side now, and unsay all that I said yesterday. Here are Mr. Diafoirus the father, and Mr. Diafoirus the son, come to visit you. How rarely will you be hope up with a son-in-law! You will see one of the best made young fellows in the world, and the wittiest too. He spoke but two words, and I was in ecstasy at 'em, and your daughter will be charmed with him.
ARGAN: *(To CLEANTHES, who makes as if he were going.)* Don't go, sir; I am upon marrying my daughter, and the person they have brought hither is her intended husband, whom she has not as yet seen.
CLEANTHES: 'Tis doing me a great deal of honour, sir, to permit me to be witness of so agreeable an interview.
ARGAN: He is son to an eminent physician, and the marriage will be performed in four days.
CLEANTHES: Very well.
ARGAN: Please to inform her music-master of it, that he may be at the wedding.
CLEANTHES: I'll not fail to do it.
ARGAN: I invite you to it likewise.
CLEANTHES: You do me a great deal of honour.
ARGAN: Come, place yourselves in order, here they are.

Scene VI

Mr. Diafoirus, Thomas Diafoirus, Argan, Angelica, Cleanthes, Toinet, Lackeys.

ARGAN: *(Putting his hand to his cap without taking it off.)* Mr. Purgon, sir, has forbid me being uncovered. You are of the faculty: you know the consequences.
MR. DIAFOIRUS: We are in all our visits to bring relief to our patients, and not to bring any inconvenience upon 'em. *(ARGAN and MR. DIAFOIRUS speak at the same time.)*
ARGAN: I receive, sir,
MR. DIAFOIRUS: We come here, sir,

ARGAN: With a great deal of joy,

MR. DIAFOIRUS: My son Thomas, and I,

ARGAN: The honour you do me,

MR. DIAFOIRUS: To declare to you, sir,

ARGAN: And I could have wished,

MR. DIAFOIRUS: The pleasure we receive,

ARGAN: To have been able to have gone to you,

MR. DIAFOIRUS: From the favour you do us,

ARGAN: To assure you,

MR. DIAFOIRUS: So kindly to admit us,

ARGAN: But you know, sir,

MR. DIAFOIRUS: To the honour, sir,

ARGAN: What it is to be a poor sick creature,

MR. DIAFOIRUS: Of your alliance,

ARGAN: Who can do no more,

MR. DIAFOIRUS: And to assure you,

ARGAN: Than to tell you here,

MR. DIAFOIRUS: That in affairs depending on our faculty,

ARGAN: That he will seek all opportunities,

MR. DIAFOIRUS: As also in all others,

ARGAN: To make you sensible, sir,

MR. DIAFOIRUS: We shall ever be ready, sir,

ARGAN: That he is entirely at your service.

MR. DIAFOIRUS: To testify our zeal for you — *(To his son.)* Come, Thomas, advance, make your compliments.

THOMAS DIAFOIRUS: *(To MR. DIAFOIRUS.)* Should not I begin with the father?

MR. DIAFOIRUS: Yes.

THOMAS DIAFOIRUS: *(To ARGAN.)* Sir, I come to salute, recognise, cherish, and revere in you a second father; but a second father, to whom, I'll be bold to say, I am more indebted than to my first. The first begat me; but you have adopted me. He received me through necessity; but you have accepted me through favour. What I have from him, is the operation of this body, what I have from you, is the operation of your will; and by how much the mental faculties are superior to the corporeal, by so much am I more indebted to you, and by so much do I hold, as more precious, this future filiation, for which I this day come to pay you beforehand, the most humble and most respectful homage.

TOINET: Prosperity to the colleges, which turn us out such ingenious persons.

THOMAS DIAFOIRUS: *(To MR. DIAFOIRUS.)* Was that well done, father?

MR. DIAFOIRUS: *Optimè.*

ARGAN: *(To ANGELICA.)* Come, pay your respects to the gentleman.

THOMAS DIAFOIRUS: *(To MR. DIAFOIRUS.)* Shall I kiss her?

MR. DIAFOIRUS: Yes, yes.

THOMAS DIAFOIRUS: *(To ANGELICA.)* Madam, 'tis with justice that Heaven has granted you the name of stepmother, since one —

ARGAN: *(To THOMAS DIAFOIRUS.)* 'Tis not my wife, 'tis my daughter you are speaking to.

THOMAS DIAFOIRUS: Where is she then?

ARGAN: She's a-coming.

THOMAS DIAFOIRUS: Shall I wait, father, till she comes?

MR. DIAFOIRUS: Always make your compliment to the young lady.

THOMAS DIAFOIRUS: Madam, just in the same manner as the statue of Memnon gave an harmonious sound, when it was illuminated by the rays of the sun: so, in like manner, do I feel myself animated with a sweet transport at the appearance of the sun of your beauty. And as the naturalists remark that the flower named the Heliotrope, turns, without ceasing, towards that star of day: so shall my heart, henceforth for ever, turn towards the resplendent stars of your adorable eyes, as to its proper pole. Permit me then, madam, now to pay, at the altar of your charms, the offering of that heart, which breathes not after, nor is ambitious of any other glory than that of being till death, madam, your most humble, most obedient, and most faithful servant, and husband.

TOINET: See what it is to study, one learns to say fine things.

ARGAN: *(To CLEANTHES.)* Heh! What say you to that?

CLEANTHES: That the gentleman does wonders, and that if he is as good a physician as he is an orator, it would be a great pleasure to be one of his patients.

TOINET: Certainly. It will be a wonderful thing, if he performs as fine cures, as he makes fine speeches.

ARGAN: Here, my chair quickly, and chairs for everybody. Sit you there, daughter. *(To MR. DIAFOIRUS.)* You see, sir, that all the world admires your son, and I think you very happy in such a young man.

MR. DIAFOIRUS: Sir, 'tis not because I am his father, but I can say I have reason to be satisfied in him, and that all who see him, speak of him as a youth who has no harm in him. He never had a very lively imagination, nor that sparkling wit which one observes in some others; but it was that, I always looked upon, as a happy presage of his judgment, a quality requisite for the exercise of our art. When he was a little one, he was never what one may call roguish, or waggish. One might always see him mild, peaceable, and taciturn, never uttering a word, and never playing at any of those little games, that we call children's-play. They had all the difficulty in the world to teach him to read, and he was nine years old before he knew his letters. Good, says I within myself; trees slow of growth, are those which bear the best fruit. One writes upon the marble with much more difficulty than one does upon the sand; but things are much longer preserved there, and that slowness of apprehension, that heaviness of imagination, is a mark of a future good judgment. When I sent him to college he was hard put to't; but he bore up obstinately against all difficulties, and his tutors always praised him to me for his assiduity and his pains. In short, by mere dint of hammering, he gloriously attained to be a licentiate; and I can say without vanity, that from the time he took his Bachelor of Physic's degree, there is no candidate that has made more noise than he in all the disputes of the schools. He has rendered himself formidable there, and not an act passes but he argues to the last extremity on the side of the contrary proposition. He is firm in a dispute, strenuous as a Turk in his principles; and pursues an argument to the farthest recesses of logic. But what pleases me above all things in him, in which he follows my example, is that he is blindly attached to the opinions of the ancients, and that he would never comprehend nor hear the reasons and experiments of the pretended discoveries of our age, concerning the circulation of the blood, and other opinions of the same stamp.

THOMAS DIAFOIRUS: *(Taking a large thesis out of his pocket rolled up, which he presents to ANGELICA.)* I have supported a thesis against the circulators, which, with the gentleman's permission, *(Bowing to ARGAN.)* I make bold to present to the young lady, as a homage I owe her of the first-fruits of my genius.

ANGELICA: Sir, 'tis a useless piece of goods for me, and I am not skilled in those sort of things.

TOINET: *(Taking the thesis.)* Give it me, give it me, 'tis always worth taking for the picture, it will serve to adorn our garret.

THOMAS DIAFOIRUS: And with the gentleman's permission also, I invite you to come and see one of these days, for your diversion, the dissection of a woman, upon which I am to read lectures.

TOINET: The diversion will be agreeable. There are some gentlemen give their mistresses a play, but to give a dissection, is something more gallant.

MR. DIAFOIRUS: As to the rest, for what concerns the requisite qualities for marriage and propagation, I do assure you that according to the rules of us doctors, he is just such as one could wish. That he possesses in a laudable degree the prolific virtue, and that he is of a temperament proper to beget, and procreate well-conditioned children.

ARGAN: Is it not your intention, sir, to push his interest at court, and procure for him a physician's place there?

MR. DIAFOIRUS: To speak frankly to you, our profession amongst your great people never appeared to me agreeable, and I always found it would be much better for us to continue amongst the commonalty. The public business is commodious. You are accountable to nobody for your actions, and provided one does but follow the beaten track of the rules of art, one gives one's self no manner of trouble about what may be the event. But what is vexatious among your great people is, that when they happen to be sick, they absolutely expect their physicians should cure them.

TOINET: That's a good jest indeed, and they are very impertinent to expect that you gentlemen should cure 'em: you don't attend them for that purpose; you only go to take your fees, and prescribe remedies, 'tis their business to cure themselves if they can.

MR. DIAFOIRUS: That's true. We are only obliged to treat people according to form.

ARGAN: *(To CLEANTHES.)* Sir, pray let my daughter sing before the company.

CLEANTHES: I waited for your orders, sir, and propose to divert the company, by singing along with miss, a scene of a little opera lately composed. *(To ANGELICA, giving her a paper.)* There's your part.

ANGELICA: I?

CLEANTHES. *(Low to ANGELICA.)* Pray don't refuse, but permit me to let you into the design of the scene we are going to sing aloud. *(Aloud.)* I have no voice for singing; but 'tis sufficient in this case if I make myself understood, you will have the goodness to excuse me, on account of the necessity I am under, to make the young lady sing.

ARGAN: Are the verses pretty?

CLEANTHES: 'Tis properly an extempore opera, and what you are to hear sung, is no more than numbered prose, or a kind of irregular verse, such as passion and necessity might suggest to two persons, who say things out of their own head, and speak off-hand.

ARGAN: Very well. Let's hear.

CLEANTHES: The subject of the scene is this. A shepherd was attentive to the beauties of a public entertainment, which was but just begun, when his attention was interrupted by a noise, on one side of him. He turns to look, and sees a brutish clown, with insolent words abusing a shepherdess. Immediately he espoused the interest of a sex to which all men owe homage; and having chastised the churl for his insolence, he comes to the shepherdess, and sees a young creature, who, from two of the finest eyes he had ever seen, was shedding tears, which he thought the most beautiful in the world. Alas! says he within himself, could anyone be capable of insulting a person so amiable: And what inhuman, what barbarous creature would not be touched with such tears? He was solicitous to stop those tears, which he thought so beautiful; and the lovely shepherdess took care at the same time, to thank him for the slight service he had done; but in a manner so charming, so tender, so passionate, that the shepherd could not resist it, but every word, every look as a flaming shaft, which he found pierced him to the heart. Is there anything, said he, can possibly deserve the lovely expressions of such an acknowledgment? And what would one not do, what service, what dangers would one not be delighted to go through, to attract but one moment the moving tenderness of so grateful a mind? The whole diversion passes without his attending to it in the least; but he complains 'tis too short, because the conclusion of it separates him from his adorable shepherdess, and from this first view, from this first moment he carried along with him all the violence of a passion of many years. He immediately suffered all the miseries of absence, and was tormented that he could no longer see what he saw for so short a time. He does everything possible to regain that sight, the dear idea of which he has in his mind by night and by day; but the great constraint under which his shepherdess is kept, deprives him of all opportunity. The violence of his passion makes him resolve to demand the adorable beauty in marriage, without whom he can no longer live, and he obtained her permission for this, by a letter which he had the dexterity to have conveyed to her hands. But at the same time he has advice that the father of this fair one has concluded a marriage with another, and that all things are disposing for celebration of the ceremony. Judge what a cruel stroke to the heart of the melancholy shepherd. See him overwhelmed with mortal sorrow. He cannot support the horrible idea of seeing all that he loves in the arms of another, and his passion being desperate makes him introduce himself into the house of his shepherdess to learn her sentiments, and know from her what destiny he is to resolve upon. He there meets with preparations for everything he fears; he there sees the unworthy rival, which the caprice of a father opposes to the tendernesses of his love. He sees this ridiculous rival, near the lovely shepherdess, triumphing, as if the conquest were sure, and this sight fills him with indignation, which he has the utmost difficulty to master. He casts a mournful look on her he adores, and both his respect for her, and the presence of her father, prevent his saying anything to her but by the eyes. But at last, he breaks through all restraint, and the transport of his passion makes him express himself in this matter *(He sings.)*

> Fair Phyllis, 'tis too much to bear,
> Break cruel silence; and your thoughts declare.
> Tell me at once my destiny,
> Shall I live, or must I die?

ANGELICA: *(Singing.)*

> With sad, dejected looks, O Thyrsis, see
> Poor Phyllis dread th' ill-fated wedding-day;
> Sighing, she lifts her eyes to Heaven and thee,
> And needs she more to say?

ARGAN: Hey, hey! I didn't know my daughter was such a mistress of the art,
> To sing at sight without hesitating.

CLEANTHES:

> Alas! my Phyllis fair,
> Can the enamoured Thyrsis be so blest,
> Your favour in the least to share,
> And find a place within that lovely breast?

ANGELICA:

> In this extreme, if I confess my love,
> Not modesty itself can disapprove,
> Yes, Thyrsis, thee I love.

CLEANTHES:

> Oh! Song enchanting to the ear!
> Did I dream, or did I hear?
> Repeat it, Phyllis, and all doubt remove.

ANGELICA:

> Yes, Thyrsis, thee I love.

CLEANTHES:

> Once more, my Phyllis.

ANGELICA:

> Thee I love.

CLEANTHES:

> A thousand times repeat, nor ever weary prove.

ANGELICA:

> I love, I love,
> Yes, Thyrsis, thee I love.

CLEANTHES:

> Ye monarchs of the earth, ye pow'rs divine,

Can you compare your happiness to mine?
But, Phyllis, there's a thought
Does my transporting joy abate,
A rival —

ANGELICA:
I, more than death, the monster hate,
And if his presence tortures you,
It does no less to Phyllis too.

CLEANTHES:
If with the match a father's power,
Would force you to comply.

ANGELICA: I'd rather, rather die than give consent,
Much rather, rather die.

ARGAN:And what says the father to all this?

CLEANTHES: He says nothing.

ARGAN: That same father was a blockhead of a father, to suffer all these foolish things, without saying anything.

CLEANTHES: *(Continuing to sing.)* Ah! my love —

ARGAN: No, no, enough of it. This play is of very bad example. The shepherd Thyrsis is an impertinent puppy, and the shepherdess Phyllis, an impudent baggage, to speak in this manner before a father. *(To ANGELICA.)* Show me the paper. Ha, ha! Where are the words then that you spoke? There's nothing writ here but the music.

CLEANTHES: Why, don't you know, sir, that they have found out an invention late, of writing the words in the very notes themselves?

ARGAN: Very well, I'm your servant, sir; adieu! We could very well have spared your impertinent opera.

CLEANTHES: I thought to divert you.

ARGAN: Impertinence never diverts. Hah! here's my wife.

Scene VII

Belina, Argan, Angelica, Mr. Diafoirus, Thomas Diafoirus, Toinet.

ARGAN: Here's Mr. Diafoirus's son, my love.

THOMAS DIAFOIRUS: Madam, 'tis with justice that Heaven has granted you the name of mother-in-law, since one sees in your face —

BELINA: Sir, I am very glad I came here apropos, that I might have the honour of seeing you.

THOMAS DIAFOIRUS: Since one sees in your face — Since one sees in your face — Madam, you interrupted me in the middle of my period, and that has disturbed my memory.

MR. DIAFOIRUS: Reserve that, Thomas, for another time.

ARGAN: I wish you had been here just now, dearie.

TOINET: Oh, madam, you have lost a great deal by not being here at the Second father, at the Statue of Memnon and the Flower named the Heliotrope.

ARGAN: Come, daughter, join hands with the gentleman, and plight him your troth, as your husband.

ANGELICA: Sir.

ARGAN: Hey, sir! What means this?

ANGELICA: For goodness' sake, don't hurry things too fast. Give us time at least to know one another, and to find the growth of that inclination in each for the other, which is so necessary to form a perfect union.

THOMAS DIAFOIRUS: As for me, madam, mine is grown already, I have no need to stay any longer.

ANGELICA: If you are so forward, sir, it is not so with me, and I confess to you that your merit has not as yet made impression enough upon my mind.

ARGAN: Hoh! well, well, that will have leisure enough to be made, when you are married together.

ANGELICA: Ah! father, pray give me time. Marriage is a chain that should never be imposed by force upon a heart, and if the gentleman is a man of honour, he should never accept a person, who must be his by constraint.

THOMAS DIAFOIRUS: *Nego consequentiam,*[9] madam; and I may be a man of honour, and yet accept you from the hands of your father.

ANGELICA: To offer violence is but a very ill way to make you beloved by anyone.

THOMAS DIAFOIRUS: We read in the ancients, madam, that their custom was to carry off the young women they were going to marry, by force from their father's house, that it might not seem to be by their consent, that they flew into the arms of a man.

ANGELICA: The ancients, sir, are the ancients, and we are moderns. Such grimaces are not necessary in our age, and when a marriage pleases us, we know very well how to go to it, without anybody's dragging us. Have patience; if you love me, sir, you ought to like everything I like.

THOMAS DIAFOIRUS: Yes, madam, as far as the interests of my love exclusively.

ANGELICA: But the great sign of love is, to submit to the will of her one loves.

THOMAS DIAFOIRUS: *Distinguo,* madam. In what regards not the possession of her, *concedo;* but in what regards that, *nego.*[10]

TOINET: 'Tis in vain to reason. The gentleman is come fire-new from college, and he'll always be too hard for you. Why should you resist so much, and refuse the glory of being tacked to the body of the faculty?

BELINA: She has some other inclination in her head perhaps.

ANGELICA: If I had, madam, it should be such as reason and honour might allow me.

ARGAN: Hey-day! I act a pleasant part here.

BELINA: If I were as you, child, I would not at all force her to marry, and I know very well what I would do.

ANGELICA: I know, madam, what you mean, and the kindness you have for me: but perhaps your counsels mayn't be lucky enough to be put into execution.

BELINA: That's because very wise and very good children like you, scorn to be obedient and submissive to the will of their fathers. That was held a virtue in times of yore.

---

[9]*Nego consequentiam:* "I deny that one thing follows from the other." Thomas's use of Latin is intended to demonstrate his pedantry.

[10]*Distinguo:* "I make a distinction." *Concedo:* "I concede." *Nego:* "I deny."

ANGELICA: The duty of a daughter has bounds, madam, and neither reason nor law extend it to all sorts of things.

BELINA: That's as much as to say you have no aversion to matrimony; but you've a mind to choose a husband to your own fancy.

ANGELICA: If my father won't give me a husband to my liking, I shall conjure him, at least, not to force me to marry one I can't love.

ARGAN: Gentlemen, I beg your pardon for all this.

ANGELICA: Everybody to their own end in marrying. For my part who would not marry a husband but really to love him, and who intend to be entirely attached to him for life, I confess to you I use some precaution in the affair. There are some persons who take husbands only to set themselves free from the restraint of their parents, and to put themselves in a condition of doing whatever they please. There are others, madam, who make marriage a commerce of pure interest; who only marry to get a jointure, to enrich themselves by those they marry; and run without scruple from husband to husband, to engross to themselves their spoils. Those people in good truth don't stand much upon ceremonies, and have little regard to the person of the man.

BELINA: You are in a mighty vein of reasoning today, and I would fain know what you mean by that.

ANGELICA: I, madam, what should I mean but what I say?

BELINA: You are such a simpleton, my dear, that there's no enduring you any longer.

ANGELICA: You would be glad, madam, to oblige me to give you some impertinent answer; but I tell you beforehand, you shan't have that advantage.

BELINA: Your insolence is not to be equalled.

ANGELICA: No, madam, your talking is in vain.

BELINA: You have a ridiculous pride, an impertinent presumption which makes you the scorn of all the world.

ANGELICA: All this will do no good, madam. I shall be discreet in spite of you, and to take away from you all hope of succeeding in what you want to be at, I shall get out of your sight.

Scene VIII

Argan, Belina, Mr. Diafoirus, Thomas Diafoirus, Toinet.

ARGAN: *(To ANGELICA who goes out.)* Harkee, there's no medium in the case. You've your choice to marry in four days' time, either this gentleman, or a convent. *(To BELINA.)* Don't give yourself any uneasiness, I'll bring her to good order.

BELINA: I'm sorry to leave you, my child, but I have an affair in the city, which can't be dispensed with. I shall come back again presently.

ARGAN: Go, love, and call upon your lawyer, that you may bid him hasten you know what.

BELINA: B'y, my little dearie.

ARGAN: B'y, jewel.

Scene IX

Argan, Mr. Diafoirus, Thomas Diafoirus, Toinet.

ARGAN: This woman loves me — 'Tis not credible how much.

MR. DIAFOIRUS: We shall take our leave of you, sir.

ARGAN: Pray, sir, tell me a little how I am.

MR. DIAFOIRUS: *(Feeling his pulse.)* Here, Thomas, take the gentleman's other arm, to see whether you can form a good judgment of his pulse. *Quid dicis?*

THOMAS DIAFOIRUS: *Dico,* that the gentleman's pulse is the pulse of a man who is not well.

MR. DIAFOIRUS: Good.

THOMAS DIAFOIRUS: That 'tis hardish, not to say hard.

MR. DIAFOIRUS: Very well.

THOMAS DIAFOIRUS: Recoiling.

MR. DIAFOIRUS: *Bene.*

THOMAS DIAFORIUS: And even a little frisking.

MR. DIAFOIRUS: *Optimè.*

THOMAS DIAFOIRUS: Which shows an intemperature in the *parenchyma splenicum,* that is to say, the spleen.

MR. DIAFOIRUS: Very well.

ARGAN: No, Dr. Purgon says, 'tis my liver that's bad.

MR. DIAFOIRUS: Why yes, he who says *parenchyma,* means both one and t'other, because of the strict sympathy they have together, by means of the *vas breve* of the *pylorus,* and sometimes the *meatus cholidici.* He orders you, doubtless, to eat roast meat.

ARGAN: No, nothing but boiled.

MR. DIAFOIRUS: Ay, yes, roast, boiled, the same thing. He orders you very prudently, and you can't be in better hands.

ARGAN: Sir, how many corns of salt should one put in an egg?

MR. DIAFOIRUS: Six, eight, ten, by even numbers; as in medicines, by odd numbers.

ARGAN: Sir, your very humble servant.

Scene X

Belina, Argan.

BELINA: I come, child, before I go abroad, to inform you of a thing, which you must take care of. As I passed by Angelica's chamber-door, I saw a young fellow with her, who immediately made his escape as soon as he saw me.

ARGAN: A young fellow with my daughter?

BELINA: Yes. Your little daughter Louison was with 'em, who can give you tidings of 'em.

ARGAN: Send her hither, lovey; send her hither. *(Alone.)* Oh! the impudent baggage! I am no longer astonished at her obstinacy.

Scene XI

Argan, Louison.

LOUISON: What do you want, papa? My mamma told me, that you want to speak with me.

ARGAN: Yes, come hither. Come nearer. Turn you. Look up. Look upon me. Heh?

LOUISON: What, papa?

ARGAN: So.

LOUISON: What?

ARGAN: Have you nothing to tell me?

LOUISON: To divert you, I'll tell you, if you please, the story of the ass's skin, or the fable of the crow and the fox, which they taught me t'other day.

ARGAN: That's not what I want.

LOUISON: What then?

ARGAN: O ye cunning hussy, you know very well what I mean.

LOUISON: Pardon me, papa.

ARGAN: Is it thus you obey me?

LOUISON: How?

ARGAN: Did not I charge you to come immediately and tell me all that you see?

LOUISON: Yes, papa.

ARGAN: Have you done so?

LOUISON: Yes, papa, I am come to tell you all that I have seen.

ARGAN: And have you seen nothing today?

LOUISON: No, papa.

ARGAN: No?

LOUISON: No, papa.

ARGAN: Indeed?

LOUISON: Indeed.

ARGAN: Hoh! very well, I'll make you see something.

LOUISON: *(Seeing ARGAN take a rod.)* Ah! papa.

ARGAN: Ha, hah! you little hypocrite, you don't tell me you saw a man in your sister's chamber.

LOUISON: *(Crying.)* Papa.

ARGAN: *(Taking her by the arm.)* Here's something will teach you to lie.

LOUISON: *(Falling down on her knees.)* Ah, papa, pray forgive me. 'Twas because my sister had bid me not to tell it you; but I'm going to tell you all.

ARGAN: You must, first of all, have the rod, for having told a lie. After that we shall consider of the rest.

LOUISON: Forgive me, papa.

ARGAN: No, no.

LOUISON: My dear papa, don't whip me.

ARGAN: You shall be whipped.

LOUISON: For Heaven's sake, papa, don't whip me.

ARGAN: *(Going to whip her.)* Come, come.

LOUISON: Oh! papa, you have hurt me. Hold, I'm dead. *(She feigns herself dead.)*

ARGAN: Hola, what's the meaning of this? Louison, Louison. Oh! bless me! Louison. Ah! my child. Oh! wretched me! My poor child's dead. What have I done, wretch! Oh! villainous rod! A curse on all rods! Oh, my dear child; my poor little Louison.

LOUISON: So, so, papa, don't cry so, I'm not quite dead.

ARGAN: D'ye see the cunning baggage? Oh, come, come, I pardon you for this time, provided you'll really tell me all.

LOUISON: Ho! yes, papa!

ARGAN: Take special care you do however, for here's my little finger knows all, and will tell me if you lie.

LOUISON: But, papa, don't tell my sister, that I told you.

ARGAN: No, no.

LOUISON: *(After seeing if anybody listened.)* Why, papa, there came a man into my sister's chamber when I was there.

ARGAN: Well?

LOUISON: I asked him what he wanted, and he told me he was her music-master.

ARGAN: *(Aside.)* Um, um. There's the business. *(To LOUISON.)* Well?

LOUISON: Afterwards my sister came.

ARGAN: Well?

LOUISON: She said to him, Begone, begone, begone, for goodness' sake! Begone, you make me in pain.

ARGAN: Very well?

LOUISON: And he wouldn't go.

ARGAN: What did he say to her?

LOUISON: He said, I don't know how many things.

ARGAN: But what was it?

LOUISON: He told her this, and that, and t'other, how he loved her dearly, and that she was the prettiest creature in the world.

ARGAN: And then?

LOUISON: And then he fell down on his knees to her.

ARGAN: And then?

LOUISON: And then he kissed her hand.

ARGAN: And then?

LOUISON: And then my mamma came to the door, and he ran away.

ARGAN: Was there nothing else?

LOUISON: No, Papa.

ARGAN: My little finger however mutters something besides. *(Putting his finger to his ear.)* Stay, Eh? ha, ha! Ay? Hoh, hoh! here's my little finger tells me something that you saw, and that you have not told me.

LOUISON: Oh! papa. Your little finger is a fibber.

ARGAN: Have a care.

LOUISON: No, papa, don't believe it, it fibs, I assure you.

ARGAN: Hoh! well, well, we shall see that. Go your way, and be sure you observe everything, go. *(Alone.)* Well! I've no more children. Oh! what perplexity of affairs! I have not leisure so much as to mind my illness. In good truth, I can hold out no longer. *(Falls down into his chair.)*

Scene XII

Beraldo, Argan.

BERALDO: Well, brother, what's the matter, how do you do?

ARGAN: Ah, brother, very ill.

BERALDO: How, very ill?

ARGAN: Yes. I am so very feeble, 'tis incredible.

BERALDO: That's a sad thing indeed.

ARGAN: I haven't even the strength to be able to speak.

BERALDO: I came here, brother, to propose a match for my niece Angelica.

ARGAN: *(Speaking with great fury, and starting out of his chair.)* Brother, don't speak to me about that base slut. She's an idle, impertinent, impudent baggage, and I'll put her in a convent, before she's two days older.

BERALDO: Hoh! 'tis mighty well. I'm very glad your strength returns to you a little, and that my visit does you good. Well, come, we'll talk of business by and by. I've brought you an entertainment here, that will dissipate your melancholy, and dispose you better for what we are to talk about. They are gipsies, dressed in Moorish habits, who perform some dances, mixed with songs, that I'm sure you will be pleased with, and this will be much better for you than one of Mr. Purgon's prescriptions. Let's go.[11]

ACT III

Scene I

Beraldo, Argan, Toinet.

BERALDO: Well, brother, what say you of this? Is not this well worth a dose of cassia?

TOINET: Ho! good cassia is an excellent thing.

BERALDO: So, shall we talk a little together?

ARGAN: A little patience, brother, I return presently.

TOINET: Hold, sir; you don't remember that you can't walk without your cane.

ARGAN: You are in the right.

Scene II

Beraldo, Toinet.

TOINET: Pray, sir, don't abandon the interest of your niece.

BERALDO: I'll try every way to obtain for her what she wishes.

TOINET: We must absolutely prevent this extravagant match, which he has got in his head, and I've thought with myself, it would be a good job, if we could introduce here a physician into our post, to disgust him and his Mr. Purgon, and cry down his conduct. But as we have nobody at hand to do it, I have resolved to play a trick of my own head.

BERALDO: How?

TOINET: 'Tis a whimsical fancy. It may be more fortunate perhaps than prudent. Let me alone with it; do you act your own part. Here's our man.

Scene III

Argan, Beraldo.

BERALDO: Will you suffer me, brother, to desire above all things, that you'll

---

[11]Beraldo thus introduced an interlude featuring dancing Moors. The actors exit, and the scene changes to an appropriate setting. After the interlude, the scenery changes back to Argan's room.

not put yourself into any heat in our conversation.

ARGAN: Done.

BERALDO: That you'd answer without any eagerness to the things I may say to you.

ARGAN: Yes.

BERALDO: And that we may reason together upon the business we have to talk of, with a mind free from all passion.

ARGAN: Lack-a-day yes. What a deal of preamble!

BERALDO: Whence comes it, brother, that having the estate which you have, and having no children but one daughter — for I don't reckon your little one — whence comes it, I say, that you talk of putting her into a convent?

ARGAN: Whence comes it, brother, that I am master of my family, but to do what I think fit?

BERALDO: Your wife does not fail advising you to get rid thus of your daughters; and I don't doubt, but that, through a spirit of charity, she would be overjoyed to see 'em both good nuns.

ARGAN: Oh! you are thereabouts. My poor wife is at once brought in play. 'Tis she does all the mischief, and all the world will have it so of her.

BERALDO: No, brother, let's let that alone; she's a woman who has the best intentions in the world for your family, and who is free from all kind of interest; who has a marvellous tenderness for you, and shows an affection and kindness for your children which is inconceivable, that's certain. We'll not talk of that, but return to your daughter. With what intention, brother, would you give her in marriage to the son of a physician?

ARGAN: With an intention, brother, to give myself such a son-in-law as I want.

BERALDO: That's no concern, brother, of your daughter's, and there's a more suitable match offered for her.

ARGAN: Yes, but this, brother, is more suitable to me.

BERALDO: But ought the husband she takes, to be for you, or for herself, brother?

ARGAN: It ought, brother, to be both for herself, and for me, and I will bring into my family people that I have need of.

BERALDO: By the same reason, if your little girl was big enough, you'd marry her to an apothecary.

ARGAN: Why not?

BERALDO: Is it possible you should always be so infatuated with your apothecaries and doctors, and resolve to be sick in spite of mankind and nature?

ARGAN: What do you mean, brother?

BERALDO: I mean, brother, that I don't see any man who's less sick than yourself, and I would not desire a better constitution than yours. 'Tis a great mark that you are well, and have a habit of body perfectly well established, that with all the pains you have taken, you've not been able yet to spoil the goodness of your constitution, and that you are not destroyed by all the medicines they have made you take.

ARGAN: But do you know, brother, 'tis that which preserves me, and that Mr. Purgon says, I should go off, if he was only three days without taking care of me.

BERALDO: If you don't take care of yourself, he'll take so much care of you, that he'll send you into the other world.

ARGAN: But let us reason a little, brother. You have no faith then in physic?

BERALDO: No, brother, and I don't find 'tis necessary to salvation, to have faith in't.

ARGAN: What! don't you think a thing true which has been established through all the world and which all ages have revered?

BERALDO: Far from thinking it true, I look on't, between us, as one of the great follies which prevails amongst men; and, to consider things philosophically, I don't know a more pleasant piece of mummery; I don't see anything more ridiculous, than for one man to undertake to cure another.

ARGAN: Why won't you allow, brother, that one man may cure another?

BERALDO: For this reason, brother, because the springs of our machines are hitherto mysteries that men scarce can see into; and because nature has thrown before our eyes too thick a veil to know anything of the matter.

ARGAN: The physicians know nothing then in your opinion?

BERALDO: True, brother. They understand for the most part polite literature; can talk good Latin, know how to call all distempers in Greek, to define, and to distinguish 'em; but for what belongs to the curing of 'em, that's what they don't know at all.

ARGAN: But nevertheless you must agree, that in this matter physicians know more than other people.

BERALDO: They know, brother, what I have told you, which won't cure any great matter; and all the excellency of their art consists in a pompous nonsense, in a special babbling, which gives you words instead of reasons, and promises instead of effects.

ARGAN: But in short, brother, there are people as wise and as learned as yourself; and we see that in sickness all the world have recourse to physicians.

BERALDO: That's a mark of human weakness, and not of the truth of their art.

ARGAN: But physicians themselves must needs believe in the truth of their art, since they make use of it themselves.

BERALDO: That's because there are some amongst 'em, who are themselves in the popular error by which they profit, and there are others who make a profit of it without being in it. Your Mr. Purgon, for example, knows no artifice; he's a thorough physician, from head to foot. One that believes in his rules, more than in all the demonstrations of the mathematics, and who would think it a crime but to be willing to examine 'em; who sees nothing obscure in physic, nothing dubious, nothing difficult, and who with an impetuosity of prepossession, an obstinacy of assurance, and a brutality void of common sense and reason, bleeds and purges at haphazard, and hesitates at nothing. He means no ill in all that he does for you, 'tis with the best principle in the world, that he will dispatch you, and he'll do no more in killing you, than what he has done to his wife and children, and what upon occasion he would do to himself.

ARGAN: That's because you have a spite against him, brother. But in short, let's come to fact. What must we do then, when we are sick?

BERALDO: Nothing, brother.

ARGAN: Nothing?

BERALDO: Nothing. We must only keep ourselves quiet. Nature herself, when we'll let her alone, will gently deliver herself from the disorder she's fallen into. 'Tis our inquietude, 'tis our impatience which spoils all, and almost all men die of their physic, and not of their diseases.

ARGAN: But you must allow, brother, that we may assist this nature by certain things.

BERALDO: Lack-a-day, brother, these are mere notions which we love to feed ourselves with; and at all times some fine imaginations have crept in amongst men which we are apt to believe because they flatter us, and that 'twere to be wished they were true. When a physician talks to you of assisting, succouring and supporting nature, of removing from her what's hurtful, and giving her what's defective, of re-establishing her, and restoring her to a full exercise of her functions; when he talks to you of rectifying the blood, refreshing the bowels, and the brain, correcting the spleen, restoring the lungs, fortifying the heart, re-establishing and preserving the natural heat, and of having secrets to lengthen out life for a long term of years; he repeats to you exactly the romance of physic. But when you come to the truth and experience of it, you find nothing of all this, and 'tis like those fine dreams which leave you nothing upon waking but the regret of having believed 'em.

ARGAN: That's to say, that all the knowledge of the world is shut up in your head; and you pretend to know more on't than all the great physicians of our age.

BERALDO: In talk, and in things, your great physicians are two sorts of people. Hear 'em talk, they are the most skilful persons in the world. See 'em act, and they're the most ignorant of all men.

ARGAN: Lack-a-day! You are a grand doctor, by what I see, and I heartily wish that some one of those gentlemen were here to pay off your arguments, and check your prating.

BERALDO: I, brother, I don't make it my business to attack the faculty, and everyone at their perils and fortune, may believe whatever they please. What I say of it is only amongst ourselves, and I could wish to have been able to deliver you a little out of the error you are in, and, to divert you, could carry you to see one of Molière's comedies upon this subject.

ARGAN: Your Molière with his comedies is a fine impertinent fellow, and I think him mighty pleasant to pretend to bring on the stage such worthy persons as the physicians.

BERALDO: 'Tisn't the physicians that he exposes, but the ridiculousness of physic.

ARGAN: 'Tis mighty proper for him to pretend to control the faculty; a fine simpleton, a pretty impertinent creature, to make a jest of consultations and prescriptions, to attack the body of physicians, and to bring on his stage such venerable persons as those gentlemen.

BERALDO: What would you have him bring there, but the different professions of men? They bring there every day princes and kings, who are of as good a family as the physicians.

ARGAN: Now by all that's terrible, if I was a physician, I would be revenged

257

of his impertinence, and, when he was sick, let him die without relief. He should say and do in vain, I would not prescribe him the least bleeding, the least small clyster, and would say to him, Perish, perish, 'twill teach you another time to make a jest of the faculty.

BERALDO: You are in a great passion at him.

ARGAN: Yes, he's a foolish fellow; and if the physicians are wise, they'll do what I say.

BERALDO: He'll be still wiser than your physicians. For he'll not ask 'em for any assistance.

ARGAN: So much the worse for him, if he has not recourse to remedies.

BERALDO: He has his reasons for not intending it, and he thinks that 'tis not proper but for vigorous and robust people, and those who have strength left to bear the physic with the disease; but for him, he has but just strength to bear his illness.

ARGAN: Very foolish reasons, those! Hold, brother, let us talk no more of that man, for it raises my choler, and you'll bring my distemper on me.

BERALDO: With all my heart, brother; and to change the discourse, I must tell you, that for a little repugnance which your daughter has discovered to you, you ought not to take the violent resolution of putting her into a convent; that in choice of a son-in-law, you should not blindly follow a passion that transports you, and that you ought in this matter to accommodate yourself a little to the inclination of your child, since 'tis for all her life, and since the whole happiness of a married state depends on it.

Scene IV

Mr. Fleurant (with a syringe in his hand), Argan, Beraldo.

ARGAN: Oh! brother, with your leave.

BERALDO: How, what would you do?

ARGAN: Take this little clyster here, 'twill be soon done.

BERALDO: You are in jest sure. Can't you be one moment without a clyster or a purge? Send it back till some other time, and take a little rest.

ARGAN: This evening, Mr. Fleruant, or tomorrow morning.

MR. FLEURANT: *(To BERALDO.)* For what reason do you pretend to oppose the prescriptions of the faculty, and to hinder the gentleman from taking my clyster? You are very pleasant to have this boldness!

BERALDO: Begone, sir, we see well enough that you have not been accustomed to speak to people's faces.

MR. FLEURANT: You ought not to make a jest of physic in this manner, and to make me lose my time. I'm not come here but on a good prescription, and I'll go tell Mr. Purgon how I've been hindered from executing his orders, and from performing my function. You'll see, you'll see —

Scene V

Argan, Beraldo.

ARGAN: Brother, you'll be the cause here of some misfortune.

BERALDO: The great misfortune of not taking a clyster which Mr. Purgon had prescribed! Once more, brother, is it possible that there should be no way of curing you of the diseases of the doctor, and will you all your lifetime lie buried in their drugs?

ARGAN: Ah, brother, you talk of it like a man that's in health; but if you were in my place, you'd soon change your language. 'Tis easy to talk against physic, when one's in full health.

BERALDO: But what distemper have you?

ARGAN: You'll make me mad. I wish that you had my distemper, to see if you would prate thus. Ah! here's Mr. Purgon.

Scene VI

Mr. Purgon, Argan, Beraldo, Toinet.

MR. PURGON: I have just now heard very pleasant news below at the door. That you make a jest of my prescriptions here, and refuse to take the remedy which I ordered.

ARGAN: Sir, 'twas not —

MR. PURGON: 'Tis a great insolence, a strange rebellion of a patient against his physician.

TOINET: That's horrible.

MR. PURGON: A clyster which I had taken the pleasure to compose myself.

ARGAN: 'Twas not I —

MR. PURGON: Invented, and made up according to all the rules of art.

TOINET: He was in the wrong.

MR. PURGON: And which would have produced a marvellous effect on the bowels.

ARGAN: My brother —

MR. PURGON: To send it back with contempt!

ARGAN: *(Pointing to BERALDO.)* 'Tis he —

MR. PURGON: 'Tis an exorbitant action.

TOINET: True.

MR. PURGON: An enormous outrage against the profession.

ARGAN: *(Pointing to BERALDO.)* He is the cause —

MR. PURGON: A crime of high treason against the faculty, which can't be enough punished.

TOINET: You're in the right.

MR. PURGON: I declare to you that I break off all commerce with you.

ARGAN: 'Tis my brother —

MR. PURGON: That I'll have no more alliance with you.

TOINET: You'll do well.

MR. PURGON: And to end all union with you, there's the deed of gift which I made to my nephew in favour of the marriage.

ARGAN: 'Tis my brother that has done all the mischief.

MR. PURGON: To condemn my clyster?

ARGAN: Let it be brought, I'll take it directly.

MR. PURGON: I should have delivered you from your malady before 'twas long.

TOINET: He doesn't deserve it.

MR. PURGON: I was going to cleanse your body, and to have discharged it entirely of all its ill humours.

ARGAN: Ah, brother!

MR. PURGON: And I wanted no more than a dozen purges, to have gone to the bottom with you.

TOINET: He's unworthy of your care.

MR. PURGON: But since you were not willing to be cured by my hands,

ARGAN: 'Tisn't my fault.

MR. PURGON: Since you have forsaken the obedience which a man owes to his physician,

TOINET: That cries for vengeance.

MR. PURGON: Since you have declared yourself rebellious to the remedies I've prescribed you,

ARGAN: Ah, not at all.

MR. PURGON: I must tell you that I abandon you to your evil constitution, to the intemperature of your bowels, the corruption of your blood, the acrimony of your bile, and the feculency of your humours.

TOINET: 'Tis very well done.

ARGAN: Oh! Heavens!

MR. PURGON: And my will is that within four days' time you enter on an incurable state.

ARGAN: Ah! mercy!

MR. PURGON: That you fall into a bradypepsia.

ARGAN: Mr. Purgon!

MR. PURGON: From a bradypepsia into a dyspepsia.

ARGAN: Mr. Purgon!

MR. PURGON: From a dyspepsia into an apepsia.

ARGAN: Mr. Purgon!

MR. PURGON: From an apepsia into a lienteria.

ARGAN: Mr. Purgon!

MR. PURGON: From a lienteria into a dissenteria.

ARGAN: Mr. Purgon!

MR. PURGON: From a dissenteria into a dropsy.

ARGAN: Mr. Purgon!

MR. PURGON: And from a dropsy into a privation of life where your folly will bring you.

Scene VII

Argan, Beraldo.

ARGAN: Ah! Heavens, I'm dead! Brother, you have undone me.

BERALDO: Why? What's the matter?

ARGAN: I can hold no longer. I feel already that the faculty is taking its revenge.

BERALDO: Faith, brother, you're a simpleton, and I would not for a great deal that you should be seen doing what you do. Pray feel your own pulse a little, come to yourself again, and don't give up so much to your imagination.

ARGAN: You see, brother, the strange diseases he threatened me with.

BERALDO: What a simple man you are!

ARGAN: He said I should become incurable within four days' time.

BERALDO: And what does it signify what he said? Is't an oracle that has spoken to you? to hear you one would think that Mr. Purgon held in his hands the thread of your days, and by supreme authority could prolong it to you, or cut it short as he pleased. Consider that the principles of your life are in yourself, and that the anger of Mr. Purgon is as incapable of killing you, as his remedies are of keeping you alive. Here's an opportunity, if you have a mind to it, to get rid o' the doctors, or if you were born not to be able to live without 'em, it is easy to have another of 'em, with whom, brother, you may run a little less risk.

ARGAN: Ah! brother, he knew all my constitution, and the way to govern me —

BERALDO: I must confess to you, that you are a man of great prepossession, and that you see things with strange eyes.

Scene VIII

Argan, Beraldo, Toinet.

TOINET: *(To ARGAN.)* Sir, there's a doctor desires to see you.

ARGAN: What doctor?

TOINET: A doctor of physic.

ARGAN: I ask thee who he is.

TOINET: I don't know him, but he's as like me as two drops of water, and if I wasn't sure that my mother was an honest woman, I should say, that this was some little brother she had given me since my father's death.

ARGAN: Let him come in.

Scene IX

Argan, Beraldo.

BERALDO: You are served to your wish. One doctor leaves you, another offers himself.

ARGAN: I much fear if you be not the cause of some misfortune.

BERALDO: Again! are you always upon that?

ARGAN: See how I have at heart all those distempers that I don't know, those —

Scene X

Argan, Beraldo, Toinet (dressed as a physician).

TOINET: Permit me, sir, to make you a visit, and to offer you my small services for all the bleedings and purgations you shall have occasion for.

ARGAN: Sir, I'm very much obliged to you. *(To BERALDO.)* By my troth, Toinet herself!

TOINET: I beg you to excuse me, sir, I had forgotten to give my servant a message, I'll return immediately.

Scene XI

Argan, Beraldo.

ARGAN: Hah! would not you say that 'tis verily Toinet?

BERALDO: 'Tis true that the likeness is very great. But this is not the first time we've seen these sort of things, and histories are full of these sports of nature.

261

ARGAN: For my part, I am astonished at it, and —

Scene XII

Argan, Beraldo, Toinet.

TOINET: What d'ye want, sir?
ARGAN: What?
TOINET: Did you not call me?
ARGAN: I? no.
TOINET: My ears must have tingled then.
ARGAN: Stay a little here, and see how much this doctor is like thee.
TOINET: Yes truly, I have other business below, and I've seen him enough.

Scene XIII

Argan, Beraldo.

ARGAN: If I hadn't seen 'em both together, I should have believed 'twas but one.
BERALDO: I have read surprising things of these kind of resemblances, and we have seen of 'em in our times, where all the world have been deceived.
ARGAN: For my part I should have been deceived by this, and should have sworn 'twas the same person.

Scene XIV

Argan, Beraldo, Toinet (in a physician's habit.)

TOINET: Sir, I ask pardon with all my heart.
ARGAN: *(Aside to BERALDO.)* This is wonderful!
TOINET: Pray, sir, don't take amiss the curiosity I had to see such an illustrious patient as you are; your reputation, which reaches everywhere, may excuse the liberty I've taken.
ARGAN: Sir, I'm your servant.
TOINET: I see, sir, that you look earnestly at me. What age d'ye really think I am?
ARGAN: I think that you may be twenty-six, or twenty-seven at most.
TOINET: Ha, ha, ha, ha, ha! I'm fourscore and ten.
ARGAN: Fourscore and ten!
TOINET: Yes. You see an effect of the secrets of my art, to preserve me thus fresh and vigorous.
ARGAN: By my troth, a fine youthful old fellow for one of fourscore and ten.
TOINET: I'm an itinerant physician, that go from town to town, province to province, kingdom to kingdom, to seek out famous matter for my capacity, to find patients worthy of employing myself on, capable of exercising the great and fine secrets which I've discovered in medicine. I disdain to amuse myself with the little fry of common diseases, with the trifles of rheumatisms and defluxions, agues, vapours, and megrims. I would have diseases of importance, good continual fevers, with a disordered brain, good purple fevers, good plagues, good confirmed dropsies, good pleurisies, with inflammations of the lungs, this is what pleases me, this is what I triumph in; and I wish, sir, that you had all

the diseases I've just now mentioned, that you were abandoned by all the physicians, despaired of, at the point of death, that I might demonstrate to you the excellency of my remedies, and the desire I have to do you service.

ARGAN: I'm obliged to you, sir, for the kind wishes you have for me.

TOINET: Let's feel your pulse. Come then beat as you should. Aha! I shall make you go as you ought. Ho! this pulse plays the impertinent; I perceive you don't know me yet. Who is your physician?

ARGAN: Mr. Purgon.

TOINET: That man's not written in my table-book amongst the great physicians. What does he say you are ill of?

ARGAN: He says that 'tis the liver, and others say that 'tis the spleen.

TOINET: They are all blockheads, 'tis your lungs that you are ill of.

ARGAN: Lungs?

TOINET: Yes, what do you feel?

ARGAN: I feel from time to time pains in my head.

TOINET: The lungs exactly.

ARGAN: I seem sometimes to have a mist before my eyes.

TOINET: The lungs.

ARGAN: I have sometimes a pain at the heart.

TOINET: The lungs.

ARGAN: I sometimes feel a weariness in all my limbs.

TOINET: The lungs.

ARGAN: And sometimes I'm taken with pains in my belly, as if 'twas the colic.

TOINET: The lungs. You have an appetite to what you eat?

ARGAN: Yes, sir.

TOINET: The lungs. You love to drink a little wine?

ARGAN: Yes, sir.

TOINET: The lungs. You take a little nap after repast, and are glad to sleep?

ARGAN: Yes, sir.

TOINET: The lungs, the lungs I tell you. What does your physician order you for your food?

ARGAN: He orders me soup.

TOINET: Ignorant!

ARGAN: Fowl.

TOINET: Ignorant!

ARGAN: Veal.

TOINET: Ignorant!

ARGAN: Broth.

TOINET: Ignorant!

ARGAN: New-laid eggs.

TOINET: Ignorant!

ARGAN: And a few prunes at night to relax the belly.

TOINET: Ignorant!

ARGAN: And above all to drink my wine well diluted.

TOINET: *Ignorantus, ignoranta, ignorantum.* You must drink your wine unmixed; and to thicken your blood which is too thin, you must eat good fat beef, good fat pork, good Dutch cheese, good rice gruel, and chestnuts and wafers, to thicken and conglutinate. Your doctor's an ass. I'll send you one of my own choice, and will come to see you from time to time, as long as I stay in this town.

ARGAN: You will very much oblige me.

TOINET: What the deuce do you do with this arm?

ARGAN: How?

TOINET: Here's an arm I'd have cut off immediately, if I were as you.

ARGAN: And why?

TOINET: Don't you see that it attracts all the nourishment to itself, and hinders this side from growing?

ARGAN: Yes, but I have occasion for my arm.

TOINET: You've a right eye there too that I would have plucked out, if I were in your place.

ARGAN: Pluck out an eye?

TOINET: Don't you find it incommodes the other, and robs it of all its nourishment? Believe me, have it plucked out as soon as possible, you'll see the clearer with the left eye.

ARGAN: There needs no hurry in this affair.

TOINET: Farewell. I'm sorry to quit you so soon, but I must be present at a grand consultation we are to have about a man who died yesterday.

ARGAN: About a man who died yesterday?

TOINET: Yes, to consider, and see what ought to have been done to have cured him. Your humble servant.

ARGAN: You know that sick folk are excused from ceremony.

Scene XV

Argan, Beraldo.

BERALDO: Truly, this doctor seems to be a very skilful man.

ARGAN: Yes; but goes a little of the fastest.

BERALDO: All your great physicians do so.

ARGAN: To cut off my arm, and pluck out my eye, that the other may be better? I'd much rather that it should not be quite so well. A pretty operation, truly, to make me at once both blind and lame.

Scene XVI

Argan, Beraldo, Toinet.

TOINET: *(Pretending to speak to somebody.)* Come, come, I'm your humble servant for that. I am not in a merry humour.

ARGAN: What's the matter?

TOINET: Your physician, troth, wants to feel my pulse.

ARGAN: Look you there, at fourscore and ten years of age.

BERALDO: Well, come, brother, since your Mr. Purgon has quarrelled with you, won't you give me leave to speak of the match, which is proposed for my niece?

ARGAN: No, brother, I'll put her in a convent, since she opposed my inclinations. I see plainly there's some intrigue in the case, and I have discovered a certain secret interview, which they don't know I have discovered.

BERALDO: Well, brother, allowing there were some little inclination, would that be so criminal, and can anything be offensive to you, when all

264

this tends only to what is very honest, as matrimony?

ARGAN: Be it what it will, brother, she shall be a nun, that I'm determined upon.

BERALDO: You will very much please a certain person.

ARGAN: I understand you. We are always harping upon that string, and my wife sticks greatly in your stomach.

BERALDO: Well, yes, brother, since I must speak frankly, 'tis your wife that I mean; and I can no more endure the infatuation you are under in respect to her, than I can your infatuation in respect to physic, nor to see you run headlong into every snare she lays for you.

TOINET: Ah, sir, don't talk of madam, she's a woman of whom there's nothing to be said; a woman without artifice, and who loves my master, who loves him — one can't express it.

ARGAN: Ask her but how fond she is of me.

TOINET: 'Tis true.

ARGAN: What uneasiness my sickness gives her.

TOINET: Most assuredly.

ARGAN: And the care, and the pains she takes about me.

TOINET: 'Tis certain. *(To BERALDO.)* Have you a mind I should convince you, and show you presently how madam loves my master? *(To ARGAN.)* Sir, let me undeceive him, and deliver him from his mistake.

ARGAN: How?

TOINET: My mistress is just returned. Clap yourself down in this chair, stretched out at your full length, and feign yourself dead. You'll see the sorrow she'll be in, when I tell her the news.

ARGAN: I'll do it.

TOINET: Yes, but don't let her continue long in despair, for she may perhaps die by it.

ARGAN: Let me alone.

TOINET: *(To BERALDO.)* Hide you yourself in this corner.

Scene XVII

Argan, Toinet.

ARGAN: Is there not some danger in counterfeiting death?

TOINET: No, no. What danger can there be? Only stretch yourself out there. 'Twill be a great pleasure to confound your brother. Here's my mistress. Steady as you are.

Scene XVIII

Belina, Argan (stretched out in his chair), Toinet.

TOINET: *(Pretending not to see BELINA.)* Oh, Heavens! oh, wretched! what a strange accident!

BELINA: What ails you, Toinet?

TOINET: Ah, madam!

BELINA: What's the matter?

TOINET: Your husband's dead.

BELINA: My husband dead?

TOINET: Alas! yes. The poor soul is defunct.

BELINA: Certainly?

TOINET: Certainly. Nobody knows of this accident as yet, I was here all alone with him. He just now departed in my arms. Here, see him laid at his full length in this chair.

BELINA: Heaven be praised. Here I am delivered from a grievous burden. What a fool art thou, Toinet, to be so afflicted at his death!

TOINET: I thought, madam, that we should cry.

BELINA: Go, go, 'tis not worth while. What loss is there of him, and what good did he do upon earth? A wretch troublesome to all the world, a filthy, nauseous fellow, never without a clyster, or a dose of physic in his guts; always snivelling, coughing, or spitting; a stupid, tedious, ill-natured creature; for ever fatiguing people, and scolding, night and day, at his maids and his footmen.

TOINET: A fine funeral oration!

BELINA: You must help me, Toinet, to execute my design, and you may depend upon it, in serving me, your recompense is sure. Since, by good luck, nobody is yet acquainted with the affair, let us carry him to his bed, and keep his death a secret till I have accomplished my business. There are some papers, and there is some money, that I have a mind to seize on, and it is not just that I should have passed the prime of my years with him, without any manner of advantage. Come, Toinet, let us first of all take all his keys.

ARGAN: *(Starting up hastily.)* Softly.

BELINA: Ah!

ARGAN: Ay, mistress wife, is it thus you love me?

TOINET: Ah, hah! the defunct is not dead.

ARGAN: *(To BELINA who makes off.)* I'm very glad to see your love, and to have heard the fine panegyric you made upon me. 'Tis a wholesome piece of advice, which will make me wise for the future, and prevent me doing a good many things.

Scene XIX

Beraldo (coming out of the place where he was hid), Argan, Toinet.

BERALDO: Well, brother, you see how 'tis.

TOINET: In good truth, I could never have believed it. But I hear your daughter; place yourself as you were, and let us see in what manner she will receive your death. 'Tis a thing which 'twill not be at all amiss to try, and since your hand is in, you'll know, by this means, the sentiments your family has for you. *(BERALDO conceals himself again.)*

Scene XX

Argan, Angelica, Toinet.

TOINET: *(Pretending not to see ANGELICA.)* Oh, Heaven! Ah! sad accident! Unhappy day!

ANGELICA: What ails you, Toinet, and what d'ye cry for?

TOINET: Alas! I've melancholy news to tell you.

ANGELICA: Eh? what?

TOINET: Your father's dead.

ANGELICA: My father dead, Toinet?

TOINET: Yes, you see him there, he died this moment of a fainting fit that took him.

ANGELICA: Oh, Heaven! what a misfortune! what a cruel stroke! Alas! must I lose my father, the only thing I had left in the world! And must I also, to increase my despair, lose him at a time when he was angry with me! What will become of me, unhappy wretch? And what consolation can I find after so great a loss?

Scene XXI

Argan, Angelica, Cleanthes, Toinet.

CLEANTHES: What's the matter with you, fair Angelica? And what misfortune do you weep for?

ANGELICA: I weep for everything I could lose most dear and precious in life. I weep for the death of my father.

CLEANTHES: Heavens! what an accident! how unexpected a stroke! Alas! after the demand I had conjured your uncle to make of you in marriage, I was coming to present myself to him, to endeavour by my respects and entreaties to incline his heart to grant you to my wishes.

ANGELICA: Ah! Cleanthes, let us talk no more of it. Let us here leave off all thoughts of marriage. After the death of my father, I'll have nothing more to do with the world, I renounce it forever. Yes, my dear father, if I have lately opposed your inclinations, I will follow one of your intentions at least, and make amends, by that, *(Kneeling.)* for the concern I accuse myself of having given you. Permit me, father, now to give you my promise of it, and to embrace you, to witness to you my resentment.

ARGAN: *(Embracing ANGELICA.)* Oh! my child!

ANGELICA: Hah!

ARGAN: Come, be not frightened, I am not dead. Come, thou art my true flesh and blood, my real daughter, and I am charmed that I have discovered thy good nature.

Scene XXII

Argan, Beraldo, Angelica, Cleanthes, Toinet.

ANGELICA: Ah! what an agreeable surprise! Since, by extreme good fortune, Heaven restores you, sir, to my wishes, permit me here to throw myself at your feet, to implore one favour of you. If you are not favourable to the inclination of my heart, if you refuse me Cleanthes for a husband; I conjure you at least, not to force me to marry another. This is all the favour I ask of you.

CLEANTHES: *(Throwing himself at ARGAN's feet.)* Ah! sir, allow yourself to be touched with her entreaties and mine; and show not yourself averse to the mutual ardours of so agreeable a passion.

BERALDO: Brother, can you withstand this?

TOINET: Can you be insensible, sir, of much love?

ARGAN: Let him turn physician, I consent to the marriage. *(To CLEANTHES.)* Yes, sir, turn physician, and I give you my daughter.

CLEANTHES: Most willingly. If it only sticks at that, sir, to become your son-in-law, I'll be a physician, and even an apothecary, if you please. That's no such a business, I should do much more to obtain the fair Angelica.

BERALDO: But, brother, a thought's come into my head. Turn a physician yourself. The conveniency will be much greater, to have all that you want within yourself.

TOINET: That's true. That's the true way to cure yourself presently; and there's no distemper so daring, as to meddle with the person of a physician.

ARGAN: I fancy, brother, you banter me. Am I of an age to study?

BERALDO: Pshaw, study! why, you are learned enough; there are a great many among 'em, who are not better skilled than yourself.

ARGAN: But one should know how to speak Latin well, to know the distempers, and the remedies proper to apply to 'em.

BERALDO: You'll learn all that by putting on the robe and cap of a physician, and you will afterwards be more skilful than you'd wish to be.

ARGAN: What! do people understand how to discourse upon distempers, when they have on that habit?

BERALDO: Yes. You have nothing to do, but to talk, with a gown and cap any stuff becomes learned, and nonsense becomes sense.

TOINET: Hold, sir, were there no more than your beard, that goes a great way already; a beard makes more than half in the composition of a doctor.

CLEANTHES. I'm ready at worst, to do everything.

BERALDO: *(To ARGAN.)* Will you have the thing done immediately?

ARGAN: How, immediately?

BERALDO: Yes, and in your own house?

ARGAN: In my own house?

BERALDO: Yes, I know a body of physicians, my friends, who will come instantly and perform the ceremony in your hall. 'Twill cost you nothing.

ARGAN: But what shall I say, what shall I answer?

BERALDO: They'll instruct you in a few words, and they'll give you in writing, what you are to say. Go dress yourself in a decent manner, I'll go send for 'em.

ARGAN: With all my heart, let's see this.

Scene XXIII

Beraldo, Angelica, Cleanthes, Toinet.

CLEANTHES: What's your intention, and what d'ye mean by this body of your friends —

TOINET: What's your design?

BERALDO: To divert ourselves a little this evening. The players have made an interlude of a doctor's admission with dances and music, I desire we may take the diversion of it together, and that my brother may act the principal character in it.

ANGELICA: But, uncle, methinks you play upon my father a little too much.

BERALDO: But niece, this is not so much playing on him, as giving into his fancies. We may each of us take a part in it ourselves, and so perform the comedy to one another. The carnival bears us out in this. Let's go quickly to get everything ready.

CLEANTHES: *(To ANGELICA.)* Do you consent to it?

ANGELICA: Yes, since my uncle conducts us.

INTERLUDE

First Entry

Upholsterers come in dancing to prepare the hall, and place the benches to music.

Second Entry

A cavalcade of physicians to the sound of instruments.

Persons bearing clyster-pipes which represent maces, enter first. After them come the apothecaries with their mortars, surgeons and doctors two by two, who place themselves on each side the stage, whilst the president ascends a chair, which is placed in the middle, and ARGAN who is to be admitted a doctor of physic, places himself on a low stool at the foot of the president's chair.

Præses.[12] Scavantissimi doctores,
Medicinæ professores,
Qui hic assemblati estis;
Et vos altri messiores,
Sententiarum facultatis
Fideles executores;
Chirurgiani and apothicari,
Atque tota compania aussi,
Salus, honor, and argentum,
Atque bonum appetitum.
Non possum, docti confreri,
In me satis admirari,
Qualis bona inventio,
Est medici professio;
How rare and choice a thing is ista
Medicina benedicta,
Quæ suo nomine solo
Marveloso miraculo
Since si longo tempore;
Has made in clover vivere
So many people omni genere.

Per totam terram videmus
Grandam vogam ubi sumus;
Et quod grandes and petiti
Sunt de nobis infatuti:
Totus mundus currens ad nostros remedios,
Nos regardat sicut deos,

---

[12]*Præses:* President. His speech, as well as the remainder of the ceremony, is presented in a hodgepodge of Latin and English — in the original, Latin and French. The effect is to make fun of physicians and at the same time to heap ridicule on Argan who seems to take the whole thing seriously; he knows enough Latin, from his associations with doctors, that he is surprised to discover that he more or less understands this learned discourse. English readers with even less Latin than Argan has will discover that, by reading the text aloud, they'll be able to pick up the gist of the ceremony. In the President's introduction, he praises medicine which has made it possible for him and his colleagues to live in the clover, he brags that even kings and princes regard physicians as gods, and he invites the other doctors to examine the candidate Argan.

Et nostris præscriptionibus
Principes and reges subjectos videtis.

'Tis therefore nostra sapientia,
Bonus sensus atque prudenita,
Strongly for to travaillare,
A nos bene conservare
In tali credito, voga and honore;
Et take care à non recevere
In nostro docto corpore
Quam personas capabiles,
Et totas dignas fillire
Has placas honorabiles.

For that nunc convocati estis,
Et credo quod findebitis
Dignam matieram medici,
In scavanti homine that there you see;
Whom in thingis omnibus
Dono ad interrogandum,
Et à bottom examinandum
Vestris capacitatibus.

First Doctor: Si mihi licentiam dat dominus præses,
Et tanti docti doctores,
Et assistantes illustres,
Learnidissimo bacheliere
Quem estimo and honoro,
Demandabo causam and rationem, quare
Opium facid dormire.

Argan: Mihi à docto doctore
Demandatur causam and rationem, quare
Opium facit dormire.
To which respondeo,
Quia est in eo
Virtus dormitiva,
Cujus est natura
Sensus stupifire.[13]

Chorus: Bene, bene, bene, bene respondere,
Dignus, dignus est intrare
In nostro docto corpore.
Bene, bene respondere.

Second Doctor: Cum permissione domini præsidis,
Doctissimæ facultatis,
Et totius his nostris actis
Companiæ assistantis,
Demandabo tibi, docte bacheliere

[13]Questioned about why opium causes sleep, Argan answers that it does so because it is its nature to do so. The doctors praise him as worthy of acceptance into the body of physicians.

Quæ sunt remedia,
Quæ in maladia
Called hydropisia
Convenit facere?

Argan: Clisterium donare,
Postea bleedare,
Afterwards purgare.[14]

Chorus: Bene, bene, bene, bene respondere,
Dignus, dignus est intrare
In nostro docto corpore.

Third Doctor: Si bonus semblatur domine præsidi,
Doctissimæ facultati
Et companiæ præsenti,
Demandabo tibi, docte bacheliere,
Quæ remedia eticis,
Pulmonicis atque asmaticis
Do you think à propos facere.

Argan: Clisterium donare,
Postea bleedare,
Afterwards purgare.

Chorus: Bene, bene, bene, bene respondere:
Dignus, dignus est intrare
In nostro docto corpore.

Fourth Doctor: Super illas maladias,
Doctus bachelierus dixit maravillas:
But if I do not tease and fret dominum præsidem,
Doctissimam facultatem,
Et totam honorabilem
Companiam hearkennantem;
Faciam illi unam quæstionem.
Last night patientus unus
Chanced to fall in meas manus:
Habet grandam fiévram cum redoublamentis
Grandum dolerem capitis,
Et grandum malum in his si-de,
Cum granda difficultate
Et pena respirare.
Be pleased then to tell me,
Docte bacheliere,
Quid illi facere.

Argan: Clisterium donare,
Postea bleedare,
Afterwards purgare.

[14]The second through fifth doctors each present a disease and ask what Argan would prescribe; in each case his prescription is the same: "Give an enema, then bleed the patient, and afterwards administer a laxative."

Fifth Doctor: But if maladia
Opiniatria
Non vult se curire,
Quid illi facere?

Argan: Clisterium donare,
Postea bleedare,
Afterwards purgare.
Rebleedare, repurgare, and reclysterisare.

Chorus: Bene, bene, bene, bene repondere:
Dignus, dignus est intrare
In nostro docto corpore.

The President: (To Argan.)
Juras keepare statuta
Per facultatem præscripta,
Cum sensu and jugeamento?

Argan: Juro.

The President: To be in omnibus
consultationibus
Ancieni aviso;
Aut bono,
Aut baddo?

Argan: Juro.

The President: That thou'lt never te servire
De remediis aucunis,
Than only those doctæ facultatis;
Should the patient burst-O
Et mori de suo malo?

Argan: Juro.

The President:[15]   Ego cum isto boneto
Venerablili and docto,
Dono tibi and concedo
Virtutem and powerantiam,
Medicandi,
Purgandi,
Bleedandi,
Prickandi,
Cuttandi,
Slashandi,
Et occidendi
Impune per totam terram.

Third Entry

The surgeons and apothecaries do reverence with music to Argan.

[15]Having received Argan's oath, he empowers him to medicate, purge, bleed, and so on.

Argan:[16]
Grandes doctores doctrinæ,
Of rhubarbe and of séné:
'Twou'd be in me without doubt one thinga folla,
Inepta and ridicula,
If I should m'engageare
Vobis loüangeas donare,
Et pretendebam addare
Des lumieras au soleillo,
Et des étoilas au cielo,
Des ondas à l'oceano,
Et des rosas to the springo.
Agree that in one wordo
Pro toto remercimento
Rendam gratiam corpori tam docto.
Vobis, vobis debeo
More than to nature, and than to patri meo;
Natura and paper meus
Hominem me habent factum:
But vos me, that which is plus,
Avetis factum medicum.
Honor, favor, and gratia,
Qui in hoc corde que voilà,
Imprimant ressentimenta
Qui dureront in sæcula.

Chorus:
Vivat, vivat, vivat, vivat, for ever vivat
Novus doctor, qui tam bene speakat,
Mille, mille annis, and manget and bibat,
Et bleedet and killat.[17]

Fourth Entry

All the surgeons and apothecaries dance to the sound of the instruments and voices, and clapping of hands, and apothecaries' mortars.

First Surgeon:
May he see doctas
Suas præscriptionas
Omnium chirurgorum,
Et apotiquarum
Fillire shopas.

Chorus:
Vivat, vivat, vivat, for ever vivat
Novus doctor, qui tam bene speakat,
Mille, mille annis, and manget and bibat,
Et bleedet and killat.

[16]Argan says he owes the college of doctors more than either nature or his father since nature and his father only made him a man, but they have made him a doctor.
[17]Live, live, live, live, forever live,
New doctor, who speaks so well,
A thousand, thousand years, and eat and drink
and bleed and kill.

Second Surgeon: May all his anni
Be to him boni
Et favorabiles,
Et n'habere jamais
Quàm plaguas, poxas,
Fiévras, pluresias
Bloody fluxies and dissenterias.

Chorus: Vivat, vivat, vivat, vivat, for ever vivat
Novus doctor, qui tam bene speakat,
Mille, mille annis, and manget and bibat,
Et bleedet and killat.

Fifth and Last Entry

While the chorus is singing, the doctors, surgeons, and apothecaries go out all according to their several ranks, with the same ceremony they entered.

THE NINETEENTH CENTURY: The Theatre of Romanticism and Melodrama

During the end of the eighteenth century and the beginning of the nineteenth, a transition took place that changed forever the way Europeans viewed and thought about theatre, art, and indeed the whole world. During these years, romanticism, a literary, artistic, and philosophical movement, took the place of classicism. At the same time, while philosophers, scholars, and artists on the cutting edge were working out the implications of romanticism, theatre professionals were entertaining massive audiences with the favorite dramatic form of the period — melodrama. Melodrama formed a link between neoclassicism and realism and motivated the development of modern stagecraft.

Political/Social/Philosophical Backgrounds

The democratic revolutions in America (1775) and France (1789) helped set the scene for romanticism. These political upheavals spelled out new rules for society: Because of them, people came to believe the individual was as important as, if not more important than, society as a whole. They accepted that all individuals, regardless of social status, are equals. They believed that the basis of human society resided in human agreement rather than divine institutions. And they accepted violent upheaval — revolution — as good rather than evil. The American Civil War in the middle of the century was in part an attempt to apply democratic principles to blacks as well as whites and in part a testing of government-by-agreement.

At the same time that political revolutions were confirming the rights of the common person, the industrial revolution and the establishment of large manufacturing centers were creating ever larger numbers of common people — the urban masses.

Furthermore, partly because of growth in scientific methodology, partly because of contact with vastly different cultures brought about by world-wide conquest, and partly because of rapid, irreversible changes in political life, people developed a different understanding of history. Whereas former ages had viewed history as cyclic or pool-like and valued the universal — that which was true of all people in all places in all times — nineteenth-century people came to see history as linear, and they began to value the uniqueness of specific, peculiar events, styles, and beliefs.

Immanuel Kant

The German philosopher Immanuel Kant (1724-1804) formulated a system of thought that helped people make sense of their new perceptions of the world and led directly into romanticism. Kant taught that there is a spiritual world which is at odds with the natural world. Human beings are

275

born in touch with the spiritual world and therefore have an innate sense of morality: their instincts are good. The natural world, however, gets in the way of the human intent to do right and, in that way, corrupts people. This idea contrasted with the neoclassical belief that the natural world is basically a good and just place; it established the romantic tendency to view humankind as good, spiritual beings cursed by a world that limits and destroys them.

Kant was the first major philosopher to make art a part of his philosophical system. He said that art is ultimately concerned with the spiritual, super-sensate world, the world of ideas and values; its purpose is to translate these perceptions into concrete, sensate reality. Friedrich von Schiller (1759-1805), the German dramatist and interpreter of Kant, put it this way: Human beings have conflicting instincts; on the one hand they have a spiritual, rational impulse which tends to make them free; on the other hand, they are bound by a natural, material impulse which limits them. Art, the play impulse, brings these two instincts into unity: "Art is that which makes man whole again." These beliefs about the purpose of art, in contrast with the neoclassical idea that art was "to teach and please," gave the romantics an almost religious feeling about art.

Kant also wrote about the manner in which artists work. He said that art is the product of genius. Genius is innate and irrational: You have it or you don't, and you can't explain it. The genius produces art without knowing how s/he does so; if s/he does understand how s/he does it, it probably isn't art. This romantic understanding of how the artist works directly contrasted with the classical belief that art is, by definition, that which is done by rational techniques and that artists can learn and improve their techniques.

Theory of Drama

The romantics attacked classicism with revolutionary zeal. They argued that, in contrast with the classical concept of art as imitation, art was instead a matter of creation, imitative neither of nature nor of great past works. The task of drama, they claimed, was not to mirror human behavior but rather to illuminate the path of ordinary folk by flashes of genius. Furthermore, while classical writers spoke of building their works like architects and carpenters, romantics said that the real art work grows like a plant, germinating and developing with living power within the artist. Plot, the careful ordering of incidents prized by classicists, was rejected by the romantics in favor of an emphasis on mood and characterization. The romantics disliked the tight, clean dramatic unity and purity of form of the classics and preferred long, uneven or fragmentary works; they prized loose, organic development and mixed forms. While the classics reached for the goal of beauty, the romantics put a premium on the powerful and the grotesque.

Rejecting the classical tradition of the seventeenth and eighteenth centuries, the romantics looked back to Shakespeare as the dramatist par excellence. They admired his sprawling plots, his use of language, his depiction of character, and his apparent disregard for the classical rules. They so revered his work that they believed his genius exceeded the capabilities of the stage, and they initiated the viewpoint, sometimes heard even today, that the plays of the theatre practitioner Shakespeare are basically unstageable.

Dramatic Literature

Seeing the physical demands of the stage as one more example of the limitations the world places on genius, the romantics turned away from theatre and focused their literary efforts instead on the novel and lyric poetry. The very term "romantic," in fact, means "novelesque." At the same time, the romantics liked the dialog form of drama. As a result, they wrote "closet dramas" — plays which were intended to be read in private rather than staged in the theatre. Samples of this kind of play include *Faust* by Johann Wolfgang von Goethe (1749-1832) and *Cain* by Lord George Gordon Byron (1788-1824). Both of these works are long, unstageable plays which focus on great souls who rebel against the world's demands.

Georg Büchner

The play *Woyzeck* and its author George Büchner (1813-37) exemplify another aspect of romantic drama. Hounded all over Europe by the German authorities because of his revolutionary pamphlets, Büchner died of typhoid fever at the age of twenty-four. He left behind a handful of fragmentary scenes which depict the ruin of Woyzeck, an unbalanced, lower-class military functionary who is destroyed by exploitation, insensitivity, and physical and mental illness. In spite of its fragmentary nature and its resultant lack of plot and form, *Woyzeck* is a powerful depiction of character and mood.

Victor-Marie Hugo and Richard Wagner

Two other romantic dramatists should be mentioned here: The French novelist Victor-Marie Hugo (1802-85) whose play *Hernani,* produced in 1830, marked the romantic victory over neoclassicism in France and Richard Wagner (1813-83) who developed a new form of opera to heighten the power of his romantic music dramas.

Melodrama

While philosophers and serious dramatists agonized over the romantic aesthetic, other theatre artists, unencumbered by theoretical shackles, were giving the urban masses the entertainment they wanted: Melodrama. The term "melodrama" indicates dramatic dialog spoken over musical accompaniment. René Charles Guilbert de Pixérécourt (1773-1819) established the form with his first play *Victor, or The Child of the Forest* in 1798, and melodrama went on to attract a huge new audience to the theatre and to dominate the nineteenth century.

Nineteenth-century melodramatic structure followed an easily recognizable formula. It began with a story-oriented plot line which was packed with incidents, often had several sub-stories, and ended with rewards for the good characters and punishment for the evil ones. Melodramatic plots usually included a lot of discoveries and reversals in the action and often made heavy use of coincidence.

The characters of melodrama, usually all middle class, tended to fit a set pattern of types.

The Villain

In the first place, a melodrama always had a villain who threatened the hero and heroine; typically, the villain had no real motivation for his or her evil beyond the fact that s/he was just born bad; furthermore, like other melodramatic characters, the villain was static in that s/he could not be reformed.

The Heroine

Secondly, melodramas had heroines — virginal, vulnerable women, as pure in their goodness as the villains were wicked.

The Hero

And third, they had heroes; frequently there were two heroes in a melodrama — a romantic hero who was somewhat ineffectual in his efforts to rescue the heroine from the villain and whose main purpose in the plot was to marry the heroine at the end of the play, and an active hero, often a comic and somewhat immoral man who, nevertheless, brought about the fall of the villain. The central melodramatic triangle of villain, heroine, and hero was frequently supplemented by other typical melodramatic characters such as the old father who represented common sense, a "lively girl" whose questionable morals supplied the spice lacking in the innocent heroine, a secondary villain who was frequently comic, and any number of ethnic types such as the stage Yankee, the stage Irishman, the stage Chinaman, and so on.

Melodramatic characters spoke prose, and the emotion of the action was heightened by instrumental background music. Stylistically, melodrama combined serious threat with comedy. Visually, melodrama offered large amounts of realistic physical action and spectacular sets and scenic effects.

In addition to the entertainment it offered, melodrama also reassured its audience that the world is basically a good place where ordinary, good people (like the audience members themselves) succeed and where evil characters (like the bankers and bosses that plagued the audience members) fall to ruin. Melodrama was also well-suited to preaching social messages.

Melodrama grew out of a dramatic tradition that began with medieval morality plays in which the Everyman-type of character was eventually rescued from the evil Vice. Shakespeare secularized this form and used it in comedies like *The Merchant of Venice* and tragedies like *Othello*. In the eighteenth century, sentimental comedy and domestic tragedies such as George Lillo's *The London Merchant* (1731) continued the tradition. And after the nineteenth century, in a somewhat sophisticated form, melodrama would continue to be the favorite drama of the twentieth century; television police dramas, action movies, Westerns, mystery thrillers, and horror movies are all direct descendants of nineteenth-century melodrama.

The writers of melodramas provided a wide variety of plays for their audiences. Samples include:

Nautical melodramas (Douglas Jerrold's *Black-Ey'd Susan* — 1829);

Spectacular melodramas (Augustin Daly's *Under the Gaslight* — 1867);

Delirium-tremens drama (William W. Pratt's *Ten Nights in a Bar Room* — 1858);

Civil War plays (William Gillette's *The Secret Service* — 1895);

Westerns (David Belasco's *The Girl of the Golden West* — 1905);

Social problem plays such as Tom Taylor's *The Ticket-of-Leave Man* (1863), about the problems of an ex-convict, and George Aiken's *Uncle Tom's Cabin.*

As audiences lost confidence in a just world and grew weary of the melodramatic formula, melodramas tended toward greater realism and sometimes had unhappy endings. A play of this type is Mrs. Henry Wood's *East Lynne* (1862).

In the twentieth century, people sneered at melodrama as a naive, artificial form, and "melodramatic" came to be a negative term applied to any overly-emotional drama or acting style. While most plays of this type seem contrived and dated and while few of them have literary merit, nevertheless they drew a huge audience to the theatre, filled a need in the frequently drab lives of the nineteenth-century masses, and provided the basis for important later developments such as the realism of Henrik Ibsen, the epic theatre of Bertold Brecht, and popular dramatic forms of the twentieth century.

Stagecraft

During the nineteenth century, the technical demands of romantic plays and melodramas, combined with changing tastes, brought about a restructuring of the stage and a new approach to stagecraft. Audiences and producers came to dislike the non-realism of neoclassical scenery with its painted perspective and wing-and-drop sets. Whereas, at one time, audiences had enjoyed watching the simultaneous shifting of wings, drops, and borders, now they felt that such technical effects detracted from the illusion of realism, and so it became the practice to close the curtains during scene shifts.

The Box Set

Eventually, wing-and-drop scenery gave way to three-dimensional sets. In order to accommodate three-dimensional scenery, the raked stages were leveled and, in the process, the now-obsolete machinery for shifting the flats was eliminated. No longer restricted to the forestage, the actors could now perform upstage within the scenery. This new, more realistic arrangement of scenery, which consisted basically of three walls, a floor and a ceiling, was called the box set.

Technology and the Set

At the same time, the romantic interest in detail plus the growing sense of historicity led the theatres to eliminate their stock sets for tragedy, comedy, and pastorals and instead to provide specific scenery for each play. Furthermore, the exotic nature of romantic plays and the attempts of melodrama to cater to audience tastes called for increasingly spectacular scenery.

Plays presented onstage horse races, locomotives, burning buildings, and sinking ships. Some productions of Shakespeare's plays featured garden sets complete with actual plants and live rabbits.

Technicians developed stage machinery to provide these effects including elevator stages, revolving stages, rolling platform stages, and panoramas — long drops which scrolled from one side of the stage to the other to give the effect of actors on stage passing by a changing background. Natural gas illumination replaced candles and permitted more realistic lighting which could be controlled and changed for different scenes. Theatre had changed drastically from Shakespeare's time when scenic effects were created in the audience's mind by the poetry of the playwright. The theatre technician had come into his own.

Performance Conventions

In performance styles, the nineteenth century saw a transition from the carefully sculpted acting of neoclassicism to a more intense, realistic manner much closer to that of twentieth-century actors. At the beginning of the period, John Philip Kemble (1757-1823) and his sister Sarah Siddon (1755-1831) set the style for acting; the best of the classical school, they brought to their roles careful preparation, control, and nobility. However, the erratic, sometimes offhand, sometimes passionate style of Edmund Kean (1787-1833) fit the romantic mood better and excited his audiences in a way the staid acting of the Kembles could no longer do. To this emotional approach, Edmund's son Charles Kean (1811-68) together with wife Ellen Tree (1806-80) added a commitment to realism and historical accuracy.

Theatrical Organization

The nineteenth century brought about two major changes in the business of theatre — the demise of the repertory company and the institution of copyright laws to protect the playwright. Since the Renaissance, professional plays had been presented by resident repertory companies — groups of actors, attached to specific theatres, who presented a large number of plays in revolving repertory. Three new practices during the nineteenth century eventually destroyed this system.

World Tours

In the first place, stars began to attract a lot of attention and eventually toured around the world performing their most famous roles with the local resident companies as supporting casts. This practice put the resident companies in subordinate roles and led audiences to lose interest in them.

Long Run Plays

Furthermore, theatre managers began to give single plays longer consecutive runs; this made it uneconomical for them to retain large companies of resident actors since they had to continue to pay some actors who did not have roles in the current long-running play.

Combination Touring Companies

Finally, combination touring companies developed — companies which combined stars, subordinate casts, and scenery and which toured a specific play across the country; this practice turned the local theatres into booking houses and further decreased the importance and frequency of local productions. By the end of the century, serious actors who wanted to work had to go to the theatrical touring hub of their country — London in England, Paris in France, and New York in America.

International Copyrights

Prior to the nineteenth century, the initial sale of a script to a theatre company meant that the playwright would have no further control over or profit from his work. But during the period under discussion, France, then England, and finally America enacted copyright laws to protect authors' rights within their own borders, and by the beginning of the twentieth century, many countries had entered into the international agreement that extended this protection worldwide.

Summary

The small number of romantic stage works and the low literary quality of nineteenth-century melodramas make it easy to consider nineteenth-century theatre primarily as transitional. The huge numbers of audience members, however, give evidence of a lively theatre scene, and the theories of romanticism, the dramaturgy of melodrama, and the stage practices of the day not only set the stage for the twentieth century but also had considerable value in themselves.

George L. Aiken

Harriet Beecher Stowe's novel *Uncle Tom's Cabin* produced many dramatizations. The best of these was written by an actor, George L. Aiken (1830-76), who was at the time in his early twenties. Aiken wrote the adaptation for George C. Howard, who was married to Aiken's cousin and who planned to feature his wife and daughter in the respective roles of Topsy and Little Eva. Aiken continued to act until 1867 and also wrote other plays, adaptations, and pulp novels. *Uncle Tom's Cabin* was far and away his greatest and most lasting success.

Uncle Tom's Cabin

The Source

Like many nineteenth-century melodramas, *Uncle Tom's Cabin* was an unauthorized adaptation. Harriet Beecher Stowe (1811-96), daughter of a Congregationalist minister and sister of the famed preacher Henry Ward Beecher, observed the plight of escaping slaves while living in southern Ohio where her father was the head of Lane Seminary. In 1850, she moved to Maine with her husband, Calvin Stowe. That same year, when Congress passed the Fugitive Slave Act which supported the slave-owners' rights to their human property, even if the escaped slaves were in free northern states, she began writing *Uncle Tom's Cabin*. She first published the story as a series of chapters in an abolitionist paper and then had the novel issued in book form by a Boston publisher in 1852. It sold 10,000 copies the first week and 300,000 the first year. It was soon translated into 37 languages and won Mrs. Stowe worldwide fame.

The author resisted attempts to dramatize her novel, but the absence of good copyright laws prevented her not only from taking effective action but also from earning a penny from any of the many popular stage versions.

In creating his dramatic version of the tragic, sentimental novel, Aiken managed to adhere to the spirit and content of the original while turning it into a melodrama. Since the book is full of dramatic events and characters who are either heroic or dastardly, Aiken's adaptation kept in most of the novel's incidents and people; even much of the dialog comes directly from the novel. Furthermore, since the world of melodrama was characterized by stark contrasts between good and evil, often expressed in religious terms, Aiken's play also preserved Mrs. Stowe's deep evangelical piety.

However, melodramas needed comedy, which was notably lacking in the steadfastly serious novel, and they also required a conclusion which handed out poetic justice. To meet the comic expectations, Aiken added characters such as the country drunk Phineas, the loser Gumption Cute, and the typical New Englander Deacon Perry as well as comic incidents such as Miss Ophelia's courtship. To provide a conclusion true to melodrama, he inserted the killing of the villain Simon Legree and the final tableau with Little Eva welcoming St. Clare and Uncle Tom into heavenly bliss.

Melodramatic Devices

In keeping with the romantic rejection of the neoclassical insistence on single story lines, melodramas often intertwined several stories in their plots. Accordingly, Aiken presents the independent stories of the George Harris family and Uncle Tom. He unites these separate strands by having minor characters like Marks and the Shelby family appear in both story lines and by jumping back and forth between the two stories. In good melodramatic fashion, he further violates the neoclassical rules of the unity of time and place by setting his scenes in the mid-West, the deep South, and New England, and by stringing the action out over several years.

Aiken's play also caters to the period's demand for spectacle by portraying Eliza's escape across the ice floes in the Ohio River, by frequent, rapid scene changes, and by calling for tableaus or "pictures," in which the actors held a dramatic pose for emotional effect. In good melodramatic fashion, the stage directions also call for specific musical accompaniment to heighten the play's moods.

The Didactic Element

The circumstances of the play's composition, the comic elements in the script, and Aiken's subsequent work all suggest that *Uncle Tom's Cabin* was written with commercial success in mind. But the play also demonstrates the persuasive power of melodrama. It portrays racial tolerance, abolitionist sentiment, Christianity, and courage as synonymous with goodness while on the other hand it equates prejudice, slavery, profanity, and cowardice with evil. It uses contemporary sexual mores to portray the villains as lecherous while the slaves and sympathetic whites are either sexually pure or corrupted in spite of themselves. The villainous slave holders earn the audience's hatred by using violence against defenseless folk while the good people turn to violence only as a last resort or, like Uncle Tom, not at all.

Production History

An abbreviated version of Aiken's play was presented at Troy, New York, in September, 1852 — the same year Mrs. Stowe's novel came out in book form. A year later it was produced in its present form in New York City. Subsequently Aiken's play and many other adaptations of Stowe's novel were performed throughout the Northern states. Together with the original novel, these plays did much to stir the abolitionist fervor that fed into the Civil War.

After the War, dramatic presentations of *Uncle Tom's Cabin* continued to be popular well into the twentieth century. Numerous companies of touring actors called "Tommers" even made careers of performing the play across the nation. *Uncle Tom's Cabin* may well be the most-performed play in American theatrical history.

Staging

The following script presents the stage directions as they occurred in nineteenth-century editions of the play. These stage directions indicate locations on stage by such abbreviations as RH, L1E, and RUE. An understanding of traditional stage terms makes these instructions easy to understand. The directions right and left on stage are always given from the perspective of an onstage actor facing the audience. Downstage means toward the audience while upstage means away from the audience. Entrances between wings on the sides of the stage were numbered starting from the proscenium arch. The proscenium itself also often had doors which were used as entrances. RH, then, means that an actor is standing to another actor's right hand side; L1E refers to the first entrance above the proscenium on the left side of the stage; and RUE means the upper entrance on the right. See the attached floor plan of a stage for clarification.

Other terms, many of which are still in use today, have the following meanings:

Closed in — flats are moved in from the wings to conceal upstage scenery while simultaneously replacing it with a setting for the next scene.

Discovered — the curtains are opened to reveal actors already on stage.

Flat — a rigid scenic component usually constructed of a wooden framework covered with canvas and painted to represent a wall. Sometimes flats would be joined together to reach all the way across the stage and would be painted with landscape scenery (See Act III, Scene 2).

Practicable — functional (as opposed to fake) and/or able to bear an actor's weight.

Quick drop — The front curtain falls quickly to conceal the stage.

Nineteenth-Century Stage Areas

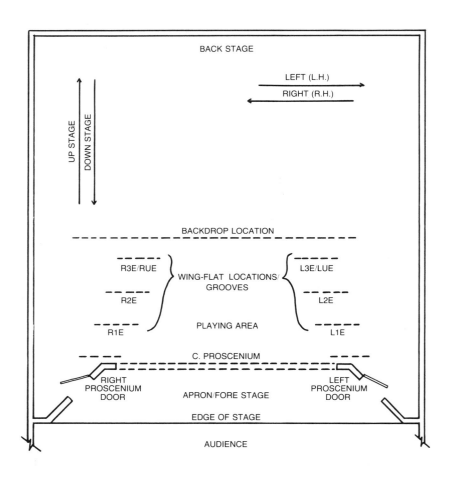

Nineteenth-Century Theatre Timeline

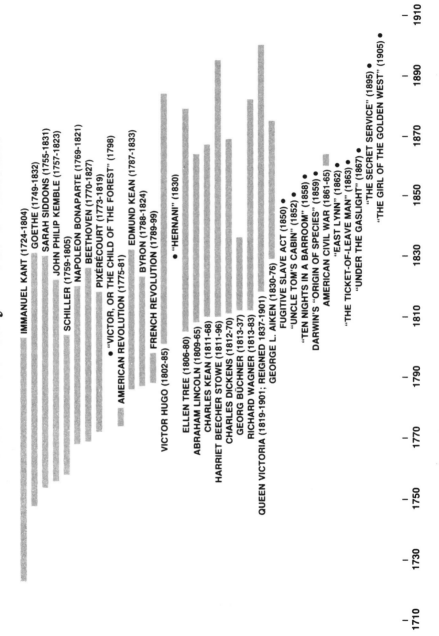

UNCLE TOM'S CABIN or LIFE AMONG THE LOWLY

A Domestic Drama in Six Acts

by GEORGE L. AIKEN

The action of the play takes place in Kentucky, Louisiana, Ohio, and Vermont around 1850.

CAST OF CHARACTERS

ELIZA
a slave belonging to Mr. Shelby

GEORGE HARRIS
Eliza's husband, a mulatto slave of Mr. Harris

MR. SHELBY
a Kentucky plantation owner

HALEY
a slave trader

HARRY
child of George and Eliza

AUNT CHLOE
a slave of Mr. Shelby

UNCLE TOM
Aunt Chloe's husband, a slave of Mr. Shelby

PHINEAS
a Kentucky farmer, in love with an Ohio Quaker woman

MARKS
a lawyer and slave-catcher

LOKER
a slave-catcher

MARIE
A New Orleans lady

EVA
Marie's daughter

ST. CLARE
Eva's father, Marie's husband

MISS OPHELIA
St. Clare's spinster cousin from Vermont

TOPSY
a slave girl purchased by St. Clare

MR. WILSON
a Southern factory owner

GUMPTION CUTE
a ne'er-do-well New Englander

MANN
A Louisiana slave owner

SIMON LEGREE
A Louisiana plantation owner

ADOLF
a slave previously belonging to St. Clare

EMMELINE
15, a quatroon (quarter-blood black) slave

SKEGGS
a New Orleans slave auctioneer

DEACON ABRAHAM PERRY
a Vermont widower

SAMBO
a slave belonging to Legree

QUIMBO
another slave belonging to Legree

CASSY
Legree's slave and concubine

GEORGE SHELBY
son of Mr. Shelby

Extras: WAITER, 3 SLAVE CATCHERS,
and AUCTION SPECTATORS

Synopsis of Scenes

ACT I

Scene 1. Eliza's cabin on the Shelby plantation in Kentucky

Scene 2. The same day, in Shelby's dining room

Scene 3. That night, outside Uncle Tom's cabin on the Shelby plantation

Scene 4. Some days later, in room in a Kentucky tavern just across the river from Ohio

Scene 5. Moments later, outside the tavern

Scene 6. Moments later, on the ice-choked Ohio River

ACT II

Scene 1. Days or weeks later, in the parlor of the St. Clare home in New Orleans

Scene 2. Some time later, in a garden on the St. Clare estate

Scene 3. Meanwhile, in the tavern in Kentucky

Scene 4. Later, in Topsy's room at the St. Clare place

Scene 5. Days later, in an Ohio Quaker home, a "station" on the underground railroad

Scene 6. Later, on a rocky pass in Ohio near the Pennsylvania line

ACT III

Scene 1. Some time later, in a room in St. Clare's home

Scene 2. That evening, by a lake on the St. Clare estate

Scene 3. Later, in a hallway outside little Eva's room

Scene 4. Soon after, in Eva's room

ACT IV

Scene 1. Days later, on a street in New Orleans

Scene 2. Meanwhile, in a "gothic chamber" in the St. Clare home

Scene 3. Less than an hour later, in a front room in St. Clare's house

Scene 4. Immediately following, in a "handsome chamber" in St. Clare's house

ACT V

Scene 1. Some weeks later, at a slave market in New Orleans

Scene 2. Meanwhile, in the garden of Ophelia's home in Vermont

Scene 3. Later, in a "rude chamber" on Simon Legree's plantation in Louisiana

Scene 4. Immediately after Scene 2, in a room in Ophelia's home

ACT VI

Scene 1. Soon after Act V, Scene 3, outside an old shed on Legree's place
Scene 2. Meanwhile, on a street in New Orleans
Scene 3. Immediately after Scene 1, in a "rough chamber" at Legree's place
Scene 4. Soon after Scene 2, on a New Orleans street
Scene 5. Later, in a room at Legree's place
Scene 6. In heaven

ACT ONE

Scene 1 — *Plain Chamber. Enter ELIZA, R.H., meeting GEORGE, L.H.*

ELIZA: Ah! George, is it you? Well, I am so glad you've come. *(GEORGE regards her mournfully.)* Why don't you smile, and ask after Harry?

GEORGE: *(Bitterly.)* I wish he'd never been born! — I wish I'd never been born myself!

ELIZA: *(Sinking her head upon his breast and weeping.)* Oh, George!

GEORGE: There now, Eliza, it's too bad for me to make you feel so. Oh! how I wish you had never seen me — you might have been happy!

ELIZA: George! George! how can you talk so? What dreadful thing has happened, or is going to happen? I'm sure we've been very happy till lately.

GEORGE: So we have, dear. But oh! I wish I'd never seen you, nor you me.

ELIZA: Oh, George! how can you?

GEORGE: Yes, Eliza, it's all misery! misery! The very life is burning out of me! I'm a poor, miserable, forlorn drudge! I shall only drag you down with me, that's all! What's the use of our trying to do anything — trying to know anything — trying to be anything? I wish I was dead!

ELIZA: Oh! now, dear George, that is really wicked. I know how you feel about losing your place in the factory, and you have a hard master; but pray be patient —

GEORGE: Patient! Haven't I been patient? Did I say a word when he came and took me away — for no earthly reason — from the place where everybody was kind to me? I'd paid him truly every cent of my earnings, and they all say I worked well.

ELIZA: Well, it *is* dreadful; but, after all, he is your master, you know.

GEORGE: My master! And who made him my master? That's what I think of? What right has he to me? I'm as much a man as he is. What right has he to make a drayhorse of me? — to take me from things I can do better than he can, and put me to work that any horse can do? He tries to do it; he says he'll bring me down and humble me, and he puts me to just the hardest, meanest and dirtiest work, on purpose.

ELIZA: Oh, George! George! you frighten me. Why, I never heard you talk so. I'm afraid you'll do something dreadful. I don't wonder at your feelings at all; but oh! do be careful — for my sake, for Harry's.

GEORGE: I have been careful, and I have been patient, but it's growing worse and worse — flesh and blood can't bear it any longer. Every chance he can get to insult and torment me he takes. He says that though I don't say anything, he sees that I've got the devil in me, and he means to bring it out; and one of these days it will come out, in a way that he won't like, or I'm mistaken.

ELIZA: Well, I always thought that I must obey my master and mistress, or I couldn't be a Christian.

GEORGE: There is some sense in it in your case. They have brought you up like a child — fed you, clothed you and taught you, so that you have a good education — that is some reason why they should claim you. But I have been kicked and cuffed and sworn at, and what do I owe? I've paid for all my keeping a hundred times over. I won't bear it — no, I *won't!* Master will find out that I'm one whipping won't tame.

My day will come yet, if he don't look out!

ELIZA: What are you going to do? Oh! George, don't do anything wicked; if you only trust in heaven and try to do right, it will deliver you.

GEORGE: Eliza, my heart's full of bitterness. I can't trust in heaven. Why does it let things be so?

ELIZA: Oh, George! we must all have faith. Mistress says that when all things go wrong to us, we must believe that heaven is doing the very best.

GEORGE: That's easy for people to say who are sitting on their sofas and riding in their carriages; but let them be where I am — I guess it would come some harder. I wish I could be good; but my heart burns and can't be reconciled. You couldn't, in my place, you can't now, if I tell you all I've got to say; you don't know the whole yet.

ELIZA: What do you mean?

GEORGE: Well, lately my master has been saying that he was a fool to let me marry off the place — that he hates Mr. Shelby and all his tribe — and he says he won't let me come here any more, and that I shall take a wife and settle down on his place.

ELIZA: But you were married to *me* by the minister, as much as if you had been a white man.

GEORGE: Don't you know I can't hold you for my wife if he chooses to part us? That is why I wish I'd never seen you — it would have been better for us both — it would have been better for our poor child if he had never been born.

ELIZA: Oh! but my master is so kind.

GEORGE: Yes, but who knows? — he may die, and then Harry may be sold to nobody knows who. What pleasure is it that he is handsome and smart and bright? I tell you, Eliza, that a sword will pierce through your soul for every good and pleasant thing your child is or has. It will make him worth too much for you to keep.

ELIZA: Heaven forbid!

GEORGE: So, Eliza, my girl, bear up now, and good by, for I'm going.

ELIZA: Going, George! Going where?

GEORGE: To Canada; and when I'm there I'll buy you — that's all the hope that's left us. You have a kind master, that won't refuse to sell you. I'll buy you and the boy — heaven helping me, I will!

ELIZA: Oh, dreadful! If you should be taken?

GEORGE: I won't be taken, Eliza — I'll *die* first! I'll be free, or I'll die.

ELIZA: You will not kill yourself?

GEORGE: No need of that; they will kill me, fast enough. I will never go down the river alive.

ELIZA: Oh, George! for my sake, do be careful. Don't lay hands on yourself, or anybody else. You are tempted too much, but don't. Go, if you must, but go carefully, prudently, and pray heaven to help you!

GEORGE: Well, then, Eliza, hear my plan. I'm going home quite resigned, you understand, as if all was over. I've got some preparations made, and there are those that will help me; and in the course of a few days I shall be among the missing. Well, now, good by.

ELIZA: A moment — our boy.

GEORGE: *(Choked with emotion.)* True, I had forgotten him; one last look, and then farewell!

ELIZA: And heaven grant it be not forever! *(Exeunt, R.H.)*

Scene 2 — A dining room. — Table and chairs c. — Dessert, wine, etc., on table. — SHELBY and HALEY discovered at table.

SHELBY: That is the way I should arrange the matter.

HALEY: I can't make trade that way — I positively can't, Mr. Shelby. *(Drinks.)*

SHELBY: Why, the fact is, Haley, Tom is an uncommon fellow! He is certainly worth that sum anywhere — steady, honest, capable, manages my whole farm like a clock!

HALEY: You mean honest, as niggers go. *(Fills glass.)*

SHELBY: No; I mean, really, Tom is a good, steady, sensible, pious fellow. He got religion at a camp-meeting, four years ago, and I believe he really did get it. I've trusted him since then, with everything I have — money, house, horses, and let him come and go round the country, and I always found him true and square in everything.

HALEY: Some folks don't believe there is pious niggers, Shelby, but *I do.* I had a fellow, now, in this yer last lot I took to Orleans — 'twas as good as a meetin' now, really, to hear that critter pray; and he was quite gentle and quiet like. He fetched me a good sum, too for I bought him cheap of a man that was 'bliged to sell out, so I realized six hundred on him. Yes, I consider religion a valeyable thing in a nigger, when it's the genuine article and no mistake.

SHELBY: Well, Tom's got the real article, if ever a fellow had. Why last fall I let him go to Cincinnati alone, to do business for me and bring home five hundred dollars. "Tom," says I to him, "I trust you, because I think you are a Christian — I know you wouldn't cheat." Tom comes back sure enough, I knew he would. Some low fellows, they say, said to him — "Tom, why don't you make tracks for Canada?" "Ah, master trusted me, and I couldn't," was his answer. They told me all about it. I am sorry to part with Tom, I must say. You ought to let him cover the whole balance of the debt and you would, Haley, if you had any conscience.

HALEY: Well, I've got just as much conscience as any man in business can afford to keep, just a little, you know, to swear by, as twere; and then I'm ready to do anything in reason to 'blige friends, but this yer, you see, is a lettle too hard on a fellow — a leetle too hard! *(Fills glass again.)*

SHELBY: Well, then, Haley, how will you trade?

HALEY: Well, haven't you a boy or a girl that you could throw in with Tom?

SHELBY: Hum! none that I could well spare; to tell the truth, it's only hard necessity makes me willing to sell at all. I don't like parting with any of my hands, that's a fact. *(HARRY runs in R.H.)* Hulloa! Jim Crow! *(Throws a bunch of raisins towards him.)* Pick that up now! *(HARRY does so.)*

HALEY: Bravo, little 'un! *(Throws an orange, which HARRY catches. He sings and dances around the stage.)* Hurrah! Bravo! What a young 'un!

That chap's a case, I'll promise. Tell you what, Shelby, fling in that chap, and I'll settle the business. Come, now, if that ain't doing the thing up about the rightest!

(ELIZA enters R.H. — Starts on beholding HALEY, and gazes fearfully at HARRY, who runs and clings to her dress, showing the orange, etc.)

SHELBY: Well, Eliza?

ELIZA: I was looking for Harry, please, sir.

SHELBY: Well, take him away, then.

(ELIZA grasps the child eagerly in her arms, and casting another glance of apprehension at HALEY, exits hastily, R.H.)

HALEY: By Jupiter! there's an article, now. You might make your fortune on that ar gal in Orleans any day. I've seen over a thousand in my day, paid down for gals not a bit handsomer.

SHELBY: I don't want to make my fortune on her. Another glass of wine. *(Fills the glasses.)*

HALEY: *(Drinks and smacks his lips.)* Capital wine — first chop. Come, how will you trade about the gal? What shall I say for her? What'll you take?

SHELBY: Mr. Haley, she is not to be sold. My wife wouldn't part with her for her weight in gold.

HALEY: Ay, ay! women always say such things, 'cause they hain't no sort of calculation. Just show 'em how many watches, feathers and trinkets one's weight in gold would buy, and that alters the case, I reckon.

SHELBY: I tell you, Haley, this must not be spoken of — I say no, and I mean no.

HALEY: Well, you'll let me have the boy tho'; you must own that I have come down pretty handsomely for him.

SHELBY: What on earth can you want with the child?

HALEY: Why, I've got a friend that's going into this yer branch of the business — wants to buy up handsome boys to raise for the market. Well, what do you say?

SHELBY: I'll think the matter over and talk with my wife.

HALEY: Oh, certainly, by all means; but I'm in a devil of a hurry and shall want to know as soon as possible, what I may depend on.

(Rises and puts on his overcoat, which hangs on a chair — takes hat and whip.)

SHELBY: Well, call up this evening, between six and seven, and you shall have my answer.

HALEY: All right. Take care of yourself, old boy! *(Exit L.H.)*

SHELBY: If anybody had ever told me that I should sell Tom to those rascally traders, I should never have believed it. Now it must come for aught I see, and Eliza's child too. So much for being in debt, heigho! The fellow sees his advantage and means to push it. *(Exit R.H.)*

Scene 3 — *Snowy landscape. — UNCLE TOM's Cabin, L.U.E. — Snow on roof. — Practicable door and window. — Dark Stage. — Music. Enter ELIZA hastily, R.U.E. with HARRY in her arms.)*

ELIZA: My poor boy! they have sold you, but your mother will save you yet!

(Goes to Cabin and taps on window. — AUNT CHLOE appears at window with a large white nightcap on.)

CHLOE: Good Lord! what's that? My sakes alive if it ain't Lizy! Get on your clothes, old man, quick! I'm gwine to open the door.

(The door opens and CHLOE enters followed by UNCLE TOM in his shirt sleeves holding a tallow candle. — TOM crosses to c.)

TOM: *(c. Holding the light towards ELIZA.)* Lord bless you! I'm skeered to look at ye, Lizy! Are ye tuck sick, or what's come over ye?

ELIZA: *(R.)* I'm running away, Uncle Tom and Aunt Chloe, carrying off my child! Master sold him!

TOM and CHLOE: *(L.)* Sold him!

ELIZA: Yes, sold him! I crept into the closet by mistress' door tonight and heard master tell mistress that he had sold my Harry and you, Uncle Tom, both, to a trader, and that the man was to take possession tomorrow.

CHLOE: The good Lord have pity on us! Oh! it don't seem as if it was true. What has he done that master should sell *him?*

ELIZA: He hasn't done anything — it isn't for that. Master don't want to sell, and mistress — she's always good. I heard her plead and beg for us, but he told her 'twas no use — that he was in this man's debt, and he had got the power over him, and that if he did not pay him off clear, it would end in his having to sell the place and all the people and move off.

CHLOE: Well, old man, why don't you run away, too? Will you wait to be toted down the river, where they kill niggers with hard work and starving? I'd a heap rather die than go there, any day! There's time for ye, be off with Lizy — you've got a pass to come and go any time. Come, bustle up, and I'll get your things together.

TOM: No, no — I ain't going. Let Eliza go — it's her right. I wouldn't be the one to say no — 'tain't in natur for her to stay; but you heard what she said? If I must be sold, or all the people on the place, and everything go to rack, why, let me be sold. I s'pose I can bar it as well as any one. Mas'r always found me on the spot — he always will. I never have broken trust, nor used my pass no ways contrary to my word, and I never will. It's better for me to go alone, than to break up the place and sell all. Mas'r ain't to blame, and he'll take care of you and the poor little 'uns! *(Overcome.)*

CHLOE: Now, old man, what is you gwine to cry for? Does you want to break this old woman's heart? *(Crying.)*

ELIZA: I saw my husband only this afternoon, and I little knew then what was to come. He told me he was going to run away. Do try, if you can, to get word to him. Tell him how I went and why I went, and tell him I'm going to try and find Canada. You must give my love to him, and tell him if I never see him again on earth, I trust we shall meet in heaven!

TOM: Dat is right, Lizy, trust in the Lord — he is our best friend — our only comforter.

ELIZA: You won't go with me, Uncle Tom?

TOM: No; time was when I would, but the Lord's given me a work among these yer poor souls, and I'll stay with 'em and bear my cross with 'em till the end. It's different with you — it's more'n you could stand, and you'd better go if you can.

ELIZA: Uncle Tom, I'll try it!

TOM: Amen! The Lord help ye!

(Exit ELIZA and HARRY, R. 1 E.)

CHLOE: What is you gwine to do, old man! What's to become of you?

TOM: *(Solemnly.)* Him that saved Daniel in the den of lions — that saved the children in the fiery furnace — Him that walked on the sea and bade the winds be still — He's alive yet! and I've faith to believe he can deliver me.

CHLOE: You is right, old man.

TOM: The Lord is good unto all that trust him, Chloe. *(Exeunt into Cabin.)*

Scene 4. — *Room in Tavern by the riverside.* — *A large window in flat, through which the river is seen, filled with floating ice.* — *Moonlight.* — *Table and chairs brought on. Enter PHINEAS, L.H.*

PHINEAS: Chaw me up into tobaccy ends! how in the name of all that's onpossible am I to get across that yer pesky river? It's a reg'lar blockade of ice! I promised Ruth to meet her tonight, and she'll be into my har if I don't come. *(Goes to window.)* Thar's a conglomerated prospect for a loveyer! What in creation's to be done? That thar river looks like a permiscuous ice-cream shop come to an awful state of friz. If I war on the adjacent bank, I wouldn't care a teetotal atom. Rile up, you old varmit, and shake the ice off your back!

(Enter ELIZA and HARRY, L.H.)

ELIZA: Courage, my boy — we have reached the river. Let it but roll between us and our pursuers, and we are safe! *(Goes to window.)* Gracious powers! the river is choked with cakes of ice!

PHINEAS: Holloa, gal! — what's the matter? You look kind of streaked.

ELIZA: Is there any ferry or boat that takes people over now?

PHINEAS: Well, I guess not; the boats have stopped running.

ELIZA: *(In dismay.)* Stopped running?

PHINEAS: Maybe you're wanting to get over — anybody sick? Ye seem mighty anxious.

ELIZA: I — I — I've got a child that's very dangerous. I never heard of it till last night, and I've walked quite a distance today, in hopes to get to the ferry.

PHINEAS: Well, now, that's onlucky; I'm re'lly consarned for ye. Thar's a man, a piece down here, that's going over with some truck this evening, if he duss to; he'll be in here to supper tonight, so you'd better set down and wait. That's a smart little chap. Say, young'un, have a chaw tobaccy? *(Takes out a large plug and a bowie knife.)*

ELIZA: No, no! not any for him.

PHINEAS: Oh! he don't use it, eh? Hain't come to it yet? Well, I have. *(Cuts off a large piece, and returns the plug and knife to pocket.)* What's the matter with the young 'un? He looks kind of white in the gills!

295

ELIZA: Poor fellow! he is not used to walking, and I've hurried him on so.
PHINEAS: Tuckered, eh? Well, there's a little room there, with a fire in it.
Take the babby in there, make yourself comfortable till that thar
ferryman shows his countenance — I'll stand the damage.
ELIZA: How shall I thank you for such kindness to a stranger?
PHINEAS: Well, if you don't know how, why, don't try; that's the teetotal.
Come, vamose! *(Exit ELIZA and HARRY, R.H.D.)* Chaw me into
sassage meat, if that ain't a perpendicular fine gal! she's a reg'lar. A
No. 1 sort of female! How'n thunder am I to get across this refrigerated
stream of water? I can't wait for that ferryman. *(Enter MARKS, L.H.)*
Halloa! what sort of a critter's this? *(Advances.)* Say, stranger, will
you have something to drink?
MARKS: You are excessively kind: I don't care if I do.
PHINEAS: Ah! he's a human. Holloa, thar! bring us a jug of whisky instantaneously, or expect to be teetotally chawed up! Squat yourself,
stranger, and go in for enjoyment. *(They sit at table.)* Who are you,
and what's your name?
MARKS: I am a lawyer, and my name is Marks.
PHINEAS: A land shark, eh? Well, I don't think no worse on you for that.
The law is a kind of necessary evil; and it breeds lawyers just as an
old stump does fungus. Ah! here's the whisky. *(Enter WAITER, with
jug and tumblers, L.H. — Places them on table.)* Here, you — take that
shin-plaster. *(Gives bill.)* I don't want any change — thar's a gal stopping in that room — the balance will pay for her — d'ye hear? —
vamose! *(Exit WAITER, L.H. — Fills glass.)* Take hold, neighbor
Marks —don't shirk the critter. Here's hoping your path of true love
may never have an ice-choked river to cross! *(They drink.)*
MARKS: Want to cross the river, eh?
PHINEAS: Well, I do, stranger. Fact is, I'm in love with the teetotalist
pretty girl, over on the Ohio side, that ever wore a Quaker bonnet.
Take another swig, neighbor. *(Fills glasses, and they drink.)*
MARKS: A Quaker, eh?
PHINEAS: Yes — kind of strange, ain't it? The way of it was this: — I used
to own a grist of niggers — had 'em to work on my plantation, just
below here. Well, stranger, do you know I fell in with that gal — of
course I was considerably smashed — knocked into a pretty conglomerated heap — and I told her so. She said she wouldn't hear a word
from me so long as I owned a nigger!
MARKS: You sold them, I suppose.
PHINEAS: You're teetotally wrong, neighbor. I gave them all their freedom,
and told 'em to vamose!
MARKS: Ah! yes — very noble, I dare say but rather expensive. This act
won you your lady-love, eh?
PHINEAS: You're off the track again, neighbor. She felt kind of pleased
about it, and smiled, and all that; but she said she could never be
mine unless I turned Quaker! Thunder and earth! what do you think
of that? You're a lawyer — come, now, what's your opinion? Don't you
call it a knotty point?
MARKS: Most decidedly. Of course you refused.

296

PHINEAS: Teetotally; but she told me to think better of it, and come tonight and give her my final conclusion. Chaw me into mince meat, if I haven't made up my mind to do it!

MARKS: You astonish me!

PHINEAS: Well, you see, I can't get along without that gal; — she's sort of fixed my flint, and I'm sure to hang fire without her. I know I shall make a queer sort of Quaker, because you see, neighbor, I ain't precisely the kind of material to make a Quaker out of.

MARKS: No, not exactly.

PHINEAS: Well, I can't stop no longer. I must try to get across that candaverous river some way. It's getting late — take care of yourself, neighbor lawyer. I'm a teetotal victim to a pair of black eyes. Chaw me up to feed hogs, if I'm not in a ruinatious state! *(Exit L.H.)*

MARKS: Queer genius, that, very! *(Enter TOM LOKER, L.H.)* So you've come at last.

LOKER: Yes. *(Looks into jug.)* Empty! Waiter! more whisky!

(WAITER enters, L.H., with jug, and removes the empty one. — Enter HALEY, L.H.)

HALEY: By the land! if this yer ain't the nearest now, to what I've heard people people call Providence! Why, Loker, how are ye?

LOKER: The devil! What brought you here, Haley?

HALEY: *(Sitting at table.)* I say, Tom, this yer's the luckiest thing in the world. I'm in a devil of a hobble, and you must help me out!

LOKER: Ugh! aw! like enough. A body may be pretty sure of that when you're glad to see 'em, or can make something off of 'em. What's the blow now?

HALEY: You've got a friend here — partner, perhaps?

LOKER: Yes, I have. Here, Marks — here's that ar fellow that I was with in Natchez.

MARKS: *(Grasping HALEY's hand.)* Shall be pleased with his acquaintance. Mr. Haley, I believe?

HALEY: The same, sir. The fact is, gentlemen, this morning I bought a young 'un of Shelby up above here. His mother got wind of it, and what does she do but cut her lucky with him; and I'm afraid by this time that she has crossed the river, for I tracked her to this very place.

MARKS: So, then, ye're fairly sewed up, ain't ye? He! he! he! it's neatly done, too.

HALEY: This young 'un business makes lots of trouble in the trade.

MARKS: Now, Mr. Haley, what is it? Do you want us to undertake to catch this gal?

HALEY: The gal's no matter of mine — she's Shelby's — it's only the boy. I was a fool for buying the monkey.

LOKER: You're generally a fool!

MARKS: Come now, Loker, none of your huffs; you see, Mr. Haley's a-puttin' us in a way of a good job. I reckon: just hold still — these yer arrangements are my forte. This yer gal, Mr. Haley — how is she? — what is she?

(ELIZA appears, with HARRY, R.H.D., listening.)

297

HALEY: Well, white and handsome — well brought up. I'd have given Shelby eight hundred or a thousand, and then made well on her.

MARKS: White and handsome — well brought up! Look here now, Loker, a beautiful opening. We'll do a business here on our own account. We does the catchin'; the boy, of course, goes to Mr. Haley — we takes the gal to Orleans to speculate on. Ain't it beautiful! *(They confer together.)*

ELIZA: Powers of mercy, protect me! How shall I escape these human bloodhounds? Ah! the window — the river of ice! That dark stream lies between me and liberty! Surely the ice will bear my trifling weight. It is my only chance of escape — better sink beneath the cold waters, with my child locked in my arms, than have him torn from me and sold into bondage. He sleeps upon my breast — Heaven, I put my trust in thee! *(Gets out of window.)*

MARKS: Well, Tom Loker, what do you say?

LOKER. It'll do!

(Strikes his hand violently on the table. — ELIZA screams. They all start to their feet. — ELIZA disappears. — Music, chord.)

HALEY: By the land, there she is now! *(They all rush to the window.)*

MARKS. She's making for the river!

LOKER: Let's after her!

(Music. — They all leap through the window. — Change.)

Scene 5 — *Snow Landscape.* — *Music. Enter ELIZA, with HARRY, hurriedly, L. 1 E.*

ELIZA: They press upon my footsteps — the river is my only hope. Heaven grant me strength to reach it, ere they overtake me! Courage, my child! — we will be free — or perish! *(Rushes off, R.H. — Music continued.)*

(Enter LOKER, HALEY and MARKS, L. 1 E.)

HALEY: We'll catch her yet; the river will stop her!

MARKS: No, it won't, for look! she has jumped upon the ice! She's a brave gal, anyhow!

LOKER: She'll be drowned!

HALEY: Curse that young 'un! I shall lose him, after all.

LOKER: Come on, Marks, to the ferry!

HALEY: Aye, to the ferry! — a hundred dollars for a boat!

(Music. — They rush off, R.H.)

Scene 6 — *The entire depth of stage, representing the Ohio River filled with Floating Ice. — Set bank on R.H. and in front. ELIZA appears, with HARRY, R.H., on a cake of ice, and floats slowly across to L.H. — HALEY, LOKER and MARKS, on bank R.H., observing. — PHINEAS on opposite.*

ACT TWO

Scene 1. — *A Handsome Parlor. MARIE discovered reclining on a sofa, R.H.*

MARIE: *(Looking at a note.)* What can possibly detain St. Clare? According to this note he should have been here a fortnight ago. *(Noise of carriage without.)* I do believe he has come at last.

(EVA runs in, L. 1 E.)

EVA: Mamma! *(Throws her arms around MARIE's neck, and kisses her.)*
MARIE. That will do — take care, child — don't you make my head ache! *(Kisses her languidly.)*

(Enter ST. CLARE, OPHELIA, and TOM, nicely dressed, L. 1 E.)

ST. CLARE: Well, my dear Marie, here we are at last. The wanderers have arrived, you see. Allow me to present my cousin, Miss Ophelia, who is about to undertake the office of our housekeeper.
MARIE: *(Rising to a sitting posture.)* I am delighted to see you. How do you like the appearance of our city?
EVA: *(Running to OPHELIA.)* Oh! is it not beautiful? My own darling home! — is it not beautiful?
OPHELIA: Yes, it is a pretty place, though it looks rather old and heathenish to me.
ST. CLARE: Tom, my boy, this seems to suit you?
TOM: Yes, mas'r, it looks about the right thing.
ST. CLARE: See here, Marie, I've brought you a coachman, at last, to order. I tell you, he is a regular hearse for blackness and sobriety, and will drive you like a funeral, if you wish. Open your eyes, now, and look at him. Now, don't say I never think about you when I'm gone.
MARIE: I know he'll get drunk.
ST. CLARE: Oh! no he won't. He's warranted a pious and sober article.
MARIE: Well, I hope he may turn out well; it's more than I expect, though.
ST. CLARE: Have you no curiosity to learn how and where I picked up Tom?
EVA: *Uncle* Tom, papa; that's his name.
ST. CLARE: Right, my little sunbeam!
TOM: Please, mas'r, that ain't no 'casion to say nothing bout me.
ST. CLARE: You are too modest, my modern Hannibal. Do you know, Marie, that our little Eva took a fancy to Uncle Tom — whom we met on board the steamboat — and persuaded me to buy him.
MARIE: Ah! she is so odd.
ST. CLARE: As we approached the landing, a sudden rush of the passengers precipitated Eva into the water —
MARIE: Gracious heavens!
ST. CLARE: A man leaped into the river, and, as she rose to the surface of the water, grasped her in his arms, and held her up until she could be drawn on the boat again. Who was that man, Eva?
EVA: Uncle Tom! *(Runs to him. — He lifts her in his arms. — She kisses him.)*
TOM: The dear soul!
OPHELIA: *(Astonished.)* How shiftless!
ST. CLARE: *(Overhearing her.)* What's the matter now, pray?
OPHELIA: Well, I want to be kind to everybody, and I wouldn't have any-

thing hurt, but as to kissing —

ST. CLARE: Niggers! that you're not up to, hey?

OPHELIA: Yes, that's it — how can she?

ST. CLARE: Oh! bless you, it's nothing when you are used to it!

OPHELIA: I could never be so shiftless!

EVA: Come with me, Uncle Tom, and I will show you about the house. *(Crosses to R.H. with TOM.)*

TOM: Can I go, mas'r?

ST. CLARE: Yes, Tom; she is your little mistress — your only duty will be to attend to her! *(TOM bows and exits, R. 1 E.)*

MARIE: Eva, my dear!

EVA. Well, mamma?

MARIE: Do not exert yourself too much!

EVA: No, mamma! *(Runs out, R.H.)*

OPHELIA: *(Lifting up her hands.)* How shiftless!

(ST. CLARE sits next to MARIE on sofa. — OPHELIA next to ST. CLARE.)

ST. CLARE: Well, what do you think of Uncle Tom, Marie?

MARIE: He is a perfect behemoth!

ST. CLARE: Come, now, Marie, be gracious, and say something pretty to a fellow!

MARIE: You've been gone a fortnight beyond the time!

ST. CLARE: Well, you know I wrote you the reason.

MARIE: Such a short, cold letter!

ST. CLARE: Dear me! the mail was just going, and it had to be that or nothing.

MARIE: That's just the way; always something to make your journeys long and letters short!

ST. CLARE: Look at this. *(Takes an elegant velvet case from his pocket.)* Here's a present I got for you in New York — a Daguerreotype of Eva and myself.

MARIE: *(Looks at it with a dissatisfied air.)* What made you sit in such an awkward position?

ST. CLARE: Well, the position may be a matter of opinion, but what do you think of the likeness?

MARIE: *(Closing the case snappishly.)* If you don't think anything of my opinion in one case, I suppose you wouldn't in another.

OPHELIA: *(Sententiously, aside.)* How shiftless!

ST. CLARE: Hang the woman! Come, Marie, what do you think of the likeness? Don't be nonsensical now.

MARIE: It's very inconsiderate of you, St. Clare, to insist on my talking and looking at things. You know I've been lying all day with the sick headache, and there's been such a tumult made ever since you came, I'm half dead!

OPHELIA: You're subject to the sick headache, ma'am?

MARIE: Yes, I'm a perfect martyr to it!

OPHELIA: Juniper-berry tea is good for sick headache; at least, Molly, Deacon Abraham Perry's wife, used to say so; and she was a great nurse.

ST. CLARE: I'll have the first juniper-berries that get ripe in our garden by the lake brought in for that especial purpose. Come, cousin, let us take a stroll in the garden. Will you join us, Marie?

MARIE: I wonder how you can ask such a question, when you know how fragile I am. I shall retire to my chamber, and repose till dinner time. *(Exit R. 2 E.)*

OPHELIA: *(Looking after her.)* How shiftless!

ST. CLARE: Come, cousin! *(As he goes out.)* Look out for the babies! If I step upon any body, let them mention it.

OPHELIA: Babies under foot! How shiftless! *(Exeunt L. 1 E.)*

Scene 2 — A Garden. TOM discovered, seated on a bank. R.U.E., with EVA on his knee — his button-holes are filled with flowers, and EVA is hanging a wreath around his neck. Music at opening of scene. Enter ST. CLARE and OPHELIA, L.U.E., observing.

EVA: Oh, Tom! you look so funny.

TOM: *(Sees ST. CLARE and puts EVA down.)* I begs pardon, mas'r, but the young missis would do it. Look yer, I'm like the ox, mentioned in the good book, dressed for the sacrifice.

ST. CLARE: I say, what do you think, Pussy? Which do you like the best — to live as they do at your uncle's, up in Vermont, or to have a house-full of servants, as we do?

EVA: Oh! of course our way is the pleasantest.

ST. CLARE: *(Patting her head.)* Why so?

EVA. Because it makes so many more round you to love, you know.

OPHELIA: Now, that's just like Eva — just one of her odd speeches.

EVA: Is it an odd speech, papa?

ST. CLARE: Rather, as this world goes, Pussy. But where has my little Eva been?

EVA: Oh! I've been up in Tom's room, hearing him sing.

ST. CLARE: Hearing Tom sing, hey?

EVA: Oh, yes! he sings such beautiful things, about the new Jerusalem, and bright angels, and the land of Canaan.

ST. CLARE: I dare say; it's better than the opera, isn't it?

EVA: Yes; and he's going to teach them to me.

ST. CLARE: Singing lessons, hey? You are coming on.

EVA: Yes, he sings for me, and I read to him in my Bible, and he explains what it means. Come, Tom. *(She takes his hand and they exit, R.U.E.)*

ST. CLARE: *(Aside.)* Oh, Evangeline! Rightly named; hath not heaven made thee an evangel to me?

OPHELIA: How shiftless! How can you let her?

ST. CLARE: Why not?

OPHELIA: Why, I don't know; it seems so dreadful.

ST. CLARE: You would think no harm in a child's caressing a large dog even if he was black; but a creature that can think, reason and feel, and is immortal, you shudder at. Confess it, cousin. I know the feeling among some of you Northerners well enough. Not that there is a particle of virtue in our not having it, but custom with us does what Christianity ought to do: obliterates the feeling of personal prejudice. You loathe them as you would a snake or a toad, yet you are indignant at their wrongs. You would not have them abused but you don't want to have anything to do with them yourselves. Isn't that it?

OPHELIA: Well, cousin, there may be some truth in this.

ST. CLARE: What would the poor and lowly do without children? Your little child is your only true democrat. Tom, now, is a hero to Eva; his stories are wonders in her eyes; his songs and Methodist hymns are better than an opera, and the traps and little bits of trash in his pockets a mine of jewels, and he the most wonderful Tom that ever wore a black skin. This is one of the roses of Eden that the Lord has dropped down expressly for the poor and lowly, who get few enough of any other kind.

OPHELIA: It's strange, cousin; one might almost think you was a *professor*, to hear you talk.

ST. CLARE: A professor?

OPHELIA: Yes, a professor of religion.

ST. CLARE: Not at all; not a professor as you town folks have it, and, what is worse, I'm afraid, not a *practicer*, either.

OPHELIA: What makes you talk so, then?

ST. CLARE: Nothing is easier than talking. My forte lies in talking, and yours, cousin, lies in doing. And speaking of that puts me in mind that I have made a purchase for your department. There's the article now. Here, Topsy! *(Whistles.)*

(TOPSY runs on, L.U.E., down c.)

OPHELIA: Good gracious! what a heathenish, shiftless looking object! St. Clare, what in the world have you brought that thing here for?

ST. CLARE: For you to educate, to be sure, and train in the way she should go. I thought she was rather a funny specimen in the Jim Crow line. Here, Topsy, give us a song, and show us some of your dancing. *(TOPSY sings a verse and dances a breakdown.)*

OPHELIA: *(Paralyzed.)* Well, of all things! If I ever saw the like!

ST. CLARE: *(Smothering a laugh.)* Topsy, this is your new mistress — I'm going to give you up to her. See now that you behave yourself.

TOPSY: Yes, mas'r.

ST. CLARE: You're going to be good, Topsy, you understand?

TOPSY: Oh, yes, mas'r.

OPHELIA: Now, St. Clare, what upon earth is this for? Your house is so full of these plagues now, that a body can't set down their foot without treading on 'em. I get up in the morning and find one asleep behind the door, and see one black head poking out from under the table — one lying on the door mat, and they are moping and mowing and grinning between all the railings, and tumbling over the kitchen floor! What on earth did you want to bring this one for?

ST. CLARE: For you to educate — didn't I tell you? You're always preaching about educating, I thought I would make you a present of a fresh caught specimen, and let you try your hand on her and bring her up in the way she should go.

OPHELIA: I don't want her, I am sure; I have more to do with 'em now than I want to.

ST. CLARE: That's you Christians, all over. You'll get up a society, and get some poor missionary to spend all his days among just such heathen; but let me see one of you that would take one into your house with you, and take the labor of their conversion upon yourselves.

OPHELIA: Well, I didn't think of it in that light. It might be a real missionary work. Well, I'll do what I can. *(Advances to TOPSY.)* She's dreadful dirty and shiftless! How old are you, Topsy?

TOPSY: Dunno, missis.

OPHELIA: How shiftless! Don't know how old you are? Didn't anybody ever tell you? Who was your mother?

TOPSY: *(Grinning.)* Never had none.

OPHELIA: Never had any mother? What do you mean? Where was you born?

TOPSY: Never was born.

OPHELIA: You musn't answer me in that way. I'm not playing with you. Tell me where you was born, and who your father and mother were?

TOPSY: Never was born, tell you; never had no father, nor mother, nor nothin'. I war raised by a speculator with lots of others. Old Aunt Sue used to take car on us.

ST. CLARE: She speaks the truth, cousin. Speculators buy them up cheap, when they are little, and get them raised for the market.

OPHELIA: How long have you lived with your master and mistress?

TOPSY: Dunno, missis.

OPHELIA: How shiftless! Is it a year, or more, or less?

TOPSY: Dunno, missis.

ST. CLARE: She does not know what a year is; she don't even know her own age.

OPHELIA: Have you ever heard anything about heaven, Topsy? *(TOPSY looks bewildered and grins.)* Do you know who made you?

TOPSY: Nobody, as I knows on, he, he, he! I spect I growed. Don't think nobody never made me.

OPHELIA: The shiftless heathen! What can you do? What did you do for your master and mistress?

TOPSY: Fetch water — and wash dishes — and rub knives — and wait on folks — and dance breakdowns.

OPHELIA: I shall break down, I'm afraid, in trying to make anything of you, you shiftless mortal!

ST. CLARE: You find virgin soil there, cousin; put in your own ideas — you won't find many to pull up. *(Exit laughing R. 1 E.)*

OPHELIA: *(Takes out her handkerchief. — A pair of gloves falls. — TOPSY picks them up slyly and puts them in her sleeve.)* Follow me, you benighted innocent!

TOPSY: Yes, missis.

(As OPHELIA turns her back to her, she seizes the end of the ribbon she wears around her waist, and twitches it off. — OPHELIA turns and sees her as she is putting it in her other sleeve. — OPHELIA takes ribbon from her.)

OPHELIA: What's this? You naughty, wicked girl, you've been stealing this?

TOPSY: Laws! why, that ar's missis' ribbon, a'nt it? How could it got caught in my sleeve?

OPHELIA: Topsy, you naughty girl, don't you tell me a lie — you stole that ribbon!

TOPSY: Missis, I declare for't, I didn't — never seed it till dis yer blessed minnit.

OPHELIA: Topsy, don't you know it's wicked to tell lies?

TOPSY: I never tells no lies, missis; it's just de truth I've been telling now and nothing else.

OPHELIA: Topsy, I shall have to whip you, if you tell lies so.

TOPSY: Laws missis, if you's to whip all day, couldn't say no other way. I never seed dat ar — it must a got caught in my sleeve. *(Blubbers.)*

OPHELIA: *(Seizes her by the shoulders.)* Don't you tell me that again, you barefaced fibber! *(Shakes her. — The gloves fall on Stage.)* There you, my gloves too — you outrageous young heathen! *(Picks them up.)* Will you tell me, now, you didn't steal the ribbon?

TOPSY: No, missis; stole de gloves, but didn't steal de ribbon. It was permis-kus.

OPHELIA: Why, you young reprobate!

TOPSY: Yes — I's knows I's wicked!

OPHELIA: Then you know you ought to be punished. *(Boxes her ears.)* What do you think of that?

TOPSY: He, he, he! De Lord, missus; dat wouldn't kill a 'skeeter. *(Runs off laughing, R.U.E. — OPHELIA follows indignantly, R.U.E.)*

Scene 3 — *The Tavern by the River. — Table and chairs. — Jug and glasses on table. — On flat is a printed placard, headed:* — "Four Hundred Dollars Reward — Runaway — George Harris!" *PHINEAS is discovered, seated at table.*

PHINEAS: So yer I am; and a pretty business I've undertook to do. Find the husband of the gal that crossed the river on the ice two or three days ago. Ruth said I must do it, and I'll be teetotally chawed up if I don't do it. I see they've offered a reward for him, dead or alive. How in creation am I to find the varmint? He isn't likely to go round looking natural, with a full description of his hide and figure staring him in the face. *(Enter MR. WILSON, L. 1 E.)* I say, stranger, how are ye? *(Rises and comes forward, R.)*

WILSON: Well, I reckon.

PHINEAS: Any news? *(Takes out plug and knife.)*

WILSON: Not that I know of.

PHINEAS: *(Cutting a piece of tobacco and offering it.)* Chaw?

WILSON: No, thank ye — it don't agree with me.

PHINEAS: Don't, eh? *(Putting it in his own mouth.)* I never felt any the worse for it.

WILSON: *(Sees placard.)* What's that?

PHINEAS: Nigger advertised. *(Advances towards it and spits on it.)* There's my mind upon that.

WILSON: Why, now, stranger, what's that for?

PHINEAS: I'd do it all the same to the writer of that ar paper, if he was here. Any man that owns a boy like that, and can't find any better way of treating him, than branding him on the hand with the letter H, as that paper states, *deserves* to lose him. Such papers as this ar' a shame to old Kaintuck! That's my mind right out, if anybody wants to know.

WILSON: Well, now, that's a fact.

PHINEAS: I used to have a gang of boys, sir — that was before I fell in love

— and I just told em: — "Boys," says I, "run now! Dig! put! jest when you want to. I never shall come to look after you!" That's the way I kept mine. Let 'em know they are free to run any time, and it jest stops their wanting to. It stands to reason it should. Treat 'em like men, and you'll have men's work.

WILSON: I think you are altogether right, friend, and this man described here is a fine fellow — no mistake about that. He worked for me some half dozen years in my bagging factory, and he was my best hand, sir. He is an ingenious fellow, too; he invented a machine for the cleaning of hemp — a really valuable affair; it's gone into use in several factories. His master holds the patent of it.

PHINEAS: I'll warrant ye; holds it, and makes money out of it, and then turns round and brands the boy in his right hand! If I had a fair chance, I'd mark him, I reckon, so that he'd carry it *one* while!

(Enter GEORGE HARRIS, disguised, L. 1 E.)

GEORGE: *(Speaking as he enters.)* Jim, see to the trunks. *(Sees WILSON.)* Ah! Mr. Wilson here?

WILSON: Bless my soul, can it be?

GEORGE: *(Advances and grasps his hand.)* Mr. Wilson, I see you remember me, Mr. Butler, of Oaklands. Shelby county.

WILSON: Ye — yes — yes — sir.

PHINEAS: Holloa! there's a screw loose here somewhere. That old gentleman seems to be struck into a pretty considerable heap of astonishment. May I be teetotally chawed up! if I don't believe that's the identical man I'm arter. *(Crosses to GEORGE.)* How are ye, George Harris?

GEORGE: *(Starting back and thrusting his hands into his breast.)* You know me?

PHINEAS: Ha, ha, ha! I rather conclude I do; but don't get riled, I an't a bloodhound in disguise.

GEORGE: How did you discover me?

PHINEAS: By a teetotal smart guess. You're the very man I want to see. Do you know I was sent after you?

GEORGE: Ah! by my master?

PHINEAS: No; by your wife.

GEORGE: My wife! Where is she?

PHINEAS: She's stopping with a Quaker family over on the Ohio side.

GEORGE: Then she is safe?

PHINEAS: Teetotally!

GEORGE: Conduct me to her.

PHINEAS: Just wait a brace of shakes and I'll do it. I've got to go and get the boat ready. 'Twon't take me but a minute — make yourself comfortable till I get back. Chaw me up! but this is what I call doing things in short order. *(Exit L. 1 E.)*

WILSON: George!

GEORGE: Yes, George!

WILSON: I couldn't have thought it!

GEORGE: I am pretty well disguised, I fancy; you see I don't answer to the advertisement at all.

WILSON: George, this is a dangerous game you are playing; I could not have advised you to it.

GEORGE: I can do it on my own responsibility.

WILSON: Well, George, I suppose you're running away — leaving your lawful master, George, (I don't wonder at it) at the same time, I'm sorry, George, yes, decidedly. I think I must say that it's my duty to tell you so.

GEORGE: Why are you sorry, sir?

WILSON: Why to see you, as it were, setting yourself in opposition to the laws of your country.

GEORGE: *My* country! What country have *I*, but the grave? And I would to heaven that I was laid there!

WILSON: George, you've got a hard master, in fact he is — well, he conducts himself reprehensibly — I can't pretend to defend him. I'm sorry for you, now; it's a bad case — very bad; but we must all submit to the indications of providence. George, don't you see?

GEORGE: I wonder, Mr. Wilson, if the Indians should come and take you a prisoner away from your wife and children, and want to keep you all your life hoeing corn for them, if you'd think it your duty to abide in the condition in which you were called? I rather imagine that you'd think the first stray horse you could find an indication of providence, shouldn't you?

WILSON: Really, George, putting the case in that somewhat peculiar light — I don't know — under those circumstances — but what I might. But it seems to me you are running an awful risk. You can't hope to carry it out. If you're taken it will be worse with you than ever; they'll only abuse you, and half kill you, and sell you down river.

GEORGE: Mr. Wilson, I know all this. I *do* run a risk, but — *(Throws open coat and shows pistols and knife in his belt.)* There! I'm ready for them. Down South I never *will* go! no, if it comes to that, I can earn myself at least six feet of free soil — the first and last I shall ever own in Kentucky!

WILSON: Why, George, this state of mind is awful — it's getting really desperate. I'm concerned. Going to break the laws of your country?

GEORGE: My country again! Sir, I haven't any country any more than I have any father. I don't want anything of *your* country, except to be left alone — to go peaceably out of it; but if any man tries to stop me, let him take care, for I am desperate. I'll fight for my liberty, to the last breath I breathe! You say your fathers did it, if it was right for them, it is right for me!

WILSON: *(Walking up and down and fanning his face with a large yellow silk handkerchief.)* Blast 'em all! Haven't I always said so — the infernal old cusses! Bless me! I hope I an't swearing now! Well, go ahead, George, go ahead. But be careful, my boy; don't shoot anybody, unless — well, you'd *better* not shoot — at least I wouldn't *hit* anybody, you know.

GEORGE: Only in self-defense.

WILSON: Well, well. *(Fumbling in his pocket.)* I suppose, perhaps, I an't following my judgement — hang it, I won't follow my judgement. So here, George. *(Takes out a pocket-book and offers GEORGE a roll of bills.)*

GEORGE: No, my kind, good sir, you've done a great deal for me, and this might get you into trouble. I have money enough, I hope, to take me as far as I need it.

WILSON: No; but you must, George. Money is a great help everywhere, can't have too much, if you get it honestly. Take it, *do* take it, *now* do, my boy!

GEORGE: *(Taking the money.)* On condition, sir, that I may repay it at some future time, I will.

WILSON: And now, George, how long are you going to travel in this way? Not long or far I hope? It's well carried on, but too bold.

GEORGE: Mr. Wilson, it is *so bold,* and this tavern is so near, that they will never think of it; they will look for me on ahead, and you yourself wouldn't know me.

WILSON: But the mark on your hand?

GEORGE: *(Draws off his glove and shows scar.)* That is a parting mark of Mr. Harris' regard. Looks interesting, doesn't it? *(Puts on glove again.)*

WILSON: I declare, my very blood runs cold when I think of it — your condition and your risks!

GEORGE: Mine has run cold a good many years; at present, it's about up to the boiling point.

WILSON: George, something has brought you out wonderfully. You hold up your head, and move and speak like another man.

GEORGE: *(Proudly)* Because I'm a *freeman!* Yes, sir; I've said "master" for the last time to any man. *I'm free!*

WILSON: Take care! You are not sure; you may be taken.

GEORGE: All men are free and equal *in the grave,* if it comes to that, Mr. Wilson.

(Enter PHINEAS, L. 1 E.)

PHINEAS: Them's my sentiments, to a teetotal atom, and I don't care who knows it! Neighbor, the boat is ready, and the sooner we make tracks the better. I've seen some mysterious strangers lurking about these diggings, so we'd better put.

GEORGE: Farewell, Mr. Wilson, and heaven reward you for the many kindnesses you have shown the poor fugitive!

WILSON: *(Grasping his hand.)* You're a brave fellow, George. I wish in my heart you were safe through, though — that's what I do.

PHINEAS: And ain't I the man of all creation to put him through, stranger? Chaw me up if I don't take him to his dear little wife, in the smallest possible quantity of time. Come, neighbor, let's vamose.

GEORGE: Farewell, Mr. Wilson. *(Crosses to L.H.)*

WILSON: My best wishes go with you, George. *(Exit, R. 1 E.)*

PHINEAS: You're a trump, old Slow-and-Easy.

GEORGE: *(Looking off, R.H.)* Look! Look!

PHINEAS: Consarn their picters, here they come! We can't get out of the house without their seeing us. We're teetotally treed!

GEORGE: Let us fight our way through them!

PHINEAS: No, that won't do; there are too many of them for a fair fight — we should be chawed up in no time. *(Looks round and sees trap door, c.)* Holloa! here's a cellar door. Just you step down here a few minutes, while I parley with them. *(Lifts trap.)*

GEORGE: I am resolved to perish sooner than surrender! *(Goes down trap.)*
PHINEAS: That's your sort! *(Closes trap and stands on it.)* Here they are!
(Enter HALEY, MARKS, LOKER and three MEN, L. 1 E.)

HALEY: Say, stranger, you haven't seen a runaway darkey about these parts, eh?
PHINEAS: What kind of a darkey?
HALEY: A mulatto chap, almost as light-complexioned as a white man.
PHINEAS: Was he a pretty good-looking chap?
HALEY: Yes.
PHINEAS: Kind of tall?
HALEY: Yes.
PHINEAS: With brown hair?
HALEY: Yes.
PHINEAS: And dark eyes?
HALEY: Yes.
PHINEAS: Pretty well dressed?
HALEY: Yes.
PHINEAS: Scar on his right hand?
HALEY: Yes, yes.
PHINEAS: Well, I ain't seen him.
HALEY: Oh, brother! Come, boys, let's search the house. *(Exeunt, R. 1 E.)*
PHINEAS: *(Raises trap.)* Now, then, neighbor George. *(GEORGE enters, up trap.)* Now's the time to cut your lucky.
GEORGE: Follow me, Phineas. *(Exit L. 1 E.)*
PHINEAS: In a brace of shakes. *(Is closing trap as HALEY, MARKS, LOKER, etc., re-enter, R. 1 E.)*
HALEY: Ah! he's down in the cellar. Follow me, boys! *(Thrusts PHINEAS aside, and rushes down trap, followed by the others. PHINEAS closes trap and stands on it.)*
PHINEAS: Chaw me up! but I've got 'em all in a trap. *(Knocking below.)* Be quiet, you pesky varmints! *(Knocking.)* They're getting mighty oneasy. *(Knocking.)* Will you be quiet, you savagerous critters! *(The trap is forced open. HALEY and MARKS appear. PHINEAS seizes a chair and stands over trap — picture.)* Down with you or I'll smash you into apple-fritters! *(Tableau — closed in.)*

Scene 4 — *A Plain Chamber.*

TOPSY: *(Without, L.H.)* You go 'long. No more nigger dan you be! *(Enters L.H. — shouts and laughter without — looks off.)* You seem to think yourself white folks. You ain't nerry one — black *nor* white. I'd like to be one or turrer. Law! you niggers, does you know you's all sinners? Well, you is — everybody is. White folks is sinners too — Miss Feely says so — but I 'spects niggers is the biggest ones. But Lor! ye ain't any on ye up to me. I's so awful wicked there can't nobody do nothin' with me. I used to keep old missis a-swarin' at me ha' de time. I 'spects I's de wickedest critter in de world. *(Song and dance introduced. Enter EVA, L. 1 E.)*
EVA: Oh, Topsy! Topsy! you have been very wrong again.
TOPSY: Well, I 'spects I have.

308

EVA: What makes you do so?

TOPSY: I dunno; I 'spects it's cause I's so wicked.

EVA: Why did you spoil Jane's earrings?

TOPSY: 'Cause she's so proud. She called me a little black imp, and turned up her pretty nose at me 'cause she is whiter than I am. I was gwine by her room, and I seed her coral earrings lying on de table, so I threw dem on de floor, and put my foot on 'em, and scrunches 'em all to little bits — he! he! he! I's so wicked.

EVA: Don't you know that was very wrong?

TOPSY: I don't car'! I despises dem what's sets up for fine ladies, when dey ain't nothing but cream-colored niggers! Dere's Miss Rosa — she gives me lots of 'pertinent remarks. T'other night she was gwine to a ball. She put on a beau'ful dress dat missis give her — wid her har curled, all nice and pretty. She hab to go down de back stairs — dem am dark — and I puts a pail of hot water on dem, and she put her foot into it, and den she go tumbling to de bottom of de stairs, and de water go all ober her, and spile her dress, and scald her dreadful bad! He! he! he! I's so wicked!

EVA: Oh! how could you!

TOPSY: Don't dey despise me cause I don't know nothing? Don't dey laugh at me 'cause I'm brack, and dey ain't?

EVA: But you shouldn't mind them.

TOPSY: Well, I don't mind dem; but when dey are passing under my winder, I trows dirty water on 'em, and dat spiles der complexions.

EVA: What does make you so bad, Topsy? Why won't you try and be good? Don't you love anybody, Topsy?

TOPSY: Can't recommember.

EVA: But you love your father and mother?

TOPSY: Never had none, ye know, I telled ye that, Miss Eva.

EVA: Oh! I know; but hadn't you any brother, or sister, or aunt, or —

TOPSY: No, none on 'em — never had nothing nor nobody. I's brack — no one loves me!

EVA: Oh! Topsy, I love you! *(Laying her hand on TOPSY's shoulder.)* I love you because you haven't had any father, or mother, or friends. I love you, I want you to be good. I wish you would try to be good for my sake. *(TOPSY looks astonished for a moment, and then bursts into tears.)* Only think of it, Topsy — *you* can be one of those spirits bright Uncle Tom sings about!

TOPSY: Oh! dear Miss Eva — dear Miss Eva! I will try — I will try. I never did care nothin' about it before.

EVA: If you try, you will succeed. Come with me. *(Crosses to R. and takes TOPSY's hand.)*

TOPSY: I will try; but den, I's so wicked! *(Exit EVA R.H., followed by TOPSY, crying.)*

Scene 5 — Chamber. Enter GEORGE, ELIZA and HARRY, R. 1 E.)

GEORGE: At length, Eliza, after many wanderings, we are united.

ELIZA: Thanks to these generous Quakers, who have so kindly sheltered us.

GEORGE: Not forgetting our friend Phineas.

ELIZA: I do indeed owe him much. 'Twas he I met upon the icy river's bank, after that fearful, but successful attempt, when I fled from the slave-trader with my child in my arms.

GEORGE: It seems almost incredible that you could have crossed the river on the ice.

ELIZA: Yes, I did. Heaven helping me, I crossed on the ice, for they were behind me — right behind — and there was no other way.

GEORGE: But the ice was all in broken-up blocks, swinging and heaving up and down in the water.

ELIZA: I know it was — I know it; I did not think I should get over, but I did not care — I could but die if I did not! I leaped on the ice, but how I got across I don't know; the first I remember, a man was helping me up the bank — that man was Phineas.

GEORGE: My brave girl! you deserve your freedom — you have richly earned it!

ELIZA: And when we get to Canada I can help you to work, and between us we can find something to live on.

GEORGE: Yes, Eliza, so long as we have each other, and our boy. Oh, Eliza, if these people only knew what a blessing it is for a man to feel that his wife and child belong to *him!* I've often wondered to see men that could call their wives and children *their own,* fretting and worrying about anything else. Why, I feel rich and strong, though we have nothing but our bare hands. If they will only let me alone now, I will be satisfied — thankful!

ELIZA: But we are not quite out of danger; we are not yet in Canada.

GEORGE: True, but it seems as if I smelt the free air, and it makes me strong!

(Enter PHINEAS, dressed as a Quaker, L. 1 E.)

PHINEAS: *(With a snuffle.)* Verily, friends, how is it with thee? — hum!

GEORGE: Why, Phineas, what means this metamorphosis?

PHINEAS: I've become a Quaker, that's the meaning on't.

GEORGE: What — you?

PHINEAS: Teetotally! I was driven to it by a strong argument, composed of a pair of sparkling eyes, rosy cheeks, and pouting lips. Them lips would persuade a man to assassinate his grandmother! *(Assumes the Quaker tone again.)* Verily, George, I have discovered something of importance to the interests of thee and thy party, and it were well for thee to hear it.

GEORGE: Keep us not in suspense!

PHINEAS: Well, after I left you on the road, I stopped at a little, lone tavern, just below here. Well, I was tired with hard driving, and after my supper I stretched myself down on a pile of bags in the corner, and pulled a buffalo hide over me — and what does I do but get fast asleep.

GEORGE: With one ear open, Phineas?

PHINEAS: No, I slept ears and all for an hour or two, for I was pretty well tired; but when I came to myself a little, I found that there were some men in the room, sitting round a table, drinking and talking; and I thought, before I made much muster, I'd just see what they were up to, especially as I heard them say something about the Quakers. Then I listened with both ears and found they were talking about you. So I kept quiet, and heard them lay off all their plans. They've got a right notion of the track we are going tonight, and they'll be down after us, six or eight strong. So, now, what's to be done?

ELIZA: What *shall* we do, George?

GEORGE: I know what I shall do! *(Takes out pistols.)*

PHINEAS: Ay — ay, thou seest, Eliza, how it will work — pistols — phitz — poppers!

ELIZA: I see; but I pray it come not to that!

GEORGE: I don't want to involve any one with or for me. If you will lend me your vehicle, and direct me, I will drive alone to the next stand.

PHINEAS: Ah! well, friend, but thee'll need a drive for all that. Thee's quite welcome to do all the fighting thee knows; but I know a thing or two about the road that thee doesn't.

GEORGE: But I don't want to involve you.

PHINEAS: Involve me! Why, chaw me — that is to say — when thee does involve me, please to let me know.

ELIZA: Phineas is a wise and skillful man. You will do well, George, to abide by his judgement. And, oh! George, be not hasty with these — young blood is hot! *(Laying her hand on pistols.)*

GEORGE: I will attack no man. All I ask of this country is to be left alone, and I will go out peaceably. But I'll fight to the last breath before they shall take from me my wife and son! Can you blame me?

PHINEAS: Mortal man cannot blame thee, neighbor George! Flesh and blood could not do otherwise. Woe unto the world because of offenses, but woe unto them through whom the offense cometh! That's gospel, teetotally!

GEORGE: Would not even you, sir, do the same, in my place?

PHINEAS: I pray that I be not tried; the flesh is weak — but I think my flesh would be pretty tolerably strong in such a case; I ain't sure, friend George, that I shouldn't hold a fellow for thee, if thee had any accounts to settle with him.

ELIZA: Heaven grant we be not tempted.

PHINEAS: But if we are tempted too much, why, consarn 'em! let them look out, that's all.

GEORGE: It's quite plain you was not born for a Quaker. The old nature has its way in you pretty strong yet.

PHINEAS: Well, I reckon you are pretty teetotally right.

GEORGE: Had we not better hasten our flight?

PHINEAS: Well, I rather conclude we had; we're full two hours ahead of them, if they start at the time they planned; so let's vamose. *(Exeunt R. 1 E.)*

Scene 6 — *A Rocky Pass in the Hills. — Large set rock and Platform, L.U.E.*

PHINEAS: *(Without, R.U.E.)* Out with you in a twinkling, everyone, and up into these rocks with me! run *now,* if you *ever* did run! *(Music. PHINEAS enters, with HARRY in his arms. — GEORGE supporting ELIZA, R.U.E.)* Come up here; this is one of our old hunting dens. Come up. *(They ascend the rock.)* Well, here we are. Let 'em get us if they can. Whoever comes here has to walk single file between those two rocks, in fair range of your pistols — d'ye see?

GEORGE: I do see. And now, as this affair is mine, let me take all the risk, and do all the fighting.

311

PHINEAS: Thee's quite welcome to do the fighting, George; but I may have the fun of looking on, I suppose. But see, these fellows are kind of debating down there, and looking up, like hens when they are going to fly up onto the roost. Hadn't thee better give 'em a word of advice, before they come up, just to tell 'em handsomely they'll be shot if they do.

(LOKER, MARKS, and three MEN enter, R. 2 E.)

MARKS: Well, Tom, your coons are fairly treed.

LOKER: Yes, I see 'em go up right here; and here's a path — I'm for going right up. They can't jump down in a hurry, and it won't take long to ferret 'em out.

MARKS: But, Tom, they might fire at us from behind the rocks. That would be ugly, you know.

LOKER: Ugh! always for saving your skin, Marks. No danger, niggers are too plaguy scared!

MARKS: I don't know why I shouldn't save my skin, it's the best I've got; and niggers do fight like the devil sometimes.

GEORGE: *(Rising on the rock.)* Gentlemen, who are you down there and what do you want?

LOKER: We want a party of runaway niggers. One George and Eliza Harris, and their son. We've got the officers here, and a warrant to take 'em too. D'ye hear? An't you George Harris, that belong to Mr. Harris, of Shelby county, Kentucky?

GEORGE: I am George Harris. A Mr. Harris, of Kentucky, did call me his property. But now I'm a freeman, standing on heaven's free soil! My wife and child I claim as mine. We have arms to defend ourselves and we mean to do it. You can come up if you like, but the first one that comes within range of our bullets is a dead man!

MARKS: Oh, come — come, young man, this ar no kind of talk at all for you. You see we're officers of justice. We've got the law on our side, and the power and so forth; so you'd better give up peaceably, you see — for you'll certainly have to give up at last.

GEORGE: I know very well that you've got the law on your side, and the power; but you haven't got us. We are standing here as free as you are, and by the great power that made us, we'll fight for our liberty till we die! *(During this, MARKS draws a pistol, and when he concludes fires at him. — ELIZA screams.)* It's nothing, Eliza; I am unhurt.

PHINEAS: *(Drawing GEORGE down.)* Thee'd better keep out of sight with thy speechifying; they're teetotal mean scamps.

LOKER: What did you do that for, Marks?

MARKS: You see, you get jist as much for him dead as alive in Kentucky.

GEORGE: Now, Phineas, the first man that advances I fire at; you take the second and so on. It won't do to waste two shots on one.

PHINEAS: But what if you don't hit?

GEORGE: I'll try my best.

PHINEAS: Creation! chaw me up if there a'nt stuff in you!

MARKS: I think I must have hit some on'em. I heard a squeal.

LOKER: I'm going right up for one. I never was afraid of niggers, and I an't a going to be now. Who goes after me?

(Music. — LOKER dashes up the rock. — GEORGE fires. — He staggers for a moment, then springs to the top. — PHINEAS seizes him. — A struggle.)

PHINEAS: Friend, thee is not wanted here! *(Throws LOKER over the rock.)*

MARKS: *(Retreating.)* Lord help us — they're perfect devils!

(Music. — MARKS and PARTY run off R. 2 E. — GEORGE and ELIZA kneel in an attitude of thanksgiving, with the CHILD between them. — PHINEAS stands over them exulting. — Tableau.)

END OF ACT TWO

ACT THREE

Scene 1 — *Chamber. Enter ST. CLARE, followed by TOM, R. 1 E.*

ST. CLARE: *(Giving money and papers to TOM.)* There, Tom, are the bills, and the money to liquidate them.

TOM: Yes, mas'r.

ST. CLARE: Well, Tom, what are you waiting for? Isn't all right there?

TOM: I'm 'fraid not, mas'r.

ST. CLARE: Why, Tom, what's the matter? You look as solemn as a judge.

TOM: I feel very bad, mas'r. I allays have thought that mas'r would be good to everybody.

ST. CLARE: Well, Tom, haven't I been? Come, now, what do you want? There's something you haven't got, I suppose, and this is the preface.

TOM: Mas'r allays been good to me. I haven't nothing to complain of on that head; but there is one that mas'r isn't good to.

ST. CLARE: Why, Tom, what's got into you? Speak out — what do you mean?

TOM: Last night, between one and two, I thought so. I studied upon the matter then — mas'r isn't good to *himself.*

ST. CLARE: Ah! now I understand; you allude to the state in which I came home last night. Well, to tell the truth, I *was* slightly elevated — a little more champagne on board than I could comfortably carry. That's all, isn't it?

TOM: *(Deeply affected — clasping his hands and weeping.)* All! Oh! my dear young mas'r, I'm 'fraid it will be *loss of all — all* body and soul. The good book says "it biteth like a serpent and stingeth like an adder," my dear mas'r.

ST. CLARE: You poor, silly fool! I'm not worth crying over.

TOM: Oh, mas'r! I implore you to think of it before it gets too late.

ST. CLARE: Well, I won't go to any more of their cursed nonsense, Tom — on my honor, I won't. I don't know why I haven't stopped long ago; I've always despised *it,* and myself for it. So now, Tom, wipe up your eyes and go about your errands.

TOM: Bless you, mas'r. I feel much better now. You have taken a load from poor Tom's heart. Bless you!

ST. CLARE: Come, come, no blessings; I'm not so wonderfully good, now. There, I'll pledge my honor to you, Tom, you don't see me so again.
(Exit TOM, R. 1 E.) I'll keep my faith with him, too.

OPHELIA: *(Without, L. 1 E.)* Come along, you shiftless mortal!

ST. CLARE: What new witchcraft has Topsy been brewing? That commotion is of her raising, I'll be bound.

(Enter OPHELIA, dragging in TOPSY, L. 1 E.)

OPHELIA: Come here now; I will tell your master.

ST. CLARE: What's the matter now?

OPHELIA: The matter is that I cannot be plagued with this girl any longer. It's past all bearing; flesh and blood cannot endure it. Here I locked her up and gave her a hymn to study; and what does she do but spy out where I put my key, and has gone to my bureau, and got a bonnet-trimming and cut it all to pieces to make dolls' jackets! I never saw anything like it in my life!

ST. CLARE: What have you done to her?

OPHELIA: What have I done? What haven't I done? Your wife says I ought to have her whipped till she couldn't stand.

ST. CLARE: I don't doubt it. Tell me of the lovely rule of woman. I never saw above a dozen women that wouldn't half kill a horse or servant, either, if they had their own way with them — let alone a man.

OPHELIA: I am sure, St. Clare, I don't know what to do. I've taught and taught — I've talked till I'm tired; I've whipped her, I've punished her in every way I could think of, and still she's just what she was at first.

ST. CLARE: Come here, Tops, you monkey! *(TOPSY crosses to ST. CLARE, grinning.)* What makes you behave so?

TOPSY: 'Spects it's my wicked heart — Miss Feely says so.

ST. CLARE: Don't you see how much Miss Ophelia has done for you? She says she has done everything she can think of.

TOPSY: Lord, yes, mas'r! old missis used to say so, too. She whipped me a heap harder, and used to pull my ha'r, and knock my head agin the door; but it didn't do me no good. I 'spects if they's to pull every spear of ha'r out o' my head, it wouldn't do no good neither — I's so wicked! Laws! I's nothin' but a nigger, no ways! *(Goes up.)*

OPHELIA: Well, I shall have to give her up; I can't have that trouble any longer.

ST. CLARE: I'd like to ask you one question.

OPHELIA: What is it?

ST. CLARE: Why, if your doctrine is not strong enough to save one heathen child, that you can have at home here, all to yourself, what's the use of sending one or two poor missionaries off with it among thousands of just such? I suppose this girl is a fair sample of what thousands of your heathen are.

OPHELIA: I'm sure I don't know; I never saw such a girl as this.

ST. CLARE: What makes you so bad, Tops? Why won't you try and be good? Don't you love any one, Topsy?

TOPSY: *(Comes down.)* Dunno nothing 'bout love; I loves candy and sich, that's all.

OPHELIA: But, Topsy, if you'd only try to be good, you might.

TOPSY: Couldn't never be nothing but a nigger, if I was ever so good. If I could be skinned and come white, I'd try then.

ST. CLARE: People can love you, if you are black, Topsy. Miss Ophelia would love you, if you were good. *(TOPSY laughs.)* Don't you think so?

TOPSY: No, she can't b'ar me, 'cause I'm a nigger — she'd's soon have a toad touch her. There can't nobody love niggers, and niggers can't do nothin'! I don't car'! *(Whistles.)*

ST. CLARE: Silence, you incorrigible imp, and begone!

TOPSY: He! he! he! didn't get much out of dis chile! *(Exit L. 1 E.)*

OPHELIA: I've always had a prejudice against negroes, and it's a fact — I never could bear to have that child touch me, but I didn't think she knew it.

ST. CLARE: Trust any child to find that out, there's no keeping it from them. But I believe all the trying in the world to benefit a child, and all the substantial favors you can do them, will never excite one emotion of gratitude, while that feeling of repugnance remains in the heart. It's a queer kind of a fact, but so it is.

OPHELIA: I don't know how I can help it — they are disagreeable to me, this girl in particular. How can I help feeling so?

ST. CLARE: Eva does, it seems.

OPHELIA: Well, she's so loving. I wish I was like her. She might teach me a lesson.

ST. CLARE: It would not be the first time a little child had been used to instruct an old disciple, if it were so. *(Crosses to L.)* Come, let us seek Eva, in her favorite bower by the lake.

OPHELIA: Why the dew is falling, she mustn't be out there. She is unwell, I know.

ST. CLARE: Don't be croaking, cousin — I hate it.

OPHELIA: But she has that cough.

ST. CLARE: Oh, nonsense, of that cough — it is not anything. She has taken a little cold, perhaps.

OPHELIA: Well, that was just the way Eliza Jane was taken — and Ellen —

ST. CLARE: Oh, stop these hobgoblin, nurse legends. You old hands get so wise, that a child cannot cough or sneeze, but you see desperation and ruin at hand. Only take care of the child, keep her from the night air, and don't let her play too hard, and she'll do well enough. *(Exeunt L. 1 E.)*

Scene 2 — *The flat represents the lake. — The rays of the setting sun tinge the waters with gold. — A large tree R. 3 E. — Beneath this a grassy bank, on which EVA (L.) and TOM (R.) are seated side by side. — EVA has a Bible open on her lap. — Music.*

TOM: Read dat passage again, please, Miss Eva?

EVA: *(Reading.)* "And I saw a sea of glass, mingled with fire." *(Stopping suddenly and pointing to lake.)* Tom, there it is!

TOM: What, Miss Eva?

EVA: Don't you see there? There's a "sea of glass mingled with fire."

TOM: True enough, Miss Eva. *(Sings.)*
Oh, had I the wings of the morning,
I'd fly away to Canaan's shore;
Bright angels should convey me home,
To the New Jerusalem.

EVA: Where do you suppose New Jerusalem is, Uncle Tom?

TOM: Oh, up in the clouds, Miss Eva.

EVA: Then I think I see it. Look in those clouds, they look like great gates of pearl; and you can see beyond them — far, far off — it's all gold! Tom, sing about 'spirits bright.'

TOM: *(Sings.)*
    I see a band of spirits bright,
    That taste the glories there;
    They are all robed in spotless white,
    And conquering palms they bear.

EVA: Uncle Tom, I've seen *them.*

TOM: To be sure you have; you are one of them yourself. You are the brightest spirit I ever saw.

EVA: They come to me sometimes in my sleep — those spirits bright —
    They are all robed in spotless white,
    And conquering palms they bear.
    Uncle Tom, I'm going there.

TOM: Where, Miss Eva?

EVA: *(Pointing to the sky.)* I'm going *there,* to the spirits bright, Tom; I'm going before long.

TOM: It's jest no use tryin' to keep Miss Eva here; I've allays said so. She's got the Lord's mark in her forehead. She wasn't never like a child that's to live — there was always something deep in her eyes. *(Rises and comes forward R. — EVA also comes forward C., leaving Bible on bank.)*

(Enter ST. CLARE, L. 1 E.)

ST. CLARE: Ah! my little pussy, you look as blooming as a rose! You are better now-a-days, are you not?

EVA: Papa, I've had things I wanted to say to you a great while. I want to say them now, before I get weaker.

ST. CLARE: Nay, this is an idle fear, Eva; you know you grow stronger every day.

EVA: It's all no use, papa, to keep it to myself any longer. The time is coming that I am going to leave you, I am going, and never to come back.

ST. CLARE: Oh, now, my dear little Eva! you've got nervous and low spirited; you mustn't indulge such gloomy thoughts.

EVA: No, papa, don't deceive yourself, I am *not* any better; I know it perfectly well, and I am going before long. I am not nervous — I am not low spirited. If it were not for you, papa, and my friends, I should be perfectly happy. I want to go — I long to go!

ST. CLARE: Why, dear child, what has made your poor little heart so sad? You have everything to make you happy that could be given you.

EVA: I had rather be in heaven! There are a great many things here that makes me sad — that seem dreadful to me; I had rather be there; but I don't want to leave you — it almost breaks my heart!

ST. CLARE: What makes you sad, and what seems dreadful, Eva?

EVA: I feel sad for our poor people; they love me dearly, and they are all good and kind to me. I wish, papa, they were all *free!*

ST. CLARE: Why, Eva, child, don't you think they are well enough off now?

EVA: *(Not heeding the question.)* Papa, isn't there a way to have slaves made free? When I am dead, papa, then you will think of me and do it for my sake?

ST. CLARE: When you are dead, Eva? Oh, child, don't talk to me so. You are all I have on earth!

EVA: Papa, these poor creatures love their children as much as you do me. Tom loves his children. Oh, do something for them!

ST. CLARE: There, there, darling; only don't distress yourself, and don't talk of dying, and I will do anything you wish.

EVA: And promise me, dear father, that Tom shall have his freedom as soon as —*(Hesitating.)* — I am gone!

ST. CLARE: Yes, dear, I will do anything in the world — anything you could ask me to. There, Tom, take her to her chamber, this evening air is too chill for her. *(Music. — Kisses her. TOM takes EVA in his arms, and exit R.U.E. Gazing mournfully after EVA.)* Has there ever been a child like Eva? Yes, there has been; but their names are always on grave-stones, and their sweet smiles, their heavenly eyes, their singular words and ways, are among the buried treasures of yearning hearts. It is as if heaven had an especial band of angels, whose office it is to sojourn for a season here, and endear to them the wayward human heart, that they might bear it upward with them in their homeward flight. When you see that deep, spiritual light in the eye when the little soul reveals itself in words sweeter and wiser than the ordinary words of children, hope not to retain that child; for the seal of heaven is on it, and the light of immortality looks out from its eyes! *(Music. — Exit R.U.E.)*

Scene 3 — *A corridor. — Proscenium doors on. — Music. — Enter TOM, L. 1 E., he listens at R. door and then lies down. Enter OPHELIA, L. 1 E., with candle.*

OPHELIA: Uncle Tom, what alive have you taken to sleeping anywhere and everywhere, like a dog, for? I thought you were one of the orderly sort, that liked to lie in bed in a Christian way.

TOM: *(Rises. — Mysteriously.)* I do, Miss Feely, I do, but now —

OPHELIA: Well, what now?

TOM: We mustn't speak loud; Mas'r St. Clare won't hear on't; but Miss Feely, you know there must be somebody watchin' for the bridegroom.

OPHELIA: What do you mean, Tom?

TOM: You know it says in Scripture, "At midnight there was a great cry made, behold, the bridegroom cometh!" That's what I'm spectin' now, every night, Miss Feely, and I couldn't sleep out of hearing, noways.

OPHELIA: Why, Uncle Tom, what makes you think so?

TOM: Miss Eva, she talks to me. The Lord, he sends his messenger in the soul. I must be thar, Miss Feely; for when that ar blessed child goes into the kingdom, they'll open the door so wide, we'll all get a look in at the glory!

OPHELIA: Uncle Tom, did Miss Eva say she felt more unwell than unsual tonight?

TOM: No; but she told me she was coming nearer — thar's them that tells it to the child, Miss Feely. It's the angels — it's the trumpet sound afore the break o' day!

OPHELIA: Heaven grant your fears be vain! *(Crosses to R.)* Come in, Tom.

317

(Exeunt R. 1 E.)

Scene 4 — *EVA's chamber. EVA discovered on a couch. — A table stands near the couch with a lamp on it. The light shines upon EVA's face, which is very pale. — Scene half dark. — UNCLE TOM is kneeling near the foot of the couch. L.H. — OPHELIA stands at the head R.H. — ST. CLARE at back. — Scene opens to plaintive Music. — After a strain enter MARIE, hastily, L. 1 E.*

MARIE: St. Clare! Cousin! Oh! what is the matter now?

ST. CLARE: *(Hoarsely.)* Hush! she is dying!

MARIE: *(Sinking on her knees, beside TOM.)* Dying!

ST. CLARE: Oh! if she would only wake and speak once more. *(Bending over EVA.)* Eva, darling! *(EVA uncloses her eyes, smiles, raises her head and tries to speak.)* Do you know me, Eva?

EVA: *(Throwing her arms feebly about his neck.)* Dear papa. *(Her arms drop and she sinks back.)*

ST. CLARE: Oh heaven! this is dreadful! Oh! Tom, my boy, it is killing me!

TOM: Look at her, mas'r. *(Points to EVA.)*

ST. CLARE: Eva! *(A pause.)* She does not hear. Oh Eva! tell us what you see. What is it?

EVA: *(Feebly smiling.)* Oh! love! joy! peace! *(Dies.)*

TOM: Oh! bless the Lord! it's over, dear mas'r, it's over.

ST. CLARE: *(Sinking on his knees.)* Farewell, beloved child! the bright eternal doors have closed after thee. We shall see thy sweet face no more. Oh! woe for them who watched thy entrance into heaven when they shall wake and find only the cold, gray sky of daily life and thou gone forever. *(Solemn music, slow curtain.)*

END OF ACT THREE

ACT FOUR

Scene 1 — *A street in New Orleans. Enter GUMPTION CUTE R., meeting MARKS L.H.*

CUTE: How do ye dew?

MARKS: How are you?

CUTE: Well, now, squire, it's a fact that I am dead broke and busted up.

MARKS: You have been speculating, I suppose!

CUTE: That's just it and nothing shorter.

MARKS: You have had poor success, you say?

CUTE: Tarnation bad, now I tell you. You see I came to this part of the country to make my fortune.

MARKS: And you did not do it?

CUTE: Scarcely. The first thing I tried my hand at was keeping school. I opened an academy for the instruction of youth in the various branches of orthography, geography, and other graphies.

MARKS: Did you succeed in getting any pupils?

CUTE: Oh, lots on 'em! and a pretty set of dunces they were too. After the first quarter, I called on the respectable parents of the juveniles, and requested them to fork over. To which they politely answered — don't you wish you may get it?

MARKS: What did you do then?

CUTE: Well, I kind of pulled up stakes and left those diggins. Well then I went into Spiritual Rappings for a living. That paid pretty well for a short time, till I met with an accident.

MARKS: An accident?

CUTE: Yes; a tall Yahoo called on me one day, and wanted me to summon the spirit of his mother — which, of course, I did. He asked me about a dozen questions which I answered to his satisfaction. At last he wanted to know what she died of — I said, Cholera. You never did see a critter so riled as he was. 'Look yere, stranger,' said he, 'it's my opinion that you're a pesky humbug! for my mother was blown up in a *Steamboat!* with that he left the premises. The next day the people furnished me with a conveyance, and I rode out of town.

MARKS: Rode out of town?

CUTE: Yes; on a rail!

MARKS: I suppose you gave up the spirits, after that?

CUTE: Well, I reckon I did; it had such an effect on my spirits.

MARKS: It's a wonder they didn't tar and feather you.

CUTE: There was some mention made of that, but when they said *feathers,* I felt as if I had wings and flew away.

MARKS: You cut and run?

CUTE: Yes; I didn't like their company and I cut it. Well, after that I let myself out as an overseer on a cotton plantation. I made a pretty good thing of that, though it was dreadful trying to my feelings to flog the darkies; but I got used to it after a while, and then I used to lather 'em like Jehu. Well, the proprietor got the fever and ague and shook himself out of town. The place and all the fixings were sold at auction and I found myself adrift once more.

MARKS: What are you doing at present?

CUTE: I'm in search of a rich relation of mine.

MARKS: A rich relation?

CUTE: Yes, a Miss Ophelia St. Clare. You see, a niece of hers married one of my second cousins — that's how I came to be a relation of hers. She came on here from Vermont to be housekeeper to a cousin of hers, of the same name.

MARKS: I know him well.

CUTE: The deuce you do! — well, that's lucky.

MARKS: Yes, he lives in this city.

CUTE: Say, you just point out the locality, and I'll give him a call.

MARKS: Stop a bit. Suppose you shouldn't be able to raise the wind in that quarter, what have you thought of doing?

CUTE: Well, nothing particular.

MARKS: How should you like to enter into a nice, profitable business — one that pays well?

CUTE: That's just about my measure — it would suit me to a hair. What is it?

MARKS: Nigger catching.

CUTE: Catching niggers! What on airth do you mean?

MARKS: Why, when there's a large reward offered for a runaway darkey, we goes after him, catches him, and gets the reward.

CUTE: Yes, that's all right so far — but s'pose there ain't no reward offered?

MARKS: Why, then we catches the darkey on our own account, sells him, and pockets the proceeds.

CUTE: By chowder, that ain't a bad speculation!

MARKS: What do you say? I want a partner. You see, I lost my partner last year, up in Ohio — he was a powerful fellow.

CUTE: Lost him! How did you lose him?

MARKS: Well, you see, Tom and I — his name was Tom Loker — Tom and I were after a mulatto chap, called George Harris, that run away from Kentucky. We traced him through the greater part of Ohio, and came up with him near the Pennsylvania line. He took refuge among some rocks, and showed fight.

CUTE: Oh! then runaway darkies show fight, do they?

MARKS: Sometimes. Well, Tom — like a headstrong fool as he was — rushed up the rocks, and a Quaker chap, who was helping this George Harris, threw him over the cliff.

CUTE: Was he killed?

MARKS: Well, I didn't stop to find out. Seeing that the darkies were stronger than I thought, I made tracks for a safe place.

CUTE: And what became of this George Harris?

MARKS: Oh! he and his wife and child got away safe into Canada. You see, they will get away sometimes though it isn't very often. Now what do you say? You are just the figure for a fighting partner. Is it a bargain?

CUTE: Well, I rather calculate our teams won't hitch, no how. By chowder, I hain't no idea of setting myself up as a target for darkies to fire at — that's a speculation that don't suit my constitution.

MARKS: You're afraid, then?

CUTE: No. I ain't, it's against my principles.

MARKS: Your principles — how so?

CUTE: Because my principles are to keep a sharp lookout for No. 1. I shouldn't feel wholesome if a darkey was to throw me over that cliff to look after Tom Loker. *(Exeunt arm-in-arm, L.H.)*

Scene 2 — *Gothic Chamber. Slow music. ST. CLARE discovered, seated on sofa, R.H. TOM, L.H.*

ST. CLARE: Oh! Tom, my boy, the whole world is as empty as an egg shell.

TOM: I know it, mas'r, I know it. But oh! if mas'r could look up — up where our dear Miss Eva is —

ST. CLARE: Ah, Tom! I do look up, but the trouble is, I don't see anything when I do. I wish I could. It seems to be given to children and poor, honest fellows like you, to see what we cannot. How comes it?

TOM: Thou hast hid from the wise and prudent, and revealed unto babes; even so, Father, for so it seemed good in thy sight.

ST. CLARE: Tom, I don't believe — I've got the habit of doubting — I want to believe and I cannot.

TOM: Dear mas'r, pray to the good Lord: "Lord, I believe; help thou my unbelief."

ST. CLARE: Who knows anything about anything? Was all that beautiful love and faith only one of the ever-shifting phases of human feeling, having nothing real to rest on, passing away with the little breath? And is there no more Eva — nothing?

320

TOM: Oh! dear mas'r, there is. I know it; I'm sure of it. Do, do, dear mas'r, believe it!

ST. CLARE: How do you know there is, Tom? You never saw the Lord.

TOM: Felt Him in my soul, mas'r — feel Him now! Oh, mas'r! when I was sold away from my old woman and the children, I was jest a'most broken up — I felt as if there warn't nothing left — and then the Lord stood by me, and He says, "Fear not, Tom," and He brings light and joy into a poor fellow's soul — makes all peace; and I's so happy, and loves everybody, and feels willin' to be jest where the Lord wants to put me. I know it couldn't come from me, 'cause I's a poor, complaining creature — it comes from above, and I know He's willin' to do for mas'r.

ST. CLARE: *(Grasping TOM's hand.)* Tom, you love me!

TOM: I's willin' to lay down my life this blessed day for you.

ST. CLARE: *(Sadly.)* Poor, foolish fellow! I'm not worth the love of one good, honest heart like yours.

TOM: Oh, mas'r! there's more than me loves you — the blessed Saviour loves you.

ST. CLARE: How do you know that, Tom?

TOM: The love of the Saviour passeth knowledge.

ST. CLARE: *(Turns away.)* Singular! that the story of a man who lived and died eighteen hundred years ago can affect people so yet. But He was no man. *(Rises.)* No man ever had such long and living power. Oh! that I could believe what my mother taught me, and pray as I did when I was a boy! But, Tom, all this time I have forgotten why I sent for you. I'm going to make a freeman of you so have your trunk packed, and get ready to set out for Kentucky.

TOM: *(Joyfully)* Bless the Lord!

ST. CLARE: *(Dryly.)* You haven't had such very bad times here, that you need be in such a rapture, Tom.

TOM: No, no, mas'r, 'tain't that; it's being a *freeman* — that's what I'm joyin' for.

ST. CLARE: Why, Tom, don't you think for your own part, you've been better off than to be free?

TOM: No, *indeed,* Mas'r St. Clare — no, indeed!

ST. CLARE: Why, Tom, you couldn't possibly have earned, by your work, such clothes and such living as I have given you.

TOM: I know all that, Mas'r St. Clare — mas'r's been too good; but I'd rather have poor clothes, poor house, poor everything, and have 'em *mine,* than have the best, if they belong to somebody else. I had *so,* mas'r; I think it's natur', mas'r.

ST. CLARE: I suppose so, Tom; and you'll be going off and leaving me in a month or so — though why you shouldn't no mortal knows.

TOM: Not while mas'r is in trouble. I'll stay with mas'r as long as he wants me, so as I can be any use.

ST. CLARE: *(Sadly.)* Not while I'm in trouble, Tom? And when will my trouble be over?

TOM: When you are a believer.

ST. CLARE: And you really mean to stay by me till that day comes? *(Smiling and laying his hand on TOM's shoulder.)* Ah, Tom! I won't keep you till that day. Go home to your wife and children, and give my love to all.

TOM: I's faith to think that day will come — the Lord has a work for mas'r.

ST. CLARE: A work, hey? Well, now, Tom, give me your views on what sort of work it is — let's hear.

TOM: Why, even a poor fellow like me has a work; and Mas'r St. Clare, that has larnin', and riches, and friends, how much he might do for the Lord.

ST. CLARE: Tom, you seem to think the Lord needs a great deal done for him.

TOM: We does for him when we does for his creatures.

ST. CLARE: Good theology, Tom. Thank you, my boy; I like to hear you talk. But go now, Tom, and leave me alone. *(Exit TOM, L. 1 E.)* That faithful fellow's words have excited a train of thoughts that almost bear me, on the strong tide of faith and feeling, to the gates of that heaven I so vividly conceive. They seem to bring me nearer to Eva.

OPHELIA: *(Outside, L. 1 E.)* What are you doing there, you limb of Satan? You've been stealing something, I'll be bound.

(OPHELIA drags in TOPSY L. 1 E.)

TOPSY: You go 'long, Miss Feely, 'tain't none o' your business.

ST. CLARE: Heyday! what is all this commotion?

OPHELIA: She's been stealing.

TOPSY: *(Sobbing.)* I hain't neither.

OPHELIA: What have you got in your bosom?

TOPSY: I've got my hand dar.

OPHELIA: But what have you got in your hand?

TOPSY: Nuffin'.

OPHELIA: That's a fib, Topsy.

TOPSY: Well, I 'spects it is.

OPHELIA: Give it to me, whatever it is.

TOPSY: It's mine — I hope I may die this bressed minute, if it don't belong to me.

OPHELIA: Topsy, I order you to give me that article; don't let me have to ask you again. *(TOPSY reluctantly takes the foot of an old stocking from her bosom and hands it to OPHELIA.)* Sakes alive! what is all this? *(Takes from it a lock of hair, and a small book, with a bit of crepe twisted around it.)*

TOPSY: Dats a lock of ha'r dat Miss Eva give me — she cut if from her own beau'ful head herself.

ST. CLARE: *(Takes book.)* Why did you wrap *this (Pointing to crepe.)* around the book?

TOPSY: 'Cause — 'cause — 'cause 'twas Miss Eva's. Oh! don't take 'em away, please! *(Sits down on stage, and, putting her apron over her head, begins to sob vehemently.)*

OPHELIA: Come, come, don't cry; you shall have them.

TOPSY: *(Jumps up joyfully and takes them.)* I wants to keep 'em, 'cause dey makes me good; I ain't half so wicked as I used to was. *(Runs off, L. 1 E.)*

ST. CLARE: I really think you can make something of that girl. Any mind that is capable of a *real sorrow* is capable of good. You must try and do something with her.

OPHELIA: The child has improved very much; I have great hopes of her.

ST. CLARE: I believe I'll go down the street a few moments, and hear the news.
OPHELIA: Shall I call Tom to attend you?
ST. CLARE: No, I shall be back in an hour. *(Exit L. 1 E.)*
OPHELIA: He's got an excellent heart, but then he's so dreadful shiftless! *(Exit R. 1 E.)*

Scene 3 — *Front Chamber. Enter TOPSY, L.H.*

TOPSY: Dar's somethin 'de matter wid me — I isn't a bit like myself. I haven't done anything wrong since poor Miss Eva went up in de skies and left us. When I's gwine to do anything wicked, I tinks of her, and somehow I can't do it. I's getting to be good, dat's a fact. I 'spects when I's dead I shall be turned into a little brack angel.

(Enter OPHELIA, L.H.)

OPHELIA: Topsy, I've been looking for you; I've got something very particular to say to you.
TOPSY: Does you want me to say the catechism?
OPHELIA: No, not now.
TOPSY: *(Aside.)* Golly! dat's one comfort.
OPHELIA: Now, Topsy, I want you to try and understand what I am going to say to you.
TOPSY: Yes, missis, I'll open my ears drefful wide.
OPHELIA: Mr. St. Clare has given you to me, Topsy.
TOPSY: Den I b'longs to you, don't I? Golly! I thought I always belong to you.
OPHELIA: Not till today have I received any authority to call you my property.
TOPSY: I's your property, am I? Well, if you say so, I 'spects I am.
OPHELIA: Topsy, I can give you your liberty.
TOPSY: My liberty?
OPHELIA: Yes, Topsy.
TOPSY: Has you got 'um with you?
OPHELIA: I have, Topsy.
TOPSY: Is it clothes or wittles?
OPHELIA: How shiftless! Don't you know what your liberty is, Topsy?
TOPSY: How should I know when I never seed 'um?
OPHELIA: Topsy, I am going to leave this place; I am going many miles away — to my own home in Vermont.
TOPSY: Den what's to become of dis chile?
OPHELIA: If you wish to go, I will take you with me.
TOPSY: Miss Feely, I doesn't want to leave you no how, I loves you I does.
OPHELIA: Then you shall share my home for the rest of your days. Come, Topsy.
TOPSY: Stop, Miss Feely; does dey hab any oberseers in Varmount?
OPHELIA: No, Topsy.
TOPSY: Nor cotton plantations, nor sugar factories, nor darkies, nor whipping nor nothing?
OPHELIA: No, Topsy.
TOPSY: By Golly! de quicker you is gwine de better den.

(Enter TOM, hastily, L.H.)

TOM: Oh, Miss Feely! Miss Feely!

OPHELIA: Gracious me, Tom! what's the matter?

TOM: Oh, Mas'r St. Clare! Mas'r St. Clare!

OPHELIA: Well, Tom, well?

TOM: They've just brought him home and I do believe he's killed.

OPHELIA: Killed?

TOPSY: Oh dear! what's to become of de poor darkies now?

TOM: He's dreadful weak. It's just as much as he can do to speak. He wanted me to call you.

OPHELIA: My poor cousin! Who would have thought of it? Don't say a word to his wife, Tom; the danger may not be so great as you think; it would only distress her. Come with me; you may be able to afford some assistance. *(Exeunt L. 1 E.)*

Scene 4 — *Handsome Chamber. ST. CLARE discovered seated on sofa. OPHELIA R.H., Tom R.H. and TOPSY L., are clustered around him. DOCTOR back of sofa feeling his pulse. Scene opens to slow music.*

ST. CLARE: *(Raising himself feebly.)* Tom — poor fellow!

TOM: Well, mas'r?

ST. CLARE: I have received my death wound.

TOM: Oh, no, no, mas'r!

ST. CLARE: I feel that I am dying — Tom, pray!

TOM: *(Sinking on his knees.)* I do, pray, mas'r! I do pray!

ST. CLARE: *(After a pause.)* Tom, one thing preys upon my mind — I have forgotten to sign your freedom papers. What will become of you when I am gone?

TOM: Don't think of that, mas'r.

ST. CLARE: I was wrong, Tom, very wrong, to neglect it. I may be the cause of much suffering to you hereafter. Marie, my wife — she — oh! —

OPHELIA: His mind is wandering.

ST. CLARE: *(Energetically.)* No! it is coming *home* at last! *(Sinks back.)* At last! at last! Eva, I come! *(Dies. Music — slow curtain.)*

END OF ACT FOUR

ACT FIVE

Scene 1 — *An Auction Mart. UNCLE TOM and EMMELINE at back — ADOLF, SKEGGS, MARKS, MANN, and various spectators discovered. MARKS and MANN come forward.*

MARKS: Hulloa, Alf! what brings you here?

MANN: Well, I was wanting a valet, and I heard that St. Clare's valet was going; I thought I'd just look at them.

MARKS: Catch me ever buying any of St. Clare's people. Spoiled niggers, every one — impudent as the devil.

MANN: Never fear that; if I get 'em, I'll soon have their airs out of them — they'll soon find that they've another kind of master to deal with than St. Clare. 'Pon my word, I'll buy that fellow — I like the shape of him. *(Pointing to ADOLF.)*

MARKS: You'll find it'll take all you've got to keep him — he's deucedly extravagant.

324

MANN: Yes, but my lord will find that he *can't* be extravagant with *me*. Just let him be sent to the calaboose a few times, and thoroughly dressed down, I'll tell you if it don't bring him to a sense of his ways. Oh! I'll reform him, up hill and down, you'll see. I'll buy him; that's flat.

(Enter LEGREE, L.H. — he goes up and looks at ADOLF, whose boots are nicely blacked.)

LEGREE: A nigger with his boots blacked — bah! *(Spits on them.)* Holloa, you! *(To TOM.)* Let's see your teeth. *(Seizes TOM by the jaw and opens his mouth.)* Strip up your sleeve and show your muscle. *(TOM does so.)* Where was you raised?

TOM: In Kintuck, mas'r.

LEGREE: What have you done?

TOM: Had care of mas'r's farm.

LEGREE: That's a likely story. *(Turns to EMMELINE.)* You're a nice-looking girl enough. How old are you? *(Grasps her arm.)*

EMMELINE: *(Shrieking.)* Ah! you hurt me.

SKEGGS: Stop that, you minx! No whimpering here. The sale is going to begin. *(Mounts the rostrum.)* Gentlemen, the next article I shall offer you today is Adolf, late valet to Mr. St. Clare. How much am I offered? *(Various bids are made. ADOLF is knocked down to MANN for eight hundred dollars.)* Gentlemen, I now offer a prime article — the quadroon girl, Emmeline, only fifteen years of age, warranted in every respect. *(Business as before. EMMELINE is sold to LEGREE for one thousand dollars.)* Now, I shall close today's sale by offering you the valuable article known as Uncle Tom, the most useful nigger ever raised. Gentlemen in want of an overseer, now is the time to bid.

(Business as before. TOM is sold to LEGREE for twelve hundred dollars.)

LEGREE: Now look here, you two belong to me. *(TOM and EMMELINE sink on their knees.)*

TOM: Heaven help us, then!

(Music — LEGREE stands over them exulting. Picture — closed in.)

Scene 2 — *The Garden of MISS OPHELIA's house in Vermont. Enter OPHELIA and DEACON PERRY, L. 1 E.*

DEACON: Miss Ophelia, allow me to offer you my congratulations upon your safe arrival in your native place. I hope it is your intention to pass the remainder of your days with us?

OPHELIA: Well, Deacon, I have come here with that express purpose.

DEACON: I presume you were not over-pleased with the South?

OPHELIA: Well, to tell you the truth, Deacon, I wasn't; I liked the country very well, but the poeple there are so dreadful shiftless.

DEACON: The result, I presume, of living in a warm climate.

OPHELIA: Well, Deacon, what is the news among you all here?

DEACON: Well, we live on in the same even jog-trot pace. Nothing of any consequence has happened — Oh! I forgot. *(Takes out his handkerchief.)* I've lost my wife; my Molly has left me. *(Wipes his eyes.)*

OPHELIA: Poor soul! I pity you, Deacon.

DEACON: Thank you. You perceive I bear my loss with resignation.

325

OPHELIA: How you must miss her tongue!

DEACON: Molly certainly was fond of talking. She always would have the last word — heigho!

OPHELIA: What was her complaint, Deacon?

DEACON: A very mild and soothing one, Miss Ophelia: she had a severe attack of the lockjaw.

OPHELIA: Dreadful!

DEACON: Wasn't it? When she found she couldn't use her tongue, she took it so much to heart that it struck to her stomach and killed her. Poor dear! Excuse my handkerchief; she's been dead only eighteen months.

OPHELIA: Why, Deacon, by this time you ought to be setting your cap for another wife.

DEACON: Do you think so, Miss Ophelia?

OPHELIA: I don't see why you shouldn't — you are still a good-looking man, Deacon.

DEACON: Ah! well, I think I do wear well — in fact, I may say remarkably well. It has been observed to me before.

OPHELIA: And you are not much over fifty?

DEACON: Just turned of forty, I assure you.

OPHELIA: Hale and hearty?

DEACON: Health excellent — look at my eye! Strong as a lion — look at my arm!! A No. 1 constitution — look at my leg!!!

OPHELIA: Have you no thoughts of choosing another partner?

DEACON: Well, to tell you the truth, I have.

OPHELIA: Who is she?

DEACON: She is not far distant. *(Looks at OPHELIA in an anguishing manner.)* I have her in my eye at this present moment.

OPHELIA: *(Aside.)* Really, I believe he's going to pop. Why, surely, Deacon, you don't mean to —

DEACON: Miss Ophelia, I do mean; and believe me, when I say — *(Looking off, R. 1 E.)* the Lord be good to us, but I believe there is the devil coming!

(TOPSY runs on, R. 1 E., with bouquet. She is now dressed very neatly.)

TOPSY: Miss Feely, here is some flowers dat I hab been gathering for you. *(Gives bouquet.)*

OPHELIA: That's a good child.

DEACON: Miss Ophelia, who is this young person?

OPHELIA: She is my daughter.

DEACON: *(Aside.)* Her daughter! Then she must have married a colored man off South. I was not aware that you had been married, Miss Ophelia?

OPHELIA: Married! Sakes alive! what made you think I had been married?

DEACON: Good gracious, I'm getting confused. Didn't I understand you to say that this — somewhat tanned — young lady was your daughter?

OPHELIA: Only by adoption. She is my adopted daughter.

DEACON: O — oh! *(Aside.)* I breathe again.

TOPSY: *(Aside.)* By Golly! dat old man's eyes stick out of 'um head dre'ful Guess he never seed anything like me afore.

OPHELIA: Deacon, won't you step into the house and refresh yourself after your walk?

DEACON: I accept your polite invitation. *(Offers his arm.)* Allow me.

OPHELIA: As gallant as ever, Deacon. I declare, you grow younger every day.

DEACON: You can never grow old, madam.

OPHELIA: Ah, you flatterer! *(Exeunt, R. 1 E.)*

TOPSY: Dar dey go, like an old goose and gander. Guess dat ole gemblemun feels kind of confectionary — rather sweet on my old missis. By Golly! she's been dre'ful kind to me ever since I come away from de South; and I loves her, I does, 'cause she takes such car' on me and gives me dese fine clothes. I tries to be good too, and I's getting 'long 'mazin' fast. I's not so wicked as I used to was. *(Looks out, L. 1 E.)* Holloa! dar's some one comin' here. I wonder what he wants now. *(Retires, observing.)*

(Enter GUMPTION CUTE, L. 1 E., very shabby — a small bundle, on a stick, over his shoulder.)

CUTE: By chowder, here I am again. Phew, it's a pretty considerable tall piece of walking between here and New Orleans, not to mention the wear of shoe-leather. I guess I'm about done up. If this streak of bad luck lasts much longer, I'll borrow six-pence to buy a rope, and hang myself right straight up! When I went to call on Miss Ophelia, I swow if I didn't find out that she had left for Varmount; so I kind of concluded to make tracks in that direction myself and as I didn't have any money left, why I had to foot it, and here I am in old Varmount once more. They told me Miss Ophelia lived up here. I wonder if she will remember the relationship. *(Sees TOPSY.)* By chowder, there's a darkey. Look here, Charcoal!

TOPSY: *(Comes forward, R.H.)* My name isn't Charcoal — it's Topsy.

CUTE: Oh! Your name is Topsy, is it, you juvenile specimen of Day & Martin?

TOPSY: Tell you I don't know nothin' 'bout Day & Martin. I's Topsy and I belong to Miss Feely St. Clare.

CUTE: I'm much obleeged to you, you small extract of Japan, for your information. So Miss Ophelia lives up there in the white house, does she? *(Points R. 1 E.)*

TOPSY: Well, she don't do nothin' else.

CUTE: Well, then, just locomote your pins.

TOPSY: What — what's dat?

CUTE: Walk your chalks!

TOPSY: By Golly! dere ain't no chalk 'bout me.

CUTE: Move your trotters.

TOPSY: How you does spoke! What you mean by trotters?

CUTE: Why, your feet, Stove Polish.

TOPSY: What does you want me to move my feet for?

CUTE: To tell your mistress, you ebony angel, that a gentleman wishes to see her.

TOPSY: Does you call yourself a gentleman! By Golly! you look more like a scar'crow.

CUTE: Now look here, you Charcoal, don't you be sassy. I'm a gentleman in distress; a done-up speculator; one that has seen better days — long time ago — and better clothes too, by chowder! My creditors are like my boots — they've no soles. I'm a victim to circumstances. I've been through much and survived it. I've taken walking exercise for the benefit of my health; but as I was trying to live on air at the same time, it was a losing speculation, 'cause it gave me such a dreadful appetite.

TOPSY: Golly! you look as if you could eat an ox, horns and all.

CUTE: Well, I calculate I could, if he was roasted — it's a speculation I should like to engage in. I have returned like the fellow that run away in Scripture; and if anybody's got a fatted calf they want to kill, all they got to do is to fetch him along. Do you know, Charcoal, that your mistress is a relation of mine?

TOPSY: Is she your uncle?

CUTE: No, no, not quite so near as that. My second cousin married her niece.

TOPSY: And does you want to see Miss Feely?

CUTE: I do. I have come to seek a home beneath her roof, and take care of all the spare change she don't want to use.

TOPSY: Den just you follow me, mas'r.

CUTE: Stop! By chowder, I've got a great idee. Say, you Day & Martin, how should you like to enter into a speculation?

TOPSY: Golly! I doesn't know what a spec — spec — cu — what-do-you-call-'um am.

CUTE: Well, now, I calculate I've hit upon about the right thing. Why should I degrade the manly dignity of the Cutes by becoming a beggar — expose myself to the chance of receiving the cold shoulder as a poor relation? By chowder, my blood biles as I think of it! Topsy, you can make my fortune, and your own, too. I've an idee in my head that is worth a million of dollars.

TOPSY: Golly! is your head worth dat? Guess you wouldn't bring dat out South for de whole of you.

CUTE: Don't you be too severe, now, Charcoal; I'm a man of genius. Did you ever hear of Barnum?

TOPSY: Barnum! Barnum! Does he live out South?

CUTE: No, he lives in New York. Do you know how he made his fortin?

TOPSY: What is him fortin, hey? Is it something he wears?

CUTE: Chowder, how green you are!

TOPSY: *(Indignantly.)* Sar, I hab you to know I' not green; I's brack.

CUTE: To be sure you are, Day & Martin. I calculate, when a person says another has a fortune, he means he's got plenty of money, Charcoal.

TOPSY: And did he make the money?

CUTE: Sartin sure, and no mistake.

TOPSY: Golly! now I thought money always growed.

CUTE: Oh, git out! You are too cute — you are cuterer than I am — and I'm Cute by name and cute by nature. Well, as I was saying, Barnum made his money by exhibiting a *woolly* horse; now wouldn't it be an all-fired speculation to show you as the woolly gal?

TOPSY: You want to make a sight of me?

CUTE: I'll give you half the receipts, by chowder!

TOPSY: Should I have to leave Miss Feely?

CUTE: To be sure you would.

TOPSY: Den you hab to get a woolly gal somewhere else, Mas'r Cute. *(Runs off, R. 1 E.)*

CUTE: There's another speculation gone to smash, by chowder! *(Exit R. 1 E.)*

Scene 3 — *A Rude Chamber. TOM is discovered, in old clothes, seated on a stool, c. — he holds in his hand a paper containing a curl of EVA's hair. The scene opens to the symphony of "Old Folks at Home."*

TOM: I have come to de dark places; I's going through de vale of shadows. My heart sinks at times and feels just like a big lump of lead. Den it gits up in my throat and chokes me till de tears roll out of my eyes; den I take out dis curl of little Miss Eva's hair, and the sight of it brings calm to my mind and I feels strong again. *(Kisses the curl and puts it in his breast — takes out a silver dollar, which is suspended around his neck by a string.)* Dere's de bright silver dollar dat Mas'r George Shelby gave me the day I was sold away from old Kentuck, and I've kept it ever since. Mas'r George must have grown to be a man by this time. I wonder if I shall ever see him again.

(Song — "Old Folks at Home." Enter LEGREE, EMMELINE, SAMBO and QUIMBO, L.H.)

LEGREE: Shut up, you black cuss! Did you think I wanted any of your infernal howling? *(Turns to EMMELINE.)* We're home. *(EMMELINE shrinks from him. He takes hold of her ear.)* You didn't ever wear earrings?

EMMELINE: *(Trembling.)* No, master.

LEGREE: Well, I'll give you a pair, if you're a good girl. You needn't be so frightened; I don't mean to make you work very hard. You'll have fine times with me and live like a lady; only be a good girl.

EMMELINE: My soul sickens as his eyes gaze upon me. His touch makes my very flesh creep.

LEGREE: *(Turns to TOM, and points to SAMBO and QUIMBO.)* Ye see what ye'd get if ye'd try to run off. These yer boys have been raised to track niggers and they'd just as soon chaw one on ye up as eat their suppers; so mind yourself. *(To EMMELINE.)* Come, mistress, you go in here with me. *(Taking EMMELINE's hand, and leading her towards R.U.E.)*

EMMELINE: *(Withdrawing her hand, and shrinking back.)* No, no! let me work in the fields; I don't want to be a lady.

LEGREE: Oh! you're going to be contrary, are you? I'll soon take all that out off you.

EMMELINE: Kill me, if you will.

LEGREE: Oh! you want to be killed, do you? Now come here, you Tom, you see I told you I didn't buy you jest for the common work; I mean to promote you and make a driver of you, and tonight ye may jest as well begin to get yer hand in. Now ye jest take this yer gal, and flog her; ye've seen enough on't to know how.

TOM: I beg mas'r's pardon — hopes mas'r won't set me at that. It's what I a'nt used to — never did, and can't do — no way possible.

LEGREE: Ye'll larn a pretty smart chance of things ye never did know before I've done with ye. *(Strikes TOM, with whip, three blows. — Music chord each blow.)* There! now will ye tell me ye can't do it?

TOM: Yes, mas'r! I'm willing to work night and day, and work while there's life and breath in me; but this yer thing I can't feel it right to do, and, mas'r, I *never* shall do it, *never!*

LEGREE: What! ye black beast! tell *me* ye don't think it right to do what I tell ye! What have any of you cussed cattle to do with thinking what's right? I'll put a stop to it. Why, what do ye think ye are? May be ye think yer a gentleman, master Tom, to be telling your master what's right and what a'nt! So you pretend it's wrong to flog the gal?

TOM: I think so, mas'r; 'twould be downright cruel, and it's what I never will do, mas'r. If you mean to kill me, kill me; but as to raising my hand agin any one here, I never shall — I'll die first.

LEGREE: Well, here's a pious dog at last, let down among us sinners — powerful holy critter he must be. Here, you rascal! you make believe to be so pious, didn't you never read out of your Bible, "Servants, obey your masters"? An't I your master? Didn't I pay twelve hundred dollars, cash, for all there is inside your cussed old black shell? An't you mine, body and soul?

TOM: No, no! My soul a'nt yours, mas'r; you haven't bought it — ye can't buy it; it's been bought and paid for by one that is able to keep it, and you can't harm it!

LEGREE: I can't? we'll see, we'll see! Here, Sambo! Quimbo! give this dog such a breaking in as he won't get over this month!

EMMELINE: Oh, no! you will not be so cruel — have some mercy! *(Clings to TOM.)*

LEGREE: Mercy? you won't find any in this shop! Away with the black cuss! Flog him within an inch of his life!

(Music — SAMBO and QUIMBO seize TOM and drag him up stage. LEGREE seizes EMMELINE, and throws her round to R.H. — She falls on her knees, with her hands lifted in supplication. — LEGREE raises his whip, as if to strike TOM. — Picture. — Closed in.)

Scene 4 — *Plain Chamber. Enter OPHELIA, followed by TOPSY, L.H.)*

OPHELIA: A person inquiring for me, did you say, Topsy?

TOPSY: Yes, missis.

OPHELIA: What kind of a looking man is he?

TOPSY: By golly! he's very queer looking man, anyway; and den he talks so dre'ful funny. What does you think? — yah! yah! he wanted to 'zibite me as de woolly gal! yah! yah!

OPHELIA: Oh! I understand. Some cute Yankee, who wants to purchase you, to make a show of — the heartless wretch!

TOPSY: Dat's just him, missis; dat's just his name. He tole me dat it was Cute — Mr. Cute Speculashum — dat's him.

OPHELIA: What did you say to him, Topsy?

TOPSY: Well, I didn't say much, it was brief and to the point — I tole him I wouldn't leave you, Miss Feely, no how.

OPHELIA: That's right, Topsy; you know you are very comfortable here — you wouldn't fare quite so well if you went away among strangers.

TOPSY: By golly! I know dat; you takes care on me, and makes me good. I don't steal any now, and I don't swar, and I don't dance breakdowns.

Oh! I isn't so wicked as I used to was.

OPHELIA: That's right, Topsy; now show the gentleman, or whatever he is, up.

TOPSY: By golly! I guess he won't make much out of Miss Feely. *(Crosses to R., and exit R. 1 E.)*

OPHELIA: I wonder who this person can be? Perhaps it is some old acquaintance, who has heard of my arrival, and who comes on a social visit.

(Enter CUTE, R. 1 E.)

CUTE: Aunt, how do ye do? Well, I swan, the sight of you is good for weak eyes. *(Offers his hand.)*

OPHELIA: *(Coldly drawing back.)* Really, sir, I can't say that I ever had the pleasure of seeing you before.

CUTE: Well, it's a fact that you never did. You see I never happened to be in your neighborhood afore now. Of course you've heard of me? I'm one of the Cutes — Gumption Cute, the first and only son of Josiah and Maria Cute, of Oniontown, on the Onion River in the north part of this here State of Varmount.

OPHELIA: Can't say I ever heard the name before.

CUTE: Well then, I calculate your memory must be a little ricketty. I'm a relation of yours.

OPHELIA: A relation of mine! Why, I never heard of any Cutes in our family.

CUTE: Well, I shouldn't wonder if you never did. Don't you remember your niece, Mary?

OPHELIA: Of course I do. What a shiftless question!

CUTE: Well, you see my second cousin, Abijah Blake, married her. So you see that makes me a relation of yours.

OPHELIA: Rather a distant one, I should say.

CUTE: By chowder! I'm *near* enough, just at present.

OPHELIA: Well, you certainly are a sort of connection of mine.

CUTE: Yes, kind of sort of.

OPHELIA: And of course you are welcome to my house, as long as you choose to make it your home.

CUTE: By chowder! I'm booked for the next six months — this isn't a bad speculation.

OPHELIA: I hope you left all your folks well at home?

CUTE: Well, yes, they're pretty comfortably disposed of. Father and mother's dead, and Uncle Josh has gone to California. I am the only representative of the Cutes left.

OPHELIA: There doesn't seem to be a great deal of *you* left. I declare, you are positively in rags.

CUTE: Well, you see, the fact is, I've been speculating — trying to get bank-notes — specie-rags, as they say — but I calculate I've turned out rags of another sort.

OPHELIA: I'm sorry for your ill luck, but I am afraid you have been shiftless.

CUTE: By chowder! I've done all that a fellow could do. You see, somehow, everything I take hold of kind of bursts up.

OPHELIA: Well, well, perhaps you'll do better for the future; make yourself at home. I have got to see to some household matters, so excuse me for a short time. *(Aside.)* Impudent and shiftless. *(Exit L. 1 E.)*

CUTE: By chowder! I rather guess that this speculation will hitch. She's a good-natured old critter; I reckon I'll be a son to her while she lives, and take care of her valuables arter she's a defunct departed. I wonder if they keep the vittles in this ere room? Guess not. I've got extensive accommodations for all sorts of eatables. I'm a regular vacuum, throughout — pockets and all. I'm chuck full of emptiness. *(Looks out, R.H.)* Holloa! who's this elderly individual coming up stairs? He looks like a compound essence of starch and dignity. I wonder if he isn't another relation of mine. I should like a rich old fellow now for an uncle.

(Enter DEACON PERRY, R. 1 E.)

DEACON: Ha! a stranger here!
CUTE: How d'ye do?
DEACON: You are a friend to Miss Ophelia, I presume?
CUTE: Well, I rather calculate that I am a leetle more than a friend.
DEACON: *(Aside.)* Bless me! what can he mean by those mysterious words?
Can he be her — no I don't think he can. She said she wasn't — well, at all events, it's very suspicious.
CUTE: The old fellow seems kind of stuck up.
DEACON: You are a particular friend to Miss Ophelia, you say?
CUTE: Well, I calculate I am.
DEACON: Bound to her by any tender tie?
CUTE: It's something more than a tie — it's a regular double-twisted knot.
DEACON: Ah! just as I suspected. *(Aside.)* Might I inquire the nature of that tie?
CUTE: Well, it's the natural tie of relationship.
DEACON: A relation — what relation?
CUTE: Why, you see, my second cousin, Abijah Blake, married her niece, Mary.
DEACON: Oh! is that all?
CUTE: By chowder, ain't that enough?
DEACON: Then you are not her husband?
CUTE: To be sure I ain't. What put that ere idee into your cranium?
DEACON: *(Shaking him vigorously by the hand.)* My dear sir, I'm delighted to see you.
CUTE: Holloa! you ain't going slightly insane, are you?
DEACON: No, no fear of that; I'm only happy, that's all.
CUTE: I wonder if he's been taking a nipper?
DEACON: As you are a relation of Miss Ophelia's, I think it proper that I should make you my confidant; in fact, let you into a little scheme that I have lately conceived.
CUTE: Is it a speculation?
DEACON: Well, it is, just at present; but I trust before many hours to make it a surety.
CUTE: By chowder! I hope it won't serve you the way my speculations have served me. But fire away, old boy, and give us the prospectus.
DEACON: Well, then, my young friend, I have been thinking, ever since Miss Ophelia returned to Vermont, that she was just the person to fill the place of my lamented Molly.
CUTE: Say, you, you couldn't tell us who your lamented Molly was, could you?

DEACON: Why, the late Mrs. Perry, to be sure.

CUTE: Oh! then the lamented Molly was your wife?

DEACON: She was.

CUTE: And now you wish to marry Miss Ophelia?

DEACON: Exactly.

CUTE: *(Aside.)* Consarn this old porpoise! if I let him do that he'll Jew me out of my living. By chowder! I'll put a spoke in his wheel.

DEACON: Well, what do you say? will you intercede for me with your aunt?

CUTE: No! bust me up if I do!

DEACON: No?

CUTE: No, I tell you. I forbid the bans. Now, ain't you a purty individual, to talk about getting married, you old superannuated Methuselah specimen of humanity! Why, you've got one foot in etarnity already, and t'other ain't fit to stand on. Go home and go to bed! have your head shaved, and send for a lawyer to make your will, leave your property to your heirs — if you hain't got any, why leave it to me — I'll take care of it, and charge nothing for the trouble.

DEACON: Really, sir, this language to one of my standing, is highly indecorous — it's more, sir, than I feel willing to endure, sir. I shall expect an explanation, sir.

CUTE: Now, you see, old gouty toes, you're losing your temper.

DEACON: Sir, I'm a deacon; I never lost my temper in all my life, sir.

CUTE: Now, you see, you're getting excited; you had better go; we can't have a disturbance here!

DEACON: No, sir! I shall not go, sir! I shall not go until I have seen Miss Ophelia. I wish to know if she will countenance this insult.

CUTE: Now keep cool, old stick-in-the-mud! Draw it mild, old timber-toes!

DEACON: Damn it all, sir what —

CUTE: Oh! only think, now, what would people say to hear a deacon swearing like a trooper?

DEACON: Sir — I — you — this is too much, sir.

CUTE: Well, now, I calculate that's just about my opinion, so we'll have no more of it. Get out of this! start your boots, or by chowder! I'll pitch you from one end of the stairs to the other.

(Enter OPHELIA, L.H.)

OPHELIA: *(Crossing to C.)* Hoity toity! What's the meaning of all these loud words?

CUTE: *(Together with DEACON.)* Well, you see, Aunt —

DEACON: *(Together with CUTE.)* Miss Ophelia, I beg —

CUTE: Now, look here, you just hush your yap! How can I fix up matters if you keep jabbering?

OPHELIA: Silence! for shame, Mr. Cute. Is that the way you speak to the deacon?

CUTE: Darn the deacon!

OPHELIA: Deacon Perry, what is all this?

DEACON: Madam, a few words will explain everything. Hearing from this person that he was your nephew, I ventured to tell him that I cherished hopes of making you my wife, whereupon he flew into a violent passion, and ordered me out of the house.

OPHELIA: Does this house belong to you or me, Mr. Cute?

CUTE: Well, to you, I reckon.

OPHELIA: Then how dare you give orders in it?

CUTE: Well, I calculated that you wouldn't care about marrying old half a century there.

OPHELIA: That's enough; I will marry him; and as for you, *(Points R.H.)* get out.

CUTE: Get out?

OPHELIA: Yes; the sooner the better.

CUTE: Darned if I don't serve him out first though.

(Music — CUTE makes a dash at DEACON, who gets behind OPHELIA. TOPSY enters, R.H., with a broom and beats CUTE around stage. — OPHELIA faints in DEACON's arms. — CUTE falls, and TOPSY butts him kneeling over him. — Quick drop.)

END OF ACT FIVE

ACT SIX

Scene 1 — *Dark Landscape. — An old, roofless Shed, R.U.E. TOM is discovered in Shed, lying on some old cotton bagging. — CASSY kneels by his side, holding a cup to his lips.*

CASSY: Drink all ye want. I knew how it would be. It isn't the first time I've been out in the night, carrying water to such as you.

TOM: *(Returning cup.)* Thank you, missis.

CASSY: Don't call me missis. I'm a miserable slave like yourself — a lower one than you can ever be! It's no use, my poor fellow, this you've been trying to do. You were a brave fellow. You had the right on your side; but it's all in vain for you to struggle. You are in the Devil's hands; he is the strongest, and you must give up.

TOM: Oh! how can I give up?

CASSY: You see *you* don't know anything about it; I do. Here you are, on a lone plantation, ten miles from any other, in the swamps; not a white person here who could testify, if you were burned alive. There's no law here that can do you, or any of us, the least good; and this man! There's no earthly thing that he is not bad enough to do. I could make one's hair rise, and their teeth chatter, if I should only tell what I've seen and been knowing to here; and it's no use resisting! Did I *want* to live with him? Wasn't I a woman delicately bred? and he! — Father in Heaven! what was he and is he? And yet I've lived with him these five years, and cursed every moment of my life, night and day.

TOM: Oh heaven! have you quite forgot us poor critters?

CASSY: And what are these miserable low dogs you work with, that you should suffer on their account? Every one of them would turn against you the first time they get a chance. They are all of them as low and cruel to each other as they can be; there's no use in your suffering to keep from hurting them?

TOM: What made 'em cruel? If I give out I shall get used to it and grow, little by little, just like 'em. No, no, Missis, I've lost everything, wife, and children, and home, and a kind master, and he would have set

334

me free if he'd only lived a day longer — I've lost everything in *this* world, and now I can't lose heaven, too: no I can't get to be wicked besides all.

CASSY: But it can't be that He will lay sin to our account; he won't charge it to us when we are forced to it; he'll charge it to them that drove us to it. Can I do anything more for you? Shall I give you some more water?

TOM: Oh missis! I wish you'd go to Him who can give you living waters!

CASSY: Go to him! Where is he? Who is he?

TOM: Our Heavenly Father!

CASSY: I used to see the picture of him, over the altar, when I was a girl but *he isn't here!* There's nothing here but sin, and long, long despair! There, there, don't talk any more, my poor fellow. Try to sleep, if you can. I must hasten back, lest my absence be noted. Think of me when I am gone, Uncle Tom, and pray, pray for me.

(Music. — Exit CASSY, L.U.E. — TOM sinks back to sleep.)

Scene 2 — *Street in New Orleans. Enter GEORGE SHELBY, R. 1 E.)*

GEORGE: At length my mission of mercy is nearly finished, I have reached my journey's end. I have now but to find the house of Mr. St. Clare, re-purchase old Uncle Tom, and convey him back to his wife and children, in old Kentucky. Some one approaches; he may, perhaps, be able to give me the information I require. I will accost him. *(Enter MARKS, L. 1 E.)* Pray, sir, can you tell me where Mr. St. Clare dwells?

MARKS: Where I don't think you'll be in a hurry to seek him.

GEORGE: And where is that?

MARKS: In the grave! *(Crosses to R.)*

GEORGE: Stay, sir! you may be able to give me some information concerning Mr. St. Clare.

MARKS: I beg pardon, sir, I am a lawyer; I can't afford to *give* anything.

GEORGE: But you would have no objections to selling it?

MARKS: Not the slightest.

GEORGE: What do you value it at?

MARKS: Well, say five dollars, that's reasonable.

GEORGE: There they are. *(Gives money.)* Now answer me to the best of your ability. Has the death of St. Clare caused his slaves to be sold?

MARKS: It has.

GEORGE: How were they sold?

MARKS: At auction — they went dirt cheap.

GEORGE: How were they bought — all in one lot?

MARKS: No, they went to different bidders.

GEORGE: Was you present at the sale?

MARKS: I was.

GEORGE: Do you remember seeing a negro among them called Tom?

MARKS: What, Uncle Tom?

GEORGE: The same — who bought him?

MARKS: A Mr. Legree.

GEORGE: Where is his plantation?

MARKS: Up in Louisiana, on the Red River; but a man never could find it, unless he had been there before.

GEORGE: Who could I get to direct me there?

MARKS: Well, stranger, I don't know of any one just at present 'cept myself, could find it for you; it's such an out-of-the-way sort of hole; and if you are a mind to come down handsomely, why, I'll do it.

GEORGE: The reward shall be ample.

MARKS: Enough said, stranger; let's take the steamboat at once. *(Exeunt R. 1 E.)*

Scene 3 — *A Rough Chamber. Enter LEGREE, L.H. — Sits.*

LEGREE: Plague on that Sambo, to kick up this yer row between Tom and the new hands. *(CASSY steals on L.H., and stands behind him.)* The fellow won't be fit to work for a week now, right in the press of the season.

CASSY: *(R.)* Yes, just like you.

LEGREE: *(L.)* Hah! you she-devil! you've come back, have you? *(Rises.)*

CASSY: Yes, I have; come to have my own way, too.

LEGREE: You lie, you jade! I'll be up to my word. Either behave yourself, or stay down in the quarters and fare and work with the rest.

CASSY: I'd rather, ten thousand times, live in the dirtiest hole at the quarters, than be under your hoof!

LEGREE: But you are under my hoof, for all that, that's one comfort; so sit down here and listen to reason. *(Grasps her wrist.)*

CASSY: Simon Legree, take care! *(LEGREE lets go his hold.)* You're afraid of me, Simon, and you've reason to be; for I've got the Devil in me!

LEGREE: I believe to my soul you have. After all, Cassy, why can't you be friends with me, as you used to?

CASSY: *(Bitterly)* Used to!

LEGREE: I wish, Cassy, you'd behave yourself decently.

CASSY: *You* talk about behaving decently! and what have you been doing? You haven't even sense enough to keep from spoiling one of your best hands, right in the most pressing season, just for your devilish temper.

LEGREE: I was a fool, it's fact, to let any such brangle come up. Now when Tom set up his will he had to be broke in.

CASSY: You'll never break *him* in.

LEGREE: Won't I? I'd like to know if I won't? He'd be the first nigger that ever come it round me! I'll break every bone in his body but he shall give up. *(Enter SAMBO, L.H., with a paper in his hand, stands bowing.)* What's that, you dog?

SAMBO: It's a witch thing, mas'r.

LEGREE: A what?

SAMBO: Something that niggers gits from witches. Keep 'em from feeling when they's flogged. He had it tied round his neck with a black string.

(LEGREE takes the paper and opens it. — A silver dollar drops on the stage, and a long curl of light hair twines around his finger.)

LEGREE: Damnation. *(Stamping and writhing, as if the hair burned him.)* Where did this come from? Take it off! burn it up! burn it up! *(Throws the curl away.)* What did you bring it to me for?

SAMBO: *(Trembling.)* I beg pardon, mas'r; I thought you would like to see um.

LEGREE: Don't you bring me any more of your devilish things. *(Shakes*

336

his fist at SAMBO who runs off L.H. — LEGREE kicks the dollar after him.) Blast it! where did he get that? If it didn't look just like — whoo! I thought I'd forgot that. Curse me if I think there's any such thing as forgetting anything, any how.

CASSY: What is the matter with you, Legree? What is there in a simple curl of fair hair to appall a man like you — you who are familiar with every form of cruelty.

LEGREE: Cassy, tonight the past has been recalled to me — the past that I have so long and vainly striven to forget.

CASSY: Has aught on this earth power to move a soul like thine?

LEGREE: Yes, for hard and reprobate as I now seem, there has been a time when I have been rocked on the bosom of mother, cradled with prayers and pious hymns, my now seared brow bedewed with the waters of holy baptism.

CASSY: *(Aside.)* What sweet memories of childhood can thus soften down that heart of iron?

LEGREE: In early childhood a fair-haired woman has led me, at the sound of Sabbath bells, to worship and to pray. Born of a hard-tempered sire, on whom that gentle woman had wasted a world of unvalued love, I followed in the steps of my father. Boisterous, unruly and tyrannical, I despised all her counsel, and would have none of her reproof, and, at an early age, broke from her to seek my fortunes on the sea. I never came home but once after that; and then my mother, with the yearning of a heart that must love something, and had nothing else to love, clung to me, and sought with passionate prayers and entreaties to win me from a life of sin.

CASSY: That was your day of grace, Legree; then good angels called you, and mercy held you by the hand.

LEGREE: My heart inly relented; there was a conflict, but sin got the victory, and I set all the force of my rough nature against the conviction of my conscience. I drank and swore, was wilder and more brutal than ever. And one night, when my mother, in the last agony of her despair, knelt at my feet, I spurned her from me, threw her senseless on the floor, and with brutal curses fled to my ship.

CASSY: Then the fiend took thee for his own.

LEGREE: The next I heard of my mother was one night while I was carousing among drunken companions. A letter was put in my hands. I opened it, and a lock of long, curling hair fell from it, and twined about my fingers, even as that lock twined but now. The letter told me that my mother was dead, and that dying she blest and forgave me! *(Buries his face in his hands.)*

CASSY: Why did you not even then renounce your evil ways?

LEGREE: There is a dread, unhallowed necromancy of evil, that turns things sweetest and holiest to phantoms of horror and afright. That pale, loving mother, — her dying prayers, her forgiving love, — wrought in my demoniac heart of sin only as a damning sentence, bringing with it a fearful looking for of judgement and fiery indignation.

CASSY: And yet you would not strive to avert the doom that threatened you.

LEGREE: I burned the lock of hair and I burned the letter; and when I saw them hissing and crackling in the flame, inly shuddered as I thought of everlasting fires! I tried to drink and revel, and wear away the memory; but often in the deep night, whose solemn stillness arraigns the soul in forced communion with itself, I have seen that pale mother rising by my bed-side, and felt the soft twining of that hair around my fingers, 'till the cold sweat would roll down my face, and I would spring from my bed in horror — horror! *(Falls in chair — After a pause.)* What the devil ails me? Large drops of sweat stand on my forehead, and my heart beats heavy and thick with fear. I thought I saw something white rising and glimmering in the gloom before me, and it seemed to bear my mother's face! I know one thing; I'll let that fellow Tom alone, after this. What did I want with his cussed paper? I believe I am bewitched sure enough! I've been shivering and sweating ever since! Where did he get that hair? It couldn't have been that! I *burn'd* that up, I know I did! It would be a joke if hair could rise from the dead! I'll have Sambo and Quimbo up here to sing and dance one of their dances and keep off these horrid notions. Here, Sambo! Quimbo! *(Exit L. 1 E.)*

CASSY: Yes, Legree, that golden tress was charmed; each hair had in it a spell of terror and remorse for thee, and was used by a mightier power to bind thy cruel hands from inflicting uttermost evil on the helpless! *(Exit R. 1 E.)*

Scene 4 — *Street. Enter MARKS R. 1 E., meeting CUTE, who enters L. 1 E., dressed in an old faded uniform.*

MARKS: By the land, stranger, but it strikes me that I've seen you somewhere before.

CUTE: By chowder! do you know now, that's just what I was a going to say?

MARKS: Isn't your name Cute?

CUTE: You're right, I calculate. Yours is Marks, I reckon.

MARKS: Just so.

CUTE: Well, I swow, I'm glad to see you. *(They shake hands.)* How's your wholesome?

MARKS: Hearty as ever. Well, who would have thought of ever seeing you again. Why, I thought you was in Vermont?

CUTE: Well, so I was. You see I went there after that rich relation of mine — but the speculation didn't turn out well.

MARKS: How so?

CUTE: Why, you see, she took a shine to an old fellow — Deacon Abraham Perry — and married him.

MARKS: Oh, that rather put your nose out of joint in that quarter.

CUTE: Busted me right up, I tell you. The Deacon did the hand-some thing though, he said if I would leave the neighborhood and go out South again, he'd stand the damage. I calculate I didn't give him much time to change his mind, and so, you see, here I am again.

MARKS: What are you doing in that soldier rig?

CUTE: Oh, this is my sign.

MARKS: Your sign?

CUTE: Yes; you see, I'm engaged just at present in an all-fired good speculation, I'm a Fillibusterow.

MARKS: A what?

CUTE: A Fillibusterow! Don't you know what that is? It's Spanish for Cuban

Volunteer; and means a chap that goes the whole perker for glory and all that ere sort of thing.

MARKS: Oh! you've joined the order of the Lone Star!

CUTE: You've hit it. You see I bought this uniform at a second hand clothing store, I puts it on and goes to a benevolent individual and I says to him, — appealing to his feelings, — I'm one of the fellows that went to Cuba and got massacred by the bloody Spaniards. I'm in a destitute condition — give me a trifle to pay my passage back, so I can whop the tyrannical cusses and avenge my brace fellow soger what got slewed there.

MARKS: How pathetic!

CUTE: I tell you it works up the feelings of benevolent individuals dreadfully. It draws tears from their eyes and money from their pockets. By chowder! one old chap gave me a hundred dollars to help on the cause.

MARKS: I admire a genius like yours.

CUTE: But I say, what are you up to?

MARKS: I am the traveling companion of a young gentleman by the name of Shelby, who is going to the plantation of a Mr. Legree of the Red River, to buy an old darkey who used to belong to his father.

CUTE: Legree — Legree? well, now, I calculate I've heard that ere name afore.

MARKS: Do you remember that man who drew a bowie knife on you in New Orleans?

CUTE: By chowder! I remember the circumstance just as well as if it was yesterday; but I can't say that I recollect much about the man, for you see I was in something of a hurry about that time and didn't stop to take a good look at him.

MARKS: Well, that man was this same Mr. Legree.

CUTE: Do you know, now, I should like to pay that critter off!

MARKS: Then I'll give you an opportunity.

CUTE: Chowder! how will you do that?

MARKS: Do you remember the gentleman that interfered between you and Legree?

CUTE: Yes — well?

MARKS: He received the blow that was intended for you, and died from the effects of it. So, you see, Legree is a murderer, and we are only witnesses of the deed. His life is in our hands.

CUTE: Let's have him right up and make him dance on nothing to the tune of Yankee Doodle!.

MARKS: Stop a bit. Don't you see a chance for a profitable speculation?

CUTE: A speculation! Fire away, don't be bashful, I'm the man for a speculation.

MARKS: I have made a deposition to the Governor of the state on all the particulars of that affair at Orleans.

CUTE: What did you do that for?

MARKS: To get a warrant for his arrest.

CUTE: Oh! and have you got it?

MARKS: Yes; here it is. *(Takes out paper.)*

CUTE: Well, now, I don't see how you are going to make anything by that bit of paper?

MARKS: But I do. I shall say to Legree, I have got a warrant against you for murder; my friend, Mr. Cute, and myself are the only witnesses who can appear against you. Give us a thousand dollars, and we will tear the warrant and be silent.

CUTE: Then Mr. Legree forks over a thousand dollars, and your friend Cute pockets five hundred of it, is that the calculation?

MARKS: If you will join me in the undertaking.

CUTE: I'll do it, by chowder!

MARKS: Your hand to bind the bargain.

CUTE: I'll stick by you thro' thick and thin.

MARKS: Enough said.

CUTE: Then shake. *(They shake hands.)*

MARKS: But I say, Cute, he may be contrary and show fight.

CUTE: Never mind, we've got the law on our side, and we're bound to stir him up. If he don't come down handsomely we'll present him with a neck-tie made of hemp!

MARKS: I declare you're getting spunky.

CUTE: Well, I reckon, I am. Let's go and have something to drink. Tell you what, Marks, if we don't get *him* we'll have his hide, by chowder! *(Exeunt, arm in arm, R. 1 E.)*

Scene 5 — *Rough Chamber. Enter LEGREE, followed by SAMBO, L.H.*

LEGREE: Go and send Cassy to me.

SAMBO: Yes, mas'r. *(Exit R.U.E.)*

LEGREE: Curse the woman! she's got a temper worse than the devil; I shall do her an injury one of these days, if she isn't careful. *(Re-enter SAMBO, R.U.E., frightened.)* What's the matter with you, you black scoundrel?

SAMBO: S'help me, mas'r, she isn't dere.

LEGREE: I suppose she's about the house somewhere?

SAMBO: No, she isn't, mas'r; I's been all over de house and I can't find nothing of her nor Emmeline.

LEGREE: Bolted, by the Lord! Call out the dogs! saddle my horse. Stop! are you sure they really have gone?

SAMBO: Yes, mas'r; I's been in every room 'cept the haunted garret and dey wouldn't go dere.

LEGREE: I have it! Now, Sambo, you just go and walk that Tom up here, right away! *(Exit SAMBO, L.U.E.)* The old cuss is at the bottom of this yer whole matter; and I'll have it out of his infernal black hide, or I'll know the reason why! I *hate* him — I *hate* him! And isn't he *mine?* Can't I do what I like with him? Who's to hinder, I wonder! *(TOM is dragged on by SAMBO and QUIMBO, L.U.E. LEGREE grimly confronting TOM.)* Well, Tom, do you know I've made up my mind to *kill* you?

TOM: It's very likely, Mas'r.

LEGREE: *I — have — done — just — that — thing,* Tom, unless you'll tell me what do you know about these yer gals? *(TOM is silent.)* D'ye hear? Speak!

TOM: I han't got anything to tell, mas'r.

LEGREE: Do you dare to tell me, you old black rascal, you don't know?

340

Speak! do you know anything?

TOM: I know, mas'r; but I can't tell anything. *I can die!*

LEGREE: Hark ye, Tom! ye think, 'cause I have let you off before, I don't mean what I say; but, this time, I have made *up my mind,* and counted the cost. You've always stood it out agin me; now, I'll *conquer ye or kill ye!* one or t'other. I'll count every drop of blood there is in you, and take 'em, one by one, 'till ye give up!

TOM: Mas'r, if you was sick, or in trouble, or dying, and I could save, I'd *give* you my heart's blood; and, if taking every drop of blood in this poor old body would save your precious soul, I'd give 'em freely. Do the worst you can, my troubles will be over soon; but if you don't repent yours won't never end.

(LEGREE strikes TOM down with the butt of his whip.)

LEGREE: How do you like that?

SAMBO: He's most gone, mas'r!

TOM: *(Rises feebly on his hands.)* There an't no more you can do. I forgive you with all my soul. *(Sinks back, and is carried off R.U.E. by SAMBO and QUIMBO.)*

LEGREE: I believe he's done for finally. Well, his mouth is shut up at last — that's one comfort. *(Enter GEORGE SHELBY, MARKS and CUTE, L. 1 E.)* Strangers! Well what do you want?

GEORGE: I understand that you bought in New Orleans a negro named Tom?

LEGREE: Yes, I did buy such a fellow, and a devil of a bargain I had of it, too! I believe he's trying to die, but I don't know as he'll make it out.

GEORGE: Where is he? Let me see him?

SAMBO: Dere he is! *(Points to TOM, R.U.E.)*

LEGREE: How dare you speak? *(Drives SAMBO and QUIMBO off L.U.E. — GEORGE exits, R.U.E.)*

CUTE: Now's the time to nab him.

MARKS: How are you, Mr. Legree?

LEGREE: What the devil brought you here?

MARKS: This little bit of paper. I arrest you for the murder of Mr. St. Clare. What do you say to that?

LEGREE: This is my answer! *(Makes a blow at MARKS, who dodges, and CUTE receives the blow — he cries out and runs off, L.H. MARKS fires at LEGREE, and follows CUTE.)* I am hit! — the game's up! *(Falls dead. QUIMBO and SAMBO return and carry him off laughing.)*

(GEORGE SHELBY enters, supporting TOM. — Music. They advance to front and TOM falls, C.)

GEORGE: Oh! dear Uncle Tom! do wake — do speak once more! look up! Here's Master George — your own little Master George. Don't you know me?

TOM: *(Opening his eyes and speaking in a feeble tone.)* Mas'r George! Bless de Lord! it's all I wanted! They hav'n't forgot me! It warms my soul; it does my old heart good! Now I shall die content!

GEORGE: You shan't die! you mustn't die, nor think of it. I have come to buy you, and take you home.

TOM: Oh, Mas'r George, you're too late. The Lord has bought me, and is

341

going to take me home.

GEORGE: Oh! don't die. It will kill me — it will break my heart to think what you have suffered, poor, poor fellow!

TOM: Don't call me, poor fellow! I *have* been poor fellow; but that's all past and gone now. I'm right in the door, going into glory! Oh, Mas'r George! *Heaven has come!* I've got the victory, the Lord has given it to me! Glory be to his name! *(Dies.)*

(Solemn music. — GEORGE covers UNCLE TOM with his cloak, and kneels over him. Clouds work on and conceal them, and then work off.)

Scene 7 — *Gorgeous clouds, tinted with sunlight. EVA, robed in white, is discovered on the back of a milk-white dove, with expanded wings, as if just soaring upward. Her hands are extended in benediction over ST. CLARE and UNCLE TOM who are kneeling and gazing up to her. Expressive music. — Slow curtain.*

THE END

NINETEENTH-CENTURY REALISM: The Beginnings of Modern Theatre

Starting with its rebirth in the Middle Ages, theatre became progressively more realistic and less stylized. Toward the end of the nineteenth century, the impact of modern science produced a new type of theatre which would have a major effect on drama in the twentieth century: realism.

Theatrical realism is the attempt to duplicate "real life" on stage for the purpose of healing society's ills. While realistic plays make subtle use of careful dramatic structure, they avoid obvious manipulation of events by the playwright, such as poetic justice, in which goodness is rewarded and evil punished. Instead, they portray the effects environment and heredity have on human beings. Realistic plays use scenery which closely approximates real environments and which shapes the lives of the characters. Realistic acting attempts to duplicate human psychology and behavior.

Political/Social/Philosophical Backgrounds

The latter half of the nineteenth century brought the beginning of a viewpoint called "modernism." Having absorbed the implications of the Renaissance, equipped with the increasingly efficient tools of science, fueled by wealth from the third world (where they dominated ancient cultures thereby demonstrating — to their own satisfaction — their superiority), nineteenth-century Europeans and Americans believed there was no riddle of nature or humanity they could not answer, no problem they could not solve. Given time, they believed they would create paradise on earth: utopia, a brave new world. Having thrown off the shackles of classicism, the art of the modern age laid aside old forms, joined with science and technology in problem solving, and gave expression to a passion for progress. As the futurist F. T. Marinetti wrote, "We affirm that the world's magnificence has been enriched by a new beauty: the beauty of speed. A racing car whose hood is adorned with great pipes, like serpents of explosive breath — a roaring car that seems to ride on grapeshot is more beautiful than the *Victory of Samothrace.*"[1]

The late nineteenth century was an optimistic age. Little dreaming of the horrors of two world wars, nuclear holocaust, brainwashing, and ecological mayhem which lay immediately ahead, these moderns put their full confidence in scientism and humanity.

Auguste Comte

Scientism and realism rested on a foundation established by the French thinker Auguste Comte (1798-1857), the philosophy of logical positivism.

---

[1]From "The Founding and Manifesto of Futurism" from SELECTED WRITINGS by F. T. Marinetti. Copyright © 1971, 1972 by Farrar, Straus and Giroux, Inc.

Two of Comte's ideas were especially important for realistic theatre. In the first place, Comte said that the best scientific research focused only on measurable data and led to a cause-and-effect explanation of reality; once the causes were known, he said, they could be manipulated to produce desired effects. Secondly, he taught that the highest and most complicated of the sciences was sociology and the other sciences were justified only insofar as they contributed to sociology's work of understanding and improving human society. In response to Comte's ideas, theatrical realists focused on material reality and believed that, by honestly portraying the ills of society, they were helping to improve the world.

Charles Darwin

The work of the biologist Charles Darwin (1809-1882) also had an important impact on realism. His book, *The Origin of Species* (1859), argued that biological species, including Homo sapiens, were the result of a natural cause-and-effect process determined by two principles: heredity and environment. This concept challenged the traditional belief that biological species were created instantaneously in their present forms. From the creationist viewpoint, human suffering had two possible causes: God's will or human wickedness. From this perspective, if any cure existed for human suffering, it was the conversion of human beings. Suffering was a problem of righteousness and sin. Darwinian evolution suggested that, instead of having a moral cause, suffering actually resulted from heredity and environment — bad genes and blighted neighborhoods. Suffering could be cured by science, which would first discover the principles of genetics and environment, and then manipulate them to improve the world. Theatrical realists believed they had a mission in the diagnostic part of this process.

Karl Marx

The ideas of Karl Marx (1818-1883) had a similar impact on theatrical realism. In his works, *The Communist Manifesto* and *Das Kapital,* he argued that governmental and economic systems carry within themselves an impetus for change. Moreover, he believed that systemic change had an observable direction that would eventually lead to a utopian society where there were no social classes and no exploitation of human beings by one another. Just as Darwin's theories suggested that science could facilitate the work of natural evolution, so Marx believed that human effort could accelerate the inevitable approach of utopia. This process would, again, involve two efforts: Research into the causes of human exploitation, and violent revolution on the part of the exploited. Partly as a result of these ideas, nineteenth-century theatrical realism tended to take sides against the controlling elements of society — the rich, the powerful, and the middle-class. And in the twentieth century, dramatists in this tradition would attempt to use theatre as a revolutionary weapon.

Sigmund Freud

Finally, the work of psychoanalyst Sigmund Freud (1856-1939) had an impact on theatre. Traditionally, people believed that deviant behavior resulted from bad moral choices — that when people did something hurtful to themselves or other people, they did so because they decided to be wicked. The way to correct this kind of behavior was to convert the "sinners" into righteous people. Freud, however, demonstrated that antisocial behavior results from psychological causes not under the deviant's control, causes that keep the deviant from making rational decisions. From this viewpoint, people aren't sinful — they're sick. Instead of punishment and conversion, they need healing.

Freudian ideas had an immense impact on theatre. For instance, theatrical realists began to portray characters as having mixed motives. Villains came to have justifiable reasons for their dastardly deeds, and it became acceptable for heroes and heroines to have moral blemishes. Also, "good," sympathetic characters might fall to ruin because of psychological problems, and "evil" characters might be healed and turn out to be "good" after all. Furthermore, because Freud demonstrated that objects in dreams and everyday life have symbolic value, realists frequently treated props, costumes, events, and even characters symbolically. Finally, the Freudian viewpoint led actors to delve into the psychology of their characters so that they could identify with them at a deep level and give "inner truth" to their words and actions.

Technology

While philosophers and theoreticians were developing these ideas, practical scientists were busy inventing thousands of technological devices from automobiles to zeppelins, from pencils to flushing toilets to cotton gins. Some of these nineteenth-century inventions would be useful in theatre. The development of gas lighting, for instance, permitted the controlled illumination of scenes; the development of incandescent, electric lighting by Thomas Edison (1847-1931) made it even easier to approximate natural lighting in the theatre; and the invention of the step-lens by the French physicist Augustine-Jean Fresnel (1788-1827) led to the Fresnel spotlight which is still used today.

Fired by optimism about the future, informed by new ideas, and equipped with a growing technology, nineteenth-century realism led theatre into the modern age.

Dramatic Literature

Realistic playwriting combined the purpose of using theatre as a sociological tool with the techniques of the "well-made play." The well-made play refers to playwriting techniques perfected by the popular French dramatist Eugène Scribe (1791-1861). Scribe and his followers devised carefully-crafted plots which began with exposition, went on to complicate the situation, and concluded by logically resolving all issues in the play. Their plays presented an ordered series of theatrical climaxes culminating in the "obligatory scene" in which all major characters of the play confronted one another. Since these plays aimed primarily at pleasing the audience with an interesting story, the playwrights did not hesitate to create characters and conclusions which, while exciting, were not true to life. Realistic playwrights, of course, refused to romanticize their characters or concoct conclusions

345

which rewarded "good" characters and punished "bad" ones, but they did use other devices from this school such as careful exposition, suspense, gripping climaxes, and clearly resolved endings.

Major realists included the Russian Anton Chekhov (1860-1904), the Irish-Englishman George Bernard Shaw (1856-1950), and the Norwegian Henrik Ibsen (1828-1906). Chekhov's major plays — *The Seagull* (1896), *Uncle Vanya* (1899), *Three Sisters* (1901), and *The Cherry Orchard* (1904) — all convey the combination of malaise and hope which brooded over Russia's middle class on the eve of the Revolution. Their realistic characterization and dialog made them especially suitable for Stanislavsky and the Moscow Art Theatre, who specialized in realistic ensemble productions. Shaw's plays, which numbered close to twenty, used comedy and surprising but believable twists of character to attack the myths and morals of the English middle class. Among his best-known plays are *Mrs. Warren's Profession* (1893), *Arms and the Man* (1894), and *Major Barbara* (1904-07). The work of Ibsen, "father of modern drama," will be dealt with later.

Naturalism and Symbolism

Realism stimulated the development of two other theatrical movements — naturalism and symbolism. Naturalism, led by French novelist and playwright Émile Zola (1840-1902), was an extreme form of realism. The naturalists rejected all conscious plotting on the part of the playwright, all use of the well-made play formula. Instead they called upon the dramatist to select a group of characters — preferably from a sociological case study — and trace their interaction, governed only by the principles of heredity and environment. They wanted theatre to present a "slice of life," a segment out of everyday life as free as possible from the artistic heightening of traditional playwriting. Perhaps the most characteristic representative of this movement is *The Lower Depths* by the Russian Maksim Gorky (1868-1936). Realism had gained a reputation for depressing treatments of sordid materials, a notoriety which was increased by naturalistic plays.

Symbolism rejected realism's concentration on surface reality. Encouraged in part by Freud's work with psychological symbols, the symbolists tried to pierce beyond the world of appearances to the mythical hopes and fears that underlie human behavior. Symbolist plays used poetic language and created dream-like worlds enveloped in mystery. Samples of symbolist plays include *Cathleen ni Houlihan* by William Butler Yeats (1865-1939), *A Dream Play* by August Strindberg (1849-1912), and *Pelléas and Mélisande* by Maurice Maeterlinck (1862-1949).

Performance Conventions

Georg II, Duke of Saxe-Meiningen (1826-1914) is usually considered to be the first theatrical director. Prior to this time, actors directed themselves; the actor-manager, who headed the company, arranged their characterizations around his own and also loosely coordinated the efforts of the costumers and set designers. The theatrical tradition and the mutual understandings which developed in a repertory company worked together to give productions a kind of informal unity. Saxe-Meiningen took a different approach. He recuited unknown actors, cast them without regard to status or "lines of business," and then prepared them with long, painstaking rehearsals in which he gave particular attention to crowd scenes and the performance of minor roles. He also unified all the other production elements into a single concept — his own. Tours of the Meiningen Players throughout Europe during the 1880s demonstrated the superior effect of ensemble playing, careful rehearsals, and a single, unifying concept. In the twentieth century, the dominating presence of the director made these ingredients a normal part of theatre.

Konstantin Stanislavsky

One of the theatre artists who was impressed by the Meiningen Players was the Russian actor and director Konstantin Stanislavsky (1863-1938). Subsequently, through his work with the Moscow Art Theatre and his writings on acting, he developed a method of acting which was ideally suited to theatrical realism. The Stanislavsky method aimed to eliminate showy, artificial acting in favor of a believable imitation of actual human behavior. The method included subordinating the actor to the character, focusing on the internal, psychological life of the character, motivating each speech and action by the character's inner life, and training the body and voice to make them adaptable to the psychological demands of a variety of characters. This approach came to be called "method acting" to distinguish it from "technique acting," which focused on external, theatricalized artistry. In the twentieth century, method acting came to be the standard for stage and movies alike.

André Antoine

Stage realism was given further impetus by André Antoine (1858-1943), also a follow of Saxe-Meiningen. In his work at Paris' Théâtre Libre, Antoine insisted that his actors behave as in real life to the extent of turning their backs on the audience and speaking up-stage when reality demanded it. He also used real objects on stage, such as real animal carcasses in scenes set in butcher shops. His practices of arranging furniture as it would be in a real, enclosed room and instructing his actors to behave as if a wall separated them from the audience reinforced what is called the "fourth wall" convention in modern theatre.

Faced with a growing variety of theatrical styles and led by directors who could shape productions according to their current concepts, early twentieth-century theatre came to be characterized by "eclecticism," in which each production devised its own style based on the script being used, the director's vision, and the performance situation.

Theatrical Organization

Two developments in the late nineteenth century had an impact on the business of theatre: The free theatre movement in Europe and the Syndicate in the United States.

The Free Theatre Movement

Because they did not cater to the entertainment-oriented appetites of mass audiences and because they frequently fell foul of censorship laws, the plays of Ibsen and other realists did not readily find a place in commercial theatres. Some producers, actors, and audience members, therefore, formed private theatre clubs to present these plays; because their primary aim was not monetary, these clubs did not need to worry about attracting large audiences, and because they were private membership organizations, censorship laws did not apply to them. The first of these theatre clubs, Antoine's Théâtre Libre, founded in 1887, set the pattern. Other important private theatres included Berlin's Freie Bühne, founded by Otto Brahm and others in 1889, and London's Independent Theatre Club, founded in 1891 by J. T. Grein. These independent theatres provided a home for realism, encouraged experimentation, and fostered the development of director-centered productions. They were the forerunners of twentieth-century experimental theatres such as London's fringe theatres and the off-off-Broadway theatres in New York.

The Theatrical Syndicate

The Theatrical Syndicate was formed in 1896 by Charles Frohman and several other New York producers with the aim of simplifying theatre organization. At this time, American theatre was centered in New York, where productions were mounted and then toured throughout the country. This touring system, known as "The Road," dominated theatre to the extent that most local theatres became booking houses, hosting road shows rather than producing their own. Local producers from all over the country would congregate in New York City each year to book their season — an inefficient process which resulted in much chaos. The Syndicate systematized the process by coordinating New York productions and bookings in road houses. Unfortunately, it soon controlled all of American theatre and established a monopoly which subordinated artistic and literary concerns to the profit motive. The Syndicate's domination lasted sixteen years before its monopoly was broken by the efforts of theatre artists such as actresses Minnie Maddern Fiske (1865-1932) and Sarah Bernhardt (1844-1923) and producer-playwright David Belasco (1859-1931). The Shubert brothers of New York, who helped to destroy the Syndicate, soon established a similar monopoly, but by that time other forces, such as the advent of film, had eliminated the road system as a significant factor in American theatre.

Henrik Ibsen

The man who was to become the father of modern drama began his working life as a pharmacist's apprentice. In his early twenties, however, he turned to theatre and writing. He spent most of the 1850s working with the Norske Teatret in Bergen. During these formative years he wrote scripts, visited theatres in Denmark and Germany, and participated in the productions of nearly 150 plays. After serving as director of two major theatres in the Norwegian capital of Christiania from 1857 to 1863, he went to Italy and lived abroad for 27 years. During this time, he wrote most of the plays which would establish his reputation and set a new direction for theatre in Europe and America.

In his early years, Ibsen experimented with a variety of historical and romantic dramas written in verse. Of the twelve plays he wrote prior to

1877, the best known are the romantic, poetic dramas *Brand* (1866) and *Peer Gynt* (1867).

In the mid-1870s, Ibsen turned to contemporary subjects, prose dialog, and realistic dramatic structures. In his first four plays of this type — *The Pillars of Society* (1877), *A Doll's House* (1879), *Ghosts* (1881), and *An Enemy of the People* (1882) — Ibsen exposed the greed, lies and narrow-minded, self-righteous assumptions which brooded beneath the surface of middle-class society.

His last eight plays, written between 1884 and 1900, focus more specifically on personal relationships and individual obsessions and make a greater use of symbolism. His best-known plays from this period are *The Wild Duck* (1884) and *Hedda Gabler* (1890).

Ibsen's plays established realism as the primary dramatic mode of modernism. They embodied realism's impulse to use drama as a scalpel which lays open the festering sores of society and to reject simplistic, moralistic solutions to the human condition. They made minimal use of coincidence and non-realistic conventions such as asides and soliloquies, and their extensive, specific stage directions treated theatrical settings as environments which molded the characters who inhabited them.

Ibsen combined this realistic perspective with technical expertise in the well-made play tradition, believable, complex characters, and an ability to give symbolic power to everyday experiences.

The independent theatres throughout Europe gradually overcame the hostile response Ibsen's plays received initially from critics and audiences until, by the end of the century, his plays and vision vitalized the theatrical scene in Europe and America. Ibsen's characters and situations still seem contemporary a century after their creation, and the realistic mode he established continues to dominate the stage and screen today.

A Doll's House

The Plot

Its dramatic structures place *A Doll's House* firmly in the tradition of melodrama and the well-made play. The first act uses expository dialog to set the scene and get the action underway; the second act complicates the situation with love interests, blackmail, and the potential of suicide; and the third act resolves all the play's conflicts and issues. Each act ends with a strong, emotional situation and speeches designed to bring the audience back to its seats after the intermission. And the third act culminates in an obligatory scene in which Helmer and Nora confront each other and, one-by-one, deal with all the conflicts of the play.

In good melodramatic fashion, the villainous Krogstad threatens the happiness of the heroine and hero — Nora and Helmer — who, on the surface, have all the purity and strength demanded of melodramatic leads. The cast even includes an old man, Dr. Rank, and a woman with a past, Mrs. Linden. Also, as is the case in typical melodramas, the outcome of the action depends on the handling of a crucial document — the forged IOU.

349

Ibsen, however, turns the melodramatic structures inside out: His heroine has a crooked deed in her past; the hero is weak and rotten at the core; the villain has a reasonable motive for his treachery and eventually converts into a decent person; rather than establish a moral center for the play, the old man has a letch for the heroine; and the "lively girl" is serious and wise.

Ideas and Attitudes

Ibsen uses these traditional structures to present new viewpoints characteristic of realism. He portrays the forces of heredity and environment as central in human society. Nora has inherited her father's essential generosity as well as his tendency to wink at the law, Dr. Rank is dying from syphilis inherited from his father, and Nora is afraid to be with her children for fear she'll pass her criminal nature on to them. The stage directions carefully establish the setting as an environment which determines Helmer and Nora's behavior, and the play's name even focuses on the locale of Nora's self-discovery. Furthermore, Krogstad's blackmail and change of heart both occur in response to changes in his environment: when people treat him badly, be becomes villainous, and when Mrs. Linden accepts him, he turns into a lamb. In the end, Nora solves her problem by rejecting Helmer's house to seek a better environment.

The attitudes of the play are also typical of realism. Religion, for instance, is portrayed as part of the problem rather than part of the solution. And the play attacks the middle class as sexist in its marital politics, phony in its concern with image, oppressive in its denigration of women, and stupid in its inability to perceive the truth.

Although the play, in good realistic fashion, focuses on diagnosing the disease which oppresses women in a middle-class society controlled by men, it also suggests some solutions: Laws need to be revised to treat women as fully human and independent, attitudes need to change so women are accepted as productive members of society, and marriage needs to be based on equality and mutuality rather than domination and paternalism. And in a conclusion which would have pleased Marx, when the downtrodden Nora understands the social realities which bind her, she revolts against her oppressor, returns the symbols of their social contract, refuses to accept any of his tainted money, and leaves — hoping against hope for the miracle of miracles; a new synthesis where she and her husband can live not as servant and master, but as equals.

Production History

A Doll's House was first presented at Copenhagen's Royal Theatre just before Christmas in 1879. In 1882, it was the first Ibsen play presented in English in the United States, and it was first produced in England in 1884. During the '80s and '90s, British and American critics were generally hostile to this and all of Ibsen's realistic plays, but by the turn of the century, Ibsen had become well-accepted. This change was due especially to the supportive efforts of Bernard Shaw and William Archer and the performances of major actresses such as Janet Achurch, Beatrice Cameron, Mrs. Fiske, and Madam Modjeska — all of whom played Nora. By the mid-

1930s, Americans considered Ibsen old-fashioned, but in the '50s and '60s they rediscovered the power of the father of realism, and in 1971 *A Doll's House*, with Claire Bloom in the role of Nora, opened the Eisenhower Theatre in Washington, DC's Kennedy Center. Today, over a hundred years after its premiere, *A Doll's House* continues to be a popular play in university and community theatres.

The Translator

William Archer (1856-1924), a theatre critic who was deeply committed to new plays and to intellectual values in drama, was the first major theatre figure to introduce Ibsen's plays in England. His translation of *A Doll's House* was first performed in London in 1889. In the years 1906 to 1908, he published all of Ibsen's works in English. A playwright himself, Archer brought to his translations a lively sense of the theatre and a desire to make the Norwegian dramatist's vision play well on the English stage. His version of *A Doll's House* remains fresh today.

All footnotes in *A Doll's House* are the work of the translator.

Turn-of-the-Century Theatre Timeline

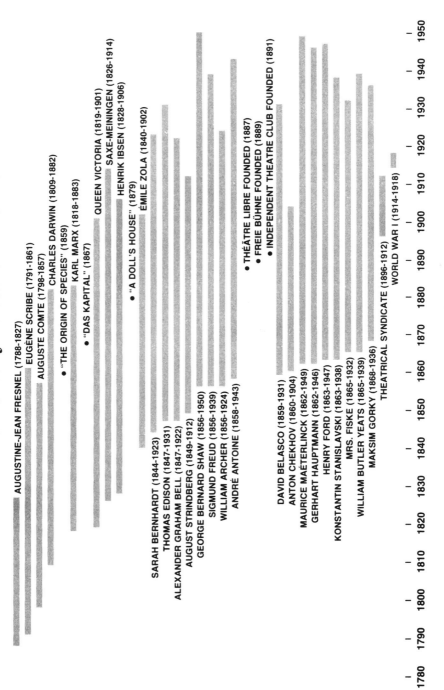

AUGUSTINE-JEAN FRESNEL (1788-1827)
EUGÈNE SCRIBE (1791-1861)
AUGUSTE COMTE (1798-1857)
CHARLES DARWIN (1809-1882)
● "THE ORIGIN OF SPECIES" (1859)
● KARL MARX (1818-1883)
● "DAS KAPITAL" (1867)
QUEEN VICTORIA (1819-1901)
SAXE-MEININGEN (1826-1914)
HENRIK IBSEN (1828-1906)
● "A DOLL'S HOUSE" (1879)
ÉMILE ZOLA (1840-1902)

SARAH BERNHARDT (1844-1923)
THOMAS EDISON (1847-1931)
ALEXANDER GRAHAM BELL (1847-1922)
AUGUST STRINDBERG (1849-1912)
GEORGE BERNARD SHAW (1856-1950)
SIGMUND FREUD (1856-1939)
WILLIAM ARCHER (1856-1924)
ANDRÉ ANTOINE (1858-1943)

● THÉÂTRE LIBRE FOUNDED (1887)
● FREIE BÜHNE FOUNDED (1889)
● INDEPENDENT THEATRE CLUB FOUNDED (1891)

DAVID BELASCO (1859-1931)
ANTON CHEKHOV (1860-1904)
MAURICE MAËTERLINCK (1862-1949)
GERHART HAUPTMANN (1862-1946)
HENRY FORD (1863-1947)
KONSTANTIN STANISLAVSKI (1863-1938)
MRS. FISKE (1865-1932)
WILLIAM BUTLER YEATS (1865-1939)
MAKSIM GORKY (1868-1936)
THEATRICAL SYNDICATE (1896-1912)
WORLD WAR I (1914-1918)

1780 1790 1800 1810 1820 1830 1840 1850 1860 1870 1880 1890 1900 1910 1920 1930 1940 1950

A DOLL'S HOUSE
(Et Dukkehjem)

by Henrik Ibsen
translated by William Archer

The action passes in Helmer's house (a flat) in Christiania.

CHARACTERS

TORVALD HELMER

NORA, his wife

DOCTOR RANK

MRS. LINDEN[1]

NILS KROGSTAD

THE HELMERS' THREE CHILDREN

ANNA[2] their nurse

A MAID-SERVANT (Ellen)

A PORTER

[1]In the original "Fru Linde."
[2]In the original "Anne-Marie."

ACT FIRST

A room, comfortably and tastefully, but not expensively, furnished. In the back, on the right, a door leads to the hall; on the left another door leads to HELMER's study. Between the two doors a pianoforte. In the middle of the left wall a door, and nearer the front a window. Near the window a round table with armchairs and a small sofa. In the right wall, somewhat to the back, a door, and against the same wall, further forward, a porcelain stove; in front of it a couple of armchairs and a rocking chair. Between the stove and the side door a small table. Engravings on the walls. A whatnot with china and bric-à-brac. A small bookcase filled with handsomely bound books. Carpet. A fire in the stove. It is a winter day.

A bell rings in the hall outside. Presently the outer door of the flat is heard to open. Then NORA enters, humming gaily. She is in outdoor dress, and carries several parcels, which she lays on the right-hand table. She leaves the door into the hall open, and a PORTER is seen outside, carrying a Christmas tree and a basket, which he gives to the MAID-SERVANT who has opened the door.

NORA: Hide the Christmas tree carefully, Ellen; the children must on no account see it before this evening, when it's lighted up. *(To the POR-TER, taking out her purse.)* How much?

PORTER: Fifty öre.[1]

NORA: There is a crown. No, keep the change. *(The PORTER thanks her and goes. NORA shuts the door. She continues smiling in quiet glee as she takes off her outdoor things. Taking from her pocket a bag of macaroons, she eats one or two. Then she goes on tip-toe to her husband's door and listens.)*

NORA: Yes; he is at home. *(She begins humming again, crossing to the table on the right.)*

HELMER: *(In his room.)* Is that my lark twittering there?

NORA: *(Busy opening some of her parcels.)* Yes, it is.

HELMER: Is it the squirrel frisking around?

NORA: Yes!

HELMER: When did the squirrel get home?

NORA: Just this minute. *(Hides the bag of macaroons in her pocket and wipes her mouth.)* Come here, Torvald, and see what I've been buying.

HELMER: Don't interrupt me. *(A little later he opens the door and looks in, pen in hand.)* Buying, did you say? What! All that? Has my little spendthrift been making the money fly again?

NORA: Why, Torvald, surely we can afford to launch out a little now. It's the first Christmas we haven't had to pinch.

HELMER: Come, come; we can't afford to squander money.

NORA: Oh yes, Torvald, do let us squander a little now — just the least little bit! You know you'll soon be earning heaps of money.

HELMER: Yes, from New Year's Day. But there's a whole quarter before my first salary is due.

[1] About sixpence. There are 100 öre in a krone or crown, which is worth thirteenpence halfpenny.

NORA: Never mind; we can borrow in the meantime.

HELMER: Nora! *(He goes up to her and takes her playfully by the ear.)* Still my little featherbrain! Supposing I borrowed a thousand crowns today, and you made ducks and drakes of them during Christmas week, and then on New Year's Eve a tile blew off the roof and knocked my brains out —

NORA: *(Laying her hand on his mouth.)* Hush! How can you talk so horridly?

HELMER: But supposing it were to happen — what then?

NORA: If anything so dreadful happened, it would be all the same to me whether I was in debt or not.

HELMER: But what about the creditors?

NORA: They! Who cares for them? They're only strangers.

HELMER: Nora, Nora! What a woman you are! But seriously, Nora, you know my principles on these points. No debts! No borrowing! Home life ceases to be free and beautiful as soon as it is founded on borrowing and debt. We two have held out bravely till now, and we are not going to give in at the last.

NORA: *(Going to the fireplace.)* Very well — as you please, Torvald.

HELMER: *(Following her.)* Come come; my little lark mustn't droop her wings like that. What? Is my squirrel in the sulks? *(Takes out his purse.)* Nora, what do you think I have here?

NORA: *(Turning round quickly.)* Money!

HELMER: There! *(Gives her some notes.)* Of course I know all sorts of things are wanted at Christmas.

NORA: *(Counting.)* Ten, twenty, thirty, forty. Oh, thank you, thank you, Torvald! This will go a long way.

HELMER: I should hope so.

NORA: Yes, indeed; a long way! But come here, and let me show you all I've been buying. And so cheap! Look, here's a new suit for Ivar, and a little sword. Here are a horse and a trumpet for Bob. And here are a doll and a cradle for Emmy. They're only common; but they're good enough for her to pull to pieces. And dress-stuffs and kerchiefs for the servants. I ought to have got something better for old Anna.

HELMER: And what's in that other parcel?

NORA: *(Crying out.)* No, Torvald, you're not to see that until this evening.

HELMER: Oh! Ah! But now tell me, you little spendthrift, have you thought of anything for youself!

NORA: For myself! Oh, I don't want anything.

HELMER: Nonsense! Just tell me something sensible you would like to have.

NORA: No, really I don't know of anything — Well, listen, Torvald —

HELMER: Well?

NORA: *(Playing with his coat buttons, without looking him in the face.)* If you really want to give me something, you might, you know — you might —

HELMER: Well? Out with it!

NORA: *(Quickly)* You might give me money, Torvald. Only just what you think you can spare; then I can buy something with it later on.

HELMER: But, Nora —

NORA: Oh, please do, dear Torvald, please do! I should hang the money in lovely gilt paper on the Christmas tree. Wouldn't that be fun?

HELMER: What do they call the birds that are always making the money fly?

NORA: Yes, I know — spendthrifts,[1] of course. But please do as I ask you, Torvald. Then I shall have time to think what I want most. Isn't that very sensible, now?

HELMER: *(Smiling.)* Certainly; that is to say, if you really kept the money I gave you, and really spent it on something for yourself. But it all goes in housekeeping, and for all manner of useless things, and then I have to pay up again.

NORA: But, Torvald —

HELMER: Can you deny it, Nora dear? *(He puts his arm round her.)* It's a sweet little lark, but it gets through a lot of money. No one would believe how much it costs a man to keep such a little bird as you.

NORA: For shame! How can you say so? Why, I save as much as ever I can.

HELMER: *(Laughing.)* Very true — as much as you can — but that's precisely nothing.

NORA: *(Hums and smiles with covert glee.)* H'm! If you only knew, Torvald, what expenses we larks and squirrels have.

HELMER: You're a strange little being! Just like your father — always on the lookout for all the money you can lay your hands on; but the moment you have it, it seems to slip through your fingers; you never know what becomes of it. Well, one must take you as you are. It's in the blood. Yes, Nora, that sort of thing is hereditary.

NORA: I wish I had inherited many of papa's qualities.

HELMER: And I don't wish you anything but just what you are — my own, sweet little songbird. But I say — it strikes me you look so — so — what shall I call it? — so suspicious today —

NORA: Do I?

HELMER: You do, indeed. Look me full in the face.

NORA: *(Looking at him.)* Well?

HELMER: *(Threatening with his finger.)* Hasn't the little sweet tooth been playing pranks today?

NORA: No; how can you think such a thing!

HELMER: Didn't she just look in at the confectioner's?

NORA: No, Torvald; really —

HELMER: Not to sip a little jelly?

NORA: No; certainly not.

HELMER: Hasn't she even nibbled a macaroon or two?

NORA: No, Torvald, indeed, indeed!

HELMER: Well, well, well; of course I'm only joking.

NORA: *(Goes to the table on the right.)* I shouldn't think of doing what you disapprove of.

HELMER: No, I'm sure of that; and, besides, you've given me your word — *(Going towards her.)* Well, keep your little Christmas secrets to yourself, Nora darling. The Christmas tree will bring them all to light, I daresay.

NORA: Have you remembered to invite Doctor Rank?

HELMER: No. But it's not necessary; he'll come as a matter of course.

[1]"Spillefugl," literally "playbird," means a gambler.

Besides, I shall ask him when he looks in today. I've ordered some capital wine. Nora, you can't think how I look forward to this evening.

NORA: And I too. How the children will enjoy themselves, Torvald!

HELMER: Ah, it's glorious to feel that one has an assured position and ample means. Isn't it delightful to think of?

NORA: Oh, it's wonderful!

HELMER: Do you remember last Christmas? For three whole weeks beforehand you shut yourself up every evening till long past midnight to make flowers for the Christmas tree, and all sorts of other marvels that were to have astonished us. I was never so bored in my life.

NORA: I didn't bore myself at all.

HELMER: *(Smiling.)* But it came to little enough in the end, Nora.

NORA: Oh, are you going to tease me about that again? How could I help the cat getting in and pulling it all to pieces?

HELMER: To be sure you couldn't, my poor little Nora. You did your best to give us all pleasure, and that's the main point. But, all the same, it's a good thing the hard times are over.

NORA: Oh, isn't it wonderful?

HELMER: Now I needn't sit here boring myself all alone; and you needn't tire your blessed eyes and your delicate little fingers —

NORA: *(Clapping her hands.)* No, I needn't, need I, Torvald? Oh, how wonderful it is to think of? *(Takes his arm.)* And now I'll tell you how I think we ought to manage, Torvald. As soon as Christmas is over — *(The hall doorbell rings.)* Oh, there's a ring! *(Arranging the room.)* That's somebody come to call. How tiresome!

HELMER: I'm "not at home" to callers; remember that.

ELLEN: *(In the doorway.)* A lady to see you, ma'am.

NORA: Show her in.

ELLEN: *(To HELMER.)* And the doctor has just come, sir.

HELMER: Has he gone into my study?

ELLEN: Yes, sir. *(HELMER goes into his study. ELLEN ushers in MRS. LINDEN, in traveling costume, and goes out, closing the door.)*

MRS. LINDEN: *(Embarrassed and hesitating.)* How do you do, Nora?

NORA: *(Doubtfully.)* How do you do?

MRS. LINDEN: I see you don't recognise me!

NORA: No, I don't think — oh yes! — I believe — *(Suddenly brightening.)* What, Christina! Is it really you?

MRS. LINDEN: Yes; really I!

NORA: Christina! And to think I didn't know you! But how could I — *(More softly.)* How changed you are, Christina!

MRS. LINDEN: Yes, no doubt. In nine or ten years —

NORA: Is it really so long since we met? Yes, so it is. Oh, the last eight years have been a happy time, I can tell you. And now you have come to town? All that long journey in mid-winter. How brave of you!

MRS. LINDEN: I arrived by this morning's steamer.

NORA: To have a merry Christmas, of course. Oh, how delightful! Yes, we will have a merry Christmas. Do take your things off. Aren't you frozen? *(Helping her.)* There; now we'll sit cosily by the fire. No, you take the armchair; I shall sit in this rocking chair. *(Seizes her hands.)* Yes, now I can see the dear old face again. It was only at the first glance — But you're a little paler, Christina — and perhaps a little thinner.

MRS. LINDEN: And much, much older, Nora.

NORA: Yes, perhaps a little older — not much — ever so little. *(She suddenly checks herself; seriously.)* Oh, what a thoughtless wretch I am! Here I sit chattering on, and — Dear, dear Christina, can you forgive me!

MRS. LINDEN: What do you mean, Nora?

NORA: *(Softly.)* Poor Christina! I forgot: you are a widow.

MRS. LINDEN: Yes; my husband died three years ago.

NORA: I know, I know; I saw it in the papers. Oh, believe me, Christina, I did mean to write to you; but I kept putting it off, and something always came in the way.

MRS. LINDEN: I can quite understand that, Nora dear.

NORA: No, Christina; it was horrid of me. Oh, you poor darling! How much you must have gone through! — And he left you nothing?

MRS. LINDEN: Nothing.

NORA: And no children?

MRS. LINDEN: None.

NORA: Nothing, nothing at all?

MRS. LINDEN: Not even a sorrow or a longing to dwell upon.

NORA: *(Looking at her incredulously.)* My dear Christina, how is that possible?

MRS. LINDEN: *(Smiling sadly and stroking her hair.)* Oh, it happens so sometimes, Nora.

NORA: So utterly alone! How dreadful that must be! I have three of the loveliest children. I can't show them to you just now; they're out with their nurse. But now you must tell me everything.

MRS. LINDEN: No, no; I want you to tell me —

NORA: No, you must begin; I won't be egotistical today. Today I'll think only of you. Oh! but I must tell you one thing — perhaps you've heard of our great stroke of fortune?

MRS. LINDEN: No. What is it?

NORA: Only think! my husband has been made manager of the Joint Stock Bank.

MRS. LINDEN: Your husband! Oh, how fortunate!

NORA: Yes; isn't it? A lawyer's position is so uncertain, you see, especially when he won't touch any business that's the least bit — shady, as of course Torvald never would; and there I quite agree with him. Oh! you can imagine how glad we are. He is to enter on his new position at the New Year, and then he'll have a large salary, and percentages. In future we shall be able to live quite differently — just as we please, in fact. Oh, Christina, I feel so lighthearted and happy! It's delightful to have lots of money, and no need to worry about things, isn't it?

MRS. LINDEN: Yes; at any rate it must be delightful to have what you need.

NORA: No, not only what you need, but heaps of money — heaps!

MRS. LINDEN: *(Smiling.)* Nora, Nora, haven't you learnt reason yet? In our schooldays you were a shocking little spendthrift.

NORA: *(Quietly smiling.)* Yes; that's what Torvald says I am still. *(Holding up her forefinger.)* But "Nora, Nora" is not so silly as you all think. Oh! I haven't had the chance to be much of a spendthrift. We have both had to work.

MRS. LINDEN: You too?

NORA: Yes, light fancy work: crochet, and embroidery, and things of that sort; *(Carelessly)* and other work too. You know, of course, that Torvald left the Government service when we were married. He had little chance of promotion, and of course he required to make more money. But in the first year after our marriage he overworked himself terribly. He had to undertake all sorts of extra work, you know, and to slave early and late. He couldn't stand it, and fell dangerously ill. Then the doctors declared he must go to the South.

MRS. LINDEN: You spent a whole year in Italy, didn't you?

NORA: Yes, we did. It wasn't easy to manage, I can tell you. It was just after Ivar's birth. But of course we had to go. Oh, it was a wonderful, delicious journey! And it saved Torvald's life. But it cost a frightful lot of money, Christina.

MRS. LINDEN: So I should think.

NORA: Twelve hundred dollars! Four thousand eight hundred crowns!¹ Isn't that a lot of money?

MRS. LINDEN: How lucky you had the money to spend!

NORA: We got it from father, you must know.

MRS. LINDEN: Ah, I see. He died just about that time, didn't he?

NORA: Yes, Christina, just then. And only think! I couldn't go and nurse him! I was expecting little Ivar's birth daily; and then I had my poor sick Torvald to attend to. Dear, kind old father! I never saw him again, Christina. Oh! that's the hardest thing I have had to bear since my marriage.

MRS. LINDEN: I know how fond you were of him. But then you went to Italy?

NORA: Yes; you see, we had the money, and the doctors said we must lose no time. We started a month later.

MRS. LINDEN: And your husband came back completely cured.

NORA: Sound as a bell.

MRS. LINDEN: But — the doctor?

NORA: What do you mean?

MRS. LINDEN: I thought as I came in your servant announced the doctor —

NORA: Oh, yes; Doctor Rank. But he doesn't come professionally. He is our best friend, and never lets a day pass without looking in. No, Torvald hasn't had an hour's illness since that time. And the children are so healthy and well, and so am I. *(Jumps up and claps her hands.)* Oh, Christina, Christina, what a wonderful thing it is to live and to be happy! — Oh, but it's really too horrid of me! Here am I talking about nothing but my own concerns. *(Seats herself upon a footstool close to CHRISTINA, and lays her arms on her friend's lap.)* Oh, don't be angry with me! Now tell me, is it really true that you didn't love your husband? What made you marry him, then?

MRS. LINDEN: My mother was still alive, you see, bedridden and helpless; and then I had my two younger brothers to think of. I didn't think it would be right for me to refuse him.

---

¹The dollar (4s. 6d.) was the old unit of currency in Norway. The crown was substituted for it shortly before the date of this play.

NORA: Perhaps it wouldn't have been. I suppose he was rich then?
MRS. LINDEN: Very well off, I believe. But his business was uncertain. It fell to pieces at his death, and there was nothing left.
NORA: And then —?
MRS. LINDEN: Then I had to fight my way by keeping a shop, a little school, anything I could turn my hand to. The last three years have been one long struggle for me. But now it is over, Nora. My poor mother no longer needs me; she is at rest. And the boys are in business, and can look after themselves.
NORA: How free your life must feel!
MRS. LINDEN: No, Nora; only inexpressibly empty. No one to live for! *(Stands up restlessly.)* That's why I could not bear to stay any longer in that out-of-the-way corner. Here it must be easier to find something to take one up — to occupy one's thoughts. If I could only get some settled employment — some office work.
NORA: But, Christina, that's such drudgery, and you look worn out already. It would be ever so much better for you to go to some watering-place and rest.
MRS. LINDEN: *(Going to the window.)* I have no father to give me the money, Nora.
NORA: *(Rising.)* Oh, don't be vexed with me.
MRS. LINDEN: *(Going to her.)* My dear Nora, don't you be vexed with me. The worst of a position like mine is that it makes one so bitter. You have no one to work for, yet you have to be always on the strain. You must live; and so you become selfish. When I heard of the happy change in your fortunes — can you believe it? — I was glad for my own sake more than for yours.
NORA: How do you mean? Ah, I see! You think Torvald can perhaps do something for you.
MRS. LINDEN: Yes; I thought so.
NORA: And so he shall, Christina. Just you leave it all to me. I shall lead up to it beautifully! — I shall think of some delightful plan to put him in a good humour! Oh, I should so love to help you.
MRS. LINDEN: How good of you, Nora, to stand by me so warmly! Doubly good in you, who knows so little of the troubles and burdens of life.
NORA: I? I know so little of —?
MRS. LINDEN: *(Smiling.)* Oh, well — a little fancy-work, and so forth. — You're a child, Nora.
NORA: *(Tosses her head and paces the room.)* Oh, come, you mustn't be so patronising!
MRS. LINDEN: No?
NORA: You're like the rest. You all think I'm fit for nothing really serious —
MRS. LINDEN: Well, well —
NORA: You think I've had no troubles in this weary world.
MRS. LINDEN: My dear Nora, you've just told me all your troubles.
NORA: Pooh — those trifles! *(Softly.)* I haven't told you the great thing.
MRS. LINDEN: The great thing? What do you mean?
NORA: I know you look down upon me, Christina; but you have no right to. You are proud of having worked so hard and so long for your mother.
MRS. LINDEN: I am sure I don't look down upon any one; but it's true I am

both proud and glad when I remember that I was able to keep my mother's last days free from care.

NORA: And you're proud to think of what you have done for your brothers, too.

MRS. LINDEN: Have I not the right to be?

NORA: Yes indeed. But now let me tell you, Christina — I, too, have something to be proud and glad of.

MRS. LINDEN: I don't doubt it. But what do you mean?

NORA: Hush! Not so loud. Only think, if Torvald were to hear! He mustn't — not for worlds! No one must know about it, Christina — no one but you.

MRS. LINDEN: Why, what can it be?

NORA: Come over here. *(Draws her down beside her on the sofa.)* Yes, Christina — I, too, have something to be proud and glad of. I saved Torvald's life.

MRS. LINDEN: Saved his life? How?

NORA: I told you about our going to Italy. Torvald would have died but for that.

MRS. LINDEN: Well — and your father gave you the money.

NORA: *(Smiling.)* Yes, so Torvald and every one believes; but —

MRS. LINDEN: But —?

NORA: Papa didn't give us one penny. It was *I* that found the money.

MRS. LINDEN: You? All that money?

NORA: Twelve hundred dollars. Four thousand eight hundred crowns. What do you say to that?

MRS. LINDEN: My dear Nora, how did you manage it? Did you win it in the lottery?

NORA: *(Contemptuously.)* In the lottery? Pooh! Any one could have done that!

MRS. LINDEN: Then wherever did you get it from?

NORA: *(Hums and smiles mysteriously.)* H'm; Tra-la-la-la!

MRS. LINDEN: Of course you couldn't borrow it.

NORA: No? Why not?

MRS. LINDEN: Why a wife can't borrow without her husband's consent.

NORA: *(Tossing her head.)* Oh! when the wife has some idea of business, and knows how to set about things —

MRS. LINDEN: But, Nora, I don't understand —

NORA: Well, you needn't. I never said I borrowed the money. There are many ways I may have got it. *(Throws herself back on the sofa.)* I may have got it from some admirer. When one is so — attractive as I am —

MRS. LINDEN: You're too silly, Nora.

NORA: Now I'm sure you're dying of curiosity, Christina —

MRS. LINDEN: Listen to me, Nora dear: haven't you been a little rash?

NORA: *(Sitting upright again.)* Is it rash to save one's husband's life?

MRS. LINDEN: I think it was rash of you, without his knowledge —

NORA: But it would have been fatal for him to know! Can't you understand that? He wasn't even to suspect how ill he was. The doctors came to me privately and told me his life was in danger — that nothing could save him but a winter in the South. Do you think I didn't try diplomacy first? I told him how I longed to have a trip abroad, like the other young wives; I wept and prayed; I said he ought to think of my condition

361

and not to thwart me; and then I hinted that he could borrow the money. But then, Christina, he got almost angry. He said I was frivolous, and that it was his duty as a huband not to yield to my whims and fancies — so he called them. Very well, thought I, but saved you must be: and then I found the way to do it.

MRS. LINDEN: And did your husband never learn from your father that the money was not from him?

NORA: No; never. Papa died at that very time. I meant to have told him all about it, and begged him to say nothing. But he was so ill — unhappily, it wasn't necessary.

MRS. LINDEN: And you have never confessed to your husband?

NORA: Good heavens! What can you be thinking of? Tell him, when he has such a loathing of debt. And besides — how painful and humiliating it would be for Torvald, with his manly self-respect, to know that he owed anything to me! It would utterly upset the relation between us; our beautiful, happy home would never again be what it is.

MRS. LINDEN: Will you never tell him?

NORA: *(Thoughtfully, half-smiling.)* Yes, some time perhaps — many, many years hence, when I'm — not so pretty. You mustn't laugh at me! Of course I mean when Torvald is not so much in love with me as he is now; when it doesn't amuse him any longer to see me dancing about, and acting. Then it might be well to have something in reserve. *(Breaking off.)* Nonsense! nonsense! That time will never come. Now, what do you say to my grand secret, Christina? Am I fit for nothing now? You may believe it has cost me a lot of anxiety. It has been no joke to meet my engagements punctually. You must know, Christina, that in business there are things called instalments, and quarterly interest, that are terribly hard to provide for. So I've had to pinch a little here and there, wherever I could. I couldn't save much out of the housekeeping, for of course Torvald had to live well. And I couldn't let the children go about badly dressed; all I got for them, I spent on them, the blessed darlings!

MRS. LINDEN: Poor Nora! So it had to come out of your own pocket money.

NORA: Yes, of course. After all, the whole thing was my doing. When Torvald gave me money for clothes, and so on, I never spent more than half of it; I always bought the simplest and cheapest things. It's a mercy that everything suits me so well — Torvald never had any suspicions. But it was often very hard, Christina dear. For it's nice to be beautifully dressed — now, isn't it?

MRS. LINDEN: Indeed it is.

NORA: Well, and besides that, I made money in other ways. Last winter I was so lucky — I got a heap of copying to do. I shut myself up every evening and wrote far into the night. Oh, sometimes I was so tired, so tired. And yet it was splendid to work in that way and earn money. I almost felt as if I was a man.

MRS. LINDEN: Then how much have you been able to pay off?

NORA: Well, I can't precisely say. It's difficult to keep that sort of business clear. I only know that I've paid everything I could scrape together. Sometimes I really didn't know where to turn. *(Smiles.)* Then I used to sit here and pretend that a rich old gentleman was in love with me —

MRS. LINDEN: What! What gentleman?

NORA: Oh, nobody! — that he was dead now, and that when his will was opened, there stood in large letters: "Pay over at once everything of which I die possessed to that charming person, Mrs. Nora Helmer."

MRS. LINDEN: But, my dear Nora — what gentleman do you mean?

NORA: Oh dear, can't you understand? There wasn't any old gentleman: it was only what I used to dream and dream when I was at my wits' end for money. But it doesn't matter now — the tiresome old creature may stay where he is for me. I care nothing for him or his will; for now my troubles are over. *(Springing up.)* Oh, Christina, how glorious it is to think of! Free from all anxiety! Free, quite free. To be able to play and romp about with the children; to have things tasteful and pretty in the house, exactly as Torvald likes it! And then the spring will soon be here, with the great blue sky. Perhaps then we shall have a little holiday. Perhaps I shall see the sea again. Oh, what a wonderful thing it is to live and to be happy! *(The hall doorbell rings.)*

MRS. LINDEN: *(Rising.)* There's a ring. Perhaps I had better go.

NORA: No; do stay. No one will come here. It's sure to be some one for Torvald.

ELLEN: *(In the doorway.)* If you please, ma'am, there's a gentleman to speak to Mr. Helmer.

NORA: Who is the gentleman?

KROGSTAD: *(In the doorway.)* It is I, Mrs. Helmer. *(MRS. LINDEN starts and turns away to the window.)*

NORA: *(Goes a step towards him, anxiously, speaking low.)* You? What is it? What do you want with my husband?

KROGSTAD: Bank business — in a way. I hold a small post in the Joint Stock Bank, and your husband is to be our new chief, I hear.

NORA: Then it is —?

KROGSTAD: Only tiresome business, Mrs. Helmer; nothing more.

NORA: Then will you please go to his study. *(KROGSTAD goes. She bows indifferently while she closes the door into the hall. Then she goes to the stove and looks to the fire.)*

MRS. LINDEN: Nora — who was that man?

NORA: A Mr. Krogstad — a lawyer.

MRS. LINDEN: Then it was really he?

NORA: Do you know him?

MRS. LINDEN: I used to know him — many years ago. He was in a lawyer's office in our town.

NORA: Yes, so he was.

MRS. LINDEN: How he has changed!

NORA: I believe his marriage was unhappy.

MRS. LINDEN: And he is a widower now?

NORA: With a lot of children. There! Now it will burn up. *(She closes the stove, and pushes the rocking chair a little aside.)*

MRS. LINDEN: His business is not of the most creditable, they say?

NORA: Isn't it? I daresay not. I don't know. But don't let us think of business — it's so tiresome. *(DR. RANK comes out of HELMER's room.)*

RANK: *(Still in the doorway.)* No, no; I'm in your way. I shall go and have a chat with your wife. *(Shuts the door and sees MRS. LINDEN.)* Oh, I beg your pardon. I'm in the way here too.

NORA: No, not in the least. *(Introduces them.)* Doctor Rank — Mrs. Linden.
RANK: Oh, indeed; I've often heard Mrs. Linden's name; I think I passed you on the stairs as I came up.
MRS. LINDEN: Yes; I go so very slowly. Stairs try me so much.
RANK: Ah — you are not very strong?
MRS. LINDEN: Only overworked.
RANK: Nothing more? Then no doubt you've come to town to find rest in a round of dissipation?
MRS. LINDEN: I have come to look for employment.
RANK: Is that an approved remedy for overwork?
MRS. LINDEN: One must live, Doctor Rank.
RANK: Yes, that seems to be the general opinion.
NORA: Come, Doctor Rank — you want to live yourself.
RANK: To be sure I do. However wretched I may be, I want to drag on as long as possible. All my patients, too, have the same mania. And it's the same with people whose complaint is moral. At this very moment Helmer is talking to just such a moral incurable —
MRS. LINDEN: *(Softly.)* Ah!
NORA: Whom do you mean?
RANK: Oh, a fellow named Krogstad, a man you know nothing about — corrupt to the very core of his character. But even he began by announcing, as a matter of vast importance, that he must live.
NORA: Indeed? And what did he want with Torvald?
RANK: I haven't an idea; I only gathered that it was some bank business.
NORA: I didn't know that Krog — that this Mr. Krogstad had anything to do with the Bank?
RANK: Yes. He has got some sort of place there. *(To MRS. LINDEN.)* I don't know whether in your part of the country, you have people who go grubbing and sniffing around in search of moral rottenness — and then, when they have found a "case," don't rest till they have got their man into some good position, where they can keep a watch upon him. Men with a clean bill of health they leave out in the cold.
MRS. LINDEN: Well, I suppose the — delicate characters require most care.
RANK: *(Shrugs his shoulders.)* There we have it! It's that notion that makes society a hospital. *(NORA, deep in her own thoughts, breaks into half-stifled laughter and claps her hands.)*
RANK: Why do you laugh at that? Have you any idea what "society" is?
NORA: What do I care for your tiresome society? I was laughing at something else — something excessively amusing. Tell me, Doctor Rank, are all the employees at the Bank dependent on Torvald now?
RANK: Is that what strikes you as excessively amusing?
NORA: *(Smiles and hums.)* Never mind, never mind! *(Walks about the room.)* Yes, it is funny to think that we — that Torvald has such power over so many people. *(Takes the bag from her pocket.)* Doctor Rank, will you have a macaroon?
RANK: What! — macaroons! I thought they were contraband here.
NORA: Yes; but Christina brought me these.
MRS. LINDEN: What! I —?
NORA: Oh, well! Don't be frightened. You couldn't possibly know that Torvald had forbidden them. The fact is, he's afraid of me spoiling my

teeth. But, oh bother, just for once! — That's for you, Doctor Rank!
(Puts a macaroon into his mouth.) And you too, Christina. And I'll
have one while we're about it — only a tiny one, or at most two. *(Walks about again.)* Oh dear, I am happy! There's only one thing in the world I really want.

RANK: Well; what's that?

NORA: There's something I should so like to say — in Torvald's hearing.

RANK: Then why don't you say it?

NORA: Because I daren't, it's so ugly.

MRS. LINDEN: Ugly!

RANK: In that case you'd better not. But to us you might — What is it you would so like to say in Helmer's hearing?

NORA: I should so love to say "Damn it all!"[1]

RANK: Are you out of your mind?

MRS. LINDEN: Good gracious, Nora —!

RANK: Say it — there he is!

NORA: *(Hides the macaroons.)* Hush — sh — sh! *(HELMER comes out of his room, hat in hand, with his overcoat on his arm.)*

NORA: *(Going to him.)* Well, Torvald dear, have you got rid of him?

HELMER: Yes; he has just gone.

NORA: Let me introduce you — this is Christina, who has come to town —

HELMER: Christina? Pardon me, I don't know —

NORA: Mrs. Linden, Torvald dear — Christina Linden.

HELMER: *(To MRS. LINDEN.)* Indeed! A school-friend of my wife's no doubt?

MRS. LINDEN: Yes; we knew each other as girls.

NORA: And only think! She has taken this long journey on purpose to speak to you.

HELMER: To speak to me!

MRS. LINDEN: Well, not quite —

NORA: You see, Christina is tremendously clever at office-work, and she's so anxious to work under a first-rate man of business in order to learn still more —

HELMER: *(To MRS. LINDEN.)* Very sensible indeed.

NORA: And when she heard you were appointed manager — it was tele-graphed, you know — she started off at once, and — Torvald, dear, for my sake, you must do something for Christina. Now can't you?

HELMER: It's not impossible. I presume Mrs. Linden is a widow?

MRS. LINDEN: Yes.

HELMER: And you have already had some experience of business?

MRS. LINDEN: A good deal.

HELMER: Well, then, it's very likely I may be able to find a place for you.

NORA: *(Clapping her hands.)* There now! There now!

HELMER: You have come at a fortunate moment, Mrs. Linden.

MRS. LINDEN: Oh, how can I thank you —?

HELMER: *(Smiling.)* There is no occasion. *(Puts on his overcoat.)* But for the present you must excuse me —

RANK: Wait; I am going with you. *(Fetches his fur coat from the hall and*

---

[1]"Död og pine," literally "death and torture"; but by usage a comparatively mild oath.

> *warms it at the fire.)*

NORA: Don't be long, Torvald dear.

HELMER: Only an hour; not more.

NORA: Are you going too, Christina?

MRS. LINDEN: *(Putting on her walking things.)* Yes; I must set about looking for lodgings.

HELMER: Then perhaps we can go together?

NORA: *(Helping her.)* What a pity we haven't a spare room for you; but it's impossible —

MRS. LINDEN: I shouldn't think of troubling you. Good-bye, dear Nora, and thank you for all your kindness.

NORA: Good-bye for the present. Of course you'll come back this evening. And you, too, Doctor Rank. What! If you're well enough? Of course you'll be well enough. Only wrap up warmly. *(They go out, talking, into the hall. Outside on the stairs are heard children's voices.)* There they are! There they are! *(She runs to the outer door and opens it. The nurse, ANNA, enters the hall with the CHILDREN.)* Come in! Come in! *(Stoops down and kisses the CHILDREN.)* Oh, my sweet darlings! Do you see them, Christina? Aren't they lovely?

RANK: Don't let us stand here chattering in the draught.

HELMER: Come, Mrs. Linden; only mothers can stand such a temperature.

(DR. RANK, HELMER, and MRS. LINDEN go down the stairs; ANNA enters the room with the CHILDREN; NORA also, shutting the door.)

NORA: How fresh and bright you look! And what red cheeks you've got! Like apples and roses. *(The CHILDREN chatter to her during what follows.)* Have you had great fun? That's splendid! Oh, really! You've been giving Emmy and Bob a ride on your sledge! — both at once, only think! Why, you're quite a man, Ivar. Oh, give her to me a little, Anna. My sweet little dolly! *(Takes the smallest from the NURSE and dances with her.)* Yes, yes; mother will dance with Bob too. What! Did you have a game of snowballs? Oh, I wish I'd been there. No; leave them, Anna; I'll take their things off. Oh, yes, let me do it; it's such fun. Go to the nursery; you look frozen. You'll find some hot coffee on the stove.

(The NURSE goes into the room on the left. NORA takes off the CHILDREN's things and throws them down anywhere, while the CHILDREN talk all together.)

> Really! A big dog ran after you? But he didn't bite you? No: dogs don't bite dear little dolly children. Don't peep into those parcels, Ivar. What is it? Wouldn't you like to know? Take care — it'll bite! What? Shall we have a game? What shall we play at? Hide-and-seek? Yes, let's play hide-and-seek. Bob shall hide first. Am I to? Yes, let me hide first.

(She and the CHILDREN play, with laughter and shouting, in the room and the adjacent one to the right. At last NORA hides under the table; the CHILDREN come rushing in, look for her, but cannot find her, hear her half-choked laughter, rush to the table, lift up the cover and see her. Loud shouts. She creeps out, as though to frighten them. Fresh shouts. Meanwhile there has been a knock at the door leading into the hall. No one has heard it. Now the

door is half opened and KROGSTAD appears. He waits a little; the game is renewed.)

KROGSTAD: I beg your pardon, Mrs. Helmer —

NORA: *(With a suppressed cry, turns round and half jumps up.)* Ah! What do you want?

KROGSTAD: Excuse me; the outer door was ajar — somebody must have forgotten to shut it —

NORA: *(Standing up.)* My husband is not at home, Mr. Krogstad.

KROGSTAD: I know it.

NORA: Then what do you want here?

KROGSTAD: To say a few words to you.

NORA: To me? *(To the CHILDREN, softly.)* Go in to Anna. What? No, the strange man won't hurt mamma. When he's gone we'll go on playing. *(She leads the CHILDREN into the left-hand room, and shuts the door behind them. Uneasy, in suspense.)* It is to me you wish to speak?

KROGSTAD: Yes, to you.

NORA: Today? But it's not the first yet —

KROGSTAD: No, today is Christmas Eve. It will depend upon yourself whether you have a merry Christmas.

NORA: What do you want? I'm not ready today —

KROGSTAD: Never mind that just now. I have come about another matter. You have a minute to spare?

NORA: Oh, yes, I suppose so; although —

KROGSTAD: Good. I was sitting in the restaurant opposite, and I saw your husband go down the street —

NORA: Well?

KROGSTAD: — with a lady.

NORA: What then?

KROGSTAD: May I ask if the lady was a Mrs. Linden?

NORA: Yes.

KROGSTAD: Who has just come to town?

NORA: Yes. Today.

KROGSTAD: I believe she is an intimate friend of yours.

NORA: Certainly. But I don't understand —

KROGSTAD: I used to know her too.

NORA: I know you did.

KROGSTAD: Ah! You know all about it. I thought as much. Now, frankly, is Mrs. Linden to have a place in the Bank?

NORA: How dare you catechise me in this way, Mr. Krogstad — you, a subordinate of my husband's? But since you ask, you shall know. Yes, Mrs. Linden is to be employed. And it is I who recommended her, Mr. Krogstad. Now you know.

KROGSTAD: Then my guess was right.

NORA: *(Walking up and down.)* You see one has a wee bit of influence, after all. It doesn't follow because one's only a woman — When people are in a subordinate position, Mr. Krogstad, they ought really to be careful how they offend anybody who — h'm —

KROGSTAD: — who has influence?

NORA: Exactly.

KROGSTAD: *(Taking another tone.)* Mrs. Helmer, will you have the kindness to employ your influence on my behalf?

NORA: What? How do you mean?

KROGSTAD: Will you be so good as to see that I retain my subordinate position in the Bank?

NORA: What do you mean? Who wants to take it from you?

KROGSTAD: Oh, you needn't pretend ignorance. I can very well understand that it cannot be pleasant for your friend to meet me; and I can also understand now for whose sake I am to be hounded out.

NORA: But I assure you —

KROGSTAD: Come, come now, once for all: there is time yet, and I advise you to use your influence to prevent it.

NORA: But, Mr. Krogstad, I have no influence — absolutely none.

KROGSTAD: None? I thought you said a moment ago —

NORA: Of course not in that sense. I! How can you imagine that I should have any such influence over my husband?

KROGSTAD: Oh, I know your husband from our college days. I don't think he is any more inflexible than other husbands.

NORA: If you talk disrespectfully of my husband, I must request you to leave the house.

KROGSTAD: You are bold, madam.

NORA: I am afraid of you no longer. When New Year's Day is over, I shall soon be out of the whole business.

KROGSTAD: *(Controlling himself.)* Listen to me, Mrs. Helmer. If need be, I shall fight as though for my life to keep my little place in the Bank.

NORA: Yes, so it seems.

KROGSTAD: It's not only for the salary: that is what I care least about. It's something else — Well, I had better make a clean breast of it. Of course you know, like every one else, that some years ago I — got into trouble.

NORA: I think I've heard something of the sort.

KROGSTAD: The matter never came into court; but from that moment all paths were barred to me. Then I took up the business you know about. I had to turn my hand to something; and I don't think I've been one of the worst. But now I must get clear of it all. My sons are growing up; for their sake I must try to recover my character as well as I can. This place in the Bank was the first step; and now your husband wants to kick me off the ladder, back into the mire.

NORA: But I assure you, Mr. Krogstad, I haven't the least power to help you.

KROGSTAD: That is because you have not the will; but I can compel you.

NORA: You won't tell my husband that I owe you money?

KROGSTAD: H'm; suppose I were to?

NORA: It would be shameful of you. *(With tears in her voice.)* The secret that is my joy and my pride — that he should learn it in such an ugly, coarse way — and from you. It would involve me in all sorts of unpleasantness —

KROGSTAD: Only unpleasantness?

NORA: *(Hotly.)* But just do it. It's you that will come off worst, for then my husband will see what a bad man you are, and then you certainly won't keep your place.

KROGSTAD: I asked whether it was only domestic unpleasantness you feared?

NORA: If my husband gets to know about it, he will of course pay you off at once, and then we shall have nothing more to do with you.

KROGSTAD: *(Coming a pace nearer.)* Listen, Mrs. Helmer: either your memory is defective, or you don't know much about business. I must make the position a little clearer to you.

NORA: How so?

KROGSTAD: When your husband was ill, you came to me to borrow twelve hundred dollars.

NORA: I knew of nobody else.

KROGSTAD: I promised to find you the money —

NORA: And you did find it.

KROGSTAD: I promised to find you the money, on certain conditions. You were so much taken up at the time about your husband's illness, and so eager to have the wherewithal for your journey, that you probably did not give much thought to the details. Allow me to remind you of them. I promised to find you the amount in exchange for a note of hand, which I drew up.

NORA: Yes, and I signed it.

KROGSTAD: Quite right. But then I added a few lines, making your father security for the debt. Your father was to sign this.

NORA: Was to —? He did sign it!

KROGSTAD: I had left the date blank. That is to say, your father was himself to date his signature. Do you recollect that?

NORA: Yes, I believe —

KROGSTAD: Then I gave you the paper to send to your father, by post. Is not that so?

NORA: Yes.

KROGSTAD: And of course you did so at once; for within five or six days you brought me back the document with your father's signature; and I handed you the money.

NORA: Well? Have I not made my payments punctually?

KROGSTAD: Fairly — yes. But to return to the point: You were in great trouble at the time, Mrs. Helmer.

NORA: I was indeed!

KROGSTAD: Your father was very ill, I believe?

NORA: He was on his death-bed.

KROGSTAD: And died soon after?

NORA: Yes.

KROGSTAD: Tell me, Mrs. Helmer: do you happen to recollect the day of his death? The day of the month, I mean?

NORA: Father died on the 29th of September.

KROGSTAD: Quite correct. I have made inquiries. And here comes in the remarkable point — *(Produces a paper.)* which I cannot explain.

NORA: What remarkable point? I don't know —

KROGSTAD: The remarkable point, madam, that your father signed this paper three days after his death!

NORA: What! I don't understand —

KROGSTAD: Your father died on the 29th of September. But look here: he has dated his signature October 2nd! Is not that remarkable, Mrs. Helmer? *(NORA is silent.)* Can you explain it? *(NORA continues silent.)* It is noteworthy, too, that the words "October 2nd" and the year are not in your father's handwriting, but in one which I believe I know. Well, this may be explained; your father may have forgotten to date his signature, and somebody may have added the date at random, before the fact of your father's death was known. There is nothing wrong in that. Everything depends on the signature. Of course it is genuine, Mrs. Helmer? It was really your father himself who wrote his name here?

NORA: *(After a short silence, throws her head back and looks defiantly at him.)* No, it was not. *I* wrote father's name.

KROGSTAD: Ah! — Are you aware, madam, that that is a dangerous admission?

NORA: How so? You will soon get your money.

KROGSTAD: May I ask you one more question? Why did you not send the paper to your father?

NORA: It was impossible. Father was ill. If I had asked him for his signature, I should have had to tell him why I wanted the money; but he was so ill I really could not tell him that my husband's life was in danger. It was impossible.

KROGSTAD: Then it would have been better to have given up your tour.

NORA: No, I couldn't do that; my husband's life depended on that journey. I couldn't give it up.

KROGSTAD: And did it never occur to you that you were playing me false?

NORA: That was nothing to me. I didn't care in the least about you. I couldn't endure you for all the cruel difficulties you made, although you knew how ill my husband was.

KROGSTAD: Mrs. Helmer, you evidently do not realise what you have been guilty of. But I can assure you it was nothing more and nothing worse that made me an outcast from society.

NORA: You! You want me to believe that you did a brave thing to save your wife's life?

KROGSTAD: The law takes no account of motives.

NORA: Then it must be a very bad law.

KROGSTAD: Bad or not, if I produce this document in court, you will be condemned according to law.

NORA: I don't believe that. Do you mean to tell me that a daughter has no right to spare her dying father trouble and anxiety? — that a wife has no right to save her husband's life? I don't know much about the law, but I'm sure you'll find, somewhere or another, that that is allowed. And you don't know that — you, a lawyer! You must be a bad one, Mr. Krogstad.

KROGSTAD: Possibly. But business — such business as ours — I do understand. You believe that? Very well; now do as you please. But this I may tell you, that if I am flung into the gutter a second time, you shall keep me company. *(Bows and goes out through hall.)*

NORA: *(Stands a while thinking, then tosses her head.)* Oh nonsense! He wants to frighten me. I'm not so foolish as that. *(Begins folding the children's clothes. Pauses.)* But —? No, it's impossible! Why, I did it for love!

CHILDREN: *(At the door, left.)* Mamma, the strange man has gone now.

NORA: Yes, yes, I know. But don't tell any one about the strange man. Do you hear? Not even papa!

CHILDREN: No, mamma; and now will you play with us again?

NORA: No, no; not now.

CHILDREN: Oh, do, mamma; you know you promised.

NORA: Yes, but I can't just now. Run to the nursery; I have so much to do. Run along, run along, and be good, my darlings! *(She pushes them gently into the inner room, and closes the door behind them. Sits on the sofa, embroiders a few stitches, but soon pauses.)* No! *(Throws down the work, rises, goes to the hall door and calls out.)* Ellen, bring in the Christmas-tree! *(Goes to table, left, and opens the drawer; again pauses.)* No, it's quite impossible!

ELLEN: *(With Christmas-tree.)* Where shall I stand it, ma'am?

NORA: There, in the middle of the room.

ELLEN: Shall I bring in anything else?

NORA: No, thank you, I have all I want. *(ELLEN, having put down the tree, goes out.)*

NORA: *(Busy dressing the tree.)* There must be a candle here — and flowers there. — That horrible man! Nonsense, nonsense! there's nothing to be afraid of. The Christmas-tree shall be beautiful. I'll do everything to please you, Torvald; I'll sing and dance, and — *(Enter HELMER by the hall door, with a bundle of documents.)*

NORA: Oh! You're back already?

HELMER: Yes. Has anybody been here?

NORA: Here? No.

HELMER: That's odd. I saw Krogstad come out of the house.

NORA: Did you? Oh, yes, by-the-bye, he was here for a minute.

HELMER: Nora, I can see by your manner that he has been begging you to put in a good word for him.

NORA: Yes.

HELMER: And you were to do it as if of your own accord? You were to say nothing to me of his having been here. Didn't he suggest that too?

NORA: Yes, Torvald; but —

HELMER: Nora, Nora! And you could condescend to that! To speak to such a man, to make him a promise! And then to tell me an untruth about it!

NORA: An untruth!

HELMER: Didn't you say that nobody had been here? *(Threatens with his finger.)* My little bird must never do that again! A song-bird must sing clear and true; no false notes. *(Puts his arm round her.)* That's so, isn't it? Yes, I was sure of it. *(Lets her go.)* And now we'll say no more about it. *(Sits down before the fire.)* Oh, how cosy and quiet it is here! *(Glances into his documents.)*

NORA: *(Busy with the tree, after a short silence.)* Torvald!

HELMER: Yes.

NORA: I'm looking forward so much to the Stenborgs' fancy ball the day after tomorrow.

HELMER: And I'm on tenterhooks to see what surprise you have in store for me.

NORA: Oh, it's too tiresome!

HELMER: What is?

NORA: I can't think of anything good. Everything seems so foolish and meaningless.

HELMER: Has little Nora made that discovery?

NORA: *(Behind his chair, with her arms on the back.)* Are you very busy, Torvald?

HELMER: Well —

NORA: What papers are those?

HELMER: Bank business.

NORA: Already!

HELMER: I have got the retiring manager to let me make some necessary changes in the staff and organization. I can do this during Christmas week. I want to have everything straight by the New Year.

NORA: Then that's why that poor Krogstad —

HELMER: H'm.

NORA: *(Still leaning over the chair-back and slowly stroking his hair.)* If you hadn't been so very busy, I should have asked you a great, great favour, Torvald.

HELMER: What can it be? Out with it.

NORA: Nobody has such perfect taste as you; and I should so love to look well at the fancy ball. Torvald, dear, couldn't you take me in hand, and settle what I'm to be, and arrange my costume for me?

HELMER: Aha! So my wilful little woman is at a loss, and making signals of distress.

NORA: Yes, please, Torvald. I can't get on without your help.

HELMER: Well, well, I'll think it over, and we'll soon hit upon something.

NORA: Oh, how good that is of you! *(Goes to the tree again; pause.)* How well the red flowers show. — Tell me, was it anything so very dreadful this Krogstad got into trouble about?

HELMER: Forgery, that's all. Don't you know what that means?

NORA: Mayn't he have been driven to it by need?

HELMER: Yes; or, like so many others, he may have done it in pure heedlessness. I am not so hard-hearted as to condemn a man absolutely for a single fault.

NORA: No, surely not, Torvald!

HELMER: Many a man can retrieve his character, if he owns his crime and takes the punishment.

NORA: Punishment —?

HELMER: But Krogstad didn't do that. He evaded the law by means of tricks and subterfuges; and that is what has morally ruined him.

NORA: Do you think that —?

HELMER: Just think how a man with a thing of that sort on his conscience must be always lying and canting and shamming. Think of the mask he must wear even towards those who stand nearest him — towards his own wife and children. The effect on the children — that's the most terrible part of it, Nora.

NORA: Why?

HELMER: Because in such an atmosphere of lies home life is poisoned and contaminated in every fibre. Every breath the children draw contains some germ of evil.

NORA: *(Closer behind him.)* Are you sure of that?

HELMER: As a lawyer, my dear, I have seen it often enough. Nearly all cases of early corruption may be traced to lying mothers.

NORA: Why — mothers?

HELMER: It generally comes from the mother's side; but of course the father's influence may act in the same way. Every lawyer knows it too well. And here has this Krogstad been poisoning his own children for years past by a life of lies and hypocrisy — that is why I call him morally ruined. *(Holds out both hands to her.)* So my sweet little Nora must promise not to plead his cause. Shake hands upon it. Come, come, what's this? Give me your hand. That's right. Then it's a bargain. I assure you it would have been impossible for me to work with him. It gives me a positive sense of physical discomfort to come in contact with such people. *(NORA draws her hand away, and moves to the other side of the Christmas-tree.)*

NORA: How warm it is here. And I have so much to do.

HELMER: *(Rises and gathers up his papers.)* Yes, and I must try to get some of these papers looked through before dinner. And I shall think over your costume too. Perhaps I may even find something to hang in gilt paper on the Christmas-tree. *(Lays his hand on her head.)* My precious little song-bird! *(He goes into his room and shuts the door.)*

NORA: *(Softly, after a pause.)* It can't be! It's impossible. It must be impossible!

ANNA: *(At the door, left.)* The little ones are begging so prettily to come to mamma.

NORA: No, no, no; don't let them come to me! Keep them with you, Anna.

ANNA: Very well, ma'am. *(Shuts the door.)*

NORA: *(Pale with terror.)* Corrupt my children! — Poison my home! *(Short pause. She throws back her head.)* It's not true! It can never, never be true!

ACT SECOND

The same room. In the corner, beside the piano, stands the Christmas-tree, stripped, and with the candles burnt out. NORA's outdoor things lie on the sofa.

NORA, alone, is walking about restlessly. At last she stops by the sofa, and takes up her cloak.

NORA: *(Dropping her cloak.)* There's somebody coming! *(Goes to the hall door and listens.)* Nobody; of course nobody will come today, Christmas-day; nor tomorrow either. But perhaps — *(Opens the door and looks out.)* — No, nothing in the letter box; quite empty. *(Comes forward.)* Stuff and nonsense! Of course he won't really do anything. Such a thing couldn't happen. It's impossible! Why, I have three little children. *(ANNA enters from the left, with a large cardboard box.)*

ANNA: I've found the box with the fancy dress at last.

NORA: Thanks; put it down on the table.

ANNA: *(Does so.)* But I'm afraid it's very much out of order.

NORA: Oh, I wish I could tear it into a hundred thousand pieces!

ANNA: Oh, no. It can easily be put to rights — just a little patience.

NORA: I shall go and get Mrs. Linden to help me.

ANNA: Going out again? In such weather as this! You'll catch cold, ma'am, and be ill.

NORA: Worse things might happen. — What are the children doing?

ANNA: They're playing with their Christmas presents, poor little dears; but —

NORA: Do they often ask for me?

ANNA: You see they've been so used to having their mamma with them.

NORA: Yes; but, Anna, I can't have them so much with me in future.

ANNA: Well, little children get used to anything.

NORA: Do you think they do? Do you believe they would forget their mother if she went quite away?

ANNA: Gracious me! Quite away?

NORA: Tell me, Anna — I've so often wondered about it — how could you bring yourself to give your child up to strangers?

ANNA: I had to when I came to nurse my little Miss Nora.

NORA: But how could you make up your mind to it?

ANNA: When I had the chance of such a good place? A poor girl who's been in trouble must take what comes. That wicked man did nothing for me.

NORA: But your daughter must have forgotten you.

ANNA: Oh, no, ma'am, that she hasn't. She wrote to me both when she was confirmed and when she was married.

NORA: *(Embracing her.)* Dear old Anna — you were a good mother to me when I was little.

ANNA: My poor little Nora had no mother but me.

NORA: And if my little ones had nobody else, I'm sure you would — Nonsense, nonsense! *(Opens the box.)* Go in to the children. Now I must — You'll see how lovely I shall be tomorrow.

ANNA: I'm sure there will be no one at the ball so lovely as my Miss Nora. *(She goes into the room on the left.)*

NORA: *(Takes the costume out of the box, but soon throws it down again.)* Oh, if I dared go out. If only nobody would come. If only nothing would happen here in the meantime. Rubbish; nobody is coming. Only not to think. What a delicious muff! Beautiful gloves, beautiful gloves! To forget — to forget! One, two, three, four, five, six — *(With a scream.)* Ah, there they come. *(Goes towards the door, then stands irresolute. MRS. LINDEN enters from the hall, where she has taken off her things.)*

NORA: Oh, it's you, Christina. There's nobody else there? I'm so glad you have come.

MRS. LINDEN: I hear you called at my lodgings.

NORA: Yes, I was just passing. There's something you must help me with. Let us sit here on the sofa — so. Tomorrow evening there's to be a fancy ball at Consul Stenborg's overhead, and Torvald wants me to appear as a Neapolitan fisher-girl, and dance the tarantella; I learned it at Capri.

MRS. LINDEN: I see — quite a performance.

NORA: Yes, Torvald wishes it. Look, this is the costume; Torvald had it made for me in Italy. But now it's all so torn, I don't know —

MRS. LINDEN: Oh, we shall soon set that to rights. It's only the trimming that has come loose here and there. Have you a needle and thread? Ah, here's the very thing.

NORA: Oh, how kind of you.

MRS. LINDEN: *(Sewing.)* So you're to be in costume tomorrow, Nora? I'll tell you what — I shall come in for a moment to see you in all your glory. But I've quite forgotten to thank you for the pleasant evening yesterday.

NORA: *(Rises and walks across the room.)* Oh, yesterday, it didn't seem so pleasant as usual. — You should have come to town a little sooner, Christina. — Torvald has certainly the art of making home bright and beautiful.

MRS. LINDEN: You too, I should think, or you wouldn't be your father's daughter. But tell me — is Doctor Rank always so depressed as he was last evening?

NORA: No, yesterday it was particularly noticeable. You see, he suffers from a dreadful illness. He has spinal consumption, poor fellow. They say his father was a horrible man, who kept mistresses and all sorts of things — so the son has been sickly from his childhood, you understand.

MRS. LINDEN: *(Lets her sewing fall into her lap.)* Why, my darling Nora, how do you come to know such things?

NORA: *(Moving about the room.)* Oh, when one has three children, one sometimes has visits from women who are half — half doctors — and they talk of one thing and another.

MRS. LINDEN: *(Goes on sewing; a short pause.)* Does Doctor Rank come here every day?

NORA: Every day of his life. He has been Torvald's most intimate friend from boyhood, and he's a good friend of mine too. Doctor Rank is quite one of the family.

MRS. LINDEN: But tell me — is he quite sincere? I mean, isn't he rather given to flattering people?

NORA: No, quite the contrary. Why should you think so?

MRS. LINDEN: When you introduced us yesterday he said he had often heard my name; but I noticed afterwards that your husband had no notion who I was. How could Doctor Rank —?

NORA: He was quite right, Christina. You see, Torvald loves me so indescribably, he wants to have me all to himself, as he says. When we were first married he was almost jealous if I even mentioned any of my old friends at home; so naturally I gave up doing it. But I often talk of the old times to Doctor Rank, for he likes to hear about them.

MRS. LINDEN: Listen to me, Nora! You are still a child in many ways. I am older than you, and have had more experience. I'll tell you something? You ought to get clear of all this with Dr. Rank.

NORA: Get clear of what?

MRS. LINDEN: The whole affair, I should say. You were talking yesterday of a rich admirer who was to find you money —

NORA: Yes, one who never existed, worse luck. What then?

MRS. LINDEN: Has Doctor Rank money?

NORA: Yes, he has.

MRS. LINDEN: And nobody to provide for?

NORA: Nobody. But —?

MRS. LINDEN: And he comes here every day?

NORA: Yes, I told you so.

MRS. LINDEN: I should have thought he would have had better taste.

NORA: I don't understand you a bit.

MRS. LINDEN: Don't pretend, Nora. Do you suppose I can't guess who lent you the twelve hundred dollars?

NORA: Are you out of your senses? How can you think such a thing? A friend who comes here every day! Why, the position would be unbearable!

MRS. LINDEN: Then it really is not he?

NORA: No, I assure you. It never for a moment occurred to me — Besides, at that time he had nothing to lend; he came into his property afterwards.

MRS. LINDEN: Well, I believe that was lucky for you, Nora dear.

NORA: No, really, it would never have struck me to ask Doctor Rank — And yet, I'm certain that if I did —

MRS. LINDEN: But of course you never would.

NORA: Of course not. It's inconceivable that it should ever be necessary. But I'm quite sure that if I spoke to Doctor Rank —

MRS. LINDEN: Behind your husband's back?

NORA: I must get clear of the other thing; that's behind his back too. I must get clear of that.

MRS. LINDEN: Yes, yes, I told you so yesterday; but —

NORA: *(Walking up and down.)* A man can manage these things much better than a woman.

MRS. LINDEN: One's own husband, yes.

NORA: Nonsense. *(Stands still.)* When everything is paid, one gets back the paper.

MRS. LINDEN: Of course.

NORA: And can tear it into a hundred thousand pieces, and burn it up, the nasty, filthy thing!

MRS. LINDEN: *(Looks at her fixedly, lays down her work, and rises slowly.)* Nora, you are hiding something from me.

NORA: You can see it in my face?

MRS. LINDEN: Something has happened since yesterday morning. Nora, what is it?

NORA: *(Going towards her.)* Christina —! *(Listens.)* Hush! There's Torvald coming home. Do you mind going into the nursery for the present? Torvald can't bear to see dressmaking going on. Get Anna to help you.

MRS. LINDEN: *(Gathers some of the things together.)* Very well; but I shan't go away until you have told me all about it. *(She goes out to the left, as HELMER enters from the hall.)*

NORA: *(Runs to meet him.)* Oh, how I've been longing for you to come, Torvald dear!

HELMER: Was that the dressmaker —?

NORA: No, Christina. She's helping me with my costume. You'll see how nice I shall look.

HELMER: Yes, wasn't that a happy thought of mine?

NORA: Splendid! But isn't it good of me, too, to have given in to you about the tarantella?

HELMER: *(Takes her under the chin.)* Good of you! To give in to your own husband? Well well, you little madcap, I know you don't mean it. But I won't disturb you. I daresay you want to be "trying on."

NORA: And you are going to work, I suppose?

HELMER: Yes. *(Shows her a bundle of papers.)* Look here. I've just come from the Bank — *(Goes towards his room.)*

NORA: Torvald.

HELMER: *(Stopping.)* Yes?

NORA: If your little squirrel were to beg you for something so prettily —

HELMER: Well?

NORA: Would you do it?

HELMER: I must know first what it is.

NORA: The squirrel would skip about and play all sorts of tricks if you would only be nice and kind.

HELMER: Come, then, out with it.

NORA: Your lark would twitter from morning till night —

HELMER: Oh, that she does in any case.

NORA: I'll be an elf and dance in the moonlight for you, Torvald.

HELMER: Nora — you can't mean what you were hinting at this morning?

NORA: *(Coming nearer.)* Yes, Torvald, I beg and implore you!

HELMER: Have you really the courage to begin that again?

NORA: Yes, yes; for my sake, you must let Krogstad keep his place in the Bank.

HELMER: My dear Nora, it's his place I intend for Mrs. Linden.

NORA: Yes, that's so good of you. But instead of Krogstad, you could dismiss some other clerk.

HELMER: Why, this is incredible obstinacy! Because you have thoughtlessly promised to put in a word for him, I am to —!

NORA: It's not that, Torvald. It's for your own sake. This man writes for the most scurrilous newspapers; you said so yourself. He can do you no end of harm. I'm so terribly afraid of him —

HELMER: Ah, I understand; it's old recollections that are frightening you.

NORA: What do you mean?

HELMER: Of course you're thinking of your father.

NORA: Yes — yes, of course. Only think of the shameful slanders wicked people used to write about father. I believe they would have got him dismissed if you hadn't been sent to look into the thing, and been kind to him, and helped him.

HELMER: My little Nora, between your father and me there is all the difference in the world. Your father was not altogether unimpeachable. I am; and I hope to remain so.

NORA: Oh, no one knows what wicked men may hit upon. We could live so quietly and happily now, in our cosy, peaceful home, you and I and the children, Torvald!

HELMER: And it is just by pleading his cause that you make it impossible for me to keep him. It's already known at the Bank that I intend to dismiss Krogstad. If it were now reported that the new manager let himself be turned round his wife's little finger —

NORA: What then?

HELMER: Oh, nothing, so long as a wilful woman can have her way —! I am to make myself a laughing-stock to the whole staff, and set people saying that I am open to all sorts of outside influence? Take my word for it, I should soon feel the consequences. And besides — there is one thing that makes Krogstad impossible for me to work with —

NORA: What thing?

HELMER: I could perhaps have overlooked his moral failings at a pinch —

NORA: Yes, couldn't you, Torvald?

HELMER: And I hear he is good at his work. But the fact is, he was a college chum of mine — there was one of those rash friendships between us that one so often repents of later. I may as well confess it at once — he calls me by my Christian name;[1] and he is tactless enough to do it even when others are present. He delights in putting on airs of familiarity — Torvald here, Torvald there! I assure you it's most painful to me. He would make my position at the Bank perfectly unendurable.

NORA: Torvald, surely you're not serious?

HELMER: No? Why not?

NORA: That's such a petty reason.

HELMER: What! Petty! Do you consider me petty!

NORA: No, on the contrary, Torvald dear; and that's just why —

HELMER: Never mind; you call my motives petty; then I must be petty too. Petty! Very well! — Now we'll put an end to this, once for all. *(Goes to the door into the hall and calls.)* Ellen!

NORA: What do you want?

HELMER: *(Searching among his papers.)* To settle the thing. *(ELLEN enters.)* Here; take this letter; give it to a messenger. See that he takes it at once. The address is on it. Here's the money.

ELLEN: Very well, sir. *(Goes with the letter.)*

HELMER: *(Putting his papers together.)* There, Madam Obstinacy.

NORA: *(Breathless.)* Torvald — what was in the letter?

HELMER: Krogstad's dismissal.

NORA: Call it back again, Torvald! There's still time. Oh, Torvald, call it back again! For my sake, for your own, for the children's sake! Do you hear, Torvald? Do it! You don't know what that letter may bring upon us all.

HELMER: Too late.

NORA: Yes, too late.

HELMER: My dear Nora, I forgive your anxiety, though it's anything but flattering to me. Why should you suppose that *I* would be afraid of a wretched scribbler's spite? But I forgive you all the same, for it's a proof of your great love for me. *(Takes her in his arms.)* That's as it should be, my own dear Nora. Let what will happen — when it comes to the pinch, I shall have strength and courage enough. You shall see; my shoulders are broad enough to bear the whole burden.

NORA: *(Terror-struck.)* What do you mean by that?

HELMER: The whole burden, I say —

NORA: *(With decision.)* That you shall never, never do!

HELMER: Very well; then we'll share it, Nora, as man and wife. That is

[1] In the original, "We say 'thou' to each other."

how it should be. *(Petting her.)* Are you satisfied now? Come, come, come, don't look like a scared dove. It's all nothing — foolish fancies. — Now you ought to play the tarantella through and practise with the tambourine. I shall sit in my inner room and shut both doors, so that I shall hear nothing. You can make as much noise as you please. *(Turns round in doorway.)* And when Rank comes, just tell him where I'm to be found. *(He nods to her, and goes with his papers into his room, closing the door.)*

NORA: *(Bewildered with terror, stands as though rooted to the ground, and whispers.)* He would do it. Yes, he would do it. He would do it, in spite of all the world. — No, never that, never, never! Anything rather than that! Oh, for some way of escape! What shall I do —! *(Hall bells rings.)* Doctor Rank —! — Anything, anything, rather than —! *(NORA draws her hands over her face, pulls herself together, goes to the door and opens it. RANK stands outside hanging up his fur coat. During what follows it begins to grow dark.)*

NORA: Good afternoon, Doctor Rank, I knew you by your ring. But you mustn't go to Torvald now. I believe he's busy.

RANK: And you? *(Enters and closes the door.)*

NORA: Oh, you know very well, I have always time for you.

RANK: Thank you. I shall avail myself of your kindness as long as I can.

NORA: What do you mean? As long as you can?

RANK: Yes. Does that frighten you?

NORA: I think it's an odd expression. Do you expect anything to happen?

RANK: Something I have long been prepared for; but I didn't think it would come so soon.

NORA: *(Catching at his arm.)* What have you discovered? Doctor Rank, you must tell me!

RANK: *(Sitting down by the stove.)* I am running down hill. There's no help for it.

NORA: *(Draws a long breath of relief.)* It's you —?

RANK: Who else should it be? — Why lie to one's self? I am the most wretched of all my patients, Mrs. Helmer. In these last days I have been auditing my life-account — bankrupt! Perhaps before a month is over, I shall lie rotting in the church-yard.

NORA: Oh! What an ugly way to talk.

RANK: The thing itself is so confoundedly ugly, you see. But the worst of it is, so many other ugly things have to be gone through first. There is only one last investigation to be made, and when that is over I shall know pretty certainly when the break-up will begin. There's one thing I want to say to you: Helmer's delicate nature shrinks so from all that is horrible: I will not have him in my sick-room —

NORA: But, Doctor Rank —

RANK: I won't have him, I say — not on any account! I shall lock my door against him. — As soon as I am quite certain of the worst, I shall send you my visiting-card with a black cross on it; and then you will know that the final horror has begun.

NORA: Why, you're perfectly unreasonable today; and I did so want you to be in a really good humour.

RANK: With death staring me in the face? — And to suffer thus for another's sin! Where's the justice of it? And in one way or another you can trace in every family some such inexorable retribution —

NORA: *(Stopping her ears.)* Nonsense, nonsense! Now cheer up!

RANK: Well, after all, the whole thing's only worth laughing at. My poor innocent spine must do penance for my father's wild oats.

NORA: *(At table, left.)* I suppose he was too fond of asparagus and Strasbourg pâté, wasn't he?

RANK: Yes; and truffles.

NORA: Yes, truffles, to be sure. And oysters, I believe?

RANK: Yes, oysters; oysters, of course.

NORA: And then all the port and champagne! It's sad that all these good things should attack the spine.

RANK: Especially when the luckless spine attacked never had any good of them.

NORA: Ah, yes, that's the worst of it.

RANK: *(Looks at her searchingly.)* H'm —

NORA: *(A moment later.)* Why did you smile?

RANK: No; it was you that laughed.

NORA: No; it was you that smiled, Doctor Rank.

RANK: *(Standing up.)* I see you're deeper than I thought.

NORA: I'm in such a crazy mood today.

RANK: So it seems.

NORA: *(With her hands on his shoulders.)* Dear, dear Doctor Rank, death shall not take you away from Torvald and me.

RANK: Oh, you'll easily get over the loss. The absent are soon forgotten.

NORA: *(Looks at him anxiously.)* Do you think so?

RANK: People make fresh ties, and then —

NORA: Who make fresh ties?

RANK: You and Helmer will, when I am gone. You yourself are taking time by the forelock, it seems to me. What was that Mrs. Linden doing here yesterday?

NORA: Oh! — you're surely not jealous of poor Christina?

RANK: Yes, I am. She will be my successor in this house. When I am out of the way, this woman will perhaps —

NORA: Hush! Not so loud! She's in there.

RANK: Today as well? You see!

NORA: Only to put my costume in order — dear me, how unreasonable you are! *(Sits on sofa.)* Now do be good, Doctor Rank! Tomorrow you shall see how beautiful I shall dance; and then you may fancy that I'm doing it all to please you — and of course Torvald as well. *(Takes various things out of box.)* Doctor Rank, sit down here, and I'll show you something.

RANK: *(Sitting.)* What is it?

NORA: Look here. Look!

RANK: Silk stockings.

NORA: Flesh-coloured. Aren't they lovely? It's so dark here now; but tomorrow — No, no, no; you must only look at the feet. Oh, well, I suppose you may look at the rest too.

RANK: H'm —

NORA: What are you looking so critical about? Do you think they won't fit me?

RANK: I can't possibly give any competent opinion on that point.

NORA: *(Looking at him a moment.)* For shame! *(Hits him lightly on the ear with the stockings.)* Take that. *(Rolls them up again.)*

RANK: And what other wonders am I to see?

NORA: You sha'n't see anything more; for you don't behave nicely. *(She hums a little and searches among the things.)*

RANK: *(After a short silence.)* When I sit here gossiping with you, I can't imagine — I simply cannot conceive — what would have become of me if I had never entered this house.

NORA: *(Smiling.)* Yes, I think you do feel at home with us.

RANK: *(More softly — looking straight before him.)* And now to have to leave it all —

NORA: Nonsense. You sha'n't leave us.

RANK: *(In the same tone.)* And not to be able to leave behind the slightest token of gratitude; scarcely even a passing regret — nothing but an empty place, that can be filled by the first comer.

NORA: And if I were to ask you for —? No —

RANK: For what?

NORA: For a great proof of your friendship.

RANK: Yes — yes?

NORA: I mean — for a very, very great service —

RANK: Would you really, for once, make me so happy?

NORA: Oh, you don't know what it is.

RANK: Then tell me.

NORA: No, I really can't, Doctor Rank. It's far, far too much — not only a service, but help and advice besides —

RANK: So much the better. I can't think what you can mean. But go on. Don't you trust me?

NORA: As I trust no one else. I know you are my best and truest friend. So I will tell you. Well then, Doctor Rank, there is something you must help me to prevent. You know how deeply, how wonderfully Torvald loves me; he wouldn't hesitate a moment to give his very life for my sake.

RANK: *(Bending towards her.)* Nora — do you think he is the only one who —?

NORA: *(With a slight start.)* Who —?

RANK: Who would gladly give his life for you?

NORA: *(Sadly.)* Oh!

RANK: I have sworn that you shall know it before I — go. I shall never find a better opportunity. — Yes, Nora, now I have told you; and now you know that you can trust me as you can no one else.

NORA: *(Standing up; simply and calmly.)* Let me pass, please.

RANK: *(Makes way for her, but remains sitting.)* Nora —

NORA: *(In the doorway.)* Ellen, bring the lamp. *(Crosses to the stove.)* Oh dear, Doctor Rank, that was too bad of you.

RANK: *(Rising.)* That I have loved you as deeply as — any one else? Was that too bad of me?

NORA: No, but that you should have told me so. It was so unnecessary —

RANK: What do you mean? Did you know —? *(ELLEN enters with the lamp; sets it on the table and goes out again.)*

RANK: Nora — Mrs. Helmer — I ask you, did you know?

NORA: Oh, how can I tell what I knew or didn't know? I really can't say — How could you be so clumsy, Doctor Rank? It was all so nice!

RANK: Well, at any rate, you know now that I am at your service, body and soul. And now, go on.

NORA: *(Looking at him.)* Go on — now?

RANK: I beg you to tell me what you want.

NORA: I can tell you nothing now.

RANK: Yes, yes! You mustn't punish me in that way. Let me do for you whatever a man can.

NORA: You can do nothing for me now. — Besides, I really want no help. You shall see it was only my fancy. Yes, it must be so. Of course! *(Sits in the rocking chair, looks at him and smiles.)* You are a nice person, Doctor Rank! Aren't you ashamed of yourself, now that the lamp is on the table?

RANK: No; not exactly. But perhaps I ought to go — for ever.

NORA: No, indeed you mustn't. Of course you must come and go as you've always done. You know very well that Torvald can't do without you.

RANK: Yes, but you?

NORA: Oh, you know I always like to have you here.

RANK: That is just what led me astray. You are a riddle to me. It has often seemed to me as if you liked being with me almost as much as being with Helmer.

NORA: Yes; don't you see? There are people one loves, and others one likes to talk to.

RANK: Yes — there's something in that.

NORA: When I was a girl, of course I loved papa best. But it always delighted me to steal into the servants' room. In the first place they never lectured me, and in the second it was such fun to hear them talk.

RANK: Ah, I see; then it's their place I have taken?

NORA: *(Jumps up and hurries towards him.)* Oh, my dear Doctor Rank, I don't mean that. But you understand, with Torvald it's the same as with papa — *(ELLEN enters from the hall.)*

ELLEN: Please, ma'am — *(Whispers to NORA, and gives her a card.)*

NORA: *(Glancing at card.)* Ah! *(Puts it in her pocket.)*

RANK: Anything wrong?

NORA: No, no, not in the least. It's only — it's my new costume —

RANK: Your costume! Why, it's there.

NORA: Oh, that one, yes. But this is another that — I have ordered it — Torvald mustn't know —

RANK: Aha! So that's the great secret.

NORA: Yes, of course. Please go to him; he's in the inner room. Do keep him while I —

RANK: Don't be alarmed; he sha'n't escape. *(Goes into HELMER's room.)*

NORA: *(To ELLEN.)* Is he waiting in the kitchen?

ELLEN: Yes, he came up the back stair —

NORA: Didn't you tell him I was engaged?

ELLEN: Yes, but it was no use.

NORA: He won't go away?

ELLEN: No, ma'am, not until he has spoken to you.

NORA: Then let him come in; but quietly. And, Ellen — say nothing about it; it's a surprise for my husband.

ELLEN: Oh, yes, ma'am, I understand. *(She goes out.)*

NORA: It is coming! The dreadful thing is coming, after all. No, no, no, it can never be; it shall not! *(She goes to HELMER's door and slips the bolt. ELLEN opens the hall door for KROGSTAD, and shuts it after him. He wears a travelling-coat, high boots, and a fur cap.)*

NORA: *(Goes towards him.)* Speak softly; my husband is at home.

KROGSTAD: All right. That's nothing to me.

NORA: What do you want?

KROGSTAD: A little information.

NORA: Be quick then. What is it?

KROGSTAD: You know I have got my dismissal.

NORA: I couldn't prevent it, Mr. Krogstad. I fought for you to the last, but it was of no use.

KROGSTAD: Does your husband care for you so little? He knows what I can bring upon you, and yet he dares —

NORA: How could you think I should tell him?

KROGSTAD: Well, as a matter of fact, I didn't think it. It wasn't like my friend Torvald Helmer to show so much courage —

NORA: Mr. Krogstad, be good enough to speak respectfully of my husband.

KROGSTAD: Certainly, with all due respect. But since you are so anxious to keep the matter secret, I suppose you are a little clearer than yesterday as to what you have done.

NORA: Clearer than you could ever make me.

KROGSTAD: Yes, such a bad lawyer as I —

NORA: What is it you want?

KROGSTAD: Only to see how you are getting on, Mrs. Helmer. I've been thinking about you all day. Even a mere money-lender, a gutter-journalist, a — in short, a creature like me — has a little bit of what people call feeling.

NORA: Then show it; think of my little children.

KROGSTAD: Did you and your husband think of mine? But enough of that. I only wanted to tell you that you needn't take this matter too seriously. I shall not lodge any information, for the present.

NORA: No, surely not. I knew you wouldn't.

KROGSTAD: The whole thing can be settled quite amicably. Nobody need know. It can remain among us three.

NORA: My husband must never know.

KROGSTAD: How can you prevent it? Can you pay off the balance?

NORA: No, not at once.

KROGSTAD: Or have you any means of raising the money in the next few days?

NORA: None — that I will make use of.

KROGSTAD: And if you had, it would not help you now. If you offered me ever so much money down, you should not get back your I.O.U.

NORA: Tell me what you want to do with it.

KROGSTAD: I only want to keep it — to have it in my possession. No outsider shall hear anythying of it. So, if you have any desperate scheme in your head —

NORA: What if I have?

KROGSTAD: If you should think of leaving your husband and children —

NORA: What if I do?

KROGSTAD: Or if you should think of — something worse —

NORA: How do you know that?

KROGSTAD: Put all that out of your head.

NORA: How did you know what I had in my mind?

KROGSTAD: Most of us think of that at first. I thought of it, too; but I hadn't the courage —

NORA: *(Tonelessly.)* Nor I.

KROGSTAD: *(Relieved.)* No, one hasn't. You haven't the courage either, have you?

NORA: I haven't, I haven't.

KROGSTAD: Besides, it would be very foolish. — Just one domestic storm, and it's all over. I have a letter in my pocket for your husband —

NORA: Telling him everything?

KROGSTAD: Sparing you as much as possible.

NORA: *(Quickly.)* He must never read that letter. Tear it up, I will manage to get the money somehow —

KROGSTAD: Pardon me, Mrs. Helmer, but I believe I told you —

NORA: Oh, I'm not talking about the money I owe you. Tell me how much you demand from my husband — I will get it.

KROGSTAD: I demand no money from your husband.

NORA: What do you demand then?

KROGSTAD: I will tell you. I want to regain my footing in the world. I want to rise; and your husband shall help me to do it. For the last eighteen months my record has been spotless; I have been in bitter need all the time; but I was content to fight my way up, step by step. Now, I've been thrust down again, and I will not be satisfied with merely being reinstated as a matter of grace. I want to rise, I tell you. I must get into the Bank again, in a higher position than before. Your husband shall create a place on purpose for me —

NORA: He will never do that!

KROGSTAD: He will do it; I know him — he won't dare to show fight! And when he and I are together there, you shall soon see! Before a year is out I shall be the manager's right hand. It won't be Torvald Helmer, but Nils Krogstad, that manages the Joint Stock Bank.

NORA: That shall never be.

KROGSTAD: Perhaps you will —?

NORA: Now I have the courage for it.

KROGSTAD: Oh, you don't frighten me! A sensitive, petted creature like you —

NORA: You shall see, you shall see!

KROGSTAD: Under the ice, perhaps? Down into the cold, black water? And next spring to come up again, ugly, hairless, unrecognisable —

NORA: You can't terrify me.

KROGSTAD: Nor you me. People don't do that sort of thing, Mrs. Helmer. And, after all, what would be the use of it? I have your husband in my pocket, all the same.

NORA: Afterwards? When I am no longer —?

KROGSTAD: You forget, your reputation remains in my hands! *(NORA stands speechless and looks at him.)* Well, now you are prepared. Do nothing foolish. As soon as Helmer has received my letter, I shall expect to hear from him. And remember that it is your husband himself who has forced me back again into such paths. That I will never forgive him. Good-bye, Mrs. Helmer. *(Goes out through the hall. NORA hurries to the door, opens it a little, and listens.)*
NORA: He's going. He's not putting the letter into the box. No, no, it would be impossible! *(Opens the door further and further.)* What's that? He's standing still; not going down stairs. Has he changed his mind? Is he —? *(A letter falls into the box. KROGSTAD's footsteps are heard, gradually receding down the stair. NORA utters a suppressed shriek, and rushes forward towards the sofa-table; pause.)* In the letter-box! *(Slips shrinkingly up to the hall door.)* There it lies. — Torvald, Torvald — now we are lost! *(MRS. LINDEN enters from the left with the costume.)*
MRS. LINDEN: There, I think it's all right now. Shall we just try it on?
NORA: *(Hoarsely and softly.)* Christina, come here.
MRS. LINDEN: *(Throws down the dress on the sofa.)* What's the matter? You look quite distracted.
NORA: Come here. Do you see that letter? There, see — through the glass of the letter-box.
MRS. LINDEN: Yes, yes, I see it.
NORA: That letter is from Krogstad —
MRS. LINDEN: Nora — it was Krogstad who lent you the money?
NORA: Yes; and now Torvald will know everything.
MRS. LINDEN: Believe me, Nora, it's the best thing for both of you.
NORA: You don't know all yet. I have forged a name —
MRS. LINDEN: Good heavens!
NORA: Now, listen to me, Christina, you shall bear me witness —
MRS. LINDEN: How "witness"? What am I to —?
NORA: If I should go out of my mind — it might easily happen —
MRS. LINDEN: Nora!
NORA: Or if anything else should happen to me — so that I couldn't be here —!
MRS. LINDEN: Nora, Nora, you're quite beside yourself!
NORA: In case any one wanted to take it all upon himself — the whole blame — you understand —
MRS. LINDEN: Yes, yes; but how can you think —?
NORA: You shall bear witness that it's not true, Christina. I'm not out of my mind at all; I know quite well what I'm saying; and I tell you nobody else knew anything about it; I did the whole thing, I myself. Remember that.
MRS. LINDEN: I shall remember. But I don't understand what you mean —
NORA: Oh, how should you? It's the miracle coming to pass.
MRS. LINDEN: The miracle?
NORA: Yes, the miracle. But it's so terrible, Christina; it mustn't happen for all the world.
MRS. LINDEN: I shall go straight to Krogstad and talk to him.
NORA: Don't; he'll do you some harm.
MRS. LINDEN: Once he would have done anything for me.

NORA: He?

MRS. LINDEN: Where does he live?

NORA: Oh, how can I tell —? Yes — *(Feels in her pocket.)* Here's his card. But the letter, the letter —!

HELMER: *(Knocking outside.)* Nora!

NORA: *(Shrieks in terror.)* Oh, what is it? What do you want?

HELMER: Well, well, don't be frightened. We're not coming in; you've bolted the door. Are you trying on your dress?

NORA: Yes, yes, I'm trying it on. It suits me so well, Torvald.

MRS. LINDEN: *(Who has read the card.)* Why, he lives close by here.

NORA: Yes, but it's no use now. We are lost. The letter is there in the box.

MRS. LINDEN: And your husband has the key?

NORA: Always.

MRS. LINDEN: Krogstad must demand his letter back, unread. He must find some pretext —

NORA: But this is the very time when Torvald generally —

MRS. LINDEN: Prevent him. Keep him occupied. I shall come back as quickly as I can. *(She goes out hastily by the hall door.)*

NORA: *(Opens HELMER's door and peeps in.)* Torvald!

HELMER: Well, may one come into one's own room again at last? Come, Rank, we'll have a look — *(In the doorway.)* But how's this?

NORA: What, Torvald dear?

HELMER: Rank led me to expect a grand transformation.

RANK: *(In the doorway.)* So I understood. I suppose I was mistaken.

NORA: No, no one shall see me in my glory till tomorrow evening.

HELMER: Why, Nora dear, you look so tired. Have you been practising too hard?

NORA: No, I haven't practised at all yet.

HELMER: But you'll have to —

NORA: Oh yes, I must, I must! But, Torvald, I can't get on at all without your help. I've forgotten everything.

HELMER: Oh, we shall soon freshen it up again.

NORA: Yes, do help me, Torvald. You must promise me — Oh, I'm so nervous about it. Before so many people — This evening you must give yourself up entirely to me. You mustn't do a stroke of work; you mustn't even touch a pen. Do promise, Torvald dear!

HELMER: I promise. All this evening I shall be your slave. Little helpless thing —! But, by-the-bye, I must just — *(Going to hall door.)*

NORA: What do you want there?

HELMER: Only to see if there are any letters.

NORA: No, no, don't do that, Torvald.

HELMER: Why not?

NORA: Torvald, I beg you not to. There are none there.

HELMER: Let me just see. *(Is going. NORA, at the piano, plays the first bars of the tarantella.)*

HELMER: *(At the door, stops.)* Aha!

NORA: I can't dance tomorrow if I don't rehearse with you first.

HELMER: *(Going to her.)* Are you really so nervous, dear Nora?

NORA: Yes, dreadfully! Let me rehearse at once. We have time before dinner. Oh, do sit down and play for me, Torvald dear; direct me and put me right, as you used to do.

HELMER: With all the pleasure in life, since you wish it. *(Sits at piano. NORA snatches the tambourine out of the box, and hurriedly drapes herself in a long parti-coloured shawl; then, with a bound, stands in the middle of the floor.)*

NORA: Now play for me! Now I'll dance! *(HELMER plays and NORA dances. RANK stands at the piano behind HELMER and looks on.)*

HELMER: *(Playing.)* Slower! Slower!

NORA: Can't do it slower!

HELMER: Not so violently, Nora.

NORA: I must! I must!

HELMER: *(Stops.)* No, no, Nora — that will never do.

NORA: *(Laughs and swings her tambourine.)* Didn't I tell you so!

RANK: Let me play for her.

HELMER: *(Rising.)* Yes, do — then I can direct her better. *(RANK sits down to the piano and plays; NORA dances more and more wildly. HELMER stands by the stove and addresses frequent corrections to her; she seems not to hear. Her hair breaks loose, and falls over her shoulders. She does not notice it, but goes on dancing. MRS. LINDEN enters and stands spellbound in the doorway.)*

MRS. LINDEN: Ah —!

NORA: *(Dancing.)* We're having such fun here, Christina!

HELMER: Why, Nora dear, you're dancing as if it were a matter of life and death.

NORA: So it is.

HELMER: Rank, stop! This is the merest madness. Stop, I say! *(RANK stops playing, and NORA comes to a sudden standstill.)*

HELMER: *(Going towards her.)* I couldn't have believed it. You've positively forgotten all I've taught you.

NORA: *(Throws the tambourine away.)* You see for yourself.

HELMER: You really do want teaching.

NORA: Yes, you see how much I need it. You must practise with me up to the last moment. Will you promise me, Torvald?

HELMER: Certainly, certainly.

NORA: Neither today nor tomorrow must you think of anything but me. You mustn't open a single letter — mustn't look at the letter-box.

HELMER: Ah, you're still afraid of that man —

NORA: Oh yes, yes, I am.

HELMER: Nora, I can see it in your face — there's a letter from him in the box.

NORA: I don't know. I believe so. But you're not to read anything now; nothing ugly must come between us until all is over.

RANK: *(Softly, to HELMER.)* You mustn't contradict her.

HELMER: *(Putting his arm around her.)* The child shall have her own way. But tomorrow night, when the dance is over —

NORA: Then you shall be free. *(ELLEN appears in the doorway, right.)*

ELLEN: Dinner is on the table, ma'am.

NORA: We'll have some champagne, Ellen.

ELLEN: Yes, ma'am. *(Goes out.)*

HELMER: Dear me! Quite a banquet.

NORA: Yes, and we'll keep it up till morning. *(Calling out.)* And macaroons, Ellen — plenty — just this once.

HELMER: *(Seizing her hand.)* Come, come, don't let us have this wild excitement! Be my own little lark again.

NORA: Oh yes, I will. But now go into the dining room; and you too, Doctor Rank, Christina, you must help me to do up my hair.

RANK: *(Softly, as they go.)* There's nothing in the wind? Nothing — I mean —?

HELMER: Oh no, nothing of the kind. It's merely this babyish anxiety I was telling you about. *(They go out to the right.)*

NORA: Well?

MRS. LINDEN: He's gone out of town.

NORA: I saw it in your face.

MRS. LINDEN: He comes back tomorrow evening. I left a note for him.

NORA: You shouldn't have done that. Things must take their course. After all, there's something glorious in waiting for the miracle.

MRS. LINDEN: What is it you're waiting for?

NORA: Oh, you can't understand. Go to them in the dining-room; I shall come in a moment. *(MRS. LINDEN goes into the dining-room. NORA stands for a moment as though collecting her thoughts; then looks at her watch.)*

NORA: Five. Seven hours till midnight. Then twenty-four hours till the next midnight. Then the tarantella will be over. Twenty-four and seven? Thirty-one hours to live. *(HELMER appears at the door, right.)*

HELMER: What has become of my little lark?

NORA: *(Runs to him with open arms.)* Here she is!

ACT THIRD

The same room. The table, with the chairs around it, in the middle. A lighted lamp on the table. The door to the hall stands open. Dance music is heard from the floor above.

MRS. LINDEN sits by the table and absently turns the pages of a book. She tries to read, but seems unable to fix her attention; she frequently listens and looks anxiously towards the hall door.

MRS. LINDEN: *(Looks at her watch.)* Not here yet; and the time is nearly up. If only he hasn't — *(Listens again.)* Ah, there he is. *(She goes into the hall and cautiously opens the outer door; soft footsteps are heard on the stairs; she whispers.)* Come in; there is no one here.

KROGSTAD: *(In the doorway.)* I found a note from you at my house. What does it mean?

MRS. LINDEN: I must speak to you.

KROGSTAD: Indeed? And in this house?

MRS. LINDEN: I could not see you at my rooms. They have no separate entrance. Come in; we are quite alone. The servants are asleep, and the Helmers are at the ball upstairs.

KROGSTAD: *(Coming into the room.)* Ah! So the Helmers are dancing this evening? Really?

MRS. LINDEN: Yes. Why not?

KROGSTAD: Quite right. Why not?

MRS. LINDEN: And now let us talk a little.
KROGSTAD: Have we two anything to say to each other?
MRS. LINDEN: A great deal.
KROGSTAD: I should not have thought so.
MRS. LINDEN: Because you have never really understood me.
KROGSTAD: What was there to understand? The most natural thing in the world — a heartless woman throws a man over when a better match offers.
MRS. LINDEN: Do you really think me so heartless? Do you think I broke with you lightly?
KROGSTAD: Did you not?
MRS. LINDEN: Do you really think so?
KROGSTAD: If not, why did you write me that letter?
MRS. LINDEN: Was it not best? Since I had to break with you, was it not right that I should try to put an end to all that you felt for me?
KROGSTAD: *(Clenching his hands together.)* So that was it? And all this — for the sake of money!
MRS. LINDEN: You ought not to forget that I had a helpless mother and two little brothers. We could not wait for you, Nils, as your prospects then stood.
KROGSTAD: Perhaps not; but you had no right to cast me off for the sake of others, whoever the others might be.
MRS. LINDEN: I don't know. I have often asked myself whether I had the right.
KROGSTAD: *(More softly.)* When I had lost you, I seemed to have no firm ground left under my feet. Look at me now. I am a shipwrecked man clinging to a spar.
MRS. LINDEN: Rescue may be at hand.
KROGSTAD: It was at hand; but then you came and stood in the way.
MRS. LINDEN: Without my knowledge, Nils. I did not know till today that it was you I was to replace in the Bank.
KROGSTAD: Well, I take your word for it. But now that you do know, do you mean to give way?
MRS. LINDEN: No, for that would not help you in the least.
KROGSTAD: Oh, help, help —! I should do it whether or no.
MRS. LINDEN: I have learnt prudence. Life and bitter necessity have schooled me.
KROGSTAD: And life has taught me not to trust fine speeches.
MRS. LINDEN: Then life has taught you a very sensible thing. But deeds you will trust?
KROGSTAD: What do you mean?
MRS. LINDEN: You said you were a shipwrecked man, clinging to a spar.
KROGSTAD: I have good reason to say so.
MRS. LINDEN: I too am shipwrecked, and clinging to a spar. I have no one to mourn for, no one to care for.
KROGSTAD: You made your own choice.
MRS. LINDEN: No choice was left me.
KROGSTAD: Well, what then?
MRS. LINDEN: Nils, how if we two shipwrecked people could join hands?
KROGSTAD: What!

MRS. LINDEN: Two on a raft have a better chance then if each clings to a separate spar.

KROGSTAD: Christina!

MRS. LINDEN: What do you think brought me to town?

KROGSTAD: Had you any thought of me?

MRS. LINDEN: I must have work or I can't bear to live. All my life, as long as I can remember, I have worked; work has been my one great joy. Now I stand quite alone in the world, aimless and forlorn. There is no happiness in working for one's self. Nils, give me somebody and something to work for.

KROGSTAD: I cannot believe in all this. It is simply a woman's romantic craving for self-sacrifice.

MRS. LINDEN: Have you ever found me romantic?

KROGSTAD: Would you really —? Tell me: do you know all my past?

MRS. LINDEN: Yes.

KROGSTAD: And do you know what people say of me?

MRS. LINDEN: Did you not say just now that with me you could have been another man?

KROGSTAD: I am sure of it.

MRS. LINDEN: Is it too late?

KROGSTAD: Christina, do you know what you are doing? Yes, you do; I see it in your face. Have you the courage then —?

MRS. LINDEN: I need some one to be a mother to, and your children need a mother. You need me, and I — I need you. Nils, I believe in your better self. With you I fear nothing.

KROGSTAD: *(Seizing her hands.)* Thank you — thank you, Christina. Now I shall make others see me as you do. — Ah, I forgot —

MRS. LINDEN: *(Listening.)* Hush! The tarantella! Go! Go!

KROGSTAD: Why? What is it?

MRS. LINDEN: Don't you hear the dancing overhead? As soon as that is over they will be here.

KROGSTAD: Oh yes, I shall go. Nothing will come of this, after all. Of course, you don't know the step I have taken against the Helmers.

MRS. LINDEN: Yes, Nils, I do know.

KROGSTAD: And yet you have the courage to —?

NORA: I know to what lengths despair can drive a man.

KROGSTAD: Oh, if I could only undo it!

MRS. LINDEN: You could. Your letter is still in the box.

KROGSTAD: Are you sure?

MRS. LINDEN: Yes; but —

KROGSTAD: *(Looking to her searchingly.)* Is that what it all means? You want to save your friend at any price. Say it out — is that your idea?

MRS. LINDEN: Nils, a woman who has once sold herself for the sake of others, does not do so again.

KROGSTAD: I shall demand my letter back again.

MRS. LINDEN: No, no.

KROGSTAD: Yes, of course. I shall wait till Helmer comes; I shall tell him to give it back to me — that it's only about my dismissal — that I don't want it read —

MRS. LINDEN: No, Nils you must not recall the letter.

KROGSTAD: But tell me, wasn't that just why you got me to come here?

MRS. LINDEN: Yes, in my first alarm. But a day has passed since then, and in that day I have seen incredible things in this house. Helmer must know everything; there must be an end to this unhappy secret. These two must come to a full understanding. They must have done with all these shifts and subterfuges.

KROGSTAD: Very well, if you like to risk it. But one thing I can do, and at once —

MRS. LINDEN: *(Listening.)* Make haste! Go, go! The dance is over; we're not safe another moment.

KROGSTAD: I shall wait for you in the street.

MRS. LINDEN: Yes, do; you must see me home.

KROGSTAD: I never was so happy in all my life! *(KROGSTAD goes out by the outer door. The door between the room and the hall remains open.)*

MRS. LINDEN: *(Arranging the room and getting her outdoor things together.)* What a change! What a change! To have some one to work for, to live for; a home to make happy! Well, it shall not be my fault if I fail. — I wish they would come. — *(Listens.)* Ah, here they are! I must get my things on. *(Takes bonnet and cloak. HELMER's and NORA's voices are heard outside, a key is turned in the lock, and HELMER drags NORA almost by force into the hall. She wears the Italian costume with a large black shawl over it. He is in evening dress and wears a black domino, open.)*

NORA: *(Struggling with him in the doorway.)* No, no, no! I won't go in! I want to go upstairs again; I don't want to leave so early!

HELMER: But, my dearest girl —!

NORA: Oh, please, please, Torvald, I beseech you — only one hour more!

HELMER: Not one minute more, Nora dear; you know what we agreed. Come, come in; you're catching cold here. *(He leads her gently into the room in spite of her resistance.)*

MRS. LINDEN: Good-evening.

NORA: Christina!

HELMER: What, Mrs. Linden! You here so late?

MRS. LINDEN: Yes, I ought to apologise. I did so want to see Nora in her costume.

NORA: Have you been sitting here waiting for me?

MRS. LINDEN: Yes; unfortunately I came too late. You had gone upstairs already, and I felt I couldn't go away without seeing you.

HELMER: *(Taking NORA's shawl off.)* Well then, just look at her! I assure you she's worth it. Isn't she lovely, Mrs. Linden?

MRS. LINDEN: Yes, I must say —

HELMER: Isn't she exquisite? Every one said so. But she's dreadfully obstinate, dear little creature. What's to be done with her? Just think, I had almost to force her away.

NORA: Oh, Torvald, you'll be sorry some day that you didn't let me stay, if only for one half-hour more.

HELMER: There! You hear her, Mrs. Linden? She dances her tarantella with wild applause, and well she deserved it, I must say — though there was, perhaps, a little too much nature in her rendering of the idea — more than was, strictly speaking, artistic. But never mind —

the point is, she made a great success, a tremendous success. Was I to let her remain after that — to weaken the impression? Not if I know it. I took my sweet little Capri girl — my capricious little Capri girl, I might say — under my arm; a rapid turn round the room, a curtsey to all sides, and — as they say in novels — the lovely apparition vanished! An exit should always be effective, Mrs. Linden; but I can't get Nora to see it. By Jove! it's warm here. *(Throws his domino on a chair and opens the door to his room.)* What! No light there? Oh, of course. Excuse me — *(Goes in and lights candles.)*

NORA: *(Whispers breathlessly.)* Well?

MRS. LINDEN: *(Softly.)* I've spoken to him.

NORA: And —?

MRS. LINDEN: Nora — you must tell your husband everything —

NORA: *(Tonelessly.)* I knew it!

MRS. LINDEN: You have nothing to fear from Krogstad; but you must speak out.

NORA: I shall not speak.

MRS. LINDEN: Then the letter will.

NORA: Thank you, Christina. Now I know what I have to do. Hush —!

HELMER: *(Coming back.)* Well, Mrs. Linden, have you admired her?

MRS. LINDEN: Yes; and now I must say good-night.

HELMER: What, already? Does this knitting belong to you?

MRS. LINDEN: *(Takes it.)* Yes, thanks; I was nearly forgetting it.

HELMER: Then you do knit?

MRS. LINDEN: Yes.

HELMER: Do you know, you ought to embroider instead?

MRS. LINDEN: Indeed! Why?

HELMER: Because it's so much prettier. Look now! You hold the embroidery in the left hand, so, and then work the needle with the right hand, in a long, graceful curve — don't you?

MRS. LINDEN: Yes, I suppose so.

HELMER: But knitting is always ugly. Just look — your arms close to your sides, and the needles going up and down — there's something Chinese about it. — They really gave us splendid champagne tonight.

MRS. LINDEN: Well, good-night, Nora, and don't be obstinate any more.

HELMER: Well said, Mrs. Linden!

MRS. LINDEN: Good-night, Mr. Helmer.

HELMER: *(Accompanying her to the door.)* Good-night, good-night; I hope you'll get safely home. I should be glad to — but you have such a short way to go. Good-night, good-night. *(She goes; HELMER shuts the door after her and comes forward again.)* At last we've got rid of her: she's a terrible bore.

NORA: Aren't you very tired, Torvald?

HELMER: No, not in the least.

NORA: Nor sleepy?

HELMER: Not a bit. I feel particularly lively. But you? You do look tired and sleepy.

NORA: Yes, very tired. I shall soon sleep now.

HELMER: There, you see. I was right after all not to let you stay longer.

NORA: Oh, everything you do is right.

HELMER: *(Kissing her forehead.)* Now my lark is speaking like a reasonable being. Did you notice how jolly Rank was this evening?

NORA: Indeed? Was he? I had no chance of speaking to him.

HELMER: Nor I, much; but I haven't seen him in such good spirits for a long time. *(Looks at NORA a little, then comes nearer her.)* It's splendid to be back in our own home, to be quite alone together! — Oh, you enchanting creature!

NORA: Don't look at me in that way, Torvald.

HELMER: I am not to look at my dearest treasure? — at all the loveliness that is mine, mine only, wholly and entirely mine?

NORA: *(Goes to the other side of the table.)* You mustn't say these things to me this evening.

HELMER: *(Following.)* I see you have the tarantella still in your blood — and that makes you all the more enticing. Listen! the other people are going now. *(More softly.)* Nora — soon the whole house will be still.

NORA: Yes, I hope so.

HELMER: Yes, don't you, Nora darling? When we are among strangers, do you know why I speak so little to you, and keep so far away, and only steal a glance at you now and then — do you know why I do it? Because I am fancying that we love each other in secret, that I am secretly betrothed to you, and that no one dreams that there is anything between us.

NORA: Yes, yes, yes. I know all your thoughts are with me.

HELMER: And then, when the time comes to go, and I put the shawl about your smooth, soft shoulders, and this glorious neck of yours, I imagine you are my bride, that our marriage is just over, that I am bringing you for the first time to my home — that I am alone with you for the first time — quite alone with you, in your trembling loveliness! All this evening I have been longing for you, and you only. When I watched you swaying and whirling in the tarantella — my blood boiled — I could endure it no longer; and that's why I made you come home with me so early —

NORA: Go now, Torvald! Go away from me. I won't have all this.

HELMER: What do you mean? Ah, I see you're teasing me, little Nora! Won't — won't! Am I not your husband —? *(A knock at the outer door.)*

NORA: *(Starts.)* Did you hear —?

HELMER: *(Going towards the hall.)* Who's there?

RANK: *(Outside.)* It is I; may I come in for a moment?

HELMER: *(In a low tone, annoyed.)* Oh, what can he want just now? *(Aloud.)* Wait a moment. *(Opens door.)* Come, it's nice of you to look in.

RANK: I thought I heard your voice, and that put it into my head. *(Looks around.)* Ah, this dear old place! How cosy you two are here!

HELMER: You seemed to find it pleasant enough upstairs, too.

RANK: Exceedingly. Why not? Why shouldn't one take one's share of everything in this world? All one can, at least, and as long as one can. The wine was splendid —

HELMER: Especially the champagne.

RANK: Did you notice it? It's incredible the quantity I contrived to get down.

NORA: Torvald drank plenty of champagne, too.

RANK: Did he?

393

NORA: Yes, and it always puts him in such spirits.

RANK: Well, why shouldn't one have a jolly evening after a well-spent day?

HELMER: Well-spent! Well, I haven't much to boast of in that respect.

RANK: *(Slapping him on the shoulder.)* But I have, don't you see?

NORA: I suppose you have been engaged in a scientific investigation, Doctor Rank?

RANK: Quite right.

HELMER: Bless me! Little Nora talking about scientific investigations!

NORA: Am I to congratulate you on the result?

RANK: By all means.

NORA: It was good then?

RANK: The best possible, both for doctor and patient — certainty.

NORA: *(Quickly and searchingly.)* Certainty?

RANK: Absolute certainty. Wasn't I right to enjoy myself after that?

NORA: Yes, quite right, Doctor Rank.

HELMER: And so say I, provided you don't have to pay for it tomorrow.

RANK: Well, in this life nothing is to be had for nothing.

NORA: Doctor Rank — I'm sure you are very fond of masquerades?

RANK: Yes, when there are plenty of amusing disguises —

NORA: Tell me, what shall we two be at our next masquerade?

HELMER: Little featherbrain! Thinking of your next already!

RANK: We two? I'll tell you. You must go as a good fairy.

HELMER: Ah, but what costume would indicate that?

RANK: She has simply to wear her everyday dress.

HELMER: Capital! But don't you know what you will be yourself?

RANK: Yes, my dear friend, I am perfectly clear upon that point.

HELMER: Well?

RANK: At the next masquerade I shall be invisible.

HELMER: What a comical idea!

RANK: There's a big black hat — haven't you heard of the invisible hat? It comes down all over you, and then no one can see you.

HELMER: *(With a suppressed smile.)* No, you're right there.

RANK: But I'm quite forgetting what I came for. Helmer, give me a cigar — one of the dark Havanas.

HELMER: With the greatest pleasure. *(Hands cigar-case.)*

RANK: *(Takes one and cuts the end off.)* Thank you.

NORA: *(Striking a wax match.)* Let me give you a light.

RANK: A thousand thanks. *(She holds the match. He lights his cigar at it.)*

RANK: And now, good-bye!

HELMER: Good-bye, good-bye, my dear fellow.

NORA: Sleep well, Doctor Rank.

RANK: Thanks for the wish.

NORA: Wish me the same.

RANK: You? Very well, since you ask me — Sleep well. And thanks for the light. *(He nods to them both and goes out.)*

HELMER: *(In an undertone.)* He's been drinking a good deal.

NORA: *(Absently.)* I daresay. *(HELMER takes his bunch of keys from his pocket and goes into the hall.)* Torvald, what are you doing there?

HELMER: I must empty the letter-box; it's quite full; there will be no room for the newspapers tomorrow morning.

NORA: Are you going to work to-night?

HELMER: You know very well I am not. — Why, how is this? Some one has been at the lock.

NORA: The lock —?

HELMER: I'm sure of it. What does it mean? I can't think that the servants —? Here's a broken hair-pin. Nora, it's one of yours.

NORA: *(Quickly.)* It must have been the children —

HELMER: Then you must break them of such tricks. — There! At last I've got it open. *(Takes contents out and calls into the kitchen.)* Ellen! — Ellen, just put the hall door lamp out. *(He returns with letters in his hand, and shuts the inner door.)*

HELMER: Just see how they accumulated. *(Turning them over.)* Why, what's this?

NORA: *(At the window.)* The letter! Oh no, no, Torvald!

HELMER: Two visiting-cards — from rank.

NORA: From Doctor Rank?

HELMER: *(Looking at them.)* Doctor Rank. They were on the top. He must just have put them in.

NORA: Is there anything on them?

HELMER: There's a black cross over the name. Look at it. What an unpleasant idea! It looks just as if he were announcing his own death.

NORA: So he is.

HELMER: What! Do you know anything? Has he told you anything?

NORA: Yes. These cards mean that he has taken his last leave of us. He is going to shut himself up and die.

HELMER: Poor fellow! Of course I knew we couldn't hope to keep him long. But so soon —! And to go and creep into his lair like a wounded animal —

NORA: When we must go, it is best to go silently. Don't you think so, Torvald?

HELMER: *(Walking up and down.)* He had so grown into our lives, I can't realise that he is gone. He and his suffering and his loneliness formed a sort of cloudy background to the sunshine of our happiness. — Well, perhaps it's best as it is — at any rate for him. *(Stands still.)* And perhaps for us too, Nora. Now we two are thrown entirely upon each other. *(Takes her in his arms.)* My darling wife! I feel as if I could never hold you close enough. Do you know, Nora, I often wish some danger might threaten you, that I might risk body and soul, and everything, everything, for your dear sake.

NORA: *(Tears herself from him and says firmly.)* Now you shall read your letters, Torvald.

HELMER: No, no; not tonight. I want to be with you, my sweet wife.

NORA: With the thought of your dying friend —?

HELMER: You are right. This has shaken us both. Unloveliness has come between us — thoughts of death and decay. We must seek to cast them off. Till then — we will remain apart.

NORA: *(Her arms around his neck.)* Torvald! Good-night! good-night!

HELMER: *(Kissing her forehead.)* Good-night, my little songbird. Sleep well, Nora. Now I shall go and read my letters. *(He goes with the letters in his hand into his room and shuts the door.)*

NORA: *(With wild eyes, gropes about her, seizes HELMER's domino,*

throws it round her, and whispers quickly, hoarsely, and brokenly.)
Never to see him again. Never, never, never. *(Throws her shawl over her head.)* Never to see the children again. Never, never. — Oh that black, icy water! Oh that bottomless —! If it were only over! Now he has it; he's reading it. Oh, no, no, no, not yet. Torvald, good-bye — ! Good-bye, my little ones —! *(She is rushing out by the hall; at the same moment HELMER flings his door open, and stands there with an open letter in his hand.)*

HELMER: Nora!

NORA: *(Shrieks.)* Ah —!

HELMER: What is this? Do you know what is in this letter?

NORA: Yes, I know. Let me go! Let me pass!

HELMER: *(Holds her back.)* Where do you want to go?

NORA: *(Tries to break away from him.)* You shall not save me, Torvald.

HELMER: *(Falling back.)* True! Is what he writes true? No, no, it is impossible that this can be true.

NORA: It is true. I have loved you beyond all else in the world.

HELMER: Pshaw — no silly evasions!

NORA: *(A step nearer him.)* Torvald —!

HELMER: Wretched woman — what have you done!

NORA: Let me go — you shall not save me! You shall not take my guilt upon yourself!

HELMER: I don't want any melodramatic airs. *(Locks the outer door.)* Here you shall stay and give an account of yourself. Do you understand what you have done? Answer! Do you understand it?

NORA: *(Looks at him fixedly, and says with a stiffening expression.)* Yes; now I begin fully to understand it.

HELMER: *(Walking up and down.)* Oh! what an awful awakening! During all these eight years — she who was my pride and my joy — a hypocrite, a liar — worse, worse — a criminal. Oh, the unfathomable hideousness of it all! Ugh! Ugh! *(NORA says nothing, and continues to look fixedly at him.)*

HELMER: I ought to have known how it would be. I ought to have foreseen it. All your father's want of principle — be silent! — all your father's want of principle you have inherited — no religion, no morality, no sense of duty. How I am punished for screening him! I did it for your sake; and you reward me like this.

NORA: Yes — like this.

HELMER: You have destroyed my whole happiness. You have ruined my future. Oh, it's frightful to think of! I am in the power of a scoundrel; he can do whatever he pleases with me, demand whatever he chooses; he can domineer over me as much as he likes, and I must submit. And all this disaster and ruin is brought upon me by an unprincipled woman!

NORA: When I am out of the world, you will be free.

HELMER: Oh, no fine phrases. Your father, too, was always ready with them. What good would it do me, if you were "out of the world," as you say? No good whatever! He can publish the story all the same; I might even be suspected of collusion. People will think I was at the bottom of it all and egged you on. And for all this I have you to thank — you whom

I have done nothing but pet and spoil during our whole married life. Do you understand now what you have done to me?

NORA: *(With cold calmness.)* Yes.

HELMER: The thing is so incredible, I can't grasp it. But we must come to an understanding. Take that shawl off. Take it off, I say! I must try to pacify him in one way or another — the matter must be hushed up, cost what it may. — As for you and me, we must make no outward change in our way of life — no outward change, you understand. Of course, you will continue to live here. But the children cannot be left in your care. I dare not trust them to you. — Oh, to have to say this to one I have loved so tenderly — whom I still —! But that must be a thing of the past. Henceforward there can be no question of happiness, but merely of saving the ruins, the shreds, the show — *(A ring; HELMER starts.)* What's that? So late! Can it be the worst? Can he —? Hide yourself, Nora; say you are ill. *(NORA stands motionless. HELMER goes to the door and opens it.)*

ELLEN: *(Half dressed, in the hall.)* Here is a letter for you, ma'am.

HELMER: Give it to me. *(Seizes the letter and shuts the door.)* Yes, from him. You shall not have it. I shall read it.

NORA: Read it!

HELMER: *(By the lamp.)* I have hardly the courage to. We may both be lost, both you and I. Ah! I must know. *(Hastily tears the letter open; reads a few lines, looks at an enclosure; with a cry of joy.)* Nora! *(NORA looks inquiringly at him.)*

HELMER: Nora! — Oh! I must read it again. — Yes, yes, it is so. I am saved! Nora, I am saved!

NORA: And I?

HELMER: You too, of course; we are both saved, both of us. Look here — he sends you back your promissory note. He writes that he regrets and apologises; that a happy turn in his life — Oh, what matter what he writes. We are saved, Nora! No one can harm you. Oh, Nora, Nora —; but first to get rid of this hateful thing. I'll just see — *(Glances at the I.O.U.)* No, I will not look at it; the whole thing shall be nothing but a dream to me. *(Tears the I.O.U. and both letters in pieces. Throws them into the fire and watches them burn.)* There! it's gone! — He said that ever since Christmas Eve — Oh, Nora, they must have been three terrible days for you!

NORA: I have fought a hard fight for the last three days.

HELMER: And in your agony you saw no other outlet but — No; we won't think of that horror. We will only rejoice and repeat — it's over, all over! Don't you hear, Nora? You don't seem able to grasp it. Yes, it's over. What is this set look on your face? Oh, my poor Nora, I understand; you cannot believe that I have forgiven you. But I have, Nora; I swear it. I have forgiven everything. I know that what you did was all for love of me.

NORA: That is true.

HELMER: You love me as a wife should love her husband. It was only the means that, in your inexperience, you misjudged. But do you think I love you the less because you cannot do without guidance? No, no. Only lean on me; I will counsel you, and guide you. I should be no true man if this very womanly helplessness did not make you doubly dear in my eyes. You mustn't dwell upon the hard things I said in my first moment of terror, when the world seemed to be tumbling about my ears. I have forgiven you, Nora — I swear I have forgiven you.

NORA: I thank you for your forgiveness. *(Goes out, to the right.)*

HELMER: No, stay —! *(Looking through the doorway.)* What are you going to do?

NORA: *(Inside.)* To take off my masquerade dress.

HELMER: *(In the doorway.)* Yes, do, dear. Try to calm down, and recover your balance, my scared little song-bird. You may rest secure. I have broad wings to shield you. *(Walking up and down near the door.)* Oh, how lovely — how cosy our home is, Nora! Here you are safe; here I can shelter you like a hunted dove whom I have saved from the claws of the hawk. I shall soon bring your poor beating heart to rest; believe me, Nora, very soon. Tomorrow all this will seem quite different — everything will be as before. I shall not need to tell you again that I forgive you; you will feel for yourself that it is true. How could you think I could find it in my heart to drive you away, or even so much as to reproach you? Oh, you don't know a true man's heart, Nora. There is something indescribably sweet and soothing to a man in having forgiven his wife — honestly forgiven her, from the bottom of his heart. She becomes his property in a double sense. She is as though born again; she has become, so to speak, at once his wife and his child. That is what you shall henceforth be to me, my bewildered, helpless darling. Don't be troubled about anything, Nora; only open your heart to me, and I will be both will and conscience to you. *(NORA enters in everyday dress.)* Why, what's this? Not gone to bed? You have changed your dress?

NORA: Yes, Torvald; now I have changed my dress.

HELMER: But why now, so late —?

NORA: I shall not sleep tonight.

HELMER: But, Nora dear —

NORA: *(Looking at her watch.)* It's not so late yet. Sit down, Torvald; you and I have much to say to each other. *(She sits at one side of the table.)*

HELMER: Nora — what does this mean? Your cold, set face —

NORA: Sit down. It will take some time. I have much to talk over with you. *(HELMER sits at the other side of the table.)*

HELMER: You alarm me, Nora. I don't understand you.

NORA: No, that is just it. You don't understand me; and I have never understood you — till tonight. No, don't interrupt. Only listen to what I say. — We must come to a final settlement, Torvald.

HELMER: How do you mean?

NORA: *(After a short silence.)* Does not one thing strike you as we sit here?

HELMER: What should strike me?

NORA: We have been married eight years. Does it not strike you that this is the first time we two, you and I, man and wife, have talked together seriously?

HELMER: Seriously! What do you call seriously?

NORA: During eight whole years, and more — ever since the day we first met

— we have never exchanged one serious word about serious things.

HELMER: Was I always to trouble you with the care you could not help me to bear?

NORA: I am not talking of cares. I say that we have never yet set ourselves seriously to get to the bottom of anything.

HELMER: Why, my dearest Nora, what have you to do with serious things?

NORA: There we have it! You have never understood me. — I have had great injustice done me, Torvald; first by father, and then by you.

HELMER: What! By your father and me? — By us, who have loved you more than all the world?

NORA: *(Shaking her head.)* You have never loved me. You only thought it amusing to be in love with me.

HELMER: Why, Nora, what a thing to say!

NORA: Yes, it is so, Torvald. While I was at home with father, he used to tell me all his opinions, and I held the same opinions. If I had others I said nothing about them, because he wouldn't have liked it. He used to call me his doll-child, and played with me as I played with my dolls. Then I came to live in your house —

HELMER: What an expression to use about our marriage!

NORA: *(Undisturbed.)* I mean I passed from father's hands into yours. You arranged everything according to your taste; and I got the same tastes as you; or I pretended to — I don't know which — both ways, perhaps; sometimes one and sometimes the other. When I look back on it now, I seem to have been living here like a beggar, from hand to mouth. I lived by performing tricks for you, Torvald. But you would have it so. You and father have done me a great wrong. It is your fault that my life has come to nothing.

HELMER: Why, Nora, how unreasonable and ungrateful you are! Have you not been happy here?

NORA: No, never. I thought I was; but I never was.

HELMER: Not — not happy!

NORA: No; only merry. And you have always been so kind to me. But our house has been nothing but a play-room. Here I have been your doll-wife, just as at home I used to be papa's doll-child. And the children, in their turn, have been my dolls. I thought it fun when you played with me, just as the children did when I played with them. That has been our marriage, Torvald.

HELMER: There is some truth in what you say, exaggerated and over-strained though it be. But henceforth it shall be different. Play-time is over; now comes the time for education.

NORA: Whose education? Mine, or the children's?

HELMER: Both, my dear Nora.

NORA: Oh, Torvald, you are not the man to teach me to be a fit wife for you.

HELMER: And you can say that?

NORA: And I — how have I prepared myself to educate the children?

HELMER: Nora!

NORA: Did you not say yourself, a few minutes ago, you dared not trust them to me?

HELMER: In the excitement of the moment! Why should you dwell upon that?

NORA: No — you were perfectly right. That problem is beyond me. There is
another to be solved first — I must try to educate myself. You are not
the man to help me in that. I must set about it alone. And that is why
I am leaving you.

HELMER: *(Jumping up.)* What — do you mean to say —?

NORA: I must stand quite alone if I am ever to know myself and my surround-
ings; so I cannot stay with you.

HELMER: Nora! Nora!

NORA: I am going at once. I daresay Christina will take me in for tonight —

HELMER: You are mad! I shall not allow it! I forbid it!

NORA: It is of no use your forbidding me anything now. I shall take with
me what belongs to me. From you I will accept nothing, either now
or afterwards.

HELMER: What madness this is!

NORA: Tomorrow I shall go home — I mean to what was my home. It will
be easier for me to find some opening there.

HELMER: Oh, in your blind inexperience —

NORA: I must try to gain experience, Torvald.

HELMER: To forsake your home, your husband, and your children! And
you don't consider what the world will say.

NORA: I can pay no heed to that. I only know that I must do it.

HELMER: This is monstrous! Can you forsake your holiest duties in this
way?

NORA: What do you consider my holiest duties?

HELMER: Do I need to tell you that? Your duties to your husband and your
children.

NORA: I have other duties equally sacred.

HELMER: Impossible! What duties do you mean?

NORA: My duties towards myself.

HELMER: Before all else you are a wife and a mother.

NORA: That I no longer believe. I believe that before all else I am a human
being, just as much as you are — or at least that I should try to become
one. I know that most people agree with you, Torvald, and that they
say so in books. But henceforth I can't be satisfied with what most
people say, and what is in books. I must think things out for myself,
and try to get clear about them.

HELMER: Are you not clear about your place in your own home? Have you
not an infallible guide in questions like these? Have you not religion?

NORA: Oh, Torvald, I don't really know what religion is.

HELMER: What do you mean?

NORA: I know nothing but what Pastor Hansen told me when I was confirmed. He explained that religion was this and that. When I get away
from all this and stand alone, I will look into that matter too. I will
see whether what he taught me is right, or, at any rate, whether it
is right for me.

HELMER: Oh, this is unheard of! And from so young a woman! But if
religion cannot keep you right, let me appeal to your conscience — for
I suppose you have some moral feeling? Or, answer me: perhaps you
have none?

NORA: Well, Torvald, it's not easy to say. I really don't know — I am all at

400

sea about these things. I only know that I think quite differently from you about them. I hear, too, that the laws are different from what I thought; but I can't believe that they can be right. It appears that a woman has no right to spare her dying father, or to save her husband's life! I don't believe that.

HELMER: You talk like a child. You don't understand the society in which you live.

NORA: No, I do not. But now I shall try to learn. I must make up my mind which is right — society or I.

HELMER: Nora, you are ill; you are feverish; I almost think you are out of your senses.

NORA: I have never felt so much clearness and certainty as tonight.

HELMER: You are clear and certain enough to forsake husband and children?

NORA: Yes, I am.

HELMER: Then there is only one explanation possible.

NORA: What is that?

HELMER: You no longer love me.

NORA: No; that is just it.

HELMER: Nora! — Can you say so!

NORA: Oh, I'm so sorry, Torvald; for you've always been so kind to me. But I can't help it. I do not love you any longer.

HELMER: *(Mastering himself with difficulty.)* Are you clear and certain on this point too?

NORA: Yes, quite. That is why I will not stay here any longer.

HELMER: And can you also make clear to me how I have forfeited your love?

NORA: Yes, I can. It was this evening, when the miracle did not happen; for then I saw you were not the man I had imagined.

HELMER: Explain yourself more clearly; I don't understand.

NORA: I have waited so patiently all these eight years; for of course I saw clearly enough that miracles don't happen every day. When this crushing blow threatened me, I said to myself so confidently, "Now comes the miracle!" When Krogstad's letter lay in the box, it never for a moment occurred to me that you would think of submitting to that man's conditions. I was convinced that you would say to him, "Make it known to all the world"; and that then —

HELMER: Well? When I had given my own wife's name up to disgrace and shame —?

NORA: Then I firmly believed that you would come forward, take everything upon yourself, and say, "I am the guilty one."

HELMER: Nora —!

NORA: You mean I would never have accepted such a sacrifice? No, certainly not. But what would my assertions have been worth in opposition to yours? — That was the miracle that I hoped for and dreaded. And it was to hinder that that I wanted to die.

HELMER: I would gladly work for you day and night, Nora — bear sorrow and want for your sake. But no man sacrifices his honour, even for one he loves.

NORA: Millions of women have done so.

HELMER: Oh, you think and talk like a silly child.

NORA: Very likely. But you neither think or talk like the man I can share my life with. When your terror was over — not for what threatened me, but for yourself — when there was nothing more to fear — then it seemed to you as though nothing had happened. I was your lark again, your doll, just as before — whom you would take twice as much care of in future, because she was so weak and fragile. *(Stands up.)* Torvald — in that moment it burst upon me that I had been living here these eight years with a strange man, and had borne him three children. — Oh, I can't bear to think of it! I could tear myself to pieces!

HELMER: *(Sadly.)* I see it, I see it; an abyss has opened between us. — But, Nora, can it never be filled up?

NORA: As I now am, I am no wife for you.

HELMER: I have strength to become another man.

NORA: Perhaps — when your doll is taken away from you.

HELMER: To part — to part from you! No, Nora, no; I can't grasp the thought.

NORA: *(Going into room on the right.)* The more reason for the thing to happen. *(She comes back with out-door things and a small travelling-bag, which she places on a chair.)*

HELMER: Nora, Nora, not now! Wait till tomorrow.

NORA: *(Putting on cloak.)* I can't spend the night in a strange man's house.

HELMER: But can we not live here, as brother and sister —?

NORA: *(Fastening her hat.)* You know very well that wouldn't last long. *(Puts on the shawl.)* Good-bye, Torvald. No, I won't go to the children. I know they are in better hands than mine. As I now am, I can be nothing to them.

HELMER: But some time, Nora — some time —?

NORA: How can I tell? I have no idea what will become of me.

HELMER: But you are my wife, now and always!

NORA: Listen, Torvald — when a wife leaves her husband's house, as I am doing, I have heard that in the eyes of the law he is free from all duties towards her. At any rate, I release you from all duties. You must not feel yourself bound, any more than I shall. There must be perfect freedom on both sides. There, I give you back your ring. Give me mine.

HELMER: That too?

NORA: That too.

HELMER: Here it is.

NORA: Very well. Now it is all over. I lay the keys here. The servants know about everything in the house — better than I do. Tomorrow, when I have started, Christina will come to pack up the things I brought with me from home. I will have them sent after me.

HELMER: All over! all over! Nora, will you never think of me again?

NORA: Oh, I shall often think of you, and the children, and this house.

HELMER: May I write to you, Nora?

NORA: No — never. You must not.

HELMER: But I must send you —

NORA: Nothing, nothing.

HELMER: I must help you if you need it.

NORA: No, I say. I take nothing from strangers.

HELMER: Nora — can I never be more than a stranger to you?

NORA: *(Taking her travelling-bag.)* Oh, Torvald, then the miracle of miracles would have to happen —

HELMER: What is the miracle of miracles?

NORA: Both of us would have to change so that — Oh, Torvald, I no longer believe in miracles.

HELMER: But *I* will believe. Tell me! We must so change that —?

NORA: That communion between us shall be a marriage. Good-bye. *(She goes out by the hall door.)*

HELMER: *(Sinks into a chair by the door with his face in his hands.)* Nora! Nora! *(He looks round and rises.)* Empty. She is gone. *(A hope springs up in him.)* Ah! The miracle of miracles —?! *(From below is heard the reverberation of a heavy door closing.)*

THE END.

ASIAN THEATRE:
The Theatres of India, China, and Japan

During Europe's Dark Ages, when no formal drama existed in the West, sophisticated, literary theatre was growing in China and India, and during Europe's late Middle Ages, while Westerners were just rediscovering the theatrical impulse, classical drama flourished in Japan. Hindu, Chinese, and Japanese theatrical traditions continue today in both written form and productions. In addition to having considerable beauty and power in itself, Asian drama, which grew up parallel to and separate from Western theatre, gives us another perspective on the human impulse toward the dramatic. Furthermore, as European and Asian cultures contacted each other during the past few centuries, their differing theatrical traditions impacted on each other, causing creative changes and renewal in drama around the world.

The history of non-Western drama stretches across centuries of time, involves countries separated by vast distances, and includes a multiplicity of different forms, theories, and traditions. The Euro-American viewpoint of this introductory anthology, *Theatre Alive!*, necessarily limits the amount of attention which can be given to theatre from the other half of the globe. However, the over-simplification which must accompany this abbreviated treatment should not obscure the intrinsic value of Asian drama — a collection of theatrical traditions which will grow in their importance to the West as Asia's leadership in global economy, politics, and thought patterns continues to increase.

Religious and Philosophical Backgrounds

Hinduism

Hinduism, the indigenous religion of India, had a major impact on the theatre of that country and the dance drama of southeast Asia. The major Hindu texts include the *Vedas,* a collection of hymns dating from around 1500 B.C., the *Upanishads,* a body of treatises on philosophical topics written after 800 B.C., and epic poems such as the fourth-century B.C. *Mahabharata.* Although the Hindu pantheon includes some 30,000,000 gods and goddesses, its major deities are the supreme god Brahma, Shiva the creator and destroyer, and Vishnu the sustainer.

Perhaps the most fundamental Hindu belief is reincarnation. According to this concept, living creatures die only to be reborn in an endless cycle of reincarnations. A person's manner of living during one incarnation determines whether he or she will be born into a higher or lower order the next time. A major goal of Hinduism is to escape the wearisome cycle of rebirths, lay aside individual identity, and be absorbed into Brahma in a state of being-in-non-being called nirvana.

Hinduism affected Indian drama in several ways. Stories about the

Hindu deities and heroes provided the subject matter for many of the Indian plays and dances and also for the dance dramas of southeast Asia. Furthermore, the act of performing a play or watching it was considered an act of worship. And finally, the unique Hindu combination of rigid discipline with lush sensuality shaped the theory and style of Indian theatre.

Buddhism

In the sixth century B.C., an Indian ascetic named Siddhartha Gautama developed a refined form of Hinduism which became a separate religion. Because he was believed to have achieved perfect spiritual enlightenment, Gautama came to be known as the Buddha, or "Enlightened One." The religion he founded is called Buddhism. Buddhism teaches that all can escape suffering and achieve enlightenment through the renunciation of desire. Some forms of Buddhism revere Gautama Buddha in god-like terms, much as Jesus Christ is worshipped in Christianity, but for the most part, the concept of God is not central to this religion. Although Buddhism did not take root in the land of its founder, it became the primary religion of the rest of eastern Asia including China, Japan, Indonesia, and the area called Indochina. Some Buddhist monks eventually produced teaching plays about the life of Gautama Buddha. Buddhism also served as a vehicle for spreading Hindu mythology to southeast Asia. And one form of the religion played a formative role in Japanese theatre.

Zen Buddhism

In Zen, the type of Buddhism practiced in Japan, worshipers seek to achieve enlightenment by looking beyond the physical realities of the world and becoming aware of their own spiritual, eternal nature. Meditation and the disciplined practices of arts such as flower arranging, archery, and gardening are processes through which Zen Buddhists attempt to shake off the chains of physical existence. The principles and aims of Zen are fundamental to the Japanese Noh theatre.

Theory of Drama

Each region of Asia developed different theories for its own theatre. The theoretical basis of classical Hindu Sanskrit theatre provides a sample of Asian dramatic theory. Two basic theoretical documents of Indian drama are the *Natyasastra,* a treatise dating from the seventh century A.D. which is ascribed to the legendary scholar Bharata, and the writings of Abhinavagupta (c. 975-c. 1025). These writings describe both the purpose and methodology of theatre.

The purpose of Indian drama is to improve the quality of the spectators' lives in a way that will assist their ascent up the reincarnational ladder. In the words of Abhinavagupta, "In drama there is the absence of the mental trace of the intention 'today I must do something practical' and the presence in its place of the intention 'today I am going to enjoy venerable sights and sounds of a non-ordinary character which arouse, in the end, a state of freedom from worldly interests.' . . . Thus the subject who enjoys it does good and avoids evil."

Rasas

According to Hindu theory, drama achieves its effect by creating and communicating one or more "rasas" or "flavors": The erotic, the comic, the pathetic, the furious, the heroic, the terrible, the odious, and the mundane. A play begins this process by creating an overwhelming combination of sense experiences including the sights and sounds of the presentation as well as — according to Abhinavagupta — the smell of incense and the services of courtesans. These sense experiences arouse a rich texture of emotional states which in their turn create *rasa*. In the words of the *Natyasastra:* "Just as flavor (rasa) comes from the combination of many spices, herbs, and other substances, so rasa (in a drama) comes from the combination of many emotional states." The Hindu dramatic masterpiece, *Shakuntala*, for instance, conveys a particular kind of the erotic rasa called "love-in-separation." To do so, it depicts such emotional states as world-weariness, anxiety, envy, fatigue, and longing.

Hindu drama, then, aims to create such an intense sensual experience that it removes the audience from their obsessions with reality. Thus liberated, the audience can experience ethical improvement in this life and the eventual attainment of nirvana.

Performance Conventions

Taken as a whole — and in striking contrast to Western drama — Oriental theatre tends to be conventional rather than realistic, theatrical rather than literary, and presentational rather than representational. An artistic convention is a basic agreement about procedures and their meanings. For instance, although in real life people face all different directions while interacting, on stage, by theatrical convention, actors almost always face the audience. While Western theatre has developed many conventions of its own, it has tended to become more and more life-like in its language, its staging, and its acting techniques. In contrast, Asian theatre typically creates its effect through a rich use of conventions. For instance, in China's Peking opera, the entire faces of some actors are painted with bright designs which symbolize their character types, and in Japanese theatre, a particular gesture with a fan indicates that the character is shooting an arrow.

We call a play highly theatrical when it places more emphasis on production elements than it does on literary elements. Furthermore, theatrical plays usually make obvious, even obtrusive use of artistic production techniques. We would expect, then, that a performance of Puccini's opera *Madame Butterfly* would be more theatrical than a performance of Ibsen's *A Doll's House*. Although the theatres of India, China, and Japan have all produced great literary masterpieces, their performances typically place primary emphasis on the work of the actors, dancers, musicians, costumers, and stage technicians. Because of this interest in theatricality, performances of Japanese Kabuki plays or Peking opera typically consist of striking scenes from several plays rather than a single, complete work.

Presentational Performances

A representational performance observes the "fourth wall convention," which suggests that the characters are not aware of the presence of the audience, and represents the story as if its events are really unfolding for the first time as the play progresses. In contrast, in a presentational performance, the actors usually acknowledge the audience and present selected aspects of the story without suggesting that either they or the audience believe they really are the characters they are portraying. Western drama has tended to become more and more representational while Asian theatre has maintained a presentational mode.

The conventional, theatrical, presentational nature of Asian theatre results in a stylized kind of performance, a performance in which the stage reality is clearly different from everyday reality. While a Western theatregoer might argue that a realistic European play more accurately portrays how people actually behave, an Asian might just as wisely argue that stylized Oriental plays deal more clearly with what is essential about human nature.

Dramatic Literature

India

India's classical plays, written between the fourth and ninth centuries in a literary language called Sanskrit, are exceedingly rich in their imagery, their use of language, their emotional qualities, and their typology. There are, in fact, ten forms or *rupakas* of Sanskrit dramas ranging from heroic comedy *(nataka)* to military spectacle *(vyayoga)*. Although they depict a variety of emotions, Hindu plays of all rupakas end happily. While they are written primarily in Sanskrit, they also use a variety of *prakrits* or "vernacular dialects," and they employ a great variety of poetic meters. *Shakuntala,* for instance, uses three prakrits in addition to Sanskrit and includes seventeen different meters.

Two important Sanskrit plays are *The Little Clay Cart* and *Shakuntala.* The former play, attributed to King Shudraka who is supposed to have lived in the fourth century A.D., is a middle-class romantic comedy about a merchant and his love for a courtesan. *Shakuntala,* a nataka and the acknowledged masterpiece of Hindu classical theatre, was written by Kalidasa (c. 350-c. 450). It tells the story of how King Dushyanta fell in love with Kalidasa, the beautiful daughter of a hermit, and how their love survived in spite of the curse of a grumpy sage.

In the twentieth century, the best-known current expressions of Indian theatre are the Western-influenced plays of Rabindranath Tagore (1861-1941), the flourishing Indian film industry, and *Kathakali,* a dance-drama still performed in southern India.

China

Chinese drama especially flourished during the Yüan Dynasty (1279-1368) founded by the Mongol conqueror Kublai Khan. Since the Mongols had no interest in classical Chinese language or literature, under their rule it became acceptable to write in the vernacular. Consequently, people began to put into script form the popular dramatic entertainments which had developed during the previous Song Dynasty (960-1279). The suspension of civil service examinations from 1237 to 1314, together with the Mongol policy of barring Chinese from service in the bureaucracy, contributed to the development of vernacular drama. These events forced displaced scholars to earn their living in "practical" professions rather than public office, and some of them therefore turned their hand to playwriting. The resulting plays emphasized stylistic excellence in poetry and music at the expense of plot structure. This emphasis reinforced the tendency among the Chinese to value the performance and production elements in theatre over the literary and textual elements.

Peking Opera

In the late eighteenth century, many elements from earlier theatre came together to form the most characteristic type of modern Chinese drama, Peking opera. Peking opera, a highly conventional form of theatre, combines operatic singing, spoken dialog, percussive music, spectacular costume and make-up, dance, and acrobatics.

In the twentieth century, under the impact of Western influences, a spoken drama grew up alongside Peking opera. After the establishment of the People's Republic in 1949, traditional dramatic forms were adapted to serve ideological purposes, and during the Cultural Revolution (1967-1972) only five specific plays and two ballets — all modern, Communist works — were permitted to be performed. Peking opera, however, continues to be performed in Taiwan and several other non-Communist Chinese countries.

Japan

Three types of traditional Japanese drama continue to be performed in the twentieth-century: *Noh,* which will be discussed below; *Kabuki;* and a puppet theatre form called *Bunraku.* Kabuki, a theatrical form combining dance and drama, developed during the early part of the seventeenth century. Throughout its history, Kabuki has had closer attachments to popular entertainments than to aristocratic culture, and it has continually expanded its traditions by adapting scripts from other genres, developing conventions to increase the emotional impact of its acting, and inventing technical devices such as trapped and revolving stages. There are three types of Kabuki scripts: domestic dramas, historical plays, and dance spectacles. However, since Kabuki emphasizes performance at the expense of literary elements, a typical Kabuki program presents excerpts from all three kinds of plays. With its large stage which includes an elevated runway cutting through the audience, its elaborate costumes, fantastic make-up, poetry, dance, technical effects, startling percussive accompaniment, and the exaggerated vocal and movement expressions of its actors, Kabuki presents a dramatic entertainment unequaled around the world for its theatricality.

Bunraku

Bunraku (or as it was originally known, *Joruri*) came into being in the late seventeenth century as a result of the combination of three popular performance forms — puppetry, playing the three-stringed *shamisen* and chanting romantic love stories. In 1685, Takemoto Gidayu, a famed chanter, enlisted the services of a Kabuki playwright, Chikamatsu Monzaemon (1653-1725) who became Japan's most famous playwright. Chikamatsu wrote his most important plays for the puppet theatre. His plays fit into two main

409

categories: romances about the merchant class, and historical plays about military figures. Both kinds of plays focus on the conflict between duty to one's self and duty to social expectations, and both tend to end unhappily. After Chikamatsu's death, the main developments in Joruri took place in puppetry techniques. Today the puppets are over four feet tall and have movable feet, fingers and eyes. A Joruri puppet is manipulated by three operators — the master, who controls the head and right arm, and two assistants who manipulate the left arm and legs. All of the puppeteers do their work in full view of the audience. In the twentieth century, Joruri is performed exclusively by Osaka's Bunraku-za, the theatre from which it now takes its name.

In the twentieth century, as a result of contact with the West, Japan developed a variety of modern theatrical expressions. These include productions of Western plays, agit-prop political theatre, a lively and influential film and video industry, and avant-garde, experimental stage plays.

In addition to India, China, and Japan, almost every other region of Asia also has its own unique dramatic tradition. These Oriental theatres present a bewildering variety reaching from Balinese dance drama and Malaysian shadow puppets to the Islamic Shi'ite passion play and modern, state-supported theatre in Turkey.

Performance

At the risk of overgeneralization, we can make several observations about the performers of Asian theatre. First, they typically enter training for their career at a very early age and focus on a single type of role. Part of the reason for these tendencies is the highly conventionalized nature of Oriental acting. While his Western counterpart need only learn to duplicate normal human behaviors on stage, the Asian actor must master a huge catalog of stylized gestures and mannerisms and frequently must learn to use his body and voice in radically distorted ways. Training the voice and body and learning to execute the conventions takes a long time and must start when the performer is young and flexible. Secondly, the Asian performer inherits, renews, and passes on a strong artistic tradition. His task is to maintain the tradition faithfully while enlivening it with his own style. Finally, in many Asian regions, the close association between religion and theatre gives the actor a kind of priestly identity. The trance-like state of the Kathakali performers and Indonesian dancers and the Noh actors' practice of Zen in their art maintains a union between religion and theatre which Western theatre has not experienced since the classical period when actors were Servants of Dionysus.

East Meets West

Oriental and Western theatre have had major impacts on each other. Sir William Jones' 1789 translation of *Shakuntala* into English triggered an interest in Sanskrit drama among European writers, including the German Romantic, Goethe. In this way, Asian drama with its loose plot structure and mingling of pathetic events with happy conclusions influenced the early-nineteenth-century Romantic revolution in theatre, art, and literature. In the present century, Bertolt Brecht (1898-1956) used Oriental dramatic techniques in some of his plays, such as *He Who Says Yes/He Who Says No* (1929-30). The "Alienation Effect," central to Brecht's Epic Theatre, adapts the presentational style of Oriental theatre for use in European political plays. Antonin Artaud (1896-1948), whose work strongly influenced experimental theatre in this century, drew inspiration from a troupe of Balinese dancers he saw in 1931. His book, *The Theatre and Its Double* (1938), proposes subordinating language to jarring visual images and aural effects similar to those used in Eastern dance drama.

At the same time, Asians were drawing new ideas from European theatre. Nobel laureate Rabindranath Tagore, for instance, combined elements of Sanskrit drama, Bengali folk plays, and Western theatre in his plays such as *The Post Office* (1913). In China, the production of European plays led to the establishment of a new "spoken drama" *(hua ju)*. This new theatre combined with traditional Chinese forms and Communist content to create a modern, ideological theatre form. In Japan, *Shimpa,* a theatrical form which combined elements of Kabuki with Western drama, came into being in the 1880s and attracted audiences throughout the twentieth century.

Asian theatre has frequently had the effect of returning Western theatre to the mythic elements and theatricality it lost during the trend toward modern theatre in the seventeenth through nineteenth centuries. The contact with Western theatre has had the opposite effect on Asian theatre and has moved it toward realism and the treatment of current, secular topics.

Today, theatre-goers can view Kathakali in southern India's Kerala State, Peking opera in Taipei, Revolutionary theatre in Peking, and — in Tokyo — a plethora of dramatic forms ranging from traditional Noh to radically experimental theatre. And in the United States, audiences can watch touring productions of Asian drama and dance as well as Oriental-style productions of Western classics. The mutual impact of the Orient and the West has enriched theatre worldwide.

Zeami

Zeami Motokiyo (1363-1443) wrote *Izutsu* ("The Well-Curb"), the play which follows. Actor, theorist, and dramatist Zeami wrote approximately one-third of the Noh scripts which are still in use today. His father, Kwannami Kiyotsugu (1333-1384), was a performer of *sarugaku,* a popular entertainment which combined dancing, acrobatics, juggling, and singing. Kwannami came to enjoy the patronage of a shogun, one of the military dictators who dominated Japan during that period, and developed a new dramatic form called Noh, meaning "skill" or "talent." Zeami spent his whole life under the patronage of a shogun named Yoshimitsu, and the sophisticated, courtly setting in which he worked contributed to the elegant form of Noh. Besides writing and performing in many Noh plays, Zeami also wrote *The Book of the Flower,* a major theoretical work which explains the aesthetic principles of the form and gives details about Noh composition, acting, direction, and production.

411

Izutsu

The Theory of Noh

A Noh play is a dramatic embodiment of medieval Zen Buddhism. Japanese Buddhists of this period believed that, while eternal truth transcends the natural world, it can only be understood through objects *in* the natural world. Therefore, Zen theatre artists, then and now, aim to deal with human events in a way which would evoke the spirit of the "other world." In contrast with most Western thought, which sees human beings as individual entities distinct from each other and the world around them, Zen understands human beings as essentially unified with each other and the world. As a result, the basic element of Western drama — conflict — has no place in Noh drama. Also, unlike Western religious and philosophical thought, Zen Buddhism has no concept of free will. Since tragedy focuses on the struggles of a free man or woman (the hero), Noh plays are not tragic. Finally, since comedy focuses on human beings as social creatures and moral agents, and since Zen does not consider social relations or moral choices as central to humanity, Noh plays are not comic. In Zen, the ideal human being has freed himself from the perishable self, is at one with himself, his enemy, and his world, and lives simultaneously in the past, present, and future. Noh plays portray this ideal.

While the text in *Izutsu* creates neither tragic nor comic effects, it does evoke a strong mood which, in spite of its power, is difficult to identify. A production of the play would intensify this effect through costumes and staging and above all through dance and music, both vocal and instrumental. According to Zeami, a Noh play must create *yugen*. This word, without exact equivalent in English, indicates a form of beauty which is obscure but still sensed, elusive yet meaningful, resigned yet sad. Yugen results from the contemplation of the Zen ideal and makes itself felt as the mood created by a play like *Izutsu*.

The Source

Zeami took the materials for *Izutsu* from two sources, the *Ise Monogatari* and the *Kokinshu*. The first of these, a ninth-century work whose title means "Tale of Ise," is supposed to have been written by Narihira himself, a major poet of the time who figures in the play. The *Kokinshu* is a tenth-century anthology of 1,100 poems.

The Story

As modified by Zeami, the story behind *Izutsu* goes as follows: The daughter of Ki-no-Aritsune and the son of a princely family, Ariwara-no-Narihira, grew up as neighbors and playmates. While playing around a well outside one of their houses, they would lean over its curb *(izutsu)* and compare their faces and long hair. As they grew older, shyness came between them, but their mutual attraction proved stronger and finally led to their marriage. Eventually Narihira became infatuated with a woman in neighboring Kawachi Province. Each night he would cross a treacherous pass to visit his mistress. Eventually, however, the faithful love of his wife overcame his infatuation, and he ended his affair to live happily with his wife.

412

Centuries later, as the play itself begins, a wandering priest visits a neglected shrine built on the site of Narihira's house. An old well-curb, hidden by brush, reminds the pilgrim of the love story, which he discusses with a young woman he meets there. He falls asleep and awakens to find that the young woman is actually the ghost of Narihira's wife. As he watches, she peers into the well and, unified with her husband, sees his face in her reflection. The ghost fades away, morning comes, and the priest awakens to find it was all a dream.

Form and Plot

A complete Noh program consists of three to five plays. The program begins with an introduction *(jo)* consisting of a *kami* Noh (god play) which features a god as its hero. The development *(ha)* of the program is made up of one to three plays from the following categories: A *shura-mono* ("Asura play"), whose hero is a famous medieval warrior; a *kazura-mono* ("female-wig play"), whose hero is a woman and which is particularly lyrical; and a Fourth Group play, which is different from any of the preceding types. In conclusion *(kyu)*, the program presents a *kiri* Noh (concluding-play) which usually features supernatural beings as main characters. *Izutsu*, a *kazura-mono*, would be the third play in a complete program.

The individual plays are divided into two parts. The first part sets the scene for the second part, and a comic monolog separates the two parts.

The personnel who present a Noh play comprise four groups: Actors, chorus, musicians, and stage attendants. The central actor, the *shite*, does most of the singing and dancing, while the secondary actor, the *waki* ("by-stander"), simply provides a character with whom the shite can interact. Since the heart of Noh is singing and dancing, the shite's performance is of supreme importance. The shite and the waki may both have attendants, and the play may also use a boy character and walk-ons. The semicomic interlude is presented by an actor called the *kyogen* who plays the role of a country person. *Izutsu* enhances the focus on the singing and dancing by using only the shite and the waki.

The chorus, consisting of eight to ten men dressed in ordinary clothing, sits in an oblong recess along the left edge of the stage; it sings the text of songs danced by the shite, comments on the action, and may dialog with the shite and waki. The musicians, who play a flute, a small hand-drum, a large hand-drum, and a horizontal drum, sit toward the back of the stage. The small and large hand-drums are particularly important to *Izutsu* because they accompany the *jo-no-mai* dance in Part Two which is central to the play's performance. The stage attendants, who sit behind the musicians in view of the audience, provide props for the actors and help them with their on-stage costume changes. One of the stage attendants, the *koken* (after-looker), is the shite's understudy and must be ready to step into his role at a moment's notice.

Staging

Noh plays are presented on a simple, formalized, traditional stage. The stage proper — a raised, roofed platform about twenty feet square —

413

thrusts out into the auditorium so that the audience sits on three sides of it. A ramp (the *hashigakari*), which leads from its up-right corner to the backstage "mirror room," gives the actors access to the stage. The stage is backed by a painting of an ancient, twisted pine tree, and three pine saplings stand between the hashigakari and the audience. Three jars, located beneath the pine-board planking of the stage, reverberate to amplify the sound of the actors' footsteps when dancing or stamping.

Each of the four on-stage pillars which support the Noh stage roof has a name. The up-right pillar is called the *shite* pillar because the shite sits beside it while not involved in the action and begins his dance from this location. Similarly, the flute-player's pillar in the up-left corner of the stage and the *waki* pillar in the down-left corner mark the locations of those performers' seats. The fourth pillar, located in the down-right corner, is called the "eye-fixing" pillar because the actors, whose vision may be obscured by their masks, use it as a landmark in positioning themselves on stage.

Noh plays use almost no specific scenery and only a limited number of conventionalized hand props; the use of the stylized well-curb set piece in *Izutsu* is, therefore, exceptional. While the stage decor of the Noh theatre is sparse, its costuming is elaborate. The actors wear costumes, wigs, and headdresses which make no attempt at historical accuracy but are rich in color, fabric, and design. The shite wears a mask, as do other actors portraying female characters and old people. Noh has over a hundred masks categorized according to the character's order of being (god/human/animal/monster), sex, and age. Many of the masks in use today were created by famous artists dating back to medieval times.

The following Noh play, *Izutsu,* comes from centuries ago and oceans away, but the emotions it depicts and the mood it evokes have an appeal unbounded by place or time.

Asian Theatre Timeline

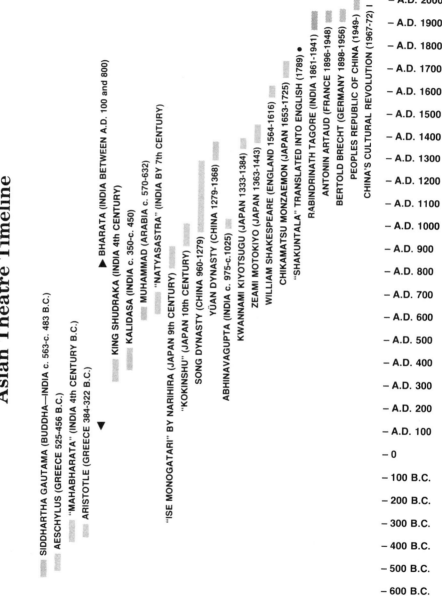

SIDDHARTHA GAUTAMA (BUDDHA—INDIA c. 563-c. 483 B.C.)
AESCHYLUS (GREECE 525-456 B.C.)
"MAHABHARATA" (INDIA 4th CENTURY B.C.)
ARISTOTLE (GREECE 384-322 B.C.)
▲ BHARATA (INDIA BETWEEN A.D. 100 and 800)
KING SHUDRAKA (INDIA 4th CENTURY)
KALIDASA (INDIA c. 350-c. 450)
MUHAMMAD (ARABIA c. 570-632)
"NATYASASTRA" (INDIA BY 7th CENTURY)
"ISE MONOGATARI" BY NARIHIRA (JAPAN 9th CENTURY)
"KOKINSHU" (JAPAN 10th CENTURY)
SONG DYNASTY (CHINA 960-1279)
YÜAN DYNASTY (CHINA 1279-1368)
ABHINAVAGUPTA (INDIA c. 975-c.1025)
KWANNAMI KIYOTSUGU (JAPAN 1333-1384)
ZEAMI MOTOKIYO (JAPAN 1363-1443)
WILLIAM SHAKESPEARE (ENGLAND 1564-1616)
CHIKAMATSU MONZAEMON (JAPAN 1653-1725)
"SHAKUNTALA" TRANSLATED INTO ENGLISH (1789) ●
RABINDRINATH TAGORE (INDIA 1861-1941)
ANTONIN ARTAUD (FRANCE 1896-1948)
BERTOLD BRECHT (GERMANY 1898-1956)
PEOPLES REPUBLIC OF CHINA (1949-)
CHINA'S CULTURAL REVOLUTION (1967-72) I

– A.D. 2000
– A.D. 1900
– A.D. 1800
– A.D. 1700
– A.D. 1600
– A.D. 1500
– A.D. 1400
– A.D. 1300
– A.D. 1200
– A.D. 1100
– A.D. 1000
– A.D. 900
– A.D. 800
– A.D. 700
– A.D. 600
– A.D. 500
– A.D. 400
– A.D. 300
– A.D. 200
– A.D. 100
– 0
– 100 B.C.
– 200 B.C.
– 300 B.C.
– 400 B.C.
– 500 B.C.
– 600 B.C.

IZUTSU
(The Well-Curb)

by Zeami Motokiyo[1]

The action of the play takes place at Ariwara Temple, Isonokami, Yamato Province[2] in the autumn.

CAST OF CHARACTERS

TRAVELING PRIEST
played by the waki[3]

MAIDEN
played by the shite[4]

MAN OF THE PLACE
played by the kyogen[5]

GHOST OF KI-NO-ARITSUNE'S DAUGHTER
played by the shite

[1]Translated by the Special Noh Committee, Japanese Classics Translation Committee of the Nippon Gakujutsu Shinkokai (The Japan Society for the Promotion of Science) and published along with nine other scripts and excellent introductory materials in *The Noh Drama: Ten Plays from the Japanese*, Tokyo: Charles E. Tuttle Company, 1960.
[2]Yamato Province is located just south of the center of the large, central island of Japan (ed. Footnotes with this designation have been provided by the anthology editor, Norman A. Bert.)
[3]waki: "by-stander" — the secondary actor in a Noh play. (ed.)
[4]shite: "performer" — the principal actor in a Noh play. (ed.)
[5]kyogen: a comic actor in a Noh play who presents entr'acte exposition. (ed.)

416

PART ONE

(Stage-attendants place on the front of the stage a square framework well-curb with a sheaf of susuki grass at one corner.)

1

(While the entrance music nanori-bue[6] is being played, the PRIEST, wearing a pointed hood, plain kimono, and broad-sleeved robe, appears and advances to the SHITE seat.[7])

PRIEST: I am a priest on pilgrimage from province to province. Of late I have visited the Seven Great Temples of Nara,[8] and now am on my way to Hatsuse.

(He looks towards the well-curb.)

When I enquired from someone about this temple, I was told it was the Ariwara Temple. I will enter the grounds and see what it is like.

(He advances to the center of the stage and faces the well-curb.)

Surely in bygone days the Ariwara Temple
Was the Isonokami home
Where Narihira and Ki-no-Aritsune's daughter
Once lived as man and wife.
Surely here too was written
"Over Tatsuta's mountain pass[9]
Perilous as storm-tossed seas . . ."

(Singing a sage-uta, a low-pitched song.)

As I stand on the site of this ancient tale,
I feel the transitoriness of life.
Now, for the sake of those twin souls,
Will I perform religious rites,
Will I perform religious rites.

(While saying the final two lines, he joins his hands in prayer and moves to the WAKI seat.[10])

2

(While the entrance music shidai is being played, a MAIDEN, wearing a

---

[6]nanori: "name-introducing" — a prose passage spoken by the waki. (ed.)

[7]Shite seat: the location in the upper-stage-right corner of the main stage, next to the bridge-way, from which the protagonist begins his dance. (ed.)

[8]The temples referred to are Todai-ji, Kofuku-ji, Gango-ji, Daian-ji, Yakushi-ji, Saidai-ji, and Horyu-ji. Some are situated in the city itself, others in the neighborhood. (tr. Footnotes with this designation have been provided by the translators of the script.)

[9]Pass crossing a hill of the same name in the mountain range between Yamato and Kawachi Provinces. The Tatsuta Shrine, one of the most ancient Shinto Temples, situated on the eastern slope of Tatsuta Hill south of Mt. Shigi, was erected in the seventh century by Imperial order and dedicated to the wind-god. The river flowing east of the hill is also called Tatsuta and has been much celebrated in ancient literature on account of the autumn tints of the maples which line its banks. (tr.)

[10]The waki seat is located in the down-stage-left corner of the main stage, diagonally opposite the shite seat. (ed.)

"young-woman" mask, wig, painted gold-patterned under-kimono, and brocade outer-kimono, appears carrying a spray of leaves[11] and stands at the SHITE seat.)

MAIDEN: *(Singing a shidai or entrance song.)* Gazing into the crystal water
    I draw each morning,
    Gazing into the crystal water I draw each morning,
    The moon, too, seems to cleanse her heart.

CHORUS:[12] *(Singing a jidori or repetition song.)* Gazing into the crystal
    water I draw each morning,
    The moon, too, seems to cleanse her heart.

MAIDEN: *(Declaiming a sashi, a recitative which precedes a song.)*
    Autumn nights are lonely anywhere,
    Yet even lonelier
    Is this old temple rarely visited,
    When the autumn winds sough through the garden pines.
    The moon sinking westward,
    The drooping eaves o'ergrown with waving ferns —
    All reminds me of the past
    Alas! How long must I still live
    And naught to hope for in the future!
    Each thing that happens leaves its mark upon the mind;
    Such is our mortal world.

(Singing a sage-uta.)

    Buddha, I cast myself on thee
    With all my heart, praying continually
    That with the unseen thread held in thy hand[13]
    Thou wilt at last lead me to Paradise!

(Continuing with an age-uta, a high-pitched song.)

    Thy vow is to enlighten those in darkness,
    Thy vow is to enlighten those in darkness.
    Although the moon at dawn
    Does surely hasten towards the western hills
    Where lies the Land of Bliss,
    Yet between here and there
    Stretches the vast and empty autumn sky
    As far as eye can reach.
    We hear the winds soughing through the pines,
    but know not whence they blow nor whither.[14]
    In this world more fleeting than the wind,
    Vain dreams deceive our minds.

[11]Or a small wooden bucket with a spray of leaves representing flowers. (tr.)
[12]The chorus, consisting of eight to ten men in normal clothing, sits in an oblong recess on the stage-left side of the stage.
[13]In Jodo-kyo, except for the Shin sect, it was customary for a dying person to hold in the left hand one end of a thread attached to a hand of the image of Amida Buddha in order that he should fix his mind on His saving power. (tr.)
[14]The metaphor seems analogous to that found in the third chapter of *St. John*, except that here the changeableness of wind is used to symbolize the uncertainty of human life. (tr.)

What call will have the power to waken us,
What call will have the power to waken us!

(While saying the final lines, the MAIDEN comes to the front of the stage, sits down, places the spray of leaves before her and joins her hands in prayer, then returns to the SHITE seat.)

3

PRIEST: *(He turns to the MAIDEN.)* While meditating in the temple grounds, I see an attractive woman draw water from a well with a wooden curb and, having poured it into a wooden vessel containing flowers, offer it reverently to a grass-covered mound. Pray, who are you?

MAIDEN: I am a woman of this neighborhood. The pious benefactor of this temple, Ariwara-no-Narihira, was a famous man and the tombstone by this mound is supposed to be his. Therefore, I offer flowers to it and pray for his salvation.

PRIEST: Yes, Narihira has left an undying name behind him. This place may indeed have been the site of his home, but since his story goes back to ancient times, I am filled with wonder that anyone, especially a woman, should thus be praying for him. Perchance you are related to him?

MAIDEN: You ask whether I am related to him? But even in his day he was called "the Ancient."[15] Now, after this long lapse of time, he belongs to the remote past. How can there still live anyone related to him?

PRIEST: You speak truth,
Yet this was once his home.

MAIDEN: Though he is long since dead, . . .

PRIEST: . . . This place remains as it was once, . . .

MAIDEN: . . . And tales that keep his fame alive . . .

PRIEST: . . . Are handed down to us.

MAIDEN: So "the Ancient" . . .

CHORUS: *(Singing an age-uta as the MAIDEN dances.)*
. . . Is still remembered,
Though time-worn is the Ariwara Temple,
Though time-worn is the Ariwara Temple.
Grass covers this mound
Shadowed by ancient pines,
And only this one bush
Of flowering susuki
Marks where he sleeps for evermore,
And might, indeed, unfold a tale
Of bygone days.
The sight of this old mound,
Hidden under lush grass
Drenched with weary dew,
Is precious to the lonely heart,

[15]Each chapter of the *Ise Monogatari* begins with the words: "In ancient times there was a man." Since the anonymous hero is understood to be Narihira, the author of the present play pretends that Narihira was called "the Ancient" in his lifetime. (tr.)

419

Is precious to the lonely heart!
(The MAIDEN sits down and weeps.)

4

PRIEST: I wish you would tell me more about Narihira.

(The MAIDEN rises, comes to the center of the stage, and sits down.)

CHORUS: *(Singing a kuri, lively piece with varying rhythms.)*
    Once Narihira, captain of the Imperial Body-guard,
    Enjoyed for many years spring flowers and autumn moons
    Here at Isonokami, then fallen into decay.
MAIDEN: *(Declaiming a sashi.)* 'Twas when he lived in wedlock
    With Ki-no-Aritsune's daughter,
    Bound each to other by strong love!
CHORUS: Later bewitched by a new love
    At Takayasu[16] in Kawachi Province,
    And loath to give up either,
    Secretly he visited her of nights.
MAIDEN: "Over Tatsuta's mountain pass, . . .
CHORUS: . . . Perilous as storm-tossed seas,
    He speeds at midnight all alone!"
    Thus sang his wife
    Fearing that treacherous pass.
    Moved by her selfless love,
    His new love withered.
MAIDEN: Since poetry alone can tell our deepest feelings, . . .
CHORUS: . . . Well might her selfless love inspire such a moving poem.

(The CHORUS continues singing an ode called a kuse.)

    Here in this province long ago
    Two households once lived side by side;
    The children, boy and girl, were playmates.
    Leaning over the well-curb beyond the gate,
    They peered together down the well
    Where mirrored lay their faces cheek to cheek,
    Their sleeves hanging o'er each other's shoulder.
    Thus used those bosom friends to play.
    In time they grew reserved and shy,
    Till the faithful-hearted youth
    Sent her a letter with a poem
    Telling his flower-like love
    In words like sparkling dew drops:
MAIDEN: "Standing against the well-curb,
    As children we compared our heights,
CHORUS: But I have grown much taller
    Since last I saw you."[17]

---

[16]Situated at the foot of a mountain of the same name in Naka-Kawachi County of that province. (tr.)
[17]Quoted from the *Ise Monogatari*, chap. xxii. (tr.)

Answering the maiden wrote:
"The hair I parted
When by the well-curb we compared our heights,
Now loose flows down my back.
For whom but you should it again be tied?"[18]
For this exchange of poems
They called her the "Lady of the Well-Curb."

5

CHORUS: *(Beginning a rongi.[19])* Listening to this ancient lovers' tale,
I am filled with wonder at your charm.
Please disclose your name!
MAIDEN: If you would know the truth,
Taking the shape of Aritsune's daughter,
By yearning moved, I have come back to my old home,
Treading under the veil of night
A road perilous as the Tatsuta Pass.
CHORUS: How wonderful!
Then you are the lady of the Tatsuta Pass?
MAIDEN: "Daughter of Ki-no-Aritsune" am I.
CHORUS: And "Lady of the Well-Curb" too.
MAIDEN: With shame I own to both those names.
CHORUS: Scarce has she revealed the name
Of her who tied the nuptial knot
When but nineteen
And made her vow before the gods,

(The MAIDEN rises.)

Than she fades away behind the well-curb,
Than she fades away behind the well-curb.

(The MAIDEN goes out.)

INTERLUDE

A MAN OF THE PLACE enters the stage, wearing a striped kimono, sleeveless robe, trailing divided skirt, and short sword. In reply to the PRIEST's request, he tells him the tale of Ki-no-Artisune's daughter.[20]

PART TWO

1

PRIEST: *(Singing a machi-utai.)* The night is growing old!
Above the temple hangs the moon,
Above the temple hangs the moon.
Wishing to dream of times gone by,

[18]Quoted from the *Ise Monogatari*, chap. xxii. (tr.)
[19]Rongi, meaning "debate," is a passage performed alternately by the chorus and the shite. It is intoned rather than sung. (ed.)
[20]The interlude narrative by the kyogen is not considered an artistic part of the Noh play itself and so is omitted from the text. This practice is similar to that of Roman comedy in which act breaks are indicated without any record of the entertainments which occurred during the interludes. (ed.)

I turn my robe inside out,[21]
And lay me down upon this bed of moss,
And lay me down upon this bed of moss.

2

(While the entrance music issei[22] is being played, the GHOST OF KI-NO-ARITSUNE'S DAUGHTER appears and stands at the SHITE seat. She wears a "young woman" mask, wig, man's ceremonial headgear, painted gold-patterned under-kimono, dancing choken robe, and embroidered kishimaki outer-kimono.)

DAUGHTER: *(Declaiming a shashi.)* "Though people call them shifty,
Yet the cherry blossoms never fail
Him who seeks my garden once a year
Less for my sake than for theirs."[23]
This poem gained for me
The name of "Friend-Awaiting Woman."
Many a year has passed with varying fortunes
Since Narihira and I played by the well-curb;
Now bereft of him, though ill-becoming,
I don this robe he gave me
And dance as he was wont to do.
CHORUS: Graceful as whirling flakes of snow,
The dancer waves her flowery sleeves.

(The DAUGHTER performs a jo-no-mai dance, a slow and elegant dance generally assigned to female spirits. After the dance, the DAUGHTER speaks:)

DAUGHTER: Hither returned, I call back time past . . .
CHORUS: . . . And on the ancient well
Of the Ariwara Temple
The moon shines brightly as of old,
The moon shines brightly as of old.

3

DAUGHTER: *(Dancing while the following lines are chanted.)*
"Is not the moon in heaven the same?
Is not the springtime as it was?"[24]

[21]It was an ancient custom for lovers to sleep with their kimono turned inside out so that they might dream of their beloved, as mentioned in a poem by Ono-no-Komachi in the *Kokinshu:*
When overwhelmed
By the yearning for the one I love,
I go to bed,
Wearing my garment inside out. (tr.)
[22]Issei is music specifically for the entrance of the shite.
[23]Quoted from the *Ise Monogatari*, chap. xvi, as attributed to the hero of the work, i.e. Narihira. The poem is also found in the *Kokinshu* where the author's name is not mentioned. (tr.)
[24]Quoted from the *Ise Monogatari*, chap. iv. The poem, which also appears in the *Kokinshu* and is a cry of a heartbroken lover whose beloved had been taken away whither he did not know, is translated in full as follows:
Is the moon changed?
Is spring no longer
What it was of yore,
While I remain my old self? (tr.)

Thus did he sing, long, long ago.
"Standing against the well-curb, . . .
CHORUS: . . . Standing against the well-curb,
   As children we compared our heights.
DAUGHTER: But I . . .
CHORUS: . . . Have grown much taller."
DAUGHTER: And much older.
CHORUS: Wearing this robe and headgear
   As Narihira did,
   It does not look like a woman,
   But a man — the living image of Narihira.

(As the CHORUS chants these lines, the DAUGHTER approaches the well, pushes aside the susuki grass, and peers down into it.)

DAUGHTER: How dear the face I see!
CHORUS: How dear the face, though it be mine!

(The DAUGHTER moves away.)

See! The ghost of the dead lady fades
Like the lingering scent of fading flowers.

(The DAUGHTER wraps the left sleeve around her arm, covers her face with the open fan, and bends forward.)

The sky is turning grey;
The Ariwara Temple's bell starts to toll,
Ushering in the morn.

(The DAUGHTER stands still as if listening to the bell.)

The garden pines awaken with the breeze;
And like the torn leaves of the basho tree[25]
The priest's dream is shattered and day dawns,
The priest's dream is shattered and day dawns.

(The DAUGHTER stamps twice at the SHITE seat indicating the end of the play.)

---

[25]Musa Basjoo, a banana-like plant with large leaves found in southern Japan. (tr.)

EARLY TWENTIETH-CENTURY THEATRE: Challenges to Realism

Even while widespread passion for science and progress were producing theatrical realism at the end of the nineteenth century, many people in the artistic and intellectual community doubted that science would bring paradise, and if progress did result in utopia, they doubted that they would want to be a part of it. During the early part of the twentieth century, political and economic events suggested they might be right. In theatre during this period, disillusionment with science, technology, and progress stimulated a variety of challenges to realism. Also during these years, theatre in the United States, which had previously been a sort of extension of European drama, came into its own as an independent, creative force.

Political/Social/Philosophical Backgrounds

Christian Liberalism

Confidence in the irresistible progress of civilization was so strong at the end of the nineteenth century that it even produced a new Christian theology: liberalism. Liberalism and its expression in the social gospel played down the supernatural elements in Christian theology and taught that the human family, by combining the teachings of Jesus with an enlightened use of technology, would soon create heaven on earth. Christian liberalism inspired a few plays such as Charles Rann Kennedy's *The Servant in the House* (1908) and Jerome K. Jerome's *Passing of the Third Floor Back* (1908). These plays combined symbolic characters and story lines with surface realism to convey the social gospel message of the fatherhood of God and the brotherhood of man.

Militarism

While theologians devised blueprints for paradise, however, the governments of Europe were using technology to build the machines of war. Militarism played a powerful counterpoint to the themes of social improvement, and in 1914 Europe exploded into the Great War which, by its conclusion four years later, had used modern technology to kill nearly 9,000,000 soldiers and an additional 28,000,000 civilians.

For vanquished Germany, armistice brought a peace that was little better than the war. Humiliated by the terms of the Treaty of Versailles (1919) and broken economically, the energetic Germans were left in political chaos that made them easy prey for demagogues. The Russian Revolution which followed World War I brought into prominence a new, disruptive political force, communism. And although people celebrated the 1920s with a kind of euphoria, beneath the facade of flapper styles, jazz music, and Charleston-type dancing brooded poverty and human oppression. Then, at the end of the 20s, the world economy collapsed into the Great Depression.

A brutal war, political turmoil, social oppression, and economic disaster brought about disillusionment with science and technology. Many people decided that progress either was an illusion or was leading human beings in destructive directions. These viewpoints found theatrical expression in nonrealistic forms such as expressionism.

Dramatic Literature

Expressionism

Theatre people sometimes use the term "expressionism" to indicate any nonrealistic style. In reality, however, expressionism was a particular kind of theatre which should not be confused with other nonrealistic twentieth-century styles such as absurdism, epic theatre, and the theatre of cruelty. Expressionism grew out of symbolism and differed from this earlier movement primarily in its ethnic connections and its impact. Expressionism originated in Germany, while symbolism centered in French-speaking countries; and while the symbolists aimed primarily to create a mood and an artistic experience, the expressionists wanted to convey a message.

Like the symbolists, expressionists disagreed with the realist belief that truth was equivalent to observable, measurable facts. They believed that the human essence was the spirit and soul, and that surface realities, the focus of sociological and psychological inquiry, frequently masked the true meaning of humanity. They attempted to peel away and eliminate the "real" veneer which hid the human soul. In this effort, they rejected realism and instead created distorted, exaggerated plays.

The plots of expressionist plays combined cause-and-effect and episodic structures. They typically began by putting their central character in a situation which emphasized his alienation from his world. The middle of the plays followed him through a series of episodes which further clarified his conflict with his world. These episodes did not necessarily grow causally out of each other, but they eventually culminated in conclusions which depicted the hero's destruction by forces beyond his control.

Expressionists typically created two-dimensional characters for their plays and gave them generic titles (The Teller, The Mother, The Gentleman with the Top Hat) instead of real names. The central characters of expressionist plays were frequently machine-like antiheroes. These flat characters typically communicated — or more often, failed to communicate — in cryptic, sparse language occasionally interspersed with wordy, lyrical passages, and the actors performed their roles in a purposefully uneven style. Distortion and exaggeration carried over into the scenery and costumes of expressionist plays. These bizarre, symbolic sets and costumes made the designer and technician especially important to expressionist productions.

German Expressionists

The best-known German expressionist playwrights included Frank Wedekind (1864-1918) with *Spring Awakening* (1906), his masterpiece about adolescent sexuality in a Victorian world; Georg Kaiser (1878-1945) who wrote *From Morn to Midnight* (1917), about a bank teller's descent to suicide; and Karel Capek (1890-1938) with his play *RUR* (1921), in which robots take over the world. Bertold Brecht wrote his early plays *Drums in the Night* (1922) and *Baal* (1923) in an expressionistic mode, and *Our Town* (1938), the American classic by Thornton Wilder (1897-1975), had expressionistic characteristics, as did his *Skin of Our Teeth* (1942).

Meanwhile, a number of playwrights continued to achieve success with plays in a realistic mode. They included the Englishmen John Galsworthy (1867-1933) and Terence Rattigan (1911-77) and the Americans Sidney Howard (1891-1939), Edward Sheldon (1886-1946), and Lillian Hellman (1905-84).

The Verse Drama Movement

In the 1930s, the British verse drama movement presented yet another challenge to realism. Stimulated by the annual Canterbury Festival, most of these plays dealt with religious subject matter. Major playwrights in the movement included T. S. Eliot (1888-1965) who wrote *Murder in the Cathedral* (1935), Dorothy Sayers (1893-1957) who wrote *The Zeal of Thy House* (1937), and Christopher Fry (1907-) who wrote *Thor, With Angels* (1948). Although these plays had a certain power and although Fry continued to write into the 1970s, the attempted return to verse dialog did not appeal to mass audiences or make much impact on other playwrights.

Musical Comedy

Another nonrealistic theatrical form which developed significantly during the first half of the twentieth century was musical comedy. *The Black Crook*, a melodramatic extravaganza which included songs and ballet, staged in New York in 1866, is usually considered to be the first musical comedy. The form, in which a dramatic story line combined spoken dialog with singing and dancing, became popular in Europe and America.

Through the first sixty years of its history, musical comedy tended to have flimsy story lines which served primarily to tie the songs and dances into a more-or-less unified whole. From World War I into the early 1940s, the form grew in popularity and also in sophistication. During this period, the contributions of American composers such as Irving Berlin (1888-1989), Jerome Kern (1885-1945), Cole Porter (1893-1964), George Gershwin (1898-1937), and Richard Rodgers (1902-79) in various combinations with book and lyric writers such as Oscar Hammerstein II (1895-1960), Ira Gershwin (1896-1983), and Lorenz Hart (1895-1943), made the United States the leading producer of musical comedy. Among the many musicals of the period were Kern and Hammerstein's *Show Boat* (1928), the Pulitzer-Prize-winning *Of Thee I Sing* (1931) by the Gershwins in collaboration with George S. Kaufman (1889-1961) and Morrie Ryskind (1895-1985), and Porter's *Anything Goes* (1934), with book by Guy Reginald Bolton (1884-1979) and P. G. Wodehouse (1881-1975).

The production of Rodgers and Hammerstein's *Oklahoma!* in 1943 became a milestone in the development of musical comedy. It featured a more sophisticated story line and brought dialog, music, dance, and staging into a tighter, more artistic unity. Rodgers and Hammerstein went on to collaborate on many more musicals, including *The Sound of Music* (1959).

Serious Musicals

In 1957, the collaboration of Leonard Bernstein (1918-90) with Stephen Sondheim (1930-) in *West Side Story* not only brought Sondheim into prominence but also helped make serious and even tragic story lines acceptable in musicals. In the 1960s and 70s, under the influence of Sondheim and the British team of Andrew Lloyd Webber (1948-) and Tim Rice (1944-), musicals focused increasingly on music, song, and dance at the expense of spoken dialog. In the last decades of the century, musicals continued to be popular with audiences and the classics were constantly restaged by high schools and community theatres. However, the immense expense of producing these spectacles on Broadway reduced the number of new contributions to the form.

Theory of Theatre

Several radical movements, related to expressionism by their attack on realistic traditions, included theatre in their theoretical manifestos. These movements — futurism, dadaism, and surrealism — tended to be anti-traditionalist, antiestablishment, antirealist, and antirational. Deeply disillusioned with a logic-based culture which could result in the madness of World War I, the people in these movements made virtues of the fragmentary, the insane, the temporary, and the socially objectionable. Since they were interested primarily in the visual arts and poetry and, at least in the case of surrealism, antagonistic to theatre, they produced no plays of lasting importance. They did, however, have an impact on theatrical performance later in the century. Their visual concepts found their way into scenic design, their irrationality fed into absurdism, and their antisocial attitude inspired some of the more radical theatre of the 1960s.

Antonin Artaud

Antonin Artaud (1895-1948) associated for a time with the surrealists and eventually had a considerable impact on theatre through a collection of his essays, *The Theatre and Its Double* (1938). In his book, Artaud said that great disasters such as the plague had a curative effect on society because they destroyed outmoded structures and stimulated the growth of new, potentially better patterns. He argued that theatre should have a similar effect on its audience. He found in Asian theatre, and particularly in Balinese dance theatre which he witnessed in 1931, elements of the kind of performance he believed would have his desired effect — performance which attacked the senses through shocking visual, aural, and emotional experiences and which bypassed or short-circuited the rational filters which kept audiences from being overpowered by the experience. He called the kind of performance he envisioned "the theatre of cruelty." Artaud's ideas provided a theoretical basis for some of the radical theatre of the 1950s and '60s including the happenings, Jean Genet's absurdist plays, and Peter Brook's 1962 production of Peter Weiss's *Marat/Sade*.

Stagecraft

Theatrical expressionism was closely related to the movement of the same name in painting and sculpture. In the visual arts, expressionists attempted to create and communicate emotional experience through the use of

428

exaggeration and distortion, powerful colors, and simplified figures. These same impulses, with the addition of clearly symbolic set pieces, characterized expressionist theatre productions. At the Bauhaus, an institution in Weimar, Germany, founded to apply functionalist and expressionist concepts to architecture and art, theatrical productions took distortion to the point of costumes which completely obscured the human figure or eliminated the human presence altogether in favor of large, dancing mobiles.

Vsevelod Meyerhold

In Russia, Vsevelod Meyerhold (1874-1940?) experimented with non-realistic approaches to performance and set design. Believing political and social revolution in his country meant that the arts would also have an opportunity to strike out in new directions, Meyerhold immediately offered his services to the government of the USSR and, in 1920, became head of the Theatre Section of the People's Commissariat for Education. The acting techniques he developed under the name bio-mechanics aimed to stimulate particular emotions in the performers and audience through stylized bodily motions which had little relation to actual human behavior.

In scenic design, with an approach he called constructivism, Meyerhold used the set as a machine for the play's action. Instead of representing actual environments, his sets provided an abstract arrangement of levels, inclines, and moving components intended to clarify or heighten the emotion of the performance. Unfortunately, Meyerhold had misjudged the artistic tastes and impulses of the USSR's leaders who came to favor a romantic propagandist style called socialist realism. He fell into disfavor, was arrested in 1938, and died under obscure circumstances in or around 1940. Meyerhold's constructivism, which used scenery almost like another performer in the play, increased the impact of nonrealistic styles on twentieth-century theatre.

Stage Lighting

The first half of the twentieth century also brought major advances in stage lighting. Ever since the Renaissance, technicians had struggled with the problem of controlling the brilliance, color, and distribution of artificial light to create the desired effect on stage. Technical advances in the nineteenth century, including Thomas Edison's invention of the incandescent electric light bulb in 1879, created new possibilities for stage lighting. Because of electricity's relative safety and ease of control, theatre technicians began to use it in place of gas lighting systems which disappeared by the end of the century. Throughout the twentieth century, theatre technicians invented successive generations of lamps, lighting instruments, and control systems which made lighting simpler, safer, and more useful as an artistic medium.

Theatrical Organization

Two developments in the United States during the early part of the twentieth century supplemented commercial theatre: The rise of educational theatre and the little theatre movement. Traditionally, colleges and universities had left theatre training in the hands of the profession. In 1905, however, George Pierce Baker (1866-1935), Harvard's first Professor of Dramatic Literature, offered a playwriting course which eventually grew into his 47 Workshop for the production of plays written under his teaching. Among Baker's students were Edward Sheldon, Sidney Howard, and Eugene O'Neill.

Educational Theatre

The success of Baker's pioneering work at Harvard, and later Yale, led other colleges and universities to initiate theatre programs. In 1936, to coordinate and improve their efforts, theatre academicians organized the American Educational Theatre Association, which was later reorganized as the American Theatre Association and then replaced by the Association for Theatre in Higher Education. Other organizations which were created to facilitate educational theatre were the American College Theatre Festival (1968-), a network of productions organized from the Kennedy Center in Washington, DC, and the University Resident Theatre Association which coordinated the semiprofessional producing companies attached to many major universities.

Educational theatre not only made good drama readily available in most American communities, but also improved the quality of professional theatre. By the late twentieth century, it became normal practice for theatre professionals to learn their craft in academic institutions.

The Little Theatre Movement

In the second decade of the century, noncommercial theatres sprang up across the United States and Canada. The locations of some of the most influential among these "little theatres" demonstrated the wide distribution of the movement: The Little Theatre of Chicago in Illinois, the Provincetown Players in Rhode Island and New York, the Arts and Crafts Theatre in Detroit, the Pasadena Playhouse in California, the Home Theatre in British Columbia, and the Hart House Theatre in Toronto.

Unhampered by commercial demands, free from the stultifying control of the Syndicate and its successors, and more interested in artistic excellence than financial success, the little theatre movement made several major contributions to theatre in America. First, these theatres gave an American home to European approaches to dramaturgy and production which came to be known as "the new stagecraft." The Pasadena Playhouse provided training for many important stage and screen actors. And the Provincetown Players and their successors produced the premieres of most of O'Neill's plays. The many community theatre groups which continued to thrive throughout the century gave millions of talented theatre amateurs a creative outlet and, in many locales, produced the only live theatre available.

Elmer Rice

Born in 1892 with the family name Reizenstein, Elmer Rice combined the practice of law with a career as a playwright. He began by writing melodramas, and his *On Trial* (1914) was the first American stage play to use the cinematic technique of the flashback. A versatile playwright, Rice not only produced *The Adding Machine*, his greatest success, but also wrote a naturalistic play about life in the slums, *Street Scene* (1929), which received a Pulitzer Prize. Elmer Rice died in 1967, three years after publishing an autobiography, *Minority Report.*

The Adding Machine

The Structures of Expressionism

The play uses a typical expressionist plot line which tells a cause-and-effect story by means of episodes which are basically complete in themselves. These episodes serve the primary purpose, not of advancing the story line, but rather of portraying the hero's situation. In good expressionistic fashion, the characters either bear generic titles (Mr. Zero, The Boss) or have fanciful names, like the barely pronounceable Shrdlu. The central character, a typical expressionistic antihero, is a loser victimized by dehumanizing technology. Rice's language has a more natural ring than that of many expressionistic plays, but he presents the dialog in nonrealistic sequences including endless monologs and the inconsequential small talk in Scene 3. The expressionistic scenery called for by the script and provided by Lee Simonson's set for the premier includes stylized wallpaper, sets that spin to express the disorientation of the characters, and a huge adding machine in the final scene with a lever almost as large as Mr. Zero himself. These exaggerated, distorted details extend to the sound effects, such as a doorbell that sounds like an adding machine, and bizarre costumes, such as that worn by Lieutenant Charles.

The Viewpoint of Expressionism

Rice's play, *The Adding Machine,* fully in tune with expressionistic disillusionment, portrays technological "progress" as a wrong direction. He also protests against stultifying, middle-class moral standards, the lack of cultural sensitivity among common folk, and racism. Repeatedly he demonstrates that, as a result of technology and cultural debasement, people don't really communicate — even at the most basic levels. In a manner which recalls *Everyman,* the allegorical characters and nonrealistic structures of this expressionist play emphasize message over action.

Production History

The Adding Machine was first produced at New York's Garrick Theatre in March, 1923, by the Theatre Guild. The Guild had been founded in 1919 with the goal of producing worthy new American and European plays which might be too risky for commercial theatre. It introduced Shaw's plays to American audiences and was a strong force in encouraging state-of-the-art theatre in the United States. Lee Simonson, who was on the Guild's board of managers and designed the scenery and costumes for *The Adding Machine,* did a great deal to popularize the new stagecraft in America. Edward G. Robinson, who played the role of Shrdlu and later became a well-known actor of stage and screen, was one of the many famous players who worked with the Guild. The Guild continued to produce plays well into the century and listed among its many successes the 1943 premier of Rodgers and Hammerstein's *Oklahoma!*

431

Early Twentieth-Century Theatre Timeline

- "THE BLACK CROOK" (1866)

FRANK WEDEKIND (1864-1918)

GEORGE PIERCE BAKER (1866-1935)

VSEVELOD MEYERHOLD (1874-1940?)

GEORG KAISER (1878-1945)

P.G. WODEHOUSE (1881-1975)

GUY REGINALD BOLTON (1884-1979)

JEROME KERN (1885-1945)

ROBERT EDMOND JONES (1887-1954)

EUGENE O'NEILL (1888-1953)

- "THE HAIRY APE" (1922)

T.S. ELIOT (1888-1965)

IRVING BERLIN (1888-1989)

GEORGE S. KAUFMAN (1889-1961)

KAREL CAPEK (1890-1938)

ELMER RICE (1892-1967)

- "THE ADDING MACHINE" (1923)

COLE PORTER (1893-1964)

LORENZ HART (1895-1943)

ANTONIN ARTAUD (1895-1948)

OSCAR HAMMERSTEIN II (1895-1960)

MORRIE RYSKIND (1895-1985)

IRA GERSHWIN (1896-1983)

THORNTON WILDER (1897-1975)

GEORGE GERSHWIN (1898-1937)

BERTOLT BRECHT (1898-1956)

RICHARD RODGERS (1902-79)

- "OKLAHOMA!" (1943)

WORLD WAR I (1914-18)

LEONARD BERNSTEIN (1918-90)

THE GREAT DEPRESSION (1929-1939)

STEPHEN SONDHEIM (1930-)

WORLD WAR II (1939-45)

TIM RICE (1944-)

ANDREW LLOYD WEBBER (1948-)

1860   1870   1880   1890   1900   1910   1920   1930   1940   1950   1960   1970   1980   1990

THE ADDING MACHINE

by Elmer Rice

The play's action takes place in an unspecified city in the early 1920s and in the world of the afterlife.

CAST OF CHARACTERS

MR. ZERO

MRS. ZERO

MESSRS. ONE, TWO THREE, FOUR, FIVE, SIX,
and their respective wives

DAISY DIANA DOROTHEA DEVORE

THE BOSS

POLICEMAN

TWO ATTENDANTS

JUDY O'GRADY

A YOUNG MAN

SHRDLU

A HEAD

LIEUTENANT CHARLES

JOE

SCENE ONE

(SCENE: A bedroom.

A small room containing an "installment plan" bed, dresser, and chairs. An ugly electric light fixture over the bed with a single glaring naked lamp. One small window with the shade drawn. The walls are papered with sheets of foolscap covered with columns of figures.

MR. ZERO is lying in the bed, facing the audience, his head and shoulders visible. He is thin, sallow, under-sized, and partially bald. MRS. ZERO is standing before the dresser arranging her hair for the night. She is forty-five, sharp-featured, gray streaks in her hair. She is shapeless in her long-sleeved cotton nightgown. She is wearing her shoes, over which sag her ungartered stockings.)

MRS. ZERO: *(As she takes down her hair)* I'm gettin' sick o' them Westerns. All them cowboys ridin' around an' foolin' with them ropes. I don't care nothin' about that. I'm sick of 'em. I don't see why they don't have more of them stories like "For Love's Sweet Sake." I like them sweet little love stories. They're nice an' wholesome. Mrs. Twelve was sayin' to me only yesterday, "Mrs. Zero," says she, "what I like is one of them wholesome stories, with just a sweet, simple little love story." "You're right, Mrs. Twelve," I says. "That's what I like, too." They're showin' too many Westerns at the Rosebud. I'm gettin' sick of them. I think we'll start goin' to the Peter Stuyvesant. They got a good bill there Wednesday night. There's a Chubby Delano comedy called "Sea-Sick." Mrs. Twelve was tellin' me about it. She says it's a scream. They're havin' a picnic in the country and they sit Chubby next to an old maid with a great big mouth. So he gets sore an' when she ain't lookin' he goes and catches a frog and drops it in her clam chowder. An' when she goes to eat the chowder the frog jumps out of it an' right into her mouth. Talk about laugh! Mrs. Twelve was tellin' me she laughed so she nearly passed out. He sure can pull some funny ones. An' they got that big Grace Darling feature, "A Mother's Tears." She's sweet. But I don't like her clothes. There's no style to them. Mrs. Nine was tellin' me she read in *Pictureland* that she ain't livin' with her husband. He's her second, too. I don't know whether they're divorced or just separated. You wouldn't think it to see her on the screen. She looks so sweet and innocent. Maybe it ain't true. You can't believe all you read. They say some Pittsburgh millionaire is crazy about her and that's why she ain't livin' with her husband. Mrs. Seven was tellin' me her brother-in-law has a friend that used to go to school with Grace Darling. He says her name ain't Grace Darling at all. Her right name is Elizabeth Dugan, he says, an' all them stories about her gettin' five thousand a week is the bunk, he says. She's sweet, though. Mrs. Eight was tellin' me that "A Mother's Tears" is the best picture she ever made. "Don't miss it, Mrs. Zero," she says. "It's sweet," she says. "Just sweet and wholesome. Cry!" she says, "I nearly cried my eyes out." There's one part in it where this big bum of an Englishman — he's a married man, too — an' she's this little simple country girl. An' she nearly falls for him, too. But she's sittin' out in the

434

garden, one day, and she looks up and there's her mother lookin' at her, right out of the clouds. So that night she locks the door of her room. An' sure enough, when everybody's in bed, along comes this big bum of an Englishman an' when she won't let him in what does he do but go an' kick open the door. "Don't miss it, Mrs. Zero," Mrs. Eight was tellin' me. It's at the Peter Stuyvesant Wednesday night, so don't be tellin' me you want to go to the Rosebud. The Eights seen it downtown at the Strand. They go downtown all the time. Just like us — nit! I guess by the time it gets to the Peter Stuyvesant all that part about kickin' in the door will be cut out. Just like they cut out that big cabaret scene in "The Price of Virtue." They sure are pullin' some rough stuff in the pictures nowadays. "It's no place for a young girl," I was tellin' Mrs. Eleven, only the other day. An' by the time they get uptown half of it is cut out. But you wouldn't go downtown — not if wild horses was to drag you. You can wait till they come uptown! Well, I don't want to wait, see? I want to see 'em when everybody else is seein' them an' not a month later. Now don't go tellin' me you ain't got the price. You could dig up the price all right, all right, if you wanted to. I notice you always got the price to go to the ball game. But when it comes to me havin' a good time then it's always: "I ain't got the price, I gotta start savin'." A fat lot you'll ever save! I got all I can do now makin' both ends meet an' you talkin' about savin'. *(She seats herself on a chair and begins removing her shoes and stockings.)* An' don't go pullin' that stuff about bein' tired. "I been workin' hard all day. Twice a day in the subway's enough for me." Tired! Where do you get that tired stuff, anyhow? What about me? Where do I come in? Scrubbin' floors an' cookin' your meals an' washin' your dirty clothes. An' you sittin' on a chair all day, just addin' figgers an' waitin' for five-thirty. There's no five-thirty for me. I don't wait for no whistle. I don't get no vacations neither. And what's more I don't get no pay envelope every Saturday night neither. I'd like to know where you'd be without me. An' what have I got to show for it? — slavin' my life away to give you a home. What's in it for me, I'd like to know? But it's my own fault, I guess. I was a fool for marryin' you. If I'd 'a' had any sense, I'd 'a' known what you were from the start. I wish I had it to do over again, I hope to tell you. You was goin' to do wonders, you was! You wasn't goin' to be a bookkeeper long — oh, no, not you. Wait till you got started — you was goin' to show 'em. There wasn't no job in the store that was too big for you. Well, I've been waitin' — waitin' for you to get started — see? It's been a good long wait, too. Twenty-five years! An' I ain't seen nothin' happen. Twenty-five years in the same job. Twenty-five years tomorrow! You're proud of it, ain't you? Twenty-five years in the same job an' never missed a day! That's somethin' to be proud of, ain't it? Sittin' for twenty-five years on the same chair, addin' up figures. What about bein' store-manager? I guess you forgot about that, didn't you? An' me at home here lookin' at the same four walls an' workin' my fingers to the bone to make both ends meet. Seven years since you got a raise! An' if you don't get one tomorrow, I'll bet a nickel you won't have the guts to go an' ask for one. I didn't pick much when I picked you, I'll tell the world. You ain't much to be proud of. *(She rises, goes to the window, and raises the shade. A few lighted windows are visible on the other side of the closed court. Looking out for a moment.)* She ain't walkin' around tonight, you can bet your sweet life on that. An' she won't be walkin' around any more nights, neither. Not in this house, anyhow. *(She turns away from the window.)* The dirty bum! The idea of her comin' to live in a house with respectable people. They should 'a' gave her six years, not six months. If I was the judge I'd of gave her life. A bum like that. *(She approaches the bed and stands there a moment.)* I guess you're sorry she's gone. I guess you'd like to sit home every night an' watch her goin's-on. You're somethin' to be proud of, you are! *(She stands on the bed and turns out the light . . . A thin stream of moonlight filters in from the court. The two figures are dimly visible. MRS. ZERO gets into bed.)*

You'd better not start nothin' with women, if you know what's good for you. I've put up with a lot, but I won't put up with that. I've been slavin' away for twenty-five years, makin' a home for you an' nothin' to show for it. If you was any kind of a man you'd have a decent job by now an' I'd be gettin' some comfort out of life — instead of bein' just a slave, washin' pots an' standin' over the hot stove. I've stood it for twenty-five years an' I guess I'll have to stand it twenty-five more. But don't you go startin' nothin' with women — *(She goes on talking as the curtain falls.)*

SCENE TWO

(SCENE: An office in a department store. Wood and glass partitions. In the middle of the room, two tall desks back to back. At one desk on a high stool is ZERO. Opposite him at the other desk, also on a high stool, is DAISY DIANA DOROTHEA DEVORE, a plain, middle-aged woman. Both wear green eye shades and paper sleeve protectors. A pendent electric lamp throws light upon both desks. DAISY reads aloud figures from a pile of slips which lie before her. As she reads the figures, ZERO enters them upon a large square sheet of ruled paper which lies before him.)

DAISY: *(Reading aloud)* Three ninety-eight. Forty-two cents. A dollar fifty. A dollar fifty. A dollar twenty-five. Two dollars. Thirty-nine cents. Twenty-seven fifty.
ZERO: *(Petulantly)* Speed it up a little, cancha?
DAISY: What's the rush? Tomorrow's another day.
ZERO: Aw, you make me sick.
DAISY: An' you make me sicker.
ZERO: Go on. Go on. We're losin' time.
DAISY: Then quit bein' so bossy.
　　　　(She reads.) Three dollars. Two sixty-nine. Eighty-one fifty. Forty dollars. Eight seventy-five. Who do you think you are, anyhow?
ZERO: Never mind who I think I am. You tend to your work.
DAISY: Aw, don't be givin' me so many orders. Sixty cents. Twenty-four cents. Seventy-five cents. A dollar fifty. Two fifty. One fifty. One fifty. Two fifty. I don't have to take it from you and what's more I won't.
ZERO: Aw, quit talkin'.

436

DAISY: I'll talk all I want. Three dollars. Fifty cents. Fifty cents. Seven dollars. Fifty cents. Two fifty. Three fifty. Fifty cents. One fifty. Fifty cents. *(She goes bending over the slips and transferring them from one pile to another. ZERO bends over his desk, busily entering the figures.)*

ZERO: *(Without looking up)* You make me sick. Always shootin' off your face about somethin'. Talk, talk, talk. Just like all the other women. Women make me sick.

DAISY: *(Busily fingering the slips)* Who do you think you are, anyhow? Bossin' me around. I don't have to take it from you, and what's more I won't. *(They both attend closely to their work, neither looking up.)*

ZERO: Women make me sick. They're all alike. The judge gave her six months. I wonder what they do in the work-house. Peel potatoes. I'll bet she's sore at me. Maybe she'll try to kill me when she gets out. I better be careful. Hello, Girl Slays Betrayer. Jealous Wife Slays Rival. You can't tell what a woman's liable to do. I better be careful.

DAISY: I'm gettin' sick of it. Always pickin' on me about somethin'. Never a decent word out of you. Not even the time o' day.

ZERO: I guess she wouldn't have the nerve at that. Maybe she don't even know it's me. They didn't even put my name in the paper, the big bums. Maybe she's been in the work-house before. A bum like that. She didn't have nothin' on that one time — nothin' but a shirt. *(He glances up quickly, then bends over again)* You make me sick. I'm sick of lookin' at your face.

DAISY: Gee, ain't that whistle ever goin' to blow? You didn't used to be like that. Not even good mornin' or good evenin'. I ain't done nothin' to you. It's the young girls. Goin' around without corsets.

ZERO: You face is gettin' all yeller. Why don't you put some paint on it? She was puttin' on paint that time. On her cheeks and on her lips. And that blue stuff on her eyes. Just sittin' there in a shimmy puttin' on the paint. An' walkin' around the room with her legs all bare.

DAISY: I wish I was dead.

ZERO: I was a goddam fool to let the wife get on to me. She oughta get six months at that. The dirty bum. Livin' in a house with respectable people. She'd be livin' there yet, if the wife hadn't o' got on to me. Damn her!

DAISY: I wish I was dead.

ZERO: Maybe another one'll move in. Gee, that would be great. But the wife's got her eye on me now.

DAISY: I'm scared to do it, though.

ZERO: You oughta move into that room. It's cheaper than where you're livin' now. I better tell you about it. I don't mean to be always pickin' on you.

DAISY: Gas. The smell of it makes me sick. *(ZERO looks up and clears his throat.)*

DAISY: *(Looking up startled)* Whadja say?

ZERO: I didn't say nothin'.

DAISY: I thought you did.

ZERO: You thought wrong. *(They bend over their work again.)*

DAISY: A dollar sixty. A dollar fifty. Two ninety. One sixty-two.

ZERO: Why the hell should I tell you? Fat chance of you forgettin' to pull down the shade!

DAISY: If I asked for carbolic they might get on to me.

ZERO: Your hair's gettin' gray. You don't wear them shirt waists any more with the low collars. When you'd bend down to pick somethin' up —

DAISY: I wish I knew what to ask for. Girl Takes Mercury After All-Night Party. Woman In Ten-Story Death Leap.

ZERO: I wonder where'll she go when she gets out. Gee, I'd like to make a date with her. Why didn't I go over there the night my wife went to Brooklyn? She never woulda found out.

DAISY: I seen Pauline Frederick do it once. Where could I get a pistol though?

ZERO: I guess I didn't have the nerve.

DAISY: I'll bet you'd be sorry then that you been so mean to me. How do I know, though? Maybe you wouldn't.

ZERO: Nerve! I got as much nerve as anybody. I'm on the level, that's all. I'm a married man and I'm on the level.

DAISY: Anyhow, why ain't I got a right to live? I'm as good as anybody else. I'm too refined, I guess. That's the whole trouble.

ZERO: The time the wife had pneumonia I thought she was goin' to pass out. But she didn't. The doctor's bill was eighty-seven dollars. *(Looking up)* Hey, wait a minute! Didn't you say eighty-seven dollars?

DAISY: *(Looking up)* What?

ZERO: Was the last you said eighty-seven dollars?

DAISY: *(Consulting the slip)* Forty-two fifty.

ZERO: Well, I made a mistake. Wait a minute. *(He busies himself with an eraser.)* All right. Shoot.

DAISY: Six dollars. Three fifteen. Two twenty-five. Sixty-five cents. A dollar twenty. You talk to me as if I was dirt.

ZERO: I wonder if I could kill the wife without anybody findin' out. In bed some night. With a pillow.

DAISY: I used to think you was stuck on me.

ZERO: I'd get found out, though. They always have ways.

DAISY: We used to be so nice and friendly together when I first came here. You used to talk to me then.

ZERO: Maybe she'll die soon. I noticed she was coughin' this mornin'.

DAISY: You used to tell me all kinds o' things. You were goin' to show them all. Just the same, you're still sittin' here.

ZERO: Then I could do what I damn please. Oh, boy!

DAISY: Maybe it ain't all your fault neither. Maybe if you'd had the right kind o' wife — somebody with a lot of common-sense, somebody refined — me!

ZERO: At that, I guess I'd get tired of bummin' around. A feller wants some place to hang his hat.

DAISY: I wish she would die.

ZERO: And when you start goin' with women you're liable to get into trouble. And lose your job maybe.

DAISY: Maybe you'd marry me.

ZERO: Gee, I wish I'd gone over there that night.

DAISY: Then I could quit workin'.

ZERO: Lots o' women would be glad to get me.

DAISY: You could look a long time before you'd find a sensible, refined girl like me.

ZERO: Yes, sir, they could look a long time before they'd find a steady meal-ticket like me.

DAISY: I guess I'd be too old to have any kids. They say it ain't safe after thirty-five.

ZERO: Maybe I'd marry you. You might be all right, at that.

DAISY: I wonder — if you don't want kids — whether — if there's any way —

ZERO: *(Looking up)* Hey! Hey! Can't you slow up? What do you think I am — a machine?

DAISY: *(Looking up)* Say, what do you want, anyhow? First it's too slow an' then it's too fast. I guess you don't know what you want.

ZERO: Well, never mind about that. Just you slow up.

DAISY: I'm gettin' sick o' this. I'm goin' to ask to be transferred.

ZERO: Go ahead. You can't make me mad.

DAISY: Aw, keep quiet. *(She reads)* Two forty-five. A dollar twenty. A dollar fifty. Ninety cents. Sixty-three cents.

ZERO: Marry you! I guess not! You'd be as bad as the one I got.

DAISY: You wouldn't care if I did ask. I got a good mind to ask.

ZERO: I was a fool to get married.

DAISY: Then I'd never see you at all.

ZERO: What chance has a guy got with a woman tied around his neck?

DAISY: That time at the store picnic — the year your wife couldn't come — you were nice to me then.

ZERO: Twenty-five years holdin' down the same job!

DAISY: We were together all day — just sittin' around under the trees.

ZERO: I wonder if the boss remembers about it bein' twenty-five years.

DAISY: And comin' home that night — you sat next to me in the big delivery wagon.

ZERO: I got a hunch there's a big raise comin' to me.

DAISY: I wonder what it feels like to be really kissed. Men — dirty pigs! They want the bold ones.

ZERO: If he don't come across I'm goin' right up to the front office and tell him where he gets off.

DAISY: I wish I was dead.

ZERO: "Boss," I'll say, "I want to have a talk with you." "Sure," he'll say, "sit down. Have a Corona Corona." "No," I'll say, "I don't smoke." "How's that?" he'll say. "Well, boss," I'll say, "it's this way. Every time I feel like smokin' I just take a nickel and put it in the old sock. A penny saved is a penny earned, that's the way I look at it." "Damn sensible," he'll say. "You got a wise head on you, Zero."

DAISY: I can't stand the smell of gas. It makes me sick. You coulda kissed me if you wanted to.

ZERO: "Boss," I'll say, "I ain't quite satisfied. I been on the job twenty-five years now and if I'm gonna stay I gotta see a future ahead of me." "Zero," he'll say, "I'm glad you came in. I've had my eye on you, Zero. Nothin' gets by me." "Oh, I know that, boss," I'll say. That'll hand him a good laugh, that will. "You're a valuable man, Zero," he'll say, "and I want you right up here with me in the front office. You're done

439

addin' figgers. Monday mornin' you move up here."

DAISY: Them kisses in the movies — them long ones — right on the mouth —

ZERO: I'll keep a-goin' right on up after that. I'll show some of them birds where they get off.

DAISY: That one the other night — "The Devil's Alibi" — he put his arms around her — and her head fell back and her eyes closed — like she was in a daze.

ZERO: Just give me about two years and I'll show them birds where they get off.

DAISY: I guess that's what it's like — a kinda daze — when I see them like that, I just seem to forget everything.

ZERO: Then me for a place in Jersey. And maybe a little Buick. No tin Lizzie for mine. Wait till I get started — I'll show 'em.

DAISY: I can see it now when I kinda half-close my eyes. The way her head fell back. And his mouth pressed right up against hers. Oh, Gawd! it must be grand! *(There is a sudden shrill blast from a steam whistle.)*

DAISY and ZERO: *(Together)* The whistle!

> *(With great agility they get off their stools, remove their eye shades and sleeve protectors and put them on the desks. Then each produces from behind the desk a hat — ZERO, a dusty derby, DAISY a frowsy straw . . . DAISY puts on her hat and turns toward ZERO as though she were about to speak to him. But he is busy cleaning his pen and pays no attention to her. She sighs and goes toward the door at the left.)*

ZERO: *(Looking up)* G'night, Miss Devore.

> *(But she does not hear him and exits. ZERO takes up his hat and goes left. The door at the right opens and the BOSS enters — middle-aged, stoutish, bald, well-dressed.)*

THE BOSS: *(Calling)* Oh — er — Mister — er —

> *(ZERO turns in surprise, sees who it is and trembles nervously.)*

ZERO: *(Obsequiously)* Yes, sir. Do you want me, sir?

BOSS: Yes. Just come here a moment, will you?

ZERO: Yes, sir. Right away, sir. *(He fumbles his hat, picks it up, stumbles, recovers himself, and approaches the BOSS, every fibre quivering.)*

BOSS: Mister — er — er —

ZERO: Zero.

BOSS: Yes, Mr. Zero. I wanted to have a little talk with you.

ZERO: *(With a nervous grin)* Yes, sir, I been kinda expectin' it.

BOSS: *(Staring at him)* Oh, have you?

ZERO: Yes, sir.

BOSS: How long have you been with us, Mister — er — Mister —

ZERO: Zero.

BOSS: Yes, Mister Zero.

ZERO: Twenty-five years today.

BOSS: Twenty-five years! That's a long time.

ZERO: Never missed a day.

BOSS: And you've been doing the same work all the time?

ZERO: Yes, sir. Right here at this desk.

BOSS: Then, in that case, a change probably won't be unwelcome to you.

ZERO: No, sir, it won't. And that's the truth.

BOSS: We've been planning a change in this department for some time.

ZERO: I kinda thought you had your eye on me.

BOSS: You were right. The fact is that my efficiency experts have recommended the installation of adding machines.

ZERO: *(Staring at him)* Addin' machines?

BOSS: Yes, you've probably seen them. A mechanical device that adds automatically.

ZERO: Sure. I've seen them. Keys — and a handle that you pull. *(He goes through the motions in the air.)*

BOSS: That's it. They do the work in half the time and a high-school girl can operate them. Now, of course, I'm sorry to lose an old and faithful employee —

ZERO: Excuse me, but would you mind sayin' that again?

BOSS: I say I'm sorry to lose an employee who's been with me for so many years —

(Soft music is heard — the sound of the mechanical player of a distant merry-go-round. The part of the floor upon which the desk and stools are standing begins to revolve very slowly.)

BOSS: But, of course, in an organization like this, efficiency must be the first consideration —

(The music becomes gradually louder and the revolutions are rapid.)

BOSS: You will draw your salary for the full month. And I'll direct my secretary to give you a letter of recommendation —

ZERO: Wait a minute, boss. Let me get this right. You mean I'm canned?

BOSS: *(Barely making himself heard above the increasing volume of sound)* I'm sorry — no other alternative — greatly regret — old employee — efficiency — economy — business — *business* — BUSINESS —

(His voice is drowned by the music. The platform is revolving rapidly now. ZERO and the BOSS face each other. They are entirely motionless save for the BOSS's jaws, which open and close incessantly. But the words are inaudible. The music swells and swells. To it is added every off-stage effect of the theatre: the wind, the waves, the galloping horses, the locomotive whistle, the sleigh bells, the automobile siren, the glass-crash. New Year's Eve, Election Night, Armistice Day, and the Mardi-Gras. The noise is deafening, maddening, unendurable. Suddenly it culminates in a terrific peal of thunder. For an instant there is a flash of red and then everything is plunged into blackness.)

(Curtain)

SCENE THREE

(SCENE: The ZERO dining room. Entrance door at right. Doors to kitchen and bedroom at left. The walls, as in the first scene, are papered with foolscap sheets covered with columns of figures. In the middle of the room, upstage, a table set for two. Along each side wall, seven chairs are ranged in symmetrical rows.

At the rise of the curtain MRS. ZERO is seen seated at the table looking alternately at the entrance door and a clock on the wall. She wears a bungalow apron over her best dress.

After a few moments, the entrance door opens and ZERO enters. He hangs his hat on a rack behind the door and coming over to the table seats himself at the vacant place. His movements throughout are quiet and abstracted.)

MRS. ZERO: *(Breaking the silence)* Well, it was nice of you to come home. You're only an hour late and that ain't very much. The supper don't get very cold in an hour. An' of course the part about our havin' a lot of company tonight don't matter.

(They begin to eat.)

Ain't you even got sense enough to come home on time? Didn't I tell you we're goin' to have a lot o' company tonight? Didn't you know the Ones are comin'? An' the Twos? An' the Threes? An' the Fours? An' the Fives? And the Sixes? Didn't I tell you to be home on time? I might as well talk to a stone wall.

(They eat for a few moments in silence.)

I guess you musta had some important business to attend to. Like watchin' the score-board. Or was two kids havin' a fight an' you was the referee? You sure do have a lot of business to attend to. It's a wonder you have time to come home at all. You gotta tough life, you have. Walk in, hang up your hat, an' put on the nose-bag. An' me in the hot kitchen all day, cookin' your supper an' waitin' for you to get good an' ready to come home!

(Again they eat in silence.)

Maybe the boss kept you late tonight. Tellin' you what a big noise you are and how the store couldn't 'a' got along if you hadn't been pushin' a pen for twenty-five years. Where's the gold medal he pinned on you? Did some blind old lady take it away from you or did you leave it on the seat of the boss's limousine when he brought you home?

(Again a few moments of silence.)

I'll bet he gave you a big raise, didn't he? Promoted you from the third floor to the fourth, maybe. Raise? A fat chance you got o' gettin' a raise. All they gotta do is put an ad in the paper. There's ten thousand like you layin' around the streets. You'll be holdin' down the same job at the end of another twenty-five years — if you ain't forgot how to add by that time.

(A noise is heard off-stage, a sharp clicking such as is made by the operation of the keys and levers of an adding machine. ZERO raises his head for a moment, but lowers it almost instantly.)

MRS. ZERO: There's the door-bell. The company's here already. And we ain't hardly finished supper.

(She rises.)

But I'm goin' to clear off the table whether you're finished or not. If you want your supper, you got a right to be home on time. Not standin' around lookin' at score-boards.

(As she piles up the dishes, ZERO rises and goes toward the entrance door.)

Wait a minute! Don't open the door yet. Do you want the company to see all the mess? An' go an' put on a clean collar. You got red ink all over it.

442

(ZERO goes toward bedroom door.)
I should think after pushin' a pen for twenty-five years, you'd learn how to do it without gettin' ink on your collar.
(ZERO exits to bedroom. MRS. ZERO takes dishes to kitchen talking as she goes.)
I guess I can stay up all night now washin' dishes. You should worry! That's what a man's got a wife for, ain't it? Don't he buy her her clothes an' let her eat with him at the same table? An' all she's gotta do is cook the meals an' do the washin' an' scrub the floor, an' wash the dishes, when the company goes. But, believe me, you're goin' to sling a mean dish-towel when the company goes tonight!
(While she is talking ZERO enters from bedroom. He wears a clean collar and is cramming the soiled one furtively into his pocket. MRS. ZERO enters from kitchen. She has removed her apron and carries a table cover which she spreads hastily over the table. The clicking noise is heard again.)
MRS. ZERO: There's the bell again. Open the door, cancha?
(ZERO goes to the entrance door and opens it. Six men and six women file into the room in a double column. The men are all shapes and sizes, but their dress is identical with that of ZERO in every detail. Each, however, wears a wig of a different color. The women are all dressed alike, too, except that the dress of each is of a different color.)
MRS. ZERO: *(Taking the first woman's hand)* How de do, Mrs. One.
MRS. ONE: How de do, Mrs. Zero.
(MRS. ZERO repeats this formula with each woman in turn. ZERO does the same with the men except that he is silent throughout. The files now separate, each man taking a chair from the right wall and each woman one from the left wall. Each sex forms a circle with the chairs very close together. The men — all except ZERO — smoke cigars. The women munch chocolates.)
SIX: Some rain we're havin'.
FIVE: Never saw the like of it.
FOUR: Worst in fourteen years, paper says.
THREE: Y'can't always go by the papers.
TWO: No, that's right, too.
ONE: We're liable to forget from year to year.
SIX: Yeh, come t' think, last year was pretty bad, too.
FIVE: An' how about two years ago?
FOUR: Still this year's pretty bad.
THREE: Yeh, no gettin' away from that.
TWO: Might be a whole lot worse.
ONE: Yeh, it's all the way you look at it. Some rain, though.
MRS. SIX: I like them little organdie dresses.
MRS. FIVE: Yeh, with a little lace trimmin' on the sleeves.
MRS. FOUR: Well, I like 'em plain myself.
MRS. THREE: Yeh, what I always say is the plainer the more refined.
MRS. TWO: Well, I don't think a little lace does any harm.
MRS. ONE: No, it kinda dresses it up.
MRS. ZERO: Well, I always say it's all a matter of taste.
MRS. SIX: I saw you at the Rosebud Movie Thursday night, Mr. One.

ONE: Pretty punk show, I'll say.
TWO: They're gettin' worse all the time.
MRS. SIX: But who was the charming lady, Mr. One?
ONE: Now don't you go makin' trouble for me. That was my sister.
MRS. FIVE: Oho! That's what they all say.
MRS. FOUR: Never mind! I'll bet Mrs. One knows what's what, all right.
MRS. ONE: Oh, well, he can do what he likes — 'slong as he behaves himself.
THREE: You're in luck at that, One. Fat chance I got of gettin' away from the
frau even with my sister.
MRS. THREE: You oughta be glad you got a good wife to look after you.
THE OTHER WOMEN: *(In unison)* That's right, Mrs. Three.
FIVE: I guess I know who wears the pants in your house, Three.
MRS. ZERO: Never mind. I saw them holdin' hands at the movie the other
night.
THREE: She musta been tryin' to get some money away from me.
MRS. THREE: Swell chance anybody'd have of gettin' any money away from
you.
          (General laughter.)
FOUR: They sure are a loving couple.
MRS. TWO: Well, I think we oughta change the subject.
MRS. ONE: Yes, let's change the subject.
SIX: *(Sotto voce)* Did you hear the one about the travellin' salesman?
FIVE: It seems this guy was in a sleeper.
FOUR: Goin' from Albany to San Diego.
THREE: And in the berth was an old maid.
TWO: With a wooden leg.
ONE: Well, along about midnight —
          (They all put their heads together and whisper.)
MRS. SIX: *(Sotto voce)* Did you hear about the Sevens?
MRS. FIVE: They're gettin' a divorce.
MRS. FOUR: It's the second time for him.
MRS. THREE: They're two of a kind, if you ask me.
MRS. TWO: One's as bad as the other.
MRS. ONE: Worse.
MRS. ZERO: They say that she —
          (They all put their heads together and whisper.)
SIX: I think this woman suffrage is the bunk.
FIVE: It sure is! Politics is a man's business.
FOUR: Woman's place is in the home.
THREE: That's it! Lookin' after the kids, 'stead of hangin' around the streets.
TWO: You hit the nail on the head that time.
ONE: The trouble is they don't know what they want.
MRS. SIX: Men sure get me tired.
MRS. FIVE: They are a lazy lot.
MRS. FOUR: And dirty.
MRS. THREE: Always grumblin' about somethin'.
MRS. TWO: When they're not lyin'!
MRS. ONE: Or messin' up the house.
MRS. ZERO: Well, believe me, I tell mine where he gets off.
SIX: Business conditions are sure bad.

444

FIVE: Never been worse.
FOUR: I don't know what we're comin' to.
THREE: I look for a big smash-up in about three months.
TWO: Wouldn't surprise me a bit.
ONE: We're sure headin' for trouble.
MRS. SIX: My aunt has gall-stones.
MRS. FIVE: My husband has bunions.
MRS. FOUR: My sister expects next month.
MRS. THREE: My cousin's husband has erysipelas.
MRS. TWO: My niece has St. Vitus's dance.
MRS. ONE: My boy has fits.
MRS. ZERO: I never felt better in my life. Knock wood!
SIX: Too damn much agitation, that's at the bottom of it.
FIVE: That's it! too damn many strikes.
FOUR: Foreign agitators, that's what it is.
THREE: They ought be run outa the country.
TWO: What the hell do they want, anyhow?
ONE: They don't know what they want, if you ask me.
SIX: America for the Americans is what I say!
ALL: *(In unison)* That's it! Damn foreigners! Damn dagoes! Damn Catholics!
　　Damn sheenies! Damn niggers! Jail 'em! shoot 'em! hang 'em! lynch
　　'em! burn 'em!
　　　(They all rise.)
ALL: *(Sing in unison)* "My country 'tis of thee,
　　Sweet land of liberty!"
MRS. FOUR: Why so pensive, Mr. Zero?
ZERO: *(Speaking for the first time)* I'm thinkin'.
MRS. FOUR: Well, be careful not to sprain your mind.
　　(Laughter.)
MRS. ZERO: Look at the poor men all by themselves. We ain't very sociable.
ONE: Looks like we're neglectin' the ladies.
　　(The women cross the room and join the men, all chattering loudly.
　　The door-bell rings.)
MRS. ZERO: Sh! The door-bell!
　　(The volume of sound slowly diminishes. Again the door-bell.)
ZERO: *(Quietly)* I'll go. It's for me.
　　(They watch curiously as ZERO goes to the door and opens it,
　　admitting a policeman. There is a murmur of surprise and excitement.)
POLICEMAN: I'm lookin' for Mr. Zero.
　　(They all point to ZERO.)
ZERO: I've been expectin' you.
POLICEMAN: Come along!
ZERO: Just a minute. *(He puts his hand in his pocket.)*
POLICEMAN: What's he tryin' to pull? *(He draws a revolver.)* I've got you
　　covered.
ZERO: Sure, that's all right. I just want to give you somethin'. *(He takes the*
　　collar from his pocket and gives it to the policeman.)
POLICEMAN: *(Suspiciously)* What's that?
ZERO: The collar I wore.
POLICEMAN: What do I want it for?

ZERO: It's got blood-stains on it.
POLICEMAN: *(Pocketing it)* All right, come along!
ZERO: *(Turning to MRS. ZERO)* I gotta go with him. You'll have to dry the dishes yourself.
MRS. ZERO: *(Rushing forward)* What are they takin' you for?
ZERO: *(Calmly)* I killed the boss this afternoon. *(Quick curtain as the POLICEMAN takes him off.)*

SCENE FOUR

(SCENE: A court of justice. Three bare white walls without door or windows except for a single door in the right wall. At the right is a jury-box in which are seated MESSRS. ONE, TWO, THREE, FOUR, FIVE and SIX and their respective wives. On either side of the jury box stands a uniformed OFFICER. Opposite the jury-box is a long, bare oak table piled high with law books. Behind the books ZERO is seated, his face buried in his hands. There is no other furniture in the room. A moment after the rise of the curtain, one of the officers rises and going around the table, taps ZERO on the shoulder. ZERO rises and accompanies the officer. The OFFICER escorts him to the great empty space in the middle of the court room, facing the jury. He motions to ZERO to stop, then points to the jury and resumes his place beside the jury-box. ZERO stands there looking at the jury, bewildered and half afraid. The JURORS give no sign of having seen him. Throughout they sit with folded arms, staring stolidly before them.)

ZERO: *(Beginning to speak haltingly)* Sure I killed him. I ain't sayin' I didn't, am I? Sure I killed him. Them lawyers give me a good stiff pain, that's what they give me. Half the time I don't know what the hell they're talkin' about. Objection sustained. Objection over-ruled. What's the big idea, anyhow? You ain't heard me do any objectin', have you? Sure not! What's the idea of objectin'? You got a right to know. What I say is if one bird kills another bird, why you got a right to call him for it. That's what I say. I know all about that. I been on the jury, too. Them lawyers! Don't let 'em fill you full of bunk. All that bull about it bein' red ink on the bill-file. Red ink nothin'! It was blood, see? I want you to get that right. I killed him, see? Right through the heart with the bill-file, see? I want you to get that right — all of you. One, two, three, four, five, six, seven, eight, nine, ten, eleven, twelve. Twelve of you. Six and six. That makes twelve. I figgered it up often enough. Six and six makes twelve. And five is seventeen. And eight is twenty-five. And three is twenty-eight. Eight and carry two. Aw, cut it out! Them damn figgers! I can't forget 'em. Twenty-five years, see? Eight hours a day, exceptin' Sundays. And July and August half-day Saturday. One week's vacation with pay. And another week without pay if you want it. Who the hell wants it? Layin' around the house listenin' to the wife tellin' you where you get off. Nix! An' legal holidays. I nearly forgot them. New Year's, Washington's Birthday, Decoration Day, Fourth o' July, Labor Day, Election Day, Thanksgivin', Christmas. Good Friday if you want it. An' if you're a Jew, Young Kipper an' the other one — I forget what they call it. The dirty sheenies — always gettin' two to the other bird's one. An' when a holiday comes on Sunday, you get Monday off. So that's fair enough. But when the Fourth o' July comes on Saturday, why you're out o' luck on account of

Saturday bein' a half-day anyhow. Get me? Twenty-five years — I'll tell you somethin' funny. Decoration Day an' the Fourth o' July are always on the same day o' the week. Twenty-five years. Never missed a day, and never more'n five minutes late. Look at my time card if you don't believe me. Eight twenty-seven, eight thirty, eight twenty-nine, eight twenty-seven, eight thirty-two. Eight an' thirty-two's forty an' — Goddam them figgers! I can't forget 'em. They're funny things, them figgers. They look like people sometimes. The eights, see? Two dots for the eyes and a dot for the nose. An' a line. That's the mouth, see? An' there's others remind you of other things — but I can't talk about them on account of there bein' ladies here. Sure I killed him. Why didn't he shut up? If he'd only shut up! Instead o' talkin' an' talkin' about how sorry he was an' what a good guy I was an' this an' that. I felt like sayin' to him: "For Christ's sake, shut up!" But I didn't have the nerve, see? I didn't have the nerve to say that to the boss. An' he went on talkin', sayin' how sorry he was, see? He was standin' right close to me. An' his coat only had two buttons on it. Two an' two makes four an' — aw, can it! An' there was the bill-file on the desk. Right where I could touch it. It ain't right to kill a guy. I know that. When I read all about him in the paper an' about his three kids I felt like a cheap skate, I tell you. They had the kids' pictures in the paper, right next to mine. An' his wife, too. Gee, it must be swell to have a wife like that. Some guys sure is lucky. An' he left fifty thousand dollars just for a rest-room for the girls in the store. He was a good guy, at that. Fifty thousand. That's more'n twice as much as I'd have if I saved every nickel I ever made. Let's see. Twenty-five an' twenty-five an' twenty-five an' — aw, cut it out! An' the ads had a big, black border around 'em; an' all it said was that the store would be closed for three days on account of the boss bein' dead. That nearly handed me a laugh, that did. All them floor-walkers an' buyers an' high-muck-a-mucks havin' me to thank for gettin' three days off. I hadn't oughta killed him. I ain't sayin' nothin' about that. But I thought he was goin' to give me a raise, see? On account of bein' there twenty-five years. He never talked to me before, see? Except one mornin' we happened to come in the store together and I held the door open for him and he said "Thanks." Just like that, see? "Thanks!" That was the only time he ever talked to me. An' when I seen him comin' up to my desk, I didn't know where I got off. A big guy like that comin' up to my desk. I felt like I was chokin' like and all of a sudden I got a kind o' bad taste in my mouth like when you get up in the mornin'. I didn't have no right to kill him. The district attorney is right about that. He read the law to you, right out o' the book. Killin' a bird — that's wrong. But there was that girl, see? Six months they gave her. It was a dirty trick tellin' the cops on her like that. I shouldn't 'a' done that. But what was I gonna do? The wife wouldn't let up on me. I hadda do it. She used to walk around the room, just in her undershirt, see? Nothin' else on. Just her undershirt. An' they gave her six months. That's the last I'll ever see of her. Them birds — how do they get away with it? Just grabbin' women, the way you see 'em do in the pictures. I've seen lots I'd like to grab like that, but I ain't got the nerve — in the

447

subway an' on the street an' in the store buyin' things. Pretty soft for them shoe-salesmen, I'll say, lookin' at women's legs all day. Them lawyers! They give me a pain, I tell you — a pain! Sayin' the same thing over an' over again. I never said I didn't kill him. But that ain't the same as bein' a regular murderer. What good did it do me to kill him? I didn't make nothin' out of it. Answer yes or no! Yes or no, me elbow! There's some things you can't answer yes or no. Give me the once-over, you guys. Do I look like a murderer? Do I? I never did no harm to nobody. Ask the wife. She'll tell you. Ask anybody. I never got into trouble. You wouldn't count that one time at the Polo Grounds. That was just fun like. Everybody was yellin', "Kill the empire! Kill the empire!" An' before I knew what I was doin' I fired the pop bottle. It was on account of everybody yellin' like that. Just in fun like, see? The yeller dog! Callin' that one a strike — a mile away from the plate. Anyhow, the bottle didn't hit him. An' when I seen the cop comin' up the aisle, I beat it. That didn't hurt nobody. It was just in fun like, see? An' that time in the subway. I was readin' about a lynchin', see? Down in Georgia. They took the nigger an' they tied him to a tree. An' they poured kerosene on him and lit a big fire under him. The dirty nigger! Boy, I'd of liked to been there, with a gat in each hand pumpin' him full of lead. I was readin' about it in the subway, see? Right at Times Square where the big crowd gets on. An' all of a sudden this big nigger steps right on my foot. It was lucky for him I didn't have a gun on me. I'd of killed him sure, I guess. I guess he couldn't help it all right on account of the crowd, but a nigger's got no right to step on a white man's foot. I told him where he got off all right. The dirty nigger. But that didn't hurt nobody, either. I'm a pretty steady guy, you gotta admit that. Twenty-five years in one job an' I never missed a day. Fifty-two weeks in a year. Fifty-two an' fifty-two an' fifty two an' — They didn't have t' look for me, did they? I didn't try to run away, did I? Where was I goin' to run to! I wasn't thinkin' about it at all, see? I'll tell you what I was thinkin' about — how I was goin' to break it to the wife about bein' canned. He canned me after twenty-five years, see? Did the lawyers tell you about that? I forget. All that talk gives me a headache. Objection sustained. Objection over-ruled. Answer yes or no. It gives me a headache. And I can't get the figgers outta my head, neither. But that's what I was thinkin' about — how I was goin' t' break it to the wife about bein' canned. An' what Miss Devore would think when she heard about me killin' him. I bet she never thought I had the nerve to do it. I'd of married her if the wife had passed out. I'd be holdin' down my job yet, if he hadn't o' canned me. But he kept talkin' an' talkin'. An' there was the bill-file right where I could reach it. Do you get me? I'm just a regular guy like anybody else. Like you birds, now.

(For the first time the JURORS relax, looking indignantly at each other and whispering.)

Suppose you was me, now. Maybe you'd 'a' done the same thing. That's the way you oughta look at it, see? Suppose you was me —

THE JURORS: *(Rising as one and shouting in unison)* GUILTY! *(ZERO falls back, stunned for a moment by their vociferousness. The JURORS right-face in their places and file quickly out of the jury-box and toward the door in a double column.)*

ZERO: *(Recovering speech as the JURORS pass out at the door)* Wait a minute. Jest a minute. You don't get me right. Jest give me a chance an' I'll tell you how it was. I'm all mixed up, see? On account of them lawyers. And the figgers in my head. But I'm goin' to tell you how it was. I was there twenty-five years, see? An' they gave her six months, see? *(He goes on haranguing the empty jury-box as the curtain falls.)*

SCENE FIVE

(SCENE: A grave-yard in full moonlight. It is a second-rate grave-yard — no elaborate tombstones or monuments — just simple headstones and here and there a cross. At the back is an iron fence with a gate in the middle. At first no one is visible, but there are occasional sounds throughout: the hooting of an owl, the whistle of a distant whippoorwill, the croaking of a bull-frog, and the yowling of a serenading cat. After a few moments two figures appear outside the gate — a man and a woman. She pushes the gate and it opens with a rusty creak. The couple enter. They are now fully visible in the moonlight — JUDY O'GRADY and a YOUNG MAN.)

JUDY: *(Advancing)* Come on, this is the place.

YOUNG MAN: *(Hanging back)* This! Why this here is a cemetery.

JUDY: Aw, quit yer kiddin'!

YOUNG MAN: You don't mean to say —

JUDY: What's the matter with this place?

YOUNG MAN: A cemetery!

JUDY: Sure. What of it?

YOUNG MAN: You must be crazy.

JUDY: This place is all right, I tell you. I been here lots o' times.

YOUNG MAN: Nix on this place for me!

JUDY: Ain't this place as good as another? Whaddya afraid of? They're all dead ones here! They don't bother you.
     (With sudden interest) Oh, look, here's a new one.

YOUNG MAN: Come on out of here.

JUDY: Wait a minute. Let's see what it says. *(She kneels on a grave in the foreground and putting her face close to headstone spells out the inscription)* Z-E-R-O. Z-e-r-o. Zero! Say, that's the guy —

YOUNG MAN: Zero? He's the guy killed his boss, ain't he?

JUDY: Yeh, that's him, all right. But what I'm thinkin' of is that I went to the hoose-gow on account of him.

YOUNG MAN: What for?

JUDY: You know, same old stuff. Tenement House Law. *(Mincingly)* Section blaa-blaa of the Penal Code. Third offense. Six months.

YOUNG MAN: And this bird —

JUDY: *(Contemptuously)* Him? He was mama's white-haired boy. We lived in the same house. Across the airshaft, see? I used to see him lookin' in my window. I guess his wife musta seen him, too. Anyhow, they went and turned the bulls on me. And now I'm out and he's in. *(Suddenly)* Say — say — *(She bursts into a peal of laughter.)*

YOUNG MAN: *(Nervously)* What's so funny?

449

JUDY: *(Rocking with laughter)* Say, wouldn't it be funny — if — if *(She explodes again)* That would be a good joke on him, all right. He can't do nothin' about it now, can he?

YOUNG MAN: Come on out of here. I don't like this place.

JUDY: Aw, you're a bum sport. What do you want to spoil my joke for?
(A cat yammers mellifluously.)

YOUNG MAN: *(Half hysterically)* What's that?

JUDY: It's only the cat. They seem to like it here all right. But come on if you're afraid. *(They go toward the gate. As they go out)* You nervous men sure are the limit.
(They go out through the gate. As they disapper ZERO's grave opens suddenly and his head appears.)

ZERO: *(Looking about)* That's funny! I thought I heard her talkin' and laughin'. But I don't see nobody. Anyhow, what would she be doin' here? I guess I must 'a' been dreamin'. But how could I be dreamin' when I ain't been asleep? *(He looks about again)* Well, no use goin' back. I can't sleep, anyhow. I might as well walk around a little. *(He rises out of the ground, very rigidly. He wears a full-dress suit of very antiquated cut and his hands are folded stiffly across his breast.)*

ZERO: *(Walking woodenly)* Gee! I'm stiff! *(He slowly walks a few steps, then stops)* Gee, it's lonesome here! *(He shivers and walks on aimlessly)* I should 'a' stayed where I was. But I thought I heard her laughin'.
(A loud sneeze is heard. ZERO stands motionless, quaking with terror. The sneeze is repeated.)

ZERO: *(Hoarsely)* What's that?

A MILD VOICE: It's all right. Nothing to be afraid of.
(From behind a headstone SHRDLU appears. He is dressed in a shabby and ill-fitting cutaway. He wears silver-rimmed spectacles and is smoking a cigarette.)

SHRDLU: I hope I didn't frighten you.

ZERO: *(Still badly shaken)* No-o. It's all right. You see, I wasn't expectin' to see anybody.

SHRDLU: You're a newcomer, aren't you?

ZERO: Yeh, this is my first night. I couldn't seem to get to sleep.

SHRDLU: I can't sleep, either. Suppose we keep each other company, shall we?

ZERO: *(Eagerly)* Yeh, that would be great. I been feelin' awful lonesome.

SHRDLU: *(Nodding)* I know. Let's make ourselves comfortable.
(He seats himself easily on a grave. ZERO tries to follow his example but he is stiff in every joint and groans with pain.)

ZERO: I'm kinda stiff.

SHRDLU: You mustn't mind the stiffness. It wears off in a few days. *(He seats himself on the grave beside ZERO and produces a package of cigarettes.)* Will you have a Camel?

ZERO: No, I don't smoke.

SHRDLU: I find it helps keep the mosquitoes away. *(He lights a cigarette.)*

SHRDLU: *(Suddenly taking the cigarette out of his mouth)* Do you mind if I smoke, Mr. — Mr. —?

ZERO: No, go right ahead.

SHRDLU: *(Replacing the cigarette)* Thank you. I didn't catch your name.

450

(ZERO does not reply.)

SHRDLU: *(Mildly)* I say I didn't catch your name.

ZERO: I heard you the first time. *(Hesitantly)* I'm scared if I tell you who I am and what I done, you'll be off me.

SHRDLU: *(Sadly)* No matter what your sins may be, they are as snow compared to mine.

ZERO: You got another guess comin'. *(He pauses dramatically)* My name's Zero. I'm a murderer.

SHRDLU: *(Nodding calmly)* Oh, yes, I remember reading about you, Mr. Zero.

ZERO: *(A little piqued)* And you still think you're worse than me?

SHRDLU: *(Throwing away his cigarette)* Oh, a thousand times worse, Mr. Zero — a million times worse.

ZERO: What did you do?

SHRDLU: I, too, am a murderer.

ZERO: *(Looking at him in amazement)* Go on! You're kiddin' me!

SHRDLU: Every word I speak is the truth. Mr. Zero. I am the foulest, the most sinful of murderers! You only murdered your employer, Mr. Zero. But I — I murdered my mother. *(He covers his face with his hands and sobs.)*

ZERO: *(Horrified)* The hell yer say!

SHRDLU: *(Sobbing)* Yes, my mother! — my beloved mother!

ZERO: *(Suddenly)* Say, you don't mean to say you're Mr. —

SHRDLU: *(Nodding)* Yes. *(He wipes his eyes, still quivering with emotion.)*

ZERO: I remember readin' about you in the papers.

SHRDLU: Yes, my guilt has been proclaimed to all the world. But that would be a trifle if only I could wash the stain of sin from my soul.

ZERO: I never heard of a guy killin' his mother before. What did you do it for?

SHRDLU: Because I have a sinful heart — there is no other reason.

ZERO: Did she always treat you square and all like that?

SHRDLU: She was a saint — a saint, I tell you. She cared for me and watched over me as only a mother can.

ZERO: You mean to say you didn't have a scrap or nothin'?

SHRDLU: Never a harsh or an unkind word. Nothing except loving care and good advice. From my infancy she devoted herself to guiding me on the right path. She taught me to be thrifty, to be devout, to be unselfish, to shun evil companions and to shut my ears to all the temptations of the flesh — in short, to become a virtuous, respectable, and God-fearing man. *(He groans)* But it was a hopeless task. At fourteen I began to show evidence of my sinful nature.

ZERO: *(Breathlessly)* You didn't kill anybody else, did you?

SHRDLU: No, thank God, there is only one murder on my soul. But I ran away from home.

ZERO: You did!

SHRDLU: Yes. A companion lent me a profane book — the only profane book I have ever read, I'm thankful to say. It was called "Treasure Island." Have you ever read it?

ZERO: No, I never was much on readin' books.

SHRDLU: It is a wicked book — a lurid tale of adventure. But it kindled in my sinful heart a desire to go to sea. And so I ran away from home.

ZERO: What did you do — get a job as a sailor?

SHRDLU: I never saw the sea — not to the day of the my death. Luckily, my mother's loving intuition warned her of my intention and I was sent back home. She welcomed me with open arms. Not an angry word, not a look of reproach. But I could read the mute suffering in her eyes as we prayed together all through the night.

ZERO: *(Sympathetically)* Gee, that must 'a' been tough. Gee, the mosquitoes are bad, ain't they? *(He tries awkwardly to slap at them with his stiff hands.)*

SHRDLU: *(Absorbed in his narrative)* I thought that experience had cured me of evil and I began to think about a career. I wanted to go in foreign missions at first, but we couldn't bear the thought of the separation. So we finally decided that I should become a proof-reader.

ZERO: Say, slip me one o' them Camels, will you? I'm gettin' all bit up.

SHRDLU: Certainly. *(He hands ZERO cigarettes and matches.)*

ZERO: *(Lighting up)* Go ahead. I'm listenin'.

SHRDLU: By the time I was twenty I had a good job reading proof for a firm that printed catalogues. After a year they promoted me and let me specialize in shoe catalogues.

ZERO: Yeh? That must 'a' been a good job.

SHRDLU: It was a very good job. I was on the shoe catalogues for thirteen years. I'd been on them yet, if I hadn't — *(He chokes back a sob.)*

ZERO: They oughta put a shot o' citronella in that embalmin'-fluid.

SHRDLU: *(He sighs)* We were so happy together. I had my steady job. And Sundays we would go to morning, afternoon, and evening service. It was an honest and moral mode of life.

ZERO: It sure was.

SHRDLU: Then came that fatal Sunday. Dr. Amaranth, our minister, was having dinner with us — one of the few pure spirits on earth. When he had finished saying grace, we had our soup. Everything was going along as usual — we were eating our soup and discussing the sermon, just like every other Sunday I could remember. Then came the leg of lamb — *(He breaks off, then resumes in a choking voice)* I see the whole scene before me so plainly — it never leaves me — Dr. Amaranth at my right, my mother at my left, the leg of lamb on the table in front of me and the cuckoo clock on the little shelf between the windows. *(He stops and wipes his eyes.)*

ZERO: Yeh, but what happened?

SHRDLU: Well, as I started to carve the lamb — Did you ever carve a leg of lamb?

ZERO: No, corned beef was our speed.

SHRDLU: It's very difficult on account of the bone. And when there's gravy in the dish there's danger of spilling it. So Mother always used to hold the dish for me. She leaned forward, just as she always did, and I could see the gold locket around her neck. It had my picture in it and one of my baby curls. Well, I raised my knife to carve the leg of lamb — and instead I cut my mother's throat! *(He sobs.)*

ZERO: You must 'a' been crazy!

SHRDLU: *(Raising his head, vehemently)* No! Don't try to justify me. I wasn't crazy. They tried to prove at the trial that I was crazy. Dr. Amaranth saw the truth! He saw it from the first! He knew that it was my sinful nature — and he told me what was in store for me.

ZERO: *(Trying to be comforting)* Well, your troubles are over now.

SHRDLU: *(His voice rising)* Over! Do you think this is the end?

ZERO: Sure. What more can they do to us?

SHRDLU: *(His tones growing shriller and shriller)* Do you think there can ever be any peace for such as we are — murderers, sinners? Don't you know what awaits us — flames, eternal flames!

ZERO: *(Nervously)* Keep your shirt on, Buddy — they wouldn't do that to us.

SHRDLU: There's no escape — no escape for us, I tell you. We're doomed! We're doomed to suffer unspeakable torments through all eternity. *(His voice rises higher and higher.)*

(A grave opens suddenly and a head appears.)

THE HEAD: Hey, you birds! Can't you shut up and let a guy sleep?

(ZERO scrambles painfully to his feet.)

ZERO: *(To SHRDLU)* Hey, put on the soft pedal.

SHRDLU: *(Too wrought up to attend)* It won't be long now! We'll receive our summons soon.

THE HEAD: Are you goin' to beat it or not? *(He calls into the grave)* Hey, Bill, lend me your head a minute.

(A moment later his arm appears holding a skull.)

ZERO: *(Warningly)* Look out! *(He seizes SHRDLU and drags him away just as THE HEAD throws the skull.)*

THE HEAD: *(Disgustedly)* Missed 'em. Damn old tabby cats! I'll get 'em next time. *(A prodigious yawn)* Ho-hum! Me for the worms!

(THE HEAD disappears as the curtain falls.)

SCENE SIX

(SCENE: A pleasant place. A scene of pastoral loveliness. A meadow dotted with fine old trees and carpeted with rich grass and field flowers. In the background are seen a number of tents fashioned of gay-striped silks and beyond gleams a meandering river. Clear air and a fleckless sky. Sweet distant music throughout.

At the rise of the curtain, SHRDLU is seen seated under a tree in the foreground in an attitude of deep dejection. His knees are drawn up and his head is buried in his arms. He is dressed as in the preceding scene.

A few minutes later, ZERO enters at right. He walks slowly and looks about him with an air of half-suspicious curiosity. He, too, is dressed as in the preceding scene. Suddenly he sees SHRDLU seated under the tree. He stands still and looks at him half fearfully. Then, seeing something familiar in him, goes closer. SHRDLU is unaware of his presence. At last ZERO recognizes him and grins in pleased surprise.)

ZERO: Well, if it ain't —! *(He claps SHRDLU on the shoulder)* Hello, Buddy!

(SHRDLU looks up slowly, then recognizing ZERO, he rises gravely and extends his hand courteously.)

SHRDLU: How do you do, Mr. Zero? I'm very glad to see you again.

ZERO: Same here. I wasn't expectin' to see you, either. *(Looking about)* This is a kinda nice place. I wouldn't mind restin' here for a while.

SHRDLU: You may if you wish.
ZERO: I'm kinda tired. I ain't used to bein' outdoors. I ain't walked so much
   in years.
SHRDLU: Sit down here, under the tree.
ZERO: Do they let you sit on the grass?
SHRDLU: Oh, yes.
ZERO: *(Seating himself)* Boy, this feels good. I'll tell the world my feet are
   sore. I ain't used to so much walkin'. Say, I wonder would it be all
   right if I took my shoes off; my feet are tired.
SHRDLU: Yes. Some of the people here go barefoot.
ZERO: Yeh? They sure must be nuts. But I'm goin' t' leave 'em off for a
   while. So long as it's all right. The grass feels nice and cool. *(He
   stretches out comfortably)* Say, this is the life of Riley all right, all
   right. This sure is a nice place. What do they call this place, anyhow?
SHRDLU: The Elysian Fields.
ZERO: The which?
SHRDLU: The Elysian Fields.
ZERO: *(Dubiously)* Oh! Well, it's a nice place, all right.
SHRDLU: They say that this is the most desirable of all places. Only the
   most favoured remain here.
ZERO: Yeh? Well, that let's me out, I guess. *(Suddenly)* But what are you
   doin' here? I thought you'd be burned by now.
SHRDLU: *(Sadly)* Mr. Zero, I am the most unhappy of men.
ZERO: *(In mild astonishment)* Why, because you ain't bein' roasted alive?
SHRDLU: *(Nodding)* Nothing is turning out as I expected. I saw everything
   so clearly — the flames, the tortures, an eternity of suffering as the
   just punishment for my unspeakable crime. And it has all turned out
   so differently.
ZERO: Well, that's pretty soft for you, ain't it?
SHRDLU: *(Wailingly)* No, no, no! It's right and just that I should be punished.
   I could have endured it stoically. All through those endless ages of
   indescribable torment I should have exulted in the magnificence of
   divine justice. But this — this is maddening! What becomes of justice?
   What becomes of morality? What becomes of right and wrong? It's
   maddening — simply maddening! Oh, if Dr. Amaranth were only here
   to advise me! *(He buries his face and groans.)*
ZERO: *(Trying to puzzle it out)* You mean to say they ain't called you for
   cuttin' your mother's throat?
SHRDLU: No! It's terrible — terrible! I was prepared for anything — any-
   thing but this.
ZERO: Well, what did they say to you?
SHRDLU: *(Looking up)* Only that I was to come here and remain until I
   understood.
ZERO: I don't get it. What do they want you to understand?
SHRDLU: *(Despairingly)* I don't know — I don't know! If I only had an
   inkling of what they meant — *(Interrupting him)* Just listen quietly
   for a moment; do you hear anything?
     (They are both silent, straining their ears.)
ZERO: *(At length)* Nope.
SHRDLU: You don't hear any music? Do you?

ZERO: Music? No, I don't hear nothin'.

SHRDLU: The people here say that the music never stops.

ZERO: They're kiddin' you.

SHRDLU: Do you think so?

ZERO: Sure thing. There ain't a sound.

SHRDLU: Perhaps. They're capable of anything. But I haven't told you of the bitterest of my disappointments.

ZERO: Well, spill it. I'm gettin' used to hearin' bad news.

SHRDLU: When I came to this place, my first thought was to find my dear mother. I wanted to ask her forgiveness. And I wanted her to help me to understand.

ZERO: An' she couldn't do it?

SHRDLU: *(With a deep groan)* She's not here! Mr. Zero! Here where only the most favoured dwell, that wisest and purest of spirits is nowhere to be found. I don't understand it.

A WOMAN'S VOICE: *(In the distance)* Mr. Zero! Oh, Mr. Zero!

(ZERO raises his head and listens attentively.)

SHRDLU: *(Going on, unheedingly)* If you were to see some of the people here — the things they do —

ZERO: *(Interrupting)* Wait a minute, will you? I think somebody's callin' me.

THE VOICE: *(Somewhat nearer)* Mr. Ze-ro! Oh! Mr. Ze-ro!

ZERO: Who the hell's that now? I wonder if the wife's on my trail already. That would be swell, wouldn't it? An' I figured on her bein' good for another twenty years, anyhow.

THE VOICE: *(Nearer)* Mr. Ze-ro! Yoo-hoo!

ZERO: No. That ain't her voice. *(Calling, savagely)* Yoo-hoo. *(To SHRDLU)* Ain't that always the way? Just when a guy is takin' life easy an' havin' a good time! *(He rises and looks off left)* Here she comes, whoever she is. *(In sudden amazement)* Well, I'll be —! Well, what do you know about that!

(He stands looking in wonderment, as DAISY DIANA DOROTHEA DEVORE enters. She wears a much-beruffled white muslin dress which is a size too small and fifteen years too youthful for her. She is red-faced and breathless.)

DAISY: *(Panting)* Oh! I thought I'd never catch up to you. I've been followin' you for days — callin' an' callin'. Didn't you hear me?

ZERO: Not till just now. You look kinda winded.

DAISY: I sure am. I can't hardly catch my breath.

ZERO: Well, sit down an' take a load off your feet. *(He leads her to the tree.)*

(DAISY sees SHRDLU for the first time and shrinks back a little.)

ZERO: It's all right, he's a friend of mine. *(To SHRDLU)* Buddy, I want you to meet my friend, Miss Devore.

SHRDLU: *(Rising and extending his hand courteously)* How do you do, Miss Devore?

DAISY: *(Self-consciously)* How do!

ZERO: *(To DAISY)* He's a friend of mine. *(To SHRDLU)* I guess you don't mind if she sits here a while an' cools off, do you?

SHRDLU: No, no, certainly not.

(They all seat themselves under the tree. ZERO and DAISY are a little self-conscious. SHRDLU gradually becomes absorbed in his

455

own thoughts.)

ZERO: I was just takin' a rest myself. I took my shoes off on account of my feet bein' so sore.

DAISY: Yeh, I'm kinda tired, too. *(Looking about)* Say, ain't it pretty here, though?

ZERO: Yeh, it is at that.

DAISY: What do they call this place?

ZERO: Why — er — let's see. He was tellin' me just a minute ago. The — er — I don't know. Some kind o' fields. I forget now. *(To SHRDLU)* Say, Buddy, what do they call this place again? *(SHRDLU, absorbed in his thoughts, does not hear him. To DAISY)* He don't hear me. He's thinkin' again.

DAISY: *(Sotto voce)* What's the matter with him?

ZERO: Why, he's the guy that murdered his mother — remember?

DAISY: *(Interested)* Oh, yeh! Is that him?

ZERO: Yah. An' he had it all figgered out how they was goin' t' roast him or somethin'. And now they ain't goin' to do nothin' to him an' it's kinda got his goat.

DAISY: *(Sympathetically)* Poor feller!

ZERO: Yeh. He takes it kinda hard.

DAISY: He looks like a nice young feller.

ZERO: Well, you sure are good for sore eyes. I never expected to see you here.

DAISY: I thought maybe you'd be kinda surprised.

ZERO: Surprised is right. I thought you was alive an' kickin'. When did you pass out?

DAISY: Oh, right after you did — a coupla days.

ZERO: *(Interested)* Yeh? What happened? Get hit by a truck or somethin'?

DAISY: No. *(Hesitantly)* You see — it's this way. I blew out the gas.

ZERO: *(Astonished)* Go on! What was the big idea?

DAISY: *(Falteringly)* Oh, I don't know. You see, I lost my job.

ZERO: I'll bet you're sorry you did it now, ain't you?

DAISY: *(With conviction)* No, I ain't sorry. Not a bit. *(Then hesitantly)* Say, Mr. Zero, I been thinkin' — *(She stops.)*

ZERO: What?

DAISY: *(Plucking up courage)* I been thinkin' it would be kinda nice — if you an' me — if we could kinda talk things over.

ZERO: Yeh. Sure. What do you want to talk about?

DAISY: Well — I don't know — but you and me — we ain't really ever talked things over, have we?

ZERO: No, that's right, we ain't. Well, let's go to it.

DAISY: I was thinkin' if we could be alone — just the two of us, see?

ZERO: Oh, yeh! Yeh, I get you. *(He turns to SHRDLU and coughs loudly. SHRDLU does not stir.)*

ZERO: *(To DAISY)* He's dead to the world. *(He turns to SHRDLU)* Say, Buddy! *(No answer)* Say, Buddy!

SHRDLU: *(Looking up with a start)* Were you speaking to me?

ZERO: Yeh. How'd you guess it? I was thinkin' that maybe you'd like to walk around a little and look for your mother.

SHRDLU: *(Shaking his head)* It's no use. I've looked everywhere. *(He relapses into thought again.)*

ZERO: Maybe over there they might know.

SHRDLU: No, no! I've searched everywhere. She's not here. *(ZERO and DAISY look at each other in despair.)*

ZERO: Listen, old shirt, my friend here and me — see? — we used to work in the same store. An' we got some things to talk over — business, see — kinda confidential. So if it ain't askin' too much —

SHRDLU: *(Springing to his feet)* Why, certainly! Excuse me!

(He bows politely to DAISY and walks off. DAISY and ZERO watch him until he has disappeared.)

ZERO: *(With a forced laugh)* He's a good guy at that.

(Now that they are alone, both are very self-conscious, and for a time they sit in silence.)

DAISY: *(Breaking the silence)* It sure is pretty here, ain't it?

ZERO: Sure is.

DAISY: Look at the flowers! Ain't they just perfect! Why, you'd think they was artificial, wouldn't you?

ZERO: Yeh, you would.

DAISY: And the smell of them. Like perfume.

ZERO: Yeh.

DAISY: I'm crazy about the country, ain't you?

ZERO: Yeh. It's nice for a change.

DAISY: Them store picnics — remember?

ZERO: You bet. They sure was fun.

DAISY: One time — I guess you don't remember — the two of us — me and you — we sat down on the grass together under a tree — just like we're doin' now.

ZERO: Sure I remember.

DAISY: Go on! I'll bet you don't.

ZERO: I'll bet I do. It was the year the wife didn't go.

DAISY: *(Her face brightening)* That's right! I didn't think you'd remember.

ZERO: An' comin' home we sat together in the truck.

DAISY: *(Eagerly, rather shamefacedly)* Yeh! There's somethin' I've always wanted to ask you.

ZERO: Well, why didn't you?

DAISY: I don't know. It didn't seem refined. But I'm goin' to ask you now, anyhow.

ZERO: Go ahead. Shoot.

DAISY: *(Falteringly)* Well — while we was comin' home — you put your arm up on the bench behind me — and I could feel your knee kinda pressin' against mine. *(She stops.)*

ZERO: *(Becoming more and more interested)* Yeh — well — what about it?

DAISY: What I wanted to ask you was — was it just kinda accidental?

ZERO: *(With a laugh)* Sure it was accidental. Accidental on purpose.

DAISY: *(Eagerly)* Do you mean it?

ZERO: Sure I mean it. You mean to say you didn't know it?

DAISY: No. I've been wantin' to ask you —

ZERO: Then why did you get sore at me?

DAISY: Sore? I wasn't sore! When was I sore?

ZERO: That night. Sure you was sore. If you wasn't sore why did you move away?

DAISY: Just to see if you meant it. I thought if you meant it you'd move up

457

closer. An' then when you took your arm away I was sure you didn't mean it.

ZERO: An' I thought all the time you was sore. That's why I took my arm away. I thought if I moved up you'd holler and then I'd be in a jam, like you read in the paper all the time about guys gettin' pulled in for annoyin' women.

DAISY: An' I was wishin' you'd put your arm around me — just sittin' there wishin' all the way home.

ZERO: What do you know about that? That sure is hard luck, that is. If I'd 'a' only knew! You know what I felt like doin' — only I didn't have the nerve?

DAISY: What?

ZERO: I felt like kissin' you.

DAISY: *(Fervently)* I wanted you to.

ZERO: *(Astonished)* You would 'a' let me?

DAISY: I wanted you to! I wanted you to! Oh, why didn't you — why didn't you?

ZERO: I didn't have the nerve. I sure was a dumb-bell.

DAISY: I would 'a' let you all you wanted to. I wouldn't 'a' cared. I know it would 'a' been wrong but I wouldn't 'a' cared. I wasn't thinkin' about right an' wrong at all. I didn't care — see? I just wanted you to kiss me.

ZERO: *(Feelingly)* If I'd only knew. I wanted to do it, I swear I did. But I didn't think you cared nothin' about me.

DAISY: *(Passionately)* I never cared nothin' about nobody else.

ZERO: Do you mean it — on the level? You ain't kiddin' me, are you?

DAISY: No, I ain't kiddin'. I mean it. I'm tellin' you the truth. I ain't never had the nerve to tell you before — but now I don't care. It don't make no difference now. I mean it — every word of it.

ZERO: *(Dejectedly)* If I'd only knew it.

DAISY: Listen to me. There's somethin' else I want to tell you. I may as well tell you everything now. It don't make no difference now. About my blowin' out the gas — see? Do you know why I done it?

ZERO: Yeh, you told me — on account o' bein' canned.

DAISY: I just told you that. That ain't the real reason. The real reason is on account o' you.

ZERO: You mean to say on account o' me passin' out —?

DAISY: Yeh. That's it. I didn't want to go on livin'. What for? What did I want to go on livin' for? I didn't have nothin' to live for with you gone. I often thought of doin' it before. But I never had the nerve. An' anyhow I didn't want to leave you.

ZERO: An' me bawlin' you out, about readin' too fast an' readin' too slow.

DAISY: *(Reproachfully)* Why did you do it?

ZERO: I don't know, I swear I don't. I was always stuck on you. An' while I'd be addin' them figgers, I'd be thinkin' how if the wife died, you an' me could get married.

DAISY: I used to think o' that, too.

ZERO: An' then before I knew it, I was bawlin' you out.

DAISY: Them was the times I'd think o' blowin' out the gas. But I never did till you was gone. There wasn't nothin' to live for then. But it wasn't so easy to do, anyhow. I never could stand the smell o' gas. An' all the while I was gettin' ready, you know, stuffin' up all the cracks, the way you read about in the paper — I was thinkin' of you and hopin' that maybe I'd meet you again. An' I made up my mind if I ever did see you, I'd tell you.

ZERO: *(Taking her hand)* I'm sure glad you did. I'm sure glad. *(Ruefully)* But it don't do much good now, does it?

DAISY: No, I guess it don't. *(Summoning courage)* But there's one thing I'm goin' to ask you.

ZERO: What's that?

DAISY: *(In a low voice)* I want you to kiss me.

ZERO: You bet I will! *(He leans over and kisses her cheek.)*

DAISY: Not like that. I don't mean like that. I mean really kiss me. On the mouth. I ain't never been kissed like that.

(ZERO puts his arms about her and presses his lips to hers. A long embrace. At last they separate and sit side by side in silence.)

DAISY: *(Putting her hands to her cheeks)* So that's what it's like. I didn't know it could be like that. I didn't know anythin' could be like that.

ZERO: *(Fondling her hand)* Your cheeks are red. They're all red. And your eyes are shinin'. I never seen your eyes shinin' like that before.

DAISY: *(Holding up her hand)* Listen — do you hear it? Do you hear the music?

ZERO: No, I don't her nothin'!

DAISY: Yeh — music. Listen an' you'll hear it.

(They are both silent for a moment.)

ZERO: *(Excitedly)* Yeh! I hear it! He said there was music, but I didn't hear it till just now.

DAISY: Ain't it grand?

ZERO: Swell! Say, do you know what?

DAISY: What?

ZERO: It makes me feel like dancin'.

DAISY: Yeh? Me, too.

ZERO: *(Springing to his feet)* Come on! Let's dance!

(He seizes her hands and tries to pull her up.)

DAISY: *(Resisting laughingly)* I can't dance. I ain't danced in twenty years.

ZERO: That's nothin'. I ain't, neither. Come on! I feel just like a kid!

(He pulls her to her feet and seizes her about the waist.)

DAISY: Wait a minute! Wait till I fix my skirt.

(She turns back her skirts and pins them above ankles.)

(ZERO seizes her about the waist. They dance clumsily but with gay abandon. DAISY's hair becomes loosened and tumbles over her shoulders. She lends herself more and more to the spirit of the dance. But ZERO soon begins to tire and dances with less and less zest.)

ZERO: *(Stopping at last, panting for breath)* Wait a minute! I'm all winded.

(He releases DAISY, but before he can turn away, she throws her arms about him and presses her lips to his.)

ZERO: *(Freeing himself)* Wait a minute! Let me get my wind!

(He limps to the tree and seats himself under it, gasping for breath. DAISY looks after him, her spirits rather dampened.)

ZERO: Whew! I sure am winded! I ain't used to dancin'.

(He takes off his collar and tie and opens the neckband of his shirt. DAISY sits under the tree near him, looking at him longingly. But

he is busy catching his breath.)
Gee, my heart's goin' a mile a minute.
DAISY:Why don't you lay down an' rest? You could put your head on my lap.
ZERO: That ain't a bad idea.
(He stretches out, his head in DAISY's lap.)
DAISY: *(Fondling his hair)* It was swell, wasn't it?
ZERO: Yeh. But you gotta be used to it.
DAISY: Just imagine if we could stay here all the time — you an' me together — wouldn't it be swell?
ZERO: Yeh. But there ain't a chance.
DAISY: Won't they let us stay?
ZERO: No. This place is only for the good ones.
DAISY: Well, we ain't so bad, are we?
ZERO: Go on! Me a murderer an' you committin' suicide. Anyway, they wouldn't stand for this — the way we been goin' on.
DAISY: I don't see why.
ZERO: You don't! You know it ain't right. Ain't I got a wife?
DAISY: Not any more you ain't. When you're dead that ends it. Don't they always say "until death do us part?"
ZERO: Well, maybe you're right about that but they wouldn't stand for us here.
DAISY: It would be swell — the two of us together — we could make up for all them years.
ZERO: Yeh, I wish we could.
DAISY: We sure were fools. But I don't care. I've got you now. *(She kisses his forehead and cheeks and mouth.)*
ZERO: I'm sure crazy about you. I never saw you lookin' so pretty before, with your cheeks all red. An' your hair hangin' down. You got swell hair. *(He fondles and kisses her hair.)*
DAISY: *(Ecstatically)* We got each other now, ain't we?
ZERO: Yeh. I'm crazy about you. Daisy! That's a pretty name. It's a flower, ain't it? Well — that's what you are — just a flower.
DAISY: *(Happily)* We can always be together now, can't we?
ZERO: As long as they'll let us. I sure am crazy about you. *(Suddenly he sits upright)* Watch your step!
DAISY: *(Alarmed)* What's the matter?
ZERO: *(Nervously)* He's comin' back.
DAISY: Oh, is that all? Well, what about it?
ZERO: You don't want him to see us layin' around like this, do you?
DAISY: I don't care if he does.
ZERO: Well, you oughta care. You don't want him to think you ain't a refined girl, do you? He's an awful moral bird, he is.
DAISY: I don't care nothin' about him. I don't care nothin' about anybody but you.
ZERO: Sure, I know. But we don't want people talkin' about us. You better fix your hair an' pull down your skirts.
(DAISY complies rather sadly. They are both silent as SHRDLU enters.)
ZERO: *(With feigned nonchalance)* Well, you got back all right, didn't you?
SHRDLU: I hope I haven't returned too soon.

ZERO: No, that's all right. We were just havin' a little talk. You know — about business an' things.

DAISY: *(Boldly)* We were wishin' we could stay here all the time.

SHRDLU: You may if you like.

ZERO and DAISY: *(In astonishment)* What!

SHRDLU: Yes. Any one who likes may remain —

ZERO: But I thought you were tellin' me —

SHRDLU: Just as I told you, only the most favored do remain. But any one may.

ZERO: I don't get it. There's a catch in it somewheres.

DAISY: It don't matter as long as we can stay.

ZERO: *(To SHRDLU)* We were thinkin' about gettin' married, see?

SHRDLU: You may or not, just as you like.

ZERO: You don't mean to say we could stay if we didn't, do you?

SHRDLU: Yes. They don't care.

ZERO: An' there's some here that ain't married?

SHRDLU: Yes.

ZERO: *(To DAISY)* I don't know about this place, at that. They must be kind of a mixed crowd.

DAISY: It don't matter, so long as we got each other.

ZERO: Yeh, I know, but you don't want to mix with people that ain't respectable.

DAISY: *(To SHRDLU)* Can we get married right away? I guess there must be a lot of ministers here, ain't there?

SHRDLU: Not as many as I had hoped to find. The two who seem most beloved are Dean Swift and the Abbé Rabelais. They are both much admired for some indecent tales which they have written.

ZERO: *(Shocked)* What! Ministers writin' smutty stories! Say, what kind of a dump is this, anyway?

SHRDLU: *(Despairingly)* I don't know, Mr. Zero. All these people here are so strange, so unlike the good people I've known. They seem to think of nothing but enjoyment or of wasting their time in profitless occupations. Some paint pictures from morning until night, or carve blocks of stone. Others write songs or put words together, day in and day out. Still others do nothing but lie under the trees and look at the sky. There are men who spend all their time reading books and women who think only of adorning themselves. And forever they are telling stories and laughing and singing and drinking and dancing. There are drunkards, thieves, vagabonds, blasphemers, adulterers. There is one —

ZERO: That's enough. I heard enough. *(He seats himself and begins putting on his shoes.)*

DAISY: *(Anxiously)* What are you goin' to do?

ZERO: I'm goin' to beat it, that's what I'm goin' to do.

DAISY: You said you liked it here.

ZERO: *(Looking at her in amazement)* Like it! Say, you don't mean to say you want to stay here, do you, with a lot of rummies an' loafers an' bums?

DAISY: We don't have to bother with them. We can just sit here together an' look at the flowers an' listen to the music.

461

SHRDLU: *(Eagerly)* Music! Did you hear music?

DAISY: Sure. Don't you hear it?

SHRDLU: No, they say it never stops. But I've never heard it.

ZERO: *(Listening)* I thought I heard it before but I don't hear nothin' now. I guess I must 'a' been dreamin'. *(Looking about)* What's the quickest way out of this place?

DAISY: *(Pleadingly)* Won't you stay just a little longer?

ZERO: Didn't yer hear me say I'm goin'? Good-bye, Miss Devore. I'm goin' to beat it.

(He limps off at the right. DAISY follows him slowly.)

DAISY: *(To SHRDLU)* I won't ever see him again.

SHRDLU: Are you goin' to say here?

DAISY: It don't make no difference now. Without him I might as well be alive.

(She goes off right. SHRDLU watches her a moment, then sighs and seating himself under the tree, buries his head on his arm. Curtain falls.)

SCENE SEVEN

(SCENE: Before the curtain rises the clicking of an adding machine is heard. The curtain rises upon an office similar in appearance to that in SCENE TWO except that there is a door in the back wall through which can be seen a glimpse of the corridor outside. In the middle of the room ZERO is seated completely absorbed in the operation of an adding machine. He presses the keys and pulls the lever with mechanical precision. He still wears his full-dress suit but he has added to it sleeve protectors and a green eye shade. A strip of white paper-tape flows steadily from the machine as ZERO operates. The room is filled with this tape — streamers, festoons, billows of it everywhere. It covers the floor and the furniture, it climbs the walls and chokes the doorways. A few moments later, LIEUTENANT CHARLES and JOE enter at the left. LIEUTENANT CHARLES is middle-aged and inclined to corpulence. He has an air of world-weariness. He is bare-footed, wears a Panama hat, and is dressed in bright red tights which are a very bad fit — too tight in some places, badly wrinkled in others. JOE is a youth with a smutty face dressed in dirty blue overalls.)

CHARLES: *(After contemplating ZERO for a few moments)* All right, Zero, cease firing.

ZERO: *(Looking up, surprised)* Whaddja say?

CHARLES: I said stop punching that machine.

ZERO: *(Bewildered)* Stop? *(He goes on working mechanically.)*

CHARLES: *(Impatiently)* Yes. Can't you stop? Here, Joe, give me a hand. He can't stop.

(JOE and CHARLES each take one of ZERO's arms and with enormous effort detach him from the machine. He resists passively — mere inertia. Finally they succeed and swing him around on his stool. CHARLES and JOE mop their foreheads.)

ZERO: *(Querulously)* What's the idea? Can't you lemme alone?

CHARLES: *(Ignoring the question)* How long have you been here?

ZERO: Jes' twenty-five years. Three hundred months, ninety-one hundred

462

and thirty-one days, one hundred thirty-six thousand —

CHARLES: *(Impatiently)* That'll do! That'll do!

ZERO: *(Proudly)* I ain't missed a day, not an hour, not a minute. Look at all I got done. *(He points to the maze of paper.)*

CHARLES: It's time to quit.

ZERO: Quit? Whaddya mean quit? I ain't goin' to quit!

CHARLES: You've got to.

ZERO: What for? What do I have to quit for?

CHARLES: It's time for you to go back.

ZERO: Go back where? Whaddya talkin' about?

CHARLES: Back to earth, you dub. Where do you think?

ZERO: Awe, go on, Cap, who are you kiddin'?

CHARLES: I'm not kidding anybody. And don't call me Cap. I'm a lieutenant.

ZERO: All right, Lieutenant, all right. But what's this you're trying to tell me about goin' back?

CHARLES: Your time's up, I'm telling you. You must be pretty thick. How many times do you want to be told a thing?

ZERO: This is the first time I heard about goin' back. Nobody ever said nothin' to me about it before.

CHARLES: You didn't think you were going to stay here forever, did you?

ZERO: Sure. Why not? I did my bit, didn't I? Forty-five years of it. Twenty-five years in the store. Then the boss canned me and I knocked him cold. I guess you ain't heard about that —

CHARLES: *(Interrupting)* I know all about that. But what's that got to do with it?

ZERO: Well, I done my bit, didn't I? That oughta let me out.

CHARLES: *(Jeeringly)* So you think you're all through, do you?

ZERO: Sure, I do. I did the best I could while I was there and then I passed out. And now I'm sittin' pretty here.

CHARLES: You've got a fine idea of the way they run things, you have. Do you think they're going to all of the trouble of making a soul just to use it once?

ZERO: Once is often enough, it seems to me.

CHARLES: It seems to you, does it? Well, who are you? And what do you know about it? Why, man, they use a soul over and over again — over and over until it's worn out.

ZERO: Nobody ever told me.

CHARLES: So you thought you were all through, did you? Well, that's a hot one, that is.

ZERO: *(Sullenly)* How was I to know?

CHARLES: Use your brains! Where would we put them all? We're crowded enough as it is. Why, this place is nothing but a kind of repair and service station — a sort of cosmic laundry, you might say. We get the souls in here by the bushelful. Then we get busy and clean them up. And you ought to see some of them. The muck and the slime. Phoo! And as full of holes as a flour-sifter. But we fix them up. We disinfect them and give them a kerosene rub and mend the holes and back they go — practically as good as new.

ZERO: You mean to say I've been here before — before the last time, I mean?

CHARLES: Been here before! Why, you poor boob — you've been here thou-

463

sands of times — fifty thousand, at least.

ZERO: *(Suspiciouly)* How is it I don't remember nothin' about it?

CHARLES: Well — that's partly because you're stupid. But it's mostly because that's the way they fix it. *(Musingly)* They're funny that way — every now and then they'll do something white like that — when you'd least expect it. I guess economy's at the bottom of it, though. They figure that the souls would get worn out quicker if they remembered.

ZERO: And don't any of 'em remember?

CHARLES: Oh, some do. You see there's different types: there's the type that gets a little better each time it goes back — we just give them a wash and send them right through. Then there's another type — the type that gets a little worse each time. That's where you belong!

ZERO: *(Offended)* Me? You mean to say I'm gettin' worse all the time?

CHARLES: *(Nodding)* Yes. A little worse each time.

ZERO: Well — what was I when I started? Somethin' big? — A king or somethin'?

CHARLES: *(Laughing derisively)* A king! That's a good one! I'll tell you what you were the first time — if you want to know so much — a monkey.

ZERO: *(Shocked and offended)* A monkey!

CHARLES: *(Nodding)* Yes, sir — just a hairy, chattering, long-tailed monkey.

ZERO: That musta been a long time ago.

CHARLES: Oh, not so long. A million years or so. Seems like yesterday to me.

ZERO: Then look here, whaddya mean by sayin' I'm gettin' worse all the time?

CHARLES: Just what I said. You weren't so bad as a monkey. Of course, you did just what all the other monkeys did, but still it kept you out in the open air. And you weren't women-shy — there was one little red-headed monkey — Well, never mind. Yes, sir, you weren't so bad then. But even in those days there must have been some bigger and brainier monkey that you kowtowed to. The mark of the slave was on you from the start.

ZERO: *(Sullenly)* You ain't very particular about what you call people, are you?

CHARLES: You wanted the truth, didn't you? If there ever was a soul in the world that was labelled slave it's yours. Why, all the bosses and kings that there ever were have left their trademarks on your backside.

ZERO: It ain't fair, if you ask me.

CHARLES: *(Shrugging his shoulders)* Don't tell me about it. I don't make the rules. All I know is you've been getting worse — worse each time. Why, even six thousand years ago you weren't so bad. That was the time you were hauling stones for one of those big pyramids in a place they call Africa. Ever hear of the pyramids?

ZERO: Them big pointy things?

CHARLES: *(Nodding)* That's it.

ZERO: I seen a picture of them in the movies.

CHARLES: Well, you helped build them. It was a long step down from the happy days in the jungle, but it was a good job — even though you didn't know what you were doing and your back was striped by the foreman's whip. But you've been going down, down. Two thousand years ago you were a Roman galley-slave. You were on one of the triremes that knocked the Carthaginian fleet for a goal. Again the whip. But you had muscles then — chest muscles, back muscles, biceps. *(He feels ZERO's arm gingerly and turns away in disgust.)* Phoo! A bunch of mush! *(He notices that JOE has fallen asleep. Walking over, he kicks him in the shin.)*

CHARLES: Wake up, you mutt! Where do you think you are? *(He turns to ZERO again)* And then another thousand years and you were a serf — a lump of clay digging up other lumps of clay. You wore an iron collar then — white ones hadn't been invented yet. Another long step down. But where you dug, potatoes grew and that helped fatten the pigs. Which was something. And now — well, I don't want to rub it in —

ZERO: Rub it in is right! Seems to me I got a pretty healthy kick comin'. I ain't had a square deal! Hard work! That's all I've ever had!

CHARLES: *(Callously)* What else were you ever good for?

ZERO: Well, that ain't the point. The point is I'm through! I had enough! Let 'em find somebody else to do the dirty work. I'm sick of bein' the goat! I quit right here and now! *(He glares about defiantly. There is a thunder-clap and a bright flash of lightning.)*

ZERO: *(Screaming)* Ooh! What's that? *(He clings to CHARLES.)*

CHARLES: It's all right. Nobody's going to hurt you. It's just their way of telling you that they don't like you to talk that way. Pull yourself together and calm down. You can't change the rules — nobody can — they've got it all fixed. It's a rotten system — but what are you going to do about it?

ZERO: Why can't they stop pickin' on me? I'm satisfied here — doin' my day's work. I don't want to go back.

CHARLES: You've got to, I tell you. There's no way out of it.

ZERO: What chance have I got — at my age? Who'll give me a job?

CHARLES: You big boob, you don't think you're going back the way you are, do you?

ZERO: Sure, how then?

CHARLES: Why, you've got to start all over.

ZERO: All over?

CHARLES: *(Nodding)* You'll be a baby again — a bald, red-faced little animal, and then you'll go through it all again. There'll be millions of others like you — all with their mouths open, squalling for food. And then when you get a little older you'll begin to learn things — and you'll learn all the wrong things and learn them all in the wrong way. You'll eat the wrong food and wear the wrong clothes and you'll live in swarming dens where there's no light and no air! You'll learn to be a liar and a bully and a braggart and a coward and a sneak. You'll learn to fear the sunlight and to hate beauty. By that time you'll be ready for school. There they'll tell you the truth about a great many things that you don't give a damn about and they'll tell you lies about all the things you ought to know — and about all the things you want to know they'll tell you nothing at all. When you get through you'll be equipped for your life-work. You'll be ready to take a job.

ZERO: *(Eagerly)* What'll my job be? Another adding machine?

CHARLES: Yes. But not one of these antiquated adding machines. It will be a superb, super-hyper-adding machine, as far from this old piece of junk as you are from God. It will be something to make you sit up and take notice, that adding machine. It will be an adding machine which will be installed in a coal mine and which will record the individual output of each miner. As each miner down in the lower galleries takes up a shovelful of coal, the impact of his shovel will automatically set in motion a graphite pencil in your gallery. The pencil will make a mark in white upon a blackened, sensitized drum. Then your work comes in. With the great toe of your right foot you release a lever which focuses a violet ray on the drum. The ray playing upon and through the white mark, falls upon a selenium cell which in turn sets the keys of the adding apparatus in motion. In this way the individual output of each miner is recorded without any human effort except the slight pressure of the great toe of your right foot.

ZERO: *(In breathless, round-eyed wonder)* Say, that'll be some machine, won't it?

CHARLES: Some machine is right. It will be the culmination of human effort — the final triumph of the evolutionary process. For millions of years the nebulous gases swirled in space. For more millions of years the gases cooled and then through inconceivable ages they hardened into rocks. And then came life. Floating green things on the waters that covered the earth. More millions of years and a step upward — an animate organism in the ancient slime. And so on — step by step, down through the ages — a gain here, a gain there — the mollusc, the fish, the reptile, the mammal, man! And all so that you might sit in the gallery of a coal mine and operate the super-hyper-adding machine with the great toe of your right foot!

ZERO: Well, then — I ain't so bad, after all.

CHARLES: You're a failure, Zero, a failure. A waste product. A slave to a contraption of steel and iron. The animal's instincts, but not his strength and skill. The animal's appetites, but not his unashamed indulgence of them. True, you move and eat and digest and excrete and reproduce. But any microscopic organism can do as much. Well — time's up! Back you go — back to your sunless groove — the raw material of slums and wars — the ready prey of the first jingo or demagogue or political adventurer who takes the trouble to play upon your ignorance and credulity and provincialism. You poor, spineless, brainless boob — I'm sorry for you!

ZERO: *(Falling to his knees)* Then keep me here! Don't send me back! Let me stay!

CHARLES: Get up. Didn't I tell you I can't do anything for you? Come on, time's up!

ZERO: I can't! I can't! I'm afraid to go through it all again.

CHARLES: You've got to, I tell you. Come on, now!

ZERO: What did you tell me so much for? Couldn't you just let me go, thinkin' everythin' was goin' to be all right?

CHARLES: You wanted to know, didn't you?

ZERO: How did I know what you were goin' to tell me? Now I can't stop thinkin' about it! I can't stop thinkin'! I'll be thinkin' about it all the time.

CHARLES: All right! I'll do the best I can for you. I'll send a girl with you to keep you company.

ZERO: A girl? What for? What good will a girl do me?

CHARLES: She'll help make you forget.

ZERO: *(Eagerly)* She will? Where is she?

CHARLES: Wait a minute, I'll call her. *(He calls in a loud voice)* Oh! Hope! Yoo-hoo! *(He turns his head aside and says in the manner of a ventriloquist imitating a distant feminine voice)* Ye-es. *(Then in his own voice)* Come here, will you? There's a fellow who wants you to take him back. *(Ventriloquously again)* All right. I'll be right over, Charlie dear. *(He turns to ZERO)* Kind of familiar, isn't she? Charlie dear!

ZERO: What did you say her name is?

CHARLES: Hope. H-o-p-e.

ZERO: Is she good-lookin'?

CHARLES: Is she good-looking! Oh, boy, wait until you see her! She's a blonde with big blue eyes and red lips and little white teeth and —

ZERO: Say, that listens good to me. Will she be long?

CHARLES: She'll be here right away. There she is now! Do you see her?

ZERO: No. Where?

CHARLES: Out in the corridor. No, not there. Over farther. To the right. Don't you see her blue dress? And the sunlight on her hair?

ZERO: Oh, sure! Now I see her! What's the matter with me, anyhow? Say, she's some jane! Oh, you baby vamp!

CHARLES: She'll make you forget your troubles.

ZERO: What troubles are you talkin' about?

CHARLES: Nothing. Go on. Don't keep her waiting.

ZERO: You bet I won't! Oh, Hope! Wait for me! I'll be right with you! I'm on my way! *(He stumbles out eagerly.)*

(JOE bursts into uproarious laughter.)

CHARLES: *(Eyeing him in surprise and anger)* What in hell's the matter with you?

JOE: *(Shaking with laughter)* Did you get that? He thinks he saw somebody and he's following her! *(He rocks with laughter.)*

CHARLES: *(Punching him in the jaw)* Shut your face!

JOE: *(Nursing his jaw)* What's the idea? Can't I even laugh when I see something funny?

CHARLES: Funny! You keep your mouth shut or I'll show you something funny. Go on, hustle out of here and get something to clean up this mess with. There's another fellow moving in. Hurry now.

(He makes a threatening gesture. JOE exits hastily. CHARLES goes to chair and seats himself. He looks weary and dispirited.)

CHARLES: *(Shaking his head)* Hell, I'll tell the world this is a lousy job! *(He takes a flask from his pocket, uncorks it, and slowly drains it.)*

CURTAIN

Copies of this play, in individual paper covered acting editions, are available from Samuel French, Inc., New York, NY or 7623 Sunset Blvd., Hollywood, Calif. 90046 or in Canada Samuel French, (Canada) Ltd., 80 Richmond Street East, Toronto M5C 1P1, Canada.

EUGENE O'NEILL
and *The Hairy Ape*

$\mathbf{E}$ugene O'Neill demonstrated that the United States was ready to make a serious contribution to the world theatre. Born in 1888 to actor James O'Neill who made a career playing the title role in a spectacular melodrama, *The Count of Monte Cristo,* Eugene lived here and there. He studied at Princeton, prospected for gold in Honduras, and worked as a seaman on merchant marine ships sailing to Africa, Europe, and South America. By the age of twenty-five, he had tried marriage and suicide and succeeded in neither. Then he contracted tuberculosis and spent six months recovering in a sanatorium. During this convalescence, he read drama and began to write plays. In 1914-15, he studied playwriting with George Pierce Baker at Harvard, and the next year he became associated with the Provincetown Players who had recently moved to New York. This company subsequently produced the premieres of many of his plays.

O'Neill's first full-length play, *Beyond the Horizon,* reached Broadway in 1920 and won a Pulitzer Prize. In the next fifteen years he achieved many successes as well as seeing many of his plays fail. Some of his best known plays from this period were the expressionistic *The Emperor Jones* (1920), the realistic plays *Anna Christie* (1921) and *Desire Under the Elms* (1924), and a powerful trilogy based on Aeschylus' *Oresteia: Mourning Becomes Electra* (1931). O'Neill received the Nobel Prize for literature in 1936.

Then for over a decade, although he continued to write, O'Neill released no plays for performance. After this hiatus, several other important O'Neill plays were produced, including *The Iceman Cometh* (1946) and *A Moon for the Misbegotten* (1947). O'Neill died in 1953. His realistic autobiographical drama, *Long Day's Journey into Night,* was produced in 1956.

O'Neill wrote around twenty-five full-length plays, plus a number of one-acts. This large body of work includes plays in a variety of styles using many experimental techniques. For instance, some of the plays, like *The Great God Brown* (1926), used masks, and some, like *Lazarus Laughed* (1928) with a cast of hundreds[1] and the ten-hour-long *More Stately Mansions* (1953), stretch the resources of theatre. The power of O'Neill's conception and ideas frequently exceeded that of his dramatic skills. Many critics have commented on the ineffectiveness of his dialog, and his plays sometimes seemed to fall short of achieving the effect he intended. However, they clearly communicated an intense struggle with major questions about human nature, and their strong, interesting characters have stimulated talented performers to do their best work.

A driven, reclusive, obsessive worker, plagued by Parkinson's disease and alcoholism, Eugene O'Neill used drama to probe relentlessly into the

---

[1]The premiere by the Pasadena Community Playhouse had 16 principal actors plus 159 extras who played about 420 roles.

dark places of human nature and to ask what makes us great, what makes us fall short of our potential, what role faith plays in human life, and what is the relationship between human beings and the spiritual forces that surround us.

The Hairy Ape

Dramaturgy

This play combined the presuppositions of realism with the disillusionment and techniques of expressionism. In good realistic fashion, O'Neill repeatedly shows Yank to be the product of debased parents plus a blighted environment. The characters speak ordinary language, made more realistic by dialects, and for the most part they are three-dimensional characters with normal names and nicknames. The play's title and the repeated references to the similarities between human beings and monkeys also recall Darwin's theory of evolution, a major impetus in realism.

However, in tune with expressionism, *The Hairy Ape* portrays progress, the goal of the realists, as destructive to human beings. For instance, it contrasts the beauty of sailing vessels and their heroic crews with the smoky filth of steamers and their animal-like stokers, and by the end of the play, Yank comes to despise the steel and speed which represent progress.

In keeping with this viewpoint, the play uses expressionistic plot structure — a chronological sequence of scenes which are only loosely connected by causality and which serve to depict Yank's situation more than to develop a story. The sets distort real locations by exaggeration, such as the over-sized price tags in the shop windows, and by symbolism, such as the cage-like structures in the ship's forecastle. This distortion carries through into the chorus-like vocal effects O'Neill called for and stylized action such as Yank's attack on the invincible, zombie-like rich folk in Scene 5. And the constant repetition of motifs like steel, fire, apes, and Rodin's "Thinker" focus attention on the play's themes and emphasize the important message in this play.

Sometimes the plotting and the writing of *The Hairy Ape* are almost as clumsy as Yank himself, and stage directions such as the last one in the play ("And, perhaps, the Hairy Ape at last belongs") seem to indicate the playwright's fear that maybe audiences will miss the point. But in spite of these problems, which are typical of O'Neill, the play also demonstrates the dramatist's power and leaves no mistake about his intention to use theatre as a tool for serious thought.

Production History

The play was first produced by the Provincetown Players in New York City on March 9, 1922. This group began performing plays at the Wharf Theatre in Provincetown, Rhode Island, in 1916. Later the same year they moved to the Playwrights' Theatre in New York City's Greenwich Village. In addition to O'Neill's plays, they also produced new works by Susan Glaspell and Edna St. Vincent Millay. The Provincetown Players, who were part of the little theatre movement, and designer Robert Edmond Jones (1887-1954), who collaborated on sets for *The Hairy Ape*, were both instrumental in introducing "the new stagecraft" to America.

THE HAIRY APE

A Comedy of Ancient and Modern Life in Eight Scenes
by EUGENE O'NEILL

The action of the play takes place on an ocean liner and in New York City around 1920.

CHARACTERS

ROBERT SMITH, "YANK"
a stoker

PADDY
another stoker

LONG
another stoker

MILDRED DOUGLAS
a rich young woman

HER AUNT

SECOND ENGINEER

A GUARD

A SECRETARY OF AN ORGANIZATION

Stokers, Ladies, Gentlemen, etc.

SCENES

Scene I: The firemen's forecastle of an ocean liner — an hour after sailing from New York.

Scene II: Section of promenade deck, two days out — morning.

Scene III: The stokehole. A few minutes later.

Scene IV: Same as Scene One. Half an hour later.

Scene V: Fifth Avenue, New York. Three weeks later.

Scene VI: An island near the city. The next night.

Scene VII: In the city. About a month later.

Scene VIII: In the city. Twilight of the next day.

471

SCENE ONE

The firemen's forecastle of a transatlantic liner an hour after sailing from New York for the voyage across. Tiers of narrow, steel bunks, three deep, on all sides. An entrance in rear. Benches on the floor before the bunks. The room is crowded with men, shouting, cursing, laughing, singing — a confused, inchoate uproar swelling into a sort of unity, a meaning — the bewildered, furious baffled defiance of a beast in a cage. Nearly all the men are drunk. Many bottles are passed from hand to hand. All are dressed in dungaree pants, heavy ugly shoes. Some wear singlets, but the majority are stripped to the waist.

The treatment of this scene, or of any other scene in the play, should by no means be naturalistic. The effect sought after is a cramped space in the bowels of a ship, imprisoned by white steel. The lines of bunks, the uprights supporting them, cross each other like the steel framework of a cage. The ceiling crushes down upon the men's heads. They cannot stand upright. This accentuates the natural stooping posture which shoveling coal and the resultant over-development of back and shoulder muscles have given them. The men themselves should resemble those pictures in which the appearance of Neanderthal Man is guessed at. All are hairy-chested, with long arms of tremendous power, and low, receding brows above their small, fierce, resentful eyes. All the civilized white races are represented, but except for the slight differentiation in color of hair, skin, eyes, all these men are alike.

The curtain rises on a tumult of sound. YANK is seated in the foreground. He seems broader, fiercer, more truculent, more powerful, more sure of himself than the rest. They respect his superior strength — the grudging respect of fear. Then, too, he represents to them a self-expression, the very last word in what they are, their most highly developed individual.

VOICES: Gif me trink dere, you!
    'Ave a wet!
    Salute!
    Gesundheit!
    Skoal!
    Drunk as a lord, God stiffen you!
    Here's how!
    Luck!
    Pass back that bottle, damn you!
    Pourin' it down his neck!
    Ho, Froggy! Where the devil have you been?
    La Touraine.
    I hit him smash in yaw, py Gott!
    Jenkins — the First — he's a rotten swine —
    And the coppers nabbed him — and I run —
    I like peer better. It don't pig head gif you.
    A slut, I'm saying! She robbed me aslape —
    To hell with 'em all!
    You're a bloody liar!
    Say dot again! *(Commotion, two men about to fight are pulled apart.)*
    No scrappin' now!

Tonight —
See who's the best man!
Bloddy Dutchman!
Tonight on the for'ard square.
I'll bet on Dutchy.
He packa da wallop, I tella you!
Shut up, Wop!
No fightin', maties. We're all chums, ain't we?
(A voice starts bawling a song.)
    "Beer, beer, glorious beer!
    Fill yourselves right up to here."

YANK: *(For the first time seeming to take notice of the uproar about him, turns around threateningly — in a tone of contemptuous authority)* Choke off dat noise! Where d'yuh get dat beer stuff? Beer, hell! Beer's for goils — and Dutchmen. Me for somep'n wit a kick to it! Gimme a drink, one of youse guys. *(Several bottles are eagerly offered. He takes a tremendous gulp at one of them; then, keeping the bottle in his hand, glares belligerently at the owner, who hastens to acquiesce in this robbery by saying)* All righto, Yank. Keep it and have another. *(YANK contemptuously turns his back on the crowd again. For a second there is an embarrassed silence. Then —)*

VOICES: We must be passing the Hook.
She's beginning to roll to it.
Six days in hell — and then Southampton.
Py Yesus, I vish somepody take my first vatch for me!
Gittin' seasick, Square-head?
Drink up and forget it!
What's in your bottle?
Gin.
Dot's nigger trink.
Absinthe? It's doped. You'll go off your chump, Froggy!
Cochon!
Whisky, that's the ticket!
Where's Paddy?
Going asleep.
Sing us that whisky song, Paddy. *(They all turn to an old, wizened Irishman who is dozing, very drunk, on the benches forward. His face is extremely monkey-like with all the sad, patient pathos of that animal in his small eyes.)*
    Singa da song, Caruso Pat!
    He's gettin' old. The drink is too much for him.
    He's too drunk.

PADDY: *(Blinking about him, starts to his feet resentfully, swaying, holding on to the edge of a bunk)* I'm never too drunk to sing. 'Tis only when I'm dead to the world I'd be wishful to sing at all. *(With a sort of sad contempt)* "Whisky Johnny," ye want? A chanty, ye want? Now that's a queer wish from the ugly like of you, God help you. But no matther. *(He starts to sing in a thin, nasal, doleful tone:)*
    "Oh, whisky is the life of man!
        Whisky! O Johnny!* (They all join in on this.)

473

Oh, whisky is the life of man!
Whisky for my Johnny! (Again chorus.)

"Oh, whisky drove my old man mad!
Whisky! Oh Johnny!
Oh, whisky drove my old man mad!
Whisky for my Johnny!"

YANK: *(Again turning around scornfully)* Aw hell! Nix on dat old sailing ship stuff! All dat bull's dead, see? And you're dead, too, yuh damned old Harp, on'y yuh don't know it. Take it easy, see. Give us a rest. Nix on de loud noise. *(With a cynical grin)* Can't youse see I'm tryin' to t'ink?

ALL: *(Repeating the word after him as one with the same cynical amused mockery)* Think! *(The chorused word has a brazen metallic quality as if their throats were phonograph horns. It is followed by a general uproar of hard, barking laughter.)*

VOICES: Don't be cracking your head wit ut, Yank.
You gat headache, py yingo!
One thing about it — it rhymes with drink!
Ha, ha, ha!
Drink, don't think!
Drink, don't think!
Drink, don't think! *(A whole chorus of voices has taken up this refrain, stamping on the floor, pounding on the benches with fists.)*

YANK: *(Taking a gulp from his bottle — good-naturedly)* Aw right. Can de noise. I got yuh de foist time. *(The uproar subsides. A very drunken sentimental tenor begins to sing.)*

"Far away in Canada,
Far across the sea,
There's a lass who fondly waits
Making a home for me —"

YANK: *(Fiercely contemptuous)* Shut up, yuh lousy boob! Where d'yuh get dat tripe? Home? Home, hell! I'll make a home for yuh! I'll knock yuh dead. Home! T'hell wit home! Where d'yu get dat tripe! Dis is home, see? What d'yuh want wit home? *(Proudly)* I runned away from mine when I was a kid. On'y too glad to beat it, dat was me. Home was lickings for me, dat's all. But yuh can bet your shoit no one ain't never licked me since! Wanter try it, any of youse? Huh! I guess not. *(In a more placated but still contemptuous tone)* Goils waitin' for yuh, huh? Aw, hell! Dat's all tripe. Dey don't wait for no one. Dey'd double-cross yuh for a nickel. Dey're all tarts, get me? Treat 'em rough, dat's me. To hell wit 'em. Tarts, dat's what, de whole bunch of 'em.

LONG: *(Very drunk, jumps on a bench excitedly, gesticulating with a bottle in his hand)* Listen 'ere, Comrades! Yank 'ere is right. 'E says this 'ere stinkin' ship is our 'ome. And 'e says as 'ome is 'ell. And 'e's right! This is 'ell. We lives in 'ell, Comrades — and right enough we'll die in it. *(Raging)* And who's ter blame, I arsks yer? We ain't. We wasn't born this rotten way. All men is born free and ekal. That's in the bleedin Bible, maties. But what d'they care for the Bible — them lazy, bloated swine what travels first cabin? Them's the ones. They dragged us down 'til we're on'y wage slaves in the bowels of a bloody ship, sweatin', burnin' up, eatin' coal dust. Hit's them's ter blame — the damned Capitalist clarss! *(There had been a gradual murmur of contemptuous resentment rising among the men until now he is interrupted by a storm of catcalls, hisses, boos, hard laughter.)*

VOICES: Turn it off!
Shut up!
Sit down!
Closa da face!
Tamn fool! *(Etc.)*

YANK: *(Standing up and glaring at LONG)* Sit down before I knock yuh down! *(LONG makes haste to efface himself. YANK goes on contemptuously)* De Bible, huh? De Cap'tlist class, huh? Aw nix on dat Salvation Army-Socialist bull. Git a soapbox! Hire a hall! Come and be saved, huh? Jerk us to Jesus, huh? Aw g'wan! I've listened to lots of guys like you, see. Yuh're all wrong. Wanter know what I t'ink? Yuh ain't no good for no one. Yuh're de bunk. Yuh ain't got no noive, get me? Yuh're yellow, dat's what. Yellow, dat's you. Say! What's dem slobs in de foist cabin got to do wit us? We're better men dan dey are, ain't we? Sure! One of us guys could clean up de whole mob wit one mit. Put one of 'em down here for one watch in de stokehole, what'd happen? Dey'd carry him off on a stretcher. Dem boids don't amount to nothin'. Dey're just baggage. Who makes dis old tub run? Ain't it us guys? Well den, we belong, don't we? We belong and dey don't. Dat's all. *(A loud chorus of approval. YANK goes on)* As for dis bein' hell — aw, nuts! Yuh lost your noive, dat's what. Dis is a man's job, get me? It belongs. It runs dis tub. No stiffs need apply. But yuh're a stiff, see? Yuh're yellow, dat's you.

VOICES: *(With a great hard pride in them)*
Righto!
A man's job!
Talk is cheap, Long.
He never could hold up his end.
Divil take him!
Yank's right. We make it go.
Py Gott, Yank say right ting!
We don't need no one cryin' over us.
Makin' speeches.
Throw him out!
Yellow!
Chuck him overboard!
I'll break his jaw for him!
(They crowd around LONG threateningly.)

YANK: *(Half good-natured again — contemptuously)* Aw, take it easy. Leave him alone. He ain't woith a punch. Drink up. Here's how, whoever owns dis. *(He takes a long swallow from his bottle. All drink with him. In a flash all is hilarious amiability again, back-slapping, loud talk, etc.)*

PADDY: *(Who has been sitting in a blinking, melancholy daze — suddenly cries out in a voice full of old sorrow)* We belong to this, you're saying? We make the ship to go, you're saying? Yerra then, that Almighty God have pity on us! *(His voice runs into the wail of a keen, he rocks back and forth on his bench. The men stare at him, startled and impressed in spite of themselves)* Oh, to be back in the fine days of my youth, ochone! Oh, there was fine beautiful ships them days — clippers wid tall masts touching the sky — fine strong men in them — men that was sons of the sea as if 'twas the mother that bore them. Oh, the clean skins of them, and the clear eyes, the straight backs and full chests of them! Brave men they was, and bold men surely! We'd be sailing out, bound down round the Horn maybe. We'd be making sail in the dawn, with a fair breeze, singing a chanty song wid no care to it. And astern the land would be sinking low and dying out, but we'd give it no heed but a laugh, and never a look behind. For the day that was, was enough, for we was free men — and I'm thinking 'tis only slaves do be giving heed to the day that's gone or the day to come — until they're old like me. *(With a sort of religious exaltation)* Oh, to be scudding south again wid the power of the Trade Wind driving her on steady through the nights and the days! Full sail on her! Nights and days! Nights when the foam of the wake would be flaming wid fire, when the sky'd be blazing and winking wid stars. Or the full of the moon maybe. Then you'd see her driving through the gray night, her sails stretching aloft all silver and white, not a sound on the deck, the lot of us dreaming dreams, till you'd believe 'twas no real ship at all you was on but a ghost ship like the *Flying Dutchman* they say does be roaming the seas forevermore widout touching a port. And there was the days, too. A warm sun on the clean decks. Sun warming the blood of you, and wind over the miles of shiny green ocean like strong drink to your lungs. Work — aye, hard work — but who'd mind that at all? Sure, you worked under the sky and 'twas work wid skill and daring to it. And wid the day done, in the dog watch, smoking me pipe at ease, the lookout would be raising land maybe, and we'd see the mountains of South Americy wid the red fire of the setting sun painting their white tops and the clouds floating by them! *(His tone of exaltation ceases. He goes on mournfully)* Yerra, what's the use of talking? 'Tis a dead man's whisper. *(To YANK resentfully)* 'Twas them days men belong to ships, not now. 'Twas them days a ship was part of the sea, and a man was part of a ship, and the sea joined all together and made it one. *(Scornfully)* Is it one wid this you'd be, Yank — black smoke from the funnels smudging the sea, smudging the decks — the bloody engines pounding and throbbing and shaking — wid divil a sight of sun or a breath of clean air — choking our lungs wid coal dust — breaking our backs and hearts in the hell of the stokehole — feeding the bloody furnace — feeding our lives along wid the coal, I'm thinking — caged in by steel from a sight of the sky like bloody apes in the Zoo! *(With a harsh laugh)* Ho-ho, divil mend you! Is it to belong to that you're wishing? Is it a flesh and blood wheel of the engines you'd be?

YANK: *(Who has been listening with a contemptuous sneer, barks out the answer)* Sure ting! Dat's me. What about it?

PADDY: *(As if to himself — with great sorrow)* Me time is past due. That a
great wave wid sun in the heart of it may sweep me over the side
sometime I'd be dreaming of the days that's gone!

YANK: Aw, yuh crazy Mick! *(He springs to his feet and advances on PADDY
threateningly — then stops, fighting some queer struggle within himself — lets his hands fall to his sides — contemptuously)* Aw, take it
easy. Yuh're aw right, at dat. Yuh're bugs, dat's all — nutty as a
cuckoo. All dat tripe yuh been pullin' — Aw, dat's all right. On'y it's
dead, get me? Yuh don't belong no more, see. Yuh don't get de stuff.
Yuh're too old. *(Disgustedly)* But aw say, come up for air onct in a
while, can't yuh? See what's happened since yuh croaked. *(He suddenly
bursts forth vehemently, growing more and more excited)* Say! Sure!
Sure! I meant it! What de hell — Say, lemme talk! Hey! Hey, you old
Harp! Hey, youse guys! Say, listen to me — wait a moment — I gotter
talk, see. I belong and he don't. He's dead but I'm livin'. Listen to me!
Sure I'm part of de engines! Why de hell not! Dey move, don't dey?
Dey're speed, ain't dey? Dey smash trou, don't dey? Twenty-five
knots a hour! Dat's goin' some! Dat's new stuff! Dat belongs! But
him, he's too old. He gets dizzy. Say, listen. All dat crazy tripe
about nights and days; all dat crazy tripe about stars and moons; all
dat crazy tripe about suns and winds, fresh air and de rest of it — Aw
hell, dat's all a dope dream! Hittin' de pipe of de past, dat's what he's
doin'. He's old and don't belong no more. But me, I'm young! I'm in
de pink! I move wit it. It, get me! I mean de ting dat's de guts of all
dis. It ploughs trou all de tripe he's been sayin'. It blows dat up! It
knocks dat dead! It slams dat offen de face of de oith! It, get me! De
engines and de coal and de smoke and all de rest of it! He can't breathe
and swallow coal dust, but I kin, see? Dat's fresh air for me! Dat's
food for me! I'm new, get me? Hell in de stokehole? Sure! It takes a
man to work in hell. Hell, sure, dat's my fav'rite climate. I eat it up!
I git fat on it! It's me makes it hot! It's me makes it roar! It's me makes
it move! Sure, on'y for me everyting stops. It all goes dead, get me?
De noise and smoke and all de engines movin' de woild, dey stop. Dere
ain't nothin' no more! Dat's what I'm sayin'. Everyting else dat makes
de woild move, somep'n makes it move. It can't move witout somep'n
else, see? Den yuh get down to me. I'm at de bottom, get me! Dere
ain't nothin' foither. I'm de end! I'm de start! I start somep'n and de
woild moves! It — dat's me! — de new dat's moiderin' de old! I'm de
ting in coal dat makes it boin; I'm steam and oil for de engines; I'm
de ting in noise dat makes yuh hear it; I'm smoke and express trains
and steamers and factory whistles; I'm de ting in gold dat makes it
money! And I'm what makes iron into steel! Steel, dat stands for de
whole ting! And I'm steel — steel — steel! I'm de muscles in steel, de
punch behind it! *(As he says this he pounds with his fist against the
steel bunks. All the men, roused to a pitch of frenzied self-glorification
by his speech, do likewise. There is a deafening metallic roar, through
which YANK's voice can be heard bellowing)* Slaves, hell! We run de
whole woiks. All de rich guys dat tink dey're somep'n, dey ain't noth-
thin'! Dey don't belong. But us guys, we're in de move, we're at de
bottom, de whole ting is us! *(PADDY from the start of YANK's speech*

has been taking one gulp after another from his bottle, at first frightenedly, as if he were afraid to listen, then desperately, as if to drown his senses, but finally has achieved complete indifferent, even amused, drunkenness. YANK sees his lips moving. He quells the uproar with a shout) Hey, youse guys, take it easy! Wait a moment! De nutty Harp is sayin' somep'n.

PADDY: *(Is heard now — throws his head back with a mocking burst of laughter)* Ho-ho-ho-ho-ho —

YANK: *(Drawing back his fist, with a snarl)* Aw! Look out who yuh're givin' the bark!

PADDY: *(Begins to sing the "Miller of Dee" with enormous good nature)*
"I care for nobody, no, not I,
And nobody cares for me."

YANK: *(Good-natured himself in a flash, interrupts PADDY with a slap on the bare back like a report)* Dat's de stuff! Now yuh're gettin' wise to somep'n. Care for nobody, dat's de dope! To hell with 'em all! And nix on nobody else carin'. I kin care for myself, get me! *(Eight bells sound, muffled, vibrating through the steel walls as if some enormous brazen gong were imbedded in the heart of the ship. All the men jump up mechanically, file through the door silently close upon each other's heels in what is very like a prisoner's lockstep. YANK slaps PADDY on the back)* Our watch, yuh old Harp! *(Mockingly)* Come on down in hell. Eat up de coal dust. Drink in de heat. It's it, see! Act like yuh liked it, yuh better — or croak yuhself.

PADDY: *(With jovial defiance)* To the divil wid it! I'll not report this watch. Let thim log me and be damned. I'm no slave the like of you. I'll be sittin' here at me ease, and drinking, and thinking, and dreaming dreams.

YANK: *(Contemptuously)* Tinkin' and dreamin', what'll that get yuh? What's tinkin' got to do wit it? We move, don't we? Speed, ain't it? Fog, dat's all you stand for. But we drive trou dat, don't we? We split dat up and smash trou — twenty-five knots a hour! *(Turns his back on PADDY scornfully)* Aw, yuh make me sick! Yuh don't belong! *(He strides out the door in rear. PADDY hums to himself, blinking drowsily.)*

CURTAIN

SCENE TWO

Two days out. A section of the promenade deck. MILDRED DOUGLAS and her aunt are discovered reclining in deck chairs. The former is a girl of twenty, slender, delicate, with a pale, pretty face marred by a self-conscious expression of disdainful superiority. She looks fretful, nervous and discontented, bored by her own anemia. Her aunt is a pompous and proud — and fat — old lady. She is a type even to the point of a double chin and lorgnettes. She is dressed pretentiously, as if afraid her face alone would never indicate her position in life. MILDRED is dressed all in white.

The impression to be conveyed by this scene is one of the beautiful, vivid life of the sea all about — sunshine on the deck in a great flood, the fresh sea wind blowing across it. In the midst of this, these two incongruous, artificial

478

figures, inert and disharmonious, the elder like a gray lump of dough touched up with rouge, the younger looking as if the vitality of her stock had been sapped before she was conceived, so that she is the expression not of its life energy but merely of the artificialities that energy had won for itself in the spending.

MILDRED: *(Looking up with affected dreaminess)* How the black smoke swirls back against the sky! Is it not beautiful?

AUNT: *(Without looking up)* I dislike smoke of any kind.

MILDRED: My great-grandmother smoked a pipe — a clay pipe.

AUNT: *(Ruffling)* Vulgar!

MILDRED: She was too distant a relative to be vulgar. Time mellows pipes.

AUNT: *(Pretending boredom but irritated)* Did the sociology you took up at college teach you that — to play the ghoul on every possible occasion, excavating old bones? Why not let your great-grandmother rest in her grave?

MILDRED: *(Dreamily)* With her pipe beside her — puffing in Paradise.

AUNT: *(With spite)* Yes, you are a natural born ghoul. You are even getting to look like one, my dear.

MILDRED: *(In a passionless tone)* I detest you, Aunt. *(Looking at her critically)* Do you know what you remind me of? Of a cold pork pudding against a background of linoleum tablecloth in the kitchen of a — but the possibilities are wearisome. *(She closes her eyes.)*

AUNT: *(With a bitter laugh)* Merci for your candor. But since I am and must be your chaperon — in appearance, at least — let us patch up some sort of armed truce. For my part you are quite free to indulge any pose of eccentricity that beguiles you — as long as you observe the amenities —

MILDRED: *(Drawling)* The inanities?

AUNT: *(Going on as if she hadn't heard)* After exhausting the morbid thrills of social service work on New York's East Side — how they must have hated you, by the way, the poor that you made so much poorer in their own eyes! — you are now bent on making your slumming international. Well, I hope Whitechapel will provide the needed nerve tonic. Do not ask me to chaperon you there, however. I told your father I would not. I loathe deformity. We will hire an army of detectives and you may investigate everything — they allow you to see.

MILDRED: *(Protesting with a trace of genuine earnestness)* Please do not mock my attempts to discover how the other half lives. Give me credit for some sort of groping sincerity in that at least. I would like to help them. I would like to be some use in the world. Is it my fault I don't know how? I would like to be sincere, to touch life somewhere. *(With weary bitterness)* But I'm afraid I have neither the vitality nor integrity. All that was burnt out in our stock before I was born. Grandfather's blast furnaces, flaming to the sky, melting steel, making millions — then father keeping those home fires burning, making more millions — and little me at the tail-end of it all. I'm a waste product in the Bessemer process — like the millions. Or rather, I inherit the acquired trait of the by-product, wealth, but none of the energy, none of the strength of the steel that made it. I am sired by gold and damned

479

by it, as they say at the race track — damned in more ways than one. *(She laughs mirthlessly.)*

AUNT: *(Unimpressed — superciliously)* You seem to be going in for sincerity today. It isn't becoming to you, really — except as an obvious pose. Be as artificial as you are, I advise. There's a sort of sincerity in that, you know. And, after all, you must confess you like that better.

MILDRED: *(Again affected and bored)* Yes, I suppose I do. Pardon me for my outburst. When a leopard complains of its spots, it must sound rather grotesque. *(In mocking tone)* Purr, little leopard. Purr, scratch, tear, kill, gorge yourself and be happy — only stay in the jungle where your spots are camouflage. In a cage they make you conspicuous.

AUNT: I don't know what you are talking about.

MILDRED: It would be rude to talk about anything to you. Let's just talk. *(She looks at her wrist watch)* Well, thank goodness, it's about time for them to come for me. That ought to give me a new thrill, Aunt.

AUNT: *(Affectedly troubled)* You don't mean to say you're really going? The dirt — the heat must be frightful —

MILDRED: Grandfather started as a puddler. I should have inherited an immunity to heat that would make a salamander shiver. It will be fun to put it to the test.

AUNT: But don't you have to have the captain's — or someone's — permission to visit the stokehole?

MILDRED: *(With a triumphant smile)* I have it — both his and the chief engineer's. Oh, they didn't want to at first, in spite of my social service credentials. They didn't seem a bit anxious that I should investigate how the other half lives and works on a ship. So I had to tell them that my father, the president of Nazareth Steel, chairman of the board of directors of this line, had told me it would be all right.

AUNT: He didn't.

MILDRED: How naïve age makes one! But I said he did, Aunt. I even said he had given me a letter to them — which I had lost. And they were afraid to take the chance that I might be lying. *(Excitedly)* So it's ho! for the stokehole. The second engineer is to escort me. *(Looking at her watch again)* It's time. And here he comes, I think. *(The SECOND ENGINEER enters. He is a husky, fine-looking man of thirty-five or so. He stops before the two and tips his cap, visibly embarrassed and ill-at-ease.)*

SECOND ENGINEER: Miss Douglas?

MILDRED: Yes. *(Throwing off her rugs and getting to her feet)* Are we all ready to start?

SECOND ENGINEER: In just a second, ma'am. I'm waiting for the Fourth. He's coming along.

MILDRED: *(With a scornful smile)* You don't care to shoulder this responsibility alone, is that it?

SECOND ENGINEER: *(Forcing a smile)* Two are better than one. *(Disturbed by her eyes, glances out to sea — blurts out)* A fine day we're having.

MILDRED: Is it?

SECOND ENGINEER: A nice warm breeze —

MILDRED: It feels cold to me.

SECOND ENGINEER: But it's hot enough in the sun —

MILDRED: Not hot enough for me. I don't like Nature. I was never athletic.

SECOND ENGINEER: *(Forcing a smile)* Well, you'll find it hot enough where you're going.

MILDRED: Do you mean hell?

SECOND ENGINEER: *(Flabbergasted, decides to laugh)* Ho-ho! No. I mean the stokehole.

MILDRED: My grandfather was a puddler. He played with boiling steel.

SECOND ENGINEER: *(All at sea — uneasily)* Is that so? Hum, you'll excuse me, ma'am, but are you intending to wear that dress?

MILDRED: Why not?

SECOND ENGINEER: You'll likely rub against oil and dirt. It can't be helped.

MILDRED: It doesn't matter. I have lots of white dresses.

SECOND ENGINEER: I have an old coat you might throw over —

MILDRED: I have fifty dresses like this. I will throw this one into the sea when I come back. That ought to wash it clean, don't you think?

SECOND ENGINEER: *(Doggedly)* There's ladders to climb down that are none too clean — and dark alleyways —

MILDRED: I will wear this very dress and none other.

SECOND ENGINEER: No offense meant. It's none of my business. I was only warning you —

MILDRED: Warning? That sounds thrilling.

SECOND ENGINEER: *(Looking down the deck — with a sigh of relief)* There's the Fourth now. He's waiting for us. If you'll come —

MILDRED: Go on. I'll follow you. *(He goes. MILDRED turns a mocking smile on her aunt)* An oaf — but a handsome, virile oaf.

AUNT: *(Scornfully)* Poser!

MILDRED: Take care. He said there were dark alleyways —

AUNT: *(In the same tone)* Poser!

MILDRED: *(Biting her lips angrily)* You are right. But would that my millions were not so anemically chaste!

AUNT: Yes, for a fresh pose I have no doubt you would drag the name of Douglas in the gutter!

MILDRED: From which it sprang. Good-by, Aunt. Don't pray too hard that I may fall into the fiery furnace.

AUNT: Poser!

MILDRED: *(Viciously)* Old hag! *(She slaps her aunt insultingly across the face and walks off, laughing gaily.)*

AUNT: *(Screams after her)* I said poser!

CURTAIN

SCENE THREE

The stokehole. In the rear, the dimly-outlined bulks of the furnaces and boilers. High overhead one hanging electric bulb sheds just enough light through the murky air laden with coal dust to pile up masses of shadows everywhere. A line of men, stripped to the waist, is before the furnace doors. They bend over, looking neither to right nor left, handling their shovels as if they were part of their bodies, with a strange, awkward, swinging rhythm. They use the shovels to throw open the furnace doors. Then from these fiery round holes in the black a flood of terrific light and heat pours full upon the men who are outlined in silhouette in the crouching, inhuman attitudes of chained gorillas. The men shovel with a rhythmic motion, swinging as on a pivot from the coal which lies in heaps on the floor behind to hurl it into the flaming mouths before them. There is a tumult of noise — the brazen clang of the furnace doors as they are flung open or slammed shut, the grating, teeth-gritting grind of steel against steel, of crunching coal. This clash of sounds stuns one's ears with its rending dissonance. But there is order in it, rhythm, a mechanical regulated recurrence, a tempo. And rising above all, making the air hum with the quiver of liberated energy, the roar of leaping flames in the furnaces, the monotonous throbbing beat of the engines.

As the curtain rises, the furnace doors are shut. The men are taking a breath-ing spell. One or two are arranging the coal behind them, pulling it into more accessible heaps. The others can be dimly made out leaning on their shovels in relaxed attitudes of exhaustion.

PADDY: *(From somewhere in the line — plaintively)* Yerra, will this divil's own watch nivir end? Me back is broke. I'm destroyed entirely.

YANK: *(From the center of the line — with exuberant scorn)* Aw, yuh make me sick! Lie down and croak, why don't yuh? Always beefin', dat's you! Say, dis is a cinch! Dis was made for me! It's my meat, get me! *(A whistle is blown — a thin, shrill note from somewhere overhead in the darkness. YANK curses without resentment)* Dere's de damn en-gineer crackin' de whip. He tinks we're loafin'.

PADDY: *(Vindictively)* God stiffen him!

YANK: *(In an exultant tone of command)* Come on, youse guys! Git into de game! She's gittin' hungry! Pile some grub in her. Trow it into her belly! Come on now, all of youse! Open her up! *(At this last all the men, who have followed his movements of getting into position, throw open their furnace doors with a deafening clang. The fiery light floods over their shoulders as they bend round for the coal. Rivulets of sooty sweat have traced maps on their backs. The enlarged muscles form bunches of high light and shadow.)*

YANK: *(Chanting a count as he shovels without seeming effort)* One — two — tree — *(His voice rising exultantly in the joy of battle)* Dat's de stuff! Let her have it! All togedder now! Sling it into her! Let her ride! Shoot de piece now! Call de toin on her! Drive her into it! Feel her move! Watch her smoke! Speed, dat's her middle name! Give her coal, youse guys! Coal, dat's her booze! Drink it up, baby! Let's see yuh sprint! Dig in and gain a lap! Dere she go-o-es. *(This last in the chanting formula of the gallery gods at the six-day bike race. He slams his furnace door shut. The others do likewise with as much unison as their wearied bodies will permit. The effect is of one fiery eye after another being blotted out with a series of accompanying bangs.)*

PADDY: *(Groaning)* Me back is broke. I'm bate out — bate — *(There is a pause. Then the inexorable whistle sounds again from the dim regions above the electric light. There is a growl of cursing rage from all sides.)*

YANK: *(Shaking his fist upward — contemptuously)* Take it easy dere, you! Who d'yuh tink's runnin' dis game, me or you? When I git ready, we move. Not before! When I git ready, get me!

482

VOICES: *(Approvingly)* That's the stuff!
Yank tal him, py golly!
Yank ain't affeerd.
Goot poy, Yank!
Give him hell!
Tell 'im 'e's a bloody swine!
Bloody slave-driver!
YANK: *(Contemptuously)* He ain't got no noive. He's yellow, get me? All de engineers is yellow. Dey got streaks a mile wide. Aw, to hell wit him! Let's move, youse guys. We had a rest. Come on, she needs it! Give her pep! It ain't for him. Him and his whistle, dey don't belong. But we belong, see! We gotter feed de baby! Come on! *(He turns and flings his furnace door open. They all follow his lead. At this instant the SECOND and FOURTH ENGINEERS enter from the darkness on the left with MILDRED between them. She starts, turns paler, her pose is crumbling, she shivers with fright in spite of the blazing heat, but forces herself to leave the ENGINEERS and take a few steps nearer the men. She is right behind YANK. All this happens quickly while the men have their backs turned.)*
YANK: Come on, youse guys! *(He is turning to get coal when the whistle sounds again in a peremptory, irritating note. This drives YANK into a sudden fury. While the other men have turned full around and stopped dumbfounded by the spectacle of MILDRED standing there in her white dress, YANK does not turn far enough to see her. Besides, his head is thrown back, he blinks upward through the murk trying to find the owner of the whistle, he brandishes his shovel murderously over his head in one hand, pounding on his chest, gorilla-like, with the other, shouting)* Toin off dat whistle! Come down outa dere, yuh yellow, brass-buttoned, Belfast bum, yuh! Come down and I'll knock yer brains out! Yuh lousy, stinkin', yellow mut of a Catholic-moidern' bastard! Come down and I'll moider yuh! Pullin' dat whistle on me, huh? I'll show yuh! I'll crash yer skull in! I'll drive yer teet' down yer troat! I'll slam yer nose trou de back of yer head! I'll cut yer guts out for a nickel, yuh lousy boob, yuh dirty, crummy, muck-eatin' son of a — *(Suddenly he becomes conscious of all the other men staring at something directly behind his back. He whirls defensively with a snarling, murderous growl, crouching to spring, his lips drawn back over his teeth, his small eyes gleaming ferociously. He sees MILDRED, like a white apparition in the full light from the open furnace doors. He glares into her eyes, turned to stone. As for her, during his speech she has listened, paralyzed with horror, terror, her whole personality crushed, beaten in, collapsed, by the terrific impact of this unknown, abysmal brutality, naked and shameless. As she looks at his gorilla face, as his eyes bore into hers, she utters a low, choking cry and shrinks away from him, putting both hands up before her eyes to shut out the sight of his face, to protect her own. This startles YANK to a reaction. His mouth falls open, his eyes grow bewildered.)*
MILDRED: *(About to faint — to the ENGINEERS, who now have her one by each arm — whimperingly)* Take me away! Oh, the filthy beast! *(She faints. They carry her quickly back, disappearing in the darkness at the left,*

rear. *An iron door clangs shut. Rage and bewildered fury rush back on YANK. He feels himself insulted in some unknown fashion in the very heart of his pride. He roars* "God damn yuh!" *and hurls his shovel after them at the door which has just closed. It hits the steel bulkhead with a clang and falls clattering on the steel floor. From overhead the whistle sounds again in a long, angry, insistent command.)*

CURTAIN

SCENE FOUR

The firemen's forecastle. YANK's watch has just come off duty and had dinner. Their faces and bodies shine from a soap-and-water scrubbing but around their eyes, where a hasty dousing does not touch, the coal dust sticks like black make-up, giving them a queer, sinister expression. YANK has not washed either face or body. He stands out in contrast to them, a blackened, brooding figure. He is seated forward on a bench in the exact attitude of Rodin's "The Thinker." The others, most of them smoking pipes, are staring at YANK half-apprehensively, as if fearing an outburst; half-amusedly, as if they saw a joke somewhere that tickled them.

VOICES: He ain't ate nothin.
Py golly, a fallar gat to gat grub in him.
Divil a lie.
Yank feeds da fire, no feeda da face.
Ha-ha.
He ain't even washed hisself.
He's forgot.
Hey, Yank, you forgot to wash.
YANK: *(Sullenly)* Forgot nothin'! To hell wit washin'.
VOICES: It'll stick to you.
It'll get under your skin.
Give yer the bleedin' itch, that's wot.
It makes spots on you — like a leopard.
Like a piebald nigger, you mean.
Better wash up, Yank.
You sleep better.
Wash up, Yank!
Wash up! Wash up!
YANK: *(Resentfully)* Aw say, youse guys. Lemme alone. Can't youse see I'm tryin' to tink?
ALL: *(Repeating the word after him as one with cynical mockery)* Think! *(The word has a brazen, metallic quality as if their throats were phonograph horns. It is followed by a chorus of hard, barking laughter.)*
YANK: *(Springing to his feet and glaring at them belligerently)* Yes, tink! Tink, dat's what I said! What about it? (They are silent, puzzled by *his sudden resentment at what used to be one of his jokes. YANK sits down again in the same attitude of "The Thinker.")*
VOICES: Leave him alone.
He's got a grouch on.
Why wouldn't he?
PADDY: *(With a wink at the others)* Sure I know what's the matther. 'Tis aisy

to see. He's fallen in love, I'm telling you.

ALL: *(Repeating the word after him as one with cynical mockery)* Love! *(The word has a brazen, metallic quality as if their throats were phonograph horns. It is followed by a chorus of hard, barking laughter.)*

YANK: *(With a contemptuous snort)* Love, Hell! Hate, dat's what. I've fallen in hate, get me?

PADDY: *(Philosophically)* 'Twould take a wise man to tell one from the other. *(With a bitter, ironical scorn, increasing as he goes on)* But I'm telling you it's love that's in it. Sure what else but love for us poor bastes in the stokehole would be bringing a fine lady, dressed like a white quane, down a mile of ladders and steps to be havin' a look at us? *(A growl of anger goes up from all sides.)*

LONG: *(Jumping on a bench — hectically)* Hinsultin' us! Hinsultin' us, the bloody cow! And them bloody engineers! What right 'as they got to be exhibitin' us 's if we was bleedin' monkeys in a menagerie? Did we sign for hinsults to our dignity as 'onest workers? Is that in the ship's articles? You kin bloody well bet it ain't! But I knows why they done it. I arsked a deck steward o' she was and 'e told me. 'Er old man's a bleedin' millionaire, a bloody Capitalist! 'E's got enuf bloody gold to sink this bleedin' ship! 'E makes arf the bloody steel in the world! 'E owns this bloody boat! And you and me, Comrades, we're 'is slaves! And the skipper and mates and engineers, they're 'is slaves! And she's 'is bloody daughter and we're al 'er slaves, too! And she gives 'er orders as 'ow she wants to see the bloody animals below decks and down they takes 'er! *(There is a roar of rage from all sides.)*

YANK: *(Blinking at him bewilderedly)* Say! Wait a moment! Is all dat straight goods?

LONG: Straight as string! The bleedin' steward as waits on 'em, 'e told me about 'er. And what're we goin' ter do, I arsks yer? 'Ave we got ter swaller 'er hinsults like dogs? It ain't in the ship's articles. I tell yer we got a case. We kin go to law —

YANK: *(With abysmal contempt)* Hell! Law!

ALL: *(Repeating the word after him as one with cynical mockery)* Law! *(The word has a brazen metallic quality as if their throats were phonograph horns. It is followed by a chorus of hard, barking laughter.)*

LONG: *(Feeling the ground slipping from under his feet — desperately)* As voters and citizens we kin force the bloody governments —

YANK: *(With abysmal contempt)* Hell! Governments!

ALL: *(Repeating the word after him as one with cynical mockery)* Governments! *(The word has a brazen metallic quality as if their throats were phonograph horns. It is followed by a chorus of hard, barking laughter.)*

LONG: *(Hysterically)* We're free and equal in the sight of God —

YANK: *(With abysmal contempt)* Hell! God!

ALL: *(Repeating the word after him as one with cynical mockery)* God! *(The word has a brazen metallic quality as if their throats were phonograph horns. It is followed by a chorus of hard, barking laughter.)*

YANK: *(Witheringly)* Aw, join de Salvation Army!

ALL: Sit down! Shut up! Damn fool! Sea-lawyer! *(LONG slinks back out of sight.)*

PADDY: *(Continuing the trend of his thoughts as if he had never been inter-*

rupted — bitterly) And there she was standing behind us, and the Second pointing at us like a man you'd hear in a circus would be saying: In this cage is a queerer kind of baboon than ever you'd find in darkest Africy. We roast them in their own sweat — and be damned if you won't hear some of thim saying they like it! *(He glances scornfully at YANK.)*

YANK: *(With a bewildered uncertain growl)* Aw!

PADDY: And there was Yank roarin' curses and turning round wid his shovel to brain her — and she looked at him, and him at her —

YANK: *(Slowly)* She was all white. I tought she was a ghost. Sure.

PADDY: *(With heavy, biting sarcasm)* 'Twas love at first sight, divil a doubt of it! If you'd seen the endearin' look on her pale mug when she shriveled away with her hands over her eyes to shut out the sight of him! Sure, 'twas as if she'd seen a great hairy ape escaped from the Zoo!

YANK: *(Stung — with a growl of rage)* Aw!

PADDY: And the loving way Yank heaved his shovel at the skull of her, only she was out the door! *(A grin breaking over his face)* 'Twas touching, I'm telling you! It put the touch of home, swate home in the stokehole. *(There is a roar of laughter from all.)*

YANK: *(Glaring at PADDY menacingly)* Aw, choke dat off, see!

PADDY: *(Not heeding him — to the others)* And her grabbin' at the Second's arm for protection. *(With a grotesque imitation of a woman's voice)* Kiss me, Engineer dear, for it's dark down here and me old man's in Wall Street making money! Hug me tight, darlin', for I'm afeerd in the dark and me mother's on deck makin' eyes at the skipper! *(Another roar of laughter.)*

YANK: *(Threateningly)* Say! What yuh tryin' do to, kid me, yuh old Harp?

PADDY: Divil a bit! Ain't I wishin' myself you'd brained her?

YANK: *(Fiercely)* I'll brain her! I'll brain her yet, wait 'n' see! *(Coming over to PADDY — slowly)* Say, is dat what she called me — a hairy ape?

PADDY: She looked it at you if she didn't say the word itself.

YANK: *(Grinning horribly)* Hairy ape, huh? Sure! Dat's de way she looked at me, aw right. Hairy ape! So dat's me, huh? *(Bursting into rage — as if she were still in front of him)* Yuh skinny tart! Yuh whitefaced bum, yuh! I'll show yuh who's a ape! *(Turning to the others, bewilderment seizing him again)* Say, youse guys. I was bawlin' him out for pullin' de whistle on us. You heard me. And den I seen youse lookin' at somep'n and I tought he'd sneaked down to come up in back of me, and I hopped round to knock him dead wit de shovel. And dere she was wit de light on her! Christ, yuh coulda pushed me over with a finger! I was scared, get me? Sure! I tought she was a ghost, see? She was all in white like dey wrap around stiffs. You seen her. Kin yuh blame me? She didn't belong, dat's what. And den when I come to and seen it was a real skoit and seen de way she was lookin' at me — like Paddy said — Christ, I was sore, get me? I don't stand for dat stuff from nobody. And I flung de shovel — on'y she'd beat it. *(Furiously)* I wished it'd banged her! I wished it'd knocked her block off!

LONG: And be 'anged for murder or 'lectrocuted? She ain't bleedin' well worth it.

YANK: I don't give a damn what! I'd be square wit her, wouldn't I? Tink I

wanter let her put somep'n over on me? Tink I'm goin' to let her git away wit dat stuff? Yuh don't know me! No one ain't never put nothin' over on me and got away wit it, see! Not dat kind of stuff — no guy and no skoit neither! I'll fix her! Maybe she'll come down again —
VOICE: No chance, Yank. You scared her out of a year's growth.
YANK: I scared her? Why de hell should I scare her? Who de hell is she? Ain't she de same as me? Hairy ape, huh? *(With his old confident bravado)* I'll show her I'm better'n her, if she on'y knew it. I belong and she don't, see! I move and she's dead! Twenty-five knots a hour, dat's me! Dat carries her but I make dat. She's on'y baggage. Sure! *(Again bewilderedly)* But, Christ, she was funny lookin'! Did yuh pipe her hands? White and skinny. Yuh could see de bones through 'em. And her mush, dat was dead white, too. And her eyes, dey was like dey'd seen a ghost. Me, dat was! Sure! Hairy ape! Ghost, huh? Look at dat arm! *(He extends his right arm, swelling out of the great muscles)* I coulda took her wit dat, wit just my little finger even, and broke her in two. *(Again bewilderedly)* Say, who is dat skoit, huh? What is she? What's she come from? Who made her? Who give her de noive to look at me like dat? Dis ting's got my goat right. I don't get her. She's new to me. What does a skoit like her mean, huh? She don't belong, get me! I can't see her. *(With growing anger)* But one ting I'm wise to, aw right, aw right! Youse all kin bet your shoits I'll git even wit her. I'll show her if she tinks she — She grinds de organ and I'm on de string, huh? I'll fix her! Let her come down again and I'll fling her in de furnace! She'll move den! She won't shiver at nothin', den! Speed, dat'll be her! She'll belong den! *(He grins horribly.)*
PADDY: She'll never come. She's had her belly-full, I'm telling you. She'll be in bed now, I'm thinking, wid ten doctors and nurses feeedin' her salts to clean the fear out of her.
YANK: *(Enraged)* Yuh tink I made her sick, too, do yuh? Just lookin' at me, huh? Hairy ape, huh? *(In a frenzy of rage)* I'll fix her! I'll tell her where to git off! She'll git down on her knees and take it back or I'll bust de face offen her! *(Shaking one fist upward and beating on his chest with the other)* I'll find yuh! I'm comin', d'yuh hear? I'll fix yuh, God damn yuh! *(He makes a rush for the door.)*
VOICES: Stop him!
He'll get shot!
He'll murder her!
Trip him up!
Hold him!
He's gone crazy!
Gott, he's strong!
Hold him down!
Look out for a kick!
Pin his arms!
(They have all piled on him and, after a fierce struggle, by sheer weight of numbers have borne him to the floor just inside the door.)
PADDY: *(Who has remained detached)* Kape him down till he's cooled off. *(Scornfully)* Yerra, Yank, you're a great fool. Is it payin' attention at all you are to the like of that skinny sow widout one drop of rale blood in her?

YANK: *(Frenziedly, from the bottom of the heap)* She done me doit! She done me doit, didn't she? I'll git square wit her! I'll get her some way! Git offen me, youse guys! Lemme up! I'll show her who's a ape!

CURTAIN

SCENE FIVE

Three weeks later. A corner of Fifth Avenue in the Fifties on a fine Sunday morning. A general atmosphere of clean, well-tidied, wide street; a flood of mellow, tempered sunshine; gentle, genteel breezes. In the rear, the show windows of two shops, a jewelry establishment on the corner, a furrier's next to it. Here the adornments of extreme wealth are tantalizingly displayed. The jeweler's window is gaudy with glittering diamonds, emeralds, rubies, pearls, etc., fashioned in ornate tiaras, crowns, necklaces, collars, etc. From each piece hangs an enormous tag from which a dollar sign and numerals in intermittent electric lights wink out the incredible prices. The same in the furrier's. Rich furs of all varieties hang there bathed in a downpour of artificial light. The general effect is of a background of magnificence cheapened and made grotesque by commercialism, a background in tawdry disharmony with the clear light and sunshine on the street itself.

Up the side street YANK and LONG come swaggering. LONG is dressed in shore clothes, wears a black Windsor tie, cloth cap. YANK is in his dirty dungarees. A fireman's cap with black peak is cocked defiantly on the side of his head. He has not shaved for days and around his fierce, resentful eyes — as around those of LONG to a lesser degree — the black smudge of coal dust still sticks like make-up. They hesitate and stand together at the corner, swaggering, looking about them with a forced, defiant contempt.

LONG: *(Indicating it all with an oratorical gesture)* Well, 'ere we are. Fif' Avenoo. This 'ere's their bleedin' private lane, as yer might say. *(Bitterly)* We're trespassers 'ere. Proletarians keep orf the grass!

YANK: *(Dully)* I don't see no grass, yuh boob. *(Staring at the sidewalk)* Clean, ain't it? Yuh could eat a fried egg offen it. The white wings got some job sweepin' dis up. *(Looking up and down the avenue — surlily)* Where's all de white-collar stiffs yuh said was here — and de skoits — *her* kind?

LONG: In church, blarst 'em! Arskin' Jesus to give 'em more money.

YANK: Choich, huh? I useter go to choich onct — sure — when I was a kid. Me old man and woman, dey made me. Dey never went demselves, dough. Always got too big a head on Sunday mornin', dat was dem. *(With a grin)* Dey was scrappers for fair, bot' of dem. On Satiday nights when dey bot' got a skinful dey could put up a bout oughter been staged at de Garden. When dey got trough dere wasn't a chair or table wit a leg under it. Or else day bot' jumped on me for somep'n. Dat was where I loined to take punishment. *(With a grin and a swagger)* I'm a chip offen de old block, get me?

LONG: Did yer old man follow the sea?

YANK: Naw. Worked along shore. I runned away when me old lady croaked wit de tremens. I helped at truckin' and in de market. Den I shipped in de stokehole. Sure. Dat belongs. De rest was nothin'. *(Looking*

488

around him) I ain't never seen dis before. De Brooklyn waterfront, dat was where I was dragged up. *(Taking a deep breath)* Dis ain't so bad at dat, huh?

LONG: Not bad? Well, we pays for it wiv our bloody sweat, if yer wants to know!

YANK: *(With sudden angry disgust)* Aw, hell! I don't see no one, see — like her. All dis gives me a pain. It don't belong. Say, ain't dere a back room around dis dump? Let's go shoot a ball. All dis is too clean and quiet and dolled-up, get me! It gives me a pain.

LONG: Wait and yer'll bloody well see —

YANK: I don't wait for no one. I keep on de move. Say, what yuh drag me up here for, anyway? Tryin' to kid me, yuh simp, yuh?

LONG: Yer wants to get back at 'er, don't yer? That's what yer been sayin' every bloomin' hour since she hinsulted yer.

YANK: *(Vehemently)* Sure ting I do! Didn't I try to get even wit her in Southampton? Didn't I sneak on de dock and wait for her by de gangplank? I was goin' to spit in her pale mug, see! Sure, right in her pop-eyes! Dat woulda made me even, see? But no chanct. Dere was a whole army of plainclothes bulls around. Dey spotted me and gimme de bum's rush. I never seen her. But I'll git square wit her yet, you watch. *(Furiously)* De lousy tart! She tinks she kin get away wit moider — but not wit me! I'll fix her! I'll tink of a way!

LONG: *(As disgusted as he dares to be)* Ain't that why I brought yer up 'ere — to show yer? Yer been lookin' at this 'ere 'ole affair wrong. Yer been actin' an' talkin' 's if it was all a bleedin' personal matter between yer and that bloody cow. I wants to convince yer she was on'y a representative of 'er clarss. I wants to awaken yer bloody clarss consciousness. Then yer'll see it's 'er clarss yer've got to fight, not 'er alone. There's a 'ole mob of 'em like 'er, Gawd blind 'em!

YANK: *(Spitting on his hands — belligerently)* De more de merrier when I gits started. Bring on de gang!

LONG: Yer'll see 'em in arf a mo', when that church lets out. *(He turns and sees the window display in the two stores for the first time)* Blimey! Look at that, will yer? *(They both walk back and stand looking in the jeweler's. LONG flies into a fury)* Just look at this 'ere bloomin' mess! Just look at it! Look at the bleedin' prices on 'em — more'n our 'ole bloody stokehole makes in ten voyages sweatin' in 'ell! And they — 'er and 'er bloody clarss — buys 'em for toys to dangle on 'em! One of these 'ere would buy scoff for a starvin' family for a year!

YANK: Aw, cut de sob stuff! T' hell wit de starvin' family! Yuh'll be passin' de hat to me next. *(With naïve admiration)* Say, dem tings is pretty, huh? Bet yuh dey'd hock for a piece of change aw right. *(Then turning away, bored)* But, aw hell, what good are dey? Let her have 'em. Dey don't belong no more'n she does. *(With a gesture of sweeping the jewelers into oblivion)* All dat don't count, get me?

LONG: *(Who has moved to the furrier's — indignantly)* And I s'pose this 'ere don't count neither — skins of poor, 'armless animals slaughtered so as 'er and 'ers can keep their bleedin' noses warm!

YANK: *(Who has been staring at something inside — with queer excitement)* Take a slant at dat! Give it de once-over! Monkey fur — two t'ousand

489

bucks! *(Bewilderedly)* Is dat straight goods — monkey fur? What de hell —?

LONG: *(Bitterly)* It's straight enuf. *(With grim humor)* They wouldn't bloody well pay that for a 'airy ape's skin — no, nor for the 'ole livin' ape with all 'is 'ead, and a body, and soul thrown in!

YANK: *(Clenching his fists, his face growing pale with rage as if the skin in the window were a personal insult)* Trowin' it up in my face! Christ. I'll fix her!

LONG: *(Excitedly)* Church is out. 'Ere they come, the bleedin' swine. *(After a glance at YANK's lowering face — uneasily)* Easy goes, Comrade. Keep yer bloomin' temper. Remember force defeats itself. It ain't our weapon. We must impress our demands through peaceful means — the votes of the on-marching proletarians of the bloody world!

YANK: *(With abysmal contempt)* Votes, hell! Votes is a joke, see. Votes for women! Let dem do it!

LONG: *(Still more uneasily)* Calm, now. Treat 'em wiv the proper contempt. Observe the bleedin' parasites but 'old yer 'orses.

YANK: *(Angrily)* Git away from me! Yuh're yellow, dat's what. Force, dat's me! De punch, dat's me every time, see! *(The crowd from church enter from the right, sauntering slowly and affectedly, their heads held stiffly up, looking neither to right nor left, talking in toneless, simpering voices. The women are rouged, calcimined, dyed, overdressed to the nth degree. The men are in Prince Alberts, high hats, spats, canes, etc. A procession of gaudy marionettes, yet with something of the relentless horror of Frankensteins in their detached, mechanical unawareness.)*

VOICES: Dear doctor Caiphas! He is so sincere!

What was the sermon? I dozed off.

About the radicals, my dear — and the false doctrines that are being preached.

We must organize a hundred per cent American bazaar.

And let everyone contribute one one-hundredth per cent of their income tax.

What an original idea!

We can devote the proceeds to rehabilitating the veil of the temple.

But that has been done so many times.

YANK: *(Glaring from one to the other of them — with an insulting snort of scorn)* Huh! Huh! *(Without seeming to see him, they make wide detours to avoid the spot where he stands in the middle of the sidewalk.)*

LONG: *(Frightenedly)* Keep yer bloomin' mouth shut, I tells yer.

YANK: *(Viciously)* G'wan! Tell it to Sweeney! *(He swaggers away and deliberately lurches into a top-hatted gentleman, then glares at him pugnaciously)* Say, who d'yuh tink yuh're bumpin'? Tink yuh own de oith?

GENTLEMAN: *(Coldly and affectedly)* I beg your pardon. *(He has not looked at YANK and passes on without a glance, leaving him bewildered.)*

LONG: *(Rushing up and grabbing YANK's arm)* 'Ere! Come away! This wasn't what I meant. Yer'll 'ave the bloody coppers down on us.

YANK: *(Savagely — giving him a push that sends him sprawling)* G'wan!

LONG: *(Picks himself up — hysterically)* I'll pop orf then. This ain't what I meant. And whatever 'appens, yer can't blame me. *(He slinks off left.)*

YANK: T' hell wit youse! *(He approaches a lady — with a vicious grin and a smirking wink)* Hello, Kiddo. How's every little ting? Got anyting on for tonight? I know an old boiler down to de docks we kin crawl into. *(The lady stalks by without a look, without a change of pace. YANK turns to others — insultingly)* Holy smokes, what a mug! Go hide yuh-self before de horses shy at yuh. Gee, pipe de heine on dat one! Say, youse, yuh look like de stoin of a ferryboat. Paint and powder! All dolled up to kill! Yuh look like stiffs laid out for de boneyard! Aw, g'wan, de lot of youse! Yuh give me de eyeache. Yuh don't belong, get me! Look at me, why don't youse dare? I belong, dat's me! *(Pointing to a skyscraper across the street which is in process of construction — with bravado)* See dat building goin' up dere? See de steel work? Steel, dat's me! Youse guys live on it and tink yuh're somep'n. But I'm *in* it, see! I'm de hoistin' engine dat makes it go up! I'm it — de inside and bottom of it! Sure! I'm steel and steam and smoke and de rest of it! It moves — speed — twenty-five stories up — and me at de top and bottom — movin'! Youse simps don't move. Yuh're on'y dolls I winds up to see 'm spin. Yuh're de garbage, get me — de leavin's — de ashes we dump over de side! Now, what 'a' yuh gotta say? *(But as they seem neither to see nor hear him, he flies into a fury)* Bums! Pigs! Tarts! Bitches! *(He turns in a rage on the men, bumping viciously into them but not jarring them the least bit. Rather it is he who recoils after each collision. He keeps growling)* Git off de oith! G'wan, yuh bum! Look where yuh're goin', can't yuh? Git outa here! Fight, why don't yuh? Put up yer mits! Don't be a dog! Fight or I'll knock yuh dead! *(But, without seeming to see him, they all answer with mechanical affected politeness* "I beg your pardon." *Then at a cry from one of the women, they all scurry to the furrier's window.)*

THE WOMAN: *(Ecstatically, with a gasp of delight)* Monkey fur! *(The whole crowd of men and women chorus after her in the same tone of affected delight* "Monkey fur!")

YANK: *(With a jerk of his head back on his shoulders, as if he had received a punch full in the face — raging)* I see yuh, all in white! I see yuh, yuh white-faced tart, yuh! Hairy ape, huh? I'll hairy ape yuh! *(He bends down and grips at the street curbing as if to pluck it out and hurl it. Foiled in this, snarling with passion, he leaps to the lamppost on the corner and tries to pull it up for a club. Just at that moment a bus is heard rumbling up. A fat, high-hatted, spatted gentleman runs out from the side street. He calls out plaintively* "Bus! Bus! Stop there!" *and runs full tilt into the bending, straining YANK, who is bowled off his balance.)*

YANK: *(Seeing a fight — with a roar of joy as he springs to his feet)* At last! Bus, huh? I'll bust yuh! *(He lets drive a terrific swing, his fist landing full on the fat gentleman's face. But the gentleman stands unmoved as if nothing had happened.)*

GENTLEMAN: I beg your pardon. *(Then irritably)* You have made me lose my bus. *(He claps his hands and begins to scream)* Officer! Officer! *(Many police whistles shrill out on the instant and a whole platoon of policemen rush in on YANK from all sides. He tries to fight but is clubbed to the pavement and fallen upon. The crowd at the window have not moved or noticed this disturbance. The clanging gong of the patrol wagon approaches with a clamoring din.)*

CURTAIN

SCENE SIX

Night of the following day. A row of cells in the prison on Blackwells Island. The cells extend back diagonally from right front to left rear. They do not stop, but disappear in the dark background as if they ran on, numberless, into infinity. One electric bulb from the low ceiling of the narrow corridor sheds its light through the heavy steel bars of the cell at the extreme front and reveals part of the interior. YANK can be seen within, crouched on the edge of his cot in the attitude of Rodin's "The Thinker." His face is spotted with black and blue bruises. A blood-stained bandage is wrapped around his head.

YANK: *(Suddenly starting as if awakening from a dream, reaches out and shakes the bars — aloud to himself, wonderingly)* Steel. Dis is de Zoo, huh? *(A burst of hard, barking laughter comes from the unseen occupants of the cells, runs back down the tier, and abruptly ceases.)*

VOICES: *(Mockingly)* The Zoo? That's a new name for this coop — a damn good name!

Steel, eh? You said a mouthful. This is the old iron house.

Who is that boob talkin'?

He's the bloke they brung in out of his head. The bulls had beat him up fierce.

YANK: *(Dully)* I musta been dreamin'. I tought I was in a cage at de Zoo — but de apes don't talk, do dey?

VOICES: *(With mocking laughter)* You're in a cage aw right.

A coop!

A pen!

A sty!

A kennel! *(Hard laughter — a pause.)*

Say, guy! who are you? No, never mind lying. What are you?

Yes, tell us your sad story. What's your game?

What did they jug yuh for?

YANK: *(Dully)* I was a fireman — stokin' on de liners. *(Then with sudden rage, rattling his cell bars)* I'm a hairy ape, get me? And I'll bust youse all in de jaw if yuh don't lay off kiddin' me.

VOICES: Huh! You're a hard boiled duck, ain't you!

When you spit, it bounces! *(Laughter)*

Aw, can it. He's a regular guy. Ain't you?

What did he say he was — a ape?

YANK: *(Defiantly)* Sure ting! Ain't dat what youse all are — apes? *(A silence. Then a furious rattling of bars from down the corridor.)*

A VOICE: *(Thick with rage)* I'll show yuh who's a ape, yuh bum!

VOICES: Ssshh! Nix!

Can de noise!

Piano!

You'll have the guard down on us!

YANK: *(Scornfully)* De guard? Yuh mean de keeper, don't yuh? *(Angry exclamations from all the cells.)*

VOICE: *(Placatingly)* Aw, don't pay no attention to him. He's off his nut

492

from the beatin'-up he got. Say, you guy! We're waitin' to hear what
they landed you for — or ain't yuh tellin'?

YANK: Sure, I'll tell youse. Sure! Why de hell not? On'y — youse won't get
me. Nobody gets me but me, see? I started to tell de Judge and all he
says was: "Toity days to tink it over." — Tink it over! Christ, dat's all
I been doin' for weeks! *(After a pause)* I was tryin' to git even wit
someone, see? — someone dat done me doit.

VOICES: *(Cynically)* De old stuff, I bet. Your goil, huh?

Give yuh the double-cross, huh?

That's them every time!

Did yuh beat up de odder guy?

YANK: *(Disgustedly)* Aw, yuh're all wrong! Sure dere was a skoit in it — but
not what youse mean, not dat old tripe. Dis was a new kind of skoit.
She was dolled up all in white — in de stokehole. I tought she was a
ghost. Sure. *(A pause.)*

VOICES: *(Whispering)* Gee, he's still nutty.

Let him rave. It's fun listenin'.

YANK: *(Unheeding — groping in his thoughts)* Her hands — dey was skinny
and white like dey wasn't real but painted on somep'n. Dere was a
million miles from me to her — twenty-five knots a hour. She was
like some dead ting de cat brung in. Sure, dat's what. She didn't
belong. She belonged in de window of a toy store, or on de top of a
garbage can, see! Sure! *(He breaks out angrily)* But would yuh believe
it, she had de noive to do me doit. She lamped me like she was seein'
somep'n broke loose from de menagerie. Christ, yuh'd oughter seen
her eyes! *(He rattles the bars of his cell furiously)* But I'll get back at
her yet, you watch! And if I can't find her I'll take it out on de gang
she runs wit. I'm wise to where dey hangs out now. I'll show her who
belongs! I'll show her who's in de move and who ain't. You watch my
smoke!

VOICES: *(Serious and joking)* Dat's de talkin'!

Take her for all she's got!

What was this dame, anyway? Who was she, eh?

YANK: I dunno. First cabin stiff. Her old man's a millionaire, dey says —
name of Douglas.

VOICES: Douglas? That's the president of the Steel Trust, I bet.

Sure. I seen his mug in de papers.

He's filthy with dough.

VOICE: Hey, feller, take a tip from me. If you want to get back at that
dame, you better join the Wobblies. You'll get some action then.

YANK: Wobblies? What de hell's dat?

VOICE: Ain't you ever heard of the I.W.W.?

YANK: Naw. What is it?

VOICE: A gang of blokes — a tough gang. I been readin' about 'em today
in the paper. The guard give me the *Sunday Times.* There's a long
spiel about 'em. It's from a speech made in the Senate by a guy named
Senator Queen. *(He is in the cell next to YANK's. There is a rustling
of paper)* Wait'll I see if I got light enough and I'll read you. Listen.
(He reads) "There is a menace existing in this country today which
threatens the vitals of our fair Republic — as foul a menace against the

very life-blood of the American Eagle as was the foul conspiracy of Cataline against the eagles of ancient Rome!"

VOICE: *(Disgustedly)* Aw, hell! Tell him to salt de tail of dat eagle!

VOICE: *(Reading)* "I refer to that devil's brew of rascals, jailbirds, murderers and cutthroats who libel all honest working men by calling themselves the Industrial Workers of the World; but in the light of their nefarious plots, I call them the Industrious *Wreckers* of the World!"

YANK: *(With vengeful satisfaction)* Wreckers, dat's de right dope! Dat belongs! Me for dem!

VOICE: Ssshh! *(Reading)* "This fiendish organization is a foul ulcer on the fair body of our Democracy —"

VOICE: Democracy, hell! Give him the boid, fellers — the raspberry! *(They do.)*

VOICE: Ssshh! *(Reading)* "Like Cato I say to this Senate, the I.W.W. must be destroyed! For they represent an ever-present dagger pointed at the heart of the greatest nation the world has ever known, where all men are born free and equal, with equal opportunities to all, where the Founding Fathers have guaranteed to each one happiness, where Truth, Honor, Liberty, Justice, and the Brotherhood of Man are a religion absorbed with one's mother's milk, taught at our father's knee, sealed, signed, and stamped upon in the glorious constitution of these United States!" *(A perfect storm of hisses, catcalls, boos, and hard laughter.)*

VOICES: *(Scornfully)* Hurrah for de Fort' of July!
Pass de hat!
Liberty!
Justice!
Honor!
Opportunity!
Brotherhood!

ALL: *(With abysmal scorn)* Aw, hell!

VOICE: Give that Queen Senator guy the bark! All togedder now — one — two — tree — *(A terrific chorus of barking and yapping.)*

GUARD: *(From a distance)* Quiet there, youse — or I'll git the hose. *(The noise subsides.)*

YANK: *(With growling rage)* I'd like to catch dat senator guy alone for a second. I'd loin him some trute!

VOICE: Ssshh! Here's where he gits down to cases on the Wobblies. *(Reads)* "They plot with fire in one hand and dynamite in the other. They stop not before murder to gain their ends, nor at the outraging of defenseless womanhood. They would tear down society, put the lowest scum in the seats of the mighty, turn Almighty God's revealed plan for the world topsy-turvy, and make of our sweet and lovely civilization a shambles, a desolation where man, God's masterpiece, would soon degenerate back to the ape!"

VOICE: *(To YANK)* Hey, you guy. There's your ape stuff again.

YANK: *(With a growl of fury)* I got him. So dey blow up tings, do dey? Dey turn tings round, do dey? Hey, lend me dat paper, will yuh?

VOICE: Sure. Give it to him. On'y keep it to yourself, see. We don't wanter listen to no more of that slop.

VOICE: Here you are. Hide it under your mattress.

YANK: *(Reaching out)* Tanks. I can't read much but I kin manage. *(He sits, the paper in the hand at his side, in the attitude of Rodin's "The Thinker." A pause. Several snores from down the corridor. Suddenly YANK jumps to his feet with a furious groan as if some appalling thought had crashed on him — bewilderedly)* Sure — her old man — president of de Steel Trust — makes half de steel in de world — steel — where I tought I belonged — drivin' trou — movin' — in dat — to make *her* — and cage me in for her to spit on! Christ! *(He shakes the bars of his cell door till the whole tier trembles. Irritated, protesting exclamations from those awakened or trying to get to sleep)* He made dis — dis cage! Steel! *It* don't belong, dat's what! Cages, cells, locks, bolts, bars — dat's what it means! — holdin' me down wit him at de top! But I'll drive trou! Fire, dat melts it! I'll be fire — under de heap — fire dat never goes out — hot as hell — breakin' out in de night — *(While he has been saying this last he has shaken his cell door to a clanging accompaniment. As he comes to the "breakin' out" he seizes one bar with both hands and, putting his two feet up against the others so that his position is parallel to the floor like a monkey's, he gives a great wrench backwards. The bar bends like a licorice stick under his tremendous strength. Just at this moment the PRISON GUARD rushes in, dragging a hose behind him.)*

GUARD: *(Angrily)* I'll loin youse bums to wake me up! *(Sees YANK)* Hello, it's you huh? Got the D.T.'s, hey? Well, I'll cure 'em. I'll drown your snakes for yuh! *(Noticing the bar)* Hell, look at dat bar bended! On'y a bug is strong enough for dat!

YANK: *(Glaring at him)* Or a hairy ape, yuh big yellow bum! Look out! Here I come! *(He grabs another bar.)*

GUARD: *(Scared now — yelling off left)* Toin de hose on, Ben! — full pressure! And call de others — and a straitjacket! *(The curtain is falling. As it hides YANK from view, there is a splattering smash as the stream of water hits the steel of YANK's cell.)*

CURTAIN

SCENE SEVEN

Nearly a month later. An I.W.W. local near the waterfront, showing the interior of a front room on the ground floor, and the street outside. Moonlight on the narrow street, buildings massed in black shadow. The interior of the room, which is general assembly room, office, and reading room, resembles some dingy settlement boys' club. A desk and high stool are in one corner. A table with papers, stacks of pamphlets, chairs about it, is at center. The whole is decidedly cheap, banal, commonplace and unmysterious as a room could well be. The SECRETARY is perched on the stool making entries in a large ledger. An eye shade casts his face into shadows. Eight or ten men, longshoremen, iron workers, and the like, are grouped about the table. Two are playing checkers. One is writing a letter. Most of them are smoking pipes. A big signboard is on the wall at the rear, "Industrial Workers of the World — Local No. 57."

YANK comes down the street outside. He is dressed as in Scene Five. He moves cautiously, mysteriously. He comes to a point opposite the door; tiptoes softly up to it, listens, is impressed by the silence within, knocks carefully, as if he were guessing at the password to some secret rite. Listens. No answer. Knocks again a bit louder. No answer. Knocks impatiently, much louder.

SECRETARY: *(Turning around on his stool)* What the hell is that — someone is knocking? *(Shouts)* Come in, why don't you? *(All the men in the room look up. YANK opens the door slowly, gingerly, as if afraid of an ambush. He looks around for secret doors, mystery, is taken aback by the commonplaceness of the room and the men in it, thinks he may have gotten in the wrong place, then sees the signboard on the wall and is reassured.)*

YANK: *(Blurts out)* Hello.

MEN: *(Reservedly)* Hello.

YANK: *(More easily)* I tought I'd bumped into de wrong dump.

SECRETARY: *(Scrutinizing him carefully)* Maybe you have. Are you a member?

YANK: Naw, not yet. Dat's what I come for — to join.

SECRETARY: That's easy. What's your job — longshore?

YANK: Naw. Fireman — stoker on de liners.

SECRETARY: *(With satisfaction)* Welcome to our city. Glad to know you people are waking up at last. We haven't got many members in your line.

YANK: Naw. Dey're all dead to de woild.

SECRETARY: Well, you can help to wake 'em. What's your name? I'll make out your card.

YANK: *(Confused)* Name? Lemme tink.

SECRETARY: *(Sharply)* Don't you know your own name?

YANK: Sure; but I been just Yank for so long — Bob, dat's it — Bob Smith.

SECRETARY: *(Writing)* Robert Smith. *(Fills out the rest of the card)* Here you are. Cost you half a dollar.

YANK: Is dat all — four bits? Dat's easy. *(Gives the SECRETARY the money.)*

SECRETARY: *(Throwing it in drawer)* Thanks. Well, make yourself at home. No introductions needed. There's literature on the table. Take some of those pamphlets with you to distribute aboard ship. They may bring results. Sow the seed, only go about it right. Don't get caught and fired. We got plenty out of work. What we need is men who can hold their jobs — and work for us at the same time.

YANK: Sure. *(But he still stands, embarrassed and uneasy.)*

SECRETARY: *(Looking at him — curiously)* What did you knock for? Think we had a coon in uniform to open doors?

YANK: Naw. I tought it was locked — and dat yuh'd wanter give me the once-over trou a peep-hole or somep'n to see if I was right.

SECRETARY: *(Alert and suspicious but with an easy laugh)* Think we were running a crap game? That door is never locked. What put that in your nut?

YANK: *(With a knowing grin, convinced that this is all camouflage, a part of the secrecy)* Dis burg is full of bulls, ain't it?

SECRETARY: *(Sharply)* What have the cops got to do with us? We're breaking no laws.

YANK: *(With a knowing wink)* Sure. Youse wouldn't for woilds. Sure. I'm wise to dat.

SECRETARY: You seem to be wise to a lot of stuff none of us knows about.

YANK: *(With another wink)* Aw, dat's aw right, see. *(Then made a bit resentful by the suspicious glances from all sides)* Aw, can it! Youse needn't put me trou de toid degree. Can't youse see I belong? Sure! I'm reg'lar. I'll stick, get me? I'll shoot de woiks for youse. Dat's why I wanted to join in.

SECRETARY: *(Breezily, feeling him out)* That's the right spirit. Only are you sure you understand what you've joined? It's all plain and above board; still, some guys get a wrong slant on us. *(Sharply)* What's your notion of the purpose of the I.W.W.?

YANK: Aw, I know all about it.

SECRETARY: *(Sarcastically)* Well, give us some of your valuable information.

YANK: *(Cunningly)* I know enough not to speak outa my toin. *(Then resentfully again)* Aw, say! I'm reg'lar. I'm wise to de game. I know yuh got to watch your step wit a stranger. For all youse know, I might be a plain-clothes dick, or somep'n, dat's what yuh're tinkin', huh? Aw, forget it! I belong, see? Ask any guy down to de docks if I don't.

SECRETARY: Who said you didn't?

YANK: After I'm 'nitiated, I'll show yuh.

SECRETARY: *(Astounded)* Initiated? There's no initiation.

YANK: *(Disappointed)* Ain't there no password — no grip nor nothin'?

SECRETARY: What'd you think this is — the Elks — or the Black Hand?

YANK: De Elks, hell! De Black Hand, dey're a lot of yellow back-stickin' Ginees. Naw. Dis is a man's gang, ain't it?

SECRETARY: You said it! That's why we stand on our two feet in the open. We got no secrets.

YANK: *(Surprised but admiringly)* Yuh mean to say yuh always run wide open — like dis?

SECRETARY: Exactly.

YANK: Den yuh sure got your noive wit youse!

SECRETARY: *(Sharply)* Just what was it made you want to join us? Come out with that straight.

YANK: Yuh call me? Well, I got noive, too! Here's my hand. Yuh wanter blow tings up, don't yuh? Well, dat's me! I belong!

SECRETARY: *(With pretended carelessness)* You mean change the unequal conditions of society by legitimate direct action — or with dynamite?

YANK: Dynamite! Blow it offen de oith — steel — all de cages — all de factories, steamers, buildings, jails — de Steel Trust and all dat makes it go.

SECRETARY: So — that's your idea, eh? And did you have any special job in that line you wanted to propose to us? *(He makes a sign to the men, who get up cautiously one by one and group behind YANK.)*

YANK: *(Boldly)* Sure, I'll come out wit it. I'll show youse I'm one of de gang. Dere's dat millionaire guy, Douglas —

SECRETARY: President of the Steel Trust, you mean? Do you want to assassinate him?

497

YANK: Naw, dat don't get yuh nothin'. I mean blow up de factory, de woiks, where he makes de steel. Dat's what I'm after — to blow up de steel, knock all de steel in de woild up to de moon. Dat'll fix tings! *(Eagerly, with a touch of bravado)* I'll do it by me lonesome! I'll show yuh! Tell me where his woiks is, how to git there, all de dope. Gimme de stuff, de old butter — and watch me do de rest! Watch de smoke and see it move! I don't give a damn if dey nab me — long as it's done! I'll soive life for it — and give 'em de laugh! *(Half to himself)* And I'll write her a letter and tell her de hairy ape done it. Dat'll square tings.

SECRETARY: *(Stepping away from YANK)* Very interesting. *(He gives a signal. The men, huskies all, throw themselves on YANK and before he knows it they have his legs and arms pinioned. But he is too flabbergasted to make a struggle, anyway. They feel him over for weapons.)*

MAN: No gat, no knife. Shall we give him what's what and put the boots to him?

SECRETARY: No. He isn't worth the trouble we'd get into. He's too stupid. *(He comes closer and laughs mockingly in YANK's face)* Ho-ho! By God, this is the biggest joke they've put on us yet. Hey, you Joke! Who sent you — Burns or Pinkerton? No, by God, you're such a bonehead I'll bet you're in the Secret Service! Well, you dirty spy, you rotten agent provocator, you can go back and tell whatever skunk is paying you blood-money for betraying your brothers that he's wasting his coin. You couldn't catch a cold. And tell him that all he'll ever get on us, or ever has got, is just his own sneaking plots that he's framed up to put us in jail. We are what our manifesto says we are, neither more nor less — and we'll give him a copy of that any time he calls. And as for you — *(He glares scornfully at YANK, who is sunk in an oblivious stupor)* Oh, hell, what's the use of talking? You're a brainless ape.

YANK: *(Aroused by the word to fierce but futile struggles)* What's dat, you Sheeny bum, yuh!

SECRETARY: Throw him out, boys. *(In spite of his struggles, this is done with gusto and éclat. Propelled by several parting kicks, YANK lands sprawling in the middle of the narrow cobbled street. With a growl he starts to get up and storm the closed door, but stops bewildered by the confusion in his brain, pathetically impotent. He sits there, brooding, in as near to the attitude of Rodin's "The Thinker" as he can get in his position.)*

YANK: *(Bitterly)* So dem boids don't tink I belong, neider. Aw, to hell wit 'em. Dey're in de wrong pew — de same old bull — soap-boxes and Salvation Army — no guts! Cut out an hour offen de job a day and make me happy! Gimme a dollar more a day and make me happy! Tree square a day, and cauliflowers in de front yard — ekal rights — a woman and kids — a lousy vote — and I'm all fixed for Jesus, huh? Aw, hell! What does dat get yuh? Dis ting's in your inside, but it ain't your belly. Feedin' your face — sinkers and coffee — dat don't touch it. It's way down — at de bottom. Yuh can't grab it, and yuh can't stop it. It moves, and everything moves. It stops and de whole woild stops. Dat's me now — I don't tick, see? — I'm a busted Ingersoll, dat's what. Steel was me, and I owned de woild. Now I ain't steel, and de woild owns me. Aw, hell! I can't see — it's all dark, get me? It's all wrong! *(He turns a bitter mocking face up like an ape gibbering at the moon)* Say, youse up dere, Man in de Moon, yuh look so wise, gimme de answer, huh? Slip me de inside dope, de information right from de stable — where do I get off at, huh?

A POLICEMAN: *(Who has come up the street in time to hear this last — with grim humor)* You'll get off at the station, you boob, if you don't get up out of that and keep movin'.

YANK: *(Looking up at him — with a hard, bitter laugh)* Sure! Lock me up! Put me in a cage! Dat's de on'y answer yuh know. G'wan, lock me up!

POLICEMAN: What you been doin'?

YANK: Enuf to gimme life for! I was born, see? Sure, dat's de charge. Write it in de blotter. I was born, get me!

POLICEMAN: *(Jocosely)* God pity your old woman! *(Then matter-of-factly)* But I've no time for kidding. You're soused. I'd run you in but it's too long a walk to the station. Come on now, get up, or I'll fan your ears with this club. Beat it now! *(He hauls YANK to his feet.)*

YANK: *(In a vague mocking tone)* Say, where do I go from here?

POLICEMAN: *(Giving him a push — with a grin, indifferently)* Go to hell.

CURTAIN

SCENE EIGHT

Twilight of the next day. The monkey house at the Zoo. One spot of clear gray light falls on the front of one cage so that the interior can be seen. The other cages are vague, shrouded in shadow from which chatterings pitched in a conversational tone can be heard. On the one cage a sign from which the word "gorilla" stands out. The gigantic animal himself is seen squatting on his haunches on a bench in much the same attitude as Rodin's "The Thinker." YANK enters from the left. Immediately a chorus of angry chattering and screeching breaks out. The gorilla turns his eyes but makes no sound or move.

YANK: *(With a hard, bitter laugh)* Welcome to your city, huh? Hail, hail, de gang's all here! *(At the sound of his voice the chattering dies away into an attentive silence. YANK walks up to the gorilla's cage and, leaning over the railing, stares in at its occupant, who stares back at him, silent and motionless. There is a pause of dead stillness. Then YANK begins to talk in a friendly confidential tone, half mockingly, but with a deep undercurrent of sympathy)* Say, yuh're some hard-lookin' guy, ain't yuh? I seen lots of tough nuts dat de gang called gorillas, but yuh're de foist real one I ever seen. Some chest yuh got, and shoulders, and dem arms and mits! I bet yuh got a punch in eider fist dat'd knock 'em all silly! *(This with genuine admiration. The gorilla, as if he understood, stands upright, swelling out his chest and pounding on it with his fist. YANK grins sympathetically)* Sure, I get yuh. Yuh challenge de whole woild, huh? Yuh got what I was sayin' even if yuh muffed de woids. *(Then bitterness creeping in)* And why wouldn't yuh get me? Ain't we both members of de same club — de Hairy Apes? *(They stare at each other — a pause — then YANK goes on slowly and bitterly)* So yuh're what she seen when she looked at me, de white-faced tart! I was you to her, get me? On'y outa de cage — broke out — free to moider her, see? Sure! Dat's what she tought. She wasn't wise dat I

499

was in a cage, too — worser'n yours — sure — a damn sight — 'cause
you got some chanct to bust loose — but me — *(He grows confused)*
Aw, hell! It's all wrong, ain't it? *(A pause)* I s'pose yuh wanter know
what I'm doin' here, huh? I been warmin' a bench down to de Battery —
ever since last night. Sure. I seen de sun come up. Dat was pretty,
too — all red and pink and green. I was lookin' at de skyscrapers —
steel — and all de ships comin' in, sailin' out, all over de oith — and
dey was steel, too. De sun was warm, dey wasn't no clouds, and dere
was a breeze blowin'. Sure, it was great stuff. I got it aw right — what
Paddy said about dat bein' de right dope — on'y I couldn't get *in* it,
see? I couldn't belong in dat. It was over my head. and I kept tinkin' —
and den I beat it up here to see what youse was like. And I waited
till dey was all gone to git yuh alone. Say, how d'yuh feel sittin' in
dat pen all de time, havin' to stand for 'em comin' and starin' at
yuh — de white-faced, skinny tarts and de boobs what marry 'em —
makin' fun of yuh, laughin' at yuh, gittin' scared of yuh — damn 'em!
*(He pounds on the rail with his fist. The gorilla rattles the bars of his
cage and snarls. All the other monkeys set up an angry chattering in
the darkness. YANK goes on excitedly)* Sure! Dat's de way it hits me,
too. On'y yuh're lucky, see? Yuh don't belong wit 'em and yuh know
it. But me, I belong wit 'em — but I don't, see? Dey don't belong wit
me, dat's what. Get me? Tinkin' is hard — *(He passes one hand across
his forehead with painful gesture. The gorilla growls impatiently.
YANK goes on gropingly)* It's dis way, what I'm drivin' at. Youse can
sit and dope dream in de past, green woods, de jungle and de rest of
it. Den yuh belong and dey don't. Den yuh kin laugh at 'em, see?
Yuh're de champ of de world. But me — I ain't got no past to tink in,
nor nothin' dat's comin', on'y what's now — and dat don't belong. Sure,
you're de best off! You can't tink, can yuh? Yuh can't talk neider. But
I kin make a bluff at talkin' and tinkin' — a'most git away wit it —
a'most! — and dat's where de joker comes in. *(He laughs)* I ain't on
oith and I ain't in heaven, get me? I'm in de middle tryin' to separate
'em, takin' all de woist punches from bot' of 'em. Maybe dat's what
dey call hell, huh? But you, yuh're at de bottom. You belong! Sure!
Yuh're de on'y one in de woild dat does, yuh lucky stiff! *(The gorilla
growls proudly)* And dat's why dey gotter put yuh in a cage, see? *(The
gorilla roars angrily)* Sure! Yuh get me. It beats it when you try to
tink it or talk it — it's way down — deep — behind — you 'n' me we
feel it. Sure! Bot' members of dis club! *(He laughs — then in a savage
tone)* What de hell! T' hell wit it! A little action, dat's our meat! Dat
belongs! Knock 'em down and keep bustin' 'em till dey croaks yuh wit
a gat — wit steel! Sure! Are yuh game? Dey looked at youse, ain't
dey — in a cage? Wanter git even? Wanter wind up like a sport 'stead
of croakin' slow in dere? *(The gorilla roars an emphatic affirmative.
YANK goes on with a sort of furious exaltation)* Sure! Yuh're reg'lar!
Yuh'll stick to de finish! Me 'n' you, huh? — bot' members of dis club!
We'll put up one last star bout dat'll knock 'em offen deir seats! Dey'll
have to make de cages stronger after we're trou! *(The gorilla is straining at his bars, growling, hopping from one foot to the other, YANK
takes a jimmy from under his coat and forces the lock on the cage door. He*

500

throws this open) Pardon from de governor! Step out and shake hands. I'll take yuh for a walk down Fif' Avenoo. We'll knock 'em offen de oith and croak wit de band playin'. Come on, Brother. *(The gorilla scrambles gingerly out of his cage. Goes to YANK and stands looking at him. YANK keeps his mocking tone — holds out his hand)* Shake — de secret grip of our order. *(Something, the tone of mockery, perhaps, suddenly enrages the animal. With a spring he wraps his huge arms around YANK in a murderous hug. There is a crackling snap of crushed ribs — a gasping cry, still mocking, from YANK)* Hey, I didn't say kiss me! *(The gorilla lets the crushed body slip to the floor; stands over it uncertainly, considering; then picks it up, throws it in the cage, shuts the door, and shuffles off menacingly into the darkness at left. A great uproar of frightened chattering and whimpering comes from the other cages. Then YANK moves, groaning, opening his eyes, and there is silence. He mutters painfully)* Say — dey oughter match him — with Zybszko. He got me, aw right. I'm trou. Even him didn't tink I belonged. *(Then, with sudden passionate despair)* Christ, where do I get off at? Where do I fit in? *(Checking himself as suddenly)* Aw, what de hell! No squawkin', see! No quittin', get me! Croak wit your boots on! *(He grabs hold of the bars of the cage and hauls himself painfully to his feet — looks around him bewilderedly — forces a mocking laugh)* In de cage, huh? *(In the strident tones of a circus barker)* Ladies and gents, step forward and take a slant at de one and only — *(His voice weakening)* one and original — Hairy Ape from de wilds of — *(He slips in a heap on the floor and dies. The monkeys set up a chattering, whimpering wail. And, perhaps, the Hairy Ape at last belongs.)*

CURTAIN

TWENTIETH-CENTURY POLITICAL DRAMA:
The Theatre of Revolution

$\mathbf{A}$fter World War I, dramatists with deep political commitments developed theatre as a political tool. This was the first time since the early-Renaissance use of morality plays in the Catholic-Protestant conflict that theatre had been used as a weapon in political debate. Twentieth-century political theatre tended to express revolutionary, antiestablishment viewpoints and to use presentational, nonrealistic techniques. This movement produced plays of lasting value and also developed dramatic structures and staging techniques which were adopted by mainstream theatrical artists. It is an important part of twentieth-century theatre.

Political/Social/Philosophical Backgrounds

Revolution

The first seven decades of the twentieth century brought a worldwide succession of wave after wave of revolution. In 1917, the Bolsheviks overthrew the czar of Russia and began a revolution that would, by 1922, establish the Union of Soviet Socialist Republics, the first nation to have a communist economic and political system based on the ideas of Karl Marx as interpreted by Nikolai Lenin (1870-1924). After World War II, as a result of agreements among the victorious allies concerning eastern Europe and civil war in China, those areas also became Communist.

During this same period of time, countries in the "Third World" — Africa, India, Asia, and Latin America — shook off their colonial subservience to European empires and became independent nations. These transitions were almost always seen as revolutions of poor, down-trodden peoples against rich and powerful oppressors. The principles of equality and self-determination which drove the English, American, French, and Russian Revolutions now spread worldwide. Because the Russian Revolution was the most recent of these European upheavals, the independence struggles of the Third World often had Marxist-Lenin associations.

Labor Unions

In the industrialized nations during this period, labor unions developed as a means for working people to get fair wages, decent working conditions, and job security. The unionization struggles again pitted poor masses against a minority whose control of capital resources gave them great economic and political power, and again these struggles were often portrayed as conflicts between communists and capitalists.

Communism

When the Great Depression spread throughout the industrialized nations in the 1930s, many people believed it demonstrated that capitalism was indeed an outmoded system. Intellectuals and artists in the United States and elsewhere began to look to Communism as a possible alternative and to admire the USSR as the only available sample of Communism in practice. For theatre artists, the Moscow Art Theatre and the work of Stanislavsky and his associates made the Russian model particularly attractive.

Also during the first half of the twentieth century, it became an accepted concept around the world that all people — regardless of race, religion, sex, national origin, age, physical ability, or economic status — had, by virtue of being human, certain basic rights. The struggles of various minorities to secure their human rights frequently used the language and tactics of revolution.

Revolution, however, was not a simple matter. It quickly became apparent that revolutionary leaders could themselves become repressive despots. Marxism produced a dizzying array of factions who battled each other with the same fervor they gave to the class struggle. Industrialized nations found ways to establish an economic domination of Third World countries which was every bit as oppressive as the old colonial empires. And tensions within and between countries became increasingly dangerous as men used modern technology to create and multiply tools of warfare with almost unimaginable destructive capabilities. It was a confusing time and an exciting one. It should be no surprise that the period produced revolutionary, political theatre.

Dramatic Theory

Twentieth-century political dramatists drew on several earlier kinds of theatre. Their intent to use theatre as a tool for correcting social and political injustice put them in the tradition of nineteenth-century realism. But they borrowed stylized, presentational techniques and theatricalism from such varied sources as medieval European drama, non-Western theatre and expressionism.

Brecht's Epic Theatre

Bertolt Brecht (1898-1956), German Marxist poet, playwright, and director, explained the basic theory of revolutionary theatre in his "Short Organum for the Theatre" (1948).[1] Brecht called his kind of drama "epic theatre" to accent its loose, narrative structure and set it apart from conventional, dramatic "Aristotelian" theatre. He said that epic theatre aimed to apply scientific method to the problem of human oppression, to reveal people's motivations and show how they affect social conditions, and to show that since societal structures are man-made, they can be changed by people. He said that this kind of theatre would entertain modern audiences because it gave them the sense of participating vicariously in decision-making. Realizing that this was not the stuff for audiences of commercial theatre, Brecht suggested seeking an audience for epic theatre among suburban workers and rejecting normal theatres in favor of factories, schools, sports arenas,

---

[1]The "Short Organum" has been published several times in English. It is available in Toby Cole, ed. *Playwrights on Playwriting* (New York: Hill and Wang, 1960) and John Willett, ed. *Brecht on Theatre: The Development of an Aesthetic* (London: Metheun, 1964).

and other nontraditional performance spaces.

Brecht said epic theatre should "alienate" the audience — distance them from the characters on stage so that, rather than becoming emotionally involved in the action, they would be able to perceive and evaluate the actions and decisions of the characters rationally. While Aristotelian theatre attempted to lull the audience to sleep and pacify them with dreams, epic theatre should awaken its audience to the truth about human behavior.

The principle of alienation should operate throughout the fabric of a play. The script should use a loose, episodic structure to prevent the audience from being caught up in the flow of the action. Epic plays should employ songs and projected titles to focus the audience's attention on the "gestus," or social event being depicted.

Brecht called for epic actors to be involved in the class struggle outside the theatre and said that plays should be cast against type to increase the alienation-effect. Instead of identifying with their characters and attempting to duplicate real, emotional behavior on stage, epic actors should rather comment on their characters through nonrealistic vocal and physical techniques. They should aim to show the audience what lies beneath their characters' behavior, rather than aiming to delude the audience into thinking they really were the characters.

In performance, off-stage actors should sit in plain view of the audience. Production devices such as lighting instruments should be placed in view of the audience, rather than concealed to create the illusion of nature.

Although Brecht focused his writing and production activities on scripted drama with traditional story lines and characters, his theories also apply, with only minor adaptations, to improvisational political theatre, and less traditional scripted forms such as documentary theatre.

Dramatic Literature

Brecht began writing plays in an expressionist mode in the early 1920s, but soon began to unite his political commitments and his art into epic theatre. He achieved his first major success in 1928 with *The Threepenny Opera* with music by Kurt Weill. This free adaptation of John's Gay's *Beggar's Opera* (1728) used projected titles and harsh ballads to portray the typical Brechtian world where good people have to be crooks to survive, the rich and powerful have gutter morals, everyone lives by their wits, and the only predictable values are greed and the profit motive. During the 1930s, Brecht wrote a number of short Lehrstücke or didactic plays, including *He Who Says Yes/He Who Says No* (1929-1930), which uses a rough adaptation of Japanese Noh form, and *The Measures Taken* (1930) which uses medieval morality structures.

Brecht wrote the plays generally considered to be his best works while in exile from Nazi Germany. These included *Mother Courage and Her Children* (1941), which chronicles the survival techniques of a merchant during the Thirty Years' War; *The Life of Galileo* (1943), which probes the mixed motives of the Renaissance astronomer; *The Good Woman of Setzuan* (1943), which shows how a woman must be corrupt in order to be good; and *The*

Caucasian Chalk Circle (1954), which again shows that justice can only be served by breaking the law.

Controversy continues over whether Brecht's theory helped or hindered his drama and whether his best plays demonstrate or disprove his theories, but his plays continue to attract audiences and the techniques he developed have become a normal part of mainstream theatre.

During the 1930s, while Brecht was working out the details of his epic theatre, American dramatists were also using theatre as a tool for political debate. One well-known sample of American revolutionary theatre is Clifford Odets' *Waiting for Lefty* which follows. At the same time, theatre people and journalists who belonged to the Federal Theatre Project, a government program during the Depression, developed the Living Newspaper, a theatrical form which used documentary sources to investigate socio-political issues. Arthur Arent wrote the texts of three famous Living Newspapers, including *Triple-A Plowed Under* (1936), about the plight of farmers; *Power* (1937), about greed in the utilities industries; and *One-Third of a Nation* (1938), which advocated government development of public housing. The success of these major productions stimulated the use of Living Newspaper techniques to treat local problems throughout the United States.

Documentary Drama

After World War II, Brechtian and Living Newspaper traditions came together in documentary drama. Sometimes called "theatre of fact," documentary drama aims to present historical data in a theatrical mode. German novelist and playwright Peter Weiss (1916-82) explained the theoretical concepts underlying this kind of theatre in his essay "The Material and the Model: Notes on Documentary Theatre" (1968).[2] According to Weiss, the documentary playwright should act as an editor who arranges factual material for stage presentation using song, poetry, spectacular scenery, symbolic action, projections, and short dramatic scenes. Two of Weiss's documentary plays include *The Investigation* (1965), based on transcripts of the 1964 Frankfurt War Crimes trial, and *Discourse on the Progress of the Prolonged War of Liberation in Viet Nam and the Events Leading Up to It As Illustration of the Necessity for Armed Resistance Against Oppression, and on the Attempts of the United States of America to Destroy the Foundations of Revolution* (1968).

Other German writers of documentary drama include Rolf Hochhuth (1931-) and Heinar Kipphardt (1922-82). Hochhuth's plays, *The Deputy* (1963) and *Soldiers* (1967), included vast amounts of documentation in their respective indictments of Pope Pius XII and Winston Churchill for their parts in World War II atrocities. Kipphardt's *In the Matter of J. Robert Oppenheimer* (1964) made effective theatrical use of facts surrounding the American nuclear physicist's trial for treason during the Red-scare witch-hunts in the early 1950s.

---

[2]Published in an English translation in *Theatre Quarterly* (January-March, 1971), pp. 41-43.

Performance Conventions and Stagecraft

Perhaps because they saw themselves primarily as partisans in a war, political theatre artists developed a rough-edged, confrontational style for their performances and productions. Rather than entertain their audiences, they aimed instead to challenge, inform, persuade, polarize, and if necessary offend them. Their argumentative acting style and jarring, symbolic staging techniques fit well into these goals.

Erwin Piscator

German director Erwin Piscator (1893-1966) contributed to the production modes of political theatre by staging partially-scripted material and adaptations, using projected slides, titles, movie clips, and cartoons along with live actors, and devising symbolic machine-like sets. In the 1960s, he directed premieres of several documentary dramas, including Hochhuth's *The Deputy,* Kipphardt's *In the Matter of J. Robert Oppenheimer,* and Weiss's *The Investigation.* Theatre artists who worked or studied with Piscator included Brecht in Germany and, in America, Tennessee Williams, Judith Malina, and Arthur Miller.

Guerilla and Agit-Prop Theatre

Some political theatre groups operated outside normal theatre spaces. In the 1960s, bands of actors might suddenly draw attention in a crowded area and confront their surprised audience with a short, partially improvised play on some topical socio-political issue. Because of these tactics, this kind of performance was called guerrilla theatre. Political drama, in or out of traditional theatre spaces, which frankly attempted to agitate revolution or spread propaganda was called agit-prop theatre.

Theatrical Organization

From the Renaissance through the nineteenth century, theatre in Europe and America was a commercial venture. As the nineteenth century ended and the twentieth began, however, the rise of the independent theatre movement, the demise of The Road, and the advent of film combined to attack the capitalistic basis of theatre. Political impulses in twentieth-century theatre further weakened the hold of investors on the art form by spawning several options to commercial theatre.

The Federal Theatre Project

In the United States, the Federal Theatre Project (1935-39) was a short-lived but important experiment in noncommercial theatre. The Federal Theatre Project began during the Depression in 1935 as an effort, under the Public Works Administration, to employ theatre people for the public good. It provided work for 10,000 theatre artists who performed for audiences numbering in the millions in forty different states. The Project performed all kinds of plays, but its Living Newspaper productions brought it special fame and notoriety. Because of the political and social criticism in these docu-dramas, the Federal Theatre drew fire from conservative politicians, and in 1939 it disbanded.

The Living Theatre

In 1951, Julian Beck and his wife Judith Malina, who had studied with Erwin Piscator, founded the Living Theatre, a group committed to producing avant-garde dramas with revolutionary social and political viewpoints. The Living Theatre produced scripted dramas, like Jack Gelber's *The Connection* (1959) about drug addiction, and Kenneth Brown's *The Brig* (1963) about the Marine Corps. They also staged highly improvisational performances, like the anarchistic *Paradise Now*. They toured in Europe and the United States and became increasingly outspoken, confrontational, and politically radical, both in their performances and in their off-stage lives. Before the Living Theatre faded out in the growing conservatism of the 1970s, the group had spawned off-shoots and radicalized theatre people around the world.

Two theatre companies who shared parts of the political vision and techniques of the Living Theatre were the Bread and Puppet Theatre (1961-) which uses large puppets and plays on mythical topics to challenge the establishment, and the Teatro Campesino (Fieldworkers' Theatre), established by Luiz Valdéz in 1965, which uses bilingual productions to support social issues of importance to Latinos.

Twentieth century political theatre has always been controversial, not only because of its political associations and the content of its plays, but also because it subordinates "pure art" to didactic purposes. In spite of its controversial nature, however, it has made genuine contributions to the dramatic repertory and also to staging and performance techniques. It represents another attempt to enliven the relationship between life and theatre — the now art.

Clifford Odets and the Group Theatre

Clifford Odets was born to Jewish parents in Philadelphia in 1906 and grew up in the Bronx, New York City. After dropping out of high school in 1923, he tried writing and acting, a profession which eventually led him to join the Group Theatre.

The Group Theatre grew out of the Theatre Guild which had been formed in 1919 for the purpose of staging serious new drama from Europe and America. In 1931, as a result of a Guild workshop, Harold Clurman, Cheryl Crawford, and Lee Strasberg formed the Group Theatre. The Group aimed to use Stanislavsky's acting method and ensemble approach, to stay free from the financial pressures of commercial theatre, and to produce works of serious social impact. Before it finally disbanded in 1949, the Group Theatre not only fostered the work of major Stanislavskian actors and directors like Elia Kazan, but also produced the plays of American playwrights, such as Paul Green and William Saroyan.

Odets joined the Group as an actor in 1931. In 1934 he joined the Communist Party and then withdrew from it several months later. In 1935 the Group Theatre produced his *Waiting for Lefty*. The Group subsequently produced at least six works by Odets, including *Awake and Sing!* (1935), about materialism in the Jewish middle-class, and *Golden Boy* (1937), in which financial pressures force a talented Italian violinist to give up his art for a career as a prize fighter.

Odets later wrote for the movies and television, an experience which led him to believe that Hollywood personified the worst in capitalism. The qualities that built Odets' reputation — humor, passion, sensitivity to social evil, familiarity with middle-class hopes and fears, and rough dramatic structure — made him an excellent political dramatist. These qualities spring to life in *Waiting for Lefty*.

Waiting for Lefty

The Situation

As the play begins, New York City's taxicab (hack) drivers are trying to decide whether or not to strike for higher wages. The play's audience represents the rank and file membership of the union, and several actors, planted throughout the audience, take part in the action. On stage, the locally-elected committee sits in a semicircle while the union's professional secretary, Harry Fatt, backed up by an armed bodyguard, harangues the membership trying to convince them not to strike. The hackies, however, do not want to make a decision until their radical, elected chairman, Lefty Costello, arrives. While they wait for Lefty, the members explain why they want to strike. Their stories, dramatized with minimal scenery, make up the play.

Didactic Plot

The play is beautifully arranged as a piece of agit-prop political theatre. First of all, without actually demanding that they participate, the play casts the audience members themselves as underprivileged hack drivers. In this way, the production leaves the audience free to enjoy the play while simultaneously asking them to become involved in the workers' plight. In good Brechtian fashion, the off-stage actors — the Committee — are seated around the perimeters of the acting space. Not only does their presence act as a distancing device, but it also permits them to offer improvised comments on the action, a chorus-like activity recommended by stage directions and by Odets' appended "Notes for Production."

Waiting for Lefty also makes excellent didactic use of melodrama. The hackies and their women are classical melodramatic heroes and heroines — morally pure, solidly middle-class and heroic in their ideals. Fatt along with the rest of the rich and powerful figures are textbook samples of melodramatic villains — foul-mouthed, selfish, bigoted, and dangerous.

Furthermore, the play presents the black-and-white world view of melodrama. The forces of evil are big money, big labor, and big government personified by the industrialist Fayette, the labor boss Fatt, and the shadowy figure of the President of the United States. The forces of good are the honest laborers. Two mighty symbols of good and evil are the USSR and the USA, and the laborers maintain their identity as patriotic Americans while clearly preferring the socialist system of Russia over the capitalism of their own country. At this point, in the mid-thirties, the growing allegiance of the USSR and the United States against Germany and Japan gave this kind of political stance a respectability which it would not have fifteen years later when the Cold War began.

Production History

First presented by the Group Theatre at New York's Longacre Theatre on March 26, 1935, the play was directed by Harold Clurman and featured the Group's actors, including Elia Kazan in the role of Agate, and Odets himself as Dr. Benjamin. Subsequently, *Waiting for Lefty* was presented on Broadway on a double bill with another Odets one-act, *Till the Day I Die,* a play about life under the Nazis. *Lefty* won Yale University's George Pierce Baker Drama Cup and the New Theatre-New Masses Theatre Contest. Throughout the thirties, it was a popular play with amateur theatre groups.

Today in an affluent America, after the Cold War has ended with the worldwide collapse of Communism, the depression setting of *Waiting for Lefty* and its optimism about Communism makes the play seem archaic, but its passion, the purity of its vision, its hopeful humanism, and its powerful use of didactic dramatic devices still make it a lively sample of political theatre.

Political Theatre Timeline

KARL MARX (1818-83)

KONSTANTIN STANISLAVSKY (1863-1938)

NIKOLAI LENIN (1870-1924)

ERWIN PISCATOR (1893-1966)

BERTOLT BRECHT (1898-1956)

"SHORT ORGANUM FOR THE THEATRE" (1948) ●

CLIFFORD ODETS (1906-63)

"WAITING FOR LEFTY" (1935) ●

ELIA KAZAN (1909-)

TENNESSEE WILLIAMS (1911-83)

WORLD WAR I (1914-18)

ARTHUR MILLER (1915-)

PETER WEISS (1916-82)

RUSSIAN REVOLUTION (1917-22)

TRANSFORMATION OF THE BRITISH EMPIRE INTO THE COMMONWEALTH (1919-49)

HEINAR KIPPHARDT (1922-82)

JULIAN BECK (1925-)

JUDITH MALINA (1926-)

THE GREAT DEPRESSION (1929-39)

THE GROUP THEATRE (1931-41)

ROLF HOCCHUTH (1931-)

FEDERAL THEATRE PROJECT (1935-39)

WORLD WAR II (1939-45)

BERLINER ENSEMBLE (1949-)

THE LIVING THEATRE (1946-75?)

BREAD AND PUPPET THEATRE (1961-)

EL TEATRO CAMPESINO (1965-)

1820 1830 1840 1850 1860 1870 1880 1890 1900 1910 1920 1930 1940 1950 1960 1970 1980 1990

Waiting for Lefty

by CLIFFORD ODETS

The action of the play takes place in New York City around 1935.

CHARACTERS

FATT
a union boss

JOE
a hack driver

EDNA
Joe's wife

MILLER
a hack driver and former lab worker

FAYETTE
an industrialist

IRV
a worker

FLORRIE
Irv's sister

SID
a hack driver, in love with Florrie

CLAYTON
a spy working for Fatt

STENOGRAPHER

PHILIPS
a cabby, formerly an actor

REILLY
a theatrical producer, played by Fatt

DR. BARNES
a senior medical doctor

DR. BENJAMIN
a cabby, formerly a medical doctor

AGATE KELLER
a popular leader among the hacks

Voices, henchmen, messengers, etc.

As the curtain goes up we see a bare stage. On it are sitting six or seven men in a semicircle. Lolling against the proscenium down left is a young man chewing a toothpick: a gunman. A fat man of porcine appearance is talking directly to the audience. In other words he is the head of a union and the men ranged behind him are a committee of workers. They are now seated in interesting different attitudes and present a wide diversity of type, as we shall soon see. The fat man is hot and heavy under the collar, near the end of a long talk, but not too hot: he is well fed and confident. His name is HARRY FATT.

FATT: You're so wrong I ain't laughing. Any guy with eyes to read knows it. Look at the textile strike — out like lions and in like lambs. Take the San Francisco tie-up — starvation and broken heads. The steel boys wanted to walk out too, but they changed their minds. It's the trend of the times, that's what it is. All we workers got a good man behind us now. He's top man of the country — looking out for our interests — the man in the White House is the one I'm referrin' to. That's why the times ain't ripe for a strike. He's working day and night —

VOICE: *(From the audience)* For who? *(The GUNMAN stirs himself.)*

FATT: For you! The records prove it. If this was the Hoover régime, would I say don't go out, boys? Not on your tintype! But things is different now. You read the papers as well as me. You know it. And that's why I'm against the strike. Because we gotta stand behind the man who's standin' behind us! The whole country —

ANOTHER VOICE: Is on the blink! *(The GUNMAN looks grave.)*

FATT: Stand up and show yourself, you damn red! Be a man, let's see what you look like! *(Waits in vain.)* Yellow from the word go! Red and yellow makes a dirty color, boys. I got my eyes on four or five of them in the union here. What the hell'll they do for you? Pull you out and run away when trouble starts. Give those birds a chance and they'll have your sisters and wives in the whore houses, like they done in Russia. They'll tear Christ off his bleeding cross. They'll wreck your homes and throw your babies in the river. You think that's bunk? Read the papers! Now listen, we can't stay here all night. I gave you the facts in the case. You boys got hot suppers to go to and —

ANOTHER VOICE: Says you!

GUNMAN: Sit down, Punk!

ANOTHER VOICE: Where's Lefty? *(Now this question is taken up by the others in unison. FATT pounds with gavel.)*

FATT: That's what I wanna know. Where's your pal, Lefty? You elected him chairman — where the hell did he disappear?

VOICES: We want Lefty! Lefty! Lefty!

FATT: *(Pounding)* What the hell is this — a circus? You got the committee here. This bunch of cowboys you elected. *(Pointing to man on extreme right end.)*

MAN: Benjamin.

FATT: Yeah, Doc Benjamin. *(Pointing to other men in circle in seated order)* Benjamin, Miller, Stein, Mitchell, Phillips, Keller. It ain't my fault Lefty took a run-out powder. If you guys —

A GOOD VOICE: What's the commitee say?

OTHERS: The committee! Let's hear from the committee! *(FATT tries to*

quiet the crowd, but one of the seated men suddenly comes to the front. The GUNMAN moves over to center stage, but FATT says:)
FATT: Sure, let him talk. Let's hear what the red boys gotta say!

(Various shouts are coming from the audience. FATT insolently goes back to his seat in the middle of the circle. He sits on his raised platform and relights his cigar. The GUNMAN goes back to his post. JOE, the new speaker, raises his hand for quiet. Gets it quickly. He is sore.)

JOE: You boys know me. I ain't a red boy one bit! Here I'm carryin' a shrapnel that big I picked up in the war. And maybe I don't know it when it rains! Don't tell me red! You know what we are? The black and blue boys! We been kicked around so long we're black and blue from head to toes. But I guess anyone who says straight out he don't like it, he's a red boy to the leaders of the union. What's this crap about goin' home to hot suppers? I'm asking to your faces how many's got hot suppers to go home to? Anyone who's sure of his next meal, raise your hand! A certain gent sitting behind me can raise them both. But not in front here! And that's why we're talking strike — to get a living wage!
VOICE: Where's Lefty?
JOE: I honest to God don't know, but he didn't take no run-out powder. That Wop's got more guts than a slaughter house. Maybe a traffic jam got him, but he'll be here. But don't let this red stuff scare you. Unless fighting for a living scares you. We gotta make up our minds. My wife made up my mind last week, if you want the truth. It's plain as the nose on Sol Feinberg's face we need a strike. There's us comin' home every night — eight, ten hours on the cab. "God," the wife says, "eighty cents ain't money — don't buy beans almost. You're workin' for the company," she says to me, "Joe! you ain't workin' for me or the family no more!" She says to me, "If you don't start . . ."

I. JOE AND EDNA

The lights fade out and a white spot picks out the playing space within the space of seated men. The seated men are very dimly visible in the outer dark, but more prominent is FATT smoking his cigar and often blowing the smoke in the lighted circle.

A tired but attractive woman of thirty comes into the room, drying her hands on an apron. She stands there sullenly as JOE comes in from the other side, home from work. For a moment they stand and look at each other in silence.

JOE: Where's all the furniture, honey?
EDNA: They took it away. No installments paid.
JOE: When?
EDNA: Three o'clock.
JOE: They can't do that.
EDNA: Can't? They did it.
JOE: Why, the palookas, we paid three-quarters.
EDNA: The man said read the contract.
JOE: We must have signed a phoney . . .
EDNA: It's a regular contract and you signed it.

JOE: Don't be so sour, Edna . . . *(Tries to embrace her.)*
EDNA: Do it in the movies, Joe — they pay Clark Gable big money for it.
JOE: This is a helluva house to come home to. Take my word!
EDNA: Take MY word! Whose fault is it?
JOE: Must you start that stuff again?
EDNA: Maybe you'd like to talk about books?
JOE: I'd like to slap you in the mouth!
EDNA: No you won't.
JOE: *(Sheepish)* Jeez, Edna, you get me sore some time . . .
EDNA: But just look at me — I'm laughing all over!
JOE: Don't insult me. Can I help it if times are bad? What the hell do you want me to do, jump off a bridge or something?
EDNA: Don't yell. I just put the kids to bed so they won't know they missed a meal. If I don't have Emmy's shoes soled tomorrow, she can't go to school. In the meantime let her sleep.
JOE: Honey, I rode the wheels off the chariot today. I cruised around five hours without a call. It's conditions.
EDNA: Tell it to the A & P!
JOE: I booked two-twenty on the clock. A lady with a dog was lit . . . she gave me a quarter tip by mistake. If you'd only listen to me — we're rolling in wealth.
EDNA: Yeah? How much?
JOE: I had "coffee and —" in a beanery. *(Hands her silver coins.)* A buck four.
EDNA: The second month's rent is due tomorrow.
JOE: Don't look at me that way, Edna.
EDNA: I'm looking through you, not at you . . . Everything was gonna be so ducky! A cottage by the waterfall, roses in Picardy. You're a four-star-bust! If you think I'm standing for it much longer, you're crazy as a bedbug.
JOE: I'd get another job if I could. There's no work — you know it.
EDNA: I only know we're at the bottom of the ocean.
JOE: What can I do?
EDNA: Who's the man in the family, you or me?
JOE: That's no answer. Get down to brass tacks. Christ, gimme a break, too! A coffee cake and java all day. I'm hungry, too, Babe. I'd work my fingers to the bone if —
EDNA: I'll open a can of salmon.
JOE: Not now. Tell me what to do!
EDNA: I'm not God!
JOE: Jeez, I wish I was a kid again and didn't have to think about the next minute.
EDNA: But you're not a kid and you do have to think about the next minute. You got two blondie kids sleeping in the next room. They need food and clothes. I'm not mentioning anything else — But we're stalled like a flivver in the snow. For five years I laid awake at night listening to my heart pound. For God's sake, do something, Joe, get wise. Maybe get your buddies together, maybe go on strike for better money. Poppa did it during the war and they won out. I'm turning into a sour old nag.
JOE: *(Defending himself)* Strikes don't work!
EDNA: Who told you?

JOE: Besides that means not a nickel a week while we're out. Then when it's over they don't take you back.

EDNA: Suppose they don't! What's to lose?

JOE: Well, we're averaging six-seven dollars a week now.

EDNA: That just pays for the rent.

JOE: That is something, Edna.

EDNA: It isn't. They'll push you down to three and four a week before you know it. Then you'll say, "That's somethin'," too!

JOE: There's too many cabs on the street, that's the whole damn trouble.

EDNA: Let the company worry about that, you big fool! If their cabs didn't make a profit, they'd take them off the streets. Or maybe you think they're in business just to pay Joe Mitchell's rent!

JOE: You don't know a-b-c, Edna.

EDNA: I know this — your boss is making suckers outa you boys every minute. Yes, and suckers out of all the wives and the poor innocent kids who'll grow up with crooked spines and sick bones. Sure, I see it in the papers, how good orange juice is for kids. But dammit, our kids get colds one on top of the other. They look like little ghosts. Betty never saw a grapefruit. I took her to the store last week and she pointed to a stack of grapefruits. "What's that!" she said. My God, Joe — the world is supposed to be for all of us.

JOE: You'll wake them up.

EDNA: I don't care, as long as I can maybe wake you up.

JOE: Don't insult me. One man can't make a strike.

EDNA: Who says one? You got hundreds in your rotten union!

JOE: The Union ain't rotten.

EDNA: No? Then what are they doing? Collecting dues and patting your back?

JOE: They're making plans.

EDNA: What kind?

JOE: They don't tell us.

EDNA: It's too damn bad about you. They don't tell little Joey what's happening in his bitsie witsie union. What do you think it is — a ping pong game?

JOE: You know they're racketeers. The guys at the top would shoot you for a nickel.

EDNA: Why do you stand for that stuff?

JOE: Don't you wanna see me alive?

EDNA: *(After a deep pause)* No . . . I don't think I do, Joe. Not if you can lift a finger to do something about it, and don't. No, I don't care.

JOE: Honey, you don't understand what —

EDNA: And any other hackie that won't fight . . . let them all be ground to hamburger!

JOE: It's one thing to —

EDNA: Take your hand away! Only they don't grind me to little pieces! I got different plans. *(Starts to take off her apron.)*

JOE: Where are you going?

EDNA: None of your business.

JOE: What's up your sleeve?

EDNA: My arm'd be up my sleeve, darling, if I had a sleeve to wear. *(Puts*

neatly folded apron on back of chair.)
JOE: Tell me!
EDNA: Tell you what?
JOE: Where are you going?
EDNA: Don't you remember my old boy friend?
JOE: Who?
EDNA: Bud Haas. He still has my picture in his watch. He earns a living.
JOE: What the hell are you talking about?
EDNA: I heard worse than I'm talking about.
JOE: Have you seen Bud since we got married?
EDNA: Maybe.
JOE: If I thought . . . *(He stands looking at her.)*
EDNA: See much? Listen, boy friend, if you think I won't do this it just
    means you can't see straight.
JOE: Stop talking bull!
EDNA: This isn't five years ago, Joe.
JOE: You mean you'd leave me and the kids?
EDNA: I'd leave *you* like a shot!
JOE: No . . .
EDNA: Yes!

*(JOE turns away, sitting in a chair with his back to her. Outside the lighted
circle of the playing stage we hear the other seated members of the strike
committee. "She will . . . she will . . . it happens that way," etc. This group
should be used throughout for various comments, political, emotional and as
general chorus. Whispering . . . The fat boss now blows a heavy cloud of
smoke into the scene.)*

JOE: *(Finally)* Well, I guess I ain't got a leg to stand on.
EDNA: No?
JOE: *(Suddenly mad)* No, you lousy tart, no! Get the hell out of here. Go
    pick up that bull-thrower on the corner and stop at some cushy hotel
    downtown. He's probably been coming here every morning and laying
    you while I hacked my guts out!
EDNA: You're crawling like a worm!
JOE: You'll be crawling in a minute.
EDNA: You don't scare me that much! *(Indicates a half inch on her finger.)*
JOE: This is what I slaved for!
EDNA: Tell it to your boss!
JOE: He don't give a damn for you or me!
EDNA: That's what I say.
JOE: Don't change the subject!
EDNA: This is the subject, the EXACT SUBJECT! Your boss makes this
    subject. I never saw him in my life, but he's putting ideas in my head
    a mile a minute. He's giving your kids that fancy disease called the
    rickets. He's making a jelly-fish outa you and putting wrinkles in my
    face. This is the subject every inch of the way! He's throwing me into
    Bud Haas' lap. When in hell will you get wise —
JOE: I'm not so dumb as you think! But you are talking like a Red.
EDNA: I don't know what that means. But when a man knocks you down
    you get up and kiss his fist! You gutless piece of boloney.

JOE: One man can't —
EDNA: *(With great joy)* I don't say one man! I say a hundred, a thousand,
a whole million, I say. But start in your own union. Get those hack
boys together! Sweep out those racketeers like a pile of dirt! Stand up
like men and fight for the crying kids and wives. Goddammit! I'm
tired of slavery and sleepless nights.
JOE: *(With her)* Sure, sure! . . .
EDNA: Yes. Get brass toes on your shoes and know where to kick!
JOE: *(Suddenly jumping up and kissing his wife full on the mouth)* Listen,
Edna. I'm goin' down to 174th Street to look up Lefty Costello. Lefty
was saying the other day . . . *(He suddenly stops.)* How about this
Haas guy?
EDNA: Get out of here!
JOE: I'll be back! *(Runs out.)*

(For a moment EDNA stands triumphant.)
*(There is a blackout and when the regular lights come up, JOE MITCHELL
is concluding what he has been saying:)*

JOE: You guys know this stuff better than me. We gotta walk out! *(Abruptly
he turns and goes back to his seat and blackout.)*

BLACKOUT

II. LAB ASSISTANT EPISODE

*Discovered: MILLER, a lab assistant, looking around; and FAYETTE, an
industrialist.*

FAY: Like it?
MILL: Very much. I've never seen an office like this outside the movies.
FAY: Yes, I often wonder if interior decorators and bathroom fixture people
don't get all their ideas from Hollywood. Our country's extraordinary
that way. Soap, cosmetics, electric refrigerators — just let Mrs. Con-
sumer know they're used by the Crawfords and Garbos — more volume
of sale than one plant can handle!
MILL: I'm afraid it isn't that easy, Mr. Fayette.
FAY: No, you're right — gross exaggeration on my part. Competition is
cut-throat today. Markets up flush against a stone wall. The astrono-
mers had better hurry — open Mars to trade expansion.
MILL: Or it will be just too bad!
FAY: Cigar?
MILL: Thank you, don't smoke.
FAY: Drink?
MILL: Ditto, Mr. Fayette.
FAY: I like sobriety in my workers . . . the trained ones, I mean. The Pollacks
and niggers, they're better drunk — keeps them out of mischief. Won-
dering why I had you come over?
MILL: If you don't mind my saying — very much.
FAY: *(Patting him on the knee)* I like your work.
MILL: Thanks.
FAY: No reason why a talented young man like yourself shouldn't string
along with us — a growing concern. Loyalty is well repaid in our

518

organization. Did you see Siegfried this morning?

MILL: He hasn't been in the laboratory all day.

FAY: I told him yesterday to raise you twenty dollars a month. Starts this week.

MILL: You don't know how happy my wife'll be.

FAY: Oh, I can appreciate it. *(He laughs.)*

MILL: Was that all, Mr. Fayette?

FAY: Yes, except that we're switching you to laboratory A tomorrow. Siegfried knows about it. That's why I had you in. The new work is very important. Siegfried recommended you very highly as a man to trust. You'll work directly under Dr. Brenner. Make you happy?

MILL: Very. He's an important chemist!

FAY: *(Leaning over seriously)* We think so, Miller. We think so to the extent of asking you to stay within the building throughout the time you work with him.

MILL: You mean sleep and eat in?

FAY: Yes . . .

MILL: It can be arranged.

FAY: Fine. You'll go far, Miller.

MILL: May I ask the nature of the new work?

FAY: *(Looking around first)* Poison gas . . .

MILL: Poison!

FAY: Orders from above. I don't have to tell you from where. New type poison gas for modern warfare.

MILL: I see.

FAY: You didn't know a new war was that close, did you?

MILL: I guess I didn't.

FAY: I don't have to stress the importance of absolute secrecy.

MILL: I understand!

FAY: The world is an armed camp today. One match sets the whole world blazing in forty-eight hours. Uncle Sam won't be caught napping!

MILL: *(Addressing his pencil)* They say 12 million men were killed in that last one and 20 million more wounded or missing.

FAY: That's not our worry. If big business went sentimental over human life there wouldn't be big business of any sort!

MILL: My brother and two cousins went in the last one.

FAY: They died in a good cause.

MILL: My mother says "no!"

FAY: She won't worry about you this time. You're too valuable behind the front.

MILL: That's right.

FAY: All right, Miller. See Siegfried for further orders.

MILL: You should have seen my brother — he could ride a bike without hands . . .

FAY: You'd better move some clothes and shaving tools in tomorrow. Remember what I said — you're with a growing organization.

MILL: He could run the hundred yards in 9:8 flat . . .

FAY: Who?

MILL: My brother. He's in the Meuse-Argonne Cemetery. Momma went there in 1926 . . .

FAY: Yes, those things stick. How's your handwriting, Miller, fairly legible?
MILL: Fairly so.
FAY: Once a week I'd like a little report from you.
MILL: What sort of report?
FAY: Just a few hundred words once a week on Dr. Brenner's progress.
MILL: Don't you think it might be better coming from the Doctor?
FAY: I didn't ask you that.
MILL: Sorry.
FAY: I want to know what progress he's making, the reports to be purely
confidential — between you and me.
MILL: You mean I'm to watch him?
FAY: Yes!
MILL: I guess I can't do that . . .
FAY: Thirty a month raise . . .
MILL: You said twenty . . .
FAY: Thirty!
MILL: Guess I'm not built that way.
FAY: Forty . . .
MILL: Spying's not in my line, Mr. Fayette!
FAY: You use ugly words, Mr. Miller!
MILL: For ugly activity? Yes!
FAY: Think about it, Miller. Your chances are excellent . . .
MILL: No.
FAY: You're doing something for your country. Assuring the United States
that when those goddam Japs start a ruckus we'll have offensive
weapons to back us up! Don't you read your newspapers, Miller?
MILL: Nothing but Andy Gump.
FAY: If you were on the inside you'd know I'm talking cold sober truth!
Now, I'm not asking you to make up your mind on the spot. Think
about it over your lunch period.
MILL: No . . .
FAY: Made up your mind already?
MILL: Afraid so.
FAY: You understand the consequences?
MILL: I lose my raise —
Simultaneously: { MILL: And my job!
FAY: And your job!
MILL: You misunderstand —
MILL: Rather dig ditches first!
FAY: That's a big job for foreigners.
MILL: But sneaking — and making poison gas — that's for Americans?
FAY: It's up to you.
MILL: My mind's made up.
FAY: No hard feelings?
MILL: Sure hard feelings! I'm not the civilized type, Mr. Fayette. Nothing
suave or sophisticated about me. Plenty of hard feelings! Enough to
want to bust you and all your kind square in the mouth! *(Does exactly
that.)*

BLACKOUT

III. THE YOUNG HACK AND HIS GIRL

Opens with girl and brother. FLORENCE waiting for SID to take her to a dance.

FLOR: I gotta right to have something out of life. I don't smoke, I don't drink. So if Sid wants to take me to a dance, I'll go. Maybe if you was in love you wouldn't talk so hard.

IRV: I'm saying it for your good.

FLOR: Don't be so good to me.

IRV: Mom's sick in bed and you'll be worryin' her to the grave. She don't want that boy hanging around the house and she don't want you meeting him in Crotona Park.

FLOR: I'll meet him anytime I like!

IRV: If you do, yours truly'll take care of it in his own way. With just one hand, too!

FLOR: Why are you all so set against him?

IRV: Mom told you ten times — it ain't him. It's that he ain't got nothing. Sure, we know he's serious, that he's stuck on you. But that don't cut no ice.

FLOR: Taxi drivers used to make good money.

IRV: Today they're makin' five and six dollars a week. Maybe you wanta raise a family on that. Then you'll be back here living with us again and I'll be supporting two families in one. Well . . . over my dead body.

FLOR: Irv, I don't care — I love him!

IRV: You're a little kid with half-baked ideas!

FLOR: I stand there behind the counter the whole day. I think about him —

IRV: If you thought more about Mom it would be better.

FLOR: Don't I take care of her every night when I come home? Don't I cook supper and iron your shirts and . . . you give me a pain in the neck, too. Don't try to shut me up! I bring a few dollars in the house, too. Don't you see I want something else out of life. Sure, I want romance, love, babies. I want everything in life I can get.

IRV: You take care of Mom and watch your step!

FLOR: And if I don't?

IRV: Yours truly'll watch it for you!

FLOR: You can talk that way to a girl . . .

IRV: I'll talk that way to your boy friend, too, and it won't be with words! Florrie, if you had a pair of eyes you'd see it's for your own good we're talking. This ain't no time to get married. Maybe later —

FLOR: "Maybe Later" never comes for me, though. Why don't we send Mom to a hospital? She can die in peace there instead of looking at the clock on the mantelpiece all day.

IRV: That needs money. Which we don't have!

FLOR: Money, Money, Money!

IRV: Don't change the subject.

FLOR: This is the subject!

IRV: You gonna stop seeing him? *(She turns away.)* Jesus, kiddie, I remember when you were a baby with curls down your back. Now I gotta stand here yellin' at you like this.

FLOR: I'll talk to him, Irv.

521

IRV: When?

FLOR: I asked him to come here tonight. We'll talk it over.

IRV: Don't get soft with him. Nowadays is no time to be soft. You gotta be hard as a rock or go under.

FLOR: I found that out. There's the bell. Take the egg off the stove I boiled for Mom. Leave us alone, Irv.

(SID comes in — the two men look at each other for a second, IRV exits.)

SID: *(Enters)* Hello, Florrie.

FLOR: Hello, Honey. You're looking tired.

SID: Naw, I just need a shave.

FLOR: Well, draw your chair up to the fire and I'll ring for brandy and soda . . . like in the movies.

SID: If this was the movies I'd bring a big bunch of roses.

FLOR: How big?

SID: Fifty or sixty dozen — the kind with long, long stems — big as that . . .

FLOR: You dope . . .

SID: Your Paris gown is beautiful.

FLOR: *(Acting grandly)* Yes, Percy, velvet panels are coming back again. Madame La Farge told me today that Queen Marie herself designed it.

SID: Gee . . . !

FLOR: Every princess in the Balkans is wearing one like this. *(Poses grandly.)*

SID: Hold it. *(Does a nose camera — thumbing nose and imitating grinding of camera with other hand. Suddenly she falls out of the posture and swiftly goes to him, to embrace him, to kiss him with love. Finally:)*

SID: You look tired, Florrie.

FLOR: Naw, I just need a shave. *(She laughs tremorously.)*

SID: You worried about your mother?

FLOR: No.

SID: What's on your mind?

FLOR: The French and Indian War.

SID: What's on your mind?

FLOR: I got us on my mind, Sid. Night and day, Sid!

SID: I smacked a beer truck today. Did I get hell! I was driving along thinking of US, too. You don't have to say it — I know what's on your mind. I'm rat poison around here.

FLOR: Not to me . . .

SID: I know to who . . . and I know why. I don't blame them. We're engaged now for three years . . .

FLOR: That's a long time . . .

SID: My brother Sam joined the navy this morning — get a break that way. They'll send him down to Cuba with the hootchy-kootchy girls. He don't know from nothing, that dumb basketball player!

FLOR: Don't you do that.

SID: Don't you worry, I'm not the kind who runs away. But I'm so tired of being a dog, Baby, I could choke. I don't even have to ask what's going on in your mind. I know from the word go, 'cause I'm thinking the same things, too.

FLOR: It's yes or no — nothing in between.

SID: The answer is no — a big electric sign looking down on Broadway!

FLOR: We wanted to have kids . . .

SID: But that sort of life ain't for the dogs which is us. Christ, Baby! I get like thunder in my chest when we're together. If we went off together I could maybe look the world straight in the face, spit in its eye like a man should do. Goddamit, it's trying to be a man on the earth. Two in life together.

FLOR: But something wants us to be lonely like that — crawling alone in the dark. Or they want us trapped.

SID: Sure, the big shot money men want us like that.

FLOR: Highly insulting us —

SID: Keeping us in the dark about what is wrong with us in the money sense. They got the power an mean to be damn sure they keep it. They know if they give in just an inch, all the dogs like us will be down on them together — an ocean knocking them to hell and back and each singing cuckoo with stars coming from their nose and ears. I'm not raving, Florrie —

FLOR: I know you're not, I know.

SID: I don't have the words to tell you what I feel. I never finished school.

FLOR: I know . . .

SID: But it's relative, like the professors say. We worked like hell to send him to college — my kid brother Sam, I mean — and look what he done — joined the navy! The damn fool don't see the cards is stacked for all of us. The money man dealing himself a hot royal flush. Then giving you and me a phoney hand like a pair of tens or something. Then keep on losing the pots 'cause the cards is stacked against you. Then he says, what's the matter you can't win — no stuff on the ball, he says to you. And kids like my brother believe it 'cause they don't know better. For all their education, they don't know from nothing.

But wait a minute! Don't he come around and say to you — this millionaire with a jazz band — listen Sam or Sid or what's-your-name, you're no good, but here's a chance. The whole world'll know who you are. Yes sir, he says, get up on that ship and fight those bastards who's making the world a lousy place to live in. The Japs, the Turks, the Greeks. Take this gun — kill the slobs like a real hero, he says, a real American. Be a hero!

And the guy you're poking at? A real louse, just like you, 'cause they don't let him catch more than a pair of tens, too. On that foreign soil he's a guy like me and Sam, a guy who wants his baby like you and hot sun on his face! They'll teach Sam to point the guns the wrong way, that dumb basketball player!

FLOR: I got a lump in my throat, Honey.

SID: You and me — we never even had a room to sit in somewhere.

FLOR: The park was nice . . .

SID: In Winter? The hallways . . . I'm glad we never got together. This way we don't know what we missed.

FLOR: *(In a burst)* Sid, I'll go with you — we'll get a room somewhere.

SID: Naw . . . they're right. If we can't climb higher than this together — we better stay apart.

FLOR: I swear to God I wouldn't care.

SID: You would, you would — in a year, two years, you'd curse the day. I seen it happen.

FLOR: Oh, Sid . . .

SID: Sure, I know. We got the blues, Babe — the 1935 blues. I'm talkin' this way 'cause I love you. If I didn't, I wouldn't care . . .

FLOR: We'll work together, we'll —

SID: How about the backwash? Your family needs your nine bucks. My family —

FLOR: I don't care for them!

SID: You're making it up, Florrie. Little Florrie Canary in a cage.

FLOR: Don't make fun of me.

SID: I'm not, Baby.

FLOR: Yes, you're laughing at me.

SID: I'm not.

(They stand looking at each other, unable to speak. Finally, he turns to a small portable phonograph and plays a cheap, sad, dance tune. He makes a motion with his hand; she comes to him. They begin to dance slowly. They hold each other tightly, almost as though they would merge into each other. The music stops, but the scratching record continues to the end of the scene. They stop dancing. He finally unlooses her clutch and seats her on the couch, where she sits, tense and expectant.)

SID: Hello, Babe.

FLOR: Hello. *(For a brief time they stand as though in a dream.)*

SID: *(Finally)* Good-by, Babe.

(He waits for an answer, but she is silent. They look at each other.)

SID: Did you ever see my Pat Rooney imitation?

(He whistles Rosy O'Grady and soft shoes to it. Stops. He asks:)

SID: Don't you like it?

FLOR: *(Finally)* No. *(Buries her face in her hands. Suddenly he falls on his knees and buries his face in her lap.)*

BLACKOUT

IV. LABOR SPY EPISODE

FATT: You don't know how we work for you. Shooting off your mouth won't help. Hell, don't you guys ever look at the records like me? Look in your own industry. See what happened when the hacks walked out in Philly three months ago! Where's Philly? A thousand miles away? An hour's ride on the train.

VOICE: Two hours!!

FATT: Two hours . . . what the hell's the difference. Let's hear from someone who's got the practical experience to back him up. Fellers, there's a man here who's seen the whole parade in Philly, walked out with his pals, got knocked down like the rest — and blacklisted after they went back. That's why he's here. He's got a mighty interestin' word to say. *(Announces TOM CLAYTON!)*

(As CLAYTON starts up from the audience, FATT gives him a hand which is sparsely followed in the audience. CLAYTON comes forward.)

Fellers, this is a man with practical strike experience — Tom Clayton from little ole Philly.

CLAYTON: *(A thin, modest individual)* Fellers, I don't mind your booing. If I thought it would help us hacks get better living conditions, I'd let you walk all over me, cut me up to little pieces. I'm one of you myself. But what I wanna say is that Harry Fatt's right. I only been working here in the big town five weeks, but I know conditions just like the rest of you. You know how it is — don't take long to feel the sore spots, no matter where you park.

CLEAR VOICE: *(From audience)* Sit down!

CLAYTON: But Fatt's right. Our officers is right. The time ain't ripe. Like a fruit don't fall off the tree until it's ripe.

CLEAR VOICE: Sit down, you fruit!

FATT: *(On his feet)* Take care of him, boys.

VOICE: *(In audience, struggling)* No one takes care of me.

(Struggle in house and finally the owner of the voice runs up on stage, says to speaker:)

SAME VOICE: Where the hell did you pick up that name! Clayton! This rat's name is Clancy, from the old Clancys, way back! Fruit! I almost wet myself listening to that one!

FATT: *(Gunman with him)* This ain't a barn! What the hell do you think you're doing here!

SAME VOICE: Exposing a rat!

FATT: You can't get away with this. Throw him the hell outa here.

VOICE: *(Preparing to stand his ground)* Try it yourself . . . When this bozo throws that slop around. You know who he is? That's a company spy.

FATT: Who the hell are you to make —

VOICE: I paid dues in this union for four years, that's who's me! I gotta right and this pussy-footed rat ain't coming in here with ideals like that. You know his record. Lemme say it out —

FATT: You'll prove all this or I'll bust you in every hack outfit in town!

VOICE: I gotta right. I gotta right. Looka *him*, he don't say boo!

CLAYTON: You're a liar and I never seen you before in my life!

VOICE: Boys, he spent two years in the coal fields breaking up any organization he touched. Fifty guys he put in jail. He's ranged up and down the east coast — shipping, textiles, steel — he's been in everything you can name. Right now —

CLAYTON: That's a lie!

VOICE: Right now he's working for that Bergman outfit on Columbus Circle who furnishes rats for any outfit in the country before, during, and after strikes.

(The man who is the hero of the next episode goes down to his side with other committee men.)

CLAYTON: He's trying to break up the meeting, fellers!

VOICE: We won't search you for credentials . . .

CLAYTON: I got nothing to hide. Your own secretary knows I'm straight.
VOICE: Sure. Boys, you know who this sonovabitch is?
CLAYTON: I never seen you before in my life!!
VOICE: Boys, I slept with him in the same bed sixteen years. HE'S MY OWN LOUSY BROTHER!!
FATT: *(After pause)* Is this true? *(No answer from CLAYTON.)*
VOICE: *(To CLAYTON)* Scram, before I break your neck!

(CLAYTON scrams down center aisle. VOICE says, watching him:)

Remember his map — he can't change that — Clancy!

(Standing in his place says:)

Too bad you didn't know about this, Fatt! *(After a pause.)* The Clancy family tree is bearing nuts!

(Standing isolated clear on the stage is the hero of the next episode.)

BLACKOUT

V. THE YOUNG ACTOR

A New York theatrical producer's office. Present are a stenographer and a young actor. She is busy typing; he, waiting with card in hand.

STEN: He's taking a hot bath . . . says you should wait.
PHILIPS: *(The actor)* A bath did you say? Where?
STEN: See that door? Right through there — leads to his apartment.
PHIL: Through there?
STEN: Mister, he's laying there in a hot perfumed bath. Don't say I said it.
PHIL: You don't say!
STEN: An oriental den he's got. Can you just see this big Irishman burning Chinese punk in the bedroom? And a big old rose canopy over his casting couch . . .
PHIL: What's that — casting couch?
STEN: What's that? You from the sticks?
PHIL: I beg your pardon?
STEN: *(Rolls up her sleeves, makes elaborate deaf and dumb signs.)* No from side walkies of New Yorkie . . . savvy?
PHIL: Oh, you're right. Two years of dramatic stock out of town. One in Chicago.
STEN: Don't tell him, Baby Face. He wouldn't know a good actor if he fell over him in the dark. Say you had two years with the Group, two with the Guild.
PHIL: I'd like to get with the Guild. They say —
STEN: He won't know the difference. Don't say I said it!
PHIL: I really did play with Watson Findlay in "Early Birds."
STEN: *(Withering him)* Don't tell him!
PHIL: He's a big producer, Mr. Grady. I wish I had his money. Don't you?
STEN: Say, I got a clean heart, Mister. I love my fellow man! *(About to exit with typed letters.)* Stick around — Mr. Philips. You might be the type. If you were a woman —
PHIL: Please. Just a minute . . . please . . . I need the job.

STEN: Look at him!

PHIL: I mean . . . I don't know what buttons to push, and you do. What my father used to say — we had a gas station in Cleveland before the crash — "Know what buttons to push," Dad used to say, "and you'll go far."

STEN: You can't push me, Mister! I don't ring right these last few years!

PHIL: We don't know where the next meal's coming from. We —

STEN: Maybe . . . I'll lend you a dollar?

PHIL: Thanks very much: it won't help.

STEN: One of the old families of Virginia? Proud?

PHIL: Oh, not that. You see, I have a wife. We'll have our first baby next month . . . so . . . a dollar isn't much help.

STEN: Roped in?

PHIL: I love my wife!

STEN: Okay, you love her! Excuse me! You married her. Can't support her. No . . . not blaming you. But you're fools, all you actors. Old and young! Watch you parade in and out all day. You still got apples in your cheeks and pins for buttons. But in six months you'll be like them — putting on an act: Phoney strutting "pishers" — that's French for dead codfish! It's not their fault. Here you get like that or go under. What kind of job is this for an adult man!

PHIL: When you have to make a living —

STEN: I know, but —

PHIL: Nothing else to do. If I could get something else —

STEN: You'd take it!

PHIL: Anything!

STEN: Telling me! With two brothers in my hair! *(MR. GRADY now enters; played by FATT.)* Mr. Brown sent this young man over.

GRADY: Call the hospital: see how Boris is. *(She assents and exits.)*

PHIL: Good morning, Mr. Grady . . .

GRADY: The morning is lousy!

PHIL: Mr. Brown sent me. *(Hands over card.)*

GRADY: I heard that once already.

PHIL: Excuse me . . .

GRADY: What experience?

PHIL: Oh, yes . . .

GRADY: Where?

PHIL: Two years in stock, sir. A year with the Goodman Theatre in Chicago . . .

GRADY: That all?

PHIL: *(Abashed)* Why no . . . with the Threatre Guild . . . I was there . . .

GRADY: Never saw you in a Guild show!

PHIL: On the road, I mean . . . understudying Mr. Lunt . . .

GRADY: What part? *(PHILIPS cannot answer.)* You're a lousy liar, son.

PHIL: I did . . .

GRADY: You don't look like what I want. Can't understand that Brown. Needa big man to play a soldier. Not a lousy soldier left on Broadway! All in pictures, and we get the nances! *(Turns to work on desk.)*

PHIL: *(Immediately playing the soldier)* I was in the ROTC in college . . . Reserve Officers' Training Corps. We trained twice a week . . .

GRADY: Won't help.

PHIL: With real rifles. *(Waits.)* Mr. Grady, I weigh a hundred and fifty-five!
GRADY: How many years back? Been eating regular since you left college?
PHIL: *(Very earnestly)* Mr. Grady, I could act this soldier part. I could build
    it up and act it. Make it up —
GRADY: Think I run a lousy acting school around here?
PHIL: Honest to God I could! I need the job — that's why I could do it! I'm
    strong. I know my business! YOU'LL get an A-1 performance. Because
    I need this job! My wife's having a baby in a few weeks. We need the
    money. Give me a chance!
GRADY: What do I care if you can act it! I'm sorry about your baby. Use
    your head, son. Tank Town stock is different. Here we got investments
    to be protected. When I sink fifteen thousand in a show I don't take
    chances on some youngster. We cast to type!
PHIL: I'm an artist! I can —
GRADY: That's your headache. Nobody interested in artists here. Get a big
    bunch for a nickel on any corner. Two flops in a row on this lousy
    street nobody loves you — only God, and He don't count. We protect
    investments: we cast to type. Your face and height we want, not your
    soul, son. And Jesus Christ couldn't play a soldier in this show . . . with
    all his talent. *(Crosses himself in quick repentance for this remark.)*
PHIL: Anything . . . a bit, a walk-on?
GRADY: Sorry: small cast. *(Looking at papers on his desk.)* You try Russia,
    son. I hear it's hot stuff over there.
PHIL: Stage manager? Assistant?
GRADY: All filled, sonny. *(Stands up; crumples several papers from the
    desk.)* Better luck next time.
PHIL: Thanks . . .
GRADY: Drop in from time to time. *(Crosses and about to exit.)* You never
    know when something — *(The STENOGRAPHER enters with paper
    to put on desk.)* What did the hospital say?
STEN: He's much better, Mr. Grady.
GRADY: Resting easy?
STEN: Dr. Martel said Boris is doing even better than he expected.
GRADY: A damn lousy operation!
STEN: Yes . . .
GRADY: *(Belching)* Tell the nigger boy to send up a bromo seltzer.
STEN: Yes, Mr. Grady. *(He exits.)* Boris wanted lady friends.
PHIL: What?
STEN: So they operated . . . poor dog!
PHIL: A dog?
STEN: His Russian Wolf Hound! They do the same to you, but you don't
    know it! *(Suddenly)* Want advice? In the next office, don't let them
    see you down in the mouth. They don't like it — makes them shiver.
PHIL: You treat me like a human being. Thanks . . .
STEN: You're human!
PHIL: I used to think so.
STEN: He wants a bromo for his hangover. *(Goes to door.)* Want that dollar?
PHIL: It won't help much.
STEN: One dollar buys ten loaves of bread, Mister. Or one dollar buys nine
    loaves of bread and one copy of The Communist Manifesto. Learn while

you eat. Read while you run . . .

PHIL: Manifesto? What's that? *(Takes dollar.)* What is that, what you said . . . Manifesto?

STEN: Stop off on your way out — I'll give you a copy. From Genesis to Revelation, Comrade Philips! "And I saw a new earth and a new heaven; for the first earth and the first heaven were passed away; and there was no more sea."

PHIL: I don't understand that . . .

STEN: I'm saying the meek shall not inherit the earth!

PHIL: No?

STEN: The MILITANT! Come out in the light, Comrade.

BLACKOUT

VI. INTERNE EPISODE

DR. BARNES, an elderly distinguished man, is speaking on the telephone. He wears a white coat.

DR. BARNES: No, I gave you my opinion twice. You outvoted me. You did this to Dr. Benjamin yourself. That is why you can tell him yourself.

(Hangs up phone, angrily. As he is about to pour himself a drink from a bottle on the table, a knock is heard.)

BARNES: Who is it?

BENJAMIN: *(Without)* Can I see you a minute, please?

BARNES: *(Hiding the bottle)* Come in, Dr. Benjamin, come in.

BENJ: It's important — excuse me — they've got Leeds up there in my place — He's operating on Mrs. Lewis — the hysterectomy — it's my job. I washed up, prepared . . . they told me at the last minute. I don't mind being replaced, Doctor, but Leeds is a damn fool! He shouldn't be permitted —

BARNES: *(Dryly)* Leeds is the nephew of Senator Leeds.

BENJ: He's incompetent as hell.

BARNES: *(Obviously changing subject, picks up lab jar)* They're doing splendid work in brain surgery these days. This is a very fine specimen . . .

BENJ: I'm sorry, I thought you might be interested.

BARNES: *(Still examining jar)* Well, I am, young man, I am! Only remember it's a charity case!

BENJ: Of course. They wouldn't allow it for a second, otherwise.

BARNES: Her life is in danger?

BENJ: Of course! You know how serious the case is!

BARNES: Turn your gimlet eyes elsewhere, Doctor. Jigging around like a cricket on a hot grill won't help. Doctors don't run these hospitals. He's the Senator's nephew and there he stays.

BENJ: It's too bad.

BARNES: I'm not calling you down either. *(Plopping down jar suddenly.)* Goddammit, do you think it's my fault?

BENJ: *(About to leave)* I know . . . I'm sorry.

BARNES: Just a minute. Sit down.

BENJ: Sorry, I can't sit.

BARNES: Stand then!

BENJ: *(Sits)* Understand, Dr. Barnes, I don't mind being replaced at the last

529

minute this way, but . . . well, this flagrant bit of class distinction —
because she's poor —
BARNES: Be careful of words like that — "class distinction." Don't belong
here. Lots of energy, you brilliant young men, but idiots. Discretion!
Ever hear that word?
BENJ: Too radical?
BARNES: Precisely. And some day like in Germany, it might cost you your head.
BENJ: Not to mention my job.
BARNES: So they told you?
BENJ: Told me what?
BARNES: They're closing Ward C next month. I don't have to tell you the
hospital isn't self supporting. Until last year that board of trustees
met deficits . . . You can guess the rest. At a board meeting Tuesday,
our fine feathered friends discovered they couldn't meet the last quar-
ter's deficit — a neat little sum well over $100,000. If the hospital is
to continue at all, it's damn —
BENJ: Necessary to close another charity ward!
BARNES: So they say . . . *(A wait.)*
BENJ: But that's not all?
BARNES: *(Ashamed)* Have to cut down on staff too . . .
BENJ: That's too bad. Does it touch me?
BARNES: Afraid it does.
BENJ: But after all I'm top man here. I don't mean I'm better than others,
but I've worked harder.
BARNES: And shown more promise . . .
BENJ: I always supposed they'd cut from the bottom first.
BARNES: Usually.
BENJ: But in this case?
BARNES: Complications.
BENJ: For instance? *(BARNES hesitant.)*
BARNES: I like you, Benjamin. It's one ripping shame.
BENJ: I'm no sensitive plant — what's the answer?
BARNES: An old disease, malignant, tumescent. We need an anti-toxin for it.
BENJ: I see.
BARNES: What?
BENJ: I met that disease before — at Harvard first.
BARNES: You have seniority here, Benjamin.
BENJ: But I'm a Jew! *(BARNES nods his head in agreement. BENJ stands
there a moment and blows his nose.)*
BARNES: *(Blows his nose)* Microbes!
BENJ: Pressure from above?
BARNES: Don't think Kennedy and I didn't fight for you!
BENJ: Such discrimination, with all those wealthy brother Jews on the board?
BARNES: I've remarked before — doesn't seem to be much difference be-
tween wealthy Jews and rich Gentiles. Cut from the same piece!
BENJ: For myself I don't feel sorry. My parents gave up an awful lot to get
me this far. They ran a little dry goods shop in the Bronx until their
pitiful savings went in the crash last year. Poppa's peddling neckties
. . . Saul Ezra Benjamin — a man who's read Spinoza all his life.
BARNES: Doctors don't run medicine in this country. The men who know

530

their jobs don't run anything here, except the motormen on trolley cars. I've seen medicine change — plenty — anesthesia, steriliza- tion — but not because of rich men — in *spite* of them! In a rich man's country your true self's buried deep. Microbes! Less . . . Vermin! See this ankle, this delicate sensitive hand? Four hundred years to breed that. Out of a revolutionary background! Spirit of '76! Ancestors froze at Valley Forge! What's it all mean! Slops! The honest workers were sold out then, in '76. The Constituion's for rich men then and now. Slops! *(The phone rings.)*

BARNES: *(Angrily)* Dr. Barnes. *(Listens a moment, looks at BENJAMIN.)* I see. *(Hangs up, turns slowly to the younger doctor.)* They lost your patient. *(BENJ stands solid with the shock of this news but finally hurls his operation gloves to the floor.)*

BARNES: That's right . . . that's right. Young, hot, go and do it! I'm very ancient, fossil, but life's ahead of you, Dr. Benjamin, and when you fire the first shot say, "This one's for old Doc Barnes!" Too much dignity — bullets. Don't shoot vermin! Step on them! If I didn't have an invalid daughter —

BARNES: *(Goes back to his seat, blows his nose in silence)* I have said my piece, Benjamin.

BENJ: Lots of things I wasn't certain of. Many things these radicals say . . . you don't believe theories until they happen to you.

BARNES: You lost a lot today, but you won a great point.

BENJ: Yes, to know I'm right? To really begin believing in something? Not to say, "What a world!", but to say, "Change the world!" I wanted to go to Russia. Last week I was thinking about it — the wonderful opportunity to do good work in their socialized medicine —

BARNES: Beautiful, beautiful!

BENJ: To be able to work —

BARNES: Why don't you go? I might be able —

BENJ: Nothing's nearer what I'd like to do!

BARNES: Do it!

BENJ: No! Our work's here — America! I'm scared . . . What future's ahead, I don't know. Get some job to keep alive — maybe drive a cab — and study and work and learn my place —

BARNES: And step down hard!

BENJ: Fight! Maybe get killed, but goddam! We'll go ahead! *(BENJAMIN stands with clenched fist raised high.)*

BLACKOUT

AGATE: LADIES AND GENTLEMEN, and don't let anyone tell you we ain't got some ladies in this sea of upturned faces! Only they're wearin' pants. Well, maybe I don't know a thing; maybe I fell outa the cradle when I was a kid and ain't been right since — you can't tell!

VOICE: Sit down, cockeye!

AGATE: Who's paying you for those remarks, Buddy? — Moscow Gold? Maybe I got a *glass eye*, but it comes from working in a factory at the age of eleven. They hooked it out because they didn't have a shield on the works. But I wear it like a medal 'cause it tells the world where I belong — deep down in the working class! We had delegates in the

531

union there — all kinds of secretaries and treasurers . . . walkin' delegates, but not with blisters on their feet! Oh no! On their fat little ass from sitting on cushions and raking in mazuma. *(SECRETARY and GUNMAN remonstrate in words and actions here.)* Sit down, boys. I'm just sayin' that about unions in general. I know it ain't true here! Why no, our officers is all aces. Why, I seen our own secretary Fatt walk outa his way not to step on a cockroach. No boys, don't think —

FATT: *(Breaking in)* You're out of order!

AGATE: *(To audience)* Am I outa order?

ALL: No, no. Speak. Go on, etc.

AGATE: Yes, our officers is all aces. But I'm a member here — and no experience in Philly either! Today I couldn't wear my union button. The damnest thing happened. When I take the old coat off the wall, I see she's smoking. I'm a sonovagun if the old union button isn't on fire! Yep, the old celluloid was makin' the most god-awful stink: the landlady come up and give me hell! You know what happened? — that old union button just blushed itself to death! Ashamed! Can you beat it?

FATT: Sit down, Keller! Nobody's interested!

AGATE: Yes they are!

GUNMAN: Sit down like he tells you!

AGATE: *(Continuing to audience)* And when I finish —

(His speech is broken by FATT and GUNMAN who physically handle him. He breaks away and gets to other side of stage. The two are about to make for him when some of the committee men come forward and get in between the struggling parties. AGATE's shirt has been torn.)

AGATE: *(To audience)* What's the answer, boys? The answer is, if we're reds because we wanna strike, then we take over their salute too! Know how they do it? *(Makes Communist salute.)* What is it? An uppercut! The good old uppercut to the chin! Hell, some of us boys ain't even got a shirt to our backs. What's the boss class tryin' to do — make a nudist colony outa us?

(The audience laughs and suddenly AGATE comes to the middle of the stage so that the other cabmen back him up in a strong clump.)

AGATE: Don't laugh! Nothing's funny! This is your life and mine! It's skull and bones every incha the road! Christ, we're dyin' by inches! For what? For the debutant-ees to have their sweet comin' out parties in the Ritz! Poppa's got a daughter she's gotta get her picture in the papers. Christ, they make 'em with our blood. Joe said it. Slow death or fight. It's war!

(Throughout this whole speech AGATE is backed up by the other six workers, so that from their activity it is plain that the whole group of them are saying these things. Several of them may take alternate lines out of this long last speech.)

You Edna, God love your mouth! Sid and Florrie, the other boys, old Doc Barnes — fight with us for right! It's war! Working class, unite and fight! Tear down the slaughter house of our old lives! Let freedom really ring.

These slick slobs stand here telling us about bogeymen. That's a new one for the kids — the reds is bogeymen! But the man who got me food in 1932, he called me Comrade! The one who picked me up where I bled — he called me Comrade too! What are we waiting for . . . Don't wait for Lefty! He might never come. Every minute —

(This is broken into by a man who has dashed up the center aisle from the back of the house. He runs up on stage, says:)

MAN: Boys, they just found Lefty!
OTHERS: What? What? What?
SOME: Shhh . . . Shhh . . .
MAN: They found Lefty . . .
AGATE: Where?
MAN: Behind the car barns with a bullet in his head!
AGATE: *(Crying)* Hear it, boys, hear it? Hell, listen to me! Coast to coast!
HELLO AMERICA! HELLO. WE'RE STORMBIRDS OF THE WORK-ING-CLASS. WORKERS OF THE WORLD . . . OUR BONES AND BLOOD! And when we die they'll know what we did to make a new world! Christ, cut us up to little pieces. We'll die for what is right! Put fruit trees where our ashes are!
(To audience) Well, what's the answer?
ALL: STRIKE!
AGATE: LOUDER!
ALL: STRIKE!
AGATE and OTHERS: *(On Stage)* AGAIN!
ALL: STRIKE, STRIKE, STRIKE!!!

CURTAIN

NOTES FOR PRODUCTION

The background of the episodes, a strike meeting, is not an excuse. Each of the committeemen shows in his episode the crucial moment of his life which brought him to this very platform. The dramatic structure on which the play has been built is simple but highly effective. The form used is the old black-face minstrel form of chorus, end men, specialty men and interlocutor.

In Fatt's scenes before the "Spy Exposé," mention should again be made of Lefty's tardiness. Sitting next to Fatt in the center of the circle is a little henchman who sits with his back to the audience. On the other side of Fatt is Lefty's empty chair. This is so indicated by Fatt when he himself asks: "Yeah, where's your chairman?"

Fatt, of course, represents the capitalist system throughout the play. The audience should constantly be kept aware of him, the ugly menace which hangs over the lives of all the people who act out their own dramas. Perhaps he puffs smoke into the spotted playing space; perhaps during the action of a playlet he might insolently walk in and around the unseeing players. It is possible that some highly gratifying results can be achieved by the imaginative use of this character.

The strike committee on the platform during the acting out of the playlets should be used as chorus. Emotional, political, musical, they have in them possibilities of various comments on the scenes. This has been indicated once in the script in the place where Joe's wife is about to leave him. In the climaxes of each scene, slogans might very effectively be used — a voice coming out of the dark. Such a voice might announce at the appropriate moments in the "Young Interne's" scene that the USSR is the only country in the world where anti-Semitism is a crime against the State.

Do not hesitate to use music wherever possible. It is very valuable in emotionally stirring an audience.

MID-TWENTIETH-CENTURY AMERICAN DRAMA: The Theatre of Consolidation

After World War II, American playwrights gathered together the various theatre traditions which had developed over the past century and pulled them together into a synthesis that helped theatre survive challenges from the growing film and television industries and from its own burgeoning costs. In just over one hundred years, Western theatre had witnessed a succession of movements: Romanticism, realism, naturalism, symbolism, expressionism, and epic theatre. In Europe, absurdism was about to burst forth, and in America in the sixties, Artaud's theatre of cruelty would post-humously rock the theatre world. In the meantime, during the forties and fifties, the plays of Arthur Miller, Tennessee Williams, and their colleagues provided theatre an opportunity to consolidate its gains before thrusting ahead with a new avant-garde.

Political/Social/Philosophical Backgrounds

The United States emerged from World War II a new nation in a new world. Economic boom times replaced the grinding poverty of the pre-War depression, and permitted Americans to achieve increasingly higher standards of living. In rural areas, electric and gas ranges replaced wood stoves and indoor plumbing replaced the privy, and on cheap land around urban centers, developers built inexpensive projects to provide houses for thousands of families who never before could have afforded their own homes. Life in America was good.

Life on the international scene was frightening. The United States found itself a major world power squared off against the Soviet Union in a cold war which would last for over forty years. The threat of nuclear holocaust tortured the dreams and thoughts of adults and children alike, and America went about constructing a series of alliances and foreign economic ventures which would eventually amount to an American empire.

Middle-Class America

After the cultural, economic, and military turmoil of the past thirty years, Americans wanted to rest and enjoy the comfort of their new homes. They wanted a progressive economy which padded the pockets of the middle class, and they feared all challenges to middle-class budgets, social mores, and cultural values. Political programs, economic ideas, social movements, and artistic expressions which challenged middle-class lifestyles were quickly branded "Communist." Americans wanted to live in solid, white families who prayed together and stayed together, who kept their debts to a minimum and their sex within the bounds of matrimony, and who tolerated nonwhite Americans as long as they kept their place. The image was everything.

The fact that large minorities of Americans were not white, not middle-class, not parts of solid family units, and the fact that the surface images of many middle-class families masked marital infidelity, homosexuality, religious doubt, alcoholism, greed, crushing debt, abusive sexual politics, and relational conflict resulted in guilt, fear, and psychological disturbances.

It was this America — trying to look comfortable on the outside while being torn internally between its desires and its fears — which produced and saw itself mirrored in the plays of Arthur Miller and Tennessee Williams.

Dramatic Literature

American plays of the forties and fifties blended realism with various nonrealistic techniques, and tended to focus on psychological studies rather than socio-political issues. Thornton Wilder (*The Matchmaker*, 1954) and Eugene O'Neill (*The Iceman Cometh*, 1946; *A Moon for the Misbegotten*, 1947) were still writing, but the major dramatists of the period were William Inge (1913-73), Arthur Miller (1915-), William Saroyan (1908-81), and Tennessee Williams (1911-83).

Arthur Miller

Miller's plays, *All My Sons* (1947) and *The Crucible* (1953), both focused on social and political criticism: *All My Sons* attacked profiteering by industrialists during the War, and *The Crucible* used the witchhunts of colonial Salem as a metaphor for the "commie" scare of the early fifties. However, Miller's *Death of a Salesman* (1949), more characteristic of its period, blended realistic dialog and characterization with expressionistic staging and flashbacks to create a moving psychological portrait of a has-been traveling salesman, Willie Loman, and his disintegrating family.

Saroyan and Inge

Novelist and playwright William Saroyan used fantasy and nonconventional dramatic structure to create his nostalgic, romanticized dramas. Probably his most important play was the Pulitzer Prize winning *The Time of Your Life* (1939), a soft-focused study on the lives of a group of saloon patrons. William Inge also created a bittersweet world of alcoholics, misfits, and dysfunctional families in his plays, which included *Come Back, Little Sheba* (1950), *Picnic* (1953), *Bus Stop* (1955), and *The Dark at the Top of the Stairs* (1957).

Tennessee Williams

The life and work of Tennessee Williams most clearly epitomizes American theatre during this period. Born in Columbus, Mississippi, Thomas Lanier Williams experienced a childhood plagued by illness, a retarded sister, and a traumatic move to the urban ugliness of St. Louis. By the time of his first Broadway success, he had earned a college degree after attending three different universities, gone through a nervous breakdown, done odd jobs from Chicago to New Orleans to Los Angeles, undergone three eye operations, and taken the pseudonym "Tennessee." Throughout his life, he battled alcoholism and a sense of alienation because of his homosexuality.

In 1945, after various small successes, he suddenly achieved real fame with *The Glass Menagerie,* a drama in which a former Southern belle tries to hold her family together in a St. Louis alley apartment. For the next two decades, Williams produced a new script almost annually. These included his two Pulitzer Prize winners about life in the deep South, *A Streetcar Named Desire* (1947) and *Cat on a Hot Tin Roof* (1955); a symbolic treatment of the Don Quixote story, *El Camino Real* (1953); the steamy, exotic *Night of the Iguana* (1961); and *Summer and Smoke* (1948), another drama of desire and repression. His last play, written about Scott and Zelda Fitzgerald in 1980, was called *Clothes for a Summer Hotel.*

Romanticism and Realism

Williams' plays blended romanticism with realism. In most of his plays, realistic characters cope with everyday problems and arrive, through a series of cause-and-effect events, at inevitable conclusions. These characters and their stories may be psychologically warped, but they are recognizable, well-rounded persons rather than types, and they inhabit a world where no *deus ex machina* reaches in to rescue them at the last minute. In these ways, Williams' plays were clearly realistic.

However, his vision of the world as a harsh, materialistic environment where the poet, the artist, the spiritual man and woman is a threatened alien was closely related to romanticism. Like the romantics, Williams created heroes and heroines who are misfits, plagued by physical or emotional diseases. These neurotic antiheroes symbolize the human spirit trampled beneath the world's iron hooves. The midcentury South which provided the setting for many of Williams' plays became a metaphor for old-world values made obsolete by a crass new age. In his language and titles, he used strong motifs that took on symbolic value. Unlike the realists, whose interests were primarily sociological and political, Williams focused on psychology and spirituality.

The sets Williams called for in his scripts embodied his blend of realism and romanticism. Like the sets of the realists, they represented actual environments which shape the characters' lives and which included realistic details. At the same time, borrowing techniques from romanticism, symbolism, and expressionism, he called for fragmented sets which presented several locales simultaneously and which expressed metaphorically the conflict between individual aspirations and societal pressures. By producing a large body of works which consistently blended realism with nonrealism, Tennessee Williams embodied the midcentury theatre of consolidation.

The Movies

The theatre for which Miller and Williams wrote found itself under pressure from the mass media. By the middle of the century, live theatre had clearly given way to the movies and television as the primary media of drama for popular audiences.

Special Effects

Nineteenth-century theatre unwittingly prepared audiences for the motion pictures. Melodramas went to great lengths to reproduce natural phenomena and spectacular technology and catastrophes on stage. These efforts included panoramas — long, massive paintings of natural scenery which could be scrolled from one side of the stage to the other to create the effect that downstage actors were actually journeying past forests or mountains. They also included the on-stage use of horses and locomotives and simulated disasters such as sinking ships and burning houses. Technicians strove to make these spectacles as realistic and believable as possible.

The presentation of such marvels created in the audiences a hunger for more spectacle, more realism. Meanwhile, acted human drama and the spoken word became subordinated to the spectacle. The dramatic scenes which tied the spectacle together became shorter, more fragmentary, and less language-centered. One short scene would cut quickly to another necessitating multiple rapid set changes. These techniques strained the capabilities of the stage to their limits — and beyond.

Just when it was apparent that the stage could not satisfy the audience's hunger for realistic spectacle, along came a medium which could present in a theatre actual natural scenery, actual locomotives and steamships, actual disasters — moving pictures. And the first commercial movies, presented between 1895 and 1902, provided just that kind of entertainment — action tableaus, short topical clips and storyettes featuring physical activity.

Through the next decade, movies developed into photo-plays: feature-length films which focused on action, melodrama, and authentic spectacle. This phase culminated in 1915 in D. W. Griffith's popular feature movie, *The Birth of a Nation.* By the late twenties, the motion picture industry had developed the technology to add spoken dialog to the film images.

Economics

Movies, of course, provided much cheaper dramatic entertainment than the stage. Unlike a stage play, after the initial production expenses, a movie could be shown repeatedly, simultaneously, nationwide, to audiences of millions, without the continued presence of the actors and production people. And while movie theatres were multiplying — they numbered over 10,000 in 1915 and doubled that figure by 1920 — the decline of The Road made live theatre progressively less available to most Americans. Television's advent in the late forties increased the threat to live theatre by making it possible for people to see drama and variety shows for free in their own homes.

Sophisticated Audiences

Cinema and television had great impact on the stage. Because of their ability to provide more popular entertainment at lower prices, they caused audiences for plays to diminish. Furthermore, they greatly increased the sophistication of audiences. Audience members who see one or two movies a week or several television comedies and dramas every day quickly become adept at following story lines, recognizing character types, and absorbing dramatic impacts. When these audience members attend a play, they catch on more quickly than their ancestors and demand more of the experience. Film and television also led dramatists to make greater use of "cinematic" techniques on stage — short, fragmentary scenes which cut rapidly to other short scenes, the elimination of transitions and exposition, and the focus on visual elements at the expense of verbal exchanges. Multimedia productions which combine live actors with projected slides, film clips, and video are another extension of filmic technique to the stage.

But perhaps most important of all, cinema and television forced theatre artists to renew their search for the essence of stage theatre, to seek those aspects of their art which make it different in kind from its younger siblings and therefore give it continued reason for being. That essence, which gives live theatre its special power and which continues to make it a vital art form, is the immediacy of live actors interacting with one another in the presence of a live audience. Theatre artists throughout the twentieth century continually sought new, lively ways to express that essence in their work.

Theatrical Organization

Perhaps the most important single development in the business of American theatre during the postwar years was the advent of Off-Broadway. Broadway, the central theatre district of New York City located on or near the thoroughfare of Broadway in midtown Manhattan, developed in the middle of the nineteenth century. By its peak in the 1920s, Broadway included about 80 theatres. A variety of forces combined, however, to weaken Broadway as a creative force in American theatre. Land values in New York escalated, causing rents in the theatre district to skyrocket. Also, during the first half of the twentieth century, theatre artists developed several unions and professional societies, such as the American Actors Equity Association. In the process of improving the wages and career security of theatre artists, these unions had the effect of increasing production costs. Caught between shrinking audiences and escalating costs, many Broadway theatres closed, and those which remained became less and less willing to take a chance on new plays which might be powerful but might not draw large audiences. By the late twentieth century, Broadway limited itself primarily to popular comedies, lavish musicals, and revivals of sure-fire plays from the past.

Off-Broadway Theatres

Faced with this situation, theatre artists interested in the continued growth of their art and the production of new, potentially risky plays developed smaller theatres outside the theatre district, particularly in the Greenwich Village area of south Manhattan. Since these theatres negotiated lower prices with the unions and occupied less expensive real estate, they were better able to take the risk of producing serious, experimental plays. Jose Quintero's revival of Tennessee Williams' *Summer and Smoke* at the Circle in the Square Theatre in 1952 drew major critical attention to the work of these "Off-Broadway" theatres.

Actors Equity eventually defined Off-Broadway theatres as spaces seating under 500 audience members and located outside the central theatre district. Off-Broadway theatres continued a healthy trend in decentralization which spanned twentieth century theatre. They helped keep the art form vital by presenting the first major productions of many important plays.

539

Cat on a Hot Tin Roof

Production History

Director Elia Kazan and the Playwrights Company presented the premiere performance of *Cat on a Hot Tin Roof* on March 24, 1955. Elia Kazan (1909-) began as an actor with the Group Theatre and played the role of Agate in the Group's production of *Waiting for Lefty*. He went on to join with Cheryl Crawford in founding the Actors Studio in 1947, a company which continued to popularize the Stanislavskian approach to acting. The premiere took place in the Morosco Theatre, a Broadway theatre which had housed the premiere of Miller's *Death of a Salesman* in 1949. The theatre was finally demolished in 1982. *Cat on a Hot Tin Roof* won the New York Drama Critics Circle Award and a Pulitzer Prize. The premiere starred Ben Gazzara as Brick, Burl Ives as Big Daddy, and Barbara Bel Geddes as Maggie.

In 1958 MGM made a movie based on the script, starring Paul Newman as Brick, Burl Ives as Big Daddy, and Elizabeth Taylor as Maggie the cat. A comparison of the stage script with the movie demonstrates the manner in which film catered to its middle-class audience. The film script eliminates all harsh language and even the suspicion of homosexuality, and it concludes happily with most of the family members, including Brick and Maggie, reconciled and at peace with each other.

Modified Realism

The play clearly portrays the conflict in postwar America between the image of solid family life and the reality of inner decay. Williams uses realistic characters and situations, a realistic set, realistic dialog, and cause-and-effect plot structure to tell his story. But he modifies this realism by calling for scenery which is both symbolic and fragmentary, and by the heavy use of symbols in dialog and action. Big Daddy's cancer, for instance, presents an excellent symbol for the rot in the gut of American family life, and the frequent repetition of the title in the dialog gives a symbolic gloss to the whole drama. And like romantic heroes of a hundred years earlier, Brick, Maggie, and Big Daddy are characters of titanic proportions who are, nevertheless, cursed by the illnesses, neuroses, and misfortunes of humanity. In both its subject matter and its form, *Cat on a Hot Tin Roof* stands as a monument to the life and theatre of postwar America and to the art of Tennessee Williams.

American Post-War Theatre Timeline

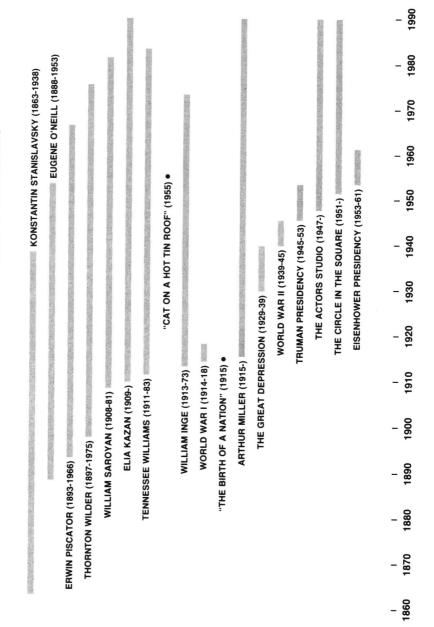

KONSTANTIN STANISLAVSKY (1863-1938)

EUGENE O'NEILL (1888-1953)

ERWIN PISCATOR (1893-1966)

THORNTON WILDER (1897-1975)

WILLIAM SAROYAN (1908-81)

ELIA KAZAN (1909-)

TENNESSEE WILLIAMS (1911-83)

"CAT ON A HOT TIN ROOF" (1955) ●

WILLIAM INGE (1913-73)

WORLD WAR I (1914-18)

"THE BIRTH OF A NATION" (1915) ●

ARTHUR MILLER (1915-)

THE GREAT DEPRESSION (1929-39)

WORLD WAR II (1939-45)

TRUMAN PRESIDENCY (1945-53)

THE ACTORS STUDIO (1947-)

THE CIRCLE IN THE SQUARE (1951-)

EISENHOWER PRESIDENCY (1953-61)

1860   1870   1880   1890   1900   1910   1920   1930   1940   1950   1960   1970   1980   1990

CAT ON A HOT TIN ROOF

by TENNESEE WILLIAMS

The action of the play takes place in a plantation home
in the Mississippi Delta in the early 1950s.

CHARACTERS

MARGARET

BRICK
her husband

MAE
sometimes called Sister Woman, Brick's sister-in-law

BIG MAMA
Brick's mother

DIXIE
Mae's daughter

BIG DADDY
Brick's father

REVEREND TOOKER

GOOPER
sometimes called Brother Man, Brick's brother

DOCTOR BAUGH
pronounced "Baw"

LACEY
a Negro servant

SOOKEY
Another

Another little girl and two small boys

(The playing script of Act III also includes TRIXIE, another little girl, also
DAISY, BRIGHTIE, and SMALL, servants.)

542

NOTES FOR THE DESIGNER

The set is the bed-sitting-room of a plantation home in the Mississippi Delta. It is along an upstairs gallery which probably runs around the entire house; it has two pairs of very wide doors opening onto the gallery; showing white balustrades against a fair summer sky that fades into dusk and night during the course of the play, which occupies precisely the time of its performance, excepting, of course, the fifteen minutes of intermission.

Perhaps the style of the room is not what you would expect in the home of the Delta's biggest cotton-planter. It is Victorian with a touch of the Far East. It hasn't changed much since it was occupied by the original owners of the place, Jack Straw and Peter Ochello, a pair of old bachelors who shared this room all their lives together. In other words, the room must evoke some ghosts; it is gently and poetically haunted by a relationship that must have involved a tenderness which was uncommon. This may be irrelevant or unnecessary, but I once saw a reproduction of a faded photograph of the verandah of Robert Louis Stevenson's home on that Samoan Island where he spent his last years, and there was a quality of tender light on weathered wood, such as porch furniture made of bamboo and wicker, exposed to tropical suns and tropical rains, which came to mind when I thought about the set for this play, bringing also to mind the grace and comfort of light, the reassurance it gives, on a late and fair afternoon in summer, the way that no matter what, even dread of death, is gently touched and soothed by it. For the set is the background for a play that deals with human extremities of emotion, and it needs that softness behind it.

The bathroom door, showing only pale-blue tile and silver towel racks, is in one side wall; the hall door in the opposite wall. Two articles of furniture need mention: a big double bed which staging should make a functional part of the set as often as suitable, the surface of which should be slightly raked to make figures on it seen more easily; and against the wall space between the two huge double doors upstage: a monumental monstrosity peculiar to our times, a *huge* console combination of radio-phonograph (Hi-Fi with three speakers), TV set *and* liquor cabinet, bearing and containing many glasses and bottles, all in one piece, which is the composition of muted silver tones, and the opalescent tones of reflecting glass, a chromatic link, this thing, between the sepia (tawny gold) tones of the interior and the cool (white and blue) tones of the gallery and sky. This piece of furniture (?!), this monument, is a very complete and compact little shrine to virtually all the comforts and illusions behind which we hide from such things as the characters in the play are faced with . . . The set should be far less realistic than I have so far implied in this description of it. I think the walls below the ceiling should dissolve mysteriously into air; the set should be roofed by the sky; stars and moon suggested by traces of milky pallor, as if they were observed through a telescope lens out of focus.

Anything else I can think of? Oh, yes, fanlights (transoms shaped like an open glass fan) above all the doors in the set, with panes of blue and amber, and above all, the designer should take as many pains to give the actors room to move about freely (to show their restlessness, their passion for breaking out) as if it were a set for a ballet.

An evening in summer. The action is continuous, with two intermissions.

("Notes for the Designer" were written by Tennessee Williams.)

ACT ONE

At the rise of the curtain someone is taking a shower in the bathroom, the door of which is half open. A pretty young woman, with anxious lines in her face, enters the bedroom and crosses to the bathroom door.

MARGARET: *(Shouting above roar of water)* One of those no-neck monsters hit me with a hot buttered biscuit so I have t' change!

(Margaret's voice is both rapid and drawling. In her long speeches she has the vocal tricks of a priest delivering a liturgical chant, the lines are almost sung, always continuing a little beyond her breath so she has to gasp for another. Sometimes she intersperses the lines with a little wordless singing, such as "Da-da-daaaa!"

(Water turns off and Brick calls out to her, but is still unseen. A tone of politely feigned interest, masking indifference, or worse, is characteristic of his speech with Margaret.)

BRICK: Wha'd you say, Maggie? Water was on s' loud I couldn't hear ya . . .

MARGARET: Well, I! — just remarked that! — one of th' no-neck monsters messed up m' lovely lace dress so I got t' — cha-a-ange . . .

(She opens and kicks shut drawers of the dresser.)

BRICK: Why d'ya call Gooper's kiddies no-neck monsters?

MARGARET: Because they've got no necks! Isn't that a good enough reason?

BRICK: Don't they have any necks?

MARGARET: None visible. Their fat little heads are set on their fat little bodies without a bit of connection.

BRICK: That's too bad.

MARGARET: Yes, it's too bad because you can't wring their necks if they've got no necks to wring! Isn't that right, honey?

(She steps out of her dress, stands in a slip of ivory satin and lace.)

Yep, they're no-neck monsters, all no-neck people are monsters . . .

(Children shriek downstairs.)

Hear them? Hear them screaming? I don't know where their voice-boxes are located since they don't have necks. I tell you I got so nervous at that table tonight I thought I would throw back my head and utter a scream you could hear across the Arkansas border an' parts of Louisiana an' Tennessee. I said to your charming sister-in-law, Mae, honey, couldn't you feed those precious little things at a separate table with an oilcloth cover? They make such a mess an' the lace cloth looks *so* pretty! She made enormous eyes at me and said, "Ohhh, noooooo! On Big Daddy's birthday? Why, he would never forgive me!" Well, I want you to know, Big Daddy hadn't been at the table two minutes with those five no-neck monsters slobbering and drooling over their food before he threw down his fork an' shouted, "Fo' God's sake, Gooper, why don't you put them pigs at a trough in th' kitchen?" — Well, I swear, I simply could have di-ieed!

Think of it, Brick, they've got five of them and number six is coming. They've brought the whole bunch down here like animals to display at a county fair. Why, they have those children doin' tricks all the time! "Junior, show Big Daddy how you do this, show Big Daddy how you do that, say your little piece fo' Big Daddy, sister. Show your dimples, Sugar. Brother, show Big Daddy how you stand on your head!" — It goes on all the time, along with constant little remarks and innuendos about the fact that you and I have not produced any children, are totally childless and therefore totally useless! — Of course it's comical but it's also disgusting since it's so obvious what they're up to!

BRICK: *(Without interest)* What are they up to, Maggie?

MARGARET: Why, you know what they're up to!

BRICK: *(Appearing)* No, I don't know what they're up to.

(He stands there in the bathroom doorway drying his hair with a towel and hanging onto the towel rack because one ankle is broken, plastered and bound. He is still slim and firm as a boy. His liquor hasn't started tearing him down outside. He has the additional charm of that cool air of detachment that people have who have given up the struggle. But now and then, when disturbed, something flashes behind it, like lightning in a fair sky, which shows that at some deeper level he is far from peaceful. Perhaps in a stronger light he would show some signs of deliquescence, but the fading, still warm, light from the gallery treats him gently.)

MARGARET: I'll tell you what they're up to, boy of mine! — They're up to cutting you out of your father's estate, and —

(She freezes momentarily before her next remark. Her voice drops as if it were somehow a personally embarrassing admission.)

— Now we know that Big Daddy's dyin' of — cancer . . .

(There are voices on the lawn below: long-drawn calls across distance. Margaret raises her lovely bare arms and powders her armpits with a light sigh.

(She adjusts the angle of a magnifying mirror to straighten an eyelash, then rises fretfully saying:)

There's so much light in the room it —

BRICK: *(Softly but sharply)* Do we?

MARGARET: Do we what?

BRICK: Know Big Daddy's dyin' of cancer?

MARGARET: Got the report today.

BRICK: Oh . . .

MARGARET: *(Letting down bamboo blinds which cast long, gold-fretted shadows over the room)* Yep, got th' report just now . . . it didn't surprise me, Baby . . .

(Her voice has range, and music; sometimes it drops low as a boy's and you have a sudden image of her playing boys' games as a child.)

I recognized the symptoms soon's we got here last spring and I'm willin' to bet you that Brother Man and his wife were pretty sure of it, too. That more than likely explains why their usual summer migration to the coolness of the Great Smokies was passed up this summer in favor of — hustlin' down here ev'ry whipstitch with their whole screamin' tribe! And why so many allusions have been made to Rainbow Hill lately. You know what Rainbow Hill is? Place that's famous for treatin' alcoholics an' dope fiends in the movies!

BRICK: I'm not in the movies.

MARGARET: No, and you don't take dope. Otherwise you're a perfect can-

didate for Rainbow Hill, Baby, and that's where they aim to ship
you — over my dead body! Yep, over my dead body they'll ship you
there, but nothing would please them better. Then Brother Man could
get a-hold of the purse strings and dole out remittances to us, maybe
get power-of-attorney and sign checks for us and cut off our credit
wherever, whenever he wanted! Son-of-a-bitch! — How'd you like that,
Baby? — Well, you've been doin' just about ev'rything in your power
to bring it about, you've just been doin' ev'rything you can think of
to aid and abet them in this scheme of theirs! Quittin' work, devoting
yourself to the occupation of drinkin'! — Breakin' your ankle last night
on the high school athletic field: doin' what? Jumpin' hurdles? At two
or three in the morning? Just fantastic! Got in the paper. *Clarksdale
Register* carried a nice little item about it, human interest story about
a well-known former athlete stagin' a one-man track meet on the
Glorious Hill High School athletic field last night, but was slightly
out of condition and didn't clear the first hurdle! Brother Man Gooper
claims he exercised his influence t' keep it from goin' out over AP and
UP or every goddam "P." But, Brick? You still have one big advantage!
*(During the above swift flood of words, Brick has reclined with contra-
puntal leisure on the snowy surface of the bed and has rolled over
carefully on his side or belly.)*
BRICK: *(Wryly)* Did you *say* something, Maggie?
MARGARET: Big Daddy dotes on you, honey. And he can't stand Brother
     Man and Brother Man's wife, that monster of fertility, Mae; she's
     downright odious to him! Know how I know? By little expressions
     that flicker over his face when that woman is holding fo'th on one of
     her choice topics such as — how she refused twilight sleep! — when
     the twins were delivered! Because she feels motherhood's an experi-
     ence that a woman ought to experience fully! — in order to fully ap-
     preciate the wonder and beauty of it! HAH!
     *(This loud "HAH!" is accompanied by a violent action such as slamming
     a drawer shut.)*
     — and how she made Brother Man come in an' stand beside her
     in the delivery room so he would not miss out on the "wonder and
     beauty" of it either! — producin' those no-neck monsters . . .
     *(A speech of this kind would be antipathetic from almost anybody but
     Margaret; she makes it oddly funny, because her eyes constantly twinkle
     and her voice shakes with laughter which is basically indulgent.)*
     — Big Daddy shares my attitude toward those two! As for me,
     well — I give him a laugh now and then and he tolerates me. In
     fact! — I sometimes suspect that Big Daddy harbors a little uncon-
     scious "lech" fo' me . . .
BRICK: What makes you think that big Daddy has a lech for you, Maggie?
MARGARET: Way he always drops his eyes down my body when I'm talkin'
     to him, drops his eyes to my boobs an' licks his old chops! Ha ha!
BRICK: That kind of talk is disgusting.
MARGARET: Did anyone ever tell you that you're an ass-aching Puritan,
     Brick?
          I think it's mighty fine that that ole fellow, on the doorstep of death,
     still takes in my shape with what I think is deserved appreciation!

And you wanta know something else? Big Daddy didn't know how many little Maes and Goopers had been produced! "How many kids have you got?" he asked at the table, just like Brother Man and his wife were new acquaintances to him! Big Mama said he was jokin', but that ole boy wasn't jokin', Lord, no!

And when they infawmed him that they had five already and were turning out number six! — the news seemed to come as a sort of unpleasant surprise . . .

(Children yell below.)

Scream, monsters!

(Turns to Brick with a sudden, gay, charming smile which fades as she notices that he is not looking at her but into fading gold space with a troubled expression.

(It is constant rejection that makes her humor "bitchy.")

Yes, you should of been at that supper-table, Baby.

(Whenever she calls him "baby" the word is a soft caress.)

Y'know, Big Daddy, bless his ole sweet soul, he's the dearest ole thing in the world, but he does hunch over his food as if he preferred not to notice anything else. Well, Mae an' Gooper were side by side at the table, direckly across from Big Daddy, watchin' his face like hawks while they jawed an' jabbered about the cuteness an' brilliance of th' no-neck monsters!

(She giggles with a hand fluttering at her throat and her breast and her long throat arched.

(She comes downstage and recreates the scene with voice and gesture.)

And the no-neck monsters were ranged around the table, some in high chairs and some on th' *Books of Knowledge,* all in fancy little paper caps in honor of big Daddy's birthday. And all through dinner, well, I want you to know that Brother Man an' his partner never once, for one moment, stopped exchanging pokes an' pinches an' kicks an' signs an' signals! — Why, they were like a couple of cardsharps fleecing a sucker. — Even Big Mama, bless her ole sweet soul, she isn't th' quickest an' brightest thing in the world, she finally noticed, at last, an' said to Gooper, "Gooper, what are you an' Mae makin' all these signs at each other about?" — I swer t' goodness. I nearly choked on my chicken!

(Margaret, back at the dressing table, still doesn't see Brick. He is watching her with a look that is not quite definable. — Amused? shocked? contemptuous? — part of those and part of something else.)

Y'know — your brother Gooper still cherishes the illusion he took a giant step up on the social ladder when he married Miss Mae Flynn of the Memphis Flynns.

(Margaret moves about the room as she talks, stops before the mirror, moves on.)

But I have a piece of Spanish news for Gooper. The Flynns never had a thing in this world but money and they lost that, they were nothing at all but fairly successful climbers. Of course, Mae Flynn came out in Memphis eight years before I made my debut in Nashville, but I had friends at Ward-Belmont who came from Memphis and they used to come to see me and I used to go to see them for Christmas and spring vacations, and so I know who rates an' who doesn't rate in Memphis society. Why, y'know ole Papa Flynn, he barely escaped doing time in the Federal pen for shady manipulations on th' stock market when his chain stores crashed, and as for Mae having been a cotton carnival queen, as they remind us so often, lest we forget, well, that's one honor that I don't envy her for! — Sit on a brass throne on a tacky float an' ride down Main Street, smilin', bowin', and blowin' kisses to all the trash on the street —

(She picks out a pair of jeweled sandals and rushes to the dressing-table.)

Why, year before last, when Susan McPheeters was singled out fo' that honor, y'know what happened to her? Y'know what happened to poor little Susie McPheeters?

BRICK: *(Absently)* No. What happened to little Susie McPheeters?

MARGARET: Somebody spit tobacco juice in her face.

BRICK: *(Dreamily)* Somebody spit tobacco juice in her face?

MARGARET: That's right, some old drunk leaned out of a window in the Hotel Gayoso and yelled, "Hey, Queen, hey, hey, there, Queenie!" Poor Susie looked up and flashed him a radiant smile and he shot out a squirt of tobacco juice right in poor Susie's face.

BRICK: Well, what d'you know about that.

MARGARET: *(Gaily)* What do I know about it? I was there, I saw it!

BRICK: *(Absently)* Must have been kind of funny.

MARGARET: Susie didn't think so. Had hysterics. Screamed like a banshee. They had to stop th' parade an' remove her from her thone an' go on with —

(She catches sight of him in the mirror, gasps slightly, wheels about to face him. Count ten.)

— Why are you looking at me like that?

BRICK: *(Whistling softly, now)* Like what, Maggie?

MARGARET: *(Intensely, fearfully)* The way y' were lookin' at me just now, befo' I caught your eye in the mirror and you started t' whistle! I don't know how t' describe it but it froze my blood! — I've caught you lookin' at me like that so often lately. What are you thinkin' of when you look at me like that?

BRICK: I wasn't conscious of lookin' at you, Maggie.

MARGARET: Well, I was conscious of it! What were you thinkin'?

BRICK: I don't remember thinking of anything, Maggie.

MARGARET: Don't you think I know that —? Don't you —? — Think I know that —?

BRICK: *(Coolly)* Know *what*, Maggie?

MARGARET: *(Struggling for expression)* That I've gone through this — hideous! — transformation, become — hard! Frantic!

(Then she adds, almost tenderly:)

— cruel!!

That's what you've been observing in me lately. How could y' help but observe it? That's all right. I'm not — thin-skinned any more, can't afford t' be thin-skinned any more.

(She is now recovering her power.)

— But Brick? Brick?

BRICK: Did you say something?
MARGARET: I was *goin'* t' say something: that I get — lonely. Very!
BRICK: Ev'rybody gets that . . .
MARGARET: Living with someone you love can be lonelier — than living
entirely *alone!* — if the one that y' love doesn't love you . . .
*(There is a pause. Brick hobbles downstage and asks, without looking
at her:)*
BRICK: Would you like to live alone, Maggie?
(Another pause: then — after she has caught a quick, hurt breath:)
MARGARET: No! — God! — I wouldn't!
*(Another gasping breath. She forcibly controls what must have been
an impulse to cry out. We see her deliberately, very forcibly, going all
the way back to the world in which you can talk about ordinary matters.)*
Did you have a nice shower?
BRICK: Uh-huh.
MARGARET: Was the water cool?
BRICK: No.
MARGARET: But it made y' feel fresh, huh?
BRICK: Fresher . . .
MARGARET: I know something would make y' feel *much* fresher!
BRICK: What?
MARGARET: An alcohol rub. Or cologne, a rub with cologne!
BRICK: That's good after a workout but I haven't been workin' out, Maggie.
MARGARET: You've kept in good shape, though.
BRICK: *(Indifferently)* You think so, Maggie?
MARGARET: I always thought drinkin' men lost their looks, but I was
plainly mistaken.
BRICK: *(Wryly)* Why, thanks, Maggie.
MARGARET: You're the only drinkin' man I know that it never seems t'
put fat on.
BRICK: I'm gettin' softer, Maggie.
MARGARET: Well, sooner or later it's bound to soften you up. It was just
beginning to soften up Skipper when —
(She stops short.)
I'm sorry. I never could keep my fingers off a sore — I wish you
would lose your looks. If you did it would make the martyrdom of
Saint Maggie a little more bearable. But no such goddam luck. I
actually believe you've gotten better looking since you've gone on the
bottle. Yeah, a person who didn't know you would think you'd never
had a tense nerve in your body or a strained muscle.
*(There are sounds of croquet on the lawn below: the click of mallets,
light voices, near and distant.)*
Of course, you always had that detached quality as if you were
playing a game without much concern over whether you won or lost,
and now that you've lost the game, not lost but just quit playing, you
have that rare sort of charm that usually only happens in very old or
hopelessly sick people, the charm of the defeated. — You look so cool,
so cool, so enviably cool.
(Music is heard.)
They're playing croquet. The moon has appeared and it's white, just

550

beginning to turn a little bit yellow . . .

You were a wonderful lover . . .

Such a wonderful person to go to bed with, and I think mostly because you were really indifferent to it. Isn't that right? Never had any anxiety about it, did it naturally, easily, slowly, with absolute confidence and perfect calm, more like opening a door for a lady or seating her at a table than giving expression to any longing for her. Your indifference made you wonderful at lovemaking — *strange?* — but true . . .

You know, if I thought you would never, never, *never* make love to me again — I would go downstairs to the kitchen and pick out the longest and sharpest knife I could find and stick it straight into my heart, I swear that I would!

But one thing I don't have is the charm of the defeated, my hat is still in the ring, and I am determined to win!

(There is the sound of croquet mallets hitting croquet balls.)

— What is the victory of a cat on a hot tin roof? — I wish I knew . . .

Just staying on it, I guess, as long as she can . . .

(More croquet sounds.)

Later tonight I'm going to tell you I love you an' maybe by that time you'll be drunk enough to believe me. Yes, they're playing croquet . . .

Big Daddy is dying of cancer . . .

What were you thinking of when I caught you looking at me like that? Were you thinking of Skipper?

(Brick takes up his crutch, rises.)

Oh, excuse me, forgive me, but laws of silence don't work! No, laws of silence don't work . . .

(Brick crosses to the bar, takes a quick drink, and rubs his head with towel.)

Laws of silence don't work . . .

When something is festering in your memory or your imagination, laws of silence don't work, it's just like shutting a door and locking it on a house on fire in hope of forgetting that the house is burning. But not facing a fire doesn't put it out. Silence about a thing just magnifies it. It grows and festers in silence, becomes malignant . . .

Get dressed, Brick.

(He drops his crutch.)

BRICK: I've dropped my crutch.

(He has stopped rubbing his hair dry but still stands hanging onto the towel rack in a white towel-cloth robe.)

MARGARET: Lean on me.

BRICK: No, just give me my crutch.

MARGARET: Lean on my shoulder.

BRICK: *I don't want to lean on your shoulder, I want my crutch!*

(This is spoken like sudden lightning.)

Are you going to give me my crutch or do I have to get down on my knees on the floor and —

MARGARET: *Here, here, take it, take it!*

(She has thrust the crutch at him.)

BRICK: *(Hobbling out)* Thanks . . .

MARGARET: We mustn't scream at each other, the walls in this house have ears . . .

(He hobbles directly to liquor cabinet to get a new drink.)

     — but that's the first time I've heard you raise your voice in a long time, Brick. A crack in the wall? — Of composure?

     — I think that's a good sign . . .

     A sign of nerves in a player on the defensive!

(Brick turns and smiles at her coolly over his fresh drink.)

BRICK: It just hasn't happened yet, Maggie.

MARGARET: What?

BRICK: The click I get in my head when I've had enough of this stuff to make me peaceful . . .

     Will you do me a favor?

MARGARET: Maybe I will. What favor?

BRICK: Just, just keep your voice down!

MARGARET: *(In a hoarse whisper)* I'll do you that favor, I'll speak in a whisper, if not shut up completely, if *you* will do *me* a favor and make that drink your last one till after the party.

BRICK: What party?

MARGARET: Big Daddy's birthday party.

BRICK: Is this Big Daddy's birthday?

MARGARET: You know this is Big Daddy's birthday!

BRICK: No, I don't, I forgot it.

MARGARET: Well, I remembered it for you . . .

(They are both speaking as breathlessly as a pair of kids after a fight, drawing deep exhausted breaths and looking at each other with faraway eyes, shaking and panting together as if they had broken apart from a violent struggle.)

BRICK: Good for you, Maggie.

MARGARET: You just have to scribble a few lines on this card.

BRICK: You scribble something, Maggie.

MARGARET: It's got to be your handwriting; it's your present, I've given him my present; it's got to be your handwriting!

(The tension between them is building again, the voices becoming shrill once more.)

BRICK: I didn't get him a present.

MARGARET: I got one for you.

BRICK: All right. You write the card, then.

MARGARET: And have him know you didn't remember his birthday?

BRICK: I didn't remember his birthday.

MARGARET: You don't have to prove you didn't!

BRICK: I don't want to fool him about it.

MARGARET: Just write "Love, Brick!" for God's —

BRICK: No.

MARGARET: You've *got* to!

BRICK: I don't have to do anything I don't want to do. You keep forgetting the conditions on which I agreed to stay on living with you.

MARGARET: *(Out before she knows it)* I'm not living with you. We occupy the same cage.

BRICK: You've got to remember the conditions agreed on.

MARGARET: They're impossible conditions!

BRICK: Then why don't you —?

MARGARET: HUSH! Who is out there? Is somebody at the door?

(There are footsteps in hall.)

MAE: *(Outside)* May I enter a moment?

MARGARET: Oh, *you!* Sure. Come in, Mae.

(Mae enters bearing aloft the bow of a young lady's archery set.)

MAE: Brick, is this thing yours?

MARGARET: Why, Sister Woman — that's my Diana Trophy. Won it at the intercollegiate archery contest on the Ole Miss campus.

MAE: It's a mighty dangerous thing to leave exposed round a house full of nawmal rid-blooded children attracted t'weapons.

MARGARET: "Nawmal rid-blooded children attracted t'weapons" ought t'be taught to keep their hands off things that don't belong to them.

MAE: Maggie, honey, if you had children of your own you'd know how funny that is. Will you please lock this up and put the key out of reach?

MARGARET: Sister Woman, nobody is plotting the destruction of your kiddies. — Brick and I still have our special archers' license. We're goin' deer-huntin' on Moon Lake as soon as the season starts. I love to run with dogs through chilly woods, run, run, leap over obstructions —

(She goes into the closet carrying the bow.)

MAE: How's the injured ankle, Brick?

BRICK: Doesn't hurt. Just itches.

MAE: Oh, my! Brick — Brick, you should've been downstairs after supper! Kiddies put on a show. Polly played the piano, Buster an' Sonny drums, an' then they turned out the lights an' Dixie and Trixie puhfawmed a toe dance in fairy costume with *spahkluhs!* Big Daddy just beamed! He just beamed!

MARGARET: *(From the closet with a sharp laugh)* Oh, I bet. It breaks my heart that we missed it!

(She reenters.)

But Mae? Why did y'give dawgs' names to all your kiddies?

MAE: *Dogs'* names?

(Margaret has made this observation as she goes to raise the bamboo blinds, since the sunset glare has diminshed. In crossing she winks at Brick.)

MARGARET: *(Sweetly)* Dixie, Trixie, Buster, Sonny, Polly! — Sounds like four dogs and a parrot . . . animal act in a circus!

MAE: Maggie?

(Margaret turns with a smile.)

Why are you so catty?

MARGARET: Cause I'm a cat! But why can't *you* take a joke, Sister Woman?

MAE: Nothin' pleases me more than a joke that's funny. You know the real names of our kiddies. Buster's real name is Robert. Sonny's real name is Saunders. Trixie's real name is Marlene, and Dixie's —

(Someone downstairs calls for her. "Hey, Mae!" — She rushes to door, saying:)

Intermission is over!

MARGARET: *(As Mae closes door)* I wonder what Dixie's real name is?

BRICK: Maggie, being catty doesn't help things any . . .

MARGARET: I know! *WHY!* — Am I so catty? — Cause I'm consumed with envy an' eaten up with longing? — Brick, I've laid out your beautiful Shantung silk suit from Rome and one of your monogrammed silk shirts. I'll put your cuff-links in it, those lovely star sapphires I get you to wear so rarely . . .

BRICK: I can't get trousers on over this plaster cast.

MARGARET: Yes, you can, I'll help you.

BRICK: I'm not going to get dressed, Maggie.

MARGARET: Will you just put on a pair of white silk pajamas?

BRICK: Yes, I'll do that, Maggie.

MARGARET: *Thank* you, thank you so *much!*

BRICK: Don't mention it.

MARGARET: *Oh, Brick!* How long does it have t' go on? This punishment? Haven't I done time enough, haven't I served my term, can't I apply for a — pardon?

BRICK: Maggie, you're spoiling my liquor. Lately your voice always sounds like you'd been running upstairs to warn somebody that the house was on fire!

MARGARET: Well, no wonder, no wonder. Y'know what I feel like, Brick?

(Children's and grownups' voices are blended, below, in a loud but uncertain rendition of "My Wild Irish Rose.")

I feel all the time like a cat on a hot tin roof!

BRICK: Then jump off the roof, jump off it, cats can jump off roofs and land on their four feet uninjured!

MARGARET: Oh, yes!

BRICK: Do it! — fo' God's sake, do it . . .

MARGARET: Do what?

BRICK: Take a lover!

MARGARET: I can't see a man but you! Even with my eyes closed, I just see you! Why don't you get ugly, Brick, why don't you please get fat or ugly or something so I could stand it?

(She rushes to hall door, opens it, listens.)

The concert is still going on! Bravo, no-necks, bravo!

(She slams and locks door fiercely.)

BRICK: What did you lock the door for?

MARGARET: To give us a little privacy for a while.

BRICK: You know better, Maggie.

MARGARET: No, I don't know better . . .

(She rushes to gallery doors, draws the rose-silk drapes across them.)

BRICK: Don't make a fool of yourself.

MARGARET: I don't mind makin' a fool of myself over you!

BRICK: I mind, Maggie. I feel embarrassed for you.

MARGARET: Feel embarrassed! But don't continue my torture. I can't live on and on under these circumstances.

BRICK: You agreed to —

MARGARET: I know but —

BRICK: — Accept that condition!

MARGARET: *I CAN'T! CAN'T! CAN'T!*
(She seizes his shoulder.)
BRICK: Let go!
(He breaks away from her and seizes the small boudoir chair and raises it like a lion-tamer facing a big circus cat.
(Count five. She stares at him with her fist pressed to her mouth, then bursts into shrill, almost hysterical laughter. He remains grave for a moment, then grins and puts the chair down.
(Big Mama calls through closed door.)
BIG MAMA: Son? Son? Son?
BRICK: What is it, Big Mama?
BIG MAMA: *(Outside)* Oh, son! We got the most wonderful news about Big Daddy. I just had t' run up an' tell you right this —
(She rattles the knob.)
    — What's this door doin' locked, faw? You all think there's robbers in the house?
MARGARET: Big Mama, Brick is dressin', he's not dressed yet.
BIG MAMA: That's all right, it won't be the first time I've seen Brick not dressed. Come on, open this door!
(Margaret, with a grimace, goes to unlock and open the hall door, as Brick hobbles rapidly to the bathroom and kicks the door shut. Big Mama has disappeared from the hall.)
MARGARET: Big Mama?
(Big Mama appears through the opposite gallery doors behind Margaret, huffing and puffing like an old bulldog. She is a short, stout woman; her sixty years and 170 pounds have left her somewhat breathless most of the time; she's always tensed like a boxer, or rather, a Japanese wrestler. Her "family" was maybe a little superior to Big Daddy's, but not much. She wears a black or silver lace dress and at least half a million in flashy gems. She is very sincere.)
BIG MAMA: *(Loudly, startling Margaret)* Here — I come through Gooper's and Mae's gall'ry door. Where's Brick! *Brick* — Hurry on out of there, son, I just have a second and want to give you the news about Big Daddy. — I hate locked doors in a house . . .
MARGARET: *(With affected lightness)* I've noticed you do, Big Mama, but people have got to have *some* moments of privacy, don't they?
BIG MAMA: No, ma'am, not in *my* house. *(Without pause)* Whacha took off you' dress faw? I thought that little lace dress was so sweet on yuh, honey.
MARGARET: I thought it looked sweet on me, too, but one of m' cute little table-partners used it for a napkin so —!
BIG MAMA: *(Picking up stockings on floor)* What?
MARGARET: You know, Big Mama, Mae and Gooper's so touchy about those children — thanks, Big Mama . . .
(Big Mama has thrust the picked-up stockings in Margaret's hand with a grunt.)
    — that you just don't dare to suggest there's any room for improvement in their —
BIG MAMA: Brick, hurry out! — Shoot, Maggie, you just don't like children.
MARGARET: I do SO like children! Adore them! — well brought up!

BIG MAMA: *(Gentle — loving)* Well, why don't you have some and bring them up well, then, instead of all the time pickin' on Gooper's an' Mae's?

GOOPER: *(Shouting up the stairs)* Hey, hey, Big Mama, Betsy an' Hugh got to go, waitin' t' tell yuh g'by!

BIG MAMA: Tell 'em to hold their hawses, I'll be right down in a jiffy!
(She turns to the bathroom door and calls out.)
Son? Can you hear me in there?
(There is a muffled answer.)
We just got the full report from the laboratory at the Ochsner Clinic, completely negative, son, ev'rything negative, right on down the line! Nothin' a-tall's wrong with him but some little functional thing called a spastic colon. Can you hear me, son?

MARGARET: He can hear you, Big Mama.

BIG MAMA: Then why don't he say something? God Almighty, a piece of news like that should make him shout. It made *me* shout, I can tell you. I shouted and sobbed and fell right down on my knees — Look!
(She pulls up her skirt.)
See the bruises where I hit my kneecaps? Took both doctors to haul me back on my feet!
(She laughs — she always laughs like hell at herself.)
Big Daddy was furious with me! But ain't that wonderful news?
(Facing bathroom again, she continues:)
After all the anxiety we been through to git a report like that on Big Daddy's birthday? Big Daddy tries to hide how much of a load that news took off his mind, but didn't fool *me*. He was mighty close to crying about it *himself!*
(Goodbyes are shouted downstairs, and she rushes to door.)
Hold those people down there, don't let them go! — Now, git dressed, we're all comin' up to this room fo' Big Daddy's birthday party because of your ankle. — How's his ankle, Maggie?

MARGARET: Well, he broke it, Big Mama.

BIG MAMA: I know he broke it.
(A phone is ringing in hall. A Negro voice answers: "Mistuh Polly's res'dence.")
I mean does it hurt him much still.

MARGARET: I'm afraid I can't give you that information, Big Mama. You'll have to ask Brick if it hurts much still or not.

SOOKEY:*(In the hall)* It's Memphis, Mizz Polly, it's Miss Sally in Memphis.

BIG MAMA: Awright, Sookey.
(Big Mama rushes into the hall and is heard shouting on the phone:)
Hello, Miss Sally. How are you, Miss Sally? — Yes, well, I was just gonna call you about it. *Shoot!* —
(She raises her voice to a bellow.)
Miss Sally? Don't ever call me from the Gayoso Lobby, too much talk goes on in that hotel lobby, no wonder you can't hear me! Now listen, Miss Sally. They's nothin' serious wrong with Big Daddy. We got the report just now, they's nothin' wrong but a thing called a — spastic! *SPASTIC!* — colon . . .
(She appears at the hall door and calls to Margaret.)

— Maggie, come out here and talk to that fool on the phone. I'm shouted breathless!

MARGARET: *(Goes out and is heard sweetly at phone)* Miss Sally? This is Brick's wife, Maggie. So nice to hear your voice. Can you hear *mine?* Well, *good!* — Big Mama just wanted you to know that they've got the report from the Ochsner Clinic and what Big Daddy has is a spastic colon. Yes. Spastic colon, Miss Sally. That's right, spastic colon. *G'bye, Miss Sally, hope I'll see you real soon!*

(Hangs up a little before Miss Sally was probably ready to terminate the talk. She returns through the hall door.)

She heard me perfectly. I've discovered with deaf people the thing to do is not shout at them but just enunciate clearly. My rich old Aunt Cornelia was deaf as the dead but I could make her hear me just by sayin' each word slowly, distinctly, close to her ear. I read her the *Commercial Appeal* ev'ry night, read her the classified ads in it, even, she never missed a word of it. But was she a mean ole thing! Know what I got when she died? Her unexpired subscriptions to five magazines and the Book-of-the-Month Club and a LIBRARY full of ev'ry dull book ever written! All else went to her hellcat of a sister . . . meaner than she was, even!

(Big Mama has been straightening things up in the room during this speech.)

BIG MAMA: *(Closing closet door on discarded clothes)* Miss Sally sure is a *case!* Big Daddy says she's always got her hand out fo' something. He's not mistaken. That poor ole thing always has her hand out fo' somethin'. I don't think Big Daddy gives her as much as he should. *(Somebody shouts for her downstairs and she shouts:)* I'm comin'!

(She starts out. At the hall door, turns and jerks a forefinger, first toward the bathroom door, then toward the liquor cabinet, meaning: "Has Brick been drinking?" Margaret pretends not to understand, cocks her head and raises her brows as if the pantomimic performance was completely mystifying to her.)

(Big Mama rushes back to Margaret:) Shoot! Stop playin' so dumb — I mean has he been drinkin' that stuff much yet?

MARGARET: *(With a little laugh)* Oh! I think he had a highball after supper.

BIG MAMA: Don't laugh about it! — Some single men stop drinkin' when they git married and others start! Brick never touched liquor before he —!

MARGARET: *(Crying out)* THAT'S NOT FAIR!

BIG MAMA: Fair or not fair I want to ask you a question, one question: D'you make Brick happy in bed?

MARGARET: Why don't you ask if he makes *me* happy in bed?

BIG MAMA: Because I know that —

MARGARET: *It works both ways!*

BIG MAMA: Something's not right! You're childless and my son drinks!

(Someone has called her downstairs and she has rushed to the door on the line above. She turns at the door and points at the bed.)

— When a marriage goes on the rocks, the rocks are *there*, right *there!*

MARGARET: *That's —*
(Big Mama has swept out of the room and slammed the door.)
— not — fair . . .
*(Margaret is alone, completely alone, and she feels it. She draws in,
hunches her shoulders, raises her arms with fists clenched, shuts her
eyes tight as a child about to be stabbed with a vaccination needle.
When she opens her eyes again, what she sees is the long oval mirror
and she rushes straight to it, stares into it with a grimace and says:
"Who are you?" — Then she crouches a little and answers herself in a
different voice which is high, thin, mocking: "I am Maggie the Cat!" —
Straightens quickly as bathroom door opens a little and Brick calls out
to her.)*
BRICK: Has Big Mama gone?
MARGARET: She's gone.
*(He opens the bathroom door and hobbles out, with his liquor glass
now empty, straight to the liquor cabinet. He is whistling softly. Margaret's head pivots on her long, slender throat to watch him.*
*(She raises a hand uncertainly to the base of her throat, as if it was
difficult for her to swallow, before she speaks:)*
You know, our sex life didn't just peter out in the usual way, it
was cut off short, long before the natural time for it to, and it's going
to revive again, just as sudden as that. I'm confident of it. That's what
I'm keeping myself attractive for. For the time when you'll see me
again like other men see me. Yes, like other men see me. They still
see me, Brick, and they like what they see. Uh-huh. Some of them
would give their — Look, Brick!
*(She stands before the long oval mirror, touches her breast and then
her hips with her two hands.)*
How high my body stays on me! — No'hing has fallen on me —
not a fraction . . .
*(Her voice is soft and trembling: a pleading child's. At this moment as
he turns to glance at her — a look which is like a player passing a ball
to another player, third down and goal to go — she has to capture the
audience in a grip so tight that she can hold it till the first intermission
without any lapse of attention.)*
Other men still want me. My face looks strained, sometimes,
but I've kept my figure as well as you've kept yours, and men admire
it. I still turn heads on the street. Why, last week in Memphis
everywhere that I went men's eyes burned holes in my clothes, at the
country club and in restaurants and department stores, there wasn't
a man I met or walked by that didn't just eat me up with his eyes
and turn around when I passed him and look back at me. Why, at
Alice's party for her New York cousins, the best lookin' man in the
crowd — followed me upstairs and tried to force his way in the powder
room with me, followed me to the door and tried to force his way in!
BRICK: Why didn't you let him, Maggie?
MARGARET: Because I'm not that common, for one thing. Not that I wasn't
almost tempted to. You like to know who it was? It was Sonny Boy
Maxwell, that's who!
BRICK: Oh, yeah, Sonny Boy Maxwell, he was a good end-runner but had a

little injury to his back and had to quit.

MARGARET: He has no injury now and has no wife and still has a lech for me!

BRICK: I see no reason to lock him out of a powder room in that case.

MARGARET: And have someone catch me at it? I'm not that stupid. Oh, I might sometime cheat on you with someone, since you're so insultingly eager to have me do it! — But if I do, you can be damned sure it will be in a place and a time where no one but me and the man could possibly know. Because I'm not going to give you any excuse to divorce me for being unfaithful or anything else . . .

BRICK: Maggie, I wouldn't divorce you for being unfaithful or anything else. Don't you know that? Hell, I'd be relieved to know that you'd found yourself a lover.

MARGARET: Well, I'm taking no chances. No, I'd rather stay on this hot tin roof.

BRICK: A hot tin roof's 'n uncomfo'table place t' stay on . . .
(He starts to whistle softly.)

MARGARET: *(Through his whistle)* Yeah, but I can stay on it just as long as I have to.

BRICK: You could leave me, Maggie.
(He resumes whistle. She wheels about to glare at him.)

MARGARET: *Don't want to and will not!* Besides if I did, you don't have a cent to pay for it but what you get from Big Daddy and he's dying of cancer!
(For the first time a realization of Big Daddy's doom seems to penetrate to Brick's consciousness, visibly, and he looks at Margaret.)

BRICK: Big Mama just said he *wasn't,* that the report was okay.

MARGARET: That's what she thinks because she got the same story that they gave Big Daddy. And was just as taken in by it as he was, poor ole things . . .

But tonight they're going to tell her the truth about it. When Big Daddy goes to bed, they're going to tell her that he is dying of cancer.
(She slams the dresser drawer.)
— It's malignant and it's terminal.

BRICK: Does Big Daddy know it?

MARGARET: Hell, do they *ever* know it? Nobody says, "You're dying." You have to fool them. They have to fool *themselves.*

BRICK: Why?

MARGARET: *Why?* Because human beings dream of life everlasting, that's the reason! But most of them want it on earth and not in heaven.
(He gives a short, hard laugh at her touch of humor.)
Well . . . *(She touches up her mascara.)* That's how it is, any-how . . . *(She looks about.)* Where did I put down my cigarette? Don't want to burn up the home-place, at least not with Mae and Gooper and their five monsters in it!
(She has found it and sucks at it greedily. Blows out smoke and continues:)
So this is Big Daddy's last birthday. And Mae and Gooper, they know it, oh, *they* know it, all right. They got the first information from the Ochsner Clinic. That's why they rushed down here with their

no-neck monsters. Because. Do you know something? Big Daddy's made no will? Big Daddy's never made out any will in his life, and so this campaign's afoot to impress him, forcibly as possible, with the fact that you drink and I've borne no children!

(He continues to stare at her a moment, then mutters something sharp but not audible and hobbles rather rapidly out onto the long gallery in the fading, much faded, gold light.)

MARGARET: *(Continuing her liturgical chant)* Y'know, I'm *fond* of Big Daddy, I am genuinely fond of that old man, I really *am*, you know . . .

BRICK: *(Faintly, vaguely)* Yes, I know you are . . .

MARGARET: I've always sort of admired him in spite of his coarseness, his four-letter words and so forth. Because Big Daddy *is* what he *is*, and he makes no bones about it. He hasn't turned gentleman farmer, he's still a Mississippi red neck, as much of a red neck as he must have been when he was just overseer here on the old Jack Straw and Peter Ochello place. But he got hold of it an' built it into th' biggest an' finest plantation in the Delta. — I've always *liked* Big Daddy . . .

(She crosses to the proscenium.)

Well, this is Big Daddy's last birthday. I'm sorry about it. But I'm facing the facts. It takes money to take care of a drinker and that's the office that I've been elected to lately.

BRICK: You don't have to take care of me.

MARGARET: Yes, I do. Two people in the same boat have got to take care of each other. At least you want money to buy more Echo Spring when this supply is exhausted, or will you be satisfied with a ten-cent beer?

Mae an' Gooper are plannin' to freeze us out of Big Daddy's estate because you drink and I'm childless. But we can defeat that plan. We're going to defeat that plan!

Brick, y'know, I've been so God damn disgustingly poor all my life! — That's the *truth*, Brick!

BRICK: I'm not sayin' it isn't.

MARGARET: Always had to suck up to people I couldn't stand because they had money and I was poor as Job's turkey. You don't know what that's like. Well, I'll tell you, it's like you would feel a thousand miles away from Echo Spring! — And had to get back to it on that broken ankle . . . without a crutch!

That's how it feels to be as poor as Job's turkey and have to suck up to relatives that you hated because they had money and all you had was a bunch of hand-me-down clothes and a few old moldy three per cent government bonds. My daddy loved his liquor, he fell in love with his liquor the way you've fallen in love with Echo Spring! — And my poor Mama, having to maintain some semblance of social position, to keep appearances up, on an income of one hundred and fifty dollars a month on those old government bonds!

When I came out, the year that I made my debut, I had just two evening dresses! One Mother made me from a pattern in *Vogue*, the other a hand-me-down from a snotty rich cousin I hated!

— The dress that I married you in was my grandmother's weddin' gown . . .

So that's why I'm like a cat on a hot tin roof!

(Brick is still on the gallery. Someone below calls up to him in a warm Negro voice, "Hiya, Mistuh Brick, how yuh feelin'?" Brick raises his liquor glass as if that answered the question.)

MARGARET: You can be young without money but you can't be old without it. You've got to be old with money because to be old without it is just too awful, you've got to be one or the other, either *young* or *with money*, you can't be old and *without* it. — That's the truth, Brick . . .
(Brick whistles softly, vaguely.)

Well, now I'm dressed, I'm all dressed, there's nothing else for me to do.
(Forlornly, almost fearfully.)

I'm dressed, all dressed, nothing else for me to do . . .
(She moves about restlessly, aimlessly, and speaks, as if to herself.)

I know when I made my mistake. — What am I —? Oh! — my bracelets . . .
(She starts working a collection of bracelets over her hands onto her wrists, about six on each, as she talks.)

I've thought a whole lot about it and now I know when I made my mistake. Yes, I made my mistake when I told you the truth about that thing with Skipper. Never should have confessed it, a fatal error, tellin' you about that thing with Skipper.

BRICK: Maggie, shut up about Skipper. I mean it, Maggie; you got to shut up about Skipper.

MARGARET: You ought to understand that Skipper and I —

BRICK: You don't think I'm serious, Maggie? You're fooled by the fact that I am saying this quiet? Look, Maggie. What you're doing is a dangerous thing to do. You're — you're — you're — foolin' with something that — nobody ought to fool with.

MARGARET: This time I'm going to finish what I have to say to you. Skipper and I made love, if love you could call it, because it made both of us feel a little bit closer to you. You see, you son of a bitch, you asked too much of people, of me, of him, of all the unlucky poor damned sons of bitches that happen to love you, and there was a whole pack of them, yes, there was a pack of them besides me and Skipper, you asked too goddam much of people that loved you, you — superior creature! — you godlike being! — And so we made love to each other to dream it was you, both of us! Yes, yes, yes! Truth, truth! What's so awful about it? I like it, I think the truth is — yeah! I shouldn't have told you . . .

BRICK: *(Holding his head unnaturally still and uptilted a bit)* It was Skipper that told me about it. Not you, Maggie.

MARGARET: I told you!

BRICK: After he told me!

MARGARET: What does it matter who —?
(Brick turns suddenly out upon the gallery and calls:)

BRICK: Little girl! Hey, little girl!

LITTLE GIRL: *(At a distance)* What, Uncle Brick?

BRICK: Tell the folks to come up! — Bring everybody upstairs!

MARGARET: I can't stop myself! I'd go on telling you this in front of them all, if I had to!

561

BRICK: Little girl! Go on, go on, will you? Do what I told you, call them!

MARGARET: Because it's got to be told and you, you! — you never let me! *(She sobs, then controls herself, and continues almost calmly.)* It was one of those beautiful, ideal things they tell about in the Greek legends, it couldn't be anything else, you being you, and that's what made it so sad, that's what made it so awful, because it was love that never could be carried through to anything satisfying or even talked about plainly. Brick, I tell you, you got to believe me, Brick, I *do* understand all about it! I — I think it was — *noble!* Can't you tell I'm sincere when I say I respect it? My only point, the only point that I'm making, is life has got to be allowed to continue even after the *dream* of life is — all — over . . . *(Brick is without his crutch. Leaning on furniture, he crosses to pick it up as she continues as if possessed by a will outside herself:)* Why I remember when we double-dated at college, Gladys Fitzgerald and I and you and Skipper, it was more like a date between you and Skipper. Gladys and I were just sort of tagging along as if it was necesary to chaperone you! — to make a good public impression —

BRICK: *(Turns to face her, half lifting his crutch)* Maggie, you want me to hit you with this crutch? Don't you know I could kill you with this crutch?

MARGARET: Good Lord, man, d' you think I'd care if you did?

BRICK: One man has one great good true thing in his life. One great good thing which is true! — I had friendship with Skipper. — You are naming it dirty!

MARGARET: I'm not naming it dirty! I am naming it clean.

BRICK: Not love with you, Maggie, but friendship with Skipper was that one great true thing, and you are naming it dirty!

MARGARET: Then you haven't been listenin', not understood what I'm saying! I'm naming it so damn clean that it killed poor Skipper! — You two had something that had to be kept on ice, yes, incorruptible, yes! — and death was the only icebox where you could keep it . . . ?

BRICK: I married you, Maggie. Why would I marry you, Maggie, if I was —?

MARGARET: Brick, don't brain me yet, let me finish! — I know, believe me I know, that it was only Skipper that harbored even any *unconscious* desire for anything not perfectly pure between you two! — Now let me skip a little. You married me early that summer we graduated out of Ole Miss, and we were happy, weren't we, we were blissful, yes, hit heaven together ev'ry time that we loved! But that fall you an' Skipper turned down wonderful offers of jobs in order to keep on bein' football heroes — pro-football heroes. You organized the Dixie Stars that fall, so you could keep on bein' team-mates forever! But somethin' was not right with it! — *Me included!* — between you. Skipper began hittin' the bottle . . . you got a spinal injury — couldn't play the Thanksgivin' game in Chicago, watched it on TV from a traction bed in Toledo. I joined Skipper. The Dixie Stars lost because poor Skipper was drunk. We drank together that night all night in the bar of the Blackstone and when cold day was comin' up over the Lake an' we were comin' out drunk to take a dizzy look at it, I said, "SKIPPER! STOP LOVIN' MY HUSBAND OR TELL HIM HE'S GOT TO LET

YOU ADMIT IT TO HIM!" — one way or another!
HE SLAPPED ME HARD ON THE MOUTH! — then turned and ran without stopping once, I am sure, all the way back into his room at the Blackstone . . .
— When I came to his room that night, with a little scratch like a shy little mouse at his door, he made that pitiful, ineffectual little attempt to prove that what I had said wasn't true . . .
(Brick strikes at her with crutch, a blow that shatters the gemlike lamp on the table.)
— In this way, I destroyed him, by telling him truth that he and his world which he was born and raised in, yours and his world, had told him could not be told?
— From then on Skipper was nothing at all but a receptacle for liquor and drugs . . .
— *Who shot cock-robin? I with my —*
(She throws back her head with tight shut eyes.)
— *merciful arrow!*
(Brick stikes at her; misses.)
Missed me! — Sorry, — I'm not tryin' to whitewash my behavior, Christ, no! Brick, I'm not good. I don't know why people have to pretend to be good, nobody's good. The rich or the well-to-do can afford to respect moral patterns, conventional moral patterns, but I could never afford to, yeah, but — I'm honest! Give me credit for just that, will you *please?* — Born poor, raised poor, expect to die poor unless I manage to get us something out of what Big Daddy leaves when he dies of cancer! But Brick?! — *Skipper is dead! I'm alive!* Maggie the cat is —
(Brick hops awkwardly forward and strikes at her again with his crutch.)
— *alive! I am alive, alive! I am . . .*
(He hurls the crutch at her, across the bed she took refuge behind and pitches forward on the floor as she completes her speech.)
— *alive!*
(A little girl, Dixie, bursts into the room, wearing an Indian war bonnet and firing a cap pistol at Margaret shouting: "Bang, bang, bang!")
(Laughter downstairs floats through the open hall door. Margaret had crouched gasping to bed at child's entrance. She now rises and says with cool fury:)
Little girl, your mother or someone should teach you — *(Gasping)* — to knock at a door before you come into a room. Otherwise people might think that you — lack — good breeding . . .
DIXIE: Yanh, yanh, yanh, what is Uncle Brick doin' on th' floor?
BRICK: I tried to kill your Aunt Maggie, but I failed — and I fell. Little girl, give me my crutch so I can get up off th' floor.
MARGARET: Yes, give your uncle his crutch, he's a cripple, honey, he broke his ankle last night jumping hurdles on the high school athletic field!
DIXIE: What were you jumping hurdles for, Uncle Brick?
BRICK: Because I used to jump them and people like to do what they used to do, even after they've stopped being able to do it . . .
MARGARET: That's right, that's your answer, now go away, little girl.
(Dixie fires cap pistol at Margaret three times.)

563

> *Stop, you stop that, monster! You little no-neck monster!*
> *(She seizes the cap pistol and hurls it through gallery doors.)*

DIXIE: *(With a precocious instinct for the cruelest thing)* You're *jealous!* — You're just jealous because you can't have babies!

(She sticks out her tongue at Margaret as she sashays past her with her stomach stuck out, to the gallery. Margaret slams the gallery doors and leans panting against them. There is a pause. Brick has replaced his spilt drink and sits, faraway, on the great four-poster bed.)

MARGARET: You see? — they gloat over us being childless, even in front of their five little no-neck monsters!

(Pause. Voices approach on the stairs.)

Brick? — I've been to a doctor in Memphis, a — a gynecologist . . .

I've been completely examined, and there is no reason why we can't have a child whenever we want one. And this is my time by the calendar to conceive. Are you listening to me? Are you? Are you LISTENING TO ME!

BRICK: Yes. I hear you, Maggie.

(His attention returns to her inflamed face.)

— But how in hell on earth do you imagine — that you're going to have a child by a man that can't stand you?

MARGARET: That's a problem that I will have to work out.

(She wheels about to face the hall door.)

Here they come!

(The lights dim.)

CURTAIN

ACT TWO

There is no lapse of time. Margaret and Brick are in the same positions they held at the end of Act I.

MARGARET: *(At door)* Here they come!

(Big Daddy appears first, a tall man with a fierce, anxious look, moving carefully not to betray his weakness even, or especially, to himself.)

BIG DADDY: Well, Brick.

BRICK: Hello, Big Daddy. — Congratulations!

BIG DADDY: — Crap . . .

(Some of the people are approaching through the hall, others along the gallery: voices from both directions. Gooper and Reverend Tooker become visible outside gallery doors, and their voices come in clearly.

(They pause outside as Gooper lights a cigar.)

REVEREND TOOKER: *(Vivaciously)* Oh, but St. Paul's in Grenada has three memorial windows, and the latest one is a Tiffany stained-glass window that cost twenty-five hundred dollars, a picture of Christ the Good Shepherd with a Lamb in His arms.

GOOPER: Who give that window, Preach?

REVEREND TOOKER: Clyde Fletcher's widow. Also presented St. Paul's with a baptismal font.

GOOPER: Y'know what somebody ought t' give your church is a *coolin'* system, Preach.

REVEREND TOOKER: Yes, siree, Bob! And y'know what Gus Hamma's family gave in his memory to the church at Two Rivers? A complete new stone parish-house with a basketball court in the basement and a —

BIG DADDY: *(Uttering a loud barking laugh which is far from truly mirthful)* Hey, Preach! What's all this talk about memorials, Preach? Y' think somebody's about t' kick off around here? 'S that it?

(Startled by this interjection, Reverend Tooker decides to laugh at the question almost as loud as he can.

(How he would answer the question we'll never know, as he's spared that embarrassment by the voice of Gooper's wife, Mae, rising high and clear as she appears with "Doc" Baugh, the family doctor, through the hall door.)

MAE: *(Almost religiously)* — Let's see now, they've had their *tyyy*-phoid shots, and their tetanus shots, their diphtheria shots and their hepatitis shots and their polio shots, they got *those* shots every month from May through September, and — Gooper! Hey! Gooper! — What all have the kiddies been shot faw?

MARGARET: *(Overlapping a bit)* Turn on the Hi-Fi, Brick! Let's have some music t' start off th' party with!

(The talk becomes so general that the room sounds like a great aviary of chattering birds. Only Brick remains unengaged, leaning upon the liquor cabinet with his faraway smile, an ice cube in a paper napkin with which he now and then rubs his forehead. He doesn't respond to Margaret's command. She bounds forward and stoops over the instrument panel of the console.)

GOOPER: We gave 'em that thing for a third anniversary present, got three speakers in it.

(The room is suddenly blasted by the climax of a Wagnerian opera or a Beethoven symphony.)

BIG DADDY: Turn that damn thing off!

(Almost instant silence, almost instantly broken by the shouting charge of Big Mama, entering through hall door like a charging rhino.)

BIG MAMA: Wha's my Brick, wha's mah precious baby!!

BIG DADDY: Sorry! Turn it back on!

(Everyone laughs very loud. Big Daddy is famous for his jokes at Big Mama's expense, and nobody laughs louder at these jokes than Big Mama herself, though sometimes they're pretty cruel and Big Mama has to pick up or fuss with something to cover the hurt that the loud laugh doesn't quite cover.

(On this occasion, a happy occasion because the dread in her heart has also been lifted by the false report on Big Daddy's condition, she giggles, grotesquely, coyly, in Big Daddy's direction and bears down upon Brick, all very quick and alive.)

BIG MAMA: Here he is, here's my precious baby! What's that you've got in your hand? You put that liquor down, son, your hand was made fo' holdin' somethin' better than that!

GOOPER: Look at Brick put it down!

(Brick has obeyed Big Mama by draining the glass and handing it to her. Again everyone laughs, some high, some low.)

BIG MAMA: Oh, you bad boy, you, you're my bad little boy. Give Big Mama a kiss, you bad boy, you! — Look at him shy away, will you? Brick never liked bein' kissed or made a fuss over, I guess because he's always had too much of it!

Son, you turn that thing off!

(Brick has switched on the TV set.)

I can't stand TV, radio was bad enough but TV has gone it one better, I mean — *(Plops wheezing in chair)* — one worse, ha ha! Now what'm I sittin' down here faw? I want t' sit next to my sweetheart on the sofa, hold hands with him and love him up a little!

(Big Mama has on a black and white figured chiffon. The large irregular patterns, like the markings of some massive animal, the luster of her great diamonds and many pearls, the brilliants set in the silver frames of her glasses, her riotous voice, booming laugh, have dominated the room since she entered. Big Daddy has been regarding her with a steady grimace of chronic annoyance.)

BIG MAMA: *(Still louder)* Preacher, Preacher, hey, Preach! Give me you' hand an' help me up from this chair!

REVEREND TOOKER: None of your tricks, Big Mama!

BIG MAMA: What tricks? You give me you' hand so I can get up an' —

(Reverend Tooker extends her his hand. She grabs it and pulls him into her lap with a shrill laugh that spans an octave in two notes.)

Ever seen a preacher in a fat lady's lap? Hey, hey, folks! Ever seen a preacher in a fat lady's lap?

(Big Mama is notorious throughout the Delta for this sort of inelegant horseplay. Margaret looks on with indulgent humor, sipping Dubonnet "on the rocks" and watching Brick, but Mae and Gooper exchange signs of humorless anxiety over these antics, the sort of behavior which Mae thinks may account for their failure to quite get in with the smartest young married set in Memphis, despite all. One of the Negroes, Lacy or Sookey, peeks in, cackling. They are waiting for a sign to bring in the cake and champagne. But Big Daddy's not amused. He doesn't understand why, in spite of the infinite mental relief he's received from the doctor's report, he still has these same old fox teeth in his guts. "This spastic thing sure is something," he says to himself, but aloud he roars at Big Mama:)

BIG DADDY: *BIG MAMA, WILL YOU QUIT HORSIN'?* — You're too old an' too fat fo' that sort of crazy kid stuff an' besides a woman with your blood-pressure — she had two hundred last spring! — is riskin' a stroke when you mess around like that . . .

BIG MAMA: *Here comes Big Daddy's birthday!*

(Negroes in white jackets enter with an enormous birthday cake ablaze with candles and carrying buckets of champagne with satin ribbons about the bottle necks.)

(Mae and Gooper strike up song, and everybody, including the Negroes and Children, joins in. Only Brick remains aloof.)

EVERYONE: Happy birthday to you.

Happy birthday to you.

Happy birthday, Big Daddy —

(Some sing: "Dear, Big Daddy!")

Happy birthday to you.
(Some sing: "How old are you?")
(Mae has come down center and is organizing her children like a chorus.
She gives them a barely audible: "One, two, three!" and they are off in
the new tune.)
CHILDREN: Skinamarinka — dinka — dink
   Skinamarinka — do
   We love you.
   Skinamarinka — dinka — dink
   Skinamarinka — do
(All together, they turn to Big Daddy.)
   Big Daddy, you!
(They turn back front, like a musical comedy chorus.)
   We love you in the morning;
   We love you in the night.
   We love you when we're with you,
   And we love you out of sight.
   Skinamarinka — dinka — dink
   Skinamarinka — do.
(Mae turns to Big Mama.)
   Big Mama, too!
(Big Mama bursts into tears. The Negroes leave.)
BIG DADDY: Now Ida, what the hell is the matter with you?
MAE: She's just so happy.
BIG MAMA: I'm just so happy, Big Daddy, I have to cry or something.
(Sudden and loud in the hush:)
   Brick, do you know the wonderful news that Doc Baugh got from
   the clinic about Big Daddy? Big Daddy's one hundred per cent!
MARGARET: Isn't that wonderful?
BIG MAMA: He's just one hundred per cent. Passed the examination with
   flying colors. Now that we know there's nothing wrong with Big Daddy
   but a spastic colon, I can tell you something. I was worried sick, half
   out of my mind, for fear that Big Daddy might have a thing like —
(Margaret cuts through this speech, jumping up and exclaiming
shrilly:)
MARGARET: Brick, honey, aren't you going to give Big Daddy his birthday
   present?
(Passing by him, she snatches his liquor glass from him.
(She picks up a fancily wrapped package.)
   Here it is, Big Daddy, this is from Brick!
BIG MAMA: This is the biggest birthday Big Daddy's ever had, a hundred
   presents and bushels of telegrams from —
MAE: *(At same time)* What is it, Brick?
GOOPER: I bet 500 to 50 that Brick don't *know* what it is.
BIG MAMA: The fun of presents is not knowing what they are till you open
   the package. Open your present, Big Daddy.
BIG DADDY: Open it you'self. I want to ask Brick somethin! Come here,
   Brick.
MARGARET: Big Daddy's callin' you, Brick.
(She is opening the package.)

BRICK: Tell Big Daddy I'm crippled.

BIG DADDY: I see you're crippled. I want to know how you got crippled.

MARGARET: *(Making diversionary tactics)* Oh, look, oh, look, why, it's a cashmere robe!

(She holds the robe up for all to see.)

MAE: You sound surprised, Maggie.

MARGARET: I never saw one before.

MAE: That's funny. — *Hah!*

MARGARET: *(Turning on her fiercely, with a brilliant smile)* Why is it funny? All my family ever had was family — and luxuries such as cashmere robes still surprise me!

BIG DADDY: *(Ominously)* Quiet!

MAE: *(Heedless in her fury)* I don't see how you could be so surprised when you bought it yourself at Loewenstein's in Memphis last Saturday. You know how I know?

BIG DADDY: I said, Quiet!

MAE: — I know because the salesgirl that sold it to you waited on me and said, Oh, Mrs. Pollitt, your sister-in-law just bought a cashmere robe for your husband's father!

MARGARET: Sister Woman! Your talents are wasted as a housewife and mother, you really ought to be with the FBI or —

BIG DADDY: QUIET!

(Reverend Tooker's reflexes are slower than the others'. He finishes a sentence after the bellow.)

REVEREND TOOKER: *(To Doc Baugh)* — the Stork and the Reaper are running neck and neck!

(He starts to laugh gaily when he notices the silence and Big Daddy's glare. His laugh dies falsely.)

BIG DADDY: Preacher, I hope I'm not butting in on more talk about memorial stained-glass windows, am I, Preacher?

(Reverend Tooker laughs feebly, then coughs dryly in the embarrassed silence.)

Preacher?

BIG MAMA: Now, Big Daddy, don't you pick on Preacher!

BIG DADDY: *(Raising his voice)* You ever hear that expression all hawk and no spit? You bring that expression to mind with that little dry cough of yours, all hawk an' no spit . . .

(The pause is broken only by a short startled laugh from Margaret, the only one there who is conscious of and amused by the grotesque.)

MAE: *(Raising her arms and jangling her bracelets)* I wonder if the mosquitoes are active tonight?

BIG DADDY: What's that, Little Mama? Did you make some remark?

MAE: Yes, I said I wondered if the mosquitoes would eat us alive if we went out on the gallery for a while.

BIG DADDY: Well, if they do, I'll have your bones pulverized for fertilizer!

BIG MAMA: *(Quickly)* Last week we had an airplane spraying the place and I think it done some good, at least I haven't had a —

BIG DADDY: *(Cutting her speech)* Brick, they tell me, if what they tell me is true, that you done some jumping last night on the high school athletic field?

BIG MAMA: Brick, Big Daddy is talking to you, son.

BRICK: *(Smiling vaguely over his drink)* What was that, Big Daddy?

BIG DADDY: They said you done some jumping on the high school track field last night.

BRICK: That's what they told me, too.

BIG DADDY: Was it jumping or humping that you were doing out there? What were you doing out there at three A.M., layin' a woman on that cinder track?

BIG MAMA: Big Daddy, you are off the sick-list, now, and I'm not going to excuse you for talkin' so —

BIG DADDY: Quiet!

BIG MAMA: — nasty in front of Preacher and —

BIG DADDY: *QUIET!* — I ast you, Brick, if you was cuttin' you'self a piece o' poon-tang last night on that cinder track? I thought maybe you were chasin' poon-tang on that track an' tripped over something in the heat of the chase — 'sthat it?

(Gooper laughs, loud and false, others nervously following suit. Big Mama stamps her foot, and purses her lips, crossing to Mae and whispering something to her as Brick meets his father's hard, intent, grinning stare with a slow, vague smile that he offers all situations from behind the screen of his liquor.)

BRICK: No, sir, I don't think so . . .

MAE: *(At the same time, sweetly)* Reverend Tooker, let's you and I take a stroll on the widow's walk.

(She and the preacher go out on the gallery as Big Daddy says:)

BIG DADDY: Then what the hell were you doing out there at three o'clock in the morning?

BRICK: Jumping the hurdles, Big Daddy, runnin' and jumpin' the hurdles, but those high hurdles have gotten too high for me, now.

BIG DADDY: Cause you was drunk?

BRICK: *(His vague smile fading a little)* Sober I wouldn't have tried to jump the *low* ones . . .

BIG MAMA: *(Quickly)* Big Daddy, blow out the candles on your birthday cake!

MARGARET: *(At the same time)* I want to propose a toast to Big Daddy Pollitt on his sixty-fifth birthday, the biggest cotton-planter in —

BIG DADDY: *(Bellowing with fury and disgust)* I told you to stop it, now stop it, quit this —!

BIG MAMA: *(Coming in front of Big Daddy with the cake)* Big Daddy, I will not allow you to talk that way, not even on your birthday, I —

BIG DADDY: I'll talk like I want to on my birthday, Ida, or any other goddam day of the year and anybody here that don't like it knows what they can do!

BIG MAMA: You don't mean that!

BIG DADDY: What makes you think I don't mean it?

(Meanwhile various discreet signals have been exchanged and Gooper has also gone out on the gallery.)

BIG MAMA: I just know you don't mean it.

BIG DADDY: You don't know a goddam thing and you never did!

BIG MAMA: Big Daddy, you don't mean that.

BIG DADDY: Oh, yes, I do, oh, yes, I do, I mean it! I put up with a whole lot of crap around here because I thought I was dying. And you thought I was dying and you started taking over, well, you can stop taking over now, Ida, because I'm not gonna die, you can just stop now this business of taking over because you're not taking over because I'm not dying. I went through the laboratory and the goddam exploratory operation and there's nothing wrong with me but a spastic colon. And I'm not dying of cancer which you thought I was dying of. Ain't that so? Didn't you think that I was dying of cancer, Ida?
(Almost everybody is out on the gallery but the two old people glaring at each other across the blazing cake.
(Big Mama's chest heaves and she presses a fat fist to her mouth.
(Big Daddy continues, hoarsely:)
    Ain't that so, Ida? Didn't you have an idea I was dying of cancer and now you could take control of this place and everything on it? I got that impression, I seemed to get that impression. Your loud voice everywhere, your fat old body butting in here and there!
BIG MAMA: Hush! The Preacher!
BIG DADDY: Rut the goddam preacher!
(Big Mama gasps loudly and sits down on the sofa which is almost too small for her.)
    Did you hear what I said? I said rut the goddam preacher!
(Somebody closes the gallery doors from outside just as there is a burst of fireworks and excited cries from the children.)
BIG MAMA: I never seen you act like this before and I can't think what's got in you!
BIG DADDY: I went through all that laboratory and operation and all just so I would know if you or me was boss here! Well, now it turns out that I am and you ain't — and that's my birthday present — and my cake and champagne! — because for three years now you been gradually taking over. Bossing. Talking. Sashaying your fat old body around the place I made! I made this place! I was overseer on it! I was the overseer on the old Straw and Ochello plantation. I quit school at ten! I quit school at ten years old and went to work like a nigger in the fields. And I rose to be overseer of the Straw and Ochello plantation. And old Straw died and I was Ochello's partner and the place got bigger and bigger and bigger and bigger and bigger! I did all that myself with no goddam help from you, and now you think you're just about to take over. Well, I am just about to tell you that you are not just about to take over, you are not just about to take over a God damn thing. Is that clear to you, Ida? Is that very plain to you, now? Is that understood completely? I been through the laboratory from A to Z. I've had the goddam exploratory operation, and nothing is wrong with me but a spastic colon — made spastic, I guess, by *disgust!* By all the goddam lies and liars that I have had to put up with, and all the goddam hypocrisy that I lived with all these forty years that we been livin' together! Hey! Ida!! Blow out the candles on the birthday cake! Purse up your lips and draw a deep breath and blow out the goddam candles on the cake!
BIG MAMA: Oh, Big Daddy, oh, oh, oh, Big Daddy!

BIG DADDY: What's the matter with you?

BIG MAMA: *In all these years you never believed that I loved you??*

BIG DADDY: Huh?

BIG MAMA: *And I did, I did so much, I did love you!* — I even loved your hate and your hardness, Big Daddy!

(She sobs and rushes awkwardly out onto the gallery.)

BIG DADDY: *(To himself)* Wouldn't it be funny if that was true . . .

(A pause is followed by a burst of light in the sky from the fireworks.)
BRICK! HEY, BRICK!

(He stands over his blazing birthday cake.

(After some moments, Brick hobbles in on his crutch, holding his glass.

(Margaret follows him with a bright, anxious smile.)

I didn't call you, Maggie. I called Brick.

MARGARET: I'm just delivering him to you.

(She kisses Brick on the mouth which he immediately wipes with the back of his hand. She flies girlishly back out. Brick and his father are alone.)

BIG DADDY: Why did you do that?

BRICK: Do what, Big Daddy?

BIG DADDY: Wipe her kiss off your mouth like she'd spit on you.

BRICK: I don't know. I wasn't conscious of it.

BIG DADDY: That woman of yours has a better shape on her than Gooper's but somehow or other they got the same look about them.

BRICK: What sort of look is that, Big Daddy?

BIG DADDY: I don't know how to describe it but it's the same look.

BRICK: They don't look peaceful, do they?

BIG DADDY: No, they sure in hell don't.

BRICK: They look nervous as cats?

BIG DADDY: That's right, they look nervous as cats.

BRICK: Nervous as a couple of cats on a hot tin roof?

BIG DADDY: That's right, boy, they look like a couple of cats on a hot tin roof. It's funny that you and Gooper being so different would pick out the same type of woman.

BRICK: Both of us married into society, Big Daddy.

BIG DADDY: Crap . . . I wonder what gives them both that look?

BRICK: Well. They're sittin' in the middle of a big piece of land, Big Daddy, twenty-eight thousand acres is a pretty big piece of land and so they're squaring off on it, each determined to knock off a bigger piece of it than the other whenever you let it go.

BIG DADDY: I got a surprise for those women. I'm not gonna let it go for a long time yet if that's what they're waiting for.

BRICK: That's right, Big Daddy. You just sit tight and let them scratch each other's eyes out . . .

BIG DADDY: You bet your life I'm going to sit tight on it and let those sons of bitches scratch their eyes out, ha ha ha . . .

But Gooper's wife's a good breeder, you got to admit she's fertile. Hell, at supper tonight she had them all at the table and they had to put a couple of extra leafs in the table to make room for them, she's got five head of them, now, and another one's comin'.

BRICK: Yep, number six is comin' . . .

BIG DADDY: Brick, you know, I swear to God, I don't know the way it happens?

BRICK: The way what happens, Big Daddy?

BIG DADDY: You git a piece of land, by hook or crook, an' things start growin' on it, things accumulate on it, and the first thing you know it's completely out of hand, completely out of hand!

BRICK: Well, they say nature hates a vacuum, Big Daddy.

BIG DADDY: That's what they say, but sometimes I think that a vacuum is a hell of a lot better than some of the stuff that nature replaces it with.

Is someone out there by that door?

BRICK: Yep.

BIG DADDY: Who?

(He has lowered his voice.)

BRICK: Someone int'rested in what we say to each other.

BIG DADDY: Gooper? — *GOOPER!*

(After a discreet pause, Mae appears in the gallery door.)

MAE: Did you call Gooper, Big Daddy?

BIG DADDY: Aw, it was you.

MAE: Do you want Gooper, Big Daddy?

BIG DADDY: No, and I don't want you. I want some privacy here, while I'm having a confidential talk with my son Brick. Now it's too hot in here to close them doors, but if I have to close those rutten doors in order to have a private talk with my son Brick, just let me know and I'll close 'em. Because I hate eavesdroppers, I don't like any kind of sneakin' an' spyin'.

MAE: Why, Big Daddy —

BIG DADDY: You stood on the wrong side of the moon, it threw your shadow!

MAE: I was just —

BIG DADDY: You was just nothing but *spyin'* an' you *know* it!

MAE: *(Begins to sniff and sob)* Oh, Big Daddy, you're so unkind for some reason to those that really love you!

BIG DADDY: Shut up, shut up, shut up! I'm going to move you and Gooper out of that room next to this! It's none of your goddam business what goes on in here at night between Brick an' Maggie. You listen at night like a couple of rutten peek-hole spies and go and give a report on what you hear to Big Mama an' she comes to me and says they say such and such and so and so about what they heard goin' on between Brick an' Maggie, and Jesus, it makes me sick. I'm goin' to move you an' Gooper out of that room, I can't stand sneakin' an' spyin', it makes me sick . . .

(Mae throws back her head and rolls her eyes heavenward and extends her arms as if invoking God's pity for this unjust martyrdom; then she presses a handkerchief to her nose and flies from the room with a loud swish of skirts.)

BRICK: *(Now at the liquor cabinet)* They listen, do they?

BIG DADDY: Yeah. They listen and give reports to Big Mama on what goes on in here between you and Maggie. They say that —

(He stops as if embarrassed.)

— You won't sleep with her, that you sleep on the sofa. Is that

true or not true? If you don't like Maggie, get rid of Maggie! — what
are you doin' there now?

BRICK: Fresh'nin' up my drink.

BIG DADDY: Son, you know you got a real liquor problem?

BRICK: Yes, sir, yes, I know.

BIG DADDY: Is that why you quit sports-announcing, because of this liquor
problem?

BRICK: Yes, sir, yes, sir, I guess so.

*(He smiles vaguely and amiably at his father across his replenished
drink.)*

BIG DADDY: Son, don't guess about it, it's too important.

BRICK: *(Vaguely)* Yes, sir.

BIG DADDY: And listen to me, don't look at the damn chandelier . . .

(Pause. Big Daddy's voice is husky.)

— Somethin' else we picked up at th' big fire sale in Europe.

(Another pause.)

Life is important. There's nothing else to hold onto. A man that
drinks is throwing his life away. Don't do it, hold onto your life. There's
nothing else to hold onto . . .

Sit down over here so we don't have to raise our voices, the walls
have ears in this place.

BRICK: *(Hobbling over to sit on the sofa beside him)* All right, Big Daddy.

BIG DADDY: Quit! — how'd that come about? Some disappointment?

BRICK: I don't know. Do you?

BIG DADDY: I'm askin' you, God damn it! How in hell would I know if you
don't?

BRICK: I just got out there and found that I had a mouth full of cotton. I
was always two or three beats behind what was goin' on on the field
and so I —

BIG DADDY: Quit!

BRICK: *(Amiably)* Yes, quit.

BIG DADDY: Son?

BRICK: Huh?

BIG DADDY: *(Inhales loudly and deeply from his cigar; then bends suddenly
a little forward, exhaling loudly and raising a hand to his forehead)*
— Whew! — ha ha! — I took in too much smoke, it made me a little
light-headed . . .

(The mantel-clock chimes.)

Why is it so *damn* hard for people to talk?

BRICK: Yeah . . .

(The clock goes on sweetly chiming till it has completed the stroke of ten.)

— Nice peaceful-soundin' clock, I like to hear it all night . . .

*(He slides low and comfortable on the sofa; Big Daddy sits up straight
and rigid with some unspoken anxiety. All his gestures are tense and
jerky as he talks. He wheezes and pants and sniffs through his nervous
speech, glancing quickly, shyly, from time to time, at his son.)*

BIG DADDY: We got that clock the summer we wint to Europe, me an' Big
Mama on that damn Cook's Tour, never had such an awful time in
my life, I'm tellin' you, son, those gooks over there, they gouge your
eyeballs out in their grand hotels. And Big Mama bought more stuff

than you could haul in a couple of boxcars, that's no crap. Everywhere she wint on this whirlwind tour, she bought, bought, bought. Why, half that stuff she bought is still crated up in the cellar, under water last spring!
(He laughs.)
That Europe is nothin' on earth but a great big auction, that's all it is, that bunch of old worn-out places, it's just a big fire-sale, the whole rutten thing, an' Big Mama wint wild in it, why, you couldn't hold that woman with a mule's harness! Bought, bought, bought! — lucky I'm a rich man, yes siree, Bob, an' half that stuff is mildewin' in th' basement. It's lucky I'm a rich man, it sure is lucky, well I'm a rich man, Brick, yep, I'm a mighty rich man.
(His eyes light up for a moment.)
Y'know how much I'm worth? Guess, Brick! Guess how much I'm worth!
(Brick smiles vaguely over his drink.)
Close on ten million in cash an' blue chip stocks, outside, mind you, of twenty-eight thousand acres of the richest land this side of the valley Nile!
(A puff and crackle and the night sky blooms with an eerie greenish glow. Children shriek on the gallery.)
But a man can't buy his life with it, he can't buy back his life with it when his life has been spent, that's one thing not offered in the Europe fire-sale or in the American markets or any markets on earth, a man can't buy his life with it, he can't buy back his life when his life is finished . . .
That's a sobering thought, a very sobering thought, and that's a thought that I was turning over in my head, over and over and over — until today.
I'm wiser and sadder, Brick, for this experience which I just gone through. They's one thing else that I remember in Europe.
BRICK: What is that, Big Daddy?
BIG DADDY: The hills around Barcelona in the country of Spain and the children running over those bare hills in their bare skins beggin' like starvin' dogs with howls and screeches, and how fat the priests are on the streets of Barcelona, so many of them and so fat and so pleasant, ha ha! — Y'know I could feed that country? I got money enough to feed that goddam country, but the human animal is a selfish beast and I don't reckon the money I passed out there to those howling children in the hills around Barcelona would more than upholster one of the chairs in this room, I mean pay to put a new cover on this chair!
Hell, I threw them money like you'd scatter feed corn for chickens, I threw money at them just to get rid of them long enough to climb back into th' car and — drive away . . .
And then in Morocco, them Arabs, why, prostitution begins at four or five, that's no exaggeration, why, I remember one day in Marrakech, that old walled Arab city, I sat on a broken-down wall to have a cigar, it was fearful hot there and this Arab woman stood in the road and looked at me till I was embarrassed, she stood stock still in the dusty hot road and looked at me till I was embarrassed. But listen to

this. She had a naked child with her, a little naked girl with her, barely able to toddle, and after a while she set this child on the ground and give her a push and whispered something to her. This child come toward me, barely able t' walk, come toddling up to me and —
Jesus, it makes you sick t' remember a thing like this! It stuck out its hand and tried to unbutton my trousers! That child was not yet five! Can you believe me? Or do you think that I am making this up? I wint back to the hotel and said to Big Mama, Git packed! We're clearing out of this country . . .

BRICK: Big Daddy, you're on a talkin' jag tonight.

BIG DADDY: *(Ignoring this remark)* Yes, sir, that's how it is, the human animal is a beast that dies but the fact that he's dying don't give him pity for others, no, sir, it —
— Did you say something?

BRICK: Yes.

BIG DADDY: What?

BRICK: Hand me over that crutch so I can get up.

BIG DADDY: Where you goin'?

BRICK: I'm takin' a little short trip to Echo Spring.

BIG DADDY: To where?

BRICK: Liquor cabinet . . .

BIG DADDY: Yes, sir, boy —
(He hands Brick the crutch.)
— the human animal is a beast that dies and if he's got money he buys and buys and buys and I think the reason he buys everything he can buy is that in the back of his mind he has the crazy hope that one of his purchases will be life everlasting! — Which it never can be . . . The human animal is a beast that —

BRICK: *(At the liquor cabinet)* Big Daddy, you sure are shootin' th' breeze here tonight.
(There is a pause and voices are heard outside.)

BIG DADDY: I been quiet here lately, spoke not a word, just sat and stared into space. I had something heavy weighing on my mind but tonight that load was took off me. That's why I'm talking. — The sky looks diff'rent to me . . .

BRICK: You know what I like to hear most?

BIG DADDY: What?

BRICK: Solid quiet. Perfect unbroken quiet.

BIG DADDY: Why?

BRICK: Because it's more peaceful.

BIG DADDY: Man, you'll hear a lot of that in the grave.
(He chuckles agreeably.)

BRICK: Are you through talkin' to me?

BIG DADDY: Why are you so anxious to shut me up?

BRICK: Well, sir, every so often you say to me, Brick, I want to have a talk with you, but when we talk, it never materializes. Nothing is said. You sit in a chair and gas about this and that and I look like I listen. I try to look like I listen, but I don't listen, not much. Communication is — awful hard between people an' — somehow between you and me, it just don't —

BIG DADDY: Have you ever been scared? I mean have you ever felt down-
right terror of something?
(He gets up.)
    Just one moment. I'm going to close these doors . . .
(He closes doors on gallery as if he were going to tell an important secret.)
BRICK: What?
BIG DADDY: Brick?
BRICK: Huh?
BIG DADDY: Son, I thought I had it!
BRICK: Had what? Had what, Big Daddy?
BIG DADDY: Cancer!
BRICK: Oh . . .
BIG DADDY: I thought the old man made out of bones had laid his cold
and heavy hand on my shoulder!
BRICK: Well, Big Daddy, you kept a tight mouth about it.
BIG DADDY: A pig squeals. A man keeps a tight mouth about it, in spite
of a man not having a pig's advantage.
BRICK: What advantage is that?
BIG DADDY: Ignorance — or mortality — is a comfort. A man don't have
that comfort, he's the only living thing that conceives of death, that
knows what it is. The others go without knowing which is the way
that anything living should go, go without knowing, without any
knowledge of it, and yet a pig squeals, but a man sometimes, he can
keep a tight mouth about it. Sometimes he —
(There is a deep, smoldering ferocity in the old man.)
— can keep a tight mouth about it. I wonder if —
BRICK: What, Big Daddy?
BIG DADDY: A whiskey highball would injure this spastic condition?
BRICK: No, sir, it might do it good.
BIG DADDY: *(Grins suddenly, wolfishly) Jesus, I can't tell you! The sky is*
open! Christ, it's open again! It's open, boy, it's open!
(Brick looks down at his drink.)
BRICK: You feel better, Big Daddy?
BIG DADDY: Better? Hell! I can breathe! — All of my life I been like a
doubled up fist . . .
(He pours a drink.)
    — Poundin', smashin', drivin'! — now I'm going to loosen these
doubled up hands and touch things *easy* with them . . .
(He spreads his hands as if caressing the air.)
    You know what I'm contemplating?
BRICK: *(Vaguely)* No, sir. What are you contemplating?
BIG DADDY: Ha ha! — *Pleasure!* — pleasure with *women!*
(Brick's smile fades a little but lingers.)
    Brick, this stuff burns me! —
    — Yes, boy. I'll tell you something that you might not guess. I
still have desire for women and this is my sixty-fifth birthday.
BRICK: I think that's mighty remarkable, Big Daddy.
BIG DADDY: Remarkable?
BRICK: *Admirable,* Big Daddy.
BIG DADDY: You're damn right it is, remarkable and admirable both. I

realize now that I never had me enough. I let many chances slip by
because of scruples about it, scruples, convention — crap . . . All that
stuff is bull, bull, bull! — It took the shadow of death to make me see
it. Now that shadow's lifted, I'm going to cut loose and have, what is
it they call it, have me a — ball!

BRICK: A ball, huh?

BIG DADDY: That's right, a ball, a ball! Hell! — I slept with Big Mama
till, let's see, five years ago, till I was sixty and she was fifty-eight,
and never even liked her, never did!

*(The phone has been ringing down the hall. Big Mama enters, exclaim-
ing:)*

BIG MAMA: Don't you men hear that phone ring? I heard it way out on
the gall'ry.

BIG DADDY: There's five rooms off this front gall'ry that you could go
through. Why do you go through this one?

(Big Mama makes a playful face as she bustles out the hall door.)

Hunh! — Why, when Big Mama goes out of a room, I can't remember what that woman looks like, but when Big Mama comes back
into the room, boy, then I see what she looks like, and I wish I didn't!

*(Bends over laughing at this joke till it hurts his guts and he straightens
with a grimace. The laugh subsides to a chuckle as he puts the liquor
glass a little distrustfully down on the table.*

(Brick has risen and hobbled to the gallery doors.)

Hey! Where you goin'?

BRICK: Out for a breather.

BIG DADDY: Not yet you ain't. Stay here till this talk is finished, young
fellow.

BRICK: I thought it was finished, Big Daddy.

BIG DADDY: It ain't even begun.

BRICK: My mistake. Excuse me. I just wanted to feel that river breeze.

BIG DADDY: Turn on the ceiling fan and set back down in that chair.

(Big Mama's voice rises, carrying down the hall.)

BIG MAMA: Miss Sally, you're a case! You're a caution, Miss Sally. Why
didn't you give me a chance to explain it to you?

BIG DADDY: Jesus, she's talking to my old maid sister again.

BIG MAMA: Well, goodbye, now, Miss Sally. You come down real soon, Big
Daddy's dying to see you! Yaisss, goodbye, Miss Sally . . .

*(She hangs up and bellows with mirth. Big Daddy groans and covers
his ears as she approaches.*

(Bursts in:)

Big Daddy, that was Miss Sally callin' from Memphis again! You
know what she done, Big Daddy? She called her doctor in Memphis
to git him to tell her what that spastic things is! Ha-*HAAAA!* — And
called back to tell me how relieved she was that — Hey! Let me in!

(Big Daddy has been holding the door half closed against her.)

BIG DADDY: Naw I ain't. I told you not to come and go through this room.
You just back out and go through those five other rooms.

BIG MAMA: Big Daddy? Big Daddy? Oh, Big Daddy! — You didn't mean
those things you said to me, did you?

(He shuts door firmly against her but she still calls.)

Sweetheart? Sweetheart? Big Daddy? You didn't mean those awful things you said to me? — I know you didn't. I know you didn't mean those things in your heart . . .
(The childlike voice fades with a sob and her heavy footsteps retreat down the hall. Brick has risen once more on his crutches and starts for the gallery again.)

BIG DADDY: All I ask of that woman is that she leave me alone. But she can't admit to herself that she makes me sick. That comes of having slept with her too many years. Should of quit much sooner but that old woman she never got enough of it — and I was good in bed . . . I never should of wasted so much of it on her . . . They say you got just so many and each one is numbered. Well, I got a few left in me, a few, and I'm going to pick me a good one to spend 'em on! I'm going to pick me a choice one, I don't care how much she costs, I'll smother her in — minks! Ha ha! I'll strip her naked and smother her in minks and choke her with diamonds! Ha ha! I'll strip her naked and choke her with diamonds and smother her with minks and hump her from hell to breakfast. *Ha aha ha ha ha!*

MAE: *(Gaily at door)* Who's that laughin' in here?

GOOPER: Is Big Daddy laughin' in there?

BIG DADDY: Crap! — them two — *drips* . . .
(He goes over and touches Brick's shoulder.)
Yes, son. Brick, boy. — I'm — *happy!* I'm happy, son, I'm happy!
(He chokes a little and bites his under lip, pressing his head quickly, shyly against his son's head and then, coughing with embarrassment, goes uncertainly back to the table where he set down the glass. He drinks and makes a grimace as it burns his guts. Brick sighs and rises with effort.)
What makes you so restless? Have you got ants in your britches?

BRICK: Yes, sir . . .

BIG DADDY: Why?

BRICK: — Something — hasn't happened . . .

BIG DADDY: Yeah? What is that!

BRICK: *(Sadly)* — the click . . .

BIG DADDY: Did you say click?

BRICK: Yes, click.

BIG DADDY: What click?

BRICK: A click that I get in my head that makes me peaceful.

BIG DADDY: I sure in hell don't know what you're talking about, but it disturbs me.

BRICK: It's just a mechanical thing.

BIG DADDY: What is a mechanical thing?

BRICK: This click that I get in my head that makes me peaceful. I got to drink till I get it. It's just a mechanical thing, something like a — like a — like a —

BIG DADDY: Like a —

BRICK: Switch clicking off in my head, turning the hot light off and the cool night on and —
(He looks up, smiling sadly.)
— all of a sudden there's — peace!

BIG DADDY: *(Whistles long and soft with astonishment; he goes back to Brick and clasps his son's two shoulders)* Jesus! I didn't know it had gotten that bad with you. Why, boy, you're — *alcoholic!*

BRICK: That's the truth, Big Daddy. I'm alcoholic.

BIG DADDY: This shows how I — let things go!

BRICK: I have to hear that little click in my head that makes me peaceful. Usually I hear it sooner than this, sometimes as early as — noon, but —

— Today it's — dilatory . . .

— I just haven't got the right level of alcohol in my bloodstream yet!

(This last statement is made with energy as he freshens his drink.)

BIG DADDY: Uh-huh. Expecting death made me blind. I didn't have no idea that a son of mine was turning into a drunkard under my nose.

BRICK: *(Gently)* Well, now you do, Big Daddy, the news has penetrated.

BIG DADDY: UH-huh, yes, now I do, the news has — penetrated . . .

BRICK: And so if you'll excuse me —

BIG DADDY: No, I won't excuse you.

BRICK:— I'd better sit by myself till I hear that click in my head, it's just a mechanical thing but it don't happen except when I'm alone or talking to no one . . .

BIG DADDY: You got a long, long time to sit still, boy, and talk to no one, but now you're talkin' to me. At least I'm talking to you. And you set there and listen until I tell you the conversation is over!

BRICK: But this talk is like all the others we've ever had together in our lives! It's nowhere, nowhere! — it's — it's *painful,* Big Daddy . . .

BIG DADDY: All right, then let it be painful, but don't you move from that chair! — I'm going to remove that crutch . . .

(He seizes the crutch and tosses it across room.)

BRICK: I can hop on one foot, and if I fall, I can crawl!

BIG DADDY: If you ain't careful you're gonna crawl off this plantation and then, by Jesus, you'll have to hustle your drinks along Skid Row!

BRICK: That'll come, Big Daddy.

BIG DADDY: Naw, it won't. You're my son and I'm going to straighten you out; now that *I'm* straightened out, I'm going to straighten out you!

BRICK: Yeah?

BIG DADDY: Today the report come in from Ochsner Clinic. Y'know what they told me?

(His face glows with triumph.)

The only thing that they could detect with all the instruments of science in that great hospital is a little spastic condition of the colon! And nerves torn to pieces by all that worry about it.

(A little girl bursts into room with a sparkler clutched in each fist, hops and shrieks like a monkey gone mad and rushes back out again as Big Daddy strikes at her.

(Silence. The two men stare at each other. A woman laughs gaily outside.)

I want you to know I breathed a sigh of relief almost as powerful as the Vicksburg tornado!

BRICK: You weren't ready to go?

BIG DADDY: GO WHERE? — Crap . . .
— When you are gone from here, boy, you are long gone and no where! The human machine is not no different from the animal machine or the fish machine or the bird machine or the reptile machine or the insect machine! It's just a whole God damn lot more complicated and consequently more trouble to keep together. Yep. I thought I had it. The earth shook under my foot, the sky come down like the black lid of a kettle and I couldn't breathe! — Today!! — that lid was lifted, I drew my first free breath in — how many years? — *God! — three . . .*
(There is laughter outside, running footsteps, the soft, plushy sound and light of exploding rockets.
(Brick stares at him soberly for a long moment; then makes a sort of startled sound in his nostrils and springs up on one foot and hops across the room to grab his crutch, swinging on the furniture for support. He gets the crutch and flees as if in horror for the gallery. His father seizes him by the sleeve of his white silk pajamas.)
Stay here, you son of a bitch! — till I say go!
BRICK: I can't.
BIG DADDY: You sure in hell will, God damn it.
BRICK: No, I can't. We talk, you talk, in — circles! We get nowhere, nowhere! It's always the same, you say you want to talk to me and don't have a ruttin' thing to say to me!
BIG DADDY: Nothin' to say when I'm tellin' you I'm going to live when I thought I was dying?!
BRICK: Oh — *that!* — Is that what you have to say to me?
BIG DADDY: Why, you son of a bitch! Ain't that, ain't that — *important?!*
BRICK: Well, you said that, that's said, and now I —
BIG DADDY: Now you set back down.
BRICK: You're all balled up, you —
BIG DADDY: I ain't balled up!
BRICK: You are, you're all balled up!
BIG DADDY: Don't tell me what I am, you drunken whelp! I'm going to tear this coat sleeve off if you don't set down!
BRICK: Big Daddy —
BIG DADDY: Do what I tell you! I'm the boss here, now! I want you to know I'm back in the driver's seat now!
(Big Mama rushes in, clutching her great heaving bosom.)
What in hell do you want in here, big Mama?
BIG MAMA: Oh, Big Daddy! Why are you shouting like that? I just cain't stainnnnnnnd — it . . .
BIG DADDY: *(Raising the back of his hand above his head) GIT!* — outa here.
(She rushes back out, sobbing.)
BRICK: *(Softly, sadly) Christ . . .*
BIG DADDY: Yeah! Christ! — is right . . .
(Brick breaks loose and hobbles toward the gallery.
(Big Daddy jerks his crutch from under Brick so he steps with the injured ankle. He utters a hissing cry of anguish, clutches a chair and pulls it over on top of him on the floor.)
Son of a — tub of — hog fat . . .
BRICK: Big Daddy! Give me my crutch.

(Big Daddy throws the crutch out of reach.)
Give me that crutch, Big Daddy.
BIG DADDY: Why do you drink?
BRICK: Don't know, give me my crutch!
BIG DADDY: You better think why you drink or give up drinking!
BRICK: Will you please give me my crutch so I can get up off this floor?
BIG DADDY: First you answer my question. Why do you drink? Why are you throwing your life away, boy, like somethin' disgusting you picked up on the street?
BRICK: *(Getting onto his knees)* Big Daddy, I'm in pain, I stepped on that foot.
BIG DADDY: Good! I'm glad you're not too numb with the liquor in you to feel some pain!
BRICK: You — spilled my — drink . . .
BIG DADDY: I'll make a bargain with you. You tell me why you drink and I'll hand you one. I'll pour you the liquor myself and hand it to you.
BRICK: Why do I drink?
BIG DADDY: Yeah! Why?
BRICK: Give me a drink and I'll tell you.
BIG DADDY: Tell me first!
BRICK: I'll tell you in one word.
BIG DADDY: What word?
BRICK: DISGUST!
(The clock chimes softly, sweetly. Big Daddy gives it a short, outraged glance.)
Now how about that drink?
BIG DADDY: What are you disgusted with? You got to tell me that, first. Otherwise being disgusted don't make no sense!
BRICK: Give me my crutch.
BIG DADDY: You heard me, you got to tell me what I asked you first.
BRICK: I told you, I said to kill my disgust!
BIG DADDY: DISGUST WITH WHAT?!
BRICK: You strike a hard bargain.
BIG DADDY: What are you disgusted with? — an' I'll pass you the liquor.
BRICK: I can hop on one foot, and if I fall, I can crawl.
BIG DADDY: You want liquor that bad?
BRICK: *(Dragging himself up, clinging to bedstead)* Yeah, I want it that bad.
BIG DADDY: If I give you a drink, will you tell me what it is you're disgusted with, Brick?
BRICK: Yes, sir, I will try to.
(The old man pours him a drink and solemnly passes it to him.)
(There is silence as Brick drinks.)
Have you ever heard the word "mendacity"?
BIG DADDY: Sure. Mendacity is one of them five dollar words that cheap politicians throw back and forth at each other.
BRICK: You know what it means?
BIG DADDY: Don't it mean lying and liars?
BRICK: Yes, sir, lying and liars.
BIG DADDY: Has someone been lying to you?
CHILDREN: *(Chanting in chorus offstage)*
We want Big Dad-dee!

We want Big Dad-dee!
(Gooper appears in the gallery door.)
GOOPER: Big Daddy, the kiddies are shouting for you out there.
BIG DADDY: *(Fiercely)* Keep out, Gooper!
GOOPER: 'Scuse *me!*
(Big Daddy slams the doors after Gooper.)
BIG DADDY: Who's been lying to you, has Margaret been lying to you, has your wife been lying to you about something, Brick?
BRICK: Not her. That wouldn't matter.
BIG DADDY: Then who's been lying to you, and what about?
BRICK: No one single person and no one lie . . .
BIG DADDY: Then what, what then, for Christ's sake?
BRICK: — The whole, the whole — thing . . .
BIG DADDY: Why are you rubbing your head? You got a headache?
BRICK: No, I'm tryin' to —
BIG DADDY: — Concentrate, but you can't because your brain's all soaked with liquor, is that the trouble? Wet brain!
(He snatches the glass from Brick's hand.)
 What do you know about this mendacity thing? Hell! I could write a book on it! Don't you know that? I could write a book on it and still not cover the subject? Well, I could, I could write a goddam book on it and still not cover the subject anywhere near enough!! — Think of all the lies I got to put up with! — Pretenses! Ain't that mendacity? Having to pretend stuff you don't think or feel or have any idea of? Having for instance to act like I care for Big Mama! — I haven't been able to stand the sight, sound, or smell of that woman for forty years now! — even when I *laid* her! — regular as a piston . . . Pretend to love that son of a bitch of a Gooper and his wife Mae and those five same screechers out there like parrots in a jungle? Jesus! Can't stand to look at 'em!
 Church! — it bores the Bejesus out of me but I go! — I go an' sit there and listen to the fool preacher!
 Clubs! — Elks! Masons! Rotary! — *crap!*
(A spasm of pain makes him clutch his belly. He sinks into a chair and his voice is softer and hoarser.)
 You I *do* like for some reason, did always have some kind of real feeling for — affection — respect — yes, always . . .
 You and being a success as a planter is all I ever had any devotion to in my whole life! — and that's the truth . . .
 I don't know why, but it is!
 I've lived with mendacity! — Why can't *you* live with it? Hell, you *got* to live with it, there's nothing *else* to *live* with except mendacity, is there?
BRICK: Yes, sir. Yes, sir there is something else that you can live with!
BIG DADDY: What?
BRICK: *(Lifting his glass)* This! — Liquor . . .
BIG DADDY: That's not living, that's dodging away from life.
BRICK: I want to dodge away from it.
BIG DADDY: Then why don't you kill yourself, man?
BRICK: I like to drink . . .

BIG DADDY: Oh, God, I can't talk to you . . .

BRICK: I'm sorry, Big Daddy.

BIG DADDY: Not as sorry as I am. I'll tell you something. A little while back when I thought my number was up —

(This speech should have torrential pace and fury.)

    — before I found out it was just this — spastic — colon, I thought about you. Should I or should I not, if the jig was up, give you this place when I go — since I hate Gooper an' Mae an' know that they hate me, and since all five same monkeys are little Maes an' Goopers. — And I thought, No — Then I thought, Yes! — I couldn't make up my mind. I have Gooper and his five same monkeys and that bitch Mae! Why should I turn over twenty-eight thousand acres of the richest land this side of the valley Nile to not my kind? — But why in hell, on the other hand, Brick — should I subsidize a goddam fool on the bottle? — Liked or not liked, well, maybe even — *loved!* — Why should I do that? — Subsidize worthless behavior? Rot? Corruption?

BRICK: *(Smiling)* I understand.

BIG DADDY: Well, if you do, you're smarter than I am, God damn it, because I don't understand. And this I will tell you frankly. I didn't make up my mind at all on that question and still to this day I ain't made out no will! — Well, now I don't have to. The pressure is gone. I can just wait and see if you pull yourself together or if you don't.

BRICK: That's right, Big Daddy.

BIG DADDY: You sound like you thought I was kidding.

BRICK: *(Rising)* No, sir, I know you're not kidding.

BIG DADDY: But you don't care —?

BRICK: *(Hobbling toward the gallery door)* No, sir, I don't care . . .

    Now how about taking a look at your birthday fireworks and getting some of that cool breeze off the river?

(He stands in the gallery doorway as the night sky turns pink and green and gold with successive flashes of light.)

BIG DADDY: WAIT! — Brick . . .

(His voice drops. Suddenly there is something shy, almost tender, in his restraining gesture.)

    Don't let's — leave it like this, like them other talks we've had, we've always — talked around things, we've — just talked around things for some rutten reason. I don't know what, it's always like something was left not spoken, something avoided because neither of us was honest enough with the — other . . .

BRICK: I never lied to you, Big Daddy.

BIG DADDY: Did I ever to *you?*

BRICK: No, sir . . .

BIG DADDY: Then there is at least two people that never lied to each other.

BRICK: But we've never *talked* to each other.

BIG DADDY: We can *now.*

BRICK: Big Daddy, there don't seem to be anything much to say.

BIG DADDY: You say that you drink to kill your disgust with lying.

BRICK: You said to give you a reason.

BIG DADDY: Is liquor the only thing that'll kill this disgust?

BRICK: Now. Yes.

BIG DADDY: But not once, huh?

BRICK: Not when I was still young an' believing. A drinking man's someone who wants to forget he isn't still young an' believing.

BIG DADDY: Believing what?

BRICK: Believing . . .

BIG DADDY: Believing *what?*

BRICK: *(Stubbornly evasive)* Believing . . .

BIG DADDY: I don't know what the hell you mean by believing and I don't think you know what you mean by believing, but if you still got sports in your blood, go back to sports announcing and —

BRICK: Sit in a glass box watching games I can't play? Describing what I can't do while players do it? Sweating out their disgust and confusion in contests I'm not fit for? Drinkin' a coke, half bourbon, so I can stand it? That's no goddam good any more, no help — time just outran me, Big Daddy — got there first . . .

BIG DADDY: I think you're passing the buck.

BRICK: You know many drinkin' men?

BIG DADDY: *(With a slight, charming smile)* I have known a fair number of that species.

BRICK: Could any of them tell you why he drank?

BIG DADDY: Yep, you're passin' the buck to things like time and disgust with "mendacity" and — crap! — if you got to use that kind of language about a thing, it's ninety-proof bull, and I'm not buying any.

BRICK: I had to give you a reason to get a drink!

BIG DADDY: You started drinkin' when your friend Skipper died.

(Silence for five beats. Then Brick makes a startled movement, reaching for his crutch.)

BRICK: What are you suggesting?

BIG DADDY: I'm suggesting nothing.

(The shuffle and clop of Brick's rapid hobble away from his father's steady, grave attention.)

— But Gooper an' Mae suggested that there was something not right exactly in your —

BRICK: *(Stopping short downstage as if backed to a wall)* "Not right"?

BIG DADDY: Not, well, exactly *normal* in your friendship with —

BRICK: They suggested that, too? I thought that was Maggie's suggestion.

(Brick's detachment is at last broken through. His heart is accelerated; his forehead sweat-beaded; his breath becomes more rapid and his voice hoarse. The thing they're discussing, timidly and painfully on the side of Big Daddy, fiercely, violently on Brick's side, is the inadmissible thing that Skipper died to disavow between them. The fact that if it existed it had to be disavowed to "keep face" in the world they lived in, may be at the heart of the "mendacity" that Brick drinks to kill his disgust with. It may be the root of his collapse. Or maybe it is only a single manifestation of it, not even the most important. The bird that I hope to catch in the net of this play is not the solution of one man's psychological problem. I'm trying to catch the true quality of experience in a group of people, that cloudy, flickering, evanescent — fiercely charged! — interplay of live human beings in the thunder-cloud of a common crisis. Some mystery should be left in the revelation of charac-

ter in a play, just as a great deal of mystery is always left in the
revelation of character in life, even in one's own character to himself.
This does not absolve the playwright of his duty to observe and probe
as clearly and deeply as he legitimately can: but it should steer him
away from "pat" conclusions, facile definitions which make a play just
a play, not a snare for the truth of human experience.

(The following scene should be played with great concentration,
with most of the power leashed but palpable in what is left unspoken.)
Who else's suggestion is it, is it *yours?* How many others thought
that Skipper and I were —

BIG DADDY: *(Gently)* Now, hold on, hold on a minute, son. — I knocked
around in my time.

BRICK: What's that got to do with —

BIG DADDY: I said 'Hold on!' — I bummed, I bummed this country till I
was —

BRICK: Whose suggestion, who else's suggestion is it?

BIG DADDY: Slept in hobo jungles and railroad Y's and flophouses in all
cities before I —

BRICK: Oh, *you* think so, too, you call me your son and a queer. Oh! Maybe
that's why you put Maggie and me in this room that was Jack Straw's
and Peter Ochello's, in which that pair of old sisters slept in a double
bed where both of 'em died!

BIG DADDY: *Now just don't go throwing rocks at —*
*(Suddenly Reverend Tooker appears in the gallery doors, his head
slightly, playfully, fatuously cocked, with a practised clergyman's smile,
sincere as a bird-call blown on a hunter's whistle, the living embodiment
of the pious, conventional lie.*
*(Big Daddy gasps a little at this perfectly timed, but incongruous,
apparition.)*
— What're you lookin' for, Preacher?

REVEREND TOOKER: The gentleman's lavatory, ha ha! — heh, heh . . .

BIG DADDY: *(With strained courtesy)* — Go back out and walk down to the
other end of the gallery, Reverend Tooker, and use the bathroom
connected with my bedroom, and if you can't find it, ask them where
it is!

REVEREND TOOKER: Ah, thanks.
(He goes out with a deprecatory chuckle.)

BIG DADDY: It's hard to talk in this place . . .

BRICK: Son of a —!

BIG DADDY: *(Leaving a lot unspoken)* — I seen all things and understood
a lot of them, till 1910. Christ, the year that — I had worn my shoes
through, hocked my — I hopped off a yellow dog freight car half a
mile down the road, slept in a wagon of cotton outside the gin — Jack
Straw an' Peter Ochello took me in. Hired me to manage this place
which grew into this one. — When Jack Straw died — why, old Peter
Ochello quit eatin' like a dog does when its master's dead, and died, too!

BRICK: Christ!

BIG DADDY: I'm just saying I understand such —

BRICK: *(Violently)* Skipper is dead. I have not quit eating!

BIG DADDY: No, but you started drinking.

(Brick wheels on his crutch and hurls his glass across the room shouting.)
BRICK: YOU THINK SO, TOO?
BIG DADDY: *Shhh!*
(Footsteps run on the gallery. There are women's calls.
(Big Daddy goes toward the door.)
    Go way! — Just broke a glass . . .
(Brick is transformed, as if a quiet mountain blew suddenly up in volcanic flame.)
BRICK: You think so, too? You think so, too? You think me an' Skipper did, did, did! — *sodomy!* — together?
BIG DADDY: Hold —!
BRICK: That what you —
BIG DADDY: — *ON* — a minute!
BRICK: You think we did dirty things between us, Skipper an' —
BIG DADDY: Why are you shouting like that? Why are you —
BRICK: — Me, is that what you think of Skipper, is that —
BIG DADDY: — so excited? I don't think nothing. I don't know nothing. I'm simply telling you what —
BRICK: You think that Skipper and me were a pair of dirty old men?
BIG DADDY: Now that's —
BRICK: Straw? Ochello? A couple of —
BIG DADDY: Now just —
BRICK: — ducking sissies? Queers? Is that what you —
BIG DADDY: Shhh.
BRICK: — think?
(He loses his balance and pitches to his knees without noticing the pain. He grabs the bed and drags himself up.)
BIG DADDY: Jesus! — Whew . . . Grab my hand!
BRICK: Naw, I don't want your hand . . .
BIG DADDY: Well, I want yours. Git up!
(He draws him up, keeps an arm about him with concern and affection.)
    You broken out in a sweat! You're panting like you'd run a race with —
BRICK: *(Freeing himself from his father's hold)* Big Daddy, you shock me, Big Daddy, you, you — *shock* me! Talkin' so —
(He turns away from his father.)
    — casually! — about a — thing like that . . .
    — Don't you know how people *feel* about things like that? How, how *disgusted* they are by things like that? Why, at Ole Miss when it was discovered a pledge to our fraternity, Skipper's and mine, did a, *attempted* to do a, unnatural thing with —
    We not only dropped him like a hot rock! — We told him to git off the campus, and he did, he got! — All the way to —
(He halts, breathless.)
BIG DADDY: — Where?
BRICK: — North Africa, last I heard!
BIG DADDY: Well, I have come back from further away than that. I have just now returned from the other side of the moon, death's country, son, and I'm not easy to shock by anything here.

(He comes downstage and faces out.)
Always, anyhow, lived with too much space around me to be
infected by ideas of other people. One thing you can grow on a big
place more important than cotton! — is *tolerance!* — I grown it.
(He returns toward Brick.)
BRICK: Why can't exceptional friendship, *real, real, deep, deep friendship!*
between two men be respected as something clean and decent without
being thought of as —
BIG DADDY: It can, it is, for God's sake.
BRICK: — *Fairies* . . .
*(In his utterance of this word, we gauge the wide and profound reach
of the conventional mores he got from the world that crowned him with
early laurel.)*
BIG DADDY: I told Mae an' Gooper —
BRICK: Frig Mae and Gooper, frig all dirty lies and liars! — Skipper and
me had a clean, true thing between us! — had a clean friendship,
practically all our lives, till Maggie got the idea you're talking about.
Normal? No! — It was too rare to be normal, any true thing between
two people is too rare to be normal. Oh, once in a while he put his
hand on my shoulder or I'd put mine on his, oh, maybe even, when
we were touring the country in pro-football an' shared hotel-rooms
we'd reach across the space between the two beds and shake hands to
say goodnight, yeah, one or two times we —
BIG DADDY: Brick, nobody thinks that that's not normal!
BRICK: Well, they're mistaken, it was! It was a pure an' true thing an'
that's not normal.
*(They both stare straight at each other for a long moment. The tension
breaks and both turn away as if tired.)*
BIG DADDY: Yeah, it's — hard t' — talk . . .
BRICK: All right, then, let's — let it go . . .
BIG DADDY: Why did Skipper crack up? Why have you?
*(Brick looks back at his father again. He has already decided, without
knowing that he has made this decision, that he is going to tell his
father that he is dying of cancer. Only this could even the score between
them: one inadmissable thing in return for another.)*
BRICK: *(Ominously)* All right. You're asking for it, Big Daddy. We're finally
going to have that real true talk you wanted. It's too late to stop it,
now, we got to carry it through and cover every subject.
(He hobbles back to the liquor cabinet.)
Uh-huh.
*(He opens the ice bucket and picks up the silver tongs with slow admir-
ation of their frosty brightness.)*
Maggie declares that Skipper and I went into pro-football after
we left "Ole Miss" because we were scared to grow up . . .
*(He moves downstage with the shuffle and clop of a cripple on a crutch.
As Margaret did when her speech became "recitative," he looks out into
the house, commanding its attention by his direct, concentrated gaze — a
broken, "tragically elegant" figure telling simply as much as he knows
of "the Truth":)*
— Wanted to — keep on tossing — those long, long! — high,

high! — passes that — couldn't be intercepted except by time, the aerial attack that made us famous! And so we did, we did, we kept it up for one season, that aerial attack, we held it high! — Yeah, but —
— that summer, Maggie, she laid the law down to me, said, Now or never, and so I married Maggie . . .
BIG DADDY: How was Maggie in bed?
BRICK: *(Wryly)* Great! the greatest!
(Big Daddy nods as if he thought so.)
She went on the road that fall with the Dixie Stars. Oh, she made a great show of being the world's best sport. She wore a — wore a — tall bearskin cap! A shako, they call it, a dyed moleskin coat, a moleskin coat dyed red! — Cut up crazy! Rented hotel ballrooms for victory celebrations, wouldn't cancel them when it — turned out — defeat . . .
MAGGIE THE CAT! Ha ha!
(Big Daddy nods.)
— But Skipper, he had some fever which came back on him which doctors couldn't explain and I got that injury — turned out to be just a shadow on the X-ray plate — and a touch of bursitis . . .
I lay in a hospital bed, watched our games on TV, saw Maggie on the bench next to Skipper when he was hauled out of a game for stumbles, fumbles! — Burned me up the way she hung on his arm! — Y'know, I think that Maggie had always felt sort of left out because she and me never got any closer together than two people just get in bed, which is not much closer than two cats on a — fence humping . . .
So! She took this time to work on poor dumb Skipper. He was a less than average student at Ole Miss, you know that, don't you?! — Poured in his mind the dirty, false idea that what we were, him and me, was a frustrated case of that ole pair of sisters that lived in this room, Jack Straw and Peter Ochello! — He, poor Skipper, went to bed with Maggie to prove it wasn't true, and when it didn't work out, he thought it *was* true! — Skipper broke in two like a rotten stick — nobody ever turned so fast to a lush — or died of it so quick . . .
— Now are you satisfied?
(Big Daddy has listened to this story, dividing the grain from the chaff. Now he looks at his son.)
BIG DADDY: Are *you* satisfied?
BRICK: With what?
BIG DADDY: That half-ass story!
BRICK: What's half-ass about it?
BIG DADDY: Something's left out of that story. What did you leave out?
(The phone has started ringing in the hall. As if it reminded him of something, Brick glances suddenly toward the sound and says:)
BRICK: Yes! — I left out a long-distance call which I had from Skipper, in which he made a drunken confession to me and on which I hung up! — last time we spoke to each other in our lives . . .
(Muted ring stops as someone answers phone in a soft, indistinct voice in hall.)
BIG DADDY: You hung up?
BRICK: Hung up. Jesus! Well —

BIG DADDY: Anyhow now! — we have tracked down the lie with which you're disgusted and which you are drinking to kill your disgust with, Brick. You been passing the buck. This disgust with mendacity is disgust with yourself.

You! — dug the grave of your friend and kicked him in it! — before you'd face truth with him!

BRICK: *His* truth, not *mine!*

BIG DADDY: His truth, okay! But you wouldn't face it with him!

BRICK: Who *can* face truth? Can *you?*

BIG DADDY: Now don't start passin' the rotten buck again, boy!

BRICK: *How about these birthday congratulations, these many, many happy returns of the day, when ev'rybody but you knows there won't be any!*

(Whoever has answered the hall phone lets out a high, shrill laugh; the voice becomes audible saying: "no, no, you got it all wrong! Upside down! Are you crazy?"

(Brick suddenly catches his breath as he realized that he has made a shocking disclosure. He hobbles a few paces, then freezes, and without looking at his father's shocked face, says:)

Let's, let's — go out, now, and —

(Big Daddy moves suddenly forward and grabs hold of the boy's crutch like it was a weapon for which they were fighting for possession.)

BIG DADDY: Oh, no, no! No one's going out. What did you start to say?

BRICK: I don't remember.

BIG DADDY: "Many happy returns when they know there won't be any"?

BRICK: Aw, hell, Big Daddy, forget it. Come on out on the gallery and look at the fireworks they're shooting off for your birthday . . .

BIG DADDY: First you finish that remark you were makin' before you cut off. "Many happy returns when they know there won't be any"? — Ain't that what you just said?

BRICK: Look, now. I can get around without that crutch if I have to but it would be a lot easier on the furniture an' glassware if I didn' have to go swinging along like Tarzan of th' —

BIG DADDY: FINISH! WHAT YOU WAS SAYIN'!

(An eerie green glow shows in sky behind him.)

BRICK: *(Sucking the ice in his glass, speech becoming thick)* Leave th' place to Gooper and Mae an' their five little same little monkeys. All I want is —

BIG DADDY: "LEAVE TH' PLACE," did you say?

BRICK: All twenty-eight thousand acres of the richest land this side of the valley Nile.

BIG DADDY: Who said I was "leaving the place" to Gooper or anybody? This is my sixty-fifth birthday! I got fifteen years or twenty years left in me! I'll outlive *you!* I'll bury you an' have to pay for your coffin!

BRICK: Sure. Many happy returns. Now let's go watch the fireworks, come on, let's—

BIG DADDY: Lying, have they been lying? About the report from th' — clinic? Did they, did they — find something? — *Cancer.* Maybe?

BRICK: Mendacity is a system that we live in. Liquor is one way out an' death's the other . . .

(He takes the crutch from Big Daddy's loose grip and swings out on

589

the gallery leaving the doors open.
(A song, "Pick a Bale of Cotton," is heard.)
MAE: *(Appearing in door) Oh, Big Daddy, the field-hands are singin' fo' you!*
BIG DADDY: *(Shouting hoarsely)* BRICK! BRICK!
MAE: He's outside drinkin', Big Daddy.
BIG DADDY: *BRICK!*
(Mae retreats, awed by the passion of his voice. Children call Brick in tones mocking Big Daddy. His face crumbles like broken yellow plaster about to fall into dust.
(There is a glow in the sky. Brick swings back through the doors, slowly, gravely, quite soberly.)
BRICK: I'm sorry, Big Daddy. My head don't work any more and it's hard for me to understand how anybody could care if he lived or died or was dying or cared about anything but whether or not there was liquor left in the bottle and so I said what I said without thinking. In some ways I'm no better than the others, in some ways worse because I'm less alive. Maybe it's being alive that makes them lie, and being almost *not* alive makes me sort of accidentally truthful — I don't know but — anyway — we've been friends . . .
— And being friends is telling each other the truth . . .
(There is a pause.)
You told *me!* I told *you!*
(A child rushes into the room and grabs a fistful of firecrackers and runs out again.)
CHILD: *(Screaming)* Bang, bang, bang, bang, bang, bang, bang, bang, bang!
BIG DADDY: *(Slowly and passionately)* CHRIST — DAMN — ALL — LYING SONS OF — LYING BITCHES!
(He straightens at last and crosses to the inside door. At the door he turns and looks back as if he had some desperate question he couldn't put into words. Then he nods reflectively and says in a hoarse voice:)
Yes, all liars, all liars, all lying dying liars!
(This is said slowly, slowly, with a fierce revulsion. He goes on out.)
— Lying! Dying! Liars!
(His voice dies out. There is the sound of a child being slapped. It rushes, hideously bawling, through room and out the hall door.
(Brick remains motionless as the lights dim out and the curtain falls.)

CURTAIN
ACT THREE

There is no lapse of time:
Mae enters with Reverend Tooker.

MAE: Where is Big Daddy! Big Daddy?
BIG MAMA: *(Entering)* Too much smell of burnt fireworks makes me feel a little bit sick at my stomach. — Where is Big Daddy?
MAE: That's what I want to know, where has Big Daddy gone?
BIG MAMA: He must have turned in, I reckon he went to baid . . .
(Gooper enters.)
GOOPER: Where is Big Daddy?
MAE: We don't know where he is!

BIG MAMA: I reckon he's gone to baid.
GOOPER: Well, then, now we can talk.
BIG MAMA: What *is* this talk, *what* talk?
(Margaret appears on gallery, talking to Dr. Baugh.)
MARGARET: *(Musically)* My family freed their slaves ten years before
    abolition, my great-great-grandfather gave his slaves their freedom
    five years before the war between the States started!
MAE: Oh, for God's sake! Maggie's climbed back up in her family tree!
MARGARET: *(Sweetly)* What, Mae? — Oh, where's Big Daddy?!
(The pace must be very quick. Great Southern animation.)
BIG MAMA: *(Addressing them all)* I think Big Daddy was just worn out.
    He loves his family, he loves to have them around him, but it's a
    strain on his nerves. He wasn't himself tonight, Big Daddy wasn't
    himself, I could tell he was all worked up.
REVEREND TOOKER: I think he's remarkable.
BIG MAMA: Yaisss! Just remarkable. Did you all notice the food he ate at
    that table? Did you all notice the supper he put away? Why, he ate
    like a hawss!
GOOPER: I hope he doesn't regret it.
BIG MAMA: Why, that man — ate a huge piece of cawn-bread with molasses
    on it! Helped himself twice to hoppin' john.
MARGARET: Big Daddy loves hoppin' john. — We had a real country dinner.
BIG MAMA: *(Overlapping Margaret)* Yais, he simply adores it! An' candied
    yams? That man put away enough food at that table to stuff a nigger
    field-hand!
GOOPER: *(With grim relish)* I hope he don't have to pay for it later on . . .
BIG MAMA: *(Fiercely)* What's *that,* Gooper?
MAE: Gooper says he hopes Big Daddy doesn't suffer tonight.
BIG MAMA: Oh, shoot, Gooper says, Gooper says! Why should Big Daddy
    suffer for satisfying a normal appetite? There's nothin' wrong with
    that man but nerves, he's sound as a dollar! And now he knows he is
    an' that's why he ate such a supper. He had a big load off his mind,
    knowin' he wasn't doomed t' — what he thought he was doomed to . . .
MARGARET: *(Sadly and sweetly)* Bless his old sweet soul . . .
BIG MAMA: *(Vaguely)* Yais, bless his heart, wher's Brick?
MAE: Outside.
GOOPER: — Drinkin' . . .
BIG MAMA: I know he's drinkin'. You all don't have to keep tellin' *me* Brick
    is drinkin'. Cain't I see he's drinkin' without you continually tellin'
    me that boy's drinkin'?
MARGARET: Good for you, Big Mama! *(She applauds.)*
BIG MAMA: Other people *drink* and *have* drunk an' will *drink,* as long as
    they make that stuff an' put it in bottles.
MARGARET: That's the truth. I never trusted a man that didn't drink.
MAE: Gooper never drinks. Don't you trust Gooper?
MARGARET: Why, Gooper don't you drink? If I'd known you didn't drink,
    I wouldn't of made that remark —
BIG MAMA: *Brick?*
MARGARET: — at least not in your presence.
(She laughs sweetly.)

591

BIG MAMA: *Brick!*

MARGARET: He's still on the gall'ry. I'll go bring him in so we can talk.

BIG MAMA: *(Worriedly)* I don't know what this mysterious family confer-
ence is about.

*(Awkward silence. Big Mama looks from face to face, then belches
slightly and mutters, "Excuse me . . ." She opens an ornamental fan
suspended about her throat, a black lace fan to go with her black lace
gown, and fans her wilting corsage, sniffing nervously and looking
from face to face in the uncomfortable silence as Margaret calls "Brick?"
and Brick sings to the moon on the gallery.)*

I don't know what's wrong here, you all have such long faces!
Open that door in the hall and let some air circulate through here,
will you please, Gooper?

MAE: I think we'd better leave that door closed, Big Mama, till after the talk.

BIG MAMA: Reveren' Tooker, will *you* please open that door?!

REVEREND TOOKER: I sure will, Big Mama.

MAE: I just didn't think we ought t' take any chance of Big Daddy hearin'
a word of this discussion.

BIG MAMA: I *swan!* Nothing's going to be said in Big Daddy's house that
he cain't hear if he wants to!

GOOPER: Well, Big Mama, it's —

*(Mae gives him a quick, hard poke to shut him up. He glares at her
fiercely as she circles before him like a burlesque ballerina, raising her
skinny bare arms over her head, janging her bracelets, exclaiming:)*

MAE: A breeze! A breeze!

REVEREND TOOKER: I think this house is the coolest house in the Delta. —
Did you all know that Halsey Banks' widow put air-conditioning units
in the church and rectory at Friar's Point in memory of Halsey?

*(General conversation has resumed; everybody is chatting so that the
stage sounds like a big bird-cage.)*

GOOPER: Too bad nobody cools your church off for you. I bet you sweat in
that pulpit these hot Sundays, Reverend Tooker.

REVEREND TOOKER: Yes, my vestments are drenched.

MAE: *(At the same time to Dr. Baugh)* You reckon those vitamin B_{12} injections are what they're cracked up t' be, Doc Baugh?

DOCTOR BAUGH: Well, if you want to be stuck with something I guess
they're as good to be stuck with as anything else.

BIG MAMA: *(At gallery door) Maggie, Maggie, aren't you comin' with Brick?*

MAE: *(Suddenly and loudly, creating a silence)* I have a strange feeling, I
have a peculiar feeling!

BIG MAMA: *(Turning from gallery)* What feeling?

MAE: That Brick said somethin' he shouldn't of said t' Big Daddy.

BIG MAMA: Now what on earth could Brick of said t' Big Daddy that he
shouldn't say?

GOOPER: Big Mama, there's somethin'—

MAE: NOW, WAIT!

*(She rushes up to Big Mama and gives her a quick hug and kiss. Big
Mama pushes her impatiently off as the Reverend Tooker's voice rises
serenely in a little pocket of silence:)*

REVEREND TOOKER: Yes, last Sunday the gold in my chasuble faded into th' purple . . .

GOOPER: Reveren', you must of been preachin' hell's fire last Sunday! *(He guffaws at this witticism but the Reverend is not sincerely amused. At the same time Big Mama has crossed over to Dr. Baugh and is saying to him:)*

BIG MAMA: *(Her breathless voice rising high-pitched above the others)* In my day they had what they call the Keeley cure for heavy drinkers. But now I understand they just take some kind of tablets, they call them "Annie Bust" tablets. But *Brick* don't need to take *nothin'*. *(Brick appears in gallery doors with Margaret behind him.)*

BIG MAMA: *(Unaware of his presence behind her)* That boy is just broken up over Skipper's death. You know how poor Skipper died. They gave him a big, big dose of that sodium amytal stuff at his home and then they called the ambulance and give him another big, big dose of it at the hospital and that and all of the alcohol in his system fo' months an' months an' months just proved too much for his heart . . . I'm scared of needles! I'm more scared of a needle than the knife . . . I think more people have been needled out of this world than — *(She stops short and wheels about.)*

OH! — here's Brick! My precious baby —

(She turns upon Brick with short, fat arms extended, at the same time uttering a loud, short sob, which is both comic and touching.

(Brick smiles and bows slightly, making a burlesque gesture of gallantry for Maggie to pass before him into the room. Then he hobbles on his crutch directly to the liquor cabinet and there is absolute silence, with everybody looking at Brick as everybody has always looked at Brick when he spoke or moved or appeared. One by one he drops ice cubes in his glass, then suddenly, but not quickly, looks back over his shoulder with a wry, charming smile, and says:)

BRICK: I'm sorry! Anyone else?

BIG MAMA: *(Sadly)* No, son. I *wish* you wouldn't!

BRICK: I wish I didn't have to, Big Mama but I'm still waiting for that click in my head which makes it all smooth out!

BIG MAMA: Aw, Brick, you — BREAK MY HEART!

MARGARET: *(At the same time)* Brick, go sit with Big Mama!

BIG MAMA: I just cain't *staiiiiiiiii-nnnnnd* — it . . . *(She sobs.)*

MAE: Now that we're all assembled —

GOOPER: We kin talk . . .

BIG MAMA: Breaks my heart . . .

MARGARET: Sit with Big Mama, Brick, and hold her hand.

(Big Mama sniffs very loudly three times, almost like three drum beats in the pocket of silence.)

BRICK: You do that, Maggie. I'm a restless cripple. I got to stay on my crutch.

(Brick hobbles to the gallery door; leans there as if waiting.

(Mae sits beside Big Mama, while Gooper moves in front and sits on the end of the couch, facing her. Reverend Tooker moves nervously into the space between them; on the other side, Dr. Baugh stands looking at nothing in particular and lights a cigar. Margaret turns away.)

BIG MAMA: Why're you all *surroundin'* me — like this? Why're you all starin' at me like this an' makin' signs at each other?

(Reverend Tooker steps back startled.)

MAE: Calm yourself, Big Mama.

BIG MAMA: Calm you'self, *you'self,* Sister Woman. How could I calm myself with everyone starin' at me as if big drops of blood had broken out on m'face? What's this all about, Annh! What—

(Gooper coughs and takes a center position.)

GOOPER: Now, Doc Baugh.

MAE: Doc Baugh?

BRICK: *(Suddenly)* SHHH! —

(Then he grins and chuckles and shakes his head regretfully.)

— Naw! — that wasn't th' click.

GOOPER: Brick, shut up or stay out there on the gallery with your liquor! We got to talk about a serious matter. Big Mama wants to know the complete truth about the report we got today from the Ochsner Clinic.

MAE: *(Eagerly)* — on Big Daddy's condition!

GOOPER: Yais, on Big Daddy's condition, we got to face it.

DOCTOR BAUGH: Well . . .

BIG MAMA: *(Terrified, rising)* Is there? Something? Something that I? Don't — Know?

(In these few words, this startled, very soft, question, Big Mama reviews the history of her forty-five years with Big Daddy, her great, almost embarrassingly true-hearted and simple-minded devotion to Big Daddy, who must have had something Brick has, who made himself loved so much by the "simple expedient" of not loving enough to disturb his charming detachment, also once coupled, like Brick's, with virile beauty.

(Big Mama has a dignity at this moment: she almost stops being fat.)

DOCTOR BAUGH: *(After a pause, uncomfortably)* Yes? — Well —

BIG MAMA: *I!!!* — want to — *knowwwwwww* . . .

(Immediately she thrusts her fist to her mouth as if to deny that statement.

(Then, for some curious reason, she snatches the withered corsage from her breast and hurls it on the floor and steps on it with her short, fat feet.)

— Somebody must be lyin'! — I want to know!

MAE: Sit down, Big Mama, sit down on this sofa.

MARGARET: *(Quickly)* Brick, go sit with Big Mama.

BIG MAMA: *What is it, what is it?*

DOCTOR BAUGH: I never have seen a more thorough examination than Big Daddy Pollitt was given in all my experience with the Ochsner Clinic.

GOOPER: It's one of the best in the country.

MAE: It's *THE* best in the country — bar *none!*

(For some reason she gives Gooper a violent poke as she goes past him. He slaps at her hand without removing his eyes from his mother's face.)

DOCTOR BAUGH: Of course they were ninety-nine and nine-tenths percent sure before they even started.

BIG MAMA: Sure of what, sure of what, sure of — *what?* — *what!*

(She catches her breath in a startled sob. Mae kisses her quickly. She thrusts Mae fiercely away from her, staring at the doctor.)

MAE: Mommy, be a brave girl!

BRICK: *(In the doorway, softly)* "By the light, by the light,
Of the sil-ve-ry mo-ooo-n . . ."
GOOPER: Shut up! — Brick.
BRICK: — Sorry . . .
(He wanders out on the gallery.)
DOCTOR BAUGH: But now, you see, Big Mama, they cut a piece off this
growth, a specimen of the tissue and —
BIG MAMA: Growth? You told Big Daddy —
DOCTOR BAUGH: Now wait.
BIG MAMA: *(Fiercely)* You told me and Big Daddy there wasn't a thing
wrong with him but —
MAE: Big Mama, they always —
GOOPER: Let Doc Baugh talk, will yuh?
BIG MAMA: — little spastic condition of —
(Her breath gives out in a sob.)
DOCTOR BAUGH: Yes, that's what we told Big Daddy. But we had this
bit of tissue run through the laboratory and I'm sorry to say the test
was positive on it. It's — well — malignant . . .
(Pause.)
BIG MAMA: — Cancer? Cancer?!
(Dr. Baugh nods gravely.
(Big Mama gives a long gasping cry.)
MAE and GOOPER: Now, now, now, Big Mama, you had to know . . .
BIG MAMA: *WHY DIDN'T THEY CUT IT OUT OF HIM? HANH? HANH?*
DOCTOR BAUGH: Involved too much, Big Mama, too many organs affected.
MAE: Big Mama, the liver's affected and so's the kidneys, both! It's gone
way past what they call a —
GOOPER: A surgical risk.
MAE: — Uh-huh . . .
(Big Mama draws a breath like a dying gasp.)
REVEREND TOOKER: Tch, tch, tch, tch, tch!
DOCTOR BAUGH: Yes, it's gone past the knife.
MAE: *That's why he's turned yellow, Mommy!*
BIG MAMA: *Git away from me, git away from me, Mae!*
(She rises abruptly.)
  I want Brick! Where's Brick! Where is my only son?
MAE: Mama! Did she say *"only* son"?
GOOPER: What does that make *me?*
MAE: A sober responsible man with five precious children! — *Six!*
BIG MAMA: I want Brick to tell me! Brick! Brick!
MARGARET: *(Rising from her reflections in a corner)* Brick was so upset
he went back out.
BIG MAMA: *Brick!*
MARGARET: Mama, let *me* tell you!
BIG MAMA: No, no, leave me alone, you're not my blood!
GOOPER: *Mama, I'm your son! Listen to me!*
MAE: Gooper's your son, he's your first-born!
BIG MAMA: Gooper never liked Daddy.
MAE: *(As if terribly shocked) That's not TRUE!*
(There is a pause. The minister coughs and rises.)

REVEREND TOOKER: *(To Mae)* I think I'd better slip away at this point.

MAE: *(Sweetly and sadly)* Yes, Doctor Tooker, you go.

REVEREND TOOKER: *(Discreetly)* Goodnight, goodnight, everybody, and God bless you all . . . on this place . . .

(He slips out.)

DOCTOR BAUGH: That man is a good man but lacking in tact. Talking about people giving memorial windows — if he mentioned one memorial window, he must have spoke of a dozen, and saying how awful it was when somebody died intestate, the legal wrangles, and so forth.

(Mae coughs, and points at Big Mama.)

DOCTOR BAUGH: Well, Big Mama . . .

(He sighs.)

BIG MAMA: It's all a mistake, I know it's just a bad dream.

DOCTOR BAUGH: We're gonna keep Big Daddy as comfortable as we can.

BIG MAMA: Yes, it's just a bad dream, that's all it is, it's just an awful dream.

GOOPER: In my opinion Big Daddy is having some pain but won't admit that he has it.

BIG MAMA: Just a dream, a bad dream.

DOCTOR BAUGH: That's what lots of them do, they think if they don't admit they're having the pain they can sort of escape the fact of it.

GOOPER: *(With relish)* Yes, they get sly about it, they get real sly about it.

MAE: Gooper and I think —

GOOPER: Shut up, Mae! — Big Daddy ought to be started on morphine.

BIG MAMA: Nobody's going to give Big Daddy morphine.

DOCTOR BAUGH: Now, Big Mama, when that pain strikes it's going to strike mighty hard and Big Daddy's going to need the needle to bear it.

BIG MAMA: I tell you, nobody's going to give him morphine.

MAE: Big Mama, you don't want to see Big Daddy suffer, you know you —

(Gooper standing beside her gives her a savage poke.)

DOCTOR BAUGH: *(Placing a package on the table)* I'm leaving this stuff here, so if there's a sudden attack you all won't have to send out for it.

MAE: I know how to give a hypo.

GOOPER: Mae took a course in nursing during the war.

MARGARET: Somehow I don't think Big Daddy would want Mae to give him a hypo.

MAE: You think he'd want *you* to do it?

(Dr. Baugh rises.)

GOOPER: Doctor Baugh is goin'.

DOCTOR BAUGH: Yes, I got to be goin'. Well, keep your chin up, Big Mama.

GOOPER: *(With jocularity)* She's gonna keep *both* chins up, aren't you Big Mama?

(Big Mama sobs.)

　　　　Now stop that, Big Mama.

MAE: Sit down with me, Big Mama.

GOOPER: *(At door with Dr. Baugh)* Well, Doc, we sure do appreciate all you done. I'm telling you, we're surely obligated to you for —

(Dr. Baugh has gone out without a glance at him.)

GOOPER: — I guess that doctor has got a lot on his mind but it wouldn't hurt him to act a little more human.

(Big Mama sobs.)

Now be a brave girl, Mommy.

BIG MAMA: It's not true, I know that it's just not true!

GOOPER: Mama, those tests are infallible!

BIG MAMA: Why are you so determined to see your father daid?

MAE: Big Mama!

MARGARET: *(Gently)* I know what Big Mama means.

MAE: *(Fiercely)* Oh, do you?

MARGARET: *(Quietly and very sadly)* Yes, I think I do.

MAE: For a newcomer in the family you sure do show a lot of understanding.

MARGARET: Understanding is needed on this place.

MAE: I guess you must have needed a lot of it in your family, Maggie, with your father's liquor problem and now you've got Brick with his!

MARGARET: Brick does not have a liquor problem at all. Brick is devoted to Big Daddy. This thing is a terrible strain on him.

BIG MAMA: Brick is Big Daddy's boy, but he drinks too much and it worries me and Big Daddy, and, Margaret, you've got to cooperate with us, you've got to cooperate with Big Daddy and me in getting Brick straightened out. Because it will break Big Daddy's heart if Brick don't pull himself together and take hold of things.

MAE: Take hold of *what* things, Big Mama?

BIG MAMA: The place.

(There is a quick violent look between Mae and Gooper.)

GOOPER: Big Mama, you've had a shock.

MAE: Yais, we've all had a shock, but . . .

GOOPER: Let's be realistic —

MAE: — Big Daddy would never, would *never,* be foolish enough to —

GOOPER: — put this place in irresponsible hands!

BIG MAMA: Big Daddy ain't going to leave the place in anybody's hands; Big Daddy is *not* going to die. I want you to get that in your heads, all of you!

MAE: Mommy, Mommy, Big Mama, we're just as hopeful an' optimistic as you are about Big Daddy's prospects, we have faith in *prayer* — but nevertheless there are certain matters that have to be discussed an' dealt with, because otherwise —

GOOPER: Eventualities have to be considered and now's the time . . . Mae, will you please get my briefcase out of our room?

MAE: Yes, honey.

(She rises and goes out through the hall door.)

GOOPER: *(Standing over Big Mama)* Now Big Mom. What you said just now was not at all true and you know it. I've always loved Big Daddy in my own quiet way. I never made a show if it, and I know that Big Daddy has always been fond of me in a quiet way, too, and he never made a show if it neither.

(Mae returns with Gooper's briefcase.)

MAE: Here's your briefcase, Gooper, honey.

GOOPER: *(Handing the briefcase back to her)* Thank you . . . Of cou'se, my relationship with Big Daddy is different from Brick's.

MAE: You're eight years older'n Brick an' always had t'carry a bigger load of th' responsibilities than Brick ever had t'carry. He never carried a thing in his life but a football or a highball.

597

GOOPER: Mae, will y' let me talk, please?

MAE: Yes, honey.

GOOPER: Now, a twenty-eight thousand acre plantation's a mighty big thing t'run.

MAE: Almost singlehanded.

(Margaret has gone out onto the gallery and can be heard calling softly to Brick.)

BIG MAMA: You never had to run this place! What are you talking about? As if Big Daddy was dead and in his grave, you had to run it? Why, you just helped him out with a few business details and had your law practice at the same time in Memphis!

MAE: Oh, Mommy. Mommy. Big Mommy! Let's be fair! Why, Gooper has given himself body and soul to keeping this place up for the past five years since Big Daddy's health started failing. Gooper won't say it, Gooper never thought of it as a duty, he just did it. And what did Brick do? Brick kept living in his past glory at college! Still a football player at twenty-seven!

MARGARET: *(Returning alone)* Who are you talking about, now? Brick? A football player? He isn't a football player and you know it. Brick is a sports announcer on TV and one of the best-known ones in the country!

MAE: I'm talking about what he was.

MARGARET: Well, I wish you would just stop talking about my husband.

GOOPER: I've got a right to discuss my brother with other members of MY OWN family which don't include *you.* Why don't you go out there and drink with Brick?

MARGARET: I've never seen such malice toward a brother.

GOOPER: How about his for me? Why, he can't stand to be in the same room with me!

MARGARET: This is a deliberate campaign of vilification for the most disgusting and sordid reason on earth, and I know what it is! It's *avarice, avarice, greed, greed!*

BIG MAMA: *Oh, I'll scream! I will scream in a moment unless this stops!*

(Gooper has stalked up to Margaret with clenched fists at his sides as if he would strike her. Mae distorts her face again into a hideous grimace behind Margaret's back.)

MARGARET: We only remain on the place because of Big Mom and Big Daddy. If it is true what they say about Big Daddy we are going to leave here just as soon as it's over. Not a moment later.

BIG MAMA: *(Sobs)* Margaret. Child. Come here. Sit next to Big Mama.

MARGARET: Precious Mommy. I'm sorry, I'm sorry, I —!

(She bends her long graceful neck to press her forehead to Big Mama's bulging shoulder under its black chiffon.)

GOOPER: How beautiful, how touching, this display of devotion!

MAE: Do you know why she's childless? She's childless because that big beautiful athlete husband of hers won't go to bed with her!

GOOPER: You just won't let me do this in a nice way, will yah? Aw right — Mae and I have five kids with another one coming! I don't give a goddam if Big Daddy likes me or don't like me or did or never did or will or will never! I'm just appealing to a sense of common decency and fair play. I'll tell you the truth. I've resented Big Daddy's partiality to Brick ever since Brick was born, and the way I've been treated like I was just barely good enough to spit on and sometimes not even good enough for that. Big Daddy is dying of cancer, and it's spread all through him and it's attacked all his vital organs including the kidneys and right now he is sinking into uremia, and you all know what uremia is, it's poisoning of the whole system due to the failure of the body to eliminate its poisons.

MARGARET: *(To herself, downstage, hissingly) Poisons, poisons! Venomous thoughts and words! In hearts and minds! — That's poisons!*

GOOPER: *(Overlapping her)* I am asking for a square deal, and I expect to get one. But if I don't get one, if there's any peculiar shenanigans going on around here behind my back, or before me, well, I'm not a corporation lawyer for nothing, I know how to protect my own interests — *OH! A late arrival!*

(Brick enters from the gallery with a tranquil, blurred smile, carrying an empty glass with him.)

MAE: Behold the conquering hero comes!

GOOPER: The fabulous Brick Pollitt! Remember him? — Who could forget him!

MAE: He looks like he's been injured in a game!

GOOPER: Yep, I'm afraid you'll have to warm the bench at the Sugar Bowl this year, Brick!

(Mae laughs shrilly.)

      Or was it the Rose Bowl that he made that famous run in?

MAE: The punch bowl, honey, It was in the punch bowl, the cut glass punch bowl!

GOOPER: Oh, that's right, I'm getting the bowls mixed up!

MARGARET: Why don't you stop venting your malice and envy on a sick boy?

BIG MAMA: *Now you two hush, I mean it, hush, all of you, hush!*

GOOPER: All right, Big Mama. A family crisis brings out the best and the worst in every member of it.

MAE: *That's* the truth.

MARGARET: *Amen!*

BIG MAMA: *I said hush!* I won't tolerate any more catty talk in my house.

(Mae gives Gooper a sign indicating briefcase.
(Brick's smile has grown both brighter and vaguer. As he prepares a drink, he sings softly:)

BRICK: *Show me the way to go home,*
    I'm tired and I wanta go to bed,
    I had a little drink about an hour ago —

GOOPER: *(At the same time)* Big Mama, you know it's necessary for me t'go back to Memphis in th' mornin' t'represent the Parker estate in a lawsuit.

(Mae sits on the bed and arranges papers she has taken from the briefcase.)

BRICK: *(Continuing the song) Wherever I may roam,*
    On land or sea or foam.

BIG MAMA: Is it, Gooper?

MAE: Yaiss.

GOOPER: That's why I'm forced to — to bring up a problem that —

MAE: Somethin' that's too important t' be put off!

GOOPER: If Brick was sober, he ought to be in on this.

MARGARET: Brick is present; we're here.

GOOPER: Well, good. I will now give you this outline my partner, Tom Bullitt, an' me have drawn up — a sort of dummy — trusteeship.

MARGARET: Oh's that's it! You'll be in charge an' dole out remittances, will you?

GOOPER: This we did as soon as we got the report on Big Daddy from th' Ochsner Laboratories. We did this thing, I mean we drew up this dummy outline with the advice and assistance of the Chairman of the Boa'd of Directors of th' Southern Plantahs Banks and Trust Company in Memphis, C. C. Bellowes, a man who handles estates for all th' prominent fam'lies in West Tennessee and th' Delta.

BIG MAMA: Gooper?

GOOPER: *(Crouching in front of Big Mama)* Now this is not — not final, or anything like it. This is just a preliminary outline. But it does provide a basis — a design — a — possible, feasible — *plan!*

MARGARET: Yes, I'll bet.

MAE: It's a plan to protect the biggest estate in the Delta from irresponsibility an' —

BIG MAMA: Now you listen to me, all of you, you listen here! They's not goin' to be any more catty talk in my house! And Gooper, you put that away before I grab it out of your hand and tear it right up! I don't know what the hell's in it, and I don't want to know what the hell's in it. I'm talkin' in Big Daddy's language now; I'm his *wife,* not his *widow,* I'm still his *wife!* And I'm talkin to you in his language an' —

GOOPER: Big Mama, what I have here is —

MAE: Gooper explained that it's just a plan . . .

BIG MAMA: I don't care what you got there. Just put it back where it came from an' don't let me see it again, not even the outside of the envelope of it! Is that understood? Basis! Plan! Preliminary! Design! I say — what is it Big Daddy always says when he's disgusted?

BRICK: *(From the bar)* Big Daddy says "crap" when he's disgusted.

BIG MAMA: *(Rising)* That's right — *CRAP!* I say *CRAP* too, like Big Daddy!

MAE: Coarse language doesn't seem called for in this —

GOOPER: Somethin' in me is *deeply outraged* by hearin' you talk like this.

BIG MAMA: *Nobody's goin' to take nothin'!* — till Big Daddy lets go of it, and maybe, just possibly, not — not even then! No, not even then!

BRICK: *You can always hear me singin' this song,*
Show me the way to go home.

BIG MAMA: Tonight Brick looks like he used to look when he was a little boy, just like he did when he played wild games and used to come home all sweaty and pink-cheeked and sleepy, with his — red curls shining . . .
(She comes over to him and runs her fat shaky hand through his hair. He draws aside as he does from all physical contact and continues the song in a whisper, opening the ice bucket and dropping in the ice cubes one by one as if he were mixing some important chemical formula.)

BIG MAMA: *(Continuing)* Time goes by so fast. Nothin' can outrun it. Death commences too early — almost before you're half-acquainted with life

600

— you meet with the other . . .
Oh, you know we just got to love each other an' stay together,
all of us, just as close as we can, especially now that such a *black*
thing has come and moved into this place without invitation.
(Awkwardly embracing Brick, she presses her head to his shoulder.
(Gooper has been returning papers to Mae who has restored them to
briefcase with an air of severely tried patience.)
GOOPER: Big Mama? Big Mama?
(He stands behind her, tense with sibling envy.)
BIG MAMA: *(Oblivious of Gooper)* Brick, you hear me, don't you?
MARGARET: Brick hears you, Big Mama, he understands what you're saying.
BIG MAMA: Oh, Brick, son of Big Daddy! Big Daddy does so love you!
Y'know what would be his fondest dream come true? If before he
passed on, if Big Daddy has to pass on, you gave him a child of yours,
a grandson as much like his son as his son is like Big Daddy!
MAE: *(Zipping briefcase shut: an incongruous sound)* Such a pity that Maggie
an' Brick can't oblige!
MARGARET: *(Suddenly and quietly but forcefully)* Everybody listen.
(She crosses to the center of the room, holding her hands rigidly to-
gether.)
MAE: Listen to what, Maggie?
MARGARET: I have an announcement to make.
GOOPER: A sports announcement, Maggie?
MARGARET: Brick and I are going to — *have a child!*
(Big Mama catches her breath in a loud gasp.)
(Pause. Big Mama rises.)
BIG MAMA: Maggie! Brick! This is too good to believe!
MAE: That's right, too good to believe.
BIG MAMA: Oh, my, my! This is Big Daddy's dream, his dream come true!
I'm going to tell him right now before he —
MARGARET: We'll tell him in the morning. Don't disturb him now.
BIG MAMA: I want to tell him before he goes to sleep, I'm going to tell him
his dream's come true this minute! And Brick! A child will make you
pull yourself together and quit this drinking!
(She seizes the glass from his hand.)
The responsibilities of a father will —
(Her face contorts and she makes an excited gesture; bursting into sobs,
she rushes out, crying.)
I'm going to tell Big Daddy right this minute!
(Her voice fades out down the hall.)
(Brick shrugs slightly and drops an ice cube into another glass. Mar-
garet crosses quickly to his side, saying something under her breath,
and she pours the liquor for him, staring up almost fiercely into his face.)
BRICK: *(Coolly)* Thank you, Maggie, that's a nice big shot.
(Mae has joined Gooper and she gives him a fierce poke, making a low
hissing sound and a grimace of fury.)
GOOPER: *(Pushing her aside)* Brick, could you possibly spare me one small
shot of that liquor?
BRICK: Why, help yourself, Gooper boy.
GOOPER: I will.

MAE: *(Shrilly)* Of course we know that this is —
GOOPER: *Be still, Mae!*
MAE: I won't be still! I know she's made this up!
GOOPER: God damn it, I said to shut up!
MARGARET: Gracious! I didn't know that my little announcement was
    going to provoke such a storm!
MAE: *That* woman isn't *pregnant!*
GOOPER: Who said she was?
MAE: *She* did.
GOOPER: The doctor didn't. Doc Baugh didn't.
MARGARET: I haven't gone to Doc Baugh.
GOOPER: Then who'd you go to, Maggie?
MARGARET: One of the best gynecologists in the South.
GOOPER: Uh huh, uh huh! — I see . . .
    (He takes out pencil and notebook.)
    — May we have his name, please?
MARGARET: No, you may not, Mister Prosecuting Attorney!
MAE: He doesn't have any name, he doesn't exist!
MARGARET: Oh, he exists all right, and so does my child, Brick's baby!
MAE: You can't conceive a child by a man that won't sleep with you unless
    you think you're —
    (Brick has turned on the phonograph. A scat song cuts Mae's speech.)
GOOPER: *Turn that off!*
MAE: We know it's a lie because we hear you in here; he won't sleep with
    you, we hear you! So don't imagine you're going to put a trick over
    on us, to fool a dying man with a —
    (A long drawn cry of agony and rage fills the house. Margaret turns
    phonograph down to a whisper.
    (The cry is repeated.)
MAE: *(Awed)* Did you hear that, Gooper, did you hear that?
GOOPER: Sounds like the pain has struck.
MAE: Go see, Gooper!
GOOPER: Come along and leave these love birds together in their nest!
    (He goes out first. Mae follows but turns at the door, contorting her
    face and hissing at Margaret.)
MAE: *Liar!*
    (She slams the door.
    (Margaret exhales with relief and moves a little unsteadily to catch
    hold of Brick's arm.)
MARGARET: Thank you for — keeping still . . .
BRICK: OK, Maggie.
MARGARET: It was gallant of you to save my face!
BRICK: — It hasn't happened yet.
MARGARET: What?
BRICK: The click . . .
MARGARET: — the click in your head that makes you peaceful, honey?
BRICK: Uh-huh. It hasn't happened . . . I've got to make it happen before I
    can sleep . . .
MARGARET: — I — know what you — mean . . .
BRICK: Give me that pillow in the big chair, Maggie.

MARGARET: I'll put it on the bed for you.

BRICK: No, put it on the sofa, where I sleep.

MARGARET: Not tonight, Brick.

BRICK: I want it on the sofa. That's where I sleep.

> *(He has hobbled to the liquor cabinet. He now pours down three shots in quick succession and stands waiting, silent. All at once he turns with a smile and says:)*
>
> There!

MARGARET: What?

BRICK: The *click* . . .

> *(His gratitude seems almost infinite as he hobbles out on the gallery with a drink. We hear his crutch as he swings out of sight. Then, at some distance, he begins singing to himself a peaceful song.*
>
> *(Margaret holds the big pillow forlornly as if it were her only companion, for few moments, then throws it on the bed. She rushes to the liquor cabinet, gathers all the bottles in her arms, turns about undecidedly, then runs out of the room with them, leaving the door ajar on the dim yellow hall. Brick is heard hobbling back along the gallery, singing his peaceful song. He comes back in, sees the pillow on the bed, laughs lightly, sadly, picks it up. He has it under his arm as Margaret returns to the room. Margaret softly shuts the door and leans against it, smiling softly at Brick.)*

MARGARET: Brick, I used to think that you were stronger than me and I didn't want to be overpowered by you. But now, since you've taken to liquor — you know what? — I guess it's bad, but now I'm stronger than you and I can love you more truly!

Don't move that pillow. I'll move it right back if you do! — Brick?

> *(She turns out all the lamps but a single rose-silk-shaded one by the bed.)*

I really have been to a doctor and I know what to do and — Brick — this is my time by the calendar to conceive!

BRICK: Yes, I understand, Maggie. But how are you going to conceive a child by a man in love with his liquor?

MARGARET: By locking his liquor up and making him satisfy my desire before I unlock it!

BRICK: Is that what you've done, Maggie?

MARGARET: Look and see. That cabinet's mighty empty compared to before!

BRICK: Well, I'll be a son of a —

> *(He reaches for his crutch but she beats him to it and rushes out on the gallery, hurls the crutch over the rail and comes back in, panting.*
>
> *(There are running footsteps. Big Mama bursts into the room, her face all awry, gasping, stammering.)*

BIG MAMA: Oh, my God, oh, my God, oh, my God, where is it?

MARGARET: Is this what you want, Big Mama?

> *(Margaret hands her the package left by the doctor.)*

BIG MAMA: I can't bear it, oh, God! Oh, Brick! Brick, baby!

> *(She rushes at him. He averts his face from her sobbing kisses. Margaret watches with a tight smile.)*

My son, Big Daddy's boy! Little Father!

> *(The groaning cry is heard again. She runs out, sobbing.)*

MARGARET: And so tonight we're going to make the lie true, and when that's done, I'll bring the liquor back here and we'll get drunk together, here, tonight, in this place that death has come into . . .
— What do you say?

BRICK: I don't say anything. I guess there's nothing to say.

MARGARET: Oh, you weak people, you weak, beautiful people! — who give up. — What you want is someone to —
(She turns out the rose-silk lamp.)
— take hold of you. — Gently, gently, with love! And —
(The curtain begins to fall slowly.)
I *do* love you, Brick, I *do!*

BRICK: *(Smiling with charming sadness)* Wouldn't it be funny if that was true?

THE CURTAIN COMES DOWN

THE END

NOTE OF EXPLANATION

Some day when time permits I would like to write a piece about the influence, its dangers and its values, of a powerful and highly imaginative director upon the development of a play, before and during production. It does have dangers, but it has them only if the playwright is excessively malleable or submissive, or the director is excessively insistent on ideas or interpretations of his own. Elia Kazan and I have enjoyed the advantages and avoided the dangers of this highly explosive relationship because of the deepest mutual respect for each other's creative function: we have worked together three times with a phenomenal absence of friction between us and each occasion has increased the trust.

If you don't want a director's influence on your play, there are two ways to avoid it, and neither is good. One way is to arrive at an absolutely final draft of your play before you let your director see it, then hand it to him saying, Here it is, take it or leave it! The other way is to select a director who is content to put your play on the stage precisely as you conceived it with no ideas of his own. I said neither is a good way, and I meant it. No living playwright, that I can think of, hasn't something valuable to learn about his own work from a director so keenly perceptive as Elia Kazan. It so happened that in the case of *Streetcar,* Kazan was given a script that was completely finished. In the case of *Cat,* he was shown the first typed version of the play, and he was excited by it, but he had definite reservations about it which were concentrated in the third act. The gist of his reservations can be listed as three points: one, he felt that Big Daddy was too vivid and important a character to disappear from the play except as an offstage cry after the second act curtain; two, he felt that the character of Brick should undergo some apparent mutation as a result of the virtual vivisection that he undergoes in his interview with his father in Act Two. Three, he felt that the character of Margaret, while he understood that I sympathized with her and liked her myself, should be, if possible, more clearly sympathetic to an audience.

It was only the third of these suggestions that I embraced wholeheartedly from the outset, because it so happened that Maggie the Cat had become steadily more charming to me as I worked on her characterization. I didn't want Big Daddy to reappear in Act Three and I felt that the moral paralysis of Brick was a root thing in his tragedy, and to show a dramatic progression would obscure the meaning of that tragedy in him and because I don't believe that a conversation, however revelatory, ever effects so immediate a change in the heart or even conduct of a person in Brick's state of spiritual disrepair.

However, I wanted Kazan to direct the play, and though these suggestions were not made in the form of an ultimatum, I was fearful that I would lose his interest if I didn't re-examine the script from his point of view. I did. And you will find included in this published script the new third act that resulted from his creative influence on the play. The reception of the playing-script has more than justified, in my opinion, the adjustments made to that influence. A failure reaches fewer people, and touches fewer, than does a play that succeeds.

It may be that *Cat* number one would have done just as well, or nearly, as *Cat* number two; it's an interesting question. At any rate, with the publication of both third acts in this volume, the reader can, if he wishes, make up his own mind about it.

TENNESSEE WILLIAMS

ACT THREE

As played in New York Production

Big Daddy is seen leaving as at the end of Act II.

BIG DADDY: *(Shouts, as he goes out DR on gallery)* ALL LYIN' — DYIN' —
LIARS! LIARS! LIARS!
   *(After Big Daddy has gone, Margaret enters from DR on gallery, into
   room through DS door. She X to Brick at LC.)*
MARGARET: Brick, what in the name of God was goin' on in this room?
   *(Dixie and Trixie rush through the room from the hall, L to gallery R,
   brandishing cap pistols, which they fire repeatedly, as they shout:
   "Bang! Bang! Bang!"*
   *(Mae appears from DR gallery entrance, and turns the children back
   UL, along gallery. At the same moment, Gooper, Reverend Tooker and
   Dr. Baugh enter from L in the hall.)*
MAE: Dixie! You quit that! Gooper, will y'please git these kiddies t'baid?
   Right now?
   *(Gooper and Reverend Tooker X along upper gallery. Dr. Baugh holds,
   UC, near hall door. Reverend Tooker X to Mae near section of gallery
   just outside doors, R.)*
GOOPER: *(Urging the children along)* Mae — you seen Big Mama?
MAE: Not yet.
   (Dixie and Trixie vanish through hall, L.)
REVEREND TOOKER: *(To Mae)* Those kiddies are so full of vitality. I
   think I'll have to be startin' back to town.
   (Margaret turns to watch and listen.)
MAE: Not yet, Preacher. You know we regard you as a member of this
   fam'ly, one of our closest an' dearest, so you just got t'be with us when
   Doc Baugh gives Big Mama th' actual truth about th' report from th'
   clinic.
   (Calls through door:)
      Has Big Daddy gone to bed, Brick?
   *(Gooper has gone out DR at the beginning of the exchange between Mae
   and Reverend Tooker.)*
MARGARET: *(Replying to Mae)* Yes, he's gone to bed.
   (To Brick)
      Why'd Big Daddy shout "liars"?
GOOPER: *(Off DR)* Mae!
   (Mae exits DR. Reverend Tooker drifts along upper gallery.)
BRICK: I didn't lie to Big Daddy. I've lied to nobody, nobody but myself,
   just lied to myself. The time has come to put me in Rainbow Hill, put
   me in Rainbow Hill, Maggie, I ought to go there.
MARGARET: Over my dead body!
   (Brick starts R. She holds him.)
      Where do you think you're goin'?
   *(Mae enters from DR on gallery, X to Reverend Tooker, who comes to
   meet her.)*
BRICK: *(X below to C)* Out for some air, I want air —
GOOPER: *(Entering from DR to Mae, on gallery)* Now, where is that old lady?

607

MAE: Cantcha find her, Gooper?
(Reverend Tooker goes out DR.)
GOOPER: *(X to Doc above hall door)* She's avoidin' this talk.
MAE: I think she senses somethin'.
GOOPER: *(Calls off L)* Sookey! Go find Big Mama an' tell her Doc Baugh an' the Preacher've got to go soon.
MAE: Don't let Big Daddy hear yuh!
(Brings Dr. Baugh to R on gallery.)
REVEREND TOOKER: *(Off DR, calls)* Big Mama.
SOOKEY and DAISY: *(Running from L to R on lawn, calling)* Miss Ida! Miss Ida!
(They go out UR.)
GOOPER: *(Calling off upper gallery)* Lacey, you look downstairs for Big Mama!
MARGARET: Brick, they're going to tell Big Mama the truth now, an' she needs you!
(Reverend Tooker appears in lawn area, UR, X C.)
DOCTOR BAUGH: *(To Mae, on R gallery)* This is going to be painful.
MAE: Painful things can't always be avoided.
DOCTOR BAUGH: That's what I've noticed about 'em, Sister Woman.
REVEREND TOOKER: *(On lawn, points off R)* I see Big Mama!
(Hurries off L and reappears shortly in hall.)
GOOPER: *(Hurrying into hall)* She's gone round the gall'ry to Big Daddy's room. Hey, Mama!
(Off)
        Hey, Big Mama! Come here!
MAE: *(Calls)* Hush, Gooper! Don't holler, go to her!
(Gooper and Reverend Tooker now appear together in hall. Big Mama runs in from DR, carrying a glass of milk. She X past Dr. Baugh to Mae, on R gallery. Dr. Baugh turns away.)
BIG MAMA: Here I am! What d'you all want with me?
GOOPER: *(Steps toward Big Mama)* Big Mama, I told you we got to have this talk.
BIG MAMA: What talk you talkin' about? I saw the light go on in Big Daddy's bedroom an' took him his glass of milk, an' he just shut the shutters right in my face.
(Steps into room through R door.)
        When old couples have been together as long as me an' Big Daddy, they, they get irritable with each other just from too much — devotion! Isn't that so?
(X below wicker seat to RC area.)
MARGARET: *(X to Big Mama, embracing her)* Yes, of course it's so.
(Brick starts out UC though hall, but sees Gooper and Reverend Tooker entering, so he hobbles through C and DS door and onto gallery.)
BIG MAMA: I think Big Daddy was just worn out. He loves his fam'ly. He loves to have 'em around him, but it's a strain on his nerves. He wasn't himself tonight, Brick —
(XC toward Brick. Brick passes her on his way out, DS.) Big Daddy wasn't himself, I could tell he was all worked up.
REVEREND TOOKER: *(USC)* I think he's remarkable.

BIG MAMA: Yaiss! Just remarkable.
(Faces US, turns, X to bar, puts down glass of milk.)
Did you notice all the food he ate at that table?
(XR a bit.)
Why he ate like a hawss!
GOOPER: *(USC)* I hope he don't regret it.
BIG MAMA: *(Turns US toward Gooper)* What! Why that man ate a huge piece of cawn bread with molasses on it! Helped himself twice to hoppin' john!
MARGARET: *(X to Big Mama)* Big Daddy loves hoppin' john. We had a real country dinner.
BIG MAMA: Yais, he simply adores it! An' candied yams. Son —
(X to DS door, looking out at Brick. Margaret X above Big Mama to her L.)
That man put away enough food at that table to stuff a fieldhand.
GOOPER: I hope he don't have to pay for it later on.
BIG MAMA: *(Turns US)* What's that, Gooper?
MAE: Gooper says he hopes Big Daddy doesn't suffer tonight.
BIG MAMA: *(Turns to Margaret, DC)* Oh, shoot, Gooper says, Gooper says! Why should Big Daddy suffer for satisfyin' a nawmal appetite? There's nothin' wrong with that man but nerves; he's sound as a dollar! An' now he knows he is, an' that's why he ate such a supper. He had a big load off his mind, knowin' he wasn't doomed to — what — he thought he was — doomed t' —
(She wavers.)
(Margaret puts her arms around Big Mama.)
GOOPER: *(Urging Mae forward)* MAE!
(Mae runs forward below wicker seat. She stands below Big Mama, Margaret above Big Mama, They help her to the wicker seat. Big Mama sits. Margaret sits above her. Mae stands behind her.)
MARGARET: Bless his ole sweet soul.
BIG MAMA: Yes — bless his heart.
BRICK: *(DS on gallery, looking out front)* Hello, moon, I envy you, you cool son of a bitch.
BIG MAMA: I want Brick!
MARGARET: He just stepped out for some fresh air.
BIG MAMA: Honey! I want Brick.
MAE: Bring li'l Brother in here so we kin talk.
(Margaret rises, X through DS door to Brick on gallery.)
BRICK: *(To the moon)* I envy you — you cool son of a bitch.
MARGARET: Brick, what're you doin' out here on the gall'ry, baby?
BRICK: Admirin' an' complimentin' th' man in the moon.
(Mae X to Dr. Baugh on R gallery. Reverend Tooker and Gooper move R UC, looking at Big Mama.)
MARGARET: *(To Brick)* Come in, Baby. They're gettin' ready to tell Big Mama the truth.
BRICK: I can't witness that thing in there.
MAE: Doc Baugh, d'you think those vitamin B_{12} injections are all they're cracked up t'be?
(Enters room to upper side, behind wicker seat.)

DOCTOR BAUGH: *(X to below wicker seat)* Well, I guess they're as good t'be stuck with as anything else.
(Looks at watch; X through to LC.)
MARGARET: *(To Brick)* Big Mama needs you!
BRICK: I can't witness that thing in there!
BIG MAMA: What's wrong here? You all have such long faces, you sit here waitin' for somethin' like a bomb — to go off.
GOOPER: We're waitin' for Brick an' Maggie to come in for this talk.
MARGARET: *(X above Brick, to his R)* Brother Man an' Mae have got a trick up their sleeves, an' if you don't go in there t'help Big Mama, y'know what I'm goin' to do —?
BIG MAMA: Talk. Whispers! Whispers!
(Looks out DR.)
      Brick! . . .
MARGARET: *(Answering Big Mama's call)* Comin', Big Mama!
(To Brick.)
      I'm going' to take every dam' bottle on this place an' pitch it off th' levee into th' river!
BIG MAMA: Never had this sort of atmosphere here before.
MAE: *(Sits above Big Mama on wicker seat)* Before what, Big Mama?
BIG MAMA: This occasion. What's Brick an' Maggie doin' out there now?
GOOPER: *(X DC, looks out)* They seem to be havin' some little altercation.
(Brick X toward DS step. Maggie moves R above him to portal DR. Reverend Tooker joins Dr. Baugh, LC.)
BIG MAMA: *(Taking a pill from pill box on chain at her wrist)* Give me a little somethin' to wash this tablet down with. Smell of burnt fireworks always makes me sick.
(Mae X to bar to pour glass of water. Dr. Baugh joins her. Gooper X to Reverend Tooker, LC.)
BRICK: *(To Maggie)* You're a live cat, aren't you?
MARGARET: You're dam' right I am!
BIG MAMA: Gooper, will y'please open that hall door — an' let some air circulate in this stiflin' room?
(Gooper starts US, but is restrained by Mae who X through C with glass of water. Gooper turns to men DLC.)
MAE: *(X to Big Mama with water, sits above her)* Big Mama, I think we ought to keep that door closed till after we talk.
BIG MAMA: I swan!
(Drinks water. Washes down pill.)
MAE: I just don't think we ought to take any chance of Big Daddy hearin' a word of this discussion.
BIG MAMA: *(Hands glass to Mae)* What discussion of what? Maggie! Brick! Nothin' is goin' to be said in th' house of Big Daddy Pollitt that he can't hear if he wants to!
(Mae rises, X to bar, puts down glass, joins Gooper and the two men, LC.)
BRICK: How long are you goin' to stand behind me, Maggie?
MARGARET: Forever, if necessary.
(Brick X US to R gallery door.)
BIG MAMA: Brick!
(Mae rises, looks out DS, sits.)

GOOPER: That boy's gone t'pieces — he's just gone t'pieces.

DOCTOR BAUGH: Y'know, in my day they used to have somethin' they called the Keeley cure for drinkers.

BIG MAMA: Shoot!

DOCTOR BAUGH: But nowadays, I understand they take some kind of tablets that kill their taste for the stuff.

GOOPER: *(Turns to Dr. Baugh)* Call 'em anti-bust tablets.

BIG MAMA: Brick don't need to take nothin'. That boy is just broken up over Skipper's death. You know how poor Skipper died. They gave him a big, big dose of that sodium amytal stuff at his home an' then they called the ambulance an' give him another big, big dose of it at th' hospital an' that an' all the alcohol in his system fo' months an' months just proved too much for his heart an' his heart quit beatin'. I'm scared of needles! I'm more scared of a needle than th' knife — *(Brick has entered the room to behind the wicker seat. He rests his hand on Big Mama's head. Gooper has moved a bit URC, facing Big Mama.)*

BIG MAMA: Oh! Here's Brick! My precious baby!

(Dr. Baugh X to bar, puts down drink. Brick X below Big Mama through C to bar.)

BRICK: Take it, Gooper!

MAE: *(Rising)* What?

BRICK: Gooper knows what. Take it, Gooper!

(Mae turns to Gooper URC, Dr. Baugh X to Reverend Tooker. Margaret, who has followed Brick US on R gallery before he entered the room, now enters room, to behind wicker seat.)

BIG MAMA: *(To Brick)* You just break my heart.

BRICK: Sorry — anyone else?

MARGARET: Brick, sit with Big Mama an' hold her hand while we talk.

BRICK: You do that, Maggie. I'm a restless cripple. I got to stay on my crutch.

(Mae sits above Big Mama. Gooper moves in front, below, and sits on couch, facing Big Mama. Reverend Tooker closes in to RC. Dr. Baugh X DC, faces upstage, smoking cigar. Margaret turns away to R doors.)

BIG MAMA: Why're you all *surroundin'* me? — like this? Why're you all starin' at me like this an' makin' signs at each other?

(Brick hobbles out hall door and X along R gallery.)

I don't need nobody to hold my hand. Are you all crazy? Since when did Big Daddy or me need anybody —?

(Reverend Tooker moves behind wicker seat.)

MAE: Calm yourself, Big Mama.

BIG MAMA: Calm you'self *you'self,* Sister Woman! How could I calm myself with everyone starin' at me as if big drops of blood had broken out on m'face? What's this all about, Annh! What?

GOOPER: Doc Baugh —

(Mae rises.)

Sit down, Mae —

(Mae sits.)

— Big Mama wants to know the complete truth about th' report we got today from the Ochsner Clinic!

(Dr. Baugh buttons his coat, faces group at RC.)

BIG MAMA: Is there somethin' — somethin' that I don't know?

611

DOCTOR BAUGH: Yes — well . . .
BIG MAMA: *(Rises)* I — want to — *knowwwww!*
> *(X to Dr. Baugh.)*
>> Somebody must be lyin'! *I want to know!*
> *(Mae, Gooper, Reverend Tooker surround Big Mama.)*
MAE: Sit down, Big Mama, sit down on this sofa!
> *(Brick has passed Margaret Xing DR on gallery.)*
MARGARET: Brick! Brick!
BIG MAMA: *What is it, what is it?*
> *(Big Mama drives Dr. Baugh a bit DLC. Others follow, surrounding Big Mama.)*
DOCTOR BAUGH: I never have seen a more thorough examination than Big Daddy Pollitt was given in all my experience at the Ochsner Clinic.
GOOPER: It's one of th' best in th' country.
MAE: It's *THE* best in th' country — bar none!
DOCTOR BAUGH: Of course they were ninety-nine and nine-tenths per cent certain before they even started.
BIG MAMA: Sure of what, sure of what, sure of what — *what?!*
MAE: Now, Mommy, be a brave girl!
BRICK: *(On DR gallery, covers his ears, sings)* "By the light, by the light, of the silvery moon!"
GOOPER: *(Breaks DR. Calls out to Brick)* Shut up, Brick!
> *(Returns to group LC.)*
BRICK: Sorry . . .
> *(Continues singing.)*
DOCTOR BAUGH: But now, you see, Big Mama, they cut a piece off this growth, a specimen of the tissue, an' —
BIG MAMA: Growth? You told Big Daddy —
DOCTOR BAUGH: Now, wait —
BIG MAMA: You told me an' Big Daddy there wasn't a thing wrong with him but —
MAE: Big Mama, they always —
GOOPER: Let Doc Baugh talk, will yuh?
BIG MAMA: — little spastic condition of —
REVEREND TOOKER: *(Throughout all this)* Shh! Shh! Shh!
> *(Big Mama breaks UC, they all follow.)*
DOCTOR BAUGH: Yes, that's what we told Big Daddy. But we had this bit of tissue run through the laboratory an' I'm sorry t'say the test was positive on it. It's malignant.
> *(Pause.)*
BIG MAMA: *Cancer! Cancer!*
MAE: Now now, Mommy —
GOOPER: *(At the same time)* You had to know, Big Mama.
BIG MAMA: *Why didn't they cut it out of him? Hanh? Hannh?*
DOCTOR BAUGH: Involved too much, Big Mama, too many organs affected.
MAE: Big Mama, the liver's affected, an' so's the kidneys, both. It's gone way past what they call a —
GOOPER: — a surgical risk.
> *(Big Mama gasps.)*
REVEREND TOOKER: Tch, tch, tch.

DOCTOR BAUGH: Yes, it's gone past the knife.

MAE: That's why he's turned yellow!

(Brick stops singing, turns away UR on gallery.)

BIG MAMA: *(Pushes Mae DS)* Git away from me, git away from me, Mae! *(X DSR)* I want Brick! Where's Brick! *Where's my only son?*

MAE: *(A step after Big Mama)* Mama! Did she say "only" son?

GOOPER: *(Following Big Mama)* What does that make me?

MAE: *(Above Gooper)* A sober responsible man with five precious children — *six!*

BIG MAMA: I want Brick! Brick! Brick!

MARGARET: *(A step to Big Mama above couch)* Mama, let *me* tell you.

BIG MAMA: *(Pushing her aside)* No, no, leave me alone. You're not my blood!

(She rushes onto the DS gallery.)

GOOPER: *(X to Big Mama on gallery)* Mama! I'm your son! Listen to me!

MAE: Gooper's your son, Mama, he's your first-born!

BIG MAMA: Gooper never liked Daddy!

MAE: That's not true!

REVEREND TOOKER: *(UC)* I think I'd better slip away at this point. Goodnight, goodnight everybody, and God bless you all — on this place.

(Goes out through hall.)

DOCTOR BAUGH: (X to DR above DS door) Well, Big Mama —

BIG MAMA: *(Leaning against Gooper, on lower gallery)* It's all a mistake, I know it's just a bad dream.

DOCTOR BAUGH: We're gonna keep Big Daddy as comfortable as we can.

BIG MAMA: Yes, it's just a bad dream, that's all it is, it's just an awful dream.

GOOPER: In my opinion Big Daddy is havin' some pain but won't admit that he has it.

BIG MAMA: Just a dream, a bad dream.

DOCTOR BAUGH: That's what lots of 'em do, they think if they don't admit they're having the pain they can sort of escape th' fact of it.

(Brick X US on R gallery. Margaret watches him from R door.)

GOOPER: Yes, they get sly about it, get real sly about it.

MAE: *(X to R of Dr. Baugh)* Gooper an' I think —

GOOPER: Shut up, Mae! — Big Mama, I really do think Big Daddy should be started on morphine.

BIG MAMA: *(Pulling away from Gooper)* Nobody's goin' to give Big Daddy morphine!

DOCTOR BAUGH: Now, Big Mama, when that pain strikes it's goin' to strike mighty hard an' Big Daddy's goin' t'need the needle to bear it.

BIG MAMA: *(X to Dr. Baugh)* I tell you, nobody's goin' to give him morphine!

MAE: Big Mama, you don't want to see Big Daddy suffer, y'know y' —

DOCTOR BAUGH: *(X to bar)* Well, I'm leavin' this stuff here

(Puts packet of morphine, etc., on bar.)

so if there's a sudden attack you won't have to send out for it.

(Big Mama hurries to L side bar.)

MAE: *(X C, below Dr. Baugh)* I know how to give a hypo.

BIG MAMA: Nobody's goin' to give Big Daddy morphine!

GOOPER: *(X C)* Mae took a course in nursin' durin' th' war.

MARGARET: Somehow I don't think Big Daddy would want Mae t'give him a hypo.

MAE: *(To Margaret)* You think he'd want *you* to do it?

DOCTOR BAUGH: Well —

GOOPER: Well, Doc Baugh is goin' —

DOCTOR BAUGH: Yes, I got to be goin'. Well, keep your chin up, Big Mama.

(X to hall.)

GOOPER: *(As he and Mae follow Dr. Baugh into the hall)* She's goin' to keep her ole chin up, aren't you, Big Mama?

(They go out L.)

    Well, Doc, we sure do appreciate all you've done. I'm telling you, we're obligated —

BIG MAMA: Margaret!

(XRC.)

MARGARET: *(Meeting Big Mama in front of wicker seat)* I'm right here, Big Mama.

BIG MAMA: Margaret, you've got to cooperate with me an' Big Daddy to straighten Brick out now —

GOOPER: *(Off L, returning with Mae)* I guess that doctor has got a lot on his mind, but it wouldn't hurt him to act a little more human —

BIG MAMA: — because it'll break Big Daddy's heart if Brick don't pull himself together an' take hold of things here.

(Brick X DSR on gallery.)

MAE: *(UC, overhearing)* Take hold of what things, Big Mama?

BIG MAMA: *(Sits in wicker chair, Margaret standing behind chair)* The place.

GOOPER: *(UC)* Big Mama, you've had a shock.

MAE: *(X with Gooper to Big Mama)* Yais, we've all had a shock, but —

GOOPER: Let's be realistic —

MAE: Big Daddy would not, would *never,* be foolish enough to —

GOOPER: — put this place in irresponsible hands!

BIG MAMA: Big Daddy ain't goin' t'put th' place in anybody's hands, Big Daddy is *not* goin' t'die! I want you to git that into your haids, all of you!

(Mae sits above Big Mama, Margaret turns R to door, Gooper X LC a bit.)

MAE: Mommy, Mommy, Big Mama, we're just as hopeful an' optimistic as you are about Big Daddy's prospects, we have faith in prayer — but nevertheless there are certain matters that have to be discussed an' dealt with, because otherwise —

GOOPER: Mae, will y'please get my briefcase out of our room?

MAE: Yes, honey.

(Rises, goes out through hall L.)

MARGARET: *(X to Brick on DS gallery)* Hear them in there?

(X back to R gallery door.)

GOOPER: *(Stands above Big Mama. Leaning over her)* Big Mama, what you said just now was not true, an' you know it. I've always loved Big Daddy in my own quiet way. I never made a show of it. I know that Big Daddy has always been fond of me in a quiet way, too.

(Margaret drifts UR on gallery. Mae returns, X to Gooper's L with briefcase.)

MAE: Here's your briefcase, Gooper, honey.
(Hands it to him.)
GOOPER: *(Hands briefcase back to Mae)* Thank you. Of cou'se, my relationship with Big Daddy is different from Brick's.
MAE: You're eight years older'n Brick an' always had t'carry a bigger load of th' responsibilities than Brick ever had t'carry; he never carried a thing in his life but a football or a highball.
GOOPER: Mae, will y'let me talk, please?
MAE: Yes, honey.
GOOPER: Now, a twenty-eight thousand acre plantation's a mighty big thing t'run.
MAE: Almost single-handed!
BIG MAMA: You never had t'run this place, Brother Man, what're you talkin' about, as if Big Daddy was dead an' in his grave, you had to run it? Why, you just had t'help him out with a few business details an' had your law practice at the same time in Memphis.
MAE: Oh, Mommy, Mommy, Mommy! Let's be fair! Why, Gooper has given himself body an' soul t'keepin' this place up fo' the past five years since Big Daddy's health started failin'. Gooper won't say it, Gooper never thought of it as a duty, he just did it. An' what did Brick do? Brick kep' livin' in his past glory at college!
(Gooper places a restraining hand on Mae's leg; Margaret drifts DS in gallery.)
GOOPER: Still a football player at twenty-seven!
MARGARET: *(Bursts into UR door)* Who are you talkin' about now? Brick? A football player? He isn't a football player an' you know it! Brick is a sports announcer on TV an' one of the best-known ones in the country!
MAE: *(Breaks UC)* I'm talkin' about what he was!
MARGARET: *(X to above lower gallery door)* Well, I wish you would just stop talkin' about my husband!
GOOPER: *(X to above Margaret)* Listen, Margaret, I've got a right to discuss my own brother with other members of my own fam'ly, which don't include *you!*
(Pokes finger at her; she slaps his finger away.)
    Now, why don't you go on out there an' drink with Brick?
MARGARET: I've never seen such malice toward a brother.
GOOPER: How about his for me? Why he can't stand to be in the same room with me!
BRICK: *(On lower gallery)* That's the truth!
MARGARET: This is a deliberate campaign of vilification for the most disgusting and sordid reason on earth, and I know what it is! *It's avarice, avarice, greed, greed!*
BIG MAMA: Oh, I'll scream, I will scream in a moment unless this stops! Margaret, child, come here, sit next to Big Mama.
MARGARET: *(X to Big Mama, sits above her)* Precious Mommy.
(Gooper X to bar.)
MAE: How beautiful, how touchin' this display of devotion! Do you know why she's childless? She's childless because that big, beautiful athlete husband of hers won't go to bed with her, that's why!
(X to L of bed, looks at Gooper.)

615

GOOPER: You jest won't let me do this the nice way, will yuh? Aw right —
(X to above wicker seat.)
  I don't give a goddam if Big Daddy likes me or don't like me or did or never did or will or will never! I'm just appealin' to a sense of common decency an' fair play! I'm tellin' you th' truth —
(X DS through lower door to Brick on DR gallery.)
  I've resented Big Daddy's partiality to Brick ever since th' goddam day you were born, són, an' th' way I've been treated, like I was just barely good enough to spit on, an' sometimes not even good enough for that.
(X back through room to above wicker seat.)
  Big Daddy is dyin' of cancer an' it's spread all through him an' it's attacked all his vital organs includin' the kidneys an' right now he is sinkin' into uremia, an' you all know what uremia is, it's poisonin' of the whole system due to th' failure of th' body to eliminate its poisons.
MARGARET: Poisons, poisons, venomous thoughts and words! In hearts and minds! That's poisons!
GOOPER: I'm askin' for a square deal an' by God I expect to get one. But if I don't get one, if there's any peculiar shenanigans goin' on around here behind my back, well I'm not a corporation lawyer for nothin'!
(X DS toward lower gallery door, on apex.)
  I know how to protect my own interests.
(Rumble of distant thunder.)
BRICK: *(Entering the room through DS door)* Storm comin' up.
GOOPER: Oh, a late arrival!
MAE: *(X through C to below bar, LCO)* Behold, the conquerin' hero comes!
GOOPER: *(X through C to bar, following Brick, imitating his limp)* The fabulous Brick Pollitt! Remember him? Who could forget him?
MAE: He looks like he's been injured in a game!
GOOPER: Yep, I'm afraid you'll have to warm th' bench at the Sugar Bowl this year, Brick! Or was it the Rose Bowl that he made his famous run in.
(Another rumble of thunder, sound of wind rising.)
MAE: *(X to L of Brick, who has reached the bar)* The punch bowl, honey, it was the punch bowl, the cut-glass punch bowl!
GOOPER: That's right! I'm always gettin' the boy's *bowls* mixed up!
(Pats Brick on the butt.)
MARGARET: *(Rushes at Gooper, striking him)* Stop that! You stop that!
(Thunder.)
(Mae X toward Margaret from L of Gooper, flails at Margaret; Gooper keeps the women apart. Lacey runs through the US lawn area in a raincoat.)
DAISY and SOOKEY: *(Off UL)* Storm! Storm comin'! Storm! Storm!
LACEY: *(Running out UR)* Brightie, close them shutters!
GOOPER: *(X onto R gallery, calls after Lacey)* Lacey, put the top up on my Cadillac, will yuh?
LACEY: *(Off R)* Yes, suh, Mistah Pollitt!
GOOPER: *(X to above Big Mama)* Big Mama, you know it's goin' to be necessary for me t'go back to Memphis in th' mornin' t'represent the Parker estate in a lawsuit.

(Mae sits on L side bed, arranges papers she removes from briefcase.)
BIG MAMA: Is it, Gooper?
MAE: Yaiss.
GOOPER: That's why I'm forced to — to bring up a problem that —
MAE: Somethin' that's too important t' be put off!
GOOPER: If Brick was sober, he ought to be in on this. I think he ought to be present when I present this plan.
MARGARET: *(UC)* Brick is present, we're present!
GOOPER: Well, good. I will now give you this outline my partner, Tom Bullit, an' me have drawn up — a sort of dummy — trusteeship!
MARGARET: Oh, that's it! You'll be in charge an' dole out remittances, will you?
GOOPER: This we did as soon as we got the report on Big Daddy from th' Ochsner Laboratories. We did this thing, I mean we drew up this dummy outline with the advice and assistance of the Chairman of the Boa'd of Directors of th' Southern Plantuhs Bank and Trust Company in Memphis, C. C. Bellowes, a man who handles estates for all th' prominent fam'lies in West Tennessee and th' Delta!
BIG MAMA: Gooper?
GOOPER: *(X behind seat to below Big Mama)* Now this is not — not final, or anything like it, this is just a preliminary outline. But it does provide a basis — a design — a — possible, feasible — *plan!*
(He waves paper Mae has thrust into his hand, US.)
MARGARET: *(X DL)* Yes, I'll bet it's a plan!
(Thunder rolls. Interior lighting dims.)
MAE: It's a plan to protect the biggest estate in the Delta from irresponsibility an'—
BIG MAMA: Now you listen to me, all of you, you listen here! They's not goin' to be no more catty talk in my house! And Gooper, you put that away before I grab it out of your hand and tear it right up! I don't know what the hell's in it, and I don't want to know what the hell's in it. I'm talkin' in Big Daddy's language now, I'm his *wife,* not his *widow,* I'm still his *wife!* And I'm talkin' to you in his language an' —
GOOPER: Big Mama, what I have here is —
MAE: Gooper explained that it's just a plan . . .
BIG MAMA: I don't care what you got there, just put it back where it come from an' don't let me see it again, not even the outside of the envelope of it! Is that understood? Basis! Plan! Preliminary! Design! — I say — what is it that Big Daddy always says when he's disgusted?
(Storm clouds race across sky.)
BRICK: *(From bar)* Big Daddy says "crap" when he is disgusted.
BIG MAMA: *(Rising)* That's right — CRAPPPP! I say CRAP too, like Big Daddy!
(Thunder rolls.)
MAE: Coarse language don't seem called for in this —
GOOPER: Somethin' in me is *deeply outraged* by this.
BIG MAMA: *Nobody's goin' to do nothin'!* till Big Daddy lets go of it, and maybe just possibly not — not even then! No, not even then!
(Thunder clap. Glass crash, off L.
(Off UR, children commence crying. Many storm sounds, L and R: barn-

yard animals in terror, papers crackling, shutters rattling. Sookey and Daisy hurry from L to R in lawn area. Inexplicably, Daisy hits together two leather pillows. They cry, "Storm! Storm!" Sookey waves a piece of wrapping paper to cover lawn furniture. Mae exits to hall and upper gallery. Strange man runs across lawn, R to L.
(Thunder rolls repeatedly.)

MAE: Sookey, hurry up an' git that po'ch furniture covahed; want th' paint to come off?
(Starts DR on gallery.
(Gooper runs through hall to R gallery.)

GOOPER: *(Yells to Lacey, who appears from R)* Lacey, put mah car away!

LACY: Cain't, Mistah Pollitt, you got the keys!
(Exits US.)

GOOPER: Naw, you got 'em, man.
(Exit DR. Reappears UR, calls to Mae:)
Where th' keys to th' car, honey?
(Runs C.)

MAE: *(DR on gallery)* You got 'em in your pocket!
(Exit DR.)
(Gooper exits UR. Dog howls. Daisy and Sookey sing off UR to comfort children. Mae is heard placating the children.
(Storm fades away.
(During the storm, Margaret X and sits on couch, DR. Big Mama X DC.)

BIG MAMA: BRICK! Come here, Brick, I need you.
(Thunder distantly.
(Children whimper, off L Mae consoles them. Brick X to R of Big Mama.)

BIG MAMA: Tonight Brick looks like he used to look when he was a little boy just like he did when he played wild games in the orchard back of the house and used to come home when I hollered myself hoarse for him! all — sweaty — and pink-cheeked — an' sleepy with his curls shinin' —
(Thunder distantly.
(Children whimper, off L. Mae consoles them. Dog howls, off.)
Time goes by so fast. Nothin' can outrun it. Death commences too early — almost before you're half-acquainted with life — you meet with the other. Oh, you know we just got to love each other, an' stay together all of us just as close as we can, specially now that such a *black* thing has come and moved into this place without invitation.
(Dog howls, off.)
Oh, Brick, son of Big Daddy, Big Daddy does so love you. Y'know what would be his fondest dream come true? If before he passed on, if Big Daddy has to pass on . . .
(Dog howls, off.)
You give him a child of yours, a grandson as much like his son as his son is like Big Daddy . . .

MARGARET: I know that's Big Daddy's dream.

BIG MAMA: That's his dream.

BIG DADDY: *(Off DR on gallery)* Looks like the wind was takin' liberties with his place.
(Lacey appears UL, X to UC in lawn area; Brightie and Small appear

UR on lawn. Big Daddy X onto the gallery.)

LACEY: Evenin', Mr. Pollitt.

BRIGHTIE and SMALL: Evenin', Cap'n. Hello, Cap'n.

MARGARET *(X to R door)* Big Daddy's on the gall'ry.

BIG DADDY: Stawm crossed th' river, Lacey?

LACEY: Gone to Arkansas, Cap'n.

(Big Mama has turned toward the hall door at the sound of Big Daddy's voice on the gallery. Now she X's DSR and out the DS door onto the gallery.)

BIG MAMA: I can't stay here. He'll see somethin' in my eyes.

BIG DADDY: *(On upper gallery, to the boys)* Stawm done any damage around here?

BRIGHTIE: Took the po'ch off ole Aunt Crawley's house.

BIG DADDY: Ole Aunt Crawley should of been settin' on it. It's time fo' th' wind to blow that ole girl away!

(Field-hands laugh, exit, UR. Big Daddy enters room, UC, hall door.)
Can I come in?

(Puts his cigar in ash tray on bar.

(Mae and Gooper hurry along the upper gallery and stand behind Big Daddy in hall door.)

MARGARET: Did the storm wake you up, Big Daddy?

BIG DADDY: Which stawm are you talkin' about — th' one outside or th' hullaballoo in here?

(Gooper squeezes past Big Daddy.)

GOOPER: *(X toward bed, where legal papers are strewn)* 'Scuse me, sir . . .

(Mae tries to squeeze past Big Daddy to join Gooper, but Big Daddy puts his arm firmly around her.)

BIG DADDY: I heard some mighty loud talk. Sounded like somethin' important was bein' discussed. What was the powwow about?

MAE: *(Flustered)* Why — nothin', Big Daddy . . .

BIG DADDY: *(X DLC, taking Mae with him)* What is that pregnant-lookin' envelope you're puttin' back in your briefcase, Gooper?

GOOPER: *(At foot of bed, caught, as he stuffs papers into envelope)* That? Nothin', suh — nothin' much of anythin' at all . . .

BIG DADDY: Nothin'? It looks like a whole lot of nothing!

(Turns US to group:)
You all know th' story about th' young married couple —

GOOPER: Yes, sir!

BIG DADDY: Hello, Brick —

BRICK: Hello, Big Daddy.

(The group is arranged in a semi-circle above Big Daddy, Margaret at the extreme R, then Mae and Gooper, then Big Mama, with Brick at L.)

BIG DADDY: Young married couple took Junior out to th' zoo one Sunday, inspected all of God's creatures in their cages, with satisfaction.

GOOPER: Satisfaction.

BIG DADDY: *(X USC, face front)* This afternoon was a warm afternoon in spring an' that ole elephant had somethin' else on his mind which was bigger'n peanuts. You know this story, Brick?

(Gooper nods.)

BRICK: No, sir, I don't know it.

BIG DADDY: Y'see, in th' cage adjoinin' they was a young female elephant in heat!

BIG MAMA: *(At Big Daddy's shoulder)* Oh, Big Daddy!

BIG DADDY: What's the matter, preacher's gone, ain't he? All right. That female elephant in the next cage was permeatin' the atmosphere about her with a powerful and excitin' odor of female fertility! Huh! Ain't that a nice way to put it, Brick?

BRICK: Yes, sir, nothin' wrong with it.

BIG DADDY: Brick says the's nothin' wrong with it!

BIG MAMA: Oh, Big Daddy!

BIG DADDY: *(X DSC)* So this ole bull elephant still had a couple of fornications left in him. He reared back his trunk an' got a whiff of that elephant lady next door! — began to paw at the dirt in his cage an' butt his head against the separatin' partition and, first thing y'know, there was a conspicuous change in his *profile* — very *conspicuous!* Ain't I tellin' this story in decent language, Brick?

BRICK: Yes, sir, too ruttin' decent!

BIG DADDY: So, the little boy pointed at it and said, "What's that?" His Mam said, "Oh, that's — nothin'!" — His Papa said, "She's spoiled!"
(Field-hands sing off R, featuring Sookey: "I Just Can't Stay Here by Myself," through following scene.)
(Big Daddy X to Brick at L.)

BIG DADDY: You didn't laugh at that story, Brick.
(Big Mama X DRC crying. Margaret goes to her. Mae and Gooper hold URC.)

BRICK: No, sir, I didn't laugh at that story.
(On the lower gallery, Big Mama sobs. Big Daddy looks toward her.)

BIG DADDY: What's wrong with that long, thin woman over there, loaded with diamonds? Hey, what's-your-name, what's the matter with you?

MARGARET: *(X toward Big Daddy)* She had a slight dizzy spell, Big Daddy.

BIG DADDY: *(ULC)* You better watch that, Big Mama. A stroke is a bad way to go.

MARGARET: *(X to Big Daddy at C)* Oh, Brick, Big Daddy has on your birthday present to him, Brick, he has on your cashmere robe, the softest material I have ever felt.

BIG DADDY: Yeah, this is my soft birthday, Maggie . . .
Not my gold or my silver birthday, but my soft birthday, everything's got to be soft for Big Daddy on this soft birthday.
(Maggie kneels before Big Daddy C. As Gooper and Mae speak, Big Mama X USRC in front of them, hushing them with a gesture.)

GOOPER: Maggie, I hate to make such a crude observation, but there is somethin' a little indecent about your —

MAE: Like a slow-motion football tackle —

MARGARET: Big Daddy's got on his Chinese slippers that I gave him, Brick. Big Daddy, I haven't given you my big present yet, but now I will, now's the time for me to present it to you! I have an announcement to make!

MAE: What? What kind of announcement?

GOOPER: A sports announcement, Maggie?

MARGARET: Announcement of life beginning! A child is coming, sired

by Brick, and out of Maggie the Cat! I have Brick's child in my body, an' that's my birthday present to Big Daddy on this birthday!
(Big Daddy looks at Brick who X behind Big Daddy to DS portal, L)
BIG DADDY: Get up, girl, get up off your knees, girl.
(Big Daddy helps Margaret rise. He X above her, to her R, bites off the end of a fresh cigar, taken from his bathrobe pocket, as he studies Margaret.)
   Uh-huh, this girl has life in her body, that's no lie!
BIG MAMA: BIG DADDY'S DREAM COME TRUE!
BRICK: *JESUS!*
BIG DADDY: *(X R below wicker seat)* Gooper, I want my lawyer in the mornin'.
BRICK: Where are you goin', Big Daddy?
BIG DADDY: Son, I'm goin' up on the roof to the belvedere on th' roof to look over my kingdom before I give up my kingdom — twenty-eight thousand acres of th' richest land this side of the Valley Nile!
(Exit through R doors, and DR on gallery.)
BIG MAMA: *(Following)* Sweetheart, sweetheart, sweetheart — can I come with you?
(Exits DR.)
(Margaret is DSC in mirror area.)
GOOPER: *(X to bar)* Brick, could you possibly spare me one small shot of that liquor?
BRICK: *(DLC)* Why, help yourself, Gooper, boy.
GOOPER: I will.
MAE: *(X forward)* Of course we know that this is a lie!
GOOPER: *(Drinks)* Be still, Mae!
MAE: *(X to Gooper at bar)* I won't be still! I know she's made this up!
GOOPER: God damn it, I said to shut up!
MAE: That woman isn't pregnant!
GOOPER: Who said she was?
MAE: She did.
GOOPER: The doctor didn't. Doc Baugh didn't.
MARGARET: *(X R to above couch)* I haven't gone to Doc Baugh.
GOOPER: *(X through to L of Margaret)* Then who'd you go to, Maggie?
  (Offstage song finishes.)
MARGARET: One of the best gynecologists in the South.
GOOPER: Uh-huh, I see —
  (Foot on end of couch, trapping Margaret:)
  May we have his name please?
MARGARET: No, you may not, Mister — Prosecutin' Attorney!
MAE: *(X to R of Margaret, above)* He doesn't have any name, he doesn't exist!
MARGARET: He does so exist, and so does my baby, Brick's baby!
MAE: You can't conceive a child by a man that won't sleep with you unless you think you're —
  (Forces Margaret onto couch, turns away C.
  (Brick starts C for Mae.)
  He drinks all the time to be able to tolerate you! Sleeps on the sofa to keep out of contact with you!
GOOPER: *(X above Margaret, who lies face down on couch)* Don't try to kid

us, Margaret —

MAE: *(X to bed, L side, rumpling pillows)* How can you conceive a child by a man that won't sleep with you? How can you conceive? How can you? How can you?!

GOOPER: *(Sharply) MAE!*

BRICK: *(X below Mae to her R, takes hold of her)* Mae, Sister Woman, how d'you know that I don't sleep with Maggie?

MAE: We occupy the next room an' th' wall between isn't soundproof.

BRICK: Oh . . .

MAE: We hear the nightly pleadin' and the nightly refusal. So don't imagine you're goin' t'put a trick over on us, to fool a dyin' man with — a —

BRICK: Mae, Sister Woman, not everybody makes much noise about love. Oh, I know some people are huffers an' puffers, but others are silent lovers.

GOOPER: *(Behind seat, R)* This talk is pointless, completely.

BRICK: How d'y'know that we're not silent lovers?

Even if y'got a peep-hole drilled in the wall, how can y'tell if sometime when Gooper's got business in Memphis an' you're playin' Scrabble at the country club with other ex-queens of cotton, Maggie and I don't come to some temporary agreement? How do you know that —?

(He X above wicker seat to above R and couch.)

MAE: Brick, I never thought that you would stoop to her level, I just never dreamed that you would stoop to her level.

GOOPER: I don't think Brick will stoop to her level.

BRICK: *(Sits R of Margaret on couch)* What is your level? Tell me your level so I can sink or rise to it.

(Rises.)

You heard what Big Daddy said. This girl has life in her body.

MAE: That is a lie!

BRICK: No, truth is something desperate, an' she's got it. Believe me, it's somethin' desperate, an' she's got it.

(X below seat to below bar.)

An' now if you will stop actin' as if Brick Pollitt was dead an' buried, invisible, not heard, an go on back to your peep-hole in the wall — I'm drunk, and sleepy — not as alive as Maggie, but still alive . . .

(Pours drink, drinks.)

GOOPER: *(Picks up briefcase from R foot of bed)* Come on, Mae. We'll leave these love birds together in their nest.

MAE: Yeah, nest of lice! Liars!

GOOPER: Mae — Mae, you jes' go on back to our room —

MAE: Liars!

(Exits through hall.)

GOOPER: *(DR above Margaret)* We're jest goin' to wait an' see. Time will tell.

(X to R of bar.)

Yes, sir, little brother, we're just goin' to wait an' see!

(Exit, hall.)

(The clock strikes twelve.)

(Maggie and Brick exchange a look. He drinks deeply, puts his glass on

622

the bar. Gradually, his expression changes. He utters a sharp exhala-
tion.
(The exhalation is echoed by the singers, off UR, who commence vocaliz-
ing with "Gimme a Cool Drink of Water Fo' I Die," and continue till
end of act.)
MARGARET: *(As she hears Brick's exhalation)* The click?
(Brick looks toward the singers, happily, almost gratefully. He XR to
bed, picks up his pillow, and starts toward head of couch, DR, Xing
above wicker seat. Margaret seizes the pillow from his grasp, rises,
stands facing C, holding the pillow close. Brick watches her with grow-
ing admiration. She moves quickly USC, throwing pillow onto bed.
She X to bar. Brick counters below wicker seat, watching her. Margaret
grabs all the bottles from the bar. She goes into hall, pitches the bottles,
one after the other, off the platform into the UL lawn area. Bottles
break, off L. Margaret re-enters the room, stands UC, facing Brick.)
   Echo Springs has gone dry, and no one but me could drive you
   to town for more.
BRICK: Lacey will get me —
MARGARET: Lacey's been told not to!
BRICK: I could drive —
MARGARET: And you lost your driver's license! I'd phone ahead and have
   you stopped on the highway before you got halfway to Ruby Lightfoot's
   gin mill. I told a lie to Big Daddy, but we can make that lie come
   true. And then I'll bring you liquor, and we'll get drunk together,
   here, tonight, in this place that death has come into! What do you
   say? What do you say, Baby?
BRICK: I admire you, Maggie.
(Brick sits on edge of bed. He looks up at the overhead light, then at
Margaret. She reaches for the light, turns it out; then she kneels quickly
beside Brick at foot of bed.)
MARGARET: Oh, you weak, beautiful people who give up with such grace.
   What you need is someone to take hold of you — gently, with love,
   and hand your life back to you, like something gold you let go of — and
   I can! I'm determined to do it — and nothing's more determined than
   a cat on a tin roof — is there? Is there, Baby?
(She touches his cheek, gently.)

CURTAIN

623

ABSURDIST
DRAMA: The Theatre of
Existentialism

In the early 1950s, the curtain rose on a new kind of drama which left audiences and critics scratching their heads in confusion. These plays showed cartoon-like characters coping with ridiculously bizarre situations. They rejected traditional dramaturgy: They started without real beginnings, continued without developing, and ended without concluding. They eliminated exposition, or else presented expository material which made no sense. Their characters spoke without communicating and shared the stage without relating. Avoiding the two most potent interest factors of drama — conflict and suspense — their dramatic structure appeared to make a virtue of boredom. These plays, which were dramatic expressions of the philosophy of existentialism, came to be known as the theatre of the absurd. They had a powerful impact on the development of theatre in the twentieth century.

Cultural and Philosophical Backgrounds

The trends which culminated in existentialism began in the Renaissance. Galileo's discovery that the earth and planets revolve around the sun instead of the sun and planets revolving around the earth eventually led to the realization that the earth is simply a minor satellite of a minor star, located on the edge of an average galaxy which is, itself, spinning through immeasurable space like millions of other galaxies with no apparent starting point or goal. Human beings, who once considered themselves the center of the universe, discovered they were, in terms of size and centrality, microscopic passengers on an insignificant speck lost in the cosmos.

Darwin increased this disillusionment by demonstrating that human beings, rather than springing from the finger of God, were actually the result of natural processes and were, biologically speaking, no different from other animals. Furthermore, the English, American, French, and Russian revolutions, together with the new science of sociology, established that government and societal order result from human actions rather than divine appointment. Freud showed that individual behavior is more a matter of sickness and health than righteousness and evil and that, in fact, rigid ethical systems contribute to mental illness.

As a result of these scientific and political discoveries, by the twentieth century, Americans and Europeans were suffering a crisis of meaning. They had lost confidence in the old belief systems which held that "God's in his heaven and all's right with the world," that mankind is the pinnacle of God's special creation, that absolute standards of right and wrong and divinely ordained institutions govern human behavior, that there is meaning in life. Furthermore, science and technology, the proudest accomplishments of twentieth-century man, had failed to create paradise on earth and had instead resulted in two world wars, brainwashing, genocide, ecological disasters, and impending nuclear holocaust.

Søren Kierkegaard

In their attempt to understand their situation, twentieth-century philosophers went back to the ideas of Søren Kierkegaard (1813-55), a Danish theologian and philosopher who argued that truth was not absolute. Rather than relying on religious dogma or searching for nonexistent absolutes, Kierkegaard taught that human beings should create their own belief systems by taking a "leap of faith."

Existentialism takes its name from its central conviction that only what exists in the present moment has any actual reality. Essences, absolutes, and ideals are all illusions. Nothing that has happened in the past can be depended upon, either to repeat itself or to cause what will happen in the future, and the future itself is only a false projection based on an inconclusive past. All philosophical, theological, and scientific systems are human constructs which people put together in order to give themselves the illusion of meaning and direction in life. When people realize the false nature of their systems and lay them aside, like a man awakening from a dream, they see reality — that life is absurd. As a result, like a person who suddenly loses his sense of balance and physical orientation, they feel the two primary emotions of existentialism — angst (anxiety) and nausea.

The absurdity of the world has implications for living. First, since accepting an uncomfortable truth is wiser than fooling oneself with a comfortable lie, existentialists resign themselves to the world's absurdity and learn to live with nausea as a fact of life. Secondly, they live fully for the moment. Since actions have no dependable effects, they do not concern themselves with the consequences of their behavior, but at the same time, since they are creating their lives by living, they must be willing to take responsibility for their behavior. Finally, although living is hard and painful, full of angst and nausea, and although the one dependable reality is death, the existentialists reject suicide as an inauthentic, cowardly escape.

Existentialism expressed itself in various intellectual and cultural movements of the midtwentieth century. It provided the philosophical viewpoint of the "beat generation" and the hippies, and also of much twentieth-century art, literature, music, and — of course — theatre.

Dramatic Theory

In 1961, Martin Esslin published his *Theatre of the Absurd*. This book not only popularized a name for existentialist drama but also clarified its dramatic principles. Esslin argued that, even though the absurdists rejected traditional dramatic structure, they had definable patterns of their own, and their dramatic form reflected their underlying existentialist philosophy.

Whereas traditional drama tends to have a linear form, to tell a story, and to follow a cause-and-effect order, absurdist plays tend to be cyclic, to present a series of images, and to be rhythmic in their structure. Absurdist plays typically begin with a situation, progress through a variety of new situations, and end by returning to the original situation. Samuel Beckett's *Waiting for Godot,* for instance, presents two days in the life of two tramps.

The end of Act Two — the second day — is essentially the same as the end of Act One, which is no different from the beginning of the play. Nothing has changed, and the play suggests that, if a third act were added, it would progress the same as the first two, without making any difference in the main characters' lives. Similarly, near the end of the same author's script titled *Play*, a stage direction dictates, "Repeat play."

Absurdist plays typically present a series of strong dramatic images instead of a connected story line. After viewing an absurdist play, an audience member may not be able to tell "what happened" in the drama, but is more likely to report a random collection of images — an old couple reaching out to each other across a room filled with empty chairs, a hobo inspecting the inside of his hat while his friend inspects the inside of his boot, two maids taking turns imitating their mistress, a woman carrying on an inane monolog while a grassy hill has devoured all but her head. And absurdist plays tend to progress from scene to scene rhythmically, in a manner similar to the progression from unit to unit in a musical composition.

The characters and dialog which provide the materials of absurdist plays are ignoble and meaningless. The characters typically lack nobility in social standing: they are bums, maids, civic functionaries. Nor do they have nobility of character. Since their world does not permit them to make real decisions or take effective action, they are incapable of demonstrating heroism. They are small people trapped in a confusing environment. And although they may talk at great length, they fail to make sense, and when their sentences do make sense, they are likely to express banalities. This is not to say that the absurdists are careless about language. On the contrary, their dialog — sometimes convoluted, sometimes minimalist — often achieves a kind of poetry.

In style, absurdist plays are nonrealistic and nonsensical. They actively defy intellectualism and rationality. Furthermore, they combine the serious with the comic, horror with hilarity. Instead of reaching out to their audience, they seem to aim at confusing, boring, or even offending their viewers.

This dramaturgy, bizarre though it may appear at first, beautifully capsulizes the existentialist world view. Instead of arguing for existentialism, these plays simply present an absurd world, devoid of meaning-creating structures. In so doing, they awaken the audience to the essential absurdity of the real world, they encourage the audience to laugh at the human predicament, and they celebrate life without a center.

Dramatic Literature

Jean-Paul Sartre (1905-80) and Albert Camus (1913-60), two major existentialist authors, both wrote plays as well as novels and essays. Sartre's plays include a retelling of the Orestes story, *The Flies* (1942), and a one-act about three people in hell, titled *No Exit* (1944). Two of Camus' plays which express his existential viewpoints are *The Misunderstanding* (1944) and *Caligula* (1945). However, while the plays of Sartre and Camus have existential content, they use traditional dramaturgy.

The major absurdist playwrights, all of whom wrote in French, were

Samuel Beckett (1906-89), Jean Genet (1910-86), and Eugène Ionesco (1912-).

Samuel Beckett

Born in Ireland, Beckett moved to Paris in 1938 and spent the rest of his life there. After spending the war years as part of the French resistance and establishing himself as a scholar and novelist, he wrote *Waiting for Godot* which premiered in Paris in 1953. *Godot* shocked the theatrical world and drew attention to absurdism. Beckett went on to write many other absurdist scripts, including *Endgame* (1957), about a blind man living in a bunker with his servant and his two aged parents whom he keeps in trash cans; *Krapps Last Tape* (1958), in which an old man repetitiously listens to audio tapes about his own life; and *Happy Days* (1961), in which a half-buried woman rattles on inconsequentially about her happy life. As Beckett continued writing, his plays became more experimental, shorter, more minimalist. His plays typically use cyclic structure to depict characters who are physically confined, obsessed about their pasts, and hopeless about their futures.

Jean Genet

Genet, an orphan who did not meet his parents until he was an adult, grew up in and out of institutions and early turned to a life of thievery. After repeatedly jailing him, the French justice system finally condemned him to life imprisonment as an incorrigible. When his writings began to win him attention, however, Sartre and other writers successfully petitioned for his release. Three of Genet's plays include *The Maids* (1947), in which two sisters (played by men) punish each other while taking turns imitating their mistress; *The Blacks* (1958), in which a black acting troupe in white masks ritualistically murders a white woman; and his most famous work, *The Balcony* (1956), in which patrons come to a brothel to act out their fantasies of grandeur. Genet's plays use political revolution and exquisite language in their investigation of the relationship between appearance and reality. His antisocial stance and the violence of his images and dramatic action show his affinity to Artaud's theatre of cruelty.

Eugéne Ionesco

The late Eugéne Ionesco was born in Rumania and spent his first thirteen years in Paris. He returned to Rumania with his family where he studied French — his native language — at the University of Bucharest. He also wrote poetry and won some local notoriety as a literary critic. He finished his studies and, in 1938 while working as a French teacher, got permission from the government to travel to Paris to do research for a monumental work on French poetry. He became a permanent resident of France, but apparently never began the project he had proposed. At the end of the war, he was living in Paris and working for a publisher.

In the late forties, Ionesco decided to learn English. The self-directed study course he used ended up having effects far beyond language acquisition. Its inane sentences, which presented such startling but irrefutable observations as the fact that the ceiling is up while the floor is down, acted as a catalyst which brought together powerful images from his youth — his love of Punch-and-Judy shows, his childhood separation from his family to attend boarding school, memories of brutality, and perceptions of the incomprehensibililty of everyday experience. With this stimulus, in 1948, he wrote a strange play which he eventually titled *The Bald Soprano*.

Although the premiere of *The Bald Soprano* by a small theatre company attracted little attention, the experience convinced Ionesco that he wanted to write for the theatre. His most characteristic works were in the form of one-acts. They included *The Lesson* (1951), in which an aged tutor uses language to brutalize a female student; *The Chairs* (1952), in which an old couple fill a room with imaginary guests to hear their philosophy of life and then fall out of windows to their deaths before the message can be delivered; and *Jack, or the Submission* (1950), in which a family subjugates their son, Jack, by forcing him to marry Roberta II, who has three noses on her face and nine fingers on her left hand.

In later full-length plays, Ionesco turned to more traditional dramaturgy. In his best-known play of this type, *Rhinoceros* (1960), all of humankind gradually turn into pachyderms. In all, Ionesco wrote over twenty plays before his death in 1994.

In Ionesco's plays, material objects proliferate at human expense: In *The Chairs*, it's chairs; in *The New Tenant* (1955), it's furniture; in *Macbett* (1972), it's the heads of guillotine victims. Ionesco portrays human beings as ordinary folk, like his reappearing antihero Berenger, who are overwhelmed by an incomprehensible world. He shows life as utterly devoid of meaning and interest. His characters speak language which, while useless in communicating meaning can still be a frightening tool for dominating the weak. Despite their bleak outlook, Ionesco's plays, which carry paradoxical subtitles such as "A Tragic Farce" and "A Grotesque Tragedy," are frequently comic.

Other Absurdist Playwrights

Many other playwrights working during the same period used absurdist structures and depicted similar world views. These included Harold Pinter (1930-) and Tom Stoppard (1937-) in England, Günter Grass (1927-) in Germany, the Spaniard Fernando Arrabal (1932-) in France, and Edward Albee (1928-) and Arthur Kopit (1938-) in the United States. Lively debates surrounded some of these playwrights concerning whether or not they were really absurdists. Some of them, like Arrabal, who calls his drama "panic theatre," disavowed connections to absurdism, or at least made no claims to belong to the movement. Some of them, like Pinter, seem to fit the descriptions of realism and absurdism equally well. Many of them include overt political comment in their scripts — subject matter foreign to the absurdism of Beckett and Ionesco.

Perhaps it is most accurate to say that, in the middle of the twentieth century, existentialism spawned a dramatic technique which, in varying degrees, affected the work of many leading playwrights. Unlike the realists and the adherents of epic theatre before them, these playwrights did not write manifestos expressing their allegiance to a particular dramatic technique. Critics like Martin Esslin, however, detected a similarity in their work and distilled from their dramaturgy characteristics which came to be called absurdism.

Theatrical Production and Organization

Although some of the absurdist plays appeared on Broadway and its European counterparts, existentialist drama seemed more at home in the smaller, more experimental, less commercial fringe theatres. This was partly due to the fact that the mass audience of commercial theatre found them uncomfortably difficult to watch and partly because they were frequently one-acts, a form that traditionally has little commercial appeal. French actor and director Roger Blin (1907-84) made a significant contribution to absurdism. He won attention by his direction of the premiere of *Waiting for Godot,* and went on to direct most of Beckett's subsequent plays as well as those of Genet.

Absurdism did not create a characteristic production style of its own. Instead, producers of these plays, attempting to provide the best mode for each individual script, selected performance and design approaches from realism, expressionism, and epic theatre. In preparing the premiere of *The Bald Soprano,* for instance, the director at first experimented with a stylized, comic acting style before deciding to do the play with serious, more-or-less realistic acting on a realistic, Ibsen-like set. Beckett became notorious for the rigidity of his prescriptions for sets and characterization. And Genet's *The Balcony* has been produced in styles ranging from rich, opulent pageantry to coarse, theatre-of-cruelty offensiveness.

The Bald Soprano

Dramaturgy

Ionesco's play illustrates almost all of the characteristics of absurdist drama. It presents six inconsistently drawn characters in a situation where absolutely nothing — not even the progression of time — can be depended upon. While these characters may carry on lively conversations, they don't really communicate with each other or relate to each other. They discuss the most banal trivia with passion, and use nonsensical language to make illogical points. The scenes and sequences which make up the plot progress in an apparently arbitrary order without cause-and-effect connections, and at its conclusion, the play returns to its beginning and replays its first lines as the curtain descends.

The play presents a world vastly different from that of realism, symbolism, expressionism, and political theatre — a world in which psychology, environment, heredity, and socio-economic structures either don't exist or are meaningless. The play intentionally disorients the audience and then leaves them on their own to construct meanings where none exist.

Production History

La Cantatrice chauve was first produced in Paris, in 1950, by an avant-garde group of young actors directed by Nicolas Bataille at the Théâtre des Noctambules. It was subsequently presented in London as *The Bald Prima Donna* (1956), and in New York, in 1958, as *The Bald Soprano.* Its bizarre comedy, its adaptability to a variety of production styles, and its effectiveness in the hands of actors of varying abilities has given it popularity with succeeding generations of community, academic, and experimental theatre groups. While it has shocked, confused, and disoriented its audiences, it has also delighted and entertained them.

Theatre of the Absurd Timeline

ANTONIN ARTAUD (1896-1948)

JEAN-PAUL SARTRE (1905-80)

SAMUEL BECKETT (1906-89)

ROGER BLIN (1907-84)

JEAN GENET (1910-86)

EUGÈNE IONESCO (1912-)

"THE BALD SOPRANO" (1950) ●

ALBERT CAMUS (1913-60)

WORLD WAR I (1914-18)

GÜNTER GRASS (1927-)

EDWARD ALBEE (1928-)

THE GREAT DEPRESSION (1929-39)

HAROLD PINTER (1930-)

FERNANDO ARRABAL (1932-)

TOM STOPPARD (1937-)

ARTHUR KOPIT (1938-)

WORLD WAR II (1939-45)

"THE THEATRE OF THE ABSURD" (1961) ●

1890 1900 1910 1920 1930 1940 1950 1960 1970 1980 1990

THE BALD SOPRANO

by EUGÈNE IONESCO
Translated by Donald M. Allen

THE CHARACTERS

MR. SMITH

MRS. SMITH

MR. MARTIN

MRS. MARTIN

MARY, *the maid*

THE FIRE CHIEF

SCENE: A middle-class English interior, with English armchairs. An English evening. Mr. Smith, an Englishman, seated in his English armchair and wearing English slippers, is smoking his English pipe and reading an English newspaper, near an English fire. He is wearing English spectacles and a small gray English mustache. Beside him, in another English armchair, Mrs. Smith, an Englishwoman, is darning some English socks. A long moment of English silence. The English clock strikes 17 English strokes.

MRS. SMITH: There, it's nine o'clock. We've drunk the soup, and eaten the fish and chips, and the English salad. The children have drunk English water. We've eaten well this evening. That's because we live in the suburbs of London and because our name is Smith.

MR. SMITH: *(Continues to read, clicks his tongue.)*

MRS. SMITH: Potatoes are very good fried in fat; the salad oil was not rancid. The oil from the grocer at the corner is better quality than the oil from the grocer across the street. It is even better than the oil from the grocer at the bottom of the street. However, I prefer not to tell them that their oil is bad.

MR. SMITH: *(Continues to read, clicks his tongue.)*

MRS. SMITH: However, the oil from the grocer at the corner is still the best.

MR. SMITH: *(Continues to read, clicks his tongue.)*

MRS. SMITH: Mary did the potatoes very well, this evening. The last time she did not do them well. I do not like them when they are well done.

MR. SMITH: *(Continues to read, clicks his tongue.)*

MRS. SMITH: The fish was fresh. It made my mouth water. I had two helpings. No, three helpings. That made me go to the w.c. You also had three helpings. However, the third time you took less than the first two times, while as for me, I took a great deal more. I ate better than you this evening. Why is that? Usually, it is you who eats more. It is not appetite you lack.

MR. SMITH: *(Clicks his tongue.)*

MRS. SMITH: But still, the soup was perhaps a little too salty. It was saltier than you. Ha, ha, ha. It also had too many leeks and not enough onions. I regret I didn't advise Mary to add some aniseed stars. The next time I'll know better.

MR. SMITH: *(Continues to read, clicks his tongue.)*

MRS. SMITH: Our little boy wanted to drink some beer; he's going to love getting tiddly. He's like you. At table did you notice how he stared at the bottle? But I poured some water from the jug into his glass. He was thirsty and he drank it. Helen is like me: she's a good manager, thrifty, plays the piano. She never asks to drink English beer. She's like our little daughter who drinks only milk and eats only porridge. It's obvious that she's only two. She's named Peggy. The quince and bean pie was marvelous. It would have been nice, perhaps, to have had a small glass of Australian Burgundy with the sweet, but I did not bring the bottle to the table because I did not wish to set the children a bad example of gluttony. They must learn to be sober and temperate.

MR. SMITH: *(Continues to read, clicks his tongue.)*

MRS. SMITH: Mrs. Parker knows a Rumanian grocer by the name of Popesco

Rosenfeld, who has just come from Constantinople. He is a great specialist in yogurt. He has a diploma from the school of yogurt-making in Adrianople. Tomorrow I shall buy a large pot of native Rumanian yogurt from him. One doesn't often find such things here in the suburbs of London.

MR. SMITH: *(Continues to read, clicks his tongue.)*

MRS. SMITH: Yogurt is excellent for the stomach, the kidneys, the appendicitis, and apotheosis. It was Doctor Mackenzie-King who told me that, he's the one who takes care of the children of our neighbors, the Johns. He's a good doctor. One can trust him. He never prescribes any medicine that he's not tried out on himself first. Before operating on Parker, he had his own liver operated on first, although he was not the least bit ill.

MR. SMITH: But how does it happen that the doctor pulled through while Parker died?

MRS. SMITH: Because the operation was successful in the doctor's case and it was not in Parker's.

MR. SMITH: Then Mackenzie is not a good doctor. The operation should have succeeded with both of them or else both should have died.

MRS. SMITH: Why?

MR. SMITH: A conscientious doctor must die with his patient if they can't get well together. The captain of a ship goes down with his ship into the briny deep, he does not survive alone.

MRS. SMITH: One cannot compare a patient with a ship.

MR. SMITH: Why not? A ship has its diseases too; moreover, your doctor is as hale as a ship; that's why he should have perished at the same time as his patient, like the captain and his ship.

MRS. SMITH: Ah! I hadn't thought of that . . . Perhaps it is true . . . And then, what conclusion do you draw from this?

MR. SMITH: All doctors are quacks. And all patients too. Only the Royal Navy is honest in England.

MRS. SMITH: But not sailors.

MR. SMITH: Naturally. *(A pause. Still reading his paper:)* Here's a thing I don't understand. In the newspaper they always give the age of deceased persons but never the age of the newly born. That doesn't make sense.

MRS. SMITH: I never thought of that!

(Another moment of silence. The clock strikes seven times. Silence. The clock strikes three times. Silence. The clock doesn't strike.)

MR. SMITH: *(Still reading his paper)* Tsk, it says here that Bobby Watson died.

MRS. SMITH: My God, the poor man! When did he die?

MR. SMITH: Why do you pretend to be astonished? You know very well that he's been dead these past two years. Surely you remember that we attended his funeral a year and a half ago.

MRS. SMITH: Oh yes, of course I do remember. I remembered it right away, but I don't understand why you yourself were so surprised to see it in the paper.

MR. SMITH: It wasn't in the paper. It's been three years since his death was announced. I remembered it through an association of ideas.

MRS. SMITH: What a pity! He was so well preserved.

MR. SMITH: He was the handsomest corpse in Great Britain. He didn't look his age. Poor Bobby, he'd been dead for four years and he was still warm. A veritable living corpse. And how cheerful he was!

MRS. SMITH: Poor Bobby.

MR. SMITH: Which poor Bobby do you mean?

MRS. SMITH: It is his wife that I mean. She is called Bobby too, Bobby Watson. Since they both had the same name, you could never tell one from the other when you saw them together. It was only after his death that you could really tell which was which. And there are still people today who confuse her with the deceased and offer their condolences to him. Do you know her?

MR. SMITH: I only met her once, by chance, at Bobby's burial.

MRS. SMITH: I've never seen her. Is she pretty?

MR. SMITH: She has regular features and yet one cannot say that she is pretty. She is too big and stout. Her features are not regular but still one can say that she is very pretty. She is a little too small and too thin. She's a voice teacher.

(The clock strikes five times. A long silence.)

MRS. SMITH: And when do they plan to be married, those two?

MR. SMITH: Next spring, at the latest.

MRS. SMITH: We shall have to go to their wedding, I suppose.

MR. SMITH: We shall have to give them a wedding present. I wonder what?

MRS. SMITH: Why don't we give them one of the seven silver salvers that were given us for our wedding and which have never been of any use to us? *(Silence.)*

MRS. SMITH: How sad for her to be left a widow so young.

MR. SMITH: Fortunately, they had no children.

MRS. SMITH: That was all they needed! Children! Poor woman. How could she have managed?!

MR. SMITH: She's still young. She might very well remarry. She looks so well in mourning.

MRS. SMITH: But who would take care of the children? You know very well that they have a boy and a girl. What are their names?

MR. SMITH: Bobby and Bobby like their parents. Bobby Watson's uncle, old Bobby Watson, is a rich man and very fond of the boy. He might very well pay for Bobby's education.

MRS. SMITH: That would be proper. And Bobby Watson's aunt, old Bobby Watson, might very well, in her turn, pay for the education of Bobby Watson, Bobby Watson's daughter. That way Bobby, Bobby Watson's mother, could remarry. Has she anyone in mind?

MR. SMITH: Yes, a cousin of Bobby Watson's.

MRS. SMITH: Who? Bobby Watson?

MR. SMITH: Which Bobby Watson do you mean?

MRS. SMITH: Why, Bobby Watson, the son of old Bobby Watson, the late Bobby Watson's other uncle.

MR. SMITH: No, it's not that one, it's someone else. It's Bobby Watson, the son of old Bobby Watson, the late Bobby Watson's aunt.

MRS. SMITH: Are you referring to Bobby Watson the commercial traveler?

MR. SMITH: All the Bobby Watsons are commercial travelers.

MRS. SMITH: What a difficult trade! However, they do well at it.

MR. SMITH: Yes, when there's no competition.

MRS. SMITH: And when is there no competition?

MR. SMITH: On Tuesdays, Thursdays, and Tuesdays.

MRS. SMITH: Ah! Three days a week? And what does Bobby Watson do on those days?

MR. SMITH: He rests, he sleeps.

MRS. SMITH: But why doesn't he work those three days if there's no competition?

MR. SMITH: I don't know everything. I can't answer all your idiotic questions!

MRS. SMITH: *(Offended)* Oh! Are you trying to humiliate me?

MR. SMITH: *(All smiles)* You know very well that I'm not.

MRS. SMITH: Men are all alike! You sit there all day long, a cigarette in your mouth, or you powder your nose and rouge your lips, fifty times a day, or else you drink like a fish.

MR. SMITH: But what would you say if you saw men acting like women do, smoking all day long, powdering, rouging their lips, drinking whisky?

MRS. SMITH: It's nothing to me! But if you're only saying that to annoy me . . . I don't care for that kind of joking, you know that very well!

(She hurls the socks across the stage and shows her teeth. She gets up.*)

MR. SMITH: *(Also getting up and going towards his wife, tenderly)* Oh, my little ducky daddles, what a little spitfire you are! You know that I only said it as a joke! *(He takes her by the waist and kisses her.)* What a ridiculous pair of old lovers we are! Come, let's put out the lights and go bye-byes.

MARY: *(Entering)* I'm the maid. I have spent a very pleasant afternoon. I've been to the cinema with a man and I've seen a film with some women. After the cinema, we went to drink some brandy and milk and then read the newspaper.

MRS. SMITH: I hope that you've spent a pleasant afternoon, that you went to the cinema with a man and that you drank some brandy and milk.

MR. SMITH: And the newspaper.

MARY: Mr. and Mrs. Martin, your guests, are at the door. They were waiting for me. They didn't dare come in by themselves. They were supposed to have dinner with you this evening.

MRS. SMITH: Oh, yes. We were expecting them. And we were hungry. Since they didn't put in an appearance, we were going to start dinner without them. We've had nothing to eat all day. You should not have gone out!

MARY: But it was you who gave me permission.

MR. SMITH: We didn't do it on purpose.

MARY: *(Bursts into laughter, then she bursts into tears. Then she smiles.)* I bought me a chamber pot.

---

*In Nicolas Bataille's production, Mrs. Smith did not show her teeth, nor did she throw the socks very far.

MRS. SMITH: My dear Mary, please open the door and ask Mr. and Mrs. Martin to step in. We will change quickly.

(Mr. and Mrs. Smith exit right. Mary opens the door at the left by which Mr. and Mrs. Martin enter.)

MARY: Why have you come so late! You are not very polite. People should be punctual. Do you understand? But sit down there, anyway, and wait now that you're here.

(She exits. Mr. and Mrs. Martin sit facing each other, without speaking. They smile timidly at each other. The dialogue which follows must be spoken in voices that are drawling, monotonous, a little singsong, without nuances.*)

MR. MARTIN: Excuse me, madam, but it seems to me, unless I'm mistaken, that I've met you somewhere before.

MRS. MARTIN: I, too, sir. It seems to me that I've met you somewhere before.

MR. MARTIN: Was it, by any chance, at Manchester that I caught a glimpse of you, madam?

MRS. MARTIN: That is very possible. I am originally from the city of Manchester. But I do not have a good memory, sir. I cannot say whether it was there that I caught a glimpse of you or not!

MR. MARTIN: Good God, that's curious! I, too, am originally from the city of Manchester, madam!

MRS. MARTIN: That is curious!

MR. MARTIN: Isn't that curious! Only, I, madam, I left the city of Manchester about five weeks ago.

MRS. MARTIN: That is curious! What a bizarre coincidence! I, too, sir, I left the city of Manchester about five weeks ago.

MR. MARTIN: Madam, I took the 8:30 morning train which arrives in London at 4:45.

MRS. MARTIN: That is curious! How very bizarre! And what a coincidence! I took the same train, sir, I too.

MR. MARTIN: Good Lord, how curious! Perhaps then, madam, it was on the train that I saw you?

MRS. MARTIN: It is indeed possible; that is, not unlikely. It is plausible and, after all, why not! — But I don't recall it, sir!

MR. MARTIN: I traveled second class, madam. There is no second class in England, but I always travel second class.

MRS. MARTIN: That is curious! How very bizarre! And what a coincidence! I, too, sir, I traveled second class.

MR. MARTIN: How curious that is! Perhaps we did meet in second class, my dear lady!

MRS. MARTIN: That is certainly possible, and it is not at all unlikely. But I do not remember very well, my dear sir!

MR. MARTIN: My seat was in coach No. 8, compartment 6, my dear lady.

MRS. MARTIN: How curious that is! My seat was also in coach No. 8, compartment 6, my dear sir!

MR. MARTIN: How curious that is and what a bizarre coincidence! Perhaps

---

*In Nicolas Bataille's production, this dialog was spoken in a tone and played in a style sincerely tragic.

we met in compartment 6, my dear lady?

MRS. MARTIN: It is indeed possible, after all! But I do not recall it, my dear sir!

MR. MARTIN: To tell the truth, my dear lady, I do not remember it either, but it is possible that we caught a glimpse of each other there, and as I think of it, it seems to me even very likely.

MRS. MARTIN: Oh! truly, of course, truly, sir!

MR. MARTIN: How curious it is! I had seat No. 3, next to the window, my dear lady.

MRS. MARTIN: Oh, good Lord, how curious and bizarre! I had seat No. 6, next to the window, across from you, my dear sir.

MR. MARTIN: Good God, how curious that is and what a coincidence! We were then seated facing each other, my dear lady! It is there that we must have seen each other!

MRS. MARTIN: How curious it is! It is possible, but I do not recall it, sir!

MR. MARTIN: To tell the truth, my dear lady, I do not remember it either. However, it is very possible that we saw each other on that occasion.

MRS. MARTIN: It is true, but I am not at all sure of it, sir.

MR. MARTIN: Dear madam, were you not the lady who asked me to place her suitcase in the luggage rack and who thanked me and gave me permission to smoke?

MRS. MARTIN: But of course, that must have been I, sir. How curious it is, how curious it is, and what a coincidence!

MR. MARTIN: How curious it is, how bizarre, what a coincidence! And well, well, it was perhaps at that moment that we came to know each other, madam?

MRS. MARTIN: How curious it is and what a coincidence! It is indeed possible, my dear sir! However, I do not believe that I recall it.

MR. MARTIN: Nor do I, madam. *(A moment of silence. The clock strikes twice, then once.)* Since coming to London, I have resided in Bromfield Street, my dear lady.

MRS. MARTIN: How curious that is, how bizarre! I, too, since coming to London, I have resided in Bromfield Street, my dear sir.

MR. MARTIN: How curious that is, well then, well then, perhaps we have seen each other in Bromfield Street, my dear lady.

MRS. MARTIN: How curious that is, how bizarre! It is indeed possible, after all! But I do not recall it, my dear sir.

MR. MARTIN: I reside at No. 19, my dear lady.

MRS. MARTIN: How curious that is. I also reside at No. 19, my dear sir.

MR. MARTIN: Well then, well then, well then, well then, perhaps we have seen each other in that house, dear lady?

MRS. MARTIN: It is indeed possible but I do not recall it, dear sir.

MR. MARTIN: My flat is on the fifth floor, No. 8, my dear lady.

MRS. MARTIN: How curious it is, good Lord, how bizarre! And what a coincidence! I too reside on the fifth floor, in flat No. 8, dear sir!

MR. MARTIN: *(Musing)* How curious it is, how curious it is, how curious it is, and what a coincidence! You know, in my bedroom there is a bed, and it is covered with a green eiderdown. This room, with the bed and the green eiderdown, is at the end of the corridor between the w.c. and the bookcase, dear lady!

MRS. MARTIN: What a coincidence, good Lord, what a coincidence! My bedroom, too, has a bed with a green eiderdown and is at the end of the corridor, between the w.c., dear sir, and the bookcase!

MR. MARTIN: How bizarre, curious, strange! Then, madam, we live in the same room and we sleep in the same bed, dear lady. It is perhaps there that we have met!

MRS. MARTIN: How curious it is and what a coincidence! It is indeed possible that we have met there, and perhaps even last night. But I do not recall it, dear sir!

MR. MARTIN: I have a little girl, my little daughter, she lives with me, dear lady. She is two years old, she's blonde, she has a white eye and a red eye, she is very pretty, her name is Alice, dear lady.

MRS. MARTIN: What a bizarre coincidence! I, too, have a little girl. She is two years old, had a white eye and a red eye, she is very pretty, and her name is Alice, too, dear sir!

MR. MARTIN: *(In the same drawling, monotonous voice)* How curious it is and what a coincidence! And bizarre! Perhaps they are the same, dear lady!

MRS. MARTIN: How curious it is! It is indeed possible, dear sir. *(A rather long moment of silence. The clock strikes 29 times.)*

MR. MARTIN: *(After having reflected at length, gets up slowly and, unhurriedly, moves toward Mrs. Martin, who, surprised by his solemn air, has also gotten up very quietly. Mr. Martin, in the same flat, monotonous voice, slighty singsong)* Then, dear lady, I believe that there can be no doubt about it, we have seen each other before and you are my own wife . . . Elizabeth, I have found you again!

(Mrs. Martin approaches Mr. Martin without haste. They embrace without expression. The clock strikes once, very loud. This striking of the clock must be so loud that it makes the audience jump. The Martins do not hear it.)

MRS. MARTIN: Donald, it's you, darling!

(They sit together in the same armchair, their arms around each other, and fall asleep. The clock strikes several more times. Mary, on tiptoe, a finger to her lips, enters quietly and addresses the audience.)

MARY: Elizabeth and Donald are now too happy to be able to hear me. I can therefore let you in on a secret. Elizabeth is not Elizabeth, Donald is not Donald. And here is the proof: the child that Donald spoke of is not Elizabeth's daughter, they are not the same person. Donald's daughter has one white eye and one red eye like Elizabeth's daughter. Whereas Donald's child has a white right eye and a red left eye, Elizabeth's child has a red right eye and a white left eye! Thus all of Donald's system of deduction collapses when it comes up against this last obstacle which destroys his whole theory. In spite of the extraordinary coincidences which seem to be definitive proofs, Donald and Elizabeth, not being the parents of the same child, are not Donald and Elizabeth. It is in vain that he thinks he is Donald, it is in vain that she thinks she is Elizabeth. He believes in vain that she is Elizabeth. She believes in vain that he is Donald — they are sadly deceived. But who is the true Donald? Who is the true Elizabeth? Who has any interest in prolonging this confusion? I don't know. Let's not try to know. Let's leave things as they are. *(She takes several steps toward the door, then returns and says to the audience:)* My real name is Sherlock Holmes. *(She exits.)*

(The clock strikes as much as it likes. After several seconds, Mr. and Mrs. Martin separate and take the chairs they had at the beginning.)

MR. MARTIN: Darling, let's forget all that has not passed between us, and now that we have found each other again, let's try not to lose each other any more, and live as before.

MRS. MARTIN: Yes, darling.

(Mr. and Mrs. Smith enter from the right, wearing the same clothes.)

MRS. SMITH: Good evening, dear friends! Please forgive us for having made you wait so long. We thought that we should extend you the courtesy to which you are entitled and as soon as we learned that you had been kind enough to give us the pleasure of coming to see us without prior notice we hurried to dress for the occasion.

MR. SMITH: *(Furious)* We've had nothing to eat all day. And we've been waiting four whole hours for you. Why have you come so late?

(Mr. and Mrs. Smith sit facing their guests. The striking of the clock underlines the speeches, more or less strongly, according to the case. The Martins, particularly Mrs. Martin, seem embarrassed and timid. For this reason the conversation begins with difficulty and the words are uttered, at the beginning, awkwardly. A long embarrassed silence at first, then other silences and hesitations follow.)

MR. SMITH: Hm. *(Silence.)*

MRS. SMITH: Hm, hm. *(Silence.)*

MRS. MARTIN: Hm, hm, hm. *(Silence.)*

MR. MARTIN: Hm, hm, hm, hm. *(Silence.)*

MRS. MARTIN: Oh, but definitely. *(Silence.)*

MR. MARTIN: We all have colds. *(Silence.)*

MR. SMITH: Nevertheless, it's not chilly. *(Silence.)*

MRS. SMITH: There's no draft. *(Silence.)*

MR. MARTIN: Oh no, fortunately. *(Silence.)*

MR. SMITH: Oh dear, oh dear, oh dear. *(Silence.)*

MR. MARTIN: Don't you feel well? *(Silence.)*

MRS. SMITH: No, he's wet his pants. *(Silence.)*

MRS. MARTIN: Oh, sir, at your age, you shouldn't. *(Silence.)*

MR. SMITH: The heart is ageless. *(Silence.)*

MR. MARTIN: That's true. *(Silence.)*

MRS. SMITH: So they say. *(Silence.)*

MRS. MARTIN: They also say the opposite. *(Silence.)*

MR. SMITH: The truth lies somewhere between the two. *(Silence.)*

MR. MARTIN: That's true. *(Silence.)*

MRS. SMITH: *(To the Martins)* Since you travel so much, you must have many interesting things to tell us.

MR. MARTIN: *(To his wife)* My dear, tell us what you've seen today.

MRS. MARTIN: It's scarcely worth the trouble, for no one would believe me.

MR. SMITH: We're not going to question your sincerity!

MRS. SMITH: You will offend us if you think that.

MR. MARTIN: *(To his wife)* You will offend them, my dear, if you think that . . .

MRS. MARTIN: *(Graciously)* Oh well, today I witnessed something extraordinary. Something really incredible.

MR. MARTIN: Tell us quickly, my dear.

MR. SMITH: Oh, this is going to be amusing.

MRS. SMITH: At last.

MRS. MARTIN: Well, today, when I went shopping to buy some vegetables, which are getting to be dearer and dearer . . .

MRS. SMITH: Where is it all going to end!

MR. SMITH: You shouldn't interrupt, my dear, it's very rude.

MRS. MARTIN: In the street, near a café, I saw a man, properly dressed, about fifty years old, or not even that, who . . .

MR. SMITH: Who, what?

MRS. SMITH: Who, what?

MR. SMITH: *(To his wife)* Don't interrupt, my dear, you're disgusting.

MRS. SMITH: My dear, it is you who interrupted first, you boor.

MR. SMITH: *(To his wife)* Hush. *(To Mrs. Martin)* What was this man doing?

MRS. MARTIN: Well, I'm sure you'll say that I'm making it up — he was down on one knee and he was bent over.

MR. MARTIN, MR. SMITH, MRS. SMITH: Oh!

MRS. MARTIN: Yes, bent over.

MR. SMITH: Not possible.

MRS. MARTIN: Yes, bent over. I went near him to see what he was doing . . .

MR. SMITH: And?

MRS. MARTIN: He was tying his shoe lace which had come undone.

MR. MARTIN, MR. SMITH, MRS. SMITH: Fantastic!

MR. SMITH: If someone else had told me this, I'd not believe it.

MR. MARTIN: Why not? One sees things even more extraordinary every day, when one walks around. For instance, today in the Underground I myself saw a man, quietly sitting on a seat, reading his newspaper.

MRS. SMITH: What a character!

MR. SMITH: Perhaps it was the same man!

(The doorbell rings.)

MR. SMITH: Goodness, someone is ringing.

MRS. SMITH: There must be somebody there. I'll go and see. *(She goes to see, she opens the door and closes it, and comes back.)* Nobody. *(She sits down again.)*

MR. MARTIN: I'm going to give you another example . . . *(Doorbell rings again.)*

MR. SMITH: Goodness, someone is ringing.

MRS. SMITH: There must be somebody there. I'll go and see. *(She goes to see, opens the door, and comes back.)* No one. *(She sits down again.)*

MR. MARTIN: *(Who has forgotten where he was)* Uh . . .

MRS. MARTIN: You were saying that you were going to give us another example.

MR. MARTIN: Oh, yes . . .

642

(Doorbell rings again.)

MR. SMITH: Goodness, someone is ringing.

MRS. SMITH: I'm not going to open the door again.

MR. SMITH: Yes, but there must be someone there!

MRS. SMITH: The first time there was no one. The second time, no one. Why do you think that there is someone there now?

MR. SMITH: Because someone has rung!

MRS. MARTIN: That's no reason.

MR. MARTIN: What? When one hears the doorbell ring, that means someone is at the door ringing to have the door opened.

MRS. MARTIN: Not always. You've just seen otherwise!

MR. MARTIN: In most cases, yes.

MR. SMITH: As for me, when I go to visit someone, I ring in order to be admitted. I think that everyone does the same thing and that each time there is a ring there must be someone there.

MRS. SMITH: That is true in theory. But in reality things happen differently. You have just seen otherwise.

MRS. MARTIN: Your wife is right.

MR. MARTIN: Oh! You women! You always stand up for each other.

MRS. SMITH: Well, I'll go and see. You can't say that I am obstinate, but you will see that there's no one there! *(She goes to look, opens the door and closes it.)* You see, there's no one there. *(She returns to her seat.)*

MRS. SMITH: Oh, these men who always think they're right and who're always wrong!

(The doorbell rings again.)

MR. SMITH: Goodness, someone is ringing. There must be someone there.

MRS. SMITH: *(In a fit of anger)* Don't send me to open the door again. You've seen that it was useless. Experience teaches us that when one hears the doorbell ring it is because there is never anyone there.

MRS. MARTIN: Never.

MR. MARTIN: That's not entirely accurate.

MR. SMITH: In fact it's false. When one hears the doorball ring it is because there is someone there.

MRS. SMITH: He won't admit he's wrong.

MRS. MARTIN: My husband is very obstinate, too.

MR. SMITH: There's someone there.

MR. MARTIN: That's not impossible.

MRS. SMITH: *(To her husband)* No.

MR. SMITH: Yes.

MRS. SMITH: I tell you *no.* In any case you are not going to disturb me again for nothing. If you wish to know, go and look yourself!

MR. SMITH: I'll go.

(Mrs. Smith shrugs her shoulders. Mrs. Martin tosses her head.)

MR. SMITH: *(Opening the door)* Oh! how do you do. *(He glances at Mrs. Smith and the Martins, who are all surprised.)* It's the Fire Chief!

FIRE CHIEF: *(He is of course in uniform and is wearing an enormous shining helmet.)* Good evening, ladies and gentlemen. *(The Smiths and the*

Martins are still slightly astonished. Mrs. Smith turns her head away, in temper, and does not reply to his greeting.) Good evening, Mrs. Smith. You appear to be angry.

MRS. SMITH: Oh!

MR. SMITH: You see it's because my wife is a little chagrined at having been proved wrong.

MR. MARTIN: There's been an argument between Mr. and Mrs. Smith, Mr. Fire Chief.

MRS. SMITH: *(To Mr. Martin)* This is no business of yours! *(To Mr. Smith)* I beg you not to involve outsiders in our family arguments.

MR. SMITH: Oh, my dear, this is not so serious. The Fire Chief is an old friend of the family. His mother courted me, and I knew his father. He asked me to give him my daughter in marriage if ever I had one. And he died waiting.

MR. MARTIN: That's neither his fault, nor yours.

FIRE CHIEF: Well, what is it all about?

MRS. SMITH: My husband was claiming . . .

MR. SMITH: No, it was you who was claiming.

MR. MARTIN: Yes, it was she.

MRS. MARTIN: No, it was he.

FIRE CHIEF: Don't get excited. You tell me, Mrs. Smith.

MRS. SMITH: Well, this is how it was. It is difficult for me to speak openly to you, but a fireman is also a confessor.

FIRE CHIEF: Well then?

MRS. SMITH: We were arguing because my husband said that each time the doorbell rings there is always someone there.

MR. MARTIN: It is plausible.

MRS. SMITH: And I was saying that each time the doorbell rings there is never anyone there.

MRS. MARTIN: It might seem strange.

MRS. SMITH: But it has been proved, not by theoretical demonstrations, but by facts.

MR. SMITH: That's false, since the Fire Chief is here. He rang the bell, I opened the door, and there he was.

MRS. MARTIN: When?

MR. MARTIN: But just now.

MRS. SMITH: Yes, but it was only when you heard the doorbell ring the fourth time that there was someone there. And the fourth time does not count.

MRS. MARTIN: Never. It is only the first three times that count.

MR. SMITH: Mr. Fire Chief, permit me in my turn to ask you several questions.

FIRE CHIEF: Go right ahead.

MR. SMITH: When I opened the door and saw you, it was really you who had rung the bell?

FIRE CHIEF: Yes, it was I.

MR. MARTIN: You were at the door? And you rang in order to be admitted?

FIRE CHIEF: I do not deny it.

MR. SMITH: *(To his wife, triumphantly)* You see? I was right. When you hear the doorbell ring, that means someone rang it. You certainly cannot say that the Fire Chief is not someone.

MRS. SMITH: Certainly not. I repeat to you that I was speaking of only the first three times, since the fourth time does not count.

MRS. MARTIN: And when the doorbell rang the first time, was it you?

FIRE CHIEF: No, it was not I.

MRS. MARTIN: You see? The doorbell rang and there was no one there.

MR. MARTIN: Perhaps it was someone else?

MR. SMITH: Were you standing at the door for a long time?

FIRE CHIEF: Three-quarters of an hour.

MR. SMITH: And you saw no one?

FIRE CHIEF: No one. I am sure of that.

MRS. MARTIN: And did you hear the bell when it rang the second time?

FIRE CHIEF: Yes, and that wasn't I either. And there was still no one there.

MRS. SMITH: Victory! I was right.

MR. SMITH: *(To his wife:)* Not so fast. *(To the Fire Chief:)* And what were you doing at the door?

FIRE CHIEF: Nothing. I was just standing there. I was thinking of many things.

MR. MARTIN: *(To the Fire Chief)* But the third time — it was not you who rang?

FIRE CHIEF: Yes, it was I.

MR. SMITH: But when the door was opened nobody was in sight.

FIRE CHIEF: That was because I had hidden myself — as a joke.

MRS. SMITH: Don't make jokes, Mr. Fire Chief. This business is too sad.

MR. MARTIN: In short, we still do not know whether, when the doorbell rings, there is someone there or not!

MRS. SMITH: Never anyone.

MR. SMITH: Always someone.

FIRE CHIEF: I am going to reconcile you. You both are partly right. When the doorbell rings, sometimes there is someone, other times there is no one.

MR. MARTIN: This seems logical to me.

MRS. MARTIN: I think so too.

FIRE CHIEF: Life is very simple, really. *(To the Smiths:)* Go on and kiss each other.

MRS. SMITH: We just kissed each other a little while ago.

MR. MARTIN: They'll kiss each other tomorrow. They have plenty of time.

MRS. SMITH: Mr. Fire Chief, since you have helped us settle this, please make yourself comfortable, take off your helmet and sit down for a moment.

FIRE CHIEF: Excuse me, but I can't stay long. I should like to remove my helmet, but I haven't time to sit down. *(He sits down, without removing his helmet.)* I must admit that I have come to see you for another reason. I am on official business.

MRS. SMITH: And what can we do for you, Mr. Fire Chief?

FIRE CHIEF: I must beg you to excuse my indiscretion *(Terribly embarrassed)* ... uhm *(He points a finger at the Martins)* ... you don't mind ... in front of them ...

MRS. MARTIN: Say whatever you like.

MR. MARTIN: We're old friends. They tell us everything.

MR. SMITH: Speak.

FIRE CHIEF: Eh, well — is there a fire here?

MRS. SMITH: Why do you ask us that?

FIRE CHIEF: It's because — pardon me — I have orders to extinguish all the fires in the city.

MRS. MARTIN: All?

FIRE CHIEF: Yes, all.

MRS. SMITH: *(Confused)* I don't know . . . I don't think so. Do you want me to go and look?

MR. SMITH: *(Sniffing)* There can't be one here. There's no smell of anything burning.*

FIRE CHIEF: *(Aggrieved)* None at all? You don't have a little fire in the chimney, something burning in the attic or in the cellar? A little fire just starting, at least?

MRS. SMITH: I am sorry to disappoint you but I do not believe there's anything here at the moment. I promise that I will notify you when we do have something.

FIRE CHIEF: Please don't forget, it would be a great help.

MRS. SMITH: That's a promise.

FIRE CHIEF: *(To the Martins)* And there's nothing burning at your house either?

MRS. MARTIN: No, unfortunately.

MR. MARTIN: *(To the Fire Chief)* Things aren't going so well just now.

FIRE CHIEF: Very poorly. There's been almost nothing, a few trifles — a chimney, a barn. Nothing important. It doesn't bring in much. And since there are no returns, the profits on output are very meager.

MR. SMITH: Times are bad. That's true all over. It's the same this year with business and agriculture as it is with fires, nothing is prospering.

MR. MARTIN: No wheat, no fires.

FIRE CHIEF: No floods either.

MRS. SMITH: But there is some sugar.

MR. SMITH: That's because it is imported.

MRS. MARTIN: It's harder in the case of fires. The tariffs are too high!

FIRE CHIEF: All the same, there's an occasional asphyxiation by gas, but that's unusual too. For instance, a young woman asphyxiated herself last week — she had left the gas on.

MRS. MARTIN: Had she forgotten it?

FIRE CHIEF: No, but she thought is was her comb.

MR. SMITH: These confusions are always dangerous!

MRS. SMITH: Did you go to see the match dealer?

FIRE CHIEF: There's nothing doing there. He is insured against fires.

MR. MARTIN: Why don't you go see the Vicar of Wakefield, and use my name?

FIRE CHIEF: I don't have the right to extinguish clergymen's fires. The Bishop would get angry. Besides they extinguish their fires themselves, or else they have them put out by vestal virgins.

MR. SMITH: Go see the Durands.

FIRE CHIEF: I can't do that either. He's not English. He's only been natural-

---

*In Nicolas Bataille's production Mr. and Mrs. Martin sniffed too.

ized. And naturalized citizens have the right to have houses, but not the right to have them put out if they're burning.

MRS. SMITH: Nevertheless, when they set fire to it last year, it was put out just the same.

FIRE CHIEF: He did that all by himself. Clandestinely. But it's not I who would report him.

MR. SMITH: Neither would I.

MRS. SMITH: Mr. Fire Chief, since you are not too pressed, stay a little while longer. You would be doing us a favor.

FIRE CHIEF: Shall I tell you some stories?

MRS. SMITH: Oh, by all means, how charming of you. *(She kisses him.)*

MR. SMITH, MRS. MARTIN, MR. MARTIN: Yes, yes, some stories, hurrah!

(They applaud.)

MR. SMITH: And what is even more interesting is the fact that firemen's stories are all true, and they're based on experience.

FIRE CHIEF: I speak from my own experience. Truth, nothing but the truth. No fiction.

MR. MARTIN: That's right. Truth is never found in books, only in life.

MRS. SMITH: Begin!

MR. MARTIN: Begin!

MRS. MARTIN: Be quiet, he is beginning.

FIRE CHIEF: *(Coughs slightly several times)* Excuse me, don't look at me that way. You embarrass me. You know that I am shy.

MRS. SMITH: Isn't he charming! *(She kisses him.)*

FIRE CHIEF: I'm going to try to begin anyhow. But promise me that you won't listen.

MRS. MARTIN: But if we don't listen to you we won't hear you.

FIRE CHIEF: I didn't think of that!

MRS. SMITH: I told you, he's just a boy.

MR. MARTIN, MR. SMITH: Oh, the sweet child! *(They kiss him.*)*

MRS. MARTIN: Chin up!

FIRE CHIEF: Well, then! *(He coughs again in a voice shaken by emotion)* "The Dog and the Cow," an experimental fable. Once upon a time another cow asked another dog: "Why have you not swallowed your trunk?" "Pardon me," replied the dog, "it is because I thought that I was an elephant."

MRS. MARTIN: What is the moral?

FIRE CHIEF: That's for you to find out.

MR. SMITH: He's right.

MRS. SMITH: *(Furious)* Tell us another.

FIRE CHIEF: A young calf had eaten too much ground glass. As a result, it was obliged to give birth. It brought forth a cow into the world. However, since the calf was male, the cow could not call him Mamma. Nor could she call him Papa, because the calf was too little. The calf was then obliged to get married and the registry office carried out all the details completely à la mode.

MR. SMITH: À la mode de Caen.

---

*In Nicolas Bataille's production, they did not kiss the Fire Chief.

MR. MARTIN: Like tripes.

FIRE CHIEF: You've heard that one?

MRS. SMITH: It was in all the papers.

MRS. MARTIN: It happened not far from our house.

FIRE CHIEF: I'll tell you another: "The Cock." Once upon time, a cock wished to play the dog. But he had no luck because everyone recognized him right away.

MRS. SMITH: On the other hand, the dog that wished to play the cock was never recognized.

MR. SMITH: I'll tell you one: "The Snake and the Fox." Once upon a time, a snake came up to a fox and said: "It seems to me that I know you!" The fox replied to him: "Me too." "Then," said the snake, "give me some money." "A fox doesn't give money," replied the tricky animal, who, in order to escape, jumped down into a deep ravine full of strawberries and chicken honey. But the snake was there waiting for him with a Mephistophelean laugh. The fox pulled out his knife, shouting: "I'm going to teach you how to live!" Then he took to flight, turning his back. But he had no luck. The snake was quicker. With a well-chosen blow of his fist, he struck the fox in the middle of his forehead, which broke into a thousand pieces, while he cried: "No! No! Four times no! I'm not your daughter."*

MRS. MARTIN: It's interesting.

MRS. SMITH: It's not bad.

MR. MARTIN: *(Shaking Mr. Smith's hand)* My congratulations.

FIRE CHIEF: *(Jealous)* Not so good. And anyway, I've heard it before.

MR. SMITH: It's terrible.

MRS. SMITH: But it wasn't even true.

MRS. MARTIN: Yes, unfortunately.

MR. MARTIN: *(To Mrs. Smith)* It's your turn, dear lady.

MRS. SMITH: I only know one. I'm going to tell it to you. It's called "The Bouquet."

MR. SMITH: My wife has always been romantic.

MR. MARTIN: She's a true Englishwoman.**

MRS. SMITH: Here it is. Once upon a time, a fiancé gave a bouquet of flowers to his fiancée, who said, "Thanks"; but before she had said, "thanks," he, without saying a single word, took back the flowers he had given her in order to teach her a good lesson, and he said, "I take them back." He said "Goodbye," and took them back and went off in all directions.

MR. MARTIN: Oh, charming! *(He either kisses or does not kiss Mrs. Smith.)*

MRS. MARTIN: You have a wife, Mr. Smith, of whom all the world is jealous.

MR. SMITH: It's true. My wife is intelligence personified. She's even more intelligent than I. In any case, she is much more feminine, everyone says so.

MRS. SMITH: *(To the Fire Chief)* Let's have another, Mr. Fire Chief.

FIRE CHIEF: Oh, no, it's too late.

---

*This story was deleted in Nicolas Bataille's production. Mr. Smith went through the gestures only, without making a sound.
**These two speeches were repeated three times in the original production.

MR. MARTIN: Tell us one, anyway.

FIRE CHIEF: I'm too tired.

MR. SMITH: Please do us a favor.

MR. MARTIN: I beg you.

FIRE CHIEF: No.

MRS. MARTIN: You have a heart of ice. We're sitting on hot coals.

MRS. SMITH: *(Falls on her knees sobbing, or else she does not do this)* I implore you!

FIRE CHIEF: Righto.

MR. SMITH: *(In Mrs. Martin's ear)* He agrees! He's going to bore us again.

MRS. MARTIN: Shh.

MRS. SMITH: No luck. I was too polite.

FIRE CHIEF: "The Headcold." My brother-in-law had, on the paternal side, a first cousin whose maternal uncle had a father-in-law whose paternal grandfather had married as his second wife a young native whose brother he had met on one of his travels, a girl of whom he was enamored and by whom he had a son who married an intrepid lady pharmacist who was none other than the niece of an unknown fourth-class petty officer of the Royal Navy and whose adopted father had an aunt who spoke Spanish fluently and who was, perhaps, one of the granddaughters of an engineer who died young, himself the grandson of the owner of a vineyard which produced mediocre wine, but who had a second cousin, a stay-at-home, a sergeant-major, whose son had married a very pretty young woman, a divorcée, whose first husband was the son of a loyal patriot who, in the hope of making his fortune, had managed to bring up one of his daughters so that she could marry a footman who had known Rothschild, and whose brother, after having changed his trade several times, married and had a daughter whose stunted great-grandfather wore spectacles which had been given him by a cousin of his, the brother-in-law of a man from Portugal, natural son of a miller, not too badly off, whose foster-brother had married the daughter of a former country doctor, who was himself a foster-brother of the son of a forrester, himself the natural son of another country doctor, married three times in a row, whose third wife . . .

MR. MARTIN: I knew that third wife, if I'm not mistaken. She ate chicken sitting on a hornet's nest.

FIRE CHIEF: It's not the same one.

MRS. SMITH: Shh!

FIRE CHIEF: As I was saying . . . whose third wife was the daughter of the best midwife in the region and who, early left a widow . . .

MR. SMITH: Like my wife.

FIRE CHIEF: . . . Had married a glazier who was full of life and who had had, by the daughter of a station master, a child who had burned his bridges . . .

MRS. SMITH: His britches?

MR. MARTIN: No his bridge game.

FIRE CHIEF: And had married an oyster woman, whose father had a brother, mayor of a small town, who had taken as his wife a blonde school-teacher, whose cousin, a fly fisherman . . .

MR. MARTIN: A fly by night?

649

FIRE CHIEF: . . . Had married another blind schoolteacher, named Marie, too, whose brother was married to another Marie, also a blonde school-teacher . . .

MR. SMITH: Since she's blonde, she must be Marie.

FIRE CHIEF: . . . And whose father had been reared in Canada by an old woman who was the niece of a priest whose grandmother, occasionally in the winter, like everyone else, caught a cold.

MRS. SMITH: A curious story. Almost unbelievable.

MR. MARTIN: If you catch a cold, you should get yourself a colt.

MR. SMITH: It's a useless precaution, but absolutely necessary.

MRS. MARTIN: Excuse me, Mr. Fire Chief, but I did not follow your story very well. At the end, when we got to the grandmother of the priest, I got mixed up.

MR. SMITH: One always gets mixed up in the hands of a priest.

MRS. SMITH: Oh yes, Mr. Fire Chief, begin again. Everyone wants to hear.

FIRE CHIEF: Ah, I don't know whether I'll be able to. I'm on official business. It depends on what time it is.

MRS. SMITH: We don't have the time, here.

FIRE CHIEF: But the clock?

MR. SMITH: It runs badly. It is contradictory, and always indicates the opposite of what the hour really is.

(Enter Mary.)

MARY: Madam . . . sir . . .

MRS. SMITH: What do you want?

MR. SMITH: What have you come in here for?

MARY: I hope, madam and sir will excuse me . . . and these ladies and gentlemen too . . . I would like . . . I would like . . . to tell you a story, myself.

MRS. MARTIN: What is she saying?

MR. MARTIN: I believe that our friends' maid is going crazy . . . she wants to tell us a story, too.

FIRE CHIEF: Who does she think she is? *(He looks at her.)* Oh!

MRS. SMITH: Why are you butting in?

MR. SMITH: This is really uncalled for, Mary . . .

FIRE CHIEF: Oh! But it is she! Incredible!

MR. SMITH: And you?

MARY: Incredible! Here!

MRS. SMITH: What does all this mean?

MR. SMITH: You know each other?

FIRE CHIEF: And how!

(Mary throws herself on the neck of the Fire Chief.)

MARY: I'm so glad to see you again . . . at last!

MR. AND MRS. SMITH: Oh!

MR. SMITH: This is too much, here, in our home, in the suburbs of London.

MRS. SMITH: It's not proper! . . .

FIRE CHIEF: It was she who extinguished my first fires.

MARY: I'm your little firehose.

MR. MARTIN: If that is the case . . . dear friends . . . these emotions are understandable, human, honorable . . .

MRS. MARTIN: All that is human is honorable.

MRS. SMITH: Even so, I don't like to see it . . . here among us . . .

MR. SMITH: She's not been properly brought up.

FIRE CHIEF: Oh, you have too many prejudices.

MRS. MARTIN: What I think is that a maid, after all — even though it's none of my business — is never anything but a maid . . .

MR. MARTIN: Even if she can sometimes be a rather good detective.

FIRE CHIEF: Let me go.

MARY: Don't be upset! . . . They're not so bad really.

MR. SMITH: Hm . . . hm . . . you two are very touching, but at the same time, a little . . . a little . . .

MR. MARTIN: Yes, that's exactly the word.

MR. SMITH: . . . A little too exhibitionistic . . .

MR. MARTIN: There is a native British modesty — forgive me for attempting, yet again, to define my thought — not understood by foreigners, even by specialists, thanks to which, if I may thus express myself . . . of course, I don't mean to refer to you . . .

MARY: I was going to tell you . . .

MR. SMITH: Don't tell us anything . . .

MARY: Oh yes!

MRS. SMITH: Go, my little Mary, go quietly to the kitchen and read your poems before the mirror . . .

MR. MARTIN: You know, even though I'm not a maid, I also read poems before the mirror.

MRS. MARTIN: This morning when you looked at yourself in the mirror you didn't see yourself.

MR. MARTIN: That's because I wasn't there yet . . .

MARY: All the same, I could, perhaps, recite a little poem for you.

MRS. SMITH: My little Mary, you are frightfully obstinate.

MARY: I'm going to recite a poem, then, is that agreed? It is a poem entitled "The Fire" in honor of the Fire Chief:

The Fire

The polypoids were burning in the wood
    A stone caught fire
    The castle caught fire
    The forest caught fire
    The men caught fire
    The women caught fire
    The birds caught fire
    The fish caught fire
    The water caught fire
    The sky caught fire
    The ashes caught fire
    The smoke caught fire
    The fire caught fire
    Everything caught fire
    Caught fire, caught fire.

(She recites the poem while the Smiths are pushing her off-stage.)

MRS. MARTIN: That sent chills up my spine . . .

MR. MARTIN: And yet there's a certain warmth in those lines . . .

FIRE CHIEF: I thought it was marvelous.

MRS. SMITH: All the same . . .

MR. SMITH: You're exaggerating . . .

FIRE CHIEF: Just a minute . . . I admit . . . all this is very subjective . . . but this is my conception of the world. My world. My dream. My ideal . . . And now this reminds me that I must leave. Since you don't have the time here, I must tell you that in exactly three-quarters of an hour and sixteen minutes, I'm having a fire at the other end of the city. Consequently, I must hurry. Even though it will be quite unimportant.

MRS. SMITH: What will it be? A little chimney fire?

FIRE CHIEF: Oh, not even that. A straw fire and a little heartburn.

MR. SMITH: Well, we're sorry to see you go.

MRS. SMITH: You have been very entertaining.

MRS. MARTIN: Thanks to you, we have passed a truly Cartesian quarter of an hour.

FIRE CHIEF: *(Moving towards the door, then stopping)* Speaking of that — the bald soprano? *(General silence, embarrassment.)*

MRS. SMITH: She always wears her hair in the same style.

FIRE CHIEF: Ah! Then goodbye, ladies and gentlemen.

MR. MARTIN: Good luck, and a good fire!

FIRE CHIEF: Let's hope so. For everybody.

(Fire Chief exits. All accompany him to the door and then return to their seats.)

MRS. MARTIN: I can buy a pocketknife for my brother, but you can't buy Ireland for your grandfather.

MR. SMITH: One walks on his feet, but one heats with electricity or coal.

MR. MARTIN: He who sells an ox today, will have an egg tomorrow.

MRS. SMITH: In real life, one must look out of the window.

MRS. MARTIN: One can sit down on a chair, when the chair doesn't have any.

MR. SMITH: One must always think of everything.

MR. MARTIN: The ceiling is above, the floor is below.

MRS. SMITH: When I say yes, it's only a manner of speaking.

MRS. MARTIN: To each his own.

MR. SMITH: Take a circle, caress it, and it will turn vicious.

MRS. SMITH: A schoolmaster teaches his pupils to read, but the cat suckles her young when they are small.

MRS. MARTIN: Nevertheless, it was the cow that gave us tails.

MR. SMITH: When I'm in the country, I love the solitude and the quiet.

MR. MARTIN: You are not old enough yet for that.

MRS. SMITH: Benjamin Franklin was right; you are more nervous than he.

MRS. MARTIN: What are the seven days of the week?

MR. SMITH: Monday, Tuesday, Wednesday, Thursday, Friday, Saturday, Sunday.*

---

*In English in the original. — Translator's note.

MR. MARTIN: Edward is a clerk; his sister Nancy is a typist, and his brother William, a shop-assistant.*
MRS. SMITH: An odd family!
MRS. MARTIN: I prefer a bird in the bush to a sparrow in a barrow.
MR. SMITH: Rather a steak in a chalet than gristle in a castle.
MR. MARTIN: An Englishman's home is truly his castle.
MRS. SMITH: I don't know enough Spanish to make myself understood.
MRS. MARTIN: I'll give you my mother-in-law's slippers if you'll give me your husband's coffin.
MR. SMITH: I'm looking for a monophysite priest to marry to our maid.
MR. MARTIN: Bread is a staff, whereas bread is also a staff, and an oak springs from an oak every morning at dawn.
MRS. SMITH: My uncle lies in the country, but that's none of the midwife's business.
MR. MARTIN: Paper is for writing, the cat's for the rat. Cheese is for scratching.
MRS. SMITH: The car goes very fast, but the cook beats batter better.
MR. SMITH: Don't be turkeys; rather kiss the conspirator.
MR. MARTIN: Charity begins at home.*
MRS. SMITH: I'm waiting for the aqueduct to come and see me at my windmill.
MR. MARTIN: One can prove that social progress is definitely better with sugar.
MR. SMITH: To hell with polishing!

(Following this last speech of Mr. Smith's, the others are silent for a moment, stupefied. We sense that there is a certain nervous irritation. The strokes of the clock are more nervous too. The speeches which follow must be said, at first, in a glacial, hostile tone. The hostility and the nervousness increase. At the end of this scene, the four characters must be standing very close to each other, screaming their speeches, raising their fists, ready to throw themselves upon each other.)
MR. MARTIN: One doesn't polish spectacles with black wax.
MRS. SMITH: Yes, but with money one can buy anything.
MR. MARTIN: I'd rather kill a rabbit than sing in the garden.
MR. SMITH: Cockatoos, cockatoos, cockatoos, cockatoos, cockatoos, cockatoos, cockatoos, cockatoos, cockatoos, cockatoos.
MRS. SMITH: Such caca, such caca, such caca, such caca, such caca, such caca, such caca, such caca, such caca.
MR. MARTIN: Such cascades of cacas, such cascades of cacas, such cascades of cacas, such cascades of cacas, such cascades of cacas, such cascades of cacas, such cascades of cacas, such cascades of cacas.
MR. SMITH: Dogs have fleas, dogs have fleas.
MRS. MARTIN: Cactus, coccyx! crocus! cockaded! cockroach!
MRS. SMITH: Incasker, you incask us.
MR. MARTIN: I'd rather lay an egg in a box than go and steal an ox.
MRS. MARTIN: *(Opening her mouth very wide)* Ah! oh! ah! oh! Let me gnash my teeth.

*In English in the original. — Translator's note.

MR. SMITH: Crocodile!
MR. MARTIN: Let's go and slap Ulysses.
MR. SMITH: I'm going to live in my cabana among my cacao trees.
MRS. MARTIN: Cacao trees on cacao farms don't bear coconuts, they yield cocoa! Cacao trees on cacao farms don't bear coconuts, they yield cocoa! Cacao trees on cacao farms don't bear coconuts, they yield cocoa.
MRS. SMITH: Mice have lice, lice haven't mice.
MRS. MARTIN: Don't ruche my brooch!
MR. MARTIN: Don't smooch the brooch!
MR. SMITH: Groom the goose, don't goose the groom.
MRS. MARTIN: The goose grooms.
MRS. SMITH: Groom your tooth.
MR. MARTIN: Groom the bridegroom, groom the bridegroom.
MR. SMITH: Seducer seduced!
MRS. MARTIN: Scaramouche!
MRS. SMITH: Sainte-Nitouche!
MR. MARTIN: Go take a douche.
MR. SMITH: I've been goosed.
MRS. MARTIN: Sainte-Nitouche stoops to my cartouche.
MRS. SMITH: "Who'd stoop to blame? . . . and I never choose to stoop."
MR. MARTIN: Robert!
MR. SMITH: Browning!
MRS. MARTIN, MR. SMITH: Rudyard.
MRS. SMITH, MR. MARTIN: Kipling.
MRS. MARTIN, MR. SMITH: Robert Kipling!
MRS. SMITH: MR. MARTIN: Rudyard Browning.*
MRS. MARTIN: Silly gobblegobblers, silly gobblegobblers.
MR. MARTIN: Marietta, spot the pot!
MRS. SMITH: Krishnamurti, Krishnamurti, Krishnamurti!
MR. SMITH: The pope elopes! The pope's got no horoscope. The horoscope's bespoke.
MRS. MARTIN: Bazaar, Balzac, bazooka!
MR. MARTIN: Bizarre, beaux-arts, brassieres!
MR. SMITH: A,e,i,o,u,a,e,i,o,u,a,e,i,o,u,i!
MRS. MARTIN: B,c,d,f,g,l,m,n,p,r,s,t,v,w,x,z!
MR. MARTIN: From sage to stooge, from stage to serge!
MRS. SMITH: *(Imitating a train)* Choo, choo, choo, choo, choo, choo, choo, choo, choo, choo, choo!
MR. SMITH: It's!
MRS. MARTIN: Not!
MR. MARTIN: That!
MRS. SMITH: Way!

*Translator's note: in the French text these speeches read as follows:
Mme Smith. — N'y touchez pas, elle est brisée.
M. Martin. — Sully!
M. Smith. — Prudhomme!
Mme Martin, M. Smith. — Francois.
Mme Smith, M. Martin. — Coppée.
Mme Martin, M. Smith. — Coppée Sully!
Mme Smith, M. Martin. — Prudhomme Francois.

MR. SMITH: It's!
MRS. MARTIN: O!
MR. MARTIN: Ver!
MRS. SMITH: Here!

(All together, completely infuriated, screaming in each others' ears. The light is extinguished. In the darkness we hear, in an increasingly rapid rhythm:)

ALL TOGETHER: It's not that way, it's over here, it's not that way, it's over here, it's not that way, it's over here, it's not that way, it's over here!*

(The words cease abruptly. Again, the lights come on. Mr. and Mrs. Martin are seated like the Smiths at the beginning of the play. The play begins again with the Martins, who say exactly the same lines as the Smiths in the first scene, while the curtain softly falls.)

---

*When produced some of the speeches in this last scene were cut or shuffled. Moreover, the final beginning again, if one can call it that, still involved the Smiths, since the author did not have the inspired idea of substituting the Martins for the Smiths until after the hundredth performance.

AFRICAN-AMERICAN DRAMA: The Theatre of Black Consciousness

In the 1960s, African-Americans created an independent theatre movement. Growing out of a long history of black performance and culture and triggered by the midcentury civil rights and black-consciousness movements, black theatre expressed the self-perceptions and revolutionary aspirations of black Americans. In later decades, African-American theatre laid aside most of its revolutionary viewpoint. By this time it had brought to prominence black writers, actors, and producers and established itself as a lively part of the American theatre scene.

Political and Social Backgrounds

When Columbus first looked on the New World in 1492, one of his crew members was Pedro Alonso Niño. There is reason to believe that Niño was black. Thirty blacks accompanied Balboa in 1513 when he trekked across the Isthmus of Panama and first gazed on the Pacific Ocean. Then, in 1517, in order to encourage emigration to America, Bishop Las Casas issued permission for Spaniards to import African slaves to the New World. For the next three centuries, black men and women were taken from their homes in Africa and sold into slavery in America. The Dutch, French, and British eventually controlled most of the slave trade, and a Dutch frigate, which landed at Jamestown in 1619 with a cargo of twenty "negars" became the first slave ship to come to the English colonies. In 1807, England and the United States both passed laws forbidding the African trade, but the smuggling of slaves continued, and it was not until after President Lincoln's Emancipation Proclamation in 1863 that slavery formally came to an end in North America.

Social customs, however, reinforced by discriminatory laws, kept Negroes from enjoying the full privileges of American citizenship for the next century. However, in spite of the prejudices of the white majority, black Americans made important contributions to their nation; black leaders included abolitionist Frederick Douglass, educator Booker T. Washington, botanist George Washington Carver, and singers Marian Anderson and Leontyne Price. In the 1920s and '30s, African Americans' experiences of slavery, freedom without rights, and World War I service came together to produce a literary and cultural movement which, named after its center in the black section of New York City, was called the Harlem Renaissance.

The Civil Rights Movement

By the late 1950s, African Americans came to believe they had a right to share the full privileges of American citizenship, and they began to find increasing support for their position from white Americans. When Rosa

Parks, an elderly black Southerner, took the unprecedented action of refusing to sit in the less desirable back seats of a bus, she sparked a social revolution. In 1960, four black students who were refused service at a lunch counter in Greensboro, North Carolina, occupied their seats until the store closed and thus initiated the sit-in technique which was to become a central method of the civil rights movement. The civil rights movement was aimed at integration. Its objective was the mingling of white and black people so that African-Americans could share the rights to education, employment, housing, respect, and affluent lifestyles. This movement culminated in the Civil Rights Act of 1964, which guaranteed equal rights to all Americans of all racial and ethnic origins.

The Black Power Movement

While many African-Americans were working for integration, however, others had no desire to associate with white Americans. Believing that they possessed a valuable, unique heritage which integration with whites would destroy, they argued for black consciousness, black separatism, black superiority — revolution. These radicals sneered at black integrationists as "Uncle Toms," who subordinated their own identities to the demands of white America, and "Oreos," who were black on the outside but white at heart. This "black power movement" became an important part of the chaos of social and political revolutionary movements which characterized the 1960s and early 1970s.

With the end of the divisive Vietnam War in 1973, however, America turned its attention to the pursuit of security and affluence. Radical movements lost energy and numbers, and conservative forces gained control of government and society. In this new America, the fires of black power burned down to embers which lay smouldering beneath society's surface, and African-Americans, although their rights were constantly threatened, went on to achieve political, social, and economic success as participants in an integrated society. As suggested in the theme song of one of the many popular television comedies which featured black life during the last decades of the century, they finally had a piece of the American pie.

Black Theatre History

Nineteenth-century America saw several attempts to exploit blacks or black culture for theatrical purposes. Perhaps the first black theatre in America was the African Grove Theatre in 1821-22. This short-lived experiment in entertainment, however, died out without having any direct impact. In 1828, Thomas Dartmouth Rice, a black impersonator, introduced a song-and-dance act which earned him the nickname "Jim Crow." Rice's success led to the development of the minstrel show in which a group of whites, made up like Negroes, sat in a semicircle on stage and entertained the audience with songs, dances, and jokes. Minstrel shows became immensely popular in America and England and eventually led to the creation of some black troupes, such as Charles Hicks' Georgia Minstrels, formed around 1865. In 1890, Sam T. Jack's Creole Show freed Negroes from the minstrel tradition and plantation image and inspired greater achievements in musical comedy.

Around 1910, theatre-going blacks in New York City began to leave the Broadway theatres for the uptown theatres of Harlem. The Anita Bush Stock Company, later known as the Lafayette Players, was established around 1915 to serve this audience. This shift culminated in the Harlem Renaissance.

A number of Negro theatres sprang up during the period between the two world wars. They included the Ethiopian Art Theatre in Chicago in 1923, W. E. B. Du Bois' Krigway Players in Harlem in 1926, the Harlem Experimental Theatre founded by Jesse Fawcett in 1928, the Harlem Suitcase Theatre spearheaded by Langston Hughes in 1937, and the American Negro Theatre organized by Abram Hill and Frederick O'Neal in 1940.

A Raisin in the Sun

In 1959, *A Raisin in the Sun* by Lorraine Hansberry (1930-65) became the first play by a black woman to be presented on Broadway. *Raisin* used realistic drama to present the story of a black family, their dreams, and their problems. It dealt with most of the issues current in the black community at the time, it drew the attention of white audiences, it attracted Negro audiences back to Broadway, and it led many black dramatists in the 1960s to write realistic plays about black family life. However, the very viewpoint which gave it its power — its integrationist protest against discrimination — led radical blacks of the 1960s to reject it as a dead end.

The Blacks

In 1959, the production of Jean Genet's violent, revolutionary spectacle *The Blacks* initiated a new mood in black theatre. This play showcased black actors, demonstrated the presence of a white audience willing to attend radical plays, and made experimental theatre forms the norm for radical black theatre.

These new possibilities came to fruition in the black theatre movement of the 1960s and '70s which was triggered by the production of LeRoi Jones' plays, *Dutchman* and *The Slave*, in 1964. These plays were racially explicit in subject matter, implied the need for violent revolution, dealt with intellectual issues, and appealed to the same audience as *The Blacks*. The subsequent work of Jones and others in Harlem sparked the birth of many black theatre companies across the country and stimulated the writing of other radical black plays.

Dramatic Theory

In the 1960s, black theatre saw itself as a revolutionary movement, not just a parallel to white theatre. It set itself two tasks, one negative and one positive. On the negative side, it aimed to eliminate cultural domination by whites. To this end, it rejected Euro-American values and white literary traditions. Black theatre artists believed Western culture focused on the individual at the expense of the community and saw art as ideally nonfunctional. They rejected this subjectivism and aestheticism. Furthermore, they believed that earlier protest theatre put blacks in the position of urging their white superiors to reassess their moral stance. Black theatre artists rejected this integrationist viewpoint and aimed instead to aggravate the conflict. They assumed that a new balance would be achieved through

659

violence, compromise, or evolution.

On the positive side, black theatre artists aimed to raise black consciousness among African-Americans. They believed a stronger self-image would better equip blacks to satisfy their material and social needs. They reached back, therefore, to their African roots, and especially the African focus on community life. In order to cultivate pride in black lifestyles, they tried to make theatre an extension of creative expressions already present in their community, such as black music, black rhetoric, black styles of dress, and black movement patterns.

Dramatic Literature

The plays of the black theatre movement took their subject matter from life within the black community and used experimental dramatic forms. The two main playwrights of the black arts movement were Ed Bullins and LeRoi Jones.

Ed Bullins

Ed Bullins (1935-) worked in black theatre in San Francisco and Harlem. In the latter location, he served as playwright-in-residence for the New Lafayette Theatre and edited the *Black Theatre Magazine* published by that organization. True to the black theatre movement, his plays focus on defining and describing the black experience. They include *Clara's Ole Man* (1965), *The Fabulous Miss Marie* (1971), and *The Taking of Miss Janie* (1974).

LeRoi Jones

LeRoi Jones (1934-) was born and raised in Newark, New Jersey. When he was nineteen, he graduated from Howard University. By the time he began writing plays, he had already begun to distinguish himself as a poet and essayist. He published a volume of poetry, *Preface to a Twenty Volume Suicide Note,* in 1961, and the nonfiction *Blues: Negro Music in White America* in 1963. He also wrote novels, such as *The System of Dante's Hell* (1965).

After the production of *Dutchman* in New York's theatre district, Jones moved his activities uptown to Harlem where he founded the Black Arts Theater. Later, believing the Harlem program was not revolutionary enough, he moved back to Newark where he became the leader of the Spirit House. In 1966, Jones changed his name to Imamu Amiri Baraka, an Arabic named meaning Spiritual Leader, Blessed Prince.

Baraka founded the Black Community Development and Defense Organization in 1968, and was one of the leaders of the separatist National Black Political Convention at Gary, Indiana, in March, 1972.

An angry, somber writer who believed there was no hope for effective communication between blacks and whites, Baraka wrote a number of plays. They included *The Toilet* (1964), about the beating of a white boy suspected of homosexual attraction to a black; a ritual drama titled *Slave Ship* (1967); an antidrug play called *Junkies Are Full of (SHHH . . .); and The Motion of History* (1977). He typically addressed a black audience and designed his plays to simultaneously arouse hatred for whites and stimulate black self-respect.

660

Theatrical Organization

A variety of theatre groups represented the different emphases of the black theatre movement. The black arts wing, which was centered in Harlem at the Harlem Black Arts Repertory Theatre and the New Lafayette Theatre, focused entirely on fostering black consciousness and separatism. The Free Southern Theatre, organized by members of the Student Nonviolent Coordinating Committee (SNCC) in 1964, worked in the deep South to educate and politicize rural blacks. And the Negro Ensemble Company, organized in New York in 1967 under the artistic direction of Douglas Turner Ward, aimed to combat racism in the profession and give black theatre artists a place to work.

The production of "A Black Quartet" in 1969 demonstrated the essential cohesiveness of the multifaceted movement. The four one-acts presented under that title included Bullins' *The Gentleman Caller*, Ben Caldwell's *Prayer Meeting, or The First Militant Preacher*, Baraka's *Great Goodness of Life (A Coon Show)*, and Ron Milner's *The Warning — A Theme for Linda*. The four plays were united by a shared spirit of revolution.

The Legacy of the Movement

The black theatre movement contributed to the revolutionary impact of experimental theatre in the 1960s. One of its lasting effects was to make the black theatre artist — writer, director, and performer — an accepted part of the theatre scene. More roles were written for African-Americans, and it became more acceptable to cast black actors in roles originally designed for white performers. The presence of a large number of black theatre companies, linked by the Black Theatre Alliance, also provided work for African-American artists. Furthermore, a growing parade of African-American dramatists provided strong scripts for the general repertory. Among these were Lonne Elder III's *Ceremonies in Dark Old Men* (1969), Ntozake Shange's *For Colored Girls Who Have Considered Suicide When the Rainbow Is Enuf* (1975), and August Wilson's Pulitzer Prize winner, *Fences* (1987). Thanks to the pioneering work of black radicals like Baraka, African-Americans made significant contributions to theatre at the end of the century.

Dutchman

Dramaturgy

The play's title refers to the legend of "the flying Dutchman," a ship's captain who, beset by contrary winds while trying to sail around Africa's Cape Horn, swore he would succeed if he had to sail for all eternity. As punishment for his blasphemy, he was doomed to wander the seas forever on a ship manned by dead sailors. According to Richard Wagner's version of the myth, the Dutchman would only be released from his curse if he found a woman who would love him to the death. This legend provides haunting overtones for Baraka's character Lula, who careens through the city's dark subways searching for the right black man.

In *Dutchman*, a white woman, Lula, intrudes on a nice, young middle-class man, Clay. She harasses and goads him until he breaks out in a long, angry defense of middle-class black life, and then she kills him. After the other passengers dutifully dispose of Clay's body, Lula watches the entrance of another young black, much like Clay, who presumably will be her next victim — or her next potential hero.

Baraka used modified realism to tell his story. Clay and Lula look, talk, and behave like real people on a real subway. While their conversation and actions might raise eyebrows among urban transit riders, they are not implausible. However, Lula's uncanny understanding of Clay, the suggestion that she is repeating an often-repeated ritual, the manner in which the robot-like passengers do her bidding, and the legendary allusion of the title — all of these set the play's world apart from reality.

The story follows a circular plot line in which the play's end could also be its own beginning. This circularity — along with the song and dance, the rhythmic dialog, and the almost automatic sequence of the murder, body disposal, and old conductor's coda — gives the play a kind of ritualistic impact.

As the central characters of the play, Baraka created two cultured, literate, intelligent people who are bound together equally by their similarities and differences. Clay is male, but passive; Lula is female and aggressive. Black Clay imitates white, middle-class living; white Lula adopts black rhetoric and dance. Unable to end either in mutual unification or in separation, their story results instead in death.

The play's language weaves a rich fabric of imagery, cultural references, and mythic allusions. In addition to the legenday inference in the title, the play also alludes to the biblical creation story in which God made man from clay and Eve seduced Adam into sharing an apple with her. The play's intellectual and mythical gymnastics cause its language to assult the mind while the visual action attacks the emotions.

Ideas

In the play, Baraka deals with the agony of the racial dilemma without offering any easy answers. He packs a huge amount of racial stereotypes, history, and arguments into his short drama. Lula seems to play the conflicting roles of playwright's mouthpiece, white liberal, and persecutor of blacks all at the same time. Clay illustrates the trapped position of the middle-class African-American. White society demands that he be black in his culture but white in his logic. If he rejects this racial schizophrenia by truly following white logic, he will wreak the vengeance that kind of reason demands. But if he instead commits himself to black culture, his dancing, singing, and poetry — which are only sublimations of his desire for violence — he will be exploited by whites. Unable to authentically stay the same and unwilling to choose between violence and sublimation, Clay dies on Lula's knife. Baraka's revolutionary play proposes three options for blacks: Live a lie, murder, or die.

Production History

Dutchman was first produced at New York City's Cherry Lane Theatre on March 24, 1964. It won its author the Obie for Best American Play of the 1963-64 season. Because of its experimental form and its violent, revolutionary viewpoint, it became a watershed play which marked the shift from integrationist to separatist plays and triggered the black theatre arts movement.

African-American Theatre Timeline

◆ COLUMBUS' VOYAGE (1492)

◆ LAS CASAS PROCLAMATION (1517)

◆ SHAKESPEARE (1564-1616)

◆ U.S. DECLARATION OF INDEPENDENCE (1776)

● SLAVE TRADE PROHIBITED IN ENGLAND & USA (1807)

FREDERICK DOUGLASS (1817-95)

BOOKER T. WASHINGTON (1856-1915)

CIVIL WAR (1861-65)

● EMANCIPATION PROCLAMATION (01/01/1863)

GEORGE WASHINGTON CARVER (c. 1864-1943)

MARIAN ANDERSON (1902-)

WORLD WAR I (1914-18)

MALCOLM X (1925-65)

LEONTYNE PRICE (1927-)

THE GREAT DEPRESSION (1929-39)

MARTIN LUTHER KING, JR. (1929-68)

LORAINE HANSBERRY (1930-65)

"A RAISIN IN THE SUN" (1959) ●

LEROI JONES/IMAMU AMIRI BARAKA (1934-)

"DUTCHMAN" (1964) ●

ED BULLINS (1935-)

WORLD WAR II (1939-45)

EISENHOWER PRESIDENCY (1953-61)

KENNEDY PRESIDENCY (1961-63)

JOHNSON PRESIDENCY (1963-69)

NIXON PRESIDENCY (1969-74)

PRODUCTION OF GENET'S "THE BLACKS" (1959) ●

CIVIL RIGHTS ACT (1964) ●

"A BLACK QUARTET" (1969) ●

WITHDRAWAL FROM VIETNAM (1973) ●

| 1790 | 1810 | 1830 | 1850 | 1870 | 1890 | 1910 | 1930 | 1950 | 1970 | 1990 |

DUTCHMAN

by IMAMU AMIRI BARAKA

The play's action takes place in the early 1960s in New York City.

CHARACTERS

CLAY
Twenty-year-old Negro

LULA
Thirty-year-old white woman

RIDERS OF COACH
White and black

YOUNG NEGRO

CONDUCTOR

In the flying underbelly of the city. Steaming hot, and summer on top, outside. Underground. The subway heaped in modern myth.

Opening scene is a man sitting in a subway seat, holding a magazine but looking vacantly just above its wilting pages. Occasionally he looks blankly toward the window on his right. Dim lights and darkness whistling by against the glass. (Or paste the lights, as admitted props, right on the subway windows. Have them move, even dim and flicker. But give the sense of speed. Also stations, whether the train is stopped or the glitter and activity of these stations merely flashes by the windows.)

The man is sitting alone. That is, only his seat is visible, though the rest of the car is outfitted as a complete subway car. But only his seat is shown. There might be, for a time, as the play begins, a loud scream of the actual train. And it can recur throughout the play, or continue on a lower key once the dialogue starts.

The train slows after a time, pulling to a brief stop at one of the stations. The man looks idly up, until he sees a woman's face staring at him through the window; when it realizes that the man has noticed the face, it begins very premeditatedly to smile. The man smiles too, for a moment, without a trace of self-consciousness. Almost an instinctive though undesirable response. Then a kind of awkwardness or embarrassment sets in, and the man makes to look away, is further embarrassed, so he brings back his eyes to where the face was, but by now the train is moving again, and the face would seem to be left behind by the way the man turns his head to look back through the other windows at the slowly fading platform. He smiles then, more comfortably confident, hoping perhaps that his memory of this brief encounter will be pleasant. And then he is idle again.

SCENE I

Train roars. Lights flash outside the windows.

LULA enters from the rear of the car in bright, skimpy summer clothes and sandals. She carries a net bag full of paper books, fruit, and other anonymous articles. She is wearing sunglasses, which she pushes up on her forehead from time to time. LULA is a tall, slender, beautiful woman with long red hair hanging straight down her back, wearing only loud lipstick in somebody's good taste. She is eating an apple, very daintily. Coming down the car toward CLAY.

She stops beside CLAY's seat and hangs languidly from the strap, still managing to eat the apple. It is apparent that she is going to sit in the seat next to CLAY, and that she is only waiting for him to notice her before she sits.

CLAY sits as before, looking just beyond his magazine, now and again pulling the magazine slowly back and forth in front of his face in a hopeless effort to fan himself. Then he sees the woman hanging there beside him and he looks up into her face, smiling quizzically.

LULA: Hello.
CLAY: Uh, hi're you?
LULA: I'm going to sit down . . . O.K.?
CLAY: Sure.

LULA: *(Swings down onto the seat, pushing her legs straight out as if she is very weary.)* Oooof! Too much weight.

CLAY: Ha, doesn't look like much to me. *(Leaning back against the window, a little surprised and maybe stiff.)*

LULA: It's so anyway. *(And she moves her toes in the sandals, then pulls her right leg up on the left knee, better to inspect the bottoms of the sandals and the back of her heel. She appears for a second not to notice that CLAY is sitting next to her or that she has spoken to him just a second before. CLAY looks at the magazine, then out the black window. As he does this, she turns very quickly toward him.)* Weren't you staring at me through the window?

CLAY: *(Wheeling around and very much stiffened.)* What?

LULA: Weren't you staring at me through the window? At the last stop?

CLAY: Staring at you? What do you mean?

LULA: Don't you know what staring means?

CLAY: I saw you through the window . . . if that's what it means. I don't know if I was staring. Seems to me you were staring through the window at me.

LULA: I was. But only after I'd turned around and saw you staring through that window down in the vicinity of my ass and legs.

CLAY: Really?

LULA: Really. I guess you were just taking those idle potshots. Nothing else to do. Run your mind over people's flesh.

CLAY: Oh boy. Wow, now I admit I was looking in your direction. But the rest of that weight is yours.

LULA: I suppose.

CLAY: Staring through train windows is weird business. Much weirder than staring very sedately at abstract asses.

LULA: That's why I came looking through the window . . . so you'd have more than that to go on. I even smiled at you.

CLAY: That's right.

LULA: I even got into this train, going some other way than mine. Walked down the aisle . . . searching you out.

CLAY: Really? That's pretty funny.

LULA: That's pretty funny . . . God, you're dull.

CLAY: Well, I'm sorry, lady, but I really wasn't prepared for party talk.

LULA: No, you're not. What are you prepared for? *(Wrapping the apple core in Kleenex and dropping it on the floor.)*

CLAY: *(Takes her conversation as pure sex talk. He turns to confront her squarely with this idea.)* I'm prepared for anything. How about you?

LULA: *(Laughing loudly and cutting it off abruptly.)* What do you think you're doing?

CLAY: What?

LULA: You think I want to pick you up, get you to take me somewhere and screw me, huh?

CLAY: Is that the way I look?

LULA: You look like you been trying to grow a beard. That's exactly what you look like. You look like you live in New Jersey with your parents and are trying to grow a beard. That's what. You look like you've been reading Chinese poetry and drinking lukewarm sugarless tea.

667

(Laughs, uncrossing and recrossing her legs.) You look like death eating a soda cracker.

CLAY: *(Cocking his head from one side to the other, embarrassed and trying to make some comeback, but also intrigued by what the woman is saying . . . even the sharp city coarseness of her voice, which is still a kind of gentle sidewalk throb.)* Really? I look like all that?

LULA: Not all of it. *(She feints a seriousness to cover an actual somber tone.)* I lie a lot. *(Smiling)* It helps me control the world.

CLAY: *(Relieved and laughing louder than the humor.)* Yeah, I bet.

LULA: But it's true, most of it, right? Jersey? Your bumpy neck?

CLAY: How'd you know all that? Huh? Really, I mean about Jersey . . . and even the beard. I met you before? You know Warren Enright?

LULA: You tried to make it with your sister when you were ten. *(CLAY leans back hard against the back of the seat, his eyes opening now, still trying to look amused.)* But I succeeded a few weeks ago. *(She starts to laugh again.)*

CLAY: What're you talking about? Warren tell you that? You're a friend of Georgia's?

LULA: I told you I lie. I don't know your sister. I don't know Warren Enright.

CLAY: You mean you're just picking these things out of the air?

LULA: Is Warren Enright a tall skinny black boy with a phony English accent?

CLAY: I figured you knew him.

LULA: But I don't. I just figured you would know somebody like that. *(Laughs.)*

CLAY: Yeah, Yeah.

LULA: You're probably on your way to his house now.

CLAY: That's right.

LULA: *(Putting her hand on CLAY's closest knee, drawing it from the knee up to the thigh's hinge, then removing it, watching his face very closely, and continuing to laugh, perhaps more gently than before.)* Dull, dull, dull. I bet you think I'm exciting.

CLAY: You're O.K.

LULA: Am I exciting you now?

CLAY: Right. That's not what's supposed to happen?

LULA: How do I know? *(She returns her hand, without moving it, then takes it away and plunges it in her bag to draw out an apple.)* You want this?

CLAY: Sure.

LULA: *(She gets one out of the bag for herself.)* Eating apples together is always the first step. Or walking up uninhabited Seventh Avenue in the twenties on weekends. *(Bites and giggles, glancing at CLAY and speaking in loose singsong.)* Can get you involved . . . boy! Get us involved, Um-huh. *(Mock seriousness.)* Would you like to get involved with me, Mister Man?

CLAY: *(Trying to be as flippant as LULA, whacking happily at the apple.)* Sure. Why not? A beautiful woman like you. Huh, I'd be a fool not to.

LULA: And I bet you're sure you know what you're talking about. *(Taking him a little roughly by the wrist, so he cannot eat the apple, then shaking the wrist.)* I bet you're sure of almost everything anybody ever asked you about . . . right? *(Shakes his wrist harder.)* Right?

CLAY: Yeah, right . . . Wow, you're pretty strong, you know? Whatta you, a lady wrestler or something?

LULA: What's wrong with lady wrestlers? And don't answer because you never knew any. Huh. *(Cynically.)* That's for sure. They don't have any lady wrestlers in that part of Jersey. That's for sure.

CLAY: Hey, you still haven't told me how you know so much about me.

LULA: I told you I didn't know anything about *you* . . . you're a well-known type.

CLAY: Really?

LULA: Or at least I know the type very well. And your skinny English friend too.

CLAY: Anonymously?

LULA: *(Sets back in seat, single-mindedly finishing her apple and humming snatches of rhythm and blues song.)* What?

CLAY: Without knowing us specifically?

LULA: Oh boy. *(Looking quickly at CLAY.)* What a face. You know, you could be a handsome man.

CLAY: I can't argue with you.

LULA: *(Vague, off-center response.)* What?

CLAY: *(Raising his voice, thinking the train noise has drowned part of his sentence.)* I can't argue with you.

LULA: My hair is turning gray. A gray hair for each year and type I've come through.

CLAY: Why do you want to sound so old?

LULA: But it's always gentle when it starts. *(Attention drifting.)* Hugged against tenements, day or night.

CLAY: What?

LULA: *(Refocusing.)* Hey, why don't you take me to that party you're going to?

CLAY: You must be a friend of Warren's to know about the party.

LULA: Wouldn't you like to take me to the party? *(Imitates clinging vine.)* Oh, come on, ask me to your party.

CLAY: Of course I'll ask you to come with me to the party. And I'll bet you're a friend of Warren's.

LULA: Why not be a friend of Warren's? Why not? *(Taking his arm.)* Have you asked me yet?

CLAY: How can I ask you when I don't know your name?

LULA: Are you talking to my name?

CLAY: What is it, a secret?

LULA: I'm Lena the Hyena.

CLAY: The famous woman poet?

LULA: Poetess! The same!

CLAY: Well, you know so much about me . . . what's my name?

LULA: Morris the Hyena.

CLAY: The famous woman poet?

LULA: The same. *(Laughing and going into her bag.)* You want another apple?

CLAY: Can't make it, lady. I only have to keep one doctor away a day.

LULA: I bet your name is . . . something like . . . uh, Gerald or Walter. Huh?

CLAY: God, no.

LULA: Lloyd, Norman? One of those hopeless colored names creeping out of New Jersey. Leonard? Gag . . .

CLAY: Like Warren?

LULA: Definitely. Just exactly like Warren. Or Everett.

CLAY: Gag . . .

LULA: Well, for sure, it's not Willie.

CLAY: It's Clay.

LULA: Clay? Really? Clay what?

CLAY: Take your pick. Jackson, Johnson, or Williams.

LULA: Oh, really? Good for you. But it's got to be Williams. You're too pretentious to be a Jackson or Johnson.

CLAY: Thass right.

LULA: But Clay's O.K.

CLAY: So's Lena.

LULA: It's Lula.

CLAY: Oh?

LULA: Lula the Hyena.

CLAY: Very good.

LULA: *(Starts laughing again.)* Now you say to me, "Lula, Lula, why don't you go to this party with me tonight?" It's your turn, and let those be your lines.

CLAY: Lula, why don't you go to this party with me tonight, huh?

LULA: Say my name twice before you ask, and no huh's.

CLAY: Lula, Lula, why don't you go to this party with me tonight?

LULA: I'd like to go, Clay, but how can you ask me to go when you barely know me?

CLAY: That is strange, isn't it?

LULA: What kind of reaction is that? You're supposed to say, "Aw, come on, we'll get to know each other better at the party."

CLAY: That's pretty corny.

LULA: What are you into anyway? *(Looking at him half sullenly but still amused.)* What thing are you playing at, Mister? Mister Clay Williams? *(Grabs his thigh, up near the crotch.)* What are *you* thinking about?

CLAY: Watch it now, you're gonna excite me for real.

LULA: *(Taking her hand away and throwing her apple core through the window.)* I bet. *(She slumps in the seat and is heavily silent.)*

CLAY: I thought you knew everything about me? What happened? *(LULA looks at him, then looks slowly away, then over where the other aisle would be. Noise of the train. She reaches in her bag and pulls out one of the paper books. She puts it on her leg and thumbs the pages listlessly. CLAY cocks his head to see the title of the book. Noise of the train. LULA flips pages and her eyes drift. Both remain silent.)* Are you going to the party with me, Lula?

LULA: *(Bored and not even looking.)* I don't even know you.

CLAY: You said you know my type.

LULA: *(Strangely irritated.)* Don't get smart with me, Buster. I know you like the palm of my hand.

CLAY: The one you eat the apples with?

LULA: Yeh. And the one I open doors late Saturday evening with. That's my door. Up at the top of the stairs. Five flights. Above a lot of Italians and lying Americans. And scrape carrots with. Also . . . *(Looks at him)* the same hand I unbutton my dress with, or let my skirt fall down. Same hand. Lover.

CLAY: Are you angry about anything? Did I say something wrong?

LULA: Everything you say is wrong. *(Mock smile.)* That's what makes you so attractive. Ha. In that funnybook jacket with all the buttons. *(More animate, taking hold of his jacket.)* What've you got that jacket and tie on in all this heat for? And why're you wearing a jacket and tie like that? Did your people ever burn witches or start revolutions over the price of tea? Boy, those narrow-shoulder clothes come from a tradition you ought to feel oppressed by. A three-button suit. What right do you have to be wearing a three-button suit and striped tie? Your grandfather was a slave, he didn't go to Harvard.

CLAY: My grandfather was a night watchman.

LULA: And you went to a colored college where everybody thought they were Averell Harriman.

CLAY: All except me.

LULA: And who did you think you were? Who do you think you are now?

CLAY: *(Laughs as if to make light of the whole trend of the conversation.)* Well, in college I thought I was Baudelaire. But I've slowed down since.

LULA: I bet you never once thought you were a black nigger. *(Mock serious, then she howls with laughter. CLAY is stunned but after initial reaction, he quickly tries to appreciate the humor. LULA almost shrieks.)* A black Baudelaire.

CLAY: That's right.

LULA: Boy, are you corny. I take back what I said before. Everything you say is not wrong. It's perfect. You should be on television.

CLAY: You act like you're on television already.

LULA: That's because I'm an actress.

CLAY: I thought so.

LULA: Well, you're wrong. I'm no actress. I told you I always lie. I'm nothing, honey, and don't you ever forget it. *(Lighter.)* Although my mother was a Communist. The only person in my family ever to amount to anything.

CLAY: My mother was a Republican.

LULA: And you father voted for the man rather than the party.

CLAY: Right!

LULA: Yea for him. Yea, yea for him.

CLAY: Yea!

LULA: And yea for America where he is free to vote for the mediocrity of his choice! Yea!

CLAY: Yea!

LULA: And yea for both your parents who even though they differ about so crucial a matter as the body politic still forged a union of love and sacrifice that was destined to flower at the birth of the noble Clay . . . what's your middle name?

CLAY: Clay.

LULA: A union of love and sacrifice that was destined to flower at the birth of the noble Clay Clay Williams. Yea! And most of all yea yea for you, Clay Clay. The Black Baudelaire! Yes! *(And with knifelike cynicism.)*

671

My Christ, My Christ.

CLAY: Thank you, ma'am.

LULA: May the people accept you as a ghost of the future. And love you, that you might not kill them when you can.

CLAY: What?

LULA: You're a murderer, Clay, and you know it. *(Her voice darkening with significance.)* You know goddamn well what I mean.

CLAY: I do?

LULA: So we'll pretend the air is light and full of perfume.

CLAY: *(Sniffing at her blouse.)* It is.

LULA: And we'll pretend the people cannot see you. That is, the citizens. And that you are free of your own history. And I am free of my history. We'll pretend that we are both anonymous beauties smashing along through the city's entrails. *(She yells as loud as she can.)* GROOVE!

Black

SCENE II

Scene is the same as before, though now there are other seats visible in the car. And throughout the scene other people get on the subway. There are maybe one or two seated in the car as the scene opens, though neither CLAY nor LULA notices them. CLAY's tie is open. LULA is hugging his arm.

CLAY: The party!

LULA: I know it'll be something good. You can come in with me, looking casual and significant. I'll be strange, haughty, and silent, and walk with long slow strides.

CLAY: Right.

LULA: When you get drunk, pat me once, very lovingly on the flanks, and I'll look at you cryptically, licking my lips.

CLAY: It sounds like something we can do.

LULA: You'll go around talking to young men about your mind, and to old men about your plans. If you meet a very close friend who is also with someone like me, we can stand together, sipping our drinks and exchanging codes of lust. The atmosphere will be slithering in love and half-love and very open moral decision.

CLAY: Great. Great.

LULA: And everyone will pretend they don't know your name, and then ... *(She pauses heavily)* later, when they have to, they'll claim a friendship that denies your sterling character.

CLAY: *(Kissing her neck and fingers.)* And then what?

LULA: Then? Well, then we'll go down the street, late night, eating apples and winding very deliberately toward my house.

CLAY: Deliberately?

LULA: I mean, we'll look in all the shop windows, and make fun of the queers. Maybe we'll meet a Jewish Buddhist and flatten his conceits over some very pretentious coffee.

CLAY: In honor of whose God?

LULA: Mine.

CLAY: Who is ...?

LULA: Me ... and you?

672

CLAY: A corporate Godhead.
LULA: Exactly. Exactly. *(Notices one of the other people entering.)*
CLAY: Go on with the chronicle. Then what happens to us?
LULA: *(A mild depression, but she still makes her description triumphant and increasingly direct.)* To my house, of course.
CLAY: Of course.
LULA: And up the narrow steps of the tenement.
CLAY: You live in a tenement?
LULA: Wouldn't live anywhere else. Reminds me specifically of my novel form of insanity.
CLAY: Up the tenement stairs.
LULA: And with my apple-eating hand I push open the door and lead you, my tender big-eyed prey, into my . . . God, what can I call it . . . into my hovel.
CLAY: Then what happens?
LULA: After the dancing and games, after the long drinks and long walks, the real fun begins.
CLAY: Ah, the real fun. *(Embarrassed in spite of himself.)* Which is . . . ?
LULA: *(Laughs at him.)* Real fun in the dark house. Hah! Real fun in the dark house, high up above the street and the ignorant cowboys. I lead you in, holding your wet hand gently in my hand . . .
CLAY: Which is not wet?
LULA: Which is dry as ashes.
CLAY: And cold?
LULA: Don't think you'll get out of your responsibility that way. It's not cold at all. You Fascist! Into my dark living room. Where we'll sit and talk endlessly, endlessly.
CLAY: About what?
LULA: About what? About your manhood, what do you think? What do you think we've been talking about all this time?
CLAY: Well, I didn't know it was that. That's for sure. Every other thing in the world but that. *(Notices another person entering, looks quickly, almost involuntarily up and down the car, seeing the other people in the car.)* Hey, I didn't even notice when those people got on.
LULA: Yeah, I know.
CLAY: Man, this subway is slow.
LULA: Yeah, I know.
CLAY: Well, go on. We were talking about my manhood.
LULA: We still are. All the time.
CLAY: We were in your living room.
LULA: My dark living room. Talking endlessly.
CLAY: About my manhood.
LULA: I'll make you a map of it. Just as soon as we get to my house.
CLAY: Well, that's great.
LULA: One of the things we do while we talk. And screw.
CLAY: *(Trying to make his smile broader and less shaky.)* We finally got there.
LULA: And you'll call my rooms black as a grave. You'll say, "This place is like Juliet's tomb."
CLAY: *(Laughs)* I might.

LULA: I know. You've probably said it before.

CLAY: And is that all? The whole grand tour?

LULA: Not all. You'll say to me very close to my face, many, many times, you'll say, even whisper, that you love me.

CLAY: Maybe I will.

LULA: And you'll be lying.

CLAY: I wouldn't lie about something like that.

LULA: Hah. It's the only kind of thing you will lie about. Especially if you think it'll keep me alive.

CLAY: Keep you alive? I don't understand.

LULA: *(Bursting out laughing, but too shrilly.)* Don't understand? Well, don't look at me. It's the path I take, that's all. Where both feet take me when I set them down. One in front of the other.

CLAY: Morbid. Morbid. You sure you're not an actress? All that self-aggrandizement.

LULA: Well, I told you I wasn't an actress . . . but I also told you I lie all the time. Draw your own conclusions.

CLAY: Morbid. Morbid. You sure you're not an actress? All scribed? There's no more?

LULA: I've told you all I know. Or almost all.

CLAY: There's no funny parts?

LULA: I thought it was all funny.

CLAY: But you mean peculiar, not ha-ha.

LULA: You don't know what I mean.

CLAY: Well, tell me the almost part then. You said almost all. What else? I want the whole story.

LULA: *(Searching aimlessly through her bag. She begins to talk breathlessly, with a light and silly tone.)* All stories are whole stories. All of 'em. Our whole story . . . nothing but change. How could things go on like that forever? Huh? *(Slaps him on the shoulder, begins finding things in her bag, taking them out and throwing them over her shoulder into the aisle.)* Except I do go on as I do. Apples and long walks with deathless intelligent lovers. But you mix it up. Look out the window, all the time. Turning pages. Change change change. Till, shit, I don't know you. Wouldn't, for that matter. You're too serious. I bet you're even too serious to be psychoanalyzed. Like all those Jewish poets from Yonkers, who leave their mothers looking for other mothers, or others' mothers, on whose baggy tits they lay their fumbling heads. Their poems are always funny, and all about sex.

CLAY: They sound great. Like movies.

LULA: But you change. *(Blankly)* And things work on you till you hate them. *(More people come into the train. They come closer to the couple, some of them not sitting, but swinging drearily on the straps, staring at the two with uncertain interest.)*

CLAY: Wow. All these people, so suddenly. They must all come from the same place.

LULA: Right. That they do.

CLAY: Oh? You know about them too?

LULA: Oh yeah. About them more than I know about you. Do they frighten you?

CLAY: Frighten me? Why should they frighten me?

LULA: 'Cause you're an escaped nigger.

CLAY: Yeah?

LULA: 'Cause you crawled through the wire and made tracks to my side.

CLAY: Wire?

LULA: Don't they have wire around plantations?

CLAY: You must be Jewish. All you can think about is wire. Plantations didn't have any wire. Plantations were big open whitewashed places like heaven, and everybody on 'em was grooved to be there. Just strummin' and hummin' all day.

LULA: Yes, yes.

CLAY: And that's how the blues was born.

LULA: Yes, yes. And that's how the blues was born. *(Begins to make up a song that becomes quickly hysterical. As she sings she rises from her seat, still throwing things out of her bag into the aisle, beginning a rhythmical shudder and twistlike wiggle, which she continues up and down the aisle, bumping into any of the standing people and tripping over the feet of those sitting. Each time she runs into a person she lets out a very vicious piece of profanity, wiggling and stepping all the time.)* And that's how the blues was born. Yes. Yes. Son of a bitch, get out of the way. Yes. Quack. Yes. Yes. And that's how the blues was born. Ten little niggers sitting on a limb, but none of them ever looked like him. *(Points to CLAY, returns toward the seat, with her hands extended for him to rise and dance with her.)* And that's how the blues was born. Yes. Come on, Clay. Let's do the nasty. Rub bellies. Rub bellies.

CLAY: *(Waves his hands to refuse. He is embarrassed, but determined to get a kick out of the proceedings.)* Hey, what was in those apples? Mirror, mirror on the wall, who's the fairest one of all? Snow White, baby, and don't you forget it.

LULA: *(Grabbing for his hands, which he draws away.)* Come on, Clay. Let's rub bellies on the train. The nasty. The nasty. Do the gritty grind, like your ol' rag-head mammy. Grind till you lose your mind. Shake it, shake it, shake it, shake it! OOOOweeee! Come on, Clay. Let's do the choo-choo train shuffle, the naval scratcher.

CLAY: Hey, you coming on like the lady who smoked up her grass skirt.

LULA: *(Becoming annoyed that he will not dance, and becoming more animated as if to embarrass him still further.)* Come on, Clay . . . let's do the thing. Uhh! Uhh! Clay! Clay! You middle-class black bastard. Forget your social-working mother for a few seconds and let's knock stomachs. Clay, you liver-lipped white man. You would-be Christian. You ain't no nigger, you're just a dirty white man. Get up, Clay. Dance with me, Clay.

CLAY: Lula! Sit down, now. Be cool.

LULA: *(Mocking him, in wild dance.)* Be cool. Be cool. That's all you know . . . shaking that wildroot cream-oil on your knotty head, jackets buttoning up to your chin, so full of white man's words. Christ. God. Get up and scream at these people. Like scream meaningless shit in these hopeless faces. *(She screams at people in train, still dancing.)* Red trains cough Jewish underwear for keeps! Expanding smells of silence. Gravy snot whistling like sea birds. Clay. Clay, you got to break out. Don't sit there dying the way they want you to die. Get up.

CLAY: Oh, sit the fuck down. *(He moves to restrain her.)* Sit down, goddamn it.

LULA: *(Twisting out of his reach.)* Screw yourself, Uncle Tom. Thomas Woolly-Head. *(Begins to dance a kind of jig, mocking CLAY with loud forced humor.)* There is Uncle Tom . . . I mean, Uncle Thomas Woolly-Head. With old white matted mane. He hobbles on his wooden cane. Old Tom. Old Tom. Let the white man hump his ol' mama, and he jes' shuffle off in the woods and hide his gentle gray head. Ol' Thomas Woolly-Head. *(Some of the other riders are laughing now. A drunk gets up and joins LULA in her dance, singing, as best he can, her "song." CLAY gets up out of his seat and visibly scans the faces of the other riders.)*

CLAY: Lula! Lula! *(She is dancing and turning, still shouting as loud as she can. The drunk too is shouting, and waving his hands wildly.)* Lula . . . you dumb bitch. Why don't you stop it? *(He rushes half stumbling from his seat, and grabs one of her flailing arms.)*

LULA: Let me go! You black son of a bitch. *(She struggles against him.)* Let me go! Help! *(CLAY is dragging her towards her seat, and the drunk seeks to interfere. He grabs CLAY around the shoulders and begins wrestling with him. CLAY clubs the drunk to the floor without releasing LULA, who is still screaming. CLAY finally gets her to the seat and throws her into it.)*

CLAY: Now you shut the hell up. *(Grabbing her shoulders.)* Just shut up. You don't know what you're talking about. You don't know anything. So just keep your stupid mouth closed.

LULA: You're afraid of white people. And your father was. Uncle Tom Big Lip!

CLAY: *(Slaps her as hard as he can, across the mouth. LULA's head bangs against the back of the seat. When she raises it again, CLAY slaps her again.)* Now shut up and let me talk. *(He turns toward the other riders, some of whom are sitting on the edge of their seats. The drunk is on one knee, rubbing his head, and singing softly the same song. He shuts up too when he sees CLAY watching him. The others go back to newspapers or stare out the windows.)* Shit, you don't have any sense, Lula, nor feelings either. I could murder you now. Such a tiny ugly throat. I could squeeze it flat, and watch you turn blue, on a humble. For dull kicks. And all these weaked-faced ofays squatting around here, staring over their papers at me. Murder them too. Even if they expected it. That man there . . . *(Points to well-dressed man.)* I could rip that *Times* right out of his hand, as skinny and middle-classed as I am, I could rip that paper out of his hand and just as easily rip out his throat. It takes no great effort. For what? To kill you soft idiots? You don't understand anything but luxury.

LULA: You fool!

CLAY: *(Pushing her against the seat.)* I'm not telling you again, Tallulah Bankhead! Luxury. In your face and your fingers. You telling me what I ought to do. *(Sudden scream frightening the whole coach.)* Well, don't! Don't you tell me anything! If I'm a middle-class fake white man . . . let me be. And let me be in the way I want. *(Through his teeth.)* I'll rip your lousy breasts off! Let me be who I feel like being. Uncle Tom. Thomas. Whoever. It's none of your business. You don't know anything except what's there for you to see. An act. Lies. Device. Not the pure heart, the pumping black heart. You don't ever know that. And I sit here, in this buttoned-up suit, to keep myself from cutting all your throats. I mean wantonly. You great liberated whore! You fuck some black man, and right away you're an expert on black people. What a lotta shit that is. The only thing you know is that you come if he bangs you hard enough. And that's all. The belly rub? You wanted to do the belly rub? Shit, you don't even know how. You don't know how. That ol' dipty-dip shit you do, rolling your ass like an elephant. That's not my kind of belly rub. Belly rub is not Queens. Belly rub is dark places, with big hats and overcoats held up with one arm. Belly rub hates you. Old bald-headed four-eyed ofays popping their fingers . . . and don't know yet what they're doing. They say, "I love Bessie Smith." And don't even understand that Bessie Smith is saying, "Kiss my ass, kiss my black unruly ass." Before love, suffering, desire, anything you can explain, she's saying, and very plainly, "Kiss my black ass." And if you don't know that, it's you that's doing the kissing.

Charlie Parker? Charlie Parker. All the hip white boys scream for Bird. And Bird saying, "Up your ass, feebleminded ofay! Up your ass." And they sit there talking about the tortured genius of Charlie Parker. Bird would've played not a note of music if he just walked up to East Sixty-seventh Street and killed the first ten white people he saw. Not a note! And I'm the great would-be poet. Yes. That's right! Poet. Some kind of bastard literature . . . all it needs is a simple knife thrust. Just let me bleed you, you loud whore, and one poem vanished. A whole people of neurotics, struggling to keep from being sane. And the only thing that would cure the neurosis would be your murder. Simple as that. I mean if I murdered you, then other white people would begin to understand me. You understand? No. I guess not. If Bessie Smith had killed some white people she wouldn't have needed that music. She could have talked very straight and plain about the world. No metaphors. No grunts. No wiggles in the dark of her soul. Just straight two and two are four. Money. Power. Luxury. Like that. All of them. Crazy niggers turning their backs on sanity. When all it needs is that simple act. Murder. Just murder! Would make us all sane. *(Suddenly weary.)* Ahh. Shit. But who needs it? I'd rather be a fool. Insane. Safe with my words, and no deaths, and clean, hard thoughts, urging me to new conquests. My people's madness. Hah! That's a laugh. My people. They don't need me to claim them. They got legs and arms of their own. Personal insanities. Mirrors. They don't need all those words. They don't need any defense. But listen though, one more thing. And you tell this to your father, who's probably the kind of man who needs to know at once. So he can plan ahead. Tell him not to preach so much rationalism and cold logic to these niggers. Let them alone. Let them sing curses at you in code and see your filth as simple lack of style. Don't make the mistake, through some irresponsible surge of Christian charity, of talking too much about the advantages of Western rationalism, or the great intellectual legacy of the white man, or maybe they'll begin to listen. And then, maybe one day, you'll find they actually do understand exactly what you are talking about, all these fantasy people. All these blues people. And on that day, as sure as shit, when you really believe you can "accept" them into your fold, as half-white trusties late of the subject peoples. With no more blues, except the very old ones, and not a watermelon in sight, the great missionary heart will have triumphed, and all of those ex-coons will be stand-up Western men, with eyes for clean hard useful lives, sober, pious and sane, and they'll murder you. They'll murder you, and have very rational explanations. Very much like your own. They'll cut your throats, and drag you out to the edge of your cities so the flesh can fall away from your bones, in sanitary isolation.

LULA: *(Her voice takes on a different, more businesslike quality.)* I've heard enough.

CLAY: *(Reaching for his books.)* I bet you have. I guess I better collect my stuff and get off this train. Looks like we won't be acting out that little pageant you outlined before.

LULA: No. We won't. You're right about that, at least. *(She turns to look quickly around the rest of the car.)* All right! *(The others respond.)*

CLAY: *(Bending across the girl to retrieve his belonging.)* Sorry, baby, I don't think we could make it. *(As he is bending over her, the girl brings up a small knife and plunges it into CLAY's chest. Twice. He slumps across her knees, his mouth working stupidly.)*

LULA: Sorry is right. *(Turning to the others in the car who have already gotten up from their seats.)* Sorry is the righest thing you've said. Get this man off me! Hurry, now! *(The others come and drag CLAY's body down the aisle.)* Open the door and throw his body out. *(They throw him off.)* And all of you get off at the next stop. *(LULA busies herself straightening her things. Getting everything in order. She takes out a notebook and makes a quick scribbling note. Drops it in her bag. The train apparently stops and all the others get off, leaving her alone in the coach.*

Very soon a young Negro of about twenty comes into the coach, with a couple of books under his arm. He sits a few seats in back of LULA. When he is seated she turns and gives him a long slow look. He looks up from his book and drops the book on his lap. Then an old Negro conductor comes into the car, doing a sort of restrained soft shoe, and half mumbling the words of some song. He looks at the young man, briefly, with a quick greeting.)

CONDUCTOR: Hey, brother!

YOUNG MAN: Hey. *(The conductor continues down the aisle with his little dance and the mumbled song. LULA turns to stare at him and follows his movements down the aisle. The conductor tips his hat when he reaches her seat, and continues out the car.)*

Curtain

THE SIXTIES AND
AFTER: Theatrical Experiment
and Synthesis

"The Sixties" have become legendary as a time of turmoil, rebellion, and experimentation. The very word conjures up images of the Beatles and the daily body count, hippies and Haight-Ashbury, Kent State and the Peace Corps, love-ins and drop-outs, Pope John XXIII, JFK, and Martin Luther King, tripping out, sitting in, and getting off, "one great step for mankind" on the moon and twisting at the disco downtown. And theatre was a part of the mix — reflecting the confusion, experiencing its own revolutions, espousing causes, changing.

During the following two decades, as the dust settled, the theatre world sifted out the lasting contributions of the sixties, consolidated its gains, and synthesized new modes. In the final decade of the century, many people worried about the race's chances for survival and wondered, if it did survive, what new shapes human interaction would take. As always, theatre reflected its world, wondering if it had a place in a technological, mass-media world and curious about what theatre would look like in the twenty-first century.

Social, Political, and Philosophical Backgrounds

During most of this period, the Cold War dominated international politics. The Soviet Union and its satellite nations in eastern Europe and Asia struggled with the capitalist countries of Europe, America, and Asia for control of the world. Both sides employed tactics such as forming ever-shifting alliances, carrying on espionage, provoking civil wars in secondary countries, waging propaganda battles, exchanging threats, and building immensely destructive arsenals. The possession of nuclear weapons by both sides with the combined capacity for destroying life on the planet greatly increased tension in the world. Repeatedly during this time, individual crises threatened to push the powers over the edge into nuclear holocaust.

Communism's Demise

By the end of the 1980s, forty years of building weapons and armies, suppressing dissent, and mismanaging economies had so drained the Soviet Union and its allies that they had to make changes. Under Mikhail Gorbachev, in its deepest changes since the Russian Revolution, the USSR began to debate its policies openly, to practice democracy, to move toward a free economy, and to release control over its satellite nations. In 1989 and '90, with unprecedented speed, country after country in eastern Europe threw its Communist leaders out of power, held elections, turned toward free economies, and began to function independently of Moscow's control. The Berlin wall, a central symbol of the Cold War, was demolished, the Warsaw Pact of Communist military alliances dissolved, and the German Democratic Republic (East Germany), eliminated its Communist leadership and united with the western German Federal Republic. Seemingly overnight, the Cold War had ended.

Back in the 1960s, the Cold War heated up in Vietnam. As American soldiers fought, killed, and died in southeast Asia, the war forced Americans at home to face many difficult questions such as: What is America's role in world politics? How dependable is a technology that cannot defeat a less sophisticated enemy? Is force of arms of any use in an ideological war? What is the implication of a white-dominated country sending its black citizens to kill and be killed by brown people? How trustworthy is logical thinking when it so easily serves the purposes of diametrically opposed factions? In a free society, does patriotism demand dissent or obedience? Is there anything really worth dying for? Is there anything really worth killing for? The American withdrawal from Vietnam in 1973, which permitted a Communist victory, not only gave the United States an unaccustomed taste of defeat, but also left many of these questions unresolved.

While the war was heating up on the other side of the world, the civil rights struggle and the assassinations of President John Kennedy, his brother Robert, and black leaders Malcolm X and Martin Luther King Jr., brought violence home to America.

Consciousness Movements

Growing out of the sixties and lasting into the eighties, various consciousness movements called attention to parts of society which democracy seemed to have overlooked. Feminists challenged the domination of politics, business, and society by white males and insisted that women be given full rights. Special populations like the sight and hearing impaired and the physically and developmentally disabled began to demand equal access to services and equal rights with the larger population. And homosexuals began to work for gay and lesbian rights and to discover a sense of personal dignity.

At the same time, Americans and Western Europeans began to realize the chaos that two centuries of technology had caused in the natural environment. They realized that their efforts to make themselves more comfortable in the world had irreparably ruined parts of the ecology, and many warned that if this trend continued, the planet would rapidly become uninhabitable.

Meanwhile, even as environmentalists were trying to put the brakes on technology and various minorities were trying to turn attention from science to human relations, computers and advances in information management and communication were causing technology to accelerate at unbelievable speed. In the span of a single, normal lifetime, like that of Thornton Wilder who lived to be 78, the western world had progressed from using horses and buggies to putting men on the moon.

Post-Modernism

As the end of the century approached, students of culture believed they detected a widespread shift in viewpoint. They called the new understanding of the world "post-modernism."

Modernism had shaped the European and American self-understanding for over a century. Modernists placed great value in progress, technology, and science. They limited truth to that which corresponded with facts, and they valued linear thinking, rationality, and logic. Modernists believed mankind to be self-determining — capable of overcoming all problems and realizing its destiny by its own willpower. They thought the present was better than the past and that the future would be better than either.

In contrast, post-modernists placed little value on progress and had little confidence that technology would provide the tools for solving mankind's most fundamental problems. They mistrusted logic and instead valued configurative thinking. They valued past cultures — including "primitive" ones — at least as much as the present. Post-modernists valued the illogical, the uncivilized, the uneven, and the unpredictable. While modernists valued the creation of original art which in some way "made sense," post-modernists frequently imitated and adapted past art works and intentionally violated principles of rationality and form.

Throughout this period, few, if any, of these events and perceptions failed to make its impact on theatre. The Cold War, Vietnam, radical life styles, feminism, gay rights, and environmentalism provided subject matter for plays, spawned special interest theatre groups, and caused shifts in dramatic structure and production approaches.

Dramatic Literature

Swiss and German Playwrights

After World War II, the world learned the full extent of the atrocities committed by the Nazi regime, including the extermination of 6,000,000 Jews. The attempts of post-war Germans to come to terms with these events stimulated some powerful drama in German-speaking countries. Two Swiss playwrights in particular made vital contributions to this drama: Max Frisch (1911-) who wrote *The Firebugs* (1958), and Friedrich Dürrenmatt (1921-) who wrote *The Visit* (1956) and *The Physicists* (1962). These playwrights used a mixture of realism and various nonrealistic modes to present the bizarre actions of their plays.

Later in the period, other Germans produced radically experimental works which tested the bounds of language, dramatic structure, and theatrical performances. These post-modern dramatists included Peter Handke (1942-) with his *Ride Across Lake Constance* (1971), and Heiner Müller (1929-) with his *Hamletmachine* (1979).

British Playwrights

In the 1950s, a new generation of British playwrights began to attack the status-quo mix of middle-class mores, Western imperialism, and nuclear politics. This movement, whose members were sometimes called "the angry young men," began with a play by John Osborn (1929-), titled *Look Back in Anger* (1956), in which the central, ne're-do-well character Jimmy rants against a whole array of symbols of the establishment ranging from his mother-in-law to the newspapers. Other plays in the "kitchen-sink realism" mode of Osborne's drama included *A Taste of Honey* (1958) by Shelagh Delaney (1939-), *Roots* (1959) by Arnold Wesker (1932-), and *Saved* (1965) by Edward Bond (1935-).

A playwright with similar viewpoints but more Marxist sympathies and Brechtian dramatic structures was John Arden (1930-), who wrote *Serjeant Musgrave's Dance* (1959). Due to their subject matter and language, some of the plays of these writers had to be presented in subscription theatres instead of publicly. This situation brought England's censorship laws under attack, and in 1968 the Licensing Act, on the books since 1737, was finally rescinded.

The new vitality in British drama continued. Peter Shaffer (1926-) used Brechtian techniques to examine the conflict between spirituality and technology in plays like *Equus* (1973). Tom Stoppard (1937-) combined absurdism and realism in varying degrees to investigate modern philosophical, psychological, social, and political perceptions. His *Rosencrantz and Guilderstern Are Dead* (1967) dealt with problems of fate and chance, his pair of one-acts, *Dogg's Hamlet/Cahoot's Macbeth* (1979) focused on language and political oppression, and *The Real Thing* (1982) was a realistic study of love and marriage.

Harold Pinter

Harold Pinter (1930-), perhaps the most influential British playwright of the century, first drew public acclaim with *The Caretaker* (1960), a harrowing play in which two young men take in an old man, befriend and harrass him, and eventually throw him out. The structures of *The Caretaker* came to be recognized as typical characteristics of a Pinter play. His characters are mysterious because the details about their backgrounds are either nonexistent or contradictory, they interact in a room which seems to be surrounded by a hostile world, and they converse in realistic dialog without effectively communicating. Other well-known plays by Pinter include *The Birthday Party* (1958), *The Dumb Waiter* (1960), *The Homecoming* (1965), and *Old Times* (1971). In his later plays like *Mountain Language* (1988), political implications which were implicit in Pinter's earlier works became more obvious. Late in the twentieth century, critics still debated whether Pinter's plays were essentially absurdist or ultra-realistic. This ambiguity, besides providing a great deal of the power of his plays, also pointed toward a perception which seemed to characterize much drama of the period: The more stringently naturalistic one's viewpoint and the more cut off from metaphysical "meaning" it is, the more absurd the world looks.

Experimental Theatre

During the 1960s, American playwrights brought new vitality to theatre in the United States by experimenting with absurdist drama and improvisational production techniques. Edward Albee (1928-) was often considered part of the absurdist movement because of plays like his *Tiny Alice* (1964). However, his major plays, *Who's Afraid of Virginia Woolf?* (1962) and *Delicate Balance* (1966) use realistic modes to examine the conflict between reality and illusion. Arthur Kopit (1938-) also exhibited absurdist connections. His *Oh Dad, Poor Dad, Momma's Hung You in the Closet, and I'm Feeling So Sad* (1960) parodied the plays of Tennessee Williams, and his *Indians* (1968) used Buffalo Bill Cody in a critique of American heroism and racism.

Jean-Claude Van Itallie (1936-) and Megan Terry (1932-), both of whom worked with the Open Theatre, were more experimental as well as more radically critical of American society. Their scripts called for a great amount of improvisation on the part of the actors and included techniques such as transformations, in which performers shifted roles instantaneously and in full view of the audience. Characteristic scripts included Van Itallie's *America Hurrah!*, produced by the Open Theatre in 1966, and Terry's *Viet Rock*, produced the same year by La Mama Experimental Club.

Realism Reappears

In the 1970s, realism, a style Americans always seemed to prefer, staged a comeback. Plays of David Rabe (1940-) like *Sticks and Bones, The Basic Training of Pavlo Hummel* (both 1971), and *Streamers* (1976) combined some cinematic techniques with basic realism to depict the social and psychological impacts of the Vietnam War. And Neil Simon (1927-), who produced his first play *(Come Blow Your Horn)* in 1961, continued to turn out popular comedies at the rate of almost one a year throughout the 1970s. Simon's large body of work, combined with his masterful technique displayed in such plays as *The Odd Couple* (1965), *The Sunshine Boys* (1972), *California Suite* (1976), and *Brighton Beach Memoirs* (1983), established him as America's leading comedy writer.

At the same time, two other Americans, Sam Shepard (1943-) and David Mamet (1947-), pushed realism to its limits. Like Pinter's drama, their almost photographic realism and their narrow focus on the lives of believable but often twisted characters gave their plays an absurdist atmosphere. Furthermore, they both wrote dialog which managed to precisely imitate American speech patterns and, simultaneously, to achieve a kind of poetic effect. Characteristic plays included Mamet's *American Buffalo* (1975) and *Speed-the-Plow* (1988), and Shepard's *Buried Child* (1978) and *A Lie of the Mind* (1985).

From the end of World War II until the end of the Cold War in 1990, the repressive governments of eastern Europe established paranoiac societies which limited the development of serious new drama in their countries. Nevertheless, some playwrights, such as Poland's Slawomir Mrozek (1930-) and Czechoslovakia's Václav Havel (1936-), wrote intriguing plays which combined absurdist techniques and thinly veiled political criticism. Examples of their plays include Mrozek's *Tango* (1965) and Havel's *The Memorandum* (1965) and *Largo Desolato* (1985).

Performance Conventions and Stagecraft

During the 1960s, experimental approaches to performance competed with realistic "method" acting, questioned the supremacy of language in the theatre, and challenged the traditional separation of audience from performers.

Jerzy Grotowski

The work of Polish director Jerzy Grotowski (1933-) at Breslau's Theatre Laboratory from around 1965 to 1976 drew a great deal of attention. Believing the essence of theatre resided in the live actor's confrontation with the audience, Grotowski de-emphasized the role of the technical and textual aspects of theatre in order to focus on the actor alone. He referred to his approach as "poor theatre," meaning theatre stripped of its "rich" accretions. His actors underwent rigorous psychological and physical training to increase their ability to control their performance. He typically synthesized performance texts from nondramatic sources or reshaped existing scripts. Grotowski's influence spread abroad by means of international tours of the Theatre Laboratory and the publication of his book, *Towards a Poor Theatre* (1968).

Happenings

"Happenings," frequently devised by painters and characteristic of the 1960s, attempted to eliminate the boundaries between theatre and the visual arts. Partially choreographed by the producers and partly improvised, happenings involved the "audience" in performance. Happenings sometimes utilized specially constructed environments, but the sequence of actions performed by the actors and audience rarely followed any story line, and the participants performed prescribed activities without taking on fictional "characters." Although some happenings were politically-motivated guerrilla theatre, many involved abstract experiences with no apparent didactic intent. Happenings permitted the artists to interact with their materials and their patrons and provided a consciousness-expanding experience for the audience/participants.

Some theatre-producing groups like the Living Theatre (discussed in the introduction to political theatre) borrowed techniques from the happenings, but this semitheatrical form disappeared soon after the end of the 1960s. The concept, however, was reborn in the 1980s as performance art.

Environmental Theatre and Found Spaces

Experimentation with the relationship between the audience and the performers in more traditional theatre led to a revival of presentation techniques which had been typical in the Middle Ages. In the twentieth century these approaches were called environmental theatre and found spaces. Environmental theatre refers to an audience arrangement which mingles the audience and the performers in the same area. Sometimes environmental theatre distributed stage areas throughout the auditorium, and sometimes it eliminated the auditorium-stage distinction altogether and interspersed seating areas and performance spaces throughout the production area. Environmental presentations often used found spaces, or already-existing buildings and natural settings which had not been designed as theatres. Partly as a response to these experiments with the audience-performer relationship, many university theatre programs built "black box" theatres or sizable rooms without fixed seating or stage areas in which directors could place the audience in varying arrangements considered most appropriate for the current productions.

Theatrical Taboos Broken

The spirit of tradition-breaking and experimentation which characterized the 1960s also led playwrights and producers to deal with subject matter and use performance techniques which had previously been considered inappropriate in public events. Plays began to deal openly with homosexuality, sexual promiscuity, and even incest. The use of obscene and profane language on stage became commonplace, and nudity, while less frequent, became an accepted part of serious theatre. Two plays in particular broke theatrical taboos: The antiwar rock musical *Hair* (1967) celebrated the sexual freedom of the 1960s' youth culture and included a scene in which the entire cast appeared nude, and the vaudeville-like revue *Oh, Calcutta* (1969) used frequent nudity to satirize current sexual attitudes and practices ranging from prudery to promiscuity.

Josef Svoboda

Perhaps more than any other designer during the 1960s, the Czech Josef Svoboda (1920-) applied the full range of modern technology and electronics to theatrical productions. Svoboda first gained international prominence at the 1958 Brussels World Fair with the *Laterna Magica,* a multimedia revue which combined live actors with a massive use of moving and still projections. Subsequently, Svoboda designed productions for many theatres both in Czechoslovakia and elsewhere. He typically used moving scenery components, projections, and innovative, spectacular lighting effects.

Dramatic Theory

During the second half of the twentieth century, theorists gave special attention to the connection between ritual and theatre. The decline of traditional religion in Europe and America provided some of the impetus for this effort. By the middle of the century, many people preferred science's explanations of the world over those traditionally supplied by religion. Most people, for instance, believed that the human race resulted from natural, evolutionary processes rather than instantaneous divine creation. Rather than leading moderns into civilized modes of conflict resolution, religious fervor had fueled two barbarous world wars and countless local wars. And debates within the Christian churches, ranging from the liberal-fundamentalist schisms of the late-nineteenth century to the death-of-God controversy of the 1960s, further weakened people's confidence in religion. Meanwhile, increased contact with Oriental cultures led many Westerners to study the Eastern religions as possible substitutes for Christianity in which they had lost faith. With a human hunger for ritual, but little confidence in their traditional religions, some turned to theatre as a kind of church for the irreligious.

Nonrealistic, experimental theatre in the 1960s seemed to provide acceptable rituals for creating temporary communities of faith. In the musical *Godspell* (1971), for instance, actors invited the audience to share bread and wine with them during intermission, and *Hair!* concluded by inviting the audience onto the stage to participate with the actors in frenzied dance.

Richard Schechner

Richard Schechner (1934-), one of the most innovative American critics and directors during the 1960s and 70s, eventually turned his creative efforts to the study of primitive ritual and its relationship to theatre. This approach was bolstered in the 1980s by "structuralism," an approach to the study of literature and theatre which focused less on content and more on formal patterns in art and their social and mythic implications. Although traditional religion seemed to enjoy a world-wide resurgence toward the end of the century, theorists continued to investigate theatre's potential for maximizing people's sense of connection with each other and with forces beyond sensory experience.

Theatrical Organization

Off-Off-Broadway

In the United States during the 1960s, the tendency for serious theatre to move away from Broadway, which had begun with the creation of Off-Broadway, continued with the development of Off-Off-Broadway theatres. By this time, the distinctions between Broadway and Off-Broadway had blurred to the extent that many people believed Off-Broadway had lost its innovative edge and sold out to commercialism. Off-Off-Broadway usually traces its beginning to a coffee house called Caffé Cino, founded by Joe Cino in 1958. By 1961, play production became a regular part of the programming at the coffee house. By the time Cino died in 1967 and the Caffé stopped producing plays, many other small theatres had developed to carry on the tradition of low-budget, experimental productions of innovative plays in informal settings. By 1972, approximately sixty-five of these groups had united to form the Off-Off-Broadway Theatre Alliance.

Probably the most influential Off-Off-Broadway theatre was Café La Mama, founded by Ellen Stewart in the basement of an Italian restaurant in 1961. La Mama began by providing a home for one-week runs of new plays. It eventually changed its name to the La Mama Experimental Theatre Club, found a permanent home in New York's Greenwich Village, and for a time had a permanent resident company. La Mama continued producing innovative, nonrealistic plays into the 1990s and also spawned many off-shoots, including La Mama theatres in Europe, South America, Australia, and Canada.

Resident Theatre Companies

During this period, American theatre outside of New York City began to experience new vitality through the development of professional, nonprofit resident theatre companies. As their designation indicates, these theatres consisted of groups of professionals who organized as nonprofit organizations. Contrary to the twentieth-century American practice of assembling a new production group for each play, many of these companies consisted of groups who produced an on-going repertory of plays with relatively little turnover in personnel. Some of the best-known regional theatres included Minneapolis' Guthrie Theatre, Los Angeles' Mark Taper Forum, Chicago's Goodman Theatre, and the Actors Theatre of Louisville. In 1961, the Theatre Communication Group organized to foster communication and cooperation among these nonprofit, professional theatres.

Minority Theatre

Partly as a result of the consciousness-raising movements of the 1960s, minority populations, such as women, gays, and the deaf, developed lively theatre communities and, in some cases, central theatre organizations. Samples included the Women's Project of New York's American Place Theatre, the National Theatre of the Deaf with its home at the O'Neill Theatre Center in Connecticut, and many gay and lesbian theatres.

Although constantly threatened by burgeoning mass entertainment media, economic pressures, and changing tastes, theatre at the end of the twentieth century continued to be a lively art. More people were studying drama, participating in plays, and earning their living in theatre than ever before, there was a greater number of theatres than ever before, and more new plays in more new styles than ever were finding productions. Constantly dying and constantly renewing itself, theatre continued to be the now-art.

Mark Medoff

After studying theatre at the University of Miami and Stanford University, Mark Medoff (1940-) joined the faculty of New Mexico State University at Las Cruces in 1966 and taught there into the 1990s. In addition to writing for theatre and screen, he also involved himself in various educational theatre activities, such as serving as chair of the Playwriting Awards Committee of the American College Theatre Festival in 1985-86. In addition to *Children of a Lesser God*, Medoff's plays include *The Kramer* (1972), *The Wager* (1972), *When You Comin' Back, Red Ryder?* (1973), *The Conversion of Aaron Weiss* (1977), *The Heart Outright* (1986), and *The Homage That Follows* (1987).

In Medoff's plays, the characters typically long for the past while trying to cope with the present. Some of his characters, like Kramer in his first play, Leeds in *The Wager,* and Teddy in *When You Comin' Back, Red Ryder?*, are psychologically vicious and physically violent, but these characters, like other Medoff people, at the same time betray a deep vulnerability.

A theatre professional whose many honors include an Obie and a Drama Critics Award, and simultaneously a committed theatre educator, Mark Medoff embodies the essential unity of educational and professional theatre in America.

Children of a Lesser God

Dramaturgy

This play typifies drama in the late twentieth century. In the first place, Medoff built into his play the kind of modified realism that characterized many plays of the period. The situation, characters, and dialog are strictly realistic, the story has the feeling of a case history, and events occur as a result of understandable social processes. But Medoff modified this realism by placing it on an essentially bare stage and by moving it from scene to short scene, fluidly and without breaks in the action.

The plot structure of *Children of a Lesser God* with many scenes, some of them very short, which progress without transitions across gaps in time and place, shows the influence of film technique on stage drama. The occasional obscenities and the play's frank treatment of the sexual aspects of interpersonal relationships resulted from the liberating impact of the 1960s. And the focus on deaf consciousness, deaf pride, and the rights of hearing-and-speech-impaired people expressed the late-twentieth-century awareness of the unique value of all people, including minorities.

Medoff provided relatively few stage directions for *Children of a Lesser God*. He indicated no set changes at all, usually did not specify whether or not the characters are signing while speaking, and frequently had characters begin speaking without dictating when or where they entered. This approach makes the play challenging reading and forces the director, designers, and actors to take an active part in shaping its performance. In fact, the production of *any* play requires that the participants make constant decisions about the delivery of every line, the shape and timing of every gesture and the appearance and location of every prop or scenic element. Medoff's omission of stage directions not only makes the necessity for these decisions more obvious, but also liberates the producers to take a fully creative role in the play.

Production History

The development of this play, typical of many successful plays in the late twentieth century, tied together various parts of the American theatre scene. It was first performed in April, 1979, in a workshop production at New Mexico State University. In the fall of the same year, it ran for over a month at the Mark Taper Forum in Los Angeles, one of the nation's leading regional theatres. On March 30, 1980, it opened at New York's Longacre Theatre with much the same cast as the California production. This Broadway production won the playwright a Tony Award for Best Play of the 1979-80 Broadway Season. The play subsequently transferred to the Albery Theatre on London's West End, England's equivalent to Broadway. This production won the Society of West End Theatre Awards for The Play of the Year, 1981.

In 1986, a film based on the play, with screenplay by Medoff and Hesper Anderson, was released by Paramount Pictures. Marlee Matlin, who played Sarah in the movie, received an Oscar for Best Actress, thus becoming the fourth actress in the history of the Academy Awards to win an Oscar for her first screen appearance. This sequence reversed the order typical of earlier twentieth-century plays in which a show first demonstrated its success on Broadway and later was produced by regional and educational theatres.

Characteristic of contemporary drama and a success in the theatre, *Children of a Lesser God* is a powerful play.

Contemporary Theatre Timeline

MAX FRISCH (1911-)
JOSEF SVOBODA (1920-)
FRIEDRICH DÜRRENMATT (1921-)
PETER SHAFFER (1926-)
NEIL SIMON (1927-)
EDWARD ALBEE (1928-)
HEINER MÜLLER (1929-)
JOHN OSBORNE (1929-)
JOHN ARDEN (1930-)
SLAWOMIR MROZEK (1930-)
HAROLD PINTER (1930-)
ARNOLD WESKER (1932-)
MEGAN TERRY (1932-)
JERZY GROTOWSKI (1933-)
RICHARD SCHECHNER (1934-)
EDWARD BOND (1935-)
JEAN-CLAUDE VAN ITALLIE (1936-)
VÁCLAV HAVEL (1936-)
"LARGO DESOLATO" (1985) ●
TOM STOPPARD (1937-)
ARTHUR KOPIT (1938-)
SHELAGH DELANEY (1939-)
MARK MEDOFF (1940-)
"CHILDREN OF A LESSER GOD" (1979) ●
DAVID RABE (1940-)
PETER HANDKE (1942-)
SAM SHEPARD (1943-)
DAVID MAMET (1947-)
CAFFÉ CINO (1958-67)
LA MAMA (1961-)

ENGLAND'S LICENSING ACT RESCINDED (1968) ●
INVASION OF CZECHOSLOVAKIA (1968) ●
U.S. WITHDRAWAL FROM VIETNAM (1973) ●
COLLAPSE OF THE RUSSIAN COMMUNIST EMPIRE (1989) ●
"BODY LEAKS" (1990) ●

1910   1920   1930   1940   1950   1960   1970   1980   1990

CHILDREN OF A LESSER GOD

by MARK MEDOFF

THE CHARACTERS

JAMES LEEDS
Thirty-ish. A speech teacher at a State School for the Deaf.

SARAH NORMAN
Mid-twenties. Deaf from birth.

ORIN DENNIS
In his twenties. Has some residual hearing; a lip reader.

MRS. NORMAN
Sarah's mother.

MR. FRANKLIN
Anywhere from his early thirties to his mid-forties.
The Supervising Teacher at the Deaf School.

LYDIA
In her late teens. Has some residual hearing; a lip reader.

EDNA KLEIN
Thirty to forty. A lawyer.

For why is all around us here
As if some lesser god had made the world,
But had not force to shape it as he would?

"Idylls of the King"
Tennyson

The play takes place in the mind of James Leeds. Throughout the events, characters step from his memory for anything from a full scene to several lines.

The stage is bare, holding only a few benches and a blackboard and permitting characters to appear and disappear easily.

As to the matter of Signed English. When James is speaking to Sarah, who is deaf and does *not* lip read, he signs what he says to her unless otherwise noted. When speaking to Orin and Lydia, who both lip read, he merely speaks directly into their faces and enunciates with some care.

Sarah speaks aloud only at the end of the play. Otherwise the notion of speech where she is concerned means strictly the use of Signed English or American Sign Language (ASL). The difference between ASL and Signed English basically is that the former is far more conceptual and pictorial than grammatical, Signed English employing a word-by-word technique.

[Brackets] indicate portions of a line which are signed but not spoken.

Because of the subtleties of American Sign Language (ASL), and the differences in technique between ASL and Signed English, an expert in these languages should be a consultant to any production.

The author insists that — in *any* professional production of this play — the roles of Sarah, Orin, and Lydia be performed by deaf or hearing impaired actors.

ACT I

James and Sarah alone, met at the climax of an argument they'll replay at the end of the play. She speaks here in ASL; were we to translate it into standard English, she would be saying: I have nothing; no hearing, no speech, no intelligence, no language. I have only you. I don't need you. I have me alone. Join, unjoined.

SARAH: Me have nothing. Me deafy. Speech inept. Intelligence — tiny block-head. English — blow away. Left one you. Depend — no. Think myself enough. Join, unjoined — *(Sarah runs off.)*

JAMES: *(Not signing)* She went away from me. Or did I drive her away? I don't know. If I did, it was because . . . I seem to be having trouble stringing together a complete . . . I mean, a speech therapist shouldn't be having difficulty with the language. All right, start in the . . . *Finish the sentence!* Start in the beginning. In the beginning there was silence and out of that silence there could come only one thing: Speech. That's right. Human speech. So, *speak! (Orin has entered the classroom area — looks at the blackboard on which is written the following:)*

ORIN: "Speech is not a specious but a sacred sanctio*na*, secured by solemn sacrifice."

JAMES: *(A together, energetic James.)* Very good, Orin.

ORIN: No, it wasn't.

JAMES: It was better. A couple of things, though —

ORIN: Mr. Leeds, remember you have to look at me when you're talking.

JAMES: Sorry. A couple of things though. Specious. Specious. It's softer, like sshhh.

ORIN: Specious.

JAMES: All right, good. And the final "n" in sanction.

ORIN: Sanctio*na.*

JAMES: Wait, please. Watch. Sanctio*n.* Un. Un.

ORIN: Sanctio*na.* That was wrong, damn it!

JAMES: That's okay, Orin . . . Watch my mouth. Cut it. Sanction. Look up in here. Sanction. "Un." *(Indicating the movement of the tongue to the roof of the mouth.)*

ORIN: Sanctio*n.*

JAMES: Yes! Good for you. How did that feel?

ORIN: How did it sound?

JAMES: It sounded beautiful.

ORIN: Then it felt all right.

JAMES: Speech.

ORIN: Speech. *(Franklin and Sarah enter.)*

FRANKLIN: Mr. Leeds . . .

JAMES: *(Indicating that Franklin should wait, keeping his focus on Orin.)* Specious.

ORIN: Specious.

JAMES: Sanction.

ORIN: Sanctio*na.*

JAMES: No.

ORIN: Sanction.

JAMES: Yes. Hello, Mr. Franklin. How are you, sir?

FRANKLIN: Just dandy, Mr. Leeds. That was very impressive, Orin.

ORIN: Thank you, Mr. Franklin.

FRANKLIN: You never worked that hard for me.

ORIN: *(Signing and speaking — the signing for Sarah's benefit.)* I never liked you, Mr. Franklin. [Asshole.]

FRANKLIN: Ah. No garlic then for Mr. Leeds — or is two weeks too soon to decide the garlic question?

ORIN: You want to smell?

FRANKLIN: No thanks. I just had an ice cream cone.

JAMES: *(Smoothing things.)* Orin, I think that'll be all for today.

ORIN: Could I see you tomorrow maybe?

JAMES: Sure, you want to have lunch with me?

ORIN: Okay. Thank you.

SARAH: *(As Orin greets her and is about to pass.)* Ass licker.	JAMES: *(To Frankilin as Orin moves away.)* Garlic?
ORIN: *(Signing only.)* [Think so? Bend over and find out.] *(She does, Orin smiles and passes her.)*	FRANKLIN: Sometimes they like to chew a little garlic for the speech therapist.

SARAH: Chicken.

ORIN: *(Signing only.)* [Later.]

(Orin leaves.)

FRANKLIN: *(Signing the following dialogue.)* Mr. Leeds, this is Sarah.

JAMES: Hello, Sarah.

FRANKLIN: Say hello to Mr. Leeds, Sarah.

SARAH: You deaf?

JAMES: Am I deaf? No. Why? *(She looks as if she may exit.)*

FRANKLIN: Stay! *(She imitates a dog "staying.")* Cute.

JAMES: Well, you did say that to her as if —

FRANKLIN: *(No longer signing.)* Pardon me, Mr. Leeds, but save the lectures for staff meeting, okay? Sarah has a certain aversion to learning speech, but she worked so hard for your predecessor that I can't imagine she won't do the same for you. So, I'd like you to take Sarah on in your spare time.

JAMES: *(A bit intimidated by her.)* Well, I wouldn't go so far as to say I *have* any spare — *(Franklin thrusts Sarah's file toward James, ending the discussion. James takes it.)* Fine.

FRANKLIN: Good. Do you play bridge?

JAMES: Yes, I do.

FRANKLIN: Good. Eight o'clock tonight, my place. *(To Sarah.)* Deaf power. Thumb up. *(Franklin goes. James speaks to Sarah as if he assumes she can lip read.)*

JAMES: Well, Sarah. Would you like to sit down? Right here. *(He sits. She remains standing.)* Okay, why don't we both stand then? *(He stands. She sits.)* I see. Very good. You got me there. *(He sits. She is inattentive.)* Could you look at me, please. Excuse me, if you don't look at me, I can't . . . *(She looks at him.)* So. You are one of the dorm assistants, is that correct? Or an apprentice instructor? *(She stares curiously at his mouth.)* Ah — no, I see it says right here you're a maid. A maid? *(She stares at his mouth.)* I can't help detecting a certain reluctance to communicate with me. Is that because you're afraid you'll be embarrassed by the sounds you make? *(She stares at his mouth.)* Are you reading my lips? I don't think you're reading my lips. *(Signing.)* Gee, that was quick of me. Okay . . . *(He loosens up his fingers and wrists and begins to sign.)* Why don't we start by signing with each other and maybe for next week we can shoot for an oral interpretation of F-i-n-n — *(Stops spelling — he mouths it carefully.)* Finnegan's Wake? Forget it, bad joke. Want to play stand up, sit down again? *(He's bombing.)* Gee, this is nice. I get the feeling Mr. Franklin is trying to play a little joke on the new teacher — putting his . . . *(Speaking it only.)* . . . delusions of grandeur — *(Signing.)* — how do you sign delusions — e-l-u-s-i-o-n-s — "dream"? *(Nothing.)* You know, the joke would be on Franklin if I just came in here and got you to speak for me. Wanna make me look good?

SARAH: Faster, huh?

JAMES: *(Thinking she's agreed to cooperate.)* Okay. Thank you.

SARAH: Faster. Move it. Fly. Speed.

JAMES: I didn't understand that.

SARAH: *(In slow Signed English.)*	JAMES: Oh, if! If! I. Do. Not. Sign.
If you do not sign faster, the hour will be over before you finish your opening speech.	Fast. Er. The hour will be over before I finish my opening speech.

(It takes him a moment to comprehend "If" — she's doing it very slowly As she goes on, her signing becomes faster, ending in a blur, James' voice trailing behind.)

JAMES: Are you doing this because I'm not deaf? I used to pretend to be deaf, if that counts. Look — you can't do this to me. I was in the Peace Corps for three years — I saved Ecuador *(It takes him a while to finger spell Ecuador.)* — so I'm scheduled for a lot of success here, if you know what I mean. *(Nope.)* Well — good — okay. Why don't you come back and see me sometime and we'll have the same fun again.

SARAH: You give up easier than most.

JAMES: I give up easier than most?

SARAH: That's smart.

JAMES: Smart. Thank you. *(She goes. After she's gone.)* Right — you can go.

MRS. NORMAN: *(Entering.)* If you don't mind, Mr. Leeds, I really don't feel like going through another interrogation about Sarah. I've come to feel like a mandatory stop in some training program for new teachers at the school.

JAMES: Mrs. Norman, your daughter's file indicates she hasn't been home here since she was eighteen.

MRS. NORMAN: That's correct.

JAMES: May I ask why?

MRS. NORMAN: We sent Sarah away to the school when she was five, Mr. Leeds. When she decided not to visit us anymore, she didn't consult me.

JAMES: But you went out there to visit her.

MRS. NORMAN: I tried. Then I stopped.

JAMES: I see.

MRS. NORMAN: Then you're unique among the teachers who've come calling here the past twenty-one years.

JAMES: Mrs. Norman, Sarah's twenty-six years old. The only reason they let her stay at the school at her age is because she works and goes through the motions of attending classes. Did you know she's a maid in the dorms?

MRS. NORMAN: No, I didn't. I'm sure you have an alternative in mind, though.

JAMES: Well, her test scores indicate exceptional intelligence.

MRS. NORMAN: Come on, now say: There's still time, there's still hope.

JAMES: There's still time, there's still hope.

MRS. NORMAN: For what?

JAMES: For her to achieve the communication skills to get into college or at least a good trade school.

MRS. NORMAN: Communication skills? In other words, you're still trying to force her to speak and lip read so she can pass for hearing.

JAMES: No, what I'm trying to *force* on her is the ability to function in the same world you and I do.

MRS. NORMAN: As if that were something to aspire to. Now, will that be all, Mr. Leeds?

JAMES: No — is Mr. Norman here? If you won't —

MRS. NORMAN: Mr. Norman went away shortly after we sent Sarah to the school. I haven't seen or heard from him in over twenty years. Now, Mr. Leeds, I will show you to the door. *(Mrs. Norman exits as Sarah enters.)*

JAMES: *(To Sarah.)* I didn't think you were going to come back. *(She holds out a note to him. He takes it.)* "Dear Sarah, Please see me tomorrow, I'll have some new routines. James Leeds." I wonder who wrote that. Want to play stand-up, sit-down again? *(She smiles a small smile.)* Careful — you're smiling. *(She frowns.)* Sorry. Are you coming in or not? *(She comes in. He writes "Sarah" on the blackboard syllabically, with accent and vowel markings.)* "Sar-ah." *(She stamps her foot to get his attention.)*

SARAH: You burn your draft card?

JAMES: I'm sorry, did I burn my what?

SARAH: Draft. Card.

JAMES: Army. Card. Oh — my draft card.

SARAH: I heard you were a radical in college.

JAMES: You heard I was a . . . in college. I'm sorry, I didn't get . . . *(He indicates "radical." She writes "RADICAL" on the blackboard opposite her name.)* Ah — you heard I was a radical in college. No. I burned my Blue Cross card.

SARAH: Why?

JAMES: I was afraid to burn my draft card. And the Blue Cross card wasn't going to be that useful in the Peace Corps.

SARAH: I don't understand.

JAMES: That's a joke.

SARAH: I don't see the humor.

JAMES: You don't see the humor? Now that we're talking, we don't seem to be understanding each other any better.

SARAH: Why should we?

JAMES: Why should we? Because I have learned all these techniques that are supposed to work. I wasn't exactly a radical. I was sort of left of liberal and right of radical.

SARAH: Where's that?

JAMES: Where's that? I still got my hair cut short before going home for major holidays.

SARAH: Why?

JAMES: Why? Well, my father scared me. He was a colonel in the army.

SARAH: Did he fight in the war?

JAMES: Not only did he fight in the war — he had billing above the title: "The United States presents Col. Walter J. Leeds in *The Vietnam War.*" *(He makes war noises.)*

SARAH: Another joke?

JAMES: Another joke, right. You're a terrific audience.

SARAH: Your timing is terrible and your signing is boring.

JAMES: My timing is terrible and my signing is boring. If you could hear, you'd think I was a scream.

SARAH: Why scream?

JAMES: Not literally "scream." That's a hearing idiom.

SARAH: But I'm deaf.

JAMES: You're deaf. I'll try to remember that.

SARAH: But you'll keep forgetting.

JAMES: I'll keep forgetting. But you'll keep reminding me.

SARAH: But you'll still forget.

JAMES: I'll still forget. But you'll still remind me.

SARAH: No. I'll give up.

JAMES: Maybe you won't have to give up.

SARAH: Why?

JAMES: Maybe I'll remember.

SARAH: I doubt it.

JAMES: We'll see.

SARAH: Right. Orin won't be so impressed when he finds out you weren't a radical.

JAMES: Orin won't be so impressed when he finds out I wasn't a radical. I'm here to teach, not to please Orin. Speaking of which . . . *(He heads for the blackboard.)* Oh, yesterday I had a really lousy visit with your mother.

SARAH: *(A burst of ASL.)* I'm a big girl now. Why do you still have to ask my mother for information?

JAMES: What's the matter? Wait a second. I'm sorry. I didn't mean to do whatever I . . . Look, what . . . what —

SARAH: What! What!

JAMES: That's my best sign. What! Look, could we stop this, please? Why don't we . . .

SARAH: What?

JAMES: . . . sneak over the wall and go into town to this little Italian restaurant I discovered last weekend.

SARAH: You're crazy.

JAMES: Just say yes or no.

SARAH: *(A beat.)* Yes.

JAMES: Good. I think. All right, I'll meet you in one hour in the trees behind the duck pond. I'll whisper your name.

SARAH: You're not funny.

JAMES: I think you *do* think I'm funny but you're afraid if you laugh you'll lose something. You know what I'm talking about? Hearing person, 1; deaf person, 0. *(Lydia has entered several lines earlier and seen the last of this from behind a corner of the blackboard. She laughs.)* Oh Christ. Are you Lydia? *(Lydia stares at him. Nods.)* How do you do. I'm Mr. Leeds, Lydia. *(He shows her his sign — an "L" in a "j" motion to his heart. Sarah and Lydia laugh.)* Hey, I'm getting some laughs here finally. Why are you laughing?

SARAH: She thinks you signed "lazy."

JAMES: She thinks I signed "lazy." *(Comparing the two signs.)* Mr. Lazy — right. Another great start.

SARAH: If you can't handle her alone, whisper my name.

JAMES: If I can't handle her alone, whisper your name. You're very funny.

SARAH: I'm funnier than you and I would be a better teacher.

JAMES: You're funnier than I am and you'd make a better teacher. If you want to be a teacher, let me help you learn to speak and lip read.

SARAH: Screw you. *(She goes, looking back.)*

LYDIA: Bye, Sarah.

JAMES: Excuse me, I know that sign! That's one of the first things I learned — how to talk dirty. *(A beat. To Lydia.)* Are you afraid of me?

LYDIA: No. Sarah.

JAMES: We're in the same boat.

LYDIA: In a boat?

JAMES: No, we're the same. She scares me too.

LYDIA: But you're the teacher.

JAMES: Teachers can't be scared?

LYDIA: Oh no. They have to teach.

JAMES: This one also has a lot to learn.

LYDIA: I'll teach you.

JAMES: I'll bet you will. Why don't you sit down right over there. "Lydia." *(He writes her name on the blackboard syllabically, with the accent and vowel markings.)*

LYDIA: Can we have our lesson in the same boat?

JAMES: What same boat?

LYDIA: On the duck pond.

JAMES: *(Doesn't know quite what she's talking about but wings it.)* Yeah. Maybe one of our lessons. Now, this is how we'll warm up for each session. Slide a little closer. *(He brushes her hair from her cheeks, revealing two large hearing aids running from her two ears into her shirt pockets, obviously she uses her hair to try to camouflage the amplifiers.)* I want you to listen, and watch my mouth, and then repeat exactly what I say. *(Sarah enters, her hair and/or attire slightly altered. She comes into the "restaurant," signifies "two," sits, looks at a menu as James and Lydia continue.)* Aaaayyyy.

LYDIA: Aaaayyyy.

JAMES: Eeeeee.

LYDIA: Eeeeee.

JAMES: Eeeeyyyyeee.

LYDIA: Eeeeyyyyeee.
JAMES: Oooohhhhh.
LYDIA: Oooohhhhh.
JAMES: Yooouuuuuu.
LYDIA: Yooouuuuuu.
JAMES & LYDIA: *(Together.)* Aaaayyyy.

JAMES: *(Joining Sarah.)* What would you like? *(She deliberates a moment, then points at something.)*

LYDIA: *(Continuing by herself.)* Ee, Eeyyee, Oohhh, Yoouu. *(Lydia leaves.)*

JAMES: Dessert? You're sure you want to start with dessert? *(Embarrassed, she quickly tries to decipher the menu again.)* Okay — wait — sure, I like the idea. We'll both start with dessert.
SARAH: Wait. *(A beat.)* Help me.
JAMES: I'd be pleased to help you. Should I suggest something?
SARAH: Yes.
JAMES: *(Not signing, to himself.)* Well, the veal piccata is nice. *(James mouthing, as for a lip reader.)* Veal piccata. *(Sarah looks away, rejecting that form of communication, forcing James to finger spell.)* I'm sorry. V-e-a-l [p-i-c-c-a-t-a.] See, by the time I finish spelling it, they may be out of it.
SARAH: What is it?
JAMES: That's veal sauteed in lemon and butter.
SARAH: What's veal?
JAMES: What's veal? Well — what the hell is veal? How do you sign calf? -a-l-f.
SARAH: Cow baby.
JAMES: Cow baby. Makes sense. Would you like some of that?
SARAH: No.
JAMES: No, I suppose cow baby sauteed in lemon and butter doesn't really sound . . .
SARAH: What I really want is pasta . . .
JAMES: What you really want is p-a — pasta. Now we're talking.
SARAH: . . . with cheese . . .
JAMES: With cheese.
SARAH: . . . garlic . . .
JAMES: And garlic.
SARAH: . . . herbs . . .
JAMES: Herbs.
SARAH: . . . meat. Stuffed inside.
JAMES: And meat. Stuffed in — Ah! You've described a dish it'll take me another hour to spell. C-a-n-n-e-l-l-o-n-i.
SARAH: Try.
JAMES: Okay. What to drink?
SARAH: Milkshake. *(The deaf sign for "milkshake" looks like the hearing symbol for "jerking off.")*
JAMES: What's that?
SARAH: Milkshake.
JAMES: Could you spell that please?
SARAH: *(Spelling.)* M-i-l-k-s-h-a-k-e.

JAMES: M-i-l-k — That's the sign for milkshake?
SARAH: Yes.
JAMES: You know, in the hearing world . . . Forget it. *(Silence. She's got it.)* You don't want that with Italian food anyway. Help me, I'm dying!
SARAH: What do I want?
JAMES: You want wine. I mean, *do* you want wine?
SARAH: Can we?
JAMES: Of course we can. Should have wine with Italian food.
SARAH: Good.
JAMES: Okay. How 'bout a nap?
SARAH: Why are you trying to be different from the other hearing teachers?
JAMES: Why am I trying to be different from the other hearing teachers? Why did I have to bring you to an Italian restaurant to get you to talk to a hearing person?
SARAH: I don't need what you want to give me. I have a language that's just as good as yours!
JAMES: You don't need what I want to give you. Your language is just as good as mine — among the *deaf,* Sarah.
SARAH: Where's the garlic bread?
JAMES: Where's the garlic bread? Over there by the salad. Come on. I'll show you. *(They rise and move to the "salad bar." She seems confused.)* You take a plate and help yourself. *(She does. He watches her.)* Wouldn't you like to be able to function in the hearing world?
SARAH: No.
JAMES: No, I mean to be able to speak and lip read like Orin?
SARAH: Orin!
JAMES: Yeah. *(She draws a grotesque picture of Orin speaking — spitting, his mouth contorted.)* Oh no, Orin doesn't look like that.
SARAH: Lydia!
JAMES: Lydia doesn't look like that either. People who are born deaf look like that sometimes.
SARAH: Always.
JAMES: Always? Oh yes, I know: Lesson number one in grad school: Very difficult to teach someone born deaf like you to speak and lip read, because you've never heard the sound of a human voice — okay? But it can be done. *(Sarah looks away. James gets her attention.)* I mean it. What's more exciting than something truly difficult? Sure, it's easier for Orin and Lydia because they can hear a little bit. All right, look, you and I can start with lip reading, whaddaya say? *(She closes him off, returns to the table. He follows.)* You like being a maid?
SARAH: Yes.
JAMES: Why?
SARAH: I like working alone. In my silence.
JAMES: Oh, come on, there are other jobs where a person can work alone and in silence.
SARAH: Not with toilet bowl cleaner.
JAMES: Not with toilet bowl cleaner. You should have told me that was the attraction. You clearly have the intelligence to — *(She concentrates on her food, closing him out again.)* Okay, I give up. What do you want to talk about?

SARAH: I want to eat so we won't have our hands.

JAMES: You want to eat so we won't have our hands. Well, I may just bury my face in the plate and keep talking. *(A beat.)*

SARAH: Talk about you.

JAMES: Talk about me. Okay. What do you want to know?

SARAH: You said before that you used to pretend to be deaf.

JAMES: I said before that I used to pretend to be deaf. So you *were* paying attention.

SARAH: How did you do that?

JAMES: How did I do that? That's easy. I just . . . *(He puts his hands over his ears.)*

SARAH: Why?

JAMES: Why? Forget it.

SARAH: Come on, come on.

JAMES: All right. My mother was Jewish; she married a Catholic who turned out to be an atheist; didn't matter because my mother turned out to be of a faith heretofore unknown to man. She designated me her confessor, complete with semi-immaculate birth and healing powers.

SARAH: How?

JAMES: How? Well, I used to . . . Demon . . . come out! You know — hands over the ears . . . *(He starts to put his hands over her ears. She pulls away. He demonstrates on himself — snapping his hands away from his ears.)* . . . like this.

SARAH: Where's the deaf part?

JAMES: Where's the deaf part? The time finally came when I had to stop hearing her, so I . . . *(He indicates shutting his mother out. A beat — he is disturbed.)* Did you ever pretend to hear?

SARAH: No . . . Yes. I used to pretend . . .

JAMES: No. Yeah? Come on, tell me.

SARAH: Dance?

JAMES: You wanna dance?

SARAH: I can hear the music.

JAMES: How do you hear the music?

SARAH: Vibrations.

JAMES: Vibrations?

SARAH: *(Deadpan.)* Through my nose.

JAMES: Through your nose? *(Sarah breaks into a smile. They move toward the dance floor.)* There's nobody else dancing. *(They dance — managing to come together physically. Perhaps out of fear, unease, whatever, she pulls back and talks to him while they continue to dance.)*

SARAH: Why did you become a speech therapist?

JAMES: Why did I get into speech therapy? I don't know. Let's dance.

SARAH: Dance and talk.

JAMES: Dance and talk. No, that's too hard. *(He pulls her to him. They dance. She pulls back.)*

SARAH: Tell me. *(They dance and talk after all.)*

JAMES: In the sixties it seemed important to do things that weren't simply self-serving.

SARAH: Isn't this self-serving?

JAMES: This is self-serving? I guess it is, in that it feels good to help people.

SARAH: But you're not helping anyone.

JAMES: I'm not helping anyone? That's your opinion.

SARAH: You're lucky.

JAMES: Why am I lucky?

SARAH: Because you believe in something you're doing, even though you're not doing it.

JAMES: Because I believe in something I'm doing, even though I'm not doing it. *(She looks at her watch. Time to go. She moves back to the table, he follows.)* You know, you too could believe in something you're not doing.

SARAH: *(Mouthing.)* Blah, blah, blah.

JAMES: Speech — right. Can I help you? *(He helps her with her sweater. They walk in silence "outdoors.")*

SARAH: So your mother told you you were God.

JAMES: So my mother told me I was God. Yes, that's correct.

SARAH: And that's why you want to make me over in your image.

JAMES: And that's why I want to make you over in my image. Okay.

SARAH: Only one problem.

JAMES: Only one problem — I thought there'd be at least two.

SARAH: I don't believe in God.

JAMES: You don't believe in . . . now, wait a minute. I thought deaf people were required to believe in God. Sure! The damned of God who must perform a lifetime of penance.

SARAH: *(Putting her hands to her ears.)* Demon, come out! Why always over the ears?

JAMES: Demon come out! Yeah. Why always over the ears? I don't know. *(She puts her hands to his head, his belly.)*

SARAH & JAMES: Why not over the head, over the belly . . .

SARAH: . . . over the mouth. *(A beat, her hand to his mouth, removed.)* Time?

JAMES: Curfew.

SARAH: Bye.

JAMES: *(Stopping her.)* I've really enjoyed this evening with you.

SARAH: Me too. *(Sarah thinks he'll kiss her but after a moment he offers his hand. They shake and part. Orin, with an Ojo de Dios, a diamond shaped piece made of multi-colored yarn strung to a wooden frame.)*

JAMES: May I come in?

ORIN: Hello, Mr. Leeds.

JAMES: You missed our session, Orin. Are you sick?

ORIN: I am busy making these to sell on Parents' Day to a lot of guilty parents who will hide them in the closet. I'm not sick, Mr. Leeds, so if that's what you came to find out . . .

JAMES: Wait a minute, is there something wrong? Between us? *(Orin focuses on his Ojo. James gets his attention.)* Orin, I need some advice on how to get Sarah Norman to speak.

ORIN: Is that what you want?

JAMES: Excuse me?

ORIN: Why did you go out to dinner with Sarah?

JAMES: How did you —

ORIN: Oh yes, we know: You want to help her.

701

JAMES: Yes, I —

ORIN: You don't fool us. You think learning to sign means you can communicate with us, that because you want to change us we want to be changed.

JAMES: Oh Orin, for Christ's —

ORIN: One of these days, Mr. Leeds, I'm going to change this system that sticks us with teachers who pretend to help but really want to glorify themselves!

JAMES: I do want to help, Orin, you have to believe that.

ORIN: No, Mr. Leeds, I don't have to. You have to. I thought you were different.

JAMES: Listen, don't lump me together with a bunch of incompetent —

ORIN: Now, if you don't mind, please leave my room.

JAMES: Orin, can't we sit down and talk this over?

ORIN: No thank you. And, oh, by the way, I have had veal piccata. Yes. And I have had other *"hearing"* food.

JAMES: "Hearing food"?

ORIN: Raw fish. Japanese. Zugee.

JAMES: No, sushi. *(Orin goes angrily.)* I'm sorry, Orin. I'm sorry.

LYDIA: *(Entering)* Hello, Mr. Leeds.

JAMES: Oh, Lydia, I'm sorry I'm late.

LYDIA: I am reading your book.

JAMES: *(Blocking it as if it might attack him.)* My old Child Psychology book!

LYDIA: Psy . . .

JAMES: Psychology. There's a good word for you. Ssss . . . *(He writes the "P" on the chalkboard.)* Sssssychology. *(He writes the rest of the word.)*

LYDIA: What does it mean?

JAMES: Cracking open people's heads. Why people do what they do.

LYDIA: Why do they?

JAMES: If I ever figure that one out, I'll let you know.

LYDIA: I'm having trouble with the first sentence.

JAMES: Ah, one of the greats. How could I forget. "Ontogeny recapitulates phylogeny." Psychology students all over the world have read those words and moved into other fields.

LYDIA: What does it mean?

JAMES: It means that . . . that we make ourselves over in our own image.

LYDIA: Oh, good.

JAMES: Want to sit down? *(Lydia sits.)*

LYDIA: Mr. Leeds . . . that other night, you ate by yourself, huh? In a restaurant in town. Boy, that's lonesome, huh, eating alone? I ate by myself in the cafeteria. I read two books. I read what you told me to practice.

JAMES: Oh really? Let me hear a little bit of it then.

LYDIA: *(Very carefully articulating.)* Thank you, Tom Turkey, for thinking of Thanksgiving.

JAMES: Hey! Good for you. You did practice.

LYDIA: I know. Will you be eating in the cafeteria on Thanksgiving?

JAMES: Maybe I will.

LYDIA: I could eat with you. I won't read a book.

JAMES: We could just talk.

LYDIA: Okay! I'll read this for tomorrow. *(She takes the book and starts to*

leave. We hear a whistle.)
JAMES: What was that noise?
LYDIA: My hearing aid. Whenever I smile, it whistles. See you soon. *(Lydia goes. We're at the "duck pond" after dinner. Sarah touches James, hands him a note.)*
JAMES: Well, at last. "Dear Sarah, Please meet me at the duck pond after dinner. I'll bring the stale bread. James Leeds." *(A beat.)* How many people did you tell about our going over the wall?
SARAH: Not many.
JAMES: Not many. Orin was very upset.
SARAH: Orin thinks he's the guardian of all us deaf children because he's an apprentice teacher and speaks.
JAMES: Orin thinks he's the guardian of all you deaf children because he's an apprentice teacher and speaks.
SARAH: And he wants to lead a revolution against the hearing world and thinks we can hardly wait to follow him.
JAMES: And he wants to lead a revolution against the hearing world and he thinks you all can hardly wait to follow him. When his revolution begins, he can have all my old Indian headbands and wire rim glasses.
SARAH: You think it's funny to want to do something for your people?
JAMES: Do I think it's funny to want to do something for my people? No, I —
SARAH: How would you like to spend your life in an institution, in a world run by people who don't understand you.
JAMES: How would I like to spend my life in an institution, in a world run by people who don't understand me? Why don't you go on the warpath with Orin?
SARAH: This isn't stale bread.
JAMES: Right, the bread is not stale. I feel good so I thought I'd bring some fresh bread.
SARAH: Why do you feel good?
JAMES: Because I missed you.
SARAH: Don't say that.
JAMES: I haven't seen you for days. You've been avoiding me. I even ate lunch in the cafeteria, thinking I'd see you.
SARAH: I've been eating in the kitchen so you wouldn't see me.
JAMES: You've been eating in the kitchen so I wouldn't see you. Well, I didn't see you. You know, I hate to say this, but you're the most mysterious, attractive, angry person I've ever met.
SARAH: Why did you miss me?
JAMES: Why did I miss you? Why do people miss each other? *(Sarah becomes conscious of Lydia who has moved in to feed the ducks too.)*
SARAH: Go! Get out of here!
JAMES: *(Calling after her.)* Wait! Oh that's all right, Lydia! Wait a . . . Come back . . . *(She's gone.)* That was a bit rough, wasn't it?
SARAH: Should I treat her like she's handicapped?
JAMES: You think the only alternative to treating someone like they're handicapped is to treat them like that?
SARAH: Yes!
JAMES: You should get out of the toilet cleaning business and give some seminars on interpersonal relationships.

SARAH: She's going to become dependent on you.

JAMES: Would that be so terrible if she became dependent on me?

SARAH: She'll fall in love with you.

JAMES: She's gonna fall in love with me? You know, all students don't automatically — Jesus Christ, that's quite a little leap you made there; from helping someone to learn something to dependency because of it, to falling in love as a result of the dependency. That's very nice, but it happens to be bullshit. You have a sign for b-u-l-l shit?

SARAH: Bullshit. *(A bull's horns with one hand, at the other end, a closed fist with the other hand, the closed fist springs open in James' face.)* You're trying to con everybody.

JAMES: Excuse me, I'm trying to what everybody?

SARAH: C-o-n everybody.

JAMES: C-o-n. No, not everybody — only you. Wait a second, I'm going to invent a little sign here. Deaf-bullshit. *(The same sign as above with one horn stuck in his ear.)*

SARAH: I have to go.

JAMES: You have to go? Fine, take your deaf-bullshit and go. *(Sarah starts to leave but James blocks her way. She forces his arms to his side and holds them there, stopping the "deaf-bullshit" sign. He kisses her. She breaks free.)*

SARAH: You didn't con me.

JAMES: It's always worked before. See, when I get in trouble, I kiss the girl and make everything better. *(She goes.)* Oh, come on, Sarah! *(He chases her.)* Sarah . . . !

FRANKLIN: *(Entering from opposite side.)* Yelling at the back of a deaf person. That's very good, Mr. Leeds . . . ! Problems?

JAMES: No. Just trying out a new technique.

FRANKLIN: What's it called — rape? . . . Mr. Leeds.

JAMES: Yes.

FRANKLIN: What are you doing here with Sarah?

JAMES: Feeding the ducks.

FRANKLIN: Ah. Why?

FRANKLIN: Because they're hun-   JAMES: Because they're hungry.
gry.

FRANKLIN: Mr. Leeds — James — Jimbo, we don't fornicate with the students. We just screw them over. If you ever get the two confused . . . you're gone. *(Franklin goes.)*

JAMES: I wasn't trying to screw her over, you damned . . . I was just trying to —

MRS. NORMAN: *(Entering.)* I usually don't get the second visit, Mr. Leeds.

JAMES: I promise if I don't strike gold this time, I'll give up like all the others.

MRS. NORMAN: I'm not sure you will. Give up, that is. There are people, I understand, who revel in failure.

JAMES: The guy who taught the Ecuadorians to grow and love brussels sprouts isn't gonna be scared off by the insults of a guilt-ridden mother.

MRS. NORMAN: I want you to leave my home.

JAMES: Look, Mrs. Norman, I know this is difficult —

MRS. NORMAN: You don't know what difficult is. Teaching speech to a retarded child deaf from birth is impossible. Give up!

JAMES: Wait a minute. Sarah is not retarded! They just thought she was until she was twelve.

MRS. NORMAN: First they said she was, then they said she wasn't. What are they saying now?

JAMES: That she's only deaf.

MRS. NORMAN: Only deaf.

JAMES: She is not retarded. She's capable of learning anything.

MRS. NORMAN: Then *you* teach her.

JAMES: That's what I'm trying to do! Help me. Please. Tell me, did Sarah ever try to speak?

MRS. NORMAN: She stopped trying when it became important to her how she looked to my friends and most of all to her sister's friends.

JAMES: How she looked?

MRS. NORMAN: Yes. She looked grotesque. She was afraid people would still think she was retarded.

JAMES: Like you did.

MRS. NORMAN: I don't know what I thought! I have stopped thinking about what I thought!

JAMES: I'm sorry. When Sarah came home on weekends, did she and her sister's friends go out together? What did they do? . . . Come on, Mrs. Norman, please. *(A beat.)*

MRS. NORMAN: There came a time when I could no longer tolerate the two of us in this house trying frantically to discover things we might do together — read, cook, sew — Here, look, see, we've having a nice, normal visit. So I asked — no, I demanded that her sister Ruth ask her boyfriend's friends to become companions for Sarah and we would owe them dearly in another life. Well, it worked. I mean, you should have seen her. These boys really liked Sarah, treated her the same way they treated Ruth, with respect and . . . and if you didn't know there was a problem, you'd have thought she was perfectly normal . . . *(A beat.)* Well, you just can't understand. *(A beat.)* You're making me pity myself now, Mr. Leeds. It's been a long time. I would appreciate it if you wouldn't come back a third time. Please. *(She goes.)*

JAMES: *(To Sarah, who is pushing a maid's cleaning cart. She begins cleaning the blackboard with a wet rag.)* Hello. I left you a note. It said: "Please see me this afternoon, I'll bring the boxing gloves." You didn't come so I ate all the gloves myself. I'm sorry to interrupt your work.

SARAH: What do you want now?

JAMES: What do I want now? Okay, I want to know if you think you *can't* learn to speak, that you're not capable?

SARAH: *(Pushing the blackboard U. out of the way.)* Not speech talk again.

JAMES: *(Helping her with the blackboard.)* Yeah, speech talk again. You're not retarded — you know that?

SARAH: Since I was twelve. *(She begins to sweep.)*

JAMES: Since you were twelve — right. But do you really believe it?

SARAH: What are you talking about?

JAMES: What am I talking about? I want to know if your hatred of hearing people has as much to do with us as it does with your hatred of you.

SARAH: That sounds like it came straight from a textbook.

JAMES: Well it did come right out of a textbook, but I think it's true anyway. Did not going home anymore after you were eighteen — did that have anything to do with your sister's friends? The boys you were going out with? *(She's silent.)* Let me help you, damn it!

SARAH: How — by showing me the joys of sex with a hearing man?

JAMES: How — by showing you the joys of sex with a hearing man? You mean you and me? I don't see you making yourself available for that kind of therapy. I think that's one language you don't speak.

SARAH: You don't know what you're talking about!

JAMES: All right, you tell it to me right so I *will* know what I'm talking about!

SARAH: You're so . . .

JAMES: I'm so what? What am I? Nosy? Stupid? Misguided? Come on — whatever it is, I can take it. *(She lets him have it.)*

SARAH: I have more than enough communication skills. You don't. They never did.

JAMES: I have more than enough communication skills. You don't. They never did. They? Who's they?

SARAH & JAMES: *(James translates now in the first person.)* Hearing boys. They could never be bothered learning my language. No — that was too difficult. I was always expected to learn to speak. Well, I don't speak! I don't do things I can't do well. The boys who did try to communicate with me got about as far as: How are you, I am fine. *(A beat.)* At first I let them have me because they would. Sex was something I could do as well as hearing girls. Better! It got to be that when I went home, the boys would be lined up on a waiting list my sister kept for me. Most of them didn't even take me for a Coke first. No introductions. No conversations. We just went straight to a dark place and [screwed]. But I liked that communication. I loved it. It made me feel a lot better than this bullshit talk you make. *(She finishes her sweep up.)*

SARAH: Now, does that explain everything?

JAMES: No, it doesn't explain everything, but it explains a little.

SARAH: That's all you're going to find out. *(She begins to rub furniture polish into a bench.)*

JAMES: No, that's not all I'm going to find out.

SARAH: I live in a place you can't enter. It's out of reach.

JAMES: You live in a place I can't enter. Out of reach? That sounds romantic.

SARAH: Deafness isn't the opposite of hearing, as you think. It's a silence full of sound.

JAMES: Deafness isn't the oppposite of hearing, as I think. It's a silence full of sound. Really? A silence full of sound?

SARAH: The sound of spring breaking up through the death of winter. *(He doesn't understand the juxtaposition of: "winter" . . . "earth" . . . "broken" . . . "growth" which is how she signs the line, yet, he is moved by it.)*

JAMES: The sound of . . . What does that mean? *(Suddenly there is a softness, a closeness between them.)*

SARAH: My secret. No hearing person has ever gotten in here to find out . . .

No person, period.

JAMES: Your secret. No hearing person has ever gotten in there to find out ... No person, period. *(She runs from him. A beat. Night. He "climbs" a "tree." He tries to get Sarah's attention at her "window" as she reenters.)* Hey! Open the window! *(She spots him in the "tree" but doesn't open the "window." James, banging onto the "tree.")* Usually, I kiss the girl and make everything better, remember? You didn't like that one, so I climbed this tree. Tough to resist a guy who climbs trees for you, isn't it?

SARAH: What if you get caught?

JAMES: What if I get caught? The hero — *(He almost falls.)* Aauugh! *(He clutches the "tree.")* The hero never gets caught on an important mission. Oh, I have another note for you. It says: "By the way, I'm terrified of heights. James Leeds." Please let me in. *(She throws the "window" open. He jumps into the room. Shy with each other but wanting to touch.)* I don't want to be like those other guys. I want to take you for a Coke first. And I want to learn to communicate with you in whatever language we both can learn to speak. I like you. I really like you.

SARAH: Why? I'm terrible to you.

JAMES: Why? You're terrible to me? No, you're delightful to me — affectionate and sympathetic to a fault. *(A beat.)*

SARAH: I thought you'd give up in the beginning.

JAMES: You thought I'd give up in the beginning. Nope.

SARAH: I knew after what I told you yesterday, I wouldn't see you again.

JAMES: You knew after what you told me yesterday, you'd never see me again. *(He indicates: Here I am.)*

SARAH: You're the nicest person I've ever known.

JAMES: I'm the nicest person you've ever known. Do you mean that?

SARAH: But you scare me.

JAMES: But I scare you? I don't mean to.

SARAH: I don't think I trust you.

JAMES: You don't think you trust me? Take a chance.

SARAH: I can't. You better go.

JAMES: *(A beat, disappointed.)* Okay ... Goodnight. *(He dives for window. She stops him. They embrace and move to the "bed." He starts to "turn the light out.")*

SARAH: Leave the light on.

JAMES: Leave the light on?

SARAH: So we can talk.

JAMES: So we can talk? During or afterward?

SARAH: Hard to talk during.

JAMES: Hard to talk during.

SARAH: Need my hands.

JAMES: You need your hands. I need my mouth.

SARAH: Silence. *(They come together.)*

ORIN: *(Entering.)* I know what is going on between you and Sarah. For weeks now half the girls' dormitory has seen you climbing in and out of her window. Of course, you might have been going in there to coach her in

707

speech.
LYDIA: *(Entering opposite.)* Mr. Leeds, hi.
JAMES: Shhh!
LYDIA: What are you doing in my tree?
JAMES: I'm not in your tree, Lydia.
LYDIA: You're not looking for Sarah.
JAMES: Sarah who? For Chrissake, shut your damn window!
LYDIA: *(To Sarah.)* He's eating at my table on Thanksgiving, you know!
    (Lydia and Sarah slam their windows at each other. Lydia goes.)
ORIN: It would not be hard for Mr. Franklin to find out what's going on.
JAMES: Look, Orin, if you're in love with Sarah, I'm sorry.
ORIN: I am not in love with anyone, Mr. Leeds.
JAMES: That's something to be proud of.
ORIN: But I need her and you don't.
JAMES: She's not going to stop being your friend just because —
ORIN: I need her for what we're going to do for deaf people.
JAMES: What you and *Sarah* are going to do?
ORIN: Believe me, I'm not some joker who burns his Blue Cross card! *(Orin
    goes as Franklin crosses U.)*
FRANKLIN: Sit down, please, Mr. Leeds.
JAMES: Orin . . . ! *(Freezing in the "tree.")*
FRANKLIN: Mr. Leeds, I've heard a rumor I'd like to share with you to give
    you an idea of the flights of fancy that deaf people are capable of.
JAMES: *(To Sarah.)* Franklin knows.
SARAH: How?
JAMES: I don't know how. Someone must have told him.
SARAH: Who?
JAMES: Orin maybe . . . ?
SARAH: No. *(Franklin crosses over again. James and Sarah take cover.)*
FRANKLIN: I'm told that if I were to station myself in the elm trees outside
    the girls' dormitory just after curfew . . .
JAMES: I can't come here anymore. Franklin would fire me if he found out.
SARAH: Who would have told him?
JAMES: Any number of people could have told him.
LYDIA: *(Entering, speaking and not signing, in effect closing Sarah out.)*
    Hi, guys. What's new?
JAMES: How are you, Lydia?
LYDIA: Oh, I'm fine.
JAMES: Good, good.
SARAH: Is it time for her lesson?
JAMES: No, she doesn't have a lesson with me today.
SARAH: Did you tell Franklin something about Mr. Leeds and me?
JAMES: Yeah.
LYDIA: I have to go to handicrafts now, Mr. Leeds. I'll see you tomorrow.
JAMES: Just a minute, answer Sarah's question. Did you tell Franklin any-
    thing —
LYDIA: I'll see you tomorrow. *(Lydia runs off.)*
SARAH: I told you she'd fall in love with you.
JAMES: Oh, she's not in love with me.
SARAH: Maybe you should climb in her window one night.

JAMES: Maybe I should climb in her window some night? You're jealous.

SARAH: *(Illustrating.)* She's dumb. Big breasts. Just what men want. Fondle her butt. Fondle her breasts.

JAMES: Is that really what men want? I'll tell you something, I happen to despise large breasts. You couldn't even give me a pair; if you had large breasts, I wouldn't be sitting here having this ridiculous —

SARAH: Pimples!

JAMES: Those are not pimples. Those are perfectly charming, more than adequate . . . Jesus Christ, you're a human being. *(As Franklin crosses this time, James slips innocently into step with him, as if they were strolling along having a conversation.)*

FRANKLIN: Lemme tell you something that I might seem out of place disclosing to you. You remember the day I brought Sarah to you I told you she'd worked so hard for the speech guy here before you . . . *(Franklin leaves. Sarah looking out her "window." James slipping up behind Sarah carrying a gift behind his back, he startles her.)*

JAMES: Sorry I'm late. I got held up.

SARAH: Robbed?

JAMES: No, not robbed. Held up. Delayed.

SARAH: How did you get in?

JAMES: How did I get in? Through the cellar window, up the back steps, and down the hall on tiptoe.

SARAH: You're crazy.

JAMES: I had to see you. *(They kiss. He hands her the gift box. She opens it. A shawl.)* I knitted it in handicrafts. *(She puts on the shawl, is delighted with it. A beat.)* Can I ask you something?

SARAH: Yes.

JAMES: Franklin was kind enough to tell me you had a relationship with the speech therapist before me.

SARAH: *(A beat.)* True.

JAMES: Franklin fired him when he found out . . . ?

SARAH: Yes.

JAMES: Was he a hearing person?

SARAH: No, hard of hearing.

JAMES: Hard of hearing. You didn't want to leave with him?

SARAH: He didn't ask me.

JAMES: He didn't ask you.

SARAH: Hard of hearing people think they're better than deaf people.

JAMES: Hard of hearing people think they're better than deaf people. Do you still carry a torch for him?

SARAH: *(She doesn't get James' sign for "torch.")* What?

JAMES: I made that up. Do you still . . . hurt?

SARAH: No. I never hurt from other people.

JAMES: No? You never hurt from other people. What if you admitted that you do hurt?

SARAH: *(A beat.)* I would shrivel up and blow away.

JAMES: You would shrivel up and blow away. *(A beat.)* Sarah, what if you and I left here together?

SARAH: What?

JAMES: What if you and I went to live in a city somewhere?

SARAH: I couldn't.
JAMES: Why couldn't you? You're scared? You'd get unscared.
SARAH: What would I do?
JAMES: You could do whatever you want to do. What do you want to do?
SARAH: I want to teach in a deaf school.
JAMES: You want to teach in a deaf school. That's possible. What else do
    you want?
SARAH: I want you.
JAMES: You've got me. What else do you want?
SARAH: House.
JAMES: A house — uh-oh.
SARAH: And car. Plant a garden and . . .
JAMES: A car. Yeah, plant a garden . . .
SARAH: So much! *(Drawing a picture with her hands.)* Microwave oven!
JAMES: So much. *(Guessing Sarah's sign after a moment of puzzlement.)* A
    microwave oven! How about a blender?
SARAH: Yes.
JAMES: *(Inventing a new sign.)* How about a food processor!
SARAH: What?
JAMES: That's a blender that's smarter than a blender.
SARAH: I want one.
JAMES: You'll have two of them! What else? Come on. Too late to stop now.
SARAH: Children.
JAMES: Children.
SARAH: Deaf children.
JAMES: Deaf children. *(A beat.)* What do you want me to say — that I want
    deaf children? I don't. But if they were, that would be all right.
SARAH: My father left us because I'm deaf.
JAMES: Your father left you because you were deaf. I am not going to do
    what your father did.
SARAH: What would you do if I went on with my schooling? Got a teaching
    certificate?
JAMES: What would I do if you went on with your schooling, got your
    teaching certificate? You mean here?
SARAH: Yes.
JAMES: I could still teach here, I guess, or I could finish my doctorate —
    What am I saying? We don't have to decide everything tonight.
SARAH: I want to.
JAMES: I know you want to, but we can't. The point is, it's all possible. And
    you know it. Say it. Say: I know it's possible. *(A beat.)*
SARAH: I know it's possible.
ORIN: *(Entering)* It won't work! It can't work!
LYDIA: *(Entering opposite side.)* Mr. Leeds, you're leaving.
JAMES: We haven't decided yet, Lydia.
ORIN: *(To Sarah.)* So you can attract a hearing man. Is that so much?
LYDIA: I want to come live with you.
JAMES: What?
ORIN: Stay here and help me.
LYDIA: You have to keep teaching me.
ORIN: Do something for someone besides yourself for a change!

LYDIA: I could sleep on your floor in a sleeping bag.

SARAH: *(Indicating Lydia.)* What?

JAMES: Lydia wants to come live with us.

SARAH: *(To Lydia.)* No!

JAMES: Oh, Sarah. *(Lydia runs off.)*

ORIN: Hey, I want to tell you something.

JAMES: Oh, Lydia, come back.

ORIN: You have no right to turn her away from us.

JAMES: I have no intention —

ORIN: You go with him and you'll still be a maid. His maid.

JAMES: *(Yelling after Orin as he goes.)* Hey! *(Franklin with a clipboard in his hand, on which his attention is focused.)*

FRANKLIN: So, will you be resigning at the end of the year?

JAMES: Resigning?

FRANKLIN: Not that I want you to leave. The bridge game needs you. And frankly, you're a promising teacher. But whether you intend it or not, you're about to uproot Sarah from the only home she's ever known.

JAMES: We're just moving across the street to faculty housing.

FRANKLIN: Not to be terribly metaphoric, Mr. Leeds, but that's a long distance. You're asking Sarah to step away from the community of the deaf.

SARAH: What's he saying?

JAMES: He's not saying anything important.

SARAH: You can't decide what I hear and don't hear.

FRANKLIN: She's right, Mr. Leeds. You can't decide what she hears and doesn't hear.

SARAH: You can't edit the conversation.

JAMES: I was not editing the conversation.

FRANKLIN: Pardon me, Mr. Leeds, it would seem you didn't like the implications I was making, so you chose not to tell Sarah.

SARAH: Now what?

JAMES: *(To Sarah.)* He should be signing. *(To Franklin.)* Mr. Franklin, would you mind —

FRANKLIN: Why don't you sign my part of the conversation for me.

JAMES: Why don't you sign your own conversation?

FRANKLIN: I've got to finish what I'm doing here, and it'll give you a little practice.

JAMES: Practice at what?

SARAH: What is he saying?

FRANKLIN: *(Not signing, forcing James to sign it.)* I'm saying I think James should get a taste of being a translator as that's one of the problems facing him each and every time the two of you venture into the hearing world. *(Franklin keeps his head to his clipboard.)*

SARAH: One of our problems! And what are the rest? Aren't you going to tell us the rest?

FRANKLIN: I'm sorry, Jimbo, what did she say?

JAMES: Oh, for Chri — She wants to know if you aren't going to forewarn us of the rest of our problems as well.

FRANKLIN: *(Forcing James to continue translating.)* I suspect neither of you wants to hear that. Well, I'm sure you've both given this a great

711

deal of thought. I've got to run. Thank you for telling me about your plans. I hope you'll invite me to the wedding. *(By the time James finishes interpreting, Franklin is long gone. James very frustrated.)*

SARAH: He's right — you will be a translator.

JAMES: He's right? Oh, that I'll be a translator. The trick is to do a better job than I just did.

SARAH: Don't hate me for not learning to speak.

JAMES: Hate you for not learning to speak? No, I'll love you for having the strength to be yourself. *(Mrs. Norman enters. She hasn't seen her daughter in eight years. She struggles to communicate with Sarah, more through gesture than sign.)*

MRS. NORMAN: Congratulations, Sarah. I'm very happy to see you. You're so grownup. You're . . . Eight years. My, a person can't digest that in . . . *(Sarah does not understand Mrs. Norman's sign.)* I don't know how to say that. *(A beat. To James.)* She didn't want to come, did she? You made her.

JAMES: You don't *make* Sarah do anything, Mrs. Norman.

SARAH: Tell me.

MRS. NORMAN: *(Managing to communicate, if haltingly.)* I said, you didn't want to come. I don't know why you've come.

SARAH: I don't either. To hurt you maybe.

MRS. NORMAN: *(To James.)* I'm sorry, I'm rusty — what did she say? *(Sarah insists on her mother's attention.)*

SARAH: *(Very slowly.)* To h-u-r-t you.   MRS. NORMAN: H.U.R. To hurt
Maybe.   me. Maybe.

SARAH: To show you I've done fine without you.

JAMES: To show you she's done fine without you. *(Silence: mother and daughter. Then Sarah breaks, begins to look around the "house.")*

MRS. NORMAN: Do your parents know?

JAMES: No, my mother's dead and my father and I haven't spoken for several years.

SARAH: Can we spend the night in my old room?

JAMES: Sarah would like to know if we can spend the night in her old room. *(A beat.)*

MRS. NORMAN: If she'll promise to make conversation with me at breakfast in the morning.

JAMES: [If you promise to make conversation with her at breakfast in the morning.] *(A beat.)*

SARAH: Try.

JAMES: She'll try.

MRS. NORMAN: Yes, I remember that sign. [Try.] *(Mrs. Norman recedes as the scene shifts.)*

SARAH: My room.

JAMES: Your old room? Bit spare.

SARAH: I threw everything out the last time I came.

JAMES: You threw everything out the last time you came. You can't destroy that time by throwing things away.

SARAH: I did. *(James picks her up and carries her into the room.)*

JAMES: Small bed.

SARAH: That's why I want to sleep in it with you.

JAMES: That's why you want to spend the night in it with me.

SARAH: No man has been in this room since I was five. That was the night before they sent me to school.

JAMES: No man has been in this room since you were five. That was the night before they sent you away to the school.

SARAH: My father stayed with me that night. He cried. I never saw him again.

JAMES: Your father stayed with you that night. He cried. You never saw him again.

SARAH: After he left, my mother put a picture of the Virgin Mary on the wall; one weekend when I came to visit, I drew a hearing aid in her ear. My mother cried.

JAMES: After he left, your mother put a picture of the Virgin Mary on the wall; one weekend when you came to visit you drew a hearing aid in her ear. Your mother cried. Yes, I can imagine.

SARAH: The next visit there was a picture of Ricky Nelson.

JAMES: The next visit there was a picture of Ricky Nelson. Makes sense. Why Ricky Nelson?

SARAH: I don't know. I never asked, she never explained.

JAMES: You never asked, she never explained.

SARAH: Nothing else on my walls.

JAMES: Nothing else on the walls.

SARAH: Just that picture: "To Sarah, Good luck, From Ricky." In my mother's handwriting.

JAMES: Just that picture: "To Sarah, Good luck, From Ricky." In your mother's handwriting. *(A beat.)* Your mother wanted very much to touch you tonight. But you . . . Maybe you wanted to touch her.

SARAH: I can't give more than I gave.

JAMES: You can't give more than you gave? I wonder. Maybe you could. You hardly ever get a second chance to . . . *(James turns away.)*

SARAH: What are you talking about?

JAMES: Nothing. Forget it. None of my business.

SARAH: Tell me.

JAMES: Just the way your mother was standing there, staring into space.

SARAH: You're hiding.

JAMES: I'm hiding? No, I'm not . . . Yes, I am. You remember I told you my mother died two years ago . . .

SARAH: Yes.

JAMES: She killed herself. My father had just left her after twenty-eight years. Just strolled away. Left me to take care of her. She lived with me for almost three years. When I raised the rent, she . . . *(A beat.)* Look, I really don't think we're gonna fit on that little bed, whudduya say?

SARAH: Tell me the rest.

JAMES: Tell you what rest. *(She lifts his hands up, encouraging him to go on.)* All right. One night, instead of sitting on her bed pretending to listen to that day's outpouring of grievances against the world, I tried a little variation on the ritual. Nothing much, I just said to her, "I can't take care of you any more. The thought of living with you one more day makes me want to put a gun to one of our heads." She was

713

very good. She picked a cracker crumb off her blanket. Helpfully, I took it from her, put it in my mouth. And she just sat there staring into space, until finally she smiled — not at me, but at some absent third party — and she said, "James can't save me; he never could. Amen." And then she turned out the light. I swallowed the cracker; she swallowed [the pills]. Her note said, "Don't blame yourself. When I see you in heaven, I'll still give you a great big Jesus hug." *(She takes him to her. He breaks.)* I'm fine. I'm sorry.

SARAH: We're not so different. We were both born to parents who would have been better off without us.

JAMES: We're not so different, huh? We were both born to parents who would have been better off without us.

SARAH: I love you.

JAMES: Oh, Sarah, I love you too. *(They cling to each other. He breaks gently, moves D.)* And the next day we were married by a Justice of the Peace, with Sarah's mother in attendance. The Justice didn't sign, of course, so I translated the ceremony for Sarah. When it was done, she said to me:

SARAH: Let no one, living or dead, absent or present, ever come between us.	JAMES: Let no one, living or dead, absent or present, ever come between us.

JAMES: And I promised

SARAH: You and me. Joined. *(James turns toward Sarah. He begins to move toward her as the lights fade to black.)*

ACT II

James watches Sarah intently. Isolated in her silence, she is "making up" her face.

JAMES: Sarah Norman Leeds. My wife. Sarah Norman Leeds is deaf. *(He puts on a pair of airplane mechanic's sound mufflers, an effort to simulate deafness somehow. He slaps them, indicating he can't hear.)* She suffers a sensory-neural deficit of unknown etiology. The osseous structures in her head conduct no sound. She has no residual hearing, derives no benefit from amplification. This profound impairment may have resulted from pre-natal rubella or from the recessive trait in her family. Sarah Norman Leeds' deafness is not correctable by surgery. It is incurable. *(Mrs. Norman and Franklin enter from opposite sides and come together.)*

SARAH: Look at me — I'm like a nervous little kid. Why should I be nervous? Are *they* nervous? No! They're going to come in and look at me like a laboratory specimen — *My* quiche! Watch — I'll ruin it and they won't be able to rave that the deafie cooked a quiche.	MRS. NORMAN: If someone had told me a year ago I'd be playing bridge with you and my daughter, I wouldn't have believed it. FRANKLIN: I explained to her she was destroying my bridge game, that she had to let him out once a week to play a couple of rubbers. To my astonishment, she informed me

James was teaching her to play, and
that we would soon meet in mortal
combat.

FRANKLIN: Do you play standard Goren? Schencken?

MRS. NORMAN: Heavens, I haven't played bridge in so long, there's no
telling what I'll play.

FRANKLIN: Great.

SARAH: *(To James)* If I make mistakes, don't get mad at me.

JAMES: I promise. If you make mistakes, I'll just smile.

FRANKLIN: *(Looking at his watch.)* Eight-oh-two!

JAMES: *(To Sarah.)* Ready to march into battle?

FRANKLIN: *(To Mrs. Norman.)* We should have started by now.

SARAH: *(To James.)* You can't embarrass me in front of them.

JAMES: I would never embarrass you in front of them — What! You're bidding that! Oh no!

FRANKLIN: *We're leaving! (James and Sarah move toward the "game."*
Franklin, to Mrs. Norman.) I've gotta have the north seat. You sit
south. It's just a little superstition of mine. *(To James.)* I thought
maybe we scared you off.

MRS. NORMAN: *(Signing only to Sarah.)* [Franklin's mean.]

JAMES: You're a bit early.

FRANKLIN: I'm not early, I'm right on the stroke of the hour.

JAMES: You're the boss. *(Mrs. Norman deals the "cards.")*

FRANKLIN: Now, no cheating, Sarah.

SARAH: Cheating?

FRANKLIN: I've seen deaf people who cheat like bandits at bridge.

MRS. NORMAN: One club.

JAMES: One diamond.

FRANKLIN: A seeming scratch of the nose — like this — six of a suit . . .
(He scratches his nose with a "six," changes to a "seven.") . . . seven.
I'm sorry, what did you say, partner?

MRS. NORMAN: One club to James' one diamond.

FRANKLIN: I'll pass. A little tug of the shirt here like this . . . *(Over the*
heart.) . . . five hearts.

SARAH: I promise I won't cheat.

MRS. NORMAN: She promises she won't cheat.

FRANKLIN: Thank you, I sign fluently.

MRS. NORMAN: Of course, I'm sorry.

SARAH: Two spades.

FRANKLIN: Two spades?

SARAH: Right.

FRANKLIN: Fine, fine.

MRS. NORMAN: Three clubs.

FRANKLIN: Three clubs?

JAMES: I double.

FRANKLIN: Uh-huh, uh-huh. Three clubs, huh?

MRS. NORMAN: Well, I thought —

FRANKLIN: *Pass.*

SARAH: Four hearts.

FRANKLIN: Four hearts?

MRS. NORMAN: Pass.
JAMES: Four spades.
FRANKLIN: Pass.
SARAH: Six spades.
FRANKLIN: Six spades!
SARAH: Right.
FRANKLIN: Fine. Terrific.
MRS. NORMAN: *(Silence. James studies his hand, looks at Sarah.)*
FRANKLIN: Ah, ah — no eye contact, please.
JAMES: Pass.
FRANKLIN: You'll forgive me for thinking that someone playing bridge for the first time isn't going to make a small slam, so — no offense — but I double.
SARAH: Redouble.
JAMES: Wait a minute. You're redoubling? Do you know how many points you're playing for?
SARAH: A lot.
JAMES: A lot — right. I'm the dummy.
MRS. NORMAN: My lead. *(They play one round of the hand. Sarah scoops up the "cards" and then James scoops her up as if the entire hand had been played.)*
JAMES: Oh, my god, she made it! I don't believe it! *(Mrs. Norman and Franklin rise to leave.)*
MRS. NORMAN: I hope we can play again sometime, Mr. Franklin.
FRANKLIN: Uh-huh.
JAMES: You amaze me!
FRANKLIN: Getting her to marry you, Jimbo, is one thing . . .
MRS. NORMAN: *(To Sarah.)* I'm very proud of you.
FRANKLIN: . . . but getting her to play bridge . . .
MRS. NORMAN: Thank you for inviting me.
FRANKLIN: I'd say the only thing more remarkable would be to get her to do the one thing you were hired to do.
JAMES: Get her to speak. I will.   FRANKLIN: Get her to speak.
MRS. NORMAN: See you again soon?
SARAH: Please.
FRANKLIN: Keep in mind — whatever your progress, I'm retiring at sixty-five. *(Mrs. Norman and Franklin go.)*
JAMES: I can't believe you played that well!
SARAH: Neither could they.
JAMES: Neither could they?
SARAH: She cooks a quiche, she bids her hand correctly.
JAMES: She cooks a quiche, she bids her hand correctly.
SARAH: They looked at me like a laboratory specimen.
JAMES: They looked at you like a laboratory specimen? I don't know about your mother, but I think Franklin was just trying to look down your dress.
SARAH: He'll expect me to speak by the end of the week.
JAMES: He'll expect you to speak by the end of the week. Well? . . . Naw, I told him dreams of a public speaking career were over — that in a moment of erotic madness I had bitten your tongue out of your mouth.

SARAH: The quiche was runny on the bottom.
JAMES: The quiche was runny on the bottom? No, it was perfect — what are you talking about?
SARAH: Don't protect me.
JAMES: Don't protect you? — Okay, it was a little runny on the bottom.
SARAH: Oh, no! — I knew it. Why?
JAMES: Did you heat the cream first?
SARAH: No.
JAMES: Try heating the cream first.
SARAH: Why didn't you tell me?
JAMES: I didn't tell you because you didn't ask me.
SARAH: Since when has that stopped you?
JAMES: Since when has that stopped me? Didn't you enjoy this evening?
SARAH: No.
JAMES: I'm sorry. I thought you did.
SARAH: *(A beat.)* I did.
JAMES: You did.
SARAH: Yes.
JAMES: Are you afraid if you let everybody know you're enjoying life in the hearing world they'll revoke your angry deaf person's license?
SARAH: Not funny.
JAMES: Not funny. I'm sorry. *(James has begun to prepare for bed. Orin enters but is unseen by either Sarah or James.)*
ORIN: All your friends across the road at the School for the Deaf — you remember the School for the Deaf — they're very impressed with you, Sarah. You have a full-time interpreter just like a United Nations diplomat.
SARAH: *(Disturbed by this evocation of Orin.)* Let's go for a walk.
JAMES: Go for a walk? Now?
SARAH: Want to?   ORIN: You drive a car . . .
JAMES: It's midnight.
SARAH: I've always wanted to go   ORIN: . . . you shop by yourself in
out after midnight without   food stores, you have a check-
worrying about curfew.   ing account. You're a regular
                                         American housewife.
JAMES: You've always wanted to go out after midnight without worrying about curfew. *(They go out into the "night.")*
ORIN: Would you care to know that I have made contact with a lawyer who is interested in the injustices being perpetrated here? *(Edna Klein — the lawyer.)*
KLEIN: Dear Mr. Dennis, I was moved by your recent letter.
ORIN: What injustices? Tell me how many deaf people teach in this institution.
KLEIN: I would be pleased to drive up and meet with you and your friend, Miss Norman.
ORIN: Don't tell me I had no right to use your name. I say I did.
KLEIN: I'm not sure what legal recourse you might have . . . *(She exits.)*
ORIN: Look at me! Don't turn your back on me, Sarah! *(He exits.)*
SARAH: I like this best — what we can do alone together.
JAMES: You like this best — what we can do alone together. We can't always

be alone . . . What's the matter? You're not unremittingly joyous about what you did tonight.

SARAH: Little bothered.

JAMES: A little bothered about what?

SARAH: I feel split down the middle, caught between two worlds.

JAMES: You feel . . . what?

SARAH: Deaf world here, hearing world here.

JAMES: Caught between the deaf and hearing worlds.

SARAH: I hope I'm strong enough to juggle both.

JAMES: You hope you're strong enough to juggle both. If you're not, I am. We're a team. We're unbeatable. Right?

SARAH: Yes.

JAMES: You didn't sign that with sufficient conviction. Try it again.

SARAH: *Yes!*

JAMES: Too much. Take it down a little bit.

SARAH: Yes.

JAMES: That's about right. *(She's still not comfortable with it all.)* I'm telling you, you're going to bridge the two worlds brilliantly. Repeat after me: Boy, am I bent on being a brilliant bridger. Boy . . .

SARAH: *(Mouthing it, no sound, no sign.)* Boy.

JAMES: Hey, what was that? That's good! All you need to do is push a little air behind that and you'll have a spoken word. Boy . . .

SARAH: You bit my tongue off.

JAMES: I bit your tongue out. Oh, Sarah, you lip read so many words. If you'd stop seeing this speaking thing as a test of wills . . .

SARAH: It's not. I'm too old to learn to speak and lip read well.

JAMES: It's not. You're too old to learn to speak and lip read well enough for *whom?*

SARAH: Me.

JAMES: For you. Yes, I know you think that.

SARAH: I've told you before — I don't do things I can't do well.

JAMES: You've told me before — you don't do things you can't do well. I still say —

SARAH: Please. I don't want to talk about this any more tonight.

JAMES: You don't want to talk about that any more tonight. What do you wanna do?

SARAH: Go home and practice my quiche.

JAMES: Go home and practice your quiche. I have a better idea. Why don't we go home and practice being alone together. Practice a particular kind of teamwork, if you follow my drift.

SARAH: I could be convinced.

JAMES: You could be convinced. What would it take to convince you?

SARAH: Nothing.

JAMES: Nothing. I love a girl who plays hard to get. *(She runs "inside," James, following.)* I was only kidding! *(The "scene" shifts into mind-space. They stare at each other from a distance.)* You amaze me. But what I don't know enough . . . I need to know what it's like in there. *(He makes the sign which Sarah used earlier to describe her silence.)* [Break-Growth.] *(Sarah covers her ears with her hands. James does the same.)* [No.] *(She puts the sound-mufflers on his head. No good.*

James takes them off. They embrace. James, unsigned, to himself:) I
need to be ingested by you. Need somehow to penetrate and twist and
burrow . . .
LYDIA: *(Entering.)* Hi, guys. Guess who came with some important news.
Mr. Franklin gave me Sarah's job.
JAMES: Yes, we heard that.
LYDIA: Now I'm the official maid.
JAMES: Congratulations.
LYDIA: You have any tips for me?
SARAH: Yes. After you clean the toilet bowl . . .
LYDIA: After you clean the toilet bowl — yeah . . . ?
SARAH: Get out before you flush.
LYDIA: Get out before you flush. What does that mean? *(To James.)* Can I
watch your new TV?
JAMES: How do you know we have a new TV?
LYDIA: Everybody knows you gave Sarah a credit card to buy new TVs.
JAMES: Ask Sarah.
LYDIA: Why do I have to ask her?
JAMES: It's her TV.
LYDIA: It's *your* TV.
JAMES: That's not right, Lydia.
SARAH: *(To Lydia.)* What are you saying?
LYDIA: It was private.
JAMES: Go on — ask her.
LYDIA: Can I watch your new TV?
SARAH: Watch in the TV lounge.
LYDIA: I don't like to watch in the TV lounge. You always have to keep
changing the volume on your hearing aid. Everyone is always fighting
about how loud the sound should be. Yesterday, I almost had a nervous
breakdown. I did. Really. *(To James, when Sarah appears unmoved.)*
Mr. Leeds . . .
JAMES: Oh, come on, Sarah, let her watch your TV. It's good for her — she
picks up the pronunciation of words.
SARAH: Fine. Go. Watch TV.
LYDIA: Yay! *(Lydia goes to watch "TV" in their "bedroom." James a bit dis-
approving of or surprised by Sarah's behavior.)*
SARAH: I don't want her hanging around here.
JAMES: You don't want her hanging around here. It's not going to hurt
Lydia if we make her feel welcome.
SARAH: It's not going to hurt me if I have my privacy. You married me, not
her.
JAMES: It's not going to hurt you if you have your privacy. I married you,
not her —
LYDIA: Mr. Leeds . . .
JAMES: *(To Sarah)* Wait a second. *(To Lydia)* What?
LYDIA: . . . can I have one of your beers from your refrigerator?
JAMES: Sure, how 'bout a beer?
LYDIA: Okay!
SARAH: Now what?
JAMES: Nothing, not important. Now, what were you saying —

SARAH: *(Mimicking James.)* Nothing, not important. *(Sarah moves away angrily.)*

JAMES: Nothing, not important. I'm sorry. I didn't mean to cut you off . . . he said loudly into the silence. *(Silence is broken by loud TV sounds.)*

LYDIA: What did you say?

JAMES: I said turn the volume on that damn thing down!

LYDIA: What?

JAMES: Turn the volume down!

LYDIA: Then I won't be able to hear it. *(Telephone rings.)*

JAMES: The phone's ringing!

LYDIA: What?

JAMES: The phone is ringing!

LYDIA: What phone?

JAMES: The one you can't hear because the TV is so goddamn loud! — *(He screams bloody murder. Sarah turns back to him.)*

SARAH: You say something?

JAMES: I screamed. The phone's ringing and the TV's going at about a hundred and ten decibels. *(Buzzer sounds.)* Ah, and there's the buzzer on the oven. *(Sarah doesn't understand.)* The buzzer on the oven! Now, if someone would fire a bazooka through the window . . .

SARAH: What?

JAMES: *(Answering "phone.")* Hello! — Would you hold on a minute, please — The buzzer on the oven — your casserole is ready — Hello, yes I'm listening, you have my undivided attention. Who the hell is this? . . . Ask him to wait a second. *(Going to Sarah at the "oven" where her casserole is smoking.)* It's for you. It's one of the dorm counselors translating a call from Che Guevara —

SARAH: Who?

JAMES: Orin. Orin. *Lydia — for crissake!*

LYDIA: Oh — *okay. (Lydia "turns down" the TV.)*

JAMES: *(Back to "phone" with Sarah in tow.)* Hello . . . Yes, Sarah's here. Is Orin there? Are you both ready, because we're both ready. Okay, this is Sarah speaking to Orin.

SARAH: I don't want to speak to you very much.

JAMES: *(Into "phone.")* I don't want to speak to you very much. *(To Sarah.)* Please. I need to see you and Jim. *(Unsigned.)* Jim — he's calling me Jim. *(Into "phone.")* No, don't translate that to Orin. I was talking to myself. *(During the exchange above, Lydia slips away.)*

SARAH: What?

JAMES: *(To Sarah.)* Please.

SARAH: You're saying please?

JAMES: No, I'm not saying please. *(Into "phone.")* Hold on. *(To Sarah.)* That was Orin saying please again. My fault — I probably sounded like me instead of like the dorm counselor sounding like Orin. Can I help you?

SARAH: I don't want to see him.

JAMES: You don't want to see him — then don't see him. *(Into "phone.")* She doesn't want —

SARAH: Please come for dinner tomorrow night.

JAMES: *(Into "phone.")* Please come for dinner tomorrow night. *(To Sarah.)* I would like that. What time should I come?

SARAH: Seven.

JAMES: *(Into "phone.")* Come at seven o'clock. *(To Sarah.)* Good, I'll see you then. *(He slams down the phone. It's quiet.)* Hey, either I've just become deaf or it's suddenly quiet in here.

SARAH: You make everything into a joke.

JAMES: I make everything into a joke? I don't see you laughing.

SARAH: Anytime things get too serious or you don't know how to fix something, you make a joke and that's supposed to make it okay.

JAMES: Anytime things get too serious or I don't know how to fix something, I make a joke and that's supposed to make it okay. I didn't know that. In other words, you're saying what? That I obfuscate the truth . . . ? How the hell do you sign "obfuscate"? *(With resignation, he tries to finger spell.)* I [o-b-f-u-s —] *(His fingers lock in a spasm.)* My hands are killing me and my brain feels like a slab of . . . Look at that — I can't even spell "slab." My brain feels like a sla*f* of . . . I'm going to put my hands into a s-a-u-n-a b-a-t-h. Hey — another bad joke! We don't even have one. I'm going to rest my hands and listen to twenty minutes of B-a-c-h. Do you know I haven't turned on my stereo since we got married? Hold it, that sounds like . . .

SARAH: Sshh.

JAMES: . . . I'm blaming you for the fact I haven't been listening to music. *(James mimes flagellating himself.)*

SARAH: Sshh. I should give you a day off once a week when you don't have to answer the phone or translate for me or sign to me when we're alone.

JAMES: You should give me a day off once a week when I don't have to answer the phone or translate for you or sign to you when we're alone. That's not what I meant. I was only saying —

SARAH: Sshh. Rest your hands, listen to your music.

JAMES: Rest my hands. Listen to my music. *(Music: Bach Double Concerto in D minor, Second movement largo ma non tanto. James gets deeply into the music, his eyes closed. Sarah in her own world, but then looking at James, happy to see him serenely involved. The following is in sign language only as she comes and rests her head in his lap.)*

SARAH: Enjoying yourself?

JAMES: [Very much. You?]

SARAH: Yes.

JAMES: [What are you doing?]

SARAH: Thinking.

JAMES: [Why don't you read a book?]

SARAH: Why don't *you* read a book?

JAMES: [Because I'm listening to music.]

SARAH: So I'm thinking.

JAMES: [About what?]

SARAH: Sorry. Sshh. Enjoy your music. *(He tries to concentrate on the music. She "busies" herself around the apartment. He can't concentrate, turns off music.)*

JAMES: *(Speaking and signing again.)* I can't.

SARAH: Why not?

JAMES: I can't enjoy my music because you can't.

SARAH: We can enjoy different things.

JAMES: Sure we can enjoy different things; but, in the case of music, you don't have a choice.

SARAH: But I *can* enjoy your music.

JAMES: But you *can* enjoy my music. How?

SARAH: Vibrations.   JAMES: Oh, yeah, vibrations through your nose.

SARAH: Really! The vibrations don't have a sound but they do have a feel. *(She demonstrates.)* Fast. Slow. Very intense. Not so intense.

JAMES: The vibrations don't have a sound but they do have a feel. Fast and slow . . .

SARAH: And when I see people dancing, I feel still more.

JAMES: And when you see people dancing, you feel still more. But you're getting it through them. That's all visual. You're missing *music.*

SARAH: No. I can feel it.

JAMES: I know you can feel it. But that's just a small part of it. You see, music is . . . *(Incredible subject to communicate.)* Music has a . . . *(But he's going to try.)* Music starts with pitches. [P-i-t-c-h-e-s.] Sounds! High and low. A whole, huge range of sounds. And each one has its own emotional life. And then when you combine them and play them together — these two and these two — it has a whole *new* life. And then you can play them on different instruments — trombones, violins, flutes and drums — The combinations are infinite! And then when you put it all together, with a beginning, a middle, and an end, it grows into a . . . It transcends mere sound and speaks directly to your heart — because you *hear* it! I don't have the signs that can . . . I can't explain it, I'm sorry.

SARAH: Don't be sorry. I could never know what music sounds like. But just watching you explain to me what you feel, I *can* understand what it means to you. And that makes me very happy.

JAMES: Don't be sorry. You could never know what music sounds like. But just watching me explain what I feel, you *can* understand what it means to me. And that makes you very happy. But it makes me sad for you, damn it!

SARAH: Sshh. No. Don't be, please.

JAMES: Don't be. All right, I'm not. There. Want to take in a vibration or two with me? *(Organ music: Bach "Toccata and fugue in D minor." James turns the volume way up. They get on the floor together.* [You feel it?] *(He tries to demonstrate the first chorus of the toccata with his hands, how they rise to crescendo.)*

SARAH: *(Rising.)* I don't like this kind of music.

JAMES: You don't like this kind of music?

SARAH: Organ music.

JAMES: That's right — it is organ music. How did you know it's organ music?

SARAH: I can go in the kitchen.

JAMES: Don't go in the kitchen! Stay here with me and I'll turn it down. *(He does.)* What have you got against organ music?

SARAH & JAMES: *(James translating in the second person.)* When we were kids in school here, on Sunday they made us go to church. They played an organ fiercely. Orin cried because he could hear just enough of it to hurt his ears. The kids with hearing aids were forbidden to turn them off. We were told it was the voice of God and should hurt.

They said we should love God for being so fierce and demanding. When Orin was nine and I was eleven, we started hiding in the trees behind the duck pond on Sunday. We pretended we were soldiers and threw dirt clods at the church and made sounds like hand grenades.

JAMES: What did they sound like?

SARAH: No.

JAMES: C'mon. You show me a deaf guy's hand grenade and I'll stop playing my organ so fiercely. *(Orin enters. He and Sarah mime "explosion" of a hand grenade, only Orin making a small sound.)*

ORIN: You remember that? That was our first rebellion. We were a really good team.

SARAH: How do you like my apartment?

ORIN: Your apartment is very nice.

JAMES: You're speaking much better, Orin.

ORIN: Thank you. I've been working very hard at it. *(To Sarah.)* I want to —

SARAH: Come see my kitchen.

ORIN: I'll see your kitchen later. I need to —

SARAH: Come. *(She moves to "kitchen.")*

ORIN: *(Following.)* Excuse me, Jim.

JAMES: Sure.

SARAH: Look at this machine. It does eleven things.

ORIN: A machine. It does eleven things.

SARAH: *(Demonstrates.)* It stirs, chops, beats, grates, mixes, grinds, crumbs, shakes, blends, purees, and liquefies. *(She "pours" it into a "glass," hands it to Orin.)*

ORIN: My mother has a blender too, Sarah. Now, can I tell you what I have to tell you — even though you don't want to hear it.

SARAH: We weren't really a good team.

ORIN: What do you mean, we weren't really a good team? We were friends. More than that — we were brother and sister.

SARAH: True, but I was never good at the kind of rebellion you wanted. But I am starting to feel I'm good at this. And happy.

ORIN: But you were never good at the kind of rebellion I wanted. But you are starting to feel you're good at this. And you're happy. I can see that. But we really need you across the street.

JAMES: May I come in? What is it you need her *for,* Orin?

KLEIN: *(Entering.)* Dear Mr. Dennis, I must confess, I never thought about discrimination against the deaf. I think you might have a legitimate complaint with the Equal Employment Opportunity Commission.

SARAH: A complaint?   JAMES: You're gonna file a complaint?

ORIN: Damn right.

KLEIN: Hiring practices are definitely open to question in your institution.

ORIN: Which is supposed to exist for our benefit.

KLEIN: Let me know if this is an area you and Miss Norman would like to enter. *(Klein goes.)*

ORIN: *(To Sarah.)* I want you with me.

SARAH: With you? Or to follow you?

ORIN: Not to follow me. With me.

SARAH: Why?

ORIN: Because you're deaf. And pure deaf. And because you're as strong as I am. Or you were.

SARAH: I'm not interested. I'm trying to do other things.

ORIN: You're not interested. You're trying to do other things. But you can't go from closing yourself in the school with your brooms and mops to closing youself in here with your TV and your blender.

SARAH: I'm not closed in here! It's not the same!

ORIN: You're not closed in here — it's not the same! What's the difference?

SARAH: Are you kidding?

ORIN: No, I'm not kidding!

SARAH: A world of difference!

ORIN: A world of difference! Listen, I didn't come here to start a fight.

JAMES: Orin, Orin, hold it!

SARAH: You have a lot of gall! Big-headed!

JAMES: Orin, excuse me for being here, but I have been cast in the role of Sarah's mentor, so lay off her, huh.

SARAH: What are you saying?

JAMES: Nothing. Between Orin and me.

SARAH: But about me.

ORIN: He's trying to protect you from me.

SARAH: Neither of you has to protect me from anyone.

JAMES & ORIN: That's right, she doesn't need either one of us to protect her from . . . *(They look at each other, stop in midsentence.)*

ORIN: Please, at least meet the lawyer. Read the research. Here.

SARAH: Maybe.

ORIN: Read it.

SARAH: Put it down. *(He puts it down.)*

ORIN: We need your help too, Jim. Will you stand with us?

JAMES: What would you want me to do?

ORIN: We'll need someone who hears and speaks to make phone calls for us for several weeks.

JAMES: Phone calls. For several weeks.

ORIN: We'll need a translator. You'll speak as if you're me —

JAMES: Oh, I know the routine. I'm already Mrs. Leeds' social secretary. You're sure you haven't got anything important I could do — something with a prefix in front of it maybe — Captain, Lord . . .

ORIN: I need someone who's isn't afraid of a fight . . . or of a little competition. *(A beat.)*

JAMES: I see. Excuse me. *(To Sarah, who is glancing at the research.)* If you're intersted, I'm interested.

ORIN: Sarah, please don't turn away from us. *(Sarah and Orin launch into an* untranslated, *totally silent argument in ASL that is beyond James' ability to keep up. A translation is printed opposite.)*

SARAH:*(ASL.)* You dirty business.	SARAH: This is a dirty thing to do.
ORIN: We need you.	ORIN: We need you.
SARAH: You never share.	SARAH: You won't share.
ORIN: ? You-two share ? "y" sweet romance last? Doubt deaf rights beat!	ORIN: Does he share with you? Do you think this little romance will last half as long as what we can accomplish for our people?

JAMES: What?

SARAH: You big-headed talk that.

ORIN: Me big-head? We-two discuss plan, will do 1-2-3-4. Thrill change.

SARAH: We-two never discuss.

ORIN. Bullshit. We-two finish talk. We-two deaf. Don't forget. We-two deaf! Period!

SARAH: You have no right to say that!

ORIN: What do you mean I have no right? We've discussed it. Planned all these things to do. Why have you changed?

SARAH: We never discussed anything.

ORIN: Bullshit. We've already discussed it. We're deaf. Don't forget it. You and I are deaf! Period!

ORIN: *(Speaking to James.)* Good night, Jim. I'll be in touch with you.

JAMES: Yeah. Fine. Sure. *(Orin leaves.)* I feel like everyone was talking in some far-northern dialect of Hungarian there. What was that all about?

SARAH: Between Orin and me.

JAMES: Between Orin and you. Hey, whudduya know, I don't like being closed out either. What was that I caught there about a "romance."

SARAH: He said our marriage won't last. It isn't as important as deaf rights.

JAMES: He said our marriage won't last. It isn't as important as deaf rights. What did you say?

SARAH: He practically accused me of being a phony hearing person.

JAMES: He practically accused you of being a phony hearing person. My God, the worst insult possible. You know what he's trying to do, don't you? It's the oldest trick in the repressed-minority handbook. He wants you to feel guilty for leaving the flock.

SARAH: I haven't left the deaf world. I haven't done anything yet.

JAMES: You haven't left the deaf world. You haven't done anything yet. Hey, hey, sit down. What you and I have to do is separate the fact that he may have a legitimate axe to grind from the fact that he's a rotten little shit.

SARAH: No more words tonight. I'm too confused and angry.

JAMES: No more words tonight. You're too confused and angry. You think silence is the best thing for confusion and anger?

SARAH: It's not silent in my head.

JAMES: It's not silent in your head. Hey, we're a team, remember? You're not the only one he insulted. I don't like being minimized any more than you do.

SARAH: What's going on between Orin and me is not about your ego.

JAMES: What's going on between Orin and you is not about my . . . *(Sarah moves off to one side.)* . . . ego. *(Miss Klein, with a note.)*

KLEIN: *(To Orin, as he enters, carefully articulating and speaking a bit loudly.)* Excuse me. Do . . . you . . . know . . . where . . . this . . . is?

ORIN: Miss Klein?

KLEIN: Yes.

ORIN: I'm Orin Dennis.

KLEIN: Oh — Orin! Hello. Finally, I had a little difficulty finding the building.

ORIN: You found it. Come on in, please. This is Sarah Norman.

SARAH: Leeds.

ORIN: Sarah Leeds — I'm sorry. Edna Klein.

KLEIN: *(Articulating carefully, a bit loudly.)* Hello Sarah, I'm so pleased to meet you finally. *(Orin translates Miss Klein's words for Sarah throughout this scene.)*

SARAH: Thank you.   ORIN: She said, thank you.

KLEIN: *(Picking up the sign.)* Thank you? *(Speaking only.)* Now then, I'm to speak directly into your faces, is that right?

ORIN: My face. She doesn't lip read. Can you understand me okay?

KLEIN: Yes. Yes, I can.

SARAH: My husband James. *(James is perusing the research.)*

ORIN: Sarah's husband James. One of our team.

KLEIN: *(Into his face.)* I'm so pleased to meet you finally.

JAMES: *(Imitating Klein's precision and loudness.)* Thank you. I am so pleased to meet you, too. Finally.

ORIN: I don't think that's very funny, Jim.

KLEIN: Am I missing something?   SARAH: *(To Orin.)* What's he doing?

JAMES: I can hear.

KLEIN: Excuse me . . . ?   ORIN: [He's pretending to be deaf.]

JAMES: I'm a hearing person. You don't have to speak directly into my face or raise your voice.

KLEIN: Was I talking loudly?

JAMES: A natural mistake.

KLEIN: *(With her back to Sarah and Orin.)* I was so sure I was going to handle this flawlessly that I suppose there was no alternative but to make an immediate fool of myself. I'm sorry.

JAMES: Forget it.   SARAH: *(To Orin.)* What are they saying?

ORIN: What is she saying?

JAMES: Nothing. I just told her I'm not deaf.

ORIN: He is a hearing person, Miss Klein. He was just making a joke.

JAMES: Yeah, I just told —

KLEIN: Yes, he told me.

JAMES: *(To Sarah, who isn't pleased.)* Sorry.

KLEIN: Well, could we, uh . . . *(Sarah gestures for them to sit.)* So, this is the young woman you wrote me about, Orin. Sarah.

SARAH: *(To Klein.)* He shouldn't have used my name without my permission —

ORIN: *(Ignoring Sarah's line above.)* Sarah, yes.

KLEIN: As I understand it, Sarah is deaf *and* dumb. *(James makes the sound of a bomb going off.)*

SARAH: I'm not deaf and dumb.   ORIN: We don't like the word "dumb"
I'm —   very much, Miss Klein.

ORIN: We are deaf or hearing impaired and we speak or we don't speak.

KLEIN: Of course. Excuse me. Sarah is deaf and doesn't speak.

SARAH: Yes. That's what I was trying to say. *(Orin ignores Sarah.)*

KLEIN: Well, unhappy as that may have made you all your life, it could be very useful to you now.

SARAH: I'm not unhappy —

ORIN: She's not unhappy being deaf, Miss Klein, that's not the point. What

726

she means is that she is often misunderstood by hearing people. She wants — *(Angry at Orin speaking for her, Sarah moves away.)* I'm sorry. I didn't mean to speak for you. I just —
SARAH: But you did! *(Orin goes.)*
KLEIN: Look, I'm sorry I appear to be so . . . Mr. Leeds, you tell her I'll do better next time.
JAMES: Right, yes, I will, I will. *(Klein goes.)* Fun evening. I thought the charades went particularly well.
SARAH: I think Klein is going to be very good.
JAMES: You think Klein is going to be very good at what?
SARAH: You were being so cute together I thought you liked her.
JAMES: We were being so cute together you thought I liked her. Why would I like her?
SARAH: She can hear and she's educated.
JAMES: She can hear, she's educated. Oh, come on, if you'd stop pretending to be deaf and listen to her, you'd know she has the remains of a bilateral lisp. *(Imitating a bilateral lisp.)* She probably sounded like this before speech therapy . . . You have no reason to be jealous of her. Am I jealous of Orin?
SARAH: Maybe.
JAMES: Maybe? Hey, I don't know which role you're playing here. Is this Sarah the Pure Deaf Person, or Sarah Norman, the old isolationist maid, or is this Sarah Leeds, teammate of James? What's eating you?
SARAH: Let's go to sleep.
JAMES: No, I don't want to go to bed. You can't just start a bonfire in the living room and then go night-night. Here, let's talk. *(He sits.)*
SARAH: I can't.
JAMES: You can't. *(She goes to the "bedroom." He follows.)* That's great. You be deaf, I'll be mute, and we'll burn our eyes out with the fire in the living room, then pray for arthritis. Not bad, huh? No hear, no speak, no see, no hands. Oh, Sarah, Sarah, let's crawl under the covers and pretend we're in a faraway place.
SARAH: We're not. We're here.
JAMES: We're not. We're here. All right, then, deal with what's bothering you!
SARAH: I don't know which role I'm supposed to play. Orin treats me like an idiot. You treat me like an idiot. Now the lady lawyer treats me like an idiot.
JAMES: You don't know which role you're supposed to play. Orin treats you like an idiot. I treat you like an idiot. Now the lady lawyers treats you — Wait a second, I don't treat you like an idiot.
SARAH: Let me be a person.
JAMES: I don't want you to be a person?
SARAH: You want me to be a *deaf* person so you can change me into a hearing person.
JAMES: I want you to be a *deaf* person so you can change into a hearing person. *(He moves away.)* Good night.
SARAH: *(Getting his attention.)* Orin doesn't want me to be a hearing person because he needs a pure deaf person.
JAMES: Orin doesn't want you to be a hearing person because he needs a

pure deaf person.

SARAH: And the lady lawyer wants me to hate being deaf so all the hearing people will feel sorry for me.

JAMES: And the lady lawyer wants you to hate being deaf so all the hearing people will feel sorry for you.

SARAH: And I just want to be me.

JAMES: And you just want to be you. And who are you? *(On Sarah's face we see confusion. She doesn't answer.)* Oh, Christ. How did we go from being Ozzie and Harriet to — *(He tries to embrace her. She pushes him away.)*

SARAH: Don't pity me.

JAMES: Don't pity you. Wait a minute! I may be just a middle-class, white, Jewish-Catholic atheist, hearing person, but I have rights too. And one of those rights is to feel sympathy for my wife even if she's an inordinate hard ass. And I don't know the sign for inordinate but I don't care. Here's "hard-ass" — it's a beauty! *(He makes to lower his pants. Sarah "turns the lights out." In the dark, the sound of Sarah crying softly. James "turns the lights on" again.)* I never heard you cry before.

SARAH: I wasn't crying.

JAMES: Yes you were. I know because I heard you. See, we don't have to look at each other or even touch to communicate . . . Let's go back to being alone together. Let's have a baby.

SARAH: A baby?

JAMES: Yes.

SARAH: No. If it were deaf, you would hate it.

JAMES: If it were deaf, I would hate it. That's a goddamn lie! If it were deaf and grew up to be as unbending as its mother, though — *(She "turns out the lights" again.)* Goddamnit! *(Music: A Handel oratorio. Lights. James listening to his stereo.)*

KLEIN: *(Entering.)* Good evening, Mr. Leeds. Are Orin and Sarah here yet?

JAMES: Huh?

KLEIN: *(Speaking over the music.)* Are Orin and Sarah here yet?

JAMES: Orin is here. Sarah is not. But I really wouldn't count on her continued participation in this . . . whatever it is.

KLEIN: Oh, I hope you're mistaken.

JAMES: I am never mistaken, Miss Klein — it's my saving grace.

KLEIN: You're very fortunate.

JAMES: Yes, I am, thank you.

KLEIN: Can I show you what I learned today and you tell me if I'm doing it right?

JAMES: Sure. What have you learned? *(She puts down her briefcase.)* Don't tell me: I'll bet you've learned some Signed English, haven't you, so you can communicate with our deaf brothers and sisters.

KLEIN: Well, I've made a start. Could we turn the Handel off, please?

JAMES: Handel?

KLEIN: I'm sorry, I thought you were listening to Handel.

JAMES: Oh, I am.

KLEIN: Oh, I thought so.

JAMES: Yes, I recall you even said so. *(Music out.)* Now.

KLEIN: How. Are. You?

JAMES: I am fine, Miss Klein. How are you?

KLEIN: Okay, I think I've got that, too. I. Am. Fine.

JAMES: You want to watch the thumb under the chin. That means *"not."* I'm *not* fine. If you're fine, you want to do *"am"* which is the letter "A," thumb under the lip . . . *(He demonstrates. Sarah has seen part of this. Klein discovers her watching.)*

KLEIN: Your wife. Hello, Sarah.

SARAH: *(To James.)* More cuteness.

JAMES: More cuteness? Where were you when I got up this morning?

KLEIN: Would you like me to wait outside?

JAMES: That's quite all right.

SARAH: What did she say?

JAMES: She wants to know if we want her to wait outside while we do our husband and wife routine.

KLEIN: Sarah, Mr. Leeds suggested you might be considering dropping out of our —

SARAH: What did she say now?

JAMES: I don't feel like telling you what she's saying. You've been gone all day — where have you been?

ORIN: Sarah, where have you been? Hello, Miss Klein.

KLEIN: Hello.

ORIN: I wanted you to be with me when I told Franklin.

FRANKLIN: *(Entering, apart from the scene.)* I think my hearing aid just blew up in my ear. You and Sarah are going to do what?

ORIN: And I wanted you to read Miss Klein's speech before she got here.

SARAH: *(Snatching the speech.)* I've got it. I'll read it.

FRANKLIN: Ask Mr. Leeds to come see me.

ORIN: Where did you go?

FRANKLIN: Tell him to see me. *(Franklin exits.)*

KLEIN: Orin, tell Sarah I want to say something to her. *(Orin taps Sarah's shoulder. She looks up.)* How. Are. You?

SARAH: Lousy.

ORIN: She's a bit perturbed, Miss Klein. How are you?

KLEIN: I. Am. Fine. Thank You. *(Sarah and Orin less than knocked out.)*

JAMES: They're bowled over, Miss Klein. *(Orin turns his attention to Sarah's perusal of Klein's speech.)*

ORIN: *(ASL only.)* [Just read it.]

KLEIN: Okay. Okay. I don't suppose that either you or they came equipped with a complete vocabulary or dancing fingers either.

JAMES: Whatever you do, Miss Klein, don't accuse them of any imperfections.

KLEIN: *(Waves for their attention.)* Orin? Sarah? What do you think of my remarks for the commission?

SARAH: Same old shit. *(James laughs.)*

KLEIN: *(To Orin.)* What did she say?

ORIN: Nothing. She thinks they're —

SARAH: *(To Orin.)* Tell her.

ORIN: Sarah, what's your problem?

KLEIN: *(To James.)* What's matter? What did Sarah say, Mr. Leeds?

JAMES: Come here, I'll tell you.

ORIN: Stay out of this, Jim.

JAMES: All right.

ORIN: The speech, Miss Klein, is okay, but it's basically what hearing people always say. We do not consider ourselves helpless in any way.

JAMES: Could I interrupt, please? Miss Klein, why don't you just let them do it themselves?

KLEIN: What do you mean? Walk out on them?

JAMES: No, sit here and give them whatever legal expertise you can but let them speak for themselves.

KLEIN: *(Excluding Orin and Sarah.)* I'm not sure that would be quite as impressive as —

JAMES: Impressive!

KLEIN: Just a minute! I had planned to call on them to answer some questions —

JAMES: Excuse me, Orin has his hand raised.

ORIN: If you don't mind, Miss Klein, I would like to participate in any discussion you're having that will affect me.

JAMES: She's saying that you, with your hard-won speaking ability, and Sarah the Pure Deaf person are going to sit silently by looking properly pathetic while Miss Klein makes your case for you.

KLEIN: Mr. Leeds, I'm perfectly capable of speaking for myself, thank you.

SARAH: Here are the two hearing people arguing while we stand and wait for you to decide what will be done *for* us.

JAMES: *(As Sarah signs.)* My wife has both her hands up now.

KLEIN: What? What is the difficulty?

ORIN: Nothing.

SARAH: *(To James.)* Tell her what I said.

JAMES: She said, Here are the two hearing people arguing while the two deaf people stand around and wonder what is to be decided *for* them.

SARAH: Same old shit.

JAMES: Same old shit.

KLEIN: So that's what it means. I see.

SARAH: Just like your speech.

JAMES: Just like your speech.

KLEIN: Yeah, I got that, thank you.

JAMES: Good, then you don't need me.

ORIN: Maybe we could suggest a few changes in your speech.

KLEIN: Yes, I think it's time you do the talking and I do the listening.

SARAH: She won't listen.

ORIN: How do you know she won't listen?

SARAH: Because none of them do!

ORIN: You can't just stand around and be cynical. That's what you've done all your life. Don't you want to do something for yourself besides spit on the deaf world and lick the ass of the hearing world?

JAMES: Hey!

SARAH: Yes.

ORIN: So, help us.

JAMES: Hey, Orin, you know talk like that doesn't make things any easier around here. *You know?*

ORIN: Making things easier for you, Jim, isn't one of my first concerns just now. *(To Sarah.)* Now, are you going to help us or not? If not, I've had enough of you.

JAMES: She's not interested! Tell them you're not interested and let's get them the hell out of our home.

SARAH: Each of you keeps making me feel — bow down.

JAMES: Each of us keeps making you feel . . . What's that? "Bow down"?

ORIN: That she owes us something.

ORIN: What? JAMES: What?

SARAH: I don't know.

ORIN: *(To Klein.)* She doesn't know. JAMES: You don't know.

SARAH: But I'm not sitting here and letting you talk about me! Who I owe something to is *me!* I want something said about me.

ORIN: But she's not going to sit JAMES: But you're not going to sit there and let us talk about . . . there — *(To Orin.)* Take it.

ORIN: Who she owes something to is her. She wants something said about her. Good.

KLEIN: *(As Orin reverses to Sarah.)* Fine. Tell her we'll sit down and I'll write something about her.

SARAH: No! No more. I'll say it myself.

ORIN: No! No more. She will say — *(He stops himself from speaking out loud what she said.)*

SARAH: And I'll write it myself!

ORIN: *(Signing only.)* [What are you talking about?]

SARAH: Tell her that!

ORIN: *(Signing and speaking.)* I'm not telling her that because you're not going to do that!

KLEIN: What is she saying? SARAH: *(To James.)* Tell her what I said!

ORIN: *(To James.)* Don't translate!

JAMES: Sarah wants to make her own speech. One that she will write herself.

SARAH: *(To Orin and Klein.)* And neither of you has anything to say about what I write.

JAMES: Neither of you has anything to say about what she writes.

SARAH: That's it — take it or leave it.

JAMES: That's it — take it or leave it.

KLEIN: *(Gathering her things.)* Well, as I'm obviously not loaded with expertise here, I guess I should gratefully take it. How do you sign "terrific"?

JAMES: *(Signing.)* [Terrific.]

KLEIN: *(Holding her coat and briefcase under her arm so she can do the two-handed sign.)* Terrific.

SARAH: Thank you.

ORIN: I'll write my own speech too, then.

SARAH: That's up to you. Nobody's going to speak for me anymore. Tell her that.

JAMES: No one is ever going to speak for Sarah again. *(Klein and Orin recede and exit.)*

SARAH: Did you hear yourself say that?

JAMES: Yes, I heard myself repeat that. What I'm a bit confused about is how we got here. Lemme see if I've got this straight. We met, we fought, we fell in love, we got married, I was happy, I thought you were happy. Now we're kicking each other's teeth in. Explain it to me.

SARAH: You think it's my fault and that you're perfect.

JAMES: I think it's your fault and that I'm perfect. What a crock of . . . *(She goes to another area of the stage to work on her speech.)*

LYDIA: *(Entering.)* Hello, Mr. Leeds, where's Sarah?

JAMES: I don't know. *(Sarah writing her speech, very into it.)*

LYDIA: She's at the duck pond — I just saw her. She told me to leave her alone. So I did. Everybody says you're giving Sarah back to the school, that you don't want her anymore.

JAMES: Everybody's saying what?

LYDIA: Yup. And frankly, I think that's a wise con . . . con-tem-pla-tion. Boy, I'm thirsty.

JAMES: Okay, one quick drink and then off you go. No TV tonight. What would you like?

LYDIA: You got a beer?

JAMES: How 'bout a beer?

LYDIA: Okay. Boy, it sure is hot, isn't it? *(She begins to fan the top of her blouse, exposing just a glimpse of breast.)*

JAMES: Oh Lydia, for Chrissake, why aren't you wearing a bra?

LYDIA: A what?

JAMES: A bra.

LYDIA: Oh . . . I forgot. Oh no.

JAMES: I think we'd better get something straight about our relationship, you and I —

LYDIA: Here it is! *(She pulls the bra from her pants pocket.)*

JAMES: No. No. No. Lydia, listen to me . . .

LYDIA: I'm sorry. Don't embarrass me, please. I'll just leave. *(Lydia runs off. James moves after Lydia a step or two, then to Sarah at the "duck pond.")*

JAMES: Working on your speech, huh?

SARAH: Yes.

JAMES: I'm through with my classes. Can I help you?

SARAH: Thanks, no.

JAMES: Throw in a few jokes?

SARAH: You're not funny in deaf, only in hearing.

JAMES: I'm not funny in deaf, only in hearing. See you at home?

SARAH: Few minutes. *(She turns her attention back to her writing.)*

FRANKLIN: *(Entering.)* Make a settlement with them!

JAMES: Yes!

FRANKLIN: They've got as much chance of —

JAMES: Aw, come on, you could make a settlement with them and they'd never have to go in front of that damned commission. A lot of embarrassment could be avoided.

FRANKLIN: The only people who're gonna be embarrassed are your wife and our friend Orin.

JAMES: Well, couldn't you spare them that?

FRANKLIN: Lemme explain the facts of life to you, James. The commission will find in their favor; they always find in favor of the downtrodden. Why not? They know they haven't got an ounce of legal power.

732

They're merely one of those liberal showcase apparatus whose opinion no one is bound to abide by. I'll make your wife and our friend Orin take me into court. If they win there, I'll appeal. I'll make them fight me for years.

JAMES: *Why?*

FRANKLIN: Because, despicable as it may seem, I won't continue in this field if the subjects of my efforts are going to tell me how to minister to them. Look, Orin is potentially a fine teacher — he has all the communication skills — but he's a rarity. Would you hire your wife to teach? What — sign? That'd be like a football team hiring a guy to do nothing but hold for extra points. *(A beat.)* All right, I'll make a settlement, Jimbo. *(James, with Franklin, watching Sarah.)*

JAMES: What did you say?

FRANKLIN: I'll make you a hero. Tell them I'll agree to hire a new deaf gym teacher and a deaf dietician. Offer them that.

JAMES: That won't be enough.

FRANKLIN: You want to know a secret? Nothing would be. Nothing would be enough. *(He exits.)*

JAMES: *(To Sarah.)* You're home from work.

SARAH: It's exciting to feel I have a job.

JAMES: It's exciting to feel you have a job. Good. I'm glad.

SARAH: Are you?

JAMES: Trying to be.

SARAH: Would you watch me practice my speech?

JAMES: Sure, I'd like to watch you practice your speech.

SARAH: But don't tell me how to make it better.

JAMES: But don't tell you how to make it better. What do you mean, don't criticize it?

SARAH: Right.

JAMES: What if your English is incorrect and I think the commission people won't understand it.

SARAH: You can tell me that.

JAMES: I can tell you that — thank you. Will you want me to translate as if I'm you?

SARAH: What do you mean?

JAMES: I mean, when we go before the commission — do you want me to translate the speech exactly —

SARAH: Do you think you're going to translate for me?

JAMES: Yes, I assumed I'd translate for you. I'll tell you a little secret. They won't understand it if I don't translate it.

SARAH: I want Orin to do it.

JAMES: You want Orin to do it? Why? Because he's hearing impaired? So you're gonna turn the tables now, and start using Orin, huh? *(A beat.)* Look, I'd like to be your translator. If you're really going to go through with this I'd like to share the experience with you.

SARAH: I can't say what I feel about being deaf through a hearing person.

JAMES: You can't say what you feel about being deaf through . . . through a hearing person.

SARAH: Does that make you angry?

JAMES: Yes, that makes me angry!

SARAH: And hurt?

JAMES: And hurt . . . ? Let me see the speech, Okay? Show me. *(He translates as if he were her.)*

SARAH & JAMES: My name is Sarah Norman Leeds, a name I wrote with my fingers faster than you can say it with your mouth. So I will not be keeping you any longer than I would if I were speaking or if, as always is the way, somebody else were speaking for me. *(He finishes some distance behind her.)*

JAMES: Good. That's very good.

SARAH & JAMES: For all my life I have been the creation of other people. The first thing I was ever able to understand was that everyone was supposed to hear but I couldn't and that was bad. Then they told me everyone was supposed to be smart but I was dumb. Then they said, oh no, I wasn't permanently dumb, only temporarily, but to be smart I had to become an imitation of the people who had from birth everything a person has to have to be good: ears that hear, mouth that speaks, eyes that read, brain that understands. Well, my brain understands a lot, and my eyes are my ears; and my hands are my voice; and my language, my speech, my ability to communicate is as great as yours. Greater, maybe, because I can communicate to you in one image an idea more complex than you can speak to each other in fifty words. For example, the sign "to connect," a simple sign — but it means so much more when it is moved between us like this. Now it means to be joined in a shared relationship, to be individual yet as one. A whole concept just like that. Well, I want to be joined to other people, but for all my life people have spoken for me. *She* says; *she* means; *she* wants. As if there were no I. As if there were no one in here who *could* understand. Until you let me be an individual, an *I*, just as you are, you will never truly be able to come inside my silence and know me. And until you can do that, I will never let myself know you. Until that time, we cannot be joined. We cannot share a relationship. *(Silence.)*

JAMES: Well, you . . . That's all very . . . that's moving — it is but . . .

SARAH: But you're pitying me.

JAMES: But I'm pitying you? Is that it? Is that it? That I'm pitying you? Maybe it is. You . . . You certainly unloaded a few of your favorite . . . You think they're really . . . that *we're* really going to — we insensitive and inarticulate hearing people — that we're really going to be able to — that one out of a million is going to care enough to even try to come inside your silence, to bend to your . . . Look, Sarah, I went to see Franklin today. I tried to get him to make a settlement with Orin — Excuse me, I should say Orin and you now, shouldn't I? I tried to save you the frustration of going before that group of hearing men who spend their lives listening to minorities vent their anger against the majority — and you know what he said?

SARAH: You tried to get him to make a settlement?

JAMES: I tried . . . Exactly right! I want to save you —

SARAH: After telling Klein to let us speak for ourselves, you went to Franklin to —

JAMES: After telling Klein to let you speak for yourselves — Hey, just a second, you're my wife — it's not like —

SARAH: Not like what? Didn't you listen to anything I just said?

JAMES: Yes I did. Yes I did, I heard every word you just said and I'm going to tell you something you're not gonna like.

SARAH: Give it to me!

JAMES: I think your real bitch — yours and Orin's — is that you are deaf and you wish you could hear.

SARAH: You didn't hear a word I said.

JAMES: I just said I heard every goddamn word you said. I also just said I think you're lying. I don't think you think being deaf is so goddamn wonderful.

SARAH: Because of people like you.

JAMES: No! Not because of people like me! Franklin, the administrators in ninety percent of the schools in the country, would never hire you. You're dreaming a dream that can't come true.

SARAH: Then I won't be a teacher.

JAMES: Then you won't be a teacher. Okay, what will you be?

SARAH: I'll go in the street with the little manual alphabet cards and beg for money.

JAMES: You'll go in the street with the little manual alphabet cards and beg for money. That's perfect!

SARAH: Or I'll be your maid.

JAMES: Or you'll be my maid. Right. And we'll have deaf children.

SARAH: Right!

JAMES: Who's going to educate them? You?

SARAH: Better me than you.

JAMES: Yeah? You think I'm going to let you change my children into people like you who so cleverly see vanity and cowardice as pride? You're going nowhere, you're achieving nothing, you're changing nothing until you change.

SARAH: Until I speak!

JAMES: Until you speak — Okay, you wanna play that one — fine with me. Goddamn right! You want to be independent of me, you want to be a person in your own right, you want people not to pity you, but you want them to understand you in the very poetic way you describe in your speech as well as the plain old, boring way *normal* people understand each other, then you learn to read my lips and you learn to use that little mouth of yours for something besides eating and showing me you're better than hearing girls in bed! Come on! Read my lips! What am I saying? Say what I'm saying! What. Am. I. Saying? *(Sarah starts to sign something. He pins her arms. The rest of this is unsigned.)* Shut up! You want to talk to me, then *you* learn *my* language! Did you get that? Of course you did. You've probably been reading lips perfectly for years; but it's a great control game, isn't it? You can cook, but you can't speak. You can drive and shop and play bridge but you can't speak. You can even make a speech but you still can't do it alone. You always have to be dependent on someone, and you always will for the rest of your life until you learn to speak. Now come on! I want you to speak to me. Let me hear it. Speak! Speak! Speak! *(She erupts like a volcano in speech. She doesn't sign.)*

SARAH: Speech! Speech! Is that it? No. You want me to be your child! You want me to be like you. How do you like my voice? Am I beautiful? Am I what you want me to be? *What about me? What I want? What I want! (She can't be sure how this sounds except by his reaction to it. It is clearly sentences, the sense of it intelligible, but it is not a positive demonstration of speech — only of passion. Only a few words are even barely understandable. She sees this in his face, knows for sure now that she does speak as badly as she has supposed she does. Silence. Close by each other. James reaches to touch her. She bolts away. They're in the same positions they were at the beginning of the play.)* Me have nothing. Me deafy. Speech inept. Intelligence — tiny blockhead. English — blow away. Left one you. Depend — no. Think myself enough. Join. Unjoined. *(She goes, but does not leave the stage. James puts his mufflers on, is alone in some silence inside there.)*

ORIN: *(Entering.)* Where's Sarah, Jim? It's time to go.

KLEIN: *(Entering.)* Mr. Leeds, the commission is waiting. Can we move along?

ORIN: You're not going to keep her from going, Jim.

KLEIN: Mr. Leeds, are you listening?

ORIN: Jim!

MRS. NORMAN: *(Entering.)* Hello, Sarah. Are you all right? How did you get here?

KLEIN: We'll have to go.

SARAH: I'm alone.

ORIN: You haven't heard the last of this, Jim. You hear me? *(They both exit.)*

MRS. NORMAN: Are you alone?

SARAH: Yes.

MRS. NORMAN: Do you want to talk?

SARAH: No. *(Sarah and her mother embrace.)*

LYDIA: *(Entering.)* Hello, Mr. Leeds. Here I am. *(A beat.)* Are you okay? Where's Sarah? Mr. Leeds, everybody says Sarah went away. But she didn't, did she? She's really here, isn't she? Hiding, huh? Like over there? Nope. Maybe over here. Nope. I wonder where she is, Jim. *(She lets "Jim" hang out there a moment. When she isn't struck by lightning:)* Jimmy. *(A beat. She touches him.)* You need a girl that doesn't go away. You need a girl that talks. *(He takes her hands, pins them together with one hand, puts his other over her mouth.)* Someone who loves — *(He presses harder.)* I — *(He presses. She's silent. They look at each other.)*

MRS. NORMAN: Hello, James.

KLEIN: *(Entering.)* We won, Mr. Leeds.

FRANKLIN: *(Entering.)* Won? Won what?

ORIN: *(Entering.)* We didn't need you and we didn't need Sarah.

FRANKLIN: Don't you understand? You've won nothing.

KLEIN: *(To James.)* Maybe I could buy you lunch someday. Perhaps if we tried talking to each other like two civilized human beings . . . *(James puts his mufflers on Klein's head and turns to Mrs. Norman.)*

JAMES: She's actually here, isn't she, Mrs. Norman? May I see her, please?

MRS. NORMAN: What if she doesn't want to see you?

JAMES: She'll have to tell me. *(To Sarah.)* Hello.

736

MRS. NORMAN: *(To Sarah.)* Would you like me to leave you alone?

JAMES: What do you think I'm going to do if you won't talk to me — exit peaceably, leaving you one of my famous notes: "Now that I actually understand *something,* I quit. James Leeds."

SARAH: *(To her mother.)* Please. *(Mrs. Norman goes, as do the others.)*

JAMES: What I did to you last night was . . . I need help. Help me.

SARAH: How can I help you?

JAMES: Teach me.

SARAH: You're the teacher.

JAMES: Yes, I'm a terrific teacher: Grow, Sarah, but not too much. Understand yourself, but not better than I understand you. Be brave, but not so brave you don't need me any more. Your silence frightens me. When I'm in that silence, I hear nothing, I feel like nothing. I can never pull you into my world of sound any more than you can open some magic door and bring me into your silence. I can say that now.

SARAH: And I can say I hurt and know I won't shrivel up and blow away.

JAMES: And you can say you hurt and you know you won't . . . *(A beat.)* Come home with me.

SARAH: No.

JAMES: Why?

SARAH: I'm afraid I would just go on trying to change you. We would have to meet in another place; not in silence or in sound but somewhere else. I don't know where that is now. I have to go it alone.

JAMES: You're afraid you would just go on trying to change me. We would have to meet in another place; not in silence or in sound but somewhere else. You don't know where that is now. You have to go it alone. *(A beat.)* But you will think about trying again with me? *(A beat.)*

SARAH: Yes. Because no matter who I am, someone inside me loves you very much.

JAMES: Yes, because no matter who you are, someone inside you . . . Well, damn it, I love you too.

SARAH: Something else.

JAMES: Something else — what?

SARAH: I don't want deaf children.

JAMES: You don't want deaf children. I'm sorry if I —

SARAH: No. I just don't have the right to demand that anyone be created in my image.

JAMES: You just don't have the right to demand that anyone be created in you image. [Me too.] *(They come together, embrace. She breaks, runs off. James alone. Signing and speaking:)* I think . . . I dream . . . And in my dream, I see her coming back to me with one last note — this one, though, not one I've written her, summoning her before me, but one she has written me. *(Sarah returns behind James.)* It is written in space with her two hands. It says:

JAMES & SARAH: *(James speaks only.)* I'll help you if you'll help me.

SARAH: Join. *(The two of them alone, James turning to her in the fading light.)*

THEATRE FOR THE 21ST CENTURY

The Future of Theatre

Where is theatre headed, and what does its future hold? A book which begins with a play about the human inability to see into the future might be excused from addressing this question, but curiosity insists on making some guesses.

In the first place, chances are that realism will continue to dominate the art. Ever since its rebirth in the Middle Ages, theatre has tended to become continually more realistic. Furthermore, in the past fifty years, realism has shown a remarkable ability to adapt to new situations by absorbing various nonrealistic elements. This flexibility makes late-twentieth-century realism less likely to stimulate the kind of rejection aroused by its more doctrinaire version a century earlier.

At the same time, theatre artists are certain to continue experimenting with new dramatic structures, new production techniques, new audience-performer relationships, and new combinations of theatre with other arts. An art form which stops experimenting is doomed to die out — or may already be dead. Some of the impetus for experimentation will probably come from the electronic media and Asia.

The Electronic Media

Film, television, and video will continue their impact on live plays. Theatre artists will be able to count on audience members who, because they have viewed many movies, television shows, and music videos, have short attention spans, a sophisticated facility at following fragmentary story lines, and the ability to absorb and respond to non-logic-based performance.

And as Japan's role in world economics and politics continues to increase, Japanese culture will likely exert increasing influence on Western art, including theatre. This influence may lead to more stylization and emphasize the mythic, ritualistic elements in Western theatre.

Finally, with the electronic and cinematic media providing easily accessible entertainment and escapism for a mass audience, theatre may be free to do in the future what it has done so well in the great moments of its past — challenge its audience intellectually and spiritually. Václav Havel, the dissident Czech playwright who became the president of his newly free country, expressed this potential for theatre.

> "My ambition is not to soothe the viewer with a merciful lie
> or cheer him up with a false offer to sort things out for him. I
> wouldn't be helping him very much if I did. I'm trying to do
> something else: to propel him, in the most drastic possible way,

into the depths of a question he should not, and cannot, avoid asking; to stick his nose into his own misery, into my misery, into our common misery, by way of reminding him that the time has come to do something about it.[1]

The following plays — Václav Havel's *Largo Desolato* and the Omaha Magic Theatre's *Body Leaks* — demonstrate some of the directions theatre is likely to take in the future.

Václav Havel

Born into a prominent middle-class family in 1936, Václav Havel grew up reading the works of Czech intellectuals and literary figures. Then, when Czechoslovakia became a Soviet satellite in 1948, his family was dispossessed. After finishing elementary school in the early 1950s, Havel worked for five years as a laboratory assistant. He applied repeatedly to study humanities at the university, but the limited number of spaces in the programs went to students from Communist backgrounds. During these years he attended night school, wrote poetry, and began to associate with intellectual groups whose activities put them on the borderline of political suspicion. From 1957 to 1958, he served in the Czech army, and while in the military he collaborated with another soldier in writing his first play, a satire about army life.

After his discharge, Havel secured a job as stagehand at the ABC Theatre, one of Prague's established companies, and after a year there, he was hired by one of the small, new experimental companies, the Theatre on the Balustrade. He remained at this theatre for the next eight years and worked at jobs ranging from stagehand to dramaturg. The Theatre on the Balustrade produced his early plays, including *The Garden Party* (1963), *The Memorandum* (1965), and *The Increased Difficulty of Concentration* (1968).

An increasing atmosphere of openness, democracy, and experimentation in Czechoslovakia led to the "Prague spring" of 1968, which ended with a brutal invasion by Warsaw Pact forces and subsequent Soviet ococupation that lasted into the 1970s. With his works banned after 1968, Havel retreated into the country, wrote, and maintained association with dissident intellectuals.

In 1977, he participated with many other Czech intellectuals in founding Charter 77, an independent human rights agency. His position as one of the three spokesmen for Charter 77 made him particularly visible and led to his arrest in 1977, and again in 1978. In 1979, he was sentenced to a four-and-a-half-year prison term. He served most of his sentence before his health broke and an international outcry resulted in his release.

After regaining his freedom, Havel wrote *Largo Desolato* (1984) — a script he completed in four days — and *Temptation* (1985). In 1989 he participated in the removal of Czechoslovakia's Communist regime, and in December of that year, he was elected president of his country.

[1]*Disturbing the Peace: A Conversation with Karel Hvízdala,* Paul Wilson, tr. (New York: Alfred A. Knopf, Inc., 1990), p. 199. Used by permission.

Believing that "a writer is the conscience of his nation,"[2] Havel focused his plays on the effects of a repressive bureaucracy. The Theatre on the Balustrade produced many absurdist plays during the 1960s, and Havel combined absurdist techniques with his own comic vision in his satirical plays.

Largo Desolato

Dramaturgy

This play draws together many strands of twentieth-century drama. It has obvious affinities to absurdism with its duplication of characters and business, its banal conversations, and its repetitive, circular plot devices. In contrast with absurdism, however, it also deals with an understandable, real-life situation and shows its hero beset by familiar pressure in both his private and his public life. Similar to expressionistic plays, *Largo Desolato* has an ineffectual, nonvolitional antihero and an obvious didactic impact. And clearly set in a paranoiac, suppressive society, the play is an expression of political theatre.

With comic actions, melodramatic villains, heroes and heroines, and a tragic denouement, *Largo Desolato* also mingles the traditional forms in characteristic contemporary fashion.

Translator

An important British playwright, Tom Stoppard was born in Czechoslovakia in 1937. His plays were much admired for their verbal gymnastics and their combinations of absurdist techniques with political and philosophical impact. Stoppard had many similarities to Havel. For instance, his pair of one-acts, *Dogg's Hamlet/Cahoot's Macbeth* created an imaginary language, as did *The Memorandum* by Havel, and *Cahoot's Macbeth* was set in Czechoslovakia. Stoppard was ideally suited by background, world view, and theatrical style to translate this recent play by Václav Havel.

---

[2]*Disturbing the Peace*, p. 72.

LARGO DESOLATO

by VACLAV HAVEL
English version by TOM STOPPARD

The play's action takes place in the mid-1980s in an eastern European capital city.

CHARACTERS

PROFESSOR LEOPOLD NETTLES

EDWARD

SUZANA

FIRST SIDNEY

SECOND SIDNEY

LUCY

BERTRAM

FIRST CHAP

SECOND CHAP

FIRST MAN

SECOND MAN

MARGUERITE

The whole play takes place in Leopold's and Suzana's living room. It is a spacious room and all the other rooms in the flat lead off it. On the left there is the front door of the flat. The door has a peep-hole. In the back wall, on the left, there is a glass-panelled door leading to a balcony. In the middle of the wall there is a glass-panelled door leading to the kitchen. To the right of that there is a small staircase leading to the door of Suzana's room. On the right hand side, opposite the front door, there is a door leading to the bathroom, and a further door leading to Leopold's room. Between the doors the walls are covered with bookcases and bookshelves. There is a hat-stand near the front door. In the right hand half of the room there is a sofa with a low table in front of it, and a few chairs. On the table there is a large bottle of rum and a glass which Leopold keeps filling up throughout the play and from which he keeps sipping. This is an old and solidly bourgeois apartment but the furnishings indicate that the occupant is an intellectual. Impressive orchestral music is heard at the beginning and the end of the play and also during the intervals between the scenes.

SCENE ONE

As the music dies away the curtain rises slowly.

LEOPOLD is alone on the stage. He is sitting on the sofa and staring at the front door. After a long pause he gets up and looks through the peep-hole. Then he puts his ear to the door and listens intently. After another long pause the curtain drops suddenly and at the same time the music returns.

SCENE TWO

As the music dies away the curtain rises slowly.

LEOPOLD is alone on the stage. He is sitting on the sofa and staring at the front door. After a long pause he gets up and looks through the peep-hole. Then he puts his ear to the door and listens intently. After another long pause the curtain drops suddenly and at the same time the music returns.

SCENE THREE

As the music dies down the curtain rises slowly.

LEOPOLD is alone on the stage. He is sitting on the sofa and staring at the front door. After a long pause he gets up, goes to the door and looks through the peep-hole and then he puts his ear to the door and listens intently. He evidently hears something which makes him jump back. At the same moment the doorbell rings. LEOPOLD hesitates for a moment and then cautiously approaches the door and looks through the peep-hole. That calms him and he opens the door. EDWARD enters.

LEOPOLD: At last!
EDWARD: Has anything happened?
LEOPOLD: No —*
EDWARD: Were you worried?
LEOPOLD: I feel better when there's someone here. Come in — *(EDWARD comes forward. LEOPOLD closes the door behind him.)*
What's it like outside?
EDWARD: Stifling —
LEOPOLD: Lots of people?
EDWARD: No more than usual —
(EDWARD goes to the door leading to the balcony.)
EDWARD: Do you mind if I open it a bit?
LEOPOLD: Go ahead —
(EDWARD opens the balcony door wide.)
What will you have?
EDWARD: Thanks, nothing for the moment —
(LEOPOLD sits down on the sofa. EDWARD takes a chair. A short pause.)
How did you sleep?
LEOPOLD: Essentially well. I would put it at six hours net. I woke up twice but only because I needed to pee —

---

*Translator's footnote: the use of dashes rather than full stops at the end of speeches is Havel's punctuation.

EDWARD: No diarrhoea?
LEOPOLD: On the contrary —
EDWARD: How about dreams?
LEOPOLD: Nothing memorable, evidently. *(Pause.)* Do you mind if I close it now?
EDWARD: Leave it open for a while. *(Pause.)* So you're all right?
LEOPOLD: At first glance I would seem to have no reason to complain today. But in all honesty I couldn't assert that I'm feeling up to the mark —
EDWARD: Nervous?
LEOPOLD: Well, I'm always nervous —
EDWARD: And the shakes you had yesterday? All gone?
LEOPOLD: I'm afraid not. In fact they're worse. It's almost as though I'd caught a chill. *(He pauses suddenly.)* Is that somebody coming? *(They both listen quietly.)*
EDWARD: Nothing. Everything's okay —
LEOPOLD: And on top of that I've got complications — a touch of vertigo, suggestion of an upset stomach, tingling in the joints, loss of appetite, and even the possbility of constipation —
EDWARD: You mean you didn't go this morning?
LEOPOLD: No —
EDWARD: Are you sure it isn't just a hangover?
LEOPOLD: My condition has some similarities to a hangover but it's not a hangover, in as much as I hardly touched a drop yesterday —
EDWARD: Well, perhaps there's something wrong with you.
LEOPOLD: No, I'm afraid not —
EDWARD: Well, that's something to be grateful for, isn't it?
LEOPOLD: Is it? I'd rather be ill than well like this. If only I could be sure they won't come today —
EDWARD: They can't be coming now —
LEOPOLD: Do you think so? Surely they can come any time —
(At that moment a key rattles in the lock. LEOPOLD is startled. SUZANA comes in through the front door carrying a full shopping bag.)
SUZANA: Hello —
(LEOPOLD and EDWARD get up.)
LEOPOLD: Hello — let me —
(LEOPOLD takes the bag from SUZANA and carries it into the kitchen.)
SUZANA: How is he?
EDWARD: The same —
(LEOPOLD returns from the kitchen.)
LEOPOLD: Did you get any meat?
SUZANA: Liver —
LEOPOLD: You didn't!
(SUZANA is going up the stairs to her room. LEOPOLD approaches her.)
Suzy —
(She stops halfway up the stairs and turns towards him.)
SUZANA: Yes?
LEOPOLD: I was up by about eight today — I felt like doing something — I

745

was thinking of making a few notes — I had a piece of paper all ready but nothing came — I wasn't feeling up to scratch again. Those shakes I had yesterday came back — so I did a bit of tidying up, wiped out the sink, took out the rubbish, dried my towel, cleaned my comb, made myself two soft boiled eggs for lunch —

SUZANA: What did you eat them with?

LEOPOLD: Well, with a teaspoon of course —

SUZANA: A silver one?

LEOPOLD: I don't know, it might have been —

SUZANA: How many times have I told you not to use the silver teaspoons for eggs — you can't get them clean properly —

LEOPOLD: Oh yes, I'm sorry, I forgot. After lunch I tried to read a bit and then Edward here turned up . . .

SUZANA: In other words, not a lot —

(She goes up another step or two.)

LEOPOLD: Suzana —

(She stops and turns towards him.)

As you've managed to get some liver why don't we have a special supper. I'll make mustard sauce, open a bottle of decent wine — we'll ask Lucy as well, and I'm sure Edward would join us. I think it would be good for me to let my hair down, take my mind off things, reminisce a little . . .

SUZANA: I'm sorry, Leopold, but I've got tickets for the cinema —

LEOPOLD: How about after the cinema?

SUZANA: That's too late for me — you know I've got to be up early —

(SUZANA goes into her room. LEOPOLD stands for a moment looking after her awkwardly, then returns slowly to his place, and sits down. Another pause.)

LEOPOLD: Edward —

EDWARD: Yes?

LEOPOLD: Will you think of me?

EDWARD: When?

LEOPOLD: Well, when I'm there —

EDWARD: You mustn't keep thinking about that all the time!

LEOPOLD: I don't keep thinking about it all the time. It just came into my head. I'm sorry —

EDWARD: Why don't you go for a walk once in a while?

LEOPOLD: Are you mad? Go out?

EDWARD: Why not?

LEOPOLD: And be a nervous wreck the whole time, not knowing what's going on back here?

EDWARD: Nothing's going on back here —

LEOPOLD: I know, but how am I going to know that if I'm gadding about somewhere else? What if they came just then?

EDWARD: They'd find you weren't at home. So what?

LEOPOLD: I couldn't possibly —

(At that moment the doorbell rings. LEOPOLD jumps up in confusion. EDWARD gets up as well. LEOPOLD goes to the peep-hole and looks through it and then turns towards EDWARD.)

LEOPOLD: *(Whispering)* What did I tell you!

746

EDWARD: *(Whispering)* Is it them?
(LEOPOLD nods. They pause, at a loss. The bell rings again.)
LEOPOLD: *(Whispering)* Should I open the door?
EDWARD: *(Whispering)* Yes, you have to —
(LEOPOLD hesitates a moment, then breathes in, goes to the door and opens it decisively. The newcomers are FIRST SIDNEY and SECOND SIDNEY.)
FIRST SIDNEY: Good afternoon, sir —
LEOPOLD: Good afternoon —
SECOND SIDNEY: Can we come in?
LEOPOLD: Do . . .
(FIRST SIDNEY and SECOND SIDNEY come forward a few paces. LEOPOLD closes the door behind them. They all remain standing and looking at each other somewhat at a loss.)
FIRST SIDNEY: You don't remember us?
LEOPOLD: I can't place you at the moment —
FIRST SIDNEY: We called on you once before, two years ago. You've obviously forgotten. I'm Sidney and he's also Sidney —
LEOPOLD: How do you do —
SECOND SIDNEY: We won't hold you up long —
LEOPOLD: *(Perplexed)* Well, do sit down —
(They all sit down, LEOPOLD on the sofa, the others on the chairs.)
FIRST SIDNEY: Is it all right to smoke?
LEOPOLD: Yes — certainly —
FIRST SIDNEY: Actually, I don't smoke myself; I was asking for Sidney here, he smokes like a chimney —
(SECOND SIDNEY is going through his pockets but can't find any cigarettes. LEOPOLD offers him one. SECOND SIDNEY takes one and lights it. There is an awkward pause.)
Do you need any paper?
LEOPOLD: Do you mean for writing on?
SECOND SIDNEY: If you need any we can get you some —
LEOPOLD: Really?
FIRST SIDNEY: Seeing as we work in a paper mill —
LEOPOLD: You do?
SECOND SIDNEY: So no problem —
(Pause. SUZANA comes out of her room and down the stairs.)
LEOPOLD: Suzana, these gentlemen are from the paper mill. It seems they've been here before —
SUZANA: Good afternoon —
FIRST SIDNEY: Good afternoon —
(SUZANA beckons to EDWARD who gets up and goes with her to the kitchen. During the following scene both of them can be seen through the glass-panelled door taking out various foodstuffs from the shopping bag, putting them where they belong and, during all this time, either discussing something in a lively way or perhaps quarrelling. Pause.)
Oh, by the way, we've got a lot of interesting stuff from the mill — minutes of meetings and so on — I'm sure you'd find it interesting —
LEOPOLD: I'm sure I would —
SECOND SIDNEY: We'll bring it to you —

(Pause.)
FIRST SIDNEY: We know everything —
LEOPOLD: Every what thing?
FIRST SIDNEY: About you —
LEOPOLD: I see —
SECOND SIDNEY: What Sidney is trying to say is, we're your fans. Not just us either —
LEOPOLD: Thank you —
FIRST SIDNEY: There's lots of people looking to you —
LEOPOLD: Thank you —
SECOND SIDNEY: We all believe that it will all turn out right for you in the end —
LEOPOLD: Well, I'm not sure —
SECOND SIDNEY: The main thing is that you mustn't weaken — we need you and we believe in you — you being the man you are —
LEOPOLD: Thank you —
(Pause.)
FIRST SIDNEY: We're not holding you up, are we?
LEOPOLD: No —
FIRST SIDNEY: Are you sure? Because if we are, you only have to say so and we'll push off —
LEOPOLD: You're not holding me up —
(Pause.)
FIRST SIDNEY: You know, I'm just an ordinary sort of bloke, a nobody, but I can spot a few things and I've got my own opinion and nobody can deny me that. And what I think is, there's a lot that could be done — certainly more than is being done at the moment —
LEOPOLD: This is it —
SECOND SIDNEY: Speaking for myself and Sidney here, we reckon — and this is partly why we're here — to our way of thinking not all the possibilities have been exhausted — I would venture to say that the most promising possibilities are still ahead of us. One has to take hold of the situation by the scruff of the neck —
LEOPOLD: What possibilities in particular did you have in mind?
FIRST SIDNEY: Well, that would require some discussion, of course —
LEOPOLD: Well, at least tell me what direction we ought to be taking.
FIRST SIDNEY: Different directions all at the same time. Surely no one knows that better than you! In short, it seems to us that it's time to take the initiative — something that would make them sit up.
LEOPOLD: I'm not sure that present circumstances differ significantly from the circumstances that have prevailed up to now, but even so I'm not *a priori* against an initiative —
FIRST SIDNEY: I'm glad we agree — who else but you could get things going again?
LEOPOLD: Well as for *me* —
SECOND SIDNEY: We realize that things are probably not easy for you at the moment. But the respect in which you're held puts you under an obligation —
LEOPOLD: I know —
FIRST SIDNEY: You'll know what's best to do, after all you're a philoso-

pher and I'm an ordinary bloke, a nobody. It goes without saying we're not forcing you — we haven't got the right, and furthermore you can't be expected to do it for everybody, all on your own, but, that said, what we think is, don't get me wrong, I'll let you have it straight, — that said, we are of the opinion that you could be doing more than you are in your place —

LEOPOLD: I'll think it over —

FIRST SIDNEY: We're only saying this because we're your fans — and not just us —

LEOPOLD: Thank you —

SECOND SIDNEY: A lot of people are looking to you —

LEOPOLD: Thank you —

FIRST SIDNEY: The main thing is that you mustn't weaken — we believe in you and we need you —

LEOPOLD: Thank you —
(Pause.)

SECOND SIDNEY: We're not holding you up, are we?

LEOPOLD: No —

SECOND SIDNEY: Are you sure? Because if we are you only have to say so and we'll push off —

LEOPOLD: You're not holding me up —
(Pause.)

SECOND SIDNEY: One could certainly do more — you just have to get hold of the situation by the scruff of the neck — and who else but you is there to get things going again?

LEOPOLD: Well, as for *me* —

FIRST SIDNEY: We have faith in you —

SECOND SIDNEY: And we need you —

LEOPOLD: Thank you —

FIRST SIDNEY: We're not holding you up, are we?

LEOPOLD: No —

FIRST SIDNEY: Are you really sure? Because if we are you only have to say so and we'll push off —

LEOPOLD: You are not holding me up. Excuse me —
(LEOPOLD gets up and walks to the balcony door, shuts it and returns to his seat.)

SECOND SIDNEY: The main thing is that you mustn't weaken —

LEOPOLD: *(Suddenly alert)* Just a moment —

FIRST SIDNEY: What's up?

LEOPOLD: I think somebody's coming —

SECOND SIDNEY: I can't hear anything —

FIRST SIDNEY: The respect in which you're held puts you under an obligation —
(At that moment the doorbell rings. That startles LEOPOLD who gets up quickly, goes to the front door and looks through the peep-hole. He calms down and turns towards the TWO SIDNEYS.)

LEOPOLD: A friend of mine —
(LEOPOLD opens the door and LUCY comes in.)

LUCY: Hello, Leo —

LEOPOLD: Come in, Lucy —

(LEOPOLD closes the door and leads LUCY to the table.)
LUCY: I see you've got company —
LEOPOLD: They're friends from the paper mill —
LUCY: Good afternoon —
FIRST SIDNEY: Good afternoon, Miss —
LEOPOLD: Sit down —
(LUCY sits down next to LEOPOLD on the sofa. There is a longer awkward pause.)
Would you like some rum?
LUCY: You know I don't drink rum —
(Pause.)
LEOPOLD: How's life?
LUCY: Depressing —
LEOPOLD: Why's that?
LUCY: Loneliness.
(Pause.)
LEOPOLD: These gentlemen think it's time to take the initiative —
LUCY: They've got something there.
(Awkward pause.)
Did I come at the wrong moment? You are obviously in the middle of discussing something —
LEOPOLD: It's all right —
(Awkward pause.)
Have you had supper?
LUCY: No —
LEOPOLD: We're having liver. Would you like to stay?
LUCY: That would be lovely —
(Another awkward pause. LUCY takes a bottle of pills out of her handbag. She puts the bottle on the table.)
I've brought you some vitamins —
LEOPOLD: You never forget —
(Awkward pause.)
I'm told it's stifling today —
LUCY: Stifling and humid —
(Awkward pause.)
LEOPOLD: Edward opened the balcony door but I closed it again — I don't like draughts —
LUCY: Is Edward here?
LEOPOLD: Yes —
(Awkward pause. LEOPOLD is becoming more and more nervous because both FIRST and SECOND SIDNEY are sitting there and not showing any signs of leaving. Several times he seems on the point of saying something but each time changes his mind. Finally he blurts out —)
LEOPOLD: Well, look how the evening's coming on —
(LUCY bursts out laughing. LEOPOLD presses her hand. Awkward pause. Both SIDNEYS sitting there apparently dumbfounded.)
I've still got a few things to do —
(LUCY bursts out laughing despite herself.)
LUCY: What have you got to do?

(She bursts out again and LEOPOLD kicks her under the table.)
LEOPOLD: *(Stammering)* Things — make some notes — some supper —
*(He relapses into a long stifling silence. Then SUZANA followed by
EDWARD, enters from the kitchen.)*
SUZANA: Lucy!
LUCY: Suzy!
(LUCY gets up at once and goes towards SUZANA and they embrace.)
Darling! How's life?
SUZANA: Never stops!
LUCY: We must have a chat — I've got so much to tell you.
SUZANA: Me too — but some other time, all right? — I'm in a rush.
LUCY: Hey, are you leaving?
SUZANA: I've got tickets for the cinema —
LUCY: What a shame — I was so looking forward to seeing you!
*(FIRST SIDNEY suddenly thumps his knees and stands up. SECOND
SIDNEY gets up as well. LEOPOLD starts getting up.)*
FIRST SIDNEY: Well, we shall look in on you soon —
LEOPOLD: Fine —
SECOND SIDNEY: And we'll bring you that writing paper —
LEOPOLD: Fine —
FIRST SIDNEY: And also the stuff from the paper mill —
LEOPOLD: Fine —
SECOND SIDNEY: The main thing is — keep your chin up!
LEOPOLD: Thank you —
FIRST SIDNEY: When are you expecting them?
LEOPOLD: All the time —
SECOND SIDNEY: We're with you — stick with it! So long —
LEOPOLD: So long —
LUCY: So long —
*(LEOPOLD accompanies the SIDNEYS to the front door and opens
the door for them. They go out. LEOPOLD closes the door behind them,
and, completely spent, leans back against the door.)*
May I ask, who that was?
LEOPOLD: I don't know. They wanted something from me. I'm not sure what.
I'm sure they mean well —
SUZANA: That sort of thing happens all the time round here — but I have
to run. *(To EDWARD)* Let's go! *(To LUCY)* Bye for now —
LUCY: Bye, Suzy —
EDWARD: Bye —
*(SUZANA and EDWARD leave. LUCY and LEOPOLD are left alone.
LUCY smiles at LEOPOLD for a moment, then takes hold of his hands,
pulls him towards her and kisses him.)*
LUCY: Do you love me?
LEOPOLD: Mm.
LUCY: Really?
LEOPOLD: Really —
LUCY: Well why don't you say so sometimes without being asked? You've
never once!
LEOPOLD: As you know, I avoid off-the-peg expressions —
LUCY: The simple truth is, you're ashamed of loving me!

LEOPOLD: Phenomenology has taught me always to beware of the propo-
sitional statement that lies outside demonstrable experience. I prefer
to say less than I feel rather than to risk saying more —
LUCY: You think loving me is not a demonstrable experience?
LEOPOLD: We may mean different things by the word love. Perhaps, though
the difference may be small, the word denotes, for me, something on
a higher plane than for you — Just a minute!
*(LEOPOLD leaves LUCY to approach the front door and looks through
the peep-hole.)*
LUCY: What is it?
LEOPOLD: I thought I heard someone coming —
LUCY: I can't hear anything —
(LEOPOLD comes back from the door and turns towards her.)
LEOPOLD: Forgive me, Lucy, but does our love have to consist solely in this
endless examination of itself?
LUCY: What do you expect when you're so evasive all the time —
LEOPOLD: It's just that like all women you long for security and men look for
something higher —
LUCY: Just my luck to keep picking lovers with a permanent crick in their
neck —
LEOPOLD: Don't be disgusting!
LUCY: What do you mean?
LEOPOLD: Please don't use the word lover! At least don't apply it to me —
LUCY: Why?
LEOPOLD: It's disgusting —
LUCY: Why?
LEOPOLD: It turns man into nothing but an ever-naked prick —
LUCY: *(Laughing)* Oh, who's being disgusting now —
LEOPOLD: Why don't you sit down?
(LUCY sits down on the sofa.)
Can I get you anything?
LUCY: Is there any wine?
LEOPOLD: I'll get some —
*(LEOPOLD goes into the kitchen and after a moment returns with a
bottle of wine, a bottle opener and two glasses. He opens the bottle,
pours wine into both glasses, takes one and LUCY takes the other.)*
Well, cheers!
LUCY: Cheers!
*(They both take a drink. LEOPOLD sits down on the sofa next to her.
Pause.)*
So tell me —
LEOPOLD: What?
LUCY: What did you do today?
LEOPOLD: I don't know —
LUCY: Did you write?
LEOPOLD: I wanted to but it wouldn't come. I wasn't feeling well —
LUCY: Did you have your depression again?
LEOPOLD: That was another thing —
LUCY: You won't get rid of it till you start writing. Everybody's waiting
for your new piece —

LEOPOLD: That's just the trouble —
LUCY: But you had it all worked out —
LEOPOLD: What do you mean?
LUCY: Well, just what you were telling me — that love is actually a dimen-
sion of being — it gives fulfilment and meaning to existence —
LEOPOLD: I couldn't have made it sound like such a cliché —
LUCY: No doubt you put it better —
LEOPOLD: It's funny but when I run out of excuses for putting off writing
and make up my mind to start, I stumble over the first banality —
pencil or pen? — which paper? — and then this thing starts —
LUCY: What thing?
LEOPOLD: The cycle thing —
LUCY: What's that?
LEOPOLD: My thoughts just start going round in a loop —
LUCY: Hm —
LEOPOLD: Look, do we have to talk about me?
LUCY: You love to talk about yourself!
LEOPOLD: That's just what you think —
*(LUCY puts her head on LEOPOLD's shoulder. He embraces her but
they both continue to look straight ahead, absorbed in thought. Pause.)*
LUCY: Leopold —
LEOPOLD: Yes —
LUCY: I can help you break out of that —
LEOPOLD: How?
LUCY: You need love — real love — mad passionate love — not that theo-
retical one, the one you write about —
LEOPOLD: I'm a bit old for that —
LUCY: You're not old, it's just that you've got an emotional block — but I'll
unblock you —
*(LUCY embraces LEOPOLD and begins to kiss his face. LEOPOLD
sits perplexed and remains quite passive. The curtain falls and the
music returns.)*

SCENE FOUR

The music fades and the curtain rises slowly.

*It is late in the evening. It is dark behind the balcony door. BERTRAM
is sitting on the sofa. LEOPOLD, who is standing in the background by the
balcony door, wears a dressing gown with nothing underneath it, and he is
rather dishevelled and seems to be cold.*

BERTRAM: How long is it since you went out?
LEOPOLD: I don't know — ages —
BERTRAM: You don't go out at all then?
LEOPOLD: No —
(Pause.)
BERTRAM: How much do you drink?
LEOPOLD: The same as everyone else —
BERTRAM: Starting in the morning?
LEOPOLD: As the case may be —
(Pause.)

BERTRAM: How do you sleep?
LEOPOLD: It varies —
BERTRAM: Do you ever dream about them? Or dream that you're already
 there?
LEOPOLD: Sometimes —
 (Pause.)
BERTRAM: Leopold —
LEOPOLD: Yes?
BERTRAM: You don't doubt, do you, that we all like you —
LEOPOLD: I know —
LUCY: *(Off stage)* Leopold —
LEOPOLD: *(Calls out)* Just a minute —
 (Pause. LEOPOLD is trembling with cold and rubbing his arms. BER-
 TRAM looks through the medicines lying on the table.)
BERTRAM: Vitamins?
LEOPOLD: Yes —
BERTRAM: Apart from vitamins are you on anything else?
LEOPOLD: Not really — why do you ask?
BERTRAM: There's some talk —
LEOPOLD: What sort of talk?
BERTRAM: Forget it —
 (Pause.)
BERTRAM: Quite a few people complain that you never answer letters —
LEOPOLD: I was never much of a letter writer —
BERTRAM: Well, there's no law about it . . . still, it's a pity that it lends
 support to the rumours —
LEOPOLD: What rumours?
BERTRAM: That you're no longer reliable, so —
LEOPOLD: I reply to anything important — perhaps something got lost in
 the post somewhere —
 (Pause.)
BERTRAM: What did you think of that collection?
LEOPOLD: What collection?
BERTRAM: The stuff I lent you the other day —
LEOPOLD: Ah yes —
BERTRAM: Have you read it?
LEOPOLD: To tell you the truth —
BERTRAM: It's essential reading —
LEOPOLD: I know — That's exactly why I couldn't just glance through it —
 There's a mood for everything — I can't just read anything any time —
 (Pause.)
BERTRAM: Leopold —
LEOPOLD: Yes?
BERTRAM: You don't doubt, do you, that we all like you?
LEOPOLD: I know —
LUCY: *(Off stage)* Leopold —
LEOPOLD: *(Calls out)* Just a minute —
 (Pause. LEOPOLD is trembling with cold and rubbing his arms.)
BERTRAM: Leopold —
LEOPOLD: Yes?

BERTRAM: It goes without saying it's your own business —
LEOPOLD: What is?
BERTRAM: You don't have to account to me —
LEOPOLD: What?
BERTRAM: I'm asking as a friend —
LEOPOLD: I know —
BERTRAM: Is it true that you're seeing Lucy?
LEOPOLD: It's not that simple —
BERTRAM: And how are things between you and Suzana?
LEOPOLD: We get along —
   (Pause.)
BERTRAM: Leopold —
LEOPOLD: Yes?
BERTRAM: You don't doubt, do you, that we all like you?
LEOPOLD: I know —
   (Pause.)
LUCY: *(Off stage)* Leopold —
LEOPOLD: *(Calls out)* Just a minute —
   (Pause. LEOPOLD is trembling with cold and is rubbing his arms.)
BERTRAM: It's terrible of course to live with this nerve-racking uncertainty — we all understand that. None of us knows how we'd stand it ourselves. That's why so many people are concerned about you. You have to understand that —
LEOPOLD: I do understand —
BERTRAM: I'm not just speaking for myself — I'm really here on behalf of everyone —
LEOPOLD: Who's everyone?
BERTRAM: Your friends —
LEOPOLD: Are you an emissary?
BERTRAM: If you want to call it that —
LEOPOLD: And what are you concerned about, specifically?
BERTRAM: How shall I put it? I don't want to be hard on you or hurt you in any way but on the other hand I wouldn't be acting as your friend if I were to be less than frank —
LEOPOLD: And what are you concerned about, specifically?
BERTRAM: How should I put it? It's not simply a general issue, it's mostly about you personally —
LEOPOLD: And what are you concerned about, specifically?
BERTRAM: How should I put it? Simply, there's growing circumstantial evidence giving rise to certain speculations —
LEOPOLD: What circumstantial evidence? What speculations?
BERTRAM: Your friends — and I won't deny I include myself — we've all — for some time — and let's hope our fears are groundless — we've all — for some time — begun to question whether you might not crack under the strain — whether you'll be able to meet all the claims which, thanks to all you've done already — the claims which are made on you — that you'll be able to fulfil the expectations which — forgive me — are rightly expected of you — if you'll be, in short, up to your mission, which is to do justice to those great obligations, to the truth, the world, to everyone for whom you set an example — set by your own

work — forgive me — but quite simply we are beginning to be slightly afraid that you might let us down and in so doing bring upon yourself — forgive me — it would be bound to be so, given your sensitivity — bring upon yourself endless agony —
(Short pause.)
You're not angry, are you, that I'm speaking so openly?
LEOPOLD: No — on the contrary —
(Pause.)
LUCY: *(Off stage)* Leopold —
LEOPOLD: *(Calls out)* Just a minute —
(Pause. LEOPOLD is trembling with cold and is rubbing his arms.)
BERTRAM: It's terrible, of course, to live with this nerve-racking uncertainty. We all understand that. None of us knows how we'd stand it ourselves. That's why so many people are concerned about you. You have to understand that —
LEOPOLD: I do understand —
BERTRAM: The more they count on you the harder it would be for them if you failed to hold out in some way —
LEOPOLD: People are calling on me all the time — not long ago a couple of lads from the paper mill showed up — typical workers — ordinary people —
BERTRAM: That's certainly excellent, but, how should I put it?
LEOPOLD: What?
BERTRAM: How should I put it?
LEOPOLD: How should you put what?
BERTRAM: The question is whether a visit from a couple of paper-mill workers — excellent though it is in itself — is simply — or might become simply — forgive me — a kind of inaction in action — a leftover from a world which is no longer the case — whether you might not be playing the role in a mechanical, superficial way to reassure yourself that you are still the person to whom that role properly belonged. What is at stake here is that a gap should not open up between you and your role in society, so that your role, which was a true reflection of your personality, becomes a crutch to prop you up — circumstantial evidence of a supposed continuity of personality — but spurious, illusory, self-deceiving — by means of which you try to assure the world and yourself that you are still the person who you in fact no longer are — in short, that your role which grew naturally out of your attitudes and your work should not become a mere substitute, and that you don't attach to that role, which has long since kept going autonomously, on its own momentum, don't attach to it the sole and lasting proof of your moral existence, and thus let your entire human identity hang on a visit from a couple of know-nothing workers from the paper mill —
(Short pause.)
You're not angry, are you, that I'm speaking so openly?
LEOPOLD: No — on the contrary —
(Pause.)
LUCY: *(Off-stage)* Leopold —
LEOPOLD: *(Calls out)* Just a minute —

(Pause. LEOPOLD is trembling with cold and rubbing his arms.)
BERTRAM: It's terrible of course to live with this nerve-racking uncertainty. We all understand that. None of us knows how we'd be able to stand it ourselves. That's why so many people are concerned about you. You have to understand that —
LEOPOLD: I do understand —
BERTRAM: You must believe me, too, that all I wish for is that we're worrying about nothing —
LEOPOLD: I do believe you —
BERTRAM: And even if this danger, which we your friends worry about, is infinitesimal, I have a duty — to you, to myself, to all of us — to confess those worries to you —
LEOPOLD: I understand —
BERTRAM: By all the things you did and have been doing up to now, you've earned our respect and our love, and in so doing you have suffered a great deal. Obviously you are not a superman, and the oppressive atmosphere in which you have had to live is bound to have left its mark. But all that said, I can't escape the awful feeling that lately something inside you has begun to collapse — as if an axis that has held you together has given way, as if the ground is collapsing under your feet — as if you've gone lame inside — that you are tending more and more to act the part of yourself instead of being yourself. Your personal life, that vital plank, is — don't be angry — in a mess, you're lacking a fixed point out of which everything inside you would grow and develop — you're losing the strength and perhaps even the will to put your affairs in order — you're erratic — you're letting yourself be tossed about by chance currents, you're sinking deeper and deeper into a void and you can't get a grip on things — you're just waiting for what is going to happen and so you're no longer the self-aware subject of your life, you're turning into its passive object — you're obviously at the mercy of great demons but they do not drive you in any direction, they merely drive about inside you — your existence seems to have become a cumbersome burden to you and you have really settled for listening helplessly to the passing of time. What happened to your perspective on things? To your humour? Your industry and persistence? The pointedness of your observations? Your irony and self-irony? Your capacity for enthusiasm, for emotional involvement, for commitment, even for sacrifice?! I fear for you, Leopold — I fear for us! We need you! You have no idea how we need you, we need you the way you used to be! So I am asking you to swear that you won't give up — Don't weaken! Keep at it! Get a grip on yourself! Pull yourself together! Straighten up! Leopold —
LEOPOLD: Yes?
BERTRAM: You don't doubt, do you, that we all like you?
LEOPOLD: I know —
BERTRAM: So I beg you — be again that brilliant Leopold Nettles whom everybody held on high!
(From LEOPOLD's room LUCY emerges quietly, dressed only in a candlewick bedspread, naked underneath it.)
LUCY: Bertram —

(BERTRAM is rather startled. He gets up quickly and looks at LUCY in astonishment.)
BERTRAM: Oh, Lucy —
LUCY: Can't you see he's cold?
BERTRAM: He never mentioned it —
LUCY: Also, it's late —
BERTRAM: Yes — of course — forgive me — I'm sorry — I didn't realize — I'm just going —
LEOPOLD: You don't have to rush — stay the night if you like —
BERTRAM: No — thank you — and so long —
LUCY: So long — and don't be offended —
BERTRAM: That's quite all right — it was presumptuous of me — so long —
LEOPOLD: Cheerio and do come again some time!
BERTRAM: Glad to —
(BERTRAM goes out through the front door. Short pause.)
LEOPOLD: You didn't have to push him out like that —
LUCY: He would have been sitting here all night — And I want you for my-self — We get so little time —
LEOPOLD: And it's not the best thing in the world that he saw you here —
LUCY: Why?
LEOPOLD: You know how much talk there'll be now —
LUCY: So what? Or are you ashamed of me?
LEOPOLD: It's not that —
LUCY: Then why do you treat me like a stranger in front of other people?
LEOPOLD: I don't, do I?
LUCY: Yes you do! I can't remember you ever taking my hand in company — touching me — not even a fond glance —
LEOPOLD: Hadn't we better go to bed?
LUCY: No —
LEOPOLD: Why?
LUCY: Because I want to have a serious talk with you —
LEOPOLD: About our relationship?
LUCY: Yes —
LEOPOLD: In that case at least fetch me a blanket —
(LUCY goes to LEOPOLD's room and returns in a moment with a blanket. LEOPOLD sits down comfortably on the sofa and wraps him-self in the blanket. Short pause.)
LUCY: I knew it wasn't going to be easy for me — you know I had to make a few sacrifices — and what I am trying to say — reluctantly but I have to say it — look, I respect your idiosyncracies —
LEOPOLD: If you mean what happened — didn't happen — I mean in there — *(He points to his room.)* then I've already explained that I haven't been feeling up to the mark today —
LUCY: That's not what I meant — and if we're going to talk about it then there's other reasons behind it —
LEOPOLD: Such as?
LUCY: You're simply blocked — you're censoring yourself — you're afraid to give in to any emotion or experience — you're controlling, observing, watching yourself every minute — you're thinking about it, so in the end it's duty instead of pleasure, and then, of course, it doesn't work —

but that's my problem — I wasn't going to talk about it now —

LEOPOLD: About what, then?

LUCY: Everything I've done for us I've done freely and willingly, I'm not complaining and I don't want anything in return — I only want you to admit what is true —

LEOPOLD: What do you mean?

LUCY: We're seeing each other — we're lovers — we love each other —

LEOPOLD: Have I ever denied it?

LUCY: Forgive me but you do everything you can to deny it, to make it invisible, to avoid acknowledging it, you behave as if it wasn't there —

LEOPOLD: I'm possibly more reserved about some things than I should be, but — forgive me — you're partly to blame —

LUCY: Me? How?

LEOPOLD: You know — I am really afraid of you —

LUCY: Me?

LEOPOLD: Your ceaseless effort to give a name to our relationship, to make your status somehow official, and the way you defend your territory while quietly but relentlessly trying to enlarge it — the way you have to discuss it endlessly — all that, quite naturally, makes me defensive. By my reserve, by wariness, perhaps even by a mild cynicism, I have been compensating for a subconscious fear of being manipulated, if not actually colonized — I reproach myself bitterly for my behaviour but I can't overcome it —

LUCY: But I ask for little of you! You must see that I live only for you and through you and all I want is for you to admit to yourself that you love me!

LEOPOLD: Hm —

LUCY: And I believe you do love me! I don't believe that you are incapable of love! I don't believe that my love is incapable of awakening love even in you! I'm on your side. Without love no one is a complete person! We only achieve an identity through the person next to us! — isn't that how you put it in your *Ontology of the Human Self?!* You'll see that if you lose your ridiculous inhibitions you'll come alive again — and even your work will go better than you can imagine!

LEOPOLD: I feel sorry for you, Lucy —

LUCY: Why?

LEOPOLD: You deserve someone better. I'm just worthless —

LUCY: I don't like you talking about yourself like that —

LEOPOLD: It's true, Lucy. I can't get rid of the awful feeling that lately something has begun to collapse inside me — as if some axis which was holding me together has broken, the ground collapsing under my feet, as if I'd gone lame inside — I sometimes have the feeling that I'm acting the part of myself instead of being myself. I'm lacking a fixed point out of which I can grow and develop. I'm erratic — I'm letting myself be tossed about by chance currents — I'm sinking deeper and deeper into a void and I can no longer get a grip on things. In truth I'm just waiting for this thing that's going to happen and am no longer the self-aware subject of my own life but becoming merely its passive object — I have a feeling sometimes that all I am doing is listening helplessly to the passing of the time. What happened to my

perspective on things? My humour? My industry and persistance? The pointedness of my observations? My irony and self-irony? My capacity for enthusiasm, for emotional involvement, for commitment, even for sacrifice? The oppressive atmosphere in which I have been forced to live for so long is bound to have left its mark! Outwardly I go on acting my role as if nothing has happened but inside I'm no longer the person you all take me for. It's hard to admit it to myself, but if *I* can all the more reason for you to! It's a touching and beautiful thing that you don't lose hope of making me into someone better than I am but — don't be angry — it's an illusion. I've fallen apart, I'm paralysed, I won't change and it would be best if they came for me and took me where I would no longer be the cause of unhappiness and disillusion —
(LUCY gets up, upset, goes quickly to the balcony door. She opens it and goes out on to the balcony and stands looking out into the night with her back to the room. Soon it becomes clear that she is crying. LEOPOLD looks at her perplexed and after a while speaks to her.)
Lucy —
(LUCY doesn't react. Pause.)
There, there, Lucy, what's the matter?
(LUCY doesn't react. Pause. LEOPOLD gets up and approaches her slowly, still wrapped up in a blanket.)
Are you crying, Lucy?
(Pause.)
Why are you crying?
(Pause.)
Don't cry!
(Pause.)
I didn't want to upset you — I didn't realize —
(He has approached LUCY and touched her carefully on the shoulder. LUCY with a tear-stained face turns suddenly to him and cries out.)
LUCY: Don't touch me!
(LEOPOLD steps back surprised. LUCY comes back into the room, wiping her eyes, sobbing quietly.)
LEOPOLD: What's the matter?
LUCY: Leave me alone —
LEOPOLD: There, there — what have I done now?
LUCY: You're a worse case than I thought —
LEOPOLD: How do you mean?
LUCY: All this talk — it's nothing but excuses! You sang a different tune the first time you got me to stay with you! You said our relationship would give you back some of your lost integrity! — That it would renew your hope — that it would put you back together emotionally! — That it would open a door into a new life! You just say what suits you! No, Leopold, you're no broken wreck, you're an ordinary bullshit-artist — you've had enough of me and now you want to get shot of me — so now you paint a picture of your ruin to make me understand that there's nothing more I can expect from you and — on top of that — to make me feel sorry for you! You're ruined all right, but not in the way you say — it's your dishonesty that shows how ruined you are! And simpleton that I am, I believed that I could awaken love in you,

that I'd give you back your zest for life, that I'd help you! You're
beyond help! Serves me right — one great illusion less —
LEOPOLD: You're being unfair, Lucy — I really am going through a crisis
— even Bertram says so —
LUCY: Please don't go on — there's no point. I'm going to get dressed —
LEOPOLD: Don't be silly, Lucy! This is no way to part —
    *(LEOPOLD tries to embrace her but she breaks free from him. At that
    moment the doorbell rings. It startles them both and they look at each
    other in confusion. Their quarrel is forgotten. LEOPOLD throws his
    blanket on the sofa, goes quickly to the front door and looks through
    the peep-hole. Then, completely rattled, turns to LUCY.)*
    (Whispering) It's them!
LUCY: *(Whispering)* What are we going to do?
LEOPOLD: *(Whispering)* I don't know — go in the bedroom — I'll let them
    in —
LUCY: I'm staying here with you!
    *(The doorbell rings again. LEOPOLD breathes in, smooths his hair,
    goes to the door and opens it decisively. The FIRST CHAP and SEC-
    OND CHAP enter.)*
FIRST CHAP: Good evening, Professor —
LEOPOLD: Good evening —
FIRST CHAP: I suppose you know who we are —
LEOPOLD: I suppose so —
SECOND CHAP: You thought we wouldn't come any more today, did you?
LEOPOLD: I realize you can come any time —
FIRST CHAP: We must apologize for the intrusion — you obviously had
    other plans for the evening —
    (The TWO CHAPS smile lecherously.)
LEOPOLD: What plans I had is my own business —
SECOND CHAP: We possibly won't keep you long, it depends on you —
FIRST CHAP: It's a pleasure to meet you. According to our colleagues you're
    a sensible chap so with luck we'll soon come to an understanding —
LEOPOLD: I don't know what there is to understand. I've got my things
    ready, I just need time to get dressed —
SECOND CHAP: What's the hurry? It may not come to the worst —
FIRST CHAP: But we must ask the lady to kindly leave —
LUCY: I'm staying!
SECOND CHAP: No, you're leaving —
    (LUCY clings on to LEOPOLD.)
LEOPOLD: My friend can't leave now —
FIRST CHAP: Why?
LEOPOLD: She's got nowhere to go —
SECOND CHAP: In that case we'll put her up for the night.
LEOPOLD: Oh no you won't!
FIRST CHAP: Watch!
    *(The FIRST CHAP opens the front door and makes a gesture towards
    the corridor. The FIRST MAN and the SECOND MAN enter smartly.
    The FIRST CHAP points toward LUCY. The FIRST and SECOND
    MAN go to her and take her by the hands. LUCY struggles against
    them and LEOPOLD clasps her in his arms.)*

LUCY: You bastards!

LEOPOLD: Don't touch her!

(The FIRST and SECOND MAN pull LUCY out of LEOPOLD's embrace and drag her towards the front door. LEOPOLD tries to prevent them but they push him roughly away.)

LUCY: *(Shouting)* Help!

(FIRST and SECOND MAN put their hands over LUCY's mouth and drag her out. The FIRST CHAP dismisses the men with a gesture and closes the door.)

FIRST CHAP: Now that wasn't necessary, was it?

(LEOPOLD remains silent.)

SECOND CHAP: You don't have to worry about your girlfriend, nobody's going to harm her. As soon as she comes to her senses we'll take her home. You don't think we'd let her run around the streets in a candlewick bedspread —

FIRST CHAP: We're not inhuman, you can be sure of that —

(LEOPOLD closes the balcony door. He picks up his blanket and wraps himself into it and sits down rebelliously on the sofa. Short pause.)

Do you mind if we sit down too?

(LEOPOLD shrugs. FIRST and SECOND CHAPS sit down on chairs. Pause.)

We're sorry about that little incident, but don't give it another thought. We're better off this way. And it wouldn't be very nice for you to have your girlfriend see this —

(Pause.)

SECOND CHAP: Miss Suzana isn't at home, then?

(LEOPOLD shrugs.)

FIRST CHAP: We know she's at the cinema —

(LEOPOLD shrugs.)

SECOND CHAP: Won't you talk to us?

(LEOPOLD shrugs.)

FIRST CHAP: What are you writing at the moment, may one ask?

LEOPOLD: What does it matter —

FIRST CHAP: No harm in asking —

(Pause.)

SECOND CHAP: When was the last time you went out?

LEOPOLD: I don't know —

FIRST CHAP: It was some time ago, wasn't it?

LEOPOLD: Hm —

(Pause. FIRST CHAP looks through the medicines which are lying on the table.)

FIRST CHAP: Vitamins?

LEOPOLD: Yes —

SECOND CHAP: Apart from vitamins are you on anything?

LEOPOLD: Not really — why?

FIRST CHAP: There's been some talk —

LEOPOLD: What sort of talk?

FIRST CHAP: Forget it —

(Pause.)

SECOND CHAP: How much do you drink?

LEOPOLD: The same as everyone else —
SECOND CHAP: Starting in the morning?
LEOPOLD: As the case may be —
(Pause.)
FIRST CHAP: Well look, Professor, we won't drag this out unnecessarily.
We're here because we've been given the job of putting a proposition
to you —
LEOPOLD: A proposition?
FIRST CHAP: Yes. As you know only too well, you're being threatened
with something unpleasant which I personally wouldn't wish upon
you and I don't suppose you are particularly looking forward to it
yourself —
LEOPOLD: In a way it might be better than —
SECOND CHAP: Now, now, Professor, no blasphemy!
FIRST CHAP: As you've been told many times before, it's not our business
to push these things to extremes — on the contrary we want to avoid
confrontations, so that — if possible — things don't come to the
worst —
SECOND CHAP: It's not in our interests —
FIRST CHAP: And in some cases, when there is no better alternative, we
even look for ways to achieve our object without having to go down
every twist and turn of the path —
SECOND CHAP: We always try to give people another chance —
FIRST CHAP: And that's why we're here. We've been given the job of notifying
you that under certain conditions this whole matter could be dropped —
LEOPOLD: Dropped? How?
SECOND CHAP: The whole thing would be declared null and void.
LEOPOLD: Under what conditions?
FIRST CHAP: As you know, what's coming to you is coming to you because
under the name of Professor Leopold Nettles you put together a certain
paper —
SECOND CHAP: An essay, as you call it —
FIRST CHAP: You never denied it and in effect therefore, you brought the
whole thing upon yourself — by this act of nondenial, you unmasked
the perpetrator —
(Brief pause.)
SECOND CHAP: As a man of wide knowledge you must be aware that if the
perpetrator isn't known one cannot proceed against him. This is known
as the Principle of the Identity of the Perpetrator —
FIRST CHAP: In a word, if you would sign, here and now, a short statement
saying that you are not Professor Leopold Nettles, author of the paper
in question, then the whole thing will be considered null and void and
all previous decisions rescinded —
LEOPOLD: If I understand you correctly you want me to declare that I am
no longer me —
FIRST CHAP: That's a way of putting it which might do for a philosopher
but of course from a legal point of view it doesn't make sense. Obviously
it is not a matter of you declaring that you are no longer you, but only
declaring that you are not the same person who is the author of that
thing — essentially it's a formality —

763

SECOND CHAP: One name being like another name —
FIRST CHAP: Or do you think that Nettles is such a beautiful name that you couldn't bear to lose it? You only have to look in the phone book to see how many equally nice names there are —
SECOND CHAP: ⎤
FIRST CHAP: ⎦ And most of them even nicer —
LEOPOLD: Do you mean that I have to change my name?
SECOND CHAP: Not at all! You can have whatever name you like, that's entirely up to you — nobody — at least in this instance — could care less. The only thing which is important here is whether you are or are not the Nettles who wrote that paper —
FIRST CHAP: If you insist on keeping your name for sentimental reasons then by all means keep it —
SECOND CHAP: Though there's no denying that it would be neater if you were to decide otherwise —
FIRST CHAP: It would be neater but it's not essential. After all there could be more than one Leopold Nettles —
SECOND CHAP: There are three just in the phone book —
FIRST CHAP: In other words, it is not so much a question of whether you are Nettles or Nichols but rather whether you are the Nettles who wrote the paper —
SECOND CHAP: You have to admit it's a good offer —
LEOPOLD: I don't understand what you'll achieve by it — or why, in that case, you're proposing it — as far as I know you never do anything without a reason —
FIRST CHAP: Our interest is to wipe this unpleasant business off the slate and give you one more chance —
LEOPOLD: What chance?
FIRST CHAP: To keep out of trouble until the next time —
LEOPOLD: I don't like it much —
FIRST CHAP: Now look, whether you like it or not is your own affair. Nobody is forcing you to do anything, and nobody can force you. But I'm telling you man to man that you'd be making a mistake if you didn't go along with it —
SECOND CHAP: It's a free gift!
FIRST CHAP: No one will know a thing so long as you don't go prattling on about it, and even if it gets around everyone will understand why you did it —
SECOND CHAP: They'd all do exactly the same —
FIRST CHAP: Many of them have already done it — and what harm has it done them? None —
SECOND CHAP: If you're hesitating then the only explanation I can think of is that you have no idea what's coming to you —
(Pause.)
LEOPOLD: Would I have to do it right this minute?
FIRST CHAP: It would be best of course —
LEOPOLD: No, — this is definitely serious enough to require some reflection —
SECOND CHAP: If you want to take the risk —
LEOPOLD: What risk?

764

FIRST CHAP: Look, we've been given the job of notifying you of what we have notified you. We don't make the decisions —

SECOND CHAP: We're small fry —

FIRST CHAP: And we can't be expected to know, of course, what the relevant authorities will make of this whole business —

SECOND CHAP: All we can do is pass on your request for time to consider —

LEOPOLD: But surely it can't make much difference to them whether it's going to be today or the day after tomorrow!

FIRST CHAP: You must understand that their goodwill is not some kind of balloon which can be expanded indefinitely —

LEOPOLD: I do understand —

(Longer pause, LEOPOLD has been rattled by all this and furthermore he's evidently becoming cold again in spite of the fact that he is wrapped up in the blanket. After a while the SECOND CHAP suddenly says in a loud voice.)

SECOND CHAP: Don't be a fool, man! Here's a chance — with one stroke of the pen — to rid yourself of everything that's piled on your head, all the shit — a chance for a completely fresh start, it's once in a lifetime! What would I give for such a chance!

(Short pause. LEOPOLD is openly trembling, either from nervousness or the cold.)

LEOPOLD: *(Whispering)* Let's have a look —

(The SECOND CHAP at once begins to go through all his pockets until finally in his back trouser pocket he finds a soiled piece of paper. He puts it on the table and straightens it out with the back of his hand. Then he gives it to LEOPOLD who holds it for a long time in his trembling hands and reads it carefully. After a while he slowly puts it back on the table and wraps himself up even more tightly in his blanket. Pause.)

FIRST CHAP: Well, what's it to be?

(The curtain falls, the music returns.)

SCENE FIVE

The music fades as the curtain rises.

LEOPOLD is alone on stage. He paces the length of the room as a prisoner might pace his cell, back and forth between the front door and the bathroom door. When he reaches the front door for the third time he pauses and looks through the peep-hole. Then he puts his ear to the door and listens intently for a moment, and then continues walking. He paces back and forth twice more and then on reaching the door he pauses, reflects a moment, then goes to one of the bookcases and from behind some books he pulls out a wooden box. He takes it to the table, sits down on a chair and opens the box. It is full of various medicines. LEOPOLD starts going through them, then he considers a moment, hesitates, and prepares himself a dose from several of the medicines. He tosses the dose back into his mouth, takes a drink of rum and swallows the lot. He shuts the box, puts it back behind the books and continues to pace. When he comes to the bathroom door for the second time he pauses, considers a moment, and then goes into the bathroom leaving the door open. There is the sound of running water and LEOPOLD gasping. Evidently he is washing his face. After a while he re-enters, his face already dry, and closes the bath-

room door and continues to pace. Reaching the front door for the third time he stops and looks through the peep-hole. He then puts his ear to the door, listening intently for a while, and then continues to pace. When he reaches the front door for the second time, he pauses, considers a moment, and then goes to the bookcase where his medicines are hidden and once more takes out his box. He takes it to the table, sits down on a chair and opens the box. He starts going through his medicines, considers a moment, hesitates, prepares himself another dose of various medicines, tosses the whole lot back into his mouth, takes a drink of rum and swallows the lot. He shuts the box, puts it back behind the books and continues to pace. When he reaches the bathroom door for the second time, he pauses, considers a moment and then goes into the bathroom leaving the door open. There is the sound of running water and LEOPOLD gasping. He is washing his face again. After a while he re-enters, his face already dry, closes the bathroom door and continues to pace. Reaching the front door for the third time he stops, considers a moment, looks through the peep-hole, steps quickly to the place where his medicines are hidden, takes out his box, takes out one bottle of medicine, empties it into his mouth and runs into the bathroom leaving the door open. There is the sound of running water and LEOPOLD gasping. LEOPOLD re-enters after a moment, closes the bathroom door and goes quickly to the front door. He puts his ear to the door, listens for a while and suddenly leaps back. At the same moment a key rattles in the lock and through the front door comes SUZANA carrying a full shopping bag.

SUZANA: Hello —
LEOPOLD: Hello —
SUZANA: Isn't Edward here?
LEOPOLD: He hasn't come yet —
    (LEOPOLD takes the shopping bag from SUZANA, carries it into the kitchen and immediately returns.)
    Did you get any vegetables?
SUZANA: A cauliflower —
LEOPOLD: You didn't!
    (SUZANA goes up the little staircase to her room. LEOPOLD approaches the staircase, hesitating for a moment.)
LEOPOLD: Suzana —
    (She stops halfway up the staircase and turns towards him.)
SUZANA: Yes?
LEOPOLD: They were here —
SUZANA: *(Surprised)* They were?
LEOPOLD: Yes —
SUZANA: When?
LEOPOLD: During the night —
SUZANA: And how come you're here?
LEOPOLD: I'll explain —
SUZANA: Did you promise them anything?
LEOPOLD: No —
SUZANA: You didn't get into trouble again in some way, did you?
LEOPOLD: No —
SUZANA: What happened, then?

LEOPOLD: When you went out to the cinema with Edward, Lucy and I cooked ourselves that liver —
SUZANA: Cooked it in what?
LEOPOLD: In a frying pan —
SUZANA: Which one?
LEOPOLD: The new one —
SUZANA: And you left it in a mess —
LEOPOLD: We scrubbed it —
SUZANA: With what?
LEOPOLD: With washing powder —
SUZANA: I might have known! You know very well you shouldn't use washing power on it —
LEOPOLD: It's all right, you can have a look — then we talked for a while and then Bertram turned up, apparently on behalf of several friends — he said they were concerned about me — that I was in a bad way — that my home life was in a mess — that I was erratic — that I wasn't doing anything —
SUZANA: I've been telling you that for ages —
LEOPOLD: When Bertram left, Lucy and I had a bit of a row —
SUZANA: What about?
LEOPOLD: It's complicated — basically she complains that I don't love her enough — that I'm evasive — that I don't make it clear in company that we belong to each other, and so on — and when I honestly tried to explain things to her she said I was making excuses —
SUZANA: Well, does that surprise you?
LEOPOLD: I know what she means but what am I supposed to do?
SUZANA: Well, if you don't know —
LEOPOLD: Before she could leave they came and then because she insisted on staying they called some men in and they dragged her away —
SUZANA: Is she out yet?
LEOPOLD: I don't know — perhaps —
SUZANA: What do you mean, you don't know? Haven't you gone to see her?
LEOPOLD: I can't possibly leave here! Not now!
SUZANA: Of course. And what about them?
LEOPOLD: Apparently I won't have to go there if I make a statement that I am not the author of that — if I simply say that I am somebody else —
SUZANA: Somebody else! That would just suit them! Denounce yourself and spit on your own work!
LEOPOLD: They are not asking me to make a value judgement, they only want a formal excuse to drop the whole thing —
SUZANA: Tsss!
LEOPOLD: They're obviously worried that once I get there it would only increase the respect in which I'm held —
SUZANA: Whereas if you were to recant you'd lose it all! Obviously that would be much more to their liking! I hope you threw them out —
LEOPOLD: I've asked for time to consider —
SUZANA: What?
LEOPOLD: There's nothing to it, surely —
SUZANA: Have you gone mad? What is there to consider? That's just showing them that they're half way to breaking you — and now they'll increase the pressure! I knew as soon as I saw you that you'd got yourself into

trouble! You wet!

LEOPOLD: It's all very well for you to talk —

SUZANA: If you can't take it you should never have got into it.

(SUZANA turns abruptly and goes towards her room.)

LEOPOLD: Suzana —

SUZANA: *(Without looking at him)* Leave me alone —

(SUZANA goes into her room. LEOPOLD nervously begins to pace his usual path. When he reaches the front door for the third time, he stops, goes to the spot where his medicines are hidden, quickly extracts his box, takes a pill out of a bottle, throws it into his mouth and swallows it. He puts the box back, then continues pacing and when he gets to the bathroom door he pauses, goes quickly to the front door, looks through the peep-hole and then runs into the bathroom leaving the door open. There is the sound of running water and LEOPOLD's gasping. Suddenly the doorbell rings. Water is still running, LEOPOLD is gasping and obviously does not hear the bell. After a while the bell rings again. The sound of running water stops, and after a moment LEOPOLD comes out of the bathroom, drying his wet hair with a towel. Drying his hair he continues to pace. When he reaches the front door for the third time he looks through the peep-hole. At that moment the bell rings again. LEOPOLD jumps, then he returns to the door and looks through the peep-hole. He calms down and looks through the door. EDWARD enters wearing a dinner jacket.)

EDWARD: At last!

LEOPOLD: Has something happened?

EDWARD: I rang three times —

LEOPOLD: I was getting myself together —

EDWARD: *(Going to the balcony door)* Can I open it a bit?

LEOPOLD: Go ahead.

(EDWARD opens the balcony door wide. LEOPOLD, the towel round his neck, walks slowly round the room. EDWARD sits down on a chair.)

EDWARD: I'm relieved to find you here —

LEOPOLD: You know, then?

EDWARD: Lucy came to see me —

LEOPOLD: So she's out —

EDWARD: What did they want?

LEOPOLD: To negotiate —

EDWARD: Did you sign anything?

LEOPOLD: I've asked for time to consider —

EDWARD: When will they be back?

LEOPOLD: They never say —

EDWARD: You ought to go and see Lucy, she's having a bad time one way and another —

LEOPOLD: I can't possibly leave here! Not now!

EDWARD: Is Suzana at home?

LEOPOLD: Yes — she was just asking for you —

(LEOPOLD goes into the bathroom and after a while returns without the towel and with his hair combed.)

Do you mind if I close it now?

EDWARD: Leave it a while —

(LEOPOLD returns to his place and sits down. Pause.)
LEOPOLD: That's a nice outfit you've got on —
EDWARD: It's a dinner jacket — my uncle lent it to me —
LEOPOLD: I know it's a dinner jacket — it's nice —
EDWARD: You know my uncle — *(PAUSE.)* How did you sleep?
LEOPOLD: Hardly at all —
EDWARD: You couldn't get them out of your mind, could you?
LEOPOLD: Well —
(Pause.)
EDWARD: Did you go this morning?
LEOPOLD: Yes —
EDWARD: Well, that's something anyway —
LEOPOLD: Not much of a thing, as it happens —
(Pause.)
EDWARD: What did you eat?
LEOPOLD: I wasn't hungry, I just ate a couple of onions and five almonds to calm myself down —
EDWARD: And did it?
LEOPOLD: Not really —
(Pause.)
EDWARD: The main thing is that you're here —
LEOPOLD: I'd rather be there than here like this! Why can't I get my life clear! It was wonderful when nobody was interested in me — when nobody expected anything from me, nobody urging me to do anything — I just browsed around the second-hand bookshops — studying the modern philosophers at my leisure — spending the nights making notes from their works — taking walks in the parks and meditating — why can't I change my name to Nichols, say, and forget everything and start a completely new life?
EDWARD: Perhaps you need some of your pills —
LEOPOLD: I splash water on my face — I don't want pills — I don't want to get dependent on them —
(Pause. LEOPOLD becomes alert, and listening.)
EDWARD: Nothing —
(At that moment the doorbell rings. LEOPOLD jumps up in confusion. EDWARD also gets up. LEOPOLD goes to the peep-hole and looks through it and leaps back from the door and runs across the room into the bathroom leaving the door open. Immediately there is the sound of running water. EDWARD is puzzled. He steps to the bathroom door. Short pause.)
(Whispering towards the bathroom) Leopold, come on —
(Short pause and the sound of water.)
(Whispering towards the bathroom) Don't be silly, Leopold, face up to it!
(Short pause and the sound of water.)
(Whispering towards the bathroom) I'll tell them you're not at home if you like but it would be better to get it over with —
(Short pause and the sound of water. The bell rings again. EDWARD doesn't know what to do. Then he makes up his mind abruptly and goes decisively to the main door, to the front door, opens it wide and gazes with surprise. FIRST SIDNEY and SECOND SIDNEY enter

each carrying a large suitcase. They put their suitcases down.)
FIRST SIDNEY: Good afternoon —
EDWARD: Good afternoon —
FIRST SIDNEY: Isn't the professor in?
(EDWARD is puzzled. Finally he nods, slowly closes the door and goes into the bathroom leaving the door half open. There is a short pause. The sound of water stops suddenly and there is some incomprehensible whispering for quite a long time off stage. FIRST SIDNEY and SEC-OND SIDNEY stand motionless next to their suitcases. Finally LEOPOLD comes out of the bathroom with his hair wet but sleekly combed. EDWARD follows him, closing the bathroom door.)
LEOPOLD: Good afternoon —
SECOND SIDNEY: Here we are, professor —
LEOPOLD: Excellent —
FIRST SIDNEY: We've got it —
LEOPOLD: What?
(FIRST SIDNEY and SECOND SIDNEY put their suitcases on the table and open them. Both suitcases are full of various documents.)
FIRST SIDNEY: *(Pointing to his suitcase)* These are blank papers — these are normal office issue — these are for carbon copies — these are carbon papers — and here we have various envelopes and files and so on —
LEOPOLD: Is that all for me?
FIRST SIDNEY: Of course —
LEOPOLD: How much do I owe you?
FIRST SIDNEY: Do me a favour, professor, what do you take us for!
LEOPOLD: Well thank you very much — I think that should last me —
SECOND SIDNEY: We're looking forward to what you'll be writing on these bits of paper —
FIRST SIDNEY: *(Pointing to the other suitcase)* Well, and this is the stuff from our plant — these are minutes of the board of management — these are minutes of meetings of all the paper-mill employees — these are specimens of factory correspondence — here we have various memos, internal regulations, information for the work-force, overtime summaries — and this is specially interesting, that's from the personnel department — personal records of employees — various complaints — returns — denunciations —
SECOND SIDNEY: I think it'll make very nice reading for you —
FIRST SIDNEY: Use it as you see fit —
SECOND SIDNEY: If you can do anything with it, it will certainly be a bombshell —
FIRST SIDNEY: Absolutely —
LEOPOLD: Thank you so —
(FIRST SIDNEY takes a sheaf of papers out of one of the suitcases and looks around.)
FIRST SIDNEY: Where do you want it?
LEOPOLD: *(Looking around)* Where? Well, in this corner, here —
(LEOPOLD points to the left-hand corner of the room, downstage. FIRST SIDNEY and SECOND SIDNEY start taking papers from the two suitcases and carrying them to the corner where they place them on the floor. After a while they are joined first by LEOPOLD and then

770

*by EDWARD. When the contents of both suitcases are in the corner,
SECOND SIDNEY closes both of the now empty cases and carries them
to the front door. Then FIRST and SECOND SIDNEY sit down at the
table. LEOPOLD sits down on the sofa. EDWARD remains standing
in the background. There is a long awkward pause.)*
LEOPOLD: There's a lot of it —
SECOND SIDNEY: For you we'd steal the whole paper mill if we had to —
LEOPOLD: Thank you —
   (Awkward pause.)
   I wasn't expecting you so soon —
FIRST SIDNEY: One must strike while the iron is hot, that's what me and
   Sidney always say —
LEOPOLD: Very well put —
   (Awkward pause.)
   I don't know how I'm ever going to repay you —
SECOND SIDNEY: What is there to repay? We've already told you that
   we're your fans — and not just us —
FIRST SIDNEY: There's lots of people looking to you —
LEOPOLD: Thank you —
   (Awkward pause.)
   I wasn't expecting you so soon —
SECOND SIDNEY: One must strike while the iron is hot, that's what me and
   Sidney always say —
LEOPOLD: Very well put —
   (Awkward pause.)
   I don't know how I'm ever going to repay you —
FIRST SIDNEY: What is there to repay? We've already told you that we're
   your fans — and not just us —
SECOND SIDNEY: There's lots of people looking to you —
   (Awkward pause.)
LEOPOLD: I don't know how I'll ever repay you —
SECOND SIDNEY: What is there to repay? We've already told you that we're
   your fans — and not just us —
LEOPOLD: Excuse me —
   *(LEOPOLD gets up and goes to the balcony door and closes it and then
   returns to his seat. SECOND SIDNEY is feeling his pockets. LEOPOLD
   offers him a cigarette.)*
SECOND SIDNEY: I've got some today —
   (SECOND SIDNEY finds his cigarettes at last and he lights one.)
   But could I ask you for something else —
LEOPOLD: I'm at your disposal —
SECOND SIDNEY: Would there be any chance of a glass of rum?
LEOPOLD: Yes — of course —
SECOND SIDNEY: Just to clarify — I'm a teetotaller — but I was asking
   for Sidney here — he drinks like a fish —
   *(LEOPOLD gets up and goes to the kitchen and comes back at once
   with a glass. He pours rum from his bottle into the glass and hands it
   to FIRST SIDNEY.)*
FIRST SIDNEY: Thanks! Cheers!
   (FIRST SIDNEY drinks the whole glass in one go and then burps,

satisfied. LEOPOLD refills his glass.)
FIRST SIDNEY: Thanks! Cheers!
(FIRST SIDNEY drinks the whole glass in one go and then burps, satisfied. LEOPOLD fills his glass again.)
Thanks! Cheers!
(FIRST SIDNEY drinks the whole glass in one go and then burps, satisfied. SUZANA comes out of her room in a long evening dress and walks down the little staircase.)
LEOPOLD: Look, Suzana, these gentlemen have brought me all this paper and all sorts of interesting stuff —
SUZANA: Where's it going to go?
LEOPOLD: I'll find somewhere — that's a nice dress.
(SUZANA makes a sign to EDWARD who accompanies her to the kitchen. During the rest of the scene both of them can be seen through the glass-panelled kitchen door taking out various foodstuffs from the shopping bag, putting them where they belong, and, during all this time either discussing something in a lively way or perhaps quarrelling. LEOPOLD notices that FIRST SIDNEY's glass is empty and fills it up again for him.)
FIRST SIDNEY: Thanks! Cheers!
(FIRST SIDNEY drinks the whole glass in one go and then burps, satisfied. LEOPOLD refills the glass.)
Thanks! Cheers!
(FIRST SIDNEY drinks the whole glass in one go and then burps, satisfied. LEOPOLD refills the glass.)
Thanks! Cheers!
(FIRST SIDNEY drinks the whole glass in one go and then burps, satisfied. LEOPOLD refills the glass.)
Thanks! Cheers!
(FIRST SIDNEY drinks the whole glass in one go and then burps, satisfied. LEOPOLD refills the glass. FIRST SIDNEY takes the glass but when he is on the point of drinking it he puts it back on the table.)
FIRST SIDNEY: Someone has to be sensible —
(Short pause.)
SECOND SIDNEY: We're not holding you up are we?
LEOPOLD: No —
FIRST SIDNEY: Are you sure? Because if we are you only have to say so and we'll push off —
LEOPOLD: You're not holding me up — excuse me —
(LEOPOLD gets up, goes to the place where his medicines are hidden, turns his back to the room so as not to be seen, pulls out his box, quickly takes out a pill, throws it into his mouth and swallows it and puts his box back and returns to his seat. Pause.)
SECOND SIDNEY: Have you thought about it yet?
LEOPOLD: About what?
FIRST SIDNEY: What we were talking about yesterday — that it's time for an initiative —
LEOPOLD: Oh yes — I haven't got round to it yet —
SECOND SIDNEY: Pity. You know, I'm an ordinary bloke, a nobody, but I can spot a few things and I've got my own opinion and nobody can

deny me that. And what I think is, there's a lot that could be done —
certainly more than is being done at the moment —

FIRST SIDNEY: One just has to get hold of the situation by the —

SECOND SIDNEY: Who else but you is there to get things going again?

(LEOPOLD is starting to get nervous. He looks discreetly at his watch.)

FIRST SIDNEY: We're not holding you up are we?

LEOPOLD: No —

SECOND SIDNEY: Are you sure? Because if we are you only have to say so
and we'll push off —

LEOPOLD: You're not holding me up. Excuse me —

*(LEOPOLD gets up and goes into the bathroom, leaving the door open.
There is the sound of running water and LEOPOLD gasping. The
sound of water stops and shortly afterwards LEOPOLD returns to his
seat.)*

FIRST SIDNEY: That thing you wrote — even if we don't fully understand
it —

SECOND SIDNEY: We're ordinary people —

FIRST SIDNEY: — and the fact that you're right behind it —

SECOND SIDNEY: — regardless of the consequences —

FIRST SIDNEY: — straight away leads one to hope that you will take the
final step —

LEOPOLD: What final step?

SECOND SIDNEY: I'm not really good at explaining myself but let me put
it like this — that whatever you're writing, you'll turn it into something that will have a practical effect —

FIRST SIDNEY: To put it simply, that you'll come up with the pay-off to all
your philosophizing —

LEOPOLD: The trouble is that opinions differ about quite what the pay-off
is —

SECOND SIDNEY: You'll find it —

FIRST SIDNEY: Who else but you is there to get things going again —

SECOND SIDNEY: I'd say that's just what people are waiting for —

LEOPOLD: What people?

FIRST SIDNEY: Everybody —

LEOPOLD: Isn't that a bit of an exaggeration?

SECOND SIDNEY: Forgive me but you probably don't realize —

LEOPOLD: What?

FIRST SIDNEY: Your responsibility —

LEOPOLD: For what?

SECOND SIDNEY: For everything —

(LEOPOLD is evidently nervous. He looks at his watch.)

FIRST SIDNEY: We're not holding you up?

LEOPOLD: No —

FIRST SIDNEY: ⎤ Are you sure? Because if we are you only have
SECOND SIDNEY: ⎦ to say so and we'll push off —

LEOPOLD: You're not holding me up. Excuse me —

*(LEOPOLD gets up and goes to the kitchen and returns shortly with
a small plate on which there are two onions and five almonds. He eats
the lot during the following dialogue.)*

SECOND SIDNEY: Sidney and I were giving it a bit of thought the other day —

FIRST SIDNEY: And we got the following idea —
LEOPOLD: What idea?
SECOND SIDNEY: We think it's quite good —
LEOPOLD: What idea?
FIRST SIDNEY: This could be exactly the step that everyone is waiting for
you to take —
LEOPOLD: What?
SECOND SIDNEY: That you should write a kind of declaration —
LEOPOLD: What kind of declaration?
FIRST SIDNEY: Quite simply a kind of general declaration covering all the
basics —
SECOND SIDNEY: It would have to be brief and easy to understand of
course —
FIRST SIDNEY: In other words you'd have to spend some time on it —
SECOND SIDNEY: You've got plenty of paper now —
*(LEOPOLD, irritated, gets up, ambles round the room and then turns
to the TWO SIDNEYS.)*
LEOPOLD: Forgive me, gentlemen, but I'm not clear about —
*(SUZANA, followed by EDWARD, comes out of the kitchen. LEOPOLD
looks at them in surprise.)*
(To SUZANA) Are you leaving?
SUZANA: Why?
LEOPOLD: I thought that we might — since you got that cauliflower —
since I need to calm down a bit — to examine everything calmly — to
discuss —
SUZANA: Forgive me, Leopold, but I've got tickets for a dance — I bought
them ages ago —
LEOPOLD: I see — I see —
SUZANA: It's my first dance this year —
LEOPOLD: I understand — I understand —
SUZANA: Not that I know what there is to discuss — I've already given you
my opinion —
LEOPOLD: I know — I only thought — but it doesn't really matter —
SUZANA: Well, so long —
EDWARD: So long, Leopold — and get to bed soon — get some sleep —
*(SUZANA and EDWARD leave through the front door. LEOPOLD
looks at them awkwardly as they leave. Pause.)*
FIRST SIDNEY: What aren't you clear about?
LEOPOLD: *(Turning round)* I beg your pardon?
SECOND SIDNEY: You were saying that you weren't clear about some-
thing —
LEOPOLD: Was I? Ah — yes — don't be angry, gentlemen, but I'm not really
quite clear about —
FIRST SIDNEY: About what?
LEOPOLD: About what exactly you want from me —
*(FIRST SIDNEY drinks the glass of rum in one go and then gets up.
SECOND SIDNEY gets up also. They both step nearer to LEOPOLD.)*
FIRST SIDNEY: Professor, you've obviously got us wrong — we don't want
anything from you —
SECOND SIDNEY: We've only taken the liberty of giving you our opinion —

FIRST SIDNEY: It's the opinion of ordinary people —
SECOND SIDNEY: Of lots of ordinary people —
FIRST SIDNEY: We only wanted to offer a suggestion —
SECOND SIDNEY: We meant well —
FIRST SIDNEY: We can't help not being able to express ourselves exactly —
SECOND SIDNEY: We're not philosophers —
FIRST SIDNEY: We just thought you might be interested in our opinion —
SECOND SIDNEY: As representing the opinion of ordinary —
LEOPOLD: I'm not saying that I'm not interested in your opinion —
FIRST SIDNEY: Well, you seem to be implying that we're confusing you —
LEOPOLD: Really I'm not suggesting anything of the sort —
SECOND SIDNEY: You were saying that you weren't clear about what we want from you —
LEOPOLD: I don't exactly know what I was saying —
FIRST SIDNEY: But we know —
(At that moment the bathroom door opens. BERTRAM is standing in the doorway talking to LEOPOLD.)
BERTRAM: I don't want to be hard on you or hurt you in any way.
(At that moment the kitchen door opens. EDWARD is standing there speaking to LEOPOLD.)
EDWARD: Were you worried?
(At that moment the door of SUZANA's room opens. SUZANA is standing there speaking to LEOPOLD.)
SUZANA: Are you sure you didn't get yourself into trouble again somehow?
BERTRAM: I'm not just speaking for myself.
EDWARD: Perhaps you should take some pills —
(At that moment the balcony door opens. LUCY is standing there in her bedspread and speaking to LEOPOLD.)
LUCY: You sang a different tune the first time you got me to stay here with you.
EDWARD: You ought to go and see Lucy.
FIRST SIDNEY: This could be what people are waiting for —
SECOND SIDNEY: You'll find a way —
SUZANA: What is there to consider, for goodness sake.
BERTRAM: And how are things between you and Suzana?
LUCY: You've had enough of me and now you want to get shot of me —
EDWARD: Did you sign anything?
FIRST SIDNEY: We've only taken the liberty of giving you our opinion —
SECOND SIDNEY: The opinion of ordinary people —
FIRST SIDNEY: Lots of ordinary people —
EDWARD: Some hero.
SUZANA: Some hero.
BERTRAM: Some hero.
LUCY: Some hero.
FIRST SIDNEY: You've had enough of me and now you want to get shot of me.
SECOND SIDNEY: Some hero.
FIRST SIDNEY: Did you sign anything?
LEOPOLD: *(Shouting)* GET OUT!
(For a moment there is complete silence and then the doorbell rings.

LEOPOLD runs into the bathroom. BERTRAM makes way for him and LEOPOLD disappears into the bathroom and immediately there is the sound of running water. All the people on stage disappear behind the doors through which they came. FIRST and SECOND SIDNEY disappear with their suitcases through the front door. They all go and all the doors except the bathroom door are closed. The only sound is running water and LEOPOLD gasping. The doorbell rings again. The curtain falls as the music begins to be heard.)

SCENE SIX

The music fades as the curtain rises.
There is no one on the stage. The bathroom door is open. There is the sound of running water and of LEOPOLD gasping. There is a short pause. Then the bell rings. The sound of water stops and LEOPOLD runs out of the bathroom. He was obviously having a shower. He is wet and is covered only by a towel wrapped round his waist. He runs to the main door, looks through the peep-hole, is taken aback, hesitates a moment and then opens the door. MARGUERITE enters.

MARGUERITE: Good evening —
LEOPOLD: *(A bit nonplussed)* Good evening —
   (Short pause.)
MARGUERITE: Professor Nettles?
LEOPOLD: Yes —
   (Short pause.)
MARGUERITE: Sorry to disturb you —
LEOPOLD: You're not disturbing me —
MARGUERITE: I won't hold you up for long —
LEOPOLD: I've got time —
   (Short pause.)
MARGUERITE: My name's Marguerite. I'm a student of philosophy —
LEOPOLD: At the university or a private student?
MARGUERITE: Both —
   (MARGUERITE walks to the middle of the room and looks round uncertainly. LEOPOLD closes the door. A short pause.)
LEOPOLD: Sit down —
MARGUERITE: Thank you —
   (MARGUERITE sits down shyly on the edge of the sofa.)
LEOPOLD: Would you like some rum?
MARGUERITE: No — thank you — I'm not used to rum —
LEOPOLD: One glass won't do you any harm —
   (LEOPOLD pours some rum into the glass which has remained on the table.)
MARGUERITE: Well, thank you —
   (MARGUERITE takes a very small sip and winces.)
LEOPOLD: Not bad is it?
MARGUERITE: No —
   (Awkward pause.)
   You'll catch cold.
LEOPOLD: Ah yes, of course —

(LEOPOLD goes quickly into the bathroom and comes back in a moment wearing a dressing gown under which he is naked. He sits down on the sofa next to MARGUERITE and smiles at her. MARGUERITE smiles back. There is a longer awkward pause.)

MARGUERITE: I know your work —

LEOPOLD: Really? Which?

MARGUERITE: *Phenomenology of Responsibility, Love and Nothingness, Ontology of the Human Self —*

LEOPOLD: You've read all those?

MARGUERITE: Several times —

LEOPOLD: Well, I am impressed —

(Pause.)

MARGUERITE: I hear *Ontology of the Human Self* got you into trouble —

LEOPOLD: It's because of that I'm supposed to go there —

MARGUERITE: What — straight there? How come?

LEOPOLD: Paragraph 511 — intellectual hooliganism —

MARGUERITE: That's awful!

LEOPOLD: That's the sort of world we're living in —

MARGUERITE: For such beautiful thoughts!

LEOPOLD: Apparently someone didn't think they were so beautiful —

MARGUERITE: And is it definite?

LEOPOLD: I could get out of it by denying that I wrote it —

MARGUERITE: Is that what they're offering you?

LEOPOLD: Yes —

MARGUERITE: They're disgusting!

(Pause. MARGUERITE takes a sip and winces. LEOPOLD promptly fills up her glass.)

Your essays have given me a great deal of —

LEOPOLD: Yes? I'm so glad —

MARGUERITE: It's because of them that I became interested in philosophy —

LEOPOLD: Really?

MARGUERITE: Somehow they opened my eyes —

LEOPOLD: You're exaggerating —

MARGUERITE: Really —

LEOPOLD: Have another drink —

(MARGUERITE has a drink and winces. LEOPOLD promptly refills her glass. Awkward pause.)

MARGUERITE: Are you writing anything?

LEOPOLD: I'm trying to —

MARGUERITE: Could you tell me — excuse my curiosity — could you tell me what you're writing?

LEOPOLD: I'm trying to think about love as a dimension of being —

MARGUERITE: You touched on that a little in the second chapter of *Love and Nothingness* —

LEOPOLD: That's right —

(Awkward pause.)

MARGUERITE: Professor —

LEOPOLD: Yes, Marguerite?

MARGUERITE: I wouldn't dare to trouble you —

LEOPOLD: You're not troubling me at all! On the contrary — I'm very pleased to have met you —

MARGUERITE: If it wasn't for the fact that I'm sure you're the only one who can help me —

LEOPOLD: What's the matter?

MARGUERITE: It's going to sound silly —

LEOPOLD: You can tell me!

MARGUERITE: I'm suddenly embarrassed —

LEOPOLD: But why, there's no need —

(MARGUERITE has a drink and winces. LEOPOLD promptly refills her glass. Short pause.)

MARGUERITE: Where should I begin? I just don't know what to do —

LEOPOLD: In your studies?

MARGUERITE: In my life —

LEOPOLD: In your life?

MARGUERITE: I find everything so stifling — all those hopeless faces in the bus queues — the endless hue and cry in the streets — people twisted out of shape in their offices and everywhere else — the general misery of life — forgive me, I know it's silly, you don't even know me — but I didn't know anyone else I could turn to —

LEOPOLD: I'm delighted that you should confide in me —

MARGUERITE: I don't get on with my parents — they're middle class types who are always watching TV — I've no boyfriend — the other students seem terribly superficial —

LEOPOLD: I know what you mean —

MARGUERITE: You're not angry?

LEOPOLD: Why do you make excuses for yourself all the time? What greater satisfaction could there be for a philosopher than to receive a visit from a reader in mid-crisis about the meaning of life?

MARGUERITE: I know that you can't solve my problem for me —

LEOPOLD: You're right in the sense that the meaning of life is not something which one can summarize or verbalize one way or the other and then hand over like a piece of information — it's not an object, it's more like an elusive spiritual state — and the more one needs it the more elusive it becomes —

MARGUERITE: Yes, yes, that's exactly —

LEOPOLD: On the other hand there is the fact — as I've already tried to show in *Ontology of the Human Self* — that there's a certain non-verbal, existential space in which — and only in which — one can get hold of something through experiencing the presence of another person —

MARGUERITE: Forgive me, it's exactly that part — it's from chapter four — which made me decide to come and see you —

LEOPOLD: There you are! But I wouldn't like to raise your hopes unduly, because the fact that I'm meditating on this subject doesn't automatically mean that I am myself capable of creating such a space —

MARGUERITE: But you've been creating it for ages — by talking to me at all — by understanding me — forgive me, I'm probably already a bit tipsy —

LEOPOLD: Not at all! Drink up —

(MARGUERITE takes a drink and winces. LEOPOLD promptly fills

up her glass.)

LEOPOLD: I'll tell you something, Marguerite — honesty deserves honesty: if I am able to understand you then it is mainly because I'm in a similar or perhaps even worse situation than you —

MARGUERITE: You? I can't believe it! You know so much — you've achieved so much — you're so wise —

LEOPOLD: That guarantees nothing —

MARGUERITE: I'm only a silly girl, but you —

LEOPOLD: You're not silly —

MARGUERITE: I am, I know it —

LEOPOLD: You're clever, Marguerite — and not only that, you're beautiful —

MARGUERITE: Me? Well, whatever next —

LEOPOLD: I'll be frank with you, Marguerite: I'm in a very bad way —

MARGUERITE: I know life has been hard on you but you seem so strong —

LEOPOLD: Alas, that's only appearance. In reality I've had the feeling for some time now that something is collapsing inside me — as if an axis holding me together has started to break — the ground crumbling under my feet — I lack a fixed point from which everything inside me could grow and develop — I get the feeling sometimes that I'm not really doing anything except listening helplessly to the time going by. Gone is the perspective I once had — my humour — my industry and persistence — the pointedness of my observations —

MARGUERITE: How beautifully you put it —

LEOPOLD: You should have known me before! It's all gone, my irony, my self-irony, my capacity for enthusiasm, for emotional involvement, for commitment, even for sacrifice! This might disappoint you, Marguerite, but for a long time I haven't been the person that you obviously take me for! Basically I'm a tired, dried out, broken man —

MARGUERITE: You mustn't speak like that, Professor! You're too hard on yourself! But even if it were all true the very fact that you are reflecting upon your situation shows that all is not lost —

LEOPOLD: You're good to me, Marguerite! And please don't call me professor, it sounds so formal! Why aren't you drinking?

(MARGUERITE has a drink and winces. LEOPOLD promptly fills up her glass. Short pause.)

MARGUERITE: So many people think so highly of you! Doesn't that alone give you strength?

LEOPOLD: On the contrary! I often say to myself how wonderful it was when nobody was interested in me — when nobody expected anything from me and nobody was urging me to do things — I used to browse around the second-hand bookshops — studying modern philosophers at my leisure — spending the nights making notes from their works — taking walks in the parks and meditating —

MARGUERITE: But it's thanks to all that that you are what you are today —

LEOPOLD: That's true, but it's also true that I've taken upon myself a heavier burden than I'm able to bear —

MARGUERITE: Leopold, I believe that you will win through!

LEOPOLD: I have a feeling that my only way out is to accept a term there — somewhere far away from my nearest and dearest — and put my hum-

779

ble trust in a higher will, to give me the chance to atone for my
guilt — to lose my apathy and regain my pride — and as a nameless
cog in a giant machine to purify myself — thus and only thus — If I
manage to drain the bitter cup with dignity — I can get back —
perhaps — something of my lost human integrity — renew the hope
inside me — reconstitute myself emotionally — open the door to a new
life —

MARGUERITE: *(Shouts)* But Leopold!

LEOPOLD: Yes?

MARGUERITE: *(Excitedly)* Don't you see that the punishment is deeply
unjust and if you try — however honourably — to turn it into a purify-
ing experience you'd just be agreeing with it and so prostrating yourself
before it. And what's more, by giving it this so-called meaning you're
hiding from yourself the fact that you're clinging to it as a kind of
escape from your life, a way out of your problems. But however far
they send you, punishment won't solve what you can't solve yourself!
Don't you understand that you've done nothing and so there is nothing
to atone! You're innocent!

LEOPOLD: Oh, Marguerite — why didn't I meet you before it was too late?
*(LEOPOLD takes hold of her hands and kisses them. MARGUERITE
is embarrassed. LEOPOLD holds her hands. She drops her eyes. Long
pause.)*

MARGUERITE: *(Whispering)* Leopold —

LEOPOLD: Yes —

MARGUERITE: Do you love anybody?

LEOPOLD: Ah, my dear girl, I really don't know if I'm capable of love —

MARGUERITE: Don't tell me that you've never felt anything towards a
woman —

LEOPOLD: Nervousness — more with some, less with others —

MARGUERITE: You need love! Mad passionate true love! Didn't you
yourself write in *Phenomenology of Responsibility* that a person who
doesn't love doesn't exist? Only love will give you the strength to stand
up to them!

LEOPOLD: That's easy for you to say, Marguerite, but where would one
find it?
(MARGUERITE takes a quick drink, winces and quietly blurts out.)

MARGUERITE: With me!

LEOPOLD: What? You?

MARGUERITE: *(Excited)* Yes! You have given me back the meaning to my
life, which is to give you the meaning back to yours! I'll save you!
(LEOPOLD strokes her hair.)

LEOPOLD: You're wonderful, Marguerite! But I can't allow you to throw
your life away on someone as worthless as myself —

MARGUERITE: On the contrary I would be fulfilling my life!

LEOPOLD: Apart from the fact that I'm an old man —

MARGUERITE: That's nonsense! I've made up my mind —

LEOPOLD: If I'd known it would come to this I'd never have told you my
problems —

MARGUERITE: Thank goodness you did! I'll give you back strength —
courage — self-confidence — joy — appetite for life! I'll bring your failing

heart back to life! I know you're capable of love! How else could you
have written those things! I'll bring you back to life and at the same
time back to philosophy!
*(LEOPOLD takes hold of MARGUERITE's arms and for a moment
looks deeply into her eyes and then begins to kiss her rapidly over her
face and neck.)*
MARGUERITE: Ah — Leopold — ah — I love you — I love your thoughts
and your words — you awoke my love a long time ago without knowing
it — without my knowing it — and now I'll awaken love in you!
(At that moment the doorbell rings. LEOPOLD jumps up at once.)
LEOPOLD: *(Whispering)* Quick — go out on the balcony!
MARGUERITE: *(Whispering)* Why?
LEOPOLD: *(Whispering)* They'll drag you off!
*(LEOPOLD takes her by the hand and hurries her to the balcony door.
He opens the door and pushes her on to the balcony and closes the door.
He runs into the bedroom leaving the door open. Pause. The doorbell
rings again. Pause. Then LEOPOLD grey-faced, emerges from the bed-
room wearing a suit and an overcoat and carrying a small military
valise. He goes to the front door. Opens it bravely. FIRST CHAP and
SECOND CHAP enter. LEOPOLD closes the door behind them.)*
FIRST CHAP: On your own today?
LEOPOLD: *(Bravely)* Gentlemen! Do your duty! I'll get ready!
SECOND CHAP: What's the hurry? It may not come to the worst —
(The FIRST CHAP goes to the balcony door, opens it and says:)
FIRST CHAP: Come in, my little one —
(MARGUERITE slowly enters the room.)
LEOPOLD: Don't you dare touch her! If you drag her off, then —
SECOND CHAP: Then what?
LEOPOLD: Then — then —
FIRST CHAP: Don't you worry, there's no need for her to go anywhere.
Today there'd be no point —
LEOPOLD: You're right. As you're obviously aware, I'm not going to sign
that statement. I'd rather die than give up my own human identity —
it's the only thing I've got!
SECOND CHAP: But Professor, why are you carrying on like this? You're
not going anywhere —
LEOPOLD: Why not? I've told you quite clearly that I'm not going to sign
anything! I'm not guilty!
FIRST CHAP: You don't have to sign anything! Your case has been ad-
journed indefinitely —
SECOND CHAP: Indefinitely for the time being.
FIRST CHAP: For the time being.
SECOND CHAP: Without signature!
LEOPOLD: What? Adjourned?
FIRST CHAP: That's right. Adjourned!
LEOPOLD: You mean no signature and no *there* either?
SECOND CHAP: For the time being, mind, for the time being —
LEOPOLD: I don't understand what it means — why don't you want my
signature any more?
FIRST CHAP: It would be just a formality. Who needs it? It's become pretty

clear by now that in your case it would be superfluous —

LEOPOLD: Are you trying to say that I am no longer me?

SECOND CHAP: You said it, not me.

(Short pause. LEOPOLD gazes at the FIRST and SECOND CHAP and then shouts.)

LEOPOLD: I don't want an adjournment! I want to go there!

(LEOPOLD suddenly falls to his knees in front of the CHAPS and starts to sob.)

I'm begging you — I beseech you — I can't go on living like this —

FIRST CHAP: It seems you'll have to —

MARGUERITE: *(Calling to him)* Leopold get up! You're not going to beg them, are you!

LEOPOLD: *(Shouting at MARGUERITE)* Leave me alone! All of you leave me alone!

(LEOPOLD collapses on the floor, banging his fists on it. The curtain falls and the music returns.)

SCENE SEVEN

The music is fading and the curtain begins to rise slowly. LEOPOLD is alone on the stage. He is sitting on the sofa staring at the front door. After a longer pause he gets up and goes to the door and looks through the peep-hole. Then he puts his ear to the door and listens intently. The lights start to come up in the auditorium and the music begins to be heard. LEOPOLD straightens up slowly, goes to the footlights and bows. At the same time all the other characters enter from the various doors and gather round LEOPOLD bowing. The curtain falls.

END

FEMINIST THEATRE

The participation of women in theatre echoes their role in society. Throughout most periods of history, women equalled or exceeded men in number; however, in most times and places, males dominated society and determined the roles women could play in the world. In general, women were expected to function mainly in the private sector — primarily the home — and their approved roles were those of mother, wife, and helper; women who ventured into the public world and took on independent roles were frequently seen as threatening not only male domination but also moral standards and even the very fabric of society. Theatre, an art which imitates life, reflected this situation.

History of Women in Theatre

Throughout much of European history, women entered the theatre only as spectators. With very few exceptions, in Greek, Roman, medieval, and early renaissance theatre, men wrote the plays, staged the productions, and played all the acting roles, including those of women characters. During this period, the great female roles — Jocasta, Medea, Desdemona, Juliet — were all created by male actors.

During the Renaissance, the Italian commedia dell'arte began changing this practice by assigning female roles to women. The Italian actresses became famous, and by touring throughout Europe, the commedia troupes spread this revolutionary new practice abroad. As a result, during the English Commonwealth period, British aristocrats, in exile in the court of France, saw women playing female roles in the plays of Molière and Racine, and when they returned to England after 1660, they brought the practice back home with them. Naturally then, when the American colonies began to stage plays, they assigned female roles to women actors. By the twentieth century, women almost always played the female roles in European and American theatre, and the very idea of male actors playing female roles had come to seem strange.

Actresses, women who dared to present themselves on the public stage, immediately shared in the ambiguous social status of their male counterparts. Just as male actors were branded "vagabonds and sturdy beggars" and were barred from burial in church cemeteries, so actresses were considered by men and women alike to be morally suspect. The life of social pioneers like the early women actors is frequently exciting but rarely easy.

Women Playwrights

While female performers gained a solid foothold in the theatre during the Renaissance, women playwrights were fewer in number and had a harder struggle gaining parity with their male counterparts. One of the earliest female playwrights, the tenth-century Benedictine nun Hrotsvitha, wrote Latin plays about saints for the instruction of her sisterhood, but as far as we know, no other medieval women continued in her footsteps. During the Renaissance, aristocratic women sometimes wrote pageants for court entertainments, but again these amateur efforts had little effect on the development of theatre.

Since the Renaissance, women writers have been most in evidence during periods of political or social upheaval. For instance, during the English Restoration, 1660 to 1720, the London theatres staged some sixty plays written by women, and Aphra Behn (1640-89) gained a reputation as the first woman writer to earn her living by her pen. Again, during the feminist period in the late nineteenth and early twentieth centuries, women playwrights moved into the spotlight; during this time, Frances Hodgson Burnett wrote the popular *Little Lord Fauntleroy* (1888) and, in the United States, Martha Morton not only wrote plays but also founded an organization for women playwrights, a forerunner of the Dramatists Guild. In fact, during the 1902-03 season in New York City, women wrote twenty-two percent of the new plays.

Women writers continued to contribute important works to theatre throughout the twentieth century. Among these leaders were Rachel Crothers (1878-1958), Lillian Hellman (1905-84), Gertrude Stein (1874-1946), Dorothy Sayers (1893-1957), and Lorraine Hansberry (1930-65). And in the early 1980s, the awarding of Pulitzer Prizes to Beth Henley (1952-) and Marsha Norman (1947-) seemed to recognize the valued place women playwrights had achieved. However, if women were really going to put their imprint on theatre, they needed more than just a succession of individual, great artists; they needed a movement.

Twentieth-Century Feminist Theatre

During the 1960s and '70s, modern feminism gave birth to a women's theatre movement that not only seemed once and for all to establish a firm foundation for women in the theatre but also produced the kind of plays and theoretical base that was likely to make a significant impact on the art form for decades to come.

During this period of time, women in all walks of life in Europe and America challenged their subordinate role in society and attempted to create a new life for themselves. They aimed to develop a confident, independent self-image, to secure more opportunities in the work place, to get equality before the law — in short, to achieve social, economic, and psychological parity in a previously male-dominated world. In this feminist atmosphere, women in the theatre demanded more acting roles and more access to all theatre trades, including playwriting. They noticed that, not only did males get the best roles, but also women had few opportunities for leadership elsewhere in theatre; for instance, between 1956 and 1975, out of 250 plays produced by London's Royal Court Theatre — an organization especially known for its championship of new works — only seventeen were written and or directed by women.

Feminist theatre artists set out to change this situation by forming women's theatre groups and by writing and producing their own plays. In keeping with an anticommercialism mood throughout theatre in the 1960s and early '70s, feminist theatre groups during this period tended to be totally female collectives which emphasized their separateness, but later, toward the beginning of the 1980s, women's groups developed a more collaborative attitude. One of these groups, which will be discussed below, was the Omaha Magic Theatre.

A Feminist Aesthetic?

Before focusing on a particular theatre, however, we need to ask the question, is there a feminist aesthetic? Or stated another way, do plays by women have characteristics which set them off as a different kind of theatre? Any attempt to define a feminist aesthetic immediately encounters the problem that many women playwrights do not consider themselves *feminist* writers; the term "feminist" has political, activist overtones that seem to commit a feminist writer to a narrow set of perspectives, content issues, and purposes. Furthermore, many women — whether or not they are a part of the feminist movement — consider creativity an androgynous impulse that encompasses the experiences of both sexes. And finally, feminists themselves have a variety of understandings about the meaning of feminism and its modes of expression that makes it difficult to describe a unified feminist dramaturgy.

At the risk, then, of offending almost everyone, here are some tendencies noted in plays written by women: First, in their manner of production, feminist plays tended to grow out of group processes; of course, many male playwrights (including Shakespeare) collaborated with others in writing plays, and the group-process approach may just be a passing result of the 1960s collectivization noted above; but those observations aside, women's plays seemed especially likely to emerge from the cooperative, improvisational efforts of groups of female artists. In terms of content, women's plays usually focused on women's issues, with the result that their cast lists had a majority of female roles. Two kinds of issues seemed particularly common in women's plays: Issues of dependence on (and independence from) men and, secondly, women's sex lives (including sexual preferences, hang-ups, practices, behaviors, and gynecological experiences). Structurally, women's plays frequently were ensemble pieces without a clearly identified central character. Women's plays also handled conflict differently; instead of the strong, obvious two-sided conflicts typical in traditional male plays, these plays tended to have diffused multifaceted tensions which seemed to suggest that conflict played a less central role here than it did in traditional European drama. Finally, women's plays tended to use a circular nondirectional development instead of the linear, chronological development typical in traditional male drama.

Many feminists considered themselves part of the post-modern culture (see pages 680-681), and the characteristics of women's drama apply almost as well to other post-modernist plays. One thing became certain: By the end of the twentieth century, women — who for centuries had served theatre as valued performers — had taken a leading role in the art. Theatre had become richer, truer, tougher — more than ever the *lively* art — thanks to feminist theatre.

Megan Terry and the Omaha Magic Theatre

Megan Terry, born in Seattle in 1932, moved to New York City and became a founding member of the Open Theatre in 1963. The Open Theatre, under the leadership of Joseph Chaikin, used collective improvisation to create nonrealistic, experimental plays which addressed various social issues; specific productions included *The Serpent* (1968) scripted by Jean-Claude Van Itallie (1936-) and *Viet-Rock* (1966) scripted by Terry.

Jo Ann Schmidman was born in Omaha, Nebraska in 1948. As a theatre student in Boston, she encountered the American avant-garde theatre movement, including the work of the Open Theatre and Megan Terry. What she discovered so energized her that she decided to return to Omaha and create an avant-garde theatre so that "Omaha and the people I care passionately about could partake of this alternative theatre." In 1968, she founded the Omaha Magic Theatre, and in 1970, spreading her efforts between New York and Omaha, she became a performing member of the Open Theatre.

When the Open Theatre disbanded in 1973, Megan Terry joined the Omaha Magic Theatre. Subsequently, she wrote most of the group's texts with Schmidman as director, designer, and lead performer. These works included *Babes in the Bighouse* (1974), *Brazil Fado* (1977), *American King's English for Queens* (1978), *Goona Goona* (1979), *Kegger* (1982), and the play which follows — *Body Leaks*.

Sora Kimberlain, born in 1954 in Cincinnati, became inspired by the expressionists, action painting, and Happenings while studying painting and sculpture in art school. In 1980, she joined the Omaha Magic Theatre as a visual artist, and by the late 1980s she was co-writing and performing with Schmidman and Terry.

Omaha Magic Theatre set itself a clear mission: A commitment to produce the works of living, working, avant-garde playwrights — especially experimental plays full of surprises, new ways of seeing, and new information. The group challenged expectations about what is relevant, pertinent, theatrical, and politically correct. They were at least as interested in engaging their audiences in dialogue as they were in entertaining them. It is perhaps significant that, although the artistic core of the OMT were women, and although their plays seemed to express feminist viewpoints, feminism was not part of their stated objective. Throughout the 1980s and '90s, the Omaha Magic Theatre not only performed in their home town, but also toured extensively, sharing their vision with enthusiastic audiences throughout North America.

Body Leaks

Production History

Body Leaks was written in 1990 as a collaborative effort between Megan Terry, Jo Ann Schmidman, and artist Sora Kimberlain with music composed by Marianne de Pury, Luigi Waites, Jeremy Arakara, and Megan Terry. Omaha Magic Theatre performed the play at their home theatre and toured it throughout the United States and Canada for two years. Schmidman, Terry, and Kimberlain performed the piece with other roles being filled by a succession of actors including Robert N. Gilmer, Susan Watts, and Holly McClay. Accompanists during these years included Luigi Waites, Jon Lindley, and Krystal Kremla.

Dramaturgy

Unlike most traditional plays which find their unity in focusing on a single event or *action*, the varied scenes and images of *Body Leaks* are loosely unified around a *thematic* core. The play focuses on various perceptions about censorship. It confronts censorship in the formal, legal sense of the word as well as the informal sense of standards imposed by society. But even more centrally, the play examines and challenges our tendency to internalize censorship, to *self*-censor, to keep ourselves from saying or doing things in order to protect ourselves and others or to control ourselves and others. *Body Leaks* is an attack on psychic and social repression.

The play follows an episodic, nonlinear structure and almost totally rejects the use of story and character. In many plays composed of a succession of short, episodic scenes (e.g. *Waiting for Lefty* or *The Bald Soprano*), the scenes themselves usually are brief stories — called "vignettes" or "sketches" — in which characters meet, develop conflicts, and achieve resolution. Most of the scenes and sequences in *Body Leaks*, however, have few elements of story. Instead of vignettes or sketches, they seem rather to be performed symbols which utilize emblematic behaviors, symbolic technical elements, and words as gestures. Rather than using performance, language, costume, props, and scenic effects to tell a story, the play uses these elements in new ways to make thematic statements.

The language used in the play is poetic, personal, and surreal — almost abstract. The occasional use of offensive language shocks the audience and challenges censorship on yet another level. *Body Leaks* tests the limits of language as a communication tool. For instance, although the line "I'll make gardenias to you between sheets of mint" uses normal sentence structure, and although it creates a feeling and maybe even a group of images, nevertheless it uses words in ways that resist translation into traditional, rational "meaning."

The play also calls for nonverbal elements — actions, costumes, props, scenery, lighting, and sound — which are abstract, symbolic, and startlingly unusual. Neon tubes hang from the ceiling in apparently random distribution; props include a toaster with rotary saw blades where the toast should be; actors scatter candy malted milk balls on the stage and then crush them; writhing colored-light effects, created right before the audience's eyes using an overhead projector and an eggbeater in a bowl of water, spread liquid images across the backdrop; polka dots, symbolizing the self leaking through, appear in dialogue, on costumes, and in visual effects.

The nonlinear plot, antirational, shocking use of language, and bombardment by unfamiliar aural and visual experiences have the effect of eliminating the rational filters through which audiences usually view theatre. The play attempts to make its impact directly on the nerve endings, the intuition, the emotions — the parts of our inner selves which are usually "censored" by our rational intellect.

Created to be performed in the theatre rather than printed between the covers of a book, *Body Leaks* is a challenging script to read; to get the most out of it, the reader needs to lay aside usual expectations about play scripts, accept the piece on its own terms, and set the mind free to imagine it on stage. Those who rise to the challenge will find inspiration and liberation in the play.

Creative, rough-edged, a slap in the face of tradition — in its manner of production, its dramatic structure, its content, its use of language, and its effect — *Body Leaks* exemplifies late-twentieth-century feminist theatre.

BODY LEAKS

by MEGAN TERRY,
JO ANN SCHMIDMAN and SORA KIMBERLAIN

music by MARIANNE DE PURY, LUIGI WAITES,
JO ANN SCHMIDMAN and MEGAN TERRY

The action of the play takes place on a stage in the present.

THE CHARACTERS

ONE
A woman

TWO
A woman

THREE
A woman or a man

FOUR
A woman

ACCOMPANIST
A musician

Left to right: Jo Ann Schmidman, Sora Kimberlain, and Hollie McClay appearing in the Omaha Magic Theatre production of Body Leaks.

PRODUCTION NOTES

Body Leaks has a single setting — the *environment* for the production. The following describes the visual installation created at Omaha Magic Theatre. The performance configuration is long (fifty-four feet right to left) and not very deep (twelve feet), similar to the vaudeville stage. A stretched screen of a lycra-like material provides the rear wall. Another nine-foot-wide by twelve-foot-high rear projection screen is angled Stage Right. This allows the presentation of performer silhouettes, often used when performers exit the stage. This screen accepts both slide and overhead projections. Four gel-covered and patterned nine-foot fluorescent light tubes hang vertically two inches from the floor. They zigzag across the performance space. Stage Left, six feet Downstage from the lycra screen, is a four-foot-high by five-foot-long wall made of glass bricks. Similarly, Stage Right, is a V-shaped fort, built also of glass bricks. At times performers make speeches from behind these places; at other times performers create images there as they disappear inside the structures and become refracted color and form, or they create an image with their bodies or properties as they emerge from the structure. Keyboards are Stage Left. Other sculptural elements and unusual properties — the lighted school desk and two light boxes used for the telephone scene, the high chair, and the lighted garbage can — are wheeled or carried on stage as needed.

At the edge of the stage, separating the audience from the performance area, a line of candles flicker in white luminary bags throughout the performance. The overhead projectors and a slide projector are on the Downstage lip of the playing area. This set-up allows the performers to alter the projected environments in full view of the audience before or during each of the scenes.

Performers in the OMT production also ran lights, including operating the switch controls for the hanging tube lights. Lighting controls were placed Stage Left of the projectors, in full view of the audience. The performers learned the technical cues at the same time they learned their lines, and they executed them as essential tasks, as the necessary teamwork of the ensemble.

Marianne de Pury wrote the music for the opening and closing songs, and Megan Terry wrote the lyrics; this music is available from the Omaha Magic Theatre. The entire sound structure of the OMT production, played on keyboards and percussion, was created during developmental workshops using both sampled and synthesized music.

There are many scenes in *Body Leaks*. There are no blackouts. We have learned to trust that the language and other sounds and visuals of the piece — the intent and content — provide ample transitions for the audience. Action moves as quickly as the human mind, from situation to situation, locale to locale, character to character. *Body Leaks* should be staged with the same random logic we use to process a situation, a thought, or to deal with the unknowns we face in any real or imagined activity of life.

It is our intent that the play be presented as a series of integrated, quick transformations between interior and exterior states as well as real or perceived places or situations. We observe audiences to be very smart and capable. When left to their own devices, if they stop worrying that they might miss something, they put tunnel vision aside and take in many events and ideas at once, just as most of us do in every moment of our conscious and dream lives. Therefore, we very purposely create a dense, multileveled theatre experience for the intense mindplay of all of us.

The visual and sound elements are meant to be interacted with by the performers. These sometimes amplify an intent of the scene or may physicalize an interior obstacle, such as the performer's inner voice, which the performer must overcome to continue. Each scene in *Body Leaks* involves a critical, life-death, personal decision for performers and audience. Audiences choose where to look, what to listen to, when to think personal thoughts, when to trust and enter the world presented — when to self-censor and hold themselves back or when to go with the flow and enjoy. We have developed this way of presentation because we find that it empowers audiences, that it gives them permission to "see" a production in "this way," if that's what they choose.

The performance mode of *Body Leaks* has evolved over the past twenty-six years of OMT's ensemble work. It has been developed and is being constantly refined by observing and listening to our audiences and incorporating discoveries made both in workshops and performances. The ideas and stories of Omaha audiences, as well as those of diverse urban and rural audiences from throughout the USA and Canada, are incorporated as we go along. The feel of the work is exuberant, energetic, intense, layered like a parfait, and passionate. This is because: (1) The artists who created and perform *Body Leaks* are committed to, believe in, and trust one another as well as the content and the form of the piece; they also trust that audiences will "get it." (2) The way the elements of *Body Leaks* are integrated; we strive to see that each of the art disciplines is equally represented and presented: Solid and light sculpture, movement, text, direct and transformed language, sound, and music. The writers, the director, the composers, and designers also perform text and gesture as well as all the technical tasks necessary to realize the performance.

We sense that the performance mode of *Body Leaks* might be similar to Shakespeare's or Molière's productions of their own community-based work. Our relationship, via our theatre, to our local and extended community, and the positive expectations we share regarding the communication of societal and personal ideologies, bridge contemporary and traditional forms. It is our goal in performance to physically communicate, in a very metaphorical (and thus broadly accessible) manner, the ideas and feelings of the script. In the following written text, we have attempted to provide as many visual descriptions as possible in order to give the reader or director a visual starting point as well as a sense of how *we* communicated the text — not necessarily "how it *must* be staged!"

Body Leaks is about self-censorship. It explores the ways we humans have of deluding ourselves even to ourselves. Conversely, it also demonstrates the secret or little-noticed techniques we develop for revealing the self. The transformational monologues, dialogue, and images reflect upon some of the eternal human questions: "Who am I?" "Who do you think I am?" "Who do I think I am?" "Am I who you think I am?" "Who is it I may not be letting myself become?"

(TWO enters to traveling music. She flirts with the audience until she arrives Center Stage. FOUR and THREE enter slowly.)
TWO: *(Sings in mock sexy torch-song style.)* I've been waiting slow
I been waiting long
For the greenhouse effect to come along.
ALL: I like it hot
I like it hot
I like it hot
Where I can see and hear and feel my dots.
TWO: I wanta take off
all my winter clothes,
and summer and spring
and autumn too.
ALL: I like it hot
I like it hot
I like it hot
I'm flying to the Amazon
Where I can see and hear and feel my dots.
TWO: Let me put my breast on
Let me strap my breast on
We're flying down, down on the Amazon.
ALL: I like it hot
I like it hot
I like it hot
Where I can get under
The rain trees *(Begin to exit.)*
Where I can see — and hear — and feel —
My dots. *(FOUR re-enters. Reflective glass-beaded glasses are mounted on a cafeteria tray which she holds as a shield and is also a radar receiver. She walks behind the flickering candle path. TWO re-enters with a small sampler that laughs when she pushes the button in response to her lines. She moves along the back wall. Both constantly look over their shoulders, suspiciously. Dots are projected. One at a time, three giant female forms, made of light, appear. TWO turns and stands in front of these forms while she begins to knead her stomach.)*
TWO: Don't look at me like that.
FOUR: *(To audience)* He gave me a long drink look.
TWO: That tight cruel mouth gives me the shivers.
FOUR: Bedroom eyes.
TWO: *(Singing)* "Eyes that I just idolize . . ."
FOUR: The eyes process seventy percent of information coming into the brain.
TWO: Twenty-twenty vision.
FOUR: Blow is just an expression, stupid.
TWO: Dirty mouth!
FOUR: Lower your eyes when talking with a superior.
TWO: Eye contact can dominate a customer, or a woman. *(Moves into another projected form.)*
FOUR: That was the evil eye.

TWO: Eyes are the windows of the soul.

FOUR: Bette Davis eyes.

TWO: He undressed me with his eyes.

FOUR: Your mouth says no, no, but your eyes say yes, yes, yes. *(Another projected form is revealed. She moves into it.)*

TWO: You have to put lipstick on your mouth so men can find it.

FOUR: What's that crunching I hear?

TWO: It's the rain eating potato chips. *(A third form appears. FOUR backs to wall with tray over her head.)*

FOUR: It's the rain cleaning her teeth.

She does it every morning and evening on my pillow.

She does it for many more minutes if there are dots.

I rest best on the crisp, dotted pillowcase I bought last week at K-Mart.

The dots are reservoirs for the rain.

TWO: Dots will beam the way out when I'm ready. *(Tube lites turn on. TWO, with her forearm in her mouth, runs around tubes. She shakes the arm in her mouth like a creature with fresh kill and exits. Black is projected. A rip appears in it, light floods through.)*

FOUR: *(In recognition, to audience)* There's an elephant without her head! I don't know what's the matter with me. I just can't seem to look her in the eyes. *(Forced laugh)* Ha ha ha ha. *(Hits self in head.)* That's not funny. *(Projection: Washing machine and dryer with people inside.)* I knew that!

My reality is on pre-wash and dry.

I went into a sleep room, a read room, and a washing machine room.

The machine room reads "pre-soaks only."

I left my sponge there and went on to the "time room."

Trash had built up around the entry way but I went in anyway.

There was a dryer there. *(Tries to say it, keeping time.)* I set it to the time *(Ticking starts. THREE enters and waits impatiently next to FOUR. THREE carries a miniature park bench with parachute men leaping from it. Both go numb.)* however many minutes it was after the hour. While waiting

for the dryer

I went to the pre-present room,

the numb room.

THREE: *(Numbly)* I sit and stare and let the

laundry build up on my body. *(FOUR exits.)*

ONE: *(Enters Stage Left.)* My sister called me at three in the morning and I told her to . . . *(Stops herself. Covers her mouth.)*

THREE: Women Who Tell It All.

ONE: A giant bird with metallic blue-green, yellow, magenta and purple dotted feathers sat on my shoulder and . . . *(Covers her mouth. THREE turns her back to audience and moves across space left with a "Women Who Tell It All" sign on her back.)* I looked into her eyes and noticed she had a reflection of the pyramids shining there. I leaned forward and . . . *(Covers her mouth and runs out. FOUR, TWO, and THREE enter on path left. Each wears earmuffs and has a metal right breast strapped on. They carry small white bags which they pierce with a*

*sharp object throughout the following. [X] indicates percussive sounds
on wood block.)*
TWO: There's this great long formation of birds. *[X]*
A shot is fired. *[X] (TWO and THREE jump or hide. FOUR picks up
a clear plexi square which she uses as a steering wheel. Polar fire and
other yellow shapes are projected. Shots continue throughout. [XXX]
A performer dribbles a large yellow ball across the stage. ONE, at
projector, squirts red dye on plexi.)*
FOUR: I was driving my tractor in Uganda around the field.
A flaming grapefruit rolls across the ground
toward me. *(Smashes plexi into face.)* It has a gash — jutted pink flesh —
leaving a track of beaded juice behind. *(To TWO and THREE)*
Coming from a heated war zone —
It has a message *(TWO, FOUR and THREE look out expectantly.)*
For the territory. *(A big splot of red is projected on performers.)*
TWO: *[X]* A bird drops. *[X]*
The formation absorbs the hole. *(All hang heads, form line and exit left.)*
THREE: *(Slips from line, moves into candlelight, confidentially to audience)*
I won't let myself use that tone of voice. *(Bites lip and exits.)*
TWO: *(Behind glass bricks)* I won't let myself cry in public *(To audience,
confidentially)* " 'cause if I did, they'd never elect me president." *(Exits.)*
FOUR: *(Re-enters left with a large tin can over her head. Takes can off and
opens it with a can opener.)* I won't let myself cry in public . . . or in
private, because it might be my mother come for a visit, and I wouldn't
want her to find out. Or, it might be the meter reader — and I wouldn't
want her to find out. *(Exits left. The effect of a blind being lowered
created on the back wall by manipulating a line-stencil on the overhead.
In this way, lines of light are cut into space. Plastic ants are thrown
onto the stencil.)*
The white frame house has no doors. *(Gasps, then sees herself.)*
I'm falling.
(On path) I'm agitating in a million swinging doors
I watch *you* through *your* reflections in *my picture window*
(Eyes front) I keep my eyes glued till a bird smashes into the glass.
(THREE at right glass brick, covers eyes.)
The reflections continue
I uncover my *eyes. (Gasps, sees self.)*
I'm falling. *(As FOUR exits, ONE and TWO enter path. They use fan
rakes to cover their faces. The rakes become human extensions. The
performers attempt to connect or break connections with their use of
the rakes. FOUR continues as she exits.)*
I uncover my ears.
Here comes the next brave bird.
First blood stain, now girl, dry up and fly off.
ONE: I've got this deadline at work and my mind's a blank.
TWO: I won't let myself be his doormat.
ONE: I won't let her pussywhip me.
TWO: I won't let myself castrate him.
ONE: I won't let them know I feel like a fraud. *(An open mouth with*

*people inside is projected. This is manipulated on the overhead with a
bright red gel, so the mouth appears to scream.)*
FOUR: *(Begins in silhouette behind right screen. She wears a high, three-
tiered, oriental headdress. Laughter explodes from her, mixed with
laughs from sampler. She emerges from behind screen and speaks.)*
I hear myself screaming,
So what — just forget it.
I plug my ears.
The ice jam breaks.
Blood is pouring from me.
The larger the puddle at my feet becomes,
The stronger I become.
Jump!
Jump up and down in the puddle.
Splash!
The red rises, it's getting tropical;
I makes my light blink on and off;
It calls to me, like starvation. *(ONE and TWO re-enter with rakes
behind left glass bricks.)*
TWO: All this is on your shoulders!
ONE: I won't let myself talk back to her and show how angry I am.
TWO: I won't let myself say anything nice, so I'm not talking.
ONE: You've turned over all the stones you could.
TWO: I won't let them know who I really am. *(To the beats of a big drum,
ONE, TWO and FOUR move across back screen as blind ones. Each
calls out a phrase.)*
ONE: Everyone
TWO: In the world
ONE: Looks up
FOUR: From what they're doing *(ONE and FOUR run to vertical tube
Right Center; TWO runs to tube Left Center. They address the audi-
ence.)*
ONE and FOUR: And points!
TWO: And thinks they know better. *(ALL begin to leave.)*
FOUR: They sneer and say,
ALL: *(Strut as they exit.)* "Oh, I could do that, I just don't choose to right now."
TWO: *(Dons a three-tiered, oriental headdress and emerges in a follow-spot
behind left glass bricks.)* I have to read! I have to read all these reports
and forecasts and comb the Wall Street Journal and listen to business
shows on TV. I wish I had a spy in Germany and another in Tokyo
and a pipeline to the Federal Reserve. The Feds — they're the ones
that set the interest rates for America. But they have secret meetings,
and you never know what they're going to do till they've done it six
weeks earlier! I can't get information on how to spend the money I
don't have fast enough! It's keeping me up nights listening to my
shortwave radio, trying to get a feel. *(Projection: Dots spiral out from
a pile.)*
FOUR: *(Enters pushing a wheelbarrow of white sand. She, calling out
lovingly, then searches in the sand.)*

Truth, truth, here truth!
(To audience) I hid it, I couldn't face it,
So I hid it, a long time ago — from me.
Now it's buried deep . . .
(Searching in sand) Where is it? *(Text is projected on back screen —*
"Every choice made excludes all other possible choices." TWO and
FOUR enter. They scoop and dump sand three times with the back of
the shovel [A Jewish burial ritual]. Each speaks a part of the following
phrase as the ritual takes place. After speaking, they form a line right
and exit. During this ritual, THREE tosses grenades of corn chips then
does military belly-crawl to them, smashes them, eats the debris and
continues to move across the front path to other side of stage. FOUR
continues.)
Every choice made

TWO: Excludes — all other possible choices. *(Exits with wheelbarrow.)*

FOUR: *(Re-enters wearing a "scratch and sniff" coat. It is high fashion,*
brightly colored and covered with emery boards and "touch of scent"
aerosols. Frenetically, she scratches and launches the smells.)
There's too much to know! —
To know it all.
It's not my responsibility.
I been worrying — just what *is* my responsibility?
I pretty regularly function as a judge.
I'm quick to *blame you* for not speaking up on my behalf.
You know or you could figure it out, I'm sure.
(She moves along back screen, covering body parts.) You can tell the
lie said, from the *truth* unspoken. *(Fiercely in left bricks)*
But you do not speak! *(Text is projected: "Scratch and sniff." TWO*
enters the dialogue. She appears in silhouette behind right screen and
speaks into a microphone. FOUR paces while scratching and pushing
"touch of scents.")
I talk loudly to myself in bus and train stations . . .

TWO: There're too many people in this line!

FOUR: . . . in airports

TWO: I should have brought my uzi.

FOUR: as I walk here to there . . .

TWO: These businessmen are already drunk!

FOUR: to here.

TWO: *(Clenched teeth)* I'm gonna have to kill one for an aisle seat.

FOUR: People are more likely to hear when they don't have to choose to
turn me on or off. *(Holds her swirling head.)* It's all in here. *(THREE*
enters right with lighted cart. She reveals a fish lying on it. She picks
up and caresses the fish. Then, she abruptly chops off its head, and
guts it while speaking harshly to the fish.)
Keep movin' the garbage 'round or it'll rot.
Shut up.

THREE: Take that — SUSHI!

FOUR: Reminds me —
The Fish Always Stinks From the Head . . . . (Exit left. THREE pushes

Body Leaks

her sushi chopped cart off right. A long blue corridor is projected. TWO enters right and runs along the back wall. She looks both ways, then looks down the corridor. [X] indicates she looks both ways before speaking. Lines are spoken as if she's using all her strength to speak after running. FOUR crosses with a tray-shield imaging a "headless guy juggling many cork heads." THREE enters and "reaches outward" in varied rhythms from behind Right Center light tube.)

TWO: I looked down a long corridor. Each door had a label on it. *[X)* The first door read "Women's Room." *[X]* The next door said "Men's Room." *(Casaba begins.)* The third door was labeled "Men's and Women's Room." *(Casaba intensifies. TWO turns and pounds on back wall.)* The last door said "Video Room — *Slash and Rape* Showing. Previews for next week, Karen Finley, Michael Jackson, Madonna and Jesse Helms starring in *How to Vogue a Senate Wimp* followed by *The Denver Yams vs. the Colorado S & L Assholes!" (FOUR re-enters with pole, parachute guys dangle from it. She makes fighter plane sounds. Overhead: text projected "Be Careful." TWO moves into candlelight, confidentially to audience)* Then there was a door I hadn't seen. I open it. *(THREE launches flying saucers.)* There are two hundred million people sitting there on folding chairs. It's the first meeting of "the adult children of war-a-holics" . . . *(Backs into wall.)* I back up and yell — Fire! *(Repeats "Fire," jammed with next speech.)*

THREE: *(Covers crotch.)* We're water. *(Bump and grind)* We retain n' retain n' retain *so much.* I'm afraid I'll burst like a hot dog cookin' too fast over an open fire. *(Hangs head, then lunges at audience. Speaks through gritted teeth.)*
I could explode right through my skin
And it might *(To audience confidentially)*
Get on you.

FOUR: *(To audience confidentially)* Leak on you

TWO: *(To audience confidentially)* Get into you.
(Picks up fly swatter and moves to back wall. She smashes giant projected flies and ants through each of her following "Don't" lines.)
No jaywalking!
Don't tell secrets to girlfriends; they'll steal your guy.
Don't gain weight!
Don't ever sing in public; you got a tin ear!

ONE: *(Enters right bravely)* I got on my bright red shirt.

TWO: Don't fart in church!

ONE: You better not come near me wearing green.

TWO: *(Gritted teeth)* Don't tell family secrets. *(Text is projected: "Take a risk, darling.")*

THREE: *(Enters left wearing three-tiered headdress and leans against back screen.)* Take a risk, darling, but show respect . . . for *Flight Distance —*

TWO: Don't scratch your crotch at the table!

THREE: The safe distance we animals need to take off — ready, set, bang . . .

TWO: It's nobody's business how much I make.

THREE: How many car lengths does it take you to stop?

TWO: *(Walks up close to stage edge, to audience)* Don't let 'em know you

799

care. *(She exits.)*

THREE: And then when you do, the highways could open up.

TWO: *(Exits.)* Don't forget to write.

THREE: *(In shock, she freezes like a rabbit surprised by headlights.)* If only I hadn't hit the brakes, *(Sobs into the wall)* I might have lived. *(THREE continues, shamefully sobbing and covering face, as she moves along wall.)* I'm not Japanese. I can't sleep that close to my relatives! *(The stage is dark. Random, very bright spots of color are projected. Sounds of constant dripping. FOUR enters, as a legless one, on a dolly. She propels herself with her hands, and she holds a lit candle in her mouth. ONE, with head bandaged, enters along wall. She speaks conversationally but thrusts a menacing toaster, rotary saw blades pop out instead of toast. She interacts with FOUR. [X] indicates a percussive sound.)*

FOUR: I feel loving because of the light. I love soft light. It makes my soul feel light and airy, as if I could float over the world on a carpet of light and rain flowers down on scenes that please me.

ONE: Are you love? *[X]*

FOUR: What makes you ask?

ONE: Floating and light sounds like love to me. *[X]*

FOUR: THAT MEANS LOVE TO YOU? *[X]*

ONE: Yeah.

FOUR: Love to me is heat, magenta, sweat, tension, flashing lights. Not soft but intense quick light, coming and going in the eyes. Breath, hot breath in my ear, a hand on my arm pulling me closer. Or sitting close at the theatre feeling the heat of my lover's body coming through my clothes. Crushed together in the back seat of a car at night. That's love to me. *(ONE turns blades onto herself.)*

THREE: *(Enters from left, moves against wall listening, then nervously turns front.)* What was all that other stuff?

FOUR: Love of nature.

THREE: Oh! I never really notice nature *[X]* unless I'm in love with a person. *[X]*

TWO: *(From mike left by keyboards — delivered as a jam with the beginning of ONE's next speech.)* Sora, *(Name of person performing ONE)* you have the most beautiful eyes . . . in Omaha *(Your town)*. Luigi Waites *(Name of your musician)* and I have this bet . . . that you have . . . the . . . most beautiful eyes in the entire United States.

ONE: *(Makes buzz sounds, while slashing air aggressively with the toaster.)* I listen.
But I don't get it.
Oh, I sorta get the idea of it.
I just don't get *it. (Jam ends.)*
I can't remember one second later what you said!
I remember how I think *they* feel about it.
I remember how I feel about it . . .
But somehow I think it's most important to remember *it*.
(Turns toaster on self and exits.) The point, the part I always miss.
(Projected polka dots dance. FOUR and THREE, shy and nervous,

come together in center; they are lovebirds, their hands sweat.)
FOUR: We were necking
THREE: on a polka dot life raft
FOUR and THREE: Then a flying saucer lands — *(Each sees saucer land in the light tube beyond the other's shoulders, then each runs to these Right and Left Center light tubes.)*
FOUR: It stays
THREE: but blows my mind away *(They back up and come together.)*
   The flying saucer is presenting — ("Canned" circus music is played.)
FOUR: THE WAY IT'S SUPPOSED TO BE.
ONE: *(Moves in and out of light tubes pushing a lawn mower.)* Sprinklers save lives! *(Tiny dots are projected, first as pinholes and then they grow larger.)*
TWO: *(Enters, vamping audience.)* Don't you think it's a little severe a-fashion-statement
   To imprint all these dots?
   Do we have to wear polka dots every season?
   Dots, polka dots — what a concept!
   Why dots can prove to the world we're open — we're free. Dots prove we got holes. *(Shows nose.)*
   Yeh, have a look. Step right up!
   See clear up into my soul, yeh!
   Yeh, polka dots are it, yeh! *("World map" is projected. She notices it.)*
   Keep your eye on these polka dots!
   See this map?
   Right, it's a map of Omaha. *(Name of your town. THREE and FOUR run through, arms in mouths, like they've just captured fresh kill. They stop and examine map.)*
   Where do you live?
   Can you find your street?
   You can't find it, can you? You know why!
   Cuz it's covered with dots! *(THREE exits.)*
   Those dots are your neighbors.
   Want to buy some spot remover? *("Neighbors" line can be adapted for specific regions, e.g. in Calgary, Canada — "Those dots are Americans"; in Tempe, AZ — "Those dots are snowbirds." Projected text: "Even numbered chairs, turn right, odd numbered, face left.")*
FOUR: *(Removes arm from mouth and lifts fist.)*
   We try to signal through the bars of our cages.
   (Bites arm and flings the flesh around like a dog.)
   We find it easier to mingle in narrow corridors.
   (To audience, in confidence)
   In my mind we relate so well.
   I get confused who's who.
   Am I me? Are you you?
   It's funny — I see me looking out
      when I look at you.
THREE: *(Over mike in silhouette behind side screen)*
   Psst, audience: Even numbered chairs, turn right . . .

FOUR: *(Ad-lib)* That's two, four, six, turn this way.

THREE: . . . odd numbers, face left.

FOUR: *(Ad-lib)* Three, THREE, seven's . . . nothing's hard, you'll just have to figure it out . . . this is a very important moment of the piece. It's called inter-audience interaction . . . If you don't know the person next to you, kind of look that person in the eyes . . . eyeball to eyeball . . . that's right, turn and look . . . *(Stops in left spot and encourages this audience action. Projection: water droplets are sprayed and projected. THREE enters with balloons by tube light, right; at [X], balloons pop.)*

ONE: *(Enters as a "seer" and stops behind left glass bricks.)* Zelda functions in any velocity of wind. Searing blades from her headgear slice the air. *(To audience)* When situations are in season, Zelda is a warrior. *(Dances from behind bricks with the projected dots as they form.)* She wears black and white polka dot dresses and carries a small white paper bag. The rains come and wash the dots off her dress. *(As "Seer")* She catches them in her bag. When the sun comes out . . . *(Dances)* the dots dance back onto her dress. *(As "Seer")* The secret of rain is carried in her bag.

TWO: *(As she enters, she ties on a white apron covered with large black polka dots, vamps like Bette Davis strutting center.)* We can't assume to know — who we — really are! Since we change . . . from moment to moment! *(Very femme)* Is it a trampoline *[X]* or a tiger trap? *[X]* *(Vamp)* Don't know! *[XX]* Don't take a chance! *[XX]* Paint it out! *(THREE, with white paint and a brush, crosses and kneels in front of TWO. She paints out the black dots on TWO's apron. Projection: An eggbeater is operated over an anatomy drawing.)*

FOUR: *(Flutters in, circles at left tube light while caressing herself all over.)* It's like we gotta monkey around, We gotta run around and around it. *(Stops; to audience)* We just gotta touch it, *(Anticipates touching her nipple)* we gotta touch and it's dangerous, *(Touches her nipple)* so, *(Pause, looks side to side)* we gotta touch when no one's looking. *(She ducks behind left glass bricks; she emerges from behind the bricks with her shirt pulled up over her head.)* "True or false — most of us would rather show our faces?" *(When all TWO's dots are painted out, she begins to snort. THREE runs off in disgust. FOUR gets malted milk balls and gleefully tosses them into the air, sometimes bowling with them. THREE re-enters with a bowling ball as her head.)*

TWO: She gives malted milk ball parties! Everyone crowds around a neon table to watch the balls. *(THREE smashes malted milk balls right then left then center. Seeing this, FOUR exits and re-enters with dustpan and whisk broom. She manically follows after THREE and sweeps up the mess.)* When the balls fall off the table, it's real funny, and everyone is supposed to laugh.

ONE: *(Lines begin nervously from Downstage projector; chattering teeth are wound up and projected. FOUR and TWO re-enter with coffee cups and saucers. They add to the "uncalm" by creating percussive sounds, "saucer hitting cup," as they try to catch the leaks with their cups.)*
Trying to be relaxed when you're not calm,
My neck cramps up. So, I have another cup of coffee.
Lips quiver — acting like you're calm — lips stick to teeth. *(ONE, wearing three-tiered wig, crosses behind right screen and speaks in silhouette into mike.)*
I'm coming home exhausted. I'm so glad to finally be able to cool out.
(ONE moves Center Stage with light box; THREE enters in candlelight with a manually generated phone which she rings.)
I'm making a package of noodles,
I sit down, by myself, in peace to eat.
The phone rings.
I decide I'm eating, I don't have to answer.
I don't want to answer it, I don't want to be disturbed at all.
But the phone keeps ringing — I keep eating.
And it rings and rings and rings.
It keeps on ringing far longer than any normal phone call rings.
Finally, to shut it up, I pick it up.
(Very curt) Hello! *(Transforming into the caller)* Is the lady of the house in? *(As herself)* Fuck you! If you ever fucking call again, I'll blow your head off! *(Slams phone; pause, phone begins ringing again; pause, unplugs phone and feeling vindicated, exits. Parade of deflated umbrellas enter. They cover over the faces of their carriers and pulse like jellyfish; they stop center. The umbrella carriers become the souls of the whales and herring. Water in constant motion is projected.)*
FOUR: *(Sneaks in, stops behind glass bricks, peeks out, ducks behind while the umbrellas open and shut like breath.)*
It wakes me several times in the night.
We are constant feeders. *(Growl)*
I can't think of a single waking moment, *(Growl)* I'm not feeding.
(Umbrellas are used abrasively with strobe-like moves.)
Through seeing, or hearing, or tasting, or touching, or feeling or whis-
    pered sensing. *(Umbrellas are lifted high and then dropped.)*
And I can really gulp down a lot of information.
I was impressed to discover that whales don't have to eat for eight months.
But when they do feed, *(Growl)*
They form a large circle and all blow bubbles. *(Umbrellas are twirled like parasols.)*
Then they turn vertical and tread water, tails down. *(Open umbrellas are raised high, dropped upside-down and twirled slowly.)*
And, of course, they're all singing at the top of their lungs — whale
    songs. *(All "sing whale sounds" with the keyboard.)*
Each one more beautiful, more siren-like, direct-to-the-heart, than the
    last. *(Everything stops.)*
The herring are freaked! *(The umbrella operators turn their backs to audience; they put closed umbrellas through their legs and rhythmically*

keep trying to open them.)
They form a tight group; "The secret society of herring."
They blow bubbles themselves and try to sing along.
They try with their whole fishy selves to follow the dancing dots.
And while they're busy singing and chattering with one another they
lose sight of themselves — they forget biological necessities, they
forget about checking their depth level, and float up. *(Open umbrellas
are slowly lifted high. When indicated by [X], umbrellas are extended
front and worked in big 360-degree circle drops.)*
Boy, those whales take a big gulp! *[X]*
They open wide *[X]* — thirteen feet wide. *[X]*
They leap straight up into space, mouths open.
Water and herring! All at once.
Once outside — in the ocean, *[X] (Then umbrellas spin on floor)* now
    inside — in the whale. *(Pause; umbrellas are twirled in front of
bodies.)*
Whales are much more developed than we realize.
They come equipped to strain, to separate — that which they should
    take in, that which they shouldn't take in.
Whales leak instinctively.
What's a strain for us, is instinct for a whale.
Whales are hemorrhoid free.
With their giant strainers they separate water from herring and under-
    sea greens. *(Umbrella carriers move left as they twirl their umbrel-
las.)*
You see, whales can tell the difference.
They know right from wrong.
They learn it young in whale school through whale ethics. *(Umbrella
carriers keep twirling, now moving right and exit.)*
They censor only the bad — what's *not good for them.*
Too much salt would make anyone throw up. *(TWO and THREE enter
haltingly and try to speak, but until the sand arrives, they can't — they
censor; FOUR wheels in a wheelbarrow of fine sand and parks it Center
Stage. TWO and THREE rush to the sand and sift it in their hands.
They try to hold onto their memories by holding the sand.)*

TWO: In the hospital, when I tried to feed my starving grandma homemade
beef and barley soup I'd made from the recipe I learned from her, she
pushed me away and said: "Quit monkeying around, Jo Ann!"

THREE: I tried to get to know my grandfather in the nursing home, but
he couldn't hear me anymore. Up till then he'd only been a birthday
check! I looked down and saw in that bed a person I longed to know,
slipping away from me just as I was waking up.

TWO: *(To THREE. Delivers lines like gunshots.)* Your father's brother was
murdered! Shot between the eyes! He was a gangster. He's got midgets
in his family. So you do too! *(Big fake smile to audience)* I trade you
my garbage for your garbage.
Let's eat up all that family garbage,
Builds layers of armor — twelve ways.

THREE: Mom burnt the lamb chops.

TWO: *(Puts on headgear made of old records.)* Not again!
THREE: He never came home; he didn't call.
    She was burnin' . . . she burnt *them.*
    (Big fake smile) The rule when I was little is today's garbage. *(TWO picks up accordion gate; THREE exits with wheelbarrow, then re-enters, joining TWO. They open and shut accordion gate facing the audience.)*
ONE: The hippos pack up and leave. They don't have to listen to this shit. They remembered why they no longer live in the ocean. *(FOUR brings in baby high chair from left, places it center behind accordion gate and sits in it.)*
FOUR: What if we're born knowing it all, but then Mom lies to protect us?
THREE: Dad ridicules her.
FOUR: They lie about some damn thing or other, like:
TWO: "If you can't say something nice, don't say anything at all."
THREE: "Stay as sweet as you are."
TWO: "Your face'll freeze like that. And your face is your fortune."
FOUR: Very young — at three or four — I discovered the *Joy of Lying.* *(A spiral binder is played like a machine gun. THREE and TWO move accordion fence in and out, and speak through smiling gritted teeth.)*
THREE: Don't eat anything larger than your head.
TWO: Your mommy got straight A's all the way through grade twelve.
THREE: Listen to that Ozzy Osbourne and you'll burn in hell!
TWO: Your mommy saved herself for your daddy.
THREE: Boys shouldn't play with Barbie dolls.
TWO: Young ladies don't walk like old cowboys.
THREE: Our children are too good to join gangs.
TWO: I want you to play "Kind and Gentle" in your sandbox just like Georgie Herbert Walker Bush.
THREE: No substitutions!
FOUR: *(Tosses spiral binder off, like a debutante, then crosses to left glass blocks.)*
    Words shoot at me, over me, through me.
    It's a good thing I'm invisible.
    (Furiously) You may have birthed me!
    (Transparently) But do you really know me?
    I used to think I knew you. *(FOUR exits and re-enters with garbage can which she bangs on in accompaniment to the following.)*
ALL: *(Sing)* I Loves Mah Babai
    I Loves Mah Babai
    I Loves Mah Babai,
    Babai, Babai — *(Giant babies are projected. "Sleep, Baby Sleep," or any lullaby, is played on the keyboard. FOUR, TWO and THREE parade out right, after baby chair. The stage is dark except for the luminaries. ONE and FOUR rush in. They lift the lid and look into the can; light floods up from can.)*
FOUR: Can you go into the center, if you shave your head?
ONE: Can you go into the center of your brain, if you shave your head?
FOUR: Can you go into the center of your body, if you shave your head?
ONE: Can you be a Barbara Hepworth sculpture with a piercing void, if

you shave your head?

FOUR: Can you see clear through to China, if you shave your head?
Can you see Hong Kong? Queen Kong?
Or is it the 270-Foot Woman?
She can crush entire cities of dickheads with a single blow!

ONE: She's touring the globe leaving no city untouched.

FOUR: It is she

ONE: that I will see,

BOTH: when I shave my head. *(They exit right with garbage can. FOUR re-enters with neon desk and sits left. At desk, she splashes water in her face, and under her arms; the water symbolizes her own sweaty discomfort. At Downstage projectors, ONE pours water into glass bowls; during the following two speeches she will beat the water with an eggbeater.)*

THREE: *(Enters by tube light right. She begins in a whisper.)* Water is sprayed. The air around it is heated up. The situation becomes steamy — if the window glass remains closed. It beads up — it sweats. *(Full voice)* And for God's sake, never let 'em see you sweat. *(High-pitched voice)* The glass is no longer transparent, beaded and sweating; it cries from the inside — longing to get through to you. *(After the next three lines, she covers her mouth and struggles to be free to speak. She speaks in her own voice.)*
S-h-h-h.
It can't say a word.
It is paralyzed.
Make a deal with yourself —
Open the window a crack. *(Puts on glasses; one lens is shattered. Raises her fist.)* Pick one of the bricks you're shitting and throw it! *(Raised fist opens and shuts as ONE enters and smashes THREE's other lens.)*

FOUR: *(As she continues to splash herself)*
How to stop up a body leak.
How to milk a body leak for all it's worth.
How a body leak can become a flood.
How to milk a body leak for all it's worth.
You are caught in a dot of white light.
What are you doing?!
(Puts on thick, black rubber gloves — hands fly up as if caught.)
"I'm changing the light bulb, it's hot!" *(ONE rocks in silhouette behind side screen, then enters in right spot. One by one, all enter and begin a self-involved rocking. Before speaking, each stops rocking and takes line, confidentially, to audience. After speaking, they rock again.)*

TWO: I won't allow myself to paint the exterior of my house anything but white.

THREE: I won't let myself watch dumb shows on TV. I cover my ears when the news comes on.

FOUR: I don't let myself hang my gigantic panties on the line to dry . . . even on the nicest days . . .

ONE: I won't allow myself to punch you when you say, "It can't be that bad — smile."

FOUR: *(Rises, crosses into left spot; rocking sound changes to a high tone.)*
When my grandma died I took off her earrings
So her body could leak.
At last free to leak in peace.
I was the last to be with her.
Now you know too.
(Frantically) Run, run for your life . . .

THREE: *(Over mike in silhouette behind side screen)* Lava picks up speed as it flows downhill. *(All run in different directions. FOUR sits back down at neon desk. Dots are projected. TWO enters slowly from left, picking invisible cake crumbs from clothes and launches them to become one of the many dots of light. THREE enters wearing grass skirt as a shawl. She places birthday cake on desk in front of FOUR and exits doing hula in silhouette with grass skirt behind screen.)*

TWO: Last summer when I visited my grandparents in Hawaii, they were so glad to see me, they panted over me like two St. Bernards. I couldn't watch TV or read a book without them saying, *(Panting)* "Whatcha watching, David? Whatcha reading, David? Let's read it together. Let's watch it together. Where ya going, David? . . . To the beach? Great! We'll go with you!" *(Panting stops.)* I didn't mean to hurt 'em when I said, "Get outta my face!" but you'da thought I'd kicked them right in the teeth.

FOUR: *(While lighting birthday candles)*
The cake man keeps picking off crumbs from his pants.
He taught me to chant the Haftorah, now he's into crumbs. *(TWO exits right.)*
I think I finally understand what I was chanting. *(FOUR exits. Projection: Images of women in negligees. THREE enters with a white box as his/her head. Party favors blow out where his/her ears would be. FOUR, also wearing a box head, joins him/her. FOUR carries a rake. Both blow party favors throughout next speech.)*

THREE: I wear a box around my face so you can't hurt me, so I can't reach my own butt to bite it. I learned this tactic from the vet. My uncle was an eye surgeon. He knew to wear gloves — soft, white cotton gloves whenever — he thought he might lose sense of where his hands were. Like he always wore them while he slept. He put them on before bedtime just in case he'd doze off, fall into oblivion, *(FOUR begins raking the wall)* and go right to it. Right to scratching and gouging and clawing at his eyes, going at it with his fingernails — scratching like a wild beast, because it feels so good. I sometimes wear these same white gloves . . . when I meet my grandmother for lunch. *(As she exits, FOUR also exits.)* When I polish the silver . . . when I don't want to leave fingerprints . . . on my slides. *(TWO walks in quickly from right, bouncing a yellow ball. FOUR re-enters left, juggling two large yellow balls.)*

FOUR: I was walking down the street and I stopped in front of this tall glass building. It's glass from top to bottom and all lit up from top to bottom with incandescent lights, not fluorescent.

TWO: But it's all lit up, like they're so rich they don't ever have to worry about the light bill. And I'm walking past all this glass and a darling older man comes up to me.

FOUR: He had white hair and blue eyes and he was wearing blue jeans and a camel hair sweater.

TWO: He walks up to me and says in a very soft and gentle voice,

FOUR: "Forgive them, Mother, for they know not what they do."

TWO: Then he looks at his feet and says . . .

FOUR: I know Christ said, "Forgive them Father," but I just can't get Mother out of my mind.

TWO: I said — "That's OK . . . neither can I." *(ONE and THREE enter to behind left and right glass bricks. When they talk of cherry pies, their earthy-Calaban-like selves speak. When they discuss hospital proce-dures, the tone is small talk, like girls who gossip.)*

THREE: It's snowing up here.

ONE: It's raining down here.

THREE: The snow's not sticking, but it might if the temperature turns colder.

ONE: We need rain. God we need rain! If we don't get enough, I'm going to have to go out there and patch up my hose and give my fruit trees a good soaking before winter hits or they'll never make it.

THREE: You still name your fruit trees?

ONE: My pie cherry is Teresa and the bing is Bruce. *(Gossip mode, they move center.)* The doctor told me I didn't have any cancer cells.

THREE: That's a break.

ONE: She had to look all the way up me through the colon into the large intestine. Maybe they even got up in there. It was weird. *(To right brick)* You remember how Grandma made that great pie crust?

THREE: *(To left brick)* You got to mix ice water into it.

ONE: Is that the secret?

THREE: She used to pour a bit of ice water on the dough and mix it lightly with a fork. She used to let us help her. I see the fork. I can feel it in my hands. Yeah.

ONE: I forgot about the ice water. *(Gossip mode, they move center.)* That thing with the light on it they put up my rectum was ice cold, let me tell you.

THREE: How'd you stand it?

ONE: My doctor's so cool. She's real straightforward. She says: "I'm going to look up inside you now. Just bear down on my instrument as if you were having a B.M." It seemed opposite of what might help. But she was right. The more I bore down with my butt muscles the higher up that snake went into my gut.

THREE: Didn't it hurt?

ONE: It wasn't a picnic. But what hurt was having to take all those lax-atives the day before.

THREE: Oh, no!

ONE: Oh, yes. I couldn't go anywhere or do anything. I was on the damned pot every THREE minutes and my poor old anus was a bleeding battered sore mess. Even the nurse was sympathetic when she saw it. She put some medicine on it before they wrangled that metal piece into me. I had to kneel on this strange operating-type contraption. You know those TV commercials you've seen of those beds you can make into zigzags for your back so you can read in bed? Well, this was like that — only you kind of kneel in it. The nurse and the doctor say: "Now grip the sides of the table and hold tight." And you lean forward with your head on one side and hang on for dear life while they raise your butt in the air. The rest is covered with a sheet. I felt sorry for my anus.

THREE: *(To left brick)* Do you mix your bings with your pie cherries when you bake?

ONE: Only for our family. For the church it's straight pie cherry. I use honey instead of sugar too. For the church social I use sugar, cuz that's what people are used to. But it's hard to get enough bings. Between the birds and the kids, I'm lucky to get enough to satisfy *me*.

THREE: *(Gossip mode, they move center.)* What'd the doctor see up inside you?

ONE: No shit. After all those laxatives and what they politely termed a "cleansing enema," my insides were cleaner than my face. The nurse was like Chickie Stewart. 'Member her — cheerleader of the football team? She kept saying: "That's it! You're doing real good — yer bearing down just fine. That's it!"

THREE: So the doctor didn't find anything?

ONE: Yeah. See, I'm busy clinging to the table and *bearing down* on you know what, but I did hear her whisper, "a lot of hemorrhoids." So back in her office I'm dressed and we're discussing my insides like they were the ninth hole of the Meadowbrook Golf Course and I ask her *what all the hemorrhoids mean*. Should I be worried? Should I do anything about it? She says, "Happens to all of us."

THREE: Me, too?

ONE: You're two years younger than me, you got two years less hems. Anyway, it seems we wasn't meant to walk on two legs. Since we do, it's the force of gravity makes all these *hemorrhoids form down in the bottom of our rectum*. Just the sheer pull of that gravity.

THREE: What if they start bleeding? *(The following lines are said as they exit.)*

ONE: Please, they haven't.

THREE: What if they do?
Do you have to do this every year?

ONE: You will too.

THREE: Never. *(TWO enters on path from left; ONE and THREE fade out as she begins to speak.)*

TWO: When I well up with love
Because I feel so much —
Well up and burst forth,
You get worried! *(Pause)*
You think I've gone too far!
You think I'll burst — then evaporate?

You think I should control it, control myself. *(Pause)*
Leaking and melting are out of control!
You think only God, babies, artists and politicians can get away with
    abandon?
It's just that I'm feeling.
Feeling emotional . . .
Feelings are a deal, a really big deal.
Feelings are what I leak — *(Stops, walks to audience and speaks even
more confidentially.)* These dots I wear allow my feelings through to
you. *(Pause)*
I'm feeling you and you and me — *(Pause)*
I feel generations of us!
Lots of garbage to sort. *(Pause)*
You feel good — you feel so good to me! *(Pause)*
I love you. *(Pause, moves behind left bricks. She remembers a voice
from her past. She's deeply touched and surprised. She cradles her
head in her hands.)*
"Oh, Jo . . . I love you, too." *(Exits left slowly.)*

THREE: *(Struts in from right.)* Hunker down and dream for a while. We
don't have to be ready yet. They'll be coming for us around eleven.
We can hug and tell stories. *(FOUR brings out a steaming bun on a
silver tray. THREE pulls it apart and places each half on FOUR's
ears.)* I have this feeling that I won't let myself try things because I
know I can't get the money to back my dreams. So I haven't been
letting myself dream the way I did when I was a kid.

ALL: *(From Off-stage)* You're not old!

THREE: *(Continues.)* That's what I mean. I've started to close down. Just
because I see other people not getting what they want, I think I can't
get what I want. Just because *they* can't. Why do I do that? I'm not
them. I have a different set of energies. I can make things happen.
(TWO and FOUR enter right.) If I can let my mind form what it is I
want to do. *(TWO is behind glass bricks left. FOUR is behind glass
bricks right. A world map is projected with dimensional dolls scattered
across it.)*

TWO: We were so close when we were kids.

FOUR: Yeah, we were.

TWO: I've missed you.

FOUR: You live three thousand miles away.

TWO: I have to. I can't make a living here.

FOUR: *(Crosses to her.)* I wish you had some kids so I could love them.

TWO: I wish I had some kids, too, but why can't you just love me?

FOUR: We're too old for that.

TWO: God, who gets too old for love?

FOUR: *(Hugs TWO; land mines begin exploding when she does this. [X])*
It's so much easier to love children. *[X]* It's natural. *[X]* *(They exit
right on path. They walk out together trying to hold one another; with
every step a land mine explodes. THREE marches in wearing a metal
hat. (S)he carries a metal corrugated sheet. An image of a gangland
shooting is projected.)*

ONE: *(Enters with breast armor from right — tough; she is uncomfortable and keeps adjusting her armor.)* So now we wear only metal hats.
We're steel plated
To match the steel in our heads.
I was a pilot in the war — fell on my head, had a metal plate put in.
A metal remembrance of war.
Is this true or false? *(THREE faces front, places metal sheet against wall.)*
Do not let it show! *(Pause. ONE and THREE bang heads into the metal sheet.)*
I saw Carol Burnett do that on TV.
That's where I learned everything. *(THREE reverses corrugated sheet to display a police shooting target pinned to crunched up chicken wire. ONE and FOUR enter with arrows. They will stab [X] the target with each line they speak. They are mildly demented.)*
FOUR: *(Dances.)* The caboose came loose
And hit me on the forehead,
But I picked myself up and went
Right back to shooting. *[X]*
ONE: I was told you were looting. *[X]*
FOUR: *[X]* Mere gossip.
ONE: Your enemies were tooting your horn? *[X]*
FOUR: Is it my fault the President *[X]* wasn't watching the store?
ONE: I think *[X]* you should quit working the streets of Los Angeles.
FOUR: That was someone else you saw.
There aren't any streets in any American cities anymore except Omaha. *[X]* *(THREE rakes the path in front of the back screen and the screen left and right of target.)*
ONE: For heaven's sake! You've painted the rake!
FOUR: I used to play the rake, but now I prefer the ukulele.
ONE: *(Sneaks forward, grabs FOUR: they struggle.)* I want to talk with you all day and all night.
FOUR: *(Still struggling; looks over shoulder to see that no one else hears.)* If you'll let me suck your fingers, I'm yours.
ONE: The lint in your belly button is a tempting soufflé. *(Stab target together.)*
FOUR: Linger on my ligaments for several hours . . .
I'll make gardenias to you between sheets of mint. *(Stab target together.)*
ONE: *(Withholding, she steps left of target.)* Today my Princess — today, to lunch and tonight — you'll come to all your senses at my petite dejeuner.
FOUR: *(Pushes through an imaginary door and then offers entry to ONE.)* I'm sinking more and more into the impression you left at the door.
ONE: I'm not content just to let you rebuild my body with your alfresco caresses. I want the monuments of your mind to find safety on the city of my tongue. *(Red is projected onto the target.)*
FOUR: *(Drags ONE to behind right bricks.)* Stairs of nightmares condense into the head of your match, while fits of laughter dress our unlimited sighs.
ONE: I'm convinced you're the right formula to take my left brain on vacation.

FOUR: Feet first we burst from eminent sheets where you'd aroused my interest on purpose.
Behind the charms of your arms
I always find the fire
Of your mind glowing
In the galaxy
Of your soul. *(ONE runs out right; FOUR follows. TWO enters. Pulls arrows from target on each line and thrusts them into her hair, under her arms, etc.)*

TWO: *(Ultra fem, she recites "the rules.")* I won't allow myself to stutter when I talk.
I won't let myself ask her for a ride home.
I won't allow myself to ask him if he wants to share my lunch.
I won't let myself ask her when her birthday is.
I won't let myself ask him to meet me on Catalina Island.
I won't let myself ask her to fix my car.
I won't let myself criticize his parents.
I won't allow myself to vote for the best person. *(Pulling out the last arrow and crossing to behind left bricks. THREE exits Christ-like with corrugated metal target on her back.)*
I won't let him know I care. *(Exits. THREE enters with Kotex absorbent jacket and birdcage on head. Projected text: "Things That Get Stuck." Also, a white hockey mask is projected with images from past and future dreams in the eyeholes. TWO and FOUR feel their way along the back screen.)*

THREE: Things That Get Stuck! *(Tiny sounds leak from TWO and FOUR and intensify. They notice it's happening but can't stop it.)*

FOUR: It's an invasion . . .

TWO: of privacy . . .

FOUR: to look at your face! *(They exit. Black is projected. A slit is ripped into it and light comes through. THREE throws snap caps on floor.)*

THREE: *(Crossing right)* Light comes out. It is dusted with flour so it can be seen. This same grain dust explodes when held *too tight — too long* in storage.

FOUR: *(Crosses left, bouncing yellow ball off back wall.)* She walks across the room feeling the heat on her back.
She slowly looks over my shoulder,
Chewing gum and dribbling the giant yellow ball with great dexterity.
Sometimes she backs up in order to remember where she's just been.
(ONE brings in wheelbarrow center. FOUR tries to hold on to the sand. ONE joins her. FOUR continues.) "When my great-grandmother was a teenager in Romania, she loved horses so much she'd often slip away to go bareback riding with the Gypsies — her long, black hair flying in the wind. No matter how the styles change, I've never wanted to cut my hair." *(TWO enters to left bricks. FOUR arranges dots on clothing, then begins polka dot dress parade: THREE joins her. The wearers of the dots walk around tubes — they walk with heads down. Occasionally, they look up, pull out a polka dot hankie and mop dots of sweat from their brows.)*

812

TWO: *(Behind bricks)* Come on in.
ONE: Is it cold?
TWO: Naw. Come on in.
ONE: How warm is it?
TWO: If it was cold, do you think I'd be in?
ONE: *(Runs to left side of brick.)* It looks cold.
TWO: I feel like a new person after a ten-minute swim. Come on in.
ONE: I don't know.
TWO: Come on in.
ONE: I'm afraid.
TWO: You know how to swim?
ONE: *(Covers face.)* My father made me take swimming at the Y.
TWO: So come on in!
ONE: But I failed the course. *(Projection: swimmers with ships as heads.)*
TWO: *(Picks up glass full of sand, careful not to leak any.)* Look, it isn't deep.
ONE: *(Also picks up a glass. Her glass leaks all its sand out through a hole in the bottom.)* I'm afraid.
TWO: *(She puts arm around ONE. They clink glasses playfully and both glasses leak sand.)* Just come in a little way and float. I'll hold you up. I can't tell you how good this feels on the skin. It goes right to the core of your body and wakes up your bones.
ONE: I don't know.
TWO: Come on in!
ONE: I'll watch *you.* You look like you're having fun.
TWO: You can too.
ONE: *(Crosses to wheelbarrow and digs into the sand.)* I'll just watch. This sand is nice and warm. Feels good to me.
TWO: *(Toasts her with leaky glass.)* You don't know what you're missing. *(Exits.)*
FOUR: Am I responsible for what she's done?
Would a tiny little surgical gown
Fit on my tongue?
ONE: Maybe tomorrow. *(Exits with wheelbarrow. Projection: Photo of young woman from the 1930s or 1940s.)*
FOUR: *(Walking path rhythmically, she speaks to herself.)* If I walk your streets with my feet,
Why is it that I cannot say the day of the week or what is the date?
Is it spring or fall?
Yes, it is. It's one or the other.
And I am breathing this fall air.
The same spring air you breathe. *(To audience, confidentially)*
I can no longer count backwards by threes from one hundred.
Oh, I once could. *(As she moves back to path)*
It's just now I've chosen to forget how.
It was not a skill I called upon often . . . .
Not in thirty years of government service!
In fact, there has not been once in the number of years I've lived in my twenties or my forties or my seventies that I have ever needed to count backwards by threes. *(Suspiciously to audience in candlelight)*

And why do you want to know now?
I sense you really don't want to know.
It's some sort of a trick,
A way to take more from me.
I don't trust you —
It's the twist of your mouth!
It's the way you smell!
I don't like your looks! *(Pause)*
And! I know where I am now!
I am not traveling now. It is Omaha, Nebraska. *(Or wherever the show is being played)*
However, when I am traveling I can never be sure of city . . . or state . . . or country.
I am usually quite certain however that my feet are on the ground.
Except of course, when I'm in the air.
(To audience, confidentially) I fly quite a bit. You don't?
I'm so sorry. (Pause)
I always seem to know I'm here.
Of course, like all of us — sometimes I must go there.
But I know now I am here with you darling —
And you are asking me silly questions.
Spell world . . . *W O R L D.*
I can spell!
So what!
I'm educated!
What are you, some sort of elitist, fascist pig?
W O R L D.
So there! So what! Spell it backwards?
D L R W O, D L W O R, *(Pause. Sincerely concerned)*
You're being ridiculous!
When one is feeling concerned with oneself, as I am now, the time is completely inappropriate to play a silly game.
You may have been taught it in school.
But, some things we learn to forget. *(Pause)*
And yes, I am angry.
And, yes, I feel I have no control.
Because I have no control
I know! You have the control!
This I see very clearly —
You and *They* have control. All my control is yours now,
And I'm mad, madder than any dog can get! *(Pause)*
A month ago would I play this silly game with you?
Maybe yes. Maybe no. I'm a Scorpio.
Maybe even years ago I wouldn't give you the answers you want.
Such a silly test. To think you could know *me* better.
I don't know me, I'm a secret society.
I've buried the important stuff deep.
So deep, I've forgotten where.

So I couldn't tell you even if I wanted to tell you.
So I say forget it.
And you have no right to ask such things of me! *(Pause)*
Spring forward, fall backward?
Fall forward, spring back!

TWO: *(In spot left, gestures with left arm.)* Look to the left!
There's a fragment. *(Turns back to audience, gestures with right arm.)*
Look to the right!
There's a whole picture.
Then I blink and only a detail of the picture remains.
I look down at my own belly button *(Pause)* and there's a lint souffle
In which suddenly — *(Pause)*
I see the whole world. *(Exits.)*

ONE: *(Enters by Right Center tube light.)* The whole thing is about being
off balance. And then when you feel safe — suddenly — the earth
quakes. Later you regain your balance but then a hurricane of emo-
tions or water hits. *Everything changes again!*
I self-censor when: "I feel this way.
But the world feels another way!
So I better try to feel the world's way."
But now it's an earthquake *inside*. And mountains form, the coastline
is changed and new rivers flow.
We deliberately put ourselves *off* balance.
It's part of our job to constantly risk our equilibrium.
(Jump front) Equal *(Very flat)* Librium:
One of those drugs that keep you stupid; on an even keel; so you don't
make waves; are agreeable; it puts you in a place where you don't
look out and you don't look in. *(Exits. Projection: Millions of dots
grow throughout final song.)*

FOUR: *(Sings.)* What I love about us women
What I love about us women
Is — we're always talking about better ways of living.
(Spoken) We're the midwives to improve our lives —
We give medical and psychiatrical and theatrical advice.
(Spoken) If loving you gives me pleasure, what business is it of yours?

ONE: *(Spoken)* Let your deepest feelings out or they'll strangle you from
the inside.

THREE: *(Spoken)* Kick him down the stairs before he kicks you.

TWO: *(Spoken)* An orgasm a day can keep depression away.

FOUR: *(Sings.)* And you never have to pay a price except — attention.

ALL: *(Sing.)* Attention, attention to prevention:
To throw off your pain
Get vain — get vain —
Get vain
About your brain.

In the main
You can beat the rain
If you say

"I love you" to your brain.

You can drown shame,
Raise depression to elation,
Give yourself the ultimate vacation.
Get off your posterior,
You're no longer inferior,
Indulge yourself on your interior.
It's all right — you have the right
To show your might.

Go on and get it on.
Go on and get it on.
Go on and get it on.

You have the right to get it off.
You have the right to get it off.
You have the right to get it off.
On —
Your own brain.

PIANIST: *(Spoken)* Let's sing it again.
ALL: *(Sing)* I'm vain about my brain!
I'm vain about my brain!
To hell with their oppressive pain;
I'm free.

I'm vain about my brain!
Let *them* drown in their acid rain.
I'm laughing with all the dots I've got
Cuz I'm vain
About my brain!

THE END

Bibliography

GENERAL REFERENCE WORKS

Bordman, Gerald, ed. *The Oxford Companion to American Theatre*. New York: Oxford University Press, 1984. (A basic encyclopedia of American theatre and drama.)

Brockett, Oscar G. *History of the Theatre*. 6th edit. Boston: Allyn and Bacon, 1991. (A thorough treatment of theatre history from the beginnings to the present, written by the dean of theatre historians.)

Connor, Billie M. and Helene Machedlover, eds. *Ottemiller's Index to Plays in Collections: An Author & Title Index to Plays Appearing in Collections Published between 1900 & 1985*. 7th ed. Metuchen, NJ: Scarecrow Press, 1988. (Because most library catalogues do not list individual plays in anthologies, this index is indispensable.)

Hartnoll, Phyllis, ed. *The Oxford Companion to the Theatre*. 4th ed. New York: Oxford University Press, 1983. (A basic encyclopedia of theatre and drama.)

THE CLASSICAL PERIOD
Other Plays to Read

Aeschylus (c. 525-456 BC). *The Oresteia*. Tr. by F. Raphael and K. McLeish. New York: Cambridge University Press, 1979. (First produced in Athens, 458 BC. These three plays, *Agamemnon, The Libation Bearers*, and *The Eumenides* make up the only complete Athenian tragic trilogy still in existence.)

Aristophanes (c. 445-385 BC). *Lysistrata*. Tr. by Jeffrey Henderson. Cambridge, MA: Focus Information Group, 1988. (First produced in 411 BC in Athens' Theatre of Dionysus by Callistratus, possibly at the Lenaean festival in January-February. Full of bawdry and criticism of contemporary politics, *Lysistrata* typifies Greek Old Comedy.)

Euripides (485?-406? BC). *Alcestis*. Tr. by William Arrowsmith. New York: Oxford University Press, 1974. (First produced in 438 BC, this tragi-comedy shows how the later New Comedy developed out of Athenian tragedy.)

Menander (c. 343-c. 290 BC). *Dyskolos (The Bad-Tempered Man)*. New American Library, 1970. (First produced in 317 BC in Athens. *Dyskolos* is the only extant sample of Greek New Comedy.)

Plautus (c. 251-c. 184 BC). *The Menaechmi*. Tr. by Frank D. Copley. New York: Bobbs-Merrill, 1956. (First produced in 186 BC in Rome, *The Menaechmi* typifies Roman comedy; Shakespeare based his *Comedy of Errors* on this play.)

Seneca, Lucius Annaeus (4 BC-AD 65). *Phaedra*. Tr. by Frederick Ahl. Ithaca, NY: Cornell University Press, 1986. (Since Seneca apparently wrote for a reading audience rather than a theater audience, *Phaedra* likely had no productions during his lifetime.)

Terence (196?-159 BC). *The Eunuch*. In Frank D. Copley, tr. *The Comedies of Terence*. New York: Bobbs Merrill, 1967. (Probably first produced at Rome in 161 BC, *The Eunuch* typifies Terence's urbane, elegant comedy.)

Contemporary Dramatic Theory

Aristotle. *Aristotle's Poetics*. Tr. by S. H. Butcher. Hill & Wang, 1961. (Aristotle's analysis of Athenian tragedy in *The Poetics* established a critical vocabulary for the study of drama and has been basic to dramatic criticism ever since.)

Horace. *The Poetic Art: A Translation of Horace's "Ars Poetica."* C. H. Sisson, ed. New York: Carcanet Press, 1975. (In this work, Horace used verse to record current ideas about drama. Renaissance theorists, who considered Rome the pinnacle of classical culture, based their concept of drama on the *Ars Poetica*.)

Modern Criticism

Arnott, Peter D. *The Ancient Greek and Roman Theatre*. New York; Random House, 1971. (This out-of-print book surveys the development of theatre buildings, stage craft, and production processes throughout the classical period.)

——— *Greek Scenic Conventions in the Fifth Century BC*. Westport, CT: Greenwood Press, 1978. (A reprint of the 1962 edition. A clear description of the Greek stage and its furnishings.)

Harsh, Philip W. *A Handbook of Classical Drama*. Stanford, CA: Stanford University Press, 1944. (A basic, playwright-by-playwright and play-by-play survey of all the Greek and Roman plays.)

Kitto, Humphrey D. F. *Greek Tragedy: A Literary Study*. 3rd rev. ed. New York: Routledge, Chapman, & Hall, 1966. (Kitto approaches his dramatic analysis of the plays with the assumption that the playwrights were in full control of their work and that the critic's task is to discover why the writers constructed their plays the way they did.)

Pickard-Cambridge, A. W. *Dithyramb, Tragedy, and Comedy*. 2nd ed. New York: Oxford University Press, 1962. (This out-of-print book carefully traces and explains the development of Greek drama; it focuses on the plays rather than the staging or theatrical organization.)

——— *The Dramatic Festivals of Athens*. 2nd ed. New York: Oxford University Press, 1968. (This out-of-print book clearly explains the organization of the festivals and the production practices in Greek theatre.)

——— *The Theatre of Dionysus in Athens*. New York: Oxford University Press, 1946. (This out-of-print book carefully traces the development of the Greek theatre building and its equipment.)

THE MEDIEVAL PERIOD

Other Plays to Read

Anonymous. *Mankind: The Macro Plays, No. 1*. (Tudor Facsimile Texts: Old English Plays: No. 3) New York: AMS Press, 1988. (Reprint of 1907 edition. First produced in London in 1472, *Mankind* is a prime sample of the psychomachia morality play in which the forces of good and evil battle over the human soul.)

Anonymous. *The Second Shepherds' Play*. Lisl Beer, ed. Boston Branden

Publishing, 1987. (This segment of the Wakefield cycle demonstrates the humor, piety, and anachronisms which characterize the medieval English mystery play.)

Heywood, John (c. 1497-1580). *Play of the Weather.* (Tudor Facsimile Texts: Old English Plays, No. 14) New York: AMS Press, 1987. (First printed in 1533, this is a sample of the secular interlude, a form mid-way between medieval moralities and English renaissance comedy.)

Gassner, John, ed. *Medieval and Tudor Drama.* New York: Applause Theatre Book Publishers, 1987. (This excellent collection includes samples of Hrotsvitha's plays, mummings, Latin religious plays, mystery plays, morality plays, interludes, and early-16th-century English comedy and tragedy.)

Hopper, Vincent F. and Gerald B. Lahey, eds. *Medieval Mystery Plays, Morality Plays, and Interludes.* Woodbury, NY: Barron's, 1962. (Includes *Abraham & Isaac, Noah's Flood,* & *The Second Shepherds' Play* [mysteries]; *The Castle of Perseverance* & *Everyman* [moralities]; and *Johan Johan* & *The Four PP.* [interludes].)

Modern Criticism

Bevington, David M. *From Mankind to Marlowe: Growth of Structure in the Popular Drama of Tudor England.* Cambridge, MA: Harvard University Press, 1962. (Shows how Elizabethan drama developed from the medieval morality play; currently out of print.)

Kolve, V. A. *The Play Called Corpus Christi.* Stanford: Stanford University Press, 1966. (This book clarifies the dramatic principles underlying the English mystery plays.)

Nicoll, Allardyce. *Masks, Mimes, and Miracles: Studies in the Popular Theatre.* New York: Cooper Square, 1963. (A reprint of a 1931 publication and itself currently out of print, this book argues for an unbroken dramatic tradition reaching from Greece to the Renaissance.)

Wickham, Glynne. *Early English Stages, 1300-1660.* 3 vols. New York: Columbia University Press, 1958-80. (Clarifies the various physical staging techniques of the Middle Ages and Renaissance.)

THE RENAISSANCE PERIOD

Other Plays to Read

Beaumont, Francis (1584-1616) and John Fletcher (1579-1625). *Philaster, or Love Lies Bleeding.* Dora Ashe, ed. Lincoln: University of Nebraska Press, 1974. (First produced in 1609, this was the first collaboration of this famous team.)

Jonson, Ben (1572-1637). *Volpone.* New York: Heinemann Educational Books, 1983. (First produced in London in 1606, probably by the King's Men at the Globe Theatre, *Volpone* typifies Jonson's cynical comedy of humors.)

Machiavelli, Niccolo (1469-1527). *Mandragola.* Tr. by Mera J. Flaumenhaft. Prospects Height, IL: Waveland Press, 1981. (First produced in Florence in 1520 at the House of Bi di Giordance. *Mandragola,* in which an old man is tricked into turning his young wife over to a lover, typifies renaissance literary comedy.)

Marlowe, Christopher (1564-93). *Doctor Faustus*. Ed. by John D. Jump. New York: Holmes & Meier, 1982. (Earliest recorded production by the Admiral's Men at London's Rose Theatre in 1587. This tragedy, with its strong central character, its blank verse, its alternation between serious and comic scenes, and its use of medieval dramatic conventions shows how medieval drama developed into renaissance drama.)

Vega Carpio, Lope Felix de (1562-1635). *Fuenteovajuna*. Victor Dixon, ed. Atlantic Highlands, NJ: Humanities Press International, 1989. (First produced in Madrid in 1612, this play by Spain's greatest dramatist shows a village rebelling against its brutal feudal overlord. In English, the title, taken from the name of the village, is *The Sheepwell*.)

Modern Criticism

Adams, John Cranford. *The Globe Playhouse: Its Design and Equipment*. 2nd rev. & enl. ed. New York: Barnes & Noble, 1966. (A painstaking, detailed reconstruction of Shakespeare's theatre.)

Baldwin, Thomas Whitfield. *The Organization and Personnel of the Shakespearean Company*. Princeton: Princeton University Press, 1927. (Currently out of print, this book explains the organizational structure of the Elizabethan acting company.)

Beckerman, Bernard. *Shakespeare at the Globe. 1599-1609*. New York: Macmillan, 1962. (Gives insights into the dramatic structures of Shakespeare's plays; currently out of print.)

Doran, Madeleine. *Endeavors of Art: A Study of Form in Elizabethan Drama*. Madison: University of Wisconsin Press, 1954. (Clarifies the theories and practices underlying Renaissance dramatic structure.)

Joseph, Bertram. *Elizabethan Acting*. 2nd ed. London: Oxford University Press, 1962. (Explains the training and methodologies of the Shakespearean actors; out of print.)

THE NEOCLASSICAL PERIOD
Other Plays to Read

Corneille, Pierre (1606-84). *Le Cid: A Translation in Rhymed Couplets*. Tr. by Vincent J. Cheng. Cranbury, NJ: University of Delaware Press, 1987. (First produced in Paris at the Théâtre du Marais in December, 1636, *Le Cid* is considered to be the first great French play.)

Lillo, George. *The London Merchant, or The History of George Barnwell*. In Ricardo Quintana, ed. *Eighteenth Century Plays*. New York: McGraw Hill, 1966. (This immensely popular domestic tragedy, first produced in London in 1731, had a great effect on the development of drama in Germany. Also in other anthologies.)

Racine, Jean (1639-99). *Phaedre*. Tr. by Richard Wilbur. San Diego, CA: Harcourt, Brace, Jovanovich, 1986. (First produced in Paris at the Hôtel de Bourgogne in 1677, this tragedy is a French classical masterpiece.)

Steele, Richard (1672-1729). *The Conscious Lovers*. Shirley S. Kenney, ed.

Lincoln: University of Nebraska Press, 1968. (First produced at London's Drury Lane Theatre in 1722, this popular sentimental comedy stimulated the development of *comédie larmoyante*.)

Wycherley (1640?-1716). *The Country Wife*. Ed. by John D. Hunt. New York: W. W. Norton & Co., 1976. (First produced in London at the Theatre Royal in Drury Lane in 1675.)

Contemporary Dramatic Theory

Collier, Jeremy (1656-1726). *A Short View of the Immorality and Profaneness of the English Stage*. 3rd ed. New York: AMS Press, n.d. (Published in 1697-98, this attack on theatre expressed middle-class, Puritan objections to Restortion comedy effectively enough that it helped bring this form of the comedy of manners to an end and paved the way for the sentimental comedy of the next century.)

Rymer, Thomas. *A Short View of Tragedy*. Totowa, NJ: Biblio Distribution Centre, 1971. (A reprint of a 1692 publication, a rigid piece of neoclassical criticism which takes Shakespeare to task for falling short of the rules.)

Modern Criticism

Duchartre, Pierre Louis. *The Italian Comedy: The Improvisation, Scenarios, Lives, Attributes, Portraits and Masks of the Illustrious Characters of the Commedia dell'Arte*. Trans. by R. T. Weaver. New York: Dover, 1966. (A reprint of a 1929 publication and a work of art in itself, this book gives a good insight into this popular dramatic form which influenced Molière's plays.)

Goldmann, Lucien. *The Hidden God: A Study of Tragic Vision in the Pensees of Pascal and the Tragedies of Racine*. Trans. by Philip Thody. London: Routledge and Kegan Paul, 1964. (A brilliant piece of Marxist criticism which elucidates the dramaturgy of Racine. Currently in print only in French.)

Kernodle, George R. *From Art to Theatre: Form and Convention in the Renaissance*. Chicago: The University of Chicago Press, 1944. (Explains the development of the main types of stage typical in the Renaissance and shows their connections with contemporary pictorial art; currently out of print.)

NINETEENTH-CENTURY ROMANTICISM & MELODRAMA

Other Plays to Read

Büchner, Georg (1813-37). *Woyzeck*. Tr. by John Mackendrick. New York: Heinemann Educational Books, 1980. (Büchner wrote the scenes that make up *Woyzeck* in 1836 and left the play unfinished at his death. It was published in 1879 and first produced at Munich's Residenztheater in 1913.)

Goethe, Johann Wolfgang von (1748-1832). *Faust*. Tr. by David Luke. New York: Oxford University Press, 1987. (Written in 1832-33, *Faust* was first produced at the Weimar Hoftheater in 1876. As was typical of many romantic plays, *Faust* was intended by its author for reading rather than staging.)

Hugo, Victor (1802-85). *The Hernani: A Tragedy in Five Acts*. Tr. by C.

Crosland (reprinted and edited from the 1887 edition) New York: Howard Fertig, 1987. (First produced at Paris's Comédie-francaise in 1830, *The Hernani* established the place of romantic theatre in France.)

Rowell, George, ed. *Nineteenth Century Plays*. 2nd ed. New York: Oxford University Press, 1972. (Ten melodramas by leading writers of the form including: Jerrold's *Black-Ey'd Susan*, Bulwer-Lytton's *Money*, Taylor and Reade's *Masks and Faces*, Boucicault's *The Colleen Bawn*, Hazlewood's *Lady Audley's Secret*, Taylor's *The Ticket of Leave Man*, Robertson's *Caste*, Albery's *Two Roses*, Lewis's *The Bells*, and Grundy's *A Pair of Spectacles*.)

Contemporary Dramatic Theory

Schiller, Friedrich von. *On the Aesthetic Education of Man*. Trans. by Reginald Snell, New York: Frederick Ungar, 1965. (In a series of letters, Schiller explains his romantic, Kantian theory of art and theatre.)

Modern Criticism

Abrams, Meyer Howard. *The Mirror and the Lamp: Romantic Theory and the Critical Tradition*. New York: Oxford University Press, 1953. (A clear explication of the romantic concept of art and its difference from the classical ideal.)

Grimsted, David. *Melodrama Unveiled: American Theatre and Culture, 1800-1850*. Berkeley: University of California Press, 1987. (Clarifies the structural principles of melodrama. Reprint of the 1968 edition.)

NINETEENTH-CENTURY REALISM

Other Plays to Read

Chekhov, Anton Pavlovich (1860-1904). *The Cherry Orchard*. In Ronald Hingley, tr. *Chekhov: Five Major Plays*. New York: Bantam, 1984. (First produced at the Moscow Art Theatre in 1904. The realistic comedies of Chekhov with their bittersweet irony and their psychological and social honesty were ideally suited to Stanislavsky's approach to acting and directing.)

Gorki, Maxim (pseudonym for Alexey Macimovich Peshkov, 1868-1936). *The Lower Depths*. Tr. by Edwin Hopkins. Boston: Branden Publishing, 1987. (First produced at the Moscow Art Theatre in 1902, *The Lower Depths* is one of the few really successful samples of naturalistic drama.)

Maeterlinck, Maurice (1862-1949). *Pelléas and Mélisande*. Trans. by R. Hovey, in Thomas H. Dickinson, ed. *Chief Contemporary Dramatists: First Series* (1915). New York: AMS Press, n.d. (First produced in Paris in 1893, this mysterious, symbolist play is Maeterlinck's masterpiece. Also printed in other anthologies.)

Shaw, George Bernard (1856-1950). *Arms and the Man*. New York: Penguin, 1950. (Premiering at London's Avenue Theatre in 1894, this popular comedy of ideas was the first of Shaw's plays to be performed.)

Strindberg, August (1849-1912). *The Father*. In Evert Sprinchorn, tr. *Selected Plays*. Minneapolis: University of Minnesota Press, 1986.

(First produced in Copenhagen at the Casino Theatre in 1887. True to the realistic tradition, *The Father* presents a devastating study of the war of the sexes.)

Contemporary Dramatic Theory

Grube, Max. *The Story of the Meininger.* Trans. by Ann Marie Koller. Coral Gables: University of Miami Press, 1963. (Max Grube acted with the Meininger from 1872 to 1888. This account was first published in German in 1926.)

Stanislavski, Konstantin. *An Actor Prepares.* Trans. by Elizabeth R. Hapgood. New York: Theatre Arts, 1989. (First published in 1936. Along with his other three books, this work sets out, in seminovelesque form, Stanislavski's method for acting. The other works are: *My Life in Art* [1924], *Building a Character* [1950], and *Creating a Role* [1961].)

Modern Criticism

Braun, Edward. *The Director and the Stage: From Naturalism to Grotowski.* New York: Holmes and Meier, 1982. (Includes discussions of the Meiningen company, Antoine, and Stanislavski as well as major nonrealistic directors.)

Valency, Maurice. *The Flower and the Castle: An Introduction to Modern Drama.* New York: Schocken Books, 1982. (Discusses the impact of Ibsen and Strindberg; currently out of print.)

ASIAN THEATRE

Other Plays to Read

Arlington, L. C. and Harold Acton, trs. and eds. *Famous Chinese Plays.* New York: Russell and Russell, 1963. (33 scripts from the following periods: San Kuo, Ming, Sung, T'ang, Lieh Kuo, Five Dynasties, and modern. Explanatory introduction, photos of modern productions, and transcriptions of some music. Currently out of print.)

Hung, Josephine Huang, tr. and ed. *Classical Chinese Plays.* Rev. ed. Taipei: Mei Ya, 1971. (Available from International Specialized Book Specialists of Portland, OR. Five Peking opera scripts with a helpful introduction and many illustrations. Scripts: *The Faithful Harlot, Two Men on a String, Twice a Bride, One Missing Head,* and *The Price on Wine.*)

Kalidasa (late fourth to early fifth century, AD). *Shakuntala.* In Arthur W. Ryder, tr. *Shakuntala and Other Writings.* New York: Dutton, 1959. (The masterpiece of all Sanskrit dramas. The English translation of *Shakuntala* in 1789 sparked European interest in Sanskrit literature.)

Contemporary Dramatic Theory

Anonymous. *Natya Sastra.* Trans. by Board of Scholars. India: SRI SATGURU Publications, 1987. (Available through Oriental Book Distributors, Livingston, NJ.)

Gnoli, Raniero. *The Aesthetic Experience According to Abhinavagupta.* Rome: Instituto per il Medio ed Estremo Oriente, 1956. (Currently out of print, this is a translation and explanation of Abhinavagupta's tenth-century work, "the most important text in the whole of Indian aesthetic thought." It clearly expresses the principles which underlie Sanskrit drama.)

Modern Criticism

Mackerras, Colin, ed. *Chinese Theatre from its Origins to the Present Day.* Honolulu: University of Hawaii Press, 1983. (Seven essays on the major periods of Chinese theatre.)

Nippon Gakujutsu Shinkokai. *The Noh Drama: Ten Plays from the Japanese.* Rutland, VT: Charles E. Tuttle, 1960. (A re-issue of the 1955 Japan Society for the Promotion of Science edition. The introduction details the types of plays in a full Noh presentation and the types of song which make up the various parts of a play; it also has a very fine illustration and explanation of a Noh stage. The translations are careful, readable, and complete with repetitions and stage directions.)

Varadpande, M. L. *Religion and Theatre.* Atlantic Highlands: Humanities Press, 1983. (Examines the religious connections of Buddhist and Hindu theatre of the present and past. Out of print.)

EARLY TWENTIETH-CENTURY THEATRE

Other Plays to Read

Eliot, T. S. (1888-1965) *Murder in the Cathedral.* San Diego: Harcourt, Brace, Jovanovich, 1964. (This tragedy about Thomas Becket, first produced in 1935, epitomizes the British verse drama movement.)

Sorge, Reinhard Johannes (1892-1916). *The Beggar.* Tr. Walter H. and Jacqueline Sokel. In Walter H. Sokel, ed., *An Anthology of German Expressionist Drama: A Prelude to the Absurd.* Garden City, NY: Anchor, 1963. pp. 22-89. (Published 1912; premiere 1917. This play's themes of youthful revolt and striving for a deeper spirituality, its episodic structure, and its experimental use of theatre technology make *Der Bettler* a prime sample of Expressionism.)

Wedekind, Frank (1864-1918). *Spring's Awakening.* Trans. by Edward Bond. Portsmouth, NH: Heinemann Educational Books, 1988. (This early sample of expressionism, first produced in 1906, shows adolescents suffering under the pressures of Victorian moral expectations.)

Wilder, Thornton (1897-1975). *Our Town.* New York: Harper & Row, 1985. (This American classic, first produced in 1938, uses expressionistic techniques.)

History, Theory and Criticism

Apollonio, Umbro. *Futurist Manifestos.* Trans. by R. W. Flint, *et al.* New York: Viking, 1973. (A collection of the major statements of leaders in the futurist movement; currently out of print.)

Artaud, Antonin. *The Theater and its Double.* Trans. Mary Caroline Richards. New York: Grove, 1958. (In this seminal work which appeared in 1938, Artaud calls for a "Theatre of Cruelty" which attacks the audience through all the senses, thereby purging it of the poisons of civilization.)

Bordman, Gerald. *American Musical Comedy: From Adonis to Dreamgirls.*

New York: Oxford University Press, 1982.

Cole, Toby, ed. *Playwrights on Playwriting: The Meaning and Making of Modern Drama.* New York: Hill and Wang, 1961. (Essays on playwriting by many modern playwrights from Ibsen to Ionesco.)

Gropius, Walter, ed. *The Theatre of the Bauhaus.* Trans. by Arthur S. Wensinger. Hanover, NH: University Press of New England, 1976.

Kirby, Michael and Victoria Nes Kirby. *Futurist Performance.* New York: PAJ, 1987. (In addition to its history and analysis of the Italian movement of Futurism, this book includes manifestos, playscripts, and illustrations.)

Macgowan, Kenneth. *Footlights Across America: Towards a National Theatre.* New York: Harcourt, Brace, and Co. 1929. (An account of America's little theatre movement by one who was deeply involved in it. Available from Kraus Reprint, Millwood, NY.)

Willett, John. *Expressionism.* London: Weidenfeld and Nicolson, 1970. (Covers expressionist tendencies in art, poetry, music, architecture, and theatre from 1900 into the 1960s. Out of print.)

POLITICAL THEATRE
Other Plays to Read

Brecht, Bertolt. *Galileo.* Trans. by Charles Laughton, New York: Grove-Weidenfeld, 1966. (Written in the USA while Brecht was in exile, *Galileo* demonstrates Brecht's quirky approach to blending humor, psychological insights, irreverence, and politics.)

Hochhuth, Rolf (1931-). *The Deputy.* Tr. by Clara and Richard Winston. New York: Grove, 1963. (First produced in 1964 in Berlin. Although its central character is fictional and its plot uses traditional, realistic dramaturgy, the basic factuality of *The Deputy* and the extensive research which Hochhuth incorporated in the script makes the play an important sample of documentary drama.

Rohan, Pierre de, ed. *Federal Theatre Plays: Three Plays.* New York: Da Capo, 1973. (Contains three scripts: *Triple-A Plowed Under* [1936], *Power* [1937], and *One-Third of a Nation* [1938]. Reprint of the 1938 edition.)

Weiss, Peter (1916-82). *The Investigation.* New York: Atheneum, 1966. (The play opened simultaneously in several theatres in East and West Germany in 1965. A stage-adaptation of transcripts of the 1964 Frankfurt War Crimes Trial, *The Investigation* epitomizes documentary drama.)

History, Theory, and Criticism

Clurman, Harold. *The Fervent Years: The Story of the Group Theatre and the Thirties.* 2nd ed. New York: Hill and Wang, 1957. (By one of the leaders of the company. Currently out of print.)

Flannigan, Haley. *Arena: The History of the Federal Theatre.* New York: Benjamin Blom, 1965. (A reprint of the 1940 book by a leader in the Federal Theatre Project. Out of print.)

Piscator, Erwin. *The Political Theatre: A History, 1914-1929.* Hugh Rorrison, tr. New York: Avon, 1978. (Written in 1929, this book is the memoirs of Piscator, a director and leader in the development of epic theatre. It includes pictures and extensive historical introductions to each chapter written by Rorrison. This version was originally published by Rowohlt Verlag in Reinbek bei Hamburg in 1963 and is currently out of print.)

Willett, John, ed. *Brecht on Theatre: The Development of an Aesthetic.* New York: Hill & Wang, 1964. (A collection of Brecht's writings including "A Short Organum for the Theatre.")

MID-TWENTIETH-CENTURY AMERICAN THEATRE

Other Plays to Read

Inge, William (1913-73). *Bus Stop.* In Inge's *Four Plays.* New York: Grove-Weidenfeld, 1990. (First produced in 1955, this is a realistic drama about ordinary people. Other plays in the book: *Come Back, Little Sheba* [1950], *Picnic* [1953], and *The Dark at the Top of the Stairs* [1957].)

Miller, Arthur (1915-). *The Death of a Salesman.* New York: Penguin, 1976. (First produced in 1949, this Pulitzer-Prize-winning tragedy of a little man combines expressionism and realism in a manner typical of the mid-twentieth century.)

Saroyan, William (1908-81). *The Time of Your Life.* In Haskell M. Block and Robert Shedd, eds. *Masters of Modern Drama.* New York: McGraw Hill, 1962. (This realistic picture of life in a city tavern, first produced in 1939, won a Pulitzer Prize. Also printed in other anthologies.)

History, Theory, and Criticism

Vardac, A. Nicholas. *Stage to Screen: Theatrical Method from Garrick to Griffith.* Cambridge: Harvard University Press, 1949. (Traces the technological and dramatic trends that led to the development of cinema. Available in a reprint edition from Ayer, Salem, NH.)

ABSURDIST DRAMA

Other Plays to Read

Beckett, Samuel. *Waiting for Godot.* New York: Grove-Weidenfeld, 1987. (First produced by Roger Blin in 1953, *Godot* established what came to be known as absurdist theatre.)

Genet, Jean (1910-86). *The Balcony.* Tr. by Bernard Frechtman. New York: Grove, 1958. (Subscription performance in London in 1956; first production in Paris at the Théâtre du Gynnase in 1960. Set in a brothel during a revolution, this major absurdist play investigates the relationship between appearances and reality.)

Sartre, Jean-Paul (1905-80). *No Exit.* In *No Exit and Three Other Plays.* New York: Random House, 1989. (First produced in 1944, this one-act uses traditional dramatic structures to tell an existentialist story of three people in hell. Other Sartre scripts in the book: *The Flies* [1942], *Dirty Hands* (1948], and *The Respectful Prostitute* [1946].)

Theory and Criticism

Esslin, Martin. *The Theatre of the Absurd.* Rev. updated ed. Garden City, NY: Doubleday, 1973. (This major study of the plays of Adamov, Becket, Genet, Ionesco, and others created the term "absurdist theatre.")

AFRICAN-AMERICAN DRAMA

Others Plays to Read

Hansberry, Lorraine (1930-65). *A Raisin in the Sun.* New York, New American Library, 1987. (First produced at New York's Ethel Barrymore Theatre in 1959. Sometimes called "the quintessential integrationist play, *A Raisin in the Sun* was the most influential African-American play of the 1950s. It drew black audiences to Broadway.)

Jones, LeRoi (Imamu Amiri Baraka) (1934-). *The Slave.* In Imamu Amiri Baraka's *Selected Plays and Prose of Amiri Baraka/LeRoi Jones.* New York; William Morrow, 1979. Also in Amiri Baraka's *Dutchman and The Slave.* New York: William Morrow, 1964. (First produced at New York's St. Mark's Playhouse in 1964. Along with *Dutchman, The Slave* initiated the Black Theatre Movement of the 1960s and 1970s.)

Riley, Clayton, ed. *A Black Quartet.* New York: New American Library/Mentor, 1970. (Currently out of print, this book includes Ed Bullins' *The Gentleman Caller,* Ben Caldwell's *Prayer Meeting or the First Militant Preacher,* LeRoi Jones's *Great Goodness of Life (A Coon Show),* and Ron Milner's *The Warning — A Theme for Linda.* Produced as a single night's entertainment in 1969, "A Black Quartet" demonstrated for the first time the black theatre movement's viability and cohesiveness.)

Wilson, August. *Fences.* New York: NAL, 1986. (First produced in 1987, this Pulitzer-Prize-winner is a good sample of African-American drama in the late twentieth century.)

History, Theory, and Criticism

Baraka, Imamu Amiri. *Raise, Race, Rays, Raze: Essays Since 1965.* New York: University Place Books, 1971. (Along with Ed Bullins, Baraka was a major leader of the black arts movement.)

Harrison, Paul Carter. *The Drama of Nommo: Black Theatre in the African Continuum.* New York: Grove, 1972. (The influence of African culture on the African-American aesthetic.)

Hill, Erroll, ed. *The Theatre of Black Americans: A Collection of Critical Essays.* 2 vols. Englewood Cliffs, NJ: Prentice-Hall, 1980. (Volume 1 contains two groups of essays: "Roots and Rituals: The Search for Identity" and "The Image Makers: Plays and Playwrights"; Volume 2 has essays on "The Presenters: Companies and Players" and "The Participators: Audiences and Critics.")

King, Woodie, Jr. *Black Theatre: Present Condition.* New York: Publishing Center of Cultural Resources, 1981. (A compilation of essays and interviews expressing the views and recounting the experiences of this leading African-American theatre producer.)

Williams, Mance. *Black Theatre in the 1960s and 1970s: A Historical-Critical*

Analysis of the Movement. Westport, CT; Greenwood, 1985. (This book begins with a good historical overview and goes on to analyze the theatre and drama of the movement using Marxist, structuralist, and realist criticism.)

THE SIXTIES AND AFTER

Other Plays to Read

Albee, Edward (1928-). *A Delicate Balance.* New York: Atheneum, 1966. (First produced in 1966 in New York's Martin Beck Theatre, this Pulitzer-Prize-winning play is considered to be Albee's best work to date. Albee was one of the few major American playwrights to emerge in the 1960s.)

Goodman, Robyn and Marisa Smith, eds. *Women Playwrights: The Best Plays of 1992.* Newbury, VT: Smith and Kraus, 1992. (Six plays written by women in the 1990s.)

Handke, Peter (1942-). *Kaspar.* In Handke's *Kaspar and Other Plays.* Trans. by Michael Roloff. New York: Farrar, Straus, & Giroux, 1970. (First produced in 1968, this play exemplifies post-modernist drama. The other plays in the book are Handke's "speak-pieces" *Offending the Audience* and *Self-Accusation* [both 1966].)

Mamet, David (1947-). *American Buffalo.* New York: Grove, 1977. (First produced in 1975 at Chicago's Goodman Theatre, Stage Two, this early play by Mamet demonstrates the playwright's ability to turn realistic dialogue into poetry and to find goodness even among the dregs of humanity.)

Miles, Julia, ed. *The Women's Project 2.* New York: Performing Arts Journal Publications, 1984. (This collection presents five plays produced by the Women's Project of New York's American Place Theatre during the first half of the '80s.)

Mrozek, Slawomir (1930-). *Tango.* In Mrozek's *Striptease, Tango, Vatzlav: Three Plays.* Trans. by Lola Gruenthal, *et al.* New York: Grove Weidenfeld, 1981. (This play, first produced in 1965, combines realism and absurdism in a political critique.)

Osborne, John (1929-). *Look Back in Anger.* New York: Penguin, 1962. (This play, first produced by the English Stage Company at London's Royal Court Theatre in 1956, initiated a new movement in British theatre which eventually eliminated the Licensing Act.)

Pinter, Harold (1930-). *The Caretaker.* New York: Grove-Weidenfeld, 1989. (First presented by London's Arts Theatre Club in 1960, this play epitomizes Pinter's dramatic mode.)

Rabe, David (1940-). *In the Boom Boom Room.* New York: Grove-Weidenfeld, 1986. (Written in 1973, this play was first produced in a revised form in London in 1976. In contemporary fashion, it combined realistic characters and situations with theatricalized effects.)

Shepard, Sam (1943-). *Buried Child.* In Shepard's *Seven Plays.* New York: Bantam, 1984. (First produced at San Francisco's Magic Theatre in 1978, this realistic play about a twisted family won a Pulitzer Prize.)

Simon, Neil (1927-). *Brighton Beach Memoirs.* New York: NAL, 1986. (First produced in 1983, this play shows Simon's comic genius at its best.)

Stoppard, Tom (born Straussler, 1937-). *Rozencrantz and Guildenstern Are Dead.* New York: Grove-Weidenfeld, 1987. (First produced professionally by the National Theatre Company at London's Old Vic Theatre in 1967, *Rozencrantz and Guildenstern* is a transitional play between absurdism and post-modernism.)

Sullivan, Victoria and James Hatch, eds. *Plays By and About Women: An Anthology.* New York: Random House, 1974. (This book, which includes Megan Terry's *Calm Down, Mother,* gives a good sampling of plays written by female authors during the first six decades of the twentieth century.)

Theory and Criticism

Abel, Lionel. *Metatheatre: A New View of Dramatic Form.* New York: Hill & Wang, 1963. (Currently out of print, this book investigates the portrayal of life as a human creation, one of the concepts of post-modern theatre.)

Brook, Peter. *The Empty Space.* New York: Macmillan, 1978. (First published in 1968, this book presents viewpoints on theatre by a major British director of the 1950s and 1960s.)

Burian, Jarka. *The Scenography of Joseph Svoboda.* Middletown: Wesleyan University Press, 1971. (A biography of the Czech designer, a statement of his design principles, and descriptions and photographs of representative productions.)

Case, Sue-Ellen. *Feminism and Theatre.* New York: Routledge, 1987. (Examines the relationship between feminism and theatre using history, stage practice and theory.)

Goodman, Lizbeth. *Contemporary Feminist Theatres: To Each Her Own.* New York: Routledge, 1993. (A historical study of British feminist artists and theatre groups during the 1970s and '80s.)

Grotowski, Jerzy. *Towards a Poor Theatre.* New York: Simon & Schuster, 1970. (An explanation, by this influential Polish director, of his theory and techniques. First published in 1968.)

Hayman, Ronald. *Theatre and Anti-Theatre: New Movements Since Beckett.* New York: Oxford Univ. Press, 1979. (Argues that the development of theatre since 1953 has been antiliterary and influenced by antiart attitudes. Out of print.)

Kirby, Michael. *Happenings: An Illustrated Anthology.* New York: E. P. Dutton, 1966. (An analysis of the history and dramatic structures of the movement plus several scenarios. Out of print.)

Schechner, Richard. *The End of Humanism: Writings on Performance.* New York: PAJ, 1982. (Essays by a leader of avant-garde theatre in the 1960s and 1970s in which he discusses the end of that period and the onset of post-modernism.)

————— and Willa Appel, eds. *By Means of Performance: Intercultural Studies of Theatre and Ritual.* New York: Cambridge University Press, 1990.

Schlueter, June. *Metafictional Characters in Modern Drama.* New York: Columbia Univ. Press, 1979. (A study of "self-conscious" characters in modern drama who frankly express their realization that they are fictive beings.)

Schmidman, Jo Ann; Sora Kimberlain; and Megan Terry. *Right Brain Vacation Photos.* Omaha, NE: The Magic Theatre Foundation and Megan Terry, 1992. (A photographic chronicle of the Omaha Magic Theatre from its beginning to 1992.)

Simard, Rodney. *Postmodern Drama: Contemporary Playwrights in America and Britain.* Lanham, MD: University Press of America, 1984. (Identifies post-modern drama as a synthesis of realism, absurdism, and epic theater.)

PRESENT-DAY THEATRE PRODUCTION

Playwriting

Smiley, Sam. *Playwriting: The Structure of Action.* Englewood Cliffs: Prentice-Hall, 1972. (Playwriting methodology and a system for analyzing dramatic structure.)

Production Management

Langley, Stephen. *Theatre Management and Production in America: Commercial, Stock, Resident, College, Community Theatre, and Presenting Organizations.* Drama Book Publishers, 1990. (A thorough handbook.)

Stern, Lawrence. *Stage Management: A Guidebook of Practical Techniques.* 2nd ed. Boston: Allyn & Bacon, 1982. (A basic handbook for stage managers; currently out of print.)

Directing

Dean, Alexander and Lawrence Carra. *Fundamentals of Play Directing.* 4th ed. New York: Holt, Rinehart, and Winston, 1980. (For fifty years, the succeeding editions of this book have provided a basic text for directors.)

Hodge, Francis. *Play Directing: Analysis, Communication, and Style.* 3rd ed. Englewood Cliffs: Prentice-Hall, 1988. (A complete, basic text.)

Acting

Benedetti, Robert L. *The Actor at Work.* 4th ed. Englewood Cliffs: Prentice-Hall, 1986. (Combines technical approaches with the Stanislavskian method.)

McGaw, Charles and Larry D. Clark. *Acting Is Believing: A Basic Method.* 5th ed. New York: Holt, Rineholt & Winston, 1987. (A basic text in the Stanislavskian tradition.)

Design and Stagecraft

Gillette, J. Michael. *Theatrical Design and Production: An Introduction to Scene Design and Construction, Lighting, Sound, Costume, and Make-up.* Palo Alto: Mayfield, 1987. (Basic and complete.)

Parker, W. Oren and R. Craig Wolf. *Scene Design and Stage Lighting.* 6th ed. New York; Holt, Rinehart, & Winston, 1990. (For years the standard text.)

Costuming

Emery, Joy Spanabel. *Stage Costume Techniques.* Englewood Cliffs: Prentice Hall, 1981. (A complete guide to costuming procedures and techniques for designers and crew members.)

Ingham, Rosemary. *The Costume Designers Handbook: A Complete Guide for Amateur and Professional Costume Designers.* Englewood Cliffs: Prentice Hall, 1983. (Focuses on the designer's tasks from script analysis through production.)

About the Editor

Norman A. Bert earned his Ph.D. at Indiana University, specializing in dramatic theory and criticism. He has taught acting, playwriting, and other theatre courses in Pennsylvania and Montana since 1975. He currently chairs the Department of Theatre and Dance at Texas Tech University, where he teaches advanced and beginning playwriting. He has been actively involved in the Playwriting Awards Committee of the American College Festival and the Playwrights Program of the Association for Theatre and Higher Education. He has written over 20 play scripts which have been produced, and has authored several books including: *One-Act Plays for Acting Students, More One-Act Plays for Acting Students, The Scenebook for Actors, New One-Act Plays for Acting Students* and *Theatre Alive!* Besides writing, teaching, and directing theatre, he enjoys traveling, cooking, and eating.

Order Form

Meriwether Publishing Ltd.
PO Box 7710
Colorado Springs CO 80933-7710
Phone: 800-937-5297 Fax: 719-594-9916
Website: www.meriwether.com

Please send me the following books:

_____ **Theatre Alive #BK-B178**   **$49.95**
by Dr. Norman A. Bert
An introductory anthology of world drama

_____ **New One-Act Plays for Acting Students**   **$19.95**
#BK-B261
edited by Norman Bert and Deb Bert
An anthology of one-act plays for one to three actors

_____ **One-Act Plays for Acting Students #BK-B159**   **$19.95**
by Dr. Norman A. Bert
An anthology of complete one-act plays

_____ **The Scenebook for Actors #BK-B177**   **$16.95**
by Dr. Norman A. Bert
Collection of great monologs and dialogs for auditions

_____ **Acting Games #BK-B168**   **$16.95**
by Marsh Cassady
A textbook of theatre games and improvisations

_____ **The Theatre and You #BK-B115**   **$17.95**
by Marsh Cassady
An introductory text on all aspects of theatre

_____ **Everything About Theatre! #BK-B200**   **$19.95**
by Robert L. Lee
The guidebook of theatre fundamentals

These and other fine Meriwether Publishing books are available at
your local bookstore or direct from the publisher. Prices subject to
change without notice. Check our website or call for current prices.

Name:_____e-mail: _____

Organization name: _____

Address: _____

City: _____ State: _____

Zip: _____ Phone: _____

❑ **Check enclosed**

❑ **Visa / MasterCard / Discover #** _____
                                                    Expiration
Signature: _____ *date:* _____
              (required for credit card orders)

Colorado residents: Please add 3% sales tax.
Shipping: Include $3.95 for the first book and 75¢ for each additional book ordered.

❑ *Please send me a copy of your complete catalog of books and plays.*